insights about the literature you read in this text. The last colum
student and professional illustrations of each approach, allowin
tain "Assumptions" lead to particular "Practices."

Practices	Examples
1. Read the text slowly, describing the responses of an ideal reader—what is anticipated, what is experienced. 2. Or, move through the text describing your own personal response. 3. Focus on details and ask how the reader's response—or your own response—would change if a detail were changed.	See pages 17–19, 41–60, 333–337, 689–691, 782–790, 955–956, 1029–1030, 1034–1037
1. Read closely. You can assume that everything is carefully calculated to contribute to the work's unity—figures of speech, point of view, diction, recurrent ideas or events, etc. 2. Determine what oppositions, tensions, ambiguities, and ironies are present in the work. 3. Say how these various elements are unified—what idea holds them together.	See pages 15–17, 71–85, 332–333, 366–369, 655–656, 664–665, 686–689, 791–792, 838–839, 954–955, 1030–1033
1. Identify the oppositions in the text, and determine which items are favored. 2. Identify what appears to be central to the text, and what appears to be marginal and excluded. 3. Reverse the text's hierarchy (the system of favoring), opening up another reading; and/or argue that what appears to be marginal is actually central.	See pages 19–21, 96–103, 341–345, 356–360, 792–793, 1045–1050
1. Identify the qualities of gender, class, race, religion, etc. of the author and/or the characters; that is, say how individuals are portrayed as members of some group. 2. Consider whether the text promotes or undermines stereotypes. 3. Imagine how the text might be read by a certain type of reader; or how a text might have been neglected by a certain type of reader.	See pages 25–27, 129–144, 329–333, 344–345, 660–664, 684–686, 691–693, 791, 957–960, 1037–1045
1. Research the author's life and relate that information, cautiously, to the work. 2. Research the author's time (the political history, economic history, intellectual history, etc.) and relate that information, cautiously, to the work. 3. Research how people reasoned during the author's lifetime, the patterns and limits involved in making sense. Relate those logical strategies to the work.	See pages 21–23, 188–209, 327–332, 337–338, 360–366, 370–372, 653–655, 664–665, 681–684, 793–794, 837–838, 950–954, 1045–1053
1. Apply a developmental concept to the work—for example, the Oedipal complex, anal retentiveness, castration anxiety, gender confusion. 2. Relate the work to psychologically significant events in the author's life. 3. Consider how repressed material may be expressed in the work's pattern of imagery or symbols.	See pages 23–25, 249–263, 332–333, 338–341, 656–660, 793, 839–841, 957–960, 1034–1037

Literature

Reading and Writing with Critical Strategies

Literature

Reading and Writing with Critical Strategies

Steven Lynn

University of South Carolina

PEARSON

Longman

New York   San Francisco   Boston
London   Toronto   Sydney   Tokyo   Singapore   Madrid
Mexico City   Munich   Paris   Cape Town   Hong Kong   Montreal

About the Cover:

We study literature (as thinkers going back to Plato have argued) because it can be a profoundly revealing imitation of life. René Magritte's *La condition humaine* (1934) certainly reminds us of this motivation, as the painting in the window appears to capture reality perfectly. Yet Magritte's work also invites a richer view of art, for the painting is within a painting: the "reality" that is captured in either case is an illusion, made of paint. The space around the window/painting becomes a fantastic trompe l'oeil, miraculously fitting the scene outside, or rather betraying the hand of the artist.

This textbook aims to inspire students to see literature in similarly rich ways: as a powerful reflection of reality, a window to reality, an opportunity to create reality, a reflection only of art, never quite getting to what's real, and much more. Such a multiplicity of meaning, such a swirling of art and life, is central to the human condition, Magritte's work suggests. It's what we're after here.

—Steven Lynn

Vice President and Editor in Chief: *Joe Terry*
Acquisitions Editor: *Erika Berg*
Development Manager: *Janet Lanphier*
Development Editor: *Barbara A. Conover*
Senior Marketing Manager: *Melanie Craig*
Senior Supplements Editor: *Donna Campion*
Production Manager: *Denise Phillip*
Project Coordination, Text Design, and
    Electronic Page Makeup: *WestWords, Inc.*

Cover Design Manager: *John Callahan*
Cover Designer: *Mary McDonnell*
Cover Image: The Human Condition, 1934,
    by Rene Magritte. © Artist's Rights Society,
    NY/Superstock
Photo Researcher: *Photosearch, Inc.*
Manufacturing Manager: *Dennis J. Para*
Printer and Binder: *Quebecor World*
Cover Printer: *Coral Graphic Services*

For permission to use copyrighted material, grateful acknowledgment is made to the copyright holders on pp. 1181—1190, which are hereby made part of this copyright page.

Library of Congress Cataloging-in-Publication Data
Lynn, Steven 1952–
    Literature: reading and writing with critical strategies / Steven Lynn.
        p. cm.
    Includes bibliographical references and index.
    ISBN 0-321-11349-7
        1. English language — Rhetoric. 2. Literature — History and criticism —
    Theory, etc. 3. Criticism — Authorship. 4. Academic writing.
        5. College readers. I. Title.
    PE1479.C7L955 2003
        808 — dc21   2003040107

Please visit our website at http://www.ablongman.com

ISBN 0-321-11349-7

1 2 3 4 5 6 7 8 9 10 — RNT — 06 05 04 03

For Annette and Anna

Brief Contents

Detailed Contents

5. Read Poetry Closely: New Criticism   67

6. Read Poetry Playfully: Deconstruction   91

7. Read Fiction Powerfully: Political Criticism   122

8. Read Fiction Contextually: Biographical, Historical, and New Historical Criticism   181

9. *Read Drama Thoughtfully: Psychological Criticism*   243

Fiction   271

10. *Elements of Fiction*   273

Poetry   567

Preface for Instructors

Critical theories are invention strategies. This realization is the starting point for *Literature: Reading and Writing with Critical Strategies*—a new kind of introduction-to-literature anthology designed to help you show your students how to think of insightful things to say about literary works, and how to shape those ideas into forceful essays.

Following the emergence of critical theory in the past few decades, today we enjoy an unprecedented consciousness about how meanings are made and articulated. While composition theory has advanced our understanding of the writing process, the teaching of literature—and writing about literature—has been relatively unaffected by theory. In the mainstream introduction-to-literature books, for all practical purposes, critical theory has been ignored, relegated to an appendix or a chapter beginning on page 2,083.

In keeping theory to ourselves, we may have been trying to save our students from bafflement and frustration. But they don't need to be soaked in Stanley Fish and Julia Kristeva, in Derrida and Foucault, to acquire a working grasp of the different kinds of critical approaches available to them. Some students intuitively discover some of these invention strategies, but most students come into our classes with fairly limited resources for making a literary text meaningful.

Literature: Reading and Writing with Critical Strategies dispels the myth that critical theory eludes the grasp of beginning-level students. Your students will find clear and accessible explanations of various critical approaches, and they will be inspired to read, think, and write *critically*. They will learn how critical essays are developed, from a blank page to questions and inklings, to rough sketches, to a finished draft. *Critical strategies are presented here as means to an end—not the object of study, but as a set of guidelines for reading and reacting more richly and rewardingly.*

Putting Invention Strategies to Work

The literature, after all, is why we're here. And in talking about literature, certain traditional terms and concepts, "the elements," have proved quite useful. Students first engage the meanings of three deceptively familiar terms—"reading," "writing," and "literature"—in the first part of this textbook. Then literary texts, critical strategies, and elements are intertwined in a series of chapters in the second part of the text. These chapters, 4 through 9, explain and illustrate some profoundly influential approaches: reader response, New Criticism, deconstruction, political criticism, historical criticism, and psychological criticism. Each of these chapters is divided into four sections:

Reflection: Here the basic principles of an approach are identified, or "reflected," in the close reading of a poem. The reader who is looking for ambiguities, and attempting to unify those tensions (employing new critical assumptions, in other words), is using quite different strategies from those used by the reader who is trying to relate the author's life and times to his work (that is, using biographical and historical criticism). Students need to understand that these different assumptions and purposes exist. Good readings don't just magically *appear.* Good readers produce interpretations, using certain tools and motivations.

Strategies: Here students learn how to use each approach's principles to write a critical essay, starting from nothing and moving through drafts to a final version. These explanations, and the evolving papers, have been classroom tested by dozens of teachers and hundreds of students for accessibility, usefulness, and interest. Each strategy is reduced to three simple yet powerful directives. (Students will also find a simplified overview of the assumptions and practices of each strategy gathered inside the front cover—for quick reference as they develop a more sophisticated understanding of each strategy.)

Elements: In traditional anthologies, the elements of literature—like critical theories—are covered in a glossarial format. But the definition of "plot" or "character" doesn't necessarily suggest to students what they might *say* about a particular plot or character. In this section the elements are defined and discussed as they function within each critical approach, giving students a richer understanding of these basic terms and concepts, and also helping them to generate an abundance of ideas.

Practice: To grasp how critical approaches work, to become comfortable applying them, to begin to blend and go beyond them, students need practice. This section therefore presents a set of texts—poems, stories, or plays—that are thematically related, encouraging students to make connections between and among them. The themes, like the works of literature, are particularly responsive to the approach. The political criticism chapter, for instance, gathers practice stories that illuminate idealism. Many students have said that their insight into—and appreciation of—literary works increased exponentially when they have tried to write one. So the "Practice" sections conclude by encouraging students to produce a literary text.

The Selections

Literature: Reading and Writing with Critical Strategies offers a balance of canonical classics, underappreciated gems, and why-haven't-I-heard-of-this-before pieces. The particular challenges and resources of each genre are considered in an "Invitation" chapter: poetry in Chapter 10, fiction in 14, and drama in 17. Each genre also has a case study chapter, giving students opportunities to explore in depth the following major writers: Robert Frost and Gwendolyn Brooks; Charlotte Perkins Gillman and Flannery O'Connor; Sophocles and Shakespeare. Students too often have been asked to produce literary criticism without having seen much of it. The critical excerpts in each of these case studies, together with the professional and student examples integrated throughout the textbook, provide an extensive array of critical models. Each genre, in addition, has a chapter presenting "More" examples—important, stimulating, wonderful readings representing the range of work in that genre. These additional works provide opportunities to extend the thematic connections established earlier.

As students engage with various recurrent themes, references, and allusions, their reading will grow in confidence and pleasure.

Portability

Most introductory anthologies of literature offer far more than could possibly be assigned in a single term. *Literature: Reading and Writing with Critical Strategies* offers an abundance of literary texts, but its heft has been limited by a more realistic selection of dramatic works. Individual plays are easy to order, and a broad selection of Penguin paperbacks can be value-packed with *Literature* at a significant discount. Discounted Penguin titles include:

Hansberry, *A Raisin in the Sun*
Hwang, *Madame Butterfly*
Miller, *Death of a Salesman*
Shakespeare, *Macbeth*
Shakespeare, *The Merchant of Venice*
Shakespeare, *Othello*
Sophocles, *The Three Theban Plays*
Wilson, *Fences*
Wilson, *Joe Turner's Come and Gone*

To review the complete list of titles available, visit www.ablongman.com/penguin and consult your Longman representative about setting up a value pack.

Supporting Materials

For Instructors:

Instructors Manual, by Steven Lynn
ISBN: 0-321-12233-X

In the expansive *Instructor's Manual,* you will find sample syllabi, tips on teaching each chapter, answers with explanations for the questions in the book, additional questions, additional writing and reading suggestions, suggestions regarding Internet resources, advice on ancillary materials, more student examples, and much more. The *Instructor's Manual* for this text is unusual in several ways. For starters, I've written it, or gathered the resources for it, myself. Still, since dozens of teachers worked with various iterations of the manuscript for this text, I'm very much indebted to many people for exercises, quiz questions, activities, background information, unexpected connections, writing assignments, exhortations, and warnings. I'm most indebted to Professor Ed Madden, my teaching partner in our teacher-training course.

Companion Website
www.ablongman.com/lynn

This text-specific companion site offers a wealth of resources for both students and instructors. Instructors will find links to sites that will further enhance the coverage of the authors featured in *Literature*, additional plays, and much more. Those same author links are available to students, as are thought-provoking Internet exercises, additional readings, and annotated links to other useful literature sites.

Video Program

An impressive selection of videotapes is available to enrich students' experience of literature. Contact your sales representative to learn how to qualify.

The Longman Electronic Testbank for Literature
Printed ISBN 0-321-14312-4
CD ISBN: 0-32114314-0

This electronic and printed testbank features various objective questions on the major works of fiction, short fiction, poetry, and drama. With this user-friendly CD-ROM, instructors simply choose questions from the electronic testbank and then print out the completed test for distribution. FREE with the adoption of Lynn's *Literature*.

Teaching Literature On-line, Second Edition
ISBN: 0-321-10618-0

Teaching Literature On-line provides instructors with strategies for incorporating electronic media into any literature classroom. Offering a range of information and examples, this manual provides ideas and activities for enhancing literature courses with the help of technology. FREE with the adoption of Lynn's *Literature*.

Coursecompass Generic Site. Longman English Resources for Introduction to Literature, Fiction, Creative Writing, and Drama Access Code Card, Second Edition
ISBN: 0-321-14311-6
Blackboard Content: 0-321-14313-2

This course management system provides a number of guides that will help students analyze literature, evaluate plays, critique and write about literature, and conduct research on-line. Also included is a journal for writing about literature, a journal for creative writing, and guides to teaching literature on-line. FREE when value-packaged with Lynn's *Literature*.

For Students:

Literature Timeline
ISBN: 0-321-14315-9

This visually appealing timeline chronicles the major literary works written throughout history. Students gain historical and contextual insights into the impact historical events have had on writers and their works. . . and vice versa. FREE when value-packaged with Lynn's *Literature: Reading and Writing with Critical Strategies*.

Responding to Literature: A Writer's Journal
ISBN: 0-321-09542-1

This journal provides students with their own personal space for writing. Helpful writing prompts for responding to fiction, poetry, and drama are included. FREE when value-packaged with Lynn's *Literature*.

Evaluating A Performance
ISBN: 0-321-09541-3

Do you ever ask your students to review a local production? This portable supplement offers students a convenient place to record their evaluations. Useful tips and suggestions of issues to consider when evaluating a production are included. FREE when value-packaged with Lynn's *Literature*.

Research Navigator for English
ISBN: 0-321-20277-5

Designed to teach students how to conduct high-quality online research and to document it properly, Research Navigator guides provide discipline-specific academic resources; in addition to helpful tips on the writing process, online research, and finding and citing valid sources. Free when packaged with any Allyn & Bacon/Longman text, Research Navigator guides include an success code to Research Navigator™- providing access to thousands of academic journals and periodicals, the NY Times Search by Subject Archive, Link Library, Library Guides, and more.

Penguin Discount Program

Longman is proud to offer a large selection of Penguin paperbacks at a significant discount when packaged with *Literature: Reading and Writing with Critical Strategies*. Penguin titles offer additional opportunities to explore contemporary and classical fiction and drama. To review the complete list of titles and discounted prices, visit http://www.ablongman.com/penguin.

Acknowledgments

This book wouldn't exist at all without the imagination, vision, and patience of Erika Berg, an extraordinary editor. It wouldn't exist in anything like its present form without the generous and thoughtful assessments of my reviewers, who have helped to guide this book through three major revisions. I'd like to thank especially Lauren Puccio, a remarkable student, whose careful reading of and enthusiasm for the manuscript in its final stages were invaluable. If this list omits any reviewers, my sincere apologies:

Barbara Barnard, Hunter College/CUNY
Dana Beckelman, University of Wisconsin—Milwaukee
Joe Benson, A&T State University
Lois Birky, Illinois Central College
Paul R. Brandt, Kent State University
Kristin Bryant, Portland Community College
James H. Clemmon, Austin Peay State University
Janice Cooke, University of New Orleans
S. Elaine Craghead, University of Rhode Island
Elizabeth H. Curtin, Salisbury State University
John L. Davis, University of Texas at El Paso
Paul M. Dombrowski, Ohio University
Elinor Flewellen, Santa Barbara City College
Randall Gloege, Eastern Montana College
James Heldman, Western Kentucky University
Barbara Hirchfelder, Santa Fe Community College
Donald Johns, University of California—Davis
Edwina Jordan, Illinois Central College
Martha E. Kendall, San Jose City College
Nancy Kennedy, Edmonds Community College
Daniel T. Kline, University of Alaska—Anchorage

Joseph E. Kruppa, University of Texas at Austin
Joseph LaBriola, Sinclair Community College
Zita M. McShane, Frostburg State University
Miriam P. Moore, University of South Carolina
Betty Jo Peters, Morehead State University
Kraft H. Rompf, Essex Community College
Melita Schaum, University of Michigan—Dearborn
John L. Schilb, University of Maryland—College Park
Susan Schiller, Sacramento City College
Ryan Schneider, San Diego State University
Susan Seyfarth, Valdosta State University
Antony Shuttleworth, Ohio State University
Phillip Sipiora, University of South Florida
Ernest J. Smith, University of Central Florida
Judith Stanford, Rivier College
Vivian Thomlinson, Cameron University
Daryl Troyer, El Paso Community College
Janet L. Warman, Elon College
Thomas A. Westerfield, University of Northern Iowa
Sharon Wilson, University of Northern Colorado
W. Potter Woodberry, Tallahassee Community College

I must also thank the dozens of teaching assistants at the University of South Carolina, who proved repeatedly that their students could indeed understand and use rewardingly different critical approaches. The Association of Canadian College and University Teachers of English provided a receptive audience at a crucial point in the evolution of this project. KC Culver provided excellent research assistance, and helped prepare many of the brief biographies. Randy Miller also adeptly researched and contributed fine questions regarding *Oedipus* and *Hamlet*. My current research assistant, Monica Hill, continues to provide cheerful and essential assistance.

A few more people deserve my particular thanks:

1. Extraordinary teachers: Karl Beason, my nomination for the greatest high school English teacher ever; Don Greiner, Bernie Dunlap, George Geckle, and Jim Garrison, who inspired me to try be an English professor of a certain kind—their kind.

2. Amazing assistants: especially Lisa Saxon, who must have cloned herself (it's the only explanation)—the most cheerful and effective administrative assistant anyone could imagine; Elizabeth Smith, who embodies courage and caring; and Modestine Redden, whose good cheer and calm efficiency keep the English department moving.

3. Patient family: Anna, who mostly left her dad alone in his study so he could finish this book, even though she had to save the Beanie Baby universe by herself sometimes; and Annette, who inspired me to win the Nobel Prize in the Special Awards category of Being Lucky Enough to Marry Annette. I'd also like to thank my brother Mike, my mother Leora, and my father Benjamin for asking—and for not asking—how the book was coming along, almost always at the right times.

4. Indefatigable development editor: Barbara Conover, whose good judgment and tactful insistence saved me from many errors and infelicities (those that remain are mine, of course).

5. Wonderful colleagues: The English department at the University of South Carolina is a supportive, fun, comfortable place to work. I'm honored to work with them.

Finally, if you have suggestions or questions, let me know. My email address is lynn@sc.edu, and I'd love to hear from you. I'm happy to respond to queries or comments from you or your students.

Steven Lynn
University of South Carolina

The Possibilities of Literary Meaning

Y ou might be featured in the following poem. Why don't you read it and see?

TOM WAYMAN (1945–)

Did I Miss Anything?

*Question frequently asked by students
after missing a class*

Nothing. When we realized you weren't here
we sat with our hands folded on our desks
in silence, for the full two hours

Everything. I gave an exam worth
40 percent of the grade for this term   5
and assigned some reading due today
on which I'm about to hand out a quiz
worth 50 percent

Nothing. None of the content of this course
has value or meaning   10
Take as many days off as you like:
any activities we undertake as a class
I assure you will not matter either to you or me
and are without purpose

Everything. A few minutes after we began last time   15
a shaft of light suddenly descended and an angel
or other heavenly being appeared
and revealed to us what each woman or man must do
to attain divine wisdom in this life and
the hereafter   20
This is the last time the class will meet
before we disperse to bring the good news to all people on earth

Nothing. When you are not present
how could something significant occur?

Everything. Contained in this classroom   25

is a microcosm of human experience
assembled for you to query and examine and ponder
This is not the only place such an opportunity has been
    gathered

but it was one place

And you weren't here

                                                          [1994]

30

We're all implicated in Wayman's poem: arriving late to a movie, getting to the ball-game six minutes into the first quarter, catching up to the tour group in the mansion's third room, we have all asked, "Did I miss anything?" Sometimes we get filled in: "See that guy in the car? He's got a frog under his hat" or "Smith sprained his ankle on the second play" or "Go back and look at the door into the first room—incredible!" Sometimes we're reassured that we haven't missed anything—but how can that be? If we haven't missed anything, then what was it that happened before we arrived?

The question is not literal, obviously. We know we missed *something*—we just wonder if we need to know what it was. But from a teacher's point of view, you can just imagine how frustrating this question is, suggesting that the work of a class hour might add up to little or nothing. To illustrate how foolish the student's question is when taken literally, the teacher offers alternating responses that are equally foolish if taken literally: the student missed "Everything" and "Nothing." We don't really believe "nothing" happened in the last class, any more than we believe "everything" happened (Dancing bears? First contact with an alien species?). Yet the poem concludes, after setting up this back-and-forth pattern of opposites, with a shift to an "Everything" that does not fit this pattern of ridicule, an "Everything" that appears to be serious. A classroom, as the poem asserts, especially a literature class, offers potentially "everything" in a sense, because it is "a microcosm of human experience." By the magic of literature and your imagination, you *could* have bear ballet, new alien friends, or anything else.

Unfortunately, as Wayman's teacher notes, the "you" in the poem wasn't "here." But you *are here,* inside this textbook right now, with many class meetings ahead of you. You have an opportunity here to "query and examine and ponder." The experience will take some patience, time, energy, organization. Don't miss a bit of it! And, if you must miss a class, you'll know to ask "*What* did I miss?"

But where exactly is "here" for you? Where are you, in terms of your attitude toward literary study? What have you encountered in English literature classrooms previously? Do you enjoy reading literature? Why? Have you read much literature? What are some of your favorite poems, short stories, plays? What do you think are your strengths and weaknesses as a reader, and as a writer? What have your teachers thought about your strengths and weaknesses? Have you ever considered a literary class to be "a microcosm of human experience"? By asking yourself such questions you're likely to have a better sense of what you need to do to get the most pleasure and satisfaction out of this opportunity. You can start to figure out where you are, with your teacher's guidance.

The first part of this text explains its "here"—where it's coming from and what philosophy it embraces. That's the purpose of the first three chapters, which examine three key terms whose meanings have evolved dramatically in the past thirty years: reading, writing, and literature. You may not experience, as in Wayman's poem, "a shaft of light" delivering "divine wisdom" in the pages that follow, but you'll be in a better position to appreciate why it's good to be "here," wherever you are.

1

Reading:
How Meaning Is Made

> "When I use a word," Humpty Dumpty said, in rather a scornful tone,
> "it means just what I choose it to mean—neither more nor less."
> "The question is," said Alice, "whether you can make words
> mean so many different things."
> "The question is," said Humpty Dumpty, "which is to be master—that's all."
>
> —Lewis Carroll, *Through the Looking Glass*

Who Makes Meaning?

Tiger Woods can "read" a putt; Judge Judy can "read" a loan agreement; Sister Jenna can "read" your palm and predict the future. What is "reading" in these diverse examples, and how is that activity—or set of activities—related to what you do when you "read" a literary work? What is going on when we read a poem, or story, or play? Is reading different when we read different kinds of things?

Consider Humpty Dumpty's own attitude toward reading poetry in *Through the Looking Glass,* the sequel to *Alice in Wonderland.* As you may recall, Humpty Dumpty offers to help

"Roger has always been text-driven."

Alice understand a particularly difficult poem, the famous "Jabberwocky." Here's the poem:

LEWIS CARROLL (1832–1898)

Jabberwocky

'Twas brillig, and the slithy toves
    Did gyre and gimble in the wabe:
All mimsy were the borogroves,
    And the mome raths outgrabe.

"Beware the Jabberwock, my son!   5
    The jaws that bite, the claws that catch!
Beware the Jubjub bird, and shun
    The frumious Bandersnatch!"

He took his vorpal sword in hand;
    Long time the manxome foe he sought—   10
So rested he by the Tumtum tree,
    And stood awhile in thought.

And, as in uffish thought he stood,
    The Jabberwock, with eyes of flame,
Came whiffling through the tulgey wood,   15
    And burbled as it came!

One, two! One, two! And through and through
    The vorpal blade went snicker-snack!
He left it dead, and with its head
    He went galumphing back.   20

"And hast thou slain the Jabberwock?
    Come to my arms, my beamish boy!
O frabjous day! Callooh, Callay!"
    He chortled in his joy.

'Twas brillig, and the slithy toves   25
    Did gyre and gimble in the wabe:
All mimsy were the borogroves,
    And the mome raths outgrabe.

[1871]

Mr. Dumpty says to Alice, "I can explain all the poems that ever were invented—and a good many that haven't been invented just yet." Although his self-assurance is brash, wouldn't it be nice to be able to approach any text with some of his confidence? Toward that end, let's consider the nature of reading, using the dramatically different views of Alice and Humpty Dumpty to mark out some useful oppositions.

For Alice, words should have stable meanings. Although a word may mean a variety of things, surely it doesn't mean, as Humpty Dumpty claims in the previous epigraph, whatever one wishes—does it? Alice has determined already that the text is a poem written backward, and that one can read it by holding it up to a mirror. She has taken, in fact, a crucial and surprisingly overlooked step. We certainly need to consider what kind of a text we're reading. In what follows you'll find essential information about the different kinds of literature—the genres of poetry, fiction, drama, and "other"—and how each of these may call for different assumptions, terms, and reading strategies. There's no magic involved—just basic information. But if you don't know what a sonnet is, or a flashback, or a narrator, you may well find a particular work almost as confusing as the backward-written "Jabberwocky." It is definitely easier to talk about a work if you control these basic concepts and terms.

Alice has also made another good series of moves, seeking out help, asking questions when she is confused, making sure she understands the words. As you read and think and talk and write about literature, you should feel free to ask questions. No question, if it's genuine, is dumb. Usually, if you're wondering about something, chances are that someone else is wondering too. What you worry might be considered a dumb question might actually be quite profound. Teachers enjoy teaching, and so they generally enjoy answering questions.

But note that Alice asks for help only after she has struggled with the work on her own. Sometimes some students apparently have so little confidence or so little discipline that their approach to reading an assigned work is to purchase a guide by someone else. These guides, which are often superficial and error-riddled, are a poor substitute for reading the work itself. Your teacher can almost always direct you to a better resource for help, if you need it. But first, read the work itself—carefully, more than once if possible. The point here sounds as if it should be spoken by one of the mad characters in *Through the Looking Glass* ("Before you try to make sense of something, be sure to read it"): If you are supposed to read a work, then make sure you read the work, not something else. Don't wait until the last minute. Don't wait until you're sleepy or exhausted. Don't "read" it while you're watching reruns of *Seinfeld*. And don't ask someone else to tell you about it. Plan ahead, find a place to concentrate, and really read it. Great literature may not always be easy to understand (although difficulty is not a measure of quality), but you get what you pay for, usually. *The price of admission to life-changing literature is reading it*.

You may, even after you've read carefully and diligently, find yourself in the same boat as Alice. Being able to decipher the words of a text, as we've all discovered at one time or another, doesn't necessarily mean that we can "read" its meaning. "Jabberwocky" in fact appears to be a particularly good example of a poem that is resistant to meaning, as the poem's famous first verse indicates:

> 'Twas brillig, and the slithy toves
>   Did gyre and gimble in the wabe:
> All mimsy were the borogoves,
>   And the mome raths outgrabe.

With any literary work, of course, it's important to look up any unfamiliar words; and sometimes even familiar words may be employed in an unexpected way. Unless you've gone through the looking glass, a dictionary will usually help. Plan to use yours liberally as you read. Mr. Dumpty fortunately is able to provide definitions, revealing that "'*Brillig*' means four o'clock in the afternoon—the time when you begin broiling things for dinner." "*Slithy*" (of course) means "lithe and slimy." By the time Humpty Dumpty has finished his dazzling explanations of the poem's vocabulary, we may well think he is right, that words *can* mean whatever one says they mean.

But notice this: Humpty Dumpty's reading does not seem entirely unfettered, unlimited. He is able to make "slithy" persuasively into a combination of "slimy" and "lithe" because parts of those words are already in "slithy." He doesn't try to make "slithy" into "consciousness" and "mole." He might be able to do that, but who knows how?

What's at stake here is huge. If the meaning of a word is, as Humpty Dumpty says, free-floating, up for grabs, subjective, then reading a whole group of words in a poem, story, play, or legal contract would seem to be entirely open to interpretation, an act of imagination. Clearly some students agree with Humpty Dumpty, complaining when teachers find their interpretations implausible, "It's just one person's opinion! How can my teacher give me a low grade because my interpretation is different? Can't I have my own opinion?" On the other hand, if the meaning of a word is grounded, stable, something we can point to firmly, then why shouldn't the meaning of a whole group of words also be fixed and transparent? From this perspective, if your teacher finds your reading of a poem implausible, then one of you—at least— is wrong. Is that right?

To think about which of these two opposing views of reading is correct, Alice's or Humpty Dumpty's, let's return to the different senses of "reading" at the beginning of this chapter. When Tiger Woods "reads" a green, it would be silly to argue that its "meaning" is whatever he says it is. Tiger may think the green breaks a little to the left, and then a lot to the right, but this reading will either be right or wrong, as he will learn when he strokes the putt. It's a matter of opinion until he tries it out. When Sister Jenna, however, reads your palm and tells you that you should follow your heart in matters of love, it is difficult to say whether she is right or wrong, or even what she means precisely. If a green doesn't mean whatever Tiger says it does, perhaps your palm does? The only way to tell, perhaps, would be to follow your heart and see what happens—although reading the direction in which your heart is pointing might take more sessions with Sister Jenna. When Judge Judy says that a lease provision allowing for pets does not include pigs because in her view a pig is not a pet, she seems to be reading a meaning that is in the words "pet" and "pig," but she is also interpreting the meaning, making it up, based on her own opinion. Her reading is "correct" because she has the authority to impose a meaning (and because the Judge Judy television show's participants have agreed not to appeal).

At this point, the issue is clearly before us, although the solution may seem to be nowhere in sight. At this point we need to leave Humpty Dumpty and Alice behind. But first, let's review what we've covered. These insights may not be amazing, but they're worth a reminder.

Suggestions for Reading

1. Consider as precisely as you can what sort of thing it is that you're reading. What are you expected to know? The information in this text about the elements of literature will help you here. Reading as many different kinds of literature as possible will also help.

2. Make sure that you do read the work carefully. Give yourself adequate time and opportunity, and don't rely on secondary sources as a substitute for the work itself, even if the work seems challenging. Your own discipline and courage will help you here. Ask your teacher for help if you're struggling.

3. Look up any words you don't understand, and remember that familiar words may have unfamiliar meanings or associations.

4. Ask questions. Don't be shy.

Are Some Readings Wrong?

If a picture is worth a thousand words, then perhaps a photograph can help clarify whether reading is the reception or the creation of meaning.

What's the meaning of this picture? Does it mean some particular thing (Alice's view), or does it mean whatever we say it means (Humpty Dumpty's view)? I have asked hundreds of students and dozens of teachers to analyze this photograph, with impressively diverse results. Some people say these two men are obviously close friends, or perhaps even father and son, in part because of their cordial expressions, their facial resemblance (not just the beards; compare their ear lobes and noses), and also simply because they are standing so near to one another. One student in fact developed a rather elaborate story based on the photo, in which the son, returning from service in the French Foreign Legion (based on the funky hat and his non-American uniform), is reuniting with his father, as the proud mother looks on. American men, as more than one person has observed, don't usually stand this close, even when they're related. So, some savvy travelers have suggested, perhaps these men are Europeans.

Other students and teachers, noting the proximity and tilt of the men's heads, have insisted that they are about to kiss, that they're gay, and that they're laughing because their cap brims are getting in the way. The older man's top shirt button is provocatively undone; the younger man is sporting a sort of Village People look (you know, the group who made famous the song "YMCA," which has become a comic kind of gay anthem). But other analysts have said that the scene seems somehow staged or unreal, and they have speculated that the men are politicians or actors (or both). One student even declared the picture to be a computer-generated fake, combining two pictures at the line of the building between the two men; the awkward placement of the woman's head, this student noted, gives the fake away. Although some of these readings seem more likely than others, is there any way to say with confidence which is correct?

Some people have argued that there is a way. They recognize these men: Ernest Hemingway, the famous American writer, on the left, with Fidel Castro, the infamous Cuban dictator. Although one student did suggest that these two must be wax figures, since Castro and Hemingway never met (according to the student), it is in fact (according to the Associated Press anyway) a picture of Hemingway and Castro in 1960, sometime after Castro assumed power in 1959, and before the Bay of Pigs in 1962. One could argue that, given this historical setting, any further "reading" of the photograph is unnecessary. *This* is the meaning of the photograph: it's Hemingway and Castro talking in 1960. But this historical fact doesn't exhaust the photograph's meaning. Since Hemingway took his own life in 1961, reportedly in despair after extended illness, the picture appears to contradict the accepted notion that his physical and mental health were failing at this point. That is another possible "meaning" of the photograph.

We've been thinking of the photograph in terms of its original historical setting, but in September of 1994 it appeared in *Newsweek* as part of an article on the Clinton administration's Cuban policies. Captioned "Tangled Up in Myths: Hemingway with the Cuban Leader in 1960," the picture accompanies Michael Elliott's essay asserting that U.S. attitudes toward Cuba are clouded by fantasies and misperceptions. Hemingway, as you may know, lived in Cuba a substantial part of his life, fishing, drinking, and entertaining buddies. When we think of Cuba, Elliott writes, we think of "romance, casinos, and marlin." "From Teddy Roosevelt to Jimmy Buffett, with contributions from Ernest Hemingway," Elliott says, Americans have formed an unrealistic myth of Cuba, thinking of it as a natural extension of the United States—our playground, our tropical resort, now sadly closed down. Within the context of Elliott's essay, the photograph points to "Hemingway's Cuba," as we have imagined it, which stands in contrast to the real Cuba, as Castro has controlled it.

In terms of an even larger context, what might Hemingway and Castro stand for, or symbolize? As an innovative creative writer, older but still vital, able to express his dreams and desires, Hemingway might embody the openness, the accomplishment, the imaginative zest for life of the United States. His casual shirt and comfortable cap contrast sharply with Castro's rigid hat and stiffly starched shirt—just as the freedom and comfort of America contrast sharply with the rigidly oppressive and impoverished regime of communist Cuba. Castro's military-style costume lacks decoration, as if he deceptively wants to suggest that he is an ordinary man. The common Cuban people, one might argue, are actually represented by the grimacing woman in the background, who is being squeezed out of the picture, just as she is being squeezed out of freedom and prosperity, ignored by her dictator. Even the background of the photo reinforces this reading, with a window and a plant behind Hemingway, and a blank wall behind Castro.

Is this the "correct" reading of this photograph? Not from the point of view of a Cuban revolutionary, loyal to Castro. From that perspective, Hemingway might be seen as a symbol of America's moral and social bankruptcy. Despite the appearance of health, America, like Hemingway, is headed toward its inevitable self-annihilation, such a viewer might argue. Years of self-indulgence will take their toll. Compare the vigor and strength of Castro, such a Castro loyalist might say. Rather than a rumpled shirt, not even buttoned, Castro is crisply attired, with a starched shirt and smart hat, reflecting the order and discipline of the Cuban people. "Where was Hemingway in 1994?"—our communist reader might say. "And where was Fidel?"

Although there is much more that could be said about this photograph, surely a commonsensical point is clear: The meaning of a thing is shaped by the context in which we place it. When we think about how to read a photograph, a story, a poem, or a life, we cannot avoid this interplay of texts and contexts. One can persuasively claim, for instance, that the photograph depicts two gay men about to kiss, if a certain context authorizing this reading can be invoked, one that allows plausible supporting evidence to emerge. When we invoke another context, that these men are Hemingway and Castro, such an interpretation becomes more implausible.

But notice that I didn't say "impossible." The world is amok, it can seem, with Hemingway impersonators; there must also be some Castro impersonators somewhere. Can we be sure that this photograph wasn't actually taken, say, during a Gay Pride March, as a reenactment of the famous photograph, and that some mischievous or lazy graphics assistant didn't substitute one photograph for the other? Sure, this reinterpretation is far-fetched, but isn't it a little bit interesting? Although we won't contemplate here the possibility that Hemingway and Castro themselves might actually have been gay or bisexual, Hemingway has been getting a good bit of attention in Gay and Lesbian Studies recently, not only for the way that he represents and reinforces a certain stereotypical masculinity, but also for the way that his masculine ideal might be designed to obscure unmanly fears and desires. This photograph might well contribute significantly to a study of Hemingway's vision of masculinity.

This section's question—"Are Some Readings Wrong?"—can be answered now: for a particular audience, in a particular context, supported by particular evidence, a reading might be considered to be wrong. But the same argument, in another context, might be considered right. Like so many things in life, the most satisfactory answer here appears to be, "It all depends."

Rather than being a source of frustration (because just about everyone yearns from time to time for clear-cut, black-and-white, right-and-wrong answers), the creativity and open-endedness involved in reading actually can be a rich resource. Once you understand how different critical strategies can be used to stimulate your thinking, how different contexts can be used to make meaning, you are likely to enjoy brainstorming lots of different readings of texts—some more plausible than others, certainly. Facing a blank screen or paper, scrambling desperately for something to say, is frustrating and unnerving. Reading is a great deal more fun when you're deciding which ideas and arguments you want to pursue. Good thinking and good writing, in other words, arise out of plentitude, out of having more ideas than you can use.

As this point—that context shapes reading—is both important and a bit abstract, let's elaborate on it. It matters greatly which of the following possibilities fits our reality:

> *There is a right reading of a text. Readings that differ from the right reading are to varying degrees wrong.* If reading works this way, then when I say "I promise to be faithful," or "My mistress' eyes are nothing like the sun," or any other thing, there is a correct way of reading the words. "I promise to be faithful" does not mean "I will be faithful except on my birthday and the last day of each month"—or it does. The phrase "My mistress' eyes" does not refer to the eyes on the potatoes under my sink—or it does.

> *Any reading is right if someone believes it. It is at least right for that person.* If reading works this way, then words may mean anything, including even contradictory things. "I promise to be faithful" might mean "I will create a statue of you every day," or it might mean "I will be true in my heart even though some parts of my body might not be." If that's what I mean when I say that, how can anyone disagree? If I say that's my opinion, who can say it isn't?

Which case represents the way things are? From a given perspective, some readings of a text are more persuasive than others. Some seem more right, and some seem clearly more wrong. If we understand our assumptions, and we're conscious of the contexts we apply, we can struggle toward an agreement on the correctness of a particular claim. We might not get to an agreement always (or ever), but we can at least (from this viewpoint) agree that such agreement is possible, and worth working toward. So the first case is looking good.

At the same time, we could argue there is no all-powerful, all-seeing perspective that we might adopt. Now, it's possible that you disagree here. You may think that you know the best set of values and goals for any given situation, and that this insight allows you to choose, in any circumstances, the correct reading of a text. Some people feel that way. If that's your feeling (which is in other words that you're always right, or that someone who's telling you how to read is always right), then this book's exploration of reading strategies will still be helpful, because it will guide you toward a better understanding of how other people make sense of things in such widely various and errant ways. We arrive at different readings, quite simply, because we are looking from different perspectives, and we are looking for different reasons, and we are different people who change over time. Thus, in a sense, when we argue about how to read something, the argument involves, at least implicitly, the question of the proper critical strategies, the proper values, the proper context to apply.

Your Right to Read and Write

It's entirely possible that everything we've considered so far makes perfect sense, and you're revved up and ready to get started. But just to make sure we're on the same page, another example certainly couldn't hurt. Rather than a traditional literary text, let's think about the First Amendment to the U. S. Constitution:

> *Congress shall make no law respecting an establishment of religion, or prohibiting the free exercise thereof; or abridging the freedom of speech or of the press; or the right of the people peaceably to assemble, and to petition the government for a redress of grievances.*

Many people think these words are elegantly clear, and that it's just about impossible to misunderstand what these words are saying, unless there is something wrong with the person reading. But making sense of this text, like any text, involves more than simply deciphering the words. We can't just receive its meaning and effects.

Consider, for example, the debate in the United States over flag-burning as a means of protest. Some people find flag-burning an intolerable abuse of free speech, and they have demanded from time to time that a law be passed against it. On the other side, people point out that a law against flag-burning would violate the First Amendment, abridging the freedom of speech. But supporters of a ban on flag-burning deny that such an act constitutes speech. For them, burning the U. S. flag is an outrageous and obscene action, not unlike spray-painting the Washington Monument, or displaying pornography on the playground, or yelling "Fire!" in a crowded theater (when there is no fire). Such behavior, in their view, deserves no protection as "speech." Those on the other side, however, argue that "free speech" isn't limited to what is literally spoken, but has always included things you write, photograph, and even do. Burning a flag, they argue, is different from yelling "Fire!" or defacing a monument. "Fire!" as an assertion has no political content, and a flag in private ownership is not a public monument.

Perhaps the whole problem here is that the wording of the Amendment is just too vague. It doesn't make clear whether flag-burning falls under its domain or not. So let's imagine the Amendment is amended to say that free speech shall not be abridged "except for burning the U.S. flag, which shall be illegal." Would that settle things? What if someone decided to burn something that looks like the U.S. flag but has fifty-two stars, or thirty-eight stripes? What if someone were to paint the flag very crudely on a piece of cardboard and burn that? What about soaking a flag in acid? What about painting a flag on the sidewalk and then washing it off in protest? How about setting fire to a field of grass painted red, white, and blue in the shape of a flag? Even if the law were to say you cannot "deface or damage anything that reasonably resembles a U. S. flag," you'd still have problems because someone would have to decide whether particular items and actions fit the definition: Does *this* resemble a flag? Is *this* defacing it?

The way we solve the problem of what this or any other Amendment (or law) means, ultimately, is that we ask those specialized textual critics known as the Supreme Court. They decide by bringing certain reading strategies to bear upon the text. They place the text into a context, and read it based upon the strategies and assumptions at work within that context. What makes the court proceedings interesting is that the justices don't all bring the same contexts to the same texts. Even when their reading strategies seem to be similar, they don't always apply them in the same way. Hence, we must have an odd number of justices (nine), and they must take a vote to decide what a law means (sometimes deciding by one vote).

The possible contexts these supreme critics might invoke are quite similar to the contexts available to literary critics.

1. **The Law Itself.** Readers might say, simply, that the only meaningful context is the text itself. The law, they might assert, is a stable object, unchanging over time. It contains within itself sufficient clues to guide its interpretation. Careful, insightful readers will understand the law in all its complexity. This approach to reading, when it's applied to literary texts, is usually called "New Criticism" or "Formalism."

2. **My Way.** From this point of view, the text has a personal meaning for the reader. The text's meaning is what the reader feels it says. Each justice has to decide for himself or herself what the text means. Since every person is different, we should expect different meanings. This approach, when used with literary texts, is usually considered a kind of reader-response criticism.

3. **Authorial Intention.** This context bases readings on what we think the authors of the text intended the words to mean. Thus, a particular reading might be supported if, say, some journal entry by James Madison, the Constitution's "Master Builder," explicitly discusses free speech or, even better, flag-burning. This sort of limiting—by referring to the author's intentions—is called an "intentionalist" view of meaning, and biographical and historical study is obviously important to this approach. But such a strategy does have its weaknesses. In the case of the First Amendment, we would have to admit that flag-burning is not mentioned in the Amendment itself, even if it were to appear in some historical documents. The evidence for an authorial intention, when it can be located, must itself be interpreted, so in a sense the situation is more complicated, with another layer of texts to read. Imagine that Madison's journal does contain some entries arguing that flag-burning shouldn't be allowed, and the law is interpreted accordingly. And then, many years later, another and later journal is found in which Madison reveals a change of heart, as he later came to think flag-burning should be allowed. In literary criticism, as you'll see, this approach would be called biographical and historical criticism.

4. **Intention Updated.** "Loose constructionists" (as they are usually called) look beyond what the Framers of the Constitution might have intended years ago; they argue instead that it makes more sense to consider what

these authors would have intended in today's world, if they were writing now. Literary critics who pursue feminist, Marxist, gay and lesbian, African-American, Native American, and other political interests are likely to find this way of looking at a text useful.

5. **Historical Reception.** Another way of looking at this matter would be to say that the text means what most readers over time have taken it to mean (a democratic or statistical view of meaning). The justices, adopting this context, would limit their interpretation by considering how a law had been interpreted in the past. Legal precedent is in fact an important consideration, and literary critics are also apt to examine the history of how a work has been received. Although judges are interested in seeing if they can conform their views to previous judgments, literary critics, who usually cannot publish or turn in a repetition of someone else's ideas, tend to value new and original readings. The problem with this sort of historical criticism, consulting the response of other readers, is of course that most readers could be wrong. You would probably not want medical treatment or car repair based on what most people think.

6. **Expert Opinion.** Rather than a majority of readers, one could say a law means in a particular case what sufficiently trained readers say it means. But that still leaves us with the problem of what to think when trained readers disagree—as they so often seem to do. It is possible that some of the experts are reading carelessly, or some are more expert than others, but differences of opinion are always possible simply because readers cannot employ precisely the same contexts, even if they want to—which is not always the case. The experts get to argue over who is the *most* expert, and some experts might even want to say that their insights are more penetrating than the author, who may not have realized what he or she meant to say. In other words, anyone who is clever enough to make an argument—any argument—can make it, because ultimately no one really knows what the text means. This view, applied in certain ways, might be termed "deconstructive," as you'll see.

Although we would often like to think of reading as the *reception* of meaning, and of texts as transparently clear, that view is ultimately inadequate, incomplete. Often we do *try* to read like other intelligent readers; often we try to see what the author intended to say. Sometimes we consider what the author would have wanted to say today. But we are always to some extent making it up, creating the meaning ourselves. Just as physicists are forced to view light in contradictory ways, as both particle and wave, so must we view reading as both a technical skill and a creative art, both receptive and creative. Ultimately, we know what the First Amendment means in much the same way that we know what a literary work means: we keep talking about it, arguing, discussing, sharing our views, reading and rereading, reading other things, consulting other readers—and ultimately writing our reading down. It's our right—to read and write. When pressed, we take a vote.

Reading is thus inextricably connected to writing. And reading literature is excellent preparation for "reading" anything. The next chapter therefore takes a closer look at how our various (literary) readings get articulated—how we get from reading to writing.

2

Writing: How Invention Strategies Shape the Process

Writing is a design, often a portrait, nearly always a revelation.

—Colette, *The Evening Star*

This chapter aims to explain how critical theories work—how they can provide the contexts that guide the process of writing about literature. The rest of the text, especially the chapters in Part II, should help you become more comfortable using various critical strategies. The idea here is simply to introduce you to using critical theories as invention strategies.

It's entirely possible that you are encountering the idea of different critical approaches (strategies, theories) for the first time, and your prior experience with literature may be limited as well. Don't be dismayed if some of the

"It's plotted out. I just have to write it."

terms and ideas are unfamiliar and even challenging. With practice, both the literature and the theories will become part of your repertoire.

The survey in this chapter doesn't deal with every theoretical approach that can be distinguished today, or even with every approach covered in this textbook, but it does cover a good sampling of the most important and interesting ones. These theories aren't presented, in this chapter or the following ones, in all their complexity or depth: what we're after is a workable, usable introduction.

To illustrate how critical theories work on literature, we need a piece of litera-ture to work upon. The following excerpt, which is taken from Brendan Gill's *Here at the New Yorker*, works nicely. It's very brief, while rich enough to sustain a hand-ful of different approaches. It can also raise interesting questions about just what "lit-erature" is.

BRENDAN GILL (1914–1997)

Brendan Gill at work at *The New Yorker*

For more than sixty years, Brendan Gill wrote for one of the most admired magazines in the world, The New Yorker. *Born in 1914, he produced fifteen books, including* Here at The New Yorker, *before his death in 1997, at age 83. Gill is pictured here in his* New Yorker *office, apparently enjoying a moment of "unshakable confidence," as he puts it in the excerpt below—although the typewriter does seem unusually large and perhaps even menacing from this angle. You can imagine Gill in this pose (after you've read the excerpt) when Gardner Bots-ford appears in his office with the dangling modifier. Miss Gould, despite her prominence in this episode, does not appear in the index to Gill's memoir, but Botsford appears repeatedly and seems to have been a lifelong friend of Gill's.*

Excerpt from Here at the New Yorker

When I started at *The New Yorker*, I felt an unshakable confidence in my talent and intelligence. I revelled in them openly, like a dolphin diving skyward out of the sea. After almost forty years, my assurance is less than it was; the revellings, such as they are, take place in becoming seclusion. This steady progress downward in the amount of one's confi-dence is a commonplace at the magazine—one might almost call it a tra-dition. Again and again, some writer who has made a name for himself in the world will begin to write for us and will discover as if for the first time how difficult writing is. The machinery of benign skepticism that surrounds and besets him in the form of editors, copy editors, and check-ers, to say nothing of fellow-writers, digs a yawning pit an inch or so beyond his desk. He hears it repeated as gospel that there are not three people in all America who can set down a simple declarative sentence correctly; what are the odds against his being one of this tiny elect?

In some cases, the pressure of all those doubting eyes upon his copy is more than the writer can bear. When the galleys of a piece are placed in front of him, covered with scores, perhaps hundreds, of pencilled hen-tracks of inquiry, suggestion, and correction, he may sense not the glory of creation but the threat of being stung to death by an army of gnats. Upon which he may think of nothing better to do than lower his head onto his blotter and burst into tears. Thanks to the hen-tracks and their conse-quences, the piece will be much improved, but the author of it will be pitched into a state of graver self-doubt than ever. Poor devil, he will type out his name on a sheet of paper and stare at it long and long, with dumb uncertainty. It looks—oh, Christ!—his name looks as if it could stand some working on.

As I was writing the above, Gardner Botsford, the editor who, among other duties, handles the copy for "Theatre," came into my office with the galleys of my latest play review in his hand. Wearing an expression of solemnity, he said, "I am obliged to inform you that Miss Gould has found a buried dangling modifier in one of your sentences." Miss Gould is our head copy editor and unquestionably knows as much about English grammar as anyone alive. Gerunds, predicate nominatives, and passive periphrastic con-jugations are mother's milk to her, as they are not to me. Nevertheless, I boldly challenged her allegation. My prose was surely correct in every way. Botsford placed the galleys before me and indicated the offending sen-tence, which ran, "I am told that in her ninth decade this beautiful woman's only complaint in respect to her role is that she doesn't have enough work to do."

I glared blankly at the galleys. Humiliating enough to have buried a dan-gling modifier unawares; still more humiliating not to be able to disinter it. Botsford came to my rescue. "Miss Gould points out that as the sentence is written, the meaning is that the complaint is in its ninth decade and has, moreover, suddenly and unaccountably assumed the female gender." I said that in my opinion the sentence could only be made worse by being corrected—it was plain that "The only complaint of this beautiful woman in her ninth decade . . ." would hang on the page as heavy as a sash-weight. "Quite so," said Botsford. "There are times when to be right is wrong, and this is one of them. The sentence stands."

[1975]

New Criticism

New Criticism (which is now decades old) focuses attention on the work itself, not the reader or the author. New Critics are not allergic to talking about the respons-es of readers or the intentions of authors, but they believe that the work itself ulti-mately must stand on its own. Talk of readers and authors is of secondary importance. The purpose of giving attention to the work itself is, first, to expose the work's unity. In a unified work, every element works together toward a theme.

Every element is essential. In addition, the "close reading" (a phrase popularized by New Critics) of a literary work reveals its complexity. Great literature, New Critics assume, contains oppositions, ambiguities, ironies, tensions; these are unified by the work—if it is successful by the standards of New Criticism.

So how does one do New Criticism? Begin by reading closely. Since everything should contribute to the work's artistic unity—figures of speech, point of view, diction, imagery, recurrent ideas or events, and so forth—then careful analysis of any aspect of the work should be revealing. Look for oppositions, tensions, ambiguities. These add complexity to the work's unity. A mediocre work might be unified but have little complexity; or it might be complex but never really come together. The New Critic, finally, shows how the various elements of a great work unify it.

My New Critical reading of this passage was developed by reading carefully, marking up the text, asking myself questions, drafting answers to the questions, brainstorming and freewriting, and putting my ideas together. Although this reading didn't just pop out of my head, it wasn't a frustrating struggle because I knew what I was trying to do, and I was confident that my assumptions and strategies would produce something interesting. Specifically, I knew that a New Critical reading would identify some tension (or irony, or opposition) in the text, and some tensions in the story do seem pretty clear:

> editor vs. writer
> the world vs. *The New Yorker*
> grammar vs. style
> confidence vs. doubt
> right vs. wrong

I also knew that such tensions must somehow be resolved if the text succeeds (by New Critical standards). Therefore, how the text ends is especially important from a New Critical perspective.

New Critics might have some trouble with the idea of an "ending" here, because the "work" I've chosen is not really a work, but rather an excerpt from a work. But for the purposes of demonstration, let's imagine this passage stands alone, entitled "Writing a Wrong." Since endings are crucial, I decided to focus on the reconciliation at the end, when Botsford pronounces "right is wrong," which is reflected in the (hypothetical) title. As a New Critic, I then had to consider, "How does this idea— 'right is wrong'—unify or resolve the work in a complex or ambiguous way?" In other words, what conflicting ideas are at work in the passage that are brought into balance and harmony by this theme?

You'll benefit most, I think, if you try to sketch out your own New Critical reading before (and perhaps after) you read mine.

The Paradoxical Unity of "Writing a Wrong"

In Brendan Gill's story of a dangling modifier, "Writing a Wrong," the editor Botsford solves the conflict between Miss Gould's rules and Gill's taste. He does so by offering a paradox that unifies Gill's story: sometimes "right is wrong," Botsford says. It turns out that Miss Gould was right to spot the error, but Gill was right to have written the sentence as he did. The irony of this solution is reinforced by various paradoxical images in the story.

For example, the dolphin in the second sentence is "diving skyward." This action simultaneously suggests a downward movement ("diving") and an upward motion ("skyward"). The description thus embodies the same sort of logic as a wrong rightness. Likewise, the "progress downward" of the writer and even his "becoming seclusion" ("becoming"—attractive and appealing to others; "seclusion"—unknown to others) convey the same kind of image. In larger terms, the writer's "unshakable confidence" quickly becomes a "dumb uncertainty"—which again suggests the kind of reversal that resolves the story.

In such an upside-down world we would expect to find imagery of struggle and violence, and we do encounter a "yawning pit" and an "army of gnats." Such tension is harmonized by Gill's brilliant conclusion: in writing, conducted properly, the demands of correctness and style are unified by the writer's poetic instincts. Similarly, the story itself is resolved by the notion of a correct error.

Reader-Response Criticism

Reader-response criticism starts from the idea that the critic's interest ultimately ought to be focused on the reader rather than on the text itself or the author. Without readers, it seems safe to say, there would be little reason to talk about literature; it is the reader who brings the text to life, who gives it meaning. Otherwise, it's just black marks on a white page.

The reader-response critic focuses on the reader's activity in one of two ways: by describing how readers *should* respond to the text or by giving the critic's own personal response. That is, either the reader-response critic is claiming to be describing what is "normal," or conventional, or ideal, or implied by the text; or the critic is expressing that which is personal, subjective, perhaps even eccentric. One could argue that reader-response critics are always engaging in subjective response, even when they think they're objectively describing "the" response. In any event, reader-response critics tend to deal with works eliciting responses that are somehow noteworthy.

How does one do reader-response criticism? If the goal is to offer a personal, subjective response, one simply reads the text and responds. As you can imagine, such a strategy has been especially popular because it really liberates the reader. It's difficult to see how any response could be wrong: who could say, No, that isn't your response? Some responses may seem richer than others; some responses may seem to deal more fully with the text; some responses may seem more authentic and honest than others. But any particular response may well help another reader to a more interesting or satisfying experience of the work.

If the idea is to describe how a reader *ought* to respond, which might better be called "reader-reception" criticism, then you'll need to try to suppress whatever is personal in your response and offer instead an "ideal" response, one that is (or rather ought to be) shared by all attentive and intelligent readers. Describing in careful detail the slow-motion progress of a hypothetical reader through the text, such "objective" or receptive reader-response criticism may consider these kinds of questions: What expectations does the text create? What happens to those expectations? (Are they met, undermined, exploited, transformed, denied?) What literary conventions does the text employ to affect the reader? How, in other words, does the text shape the reader's response?

Although these two versions of reader-response criticism are being presented as oppositions, flip sides of a single coin, it may be more accurate and helpful to see them in terms of a progression. Reader-response critics unavoidably must use their own personal responses as a starting point for talking about how the ideal, or implied, or common reader responds; but the close examination of such "ideal" responses would seem inevitably to reveal some personal and subjective features.

At this point, before we get any deeper into the question of whether reader-response criticism is unavoidably subjective, let's see how the theory applies to our passage.

The following essay tries to present a record of my movement through this passage. It was fairly easy and fun to write because I simply read through the passage slowly and asked myself, "Okay, how am I responding now? What does this make me think? What am I expecting next?" Although I decided that the passage was continually surprising me, I would not argue that surprise is the only or the correct response: I might have focused on the passage's humor, on a pervading sense of doom, or something else. That's the beauty of reader-response criticism: different responses. As a piece of reader-response criticism, this essay strives to be neither rabidly subjective nor dogmatically objective. I focus on my personal response, but I also try to play the reader's role that I believe Gill has imagined. I quote the text repeatedly, trying to show my reader exactly what I'm responding to.

The Reader's Surprise in an Excerpt from Here at *The New Yorker*

Beginning with its first sentence, the story of the buried dangling modifier in Brendan Gill's *Here at The New Yorker* is continually surprising, setting up expectations and then knocking them down. Gill begins the first sentence with "When I started at *The New Yorker*," and I naturally expect him to talk about how nervous and insecure he was starting off at one of the largest and most famous magazines in the world. Instead, Gill refers to his "unshakable confidence." The third sentence begins with "After almost forty years," leading me to expect some explanation of how his joy at the magazine has grown. But forty years of experience, it turns out, have not developed Gill's confidence and happiness. Instead, his "assurance is less than it was." How, I must wonder, has he managed to work there for forty years and yet grow less confident?

Expecting Gill to explain the oddity of his deteriorating confidence, I find, surprisingly, that such an effect "is a commonplace at the magazine," a "tradition" even. Since the loss of confidence occurs for everyone, we might then expect that *The New Yorker* staff sticks together, sharing insecurities and supporting each other. Such is hardly the case, as Gill continues to surprise me by tracing one imaginary writer's loss of confidence to the point of what appears to be a nervous breakdown. The writer, who is said to have "made a name for himself in the world," is reduced to weeping on his blotter and trying to revise his name. Such is not what I expect from a famous writer.

   Given this tradition of disaster, it seems clear to me that Gardner Botsford is appearing in the third paragraph to star in the story of Gill's own downfall. Botsford points to a major error Gill has made, and Gill's assertion that he "boldly challenged" the allegation seems to set him up for a major humiliation. "Unshakable" confidence and bold challenges certainly seem unwarranted in the atmosphere of *The New Yorker*. But, once more, Gill crosses me up and provides a story of triumph. Rather than undermining his confidence, which is what everything in the story suggests will happen, Botsford becomes Gill's champion. "The sentence stands," he says, as the last reversal provides a happy ending.

Deconstructive Criticism

Think, for starters, of deconstructive criticism as the mirror image of New Criticism: whereas New Criticism aims to reveal the coherence and unity of the work, deconstruction aims to expose the gaps, the incoherences, the contradictions of the text. Deconstructive critics assume these gaps are present because of what they assume about the nature of language. Specifically, they notice that language makes meaning by oppositions: we know what "good" means because it is the opposite of "bad"; "tired" means something to us because it is the opposite of "rested." So words make sense because of their relationship *to other words,* not because of any "natural" grounding in reality. Although we may like to think "bad" and "rested" refer to something solid and real, they don't. "Bad" has come to mean "good" in certain contexts. It could come to mean "blue," or "hungry," or anything. "Rested" with regard to a fighter pilot during combat may mean "having had three hours of sleep in the last twenty-four." Meaning is relative and relational.

   Deconstruction aims (among other things) to remind us of the arbitrary and unstable nature of language by taking texts apart—undoing them until we see how a text inevitably contradicts itself, containing traces of its opposite or "other." Any effort to explain deconstruction is therefore doomed according to the theory itself. Any effort to say *anything,* in fact, must go astray. Such an assumption could be dismaying, but many deconstructive critics have chosen to adopt a mischievously comic and even shocking stance. Although deconstructive criticism can be very difficult to read (perhaps as an illustration of how language eventually fails?), it can also be amusing and engaging.

   Thus, deconstructing a text calls for careful reading and a bit of creativity, but it's often revealing and even fun. One way to think of your goal as a deconstructive

critic is that you're trying to turn the text against itself. For instance, Botsford's concluding decision, "The sentence stands," may appear to be reassuring. Here is a case
where a writer makes a mistake, but the mistake turns out to be okay. If we were to
press this reading, however, asking if the text might say something other than what
it appears to say, we may begin to move into the realm of deconstruction. If you are
a student in a writing-about-literature class, Gill's passage may be only superficially
comforting. If a writer at *The New Yorker* can't always tell whether a sentence is
right or wrong—if in fact the rules of writing are so complex that not even three
people in America "can set down a simple declarative sentence correctly"—then
how is a college student to feel? If a grown man and an established writer is weeping onto his desk blotter and considering revising his name, then how can the ordinary student hope to write an error-free paper—especially when the rules seem to
apply in one case and not in another, and the rules for determining such exceptions
don't seem to exist but are instead invented and applied by those who happen to
be in charge? Writing becomes a nightmare.

In fact, Botsford's "reassuring" vindication is deceptive, for he does not actually
say that sometimes right is wrong and wrong is right. He only says that sometimes
"right is wrong." Isn't wrong also usually wrong? But Botsford's apparent reversal of
the dismantling of authors at *The New Yorker* is finally ambiguous, since we never
know if the writer is ever correct, no matter what he does: "The sentence stands"
indeed, but it stands with its error intact, a monument to Gill's inability to correct it
and to the inevitable errors of writing. A monument to the way language masters us.

Although deconstructive critics may well deal with obviously major features of a
text, like its ending, they may also choose some marginal element of the text and vigorously explore its oppositions, reversals, and ambiguities. In fact, for some critics,
deconstruction is simply a name for "close reading" of an especially rigorous kind. The
deconstructive critic, for example, might well decide to concentrate on the assertion
that because of the editors' merciless correction, "the piece will be much improved." A
New Critic would not be very likely to consider this assertion central, the key to the
passage. But a deconstructive critic might. Here is what happened when I turned
around the idea that "the piece will be much improved" and questioned it.

"The Sentence Stands" Triumphant:
A Deconstructive Reading

Gill's anecdote clearly sets the world's writers against
the editors, and the latter control the game. The editors
and their accomplices, the checkers and copy editors, get to
say what is wrong. They get to dig the "yawning pit" in
front of the helpless writer's desk; they determine the
"tiny elect" who can write correctly; they make the scores
and hundreds of "hen-tracks" on the writer's manuscript,
which serve as testimony to the incompetence of writers, the
near-impossibility of writing, and the arbitrary power of
the editor.

To be sure, it is acknowledged that these editorial
assaults upon the writer serve their purpose, for "thanks to
the hen-tracks and their consequences, the piece will be
much improved." But the cost is terrible. Not only is the

writer unable to write his own name with any confidence; he has become a "poor devil," outside "the elect." In delivering his writing over to the editors, conceding their dominance, the writer inevitably places his own identity, perhaps even his very soul, in jeopardy. Thus, the cry, "oh Christ!" comes to be an invocation to the only power who can save the writer from the devil and the editor's destructive forces.

In fact, this story of the errors of writing actually reveals that the kingdom of editors is based upon a lie: it simply is not true, despite the beleaguered writer's admission under torture, that "the piece will be much improved" by editorial intervention. Miss Gould's enormous grammatical lore does not improve the piece at all; her effort nearly made it "worse." And Botsford's contribution involves simply leaving the piece as it was written—a strange method of improvement. This instance, in other words, suggests that the writer need not approach falling apart in order to compose his writing.

At the same time, Gill can never again become like the gill-less dolphin of the first paragraph, confidently "diving skyward," because the dangling modifier remains: it is a part of the sea of language the author cannot leave. In the end, both writer and editor are defeated by their inability to control their language. The status of the writer at *The New Yorker* becomes a paradigm for the alarming status of writing itself: deceptive, mute, and intractable, "the sentence stands," neither improved nor made worse, standing really for nothing.

Biographical, Historical, and New Historical Criticism

Biographical and historical critics begin from the commonsensical notion that there is certainly something "outside the text" and that these biographical and historical facts help us to make sense of literature. Biographical and historical critics have at least two compelling reasons to exist. First, such criticism is often fascinating. We want to know what authors were like as persons, what kinds of lives they led, even if such information doesn't directly help us understand their works—although often it does. Second, we cannot take for granted that we know what authors might reasonably expect their initial audiences to know. By reconstructing the past, understanding the historical context of a work, we're able to see more clearly through the lens of the author's time.

Biographical and historical criticism thus seeks rather direct connections between authors and works, between historical events and works: this happened, which affected this, which affected that. New historical criticism starts from a different (a new) view of history, one much more compatible with Jacques Derrida's assertion that "there is nothing outside the text." Historical events, new historicists observe, are nothing more than texts now. Any event has meaning because of its place within a system of meaning. Rather than moving through time, showing us how one thing led to another, new historicists are more likely to take a slice of time and analyze it as a system, studying the relationship of one thing to another. If you think of history as a movie, biographical and historical critics watch the movie in the usual fashion, trying to figure out the plot, keeping track of the characters. A new historical critic may select one frame of the film, carefully analyzing minute details, and then compare that frame to another one ten minutes later, showing the radical differences between the two. Whereas traditional historians see connections, new historians see ruptures and revolutions.

Let's look briefly at the way that history can be used to write about literature by employing a biographical stance.

On Brendan Gill's Career and an Excerpt from Here at The New Yorker

This passage from Brendan Gill's *Here at The New Yorker* is a kind of meditation on his own career. Gill begins with confidence yet seems to deteriorate, like everyone else who writes at the magazine, into profound self-doubt. According to the entry on Gill in *Contemporary Authors,* he started his career at *The New Yorker* in 1936—"almost forty years ago," as he says in the passage, published in 1975. Thus, his "unshakable" optimism seems even more remarkable for arising in the midst of the Depression, with failure and fear of failure rampant all around him.

When Gill begins to tell in detail how his "assurance is less than it was," he shifts to third person, seemingly illustrating his own fortunes at the same time that he shows us everyone else's. It is not, however, Gill who has his head on the blotter in the second paragraph, but the hypothetical writer. Some investigation into Gill's life suggests, in fact, that this hypothetical writer does not stand for Gill, even though that may seem at first to be the case. Gill only says "my assurance is less than it was"; he doesn't say "I was reduced to tears."

Elsewhere in *Here at The New Yorker,* Gill writes, "I am always so ready to take a favorable view of my powers that even when I am caught out and made a fool of, I manage to twist this circumstance about until it becomes a proof of how exceptional I am" (62). This statement fits the story of the dangling modifier nicely. Although Gill says he is humiliated by his error, such a reaction seems unreasonable and unlikely. He does manage to twist his error around to be "a proof" of his "exceptional" ability: his error is an exception, a correct error. Gill's use of "humiliating" thus appears, especially in light of this other statement, to be an exaggeration for comic effect.

Another comment by Gill, reflecting on his career, further suggests that his story of profound self-doubt and

```
       humiliation is not to be taken literally: "I started out at
       the place where I wanted most to be and with much pleasure
       and very little labor have remained here since"(1). The
       writer with "hundreds" of "hen-tracks of inquiry," endlessly
       revising even his name, does not seem to be experiencing
       "much pleasure" or "very little labor." Gill's
       autobiographical "Foreword" to A New York Life also
       indicates that his troubles in the passage under
       consideration are largely for effect. For one thing, Gill
       explains in the "Foreword" how the metaphorical nature of
       language so delighted him as a child that he perceived at
       age "five or six" that he would be a writer. He was thrilled
       to find, he says, that the "ladyfingers" his mother served
       weren't really ladies' fingers. Gill's real outlook, as he
       presents it, seems more like that of the dolphin in his
       opening paragraph than that of the poor anxiety-driven
       writer. Reference to Gill's life thus emphasizes for us the
       hypothetical (not historical) and comic (not tragic) nature
       of the writer's struggles in the passage.
```

Psychological Criticism

Anyone whose writing is evaluated will be intrigued by what Gill's passage implies about the psychological effects of criticism. You too may have felt at some point the discomfort of "pencilled hen-tracks of inquiry, suggestion, and correction." The passage provides a good opportunity to consider how such feelings arise and what purpose, if any, they serve. You don't, in other words, have to be a psychologist in order to do psychological criticism. Common sense and an interest in human thinking and behavior are the only essentials.

Still, psychological concepts can be valuable and stimulating in writing about literature. Take, for instance, the idea put forward by Sigmund Freud that creative writing is like dreaming: both allow wishes or fears to be fulfilled that would otherwise be suppressed. A desire or a fear too powerful to be confronted directly can be disguised by the unconscious and expressed by the author or dreamer, Freud said. One possible task of the psychological critic, then, like the psychologist, would be to decode what is being disguised. The critic may make educated guesses about what has been repressed and transformed by the author, or by characters, or even by other readers.

Another useful psychological concept is the idea that there are basic patterns of human development, even though everyone's formative history is different in particulars. One of the most famous and controversial of these developmental concepts is Freud's idea of the Oedipus complex. In Greek myth, Oedipus was the man who unknowingly murdered his father and married his mother. For Freud, this myth depicted the infantile desire experienced by all little boys, who want to see the mother as the principal object of their affections and resent sharing her with the father. The Oedipus complex comes about when this sensual desire for the mother is not suppressed. And the vehicle for this suppression, Freud argued, is the young boy's recognition that the father is more powerful. Rather than lose his capability for pleasure, the boy pulls back from his focus on the mother and eventually turns his desires elsewhere. At its most instinctual level, Freud maintained, the threat to the boy's sexuality is perceived as a threat to that which determines his sex: it is ultimately a fear of castration that motivates the boy's withdrawal.

Although many of Freud's ideas, including the Oedipus complex, have been vigorously challenged or revised, his work did form the basis for modern psychology. Many of his ideas are so well known that any educated person can be expected to be familiar with them. It would be difficult to go very far toward understanding psychology or psychological criticism today without some awareness of Freud, who relied heavily on literature in developing his ideas. By no means, however, should you infer that psychological criticism means Freudian criticism. Other approaches are welcome. But since an introduction to psychology isn't practical here, we will discuss simply how psychological concepts can be applied by using Freud, who is arguably the most important single figure. If you can apply Freud, you can apply Abraham Maslow or Carl Rogers or whomever.

The following essay was developed primarily by applying Freud's central theory of the Oedipus complex to Gill's passage.

A Psychological Reading of Gill's Passage

Writers are brought into the world by editors, and Brendan Gill is thus in a sense the product of Miss Gould and Gardner Botsford's union. Gardner Botsford imposes the grammatical law in a fatherly enough way, but his counterpart, Miss Gould, functions only as a kind of uncreating anti-mother: she is a "Miss," and her notion of "mother's milk" is truly indigestible—"gerunds, predicate nominatives, and passive periphrastic conjugations." She nurtures neither writing nor writer.

But, at the same time, the well-being of the writers at *The New Yorker* depends on her approval because, like Gill, they have accepted the criterion of correctness as the law of the father. Miss Gould imposes that law to the letter, undermining the writer's self-esteem until finally his very identity is threatened, plunging him into such "self-doubt" that his name is called into question. He may then become an orphan; his work may be abandoned.

In fact, the source of the writer's neurotic breakdown seems to be the linking of self to writing. Although the many corrections are imprinted upon the paper, Gill shifts them to the writer and transforms them from "pencilled hentracks" into stings. It is not, as we might suppose, the particular work that may be attacked so much that it dies, but rather *the writer* who may be "stung to death by an army of gnats." Gnats do not, so far as I know anyway, have stingers; they bite. The displacement here, one might argue, is the result of the writer's sense of personal vulnerability, making the threat more plausible since being bitten to death by gnats sounds absurd, while being stung is more ominous.

The more serious threat to Gill's identity is posed by Botsford, his editor and symbolic father. Botsford enters the scene with Gill's review "in his hand." Part of the review has been illegally "buried" and may subsequently be removed. This threat to Gill's writing is a disguised fear of castration because the writer identifies with his writing. The writer's identity, his name, is crucial to his potency. His name is the key to his ability to reproduce and promulgate himself. Yet, his name "looks as if it could stand some working on."

Gill recognizes then that his editorial parent may correct and improve his "piece," but the cost may be terrible, for the piece may be taken over by the authorities who control the emissions of his pen. Gill's image for what he has lost, the dolphin, thus becomes a rather blatant phallic symbol, reemerging as the pen (the grammatical penis) that the "dumb" writer loses. In other words, the writer must give up his "piece" to be published, to survive as a writer, but he is no longer the writer.

We now may see the psychological fittingness of the error Miss Gould finds: it is a structure that is "dangling." The writer may see his own fate in the sentence that sticks out, for it has suddenly "assumed the female gender." The writer's castration anxiety emerges here: he has desired to please Miss Gould, but focusing on grammar and correctness will render him impotent and emasculated. Thus, Gill's story works to resolve his Oedipus complex by pointing out the advantages of accepting the values of the father (Botsford) and shifting his desire from Miss Gould to a more appropriate object: the reader. Gill evades symbolic castration. "The sentence stands," the father says, saving the writer's pen(is).

Feminist Criticism

Feminist criticism generally assumes, like reader-response criticism, that a literary work is shaped by our reading of it, and this reading is influenced by our own status, which significantly includes gender, or our attitude toward gender. But, as feminists point out, since the production and reception of literature have been controlled largely by men, the role of gender in reading and writing has been slighted. The interests and achievements of half of the human race have been neglected—or appreciated largely from only one sex's point of view.

You don't have to consider yourself a feminist to benefit from feminist criticism. Simply taking gender into account, regardless of your social and political views, is likely to open your eyes to important works, authors, and issues you would have missed otherwise.

Although it is difficult to generalize, given the diversity and development of feminist criticism in recent decades, there are some basic strategies you can adopt. You'll want to consider the significance of the gender of the author and the characters. You'll want to observe how sexual stereotypes might be reinforced or undermined in the work. How does the work reflect or alter the place of women (and men) in society? Perhaps most powerful, imagine yourself reading the work as a woman. If you happen to be female, this last suggestion may seem easy enough; but feminist critics point out that women have long been taught to read like men or to ignore their own gender. So, reading as a woman, even if you are a woman, may be easier said than done.

I developed the following feminist reading of Gill's passage by noticing references to gender and paying attention to any potential stereotypes.

A Feminist Reading of the Gill Passage

We know not all the writers at *The New Yorker* were men, even during the period Brendan Gill discusses in this passage from *Here at The New Yorker*. When he speaks of "some writer who has made a name for himself in the world," and about the editorial "machinery" that besets "him," Gill is of course referring to writers in the generic sense. One may still assert today, although with less assurance than in 1975, that "himself" and "him" in this passage include "herself" and "her."

Such a claim, that one sexual marker includes its opposite, may seem absurd—as if "white" included "black" or "communist" included "democratic." But the motivations for such a claim are suggested even in this brief passage, for Gill's story not only contains this obvious bias in pronouns, still accepted by some editors and writers; the story also conveys more subtle messages about sexuality and sexual roles.

For example, Miss Gould functions as a familiar stereotype: the finicky spinster, a Grammar Granny, who has devoted her life to "English grammar" and its enforcement. She is a copy editor, subservient to the male editor and writer, and her lack of imagination and taste, as Gill presents them, seem to testify to the wisdom of this power structure.

This division of labor—male/creative, female/menial—is subtly reinforced by the reference to the "hen-tracks" that cover the writer's galley. Petty correction is the realm of the hen, the feminine. But these "*hen*-tracks" (they could not be rooster tracks) are more than aggravating correction; they come to threaten the writer's very identity. In attempting to produce "his copy," the writer is in a sense attempting to reproduce himself. The "glory of creation" is his literary procreation, and thus Miss Gould's effort to remove a particular sentence is a symbolic threat to cut off some more essential part of the writer. It is, after all, a "dangling modifier" that she has located; and this dangling structure is in danger of being fed to the "yawning pit," symbolic of the feminine editing and its excising dangers. Thus, men should fear women, the passage suggests. Do not give women power.

Because Gill's initial image for the writer starting out at the magazine, the dolphin in the sea, derives some of its power from the well-established association of the ocean and the womb, the images of the "yawning" pit, not to mention the poisonous "mother's milk," become more telling. Even the error itself is subtly connected to the feminine, for the problem with the sentence is that part of it has "assumed the female gender." That part, in the context of nagging copy editors who chop up one's prose, can only be a "complaint."

The nonagenarian's complaint itself seems significant: in the mode of feminine busybodies like Miss Gould, she laments not having "enough work to do." Miss Gould, similarly overzealous, has herself done more work than is reasonable, and Botsford's pronouncement that "The sentence stands" returns her to her place, negating her feminine fussiness.

Other Approaches

The critical universe is rich and varied. Lots of other approaches are mentioned below, and might have been featured in this chapter, such as:

- Critical strategies that focus on the economic and class structures involved in literature—usually called Marxist or materialist criticism.
- Critical strategies that highlight the moral, ethical, and religious implications of literature.
- Critical strategies that give special attention to African-American issues, or texts by African Americans—or other ethnic groups and minorities.
- Critical strategies that attend to gay and lesbian concerns, exposing stereotypes, illuminating neglected texts.

Fortunately, it's not necessary to cover every possible critical strategy. Once you understand how theory drives practice—that is, how critical assumptions shape our insights—then you'll be able to evolve your own approach, drawing on various critical moves, inventing your own. Although some readers, sometimes, may be self-consciously employing a particular critical approach, most readers most of the time are focused upon saying something interesting, revealing, useful about a text. Using an ability without thinking about it involves what Michael Polanyi calls a "tacit knowledge" of that capacity. Consider playing the piano, for instance: the performer who is thinking consciously about which notes to play, who is consciously instructing this finger to play that note, and this finger to go there—that's someone who isn't playing adeptly. The performer wants to think about the piece of music as a whole; or rather, the performer in a sense doesn't want to *think* at all: he or she wants *to play*.

As you write about various kinds of literary texts, your goal should be achieving that same sort of tacit awareness of critical strategies: when you are so comfortable with the theories and strategies here that you're not really thinking about them, that's when you'll be able to write about literature most comfortably and effectively. This book will have served its purpose best, in a sense, when you've forgotten about it.

Pianists study the notes and rhythms and fingering techniques in order to forget about them and play the music. It would be silly to say that such preparatory study gets in the way of playing the music. It's the essential preparation. Likewise, your study here in this text—of literary elements, critical theories, traditions, and themes— is not an end in itself. You're making meaning, contributing to the construction and reinvention of our culture in all its harmonies and diversities.

It may sound perhaps as if I am making too much of literature, or your contribution to its study. What difference does it make if you're able to write a more sophisticated analysis of a Shakespearean sonnet or a Keatsian ode or any other sort of text? No mortal can know at this point what difference anything you do or say will make in the world. But will it matter if your life is richer, your understanding more complex and sophisticated, your grasp of literature and culture deeper? Will it matter, indeed, that you are here? I suspect it will matter a great deal to you—and to those around you, too.

3

Literature: Why It Matters

> Spock: "Your use of language has altered since our arrival.
> It is currently laced with, shall I say, more colorful metaphors.
> 'Double dumbass on you!' and so forth."
> Kirk: "You mean the profanity."
> Spock: "Yes."
> Kirk: "That's simply the way they talk here. Nobody pays any attention to you
> unless you swear every other word. You'll find it in all the literature of the period."
> Spock: "For example?"
> Kirk: "The collected works of Jacqueline Susanne.
> The novels of Harold Robbins."
> Spock: "Ah. The giants."
> —From *Star Trek IV: The Voyage Home*

What Isn't Literature?

In writing about anything, it's useful to think about what "the thing" is, but in the case of literature such defining is particularly difficult—but also particularly revealing. "Literature, in the widest sense," as one popular anthology says, "is just about anything written," including even "what you receive in the mail if you send for free information about a weight-reducing plan." That anthology, however, as you might expect, doesn't include any weight-reducing pamphlets—just fiction, poetry, and drama. Another

"Is there a doctor of literature in the house?"

popular anthology begins by saying that literature offers "a unique view of experience, one that has significance beyond the moment." Does this mean that the poem I wrote for my third-grade teacher, which without a doubt offers a unique view, and certainly holds significance for me "beyond the moment," is "literature"? Does it mean that Pope's *Essay on Man*, which offers a rather conventional outlook, taken by Pope from Bolingbroke and other sources, and which seemed to have little enduring significance for most of my students the last time I taught it, is not literature?

Even the commonsense assertion that literature consists of poetry, fiction, and drama seems problematic for at least two reasons. Pope's *Essay on Man,* as you may know, is actually a poem; but what about genuine essays? Are they excluded from "literature"? Some introduction to literature anthologies include essays; some don't. Why? What about biographies? Boswell's great *Life of Johnson* is a mainstay in eighteenth-century literature classes, but few if any any biographical writings appear in introduction to literature anthologies. What about history or science? Is it impossible to produce "literature" in those genres? What if a work that has been admired for years as a historical account, and therefore not literature, suddenly is discovered to be a work of fiction—a work of the imagination, not fact? George Orwell's famous piece, "Shooting an Elephant," has for many years appeared in collections of essays. But some Orwell scholars have recently argued that the essay is actually a work of fiction. It's interesting to think that "Shooting an Elephant," without a single word being changed, could transform from an essay to a short story, from a work of expository prose to "literature."

Here's the second problem with saying that "literature" equals poetry, fiction, and drama: what about really, really bad poetry, fiction, and drama? Greeting card verse looks like poetry on the page; it's published; it even rhymes. Should we study it in literature classes? One could argue that awful poetry ought to be studied somewhere—that more people have probably read greeting cards than have read Milton's *Paradise Lost.* But is it literature?

So perhaps we should say that "literature" means "good" poetry and fiction and drama and sometimes other things. But then the category becomes an argument about quality. Who is to say what the "Literature" of the future (capital "L") will be? It might include, as Kirk and Spock note in this chapter's epigraph, Jacqueline Susanne—or even weight-reducing plans! After all, Shakespeare's plays were once dismissed by the literary establishment as mere popular entertainments.

Some years ago my colleague, the great literary theorist and critic Morse Peckham, was in the Hirschorn Museum of Modern Art admiring a new exhibition when he came upon what he considered to be an extremely witty and stunningly realistic work. Peckham saw, hanging on the wall amid an emotional orgy of angry abstract sculptures and intricate jumbles of color-splashed fabrics, what appeared to be a perfect replica of a red fire extinguisher, ironically commenting, obviously, on the heated artistic frenzy around it, brilliantly taking Andy Warhol's paintings of soup cans a step further, calling into question the line between art and life. But as Peckham looked underneath the work to note the artist's name, he suddenly realized that this work of art wasn't signed; that it had no title card; that in fact it appeared *actually to be a fire extinguisher.* It wasn't art, at least not until Peckham put it in the exhibition. (I do not know how long the index card that Peckham wedged underneath the extinguisher—"Fire Extinguisher" by Morse Peckham— remained there.)

We've managed at this point to sneak up on an insight: Literariness is not in fact a quality strictly within texts but is rather, to some degree, the product of a reader's attention. We are used to calling some things literature, and texts that are formatted in certain ways on the page are expected to be literature—until they prove otherwise. But "Literature" clearly can occur (like "Art") whenever a reader looks at a work as if it is Literature (or Art)—that is, with a certain kind of attentiveness, in other words. If "Literature" is a quality in the reader as much as it is in the text, then perhaps the right question to ask is not "What is literature?" but rather "What kind of attention do people bring to literature?" What do people do when they say "this is literature"? Why do they want to do that? What, in other words, have people said about what they have termed to be "literature"?

Given this shift in the question, we might say provisionally, as a starting point, that "literature" seems to include those works that readers particularly value. Of course, you may particularly value your physics text, but your English teacher probably won't include it on the syllabus in a literature course. Literature, we might say, includes those works that readers particularly value for reasons beyond the information the work conveys. Such works have often been poetry, fiction, and drama—perhaps because those works may more readily lend themselves to a significance beyond a particular time and place—but what readers have wanted to study as "literature" has extended beyond these genres.

If "literature" does consist of works that informed readers believe have enduring value, and that we want to read with particular care, then it is easy to see why literature often seems challenging. It is the richest, most rewarding, most stimulating writing we have. Literature is writing that readers have decided to look at with a certain kind of attentiveness and passion. If a work is simple-minded, obvious, easy to fully comprehend, then it is unlikely to be valued by readers again and again. It may be seen as "literature" in a general sense but not as "Literature" of the sort that is studied by succeeding generations. However, any work, theoretically, could be studied *as if it were literature*. If other readers were to accept that designation, then the work arguably would *be* literature (at least for those readers who take it to be). In theory, then, one might justify studying *anything* in a "literature" class, although in practice certain texts seem to be in the starting lineup again and again. Different critical approaches are, in fact, more likely to encourage the study of one work over another. A feminist critic, for instance, might well be interested in private diaries, or hard-boiled detective stories, because these may reveal something interesting about the construction of gender; whereas a New Critic might find these works artistically lacking in rich ambiguities, and hence less interesting, and turn more often to lyric poetry.

Although this way of defining "literature" (as whatever people view as literature) may seem to confirm your worst fears about the elusiveness if its meaning, isn't every other word actually in the same situation? Even what we may think of as natural categories, like "granite" and "arthropod," are ultimately man-made in the sense that human beings use and adapt the language that creates these categories. It seems reasonable, for instance, to think of all dogs as belonging to a single natural, biological class. But what about wolves? Are they dogs? What about the offspring of a dog and a wolf? Is it a dog? What about a dog that has been genetically altered to look like a turtle, or to grade English papers? Is it still a dog?

The simple truth is that language does not map perfectly onto the world. It is artificial, and it changes as time changes; it even varies from person to person. Although this openness can be more than a little annoying at times, it also offers us tremendous potential for growth and change and enlightenment—and entertainment. Literature, along with everything else within language, is "open" to interpretation. We're always guessing about what someone or something means. Literature indeed often seems to be about how meaning goes astray. Literature is the most fruitful way we continually learn how to make more sense out of our language, how to improve and enrich our guessing, how to learn new tricks, how to rethink the boundaries of our words—including the word "literature."

What Is Literature?

Let's look at the certain kind of thinking that creates a literary work, and see how far we can go with the idea of literature as a kind of behavior. Consider this statement:

> *The play seems out for an almost infinite run.*

Is that literature? What if we add another statement?

> *The play seems out for an almost infinite run.*
> *Don't mind a little thing like the actors fighting.*

Perhaps this is a note, from the business manager of a theatre company, say. Surely it isn't literature, is it? But what if we add two more statements?

> *The play seems out for an almost infinite run.*
> *Don't mind a little thing like the actors fighting.*
> *The only thing I worry about is the sun.*
> *We'll be all right if nothing goes wrong with the lighting.*

In many workshops I have written these lines on a blackboard, one at a time, asking a roomful of students to record their thoughts as each line appears. After the third line, a few students usually notice the run/sun rhyme; and by the fourth line, most of them (but not all) suspect it is a poem. But their way of looking at the lines undergoes a dramatic change when I write something before and after the group of lines:

It Bids Pretty Fair

The play seems out for an almost infinite run.
Don't mind a little thing like the actors fighting.
The only thing I worry about is the sun.
We'll be all right if nothing goes wrong with the lighting.

—Robert Frost

Robert Frost is recognized worldwide as a major poet. Although he was born in San Francisco, he moved to New England at age 11, and his work is often rooted in New England rural life. The winner of four Pulitzer Prizes, Frost had established himself as the leading American poet by the 1920s, and his reputation increased throughout his life.

Now *this* is literature, isn't it? Usually almost all the students will agree that it is; yet one or two may still say it isn't, that it really isn't a poem by Robert Frost. But it really is a poem by Robert Frost; and if a poem by Robert Frost isn't literature, then I don't know what is. And when the students see that the poem actually appears in *The Collected Poems of Robert Frost*, then everyone agrees (sometimes after making sure I haven't somehow sewn that page into the book): it is literature.

Having made that identification, the students invariably look again at the lines, reading them as if they were literature, and they find that the lines do indeed respond to a "literary" reading. Although the lines may seem at first to refer only to a theatre production, there is something a little funny about the speaker's worry over the sun and the lighting. If the play is outdoors, in the sun, it seems a little strange to worry about the lighting—but not unthinkable. "Almost infinite" must be, of course, an exaggeration. Even *Cats* was not infinite. It is not impossible to take these lines literally, at face value; but by granting that they are part of a poem, readers become willing to look for more meaning. And at some point, most readers consider that "the play" might be a reference to life on earth ("all the world's a stage," as Shakespeare says). Human beings, "the actors" in our global drama, do seem always to be fighting somewhere at any given moment, but perhaps this fighting isn't as serious as we think. Maybe we should be worrying about a bigger problem: the "lighting" for our drama, "the sun." The title does say "It Bids Pretty Fair," but when one considers the kinds of problems we would have if something were to happen to the sun, "pretty fair" is pretty terrifying.

But what exactly does the poem suggest that we worry about? Is the sun going to blow up? Burn out? If life is like a play, it may *seem* to be out for "an almost infinite run," but is it? There are no guarantees in the theatre: the producer might get fed up with the whole thing, or interested in something else, and might decide to pull the plug, cutting off the play prematurely. Thus, in only four lines, Frost acutely focuses the literary reader's attention on the fragility, tenuousness, even the helplessness of human life. This little poem puts all of human history into a cosmic perspective, and it seems small and insubstantial—no more than a play, not real or permanent. As one student wrote after contemplating this poem: "Nothing is forever. Not even nothing. Not even forever." The poem's haunting irony is that it conveys this unsettling message in a mostly optimistic package: it bids, after all, pretty fair.

If Frost's four lines become literature in the act of reading them imaginatively, as if they were literature, then what about these four lines?

> Mary had a little lamb.
> Its fleece was white as snow.
> And everywhere that Mary went,
> The lamb was sure to go.

Many people would agree that this isn't truly literature; it's a nursery rhyme—or, more precisely, part of a classic nursery rhyme. Nursery rhymes are not the sort of things we study in literature classes—are they?—because we don't expect them to repay our imaginative reading. We don't expect them to give forth more meaning as we read them more attentively. This is a poem about Mary and a lamb, and that's it. It has a nice sing-song sound, but it doesn't really "mean" much of anything. To do an interpretation of "Mary Had a Little Lamb" would seem weird, wouldn't it? But if "literature" occurs when a reader interacts with a text in a certain way, then it ought to be possible, in theory at least, to adopt a "literary" stance toward any text. What happens if we decide to read this text imaginatively—as if it were literature, as if we expected more meaning to emerge?

Is there any meaning beyond the literal, the surface? Does this poem repay a literary attentiveness? Sure, if we can think it up. How might this poem become more complex, meaning more than it appears at first glance to mean? Could "Mary," for instance, refer to someone other than a little girl? What other Marys are there? We might consider the Mary who appears in another nursery rhyme (the one who's "quite contrary"), or Mary Queen of Scots, but neither really illuminates anything. Any other ideas? There is of course Mary the wife of Joseph, the mother of Jesus. Did she have "a little lamb"? If you know anything of Christian theology, at this point you may be able to see another level of this little poem beginning to open up. Jesus has been traditionally compared to a lamb, and mainstream Christian doctrine teaches that Jesus sacrificed himself to win forgiveness of his followers' sins, much as unblemished lambs and other creatures were sacrificed by the Hebrews in Old Testament times. Being without sin, Jesus is like a lamb whose "fleece was white as snow." The last two lines could then refer to the ever-present Holy Spirit, the continuation of Jesus's presence upon earth after his resurrection. Thus "the lamb" continues to go wherever Mary goes.

This symbolic reading thus gives the poem complexity (it has a hidden meaning) and unity (it conveys basic Christian tenets regarding the Holy Spirit). Such is essentially a New Critical view of the "poem." Another way of thinking about literature, namely as the occasion for a personal response, would produce a different "reading"— like this one, for instance, written by another student:

> This poem is uplifting because it tells us about a faithful pet. The extraordinary lamb with its perfectly white fleece dutifully follows Mary. We need little poems like this to remind us that some things are still good and true. Mary's lamb reminds me that some things are unspoiled and pure, if only in our imaginations.

Or like this one, by yet another student:

> I don't need this poem. I already know that people can't have anything forever. Everything passes away. Even the most faithful, most white lamb in the world, must go off to the slaughter. We see that Mary had the little lamb. It followed her everywhere. But we do not need to ask where the lamb is now. It is gone. Mary had it once, but like everything else in this rotten stinking world, it could not last.

How did two readers arrive at such different interpretations? By taking the poem as the occasion for a subjective response—by performing, in other words, as reader-response critics.

Another critical stance might consider what difference it makes that Mary is (most likely) a female, probably a young girl? (It is possible that a man could be named Mary, and a grown woman could have a little lamb, but social conventions make that less likely.) How then does the poem depict Mary as a female? What does the poem teach female readers about themselves? How might the poem be different if it featured John or Henry? Such questions might lead us to notice that Mary does not have a pit bull, a snake, a lizard, a popgun. She has a lamb—a little lamb. Why? Could it be because lambs are gentle, docile creatures? And doesn't the poem therefore reinforce the idea of girls as gentle and docile, desiring to play with a pet that reflects their own nature? Why is the purity of the lamb's fleece noted? What does that convey to female readers? Perhaps it indirectly conveys to them the value of keeping clean, of not playing rough, of being "pure." And what about the last two lines, praising a mindless fidelity? Doesn't it teach little girls to follow faithfully wherever they are led by *their* masters—while keeping themselves pure and innocent?

Another way of thinking about literature might try to dissect the text, taking it apart to see how it works. It would seem to be obvious that Mary is the favored member here. She *has* the lamb. Yet Mary figures in only two of the lines, while the lamb is mentioned in three. Is the poem about Mary or about the lamb? Two qualities—its whiteness, its faithfulness—are celebrated in the poem, and both belong to the lamb. The poem finds it worth remarking that the lamb follows Mary everywhere. Apparently the lamb could have chosen otherwise. If not, why would the poem mention its faithfulness? So if the lamb can choose where it wishes to go, and it chooses to follow Mary, who is really in charge? Can Mary likewise choose where she wants to go? Or does Mary have to go wherever she has to go? And the lamb freely decides to come along? It is becoming clear that it is unclear what this poem means—from a deconstructive point of view anyway.

Another critical stance might consider the psychology revealed in the poem. Imagine for instance that this rhyme was written by a 48-year-old woman whose 23-year-old daughter has married an accountant and moved across the country. We could speculate that the woman might not want to admit consciously that she would prefer her daughter to be like a lamb, doing everything she says, going everywhere she goes, never getting herself "soiled" in any way. Consciously, the mother wants to give her child freedom. She even wants to get her out of the house. Still, perhaps the poem represents her unconscious desire to think of her daughter as "Mary," a little girl with a pure "little lamb" who will never leave her.

Another kind of literary attentiveness might assert that this rhyme is designed to teach little girls the desirability of ownership. One could argue that there is a hint of class snobbery in the observation that Mary's lamb has fleece as white as snow. The implication is that other lambs with other-colored coats are not as valuable, nor their owners as good. Brown fleece or spotted fleece no doubt would keep someone as warm as all-white fleece. Thus, the racial aspects of the celebration of all-white fleece might become part of the social implication here—if one chooses to make that argument. Alternately, we might argue that the poem refers to an idealistic and rural past when little girls had faithful lambs rather than repetitive wool-spinning or sewing jobs, a time before smokestacks and pollution, a time when a lamb might have white wool. Mary then becomes a symbol for modern industrial culture, which "had" pristine lambs and lost them.

Are the first four lines of "Mary Had a Little Lamb" now a literary work? Reading a work *as if it were literature* doesn't automatically make it literature, anymore than eating dirt *as if it were food* would transform it into cuisine. You could describe the taste and texture of dirt, and various ways of preparing it and presenting it on a plate, but dirt would still be dirt (wouldn't it?). The category "literature" is constructed by a certain kind of behavior, but there is also an element of consensus involved: other readers, it would seem, will have to share the assumption that a work is literature, in order for it to be literature (for other readers). Those works that are generally perceived to be literature, that educated readers generally agree they ought to be familiar with, form what is called "the canon." "The canon" is an ongoing discussion or even argument about what we ought to read. In the past few decades, literary works by women and minorities have increasingly received scholarly attention, and have increasingly been read by all sorts of readers, and have increasingly been included in literature anthologies such as this one.

As you respond or fail to respond to the literary works presented in this text, sharing your reactions with your classmates and your teacher, you're participating in the greater cultural discussion that is ceaselessly determining what we'll read and what we'll ignore; what will be collected and published and studied as literature in the future, and what will sink out of view.

Literature is what speaks to us. Literature is what we choose to think most deeply about. Literature is an important part of what connects us to the past, helps us grasp our present, sparks us to shape the future. We can't pin it down. But it's what awaits you here.

Critical Strategies at Work

4

Read Poetry Creatively: Reader-Response Criticism

> Unless there is a response on the part of somebody,
> there is no significance, no meaning.
>
> —Morse Peckham

Reflection:
The Creative Reader

The meaning of anything is the response to that thing.[1] If there's no response, there's no significance, no meaning. In a sense, then, the reader must create—or try to re-create—the poem. Notice how this idea plays into the following out-of-the-ordinary poem, which is ultimately about poetry, an image of itself, a reflection. It's a poem that tells us how to read a poem.

"By God, for a minute there it suddenly all made sense!"

© The New Yorker Collection 1986 Gahan Wilson from cartoonbank.com. All Rights Reserved.

[1]See Morse Peckham *Explanation and Power: The Control of Human Behavior* (New York: Seabury Press, 1979).

39

DAVID WAGONER (1926–)

This Is a Wonderful Poem

Come at it carefully, don't trust it, that isn't its right name,
It's wearing stolen rags, it's never been washed, its breath
Would look moss-green if it were really breathing,
It won't get out of the way, it stares at you
Out of eyes burnt gray as the sidewalk,   5
Its skin is overcast with colorless dirt,
It has no distinguishing marks, no I.D. cards,
It wants something of yours but hasn't decided
Whether to ask for it or just take it,
There are no policemen, no friendly neighbors,   10
No peacekeeping busybodies to yell for, only this
Thing standing between you and the place you were headed,
You have about thirty seconds to get past it, around it,
Or simply to back away and try to forget it,
It won't take no for an answer: try hitting it first   15
And you'll learn what's trembling in its torn pocket.
Now, what do you want to do about it?

—from *Collected Poems 1956–76*

Poets often talk, as Wagoner does here, as if poems could come to life. Shakespeare, as you may know, concludes one of his most famous sonnets with this couplet: "So long as men can breathe or eyes can see,/ So long lives this, and this gives life to thee." It is a nice thought, but clearly the person being addressed in this poem has not ordered any pizza lately. We do not even know her name, or if the addressee was in fact a woman, or even a real person. Wagoner is, among other things, having fun with this idea of a poem coming to life. Here, the poem becomes a frightening robber, a menacing streetperson, an unknown but troubling presence. Some assertions fit both the act of reading the poem and encountering a frightening person on the street: for instance, "You have about thirty seconds to get past it, around it,/ Or simply to back away and try to forget it." But the contrast between the two situations—reading the poem, encountering a person—is also amusing, as in the assertions that "It won't get out of the way, it stares at you." An unwashed smelly person in stolen rags who won't get out of your way is disturbing, but the poem won't get out of the way, of course, because it's sitting on the page there. It is staring at you only if you imagine that it's staring. A poem can't harm you—well, not in the same sense, at least.

Again, a potential thief who "won't take no for an answer" is one thing. The poem "won't take no" because it is inanimate (it can't), but Wagoner is able to suggest that this poem is going to be troubling us too—as the poem's very first words indicate: "Come at it carefully." The poem has, so it says, a hidden threat: "try hitting it first/ And you'll learn what's trembling in its torn pocket." In the case of the frightening person, this trembling thing in a pocket is, we would fear, a knife, a gun, a blackjack; and this poem, despite its humor, also manages to conjure up a rather vivid scene of urban terror. But what is the corresponding secret of the poem? What is hidden in its pocket? And what does the line mean, "try hitting it first," with regard to the poem? Does that line apply only to the other scenario? How would it be possible to "hit" this poem "first"? How could it possibly "hit" us?

We might decide that the poem is a clever joke, but it can only be pushed so far, and these questions can't be answered. The comparison doesn't work perfectly. We might as well close the book on this poem. But wait: wouldn't closing the book be one way of hitting the poem, in a sense, as the opposite page hits the poem? If we do "hit" it first, what is the trembling secret? Is there a trick here? The poem's tricks, that we should come at carefully, did begin with the title, which tells us "This Is a Wonderful Poem." As we quickly learn, "that isn't its right name, / It's wearing stolen rags." The poem brashly announces "This Is a Wonderful Poem," yet its opening lines say "that isn't its right name." But, if this is a wonderfully clever and interesting poem, then is it really wearing the wrong name? And here, one might argue, is how the poem "hits" its readers, as we suddenly realize how it puts us on the spot. If we believe its title, then we must disagree with its opening lines: if we put it away without getting the joke of its title, without realizing the way the poem puts us on the spot, is it a wonderful poem or not? As the poem amusingly asks in the end, "What do you want to do about it?"

For readers who believe that poems exist only when someone responds, Wagoner's poem is simply more explicit about the nature of poetry than most poems. All poems, reader-response critics would say, put us on the spot, accosting us, trying to make us have some response. They get between us and some other place we were headed; they ask us to rethink our situation. Literature asks us "what are you going to do about it?" in the hopes that our answer will be: "respond."

Ecology is that branch of biology that deals with the responses of living things to the world around them; ecology studies the interactions of organisms and their environments. Without environments, life cannot exist. An ecology of reading would examine the interactions of texts and their readers: without readers (the environments texts inhabit), literature doesn't exist. This chapter thus aims to introduce you to an ecology of reading—to an understanding of how texts and readers interact, according to one particular critical approach: reader-response criticism. The ecological theme also works for this chapter, as you'll also notice, because the poems all deal in some way with nature and its significance.

Strategies: Using Reader-Response Criticism

Reader-response criticism is among the easiest things in the world to do. You read a work, and you respond. There are people who will give you advice on how to breathe and how to walk, and it turns out in fact that some easy and natural things can be done even better with some guidance. This "Strategies" section offers some guidance on how to respond, and how to evolve responses to literature into interesting and illuminating essays. The best way to proceed will be to observe some real readers interacting with a particular poem.

The poem below is mysterious and challenging enough to allow you to see how one might develop a response. On a first reading, you may find this poem to be crystal-clear; or it may leave you puzzled, even dazed. The important thing is to have a process for working through this initial response and getting to whatever sort of completed response you need—whether that is a few sentences or a full-fledged essay. I urge you to articulate *some response,* in a reading notebook, in the margins, on a napkin: reacting to a work *creates* the meaning of that work (for you, for now).

This poem first appeared in *The New Yorker,* a popular and influential magazine aimed at relatively sophisticated readers. If you're a college-educated reader (or in the process of becoming one), then you're in (or aspiring to be in) this community. The poetry editor at that magazine apparently believed that a substantial audience would have a favorable response to this poem. Let's see what you think. Read it carefully and patiently; don't expect that everything will make perfect sense the first or the fifth time through the poem. Think about whatever is puzzling, and enjoy the speculation.

JOHN BURNSIDE (1955–)

The Sand Merchant's Wife

There is a logic in the sea
that fishes understand,
a pattern that rests in the spine, a gloved assent
revealed by the sweep and turn
of the changing tide,   5

and air is a river of language,
skylarks and barn owls
calling and spinning aside,
a blue domain of semaphore and noise
drifting through rain,   10
leached through our faint receivers. From the first,

our element was stone:
it lay beneath us like a darker form
of gravity, a drift we could not mine,
the local shifts and flickers in the rock,   15
stitches and hair streaks no one could read or interpret,
and we were its echoes, rendered for the light,
moving, being, wreathed in love and fear,
that stillness at the center of our house
a shape the wind revealed by the purest chance   20
then covered, like the secret veins and seams
that harden in the bloodlines of our children.

[1995]

Inventing

It seems sensible to say that before you can respond to a poem, you need to become familiar with it, to have some clear idea what it is saying. The truth is often stranger than what is sensible, however; and you are likely to find that things you don't understand will become clearer as you begin to respond. The trick is to avoid becoming locked into your first reaction, but rather to continue to read and reread the poem, letting your response evolve. Give the poem an environment in your head in which a response can grow. You may, in fact, never understand all of a particular poem, but you can still respond to ambiguity and obscurity. And you can enjoy a poem even if you're not sure you understand it completely. One of the most appealing things about reader-response criticism is precisely this emphasis on response rather than meaning. Simply articulating what is unclear is often quite valuable.

Indeed, some of your favorite poems may include parts that don't quite make sense to you, yet keep calling you back to read and contemplate them again. Even very experienced and accomplished readers don't immediately or even eventually comprehend every aspect of every poem they read.

To get you started thinking about how to develop a response to a poem, look over the following initial reactions, each one written by someone who had read the poem several times:

Response by Dorothy Williams:

Hard poem. But interesting. Much I don't get. I like the start of the poem, beginning in the sea. I have always felt some kind of really primitive connection with the ocean, as if it really is the first home of all life, and my first home too somehow. I know other people who also feel this connection to the ocean and to water, but it's really strong with me. The lines about "the sweep and turn/ of the changing tide" are especially good. I can see the ocean moving around, almost feel it, as if I'm swimming down in it. But "gloved assent" doesn't hold any meaning for me. What does he mean by "a pattern that rests in the spine"? Maybe that will mean something by the end, as I think about it.

"Leached" is an interesting word. But how's it connected to the rest of the poem? With "local shifts and flickers in the rock," I'm starting to think the poem has something to do with an archeological dig. No, maybe not. That doesn't seem to work with the first two parts. The last section is really interesting. There is something moving about the last lines: "harden in the bloodlines of our children" seems really deep, profound, especially in light of the grand view of the sea and the air. There's some kind of monumental statement being made here. What, I don't know.

"Wreathed in love and fear" seems like a phrase the poet had in a notebook somewhere and wanted to use in a poem. It doesn't seem to fit here, does it? For some reason I keep thinking there is an allusion to some archeological dig after all? I don't know why. Oh, I see now that "gloved assent" means "gloved agreement" or "gloved approval"; I was thinking of "ascent," as if the fish rose up in the water with gloves on. No wonder it didn't make sense. It doesn't make much more sense now, though, really. The line just slides by without making sense to me. Like a fish! I'm not sure why I like this poem since it makes so little sense to me. Help!

Response by Cindy Connell:

The poem talks about people and their relationship with nature. In the beginning, the poet talks about fish and about the sea, yet he imposes human judgment on the sea— "there is a logic," he says. As the poem progresses, the narrator refers to "our" element and "our" house. I think the central line in the poem is "and we were its echoes, rendered for the light." I think the poem is relating human life to sand—our lives are "a shape the wind revealed by purest chance." Nature shapes everything; human beings can only be bought and sold by the sand merchant, and they are at the mercy of the sand merchant's wife—her whims and desires. There is a logic, but we cannot read it or interpret it. I agree with this idea.

Response by Jamie Smith:

The first thing that caught my attention in this poem is that it is divided into four major parts. The first stanza describes the sea. The speaker states that there is a "logic in the sea/ that fishes understand." The fishes understand their environment for they are accustomed to it. It is in the fishes' nature, and by instinct that the fish lives in his ocean environment.

The second stanza concerns the sky. The speaker describes the "air as a river of language." The birds know how to communicate with one another through their own instinctive language that fills the air with noise.

The third stanza is concerned with stone. The word "stone" reminds me of the "foundation," so I interpret this stanza as describing the foundation for life. The speaker mentions "stitches and hair streaks no one could read or interpret." Are these the ancient pictographs and early forms of writing that have been preserved in the stone over the centuries? In the past two stanzas, the speaker has described the language of birds and the instincts in fish. Both the fish and birds understand one another and communicate effectively with one another because there is "a pattern that rests in the spine" (i.e. they instinctively know how to communicate). But humans do not understand their language. Nor do we understand the languages of the most ancient civilizations.

However, in the fourth stanza the speaker states, "and we were its echoes rendered for the light." We are the echoes of the past? Time has moved on. The speaker goes on to say that the center of the house is "a shape the wind revealed by purest chance." Is the speaker implying that we exist only by chance, and that we like the birds only understand each other by chance? The speaker then goes on to say that the house is covered "like the secret veins and seams/ that harden in the bloodlines of our children."

This concluding statement provokes many thoughts in my head. So far the speaker has described the language of nature (instinct) and the element of stone (or foundation). These three things are building blocks needed for a civilization to occur. When a civilization becomes "covered," one can only learn from the past civilization by examining the artifacts and written documents. But what if one cannot understand the past because of "the stitches and hair streaks no one could read or interpret"? If this happens the children will not be able to know their past. If the bloodlines of the children harden, does this mean that they no longer care or want to know of their ancestors?

The title of this poem is a little strange. Why did the author choose this title? At the end of the poem, the speaker does say "our house," so perhaps he is referring to his wife and he is a sand merchant. Is that someone who deals in sand? Maybe there is a connection between a sand merchant and history. When did sand merchants first begin? Today we can buy sand for a sandbox, or for landscaping, or to make concrete. Was sand for sale in the past?

How are these three readers responding? What is each one trying to do with the poem? And how (to come to our purpose here) might these responses be developed into essays?

Dorothy's goal in responding seems pretty clear-cut: to point out what she likes, what she finds "interesting"; and also to point out what she doesn't understand, and therefore (we assume) does not like. The two responses (interesting versus confusing; like versus don't like) seem to be closely related: even when Dorothy finds something interesting ("leached" and the last section, for instance), she continues to wonder about its meaning (How is "leached" related to the poem? How does "wreathed in love and fear" work in the last section?). Like most readers, Dorothy seems to enjoy thinking about suggestive and not-immediately-clear statements; it is only when these statements seem completely obscure that she is not pleased or not "interested." She likes what she can decipher.

For Cindy, the main task seems to be finding the poem's center of gravity: what is it really about? As her response emerges, she tries out a number of different themes, formulating and reformulating: The poem, she says first, is "about people and their relationship with nature"; then, she theorizes that the "central line" in the poem is "and we were its echoes, rendered for the light"; next she considers that "the poem is relating human life to sand"; finally she surmises that the poem is really about how human beings are "at the mercy of the sand merchant's wife—her whims and desires."

Jamie's goal in responding is clearly different from Dorothy's or Cindy's: rather than evaluating what she likes and understands, or looking for the poem's core meaning, she is interested in the structure of the poem—how many parts it has, and what each one is concerned with. She moves through the poem, section by section, thinking about the details of the poem as it unfolds.

There is nothing wrong with the initial goals of these readers. It's true that we don't get much sense of how the poem affects Jamie or Cindy, but neither one is really focused on conveying that information. In Dorothy's response, we don't get much sense of why some parts are interesting to her and why others are not clear. She does not seem to be especially focused upon informing her reader. All three of these readers, as you'll see in a moment, can enrich their engagements with "The Sand Merchant's Wife" by drawing on reader-response criticism.

Varieties of Reader Response   So far, we've approached reader-response criticism as if it were a single entity. Actually, there are different kinds: At one end of the spectrum, an "associative" version of reader-response criticism encourages the reader to use the poem as the inspiration or starting point for self-expression. The reader asks, "What does this poem remind me of, or suggest to me?" The initial goals of these readers are reasonable and useful. At the other end of the spectrum, the "receptive" version of reader-response criticism assumes that the reader should try to describe how the poem is supposed to affect any careful, informed reader. In saying how a poem ought to be received, receptive reader-response criticism does suggest that some responses are off-target, eccentric, even wrong. Some descriptions of how readers should react may be more plausible than others, at least from this receptive perspective.

In the middle, the "interactive" version of reader-response aims to work somewhere between personal self-expression, on the one hand, and a description of how all readers should respond, on the other hand—thus balancing the role of the reader and the text. The interactive reader may make personal connections to the poem, but these won't veer entirely away from the poem, with the reader's attention turning ultimately to self-expression; the interactive reader may attend carefully to how the poem is designed to affect its readers, without insisting that every reader should have the same response.

Shaping

The most obvious way to develop Dorothy's essay, as her teacher indicated, would be to elaborate on why some parts of the poem were interesting, and also to try to make some sense of the unclear parts—an interactive version of reader-response strategies, in other words. One technique involves simply highlighting those words and phrases that seem especially significant, interesting, or troubling, and then brainstorming about them. It's often easier to think through something on paper, in a sense, rather than keeping everything in one's head. Here is Dorothy's application of that strategy, aimed at providing materials to develop her first response.

The Sand Merchant's Wife

There is a logic in the sea
that fishes understand,
a pattern that rests in the spine, a gloved assent
revealed by the sweep and turn
of the changing tide,   5

and air is a river of language,
skylarks and barn owls
calling and spinning aside,
a blue domain of semaphore and noise
drifting through rain,   10
leached through our faint receivers. From the first,

our element was stone:
it lay beneath us like a darker form
of gravity, a drift we could not mine,
the local shifts and flickers in the rock,   15
stitches and hair streaks no one could read or interpret,

and we were its echoes, rendered for the light,
moving, being, wreathed in love and fear,
that stillness at the center of our house
a shape the wind revealed by the purest chance   20
then covered, like the secret veins and seams
that harden in the bloodlines of our children.

- "a pattern that rests in the spine"—okay, what's the pattern resting in the spine? Well, the pattern, the logic in the sea, the pattern that the fishes understand, is not a human kind of logic, something conscious in the brain. Instead, it is a logic the fish have in their spine, part of their bodies, not something they think about. They "understand" it without thinking about it. It's in the spine, not the brain. That makes sense.
- "a gloved assent"—what can "assent" refer to here? I can only think that it substitutes for "pattern," which substitutes for "logic." So the logic, the pattern, is "gloved," and it is a kind of agreement. What is there that is around the logic or pattern? If the fish's spine contains the pattern, then the fish itself is the glove. Okay. But the pattern is not only in the spine; it is also in the sea, as the first line says. So the glove could be the ocean too? At any rate, the "assent," the saying of "yes," is hidden by the glove, whatever it is. The logic is hidden, revealed only by the tide.
- "a blue domain of semaphore and noise"—the semaphore, a signaling system (my dictionary says), makes sense of the air, which is a river of language. Like the sea and its logic, the air also is meaningful. The logic of the sea is hidden, and revealed only by the tide. The language of the air is also hidden, as it drifts through the rain, leaching or seeping into human awareness. Like the logic of the sea, we do not clearly see the air's language, but skylarks and barn owls do. Their spinning in the air, and the drifting, reminds me of the "sweep and turn of the changing tide."
- "drift"—the idea of drifting comes across in all three parts, relating to sea, air, and stone. You think of drift in the sea and the air, but not in stone. Maybe geologists do, but I do not. The whole poem does have some kind of scientific quality.
- "stitches and hair streaks"—"stitches" is like "gloved." It is odd. I think of clothing and stitches holding them together. The idea of hair streaks in the stone is weird also. Stone is our element, the poem says, but in a way human elements can be seen in the stone, if it has hair streaks.
- "echoes"—we are echoes of the stone, but the hair streaks in the stone are a kind of echo of us.
- "that stillness at the center of our house"—everything in the poem is seen to be in motion, even the stone. The exception is the "stillness at the center of our house," which is, I think, "love and fear." The stillness could be the echoes, but it makes more sense as love and fear, to me.
- "a shape the wind revealed"—in every element, sea, air, stone, something is revealed faintly, in a glimpse: in the sea, a gloved assent (a pattern, a logic) is revealed by the tide's motion; in the sky, the air's river of language, the blue domain of semaphore and noise, is leached to us; in our realm, the realm of stone, it is the love and fear, the

stillness, that is momentarily seen and then "covered." Is the element of stone different from or similar to the elements of sea and air? Well, I do not know. Maybe it is different, because the fish understand the sea's logic, and the birds fly in a river of language (air makes sense to them), but "no one could read or interpret" the signs in the rock. This difference seems important to me. Maybe it is the key to the poem; maybe that is what I like about it—the way it preserves the mystery of human life, while suggesting that animals are more insightful than we might think.

- "like the secret veins and seams"—the reference to "seams" here might connect to the glove and the stitches before. But I do not see how. It is funny how such natural things are described in terms of human clothing, which just seems to emphasize how unnatural our relationship with nature is.
- "bloodlines of our children"—"bloodlines" could refer to the arteries and veins of the children, but that would be strange, especially since the poem would then say that "the secret veins harden in the veins." "Bloodlines" suggests instead here "ancestry," "family." So, the love and fear, which is "that stillness at the center of our house," hardens—much like stone. We only glimpse it, and then it is gone—hardened, buried, hidden, like the logic of the sea, which is "gloved" within the fishes' spines; or merely "leached" to us, like the language of the air. Perhaps we are not so different from the fish and the birds: whereas the sea's logic "rests in the spine" of the fish, our center of stillness (love and fear) is shown to us by the wind and "by purest chance," and then hardens "in the bloodlines." I see that it is the logic in the stone itself that "no one could read or interpret." But we are the "echoes" of the stone; we are "rendered for the light," so maybe that's why the logic or language of stone can be revealed, through us.
- "The Sand Merchant's Wife"—Is there a connection between stone and sand? Is it related to Pound's "The River Merchant's Wife"? I'll see.

Drafting

We'll limit ourselves here to following how Dorothy's ideas become an essay, since roughly the same process was followed by all three writers, and also because Dorothy's response is especially interesting. Jamie, to evolve her essay, decided to adopt a more receptive stance, and to attempt to say what effect Burnside tries to create in each section of the poem. Cindy elected to work on pinning down the poem's main point, and then to meditate on its value—with some further references to the poem.

In her comments on the poem's closing lines, Dorothy seems to be approaching an insight, a main idea that might be used to structure an essay. What seems "most important," she says at first, as she works through the poem's words and phrases, is the idea that the element of stone is different from the sea and the air. While the inhabitants of the air and sea understand the logic and language of their "element," the inhabitants of the realm of stone do not understand its "stitches and hair streaks." But this difference, Dorothy goes on to see, is dissolved by the wind and by chance, which reveal the "echoes" of the stone—our "love and fear." We cannot "read" the stone, but we can see its echo.

Dorothy might have continued to respond freely to the poem, or to meditate on various words and phrases, but she decided at this point she was ready to sketch out an essay. Sketching out an essay is a bit like making an outline, except looser: you don't have to fill in the details, and you don't have to stick to the sketch. A sketch is just a listing of the main points you think you want to make—a way of thinking through the essay before you actually try to write it.

In adopting an interactive stance, Dorothy's goal was to describe her own personal response to the poem, taking care to show that her response was in fact based on something in the poem (and not just her own imagination). She felt she had a pretty good understanding of the poem—as good as she was likely to get. Up to this point, she had been working so hard to make the poem mean something that she really had not thought much about her response. In this first groping toward an essay, Dorothy starts to think about how the poem affects her, putting her insights in the form of what the poem says, followed by her response:

1. The poem says: Fish understand the sea's logic.
1a. My response: It is reassuring to think that there is a logic in the sea, but it is also humbling to think that fish understand it, in their spines somehow, and we don't. The poem seems to rub it in regarding my inability to understand things, with a phrase like "gloved assent."
2. The poem says: Birds understand their element, because it is to them a river of language.
2a. My response: Again, it is reassuring and inspiring even to think of the skylarks and barn owls "calling and spinning aside" in the air; and again, it is also humbling to realize that we don't really get this language, which is merely "leached through our faint receivers."
3. The poem says: We do not understand our element, which is stone. It is like "a darker form of gravity," and we certainly don't understand gravity. Stone has markings in it "no one could read or interpret."
3a. My response: If fish and birds can understand their elements, then why can't we? Are we inferior in this respect to birds and fish? There is something wrong, or at least disturbing, I think, with the idea that fish and birds are more insightful than we are, if that is the poem's idea. The fish and birds are more in tune with their environments than we are, according to the poem.
4. The poem says: We do know about stone indirectly, since we are "its echoes," and the shape of our "love and fear" is revealed by the wind "by purest chance." And then this shape is covered over.
4a. My response: I do not see how the wind can reveal the shape of love and fear, so on a literal level the poem appears to make no sense. Nor do I see how we can be echoes of stone. So my response is to want to argue with the poem, to question

its reasonableness. I doubt this is the effect Burnside is
aiming for. I'll continue to think about this aspect.

5. The poem says: The shape the wind revealed is "covered," and
in this respect it is "like the secret veins and seams/ that
harden in the bloodlines of our children."

5a. My response: The poem is trying to get us to connect the
element of stone to the children. Stone has veins and seams,
and so that does connect; but what is the hardening? That
may suggest the children are returning to stone. But
children do not have "seams," do they, not even in their
bloodlines? What bothers me most, as I try to respond
adequately to the poem, is that the assumption seems flat-
out wrong. Is stone really our element? We don't live in it,
the way fish live in the sea, or birds in the air. The poem
seems to make a profound statement, but what is it saying?
So my response, ultimately, is one of aggravation and
yearning for some meaning. Is that what Burnside wanted?

At this point, Dorothy has not begun her actual essay, and she may in fact seem
to be very far from beginning it; she still has fundamental questions. Yet, as it turns
out, it is pretty much already done, since she has generated so much material thinking about the poem. Dorothy has decided that her response to the poem is mainly
one of frustration, that the poem doesn't make sense as a whole, although parts of it
are very interesting. Her goal, then, will be to explain clearly why the poem isn't
ultimately clear. Her title seemed easy enough to come up with, since the poem itself
has a line about the inability to read something. Her sketch, after a few drafts (circulated to her classmates and teacher), evolved into the following essay. Note the way
that Dorothy is able to use her uncertainties in her essay. Mostly, Dorothy filled in
quotations and comments supporting the ideas she had already brainstormed.

Dorothy Williams
Dr. Lynn
English 102

"No One Could Read or Interpret":
The Meaning of "The Sand Merchant's Wife"

To any experienced reader of poems, John Burnside's "The
Sand Merchant's Wife" would appear to be related to Ezra
Pound's famous poem, "The River Merchant's Wife." It may
indeed somehow be related to Pound's simple story of a lover
who goes away and is longed for, but I can see no connection.
Such a hint at meaning that does not appear is typical for
this poem, which does not mention sand, or a merchant, or a
wife. The poem does talk about logic, about language, and

about a meaningful shape. None of these, the poem suggests, can be understood; and the poem leaves me feeling that if it is about anything, it is about how hard it is to make sense of the world. I knew that before I read the poem.

In the opening stanza, I am immediately comforted by the assertion that "There is a logic in the sea/ that fishes understand." The sea does seem to be quite random, with waves sloshing back and forth, no one quite like another one, with currents flowing here and there. If there is a logic, and fish understand it, then I feel better. But the next few lines complicate my assurance, because they say that the logic is "a pattern that rests in the spine, a gloved assent/ revealed by the sweep and turn/ of the changing tide." Assume for the moment that I know what "a gloved assent" means. If the logic of the sea is a pattern in the spine of the fish, then I am not sure how they "understand" it in any sense that I can understand. I am sure I have patterns in my spine too, but I cannot understand them without a medical education. Although fish do have "schools," so far as I know they do not study medicine in them. I do not in fact know what "gloved assent" means, despite much deliberation, and so the stanza drifts off into more confusion for me.

The second stanza also begins with a positive statement: "and air is a river of language." I find this to be a wonderful image, even more uplifting perhaps than asserting the logic of the sea, as I think about "skylarks and barn owls/ calling and spinning aside." In the rest of the stanza, however, this river of language becomes less clear. Air is, the poem says in the next line, "a blue domain of semaphore and noise." Communication by semaphore is of course silent, so semaphore would appear not to be part of the birds' "calling." "Noise" usually does not suggest communication, and the next line, "drifting through rain," suggests that the river of language is not one we can navigate. The final line of the stanza confirms that we are not able to understand, since something is "leached through our faint receivers." I say "something" because it is not clear what is drifting through the rain and is leached: the air, the river of language, the calling, the blue domain, or the semaphore and noise—these are all possibilities.

The third stanza gets to "our element," which has always been, according to the poem, stone. Not only do we fail to understand the logic of the sea and the language of the air, we do not understand our own element, which "lay beneath us like a darker form/ of gravity, a drift we could not mine,/ the local shifts and flickers in the rock,/ stitches and hair streaks no one could read or interpret." Obviously, gravity is something we cannot see at all; a "darker form/ of gravity" must be especially invisible. Not only can "no one read or interpret" the markings in the rock, I cannot imagine why they are called "stitches and hair streaks." I would like to relate "stitches" to the references to "seams" or even to a glove, but I cannot.

The final stanza is the most obscure, and most clearly indicates that the poem may be about mystery and the failure of meaning. The idea that "we" were the "echoes" of stone is a striking one, but in what sense are we made of stone? Literally, if human beings are the "we" here, our bodies are more water than anything else. I do not know why we should be considered echoes of stone any more than we should be thought of as echoes of light, or energy, or water, or air, or dust, or whatever.

We are, the poem goes on to say, "wreathed in love and fear,/ that stillness at the center of our house." If the "our" is the river merchant and his wife; and if the stillness is the love and fear; then the "shape" of their love and fear is revealed by the wind "by purest chance."

But, whatever it is that is revealed, there is quite a contrast here between "us" on the one hand and the fish and birds on the other. We understand (whatever it is that we understand) only by chance.

Even this accidentally glimpsed shape is "covered, like the secret veins and seams/ that harden in the bloodlines of our children." It seems clear at this point that the poem is trying to get its readers to connect the element of stone to the children. Stone has veins and seams, and so that part does connect; but the hardening? That may suggest the children are returning to stone. But children do not have "seams," do they, not even in their bloodlines? And it seems impossible to think of love and fear as somehow hardening in bloodlines.

But what bothers me most, as I try to respond adequately to the poem as it ends, is that its basic assumption seems flat-out wrong. Is stone really our element? We don't live in it, the way fish live in the sea, or birds in the air. The poem seems to make a profound statement, but what is it saying? So my response, ultimately, is one of aggravation and yearning for some meaning. Is that what Burnside wanted? Have I just confirmed that I do not understand my own element?

This paper is an especially useful and unusual instance of reader-response criticism because it illustrates how a reader can meaningfully respond to a work he or she does not fully understand or even like. Sometimes the only response you may have to a work is "I don't get it"—but you probably need a bit more material than that to write an essay. Dorothy's writing process indicates how to start from such a point of confusion and work toward a rich response, even if that response can only describe lucidly why you don't get it. And that, after all, is the real beauty of reader-response criticism, because it allows us to talk honestly about how we read and what it means to us. Burnside's poem seems to be about the mystery of human life, and so Dorothy's response is quite insightful to me. Unlike fish and birds, who glide through mediums they comprehend, humans cannot really inhabit their "element": we cannot live in stone, the way fish can live in water, and birds can live in the air. Yet the poem suggests the mystery of human life, as stone seems to live in us, in "the secret veins and seams/ that harden in the bloodlines of our children"; and we seem to live on and around the stone somehow, with its "stitches and hair streaks no one can read or interpret."

✔ Checklist: Using Reader-Response Criticism

❑ Read actively—make notes, ask questions, respond and record.
❑ Focus on details and ask how your response would change if the detail were changed.
❑ Decide on your purpose: a subjective, an interactive, or a receptive response.

Useful Terms for Reader-Response Criticism

Affect: In discussing your response, you may well talk about how something affects you. Be sure to distinguish the spelling of this word from the following one:

Effect: This word refers (usually) to what the work creates in you: the effect of the work comes from how it affects you. "Affect" is usually a verb, and "effect" a noun—although there are exceptions. Psychiatrists, for instance, talk about the "affect" of someone, referring to that person's emotions and demeanor: "He has a flat affect" means that his emotions appear to be flat. Also, "effect" can be used as a verb, meaning "to bring something into being." For instance, "we are going to effect some changes in the retirement plan" means that we are going to bring about changes.

Expectation, anticipation: In describing your response you're likely to talk about how the text prepares you for something and then surprises or satisfies you.

Implied reader: The reader that you think the author had in mind. In trying to respond as the implied reader, you aim to put aside your own idiosyncrasies and try to play the role of the reader the author was addressing. Obviously, the implied reader is a fiction, a composite of lots of real readers.

Subjective response: This stance involves letting your own personality figure freely into your response. With a subjective response, you're not trying to be the implied reader (as in a receptive stance). Instead, you're trying to respond authentically, honestly, richly, personally.

Elements: Symbol and Image; Personification, Allegory, and Allusion

Symbol, Image   In 1913, Gertrude Stein wrote one of her most famous sentences, which is this one: "Rose is a rose is a rose is a rose." There are people who claim that this sentence means something, and, furthermore, they know what that something is. In the spirit of reader-response criticism, I invite you to make up your own interpretation. Here is mine:

> *Stein, fed up with critics who read all sorts of preposterous meanings into things, is insisting vehemently that a rose simply stands for a rose, and nothing else. A rose is a rose, which is a rose, WHICH IS A ROSE I TOLD YOU, and that's all there is to it.*

If that is by any chance what Stein meant, we can certainly understand her frustration at overly creative readers. But a rose is almost always something more than just a rose, isn't it? Red roses as a gift signify "I love you," or "I really like you," or at least "I want you to think I really like you." Black roses, at least in some gangster movies, mean "You're about to get killed." A white rose worn on the lapel on Mother's or Father's Day signifies that one's mother or father (depending on the day) is deceased; and a red rose signifies that the parent is still alive. In the fifteenth century, a white rose was the badge of the House of York, and a red rose was the badge of the House of Lancaster; as these two Houses battled each other for the throne of England, in the War of the Roses of course, a white or a red rose indicated one's allegiance. Today, the rose is the official emblem of England; and so at official ceremonies, roses symbolically stand for the country. If you are in New York state, or Iowa, or North Dakota, or the District of Columbia, which have all adopted various kinds of roses as the state or district flower, then a rose may stand for the state.

When an object stands for something else, we may call the object a *symbol.* This word comes from a Greek noun, *symbolon,* which means "mark," "emblem," "token," or "sign." The Greek verb *symballein* is also related to "symbol": it means "to throw together," which suggests the way that the object and what it represents are joined or "thrown" together. By adopting the rose as their emblem, rather than, say, pigweed or nutgrass or slime mold, these people are trying to associate themselves with their symbol, throwing the two together, using one as a token of the other: England (or New York, Iowa, North Dakota, D.C.) wants to suggest that it is sweet, beautiful, enduring (roses have been around a long time), and so forth, like its emblem.

The symbols mentioned thus far have been what are usually called conventional symbols, which have a shared and relatively stable meaning. Another kind of symbol, a contextual symbol, takes on its meanings within a particular setting or context. If a novelist, for instance, were to work in references to roses whenever a character's sanity deteriorated, then roses might be taken as a symbol of insanity, within the context of that novel—"might be taken" because contextual symbols are often richly suggestive; that is, they are often hard to pin down. Most readers agree that the green light in F. Scott Fitzgerald's *The Great Gatsby* symbolizes something, but few are sure exactly what—and those few tend to find themselves disagreeing. Moby Dick, the white whale in Herman Melville's great *Moby Dick,* surely stands for something; but, as Eudora Welty noted, only a whale would be large enough to hold all the meanings that critics have found in him. Thus, symbols can be quite powerful, but they can also be quite elusive.

For some inexperienced readers, every object in a poem stands for something else, and nothing stands for itself; as a result, imaginative symbol hunting seems to become a substitution for careful and sensible reading. Likewise, any object in a literary work can be called an *image,* and patterns of imagery are often traced in works: decay and illness in Shakespeare's *Hamlet* for instance. "Imagery," for most literary critics, includes more than visual objects, allowing any sensory perception (taste, touch, smell, hearing) to be called an image. So how can we tell when an image, even a pattern of imagery, has become a symbol? Are the gigantic buildings in Ridley Scott's science fiction classic *Blade Runner* images that help create the sense of a crowded, impersonal, high-tech future, or are they symbols of such a concept? Symbols highlight an interesting issue for reader-response criticism: if the meaning of something is the reader's response to it, then how can a reader know whether to believe in a particular instance that a rose really is just a rose (is a rose), or to search for some hidden meaning within the rose? A reader's response that is entirely individual and idiosyncratic, while it may well be a stimulating starting point, would seem to have a limited value for other readers. At some point, unless you're writing a response strictly for yourself, you have to take into account what other readers will find plausible. But how can anyone possibly know what other readers will find plausible?

This question focuses on the way in which reader-response criticism, however personal and subjective it may be, naturally moves toward a communal and receptive reading. We can ascertain plausibility in interpretation (whether this rose might stand for Roseville, a town near Detroit, say) by understanding the intellectual community within which the author wrote the work, and the community in which the reader is responding. With more knowledge, with more reading experience in other words, your responses will become richer and more persuasive. While true of any aspect of response, this assertion seems especially revealing for the kinds of layers of meaning involved in symbols and allusions. An image, then, is a symbol if some reader says it is, and (we might add) can persuade other readers to that effect.

Allegory, Personification, Allusion   When the symbolism in a work becomes so extensive that the story seems to be a vehicle for this second layer of meaning, then we have an ***allegory.*** In that part of *The Romance of the Rose* written by Guillaume de Lorris, the hero in this medieval classic wants to possess a beautiful rose, but characters who are named "Shame," "Jealousy," and "Reason" keep getting in the way, although "Fair Welcome" provides some key assistance. The characters here are mostly concepts that have been turned into persons—***personifications.*** The story exists to tell us something about the ideas. Some allegories are not so obviously allegorical, but almost any story might be read in an allegorical fashion, if its elements can persuasively be shown to convey another conceptual level.

Here is a particularly interesting poem that focuses on the symbolic nature of the rose's relative, the carnation, which is not always just a carnation.

GJERTRUD SCHNACKENBERG (1953–)

Supernatural Love

My father at the dictionary-stand
Touches the page to fully understand
The lamplit answer, tilting in his hand

His slowly scanning magnifying lens,
A blurry, glistening circle he suspends   5
Above the word "Carnation." Then he bends

So near his eyes are magnified and blurred,
One finger on the miniature word,
As if he touched a single key and heard

A distant, plucked, infinitesimal string,   10
"The obligation due to every thing
That's smaller than the universe." I bring

My sewing needle close enough that I
Can watch my father through the needle's eye,
As through a lens ground for a butterfly   15

Who peers down flower-hallways toward a room
Shadowed and fathomed as this study's gloom
Where, as a scholar bends above a tomb

To read what's buried there, he bends to pore
Over the Latin blossom. I am four,   20
I spill my pins and needles on the floor

Trying to stitch "Beloved" X by X.
My dangerous, bright needle's point connects
Myself illiterate to this perfect text

I cannot read. My father puzzles why   25
It is my habit to identify
Carnations as "Christ's flowers," knowing I

Can give no explanation but "Because."
Word-roots blossom in speechless messages
The way the thread behind my sampler does   30

Where following each X I awkward move
My needle through the word whose root is love.
He reads, "A pink variety of Clove,

Carnatio, the Latin, meaning flesh."
As if the bud's essential oils brush   35
Christ's fragrance through the room, the iron-fresh

Odor carnations have floats up to me,
A drifted, secret, bitter ecstasy,
The stems squeak in my scissors, *Child, it's me,*

He turns the page to "Clove" and reads aloud: 40
"The clove, a spice, dried from a flower-bud."
Then twice, as if he hasn't understood,

He reads, "From French, for *clou,* meaning a nail."
He gazes, motionless. "Meaning a nail."
The incarnation blossoms, flesh and nail,   45

I twist my threads like stems into a knot
And smooth "Beloved," but my needle caught
Within the threads, *Thy blood so dearly bought,*

The needle strikes my finger to the bone.
I lift my hand, it is myself I've sewn,   50
The flesh laid bare, the threads of blood my own,

I lift my hand in startled agony
And call upon his name, "Daddy daddy" —
My father's hand touches the injury

As lightly as he touched the page before,   55
Where incarnation bloomed from roots that bore
The flowers I called Christ's when I was four.

[1985]

The father in the opening lines is using a magnifying lens to look up the word
"carnation." It is possible that the father is using a magnifying glass because his
vision is impaired, but notice that he has his finger "on the miniature word." We
might suspect therefore that he is using a tiny-print edition of the *Oxford English
Dictionary,* a fascinating dictionary that explains not only what a word means, but
also what it has meant throughout its history. (The *OED* is available, in a regular-size
print, in any major library, and may also be available online through your library.
You'll find it to be a valuable resource. The father appears to be using the two-volume,
microprint edition, much more affordable for home use, which comes with its own

magnifying glass.) We get the sense certainly that the father is a scholar, or at least a serious reader: he has a "dictionary-stand," and he is attempting to "fully understand" this word. He is in fact trying, the poem hints, to find in this word some key to the universe, as if the word is "a single key" which links him to "A distant, plucked, infinitesimal string." This image is so strange that you may wonder if there is more to it. You may argue that it is in fact a subtle reference, an **allusion,** to the ancient idea of the music of the spheres—the idea that the planets and other heavenly bodies vibrated in such a way to produce a cosmic harmony. Perhaps the father is peering so intently at this word because he is trying to read this celestial music, which resonates with "The obligation due to every thing/ That's smaller than the universe."

From this opening image of the father at the dictionary-stand, the daughter's attention shifts to a different view of the same scene, as she uses her needle's eye, in imitation of her father's peering, to frame her father. In a remarkable bit of imagining, the daughter thinks of herself as looking "through a lens ground for a butterfly/ Who peers down flower-hallways," and her butterfly point of view seems especially appropriate, as it emphasizes the textual flower that her father is seeing. Subsequent readings of this poem (like most) will no doubt produce a richer response, but even the first time through it is possible to wonder if the needle's eye is not also an allusion, referring to something else. And once references to Christ do appear in the poem, the child looking through the eye of a needle seems undeniably allusive: the reader familiar with the New Testament will naturally think of Christ's assertion that it is easier for a camel to get through the eye of a needle, than for a rich man to get into heaven; and the image thus also would seem to allude to Christ's related statement that one must become like a child in order to enter heaven (Matthew 19:24; 18:3).

Christian imagery pervades the poem because the mystery that Schnackenberg unfolds is that the little girl somehow, through luck or intuition or something else, perceives the carnation to be a symbol for Christ. Her father comes to see the girl's association of Christ and carnations only by studying the roots of "carnation." "Carnation," which comes from the Latin for "flesh," is a variety of "clove," which means "nail" in French. For the father, "flesh" and "nail" brought together constitute an indirect reference, an allusion, to Christ. Not everyone would see this connection, even after looking up "carnation" and "clove." By definition, an allusion depends on the reader drawing on some shared knowledge; in this case, if the reader knows nothing about the Christian tradition, has never heard of the crucifixion of Christ, then "flesh" and "nail" are not seen as an allusion to Christ and remain no doubt puzzling. Allusion thus highlights, in a sense, the value of reader-response criticism, since meaning is so clearly a function of the reader's activity: the meaning is not *in* the poem so much as it is *created* by the reader, using the poem's materials. For the little girl, the carnation is a symbol of Christ, but not an allusion for her in the same way as for the father. For the girl, the stems of the carnation, being cut in her scissors, squeak *Child, it's me.*" For the father, "carnation" makes an indirect reference to an event and a person.

There are other allusions in the poem—when the speaker recalls sticking her finger with a needle (an allusion to the piercing of Christ's flesh as he was being crucified), and when the father appears to be bending over a tomb (an allusion to Christ's burial), for example. Even the "X" that the little girl stitches alludes to the Greek letter Chi, which looks like an X, and which makes the first letter of "Christ" in Greek. It was used by the early Christians as a symbol of their faith; even today, an

"X" is sometimes used in "Christmas" as "Xmas"—which is not, as some people think, an irreverent abbreviation, but is rather an ancient and reverent practice, if one understands what the X stands for, allusively.

How can you tell where to stop when looking for symbols and allusions? Does the dictionary itself in "Supernatural Love" symbolize something? Is the dictionary-stand an allusion to anything? If there were a clear-cut answer to these questions, then reading poetry would be a science, not an art. Even with conventional symbols (those shared by a community, which contrast with contextual symbols), we must decide if *this* black cat or *that* broken mirror represents something else as well, or if it's just a black cat, just a broken mirror. And how do you decide? You must look carefully at the poem, using good sense and imagination at the same time, weighing the evidence before you jump, symbolically or allusively or allegorically, to any conclusions. But making sense is always a little magical: like the little girl who knows about carnations, you'll know.

For a very different view of how we relate to nature and the concept of God, consider the following poem. In thinking about your response, pay particular attention to the possible roles played by the elements discussed in this section: image, symbol, personification, allegory, allusion.

MARGARET CAVENDISH (1623–1673)

Earth's Complaint

O *Nature, Nature,* hearken to my *Cry,*
Each *Minute* wounded am, but cannot die.
My *Children* which *I* from my *Womb* did bear,
Do dig my *Sides,* and all my *Bowels* tear:
Do plow deep *Furrows* in my very *Face,*   5
From *Torment, I* have neither time, nor place.
No other *Element* is so abused,
Nor by *Mankind* so cruelly is used.
Man cannot reach the *Skies* to plow, and sow,
Nor can they set, or mark the *Stars* to grow.   10
But they are still as *Nature* first did plant,
Neither *Maturity,* nor *Growth* they want.
They never die, nor do they yield their place
To *younger Stars,* but still run their own *Race.*
The *Sun* doth never groan *young Suns* to bear,   15
For he himself is his own *Son,* and *Heir.*
The *Sun* just in the *Center* sits, as *King,*
The *Planets* round about encircle him.
The slowest *Orbs* over his *Head* turn slow,
And underneath, the *swiftest Planets* go.   20
Each several *Planet,* several measures take,
And with their *Motions* they sweet *Musick* make.
Thus all the *Planets* round about him move,
And he returns them *Light* for their kind *Love.*

[1653]

Questions

1. Who is speaking to whom? What role does personification play in this poem?

2. Explain the image at work in the first six lines. What is going on at the literal and symbolic levels? How effective is this comparison?

3. Why does Cavendish say that the sky and the stars are unchanged? How would Cavendish change her assertions if she were writing today?

4. What is the allusion in the reference to "Musick" in line 22?

5. Do you think there is any significance in the genders Cavendish chooses for the earth or the sun?

6. How do you respond to the ending? Does Cavendish lose sight of the first part of the poem, or does she prepare somehow for the ending? What is the significance in particular of the poem's last word?

Margaret Lucas Cavendish, Duchess of Newcastle

Practice: Environments

Here are poems, ecologically intriguing in some way, to practice reading and responding.

MARK STRAND (1934–)

The Garden

for Robert Penn Warren

It shines in the garden,
in the white foliage of the chestnut tree,
in the brim of my father's hat
as he walks on the gravel.
In the garden suspended in time   5
my mother sits in a redwood chair;
light fills the sky,
the folds of her dress,
the roses tangled beside her.
And when my father bends   10
to whisper in her ear,
when they rise to leave
and the swallows dart

and the moon and stars
have drifted off together, it shines.
Even as you lean over this page,   15
late and alone, it shines; even now
    in the moment before it disappears.

[1978]

Questions

1. What emotions or feelings do the images in this poem convey to you? How
   do you respond to the pictures presented here?

2. Mark Strand's poems often have an eery dreamlike quality. Does anything in
   this poem seem unreal, like a dream? (For instance, where—or perhaps I
   should say "when"—is the garden?)

3. After the first section of this poem, what do you think "It" is or might be?
   What do you learn about "it" in the rest of the poem? Exactly when does "it"
   disappear?

4. How is your response affected by the obscurity of what "it" is?

JOY HARJO (1951–)

For Anna Mae Aquash* Whose Spirit Is Present Here and in the Dappled Stars

For we remember the story and must tell it again so we may all live
Beneath a sky blurred with mist and wind,
I am amazed as I watch the violet
heads of crocuses erupt from the stiff earth
after dying for a season,   5
as I have watched my own dark head
appear each morning after entering
the next world
to come back to this one,
amazed.   10
It is the way in the natural world to understand the place
the ghost dancers named
after the heart-breaking destruction.
Anna Mae,
everything and nothing changes   15
You are the shimmering young woman
who found her voice
when you were warned to be silent, or have your body cut away
from you like an elegant weed.
You are the one whose spirit is present in the dappled stars.   20
(They prance and lope like colored horses who stay with us
through the streets of these steely cities. And I have seen them

---

*Anna Mae Aquash, a young Micmac Indian activist, was mysteriously murdered in February 1976
on the Pine Ridge Reservation in South Dakota.

nuzzling the frozen bodies of tattered drunks
on the corner.)
This morning when the last star is dimming   25
and the buses grind toward
the middle of the city, I know it is ten years since they buried
you the second time in Lakota, a language that could
free you.
I heard about it in Oklahoma, or New Mexico,   30
how the wind howled and pulled everything down
in a righteous anger.
(It was the women who told me) and we understood wordlessly
the ripe meaning of your murder.
As I understand ten years later after the slow changing   35
of the seasons
that we have just begun to touch
the dazzling whirlwind of our anger,
we have just begun to perceive the amazed world the ghost
dancers entered   40
crazily, beautifully.

                                                                                   [1990]

Joy Harjo

Questions

1. Joy Harjo (or the speaker in this poem) says "the wind howled and pulled everything down/ in a righteous anger." Does the poem make you feel angry? Do you think Harjo is attempting simply to stir up our indignation? What emotions does the poem arouse?

2. What role do the following play in the speaker's response? In your own response?

   amazement
   the stars (note the title)
   the wind
   death and rebirth

CAROLINE FRASER

All Bears

Are Dangerous. Enjoy Them—
say signs—At a Distance. What they want

is huckleberries,
salmonberries, bearberries,

areas of dense brush, heavy   5
forage, golden-

mantled ground squirrels, spawning
salmon full of eggs, corn

spilled from freight cars
on the Continental Divide, canned   10

spaghetti, freeze-dried
beef Stroganoff, anything

you've got. They want to know
whether you're predator

or prey, but what they really   15
prefer is carrion. They like

to roll in it. They may run off
and then return and pull you

out of a tree
like fruit and eat part   20

and stash the rest
for later. But remember:

it's not you
they're after—not the camper lying

zipped in his tent   25
in the rain, hearing the drops splashing

overhead like cloth
tearing, not the girl

cramped on the front seat
of the car, staring   30

into the black, seeing the thick
trunks rear up

and walk bipedally; not your watch,
not your wallet, not your waterproof

down coat. The bears, they could take you   35
or leave you alone

but for the fact
of what they can smell.

[1991]

Questions

1. Consider how the ending affects your response. Specifically, what is suggested by the assertion that "The bears, they could take you or leave you alone"? How is that effect altered by the last two lines?

2. Is there any logical order to the list of "What they want" (beginning in line 2, ending with "anything/ you've got")? How does the list progress, and how is your response affected?

3. How comforting are the lines following the assertion "it's not you/ they're after"?

4. Consider how the following people might respond to this poem: an environmentalist; a hunter; a scoutmaster; a comedian; you.

EMILY DICKINSON (1830–1886)

Through the Dark Sod

Through the Dark Sod—as Education—
The Lily passes sure—
Feels her white foot—no trepidation—
Her faith—no fear—

Afterward—in the Meadow—   5
Swinging her Beryl Bell
The Mold-life—all forgotten—now—
In Ecstasy—and Dell—

[before 1886]

Questions

1. Attempt to make this poem into an allegory. What happens?

2. How does "Education" affect your response?

3. What does the word "foot" do? How does it affect your view of the Lily? (What is this device called?)

4. Is "faith" a significant word here, for a Lily? Is the Lily a symbol?

5. What is the "Mold-life"? Be sure you know the meaning of "Beryl Bell" and "Dell." (This may be a good time to use your dictionary.) How would the

effect upon the reader be different if the last line were reversed? (That is, if "Ecstasy" and not "Dell" ended the poem?) Which word would you expect to come last?

ROBINSON JEFFERS (1887–1962)

Carmel Point

The extraordinary patience of things!
This beautiful place defaced with a crop of suburban houses—
How beautiful when we first beheld it,
Unbroken field of poppy and lupin walled with clean cliffs;
No intrusion but two or three horses pasturing,   5
Or a few milch cows rubbing their flanks on the outcrop rockheads—
Now the spoiler has come: does it care?
Not faintly. It has all time. It knows the people are a tide
That swells and in time will ebb, and all
Their works dissolve. Meanwhile the image of the pristine beauty   10
Lives in the very grain of the granite,
Safe as the endless ocean that climbs our cliff. —As for us:
We must uncenter our minds from ourselves;
We must unhumanize our views a little, and become confident
As the rock and ocean that we were made from.   15

[1928]

Questions

Hawk Tower, built by Jeffers himself on the coast of Carmel

1. How is it possible (perhaps easy, or even inevitable) to misread the third line? What do you think Jeffers is saying, and what does it turn out, as you proceed further, that he *is* saying? Why does Jeffers do this?

2. Is "crop" an interesting word? What other words are significant, and why?

3. What do you expect to happen in the poem after the assertion, "Now the spoiler has come"? Would you expect "it" to care? What is "it" in line 7?

4. What do you think about the phrase "Their works dissolve"? Why isn't it "Our works dissolve"? How does "Their" affect your response?

5. Why is the ocean "endless"? How does that word contribute (subtly perhaps) to the poem's effect?

6. What precisely is the "image" referred to in line 10? Why is it "pristine"?

7. Why should we "uncenter" and "unhumanize"? Do you agree?

Suggestions for Writing

One of the best ways to understand and appreciate the work of a fine chef is to attempt to reproduce some of his or her recipes. Likewise, if you want to understand jazz, or bluegrass, or polka, you should ideally get an instrument and play some. If you want to see life the way a painter sees it, or a sculptor, or an architect, wouldn't it be helpful to try to paint, or sculpt, or design something? Thus an excellent way to enhance your understanding of poetry would be to try to write a poem. Why not give it a try?

For some students, the idea of writing a poem is unappealing, if not unnerving. If that's the way you feel, then try to lower your standards and expectations and have a good time with this. I'm not saying that you shouldn't give it some effort. Instead, set aside harsh self-judgment, insecurities, and fear, and focus on trying to say something. This chapter is about responding to literature, and this little exercise encourages you to respond *with* literature.

Most importantly, take your time; put yourself into this task; and you're likely to find it rewarding, and probably even enjoyable.

Here are a few suggestions.

1. Write a poem that responds to one of the poems above. You may want to add a sequel, take another point of view, disagree somehow, or simply imagine that the poem has a section or two mysteriously left out, and now you're supplying it.
2. James Dickey used to give his students a fruit or a vegetable and tell them to carry it with them for an entire day, studying it. Then he asked them to write a poem about it, considering what it might symbolize. Try Dickey's experiment. (You may want to pick your own fruit or vegetable, or have someone assign one to you.)
3. Literature allows us to imagine the viewpoint of any person (or even place, or thing!). Try writing a poem that inhabits the point of view of someone who is involved in converting part of the Amazonian rain forest to farmland.
4. Try writing a poem that inhabits the point of view of a "deep" environmentalist, someone who is so committed to protecting the environment that he or she would be willing to place spikes in trees, even though loggers might be injured.
5. Pick any natural object and study it carefully. Personify the object and allow it to speak. What does it say?
6. Try your hand at an allegory.

5

Read Poetry Closely: New Criticism

The study of literature means the study of literature, not of biography nor of literary history (incidentally of vast importance), not of grammar, not of etymology, not of anything except the works themselves, viewed as their creators wrote them, viewed as art, as transcripts of humanity—not as logic, not as psychology, not as ethics.

—Martin Wright Sampson

But the elements of a poem are related to each other, not as blossoms juxtaposed in a bouquet, but as the blossoms are related to the other parts of a growing plant. The beauty of the poem is the flowering of the whole plant, and needs the stalk, the leaf, and the hidden roots.

—Cleanth Brooks, *"Irony as a Principle of Structure" (1951)*

Reflection: The Organic Text

In the two epigraphs at the beginning of this chapter, Martin Sampson and Cleanth Brooks are articulating two key ideas for modern literary criticism. At their appearance, these related ideas were perceived to be revolutionary and controversial—so much so that the critical strategies that evolved came to be called the "New Criticism." Today these ideas seem to many people so unremarkable and perhaps even obvious at least in part because they have been so widely

"Really? 'Happy Hour' is meant ironically? And you say everybody knows this?"

adopted. It would be hard to find someone who has studied literature and taken an English class in the last fifty years or so who has not been influenced by these two notions:

1. Literature classes focus primarily on literary works, not history or biography or ethics or grammar or taste or anything else.
2. This focus on literary works themselves assumes that a work is in some sense like a living thing: every part contributes to the whole, and so careful study of any and every part helps to reveal the beauty, the wonder, the unity, and the complexity of the whole.

Although "New" Criticism is itself pretty old at this point, the assumptions that Sampson and Brooks are using go back much further. Aristotle's ancient idea (Fourth Century BCE) that beauty is the result of variety in unity is crucial, for instance. Samuel Taylor Coleridge, writing in the nineteenth century, expresses much the same notion when he says that a work is "rich in proportion to the variety of parts which it holds in unity." But rather than elaborate on these principles as they appear in literary critics and philosophers, let's see how this view of literature inhabits a particular poem. Poetry, for New Critics, *is* in a sense literature; the *poetic* qualities in fiction and drama, New Critics say, make stories and plays literary. The poem we are about to examine, therefore, is especially appropriate because it is a poem about the nature of poetry, and hence the nature of literature, from (as you'll see) a New Critical perspective. Note that this very famous poem by Archibald MacLeish, "Ars Poetica" (which means "the art of poetry"), was published in 1926, when the ideas underlying New Criticism were being formulated. What you're about to encounter, then, is a New Critical reading of a poem about poetry that promotes New Critical readings.

ARCHIBALD MACLEISH (1892–1982)

Ars Poetica

A poem should be palpable and mute
As a globed fruit,

Dumb
As old medallions to the thumb,

Silent as the sleeve-worn stone   5
Of casement ledges where the moss has grown—

A poem should be wordless
As the flight of birds.

A poem should be motionless in time
As the moon climbs,   10

Leaving, as the moon releases
Twig by twig the night-entangled trees,

Leaving, as the moon behind the winter leaves,
Memory by memory the mind—

A poem should be motionless in time   15
As the moon climbs.

A poem should be equal to:

Not true.

For all the history of grief

An empty doorway and a maple leaf.   20

For love

The leaning grasses and two lights above the sea—

A poem should not mean

But be.

[1926]

This poem is startling from its opening lines (isn't it?), asserting that a poem should be "palpable and mute." How can a poem possibly be "palpable," or "capable of being handled, touched, or felt" (*American Heritage Dictionary*)? Whether we think of a poem as an idea, or a group of ideas, or the writing on a piece of a paper, or a group of spoken words, none of these seems to be the sort of thing we can handle. And how can a poem be "mute"? Isn't a poem made of words? Don't we at least *imagine* a voice speaking the words? Suggesting that a poem be mute seems a bit like suggesting that a movie be invisible, or a song be inaudible, or a sculpture be without shape.

But MacLeish reiterates these strange ideas in subsequent lines, saying explicitly that a poem should be "Dumb," "Silent," and even "wordless" (lines 3, 5, and 7). He uses comparisons that reinforce particularly the idea of being "palpable." In comparing the poem to a "fruit," for instance, MacLeish suggests that the poem should be a real thing, having substance. The idea that it should be "globed" (a "globed" fruit) emphasizes the three-dimensionality that MacLeish desires: like a globe, the poem should have more extension in time and space than a map or a picture. Not just a depiction of a fruit, it should *be* a "globed" fruit. Likewise, "old medallions to the thumb" and "the sleeve-worn stone/ Of casement ledges where the moss has grown" are both not only "silent" or "dumb," but they also have an enduring solidity, a tangible reality. These images of fruit, old medallions, and worn ledges may also seem a bit mysterious, like "the flight of birds" (line 8), which in some "wordless," seemingly magical way is organized and orchestrated—as anyone knows who's ever seen a flock of birds rise together and move as one, silently.

From lines 1–8, then, we draw our first principle of New Criticism:

1. A poem should be seen as an object—an object of an extraordinary and somewhat mysterious kind, a silent object that is not equal to the words printed on a page.

Lines 8–16 articulate another idea, that "A poem should be motionless in time." This idea seems easy enough to understand: MacLeish believes that poems shouldn't change. Aren't Shakespeare's sonnets the same today as when they were written? ("So long as men can breathe or eyes can see,/ So long lives this, and this gives life to thee," as Sonnet 18 says.) But MacLeish's comparison, "As the moon climbs," is not so easy to grasp: how can the moon be "climbing" through the sky, yet "motionless in time"? Perhaps the answer lies in the repeated idea that the moon, like the poem, should be "Leaving, as the moon releases/ Twig by twig the night-entangled trees" (lines 11–12); it should be "Leaving, as the moon behind the winter leaves/ Memory by memory the mind" (lines 13–14). Something that is "leaving" is neither fully here nor fully gone; it is caught in an in-between contradictory timespace. We do not notice a memory deteriorating: it is there, unchanging; then it is only partly there; then it may be gone. The moon climbing in the sky does seem like this: it appears to sit there, motionless in time, yet it is leaving and will "release" the trees.

MacLeish repeats lines 8-9 in lines 15-16, as if his own poem is motionless, continuing on but remaining in the same place it was. This paradox adds to the mystery of the earlier lines, and also suggests a second principle:

2. The poem as silent object is unchanging, existing somehow both within and outside of time, "leaving" yet "motionless."

Lines 17-18 offer a third surprising idea: "A poem should be equal to:/ Not true." It's difficult to believe that MacLeish is saying that poems should lie. But what is he saying? Lines 19-22 appear to explain his point, but these lines seem particularly difficult. What can these lines possibly mean—ignoring for the moment the concluding assertion of lines 23-24, which seems to be that poems ought not have meanings? The lines are obscure basically because the verbs are missing, so our task of making sense must include imagining what has been left out.

First MacLeish says, "For all the history of grief/ An empty doorway and a maple leaf" (19-20). If we look closely at this statement, its form is familiar and clear enough: "For X, Y." Or, adding a verb, "For X, substitute Y." Thus, no doubt these lines mean simply that instead of recounting "all the history of grief," the poet should present instead "An empty doorway and a maple leaf." An empty doorway can speak to us of someone departed, conveying an emptiness and an absence that may be more compressed and intense than an entire history of grief. A maple leaf, perhaps lying on the ground, bursting with fall colors inevitably turning to brown and crumbling, may tell us something about loss more directly and powerfully and concisely than any history book.

The next two lines are similarly structured: "For love/ The leaning grasses and two lights above the sea." That is, "For love," an abstraction, impossible to grasp, the poet should present something concrete: "The leaning grasses and two lights above the sea." Although we can't say precisely how the grasses and lights here stand for love, somehow as images they do seem romantic, mysterious, moving. This principle of selecting something concrete to stand for an abstraction had already been advocated by T. S. Eliot in 1919, in what turned out to be an extremely influential opinion for the formation of New Criticism: "The only way of expressing emotion in the form of art," Eliot said, "is by finding an 'objective correlative'; in other words, a set of objects, a situation, a chain of events which shall be the formula of that particular emotion." Not surprisingly, throughout its history New Criticism has been especially concerned with analyzing the imagery of particular works, noticing how a poem's "objective correlatives" structure its ideas.

It is not then that the poem should lie, but rather that it does not strive to tell the truth in any literal or historical or prosaic way. Poetry, MacLeish is saying, should speak metaphorically, substituting evocative images for the description of emotions, or historical details, or vague ideas. Instead of telling us about an idea or emotion, literature confronts us with something that may spark emotions or ideas. A poem is an experience, not a discussion of an experience. The final two lines summarize this point in a startling way: "A poem should not mean/ But be."

Ordinarily we assume that words are supposed to convey a meaning, transferring ideas from an author to a reader. But the images that MacLeish's poem has given us—the globed fruit, the old medallions, the casement ledges, the flight of birds, the moon climbing, the empty doorway and the maple leaf, the leaning grasses and the two lights—these do not "mean" anything in a literal, historical, scientific way. What is the meaning, for example, of a flight of birds? Of a casement ledge where some moss has grown? These things just are. They are suggestive and even moving, but their meaning is something we impose on them; they simply exist, and we experience their being more powerfully than any abstract idea. It would be a mistake to think an empty doorway is somehow a translation of all the history of grief.

In much the same way, poems (MacLeish is asserting) do not mean, but rather have an existence—which takes us to the third principle:

3. Poems as unchanging objects represent an organized entity, not a meaning. In this way, poems are therefore fundamentally different from prose: prose strives to convey meaning; but poems cannot be perfectly translated or summarized for they offer a complex and mysterious being, an existence, an experience perhaps—but not a meaning.

Strategies: Using New Criticism

Starting from the assumptions of New Criticism, underlying MacLeish's poem, how can we approach a particular literary work? Here's a simple three-step procedure:

1. Read closely, identifying the work's oppositions, tensions, paradoxes, ironies.
2. Read closely, assuming that everything in the work—figures of speech, point of view, diction, recurrent ideas or images, everything—is carefully calculated to contribute to the work's unity.
3. Read closely, determining how the poem's various elements create complex unity.

These steps, may seem quite abstract. To say that they fully and accurately describe the practice of New Criticism would be an exaggeration. The critics that we think of as New Critics today are in fact a diverse group, including even some who would deny that they are New Critics. Other books can fill in a more detailed sense of New Criticism's diversity and historical development. The task here is simply to show you how some basic New Critical assumptions and strategies can help you generate useful insights.

To see how New Criticism works, let's apply its strategies to a poem, a poem that engages one of the most controversial and emotional topics of our day. Read the poem carefully several times, writing down any comments or questions that occur to you, and noting any tensions, ambiguities, or oppositions that you see.

Gwendolyn Brooks (1917–2000)

The Mother

Abortions will not let you forget.
You remember the children you got that you did not get,
The damp small pulps with a little or with no hair,
The singers and workers that never handled the air.
You will never neglect or beat   5
Them, or silence or buy with a sweet.
You will never wind up the sucking-thumb
Or scuttle off ghosts that come.
You will never leave them, controlling your luscious sigh,
Return for a snack of them, with gobbling mother-eye.   10
I have heard in the voices of the wind the voices of my dim killed
    children.

I have contracted. I have eased
My dim dears at the breasts they could never suck.
I have said, Sweets, if I sinned, if I seized
Your luck   15
And your lives from your unfinished reach,
If I stole your births and your names,
Your straight baby tears and your games,
Your stilted or lovely loves, your tumults, your marriages, aches, and
     your deaths,
If I poisoned the beginnings of your breaths,   20
Believe that even in my deliberateness I was not deliberate.
Though why should I whine,
Whine that the crime was other than mine?—
Since anyhow you are dead.
Or rather, or instead,   25
You were never made.
But that too, I am afraid,
Is faulty: oh, what shall I say, how is the truth to be said?
You were born, you had body, you died.
It is just that you never giggled or planned or cried.   30
Believe me, I loved you all.
Believe me, I knew you, though faintly, and I loved, I loved you
All.

[1987]

Your questions and comments and notes may or may not be similar to those following, which deal only with the first ten lines. At this point, the important thing is to see how this material emerges from reading the poem closely, looking for oppositions and ambiguities, and thinking about how these tensions in the poem might be unified. If you've ever stared at a blank sheet of paper and wondered how in the world to write an essay on a poem, then it's very important to realize that notes, ideas, questions, comments, quotations, musings, and so forth must come first. Writers need to invent materials before they embark upon writing an essay. You will notice in the following notes that the reader is on the lookout for ambiguities, oppositions, contradictions, and paradoxes. The reader is looking for things that are puzzling, in other words, assuming (on faith) that they will appear, if sought.

Inventing

Here are some sample notes on the first ten lines of "The Mother":

```
     Line 1: The speaker says "Abortions will not let you
forget," as if abortions could actively do something. I know
what the speaker means, but an abortion is a medical
procedure; it can't make "you" remember or keep you from
forgetting. Assuming that this phrasing is significant, why
doesn't the speaker just say "You can't forget about your
abortion"? This question raises another one: why does the
speaker say "you" rather than "me," especially since the
second section reveals that she has had abortions?
```

Line 2a: The reference to children "you got that you did not get" seems contradictory. Either you got them or you didn't, it would seem.

Line 2b: The ambiguous status of these children makes me wonder why the poem is called "The Mother" if she has had abortions? Does the title perhaps refer to her other children, or to the abortions? This is probably an important ambiguity. It is, after all, the title. Any idea that ties the poem together, that unifies it, will have to include the title, won't it?

Lines 3 and 4: There is a conflict here. In line 3 "the children" are simply "damp small pulps with a little or with no hair." A "pulp" isn't alive, isn't a person, so removing a hairless (or nearly hairless) pulp isn't a big deal. But line 4 refers to the children or abortions in a strikingly different way, as "singers and workers that never handled the air." As singers and workers, the children are real, and their loss is tragic: they did not even get a chance to handle the air—which seems to me a wonderful and surprising description of living. We are all, as singers and workers, handling the air.

Lines 5ff: Another opposition shapes the next few lines. Lines 5-6 suggest that the abortions were in some respects a good thing: "You will never neglect or beat/ Them." The next image, never "silence or buy with a sweet," is perhaps faintly negative or even neutral: it doesn't sound good to think of silencing or buying children, and giving them "a sweet" probably isn't the greatest thing to do, but almost every parent resorts to such strategies at times, I suppose. And the next image moves into the realm of tenderness: to wind up "the sucking thumb" or "scuttle off ghosts that come"—these are acts of kindness. So the lines move from abuse, which places the abortions in a more positive light, to parental care, which makes the abortions seem more tragic.

Line 9: With "them" there is another indication that the speaker is talking about more than one abortion. I can understand, maybe, one mistake. But it is hard for me to have sympathy for someone who is having multiple abortions, apparently learning nothing, or just not caring what happens. But here is another ambiguity or paradox, because the speaker clearly does feel pain and care. The puzzle is this: how she is having more than one abortion if she really does care about the aborted babies?

Line 10: The idea of eating up the children in line 10 is strange ("a snack of them, with gobbling mother-eye").

As you think about the poem, putting your ideas on paper, you might reasonably wonder how much you need to know about 1945, when the poem was published; how much about the history of the debate over abortion; how much about Gwendolyn Brooks's life; how much about her career as a poet and about her other poems; and on and on. All these things would be good to know, but you could end up spending a semester on this poem. By adopting a New Critical stance, one can assume that the poem itself will reveal whatever it is essential for a reader to know. Of course, it probably isn't really all that helpful just to say, "Concentrate on the poem itself and read it closely." You need guidelines that tell you what to look for as you read closely. To put it simply, what you are looking for, as a New Critic, is the complexity and the unity of the work. Great works, New Criticism assumes, contain a unified ambiguity; second-rate works see things simply or in fragments.

Once you've used a New Critical stance to generate some oppositions, some ideas regarding the work's complexity, some notions of its controlling or unifying idea, how do you get to a finished essay?

Shaping

What would you say is the unifying idea of "The Mother"? What holds it together? Those questions are crucial to a New Critical reading because they lead to your thesis, which will shape and control the development of your essay. Even in the few notes reproduced here, it seems clear that the title points us toward the poem's complexity: the speaker, as the title identifies her, is "The Mother," and yet she speaks only of the children she does not have, the children who have been aborted. So how can she be a mother without any children? How can she love her children, or have aborted them, if they don't exist? That is one way of saying what the poem struggles through. The theme or unifying idea, holding together the ambiguous status of the speaker, can be stated in any number of ways, and you might try out your way of expressing it. Here's one way to put it:

> Although her children do not exist, and may have never
> existed, the speaker is a mother because she loves her
> "children."

This theme emphasizes the way the poem ends. Generally that's where the oppositions in a work are resolved. In this case, the ambiguity between the speaker as mother and non-mother is resolved at the end of the poem with her declaration of her love. She could not love the children if they did not have some kind of existence, and if they exist in some way, then she is some kind of "mother." But her status is by no means simple. Likewise, she "knew" them, she says, even if it was "faintly"; and, again, it would seem she could not know them if they did not exist, if they were not her "children," in some sense.

The strategy of a New Critical reading, then, would involve showing how the details of the poem support and elaborate this complex or ironic unity. The structure of a New Critical reading emerges from arranging this evidence in a coherent way, grouping kinds of details perhaps, or moving logically through the poem. Throughout the poem, in other words, a New Critical reading would find oppositions reinforcing and supporting in some way the poem's central ambiguity. Line 21 would be seen, for example, as a reflection of the central opposition. The speaker says "even in my deliberateness I was not deliberate." Just as the children who are aborted are not children; just as the woman abandons her motherhood by having an abortion and nonetheless retains her claim to be a "mother." By the same token, the speaker's "deliberateness is not deliberate." Her decision to have the abortion was made with "deliberateness," and for such thoughtful decisions we are more accountable, by some measures anyway, than for impulsive decisions. But the mother's culpability is qualified by the rest of the sentence, which says that the deliberateness was not "deliberate." She carefully decided something she did not carefully decide, so it seems.

Drafting

After you've worked your way through the poem, noting oppositions, tensions, ambiguities, paradoxes, and considering how these relate to the poem's unity, then it's time for a draft. Here is a first draft developed out of the annotations given; it's been polished up a bit, and there are annotations in the margin to help you see what is going on.

Golpi Watun
Dr. MacNicholas
English 2

The Mother Without Children:
A Reading of Gwendolyn Brooks's
"The Mother"

Gwendolyn Brooks's "The Mother" points to a

From the notes: this tension seems to unify to poem.

paradox with its first word, "Abortions." Although the speaker is called "the mother" in the title, she quickly reveals that "the children" have actually been aborted. How can she be a mother if her children never existed?

This introduction sets up the essay's form: mother vs. not-mother.

Her opening line asserts that "Abortions will not let you forget," but what is there for her to remember? The rest of the poem shows the "mother's" struggle with this problem: how to remember "the children that you did not get" (line 2). On the one hand, the speaker realizes

This paragraph elaborates on the two possibilities: children or not.

the children are nothing more than "damp small pulps with a little or with no hair" (3), but the rest of this sentence sees them as "singers and workers that never handled the air" (4). If they can be called "singers and workers," then they must have some existence. But if they never "handled the air," they did not work and sing, and so their status as workers and singers is problematic, to say the least. This question is what is distressing the "mother," because if these fetuses were children, then her statement in line 17 is accurate: "I stole your births and your names." But the line does begin with an "If," and it is this uncertainty that provides the speaker with some comfort.

The two possibilities come together in the uncertainty.

The comfort takes two forms. The mother first eases her pain by pointing to the uncertainty of her decision to have the abortions: "even in my deliberateness I was not deliberate" (21). Since she is uncertain about the status of what is being aborted, she decided without knowing what she was deciding. Regarding such an emotional decision, it is easy to see how one could not be entirely deliberate. And, in truth, she still does not know what her decision means: no one can say with authority, to everyone's satisfaction, when life begins, or when fetuses become persons, when they are still unviable tissue masses, "pulps" (3).

This point explains how the uncertainty comforts the mother.

More importantly, the speaker is also comforted in the end by declaring her love, even though this expression paradoxically sustains her pain and mourning. She clings to the idea of her "dim killed children" (11-12), refusing to let them become "pulps," because she can love them only if they actually existed. So she must say that she "knew" them, even while admitting it was only "faintly" (32). She does claim her status as "the mother," as the title says, even though it causes her pain. As she says in the opening line, "Abortions will not let you forget," but perhaps

This point began to emerge in the notes: the mother's pain suggests her love, which is explicitly declared later on.

Still relying on the opposition: mother/not; children/not.

From the notes, balancing the title and the first line.

Resolving the problem set up in the intro.

only if you continue to see yourself as a mother, even though you have no children. Thus, the poem balances the speaker's two visions of herself, as murderer and as mother; and it resolves this conflict in the final lines, as the mother is able to atone for her decision, in some measure, by suffering with her memory always, saying "I loved you, I loved you/ All" (32-33).

Notice that this essay doesn't explicate every detail that supports its thesis. Rather, the essay brings forth enough evidence to be persuasive. How much evidence is needed to make a close reading convincing will vary depending on the work and the thesis, and perhaps your audience. Follow your common sense and the guidance of your teacher.

Finally, as you apply New Criticism on your own, notice how two factors helped the sample essay develop smoothly.

1. *Thorough preparation.* The essay, for the most part, arranges and connects the extensive notes on the poem. You want too much material rather than too little. The process of selecting from an abundance of ideas is much more pleasant than struggling for something to say.
2. *Theoretical awareness.* Starting out with a particular approach in mind allows you to look for certain things in the work. Assuming a New Critical stance, you're looking for ideas or images in opposition; complexity or ambiguity; the unifying idea or theme. In addition, assuming a particular approach guides the development of your essay because it imposes a certain task. Within a New Critical context, an essay has to show how the parts add up to a complex, paradoxical, yet unified whole. It doesn't matter whether Gwendolyn Brooks might have intended to say this or that; it doesn't matter what your own opinion is about abortion. Even your own personal reaction to the work is not the point. Your job as a New Critic is simple: show how the unifying idea holds together the work's conflicting parts. By being aware of the theoretical stance you are evolving or adopting, you clarify for yourself what you're doing and how to do it. You can also expand beyond a particular stance. You can even evolve your own approach.

It's probably unlikely that one example will make New Criticism crystal clear for you. Even when you're quite comfortable with the theory, putting it into practice will always require some creativity and patience. Some poems unfold nicely with New Critical moves; others seem more resistant. That's the great thing about becoming familiar with a variety of different approaches. You'll have a wealth of strategies to apply.

To help you become more comfortable with New Criticism, have a go at the next poem, Lucille Clifton's "forgiving my father," which is followed by some questions intended to guide your analysis. After working through Clifton's poem, we'll take up some useful terms and concepts for writing about poetry.

LUCILLE CLIFTON (1936–)

forgiving my father

it is friday. we have come
to the paying of the bills.
all week you have stood in my dreams
like a ghost, asking for more time
but today is payday, payday old man,   5
my mother's hand opens in her early grave
and i hold it out like a good daughter.

there is no more time for you. there will
never be time enough daddy daddy old lecher
old liar. i wish you were rich so i could take it all   10
and give the lady what she was due
but you were the son of a needy father,
the father of a needy son,
you gave her all you had
which was nothing. you have already given her   15
all you had.

you are the pocket that was going to open
and come up empty any friday.
you were each other's bad bargain, not mine.
daddy old pauper old prisoner, old dead man   20
what am i doing here collecting?
you lie side by side in debtor's boxes
and no accounting will open them up.

[1969]

Questions

1. How does the title relate to the poem? That is, how is the title at odds with what the poem says? List the statements in the poem that do not sound "forgiving."
2. What is the significance of "collecting" in line 21? How is this word like "accounting" and "open" in line 24? In what sense is the speaker "collecting"?
3. What reasons does the poem offer for forgiving the father?
4. How is the poem's conflict resolved? Is the phrase "forgiving a debt" relevant to this poem?
5. How would you state the theme of this poem in one sentence? Try a two-part sentence: "Although x, y."

Elements: Voice, Speaker, Tone, Point of View, and Irony

Although many textbooks struggle to define what "poetry" is, few students seem truly worried about this. What students are often concerned about is how to read poetry, how to make sense of it and enjoy it—not how to find it. But the question of why poetry is so hard is actually related to the question of what poetry is. Poetry is challenging—for all readers, not just students—because "poems" represent what we consider to be the richest and most intense uses of our language. Poems can draw upon all of language's resources: rhythm, rhyme, spacing, word choice, form: whatever language can do, poems attempt to do it, and often even more. If "literature" refers to those works we particularly value, for reasons beyond the information they convey, then "poetry" points to literature distilled, we might say. Every single word counts in a poem. Poems are usually arranged on the page in a way that calls implicitly for this heightened attentiveness: even if you don't know a word of French, you can likely guess whether a particular book in French is a collection of poetry or something else. Because there is usually more white space on the page, the words of the poem naturally seem more important.

Not all poems are teeth-grindingly difficult, and some are quite simple. But even the simplest poems attempt to do something extraordinary with language, and so poetic readers have to be alert in order not to miss it. When you do catch onto a poem, "when you really feel it," as James Dickey puts it, "a new part of you happens, or an old part is renewed, with surprise and delight at being what it is" (from "How to Enjoy Poetry"). You'd think more people would read poetry; you'd think people would wake up in the morning and go out in the driveway to pick up the morning poetry. Unfortunately, Newton's laws of motion seem to apply to our brains, and objects at rest tend to stay at rest, unless an external force acts upon them: thinking is hard work, and engaging with the external force of a poem can be tough. It's not easy to make a new part of yourself happen, or to renew an old part. The number of people who read poetry regularly may be relatively small. But the payoff—your mind in motion—can be huge.

There are indeed practical rewards for reading and writing poetry, beyond discovering and renewing parts of yourself. Consider, for instance, this letter to a particularly well-known director of dermatology at a medical school (whose name has been changed to protect the guilty):

```
Dear Dr. Skin:

    It has come to the attention of this office that the

    lectures scheduled to be delivered September 11 and 18 were

    not given. These lectures are an integral part of the

    residents' training program. Please consult your schedule

    carefully and arrange to have the upcoming lectures

    delivered.
```

How would you describe the **voice** in this letter? It's not friendly. In fact, it sounds distant, impersonal, and self-important. The information actually didn't come to "this office"; it came to some person, but that person has transformed himself into an object. The disembodied voice of this office does not reveal the source of its information, which did not come on its own power, and which turned out to be inaccurate. The information sounds as if it just appears, almost as if this entity extends its consciousness in a God-like way and receives data. If the first sentence is cold, the second is patronizing. It seems unlikely that the letter's recipient really does not know that these lectures are important, and that they are part of the residents' training. The sentence isn't trying to be informative, either. If you read this letter aloud, you might find it hard not to sound like a scolding father. The final sentence, although superficially polite with its initial "Please," sounds like a stiff and threatening command, given to an underling of questionable intelligence: consult *carefully* (reading your own schedule is no doubt difficult for you) and arrange—or else.

Compare this letter:

```
Susan,

     Is there some problem with your lecture schedule? One of

the residents happened to mention to me that you had

cancelled the last two, and so I thought I'd better check.

I'm always hearing from the students and residents about how

valuable your Derm lectures are for them, so I'm especially

eager to do whatever we can to make sure they get to hear

your lectures. Let me know.
```

Which letter would you prefer to receive? Which letter would you prefer to have written? Which letter seems more appropriate for gathering information about something that might be a problem, but that is at this point an unknown quantity? How would you feel if you wrote the first letter and then discovered that the recipient has recently been diagnosed with cancer, or her mother had been deathly ill, or—as turned out to be the case—the person had actually given the lectures, but not in the place that one resident had written on her calendar, erroneously?

To be sure, in some situations, a cold and distant voice may be exactly what you want to project. But too many writers have little or no sense of how they are presenting themselves on paper. They cannot hear the voice, or the tone of voice, that comes across. This tone deafness is so common and so difficult to overcome, that in email messages certain symbols have evolved (they're usually called emoticons) to indicate the writer's intended tone—a stylized wink, a smiley face, a sad face, and a good many more.

How can you develop your sensitivity to the voices that words imply? How can you avoid writing letters that make people unnecessarily mad and offended— and that you have to apologize for later? One powerful way—as you may have suspected—is by studying poetry. Whereas fiction and drama often provide lots of clues about a speaker's tone, telling who and where and when and under what circumstances someone is speaking, poems often give us only the speaker's words. We have to imagine everything else, which can make reading poetry challenging, but also terrific training for hearing the voice that a text is projecting. New Criticism in particular, because it focuses upon the text itself for meaning and not upon historical and biographical information, is especially good practice for "hearing" what is written.

In this section we shall consider some of the various aspects of poetry that make engaging attentively with poetry difficult; similar sections in subsequent chapters will deal with other challenging aspects. Let's begin with speaker and some related concepts.

Here is a wonderful poem, winner of the prestigious Pushcart Prize in 1982-1983. Read it several times, and consider who is the speaker, and how the speaker's voice contributes to the poem.

STEPHEN SHU-NING LIU (1930–)

My Father's Martial Art

When he came home Mother said he looked
like a monk and stank of green fungus.
At the fireside he told us about life
at the monastery: his rock pillow,
his cold bath, his steel-bar lifting   5
and his wood-chopping. He didn't see
a woman for three winters, on Mountain O Mei.

"My Master was both light and heavy.
He skipped over treetops like a squirrel.
Once he stood on a chair, one foot tied   10
to a rope. We four pulled; we couldn't
move him a bit. His kicks could split
a cedar's trunk."

I saw Father break into a pumpkin
with his fingers. I saw him drop a hawk   15
with bamboo arrows. He rose before dawn, filled
our backyard with a harsh sound *hah, hah, hah*:
there was his Black Dragon Sweep, his Crane Stand,
his Mantis Walk, his Tiger Leap, his Cobra Coil . . .
Infrequently he taught me tricks and made me   20
fight the best of all the village boys.

From a busy street I brood over high cliffs
on O Mei, where my father and his Master sit:
shadows spread across their faces as the smog
between us deepens into a funeral pyre.   25

But don't retreat into night, my father.
Come down from the cliffs. Come
with a single Black Dragon Sweep and hush
this oncoming traffic with your *hah, hah, hah.*

[1982]

It might seem obvious that the answer to the question "Who is speaking in the poem?" is Stephen Shu-ning Liu. And if you wonder "who is that?" a web search of his name will take you to the University of Nevada Press and this biographical tidbit: "Stephen Shu-ning Liu is a unique figure in contemporary letters—a native of China, from a family of scholars, who left his country as a young man and now writes in English, a language he learned only after emigrating." Clearly, it would be interesting to know more, but New Criticism, you will recall, assumes that the author's biography is not an essential tool for understanding and appreciating the author's work. Our focus as readers, at least while reading as New Critics, should ultimately be upon the work itself. Such a distinction is easy to make when, for example, a middle-aged man writes a poem in which the speaker is a young girl. The middle-aged man may or may not like to play with dolls; we'd be making a mistake if we ventured a guess based on the poem.

But why do we need to make this distinction between the author and the speaker when the two seem, as in this poem, suggestively to be the same, or thereabouts? For one thing, from a New Critical perspective, if we think of the first-person speaker as the voice of Shu-ning Liu, the flesh and blood author, whose father really may have been in a monastery, our attention may begin to leak away from the poem. We naturally may want to find out all we can about Shu-ning Liu's father, for instance: which monastery was he in, did he really have a master who could skip over the treetops like a squirrel, how can anyone sink his fingers into a pumpkin, and what were the tricks he showed his son? New Critics are not opposed to such investigation; their point is just that you're not doing literary criticism in that case; you're doing something else. What *is* essential to a reading of the poem, as New Critics see it anyway, is careful analysis of the poem itself. We don't have to worry about whether the facts in the poem agree with the facts of Shu-ning Liu's life, and whether the voice in the poem belongs to a character (even a character with the same name as the poet) or the real-life poet himself. The voice in the poem belongs to the speaker, we can say, and get on with our analysis.

The voice in this poem is an intimate one, not bothering to explain who "he" and "Mother" are in the first line, but revealing how his father smelled, according to his mother, and how long his father went without seeing a woman. Such immediacy is not unusual in poetry, especially in lyric poetry, which is characterized in part by its goal of expressing the ideas and emotions of a speaker. Although there are hints of stories in this poem (the father's time at the monastery, the father's time with the growing son, the son's call for his father), it does not really tell a tale, with a beginning, middle, and end. Therefore, this poem would be classed as a **lyric poem**, not **a narrative poem**, and the focus upon the speaker's personal emotions is thus what the poem is all about.

The speaker's voice, then, which is essential to the poem's task, seems disciplined and restrained, laying out the facts in the first section without embellishment: he looked like a monk and stank; he told about his harsh regimen; he didn't see a woman for three years. The speaker's **tone** seems matter of fact. But the first-person speaker, the "I" who speaks so closely to us, and tells us bits and pieces of his father's life, is not, we should notice, the only speaker in the poem. The second section is enclosed in quotation marks, indicating (it would seem) that the speaker is quoting someone else. Shu-ning Liu might have chosen to have this speech reported, as in the first stanza ("My father used to say that his Master was both light and heavy . . ."), but the direct presentation of the father's voice shifts the point of view and the emphasis of the poem momentarily. Rather than the speaker filtering his father's memories, the quotation gives us the father's reminiscence directly.

The father's voice seems even more disciplined and efficient than the son's, providing startling information in short simple sentences, without expressions of awe or wonder. The son's tone in the third stanza echoes the father's tone: the father merely lists his Master's exploits ("His kicks could split a cedar's trunk"); likewise, the son lists his father's amazing deeds in spare yet precise language ("I saw Father break into a pumpkin/ with his fingers"). Against this simplicity, the names of the father's postures seem particularly strange and exotic: "his Black Dragon Sweep, his Crane Stand,/ his Mantis Walk, his Tiger Leap, his Cobra Coil."

But the tone of the poem is complicated by one word in line 20: "Infrequently." The significance of this word is ambiguous, but it does suggest the possibility that the son feels some neglect from the father. The father did leave home for an extended period during the crucial years of the son's childhood. Does the son long for more frequent contact with the father? Does he wish the father taught him tricks more often? If there is any feeling of neglect, any anger, it does not emerge clearly in the poem, but there is a further ambiguity in the assertion in line 21 that the father made the son "fight the best of all the village boys." Does he mean that the father showed him, even with infrequent coaching, how to fight better than all the village boys? In that case, the son might naturally feel appreciation. Or does he mean that the father, even though he rarely taught him anything, made him fight against the best of the village boys (to make him tougher we suppose)? In that case, the son might naturally feel resentment.

The poem's ambiguity, made possible by the speaker's restraint, continues to the end. The son's **point of view**, literally the place from which he is speaking, is clarified in line 22, when we learn that he is speaking from "a busy street." Until this point, the speaker has not revealed that he is physically as well as temporally removed from his father. The son's brooding takes his attention to the mountain O Mei, "where my father and his Master sit." Although it may appear at first that the father has again left his family to be with his Master, the reference to the shadows spreading across their faces, and the smog becoming "a funeral pyre" suggests that the father is actually dead. In what sense then does the son see the father? If the son's tone had been hysterical or irrational, one might think that he is having a vision, that he really believes he sees his father and his Master over the high cliffs. But it seems more likely, given the level tone, that he is simply imagining his father, without losing touch with reality.

The complexity of the final paragraph depends upon the meaning of the son's final plea to the father. After imploring him, "don't retreat into night, my father," the son asks him to "Come down from the cliffs. Come/ with a single Black Dragon Sweep and hush/ this oncoming traffic with your *hah, hah, hah*." These lines may simply mean that the son misses the father sorely, imagines him sitting with his Master in the afterlife, and wishes for the father to come back. The absence of the father is made more dramatic, I think, by the speaker's physical position: it appears that he is not in the village; he's not literally facing the cliffs of O Mei. He is somewhere in a large city—enduring a "busy street," "smog," and "oncoming traffic"—removed from his father in every way. But what is not revealed here, explicitly, is how the son feels about the father's absence. That "Infrequently" may haunt the poem, and it is possible that the closing lines are not literal, but ironic: that is, that the son, resentful of his father's neglect, is ridiculing his power. The father cannot avoid retreating into the night: he isn't even there. He cannot come down from the cliffs, and the son is simply taunting his memory by asking him to "hush/ this oncoming traffic with your *hah, hah, hah*." No martial arts moves I have ever seen, even in Jackie Chan's kung fu movies, will stop city traffic on a busy street.

This New Critical reading, exposing the poem's ambiguity and complexity, relies as you have seen upon paying attention to the poem's voices, the speaker's point of view, tone, and possible irony. For New Critics, **irony** is a particularly important term, because it refers to the potential for words to mean more than one thing. If I say "wow, what a nice day!" in the middle of a driving cold rainstorm, I either have an unusual view of the weather, or I am being ironic. Ordinarily, if it's unclear whether I'm ironic or weird, then my language has failed. But New Critics celebrate such ambiguity in poetry, such richness of language: it's the key to great literature.

✔ Checklist for New Criticism

- ❏ Read closely, identifying the work's oppositions, tensions, paradoxes, ironies.
- ❏ Read closely, assuming that everything in the work—figures of speech, point of view, diction, recurrent ideas or images, everything—is carefully calculated to contribute to the work's unity.
- ❏ Read closely, determining how the poem's various elements create unity.

Useful Terms for New Criticism

Let's review briefly the terms introduced in this section before applying them to another moving poem:

Voice: The voice is what we don't actually hear, but must imagine that we hear in order to read poetry effectively. In fiction, we are usually given information about who is speaking. In drama, when it is performed anyway, we can actually see and hear the characters speaking. But in poetry, the reader often has to invent the voice out of clues in the work. Oftentimes, readers of poetry are not told directly who is speaking, to whom, from where, on what occasion. We have to figure that out, and that effort helps us to imagine the voices we should hear in the poem.

Speaker: The person speaking in the poem is not equivalent to the author. Even if the poem's speaker has the same name as the author, we should not assume that this speaker is the author. The speaker within the poem is a presentation, a kind of character.

Tone: Tone means pretty much the same thing in critical circles that it means in everyday life. It's the way something is said. What is interesting about texts, again, is that they have no tone until we supply it, and we do so based upon the clues of the text, as we read them. This invention is often not easy, necessitating careful attention. Many readers find it helpful to read a poem aloud, to hear the tone of the work. But note that you cannot simply read the poem aloud in order to create an interpretation of it; you really need an interpretation in order to read it aloud appropriately. Finding the right tone for a speaker in a poem is a process of trial and error. As you read the work, evolve your understanding of the way something is being said. Tone is potentially complex—since there are more ways than one to say what is being said.

Point of View: Everyone has to be somewhere, and point of view is simply that place from which a voice is speaking. Stories may be told by a *first-person narrator*, an "I" who tells us what happened. This "I" may be a participant in what happened, or not. The **narrator** (or speaker, if there doesn't seem to be a story to narrate) can also be a voice standing outside the story. Instead of saying "I thought John was going" (first person), the narrator could say "Sam thought John was going" (*third-person narrator*). If the third-person narrator seems to know everything, then we say the narrator is *omniscient*; if the third-person narrator knows more than any person or other entity could (for instance, what other characters are thinking), but not everything, then we have a "*limited omniscient narrator.*" Of course, if the narrator is a telepath, then we have a first-person narrator with extraordinary powers.

Irony: Irony calls for the reader to create, in a sense, a certain kind of mask for the speaker. When the reader identifies irony, the reader says, in effect, "I see two of you: a false you who's saying something that I'm supposed to see through; and another more true you who is really saying something different from what you appear on the surface to be saying." The mask may be serious; the face underneath may be kidding. For New Critics, irony is a key term, pointing to the multiple meanings of a single assertion. A text with irony is complex, meaning potentially more than one thing.

Here is another poem dealing with fatherhood. Read it, think about it, and discuss it in terms of voice, speaker, tone, point of view, and irony. Specifically, consider who is speaking and the nature of the voice(s) you hear. Where is the speaker located in space and time? What is the relationship (space, time, emotions) of the speaker to any events and people mentioned? That is, what is the speaker's point of view? Tone? Do you detect any irony in the speaker's words?

SEAMUS HEANEY (1939–)

Digging

Between my finger and my thumb
The squat pen rests; snug as a gun.

Under my window, a clean rasping sound
When the spade sinks into gravelly ground.
My father, digging. I look down   5

Till his straining rump among the flowerbeds
Bends low, comes up twenty years away
Stooping in rhythm through potato drills
Where he was digging.

The coarse boot nestled on the lug, the shaft   10
Against the inside knee was levered firmly.
He rooted out tall tops, buried the bright edge deep
To scatter new potatoes that we picked
Loving their cool hardness in our hands.

By God, the old man could handle a spade.   15
Just like his old man.

My grandfather cut more turf in a day
Than any other man on Toner's bog.
Once I carried him milk in a bottle
Corked sloppily with paper. He straightened up   20
To drink it, then fell to right away

Nicking and slicing neatly, heaving sods
Over his shoulder, going down and down
For the good turf. Digging.

The cold smell of potato mould, the squelch and slap   25
Of soggy peat, the curt cuts of an edge
Through living roots awaken in my head.
But I've no spade to follow men like them.

Between my finger and my thumb   30
The squat pen rests.
I'll dig with it.

[1966]

Practice: Ties That Bind

Here are some more poems drawing your close attention to the bonds between
parents and children.

RICHARD WILBUR (1921–)

The Writer

In her room at the prow of the house
Where light breaks, and the windows are tossed with linden,
My daughter is writing a story.

I pause in the stairwell, hearing
From her shut door a commotion of typewriter-keys   5
Like a chain hauled over a gunwale.

Young as she is, the stuff
Of her life is a great cargo, and some of it heavy:
I wish her a lucky passage.

But now it is she who pauses,   10
As if to reject my thought and its easy figure.
A stillness greatens, in which

The whole house seems to be thinking,
And then she is at it again with a bunched clamor
Of strokes, and again is silent.   15

I remember the dazed starling
Which was trapped in that very room, two years ago;
How we stole in, lifted a sash

And retreated, not to affright it;
And how for a helpless hour, through the crack of the door, 20
We watched the sleek, wild, dark

And iridescent creature
Batter against the brilliance, drop like a glove
To the hard floor, or the desk-top.

And wait then, humped and bloody,   25
For the wits to try it again; and how our spirits
Rose when, suddenly sure,

It lifted off from a chair-back,
Beating a smooth course for the right window
And clearing the sill of the world.   30

It is always a matter, my darling,
Of life or death, as I had forgotten. I wish
What I wished you before, but harder.

                                            [1976]

Questions

1. In line 11, the speaker refers to his "easy figure." A "figure" in this sense is
   a metaphor, a comparison. What is the metaphor? (See "prow," "tossed,"
   "gunwale," "cargo," "passage.") The speaker imagines that she rejects his
   metaphor, but what happens to the image as the poem unfolds?

2. Who is speaking in the poem, and how would you describe his tone? Does
   the speaker's tone change? When he says "my darling" in line 31, to whom is
   he speaking?

3. In what sense does the story of the starling conflict or contrast with what is
   actually going on in the house? In what sense does the starling's story illuminate and reveal what is going on in the house? How does the starling contribute to the poem's complexity?

4. Pick three or four interesting words in the poem—words that strike you as
   unexpected, or as words you might not have used if you were writing the
   poem. Ponder how these words work, and what they do for the poem.

The Prodigal Son (*Luke 15: 11–32, King James Version*)

11 ¶And he said, A certain man had two sons:

12 And the younger of them said to *his* father, Father, give me the portion
of goods that falleth *to me*. And he divided unto them *his* living.

13 And not many days after the younger son gathered all together, and
took his journey into a far country, and there wasted his substance   5
with riotous living.

14 And when he had spent all, there arose a mighty famine in that land;
and he began to be in want.

15 And he went and joined himself to a citizen of that country; and he
sent him into his fields to feed swine.   10

16 And he would fain have filled his belly with the husks that the swine
did eat: and no man gave unto him.

17 And when he came to himself, he said, How many hired servants of my
father's have bread enough and to spare, and I perish with hunger!

18 I will arise and go to my father, and will say unto him, Father, I have   15
sinned against heaven, and before thee,

19 And am no more worthy to be called thy son: make me as one of thy
hired servants.

20 And he arose, and came to his father. But when he was yet a great way
off, his father saw him, and had compassion, and ran, and fell on his   20
neck, and kissed him.

21 And the son said unto him, Father, I have sinned against heaven, and in
thy sight, and am no more worthy to be called thy son.

22 But the father said to his servants, Bring forth the best robe, and put *it*
on him; and put a ring on his hand, and shoes on *his* feet: 25

23 And bring hither the fatted calf, and kill *it;* and let us eat, and be merry:

24 For this my son was dead, and is alive again; he was lost, and is found.
And they began to be merry.

25 Now his elder son was in the field: and as he came and drew nigh to
the house, he heard musick and dancing.   30

26 And he called one of the servants, and asked what these things meant.

27 And he said unto him, Thy brother is come; and thy father hath killed
the fatted calf, because he hath received him safe and sound.

28 And he was angry, and would not go in: therefore came his father out,
and intreated him.   35

29 And he answering said to *his* father, Lo, these many years do I serve
thee, neither transgressed I at any time thy commandment: and yet
thou never gavest me a kid, that I might make merry with my friends:

30 But as soon as this thy son was come, which hath devoured thy living
with harlots, thou hast killed for him the fatted calf.   40

31 And he said unto him, Son, thou art ever with me, and all that I have is
thine.

32 It was meet that we should make merry, and be glad: for this thy
brother was dead, and is alive again; and was lost, and is found.

Questions

1. The speaker of this story (or parable) is of course Jesus, as reported in *The Gospel
of Luke*, and the context is that Jesus has been accused by "the Pharisees and

scribes" of "welcoming sinners" and even eating with them. The parable apparently answers this charge—that Jesus spends time in the company of sinners. Does an awareness of that context affect your reading of the parable? How?

2. What irony do you find in the story?
3. How does a phrase like "the fatted calf" (in this translation) affect the tone of this parable? What other words and phrases do you find that contribute to the voice here?
4. What is the unifying idea of this parable?

THEODORE ROETHKE (1908–1963)

My Papa's Waltz

The whiskey on your breath
Could make a small boy dizzy;
But I hung on like death:
Such waltzing was not easy.

We romped until the pans   5
Slid from the kitchen shelf;
My mother's countenance
Could not unfrown itself.

The hand that held my wrist
Was battered on one knuckle;   10
At every step you missed
My right ear scraped a buckle.

You beat time on my head
With a palm caked hard by dirt,
Then waltzed me off to bed   15
Still clinging to your shirt.

[1948]

Questions

1. Who is speaking? When? What is his tone?
2. The tension in this poem, obviously, concerns how we take this event: is it an affectionate moment, rough-housing play of father and son? Is it drunken indulgence, bordering perhaps on abuse even? In two columns, put down the evidence you see for each side.
3. How is the poem unified? In what sense is the affection-versus-abuse equation too simple? Why is the boy "still clinging" at the end?

GREGORY DJANIKIAN (1949–)

Immigrant Picnic

It's the Fourth of July, the flags
are painting the town,
the plastic forks and knives
are laid out like a parade.

And I'm grilling, I've got my apron,   5
I've got potato salad, macaroni, relish,
I've got a hat shaped
like the state of Pennsylvania.

I ask my father what's his pleasure
and he says, "Hot dog, medium rare,"   10
and then, "Hamburger, sure,
what's the big difference,"
as if he's really asking.

I put on hamburgers *and* hot dogs,
slice up the sour pickles and Bermudas,   15
uncap the condiments. The paper napkins
are fluttering away like lost messages.

"You're running around," my mother says,
"like a chicken with its head loose."

"Ma," I say, "You mean *cut off,*   20
loose and *cut off* being as far apart
as, say, *son* and *daughter*."

She gives me a quizzical look as though
I've been caught in some impropriety.
"I love you and your sister just the same," she says.   25
"Sure," my grandmother pipes in,
"You're both our children, so why worry?"

That's not the point I begin telling them,
and I'm comparing words to fish now,
like the ones in the sea at Port Said,   30
or like birds among the date palms by the Nile,
unrepentantly elusive, wild.

"Sonia," my father says to my mother,
"what the hell is he talking about?"
"He's on a ball," my mother says.   35

"That's *roll!*" I say, throwing up my hands,
"as in hot dog, hamburger, dinner roll. . . ."

"And what about *roll out the barrels?*" my mother asks,
and my father claps his hands, "Why sure," he says,
"let's have some fun," and launches   40
into a polka, twirling my mother
around and around like the happiest top,

and my uncle is shaking his head, saying
"You could grow nuts listening to us,"

and I'm thinking of pistachios in the Sinai   45
burgeoning without end,
pecans in the South, the jumbled
flavor of them suddenly in my mouth,
wordless, confusing,
crowding out everything else.   50

[1999]

Questions

1. What is the most obvious tension or opposition in this poem? Are there others? See how many you can list.
2. In the first four lines, inanimate objects seem to come alive. (It's a wonderful opening, isn't it?) How do words and things seem to take on lives of their own in the rest of the poem?
3. How do the different voices quoted in the poem contrast with the speaker's voice? How does this contrast contribute to the poem?
4. How is the opposition between, for instance, the Sinai and the South, resolved by the ending of the poem?

Suggestions for Writing

The idea here is to write a poem that has something to do with parenting. That's pretty vague and wide open, which is just what we want. The key to a good poem, like a good essay, is preparation. There are hundreds, maybe thousands of exercises that creative writing teachers use to get students started. Here are a few for you to try:

1. **Automatic Writing.**   This trick is usually called "freewriting" when it's being used to develop an essay. You've probably used it before. It's very simple and effective. You just start writing and don't stop. You don't worry about the quality of what you're saying, about the grammar, about the logic, about anything. Just keep writing. In this case, you focus your mind on parenting—perhaps thinking of some particular event that relates to parenting, and you're off. If you find yourself getting off the topic, don't worry about it; just pull yourself back to the topic and keep going. After you have a good bit of material, read back over it and see if there is anything worth saving. Then go again. After a while, you're bound to have some stuff you can use to develop a poem. From a New Critical perspective, of course, the "stuff" you are looking for would be ideas, words, and phrases that create some tension, conflict, ambiguity, etc.

2. **Rich Words.**   This technique is also easy. Just list some interesting words. Some should relate to parenting in some way, but they don't all have to. Then see how many of these interesting words you can work into a poem. Why does this often work? Because the words themselves spark ideas, and the mind naturally brainstorms to make connections.

3. **Three more suggestions:**   First, try to show your reader, rather than telling. In James Dickey's "Cherrylog Road," instead of saying "I was really nervous," Dickey writes "I popped with sweat." Second, try to get some people talking in your poem: quote someone. Dialogue usually enlivens a work. Third, be gentle with yourself and your classmates. Don't lie, but be as appreciative as you can be when reading someone else's poetry.

6

Read Poetry Playfully: Deconstruction

> "To do deconstruction, just jump up in the air and stay there."
> —Hans Aarsleff, *in a conversation at the Folger Library, sometime in 1986*

Deconstruction is like Elvis. Both have been declared dead, yet that status seems not to have interfered much with their influence or fascination. Deconstructive ways of thinking have profoundly influenced and are still influencing fields as diverse as theology and fashion design, architecture and music videos. If Elvis is alive, there's a good chance he's heard of deconstruction, which has altered the critical landscape, and lives on under a variety of other names.

Like any term that enters popular culture, "deconstruction" has been used in many different ways—sometimes with little apparent understanding of the word's history or reference. In a recent *Coffee Journal,* an article entitled "Deconstructing Starbucks" seems to use "deconstructing" as a synonym for "analyzing carefully." In a recent *Chronicle of Higher Education,* a regular feature called "Deconstruct This" seems simply to ask several academic experts to comment on a particular topic: in one issue, three professors offer different perspectives on the popularity of competitive shows like *Survivor* and on the role of competition in society. Careful analysis and differing perspectives would not seem to call for a new word, and so you may wonder what is distinctive about "deconstruction." What exactly does it mean?

An esteemed authority on deconstruction once responded to this question ("What exactly does 'deconstruction' mean?"), after a very long pause, in this way: "I'm not going to fall into that trap." "If you really understood deconstruction," Professor Deepthinker might say, "you wouldn't try to explain it, especially not to undergraduates. You'll have to distort and simplify grossly." But deconstruction (and here my explanation of it begins) holds that all explanations ultimately fail. Nothing that is put into language can be entirely successful and complete because language always distorts or leaves something out, and what turns out to be missing can be shown to be crucial. Since an explanation is doomed to fail, why not illustrate deconstruction brilliantly by constructing a simple and careful explanation that nonetheless fails to make its point? If deconstruction itself can be deconstructed, we might say that its point is simply that every text always makes its point.

Deconstruction is an interpretive strategy that is ultimately skeptical about interpreting. This lack of faith in our ability to make coherent sense out of texts, while it has been disturbing and even depressing for some people, has often proved to be stimulating, liberating, even entertaining. To see why, and to see how deconstruction works, let's start with this idea: a map of a mountain is not the same thing as the mountain itself. No matter how detailed the map is, some aspects of the mountain must be left out. Even a photograph of the mountain would be different from the mountain, even if the photograph were exactly the same size as the mountain, in incredible detail. Even if we decided to make a three-dimensional map of the mountain, a replica of it, the two would not be identical: by the time we finished making our "map," the real mountain would no doubt have changed. I can imagine the construction of another mountain that would be exactly like the first mountain at its completion, a perfect copy that would change over time in exactly the same way as the first mountain. But I can't imagine any human force performing this, nor can I see in what sense that second mountain would be a "map." A map is a representation of something, and to be useful, a representation simplifies and organizes the thing it represents.

Language is one of the tools we use to map our world. Unavoidably, language imposes an order and a simplicity on whatever it describes. Deconstruction aims to call our attention to what our various linguistic maps of the world leave out or distort. Deconstruction is therefore unsettling and aggravating to many people, especially to those who think they already have something (or everything) figured out and don't want to think about it anymore. Deconstruction comes up to someone who has figured out where they are, points at their map and says, "Are you sure that's where you are? I think maybe you're over here. No, wait, I think you've got the map upside down. No, actually, I think that's the wrong map!"

Of what possible use could such a smart-alecky, no-matter-what-you-say-you're-wrong attitude be? For one thing, deconstruction's deep skepticism may help to unravel our closed-minded complacency. It opens up our thinking and challenges us to look at things from another point of view. And another. And another. Such freedom can be quite healthy and exciting. It is a freedom that, when we take notice of it, obliges us to play in the fields and forests of language, to look up from our maps and become explorers on our own.

But there are at least two limits on deconstruction's freedom. First limit: practically speaking, most people can't explore and play indefinitely all the time. Although deconstruction tells us that something is always left out, and that more could always be said on any topic, we can't go on forever talking and rethinking about everything. Sometimes, in some matters, we have to decide; we have to take a stand, to write the last sentence, and to end that sentence somewhere, even though we know we might say more, see the problem more complexly, or even change our minds, or just go on and on like maybe you think this sentence is going to do (but it isn't; it can't). Still, after some experience with deconstruction, the choice you have to make might be based on a richer evaluation; and, after deconstruction, you are more likely to view your decision with a more open mind, realizing that you could always go back and reconsider—simply because you understand something about the way language and reasoning work.

The second limit: some ideas or positions seem so abhorrent, so despicable to us, that another, alternative viewpoint seems impossible or at least irresponsible. Does deconstruction require us to take another view of Nazism, to see the Ku Klux Klan differently? Jacques Derrida (who is usually credited with inventing deconstruction) contributed in 1986 to a collection honoring Nelson Mandela (published in English as *For Nelson Mandela,* edited by Derrida [New York: Holt, 1987]). In his essay, Derrida refuses to deconstruct apartheid or to place in question Mandela's great contribution to dismantling South Africa's racist policies. There are just some concepts and values, Derrida asserted, that we may choose to exempt from our scrutiny. So, deconstruction does not require us to deconstruct anything. It only claims that given the nature of language, any system of ideas may be questioned—if we are clever enough, and if we choose to do so.

One could argue, in fact, that subjecting Mandela's ideas to deconstruction might produce something valuable, and that Derrida is simply being closed-minded in this area. And he is. But applying deconstruction to apartheid or to Mandela would not produce any stable truth, any solid ground to stand on anyway; it would only produce understanding—or rather, an understanding of the incompleteness of our understanding, and Derrida chooses not to expose the incompleteness of Mandela and the opposition to apartheid. There will always be some reality out there beyond our words, as in the "Presidential Post-Modernism" cartoon. Although "Bill" says, "Who's to say 'We' 'are' 'even' 'here'?"—we may notice that there is, in fact, someone peeking around the door—a reality not subject to his fast talking. Deconstruction is a tool to investigate language; language is not reality, but language is a tool that we use to interact with or understand or evade reality.

To deconstruct Starbucks, or the idea of competition, or a poem, means then that we subject it to a skeptical and playful scrutiny. The easiest way to apply this deep scrutiny to something is simply to stand the thing on its head, or turn it inside out. If the *Survivor* show's popularity seems like a disturbing sign of competition gone wild in the early twenty-first century, one might argue that the show also showcases cooperation, or that those who compete fiercely don't usually win, or that the show's version of competition is irrelevant to real life.

The limits of deconstruction, in other words, don't cancel out its value; they illuminate it. The limits of deconstruction help us to see more clearly what its virtues are. It is in theory without end and without morals; but in practice, deconstruction may help us to a better understanding of our own chosen ends and morals.

Reflection: An Open Space

A playfulness with language is especially prominent in John Ashberry's poems, which often seem to be turning around and looking at themselves, talking about themselves, flirting with doing what language cannot do. Here is a poem that seems to be dealing with some of the basic issues of deconstruction.

JOHN ASHBERRY (1927–)

Paradoxes and Oxymorons

The poem is concerned with language on a very plain level.
Look at it talking to you. You look out a window
Or pretend to fidget. You have it but you don't have it.
You miss it, it misses you. You miss each other.   5

The poem is sad because it wants to be yours, and cannot.
What's a plain level? It is that and other things,
Bringing a system of them into play. Play?
Well, actually, yes, but I consider play to be

A deeper outside thing, a dreamed role-pattern,   10
As in the division of grace these long August days
Without proof. Open-ended. And before you know
It gets lost in the steam and chatter of typewriters.

It has been played once more. I think you exist only
To tease me into doing it, on your level, and then you aren't there   15
Or have adopted a different attitude. And the poem
Has set me softly down beside you. The poem is you.

[1981]

Ashberry's first four lines tell us that even though "the poem is concerned with language on a very plain level," it doesn't link up with its reader: "You miss it, it misses you." This gap between the poem and the reader is unavoidable, according to deconstruction's assumptions, which insist that we will always "miss" the poem given the slipperiness and arbitrariness of language. The second stanza, immediately following the assertion "You miss each other," seems to illustrate this gap by shifting the meaning of "miss" from "not connecting" to include "wishing you were here." We have indeed, reading backward, "missed" the poem.

To be sure, Ashberry says "The poem is concerned," which might mean "this particular poem" or *any* poem (the poem as a genre). And Ashberry's poem actually does not say it is trying to speak to us on a "very plain level," but rather that it is "concerned with" language on a plain level. Is Ashberry using very plain language, or *analyzing* the use of very plain language? Obviously, the second possibility would be much more demanding; and with line six, this more difficult topic seems more likely. Responding to its own question, "What's a plain level?" the poem says, enigmatically, "It is that and other things,/ Bringing a system of them into play." As readers, we might well wonder "It is *that* what? You didn't say what *that* is!" From a deconstructive point of view, however, it doesn't matter so much what "that" is, since it is "other things" too. Even if the "that" were specified, we wouldn't have pinned it down very much, since anything is always "that" and other things too, since language can't really pin anything down ultimately, finally, completely.

Ashberry's acceptance of deconstructive assumptions seems especially evident in the suggestion that this uncertainty extends beyond particular words or sentences, since "a system of them" (whatever "them" refers to) is brought "into play." The mysterious third quatrain defines what the speaker considers "play to be":

> A deeper outside thing, a dreamed role-pattern,
> As in the division of grace these long August days
> Without proof.

This definition seems to create more of a feeling than a meaning. Something "deeper" would seem to be inside, but "play" here is a "deeper outside thing." Deconstructive critics have often revealed a desire to get outside the boundaries of language, or at least to write "on the margins" of language if we cannot think beyond it. It is very difficult if not impossible to think of how "grace" might be divided: we can say it, but can we think it? The idea that this "division of grace" occurs "Without proof" just seems to emphasize Ashberry's effort to try to say something outside the strict logic of serious language: "play" operates in the realm that is "Without proof." The playfulness of language that deconstruction so often embraces is, as Ashberry says, "Open-ended."

In the final four lines Ashberry's poem seems to step outside itself and comment on what has been happening: "It has been played once more." The poem's "I" and "you" seem to refer to Ashberry and the reader ("me" at the moment), but the poem says that "you" (the reader) "aren't there." I assure you that I am here right now, as I type this, but there is no "here" as you read this. And you're not "there" in a sense, either. The poem's "I," on the other hand, who really is the one who isn't there, at least from our perspective, is said to be set down softly "beside you." You can look around the room you're in all you want, but I bet you cannot find the poem's "I" sitting anywhere softly. The only thing sitting softly beside me, as I write, is this poem. But perhaps that is what the poem means: that the "I" exists only on the page. The "I" of language is sitting beside the "you" of language.

Yet the last sentence collapses the "I" of the poem, the poem itself, and "you": "The poem is you," it says. This claim is consistent with deconstruction's vision of the way language shapes us, as we inhabit its various systems of meaning (we are the poem as we read it); and this claim is also consistent with deconstruction's vision of the way that we may shape language, as we attempt to read differently, opening up the play of language. As Ashberry's title indicates, the poem, you, I, and our language—everything—is made of "Paradoxes and Oxymorons," of contradictions and differences, in other words, coming apart.

Here are some of the qualities of deconstruction we noticed in this poem:

- Even on a very plain level, a poem misses what it aims at.
- A poem is open-ended.

- A poem is part of a system of meaning that is in play.
- A poem tries to get outside logic and proof.
- We are made of language.

These ideas may still seem rather vague and abstract. Let's see how to apply deconstruction to a poem, step by step.

Strategies: Using Deconstructive Criticism

Here is a simple three-step strategy for performing a deconstructive reading. It is offered in the spirit of deconstructing deconstruction, which could only be reduced to such a recipe as a deconstructive act:

1. Because language inevitably makes meaning in terms of oppositions, dividing life into black and white, man and woman, pro and con, in and out, day and night, etc., you can begin to challenge this meaning-making by identifying the oppositions in a text and determining which ones are favored. (In any binary, one is always favored in some way.)
2. Because the ranking of the oppositions (often called "privileging") is arbitrary, you can turn it around, upside-down, inside-out, if you're clever and lucky enough. So, try to reverse the text's oppositions. Make the text say the opposite of what it appears to say, or make it focus upon something that might seem at first to be marginal or unimportant.
3. Assert how this reversal suggests the arbitrariness of the text's apparent claims. (This step is not always necessary or prudent. The text's instability may already be apparent.)

This strategy may, as many critics have noted, look a good bit like New Criticism distorted. Instead of finding the work's unity, showing how the work's oppositions are unified, the deconstructive critic shows how these oppositions pull the work apart, thereby exposing its self-contradictions. New Critics see paradoxes and oxymorons that are ultimately harmonized; deconstructive critics see paradoxes and oxymorons that reveal the unavoidable and inescapable contradictions inherent in language itself.

Let's work on a particular poem. What oppositions or tensions do you see in the following poem?

LANGSTON HUGHES (1902–1967)

Cross

My old man's a white old man
And my old mother's black.
If ever I cursed my white old man
I take my curses back.

If ever I cursed my black old mother   5
And wished she were in hell,
I'm sorry for that evil wish
And now I wish her well.

My old man died in a fine big house.

My ma died in a shack.
I wonder where I'm gonna die,
Being neither white nor black?

10

[1936]

You may have no-
ticed the following oppo-
sitions in this poem:

> white versus black
> rich versus poor
> father versus mother
> hatred versus
>   forgiveness
> the parents versus
>   the son
> knowing versus
>   wondering

Let's see first how the
poem puts these opposi-
tions together. How are
these tensions resolved
by the poem?

In New Critical
readings, titles are often
crucial keys to the work's
unity. What might "Cross"
mean? You will rarely
want to quote from a
dictionary as evidence
in an essay, since most
readers know the mean-
ings of most words, and
since such a strategy is
overused by students; but
you will certainly want to
use a dictionary to clarify
unfamiliar words and to

Langston Hughes, about 1927 (a little after "Cross"),
is standing between Jessie Fauset (right), an important editor and writer, and the great writer Zora
Neale Hurston. Behind them is the statue of Booker T.
Washington at Tuskegee University.

suggest meanings you might not have thought of. Look in any good dictionary and
note the rich variety of definitions for "cross." How many of this word's meanings
might be contributing to this poem?

Here are a student's notes as he brainstorms about the different meanings of
"cross," attempting to tie some of the poem's oppositions together.

```
    A cross between two kinds—a cross breed.
    Normally used to talk about animals. Why would the
speaker talk about himself that way? Does his mixed race
lead him to think of himself as subhuman?
    The state of anger: he (or is it a he?) was "cross" with
his parents, but now forgives them.
```

A burden to bear: just as Christ had to suffer
crucifixion.

Starting from these ideas, which may seem rather slim, the student evolved the following essay:

Race and Anger: Langston Hughes's "Cross"

Langston Hughes's poem "Cross" is only twelve lines long, but it packs a lifetime of resentment and reconciliation into its few verses. The speaker of the poem is the child of a black mother and white father: Hughes establishes this in the first two lines of the poem. We know nothing else about the persona, not even his gender. Hughes withholds this information from his readers to focus their attention on the speaker's racial ambiguity. We can infer, however, that the persona is at least middle-aged: the depth and maturity of his reflections suggest that this person has spent many years contemplating the circumstances and consequences of his birth.

The ambiguous title of the poem—"Cross"—reflects the racial ambiguity of the speaker. One meaning of "cross" is "a crossbred individual." The persona is a cross in this sense of the word, but nevertheless it seems clumsy to say this about a human being: usually, "cross" denotes an animal, not a person. The speaker's usage of "cross" here underscores the self-hatred which is evident in the anger he shows toward his parents. The anger is the second meaning of the title: the speaker as a younger person was "cross," or angry, about his heritage. The speaker suffered as a young person and tells us that his parents were the scapegoats for his pain. As a mature adult, however, the persona realizes that his anger was destructive and misdirected: "I take my curses back" he says of his father (4); of his mother, "I'm sorry for that evil wish/And now I wish her well"(7-8).

In the narrative present of the poem, the speaker understands that society, not his family, is the source of

```
his problems. The final stanza introduces race as a social
issue: the speaker wistfully contrasts his father's "fine big
house" with his mother's "shack" (9, 10). The persona now
knows that his parents were subjected to the same societal
forces that affect his own life, and this understanding makes
him wiser. The speaker finally realizes that the problem of
race prejudice cannot be blamed on his parents. Rather, it is
his personal burden: his cross to bear.
```

In this unifying reading of Hughes's poem, the speaker takes up the cross of being between races, of being a "cross." He (let us assume the speaker shares Hughes's gender) forgives his parents for having him (he is no longer "cross"); he acknowledges the social and financial gulf between his mother and father; and he accepts the state of uncertainty he cannot escape, since he has no clear place in either race.

But another view of a poem is always possible, deconstruction tells us. As we have noted before, one way of suggesting the uncertainty and openness of a text is simply to reverse the most obvious or conventional reading. Such mental acrobatics often require some imagination and patience: you may have to try a handful of reversals before you find one that will work. Notice how these notes on part of the poem push on just about every line to see if it will slip-slide around and mean something else.

My old man's a white old man

```
    Could I argue that his old man really isn't a white old
man? How does he know who his father really is anyway? I
guess I can't do much with this.
```

And my old mother's black.

```
    I don't know how I can question this. I mean, if he says
his mother is black and his father white, then how can I say
he's wrong? He ought to be able to tell, I guess, whether a
parent is white or black. But wait a minute: there are lots of
people that it isn't so easy to tell what their racial
background is. What does "white" or "black" mean anyway? What
if his dad had some black heritage, or if his mom had some
Caucasian blood? How could he know for sure that both parents
weren't already of mixed blood? What is the legal definition
of "black" or "white"? Is there a legal definition? There must
be, since I've seen articles in the newspaper about the courts
deciding whether white families can adopt black babies. I'll
do some research on this. What is a mulatto legally? White or
black? Is that the right term for a person of mixed race?
```

If ever I cursed my white old man
I take my curses back.

```
    This is weird. Why doesn't he know whether he has cursed
his father? The only reason I can think of is that he isn't
really mad. He doesn't know because it isn't that big of a
deal. He'd know if he were really suffering with his
```

feelings, wouldn't he? Maybe he thinks he ought to be angry. He's saying, hey, maybe I cursed you, I don't know, but I take it back. This really is weird. Another idea for reversing: he doesn't really take it back. He says he does, but he is giving his dad one more curse with this poem. He hates him, but he can't admit it. He doesn't even want to admit he has cursed his father? Yes?

If ever I cursed my black old mother
And wished she were in hell,
I'm sorry for that evil wish
And now I wish her well.

Same things apply here as for the father, pretty much. He may be tougher on the mother, for some reason, wishing she'd go to hell, while he just cursed his father. But he's not sure about either one, it appears.

My old man died in a fine big house.
My ma died in a shack.
I wonder where I'm gonna die,
Being neither white nor black?

The logical answer to this question would be somewhere in the middle, wouldn't it? Is it the father's whiteness that puts him in a fine big house? Why isn't he mad at the father, if he's in a fine house, while his mother's in a shack? Or is the problem sex? Does the mother's blackness put her in a shack, or her status as a woman? Or both? It seems, clearly, to be race, in the speaker's mind, given the last question here. But maybe the speaker really is mistaken? After all, even in Hughes's day, there were many affluent blacks who lived in fine big houses, and many poor whites who lived in shacks. Yet the speaker seems to assume in this stanza that his race would determine where he would die—his social position in other words—if he only knew what that race is. Maybe Hughes does not agree with the speaker's acceptance and complacency. Maybe he thinks the final question is dumb and he is exposing the speaker here?

Question: what color was Hughes? Look this up in the *Oxford Companion to American Literature*. Look up "race" in the *Encyclopedia Britannica*.

Using such notes, which attempt a deconstructive stance, along with a little research, the student wrote another essay. Notice how the following essay not only reverses the obvious reading, but it also suggests that Hughes is taking a deconstructive step toward calling into question the basic opposition of the poem, white versus black.

Racial Acquiescence: A "Cross" Reading

Langston Hughes's poem "Cross" appears to chart the maturing of a mulatto man as he deals with his hatred for his parents. Hughes was himself of European and African heritage, and the poem may seem to be part of an effort to heal his own childhood wounds. But the speaker, who is divided between white and black, may also be divided from Hughes. If the speaker seems at first to be moving toward peace and reconciliation, another look reveals that Hughes's view of the speaker is not necessarily sympathetic. Is the speaker dealing with the problem of his parents' race, or simply evading it?

A sharp opposition between the races is the distinctive hallmark of American racial history. Even in South Africa there are intermediate racial categories between white and black. The American person of mixed race is in a peculiar position, since his government apparently cannot allow for any ambiguity. The United States' legal standard for whiteness, which is still on the books, is that a person must be less than one seventy-second black to be white. This law is of course absurd at first glance: how can a person be one seventy-second of anything, since that number is not a power of two? Moreover, if a half-black person, like the speaker of the poem, is nevertheless legally one hundred percent black, does that not logically imply that anyone who has any trace of African heritage is black? The poem's speaker wonders where he belongs, with whites or blacks, but Hughes himself did not have such a question, at least not legally: he was black.

Hughes does not sympathize with the complacent speaker of the poem, who forgives his parents and ponders his future. The speaker, who is the crossing of his father and mother, ought to be cross over his situation. He is deprived of both father and mother, since he can identify with neither. He can only hate his parents for placing him in no-man's land, but in the poem he even gives up that hatred. Hughes suggests clearly that the speaker ought to be outraged: "My old man died in a big fine house./ My ma died in a shack."

Yet the speaker does not question the injustice of this arrangement, which must strike any reader as odd. He merely retreats into the numb detachment of the last two lines: "I wonder where I'm gonna die,/ Being neither white nor black." The speaker gives in to his society's racism.

The misdirected anger revealed in the first eight lines is hardly a healthy attitude, but at least it is intellectually honest. The angry young man realizes that he has been wronged, but does not identify the culprit: the racism of his society. His parents are only agents of this prejudice. The complacent older man should have understood these issues, Hughes implies; instead, he refuses to express any problem at all with society. Rather, he sees himself as the problem, wondering where he fits in. But it is his society, which refuses to make a place for him. Or perhaps, the problem is in part his own, as he accepts his society's racial division, considering himself "neither white nor black" rather than *both* white *and* black. Hughes thus not only exposes the shallowness of the speaker, he also questions dividing people into whites and blacks. Someone who is supposedly half-white and half-black cannot be divided.

✔ Checklist for Deconstruction

- ❑ Identify the oppositions in the text and determine which ones are favored.
- ❑ Reverse the oppositions, making the text say the opposite of what it appears to say, or making it focus upon something that might seem at first to be marginal or unimportant.
- ❑ Assert how this reversal suggests the text's arbitrariness, calling its meaning into question. Continue exposing uncertainties until the text's instability is clear.

Useful Terms for Deconstruction

Let's review briefly the terms discussed in this section.

Arbitrariness: Language, deconstruction assumes, is ultimately arbitrary. It could be different from what it is; indeed, languages change and evolve and become different as time goes on. Different languages divide up the universe differently, and each language is itself something constructed: if all English speakers decided that black dogs weren't actually dogs, and should be called "gringats" from now on, then black dogs and other kinds of dogs, according to our language, would be distinct things. Deconstruction wants to highlight this arbitrariness in order to remind us that texts are open to interpretation, and meaning is not fixed.

Binary: Language is based, structuralists and poststructuralists say, on oppositions: "bad" only has meaning because we can contrast it to "good"; "man" takes on its meaning in opposition to "woman," or "animal," or "boy," or some other opposing term. This opposing nature of language means that it is binary—that is, having two parts, two alternatives. Deconstruction recognizes that within this binary nature, one alternative is always suppressed, falsely simplifying reality.

Difference: See *différance*.

Différance: This difficult term was made up by Derrida to indicate two meanings at once: difference and deferral. "Difference" is an important idea in deconstruction, which seeks to show how a text contains within itself a trace of its own contradiction. The idea that something differs from itself may seem at first insane; but we've all heard someone say, "I'm not myself today." "Difference," as deconstruction sees things, is unavoidable: we are always not entirely and strictly ourselves. The related idea of "deferral" is important too; whereas "difference" seems to be a spatial idea, dividing an apparent unity, "deferral" refers to time—specifically to the idea of putting something off. "I'm going to defer a decision on that matter today," one might say. From a deconstructive point of view, when we move through time we never quite get where we're going: the point in time we aim for is always deferred. Likewise, if we want to see what something means by traveling back to its origin, we can never pinpoint this origin: there is always some prior beginning.

Think of the story of Adam and Eve, for instance: it is a story about "in the beginning," explaining the meaning of evil and suffering, which are (in the traditional reading) the effects of the first man and woman's sin, the fall from grace and innocence. But this story does not reveal the origin of the most important agent in the story: God. Why did God create Eden in the way that he did? What is the origin of the serpent who tempts Adam and Eve? Did God create him? If so, why? If not, where did the serpent come from? Thus, the deeper meaning of the story, the origin of the origin, can always be deferred if the analysis is pressed.

Dispersal: Deconstruction does not suggest simply that meanings can be reversed, end of story. Rather, the reversal of oppositions is a gesture designed to suggest the arbitrariness of meanings. Ultimately, a text could be analyzed until its essential uncertainty resulted in its unraveling—the dispersal or scattering of its meaning.

Opposition: See "binary."

Privilege: In an opposition, one term is unavoidably favored over the other in some way, since a perfect balance in every sense seems unlikely if not impossible. Deconstruction emphasizes how one term is "privileged" over another by reversing or subverting the apparent meaning.

Elements: Figures and Forms

Metaphor, Simile   In most science fiction, human beings seem to have little trouble communicating with alien beings. They always learn our language rather quickly, if they don't already somehow mysteriously know it. But what if we really were to encounter a truly alien civilization? Would we be able to communicate with them? Maybe, but only if we were able somehow to relate their language to our own. It is easy to imagine aliens so completely unlike ourselves that communication would be very difficult—beings who communicate perhaps by emitting a sequence of odors, electrical pulses, and infrared flashes, or by flicking their three tails around in different patterns. But we could probably eventually convert these signals into our language, and vice-versa. For communication to be impossible, the alien beings would have to be doing something that we can't detect or even imagine, because as long as we can relate something new to something already known, we can make some sense of it ("When the green blob emits 2.547 milligrams of sulphur and carbon in a slow stream over 1.4 seconds, it's saying Hello, I'd like a cheeseburger with fries, hold the mayo").

Thus, comparison is both powerful and necessary in expanding our thinking, allowing us to see something new, or to see something old in a new light. Sometimes we use "like" or "as" in relating the two things ("rattlesnake tastes like chicken"), and sometimes we do not ("For real cowboys, rattlesnake meat is just free-range chicken in a tube"). It's not a great imaginative stretch to compare rattlesnake and chicken as entrees (there are lots of things that taste, supposedly, "just like chicken"), but the human imagination can compare almost any two things. When a comparison uses "like" or "as," we say it's a *simile,* as you probably already know: "His ego is as fragile as an eggshell." When the comparison doesn't use "like" or "as," we say it's a *metaphor:* "I've had enough of his eggshell ego."

Such language that is not *literal* (the speaker doesn't mean that his ego is literally made of eggshell) is said to be *figurative.* And if we extend the metaphor, taking say six aspects of his personality and comparing them to six aspects of eggshells, then we have an *analogy*—which is an extended metaphor. (We don't call a metaphor "a compressed analogy," for some reason.)

Deconstruction, which avowedly aims to expand our thinking, begins from the observation that language itself is metaphorical, as we noted: language does not form a simple system for naming objects that already exist; rather, language is an invented system that we are constantly comparing to reality, shaping that reality as we attempt to apprehend it. Deconstruction thus hits us over the head with the possibilities of a text, urging us to open it up in a radical way.

Here is a poem that makes powerful use of figurative language, using some startling comparisons to do some deconstructing of its own:

DEREK WALCOTT (1930–)

Frederiksted, Dusk

Sunset, the cheapest of all picture-shows,
was all they waited for; old men like empties
set down from morning outside the almshouse,
to let the rising evening brim their eyes,
and, in one row, return the level stare   5
of light that shares its mortal properties
with the least stone in Frederiksted, as if
more than mortality brightened the air,
like a girl tanning on a rock alone
who fills with light. Whatever it is   10
that leaves bright flesh like sand and turns it chill,
not age alone, they were old, but a state
made possible by their collective will,

would shine in them like something between life
and death, our two concrete simplicities,   15
and waited too in, seeming not to wait,
substantial light and insubstantial stone.

[1976]

The first line in "Frederiksted, Dusk" compares the sunset to a movie, two things literally different, and so the comparison must be considered figurative—a metaphor,
to be specific, since neither "like" nor "as" is used. The comparison, by associating the
sunset with "the cheapest of all picture shows," may seem to diminish the natural
event: it's just entertainment, the cheapest of a certain kind. Notice that Walcott uses
"picture shows" rather than "movies" or "films." Why? Does it make a difference?
(This experiment is a good way to assess the word choice of any work: pick a word
and imagine how it would change the work to use another word.) The term "picture
show" is an old-fashioned name, the sort of thing the old men might say, and so the
poem begins by including what might be their point of view. But if the sunset is "all
they waited for," then perhaps it is more than cheap entertainment, if it gives meaning to their lives. Is it all they waited for because it is so glorious and fulfilling, or
because their lives are so empty that they have nothing better to do than wait
around for the sunset? The poem suggests immediately that emptiness motivates
them in this dramatic simile: "old men like empties/ set down from morning outside
the almshouse." The word "empties" is a wonderful choice, I think, because it suggests that the men have been used up, like empty beer bottles lined up, or empty
milk bottles, waiting to be retrieved. It's unclear whether the men are actually outside the poorhouse, or if they are being compared to bottles outside the almshouse
(the first seems more likely to me), but in either case the reference adds another
layer of poverty and deprivation.

The poem quickly begins to undermine this implication, as the old men are said
to be there "to let the rising evening brim their eyes." This reference is a metaphor so
compressed that it may be hard to follow, but I think Walcott is saying that the
evening will fill their eyes up to the brim. The evening is thus (to our surprise) "rising" in two senses: rising, as the evening grows; and rising, as it "brims" or fills the
men up. The comparison of the men to "empties" (milk, beer, whatever) is thus being
subtly extended, as they become empties that the evening will fill. Are the men
impoverished or blessed? We may think that they are blessed in their poverty by the
way they interact with the light: lined up, "in one row," they "return the level stare/
of light that shares its mortal properties," according to lines 5 and 6.

The image of light staring, as if it were alive, is interesting, reversing what seems
to be the case: the men are staring at the light. But the end of line 6 is not the end of
this sentence, and Walcott delightfully twists and turns the poem's sense around,
using line endings to set up one meaning that is altered by the sentence's continuation in the next line. Line 7 does not tell us that the light "shares its mortal properties"
with the men; rather, it "shares its mortal properties/ with the least stone in Freder-
icksted." If we thought the men were special, communing with the light staring at
them, they are no more special than "the least stone."

What are the "mortal properties" of light anyway? What does that mean? Walcott
(or the poem's speaker) is imagining that light is alive: figuratively, it has "mortal"
properties. Perhaps it also has immortal properties, or nonmortal properties too, but
light (so far as we know) is not capable literally of dying—although that metaphor is
indeed common. If the assertion that the light is shared not only with the men but
also with the least stone diminishes the old men's activity, the next lines once again

complicate the poem, undoing what the poem has just done. The light shares its mortal properties, we read, "as if more than mortality brightened the air,/ like a girl tanning on a rock alone/ who fills with light." What, except for immortality, is "more than mortality"? The poem is suggesting, it appears, that there is something super-natural and amazing about the light—or at least that it seems that way: it is "as if" something beyond mortality brightens the air. The simile that follows in lines 9 and 10 is arresting: just imagine a girl tanning on a rock "who fills with light." To under-stand what this comparison contributes to the poem's meaning, you will likely have to think carefully about Walcott's sentence: the syntax (the sentence structure) is so complex that you probably need to look for the main parts. What is being said? Find the subject and verb: the old *men . . . return* the level stare of light . . . like a girl tanning on a rock who fills with light.

If we are trying to decide if the old men are empty and pitiful, or filling and glo-rious, the girl on the rock suggests that the old men are quite fortunate, for they are being filled to the brim with a magical kind of light, the sort of supernatural light that can fill a tanning girl. But the poem does not end here, and what follows com-plicates even further the poem's whirling sense. Again, it's helpful (or rather essen-tial) to find the subject and verb of the sentence that comprises the rest of the poem: the subject is "Whatever it is" and the verbs are "would shine" and "waited." There is something, the poem says, that "leaves bright flesh like sand and turns it chill." "Bright flesh" metaphorically imagines that flesh is like some substance that can give off heat and light, but when this awful something, this "Whatever it is," shines in the old men, it has an un-shining effect. The anti-shining shining, the "what-ever it is," is "not age alone," the poem says. The men are old, the poem acknowl-edges, but the enabling factor is "a state/ made possible by their collective will." The men, in other words, are themselves responsible "by their collective will" for this unnamed stuff that leaves them "like sand."

Amazingly, the poem goes on to complicate this apparently negative quality of the shining "Whatever it is," which "would shine in them like something between life/ and death." This odd comparison challenges, I think, the boundaries of sense: how can the stuff that makes flesh into sand shine in the men "*like* something between life/ and death"? For something to shine in the old men, I would think that it would have to be *literally* between life and death, and not figuratively "like" some-thing between life and death. The old men are not dead (we know) because they are said to be waiting in the second line. Line 15 refers to "life/ and death" as "our two concrete simplicities," but life and death seem neither concrete nor simple here. The light has mortal properties that it is sharing, but it seems as if "more than mortality" brightens the air. There is something like death, or at least something that turns bright flesh into dead sand, shining in the men's living will. The poem in other words seems to be deconstructing our easy assumption that we know what is alive and what isn't; what is empty and what isn't; what can shine and what can't. In closing, the poem says that the "whatever it is" waited and at the same time seemed not to wait. Which is it? The final line confounds such questions of "this or that" by undo-ing what we know about light and stone: the transforming stuff waits (and seems not to) in "substantial light and insubstantial stone."

Is the ending nonsense, a simple reversal that undoes any meaning? Not really: all along Walcott has been playing with our easy complacencies; and making light into substance, and stone into something insubstantial, seems consistent with the poem's exploration of meaning. In the dusk of Frederiksted, the men may seem like ghosts, empty, without substance, filling up with light, waiting and not waiting, inconsequential and yet full of something transforming. The poem conveys, I would say, the sense that there is something remarkable hidden in ordinary things like sunsets, but that something is not easily pinned down. Metaphor and simile play a crucial role in the poem's magic, but you may not have noticed, at least not consciously, that rhyme also contributes to the poem. The sequence of the poem's rhymes is as unpredictable as its meaning, and not every line has a rhyme, but the rhymes are there: "empties" (2), "properties" (6), and "simplicities" (15); "stare" (5) and "air" (8); "alone" (9) and "stone" (17); "chill" (11) and "will" (13); "state" (12) and "wait" (16). These erratic rhymes help provide the sense, in my view, that the poem's language is above and beyond the ordinary. You might notice also that the lines all seem to have similar rhythms, as Walcott is using a five-stress, or pentameter line, which also contributes to the poetic feel. (Try marking stressed words with a slash and unstressed words with a hyphen: see the lines with five stresses?)

Metaphor   Metaphor and simile, as we have seen, depend upon comparison, as we come to see one thing in terms of another. A key insight of deconstruction, as a matter of fact, is that such acts of comparison pervade language: all language is figurative; all language depends upon a network of comparisons. There is no positive connection, no perfect link, between words and things; there are only relationships between and among words, and so language itself is in a sense metaphorical. The signifier, or the word that points (say, the word "pizza"), is compared to what is signified, or the thing pointed at (the slice of Italian food that is on my desk right now, for instance). As you are reading this sentence, it may well be that there is no pizza slice on my desk (at any moment, however, the probability is surprisingly high). You cannot see my desk, or even confirm that I have one. There is an inevitable gap between the signifier and signified: all language is figurative, in a sense.

The starting point for deconstruction (which would seek of course to undermine the whole idea of a starting *point*) might be said to be the **structuralist** work of Ferdinand de Saussure, whose lectures were published in 1916 as the *Cours de linguistique generale* (*Course in General Linguistics*). We make sense out of the world, structuralists maintain, by means of a system of differences: "boy" means something because it is not "girl"; we know what "love" means because we oppose it to "hate"; our understanding of "speech" depends upon our understanding of "writing." The system of meaning is of course more complex than this ("boy" is also not "man"), but its essential structure is binary, a whole system of binary relationships, not unlike the on/off or 0/1 switches that drive computers.

Given this underlying system of meaning-making, structuralists have looked in all sorts of places for underlying structures: How, for example, are the plots of fairy tales structured? What is the underlying system of meaning in detective stories? How are marriage rituals structured in different cultures? Is there some underlying pattern, or set of patterns? How do different cultures handle the system of kinship, of knowing who is related to whom? Do scripted wrestling matches follow a certain underlying pattern? Although structuralists have been able to produce some fascinating work, deconstruction grows out of a fundamental challenge to structuralism. This fundamental challenge has usually been called "*poststructuralism.*"

The problem with structuralism, poststructuralists like Derrida, Kristeva, and Foucault have said, is that the binary-based systems of meaning are ultimately arbitrary: they are influenced and shaped by political and social power, by the unconscious mind, by prejudice, accident, and whim. In the late 1960s and 1970s, many structuralists became poststructuralists, as they questioned the inevitability of the underlying structures they were analyzing. Jacques Derrida's dismantling of various systems of meaning was particularly intoxicating, as he reversed and then exploded our assumptions: we may have thought that writing was an offshoot of speech, but Derrida showed how speech could be usefully seen as a derivative of writing. We might assume that masturbation is a substitute for intercourse, but Derrida argued persuasively just the opposite: masturbation is the initial and primary form of sexual expression, from which our understanding of intercourse is derived.

Deconstruction is therefore a particular analytical technique, based upon the broader skepticism of poststructuralism. And poststructuralism is itself a philosophical outgrowth of a larger cultural reaction against confidence and truth usually called **postmodernism.**

It is possible to think that postmodernism, which embraces parody, irony, playfulness, superficiality (because there are no objective truths or realities), is entirely an unhealthy force. Jean-Francois Lyotard in particular, in *The Postmodern Condition* (1984), has attacked the social irresponsibility of a position that would allow one to deny that the Holocaust occurred, or to say that modern science has not advanced our understanding of the natural world. From this perspective, looking only at the dark side, the meaning of "deconstruction" seems to be pretty much the same as "destruction." And there is an element of truth in this view: deconstruction is about undermining confident certainties, loosening up hardened dogmas, forcing us to take another look and consider thinking otherwise. But no one, not even deconstruction's most enthusiastic adherent, can inhabit a fully deconstructive world, relentlessly dismantling meaning. Deconstruction is then a potentially liberating tool that opens up texts, and hence opens up meaning. We may choose to believe precisely what we believed before we deconstructed what we believed in: but after deconstruction, we have a much clearer vision of the act of choosing. Deconstruction seeks to expose and expand the freedom we have in making sense of things.

In this endeavor deconstruction and metaphorical language share a common goal of expanding and challenging the boundaries of meaning. Some metaphors are so vividly meaningful, so effective in conveying an idea, that they are widely embraced. At some point, the effectiveness of such a comparison becomes its doom: a dead metaphor, a cliché ("cool as a cucumber," for instance) makes a comparison that generally fails to expand our understanding. The phrase has been drained of power by its familiarity; we no longer think of a cucumber and make the comparison. For someone who has never heard a particular cliché before, it is not a cliché: "cool as a cucumber" may be a startling comparison. Walcott's notion of the old men as "empties" is not a cliché: it's an arresting idea. When Walcott imagines these men as being filled with the sunset's light, he begins an imaginative line of thinking that calls into question what we think we know about mortality, meaning, substantiality. His poem is deconstructive in the sense that it plays with our ordinary way of organizing the world.

Hyperbole, Understatement; Metonymy, Synecdoche   Deconstruction reminds us that there is a gap or absence or aporia (as Derrida puts it) embedded in language itself. As we've noted, words like "active," "productive," "full," "mortal," have meanings because they are silently (usually) opposed to ideas like "inactive," "retired," "empty," "inanimate"; yet these opposing ideas are porous, allowing us to show how emptiness can be in some sense a fullness, or the inanimate can be seen as somehow mortal, or the inactive may be actually doing something. We talk commonly about reading between the lines, where there is of course nothing to read, only empty space—but perhaps deconstruction articulates our intuition that meaning is being created in this empty in-between. Although this may sound weird, perhaps deconstruction is not so odd after all, but is only a reminder of how slippery language is, and how hard we must work to make sense of things.

Sometimes the gap between what someone says and reality is so hugely obvious that we don't need any analytical strategy at all to notice it. If I say "The running back Ryan Brewer exploded up the middle for forty yards," you can be confident that "exploded" is a figurative overstatement. Few people would want to be running backs if you could really explode. We have a particular term to designate exaggerations that reach a certain proportion of absurdity: *hyperbole.*

Whether a particular statement is a mere exaggeration or a hyperbole is a matter of judgment. Naming a statement a hyperbole is a way of saying that the comparison is a rash overstatement, an extravagant exaggeration. To say "Ryan Brewer exploded like ten super-novas up the middle" would surely be hyperbole. The opposing term for hyperbole is *understatement:* "Ryan Brewer is not disliked by Gamecock fans," for example, would be perceived by informed fans as a deliberate understatement. The guy was so beloved after South Carolina won its first bowl game in school history that he could have been elected governor. The statement is thus figurative, telling us "he's really appreciated" by creating such a dramatic gap between what is said and what is perceived to be the reality. This particular kind of understatement, in which something positive is said (he's beloved) by denying its opposite (he's not disliked) is called a *litotes.*

Whereas hyperbole may seem to encourage skepticism, understatement often seems to be an effective strategy for deflating skepticism. Parents would sound silly, when asked how they like their newborn baby, if they were to say, "we love her more than the world itself," or "we would gladly kill a million people to save her." Hyperbole invites us to read between the lines, to question what we're hearing, and so it's a good idea to use hyperbole carefully. Likewise, parents might more plausibly say, about a newborn, "we think we'll keep her." Such understatement (one certainly hopes) invites us to perceive the gap between what they say and what they mean. Hyperbole and understatement are of course common strategies in poetry, especially in love poetry. Let's see, for instance, how the speaker in this Shakespearean sonnet uses the anticipated charge of hyperbole as a strategy:

WILLIAM SHAKESPEARE (1564–1616)

Sonnet 17

Who will believe my verse in time to come,
If it were filled with your most high deserts?
Though yet, heaven knows, it is but as a tomb
Which hides your life and shows not half your parts.
If I could write the beauty of your eyes   5
And in fresh numbers number all your graces,
The age to come would say "This poet lies!
Such heavenly touches ne'er touched earthly faces."
So should my papers, yellowed with their age,
Be scorned, like old men of less truth than tongue,   10
And your true rights be termed a poet's rage
And stretched metre of an antique song:
    But were some child of yours alive that time,
    You should live twice, in it and in my rhyme.

[1609]

The speaker here laments that he cannot tell the truth about his beloved because future readers would consider it hyperbole. If the speaker were able to describe her eyes (I'm assuming the addressee is a woman) and number her graces, "The age to come would say 'This poet lies!/ Such heavenly touches ne'er touched earthly faces.'" This is clever: the poet declares he will avoid trying to articulate what might be perceived as hyperbole, even though it is the truth. He is therefore able to slip in under the radar what might well be considered hyperbole. It's the old antihyperbole hyperbole ruse. Can we believe that she really is so beautiful that a truthful description of her in words would be declared a blatant lie? Is she so beautiful that no human being has enjoyed such beauty, that she must be seen as a heavenly being?

Notice how the speaker exaggerates even the failure of his poetic attempts to describe her beauty: they have been so far short of the truth they seem "but as a tomb"—a dramatic simile that sets up the poem's ending reference to her immortality, which will be accomplished in part by this poetry, which has already been depicted as a tomb. How can a tomb regenerate life? Or perhaps, we should ask what sort of life a poetic tomb can engender, because the subject of this poem can be questioned: is the poem about the person being addressed? It begins with a reference to "my verse" and ends with "my rhyme," and in between the poem is at least as much about poetry as it as about the woman being addressed.

At line 9, in fact, the speaker's overriding concern for his poetry comes forward. If he writes about her beauty faithfully, then the horrible consequence will be that his poetry will be belittled:"So should my papers, yellowed with their age,/ Be scorned, like old men of less truth than tongue." He is not, we can assume, really worried about the reputation of his actual papers, but about what he has written upon them. Such a substitution of item A (papers) for an associated item B (the poetry) is called *metonymy,* and the figure of speech works especially well here because it suggests another aging and yellowing that promotes the speaker's cause. Although the papers are "yellowed with age," the poem has worked hard to link the woman with the poetry that is trying to capture her. The poem has certainly reinforced the idea that the woman is valued because of her amazing beauty, so extraordinary it will not be believed in print: what will she be worth when that beauty has "yellowed with age"? His papers will be like "old men," scorned for their lack of truth, and she will be an old woman, similarly scorned, we may presume, for her lack of beauty. (Poems are judged for truthfulness; women for beauty.) Her "true rights," her claim to be or to have been once beautiful, will be considered nothing more than the "stretched metre of an antique song." This figure, which collapses a whole into a part (or, to think of it another way, uses a part to signify a whole), is called a *synecdoche,* and again subtly promotes fears of aging and insignificance: if her value resides in her beauty, and then she becomes an "antique" with stretchmarks and wrinkles, then she is as worthless as untruthful yellowed paper.

The poem seems to have arrived at a crisis, and experienced readers of poetry will have some expectation at this point, line 12, the crisis is about to be solved. Shakespeare's reference to the "metre of an antique song" may remind us that this poem does use a form that was already well-established by Shakespeare's time. It is of course a **sonnet**, a fourteen-line, single-stanza poem, exhibiting one of several sonnet rhyme schemes. The rhymes in this poem (which don't seem "stretched" or strained at all) follow this pattern: abab cdcd efef gg. (The first line, in other words, rhymes with the third, and the second with the fourth: abab.)

Poems following this pattern are called Shakespearean sonnets, simply because Shakespeare made them most famous. Readers get a certain satisfaction from rhyming lines (even children delight when the rhyme plunks down into place), but there is an additional pleasure in anticipating the unfolding of a sonnet, if you know what to expect. The rhyming patterns of a sonnet contribute to their structural patterns of meaning: as you can see, there are three natural separations in a Shakespearean sonnet, between lines 4 and 5, 8 and 9, 12 and 13. The sentence structures in this sonnet reflect this grouping, with sentences ending at the ends of lines 4, 8, and 12. Usually in a sonnet there is no dramatic shift in sense between the fourth and fifth lines, but there is almost always some kind of "turn" in the poem's direction after line 8, or 12, or both. In this sonnet, the attention turns to the papers in line 9, but the most striking shift comes with the final couplet, for the poem posits, as I've said, a crisis, and then offers a solution in the last two lines: "But were some child of yours alive that time,/ You should live twice, in it and in my rhyme."

How is the woman going to get a child? The poem doesn't say, but if you cannot imagine, then you're not ready to be dating. The purpose of poetry, at least according to the English teacher in *The Dead Poets Society* (played by Robin Williams), is to woo women, and this sonnet offers to extend a kind of metonymy and synecdoche beyond the poem's boundaries: the lady's child, the speaker says, a synecdochic part of her, will live on; his poems, a metonymic substitution for her, will also live for her. An appealing offer, perhaps, but a bit of deconstructive analysis might come in handy, opening up the question of whether the poet's work is a device for life extension or a tomb, as he says himself (the identity of the woman, her graces, her thoughts, her significance—these all seem to be submerged, buried, in the poem).

We might also wonder how much to trust a speaker who imagines himself being considered a liar if he attempts to tell the truth. Is he now lying in order to be perceived as telling the truth? Of course, it is even possible to wonder if the speaker hasn't already anticipated such objections: perhaps he is revealing so blatantly the unavoidable hyperbole of telling the truth when one is in love? Should the poem's deconstruction be deconstructed? And just precisely what does the speaker mean by "were some child of yours alive"? Is it a trick (of language)?

Obviously, there are too many poetic forms to be covered conveniently here, but we do need to raise the issue. Now you've been introduced or (more likely) reminded of the sonnet, and other forms will be noted as you move through the readings your teacher assigns. You certainly don't have to know that a poem is in the form of a villanelle to get something out of it, or even what a villanelle is. But it is often useful to know the terminology and the forms. Just as you are more likely to notice instances of metaphor, simile, hyperbole, understatement, metonymy, and synecdoche if you know these terms, you are by the same token more likely to notice how the poem's structure works if you know it's a recognized form with a name. The most common terms are described in the glossary here (in the back of this book). In a way, poetic forms highlight the extraordinary nature of what we're reading: "this isn't everyday language," the form says; "pay particular attention, and don't take this literally, necessarily." We usually don't get a jury summons, or a request for a donation, or directions for assembling a bookcase in the form of a sonnet (those kinds of texts have their own distinctive forms). What deconstruction insists upon (and it's a useful reminder) is that there is no such thing as "ordinary"

language, if we mean by that "language that maps unproblematically onto reality."
All language, deconstruction assumes, is somehow metaphorical, and everything we
say is in some "form" that unavoidably distorts the world we seek. Deconstruction
encourages, therefore, a certain skepticism, humility, and tolerance. These aren't
always easy or comfortable (or even sometimes practical) postures to assume. But
they are often healthy correctives to dogmatic overconfidence and intolerance.

Practice: Good and Evil

Here are poems that will encourage you to witness deconstruction, practice deconstruction, or both. The poems raise ethical questions—questions of good and evil—
that seem especially interesting in the context of deconstruction, which asks us to
rethink our foundational ideas. Each poem also features some or all of the figures
discussed here. The questions are designed to help guide you, but don't let them
limit your thinking.

LINDA PASTAN (1932–)

Ethics

In ethics class so many years ago
our teacher asked this question every fall:
if there were a fire in a museum
which would you save, a Rembrandt painting
or an old woman who hadn't many
years left anyhow? Restless on hard chairs   5
caring little for pictures or old age
we'd opt one year for life, the next for art
and always half-heartedly. Sometimes
the woman borrowed my grandmother's face
leaving her usual kitchen to wander   10
some drafty, half imagined museum.
One year, feeling clever, I replied
why not let the woman decide herself?
Linda, the teacher would report, eschews
the burdens of responsibility.   15
This fall in a real museum I stand
before a real Rembrandt, old woman,
or nearly so, myself. The colors
within this frame are darker than autumn,
darker even than winter—the browns of earth,   20
though earth's most radiant elements burn
through the canvas. I know now that woman
and painting and season are almost one
and all beyond saving by children.

[1981]   25

Questions

1. Consider how these oppositions work within the poem: the adult speaker versus the child in ethics class; the Rembrandt versus the old woman; accepting responsibility versus avoiding it; the students versus the teacher; the Rembrandt's colors versus autumn's colors; half-imagining versus vividly imagining; childhood versus old age. How are these oppositions related? (Try making a chart with one kind of item on one side, the other kind on the other.)

2. In what sense does the poem itself deconstruct these oppositions? How does the ending, in other words, affect the teacher's ethics question?

3. Does the poem itself undermine or support the assertion that woman, painting, and season are "beyond saving by children"? What does Pastan mean when she says that the woman, painting, and season "are almost one"? Do you agree? Does that make sense?

4. What do you think of Linda's "clever" response in line 14? How is it different from the response she would later make as a "nearly" old woman, viewing a Rembrandt herself? (Is it really different?)

5. Perhaps this poem, despite its title, isn't really about "Ethics." What else could it be about? What theme seems to be raised, for instance, by the ending? Is the speaker's age significant? What difference does it make that the three items are "almost one" but not exactly one? What difference does it make that the items are beyond saving by children? Was the teacher literally asking the children to save one or the other?

ROBERT LOWELL (1917–1977)

For the Union Dead

"Relinquunt Omnia Servare Rem Publicam."[1]

The old South Boston Aquarium stands
in a Sahara of snow now. Its broken windows are boarded.
The bronze weathervane cod has lost half its scales.
The airy tanks are dry.

Once my nose crawled like a snail on the glass;   5
my hand tingled
to burst the bubbles
drifting from the noses of the cowed, compliant fish.

My hand draws back. I often sigh still
for the dark downward and vegetating kingdom   10
of the fish and reptile. One morning last March,
I pressed against the new barbed and galvanized

fence on the Boston Common. Behind their cage,
yellow dinosaur steamshovels were grunting
as they cropped up tons of mush and grass   15
to gouge their underworld garage.

Parking spaces luxuriate like civic
sandpiles in the heart of Boston.

[1] They give up everything to serve the Republic (Latin).

A girdle of orange, Puritan-pumpkin colored girders
braces the tingling Statehouse,   20

shaking over the excavations, as it faces Colonel Shaw
and his bell-cheeked Negro infantry
on St. Baudens' shaking Civil War relief,
propped by a plank splint against the garage's earthquake.

Two months after marching through Boston,   25
half the regiment was dead;
at the dedication,
William James could almost hear the bronze Negroes breathe.

Their monument sticks like a fishbone
in the city's throat.   30
Its Colonel is as lean
as a compass-needle.

He has an angry wrenlike vigilance,
a greyhound's gentle tautness;
he seems to wince at pleasure,   35
and suffocate for privacy.

He is out of bounds now. He rejoices in man's lovely,
peculiar power to choose life and die—
when he leads his black soldiers to death,
he cannot bend his back.   40

On a thousand small town New England greens,
the old white churches hold their air
of sparse, sincere rebellion; frayed flags
quilt the graveyards of the Grand Army of the Republic.

The stone statues of the abstract Union Soldier   45
grow slimmer and younger each year—
wasp-wasted, they doze over muskets
and muse through their sideburns . . .

Shaw's father wanted no monument
except the ditch,   50
where his son's body was thrown
and lost with his "niggers."

The ditch is nearer.
There are no statues for the last war here;
on Boylston street, a commercial photograph   55
shows Hiroshima boiling

over a Mosler Safe, the "Rock of Ages"
that survived the blast. Space is nearer.
When I crouch to my television set,
the drained faces of Negro school-children rise like balloons.   60

Colonel Shaw
is riding on his bubble,
he waits
for the blesséd break.

The Aquarium is gone. Everywhere,   65
giant finned cars nose forward like fish;

a savage servility
slides by on grease.

[1960]

Questions

1. The poem's title indicates it is "for" the Union dead. What do you take that to mean? How many meanings can you imagine?
2. How much of the poem is actually devoted to talking about the Civil War in general and the Union soldiers in particular? Does the poem focus on all Union soldiers, or a segment of them?
3. If we were to reject the accuracy of Lowell's title, who or what else might the poem be "for"?
4. Does the speaker celebrate the involvement of the Black Union soldiers? Explain your answer, then look for evidence for the contrary point of view.
5. What opposition does the last stanza reinforce? Which era does Lowell favor, the past time of the Aquarium or the present time of the "giant finned cars" nosing "forward like fish"? How do you know? What does this opposition have to do with the Union dead?
6. The speaker suggests that he misses the Aquarium. What was appealing about it to him? Why does he say the fish were "cowed" and "compliant"? What sort of person would enjoy viewing cowed and compliant beings? What other groups mentioned or alluded to in the poem might be considered cowed and compliant? How does the speaker's affection for the aquarium relate to the Union dead and their struggle?
7. How does the speaker feel about the ongoing construction project? To what does that passage relate? To the Union dead?

ELI MANDEL (1922–1990)

Houdini

I suspect he knew that trunks are metaphors,
could distinguish between the finest rhythms
unrolled on rope or singing in a chain
and knew the metrics of the deepest pools

I think of him listening to the words   5
spoken by manacles, cells, handcuffs,
chests, hampers, roll-top desks, vaults,
especially the deep words spoken by coffins

escape, escape: quaint Harry in his suit
his chains, his desk, attached to all attachments   10
how he'd sweat in that precise struggle
with those binding words, wrapped around him
like that mannered style, his formal suit

and spoken when? by whom? What thing first said
"there's no way out?"; so that he'd free himself,   15
leap, squirm, no matter how, to chain himself again,
once more jump out of the deep alive

with all his chains singing around his feet
like the bound crowds who sigh, who sigh.

[1967]

Questions

1. Explain the first line. The speaker suspects that the most famous escape
   artist ever, Harry Houdini, knew "that trunks are metaphors." What do you
   think trunks are a metaphor for? What might they stand for?
2. How is Houdini, as Mandel presents him, like a literary critic? What sort of
   thing is Houdini "reading"? How is his escape like (or unlike) the feats of a literary critic? Or does the comparison work better if we think of Houdini as a
   writer?
3. In the following phrases, the italicized word seems particularly interesting, surprising, odd, significant. Explore these phrases: "*quaint* Harry" (line 9); "*binding*
   words" (12); "chains *singing*" (18); "*bound* crowds who *sigh*, who *sigh*" (19).
4. How is Houdini a kind of deconstructionist? What does he dismantle, call
   into question, reverse? How do Mandel's references to language (to "the
   words/ spoken by manacles" for instance) support the idea of Houdini as
   master deconstructionist?

JOHN DONNE (1572–1631)

Death Be Not Proud

Death be not proud, though some have callèd thee
Mighty and dreadful, for thou art not so;
For those whom thou think'st thou dost overthrow
Die not, poor death, nor yet canst thou kill me.
From rest and sleep, which but thy pictures be,   5
Much pleasure; then from thee much more must flow,
And soonest our best men with thee do go,
Rest of their bones, and soul's delivery.
Thou art slave to fate, chance, kings, and desperate men,
And dost with poison, war, and sickness dwell;   10
And poppy, or charms can make us sleep as well,
And better than thy stroke; why swell'st thou then?
One short sleep past, we wake eternally,
And death shall be no more; Death, thou shalt die.

[1610?]

Questions

1. What kind of poem is this? What is its form? What is the rhyme scheme?
   How does the rhyme scheme reinforce (or fail to reinforce) the sense?
2. What is the key reversal driving this poem? What sense does it make? That
   is, what assumptions would one have to hold in order to make the claim that
   Donne makes here?
3. The poem is addressed to Death, at least ostensibly, directing Death not to
   assume a certain stance of pride. Is the poem truly and only addressed to

Death? Who might be the audience? Here's another way to think about this issue: why should we care what Death feels?

4. Take one line and see if you can complicate it: for instance, "Thou art slave to fate, chance, kings, and desperate men." This statement is applied, by the speaker, to death. Why is that a problematic assertion? (Who is—or who else is—a slave to these things? Is Death alive? Can one be a slave and be dead— or be Death?) Explain how this line involves a reversal and, if pressed, a dispersal of meaning.

JOHANNES VERMEER (1632–1675)

Johannes Vermeer grew up as a Protestant in Delft, Holland, but married into a Catholic family in 1653, and apparently converted to Catholicism to please his mother-in-law. His father was a weaver of fine satins, and he also appears to have sold fine art. Vermeer's early paintings were religious and mythological scenes, large and ambitious, but his later work focused on scenes in Delft. He was not a prolific artist—only thirty-five or so works are known, but his paintings are exquisitely crafted. Recent scholarship has speculated about his use of the camera obscura, a kind of primitive projector, in his work. With his artistic reputation virtually limited to his hometown, Vermeer's early death left his wife and eleven children deeply in debt. Today he is one of the world's most renowned artists.

Johannes Vermeer, *Woman Holding a Balance*, c. 1664,
National Gallery of Art, Widener Collection

Questions

1. No reproduction in a book can pretend to do much justice to a painting. If you ever visit Washington, D.C., you must visit the National Gallery of Art and see this painting and everything else on display. The National Gallery has a good website, and the painting is available there; any search engine, given "Vermeer *Woman Holding a Balance*" will take you to it, and I suggest you supplement this textbook's image with the one you'll find there. You might reasonably think the darkness of the painting is the result of poor reproduction here, but the painting, which has recently been restored, is quite dark. The lower left-hand corner is shrouded in darkness, which makes the play of light, from the upper left-hand corner sweeping down to the woman and the balance, quite dramatic. Visiting the National Gallery recently, I found myself wanting to turn up the lights. Is the painting's use of light in any way suggestive of deconstruction? Vermeer offers us a very detailed realism, yet at the same time he obscures in darkness a good portion of the painting. Does darkness ever illuminate?

2. According to one critic, "the image embodies a spiritual principle that is often manifest in Vermeer's work: the need to lead a balanced life" (National Gallery website: http://www.nga.gov/feature/vermeer/composition1.html). Do you agree? Can you open up this reading of the painting, perhaps arguing that it is about something else, or that it does not so much embody this principle as call it into question? Here's a possible starting point: the balance appears to be empty, yet it is not perfectly balanced. To provide more material for you to work with, here are some "facts" from the National Gallery discussion:

   Regarding the pearls on the desk: "Symbolically, pearls have been associated with vanity and worldly concerns," but they "can also represent purity."

   Regarding the mirror, just below the window: "Mirrors in art often symbolize vanity or self-knowledge."

   Regarding the light: "Artists often use light to denote supernatural events and spiritual enlightenment."

   Regarding the painting of The Last Judgment behind the woman: "Christ in majesty judges the souls below in this violent and fearsome final reckoning of mankind. The woman's head obscures the place where Saint Michael customarily would be weighing souls in the balance. The figure of Christ appears immediately above the woman's head, reinforcing the interpretation that her mundane act is intended to parallel the weighing of souls in The Last Judgment. While the day of judgment is violent and final, the woman seems serene and contemplative."

   Regarding the woman's dress and figure: "Golden light falls on her ample belly, further emphasized by a yellow streak. Some contemporary authors speculate that the woman is pregnant, while others conclude that her costume— a short jacket, a bodice, and a thickly padded skirt—reflects a style of dress current in the early to mid-1660s."

LINDA PASTAN

Woman Holding a Balance, *Vermeer, 1664*

The picture within
the picture is The Last

Judgment, subdued
as wallpaper in the background.
And though the woman   5
holding the scales
is said to be weighing
not a pearl or a coin
but the heft of a single soul,
this hardly matters.   10
It is really the mystery
of the ordinary
we're looking at—the way
Vermeer has sanctified
the same light that enters   15
our own grimed windows
each morning, touching
a cheek, the fold
of a dress, a jewelry box
with perfect justice.   20

[1998]

Questions

1. Compare Pastan's "Ethics" (p. 112) with this poem. What do the two poems have in common? How might one illuminate the other?
2. Does Pastan's poem confirm, open up, complicate, or challenge your "reading" of the painting?
3. When the poem's speaker says "this hardly matters," what is startling about that assertion? Do you agree? See if you can make the case either way (it does matter greatly; it hardly matters).
4. What is the relationship of the picture within the picture to the scene that is depicted?
5. How much of the painting is empty, in some sense?

MARGARET ATWOOD (1939–)

Spelling

My daughter plays on the floor
with plastic letters,
red, blue & hard yellow,
learning how to spell,
spelling,   5
how to make spells.

I wonder how many women
denied themselves daughters,
closed themselves in rooms,
drew the curtains
so they could mainline words.   10

A child is not a poem,

a poem is not a child.
There is no either / or.
However.   15
.
I return to the story
of the woman caught in the war
& in labour, her thighs tied
together by the enemy
so she could not give birth.   20

Ancestress: the burning witch,
her mouth covered by leather
to strangle words.

A word after a word
after a word is power.   25
.
At the point where language falls away
from the hot bones, at the point
where the rock breaks open and darkness
flows out of it like blood, at
the melting point of granite   30
when the bones know
they are hollow & the word
splits & doubles & speaks
the truth & the body
itself becomes a mouth.   35

This is a metaphor.
.
How do you learn to spell?
Blood, sky & the sun,
your own name first,
your first naming, your first name,   40
your first word.

                                                                    [1981]

Questions

1. Atwood plays with language in this poem, repeating words in shifting meanings. Identify some of these shifts. Why is this maneuver especially appropriate in this poem?
2. The poem says "There is no either / or." The aim of deconstruction, according
   to many critics, involves replacing "either/or" with "both/and." What is the
   "either/or" here? (The second section holds the answer to this question.)
   Does Atwood argue for a "both/and" in this apparent conflict? In what way
   does "However" in line 15 complicate this apparent rejection of either/or?
3. What does the "this" in line 36 mean? To what does the "this" refer?
4. The daughter's learning contrasts starkly with the other instances of women
   in the poem. Meditate on the significance of the "woman caught in the war"
   and "the burning witch." How do they reflect on the speaker's situation? Do
   these examples in any way reinforce men's fears regarding women—fears
   that may have led men to keep language and metaphor away from women?
   (In other words, how is "spelling" threatening to men, reinforcing a negative
   stereotype of women that the poem, in most ways, challenges.)

Suggestions for Writing

1. Your creative assignment for this chapter might be to apply your deep skepticism to an advertisement, showing deconstructively how an ad can be made to fall apart. Since advertisements are designed somehow to convince us to buy some product, the simplest strategy would be to set out to show how the advertisement also attempts unsuccessfully to suppress a message that would dissuade us from buying.

2. You or your teacher may prefer creating a deconstructive poem, one that calls into question some supposedly established system of meaning.

3. You might want to create an advertisement that deconstructs a product, or even a deconstructive advertisement for poetry. Just remember: deconstruction is supposed to be playful.

7

Read Fiction Powerfully: Political Criticism

> Every body continues in its state of rest, or of uniform motion in a right [straight] line, unless it is compelled to change that state by a force impressed upon it.
>
> —Sir Isaac Newton, *The First Law of Motion*

Reflection: The Useful Text

True story: my daughter, age five, trips and falls on the driveway, skinning her knees. I bop over quickly, pat her on the back, and say, "Let's go inside and get that fixed up." My daughter looks up at me, tears flowing, and says in amazed disgust, "What can you do? You're just a literature doctor! I want my mommy, the real doctor!"

What indeed can literature doctors—and their students—do? What does literature itself do, for that matter? Is there any practical value in doing literary criticism? With all the skinned knees in the world, not to mention hunger, disease,

"This artist is a deeply religious feminist and anti-smoking advocate, who made a lot of money in the computer industry before going off to paint in Paris, where she now lives with her husband and two little girls."

poverty, oppression, racism, sexism, child abuse, isn't the study of poetry, fiction, and drama a huge self-indulgence? Don't we have much better things to do?

To be sure, we can't eat poetry (but see Mark Strand's "Eating Poetry" in Chapter 13, and nothing I could say, however insightful, would disinfect and bandage my daughter's knee (although she did laugh as I recited Carroll's "Jabberwocky" while she was getting cleaned up). We say "The pen is mightier than the sword," but I'd rather have a sword sometimes. Still, as Christopher Hitchens puts it in his recent book on the political impact of literature, *Unacknowledged Legislation,* "there are things that pens can do, and swords cannot" (xiv). Hitchens's title refers to Percy Bysshe Shelley's famous claim that "Poets are the unacknowledged legislators of the world"; and for Hitchens, a good example of literature's legislative power is the collapse of the Soviet Union's empire, the consequence in large part, especially in Eastern Europe, of "a civil opposition led by satirical playwrights, ironic essayists, Bohemian jazz players and rock musicians, and subversive poets."

The approaches discussed in this chapter in fact all insist that literature and literary study can have enormous practical value, raising our awareness of oppression and bias, showing us how all sorts of exclusions, suppressions, and exploitations are invented, reinvented, and perpetuated. Whether we are talking about gender, sexuality, economic status, ethnicity, or race, we may reasonably assume that literary works not only unavoidably reflect the politics of the world we inhabit, but they also inevitably influence that world. There are obvious examples of literary works that have had a direct and dramatic impact upon society: Harriet Beecher Stowe's *Uncle Tom's Cabin* clearly fueled antislavery sentiments leading up to the American Civil War. When Abraham Lincoln met Ms. Stowe, he remarked, "So this is the little lady who made this big war!" But the political significance of a particular literary work is often more subtle, complex, and dependent upon interpretation. To get you started thinking about the intersection of literature and politics, let's focus on the evocative story that follows. After you've read it, before you proceed on to my commentary, ask yourself this question: "What is most striking and significant about this story?" Why don't you take a few minutes to write down your response.

Elizabeth Tallent (1955–)

Elizabeth Tallent teaches creative writing at Stanford. She has published Museum Pieces, *a novel, and three short-story collections, placing her work in* The New Yorker, Esquire, Harper's, *and other excellent venues.*

No One's a Mystery

For my eighteenth birthday Jack gave me a five-year diary with a latch and a little key, light as a dime. I was sitting beside him scratching at the lock, which didn't seem to want to work, when he thought he saw his wife's Cadillac in the distance, coming toward us. He pushed me down onto the dirty floor of the pickup and kept one hand on my head while I inhaled the musk of his cigarettes in the dashboard ashtray and sang along with Rosanne Cash on the tape deck. We'd been drinking tequila and the bottle was between his legs, resting up against his crotch, where the seam of his Levi's was bleached linen-white, though the Levi's were nearly new. I don't know why his Levi's always bleached like that, along the seams and at the knees. In a curve of cloth his zipper glinted, gold.

"It's her," he said. "She keeps the lights on in the daytime. I can't think of a single habit in a woman that irritates me more than that." When he saw that I was going to stay still he took his hand from my head and ran it through his own dark hair.

"Why does she?" I said.

"She thinks it's safer. Why does she need to be safer? She's driving exactly fifty-five miles an hour. She believes in those signs: 'Speed Monitored by Aircraft.' It doesn't matter that you can look up and see that the sky is empty."

"She'll see your lips move, Jack. She'll know you're talking to some- 5 one."

"She'll think I'm singing along with the radio."

He didn't lift his hand, just raised the fingers in salute while the pressure of his palm steadied the wheel, and I heard the Cadillac honk twice, musically; he was driving easily eighty miles an hour. I studied his boots. The elk heads stitched into the leather were bearded with frayed thread, the toes were scuffed, and there was a compact wedge of muddy manure between the heel and the sole—the same boots he'd been wearing for the two years I'd known him. On the tape deck Rosanne Cash sang, "Nobody's into me, no one's a mystery."

"Do you think she's getting famous because of who her daddy is or for herself?" Jack said.

"There are about a hundred pop tops on the floor, did you know that? Some little kid could cut a bare foot on one of these, Jack."

"No little kids get into this truck except for you." 10

"How come you let it get so dirty?"

"'How come,'" he mocked. "You even sound like a kid. You can get back into the seat now, if you want. She's not going to look over her shoulder and see you."

"How do you know?"

"I just know," he said. "Like I know I'm going to get meat loaf for supper. It's in the air. Like I know what you'll be writing in that diary."

"What will I be writing?" I knelt on my side of the seat and craned 15 around to look at the butterfly of dust printed on my jeans. Outside the window Wyoming was dazzling in the heat. The wheat was fawn and yellow and parted smoothly by the thin dirt road. I could smell the water in the irrigation ditches hidden in the wheat.

"Tonight you'll write, 'I love Jack. This is my birthday present from him. I can't imagine anybody loving anybody more than I love Jack.'"

"I can't."

"In a year you'll write, 'I wonder what I ever really saw in Jack. I wonder why I spent so many days just riding around in his pickup. It's true he taught me something about sex. It's true there wasn't ever much else to do in Cheyenne.'"

"I won't write that."

"In two years you'll write, 'I wonder what that old guy's name was, the 20 one with the curly hair and the filthy dirty pickup truck and time on his hands.'"

"I won't write that."

"No?"

"Tonight I'll write, 'I love Jack. This is my birthday present from him. I can't imagine anybody loving anybody more than I love Jack.'"

"No, you can't," he said. "You can't imagine it."

    "In a year I'll write, 'Jack should be home any minute now. The table's   25
set—my grandmother's linen and her old silver and the yellow candles left
over from the wedding—but I don't know if I can wait until after the trout
à la Navarra to make love to him.'"

    "It must have been a fast divorce."

    "In two years I'll write, 'Jack should be home by now. Little Jack is hun-
gry for his supper. He said his first word today besides "Mama" and "Papa."
He said "kaka."'"

    Jack laughed. "He was probably trying to finger-paint with kaka on the
bathroom wall when you heard him say it."

    "In three years I'll write, 'My nipples are a little sore from nursing Eliza
Rosamund.'"

    "Rosamund. Every little girl should have a middle name she hates."   30

    "'Her breath smells like vanilla and her eyes are just Jack's color of
blue.'"

    "That's nice," Jack said.

    "So, which one do you like?"

    "I like yours," he said. "But I believe mine."

    "It doesn't matter. I believe mine."   35

    "Not in your heart of hearts, you don't."

    "You're wrong."

    "I'm not wrong," he said. "And her breath would smell like your milk,
and it's kind of a bittersweet smell, if you want to know the truth."

                                                        [1985]

    There's no correct answer to the question ("What is most striking and signifi-
cant about this story?"), but what many people find most striking and significant
about this story is the stark contrast between the two main characters, Jack and the
narrator. The narrator believes—in her "heart of hearts" she says—that in the next
year Jack is going to leave his wife and marry her. Jack in no way confirms this fantasy, and his response to her vision of preparing a romantic meal for him next year,
as she waits for him to come home, is simply "It must have been a fast divorce." Moreover, the narrator believes that within three years they will have two children together. Jack imagines, in contrast, that in two years she will be unable to remember his
name, recalling him only as the guy "with the curly hair and the filthy dirty pickup
truck and time on his hands." He imagines that time on her hands also motivates the
narrator, as he imagines her writing "there wasn't ever much else to do in
Cheyenne." And he also imagines her writing in her journal, "It's true he taught me
something about sex." But it is clear that for her the relationship is not about avoiding boredom or achieving sexual tutelage from the master-lover Jack. She is involved
in this relationship, in her own mind, because it is true love: she says she can't even
imagine loving anybody more than she loves Jack. Jack does not say, "I feel the same
way," or "I love you too." Instead, he simply agrees, "You can't imagine it." He appears
to recognize that she lacks the maturity, the life experience, to be able to envision
something better.

    Or, perhaps she cannot imagine loving anyone more because the current rela-
tionship is more a product of her imagination than a reality. Dreaming about marriage and procreation, she naturally thinks of the danger to little children posed
by the hundreds of pop tops on the floor of his truck. Some "little kid could cut a
bare foot," she says. In a truck going eighty, with a bottle of tequila resting against
the crotch of the driver, who has some portion of the tequila already inside him,

the pop tops would seem to be a trivial concern for any nonexistent children. It is indeed reassuring to hear Jack say "No little kids get into this truck except for you." He may be teasing her when he calls her a "little kid," but he clearly does not view her as an equal. She appears, after all, to be eighteen, since the journal is Jack's present for her eighteenth birthday, and it would be odd to write "This is my birthday present from him" if she had been writing in the journal for some time. The narrator reveals she has known Jack for two years—he's worn the same boots all that time—and so their relationship began, we surmise, when she was sixteen. It seems reasonable to assume that he does think of her as a kid at some level.

That's disturbing (even if you don't have a daughter) because most people would agree that teenage girls are not ready to have affairs with much older, married men. The distance between Jack and the narrator is emphasized by the story's ending, in which Jack says firmly that they have no future together ("I'm not wrong"), and that the baby's breath would not smell "like vanilla." The baby's breath, he tells her, "would smell like your milk, and it's kind of a bittersweet smell, if you want to know the truth." How does Jack know what a baby's breath smells like? How does he know what her milk smells like? These are troubling questions raised by the story's last lines, and it seems most likely Jack knows from the experience of his own children and his wife's milk.

Although we might view Jack and the narrator as depictions of unique individuals, with a unique relationship, few if any readers will be able to resist relating these two characters and their stories to other characters, real and imaginary, and their stories. Do you know, or have you read about, or have you seen in a movie or television show anyone at all like the narrator? Does she fit into any sort of categories? Is she a type of anything? How about Jack? Is he in any way familiar? Is every fact we learn about Jack equally surprising, or do we at some point begin to form expectations that are confirmed in one way or another as the story unfolds? Are these expectations in any way influenced by our notion that Jack is not entirely unique—that he fits into a pattern?

All the critical approaches discussed in this chapter (and others in this same family of approaches) involve assessing how particular individuals relate to certain socially and politically significant categories. In "No One's a Mystery," the most obvious categorical distinction between Jack and the narrator is their sexual difference: he's male; she's female. Although their age difference is also important, we might argue that Jack, to the extent that he is recognizable as a type, represents a certain type of man at a certain age. He has little respect for the narrator, pushing her down "onto the dirty floor of his pickup," holding her there until he sees she's going to be still—as if she's a dog that he's stealing. He ridicules his wife for driving with her lights on, observing the speed limit, and believing aircraft you can't see can monitor your speed. There is more to Jack's imperfection than his lack of respect for the women in his life, but that is certainly a key part of his scumbag status. Likewise, the narrator's values arguably represent those of a certain kind of woman, at a certain level of developmental maturity. Not that the narrator is typical of all eighteen-year-old women, any more than Jack is typical of all married adult men. But they are understandable within a particular cultural setting as stereotypes.

To see whether you agree, imagine the story retold with Jacqueline driving the speeding truck, the tequila stuck between her legs. Jackie is much older than the narrator, a young boy, whom she pushes down onto the filthy floor of the truck when she sees her husband approaching in his Cadillac, holding the boy's head down until she's sure he's going to stay put. The young boy telling the story notices that Jackie's well-worn boots have a wedge of muddy manure, and the floor is littered with her pop tops, which he worries might pose a danger to any children riding in the truck. She and the young boy, who has been her lover since he was sixteen, discuss what he will write in the diary she has given him for his birthday. He imagines a future in which they have children, and he will have prepared a lovely romantic dinner for her, waiting for her to come home, wondering if he will be able to wait until after the trout à la Navarra to make love to her. She has a different view of the future, thinking that in two years the diary entry will say, "I wonder what that old woman's name was, the one with the curly hair and the filthy pickup truck and time on her hands." But he believes that a future diary entry will talk about how his nipples are a little sore from nursing their second child.

The boy's sore nipples are of course absurd, unless we're entering the realm of science fiction, but most readers find the entire sex reversal almost as implausible. Not that there is anything more or less inappropriate about a relationship between an older woman and a teenage boy. Nor might there be anything wrong with a teenage boy who appreciates his grandmother's linen, old silver, and yellow wedding candles, and who knows how to make trout à la Navarra. However, most readers, in English-speaking countries at the outset of the twenty-first century, will understand what Tallent's narrator says and does in terms of her feminine status. How we read the narrator, in other words, is a function of our understanding of what it means to be an eighteen-year-old woman. We understand Jack, likewise, in terms of our experience, in life and fiction (in various media), with mature, adulterous, fast-driving, hard-drinking, self-assertive men willing to lure teenagers into sexual relationships.

If you agree that it makes sense to read this story in terms of what it reveals about men and women, about older men and younger women (the way men and women view themselves and each other), then you're already entering the realm of feminist criticism. Is the narrator, in your opinion, motivated by her biological difference, which compels her to express her maternal instincts, which makes her vulnerable to Jack's "charms"? Do women naturally think in romantic terms of latching onto one man, having his children, and creating beautiful table settings and sophisticated trout dishes? Is Jack, by the same token, simply expressing a natural male desire to spread his genetic code as widely as possible? On the other hand, perhaps the narrator is not the product of her biological nature, but rather has absorbed her values and desires from the culture she has inhabited. Where indeed has she gotten these notions of a transforming love that overcomes all obstacles, of romantic candle-lit dinners, of sore nipples from nursing a child, whose "breath smells like vanilla"? It seems implausible that such ideas are entirely the result of some hardwiring in her brain, and so the role of culture in creating and perpetuating such systems of meaning would seem to demand investigation—to demand, in other words, feminist criticism.

Here, then, is the crucial assumption that underlies one form of political criticism: men and women are different, and we need to understand this difference—its origin, its nature, its diversity—because we want to intervene in the deforming process of prejudice and oppression. One manifestation of power, and its unequal distribution by sex, is certainly literacy, and if men and women are different— because of biology, or culture, or both—then their differences may well be reflected in the differing ways they write and read. The greatest historical difference in women's writing and reading has stemmed from the greater access men have enjoyed. "No One's a Mystery" reflects obliquely this long-standing struggle by women to write and be heard: Jack has given the narrator a diary, which represents a genre of writing historically open to women, but is also a means of self-expression that tends in its privacy and immediacy to limit and contain the effects of expression.

Jack gives her a diary, not so that she can convey her thoughts to him or a larger audience, but so that she can keep her thoughts to herself. The diary's lock (which doesn't seem to work: it's probably cheap) would keep other people out, which may appear to give the narrator power over her thoughts, but also keeps her thoughts safely tucked away. Jack presumes his knowledge and power even extend to what she is going to write, if she is going to be truthful. The title of "No One's a Mystery" thus may refer to Jack's belief that he understands himself, his wife, and (better than she understands herself) the narrator. But knowledge, self-awareness, so feminist critics believe, is empowering, and we may notice that Tallent's story is after all told by the narrator. If no one is a mystery, then perhaps the narrator, in penning this story, is solving the mystery of Jack, exposing his arrogance and her own naïveté through the enlightening power of writing. It would be nice to think that this story is the actual entry in her diary, and that Jack's gift turns out to be the impetus for her to see him clearly—and drop him.

Every story has more than one side of course, and the feminist stance on Tallent's story might be balanced by a masculine point of view. Men's Studies, which might be thought of as a subset of Women's Studies, or as everything that isn't Women's Studies (depending on your outlook), looks at how our notions of masculinity are constructed and perpetuated, at what it means to be a man. Tallent is a woman, and it would be possible to ask why she has constructed this unflattering view of Jack: whose interest is served by this portrayal?

The other approaches explained in this chapter might appear to be less obviously relevant to this particular story, but they employ strategies that are fundamentally similar. Instead of thinking in terms of male and female, for instance, gay and lesbian studies asks us to think in more complicated ways about sexuality, and to think about the representation of same-sex desire. Some works seem to respond easily to one approach and resist another, and there might appear to be little that gay and lesbian approaches could do with "No One's a Mystery," given the apparent heterosexuality of Jack and the narrator: it is hard to talk about the representation of gay and/or lesbian people when there aren't any in the story. But one could talk, perhaps, about the story's depiction of heterosexuality as a way of beginning to illuminate representations of gay and lesbian relationships. By the same token, African American studies, Native American studies—any approach focusing upon race or ethnicity—would seem to have little to work with here: these approaches consider the political interests of groups that appear to be absent from the story.

It is possible to examine a work for what is missing, but such analysis works best as a way of contrasting examples in which certain features are present. We might ask, for instance, if readers make any assumptions about the race of Jack and the narrator, and consider precisely what clues we are using to make such inferences. What difference—if any—do such assumptions make in our reading? Likewise, materialist criticism looks at literary works in terms of class and economics, and we can make, I think, some educated guesses about Jack's material status. What economic markers are present in the story, and what do they suggest about the values of the society Jack and the narrator inhabit? Indeed, Tallent's title might be seen as a slogan for the approaches considered in this chapter, because they all seek to understand individuals in terms of their membership in some sexual, economic, racial, or ethnic group. No one's a mystery, these theories attempt to show, if we bring the right theoretical tools to the job. In practice, these critical strategies are often used in concert, as, say, African American and feminist concerns are taken up at the same time, or gay and lesbian approaches are linked to materialist investigations.

We've raised the issues with this analysis of Tallent's story. Let's see more precisely how these various theories can be put to work.

Strategies: Using Political Criticism

To do political criticism, you should read literature with an awareness of its political implications. "Political" is one of those words that books can be written about, but everyone has some notion of what it means. It points to that arena in which people negotiate meaning and value, organizing themselves into groups, pursuing power and control. I have ideas; you have ideas; if I try to get you to accept my ideas, then we're moving into the realm of politics, especially if my ideas have some social consequences. We are not born with an understanding of "man" and "woman," or "white" and "black," or "work" and "leisure," or "heterosexual" and "gay," or any of the categories we use to make sense of the world. We absorb and adapt and alter such conceptions from the culture we create and inhabit, and political criticism therefore considers how our social landscape is invented and passed on; how certain ideas persist and others are changed. Although fiction, poetry, and drama play important roles in the continual reinvention of culture in all its amazing diversity and conflict, popular culture is also an important subject for political criticism. Advertisements, films, fashion, songs, amusement parks—in short, anything that can be viewed as a "text" and analyzed for its social effects—might be the occasion for some kind of political criticism.

To get things done in politics, in this scramble for alliances and power, people who share at least some values (or who believe they share them) may work together, conceiving of themselves in some sense, for some moment of time, to some degree, as a group. In politics, there is always "us" and "them," in other words. As human beings struggle to make things happen, whether it is keeping the fire burning all night or putting a man on the moon, we interact with each other in terms of these categories we have created. These categories, like any human tool, can be used for better or worse, attempting to make our group's vision of the world come true. Political criticism in all its varieties thus tries to alert us to how these categories are being used—especially when they are being used to oppress, limit, exclude, or exploit a particular group. As this explanation is still pretty vague, let's look at some specific examples.

Feminist criticism is the form of political criticism that has been the most spectacularly successful in the last thirty years. Like feminism, feminist criticism looks for sexual oppression, exposing those assumptions and ways of thinking that have been deleterious to women. The most obvious such assumption in literary history has been that it was inappropriate or implausible for women to write significant literature. This prejudice did not keep women from writing, fortunately, and feminist critics have recovered an astonishing wealth of great literature by women. This expansion of the **canon** (that is, those works considered worthy of everyone's attention) has been accomplished in part by enlarging the kinds of works thought of as literature (including diaries, journals, letters), and in part simply by tracking the works down and publishing them—in anthologies, in separate editions.

In addition to seeing what women have written, feminist critics have also paid attention to the way women have been written—that is, to the way they have been depicted in texts. As Simone de Beauvoir argued in 1949 in her ground-breaking *Second Sex,* women have been depicted as either Mary or Eve, the angelic mother or the evil seductress. Such idealization (woman as saint) and misogyny (woman as monster) together represent pernicious stereotypes, which feminist criticism strives to expose. A key idea in the struggle to expose and undo limiting conceptions of women has been the distinction between *sex* and *gender.* Sex is a biological category. Although sex is not as clearly delineated as we might think (some people are born with both sex organs, or have the anatomy of one sex and the biochemistry of the other, or have the physiology of one sex yet perceive themselves to be "naturally" the other), it is assumed to have an origin in nature. Gender, on the other hand, is socially constructed. We may think of wearing makeup as feminine, and hunting as a male endeavor, but these activities could be distributed differently. Most cultures have been patriarchal (with the patriarch, or father figure, in charge) because we have constructed this way of thinking. Because writing and reading have been controlled by a patriarchal system (by men, that is, as they have imagined themselves somehow placed in charge of society, just as the father, or patriarch, has been thought of as the head of the household), the responses of women to texts have been ignored, or assumed to be essentially the same as men. Feminist criticism, not surprisingly, has explored what it means to read as a woman—and not as a woman trying to read like a man.

To do feminist criticism you may undertake the following:

1. Consider how the writer's sex has influenced the work.
2. Look for stereotypes based on sex and gender.
3. Imagine how the work might be read differently by women readers.

Gay and lesbian approaches   obviously share with feminist criticism a commitment to identifying and challenging oppressive stereotypes and destructive assumptions. Just as feminist criticism proceeds from the recognition that men and women are different, gay and lesbian approaches proceed from the idea that same-sex desire, opposed to heterosexual desire, has been differently represented and valued. Just as feminist criticism has struggled to determine the role that biology and culture play in constructing what it means to be a woman, so have gay and lesbian studies argued over the essentialist (biologically imprinted) versus constructionist (socially transmitted) nature of same-sex desire. Recovering works by gay and lesbian writers has meant not only (as with feminist criticism) uncovering and publishing neglected or unknown works by women; the "recovery" has also involved assessing the sexual orientation of various writers who may have hidden or suppressed their gay or lesbian status. "Gay" is a strategic term, meant to displace "homosexual," which suggests deviancy or illness. The need to distinguish "lesbian" studies from "gay" studies arose in part because gay women confront two layers of bias, sexuality and gender, which makes their position significantly different from that of gay men.

Queer theory   responds to the perception of a problem with gay and lesbian studies: they still adhere to a binary model of sexuality. In recent years, queer theory has emerged to challenge the limitations of sexual prejudice left intact by gay and lesbian studies. "Queer" is again a strategic choice, meant to embrace and defuse a formerly derisive term. Queer theory can be seen as the third step in the process of undoing sexual prejudice: feminist criticism seeks to expose and challenge bias against one sex; gay and lesbian approaches seek to expose and challenge bias against a sexual preference; and queer theory seeks to expose and challenge all assumptions about sexuality. Why do we think in terms of only two sexes, queer theorists ask? What authorizes the exclusion of bisexual, transsexual, and transgendered people? Again, it's easy, at least in theory, to engage in gay, lesbian, and queer strategies:

1. Consider how the writer's sexual preference has influenced the work.
2. Look for stereotypes based on sexual preference.
3. Imagine how the work might be read differently by readers with different sexual desires.

Economic, materialist, and Marxist criticism   all draw attention to the economic circumstances represented in literary works, as well as the ideology (the set of beliefs) that justify and support these circumstances. Marxist criticism explicitly uses the ideas of Karl Marx (1818–1883), who divided society into the aristocracy, the bourgeoisie, and the proletariat, and argued that in modern times, in capitalist societies, the bourgeoisie have exploited the proletariat (and the aristocracy have dwindled in number and influence). In other words, Marx imagines an upper class, owners of business and land, who oppress and use the lower class, who do the work but do not share proportionately in the rewards.

As a political philosophy, Marxism has turned out to be a massive failure, ignoring the personal identity that motivates most people, and the opportunities offered by capitalism for class movement up and down. But as a critical strategy, Marxism is more successful because it focuses upon the set of beliefs (the ideology) that structure value and desire in a society. An ideology makes our various social roles appear to be natural and inevitable. When a culture is in turmoil, when social roles for significant numbers of people are unclear, it is because there is no shared ideology. The members of the society do not agree on the purpose of the society.

Materialist criticism can be distinguished from Marxist criticism by its emphasis upon the material circumstances depicted in a text: where do people live, what do they eat, how are they educated, under what conditions do they work? By distinguishing these material conditions, we can address the belief system that creates them, and perhaps even move toward improving the material existence of people. Economic criticism is a looser term that refers simply to any criticism that pays particular attention to the economic conditions portrayed in or related to a text. Marxist and materialist strategies may be used by economic criticism, but other economic theories and interests are also available. Like feminist and gay/lesbian/queer approaches, these economic theories aim to see how people in a particular group (women, gays and lesbians, the lower class) are portrayed: how does literature contribute to maintaining or changing the dominant ideology? How can literary criticism be a tool for positive change?

Race and ethnicity   can also be the motivating factors in distinctive critical approaches, employing the same sort of strategies used by other kinds of political criticism. An African American approach, or a Native American approach seeks (as with feminist criticism) to recover and appreciate neglected or unknown works by members of that group, noting the special contribution made possible by a different perspective. Whether race or ethnicity is the distinguishing factor, the assumption is that members of this group read and write differently, and that our cultural life will be richer if we engage with this difference. Henry Louis Gates, for instance, in his influential book *The Signifying Monkey,* has explored the way African Americans have transformed language for their own purposes, signifying in ways that subvert and resist the oppression they have encountered. Such racial and ethnic approaches seek not only to see how members of a group have written, but also (again, as with feminist criticism) to see how they have been written. How have people from Africa, or China, or the Middle East been represented in fiction? What stereotypes of Native Americans, or Jews, or Quakers have been employed and resisted in American films?

Feminist critics, as we have seen, confront the difficulty of saying what it means to be female: is this a biological (sexual) or a cultural (gendered) category? Gay/lesbian/queer theories confront a similar difficulty: are we talking about socially constructed desires or "natural" instincts? Even economic approaches must struggle with defining the groups being analyzed or spoken for: are there really only two classes, or three, or six? Where does each begin and end, and what are their features? By the same token, race and ethnicity are increasingly becoming contested categories, as most anthropologists and biologists agree that the concept of "race" is hopelessly untenable. Groups of people may identify themselves as belonging to a particular race, but we are unable to draw distinct lines between the races: instead, we blend together at the edges, and even in the middle—whatever these spatial metaphors mean in racial terms. Ethnic groups are even more porous, sharing customs, languages, religions, geographical origins—but not necessarily physiological tendencies.

Such necessary struggles to define and demarcate this or that political entity serves, perhaps surprisingly, a dual function: by creating a better understanding of a particular group, by those within it and those outside, critics can serve as political agents for change. It is much harder, for most people, to oppress, exploit, abuse, or ignore someone if you understand who that person is—if you have a deep understanding of what life looks like from that person's point of view. It is also much easier, with greater understanding, to see how we are all more similar than we may have thought, and how justice and opportunity should be extended to every human. The power of reading literature, which political criticism seeks to seize and promote, is simply that we are allowed to examine, in a limited sense admittedly, life inside other bodies, from within other social positions. It's hard to do that, and to practice political criticism, without growing as a person in some way.

Let's turn now to a particular literary work and see what these approaches might offer. Here's a very short story, which is actually part of a sequence of stories.

ERNEST HEMINGWAY (1899–1961)

In his early career, Ernest Hemingway was a reporter, an ambulance unit member, and the recipient of a World War I medal for heroism (he was wounded in 1918). His passion for adventure and his careful observation of human struggle and suffering were transformed into some of the most celebrated novels and short stories in American literature. Hemingway went on to win the Pulitzer and Nobel Prizes, among many others, for works such as A Farewell to Arms *(1929),* Death in the Afternoon *(1932),* For Whom the Bell Tolls *(1940), and* The Old Man and the Sea *(1952). He participated in the D-Day landings of World War II (1944) as a war correspondent. A hunter, fisherman, and bullfighting fan, Hemingway spent much of his time in Cuba until the 1960 revolution. He and his fourth wife were living on a ranch near Ketchum, Idaho, when Hemingway, depressed by illness and by fears of illness, committed suicide with a shotgun in 1961.*

A Very Short Story

One hot evening in Padua they carried him up onto the roof and he could look out over the top of the town. There were chimney swifts in the sky. After a while it got dark and the searchlights came out. The others went down and took the bottles with them. He and Luz could hear them below on the balcony. Luz sat on the bed. She was cool and fresh in the hot night.

Luz stayed on night duty for three months. They were glad to let her. When they operated on him she prepared him for the operating table; and they had a joke about friend or enema. He went under the anesthetic holding tight on to himself so he would not blab about anything during the silly, talky time. After he got on crutches he used to take the temperatures so Luz would not have to get up from the bed. There were only a few patients, and they all knew about it. They all liked Luz. As he walked back along the halls he thought of Luz in his bed.

Before he went back to the front they went into the Duomo and prayed. It was dim and quiet, and there were other people praying. They wanted to get married, but there was not enough time for the banns, and neither of them had birth certificates. They felt as though they were married, but they wanted everyone to know about it, and to make it so they could not lose it.

Luz wrote him many letters that he never got until after the armistice. Fifteen came in a bunch to the front and he sorted them by the dates and read them all straight through. They were all about the hospital, and how much she loved him, and how it was impossible to get along without him, and how terrible it was missing him at night.

After the armistice they agreed he should go home to get a job so they might be married. Luz would not come home until he had a good job and could come to New York to meet her. It was understood he would not drink, and he did not want to see his friends or anyone in the States. Only to get a job and be married. On the train from Padua to Milan they quarreled about her not being willing to come home at once. When they had to say goodbye, in the station at Milan, they kissed goodbye, but were not finished with the quarrel. He felt sick about saying goodbye like that.

He went to America on a boat from Genoa. Luz went back to Pordenone to open a hospital. It was lonely and rainy there, and there was a battalion of arditi quartered in the town. Living in the muddy, rainy town in the winter, the major of the battalion made love to Luz, and she had never known Italians before, and finally wrote to the States that theirs had been only a boy and girl affair. She was sorry, and she knew he would probably not be able to understand, but might someday forgive her, and be grateful to her, and she expected, absolutely unexpectedly, to be married in the spring. She loved him as always, but she realized now it was only a boy and girl love. She hoped he would have a great career and believed in him absolutely. She knew it was for the best.

The major did not marry her in the spring, or any other time. Luz never got an answer to the letter to Chicago about it. A short time after he contracted gonorrhea from a salesgirl in a loop department store while riding in a taxicab through Lincoln Park.

[1925]

How this story shapes the reader's response has already been suggested by Robert Scholes in *Semiotics and Interpretation.* As Scholes observes, the point of view in the story is technically third person (if it were **first-person narration,** it would read this way:"One hot evening in Padua they carried me up on the roof . . .").But the viewpoint, Scholes says, seems to be closer to the unnamed man than to Luz. If the narrator were equally distanced from both characters, they would both have names. But "he" apparently doesn't need a name. The reader is told in the first and second sentences what "he" could see. Also, as Scholes notes, the assertion "She was cool and fresh in the hot night" really makes sense only from his perspective: *to him,* she seemed cool and fresh. This point of view thus plays an important role in the reader's response. Let's elaborate on Scholes's view of the story by tracing out in some detail "the reader's" experience, as it is shaped by the story's implicitly male perspective.

For starters, we might consider how the reader responds to Hemingway's opening paragraph. Our response must be problematic at that point because we know so little: important information is being left out. But we do know something. We know "he" is in Padua, but we don't know what he is doing there or who he is. We learn that "they" carried him to the roof, but we don't know who "they" are or why he has to be carried: is he sick or injured? Does he have a handicap? The reference to searchlights in the third sentence probably suggests to most readers that the story may be taking place during wartime: these are probably searchlights looking for attacking planes. If that's the case, then perhaps he is being carried because he is wounded. We also learn that he and Luz are somehow close: "they" leave them alone on the roof, and Luz sits on his bed, appearing "cool and fresh."

In the second paragraph, the implied point of view is made clearer, and additional clues are offered. The notion that he is in a hospital is confirmed here. Luz is on night duty, so she would seem to be a nurse—an inference further supported by her preparation of him for the operating table. The reader may notice, as Scholes points out, that the male character's reticence is much like the story's own restraint. He doesn't want to blab, and neither apparently does the story's narrator, telling us only the minimum. As Scholes puts it, "Logorrhea and diarrhea are equally embarrassing." Keeping one's emotions in, not blabbing—these are, within the soldier's culture at least, distinctly masculine traits. (Think of all the action heroes who don't say much.)

Even if the reader finds the male character's fear of talking about anything troubling, the embodiment of a dumb macho stereotype, the strong silent man, we must be softened by his kindness in taking the temperatures. Here he is on crutches, and yet he gets up so Luz won't have to. What is not said by the narrator is what Luz is doing in his bed, but this is a blank that the reader easily fills in. The reader can easily imagine that the "it" that the few patients "all knew about" must be an affair "he" and Luz are having. Why else would the narrator present the revelation that "they all knew about it" as if it were a kind of secret? The wounded man's nighttime nursing is thus an extraordinary marker of his affection for Luz: he is wounded himself, yet he nurses others; he is a man, yet he is willing to assume the definitively feminine role (in 1925) of nursing.

Recognizing what "it" is, most readers will probably acknowledge that a nurse sleeping with her patient probably does not represent the highest ethical standards. And recognizing this response perhaps makes clear why Hemingway has the narrator immediately tell us "They all liked Luz": their affection for Luz is designed to qualify the reader's assumed disapproval. With the paragraph's final sentence, the reader must also realize, as "he" thinks of Luz in his bed, that she apparently means a lot to a recovering man, a wounded soldier. Having immersed ourselves in "his" point of view, readers may not notice, without some consideration, that we do not know what Luz is thinking.

In the third paragraph we learn for certain that he is in fact a soldier because he goes back to the front. We learn that he and Luz pray together in church, and the narrator tells us they wish they could be married, and feel as if they are married. If this feeling really is mutual, the reader may wonder about their plan. Why doesn't

Luz return with him rather than waiting on his "good job"? Doesn't this condition make her seem a bit mercenary? Also, why are the restrictions on him seemingly so severe? Perhaps it makes sense that he will not drink, especially if he has a problem with drinking. But why does he not want to see his friends? In fact, he doesn't want to see anyone at all, according to their understanding. Does Luz not trust him? Does he not trust himself? The reader cannot be sure, the way this understanding is phrased, whether Luz imposes these conditions or he volunteers them; but since they restrict his behavior, the reader may naturally assume the rules are Luz's idea.

Such subtle shaping prepares us for the bombshell in the fifth paragraph: she dumps him. Consider (among other things) the effect of the information that "she had never known Italians before." The passage seems to offer this fact as a kind of explanation of her behavior, but it is an excuse that makes Luz seem worse, as if she wants to try Italians the way one might try a new flavor of ice cream. Hemingway does not say this excuse is disgustingly inadequate, but he sets up the story so that we easily come to such a conclusion. Her letter is not quoted, but is filtered through his perspective; from that vantage point, it seems reasonable to assume that Luz has shamefully betrayed him.

There are in fact aspects of the letter, as it is reported, that seem so unfeeling they appear to be cruel. It is difficult to imagine what could be more devastating to the soldier than hearing Luz's view that the love of his life was actually, in her view, "only a boy and girl affair." To say "she loved him as always" similarly demeans their relationship. "I thought we were in love," she is in effect saying, "but now that I've been with this Italian, I see we were just playing like children." Her love hasn't changed, just her understanding of what that love was. Finally, to say she "believed in him absolutely" after refusing to come to America before he had a "good" job seems to embody hypocrisy and coldness.

How do we respond to the conclusion? Hemingway has led the reader, it may seem, to see Luz's own jilting by the major as just what she deserves. He adds "or any other time" to prevent the reader from assuming that Luz and the Italian had some problems but later worked them out. The affair *she said* she thought was the real thing, in comparison to their boy and girl thing, does not turn out to be real after all. But did she really believe the Italian was different? Is Luz a "loose" woman? Is that the significance of her name?

By telling us that Luz never got an answer to her letter, Hemingway conveys the soldier's pain. We imagine he is so hurt, so disgusted, that he can't even respond. The final sentence deepens the reader's perception of his pain. As Scholes points out, first Luz wounds his heart; then the salesgirl wounds him in a different place. The reader naturally assumes that he wouldn't have been fooling around recklessly and decadently, if not for Luz. The narrator does not say it is Luz's fault that he gets gonorrhea, but that is the implication: when he loses Luz, he loses everything. "A short time after" here implies loosely some connection. First the war wound; then Luz's; then the salesgirl's.

In moving through the story, we are carrying out and elaborating on the reading Scholes suggests. About the reader's response to this story—that is, the implied response that Hemingway marks out—Scholes says the following:

Most male students sympathize with the protagonist and are very critical of Luz—as indeed [the story] asks them to be. Many female students try to read the story as sympathetic to Luz, blaming events on the "weakness" of the young man or the state of the world. This is a possible interpretation, but it is not well supported by the text. Thus the female student must either

Hemingway, recovering from his World War I injury (1918), stands next to
Agnes von Kurowsky (to his right). The events in "A Very Short Story" are
based on Hemingway's affair with Agnes. In the 1925 edition of *In Our Time*
(Boni and Liveright), the nurse is called "Ag." For the 1930 edition, published by Scribner's, Hemingway changed her name to "Luz," and he also
changed the names of the cities.

"misread" the work (that is, she must offer the more weakly supported of
two interpretations) or accept one more blow to her self-esteem as a
woman. Faced with this story in a competitive classroom, women are put at
a disadvantage. They are, in fact, in a double bind. (120–121)

The discussion thus far has elaborated upon this analysis of the implied reader's
response. The text, in Scholes's opinion, makes the case against Luz. Although taking
Luz's side is "a possible interpretation," Scholes says, it seems more difficult to him, a
misreading. Scholes does place "misread" inside quotation marks, indicating his awareness of alternatives. But in truth, Scholes sees the reader—the male reader anyway—
as being pulled toward one best response.

Not only does Scholes implicitly assume the text is a stable structure, marking out
a particular response, he also assumes that "most" males will naturally take the soldier's

side, and females will naturally try to take Luz's side. But one of the beauties of the variety of political criticism is that we can take advantage of the diversity of readers in the world, reminding us of the treacherousness of generalizations about them. Although there may be profitable uses here for economic, gay/lesbian/queer, and even racial and ethnic approaches, the most obvious dynamic at work in Hemingway's story concerns the representation of gender. The portrait of Luz reinforces the stereotype of woman as Eve—vulnerable, weak, untrustworthy, subject to temptation, the doom of man. Feminist criticism would seem to be the most appropriate political stance to use to revitalize this text we think we already have learned how to read.

Inventing

What seems more difficult to Scholes (that is, taking Luz's side) seems to me in fact more compelling. I felt the first time I read this story that Luz was getting a raw deal, both from the soldier and from the narrator. Does that mean I am responding from a woman's point of view? And is that point of view necessarily "at a disadvantage"? Even if we assume that women tend to side with Luz, and that the evidence for doing so is weaker than the evidence against Luz, we should still note that what is most obvious is oftentimes not very interesting in literary criticism. Making the case for Luz against the soldier is generally a more interesting endeavor than showing how Luz is cruel to the soldier.

Thus, I would argue that Hemingway creates such apparent bias against Luz in order to expose it: that is, the soldier is so obviously being made into a martyr, and Luz into a villain, that the thoughtful reader's response ought to resist this bias and look more carefully at the text, seeing past the narrator's obscuring point of view.

To give you an idea how one student developed this response into an essay, let's look at his notes and then the essay that resulted from them. Before examining these documents, you might want to sketch out your own response to Hemingway's story. What does it say to you?

```
    Make clear that the narrator clearly takes his side:
Hemingway is reminding us to consider the source. You can't
let the player's coach call the balls in or out, and the
narrator in this case is on the soldier's team.
    I could make Hemingway into the villain who tries to
cover for the soldier, making Luz into an Eve figure. Or, I
could argue that Hemingway has the narrator make those moves,
thus exposing him. I think the latter would be more fun.
    What is the absolute worst evidence against Luz? Probably
the reason she gives for the break-up. Focus on that reason:
"theirs had been only a boy and girl affair." The reader
assumes, in the context created by the soldier's spokesman,
that this excuse is cruel and cold. But maybe it isn't a
rationalization, a way of justifying her fling with an
Italian major. Consider the possibility that Luz is right:
they are immature; it is a boy/girl affair. Any evidence?
    The soldier does reveal his immaturity after Luz breaks
it off: having sex in a taxicab, getting an S.T.D.—now
that's really mature.
    We also must wonder about his decision not to respond to
Luz's last letter. If he really loved Luz, wouldn't he
consider forgiving her? Doesn't everyone make mistakes?
```

Isn't it possible that Luz just got confused and mistook infatuation with the major for love? At such a distance from the soldier, in such bleak circumstances, she simply erred. But the soldier is such an immature hothead that the idea of forgiving her never occurs to him.

What is the basis of the soldier's relationship with Luz? If she is wrong, if it is more than a boy/girl affair, what evidence is there in the story of his maturity and the depth of his love? The story in fact tells us nothing that suggests any great passion on his part. He seems perfectly willing to leave her behind while he goes to the U.S. to get a job. What does he think of Luz? We know only two things, really: She was "cool and fresh" and "he thought of Luz in his bed." So far as we can tell, the relationship is based on sex, which isn't the strongest foundation for marriage.

What is the evidence that Luz is a bad person? She does have sex with the soldier while he's a patient. She sleeps in his bed. She lets him get up and take the temperatures. But none of this makes her evil. He is a wounded soldier in a foreign country about to go back to the front. She is comforting him. She offers him love and affection. She is the nurse every wounded soldier no doubt dreams of. In letting the soldier get up and take the temperatures, Luz is arguably letting him act as her protector, strengthening his ego, which is likely to be fragile after his injury.

Why is there an understanding that he won't drink and won't hang around with his friends? Is Luz being mean? Hemingway leaves this meaningful gap in the story, when he could have easily filled it in. Perhaps the soldier has a drinking problem. Early in the story other people do take away the bottles. The story doesn't say that Luz imposed this "no drinking" policy on him; perhaps he imposed it on himself to indicate his seriousness and trustworthiness to Luz.

What does it mean when Luz breaks it off? Had there been a formal proposal, an acceptance, a ring, an engagement? All the reader knows is that the two are sleeping together, and that they come to view each other as married—at least from the soldier's perspective. Hemingway says the understanding is that "he should go home so they might be married." What does "might" mean here? If they wanted to get married before he went back to the front, why didn't they arrange it when he returned? Such unexplained gaps must lead the reader to wonder about the facts. Has the soldier come to assume something that just isn't the case: he assumes, because they are sleeping together, they're going to get married; and poor Luz, feeling sorry for his wounds and his inevitable return to danger doesn't have the heart to tell him it just isn't that serious.

If they really were in love, why might Luz fall for the Italian major? The reader isn't told anything about what things look like from her perspective. Does he write letters? Does he get a job? Does he follow through on his "no drinking" pledge? If he *does* get a job, then why hasn't

Luz already come over? It seems likely, in fact, the more one thinks about it, that something is seriously wrong on his end. Hemingway, by withholding vital information, allows the reader to jump to conclusions—conclusions the careful reader must eventually withdraw. The reader leaps to conclusions, much like the soldier. Hemingway, the feminist, is teaching us to be more careful in judging women.

Shaping

Based on these notes, which meditated on the possibility that Luz is being set up, and that we ought to see through this unfair treatment, the student sketched out a draft of the main points to make in articulating his response. Here's what he wrote:

Main point: Luz is right. It was a boy and girl affair.

Evidence

1. Their relationship is apparently based on sex; plus, some questionable ethics are involved in their affair.

2. The soldier appears to be unreliable: Luz is afraid he won't get a job, but will just drink and run around. Since she doesn't come to the U.S., it appears that she may have been right.

3. Luz obviously wasn't ready to get married, or she would have married him when he returned to the front, before he returned to the States. She just couldn't break his heart so soon after the war.

4. He doesn't respond to her last letter; he doesn't try to win her back. Instead he responds with reckless indulgence. Our first impulse is to feel sorry for him; our more reasoned response is to fault him.

Problems

1. If Luz has no intention to marry him, it is only momentarily kind to string him along.

2. If Luz aims to get him to the States, where he'll slowly forget about her, then why do they have this understanding about his drinking and socializing?

Drafting

At this point, he was ready to write a draft. He didn't have everything worked out, but we write drafts to learn and discover. After several tries, and some rewriting and rethinking, here is the essay he produced.

The Longer View of Hemingway's "A Very Short Story"

Most readers of Hemingway's "A Very Short Story" will naturally pity the poor nameless soldier. He is wounded in the war, and then his fiancé breaks off their relationship when she falls for an Italian major. Her name, Luz, which might be pronounced like "lose," points to his fate: where women are involved, he will lose. As a final indignity and injury, another woman gives him gonorrhea, emphasizing his status as a victim and a loser—because of women. Although the main villain is Luz, his experience with the salesgirl, who wounds him in a different way, suggests quite simply that women are untrustworthy, evil, dangerous—as bad as the war, it seems.

But this immediate reaction of pity is only the effect of our point of view, and our reliance upon certain pervasive and destructive stereotypes of women. Although the story is told in third-person, Hemingway actually gives us, as Robert Scholes points out in *Semiotics and Interpretation* (New Haven, CN: Yale UP, 1982), what is essentially the soldier's point of view. Repeatedly in the brief story, we are told what he experiences and what he is thinking. In the opening, for instance, we are told that "he could look out over the top of the town." We learn that Luz "was cool and fresh in the hot night"—a perception that clearly is his. We know his motivation for trying not to talk under anesthetic (he does not want to "blab"), and we know how many letters he received and what was in them. We never know, however, what Luz could see, what she was really thinking, and we learn the content of her letters from his perspective, when he reads them. The real context of Luz's writing is hidden from the reader, controlled by the soldier and the narrator.

But Hemingway gives the careful reader plenty of clues that suggest we should look closer, overcoming the bias and limitation of the narrative's point of view. Is Luz in fact entirely the villain, and the soldier purely the innocent victim? Or does this reaction reveal a prejudice?

Our opinion of Luz is of course influenced by the fact that in falling for the Italian major, she betrays the American soldier. There is little question that Luz made a mistake, misjudging the Italian's sincerity or trustworthiness, but it is also clear that she pays for her mistake, for "The major did not marry her in the spring, or any other time." Her story, in a sense, might not be that different from the solder's, if it were told. And when Luz writes to the soldier about the major's departure, she is perhaps attempting to resurrect her relationship with the soldier, but he fails to respond. The soldier cannot forgive her, apparently.

Nor, it seems, can those readers who rely upon stereotypes and assumptions. The most important criticism of Luz clearly has to do with the letter breaking off her relationship with the soldier. Specifically, her assertion that "theirs had been only a boy and girl affair" seems especially thoughtless and cruel. It is bad enough to be dumped for an Italian stallion, but it is even worse to learn that your own relationship was, in your partner's view, immature and superficial. But before we damn Luz's insensitivity, we ought not dismiss the possible validity of her remark. In other words, is she possibly right? Was their relationship only a boy and girl affair?

What in fact is the basis of their relationship? It appears to be only physical. All we know of his view of Luz is that she is "cool and fresh." She sounds more like a soft drink or a vegetable than a partner for life. Luz is after all sleeping in the hospital with one of her patients, and another pronunciation of her name, as "loose," may also be appropriate. When she says their relationship was immature, perhaps she accurately assesses her own behavior—as well as the soldier's. The conditions, to be sure, were extraordinary: it is wartime, and the wounded soldier is returning to the front. I can understand Luz's looseness, but I can also agree that she is immature.

Her assessment of the soldier's maturity also seems accurate to me. Just look at his response to her last letter. He goes from hospital-bed sex to taxicab sex.

Hemingway provides the tawdry details to emphasize his poor judgment: "A short time after [her letter] he contracted gonorrhea from a sales girl in a loop department store while riding in a taxicab through Lincoln Park." The poor soldier is wounded again in "combat," but surely this problem is his own fault. It is not Luz's fault, nor even the salesgirl's fault, is it? Even if we grant that mature and thoughtful people might contract a sexually transmitted disease, and that things were much different back then, the circumstances here still do not suggest responsible behavior. In fact, it is hard for me to imagine how he could be more immature, unless perhaps he had sex on the sidewalk with a prostitute.

I also notice the soldier's promise not to drink, nor to see "his friends or anyone." Given the reference early in the story to drinking on the roof, I have to wonder if he has a drinking problem. I wonder why they did not marry when he returned from the front. There was not sufficient time before he left, but surely there was enough time when he got back. It seems fair to suspect that the lack of time was just a convenient excuse. Likewise, why does he go ahead and leave Luz if he is unhappy with the arrangement? How long does it take him to get a job? Does he in fact get one? If so, then why is Luz still overseas? We are not told many things we need to know to evaluate his responsibility, but what is left out, together with what we do know, does suggest to me that Luz's view may not be thoughtless or cruel, but simply accurate. Hemingway allows us, in other words, if we are thoughtful and aware of our prejudices, to see the other side. Theirs was indeed a boy and girl affair. At least Luz is perceptive enough to see it.

✔ Checklist for Political Criticism

- ❑ Consider how the writer's sex, race, class, or other identity has influenced the work.
- ❑ Look for stereotypes based on sex, gender, race, class, or other convention.

❑ Imagine how the work might be read differently by a reader of a particular sex, class, race, or other identity.

Useful Terms for Political Criticism

Canon: The canon is that group of works that are usually reprinted, read, assigned, written about, and taken most seriously. Feminist criticism has been particularly effective in arguing that some works are included and others ignored on largely political grounds. Historically, women as a rule have had few opportunities to write; and when they have somehow managed to produce works of merit, these often have not been appreciated or understood (some women writers have adopted male pseudonyms in order to get a fair reading). Critics have similarly pressed to open the canon to African American, American Indian, and other neglected writers.

Constructed: This term is particularly powerful because it reminds us that any representation of a particular ethnic or racial or sexual group is something that is made up. It is not inevitable, nor does it fully (or even partially) depict reality. Our notions, in other words, of women, or African Americans, or American Indians, or gay men, or any other segment of society are just that: our notions.

Double-voiced: A member of an oppressed group, attempting to speak to and through the dominant culture, faces a tricky situation: how to speak one's mind without being silenced? One strategy is to write with two voices, saying what can be taken on the surface in a nonthreatening way, and on a deeper level in a subversive or challenging way. Because the various strands of political criticism often look at the way an oppressed group represents itself in a text, teasing out a text's double-voicing has been a recurrent critical activity.

Exclusion: What we value as great literature depends on what values we bring to our reading. Since white European males have dominated the worlds of publishing and criticism, it is not surprising that white European males have dominated the canon of literature. Some works may have been excluded from study because of the status of their authors; others may have been excluded because their virtues are not appreciated by established literary values.

Gender: "Gender" refers to the cultural aspects of sexuality. In other words, gender includes not just biological factors, but also psychological and social factors as well. We are still trying to discover just how much of "maleness" and "femaleness" can be attributed to biology, and how much to other factors. It seems clear that gender is not entirely constructed by cultural influences, that there are some differences between the sexes (surprise!). But the wide range of variation within "male" and "female" makes it difficult to say definitively what those differences always are, and thus how "gender" (the construction of male and female) relates to "sex" (the biological status).

Marxist: Because Marx considered issues of economy and class to be fundamental, shaping everything, literary criticism that focuses on economy and class is often termed "Marxist," even when the critic does not embrace the same principles as Karl Marx. This way of reading, attaching primary importance to the material sources of a work in class and money, is also sometimes called "materialist," especially when the physical conditions and circumstances are the focus.

Materialist: See *Marxist.*

Patriarchy: Literally, "father-ruled," the term points to the superior status of men within a culture. The opposite term, "matriarchy," refers to a culture in which women are superior.

Sex: See *Gender.*

Sexist: Assuming that someone has certain characteristics because of his or her sex is sexist. Usually, the term is used to describe pejorative characterizations of women as a group, or of individual women as representative types of that group.

Elements: Character, Setting, and Theme

The following story is one of the most celebrated, reprinted, and analyzed short stories in literary history. If you're not already familiar with it, you're in for a treat. If you do know this story, read it carefully again, looking for things you haven't noticed before. It's a story that is rich enough, as many readers have found, to sustain many satisfying readings. This story will be the focus for the discussion of character, setting, and theme, which are all familiar terms meaning roughly the same thing in literary criticism that they mean in ordinary conversation. The characters are the actors, usually people (although animals, or aliens, or robots, or ghosts, or just about anything can be a character); the setting is where the action takes place; and the theme is what the story adds up to—the main idea that seems to hold the story together. By considering these elements in Faulkner's story, we will fill out each of these concepts a bit, as well as consider how different critical perspectives put them to different kinds of uses.

WILLIAM FAULKNER (1897–1962)

*William Faulkner lived most of his life in Oxford, Mississippi. He left high school to serve with the British Royal Air Force in World War I, and returned to the University of Mississippi first as a student, then as its postmaster. Faulkner switched from poetry (*The Marble Faun *in 1924) to fiction while working as a journalist and was encouraged by Sherwood Anderson. With Sartoris *in 1929, Faulkner began creating the fictional Yoknapatawpha County that would be the backdrop for major works such as* The Sound and the Fury *(1929),* Light in August *(1932),* Absalom, Absalom! *(1936), and others. He also worked on movie scripts in Hollywood occasionally. He won the Nobel Prize for literature in 1949 and the Pulitzer in 1954.*

A Rose for Emily

I

When Miss Emily Grierson died, our whole town went to her funeral: the men through a sort of respectful affection for a fallen monument, the women mostly out of curiosity to see the inside of her house, which no one save an old manservant—a combined gardener and cook—had seen in at least ten years.

It was a big, squarish frame house that had once been white, decorated with cupolas and spires and scrolled balconies in the heavily lightsome style of the seventies, set on what had once been our most select street. But garages and cotton gins had encroached and obliterated even the august names of that neighborhood; only Miss Emily's house was left, lifting its stubborn and coquettish decay above the cotton wagons and the gasoline pumps—an eyesore among eyesores. And now Miss Emily had gone to join the representatives of those august names where they lay in the cedar-bemused cemetery among the ranked and anonymous graves of Union and Confederate soldiers who fell at the battle of Jefferson.

Alive, Miss Emily had been a tradition, a duty, and a care; a sort of hereditary obligation upon the town, dating from that day in 1894 when Colonel Sartoris, the mayor—he who fathered the edict that no Negro woman should appear on the streets without an apron—remitted her taxes, the dispensation dating from the death of her father on into perpetuity. Not that Miss Emily would have accepted charity. Colonel Sartoris invented an involved tale to the effect that Miss Emily's father had loaned money to the town, which the town, as a matter of business, preferred this way of repaying. Only a man of Colonel Sartoris' generation and thought could have invented it, and only a woman could have believed it.

William Faulkner (left) sits with other honorees at the formal Nobel Prize dinner in Stockholm in 1950.

When the next generation, with its more modern ideas, became mayors and aldermen, this arrangement created some little dissatisfaction. On the first of the year they mailed her a tax notice. February came, and there was no reply. They wrote her a formal letter, asking her to call at the sheriff's office at her convenience. A week later the mayor wrote her himself, offering to call or to send his car for her, and received in reply a note on paper of an archaic shape, in a thin, flowing calligraphy in faded ink, to the effect that she no longer went out at all. The tax notice was also enclosed, without comment.

They called a special meeting of the Board of Aldermen. A deputation waited upon her, knocked at the door through which no visitor had passed since she ceased giving china-painting lessons eight or ten years earlier. They were admitted by the old Negro into a dim hall from which a stairway mounted into still more shadow. It smelled of dust and disuse—a close, dank smell. The Negro led them into the parlor. It was furnished in heavy, leather-covered furniture. When the Negro opened the blinds of one window, they could see that the leather was cracked; and when they sat down, a faint dust rose sluggishly about their thighs, spinning with slow motes in the single sun-ray. On a tarnished gilt easel before the fireplace stood a crayon portrait of Miss Emily's father.

They rose when she entered—a small, fat woman in black, with a thin gold chain descending to her waist and vanishing into her belt, leaning on an ebony cane with a tarnished gold head. Her skeleton was small and spare; perhaps that was why what would have been merely plumpness in another was obesity in her. She looked bloated, like a body long submerged in motionless water, and of that pallid hue. Her eyes, lost in the fatty ridges of her face, looked like two small pieces of coal pressed into a lump of dough as they moved from one face to another while the visitors stated their errand.

5

She did not ask them to sit. She just stood in the door and listened quietly until the spokesman came to a stumbling halt. Then they could hear the invisible watch ticking at the end of the gold chain.

Her voice was dry and cold. "I have no taxes in Jefferson. Colonel Sartoris explained it to me. Perhaps one of you can gain access to the city records and satisfy yourselves."

"But we have. We are the city authorities, Miss Emily. Didn't you get a notice from the sheriff, signed by him?"

"I received a paper, yes," Miss Emily said. "Perhaps he considers himself   10
the sheriff . . . I have no taxes in Jefferson."

"But there is nothing on the books to show that, you see. We must go by the—"

"See Colonel Sartoris. I have no taxes in Jefferson."

"But, Miss Emily—"

"See Colonel Sartoris." (Colonel Sartoris had been dead almost ten years.) "I have no taxes in Jefferson. Tobe!" The Negro appeared. "Show these gentlemen out."

II

So she vanquished them, horse and foot, just as she had vanquished their   15
fathers thirty years before about the smell. That was two years after her father's death and a short time after her sweetheart—the one we believed would marry her—had deserted her. After her father's death she went out very little; after her sweetheart went away, people hardly saw her at all. A few of the ladies had the temerity to call, but were not received, and the only sign of life about the place was the Negro man—a young man then—going in and out with a market basket.

"Just as if a man—any man—could keep a kitchen properly," the ladies said; so they were not surprised when the smell developed. It was another link between the gross, teeming world and the high and mighty Griersons.

A neighbor, a woman, complained to the mayor, Judge Stevens, eighty years old.

"But what will you have me do about it, madam?" he said.

"Why, send her word to stop it," the woman said. "Isn't there a law?"

"I'm sure that won't be necessary," Judge Stevens said. "It's probably   20
just a snake or a rat that nigger of hers killed in the yard. I'll speak to him about it."

The next day he received two more complaints, one from a man who came in diffident deprecation. "We really must do something about it, Judge. I'd be the last one in the world to bother Miss Emily, but we've got to do something." That night the Board of Aldermen met—three graybeards and one younger man, a member of the rising generation.

"It's simple enough," he said. "Send her word to have her place cleaned up. Give her a certain time to do it in, and if she don't . . ."

"Dammit, sir," Judge Stevens said, "will you accuse a lady to her face of smelling bad?"

So the next night, after midnight, four men crossed Miss Emily's lawn and slunk about the house like burglars, sniffing along the base of the brickwork and at the cellar openings while one of them performed a regular sowing motion with his hand out of a sack slung from his shoulder. They broke open the cellar door and sprinkled lime there, and in all the out-buildings. As they recrossed the lawn, a window that had been dark was lighted and Miss Emily sat in it, the light behind her, and her upright torso motionless as that of an idol. They crept quietly across the lawn and into the shadow of the locusts that lined the street. After a week or two the smell went away.

That was when people had begun to feel really sorry for her. People in our town, remembering how old lady Wyatt, her great-aunt, had gone completely crazy at last, believed that the Griersons held themselves a little too high for what they really were. None of the young men were quite good enough for Miss Emily and such. We had long thought of them as a tableau, Miss Emily a slender figure in white in the background, her father a spraddled silhouette in the foreground, his back to her and clutching a horsewhip, the two of them framed by the back-flung front door. So when she got to be thirty and was still single, we were not pleased exactly, but vindicated; even with insanity in the family she wouldn't have turned down all of her chances if they had really materialized.

When her father died, it got about that the house was all that was left to her; and in a way, people were glad. At last they could pity Miss Emily. Being left alone, and a pauper, she had become humanized. Now she too would know the old thrill and the old despair of a penny more or less.

The day after his death all the ladies prepared to call at the house and offer condolence and aid, as is our custom. Miss Emily met them at the door, dressed as usual and with no trace of grief on her face. She told them that her father was not dead. She did that for three days, with the ministers calling on her, and the doctors, trying to persuade her to let them dispose of the body. Just as they were about to resort to law and force, she broke down, and they buried her father quickly.

We did not say she was crazy then. We believed she had to do that. We remembered all the young men her father had driven away, and we knew that with nothing left, she would have to cling to that which had robbed her, as people will.

III

She was sick for a long time. When we saw her again, her hair was cut short, making her look like a girl, with a vague resemblance to those angels in colored church windows—sort of tragic and serene.

The town had just let the contracts for paving the sidewalks, and in the summer after her father's death they began the work. The construction company came with niggers and mules and machinery, and a foreman named Homer Barron, a Yankee—a big, dark, ready man, with a big voice and eyes lighter than his face. The little boys would follow in groups to hear him cuss the niggers, and the niggers singing in time to the rise and fall of picks. Pretty soon he knew everybody in town. Whenever you heard a lot of laughing anywhere about the square, Homer Barron would be in the center of the group. Presently we began to see him and Miss Emily on Sunday afternoons driving in the yellow-wheeled buggy and the matched team of bays from the livery stable.

At first we were glad that Miss Emily would have an interest, because the ladies all said, "Of course a Grierson would not think seriously of a Northerner, a day laborer." But there were still others, older people, who said that even grief could not cause a real lady to forget *noblesse oblige*— without calling it *noblesse oblige*.* They just said, "Poor Emily. Her kinsfolk should come to her." She had some kin in Alabama; but years ago her father had fallen out with them over the estate of old lady Wyatt, the crazy woman, and there was no communication between the two families. They had not even been represented at the funeral.

And as soon as the old people said, "Poor Emily," the whispering began. "Do you suppose it's really so?" they said to one another. "Of course it is. What else could . . ." This behind their hands; rustling of craned silk and satin behind jalousies closed upon the sun of Sunday afternoon as the thin, swift clop-clop-clop of the matched team passed: "Poor Emily."

She carried her head high enough—even when we believed that she was fallen. It was as if she demanded more than ever the recognition of her dignity as the last Grierson; as if it had wanted that touch of earthiness to reaffirm her imperviousness. Like when she bought the rat poison, the arsenic. That was over a year after they had begun to say "Poor Emily," and while the two female cousins were visiting her.

"I want some poison," she said to the druggist. She was over thirty then, still a slight woman, though thinner than usual, with cold, haughty black eyes in a face the flesh of which was strained across the temples and about the eye-sockets as you imagine a lighthouse-keeper's face ought to look. "I want some poison," she said.

"Yes, Miss Emily. What kind? For rats and such? I'd recom—"   35

"I want the best you have. I don't care what kind."

The druggist named several. "They'll kill anything up to an elephant. But what you want is—"

"Arsenic," Miss Emily said. "Is that a good one?"

"Is . . . arsenic? Yes, ma'am. But what you want—"

"I want arsenic."   40

The druggist looked down at her. She looked back at him, erect, her face like a strained flag. "Why, of course," the druggist said. "If that's what you want. But the law requires you to tell what you are going to use it for."

Miss Emily just stared at him, her head tilted back in order to look him eye for eye, until he looked away and went and got the arsenic and wrapped it up. The Negro delivery boy brought her the package; the druggist didn't come back. When she opened the package at home there was written on the box, under the skull and bones: "For rats."

IV

So the next day we all said, "She will kill herself"; and we said it would be the best thing. When she had first begun to be seen with Homer Barron, we had said, "She will marry him." Then we said, "She will persuade him yet," because Homer himself had remarked—he liked men, and it was known that he drank with the younger men in the Elks' Club—that he was not a marrying man. Later we said, "Poor Emily," behind the jalousies as they passed on Sunday afternoon in the glittering buggy, Miss Emily with her

noblesse oblige: the obligation of a member of the nobility to behave with honor and dignity.

head high and Homer Barron with his hat cocked and a cigar in his teeth, reins and whip in a yellow glove.

Then some of the ladies began to say that it was a disgrace to the town and a bad example to the young people. The men did not want to interfere, but at last the ladies forced the Baptist minister—Miss Emily's people were Episcopal—to call upon her. He would never divulge what happened during that interview, but he refused to go back again. The next Sunday they again drove about the streets, and the following day the minister's wife wrote to Miss Emily's relations in Alabama.

So she had blood-kin under her roof again and we sat back to watch developments. At first nothing happened. Then we were sure that they were to be married. We learned that Miss Emily had been to the jeweler's and ordered a man's toilet set in silver, with the letters H.B. on each piece. Two days later we learned that she had bought a complete outfit of men's clothing, including a nightshirt, and we said, "They are married." We were really glad. We were glad because the two female cousins were even more Grierson than Miss Emily had ever been.   45

So we were not surprised when Homer Barron—the streets had been finished some time since—was gone. We were a little disappointed that there was not a public blowing-off, but we believed that he had gone on to prepare for Miss Emily's coming, or to give her a chance to get rid of the cousins. (By that time it was a cabal, and we were all Miss Emily's allies to help circumvent the cousins.) Sure enough, after another week they departed. And, as we had expected all along, within three days Homer Barron was back in town. A neighbor saw the Negro man admit him at the kitchen door at dusk one evening.

And that was the last we saw of Homer Barron. And of Miss Emily for some time. The Negro man went in and out with the market basket, but the front door remained closed. Now and then we would see her at a window for a moment, as the men did that night when they sprinkled the lime, but for almost six months she did not appear on the streets. Then we knew that this was to be expected too; as if that quality of her father which had thwarted her woman's life so many times had been too virulent and too furious to die.

When we next saw Miss Emily, she had grown fat and her hair was turning gray. During the next few years it grew grayer and grayer until it attained an even pepper-and-salt iron-gray, when it ceased turning. Up to the day of her death at seventy-four it was still that vigorous iron-gray, like the hair of an active man.

From that time on her front door remained closed, save for a period of six or seven years, when she was about forty, during which she gave lessons in china-painting. She fitted up a studio in one of the downstairs rooms, where the daughters and granddaughters of Colonel Sartoris' contemporaries were sent to her with the same regularity and in the same spirit that they were sent to church on Sundays with a twenty-five-cent piece for the collection plate. Meanwhile her taxes had been remitted.

Then the newer generation became the backbone and the spirit of the town, and the painting pupils grew up and fell away and did not send their children to her with boxes of color and tedious brushes and pictures cut from the ladies' magazines. The front door closed upon the last one and remained closed for good. When the town got free postal delivery, Miss   50

Emily alone refused to let them fasten the metal numbers above her door and attach a mailbox to it. She would not listen to them.

Daily, monthly, yearly, we watched the Negro grow grayer and more stooped, going in and out with the market basket. Each December we sent her a tax notice, which would be returned by the post office a week later, unclaimed. Now and then we would see her in one of the downstairs windows—she had evidently shut up the top floor of the house—like the carven torso of an idol in a niche, looking or not looking at us, we could never tell which. Thus she passed from generation to generation—dear, inescapable, impervious, tranquil, and perverse.

And so she died. Fell ill in the house filled with dust and shadows, with only a doddering Negro man to wait on her. We did not even know she was sick; we had long since given up trying to get any information from the Negro. He talked to no one, probably not even to her, for his voice had grown harsh and rusty, as if from disuse.

She died in one of the downstairs rooms, in a heavy walnut bed with a curtain, her gray head propped on a pillow yellow and moldy with age and lack of sunlight.

V

The Negro met the first of the ladies at the front door and let them in, with their hushed, sibilant voices and their quick, curious glances, and then he disappeared. He walked right through the house and out the back and was not seen again.

The two female cousins came at once. They held the funeral on the second day, with the town coming to look at Miss Emily beneath a mass of bought flowers, with the crayon face of her father musing profoundly above the bier and the ladies sibilant and macabre; and the very old men—some in their brushed Confederate uniforms—on the porch and the lawn, talking of Miss Emily as if she had been a contemporary of theirs, believing that they had danced with her and courted her perhaps, confusing time with its mathematical progression, as the old do, to whom all the past is not a diminishing road but, instead, a huge meadow which no winter ever quite touches, divided from them now by the narrow bottleneck of the most recent decade of years.

Already we knew that there was one room in that region above stairs which no one had seen in forty years, and which would have to be forced. They waited until Miss Emily was decently in the ground before they opened it.

The violence of breaking down the door seemed to fill this room with pervading dust. A thin, acrid pall as of the tomb seemed to lie everywhere upon this room decked and furnished as for a bridal: upon the valance curtains of faded rose color, upon the rose-shaded lights, upon the dressing table, upon the delicate array of crystal and the man's toilet things backed with tarnished silver, silver so tarnished that the monogram was obscured. Among them lay collar and tie, as if they had just been removed, which, lifted, left upon the surface a pale crescent in the dust. Upon a chair hung the suit, carefully folded; beneath it the two mute shoes and the discarded socks.

The man himself lay in the bed.

55

For a long while we just stood there, looking down at the profound and fleshless grin. The body had apparently once lain in the attitude of an embrace, but now the long sleep that outlasts love, that conquers even the grimace of love, had cuckolded him. What was left of him, rotted beneath what was left of the nightshirt, had become inextricable from the bed in which he lay; and upon him and upon the pillow beside him lay that even coating of the patient and biding dust.

Then we noticed that in the second pillow was the indentation of a head.   60
One of us lifted something from it, and leaning forward, that faint and invisible dust dry and acrid in the nostrils, we saw a long strand of iron-gray hair.

[1931]

Who we are cannot easily be separated from what we have done and experienced. Plot (the succession of events in a story) reveals character (the attributes of a person, real or imaginary). Literary critics do however often distinguish plot and character for convenience: it is impossible to talk about everything at once. Likewise, the setting of a story is also intimately related to character and plot, as the circumstances of the story are revealed in part by what the characters do and experience. The purpose of creating characters in a particular setting, critics have traditionally assumed, is to convey some theme—some central idea that drives the story. Let's think for a moment about each of these three separate elements, which are so intimately connected in practice.

Character   Perhaps the most obvious thing to say about character is that a character is not a person (even in biography or autobiography), although a good writer may make it seem so. A **character** is a textual entity, an imaginary person, constructed out of various statements, actions, and descriptions. To appreciate the construction of a character, we take account, of course, of what the character says, is reported to say, does, and experiences. We can consider the role of a particular character in a story, asking ourselves why the author needs this particular character. We might also think about how a particular character is like other characters in other stories, or is like some real person.

Having noted that characters are not real persons, we might observe that our notions of real people are also constructed to some degree out of various statements, actions, and descriptions. Assessing the hidden motivations, the hidden histories of artificial persons, thus involves you in practicing and refining the very valuable ability to understand real people and their behaviors. The pursuit of such understanding in the study of character involves us inevitably in the sort of analysis that enables political criticism, as we examine other lives, other points of view. Hundreds of thousands, perhaps millions of student essays have been written about the character of Emily Grierson, and we might ponder what teachers have sought to accomplish by such an assignment, and how they have imagined students would go about it.

Traditionally, characters have been divided into **round** and **flat,** depending upon their complexity. Emily is a mysterious and fascinating character, so richly described that she would probably be considered a rounded character, although such a designation could be challenged by arguing that all her actions can be traced back to a simple motivation. This distinction has often been taken to mean that flat characters are inferior to rounded ones, but some characters who are marked by a particular trait or feature, and are therefore considered flat, may still be quite essential and intriguing.

Characters have also traditionally been divided into **static** and **dynamic,** depending upon whether they change over time. Faulkner's story shows us an Emily

who certainly evolves in appearance, but what is most interesting about her character is how her thinking has changed over time. How did she get to the point that she
denies her father is dead, for three days? And how does she get from that point to
poisoning Homer and then, years after his death, apparently lying in the same bed
with his decayed corpse? Does the story provide us with enough information to
allow for convincing speculation?

Most readers would say "yes," and in asking students to analyze Emily Grierson's
character, teachers have no doubt hoped for essays that organize the complex data the
story gives us into a plausible explanation of why Emily becomes what she does. Such
terms as "round" and "dynamic," while handy, do not go very far in helping us think of
revealing things to say about character. In fact, Gregory Jay asserts, in *America the
Scrivener*, that "the death of literary study begins when students start memorizing terms
like 'personification' and 'catharsis' with no sense of their intellectual, psychological,
historical, or ideological functions" (335). We need to place "character" (along with
other elements), in other words, within the context of various critical approaches.

So, how can you begin to think about analyzing character strategically? First,
consider what the character does that requires explanation, in terms of character;
then begin to gather the clues that might allow for an explanation; and then consider how different approaches might make sense of this data. It is safe to say that every
reader of "A Rose for Emily" who understands the significance of that "long strand of
iron-gray hair" on the pillow at the end, has wondered: why? That's one question that
an analysis of character might focus upon.

Different critical approaches will provide for different paths to an answer. A New
Critical stance, looking for the unifying idea in tensions and ambiguities, may lead
readers to notice, for instance, that Emily is thought by the townspeople to be
extremely prideful, like all the Griersons. Emily believes herself to be above the ordinary folk: she does not pay taxes. She does not need a mailbox or numbers over her
house. She does not need to supply an explanation for why she needs poison. At the
same time, Emily lives in a decaying house, in a decayed neighborhood. She is apparently impoverished; although she somehow affords a manservant, the town understands that she has been left only the house. This conflict, between her pride and her
circumstances, is resolved ultimately by her break with reality: she denies the flow of
time, referring the tax delegation to a man who has been dead ten years, refusing to
let go of her father, and even more persistently refusing to let go of Homer. Similar
conflicts in her character could be pursued from this focus on pride (for instance, her
father's antagonism toward suitors, and her own shocking looseness later with
Homer; her Southern roots versus her attraction to a Northern gentleman), with the
aim of finding a unifying thread in her character to pull these conflicts together.

Reader-response criticism would encourage an experiential approach to Emily's
character, and the way that Faulkner unfolds Emily and her story is indeed masterful.
How Faulkner shapes our response to Emily can be suggested simply by observing
how the story begins. Emily is already dead in the opening sentence, with "our whole
town" attending the funeral. That's a mystery, which is compounded by the reasons
people attended: for the men, she is "a fallen monument," and for the women, she is
the object of curiosity—or rather, her house is. No one except for her servant has
seen the inside, we are told, "in at least ten years," and so Faulkner arouses our curiosity (we are like the women in the story, I think). This desire to know what is inside
will build until the story's final sentence, when we penetrate to the house's most interior room. The experience of Emily's house in the second paragraph—which we see
only from the outside at this point—frames our experience of Emily: "stubborn and
coquettish decay" applies to her house and to her.

Different readers are likely, however, to respond differently to Emily. Whereas a New Critical view of character assumes that a close reading will reveal the unifying features, one reader may see Emily as a cold-blooded murdering psychopath, while another may see her as a kindly grandmotherly type. Such divergent responses to character, when supported by textual evidence, can be usefully enriching when taken together. Rather than reject such a response, denying that Emily is an endearing figure, we might notice certain details in this light: it is perhaps easy to forget Emily teaching neighborhood children how to paint china, but that information may alter the way we think about Emily's sense of beauty and delicacy, her nurturing and care-taking features, which emerge in the preparations she makes to "care for" Homer, with a toiletry set and new clothes, arranged in an elegant bedroom.

Such diversity of response is explained from a deconstructive vantage point by the text's ultimate incoherence. Emily's character is not expected to make sense, but remains at some level contradictory. If she has lost touch with reality, denying her father's death and the reality of taxes, then why does she not simply deny that Homer will not marry her? How can she poison Homer and yet believe he is alive enough to sleep with? There is simply a gap in the explanation, and it is naïve (from a deconstructive perspective) to assume Emily's thinking will make coherent sense.

The political approaches considered in this chapter, focusing upon character, would all have much to work with in this story. Emily is the victim of her father's oppression, as the memorable "tableau" of her father fending off suitors suggests. In Judith Fetterley's famous feminist reading of Emily's character, in *The Resisting Reader*, Emily is motivated by a kind of revenge upon her father: "Having been consumed by her father, Emily in turn feeds off Homer Barron, becoming, after his death, suspiciously fat" (83). The violence of her father, which "thwarted her," is "reenacted upon Homer Barron." Emily's character is thus a tragic study in the consequences of oppressing women: Emily has no way to support herself, no way to pay her taxes, as her father's sheltering of her has made her helpless. The limited social roles available to women become literally a poison that returns upon a representative male, who has refused his role as husband and protector. Emily thus exposes the fragility of this society, which functions only if everyone, from maids to mayors, occupies their proper position. Colonel Sartoris's odd edict, "that no Negro woman should appear on the streets without an apron," reflects the urgent importance of this social stasis.

The question of why Homer scandalously refuses to marry Emily opens up some possibilities for an analysis of his character—and his sexuality. Here the most interesting sentence might be:

> Then we said, "She will persuade him yet," because Homer himself had remarked—he liked men, and it was known that he drank with the younger men in the Elks' Club—that he was not a marrying man.

What does the narrator mean by "he liked men"? Any assertion that Homer is gay probably lacks sufficient evidence, but these three statements, in the same sentence, are certainly suggestive: "he liked men"; "it was known that he drank with the younger men in the Elks' Club"; and "he was not a marrying man." Is he not a marrying man because he likes being with men so much? Why is it, in the eyes of the ladies of the town, such a "disgrace" for Emily to ride around "with her head high," in the "glittering buggy" with Homer, "his hat cocked and a cigar in his teeth, reins and whip in a yellow glove"? Why would the town ladies be so offended by a middle-aged woman, unmarried, riding around with an unmarried man? It would seem unreasonable for Emily and Homer to have a chaperone. It is hard to see what taboo

is being violated here. But if Homer "likes" men, is not a marrying man; if it is significant that the buggy is "glittering," that he has a phallic cigar in his mouth, and wears
an effeminate yellow glove—if, in other words, Homer is widely known by the
townspeople to be gay, then perhaps it would make sense for the women to be scan-
dalized: Emily is being made a public fool, in this case. Gay and lesbian studies are
certainly concerned with much more than outing unsuspected gay and lesbian characters and authors, but the notion that Homer is possibly gay is, certainly, interesting
because it accounts for the story's events in another way.

Clearly issues of class and economy are heavily involved in Faulkner's story.
Emily's character might well be explained in terms of the gap between her self-
image and her actual circumstances. Her break with reality, denying the death of her
father and Homer, might be seen to originate in her self-delusion of class and money.
Likewise, race would seem to be a fertile area for investigating Emily's character, if
only because the town is so acutely aware of racial politics. As Gregory Jay has in
fact argued, Emily is "identified with the enforcers of subjection, as a train of imagery
and incident shows" (333). That is, Emily is aligned with "the racist patriarchal master," yet at the same time her fate is linked to that of the blacks in the town. Emily is
a "sort of hereditary obligation upon the town," which is also the paternalistic way
the town fathers view the dependent blacks. When Colonel Sartoris dictates that
black women must wear aprons in public, he is attempting to stabilize the racial and
class hierarchy: black women must be maids, even if they are not maids. It is a mystery why Emily's servant stays with her (can she pay him? Does he think he's her
slave?) but his presence helps continue her illusion that she is still part of the
wealthy upper class.

Setting   In thinking about **setting**, you may consider how the place affects what
happens and, more importantly, our perception of what happens. A marriage
proposal offered by candlelight in an elegant restaurant is significantly different
from the same proposal offered in a butcher's shop, picking out hamburger. The
setting may reinforce the action, or contradict it, or stand in an ironic relationship, or play some other more complex role. The setting includes not only the
place but also the time. In "A Rose for Emily," the town and the era are clearly crucial. The description of Emily's house in the second paragraph brilliantly places
the story in an environment of decay: the Old South lingers on, but it is increasingly out of place. Its elegance, like the cupolas and spires and scrolled balconies
of Emily's house, is disappearing—and even at its zenith was hiding monstrous
cruelties.

The reference to the "cedar-bemused cemetery," where Emily's body will join
"the ranked and anonymous graves of Union and Confederate soldiers who fell at
the battle of Jefferson," grounds the story in a present that is linked to struggles of
the Civil War. Emily does not go to join the lawyers, bankers, librarians, mothers,
fathers, schoolteachers of the town, who are no doubt also in the cemetery. She goes
to join the Civil War soldiers, as Faulkner uses this aspect of the setting to underscore the appearance of Homer Barron later as an interloper from the North—who
arrives in Jefferson to modernize the city with sidewalks, and to scandalize the
women of the town with his apparent courtship of Miss Emily.

Like any other element, setting can be approached differently by different
critical strategies. New Criticism is especially alert to the way the setting may contribute to the work's complex unity: the "coquettish decay" of Emily's house nicely
suggests the grotesque romance that resolves the story. The setting is often crucial
in shaping the reader's response; but from a deconstructive stance, the setting may

complicate the reader's response, providing some conflict or uncertainty that is not fully resolved. The "rose color" of the curtains, and the "rose-shaded lights" in the room with Homer's remains, for instance, might be used to launch a deconstruction of the story's title. "Rose" seems significant, but in what sense? Is the story a tribute to Emily, a "rose" given in her honor? Is it a pun, as my high school English teacher suggested, on "arose"? (Who rises from the dead in this story?) Or is the title, like the color of the curtains and lights, resistant to deeper meaning—tantalizing but ultimately just there? Critical strategies attentive to economy are of course especially interested in the setting and what it reveals about social class and material conditions.

Theme   **Theme** is usually understood as the main idea of a work of literature. The purpose of literature, according to the philosopher George Santayana, is to transform events into ideas, but precisely what idea is represented by a particular story seems always to be a matter of contention. For Ernest Hemingway, in fact, the whole enterprise of explaining what a work means is a creative endeavor: "Read anything I write," Hemingway said, "for the pleasure of reading it. Whatever else you find will be the measure of what you brought to the reading." From the vantage point of political approaches, Hemingway's comment is hardly a deterrent to interpretation: of course the meaning that we find is a function of what we bring to the text. We use literature as a tool, exploring and shaping the intellectual world. Students sometimes wonder (teachers too perhaps) why writers don't just tell us what a story is about: why not attach an explicit statement of a work's theme to its ending? With Aesop's fables, that is precisely what we have. Here is the fable, for instance, of "The Fox and the Grapes":

AESOP

A storyteller named "Aesop" may have existed in the sixth century B.C., but the fables attributed to him are most likely a gathering of stories from various sources.

The Fox and the Grapes

There was a time when a fox would have searched as diligently for a bunch of grapes as for a shoulder of mutton. And so it was that a hungry Fox stole one day into a vineyard where bunches of grapes hung ripe and ready for eating. But as the Fox stood licking his chops under an especially juicy cluster of grapes, he realized that they were all fastened high upon a tall trellis. He jumped, and paused, and jumped again, but the grapes remained out of his reach. At last, weary and still hungry, he turned and trotted away. Looking back at the vineyard, he said to himself: "The grapes are sour!"

There are those who pretend to despise what they cannot obtain.

We know, with the explicit statement of the moral, what this story means. The theme is clear: "There are those who pretend to despise what they cannot obtain." If Faulkner had simply attached such a sentence at the end of "A Rose for Emily," telling us what it means, he might have saved his readers much effort (not to mention ink and paper). But when Faulkner was asked, in an interview in 1959, about the meaning of his title, he responded this way:

Oh, it's simply the poor woman had no life at all. Her father had kept her more or less locked up and then she had a lover who was about to quit her, she had to murder him. It was just "A Rose for Emily"— that's all. (From *Faulkner in the University,* ed. F. Gwynn and Joseph Blotner)

I think most teachers would agree that as a response to an exam question like "Explain the significance of Faulkner's title," Faulkner would get a rather poor grade. Asked also if Homer represented the North, and Emily symbolized the South, Faulkner responded "I don't know"—that he had no intention of saying that, but at the same time "I don't say that's not valid and not there."

Although Faulkner, like other writers, may have enjoyed occasionally misleading his critics, his deflection of requests to reveal a work's meaning is widely reiterated by other writers. Joyce Carol Oates, not only a great fiction writer but also an admired literary critic herself, has said she makes "a special effort to guard against a tug toward philosophical abstractions." Oates tries, she says, to avoid letting her story become reduced to a message, a theme, by "grounding the story securely in the here and now" (in Jay Woodruff, *A Piece of Work*, 169). When Ellen Malphrus was asked about the theme of "Thanksgiving on the Chicken Bone Express" (see Chapter 8), she replied simply, "I don't know. I was just trying to tell the story." And yet, the impulse to try to reduce a story to a meaning, to a theme, is just about irresistible. We want what happens—whether it is in a work of fiction, in the news, in our own lives—to add up to something. So why do readers sometimes fail to see any theme in a story, or disagree about what that theme is? Why do writers deny the existence of a theme in the first place? Do some readers just read poorly, and some authors don't know what they're talking about, even when it's their own work? Perhaps instead there is something amiss in the usual concept of "theme." When textbooks talk about "the" theme that is "in" a story, just exactly what do they mean? In what sense is "the" theme "in" a work?

If we look more closely at the theme that is "in" the fable of "The Fox and the Grapes," something interesting emerges. The moral of the story, the theme, seems unproblematic: there it is, at the end. We know what that little story means. But there are slightly different versions of Aesop's fables, and the moral is stated differently. The moral cited, "There are those who pretend to despise what they cannot obtain," comes from the Puffin edition of the fable, without attribution to a particular translator or editor. Paul Galdone, however, in his edition of *Three Aesop Fox Fables,* offers this moral at the end of "The Fox and the Grapes": "It is easy to scorn what you cannot get." Although these morals may seem at first glance very similar, the Puffin version says that those who cannot get something will *pretend* to despise it. They do not really despise whatever is unobtainable, but they put up a front. The fox still wants those grapes, but he pretends not to. Galdone's version makes no mention of pretense: those who cannot get something really do scorn it—easily. The fox, for Galdone, doesn't want those grapes anymore: with little effort at all, he has talked himself out of that desire. Obviously, these two morals are substantially different. Which is correct? Is it easy to scorn what we cannot get, or do we work to pretend to despise the unobtainable? Is the fable about hypocrisy or self-deception?

Now it might occur to you that the best way to settle this issue would be to see what Aesop originally said, in his ancient Greek. Unfortunately, most scholars agree that no standard text of these fables ever existed, and they have evolved over time as they have been retold and recirculated and reprinted. Even if there were an original text, with an original moral by Aesop himself, it is possible that his moral might seem unconvincing to us, and that a later articulation would appear to capture the story's moral better. What if we discover an ancient manuscript of this fable with this moral: "If at first you don't succeed, quit before you're exhausted." Or this one: "Make sure that what you seek is worth your effort before you get started." Or this one: "If you do not succeed, then your goal was not meant to be." Or this: "To be happy, curb your desires." Even if we agree that the moral is one of these possibilities, then isn't it possible that readers will disagree about what *that moral* really means?

The point here is that the idea of a single correct theme, inevitably embedded "in" the story, is problematic *even for a fable,* a story ostensibly devoted to conveying a theme. Any story can spark any number of meanings—some more plausible than others, to some readers. Although this state of affairs may be frustrating to students who wish someone would just tell them what the theme of a story is, it is also an essential part of why we find literature so rewarding. What a story means depends upon what we say it means, and what we can persuade other people to agree that it means. The work of the reader is therefore necessary, creative, and challenging. Although an author certainly may shape a story to support some themes better than others, some reader, employing some critical set of assumptions, must make some sense out of it. Literary criticism (to repeat one of this textbook's fundamental ideas), far from ruining a story or detracting from it (as if one could analyze a story to pieces, or harm it by thinking about it), actually adds essential meaning to a work, completing it in a sense.

Critical strategies and our own creativity then help determine what the theme of a particular work is. A theme is a complete sentence, an assertion (and not just a topic, like "The North versus The South"). For a New Critic, the theme unifies the story's complexity: "Although Emily appears to be a victim of her father, the town, Homer Barron, and the decay of the Old South, she ultimately triumphs by violating their restrictive values." For an African American reading, the theme might be this: "The departure of Emily's 'Negro' manservant at the end symbolizes the faithfulness and dignity that is missing from the dominant culture of Jefferson, which is as doomed in its oppression and prejudice as both Emily and Homer." The theme is not "in" the story: it is "in" your head as you read the story and create it, employing whatever critical strategies seem to you most appropriate and effective, and your own attentive intelligence and ingenuity.

Practice: Idealisms

Here are stories that will respond well to political strategies.

LANGSTON HUGHES (1902–1967)

Langston Hughes's parents separated shortly after he was born in Joplin, Missouri, leaving his grandmother to raise him in Lawrence, Kansas. His famous poem, "The Negro Speaks of Rivers," was written the summer after his high school graduation. After a brief stay at Columbia University, working as a hotel busboy, Hughes advanced his poetic career by slipping three of his poems into the luggage of famous poet Vachel Lindsay. Lindsay helped Hughes win a scholarship to Lincoln University, and by 1930 Hughes had published three books and earned his degree. Hughes went on to create many enduring poems, powerful stories, an opera, and a public presence that made him a leading member of the Harlem Renaissance, a flowering of creative achievement in the 1920s in New York City.

Thank You, M'am

She was a large woman with a large purse that had everything in it but a hammer and nails. It had a long strap, and she carried it slung across her shoulder. It was about eleven o'clock at night, dark, and she was walking alone, when a boy ran up behind her and tried to snatch her purse. The strap broke with the sudden single tug the boy gave it from behind. But the boy's weight and the weight of the purse combined caused him to lose his balance. Instead of taking off full blast as he had hoped, the boy fell on his back on the sidewalk and his legs flew up. The large woman simply turned around and kicked him right square in his blue-jeaned sitter. Then she reached down, picked the boy up by his shirt front, and shook him until his teeth rattled.

After that the woman said, "Pick up my pocketbook, boy, and give it here."

She still held him tightly. But she bent down enough to permit him to stoop and pick up her purse. Then she said, "Now ain't you ashamed of yourself?"

Firmly gripped by his shirt front, the boy said, "Yes'm."

The woman said, "What did you want to do it for?"   5

The boy said, "I didn't aim to."

She said, "You a lie!"

By that time two or three people passed, stopped, turned to look, and some stood watching.

"If I turn you loose, will you run?" asked the woman.

"Yes'm," said the boy.   10

"Then I won't turn you loose," said the woman. She did not release him.

"Lady, I'm sorry," whispered the boy.

"Um-hum! Your face is dirty. I got a great mind to wash your face for you. Ain't you got nobody home to tell you to wash your face?"

"No'm," said the boy.

"Then it will get washed this evening," said the large woman, starting   15
up the street, dragging the frightened boy behind her.

He looked as if he were fourteen or fifteen, frail and willow-wild, in tennis shoes and blue jeans.

The woman said, "You ought to be my son. I would teach you right from wrong. Least I can do right now is to wash your face. Are you hungry?"

"No'm," said the being-dragged boy. "I just want you to turn me loose."

"Was I bothering *you* when I turned that corner?" asked the woman.

"No'm."   20

"But you put yourself in contact with *me*," said the woman. "If you think that that contact is not going to last awhile, you got another thought coming. When I get through with you, sir, you are going to remember Mrs. Luella Bates Washington Jones."

Sweat popped out on the boy's face and he began to struggle. Mrs. Jones stopped, jerked him around in front of her, put a half nelson about his neck, and continued to drag him up the street. When she got to her door, she dragged the boy inside, down a hall, and into a large kitchenette-furnished room at the rear of the house. She switched on the light and left the door open. The boy could hear other roomers laughing and talking in the large house. Some of their doors were open, too, so he knew he and the woman were not alone. The woman still had him by the neck in the middle of her room.

She said, "What is your name?"

"Roger," answered the boy.

"Then, Roger, you go to that sink and wash your face," said the woman, whereupon she turned him loose—at last. Roger looked at the door— looked at the woman—looked at the door—*and went to the sink.* 25

"Let the water run until it gets warm," she said. "Here's a clean towel."

"You gonna take me to jail?" asked the boy, bending over the sink.

"Not with that face, I would not take you nowhere," said the woman. "Here I am trying to get home to cook me a bite to eat, and you snatch my pocketbook! Maybe you ain't been to your supper either, late as it be. Have you?"

"There's nobody home at my house," said the boy.

"Then we'll eat," said the woman. "I believe you're hungry—or been hungry—to try to snatch my pocketbook!" 30

"I want a pair of blue suede shoes," said the boy.

"Well, you didn't have to snatch *my* pocketbook to get some suede shoes," said Mrs. Luella Bates Washington Jones. "You could of asked me."

"M'am?"

The water dripping from his face, the boy looked at her. There was a long pause. A very long pause. After he had dried his face, and not knowing what else to do, dried it again, the boy turned around, wondering what next. The door was open. He could make a dash for it down the hall. He could run, run, run, *run!*

The woman was sitting on the daybed. After a while she said, "I were young once and I wanted things I could not get." 35

There was another long pause. The boy's mouth opened. Then he frowned, not knowing he frowned.

The woman said, "Um-hum! You thought I was going to say *but,* didn't you? You thought I was going to say, *but I didn't snatch people's pocketbooks.* Well, I wasn't going to say that." Pause. Silence. "I have done things, too, which I would not tell you, son—neither tell God, if He didn't already know. Everybody's got something in common. So you set down while I fix us something to eat. You might run that comb through you hair so you will look presentable."

In another corner of the room behind a screen was a gas plate and an icebox. Mrs. Jones got up and went behind the screen. The woman did not watch the boy to see if he was going to run now, nor did she watch her purse, which she left behind her on the daybed. But the boy took care to sit on the far side of the room, away from the purse, where he thought she could easily see him out of the corner of her eye if she wanted to. He did not trust the woman *not* to trust him. And he did not want to be mistrusted now.

"Do you need somebody to go to the store," asked the boy, "maybe to get some milk or something?"

"Don't believe I do," said the woman, "unless you just want sweet milk   40
yourself. I was going to make cocoa out of this canned milk I got here."

"That will be fine," said the boy.

She heated some lima beans and ham she had in the icebox, made the
cocoa, and set the table. The woman did not ask the boy anything about
where he lived, or his folks, or anything else that would embarrass him.
Instead, as they ate, she told him about her job in a hotel beauty shop that
stayed open late, what the work was like, and how all kinds of women came
in and out, blondes, redheads, and Spanish. Then she cut him a half of her
ten-cent cake.

"Eat some more, son," she said.

When they were finished eating, she got up and said, "Now here, take
this ten dollars and buy yourself some blue suede shoes. And next time, do
not make the mistake of latching onto *my* pocketbook *nor nobody else's*—
because shoes got by devilish ways will burn your feet. I got to get my rest
now. But from here on in, son, I hope you will behave yourself."

She led him down the hall to the front door and opened it. "Good   45
night! Behave yourself, boy!" she said, looking out into the street as he went
down the steps.

The boy wanted to say something other than, "Thank you, M'am," to Mrs.
Luella Bates Washington Jones, but although his lips moved, he couldn't
even say that as he turned at the foot of the barren stoop and looked up at
the large woman in the door. Then she shut the door.

[1958]

Questions

1. How does Hughes use italics to enhance theme and character in this story?
2. How does Hughes use comedy in this story?
3. Does Hughes tell us the race of the boy and woman? What role does race play
   in this story? Does this story reinforce stereotypes, undermine them, or both?
4. Although Hughes might well say "I'm just trying to tell a good story," what
   political consequence would you say this story is after? How might this story
   alter our perceptions? What might this story encourage us to do (as a community, state, nation)?

TOBIAS WOLFF (1945–)

*Tobias Wolff is a celebrated author of short stories and memoirs, having won the PEN/
Faulkner Award, Saint Lawrence Award, O. Henry Award, American Academy of Arts and
Letters Award in Literature, and others. This Boy's Life, the story of his youth in Washington
state, was made into a major motion picture; Pharoah's Army is the dramatic story of his
service in Vietnam. A professor at Stanford since 1997, he became director of Stanford's creative writing program in 2000.*

Say Yes

They were doing the dishes, his wife washing while he dried. He'd
washed the night before. Unlike most men he knew, he really pitched in
on the housework. A few months earlier he'd overheard a friend of his
wife's congratulate her on having such a considerate husband, and he

thought, *I try.* Helping out with the dishes was a way he had of showing
how considerate he was.

They talked about different things and somehow got on the subject of
whether white people should marry black people. He said that all things
considered, he thought it was a bad idea.

"Why?" she asked.

Sometimes his wife got this look where she pinched her brows together and bit her lower lip and stared down at something. When he saw her
like this he knew he should keep his mouth shut, but he never did. Actually it made him talk more. She had that look now.

"Why?" she asked again, and stood there with her hand inside a bowl,   5
not washing it but just holding it above the water.

"Listen," he said, "I went to school with blacks, and I've worked with
blacks and lived on the same street with blacks, and we've always gotten along
just fine. I don't need you coming along now and implying that I'm a racist."

"I didn't imply anything," she said, and began washing the bowl again,
turning it around in her hand as though she were shaping it. "I just don't see
what's wrong with a white person marrying a black person, that's all."

"They don't come from the same culture as we do. Listen to them
sometime—they even have their own language. That's okay with me, I *like*
hearing them talk"—he did; for some reason it always made him feel
happy—"but it's different. A person from their culture and a person from
our culture could never really *know* each other."

"Like you know me?" his wife asked.

"Yes. Like I know you."   10

"But if they love each other," she said. She was washing faster now, not
looking at him.

Oh boy, he thought. He said, "Don't take my word for it. Look at the statistics. Most of those marriages break up."

"Statistics." She was piling dishes on the drainboard at a terrific rate,
just swiping at them with the cloth. Many of them were greasy, and there
were flecks of food between the times of the forks. "All right," she said,
"what about foreigners? I suppose you think the same thing about two foreigners getting married."

"Yes," he said, "as a matter of fact I do. How can you understand someone who comes from a completely different background?"

"Different," said his wife. "Not the same, like us."   15

"Yes, different," he snapped, angry with her for resorting to this trick of
repeating his words so that they sounded crass, or hypocritical. "These are
dirty," he said, and dumped all the silverware back into the sink.

The water had gone flat and gray. She stared down at it, her lips pressed
tight together, then plunged her hands under the surface. "Oh!" she cried,
and jumped back. She took her right hand by the wrist and held it up. Her
thumb was bleeding.

"Ann, don't move," he said. "Stay right there." He ran upstairs to the
bathroom and rummaged in the medicine chest for alcohol, cotton, and a
Band-Aid. When he came back down she was leaning against the refrigerator with her eyes closed, still holding her hand. He took the hand and
dabbed at her thumb with the cotton. The bleeding had stopped. He
squeezed it to see how deep the wound was and a single drop of blood
welled up, trembling and bright, and fell to the floor. Over the thumb she

stared at him accusingly. "It's shallow," he said. "Tomorrow you won't even know it's there." He hoped that she appreciated how quickly he had come to her aid. He'd acted out of concern for her, with no thought of getting anything in return, but now the thought occurred to him that it would be a nice gesture on her part not to start up that conversation again, as he was tired of it. "I'll finish up here," he said. "You go and relax."

"That's okay," she said. "I'll dry."

He began to wash the silverware again, giving a lot of attention to the   20
forks.

"So," she said, "you wouldn't have married me if I'd been black."

"For Christ's sake, Ann!"

"Well, that's what you said, didn't you?"

"No, I did not. The whole question is ridiculous. If you had been black we probably wouldn't even have met. You would have had your friends and I would have had mine. The only black girl I ever really knew was my part- ner in the debating club, and I was already going out with you by then."

"But if we had met, and I'd been black?"   25

"Then you probably would have been going out with a black guy." He picked up the rinsing nozzle and sprayed the silverware. The water was so hot that the metal darkened to pale blue, then turned silver again.

"Let's say I wasn't," she said. "Let's say I am black and unattached and we meet and fall in love."

He glanced over at her. She was watching him and her eyes were bright. "Look," he said, taking a reasonable tone, "this is stupid. If you were black you wouldn't be you." As he said this he realized it was absolutely true. There was no possible way of arguing with the fact that she would not be herself if she were black. So he said it again: "If you were black you wouldn't be you."

"I know," she said, "but let's just say."

He took a deep breath. He had won the argument but he still felt cor- nered. "Say what?" he asked.

"That I'm black, but still me, and we fall in love. Will you marry me?"   30

He thought about it.

"Well?" she said, and stepped close to him. Her eyes were even brighter. "Will you marry me?"

"I'm thinking," he said.

"You won't, I can tell. You're going to say no."

"Let's not move too fast on this," he said. "There are lots of things to   35
consider. We don't want to do something we would regret for the rest of our lives."

"No more considering. Yes or no."

"Since you put it that way—"

"Yes or no."

"Jesus, Ann. All right. No."

She said. "Thank you," and walked from the kitchen into the living   40
room. A moment later he heard her turning the pages of a magazine. He knew that she was too angry to be actually reading it, but she didn't snap through the pages the way he would have done. She turned them slowly, as if she were studying every word. She was demonstrating her indifference to him, and it had the effect he knew she wanted it to have. It hurt him.

He had no choice but to demonstrate his indifference to her. Quietly, thor- oughly, he washed the rest of the dishes. Then he dried them and put them away. He wipcd the counters and the stove and scoured the linoleum where the drop of blood had fallen. While he was at it, he decided, he might as well mop the whole floor. When he was done the kitchen looked new, the way it looked when they were first shown the house, before they had ever lived here.

He picked up the garbage pail and went outside. The night was clear and he could see a few stars to the west, where the lights of the town didn't blur them out. On El Camino the traffic was steady and light, peaceful as a river. He felt ashamed that he had let his wife get him into a fight. In another thirty years or so they would both be dead. What would all that stuff matter then? He thought of the years they had spent together, and how close they were, and how well they knew each other, and his throat tightened so that he could hardly breathe. His face and neck began to tingle. Warmth flooded his chest. He stood there for a while, enjoying these sensations, then picked up the pail and went out the back gate.

The two mutts from down the street had pulled over the garbage can again. One of them was rolling around on his back and the other had something in her mouth. Growling, she tossed it into the air, leaped up and caught it, growled again and whipped her head from side to side. When they saw him coming they trotted away with short, mincing steps. Normally he would heave rocks at them, but this time he let them go.

The house was dark when he came back inside. She was in the bathroom. He stood outside the door and called her name. He heard bottles clinking, but she didn't answer him. "Ann, I'm really sorry," he said. "I'll make it up to you, I promise."

"How?" she asked.

He wasn't expecting this. But from a sound in her voice, a level and definite note that was strange to him, he knew that he had to come up with the right answer. He leaned against the door. "I'll marry you," he whispered.   45

"We'll see," she said. "Go on to bed. I'll be out in a minute."

He undressed and got under the covers. Finally he heard the bathroom door open and close.

"Turn off the light," she said from the hallway.

"What?"

"Turn off the light."

He reached over and pulled the chain on the bedside lamp. The room went dark. "All right," he said. He lay there, but nothing happened. "All right," he said again. Then he heard a movement across the room. He sat up, but he couldn't see a thing. The room was silent. His heart pounded the way it had on their first night together, the way it still did when he woke at a noise in the darkness and waited to hear it again—the sound of someone moving through the house, a stranger.   50

[1985]

Questions

1. Explain the story's last sentence. Why does it end with the word "stranger"?
2. Why does Ann pursue this question? Did the husband come up with the right answer? Explain. Why does Ann ask her husband to turn off the light?

3. Is the husband a sexist? A racist? How would you describe him? How does Wolff want us to see him? How might this story affect a reader opposed to interracial marriage?

4. How do the small details of washing the dishes contribute to the story? Consider, for instance, the still-greasy dishes, the color of the washing water, the injury to Ann. Consider especially the husband's decision to mop, and the way he describes the floor.

JOHN UPDIKE (1932–)

John Updike, born in Shillington, Pennsylvania, is an extraordinarily versatile and prolific novelist, short story writer, poet, essayist, and critic. Updike suffered in childhood from stammering and psoriasis, but he read widely and attended Harvard, graduating in English in 1954, and then working for The New Yorker *(1955–1957). His series of "Rabbit" novels, chronicling the life of one of literature's most vividly realized characters, Harry Angstrom, have been especially popular. His spin-off from Shakespeare's* Hamlet *(see Chapter 18) appeared in 2000. Updike has won many awards, and "A&P" is one of the twentieth century's most anthologized stories.*

A & P

In walks three girls in nothing but bathing suits. I'm in the third check-out slot, with my back to the door, so I don't see them until they're over by the bread. The one that caught my eye first was the one in the plaid green two-piece. She was a chunky kid, with a good tan and a sweet broad soft-looking can with those two crescents of white just under it, where the sun never seems to hit, at the top of the backs of her legs. I stood there with my hand on a box of HiHo crackers trying to remember if I rang it up or not. I ring it up again and the customer starts giving me hell. She's one of these cash-register-watchers, a witch about fifty with rouge on her cheekbones and no eyebrows, and I know it made her day to trip me up. She'd been watching cash registers for fifty years and probably never seen a mistake before.

By the time I got her feathers smoothed and her goodies into a bag— she gives me a little snort in passing, if she'd been born at the right time they would have burned her over in Salem—by the time I get her on her way the girls had circled around the bread and were coming back, without a pushcart, back my way along the counters, in the aisle between the check-outs and the Special bins. They didn't even have shoes on. There was this chunky one, with the two-piece—it was bright green and the seams on the bra were still sharp and her belly was still pretty pale so I guessed she just got it (the suit)—there was this one, with one of those chubby berry-faces, the lips all bunched together under her nose, this one, and a tall one, with black hair that hadn't quite frizzed right, and one of these sunburns right across under the eyes, and a chin that was too long—you know, the kind of girl other girls think is very "striking" and "attractive" but never quite makes it, as they very well know, which is why they like her so much—and then the third one, that wasn't quite so tall. She was the queen. She kind of led them, the other two peeking around and making their shoulders round. She didn't look around, not this queen, she just walked straight on slowly, on these long white prima-donna legs. She came down a little hard on her heels, as if she didn't walk in her bare feet that much, putting down her

heels and then letting the weight move along to her toes as if she was testing the floor with every step, putting a little deliberate extra action into it.
You never know for sure how girls' minds work (do you really think it's a
mind in there or just a little buzz like a bee in a glass jar?) but you got the
idea she had talked the other two into coming in here with her, and now
she was showing them how to do it, walk slowly and hold yourself straight.

She had on a kind of dirty-pink—beige maybe, I don't know—bathing
suit with a little nubble all over it and, what got me, the straps were down.
They were off her shoulders looped loose around the cool tops of her
arms, and I guess as a result the suit had slipped a little on her, so all around
the top of the cloth there was this shining rim. If it hadn't been there you
wouldn't have known there could have been anything whiter than those
shoulders. With the straps pushed off, there was nothing between the top
of the suit and the top of her head except just *her,* this clean bare plane of
the top of her chest down from the shoulder bones like a dented sheet of
metal tilted in the light. I mean, it was more than pretty.

She had sort of oaky hair that the sun and salt had bleached, done up in
a bun that was unraveling, and a kind of prim face. Walking into the A & P
with your straps down, I suppose it's the only kind of face you *can* have. She
held her head so high her neck, coming up out of those white shoulders,
looked kind of stretched, but I didn't mind. The longer her neck was, the
more of her there was.

She must have felt in the corner of her eye me and over my shoulder   5
Stokesie in the second slot watching, but she didn't tip. Not this queen. She
kept her eyes moving across the racks, and stopped, and turned so slow it
made my stomach rub the inside of my apron, and buzzed to the other two,
who kind of huddled against her for relief, and they all three of them went
up the cat-and-dog-food-breakfast-cereal-macaroni-rice-raisins-seasonings-
spreads-spaghetti-soft-drinks-crackers-and-cookies aisle. From the third slot
I look straight up this aisle to the meat counter, and I watched them all the
way. The fat one with the tan sort of fumbled with the cookies, but on second
thought she put the packages back. The sheep pushing their carts down the
aisle—the girls were walking against the usual traffic (not that we have one-
way signs or anything)—were pretty hilarious. You could see them, when
Queenie's white shoulders dawned on them, kind of jerk, or hop, or hiccup,
but their eyes snapped back to their own baskets and on they pushed. I bet
you could set off dynamite in an A & P and the people would by and large
keep reaching and checking oatmeal off their lists and muttering "Let me see,
there was a third thing, began with A, asparagus, no, ah, yes, applesauce!" or
whatever it is they do mutter. But there was no doubt, this jiggled them. A few
houseslaves in pin curlers even looked around after pushing their carts past
to make sure what they had seen was correct.

You know, it's one thing to have a girl in a bathing suit down on the
beach, where what with the glare nobody can look at each other much anyway, and another thing in the cool of the A & P, under the fluorescent lights,
against all those stacked packages, with her feet padding along naked over
our checkerboard green-and-cream rubber-tile floor.

"Oh Daddy," Stokesie said beside me. "I feel so faint."

"Darling," I said. "Hold me tight." Stokesie's married, with two babies
chalked up on his fuselage already, but as far as I can tell that's the only difference. He's twenty-two, and I was nineteen this April.

"Is it done?" he asks, the responsible married man finding his voice. I forgot to say he thinks he's going to be manager some sunny day, maybe in 1990 when it's called the Great Alexandrov and Petrooshki Tea Company or something.

What he meant was, our town is five miles from a beach, with a big   10
summer colony out on the Point, but we're right in the middle of town, and the women generally put on a shirt or shorts or something before they get out of the car into the street. And anyway these are usually women with six children and varicose veins mapping their legs and nobody, including them, could care less. As I say, we're right in the middle of town, and if you stand at our front doors you can see two banks and the Congregational church and the newspaper store and three real-estate offices and about twenty-seven old freeloaders tearing up Central Street because the sewer broke again. It's not as if we're on the Cape; we're north of Boston and there's people in this town haven't seen the ocean for twenty years. The girls had reached the meat counter and were asking McMahon something. He pointed, they pointed, and they shuffled out of sight behind a pyramid of Diet Delight peaches. All that was left for us to see was old McMahon patting his mouth and looking after them sizing up their joints. Poor kids, I began to feel sorry for them, they couldn't help it.

Now here comes the sad part of the story, at least my family says it's sad but I don't think it's sad myself. The store's pretty empty, it being Thursday afternoon, so there was nothing much to do except lean on the register and wait for the girls to show up again. The whole store was like a pinball machine and I didn't know which tunnel they'd come out of. After a while they come around out of the far aisle, around the light bulbs, records at discount of the Caribbean Six or Tony Martin Sings or some such gunk you wonder they waste the wax on, six-packs of candy bars, and plastic toys done up in cellophane that fall apart when a kid looks at them anyway. Around they come, Queenie still leading the way, and holding a little gray jar in her hand. Slots Three through Seven are unmanned and I could see her wondering between Stokes and me, but Stokesie with his usual luck draws an old party in baggy gray pants who stumbles up with four giant cans of pineapple juice (what do these bums *do* with all that pineapple juice? I've often asked myself) so the girls come to me. Queenie puts down the jar and I take it into my fingers icy cold. Kingfish Fancy Herring Snacks in Pure Sour Cream: 49¢. Now her hands are empty, not a ring or a bracelet, bare as God made them, and I wonder where the money's coming from. Still with that prim look she lifts a folded dollar bill out of the hollow at the center of her nubbled pink top. The jar went heavy in my hand. Really, I thought that was so cute.

Then everybody's luck begins to run out. Lengel comes in from haggling with a truck full of cabbages on the lot and is about to scuttle into that door marked MANAGER behind which he hides all day when the girls touch his eye. Lengel's pretty dreary, teaches Sunday school and the rest, but he doesn't miss that much. He comes over and says, "Girls, this isn't the beach."

Queenie blushes, though maybe it's just a brush of sunburn I was noticing for the first time, now that she was so close. "My mother asked me to pick up a jar of herring snacks." Her voice kind of startled me, the way voices do when you see the people first, coming out so flat and dumb yet kind of tony, too, the way it ticked over "pick up" and "snacks." All of a sudden I slid right down her voice into her living room. Her father and the other men were standing around in ice-cream coats and bow ties and the women were in sandals picking up herring snacks on toothpicks off a big plate and they were all holding drinks the color of water with olives and sprigs of mint in them. When my parents have somebody over they get lemonade and if it's a real racy affair Schlitz in tall glasses with "They'll Do It Every Time" cartoons stencilled on.

"That's all right," Lengel said. "But this isn't the beach." His repeating this struck me as funny, as if it had just occurred to him, and he had been thinking all these years the A & P was a great big dune and he was the head lifeguard. He didn't like my smiling—as I say he doesn't miss much—but he concentrates on giving the girls that sad Sunday-school-superintendent stare.

Queenie's blush is no sunburn now, and the plump one in plaid, that I   15
liked better from the back—a really sweet can—pipes up, "We weren't doing any shopping. We just came in for the one thing."

"That makes no difference," Lengel tells her, and I could see from the way his eyes went that he hadn't noticed she was wearing a two-piece before. "We want you decently dressed when you come in here."

"We *are* decent," Queenie says suddenly, her lower lip pushing, getting sore now that she remembers her place, a place from which the crowd that runs the A & P must look pretty crummy. Fancy Herring Snacks flashed in her very blue eyes.

"Girls, I don't want to argue with you. After this come in here with your shoulders covered. It's our policy." He turns his back. That's policy for you. Policy is what the kingpins want. What the others want is juvenile delinquency.

All this while, the customers had been showing up with their carts but, you know, sheep, seeing a scene, they had all bunched up on Stokesie, who shook open a paper bag as gently as peeling a peach, not wanting to miss a word. I could feel in the silence everybody getting nervous, most of all Lengel, who asks me, "Sammy, have you rung up this purchase?"

I thought and said "No" but it wasn't about that I was thinking. I go   20
through the punches, 4, 9, GROC, TOT—it's more complicated than you think, and after you do it often enough, it begins to make a little song, that you hear words to, in my case "Hello (*bing*) there, you (*gung*) hap-py *pee*-pul (*splat*)!"—the *splat* being the drawer flying out. I uncrease the bill, tenderly as you may imagine, it just having come from between the two smoothest scoops of vanilla I had even known were there, and pass a half and a penny into her narrow pink palm, and nestle the herrings in a bag and twist its neck and hand it over, all the time thinking.

The girls, and who'd blame them, are in a hurry to get out, so I say "I quit" to Lengel quick enough for them to hear, hoping they'll stop and watch me, their unsuspected hero. They keep right on going, into the electric eye; the door flies open and they flicker across the lot to their car, Queenie and Plaid and Big Tall Goony-Goony (not that as raw material she was so bad), leaving me with Lengel and a kink in his eyebrow.

"Did you say something, Sammy?"

"I said I quit."

"I thought you did."

"You didn't have to embarrass them."   25

"It was they who were embarrassing us."

I started to say something that came out "Fiddle-de-doo." It's a saying of my grandmother's, and I know she would have been pleased.

"I don't think you know what you're saying," Lengel said.

"I know you don't," I said. "But I do." I pull the bow at the back of my apron and start shrugging it off my shoulders. A couple customers that had been heading for my slot begin to knock against each other, like scared pigs in a chute.

Lengel sighs and begins to look very patient and old and gray. He's   30
been a friend of my parents for years. "Sammy, you don't want to do this to your Mom and Dad," he tells me. It's true, I don't. But it seems to me that once you begin a gesture it's fatal not to go through with it. I fold the apron, "Sammy" stitched in red on the pocket, and put it on the counter, and drop the bow tie on top of it. The bow tie is theirs, if you've ever wondered. "You'll feel this for the rest of your life," Lengel says, and I know that's true, too, but remembering how he made that pretty girl blush makes me so scrunchy inside I punch the No Sale tab and the machine whirs "pee-pul" and the drawer splats out. One advantage to this scene taking place in summer, I can follow this up with a clean exit, there's no fumbling around getting your coat and galoshes, I just saunter into the electric eye in my white shirt that my mother ironed the night before, and the door heaves itself open, and outside the sunshine is skating around on the asphalt.

I look around for my girls, but they're gone, of course. There wasn't anybody but some young married screaming with her children about some candy they didn't get by the door of a powder-blue Falcon station wagon. Looking back in the big windows, over the bags of peat moss and aluminum lawn furniture stacked on the pavement, I could see Lengel in my place in the slot, checking the sheep through. His face was dark gray and his back stiff, as if he'd just had an injection of iron, and my stomach kind of fell as I felt how hard the world was going to be to me hereafter.

[1961]

Questions

1. Is Sammy's dramatic gesture at the end heroic and admirable? Or is it just impulsive? Or is it both? What is motivating Sammy?
2. Examine the description of Queenie. What is her social standing? How are we supposed to view her? Can you imagine Sammy and Queenie getting together later?
3. Why is the world going to be "hard" for Sammy? Is he right about that?
4. Does this story shed light on the social and gender gaps in American culture in 1961? How about today? What, in other words, is the story's theme?

NATHANIEL HAWTHORNE (1804–1864)

Nathaniel Hawthorne was born in Salem, Massachusetts. After graduating from Bowdoin College, he spent almost every daylight hour for twelve years isolated in his uncle's house attempting to master the art of writing. After burning his first series of stories, Hawthorne published Twice-Told Tales *in 1837. His most famous novel,* The Scarlet Letter, *was published in 1850, followed by* The House of Seven Gables *in 1851, then several other important novels, a biography, and stories for children.*

The Birthmark

In the latter part of the last century there lived a man of science, an eminent proficient in every branch of natural philosophy, who not long before our story opens had made experience of a spiritual affinity more attractive than any chemical one. He had left his laboratory to the care of an assistant, cleared his fine countenance from the furnace smoke, washed the stain of acids from his fingers, and persuaded a beautiful woman to become his wife. In those days when the comparatively recent discovery of electricity and other kindred mysteries of Nature seemed to open paths into the region of miracle, it was not unusual for the love of science to rival the love of woman in its depth and absorbing energy. The higher intellect, the imagination, the spirit, and even the heart, might all find their congenial ailment in pursuits which, as some of their ardent votaries believed, would ascend from one step of powerful intelligence to another, until the philosopher should lay his hand on the secret of creative force and perhaps make new worlds for himself. We know not whether Aylmer possessed this degree of faith in man's ultimate control over Nature. He had devoted himself, however, too unreservedly to scientific studies ever to be weaned from them by any second passion. His love for his young wife might prove the stronger of the two; but it could only be by intertwining itself with his love of science, and uniting the strength of the latter to his own.

Such a union accordingly took place, and was attended with truly remarkable consequences and a deeply impressive moral. One day, very soon after their marriage, Aylmer sat gazing at his wife with a trouble in his countenance that grew stronger until he spoke.

"Georgiana," said he, "has it never occurred to you that the mark upon your cheek might be removed?"

"No, indeed," said she, smiling; but perceiving the seriousness of his manner, she blushed deeply. "To tell you the truth it has been so often called a charm that I was simple enough to imagine it might be so."

"Ah, upon another face perhaps it might," replied her husband;

Nathaniel Hawthorne meets with William Ticknor and James Fields, prominent publishers not only of Hawthorne, but also of other New England authors of the day.

5

"but never on yours. No, dearest Georgiana, you came so nearly perfect from the hand of Nature that this slightest possible defect, which we hesitate whether to term a defect or a beauty, shocks me, as being the visible mark of earthly imperfection."

"Shocks you, my husband!" cried Georgiana, deeply hurt; at first reddening with momentary anger, but then bursting into tears. "Then why did you take me from my mother's side? You cannot love what shocks you!"

To explain this conversation it must be mentioned that in the center of Georgiana's left cheek there was a singular mark, deeply interwoven, as it were, with the texture and substance of her face. In the usual state of her complexion—a healthy though delicate bloom—the mark wore a tint of deeper crimson, which imperfectly defined its shape amid the surrounding rosiness. When she blushed it gradually became more indistinct, and finally vanished amid the triumphant rush of blood that bathed the whole cheek with its brilliant glow. But if any shifting motion caused her to turn pale, there was the mark again, a crimson stain upon the snow, in what Aylmer sometimes deemed an almost fearful distinctness. Its shape bore not a little similarity to the human hand, though of the smallest pygmy size. Georgiana's lovers were wont to say that some fairy at her birth hour had laid her tiny hand upon the infant's cheek, and left its impress there in token of the magic endowments that were to give her such sway over all hearts. Many a desperate swain would have risked life for the privilege of pressing his lips to the mysterious hand. It must not be concealed, however, that the impression wrought by this fairy sign manual varied exceedingly, according to the difference of temperament in the beholders. Some fastidious persons—but they were exclusively of her own sex—affirmed that the bloody hand, as they chose to call it, quite destroyed the effect of Georgiana's beauty, and rendered her countenance even hideous. But it would be as reasonable to say that one of those small blue stains which sometimes occur in the purest statuary marble would convert the Eve of Powers to a monster. Masculine observers, if the birthmark did not heighten their admiration, contented themselves with wishing it away, that the world might possess one living specimen of ideal loveliness without the semblance of a flaw. After his marriage,—for he thought little or nothing of the matter before,—Aylmer discovered that this was the case with himself.

Had she been less beautiful,—if Envy's self could have found ought else to sneer at,—he might have felt his affection heightened by the prettiness of this mimic hand, now vaguely portrayed, now lost, now stealing forth again and glimmering to and fro with every pulse of emotion that throbbed within her heart; but seeing her otherwise so perfect, he found this one defect grow more and more intolerable with every moment of their united lives. It was the fatal flaw of humanity which Nature, in one shape or another, stamps ineffaceably on all her productions, either to imply that they are temporary and finite, or that their perfection must be wrought by toil and pain. The crimson hand expressed the ineludible gripe* in which mortality clutches the highest and purest of earthly mold, degrading them into kindred with the lowest, and even with the very brutes, like whom their visible frames return to dust. In this manner, selecting it as the symbol of his wife's liability to sin, sorrow, decay, and death, Aylmer's somber imagination was not long in rendering the birthmark a frightful object, causing him more trouble and horror than ever Georgiana's beauty, whether of soul or sense, had given him delight.

*gripe: Grip.

At all the seasons which should have been their happiest, he invariably and without intending it, nay, in spite of a purpose to the contrary, reverted to this one disastrous topic. Trifling as it at first appeared, it so connected itself with innumerable trains of thought and modes of feeling that it became the central point of all. With the morning twilight Aylmer opened his eyes upon his wife's face and recognized the symbol of imperfection; and when they sat together at the evening hearth his eyes wandered stealthily to her cheek, and beheld, flickering with the blaze of the wood fire, the spectral hand that wrote mortality where he would fain have worshiped. Georgiana soon learned to shudder at his gaze. It needed but a glance with the peculiar expression that his face often wore to change the roses of her cheek into a deathlike paleness, amid which the crimson hand was brought strongly out, like a bas-relief of ruby on the whitest marble.

Late one night when the lights were growing dim, so as hardly to betray the stain on the poor wife's cheek, she herself, for the first time, voluntarily took up the subject.   10

"Do you remember, my dear Aylmer," said she, with a feeble attempt at a smile, "have you any recollection of a dream last night about this odious hand?"

"None! none whatever!" replied Aylmer, starting; but then he added, in a dry, cold tone, affected for the sake of concealing the real depth of his emotion, "I might well dream of it; for before I fell asleep it had taken a pretty firm hold of my fancy."

"And did you dream of it?" continued Georgiana hastily, for she dreaded lest a gush of tears should interrupt what she had to say. "A terrible dream! I wonder that you can forget it. Is it possible to forget this one expression?— 'It is in her heart now; we must have it out!' Reflect, my husband; for by all means I would have you recall that dream."

The mind is in a sad state when Sleep, the all-involving, cannot confine her specters within the dim region of her sway, but suffers them to break forth, affrighting this actual life with secrets that perchance belong to a deeper one. Aylmer now remembered his dream. He had fancied himself with his servant Aminadab, attempting an operation for the removal of the birthmark; but the deeper went the knife, the deeper sank the hand, until at length its tiny grasp appeared to have caught hold of Georgiana's heart; whence, however, her husband was inexorably resolved to cut or wrench it away.

When the dream had shaped itself perfectly in his memory, Aylmer sat in his wife's presence with a guilty feeling. Truth often finds its way to the mind close muffled in robes of sleep, and then speaks with uncompromising directness of matters in regard to which we practice an unconscious self-deception during our waking moments. Until now he had not been aware of the tyrannizing influence acquired by one idea over his mind, and of the lengths which he might find in his heart to go for the sake of giving himself peace.   15

"Aylmer," resumed Georgiana solemnly, "I know now what may be the cost to both of us to rid me of this fatal birthmark. Perhaps its removal may cause cureless deformity; or it may be the stain goes as deep as life itself. Again: do we know that there is a possibility, on any terms, of unclasping the firm grip of this little hand which was laid upon me before I came into the world?"

"Dearest Georgiana, I have spent much thought upon the subject," hastily interrupted Aylmer. "I am convinced of the perfect practicability of its removal."

"If there be the remotest possibility of it," continued Georgiana, "let the attempt be made at whatever risk. Danger is nothing to me; for life, while this hateful mark makes me the object of your horror and disgust,—life is a burden which I would fling down with joy. Either remove this dreadful hand, or take my wretched life! You have deep science. All the world bears witness of it. You have achieved great wonders. Cannot you remove this little, little mark, which I cover with the tips of two small fingers? Is this beyond your power, for the sake of your own peace, and to save your poor wife from madness?"

"Noblest, dearest, tenderest wife," cried Aylmer rapturously, "doubt not my power. I have already given this matter the deepest thought—thought which might almost have enlightened me to create a being less perfect than yourself. Georgiana, you have led me deeper than ever into the heart of science. I feel myself fully competent to render this dear cheek as faultless as its fellow; and then, most beloved, what will be my triumph when I shall have corrected what Nature left imperfect in her fairest work! Even Pygmalion, when his sculptured woman assumed life, felt not greater ecstasy than mine will be."   20

"It is resolved, then," said Georgiana, faintly smiling. "And, Aylmer, spare me not, though you should find the birthmark take refuge in my heart at last."

Her husband tenderly kissed her cheek—her right cheek—not that which bore the impress of the crimson hand.

The next day Aylmer apprised his wife of a plan that he had formed whereby he might have opportunity for the intense thought and constant watchfulness which the proposed operation would require; while Georgiana, likewise, would enjoy the perfect repose essential to its success. They were to seclude themselves in the extensive apartments occupied by Aylmer as a laboratory, and where, during his toilsome youth, he had made discoveries in the elemental powers of Nature that had roused the admiration of all the learned societies in Europe. Seated calmly in this laboratory, the pale philosopher had investigated the secrets of the highest cloud region and of the profoundest mines; he had satisfied himself of the causes that kindled and kept alive the fires of the volcano; and had explained the mystery of fountains, and how it is that they gush forth, some so bright and pure, and others with such rich medicinal virtues, from the dark bosom of the earth. Here, too, at an earlier period, he had studied the wonders of the human frame, and attempted to fathom the very process by which Nature assimilates all her precious influences from earth and air, and from the spiritual world, to create and foster man, her masterpiece. The latter pursuit, however, Aylmer had long laid aside unwilling recognition of the truth—against which all seekers sooner or later stumble—that our great creative Mother, while she amuses us with apparently working in the broadest sunshine, is yet severely careful to keep her own secrets, and, in spite of her pretended openness, shows us nothing but results. She permits us, indeed, to mar, but seldom to mend, and, like a jealous patentee, on no account to make. Now, however, Aylmer resumed these half-forgotten investigations,—not, of course, with such hopes or wishes as first suggested them, but because they involved much physiological truth and lay in the path of his proposed scheme for the treatment of Georgiana.

As he led her over the threshold of the laboratory, Georgiana was cold and tremulous. Aylmer looked cheerfully into her face, with intent to reassure her, but was so startled with the intense glow of the birthmark upon the whiteness of her cheek that he could not restrain the strong convulsive shudder. His wife fainted.

"Aminadab! Aminadab!" shouted Aylmer, stamping violently on the floor.

Forthwith there issued from an inner apartment a man of low stature,   25
but bulky frame, with shaggy hair hanging about his visage, which was

grimed with the vapors of the furnace. This personage had been Aylmer's underworker during his whole scientific career, and was admirably fitted for that office by his great mechanical readiness, and the skill with which, while incapable of comprehending a single principle, he executed all the details of his master's experiments. With his vast strength, his shaggy hair, his smoky aspect, and the indescribable earthiness that encrusted him, he seemed to represent man's physical nature; while Aylmer's slender figure, and pale, intellectual face, were no less apt a type of the spiritual element.

"Throw open the door of the boudoir, Aminadab," said Aylmer, "and burn a pastille."

"Yes, master," answered Aminadab, looking intently at the lifeless form of Georgiana; and then he muttered to himself, "If she were my wife, I'd never part with that birthmark."

When Georgiana recovered consciousness she found herself breathing an atmosphere of penetrating fragrance, the gentle potency of which had recalled her from her deathlike faintness. The scene around her looked like enchantment. Aylmer had converted those smoky, dingy, somber rooms, where he had spent his brightest years in recondite pursuits, into a series of beautiful apartments not unfit to be the secluded abode of a lovely woman. The walls were hung with gorgeous curtains, which imparted the combination of grandeur and grace that no other species of adornment can achieve; and as they fell from the ceiling to the floor, their rich and ponderous folds, concealing all angles and straight lines, appeared to shut in the scene from infinite space. For aught Georgiana knew, it might be a pavilion among the clouds. And Aylmer, excluding the sunshine, which would have interfered with his chemical processes, had supplied its place with perfumed lamps, emitting flames of various hue, but all uniting in a soft, empurpled radiance. He now knelt by his wife's side, watching her earnestly, but without alarm; for he was confident in his science, and felt that he could draw a magic circle round her within which no evil might intrude.

"Where am I? Ah, I remember," said Georgiana faintly; and she placed her hand over her cheek to hide the terrible mark from her husband's eyes.

"Fear not, dearest!" exclaimed he. "Do not shrink from me! Believe me, Georgiana, I even rejoice in this single imperfection, since it will be such a rapture to remove it."

"Oh, spare me!" sadly replied his wife. "Pray do not look at it again. I never can forget that convulsive shudder."

In order to soothe Georgiana, and, as it were, to release her mind from the burden of actual things, Aylmer now put in practice some of the light and playful secrets which science had taught him among its profounder lore. Airy figures, absolutely bodiless ideas, and forms of unsubstantial beauty came and danced before her, imprinting their momentary footsteps on beams of light. Though she had some indistinct idea of the method of these optical phenomena, still the illusion was almost perfect enough to warrant the belief that her husband possessed sway over the spiritual world. Then again, when she felt a wish to look forth from her seclusion, immediately, as if her thoughts were answered, the procession of external existence flitted across a screen. The scenery and the figures of actual life were perfectly represented, but with that bewitching, yet indescribable difference which always makes a picture, an image, or a shadow so much more attractive than the original. When wearied of this, Aylmer bade her cast her eyes upon a vessel containing a quantity of earth. She did so, with little interest

30

at first; but was soon startled to perceive the germ of a plant shooting upward from the soil. Then came the slender stalk; the leaves gradually unfolded themselves; and amid them was a perfect and lovely flower.

"It is magical!" cried Georgiana. "I dare not touch it."

"Nay, pluck it," answered Aylmer: "pluck it, and inhale its brief perfume while you may. The flower will wither in a few moments and leave nothing save its brown seed vessels; but thence may be perpetuated a race as ephemeral as itself."

But Georgiana had no sooner touched the flower than the whole plant   35
suffered a blight, its leaves turning coal-black as if by the agency of fire.

"There was too powerful a stimulus," said Aylmer thoughtfully.

To make up for this abortive experiment, he proposed to take her portrait by a scientific process of his own invention. It was to be effected by rays of light striking upon a polished plate of metal. Georgiana assented; but, on looking at the result, was affrighted to find the features of the portrait blurred and indefinable; while the minute figure of a hand appeared where the cheek should have been. Aylmer snatched the metallic plate and threw it into a jar of corrosive acid.

Soon, however, he forgot these mortifying failures. In the intervals of study and chemical experiment he came to her flushed and exhausted, but seemed invigorated by her presence, and spoke in glowing language of the resources of his art. He gave a history of the long dynasty of the alchemists, who spent so many ages in quest of the universal solvent by which the golden principle might be elicited from all things vile and base. Aylmer appeared to believe that, by the plainest scientific logic, it was altogether within the limits of possibility to discover this long-sought medium; "but," he added, "a philosopher who should go deep enough to acquire the power would attain too lofty a wisdom to stoop to the exercise of it." Not less singular were his opinions in regard to the elixir vitae. He more than intimated that it was at his option to concoct a liquid that should prolong life for years, perhaps interminably; but that it would produce a discord in Nature which all the world, and chiefly the quaffer of the immortal nostrum, would find cause to curse.

"Aylmer, are you in earnest?" asked Georgiana, looking at him with amazement and fear. "It is terrible to possess such power, or even to dream of possessing it."

"Oh, do not tremble, my love," said her husband. "I would not wrong   40
either you or myself by working such inharmonious effects upon our lives; but I would have you consider how trifling, in comparison, is the skill requisite to remove this little hand."

At the mention of the birthmark, Georgiana, as usual, shrank as if a red-hot iron had touched her cheek.

Again Aylmer applied himself to his labors. She could hear his voice in the distant furnace-room giving directions to Aminadab, whose harsh, uncouth, misshapen tones were audible in response, more like the grunt or growl of a brute than human speech. After hours of absence, Aylmer reappeared and proposed that she should now examine his cabinet of chemical products and natural treasures of the earth. Among the former he showed her a small vial, in which, he remarked, was contained a gentle yet most powerful fragrance, capable of impregnating all the breezes that blow across a kingdom. They were of inestimable value, the contents of that little vial, and, as he said so, he threw some of the perfume into the air and filled the room with piercing and invigorating delight.

"And what is this?" asked Georgiana, pointing to a small crystal globe containing a gold-colored liquid. "It is so beautiful to the eye that I could imagine it the elixir of life."

"In one sense it is," replied Aylmer; "or rather, the elixir of immortality. It is the most precious poison that ever was concocted in this world. By its aid I could apportion the lifetime of any mortal at whom you might point your finger. The strength of the dose would determine whether he were to linger out years, or drop dead in the midst of a breath. No king on his guarded throne could keep his life if I, in my private station, should deem that the welfare of millions justified me in depriving him of it."

"Why do you keep such a terrific drug?" inquired Georgiana in horror.   45

"Do not mistrust me, dearest," said her husband, smiling; "its virtuous potency is yet greater than its harmful one. But see! here is a powerful cosmetic. With a few drops of this in a vase of water, freckles may be washed away as easily as the hands are cleansed. A stronger infusion would take the blood out of the cheek, and leave the rosiest beauty a pale ghost."

"Is it with this lotion that you intend to bathe my cheek?" asked Georgiana, anxiously.

"Oh, no," hastily replied her husband; "this is merely superficial. Your case demands a remedy that shall go deeper."

In his interviews with Georgiana, Aylmer generally made minute inquiries as to her sensations and whether the confinement of the rooms and the temperature of the atmosphere agreed with her. These questions had such a particular drift that Georgiana began to conjecture that she was already subjected to certain physical influences, either breathed in with the fragrant air or taken with her food. She fancied likewise, but it might be altogether fancy, that there was a stirring up of her system—a strange, indefinite sensation creeping through her veins, and tingling, half painfully, half pleasurably, at her heart. Still, whenever she dared to look into the mirror, there she beheld herself pale as a white rose and with the crimson birthmark stamped upon her cheek. Not even Aylmer now hated it so much as she.

To dispel the tedium of the hours which her husband found it neces-   50
sary to devote to the processes of combination and analysis, Georgiana turned over the volumes of his scientific library. In many dark old tomes she met with chapters full of romance and poetry. They were the works of the philosophers of the middle ages, such as Albertus Magnus, Cornelius Agrippa, Paracelsus, and the famous friar who created the prophetic Brazen Head. All these antique naturalists stood in advance of their centuries, yet were imbued with some of their credulity, and therefore were believed, and perhaps imagined themselves to have acquired from the investigation of Nature a power above Nature, and from physics a sway over the spiritual world. Hardly less curious and imaginative were the early volumes of the Transactions of the Royal Society, in which the members, knowing little of the limits of natural possibility, were continually recording wonders or proposing methods whereby wonders might be wrought.

But to Georgiana the most engrossing volume was a large folio from her husband's own hand, in which he had recorded every experiment of

his scientific career, its original aim, the methods adopted for its development, and its final success or failure, with the circumstances to which
either event was attributable. The book, in truth, was both the history and
emblem of his ardent, ambitious, imaginative, yet practical and laborious
life. He handled physical details as if there were nothing beyond them; yet
spiritualized them all, and redeemed himself from materialism by his strong
and eager aspiration towards the infinite. In his grasp the veriest clod of
earth assumed a soul. Georgiana, as she read, reverenced Aylmer and loved
him more profoundly than ever, but with a less entire dependence on his
judgment than heretofore. Much as he had accomplished, she could not but
observe that his most splendid successes were almost invariably failures, if
compared with the ideal at which he aimed. His brightest diamonds were
the merest pebbles, and felt to be so by himself, in comparison with the
inestimable gems which lay hidden beyond his reach. The volume, rich
with achievements that had won renown for its author, was yet as melancholy a record as ever mortal hand had penned. It was the sad confession
and continual exemplification of the shortcomings of the composite man,
the spirit burdened with clay and working in matter, and of the despair that
assails the higher nature at finding itself so miserably thwarted by the earthly part. Perhaps every man of genius in whatever sphere might recognize
the image of his own experience in Aylmer's journal.

So deeply did these reflections affect Georgiana that she laid her face
upon the open volume and burst into tears. In this situation she was found
by her husband.

"It is dangerous to read in a sorcerer's books," said he with a smile,
though his countenance was uneasy and displeased. "Georgiana, there are
pages in that volume which I can scarcely glance over and keep my senses.
Take heed lest it prove as detrimental to you."

"It has made me worship you more than ever," said she.

"Ah, wait for this one success," rejoined he, "then worship me if you   55
will. I shall deem myself hardly unworthy of it. But come, I have sought
you for the luxury of your voice. Sing to me, dearest."

So she poured out the liquid music of her voice to quench the thirst of
his spirit. He then took his leave with a boyish exuberance of gaiety, assur-
ing her that her seclusion would endure but a little longer, and that the
result was ready certain. Scarcely had he departed when Georgiana felt irre-
sistibly impelled to follow him. She had forgotten to inform Aylmer of a
symptom which for two or three hours past had begun to excite her attention. It was a sensation in the fatal birthmark, not painful, but which
induced a restlessness throughout her system. Hastening after her husband,
she intruded for the first time into the laboratory.

The first thing that struck her eye was the furnace, that hot and feverish worker, with the intense glow of its fire, which by the quantities of soot
clustered above it seemed to have been burning for ages. There was a distilling apparatus in full operation. Around the room were retorts, tubes,
cylinders, crucibles, and other apparatus of chemical research. An electrical
machine stood ready for immediate use. The atmosphere felt oppressively
close, and was tainted with gaseous odors which had been tormented forth
by the processes of science. The severe and homely simplicity of the apartment, with its naked walls and brick pavement, looked strange, accustomed

as Georgiana had become to the fantastic elegance of her boudoir. But what chiefly, indeed almost solely, drew her attention, was the aspect of Aylmer himself.

He was pale as death, anxious and absorbed, and hung over the furnace as if it depended upon his utmost watchfulness whether the liquid which it was distilling should be the draught of immortal happiness or misery. How different from the sanguine and joyous mien that he had assumed for Georgiana's encouragement!

"Carefully now, Aminadab; carefully, thou human machine; carefully, thou man of clay!" muttered Aylmer, more to himself than his assistant. "Now, if there be a thought too much or too little, it is all over."

"Ho! ho!" mumbled Aminadab. "Look, master! look!"   60

Aylmer raised his eyes hastily, and at first reddened, then grew paler than ever, on beholding Georgiana. He rushed towards her and seized her arm with a gripe that left the print of his fingers upon it.

"Why do you come hither? Have you no trust in your husband?" cried he impetuously. "Would you throw the blight of the fatal birthmark over my labors? It is not well done. Go, prying woman, go!"

"Nay, Aylmer," said Georgiana with the firmness of which she possessed no stinted endowment, "it is not you that have a right to complain. You mistrust your wife; you have concealed the anxiety with which you watch the development of this experiment. Think not so unworthily of me, my husband. Tell me all the risk we run, and fear not that I shall shrink; for my share in it is far less than your own."

"No, no, Georgiana!" said Aylmer impatiently; "it must not be."

"I submit," replied she calmly. "And, Aylmer, I shall quaff whatever   65 draught you bring me; but it will be on the same principle that would induce me to take a dose of poison if offered by your hand."

"My noble wife," said Aylmer, deeply moved, "I knew not the height and depth of your nature until now. Nothing shall be concealed. Know, then, that this crimson hand, superficial as it seems, has clutched its grasp into your being with a strength of which I had no previous conception. I have already administered agents powerful enough to do aught except to change your entire physical system. Only one thing remains to be tried. If that fails us we are ruined."

"Why did you hesitate to tell me this?" asked she.

"Because, Georgiana," said Aylmer in a low voice, "there is danger."

"Danger? There is but one danger—that this horrible stigma shall be left upon my cheek!" cried Georgiana. "Remove it, remove it, whatever be the cost, or we shall both go mad!"

"Heaven knows your words are too true," said Aylmer sadly. "And now,   70 dearest, return to your boudoir. In a little while all will be tested."

He conducted her back and took leave of her with a solemn tenderness which spoke far more than his words how much was now at stake. After his departure Georgiana became rapt in musings. She considered the character of Aylmer, and did it completer justice than at any previous moment. Her heart exulted, while it trembled, at his honorable love—so pure and lofty that it would accept nothing less than perfection nor miserably make itself contented with an earthlier nature than he had dreamed of. She felt how much more precious was such a sentiment than that meaner kind which would have borne with the imperfection for her sake and have been guilty of treason to holy love by degrading its perfect idea to the level of the actual; and with her whole spirit she prayed that, for a single moment, she might satisfy his highest and deepest conception. Longer than one moment she well knew it could not be; for his spirit was ever on the march, ever ascending, and each instant required something that was beyond the scope of the instant before.

The sound of her husband's footsteps aroused her. He bore a crystal goblet containing a liquor colorless as water, but bright enough to be the draught of immortality. Aylmer was pale; but it seemed rather the consequence of a highly wrought state of mind and tension of spirit than of fear or doubt.

"The concoction of the draught has been perfect," said he, in answer to Georgiana's look. "Unless all my science have deceived me, it cannot fail."

"Save on your account, my dearest Aylmer," observed his wife, "I might wish to put off this birthmark of mortality by relinquishing mortality itself in preference to any other mode. Life is but a sad possession to those who have attained precisely the degree of moral advancement at which I stand. Were I weaker and blinder it might be happiness. Were I stronger, it might be endured hopefully. But, being what I find myself, methinks I am of all mortals the most fit to die."

"You are fit for heaven without tasting death!" replied her husband. 75 "But why do we speak of dying? The draught cannot fail. Behold its effect upon this plant."

On the window seat there stood a geranium diseased with yellow blotches, which have overspread all its leaves. Aylmer poured a small quantity of the liquid upon the soil in which it grew. In a little time, when the roots of the plant had taken up the moisture, the unsightly blotches began to be extinguished in a living verdure.

"There needed no proof," said Georgiana quietly. "Give me the goblet. I joyfully stake all upon your word."

"Drink, then, thou lofty creature!" exclaimed Aylmer, with fervid admiration. "There is no taint of imperfection on thy spirit. Thy sensible frame, too, shall soon be all perfect."

She quaffed the liquid and returned the goblet to his hand.

"It is grateful," said she, with a placid smile. "Methinks it is like water 80 from a heavenly fountain; for it contains I know not what of unobtrusive fragrance and deliciousness. It allays a feverish thirst that had parched me for many days. Now, dearest, let me sleep. My earthly senses are closing over my spirit like the leaves around the heart of a rose at sunset."

She spoke the last words with a gentle reluctance, as if it required almost more energy than she could command to pronounce the faint and lingering syllables. Scarcely had they loitered through her lips ere she was lost in slumber. Aylmer sat by her side, watching her aspect with the emotions proper to a man the whole value of whose existence was involved in the process now to be tested. Mingled with his mood, however, was the philosophic investigation characteristic of the man of science. Not the minutest symptom escaped him. A heightened flush of the cheek, a slight irregularity of breath, a quiver of the eyelid, a hardly perceptible tremor through the frame,—such were the details which, as the moments passed, he wrote down in his folio volume. Intense thought had set its stamp upon every previous page of that volume, but the thoughts of years were all concentrated upon the last.

While thus employed, he failed not to gaze often at the fatal hand, and not without a shudder. Yet once, by a strange and unaccountable impulse, he pressed it with his lips. His spirit recoiled, however, in the very act; and Georgiana, out of the midst of her deep sleep, moved uneasily and murmured as if in remonstrance. Again Aylmer resumed his watch. Nor was it without avail. The crimson hand, which at first had been strongly visible upon the marble paleness of Georgiana's cheek, now grew more faintly outlined. She remained not less pale than ever; but the birthmark, with every breath that came and went, lost somewhat of its former distinctness. Its presence had been awful; its departure was more awful still. Watch the stain of the rainbow fading out of the sky, and you will know how that mysterious symbol passed away.

"By Heaven! it is well-nigh gone!" said Aylmer to himself, in almost irrepressible ecstasy. "I can scarcely trace it now. Success! success! And now it is like the faintest rose color. The lightest flush of blood across her cheek would overcome it. But she is so pale!"

He drew aside the window curtain and suffered the light of natural day to fall into the room and rest upon her cheek. At the same time he heard a gross, hoarse chuckle, which he had long known as his servant Aminadab's expression of delight.

"Ah, clod! ah, earthly mass!" cried Aylmer, laughing in a sort of frenzy, "you have served me well! Matter and spirit—earth and heaven—have both done their part in this! Laugh, thing of the senses! You have earned the right to laugh." ₈₅

These exclamations broke Georgiana's sleep. She slowly unclosed her eyes and gazed into the mirror which her husband had arranged for that purpose. A faint smile flitted over her lips when she recognized how barely perceptible was now that crimson hand which had once blazed forth with such disastrous brilliancy as to scare away all their happiness. But then her eyes sought Aylmer's face with a trouble and anxiety that he could by no means account for.

"My poor Aylmer!" murmured she.

"Poor? Nay, richest, happiest, most favored!" exclaimed he. "My peerless bride, it is successful! You are perfect!"

"My poor Aylmer," she repeated, with a more than human tenderness, "you have aimed loftily; you have done nobly. Do not repent that with so high and pure a feeling, you have rejected the best the earth could offer. Aylmer, dearest Aylmer, I am dying!"

Alas! it was too true! The fatal hand had grappled with the mystery of life and was the bond by which an angelic spirit kept itself in union with a mortal frame. As the last crimson tint of the birthmark—that sole token of human imperfection—faded from her cheek, the parting breath of the now perfect woman passed into the atmosphere, and her soul, lingering a moment near her husband, took its heavenward flight. Then a hoarse, chuckling laugh was heard again! Thus ever does the gross fatality of earth exult in its invariable triumph over the immortal essence which, in this dim sphere of half development, demands the completeness of a higher state. Yet, had Aylmer reached a profounder wisdom, he need not thus have flung away the happiness which would have woven his mortal life of the self-same texture with the celestial. The momentary circumstance was too strong for him; he failed to look beyond the shadowy scope of time, and, living once for all eternity, to find the perfect future in the present.

[1843]

Questions

1. Is Aylmer a stereotypical scientist? Does Hawthorne depict both the virtues and the dangers of science? Is Aylmer's version of science distinctly masculine?
2. Is Georgiana a stereotypical woman? Would she be out of place in the twenty-first century—or right at home?
3. Who is at fault? Where is the source of evil in the story? What happens if you imagine this story as a fable?
4. Imagine that this story is the inspiration for a nonprofit organization you will invent. What would be the organization?
5. Why does Hawthorne describe Aylmer's laboratory and his previous experiments?

Suggestions for Writing

You are, like everyone else on the planet, a political animal. What gets you worked up? What do you feel strongly about? If you were elected king, what edicts would you enact?

Try writing a very short story, no more than two typed pages, in which you capture a moment in someone's life that has political implications. Readers usually will resist a heavy-handed approach, so your challenge here is to convey a political message without banging your reader over the head with it. Have fun with this!

8

Read Fiction Contextually: Biographical, Historical, and New Historical Criticism

We know somewhat, and we imagine the rest.

—Samuel Johnson

Reflection: Real Life

Even the most rigorously formal New Critic or the most sensitively responding reader may make some use of biographical or historical information. It's only natural to wonder who wrote a particular work, and when, and how, and in what circumstances. It also makes sense to wonder, once we have such biographical and historical facts, whether they can enhance our understanding and appreciation of a work. Some readers have argued that the work itself should stand alone—that we shouldn't have to study the author's life and the author's world to get the most out of a story, poem, or play. On the other hand, other readers have argued that we often do not know today

"More port for Dr. Johnson. And more ink for Mr. Boswell."

what an author's initial audience took for granted. It therefore makes sense to reconstruct what happened to an author intellectually and personally (biography), and what happened in the world around the writer, politically, culturally, economically, and so forth (history). Obviously, these two pursuits, biography and history, blend into one another.

The issue here concerns what literary study is really about: literature, life, or both. Whether we look at Samuel Johnson's eighteenth-century *Lives of the Poets*, or Arnold Rampersad's recent two-volume biography of Langston Hughes, the assumption remains that biography and history are not only interesting, but that they contribute to the study of literature. Finding out about biography and history, and relating such findings to literature, would appear to be a fairly straightforward pursuit. But with the advent of deconstruction, altering all our notions of language and knowledge, we also have new conceptions of authorship and historical circumstances. Thus, this chapter not only considers traditional biographical and historical approaches, but it also takes up the so-called "new historicism," which treats history and biography as texts (rather than "facts").

Let's begin our exploration of these approaches—biographical, historical, and new historical—by looking carefully at the following story.

CHARLES JOHNSON (1948–)

Charles Johnson, born in Evanston, Illinois, attended Southern Illinois University, studying philosophy but also taking courses with the novelist John Gardner. Before graduating, Johnson had a drawing show on PBS, "Charley's Pad," and he worked as an editorial cartoonist, publishing two collections of drawings. He also wrote six novels that remain unpublished, but in 1974 he published his first novel, as well as Faith and the Good Thing, *a combination of philosophy and homespun wisdom. Johnson's breakthrough, after another well-received novel and a collection of short stories, came with* Middle Passage *(1990), the best-selling story of a freed slave who finds himself on a slave ship and sides with the mutinous slaves. This book, which is surprisingly generous in its treatment of slavery's causes, won the National Book Award and established Johnson as a major modern author. A professor at the University of Washington, Johnson has recently published* Dreamer, *a novel about Martin Luther King Jr.'s last days.*

Moving Pictures

You sit in the Neptune Theatre waiting for the thin, overhead lights to dim with a sense of respect, perhaps even reverence, for American movie houses are, as everyone knows, the new cathedrals, their stories better remembered than legends, totems, or mythologies, their directors more popular than novelists, more influential than saints—enough people, you've been told, have seen the James Bond adventures to fill the entire country of Argentina. Perhaps you have written this movie. Perhaps not. Regardless, you come to it as everyone does, as a seeker groping in the darkness for light, hoping something magical will be beamed from above, and no matter how bad this matinee is, or silly, something deep and maybe even too dangerous to talk loudly about will indeed happen to you and the others before this drama reels to its last transparent frame.

Naturally, you have left your life outside the door. Like any life, it's a messy thing, hardly as orderly as art, what some call life in the fast lane—: the Sanka and sugar-donut breakfasts, bumper-to-bumper traffic downtown, the business lunches, and a breakneck schedule not to get ahead but simply to stay in one place, which is peculiar, because you grew up in the sixties speeding on Methadone and despising all this, knowing your Age (Aquarian) was made for finer stuff. But no matter. Outside, across town, you have put away for ninety minutes the tedious, repetitive job that is, obviously, beneath your talents, sensitivity, and education (a degree in English), the once beautiful woman—or wife—a former model (local), college dancer, or semiprofessional actress named Megan or Daphne, who has grown tired of you, or you of her, and talks now of legal separation and finding herself, the children from a former, frighteningly brief marriage whom you don't want to lose, the mortgage, alimony, IRS audit, the aging, gin-fattened face that once favored a rock star's but now frowns back at you in the bathroom mirror, the young woman at work, born in 1960 and unable to recall John Kennedy, who after the Christmas party took you to bed in her spacious downtown loft, perhaps out of pity because your mother, God bless her, died and left you with a thousand dollars in debt before you could get the old family house clear—all that shelved, mercifully, as the film starts: first that frosty mountaintop ringed by stars, or a lion roaring, or floodlights bathing the tips of buildings in a Hollywood skyline: stable trademarks in a world of flux, you think, sure-fire signs that whatever follows—tragedy or farce—is made by people who are accomplished dream-merchants. Perhaps more: masters of vision, geniuses of the epistemological Murphy.

If you have written this film, which is possible, you look for your name in the credits, and probably frown at the names of the Crew, each recalling some disaster during the production, first at the studio, then later on location for five weeks in Oklahoma cowtowns during the winter, which was worse than living on the moon, the days boiling and nights so cold. Nevertheless, you'd seen it as a miracle, an act of God when the director, having read your novel, called, offering you the project—a historical romance—then walked you patiently through the first eight drafts, suspicious of you at first (there was real money riding on this, it wasn't poetry), of your dreary, novelistic pretensions to Deep Profundity, and you equally suspicious of him, his background in sitcoms, obsession with "keeping it sexy," and love of Laurel and Hardy films. For this you wrote a dissertation on Derrida? Yet, you'd listened. He was right, in the end. He was good, you admitted, grudgingly. He knew, as you—with your liberal arts degree—didn't, the meaning of Entertainment. You'd learned. With his help, you got good, too. You gloated. And lost friends. "A movie?" said your poet friends, "that's wonderful, it's happening for you," and then they avoided you as if you had AIDS. What *was* happening was this:

You'd shelved the novel, the Big Book, for bucks monitored by the Writers Guild (West), threw yourself into fast-and-dirty scripts, the instant gratification of quick deadlines and fat checks because the Book, with its complexity and promise of critical praise, the Book with its long-distance demands and no financial reward whatsoever, was impossible, and besides, you didn't have it anymore, not really, the gift for narrative or language, while the scripts were easy, like writing shorthand, and soon—way sooner than you thought—the films, with their lifespan shorter than a mayfly's, were all you could do. It's a living, you said. Nothing lasts forever. And you pushed on.

The credits crawl up against a montage of Oklahoma farmlife, and in   5
this you read a story, too, even before the film begins. For the audience, the
actors are stars, the new Olympians, but oh, you know them, this one—the
male lead—whose range is boundless, who could be a Brando, but who hadn't
seen work in two years before this role and survived by doing voice-overs
for a cartoon villain in *The Smurfs;* that one—the female supporting role—
who can play the full scale of emotions, but whose last memorable performance was a commercial for Rolaids, all of them; all, including you,
fighting for life in a city where the air is so corrupt joggers spit black after a
two-mile run; failing, trying desperately to keep up the front of doing-well,
these actors, treating you shabbily sometimes because your salary was bigger than theirs, even larger than the producer's, though he wasn't exactly
hurting—no, he was richer than a medieval king, a complex man of remarkable charm and cunning, someone to both admire for his Horatio Alger
orphan-boy success and fear for his worship at the altar of power. You won't
forget the evening he asked you to his home after a long conference, served
you Scotch, and then, from inside a drawer in his desk removed an envelope,
dumped its contents out, and you saw maybe fifty snapshots of beautiful,
naked women on his bed—all of them second-rate actresses, though the
female supporting role was there, too—and he watched you closely for your
reaction, sipping his drink, smiling, then asked, "You ever sleep with a
woman like that?" No, you hadn't. And, no, you didn't trust him either. You
didn't turn your back. But, then again, nobody in this business did, and in
some ways he was, you knew, better than most.

You'd compromised, given up ground, won a few artistic points, but
generally you agreed to the producer's ideas—it *was* his show—and then
the small army of badly-paid performers and production people took over,
you trailing behind them in Oklahoma, trying to look writerly, wearing a
Panama hat, holding your notepad ready for rewrites, surviving the tedium
of eight or nine takes for difficult scenes, the fights, fallings-out, bad catered
food, and midnight affairs, watching your script change at each level of
interpretation—director, actor—until it was unrecognizable, a new thing
entirely, a celebration of the Crew. Not you. Does anyone suspect how bad
this thing really looked in roughcut? How miraculous it is that its rags of
shots, conflicting ideas, and scraps of footage actually cohere? You sneak a
look around at the audience, the faces lit by the glow of the screen. No one
suspects. You've managed to fool them again, you old fox.

No matter whether the film is yours or not, it pulls you in, reels in your
perception like a trout. On the narrow screen, the story begins with an
establishing wideshot of an Oklahoma farm, then in close-up shows the
face of a big towheaded, brown-freckled boy named Bret, and finally settles
on a two-shot of Bret and his blonde, bosomy girlfriend, Bess. No margin for
failure in a formula like that. In the opening funeral scene at a tiny, whitewashed church, camera favors Bret, whose father has died. Our hero must
seek his fortune in the city. Bess just hates to see him go. Dissolve to cemetery gate. As they leave the cemetery, and the coffin is lowered, she
squeezes his hand, and something inside you shivers, the sense of ruin you
felt at your own mother's funeral, the irreversible feeling of abandonment.
There was no girl with you, but you wished to heaven there had been, the
one named Sondra you knew in high school who wouldn't see you for
squat, preferring basketball players to weird little wimps and geeks, which

is pretty much what you were back then, a washout to those who knew you, but you give all that to Bret and Bess, the pain of parental loss, the hopeless, quiet love never to be, which thickens the screen so thoroughly that when Bess kisses Bret your nose is clogged with tears and mucus, and then you have your handkerchief out, honking shamelessly, your eyes streaming, locked—even you—in a cycle of emotion (yours), which their images have borrowed, intensified, then given back to you, not because the images or sensations are sad, but because, at bottom, all you have known these last few minutes are the workings of your own nervous system. You yourself have been supplying the grief and satisfaction all along, from within. But even that is not the true magic of film.

As Bret rides away, you remember sitting in the studio's tiny editing room amidst reels of film hanging like stockings in a bathroom, the editor, a fat, friendly man named Coates, tolerating your curiosity, letting you peer into his viewer as he patched the first reel together, figuring he owed you, a semifamous scriptwriter, that much. Each frame, you recall, was a single, frozen image, like an individual thought, complete in itself, with no connection to the others, as if time stood still; but then the frames came faster as the viewer sped up, chasing each other, surging forward and creating a linear, continuous motion that outstripped your perception, and presto: a sensuously rich world erupted and took such nerve-knocking reality that you shielded your eyes when the harpsichord music came up and Bret stepped into a darkened Oklahoma shed seen only from his point-of-view—oh yes, at times even your body responded, the sweat glands swaling, but it was lunchtime then and Coates wanted to go to the cafeteria for coffee and clicked off his viewer; the images flipped less quickly, slowed finally to a stop, the drama disappearing again into frames, and you saw, pulling on your coat, the nerve-wracking, heart-thumping vision for what it really was: the illusion of speed.

But is even that the magic of film? Sitting back in your seat, aware of your right leg falling asleep, you think so, for the film has no capacity to fool you anymore. You do not give it your feelings to transfigure. All that you see with godlike detachment are your own decisions, the lines that were dropped, and the microphone just visible in a corner of one scene. Nevertheless, it's gratifying to see the audience laugh out loud at the funny parts, and blubber when Bret rides home at last to marry Bess (actually, they hated each other on the set), believing, as you can't, in a dream spun from accelerated imagery. It almost makes a man feel superior, like knowing how Uri Geller bends all those spoons.

And then it is done, the theatre emptying, the hour and a half of illusion over. You file out with the others, amazed by how so much can be projected onto the *tabula rasa* of the Big Screen—grief, passion, fire, death—yet it remains, in the end, untouched. Dragging on your overcoat, the images still an afterglow in your thoughts, you step outside to the street. It takes your eyes, still in low gear, a moment to adjust to the light of late afternoon, traffic noise, and the things around you as you walk to your Fiat, feeling good, the objects on the street as flat and dimensionless at first as props on a stage. And then you stop.

The Fiat, you notice, has been broken into. The glove compartment has been rifled, and this is where you keep a checkbook, an extra key to the

10

house, and where—you remember—you put the report due tomorrow at nine sharp. The glove compartment, how does it look? Like a part of your body, yes? A wound? From it spills a crumpled photo of your wife, who has asked you to move out so she can have the house, and another one of the children, who haven't the faintest idea how empty you feel getting up every morning to finance their lives at a job that is a ghastly joke, given your talents, where you can't slow down and at least four competitors stand waiting for you to step aside, fall on your face, or die, and the injustice of all this, what you see in the narrow range of radiation you call vision, in the velocity of ideation, is necessary and sufficient—as some logicians say—to bring your fists down again and again on the Fiat's roof. You climb inside, sit, furiously cranking the starter, then swear and lower your forehead to the steering wheel, which is, as anyone in Hollywood can tell you, conduct unbecoming a triple-threat talent like yourself: producer, star, and director in the longest, most fabulous show of all.

[1985]

    If we think of a literary work primarily as a personal achievement, the accomplishment of a great mind, then biographical criticism offers to help us understand both the work and its creator, as we relate one to the other. We read Shakespeare's plays, in this line of thinking, in part to get inside Shakespeare's great mind; and the more we can learn about Shakespeare, the more we can appreciate his genius, and perhaps even begin to emulate his thinking. Of course, although Shakespeare's biography may help us somehow to appreciate Prospero in *The Tempest*, who is a creator of magic and illusions, and according to legend was sometimes played by Shakespeare, we certainly should not equate the two.

    Charles Johnson's "Moving Pictures" is also about the creation of illusions, on several levels, and the narrator points out insistently that the fiction we see is not real. In the movie, "Bret rides home to marry Bess," but the two stars actually "hated each other on the set." Although the movie "reels in your perception like a trout," making you think it is real, you can see a microphone in the corner of one scene, and the whole thing is made out of "rags of shots, conflicting ideas, and scraps of footage." It is "miraculous" that it somehow can "actually cohere." Johnson's story thus suggests that the work of art is an illusion; to enjoy the work, we lose sight of the real life outside the illusion; as the narrator says, he and the audience are "believing," drawn in by "the illusion of speed" that is the film. A film, after all, is simply a series of still pictures, run through a projector, resulting in the illusion of "moving pictures"—the illusion of speed.

    If this take on the relationship between literature and life is correct, that an awareness of the life behind the work of art impairs our appreciation of the work, then perhaps the New Critics have it right: we should attend to the work itself, leaving aside the author's life and intentions, unless we just happen to be curious. But Johnson's story does not allow such a simple reading, divorcing art and life, because the narrator also reveals that he has in fact put his own life into the screenplay: the cemetery scene in the movie arouses in him "the sense of ruin you felt at your own mother's funeral, the irreversible feeling of abandonment." All the narrator's "pain of parental loss, the hopeless quiet love never to be," he has given, he says, to the characters, Bret and Bess. And this connection between real life and reel life provides for the narrator the emotional response he experiences—his "nose clogged with tears and mucus," "honking shamelessly," "eyes streaming." Without this personal connection of life to work, the movie appears to be substantially drained of its affective power.

Thus, the issue that Johnson's story raises can be isolated in the second paragraph's opening: "Naturally, you have left your life outside the door." When we enter a movie theater, just as when we enter a story, poem, or play, we leave the real world behind, in a sense. Or do we? The paragraph in fact goes on to take back that assertion: "Like any life," the narrator says, "it's a messy thing, hardly as orderly as art, what some call life in the fast lane"—and he proceeds to detail a host of troubles, including (to take a little slice out of the rolling wave of a sentence of woes) "the mortgage, alimony, IRS audit, the aging, gin-fattened face that once favored a rock star's but now frowns back at you in the bathroom mirror." Although the narrator says "all that" is "shelved, mercifully, as the film starts," clearly it is not. Johnson's story, then, might be seen as an assertion of the inextricable connection between life and art, between history and literature, thereby implicitly endorsing biographical and historical interests.

But there is something peculiar about this story and what it suggests. The "you" that we take to be the narrator is unusual. When the story begins, "You sit in the Neptune Theatre waiting for the thin, overhead lights to dim." This "you" is not literally the reader, is it? It's not quite the narrator either, as it draws both the reader and the narrator together, as if the narrator is addressing himself, but the reader is also expected to imagine himself in that position. The related uncertainty over who has written the movie is also odd, as we read in the first paragraph, "Perhaps you have written this movie. Perhaps not." And a paragraph later: "If you have written this film, which is possible, you look for your name in the credits. . . ." If the narrator were an ordinary narrator, we would expect him to know whether he has written a movie that he is going to see, or not. The narrator's odd second-person point of view is an imperfect illusion, a fiction that complicates and draws attention to the "reality" behind it, or outside of it.

It is easy to imagine Charles Johnson inventing this narrator as he goes along inventing the story. The narrator can't entirely believe in the movie, except when he finds his own life reflected in it. We resist the illusion of the narrator's existence, even though he involves us in so many compelling details. Johnson thus involves the reader in a sort of relativity of reality. The reality inside the movie is certainly an illusion, although the narrator finds himself swept along by its engrossing emotions—or rather by his own emotions, projected onto the movie screen. The reality of the film crew making the movie, and the narrator watching the movie, seems more real by contrast. Yet when the narrator exits the theatre, the world outside the movie—the movie that it seems he has helped to make and view—seems more like a movie than a reality:

> It takes your eyes, still in low gear, a moment to adjust to the light of late afternoon, traffic noise, and the things around you as you walk to your Fiat, feeling good, the objects on the street *as flat and dimensionless at first as props on a stage.* (emphasis added)

The break in of his car seems real enough, and yet at the same time seems unreal, as the glove compartment is compared to a part of his body—a wound, which spills photographs, and which brings out more information about the narrator's life. In moments of extreme emotion, to be sure, after such vandalism for instance, reality does seem to have an unreal quality about it, and thus Johnson in many ways is complicating our notions of what is real and what is fiction, and how one affects our perception of the other.

Indeed, the reference to "the narrow range of radiation you call vision" highlights the artificiality of what we think is real, reminding us that what we experience is such a small part of what is "there." With our eyes, with our imaginations, we see (as Johnson's title says) "Moving Pictures," and the closing image of the narrator lowering his forehead to the steering wheel is a scene right out of any number of movies. According to the narrator, this scene is too obvious, "as anyone in Hollywood can tell you"; it is "conduct unbecoming a triple-threat talent like yourself: producer, star, and director in the longest, most fabulous show of all." That show is life—and this closing sentence dissolves once more the distinction between reality and the show. The narrator, we notice, says he has written a dissertation on Derrida, and the story he tells strikingly illustrates Derrida's sense of the textual and tentative nature of what we consider real.

Johnson's story, then, directs our attention to the strategies presented in this chapter: biographical and historical criticism, in which an awareness of the author's life and times enriches the artistic work, and vice-versa; and new historical criticism, which emphasizes the overlapping and interactive character of fiction and history, which are both artistic constructions.

Let's see how these approaches work.

Strategies: Using Biographical, Historical, and New Historical Criticism

To do biographical and historical criticism, you need to know as much as you can about the life and times of the author, and then apply that knowledge, exploring how your understanding and appreciation of the work might be enlarged. New Historicism complicates things a bit, because you ought to know the author's biography—even though the author's personality is a cultural construct, a textual effect. You also ought to know history (or histories)—even though the "facts" are always subject to questioning, supplementation, opposition. There is no telling what else you ought to know, since any and every discipline may shed some productive light on the literary work. Since you can't know everything, follow your instincts and your interests: useful connections or disconnections may be identified anywhere.

To put these strategies into a sequence:

1. Determine the historical setting of the work. Investigate the author's biography.
2. Consider how the historical or biographical background helps us to understand the work. Or, consider how the work contradicts or stands apart from the usual historical or biographical background.
3. Consider what other texts of the same time might be related to the text. Identify the ideology that is shaping this system of texts.

Although these approaches require some research and patience, they are interesting and often very rewarding.

Inventing

In this section let's focus on a compelling short story, first published in the October 27, 1962, issue of *The New Yorker.*

JOHN CHEEVER (1912–1982)

John Cheever was born in Quincy, Massachusetts. His father abandoned his family after losing his shoe factory in the 1929 stock market crash. His first published story, "Expelled" (1930), was based on his own experience (he was expelled for smoking). Cheever's formal schooling ended when he was seventeen. Living in New York, he became friends with a circle of writers, including John Dos Passos and James Agee, as he published short stories in excellent magazines, including The New Yorker. *Cheever (and his family) suffered from his alcoholism and from his guilt associated with his bisexuality. His stories and novels did bring fame and awards, including a Guggenheim, a Pulitzer, and a National Book Award.*

Reunion

The last time I saw my father was in Grand Central Station. I was going from my grandmother's in the Adirondacks to a cottage on the Cape that my mother had rented, and I wrote my father that I would be in New York between trains for an hour and a half and asked if we could have lunch together. His secretary wrote to say that he would meet me at the information booth at noon, and at

John Cheever in his study.

twelve o'clock sharp I saw him coming through the crowd. He was a stranger to me—my mother divorced him three years ago, and I hadn't been with him since—but as soon as I saw him I felt that he was my father, my flesh and blood, my future and my doom. I knew that when I was grown I would be something like him; I would have to plan my campaigns within his limitations. He was a big, good-looking man, and I was terribly happy to see him again. He struck me on the back and shook my hand. "Hi, Charlie," he said. "Hi, boy. I'd like to take you up to my club, but it's in the Sixties, and if you have to catch an early train I guess we'd better get something to eat around here." He put his arm around me, and I smelled my father the way my mother sniffs a rose. It was a rich compound of whiskey, after-shave lotion, shoe polish, woolens, and the rankness of a mature male. I hoped that someone would see us together. I wished that we could be photographed. I wanted some record of our having been together.

We went out of the station and up a side street to a restaurant. It was still early, and the place was empty. The bartender was quarreling with a delivery boy, and there was one very old waiter in a red coat down by the kitchen door. We sat down, and my father hailed the waiter in a loud voice. *"Kellner!"* he shouted. *"Garçon! Cameriere! You!"* His boisterousness in the empty restaurant seemed out of place. "Could we have a little service here!" he shouted. "Chop-chop." Then he clapped his hands. This caught the waiter's attention, and he shuffled over to our table.

"Were you clapping your hands at me?" he asked.

"Calm down, calm down, *sommelier*," my father said. "If it isn't too much to ask of you—if it wouldn't be too much above and beyond the call of duty, we would like a couple of Beefeater Gibsons."

"I don't like to be clapped at," the waiter said.   5

"I should have brought my whistle," my father said. "I have a whistle that is audible only to the ears of old waiters. Now, take out your little pad and your little pencil and see if you can get this straight: two Beefeater Gibsons. Repeat after me: two Beefeater Gibsons."

"I think you'd better go somewhere else," the waiter said quietly.

"That," said my father, "is one of the most brilliant suggestions I have ever heard. Come on, Charlie, let's get the hell out of here."

I followed my father out of that restaurant into another. He was not so boisterous this time. Our drinks came, and he cross-questioned me about the baseball season. He then struck the edge of his empty glass with his knife and began shouting again. "*Garçon! Kellner! You!* Could we trouble you to bring us two more of the same."

"How old is the boy?" the waiter asked.   10

"That," my father said, "is none of your goddamned business."

"I'm sorry, sir," the waiter said, "but I won't serve the boy another drink."

"Well, I have some news for you," my father said. "I have some very interesting news for you. This doesn't happen to be the only restaurant in New York. They've opened another on the corner. Come on, Charlie."

He paid the bill, and I followed him out of that restaurant into another. Here the waiters wore pink jackets like hunting coats, and there was a lot of horse tack on the walls. We sat down, and my father began to shout again. "Master of the hounds! Tallyhoo and all that sort of thing. We'd like a little something in the way of a stirrup cup. Namely, two Bibson Geefeaters."

"Two Bibson Geefeaters?" the waiter asked, smiling.   15

"You know damned well what I want," my father said angrily. "I want two Beefeater Gibsons, and make it snappy. Things have changed in jolly old England. So my friend the duke tells me. Let's see what England can produce in the way of a cocktail."

"This isn't England," the waiter said.

"Don't argue with me," my father said. "Just do as you're told."

"I just thought you might like to know where you are," the waiter said.

"If there is one thing I cannot tolerate," my father said, "it is an impu-   20
dent domestic. Come on, Charlie."

The fourth place we went to was Italian. "*Buon giorno,*" my father said. "*Per favore, possiamo avere due cocktail americani, forti, forti. Molto gin, poco vermut.*"

"I don't understand Italian," the waiter said.

"Oh, come off it," my father said. "You understand Italian, and you know damned well you do. *Vogliamo due cocktail americani. Subito.*"

The waiter left us and spoke with the captain, who came over to our table and said, "I'm sorry, sir, but this table is reserved."

"All right," my father said. "Get us another table."   25

"All the tables are reserved," the captain said.

"I get it," my father said. "You don't desire our patronage. Is that it? Well, the hell with you. *Vada all' inferno.* Let's go, Charlie."

"I have to get my train," I said.

"I'm sorry, sonny," my father said. "I'm terribly sorry." He put his arm around me and pressed me against him. "I'll walk you back to the station. If there had only been time to go up to my club."

"That's all right, Daddy," I said.

"I'll get you a paper," he said. "I'll get you a paper to read on the train."   30

Then he went to a newsstand and said, "Kind sir, will you be good enough to favor me with one of your goddamned, no-good, ten-cent afternoon papers?" The clerk turned away from him and stared at a magazine cover. "Is it asking too much, kind sir," my father said, "is it asking too much for you to sell me one of your disgusting specimens of yellow journalism?"

"I have to go, Daddy," I said. "It's late."

"Now, just wait a second, sonny," he said. "Just wait a second. I want to get a rise out of this chap."

"Goodbye, Daddy," I said, and I went down the stairs and got my train,   35
and that was the last time I saw my father.

[1962]

In what follows we turn from the literary text to other texts, seeking connections. These connections might be used to argue for the story's unity or disjunction, or to explain the psychology of the characters, or to do any number of other things. But here we'll focus primarily on how the story might reflect Cheever's personal history and feelings, in the first example, and how the story is shaped by a system of ideas regarding prestige, identity, suicide, and alcohol in the second example.

John Cheever at play with his dogs.

A Biographical Essay

Inventing

Let's follow one illustrative student through the process of developing a biographical essay. A search of the electronic card catalog at Alisha's school's library revealed thirteen books with John Cheever as their subject. She retrieved the seven that weren't checked out and requested the others to be held. Then Alisha started skimming and reading, looking especially for materials relating to "Reunion," but also learning as much about Cheever as possible. Here is a sampling of the notes she took:

From *John Cheever* by Lynne Waldeland (Boston: Twayne, 1979):

- "Reunion is from *The Brigadier and the Golf Widow*, Cheever's "best volume of short stories," according to William Peden (91).

From *The Letters of John Cheever*, edited by Cheever's son, Benjamin (New York: Simon and Schuster, 1988):

- Regarding the original publication of "The Brigadier and the Golf Widow," the title story of the volume in which "Reunion" would later appear: Cheever writes to a friend that he went into *The New Yorker* offices to correct the galleys (the trial printing) of the story and found that Bill Maxwell had cut the story "in half." Cheever went along, he says, with the cut in the office but then later called from a bar and cursed Maxwell, who was at home entertaining "Elizabeth Bowen and Eudora Welty" (two famous writers), telling Maxwell that if he cut the story "I'll never write another story for your [sic] or anybody else" (232).

- Cheever's letter concludes this way: "Anyhow the magazine has gone to press and they had to remake the whole back of the book and stay up all night but they ran it without the cut" (232–233).

Maxwell's recollection, reported by Benjamin, is very different: Maxwell says he thought the story had two endings, and so he was going to see how Cheever liked it with only one. He had no plan to cut the story at all without Cheever's approval; the story wasn't about to go to press (Cheever had found it on Maxwell's desk), and there was no all-night reworking; Bowen and Welty had visited his house, but never at the same time (233).

How can Cheever have the story so wrong? Does he have no allegiance to the truth, preferring to spin a good tale? The letter seems to have been written immediately afterward: how could his memory be so immediately faulty? Intrigued by this problem, Alisha turned to the introduction to the volume of letters, written by Cheever's son, Benjamin. Benjamin Cheever makes clear that "my father's interest in telling a good story was greater than his interest in what we might consider the facts" (20). Cheever's letters thus become a kind of rehearsal for his fiction, as he practices shaping reality into better narrative material. Benjamin notes that he has "included excerpts from his journals and his fiction, so that one can see the life—sometimes the same incident—reflected differently through the prism of his prose" (20).

The implications here are clear: we should be particularly cautious regarding the "facts," especially as reported by Cheever; at the same time, we should be aware that Cheever does work his life into his stories, apparently sometimes in rather direct ways.

The following passages also caught her attention:

- Benjamin writes:
  "The most difficult part for me, as a son, was the extent of my father's homosexuality. It's impossible for me to be objective about this, or to separate his fears from my own, but he was certainly troubled by the issue" (16).

- Benjamin writes:
  "He used to say that I must wish I had a father who didn't drink so much, and I'd always say no. I suppose this makes me what Alcoholics Anonymous would call an enabler, somebody who makes it all right for the alcoholic to destroy himself. Maybe so, but I thought then and think now that you have to take the people you love pretty much the way you find them. Their worst qualities are often linked with their very best ones" (18).

- Also, reminding me of the father's smells in "Reunion," Benjamin writes:
  "It remains that while I am not a heavy drinker myself, or a smoker, I still find the smell of gin and tobacco a delicious combination" (18).

- Benjamin Cheever also says:
  "The connection between his life and his work was intimate, but it was also mysterious. My father was fond of saying that fiction was 'crypto-autobiography.' One obvious reason for this statement is that it protected him from the attacks of friends and family who felt that they'd been libeled in his prose" (21).

From the first chapter of *John Cheever* by Samuel Coale, "Cheever's Life" (New York: Frederick Ungar, 1977):

- Cheever's father was a shoe salesman who was out of work late in life, and his mother opened a shop for the family to survive, selling first their own belongings. Cheever's father resented, apparently, her independence and competence and his own helplessness.

From *Home Before Dark,* a biography of Cheever by his daughter, Susan (Boston: Houghton, 1984):

- e. e. cummings was Cheever's "first model" (59). Susan Cheever remembers attending with her father a poetry reading by cummings. When cummings saw Cheever, "The force and openness of their affection for one another seemed to shake that airless, heavily draped room" (60). Susan remembers particularly, she says, sitting with her father as cummings read "my father moved through dooms of love" (60), the elegy to cummings's father.

- cummings died in 1962, the same year "Reunion" was published.

- Compare the father's use of foreign language to attract
  waiters in "Reunion":

> Although he spoke minimal French, he always called
> the French classics by their original names: *Les
> Faux-Monnayeurs, La Chartreuse de Parme, Le Rouge et
> le Noir.* In his last years—a time when he was so well
> respected that a lot of people assumed he spoke two
> or three languages—he began dropping French words
> into his conversation. When he was sent his own books
> in French translations, he kept them on the desk or
> his bedside table. With Italian, he was even worse.
> He spoke a stilted, conversational Italian, but he
> used it at every opportunity, and he even insisted on
> re-Italianizing all Americanized Italian words or
> names. (He always insisted on calling my editor Nan
> Talese "Nan Talayzee," for instance.)
>
> "Che cosa di buona oggi?" he would ask any dark-
> haired waiter, whether he was at the Four Seasons or
> the Highland Diner on Route 9 in Ossining. They were
> always very polite (113-114).

- Compare Charlie's awareness of the smell of his father:

> "There is the presence of a father—stern,
> unintelligent and with a gamey odor—but a force of
> counsel and support that would have carried one into
> manhood," my father wrote in his journal. "One does
> not invest the image with brilliance or wealth; it is
> simply a man in a salt and pepper tweed, sometimes
> loving, sometimes irascible and sometimes drunk but
> always responsible to his son." My father didn't have
> this ideal, tweedy parent he dreamed of in his journal
> who would have "equipped him for manhood." He spent
> much of his life looking for counsel and support from
> surrogate fathers and ultimately, painfully, rejecting
> them (128).

- Late in Cheever's life, when he had achieved some fame:

> He dropped names shamelessly. It was no longer safe
> to tease him about favorable reviews. In restaurants,
> he let headwaiters know that he was someone important.
> Since this kind of behavior was new to him, he wasn't
> particularly graceful about it. Walking down Park
> Avenue with him once, after a lunch at the Four Seasons
> ("Che cosa di buona oggi?"), I noticed that he was
> smiling his public smile at everyone who passed—just in
> case they recognized him, I suppose (210-211).

From Scott Donaldson's biography, *John Cheever* **(New York: Random, 1988):**

- Cheever's mother told him he was a mistake: "If I hadn't
  drunk two Manhattans one afternoon, you never would have
  been conceived" (19). And his father wanted him aborted,

even inviting the abortionist to dinner, an event that appears in both *The Wapshot Chronicle* and *Falconer*.

- In the story "National Pastime," the father won't teach the son to play baseball, which causes the son real embarrassment and trauma (20).

From *The Journals of John Cheever,* edited by Robert Gottlieb (New York: Knopf, 1991):

- Cheever writes:
"Having drunk less than usual, having, as my father would say, gone light on the hooch, I find myself, for the first time in a long time, free of the cafarde. Quarter to nine. Eastern day-light-saving time. It would be pleasant to consider this a simple matter of self-discipline. Thunder and rain in the middle of the afternoon; the first of the month. Our primordial anxiety about drought and its effect on the crops, the crops in this case being three acres of lawn and forty-two rosebushes" (135–136).
"I dislike writing here about boozefighting, but I must do something about it. A friend comes to call. In my anxiety to communicate, to feel the most in warmth and intimacy, I drink too much, which can be two drinks these days. In the morning I am deeply depressed, my insides barely function, my kidney is painful, my hands shake, and walking down Madison Avenue I am in fear of death. But evening comes or even noon and some combination of nervous tensions obscures my memories of what whiskey costs me in the way of physical and intellectual well-being. I could very easily destroy myself. It is ten o'clock now and I am thinking of the noontime snort" (103).
"Year after year I read in here that I am drinking too much, and there can be no doubt of the fact that this is progressive. I waste more days, I suffer deeper pangs of guilt, I wake up at three in the morning with the feelings of a temperance worker. Drink, its implements, environments, and effects all seem disgusting. And yet each noon I reach for the whiskey bottle. I don't seem able to drink temperately and yet I don't seem able to stop" (103).
"Never having known the love of a father has forced me into love so engulfing and passionate that there is no margin of choice" (177).

At this point the student had invested about twelve hours in doing research—skimming, reading, taking notes. She decided to move on to the next phase: organizing this material and relating it to "Reunion."

Shaping

Simply by selecting some observations rather than others, she was already in a sense organizing the materials. She spent some time reading over her notes and looking for links and patterns. For each note, Alisha tried to think of some words or phrases that would characterize the material. The following topics seemed the most obvious:

1. Fiction as "crypto-autobiography."
2. The need for the father's love.
3. Alcoholism.
4. The father's smells.
5. The father's coldness.
6. The father's love.
7. The father's failure.
8. Foreign languages (and name-dropping).

Next, Alisha went through the materials again and numbered them according to the list above, thus allowing her to group together all the materials that dealt, for instance, with the relationship of Cheever's fiction to his life.

At this point, to see how to arrange these materials, Alisha needed a main idea. Employing a biographical stance, she was trying to determine how our understanding of Cheever's life enlarges or affects our understanding of his story. In Cheever's case, such an approach seems especially promising, given Cheever's own acknowledgment of the intimate relationship between his life and art.

But how would one characterize that relationship? At this point, before we launch into that speculation, you may want to take a few moments and see how you'd apply the biographical information to the story. What would your main idea be?

One striking finding is that Cheever and the father in "Reunion" resemble each other: each is an alcoholic father who may be neglecting or hurting his children. Cheever struggles not to drink before noon and then, losing that battle, struggles not to get out of control. The father in the story also seems to be fixated on his drinking, forgetting apparently about feeding Charlie lunch. After only one drink with Charlie, he orders "Bibson Geefeater," suggesting perhaps that he has already been drinking beforehand. The father in the story also seems to be like Cheever in his desire to show off his knowledge of foreign languages, and the father also does a bit of name-dropping. Although Cheever and his wife never divorced, they seem to have lived most of their lives on the edge of that gulf. Seeing Cheever in the father, seeing Cheever's awareness of his own shortcomings reflected in the father, one may tend to have more sympathy for the father.

But there are also significant ways in which the young boy, Charlie, is like Cheever. Cheever felt distanced from his father, even as he longed for his love. He felt his father to be mysteriously cold—"the greatest and most bitter mystery in my life." Even Cheever's sensitivity to the way his father smelled, recorded in his journal, is a trait we see in Charlie. Cheever did not have a secretary, but his father did, at least until he lost his job. We know that Cheever felt his father neglected him, just as Charlie's father, who has not seen him in three years, is "a stranger." In fact, Cheever believed his father wanted him aborted.

But so what if Charlie's father is like Cheever's father, and like Cheever? And Charlie is also like Cheever and perhaps like Cheever's son? What do these parallels explain? Well, what *needs* to be explained? What do you find most remarkable or puzzling about the story? For Alisha, two things are strange:

1. Charlie says his father will be "my future and my doom." Why will his father be his doom? How does he know "that when I was grown I would be something like him"?

2. Charlie provides a portrait of his father that is at first perhaps a bit amusing but is ultimately grotesque. In the end Charlie's father seems to be a kind of monster, obsessed with getting "a rise" out of the newsstand clerk while the son he hasn't seen in three years is leaving. Why does Charlie, after telling us how "terribly happy" he was to see his father, reveal nothing of his feelings? We can guess how Charlie felt, but we do not know. Why the absence of feeling—at least in the telling (which may not be truthful)?

Does Cheever's relationship to the two characters offer any sort of explanation to both questions? Alisha thinks so, and that idea becomes her tentative thesis:

> Cheever resented his father's alcoholism and inattention and at the same time longed for his love; he desired to turn away from his father, putting the pain of his neglect behind him, and at the same time he wanted to turn toward his father, to bridge their distance. This love/hate conflict is intensified by Cheever's awareness that he is in certain crucial ways like his father. In "Reunion" Charlie does not directly express his disgust and rage at his father because his position is essentially the same as Cheever's: in hating his father, Charlie (like Cheever) is closing off the possibility of resolution; in hating his father, Charlie (like Cheever) is hating himself.

This thesis, as is usually the case, suggests an organization for the essay:

1. Cheever's fiction meaningfully echoes his life: thesis.
2. Charlie's father and Cheever's father.
3. Charlie and Cheever.
4. Charlie's father and Cheever himself.
5. Conclusion.

Drafting

You might want to sketch out your own draft of an essay based on the plan above before you read the one that follows.

John Cheever's "Reunion" as "Crypto-Autobiography"

The intro sets up the problem: why is Charlie's father unsympathetically portrayed?

In John Cheever's "Reunion," the portrait of Charlie's father seems in the final analysis harsh and unforgiving. Not having seen his son in three years, the father proceeds at their meeting to drink himself into an abusive, obsessive state. He is never overtly mean to Charlie to be sure, but he is also far from attentive. Before the meeting, he did not respond personally to his son's letter asking about the lunch, letting his secretary arrange it instead; and throughout the visit, he seems intent only on getting drinks and exerting his authority over waiters, showing little or no interest in the well-being of his son. As Charlie leaves, his father is unable even to say goodbye appropriately because he is so intent on getting "a rise" out of the newspaper clerk.

Yet Charlie's opinion is not explicitly presented.

And yet, despite his father's distressing behavior, Charlie does not directly express his feelings about the day's events. In the first paragraph he tells us that he was "terribly happy" to see his father, that he even wished they could be photographed together, but at the same time he says he immediately knew, the moment he saw his father, that he was "my future and my doom." Even with this emotional load, Charlie appears simply to report what happened without betraying his own reaction. But much is left out, leaving the reader to guess what Charlie is feeling, how this event has affected him, why this was the "last time I saw my father." Was he so outraged, hurt, saddened, confused, embarrassed, or something else that he determined never to see him again? Or did his father die soon afterward? The story is so brief that it is difficult to speculate with any confidence on Charlie's motivations, or even on his accuracy, yet it is so vividly told that it is difficult not to speculate.

Thesis is introduced here.

Perhaps this distancing is precisely what Cheever wanted: to tell a story about a father and a son, presenting deeply moving events without really exposing what they mean. To understand Cheever's purpose, and thereby understand his story better, we need to look at Cheever's own experience of father-son relationships. The justification for relating life to fiction is particularly strong in Cheever's case since the same incident oftentimes is recounted in his letters and journals and then employed in his fiction. Even when Cheever was supposedly reporting a real event, his "interest in telling a good story was greater than his interest in what we might consider the facts," as his son Benjamin put it (20). As Benjamin wrote, "The connection between his life and his work was intimate," and Cheever was even "fond of saying that fiction was 'crypto-autobiography'" (21). In fact there are obvious autobiographical elements in "Reunion," and decoding them does shed some light on the story.

Cheever's life connects to the story.

Cheever's father and Charlie's father.

First, we should note that Cheever was profoundly troubled by his relationship to his father: late in life he called his father "the

greatest and the most bitter mystery in my life,"
and he revealed that the problem of learning to
love a father "appears in all the books and
stories" (qtd. Susan Cheever 209–210). We do not
need to know much about Cheever's childhood to
imagine why he kept trying to sort it out. Not
only did Cheever's mother tell him he was a
mistake ("If I hadn't drunk two Manhattans one
afternoon, you never would have been conceived"),
but also, as Scott Donaldson's biography says,
"his father wanted him aborted, even inviting the
abortionist to dinner, an event that appears in
both *The Wapshot Chronicle* and *Falconer*" (19).
Charlie's father is in some crucial aspects like
Cheever's father: alcoholic, insecure, sarcastic,
self-centered. Unlike Charlie's father, Cheever's
father was not divorced, but there were
tremendous hostilities between his parents,
leading to drunken infidelities, threatened
suicides, and violent arguments—which formed much
of the substance of Cheever's fiction.

Charlie and Cheever.

　　If Charlie's father is like Cheever's
father, Charlie is also a reflection of Cheever.
Charlie, like Cheever, wants to love his father,
but he finds a man who is apparently
uninterested in him and careening out of
control. In his hunger for love, Charlie tries
to connect with his father on some more
primitive level, smelling his father "the way my
mother sniffs a rose" and finding "a rich
compound of whiskey, after-shave lotion, shoe
polish, woolens, and the rankness of a mature
male." Cheever was also extraordinarily moved by
smells, telling his publisher at one point that
he was "a very olfactory fellow," and not to try
to remove any of the smells in his book.

Cheever and his father.

　　But Cheever does not seem to express his
rage and disappointment very directly through
Charlie. Surely part of the obstruction is
Cheever's realization that he is in many ways
like his father, Frederick Cheever, a shoe
salesman who became unemployed and bitter in the
mid-1920s. John Cheever was not technically out
of work, but he did not have a regular job, and
he struggled for much of his life to make ends
meet. Most obviously, like his father (like
Charlie's father) Cheever could not control his
drinking. In an entry from the early journals
(late forties and fifties), Cheever writes,
"Year after year I read in here [in his journal]
that I am drinking too much, and there can be no
doubt of the fact that this is progressive"

(103). Although Cheever finds everything about his drinking "disgusting," still "each noon I reach for the whiskey bottle." Cheever was evidently aware of the effect of such behavior on a son, as Cheever's own son, Benjamin, writes (in *The Letters of John Cheever*), "He used to say that I must wish I had a father who didn't drink so much, and I'd always say no" (18).

Cheever and Charlie's father.

In fact, Charlie's father's habit of baiting waiters in foreign tongues may have been modeled on Cheever's own behavior, as a passage from Susan Cheever's biography of her father reveals. After commenting on how Cheever, even though "he spoke minimal French," began "dropping French words into his conversation," she goes on to say, "With Italian, he was even worse," using it "at every opportunity," especially in restaurants (113).

Summary

Thus Charlie's statement that his father was "my future and my doom" resonates on several levels. Cheever, the model for Charlie, had become "something like" his father. And Cheever's father was "something like" Charlie's father, just as Charlie would become "something like" Cheever himself. For Charlie to hate his father would involve hating himself, his own future self; yet he could hardly approve affectionately of his father. But more than that: for Charlie to express his hatred toward his father, Cheever would have to acknowledge his own hatred for his father, which would likewise involve a self-destructive disgust. Cheever could not find a way to love his father, but he could not find a way to hate him either. And so he was driven to write about him endlessly, searching for a way to describe the relationship and resolve it.

Works Cited

Cheever, John. *The Brigadier and the Golf Widow*. New York: Harper, 1964.
———. *The Journals of John Cheever*. Ed. Robert Gottlieb. New York: Knopf, 1991.
———. *The Letters of John Cheever*. Ed. Benjamin Cheever. New York: Simon & Schuster, 1988.
Cheever, Susan. *Home Before Dark*. Boston: Houghton, 1984.
Donaldson, Scott. *John Cheever*. New York: Random, 1988.

A New Historical Essay

Inventing

Where could I look for some clues to the ideology shaping Cheever's story? I decided that one place to look, thinking of "Reunion" as part of a cultural system, would be *The*

New Yorker magazine in which the story was first published. Knowing the story came out in 1962, I found it in the October 27th issue: the whole story appears on page 45.

I studied the magazine, trying to absorb the culture of 1962, the book and movie reviews, the current events, the articles, the advertisements, time-traveling back to that year. I did not imagine one issue of one magazine could contain an entire culture, but I did assume that a close inspection of one issue might suggest a great deal about the world *The New Yorker* presented to its readers. I tried to imagine myself as an anthropologist studying a foreign and unknown culture—in this case, the culture of *The New Yorker's* writers, advertisers, and readers. In reading through the magazine, I was struck very quickly by two messages, which seemed to appear relentlessly in various ways. Both messages arguably still permeate our culture, but they seemed especially prominent in this "foreign" setting. Perhaps I was simply paying close attention to what I ordinarily try to ignore.

Put bluntly, I found the magazine telling its readers again and again to consume— to purchase, to view, to possess, to ingest—and to display the quality of their discerning consumption. Most insistently, it seemed that readers were being told to consume superior alcoholic beverages: directly in some thirty-six ads and indirectly in ads for other products. An ad for Japan Airlines pictured a happy couple in the act of taking drinks from an attentive hostess; another for Caron perfumes depicted a beautiful woman clinking a brandy glass with her lover.

I was also struck by the exhortations to wear superior clothing, urging readers to display their wealth and excellent taste. Such exhibition was motivated, sometimes blatantly, sometimes subtly, by the promise of acceptance and affection. These messages—consume and display—appeared most obviously in the advertisements, but they could also be discerned in the articles and even the cartoons. They often appeared together.

Shaping

If we recognize that Cheever's story appears in a context saturated with recurrent encouragements to drink (for status and success) and to display one's status and success, what difference does it make? How does this context affect our reading of the story? How does the story affect our reading of the context, for that matter?

One effect might be to reconsider our assessment of Charlie's father's drinking. In new historicist fashion, stressing ideology over individuals, I would argue that Charlie's father is not an autonomous agent, fully responsible for his failures. Rather, Charlie's father is to some degree a product of a value system he has learned too well. He has simply learned to seek affection and status in alcohol. His efforts to display his sophistication in languages and to demonstrate his dominance over the various waiters are also the effect of a powerful (but pitiful) desire for status.

This view of the father's fundamental insecurity and loneliness, which he attempts to erase by drinking and asserting himself, reminds me of some passages in Cheever's journal.

Writing about his inability to control his drinking, Cheever writes: "I could very easily destroy myself" (103). Charlie's father, like Cheever, is destroying himself slowly. Cheever and his character are being driven by emotional pain and insecurity to seek relief in the way that their culture has prescribed—asserting their status, consuming alcohol.

We do not know in "Reunion" why Charlie's father and mother were divorced, and we may assume that Charlie has not seen his father for three years because his father is uncaring. Cheever's journal may help us to consider other possibilities consistent with the facts of the story—namely that Charlie's mother may have prevented his father from seeing him. Perhaps she considered his father so worthless that she did not want Charlie to see him again. Perhaps Charlie's father feels so guilty that he considers himself unworthy of his son's attention.

Finally, I should mention one more journal entry in which Cheever records the visit of a friend: "in my anxiety to communicate, to feel the most in warmth and intimacy, I drink too much, which can be two drinks these days" (103). The advertisements and cartoons link intimacy and affection to alcohol, and Cheever does the same thing here. Again, Charlie's father's behavior needs to be reconsidered.

At this point, it seems clear that I have way too much material for a brief essay—which means that I'm in good shape. But don't I need to dig further, examining all *The New Yorker* issues of 1962, and *Good Housekeeping* and *Reader's Digest* also, and everything else that can be recovered? Not really, although it's always nice to know as much as you can. My claim is simply that a certain community (the readers of *The New Yorker*) at a certain slice of time (1962) were being exposed to a certain set of messages. Rather than having to dig up a whole city, the new historicist can construct a tentative system of meaning from the close analysis of selected artifacts. The point is not that one document influenced another, but rather that at this moment within this community all documents participated in certain common assumptions.

So, looking over my notes, freewriting and brainstorming, I come back to my focus on Charlie's father as a reflection of a system of meaning. I try organizing my material in the following way:

> *The emotional view: Charlie's father as a deviant jerk.*
>
> *Thesis: The analytical view: Charlie's father as a product of his time.*
>
> *Advertisements and cartoons suggest alcohol confers status and affection: manliness.*
>
> *Cheever and Charlie's father: drowning self and pain in drink.*

Drafting

You might wish to draft an essay yourself at this point, then compare your application of the materials to mine.

How to Make an Alcoholic Drink: Cheever's "Reunion" in Its Context

The opening orients the reader to the story and the issue: the father's lack of affection.

In John Cheever's "Reunion," Charlie's father appears to be the worst sort of parent. After three years of separation (following a divorce), the father doesn't respond to his son's letter but rather has his secretary arrange their meeting. He greets his son in a strange way, with no apparent affection:

> "Hi Charlie," he said. "Hi, boy. I'd like to take you up to my club, but it's in the Sixties, and if you have to catch an early train I guess we'd better get something to eat around here."

Although he puts his arm around Charlie, his subsequent behavior seems to confirm his callous self-absorption, as he apparently forgets about lunch and thinks only of drinking and insulting waiters. The visit ends with Charlie saying goodbye, for the last time, to a father who seems interested only in harassing a newsstand clerk.

But before we entirely dismiss Charlie's father, we might consider his motivation. What does he think he is doing? Where has he learned such behavior? Certainly Charlie is a victim of his father's indulgent inattention; but is Charlie's father also a victim in any way? In *The New Yorker* magazine in which "Reunion" first appeared, we find a set of directives that helps to explain the behavior of Charlie's father, which may well be motivated not by any sort of disregard or animosity toward Charlie, but rather by the desire for status and affection. This desire is fueled by a system of values reflected in and even shaped by *The New Yorker*.

Again and again advertisements in the October 26th issue of 1962 convey to the readers the paramount importance of status, rank, superiority. One of the most blatant of these ads asks the question "Are you a status seeker?" If you like "Italian restaurants," the ad continues, "foreign cars," "antique furniture," and finally "Lord Calvert" whiskey, then you apparently are a status seeker (as you should be, the ad implies). The association of alcoholic beverages with nobility, and therefore "status," is a recurrent theme. Grand Marnier is "The Emperor of Liqueurs," and another scotch is named "House of Lords." Old Hickory is drunk by "all the nicest people," and several couples in formal evening attire are depicted. The drink identifies you as a superior being, among "the nicest people," which does not in this context seem to mean the most polite or philanthropic.

Other ads for nonalcoholic products also reinforce this desire for status. One ad pictures an aristocratic man, sneering slightly, in an overcoat, standing behind a large, exotic-looking dog, with the caption "Which has the pedigree?" Of course, it isn't the dog, or the man; it's the coat. Buying this coat, the ad implies, gives you a pedigree you can wear. This anxiety about the status of one's clothing, or how one's clothing expresses one's status, is also employed by advertisements for alcoholic

This paragraph introduces a possible explanation: the father's values are shaped by his culture.

Evidence: Ads for alcoholic beverages focus on status.

Other ads and status.

Clothing and status.

drinks. One ad depicts a man from the neck down, dressed in a tuxedo, carrying a fur coat with a large label clearly exposed. The caption says, "When a label counts, it's Imported O.F.C.," and we can easily see that the label in the fur coat is the same as the label on the bottle of whiskey to the right of the text.

Here the focus on labels is applied to clothing and whiskey.

When does a label count? When one is concerned about the display of status and superiority, a concern that this and many other ads serve to amplify and exploit. A tuxedo and a fur coat represent the pinnacle of fashion, and we can imagine that the physically fit man, draping the fur coat over his arm, is waiting for his companion to come claim the coat. The man's head is not pictured because with the right label, his appearance doesn't really matter—and the reader can imagine his own head on that body. Tellingly, the ad says almost nothing about how the whiskey tastes ("Rich. Light.") but stresses rather that it is "In immaculate good taste." This designer whiskey confers status, prestige, and even companionship; who cares what it tastes like?

The claim: Charlie's father is motivated by anxiety, created in part by these cultural values.

This anxiety about one's status and the implication that drinking alcoholic beverages will elevate it, which pervade the advertisements and even the cartoons in *The New Yorker*, arguably shape the character of Charlie's father, and Cheever as well. Charlie's father has his secretary make the arrangements for meeting his son in order to establish that he has a secretary. He wants his son to realize that he has status—because he has absorbed the cultural lesson that his self-worth depends on it. He mentions "my club" for the same reason, I would argue: to convey that he has a club, even though it is conveniently too distant to be used. Likewise, his display of foreign languages and his manic rudeness toward the various waiters are pitiful efforts to impress his son with his sophistication and power. At the end, as he struggles to "get a rise" out of the newsstand clerk, he is trying desperately to show his son how clever and superior he is. That is why he says "just wait a second, sonny": he is putting on this performance for his son, not for his own amusement. His interest in his son and his excitement are subtly suggested by his arrival "at twelve o'clock sharp." He's eager to see his son; he simply does not know how to impress his son, and his response is an effort to establish his status.

Even his alcoholism is related.   Even Charlie's father's desperate pursuit of alcohol reflects his anxiety about his status. Not only can we speculate that his nervousness drives him to medicate himself with liquid depressants; we can also see how his pursuit of drinks reflects his awareness of the association, created in advertisements and other cultural messages, between alcoholic consumption and affection. Charlie's father is seeking to create a bond with Charlie in a way that advertisements even today continue to promote. Charlie's father wants to create an "it-doesn't-get-any-better-than-this" moment; when the second waiter refuses to serve Charlie, his father immediately leaves because he wants more than a drink for himself; he hopes the drinks will lead to affection and bonding.

Conclusion: these values are destructive.   But he is really self-destructive, as Cheever makes clear. Charlie's father does not establish his status, and his quest for drinks does not create a bond. Instead, the day's events extinguish the contact between father and son, just as the father's drinking represents a slow self-extinction. Cheever has exposed the lie in the advertisements surrounding his story.

✔ Checklist for Biographical and Historical Criticism

❑ Research the author's life and relate that information to the work. (But do not assume that any character in the work simply stands for the author).

❑ Research the author's time (political history, intellectual history, economic history, etc.) and relate that information to the work.

❑ Research the systems of meaning available to the author and relate those systems to the work.

Useful Terms and Sources for Biographical, Historical, and New Historical Criticism

Author: Perhaps the most important thing to gain from this chapter is an awareness of the radically different ways an author is viewed by different critical approaches. For New Criticism, with its close analysis of the work itself, an author has little authority. The lives of authors may be intriguing, but it's the text itself that counts. For reader-oriented approaches, the reader's reaction to the text is what counts—and the authors is again peripheral.

Biographical criticism, however, assumes that it matters who wrote something, and under what conditions it was written. Studying the life of a writer is intrinsically interesting and useful—probably anyone's life holds instructive insights; but the purpose of literary biography, ultimately, is to shed some light on an author's work. The risks of biographical criticism are thus fairly transparent, but it is nonetheless important to keep them in mind: First, there's the problem of recovering the author's life and times. For some writers, biographical information is sparse or suspect: for J. D. Salinger (fiercely reclusive) or Homer (perhaps not even a single person), we'd like to know a whole lot more. For other writers, there is a wealth of information, sometimes contradictory and confusing: to understand Samuel Johnson for instance, you'd need to study Boswell's magnificent and massive *Life of Johnson* (five volumes in the standard edition), as well as at least a dozen other biographies and memoirs, not to mention the life and works of those around Johnson (not to mention Boswell's drafts and notebooks, which have some surprising differences with what he published), and so on.

Second, once we think we have biographical information, there's the problem of how to use it to illuminate creative work. We know Hemingway was wounded in World War I, and "A Very Short Story" features a soldier who was wounded, so can we conclude that the soldier is Hemingway? No, we can't. What if the soldier in the story is recovering in the same town in which Hemingway recovered, and is involved with a nurse who sounds a bit like a nurse Hemingway was involved with? We would still diminish the literary work, rather than enhance it, if we assume that Hemingway's story is simply covert autobiography. By insisting on a distinction between the author and his creations, we're in a better position to appreciate the literary work and the artistic choices the author made in crafting it. At the same time, even as we acknowledge the difficulties and risk of recovering an author's life, we can certainly learn much that adds interest and insight to the literary work. We shouldn't naïvely draw a one-to-one parallel between Hemingway and the wounded soldier, but we also shouldn't pretend that literary biography doesn't enrich our understanding of and interest in a work, and vice-versa.

A larger historical perspective sees the work of an author within the context of his time and place. Hemingway and his work can be illuminated by a better understanding of World War I, of its battles, its hospitals and medical practices, and of the values and ideas at work in Hemingway's culture. From a new historical perspective, the author is indeed so much a function of the time and place he or she inhabits, that the author as individual tends to dissolve. From this viewpoint, the language and the patterns of thinking available to an author, at a particular time and place, determine what he or she will say—so thoroughly that it is possible to speak (as Roland Barthes has) of "the death of the author." It's more reasonable, within new historical assumptions at least, to think about an "author" as a part of a system of discourse (language, logic, values, assumptions, etc.), rather than as an individual entity or freestanding agent.

Autobiography: A writer's story of his or her own life—an autobiography—offers (potentially) an especially interesting version of what happened. But it's important to remember that the use of autobiographical material in literary study is subject to the same scrutiny as the use of biographical material. Sometimes we forget what happened, or we only thought we understood what happened, or we decide to place what happened in a certain light, or we may just flat-out lie. Interestingly, autobiographies are rather rare prior to the seventeenth century, when there was a rapid expansion of interest in self-analysis and introspection.

Confessional: In some literary works, the writer seems to express his or her strong emotional feelings directly, in his or her own voice and person. We call such works "confessional" because they appear to be about the writer's life, and they often explore uncomfortable, ordinarily private issues (as in a "confession"). The speaker in a poem and the creator of that poem may seem to be united. For some critics, such apparent self-exposure is daring and exhilarating; for others, the work and the life disturbingly collapse into one another, blurring the critic's function. Is the critic judging the writer's life or work? Are we engaging in artistic or aesthetic assessment or psychological analysis? On the other hand, one might argue that confessional works simply expose the personal character that is inevitable in all expressions, insisting that we unite the person and the work, violating the usual critical assumption that the speaker and the author are distinct.

Culture: Biographical and historical approaches to literary works assume that it is possible to make some meaningful generalizations, not only about an individual but about the society around him or her. "Culture" refers to the whole of a particular society—the beliefs, habits, facts, laws, values, and more that we may use to distinguish one group of people from another. It certainly makes sense to distinguish one culture from another: early seventeenth-century English culture is different from early twenty-first century English culture; Islamic culture is different from Jewish culture. To understand better a literary work written in an Islamic culture, one should seek a better understanding of that culture. And yet, every individual within a culture does not, or course, embrace every aspect of that culture. Any attempt to describe anything so complicated as a "culture" is bound to be partial—a construct of imagination, to some degree.

Despite such difficulties, the study of literature and culture together is powerfully appealing, as we strive to see how literature and culture shape and influence each other.

Discourse: Literary critics who employ biographical and historical materials have found "discourse" to be a particularly useful term because it allows them to make useful connections between the writer and the work. If one individual is speaking to another one who can be reasonably expected to understand the speaker, then they share, to some degree, a discourse. They are participants in a conversation, which means that they share (for starters) a language. "Discourse" refers to more than just language, including the assumptions and protocols shared by a community. So it's possible for critics to talk about "the discourse of nineteenth-century biology," or "the discourse of the eighteenth-century penal system," or "the discourse of the late twentieth-century capitalism." Particular writers and their works can then be made sense of within these discourses.

Implied Author: This term distinguishes usefully between the real-life person who writes (who may be sitting in his pajamas, worried about his mortgage, with children yelling in the background, with a slight hangover and a sore throat) and the written construction of that person (which might project calm, confidence, energy). This term can be compared to "the implied reader"—an idea distinguishing the reader that the author seems to have imagined from the real-life person who is experiencing the text. The implied reader for some eighteenth-century works, for instance, might well be someone who has some familiarity with the history of armed conflict between France and England, and who has a working knowledge of Latin. A real reader, sitting in his or her twenty-first century living room, might be very different from this implied reader. By the same token, the real author might be very different from the implied author, as he or she is reflected in the text.

Influence: Historical critics are often interested in seeing how some prior work (or body of works) has affected another work (or body of works). Themes, strategies, forms, words, plot devices—anything might be picked up from a prior work and reused by an author. More recently, the idea of influence has gotten renewed attention because of the work of Walter Jackson Bate and Harold Bloom, who drew attention to the way some writers confront "the burden of the past" (Bate) or "the anxiety of influence" (Bloom). Rather than following after a prior writer, accepting an influence, a writer (Bate and Bloom argued) may struggle to hide or overcome an influence, attempting to assert his or her originality.

Intention: Biographical criticism brings the problematic relationship between intention and meaning to the forefront. If the meaning of a text depends on what the

author meant to say (a reasonable enough assumption, it would seem), then biographical criticism may hold powerful keys to meaning. As we become removed in
time from an author, we face greater difficulties in discerning what he or she might
have meant, and biographical information may offer help. Intention is, however, a
controversial basis for meaning: how can we know for sure what another person
meant? After Freud, how can another person know what he or she meant—there
may be unconscious motivations at work. It seems problematic to assume that we
can say with any confidence what an author intended. Thus intention is an especially fruitful ground for literary argument and engagement.

Literary History: Literary history not only describes the nature of individual
texts but inevitably makes some generalizations about groups of texts. If we
have simply a succession of random, unrelated events, then we can't realistically be said to have "history," which connects and relates discrete events. Likewise,
literary history aims to connect and relate certain works. In this endeavor, the
construction of distinct literary periods is helpful.

Paradigm: This term and any number of related ones ("worldview," "episteme,"
"ideology") draw our attention to a complex set of assumptions at work within
a particular culture at a particular time. A solar eclipse means something very
different from within the paradigm of the ancient Egyptians, on the one hand,
and the paradigm of a modern astronomer, on the other hand. We may read individual literary works, if we employ historical approaches, in order to make sense
of the different paradigms that people have inhabited. At any one moment, in
any one place, however, it is quite likely that different people will hold conflicting and overlapping paradigms in their heads—the same person may even have
access to conflicting paradigms. A paradigm, in other words, might be thought
of as a set of instructions for making meaning. As more people accept this way
of making sense, the paradigm grows in importance.

Period: For convenience, we divide history of all sorts, including literary history, into segments or periods. Although these divisions are based on evidence,
they are ultimately arbitrary. There are useful generalizations about medieval
literature, and about how renaissance literature differs from medieval literature; but like all generalizations, they're subject to exceptions and challenges.
The study of eighteenth-century literature has traditionally been distinct from
the study of nineteenth-century literature, but it would be unreasonable to
think that writers uniformly adjusted their ideas and styles and goals as the
calendar shifted. The idea of a period, in other words, is a useful convenience
(most useful, perhaps, as you begin to see the limitation of any particular set
of generalizations).

Tradition: Just as we divide literary history into distinct periods, we also connect
literary works across time with the idea of a "tradition." The most visible sort of
tradition is probably that of genre: Milton's *Paradise Lost* can hardly be understood without some sense of the epic tradition, for example. Shakespeare's sonnets are part of a tradition of sonnets. The idea of tradition highlights the limits
of formal analysis in New Criticism (and the power of biographical and historical
approaches): the text itself is rarely meant to stand by itself. Writers inevitably
position their works in one or more traditions of literary effort.

Sources for Biographical Research

❑ For convenient access to essential facts about the life of a major figure—
consult the *Encyclopedia Brittanica* (now available on the Internet) or

another major encyclopedia. As a rule, however, you don't want to cite general encyclopedias in your essay; just use them to get started.

❑ For more details—see the *Dictionary of National Biography* (for British figures), the *Dictionary of American Biography,* or the *Dictionary of Literary Biography.*

❑ For information on contemporary authors—see *Contemporary Authors.*

❑ Also useful—*Biography Index, Oxford Companion to English Literature, Oxford Companion to American Literature,* and the other *Oxford Companions.* An especially appealing resource is *The Atlantic Brief Lives,* which offers brief and often brilliant biographies of writers and other artists by authoritative scholars.

❑ For book-length biographies—check the catalog in your library. Do be sure to check the publication date of the biography; new facts and resources are coming to light all the time, although a newer biography is not necessarily a better one. Also, book reviews can help you evaluate a particular biography: *Book Review Index* (covers the most sources), *Book Review Digest* (includes excerpts from the reviews).

Sources for Historical Research

❑ For detailed surveys of literary history—try the *Oxford History of English Literature* (13 volumes); F. E. Halliday, *A Concise History of England, from Stonehenge to the Atomic Age;* or Robert Adams, *The Land and Literature of England.* A delightful mini-view of American literature appears in the first chapter of *An Incomplete Education.* The standard heavy-duty history of American literature is *The Literary History of the United States* (2 volumes).

Sources for New Historical Research

Some suggestions for places to look for materials:

❑ Popular or noncanonical literature: children's stories, adolescent fiction, romances, adventure stories, and so forth.

❑ Primary materials for other disciplines: music theory, psychology, criminology, architecture, and so forth.

❑ Newspapers and magazines. These can offer you descriptions of events and leads to other texts.

❑ Artifacts from the period. Think like an archeologist trying to make sense of the physical remains of a particular time. For instance, a delicate and ornate snuffbox from the eighteenth century may illuminate the sort of cultural environment in which, say, Mozart's delicate and ornate music could be written.

Elements: Plot and Structure

The definition of "plot" that most people agree upon—"the sequence of events in a narrative"—offers little clue as to why the concept has received so much attention from literary critics and theorists in the last few decades. To understand the recent fascination with "plot," and its importance as a concept, we need to distinguish "plot" from "story" and "narrative." To make such a distinction, let's again look at an example.

ELLEN MALPHRUS (1964–)

Ellen Malphrus lives in Bluffton, South Carolina, and teaches at the University of South Carolina at Beaufort.

Thanksgiving on the Chicken Bone Express

There is turkey everywhere. On the train coming up the club car special is a turkey sandwich with cranberry jelly, your choice of chips, and a medium coke, $3.95. The restaurant where they now sit is serving escalloped breast of tender young free range turkey with a fresh cranberry glaze, etc., etc., $13.95. She is not interested in turkey. Thanksgiving is not even until tomorrow. When she is recited the offerings of the evening she laughs out loud and her mother and the waiter look at her. It's a communist plot, she says. Of course neither her mother nor the waiter understand.

The restaurant is on South Street in Philadelphia. It was apparently a church once, with the stained glass still intact. More likely replaced. It's like a circus, her mother told her the first time she brought her to South Street, and indeed it is. Not only because of the jugglers and mimes and bizarre outfits, but also because of the electric air buzz that never shuts down—the energy that floats around everything like a child shading in the background of a kindergarten picture.

She likes South Street. People laugh there, and escape, she supposes. And South Philly too, with its deep food smells. She always buys a gallon of Colavita olive oil which she cannot get at home to take back on the train. Even downtown is okay. She can spend half the day at the Reading Terminal, and she doesn't mind stepping over the street people nearly as much as she does driving through the mile after mile of row house upon ever more depressing row house on the way to her mother's apartment.

The stained glass reminds her of her best kaleidoscope. She collects them now. She makes up crazy pictures in her head too. That's how she gets by. The kaleidoscope she is thinking of has brilliant cobalt blue glass pieces inside where she can lose herself for long, long minutes. It is packed in her suitcase in the trunk of her mother's car. They have just come from the train station.

Her mother has been working on graduate degrees at Bryn Mawr College since her parents finally put their marriage out of its misery several years back. The year she got married in fact.   5

When the waiter comes with the appetizers, butternut soup for her mother and a steamed artichoke for her, she orders another extra dry Absolut martini with olives. She might as well have asked for straight vodka with olives since the two are one and the same, but she knows well that anytime anyone orders anything straight somebody is bound to think something.

She has debated with herself on the train as to whether she should tell her mother tonight or wait until later in the visit or even Sunday when she gets ready to leave. If she tells her tonight, it will be over and done with. Her mother will be sad but she will understand and they can get over it and enjoy the rest of the weekend. If she waits until Sunday she will have it on her mind tonight and tomorrow night, and the next, and the next.

Then again, if she tells her mother tonight, it will put a damper on Thanksgiving and she will be plagued by a thousand sad questions for days to come. If she waits, though, there will be the reminiscences of Thanksgivings past. That will mean a thousand other questions, happy ones, equally as hard to answer. It is confusing to think about and she is weary from confusion. She sinks back into the seat and decides it can wait.

The train which she rides up to see her mother is officially called the Southern Crescent, but is nicknamed "the Chicken Bone Express" because so many people ride it to Washington or New York but mostly Philly where they have family, and they always seem to bring along fried chicken packed in big baskets with striped dish towels over the top. The conductor rags them about what's left behind when they get off. He is the one who came up with the name, and now anyone who's ridden the train before calls it that, sort of like a club.

She had flown when her mother first moved to Philadelphia, but once she settled in for the twelve hours of beautiful train ride void, where she can be anyone or no one, she knew she would come this way from now on. The motion is stronger on a train, and looking out into the blur of woods and clotheslines she can almost see her freedom from across the way.

They order a bottle of wine with dinner, the free rambling turkey for her mother and salmon with dill sauce for her, and talk about her work at the museum and her mother's classes and job at the mental health center. She has gingerly avoided all else and decides that's definitely the better plan for now.

For dessert she orders dark chocolate mousse with raspberries and Sambuca, and her mother has pumpkin sorbet. She has made a deal with her mother that they will not have turkey and dressing tomorrow and now she feels badly that her mother is having to eat a subterfuge Thanksgiving meal.

She begins to think about driving home through the row houses. She pities most of them, whoever there is inside, but feels something darker for the ones who plant plastic flowers in the window boxes or place big outdoor statuary of girls with umbrellas on the raw patches of six-by-eight ground that gape before some of the buildings. Little gray girls holding up cement umbrellas to ward off the world. They will ride out into Lancaster County tomorrow and the long curved fields will soothe her.

"I'm leaving Patrick," she says, and wonders if she meant to say it aloud.

Her mother looks at her, spoon hovering over the sorbet, and says nothing.

The absence of a thousand questions makes her feel she wants to explain. She has made certain, as best she could, that no one in her family has had to know. It is amazing, the things you can cover up, the things no one really wants to see anyway.

"You silly little fool," her mother says.

A reaction she does not expect.

"You silly little fool," her mother says again. "You don't know how good you've got it."

Strange, she thinks, remembering the day she and Patrick told her mother they planned to be married. Oh my God, her mother had said, live together, see the world, find yourself, do anything, but for God's sake don't get married so young. She had just graduated from college and Patrick had been out for two years. They were good together. In private her mother had begged her not to do it. Begged her until the silken web came down across her bridal face.

There had been a thousand questions then, but now there are none. That is odd to her. Very strange. She wishes that the waiter would come with the check. Wishes for the blue kaleidoscope wrapped inside her black sweater.

How good you've got it. The echo of her mother's words slap at her from across the silent table. Slap at her like a mime, she thinks, imagining the white faced tricksters out on the street. Her mind shoots off to a picture of the mimes juggling drumsticks on the Chicken Bone Express, steaming down the tracks with boxcars full of Butterball turkeys.

Oh yes, her mother *should* know, she thinks, standing in the middle of the tracks, listening to the train come, as the concrete umbrellas close down dark around her.

[1997]

Determining what constitutes an "event" in this or any story is somewhat of an arbitrary decision. I've divided this story into twenty-three "events," but you might think there are twenty-eight or eighteen. The sequence of events listed here is simply a convenience to allow us to talk about the ordering of the story. First, here are the events of the story in chronological order. Some events are explicitly described, and others are referred or alluded to. (The event in brackets is not explicitly presented, but is clearly implied.)

1. Her mother privately begs her not to marry Patrick.
2. Her mother and father are divorced; she and Patrick in the same year get married.
3. There are thousands of questions from her mother about marrying Patrick.
4. When her mother moves to Philadelphia, she flies there.
5. Her mother takes her to South Street in Philadelphia, telling her it's a circus; she likes it.
6. [She decides to leave her husband,] and she "gets by" by making up "crazy pictures in her head" and looking in her kaleidoscopes.
7. She comes up on the Chicken Bone Express (named earlier by the conductor) the day before this Thanksgiving, finding turkey everywhere.
8. The conductor (as usual) teases people about how much food is left behind.
9. She debates on the train when to tell her mother about leaving her husband.
10. They go to talk in a restaurant, on South Street in Philly, the same day she comes in on the train.
11. The waiter recites the menu, and she makes a joke the waiter and her mother don't get.
12. The waiter serves appetizers and she orders another drink.
13. She decides to wait to tell her mother.
14. They order wine, turkey (for her mother), salmon (for her).
15. She avoids all topics except her work and her mother's work and classes, realizing that waiting is right.
16. She regrets making her mother eat a subterfuge Thanksgiving meal.
17. She thinks about the drive home and the statuary of little girls with umbrellas.
18. She tells her mom about leaving Patrick, unsure that she meant to say it aloud.
19. Her mother does not approve, calling her a "silly fool."
20. There are no questions from her mother about leaving Patrick.
21. She wants to leave, to look at her kaleidoscope.
22. She imagines her mother's words slap at her like a mime; then she imagines mimes juggling drumsticks on the train, with boxcars of turkeys.
23. She is standing in the middle of the tracks, listening to the train come, as concrete umbrellas close down on her.

That's the chronological ordering of the story's events. Now compare that sequence to the way the events are revealed to the reader. We'll use the numbering from the previous list just to indicate clearly the difference:

7a. The narrator comes up on the train the day before this Thanksgiving, finding turkey everywhere.

10. They go to a restaurant, on South Street in Philly (the same day she comes in on the train).

11. The waiter recites the menu, and she makes a joke the waiter and her mother don't get.

5. Her mother takes her to South Street in Philadelphia, telling her it's a circus; she likes it.

6a. She "gets by" by making up "crazy pictures in her head" and looking in her kaleidoscopes.

2. Her mother and father are divorced; she and Patrick in the same year get married.

12. The waiter serves appetizers and she orders another drink.

9a. She debates on the train when to tell her mother something.

13. She decides to wait to tell her mother.

7b. The Chicken Bone Express is named earlier by the conductor.

8. The conductor (as usual) teases people about how much food is left behind.

4. When her mother moves to Philadelphia, she flies there.

14. They order wine, turkey (for her mother), salmon (for her).

15. She avoids all topics except her work and her mother's work and classes, realizing that waiting is right.

16. She regrets making her mother eat a subterfuge Thanksgiving meal.

17. She thinks about the drive home and the statuary of little girls with umbrellas.

18. She tells her mom about leaving Patrick, unsure that she meant to say it aloud.

6b. She decides to leave her husband.

9b. [She debates on the train whether to tell her mother] about leaving Patrick.

19. Her mother does not approve, calling her a "silly little fool."

20. There are no questions from her mother about leaving Patrick.

1. Her mother privately begs her not to marry Patrick.

3. There are thousands of questions from her mother about marrying Patrick.

21. She wants to leave, to look at her kaleidoscope.

22. She imagines her mother's words slap at her like a mime; then she imagines mimes juggling drumsticks on the train, with boxcars of turkeys.

23. She is standing in the middle of the tracks, listening to the train come, as concrete umbrellas close down on her.

Obviously, the reconstructed order of what occurred is quite different from the order of events as they are revealed to the reader. Which of these two sequences is referred to by the term "plot"? Plot is, according to one textbook, "the pattern of events in a story"; according to another, plot is "the way in which the events of a story are arranged"; and another representative text says that plot is "the significant order of events in a narrative."[1] These definitions, from excellent textbooks, don't really make clear whether "story" and "narrative" mean "what really occurred" or "the presentation (possibly in a different order) of what really occurred." The difference, of course, could be huge. Furthermore, "story" is one of

[1]The quotations come from Hans Guth and Gabrielle Rico, *Discovering Literature* (Upper Saddle River, NJ: Prentice-Hall, 1999), p. 1608; Steven Kirzner and Laurie Mandell, *Literature* (Boston: Dryden Press, 2000), p. 1807; Arthur Biddle and Toby Fulwiler, *Reading, Writing, and the Study of Literature* (Boston: McGraw-Hill, 1998), p. 1780.

those many familiar words that mean lots of different things: we refer to the text of a work of short fiction as "a story," but we also refer to "the story" that readers piece together by reading such a work: again, the two meanings confuse "what happened" and "what we are told." Thus, "plot," one of the most basic terms of literary analysis, seems to be a pretty fuzzy term.

In fact, the recent interest that literary critics have shown in "plot" has stemmed in part from thinking productively about this fuzziness. Generally, with some significant exceptions, critics and scholars have agreed in recent years to use the term **story** for "what actually happened," and the term **narrative** for "the presentation of what actually happened." The term **plot**, then, as the narrative theorist Peter Brooks puts it, "cuts across [this] . . . distinction in that to speak of plot is to consider both story elements and their ordering." And this "cutting across" is precisely why plot is so interesting to think about, because its consideration takes us directly to the heart of the writer's crafting: thinking about plot in both these senses (story and narrative, what happened and the telling of what happened), we are led to consider how the writer has shaped "what happened" into "what is told." We are led to ask, for instance, why the author has rearranged the sequence of events, and why the author may have omitted crucial events even, leaving them to our inference, while selecting, perhaps even lingering upon, other seemingly minor events. These are often very revealing questions to pursue.

We might ask, for example, why Malphrus begins her story in the middle of things (which is often called *in medias res*—Latin for "in the middle of things"), starting with the observation "There is turkey everywhere." How does this beginning compare to the way stories usually begin? How do readers expect stories to begin and unfold?

Experienced readers, it's usually assumed, expect an initial **conflict,** followed by **complications,** leading eventually to a **crisis** or **climax.** This movement, from conflict to crisis, is usually called the **rising action,** and it includes along the way **exposition,** which is the background information that allows the reader to make sense of what is going on. If the main character, as the story unfolds, has a breakthrough insight, then that moment of awareness can be called an **epiphany.** If this rising action involves growing up, or "coming of age," then the story may be considered an **initiation story** (or a **Bildungsroman**). Whatever the nature of the rising action and crisis, the ensuing resolution of the story is often called the **dénoument.** Readers ordinarily expect this solving of the story's conflicts to bring the sense of an ending, or **closure.** The whole sequence, then, potentially looks like this:

Conflict > Complications > Crisis > Climax > Dénoument > Closure

Malphrus's opening sentence, "There is turkey everywhere," immediately involves the experienced reader in a potential problem. Perhaps there has been a terrible accident, an explosion at the turkey factory, and turkey is everywhere. Perhaps there has been a riot at the prison on Thanksgiving (hence the title) and the inmates have thrown turkey all over the cafeteria. Readers do not ordinarily pause and contemplate, of course, what might be about to happen, but our brains are amazingly agile, and Malphrus's opening assertion does suggest that something is wrong. In most situations, anyway, turkey is not supposed to be "everywhere."

Readers quickly realize turkey really isn't *everywhere*, and the daughter soon laughs at the menu. But suspense and complication are already building, because the mother and the waiter don't share in the humor, and readers don't really see it either (do we?). The feeling that something is wrong might be traced back to the title: it's the Chicken Bone Express, but there is *turkey* everywhere? Chickens at Thanksgiving? Something doesn't fit, and the story will continue to exploit the notion that various things don't fit together: chickens and turkeys, mother and daughter, mother and father, daughter and husband.

Malphrus structures the plot, we could argue, to maximize the effect of the daughter's revelation of one particular incongruity: "I'm leaving Patrick." Readers are, like the mother, caught off guard since the plot gives no indication that the daughter has decided to reveal her secret, the substance of which has been withheld from the reader. This surprise, although surprising, is a structure that readers have encountered before, so that we are in the interesting position of expecting to be surprised.

In terms of character, one might think that the logical starting point for Malphrus's story is her decision to marry Patrick, since this story brings that plot line to some closure. Or, we could argue that the decision to *leave* Patrick is the logical starting point. Malphrus instead structures the plot to focus upon the daughter's character, and not upon the break-up with Patrick. Psychologists have made it common knowledge that many people find the major holidays difficult, even depressing, and from the outset it is clear that the daughter is finding this Thanksgiving oppressive. She feels surrounded by turkey, by the props of Thanksgiving, and her feeble joke, that the turkey everywhere is "a communist plot," further suggests her fear: she is being threatened by totalitarian regimes—the Thanksgiving tradition, her mother, Patrick. Malphrus's opening thus **foreshadows** the story's ending, where the idea of being contained or surrounded by turkey has become something much more ominous—a train bearing down upon her, and "concrete umbrellas" that "close down around her." These beginning and ending images of enclosure and oppression reveal much about the character of the daughter, and they also contrast dramatically with her desires within the narrative to "lose herself," in the South Street "circus," in her kaleidoscopes, in the "freedom" she can almost see "across the way" from the train. The story thus becomes structured at some level by the character's drive to escape that which is closing in.

With the final paragraph, the plot immerses the narrator in the daughter's experience. It seems clear in the next-to-the-last paragraph, that the daughter's imagination is creating the mimes juggling drumsticks, the train full of turkeys (returning us again to the opening):

> The echo of her mother's words slap at her from across the silent table. Slap at her like a mime, she thinks, imagining the white-faced tricksters out on the street. Her mind shoots off to a picture of the mimes juggling drumsticks on the Chicken Bone Express, steaming down the tracks with boxcars full of Butterball turkeys.

But with the final paragraph, this grip on what is "real" seems to slip. In this concluding scene, is she actually standing on the tracks, waiting on the train, committing suicide as she imagines the concrete umbrellas? Or is she really still in the restaurant, imagining both the train and the umbrellas?

> Oh yes, her mother *should* know, she thinks, standing in the middle of the tracks, listening to the train come, as the concrete umbrellas close down dark around her.

Malphrus might have employed **flashbacks**, moving us back in time to show us prior moments with Patrick or the mother, but such information might clarify the situation, and thus ruin the concluding ambiguity. But ambiguity is built into the story from its title: the daughter does not, it appears, spend "Thanksgiving on the Chicken Bone Express"; she spends *the day before* Thanksgiving on the train. Perhaps the daughter will indeed spend Thanksgiving on the Chicken Bone Express because she will be returning home on it the next day, electing after her mother's response not to stay any longer. Or, perhaps, the daughter will spend Thanksgiving on the Chicken Bone Express in a more tragic sense, standing the next day on the train track, being struck by the train. Whether the last scene is entirely in her imagination, while John is still at the restaurant, or the last scene shifts forward to the next day on the train track, in either case the title arguably becomes, in an interesting sense, the last event in the plot.

"Plot" and "character" are especially important in biographical and historical criticism because, quite simply, we unavoidably see biographies and histories as stories. Fact and fiction are both shaped by overlapping expectations, which are most visible in terms of plot and character: stories will start at some significant point, and they will unfold in ways that build to a climax, which will be resolved; and in this unfolding, character will be revealed.

Here, as a kind of review, are some questions you should find helpful in thinking about plot and structure:

1. Is the ordering of the narrative different from the ordering of the story? What difference does this difference make? Is there a real-life incident on which the story is based? If so, is the biographical/historical event altered in the story? How, and why?
2. Where in time is the speaker located? Does the plot move about in time, with flashbacks and foreshadowings, or is the story straightforward? How does the temporal sequence affect the story? How does the setting (time and space) of the story relate to the author's time and space?
3. Where is the conflict in the story? How does the plot expose this conflict? Is there anything in the writer's life in particular or history in general that would draw attention to this conflict?
4. Can you identify a crucial moment in the plot, a moment of decision, when the story's crisis is resolved? Why is that moment the climax?
5. Are there events missing from the narrative—events that we can conjecture must have occurred but are not revealed? Why are they omitted?
6. Do the events mean something to the reader that they do not mean to the characters? (Is there, in other words, dramatic irony in the plot?)
7. Are there developments in the story that seem arbitrary or implausible, or does the plot proceed convincingly? Explain.
8. Are there events in the plot that seem marginal but might be considered central, reversing or unsettling the plot's apparent structure?

Practice: Missing Persons

You can practice biographical, historical, and new historical criticism with any of the works in this textbook, of course. But this textbook can't possibly provide you with all the materials you might need—and remain small enough for you to carry around. Here, therefore, are two stories by John Cheever since you already have access to the materials used in reading "Reunion." These are great stories by a master of short fic-

John and Mary Cheever with John and Mary Updike

tion, and the earlier biographical and historical materials should enhance your appreciation of them.

JOHN CHEEVER (1912–1982)

The Swimmer

It was one of those midsummer Sundays when everyone sits around saying, "I *drank* too much last night." You might have heard it whispered by the parishioners leaving church, heard it from the lips of the priest himself, struggling with his cassock in the *vestiarium,* heard it from the golf links and the tennis courts, heard it from the wild-life preserve where the leader of the Audubon group was suffering from a terrible hangover. "I *drank* too much," said Donald Westerhazy. "We all *drank* too much," said Lucinda Merrill. "It must have been the wine," said Helen Westerhazy. "I *drank* too much of that claret."

This was the edge of the Westerhazys' pool. The pool, fed by an artesian well with a high iron content, was a pale shade of green. It was a fine day. In the west there was a massive stand of cumulus cloud so like a city seen from a distance—from the bow of an approaching ship—that it might have had a name. Lisbon. Hackensack. The sun was hot. Neddy Merrill sat by the green water, one hand in it, one around a glass of gin. He was a slender man—he seemed to have the especial slenderness of youth—and while he was far from young he had slid down his banister that morning and given the bronze backside of Aphrodite on the hall table a smack, as he jogged toward the smell of coffee in his dining room. He might have been compared to a summer's day, particularly the last hours of one, and while he lacked a tennis racket or a sail bag the impression was definitely one of youth, sport, and clement weather. He had been swimming and now he was breathing deeply, stertorously as if he could gulp into his lungs the components of that moment, the heat of the sun, the intenseness of his pleasure. It all seemed to flow into his chest. His own house stood in Bullet Park, eight miles to the south, where his four beautiful daughters would have had their lunch and might be playing tennis. Then it occurred to him that by taking a dogleg to the southwest he could reach his home by water.

His life was not confining and the delight he took in this observation could not be explained by its suggestion of escape. He seemed to see, with a cartographer's eye, that string of swimming pools, that quasi-subterranean stream that curved across the county. He had made a discovery, a contribution to modern geography; he would name the stream Lucinda after his wife. He was not a practical joker nor was he a fool but he was determinedly original and had a vague and modest idea of himself as a legendary figure. The day was beautiful and it seemed to him that a long swim might enlarge and celebrate its beauty.

He took off a sweater that was hung over his shoulders and dove in. He had an inexplicable contempt for men who did not hurl themselves into pools. He swam a choppy crawl, breathing either with every stroke or every fourth stroke and counting somewhere well in the back of his mind the one-two one-two of a flutter kick. It was not a serviceable stroke for long distances but the domestication of swimming had saddled the sport with some customs and in his part of the world a crawl was customary. To be embraced and sustained by the light green water was less a pleasure, it seemed, than the resumption of a natural condition, and he would have liked to swim without trunks, but this was not possible, considering his project. He hoisted himself up on the far curb—he never used the ladder—and started across the lawn. When Lucinda asked where he was going he said he was going to swim home.

The only maps and charts he had to go by were remembered or imaginary but these were clear enough. First there were the Grahams, the Hammers, the Lears, the Howlands, and the Crosscups. He would cross Ditmar Street to the Bunkers and come, after a short portage, to the Levys, the Welchers, and the public pool in Lancaster. Then there were the Hallorans, the Sachses, the Biswangers, Shirley Adams, the Gilmartins, and the Clydes. The day was lovely, and that he lived in a world so generously supplied with water seemed like a clemency, a beneficence. His heart was high and he ran across the grass. Making his way home by an uncommon route gave him the feeling that he was a pilgrim, an explorer, a man with a destiny, and he knew that he would find friends all along the way; friends would line the banks of the Lucinda River.

He went through a hedge that separated the Westerhazys' land from the Grahams', walked under some flowering apple trees, passed the shed that housed their pump and filter, and came out at the Grahams' pool. "Why, Neddy," Mrs. Graham said, "what a marvelous surprise. I've been trying to get you on the phone all morning. Here, let me get you a drink." He saw then, like any explorer, that the hospitable customs and traditions of the natives would have to be handled with diplomacy if he was ever going to reach his destination. He did not want to mystify or seem rude to the Grahams nor did he have the time to linger there. He swam the length of their pool and joined them in the sun and was rescued, a few minutes later, by the arrival of two carloads of friends from Connecticut. During the uproarious reunions he was able to slip away. He went down by the front of the Gra-

5

hams' house, stepped over a thorny hedge, and crossed a vacant lot to the Hammers'. Mrs. Hammer, looking up from her roses, saw him swim by although she wasn't quite sure who it was. The Lears heard him splashing past the open windows of their living room. The Howlands and the Crosscups were away. After leaving the Howlands' he crossed Ditmar Street and started for the Bunkers', where he could hear, even at that distance, the noise of a party.

The water refracted the sound of voices and laughter and seemed to suspend it in midair. The Bunkers' pool was on a rise and he climbed some stairs to a terrace where twenty-five or thirty men and women were drinking. The only person in the water was Rusty Towers, who floated there on a rubber raft. Oh, how bonny and lush were the banks of the Lucinda River! Prosperous men and women gathered by the sapphire-colored waters while caterer's men in white coats passed them cold gin. Overhead a red de Haviland trainer was circling around and around and around in the sky with something like the glee of a child in a swing. Ned felt a passing affection for the scene, a tenderness for the gathering, as if it was something he might touch. In the distance he heard thunder. As soon as Enid Bunker saw him she began to scream: "Oh, look who's here! What a marvelous surprise! When Lucinda said you couldn't come I thought I'd *die*." She made her way to him through the crowd, and when they had finished kissing she led him to the bar, a progress that was slowed by the fact that he stopped to kiss eight or ten other women and shake the hands of as many men. A smiling bartender he had seen at a hundred parties gave him a gin and tonic and he stood by the bar for a moment, anxious not to get stuck in any conversation that would delay his voyage. When he seemed about to be surrounded he dove in and swam close to the side to avoid colliding with Rusty's raft. At the far end of the pool he bypassed the Tomlinsons with a broad smile and jogged up the garden path. The gravel cut his feet but this was only unpleasantness. The party was confined to the pool, and as he went toward the house he heard the brilliant, watery sound of voices fade, heard the noise of a radio from the Bunkers' kitchen, where someone was listening to a ball game. Sunday afternoon. He made his way through the parked cars and down the grassy border of their driveway to Alewives Lane. He did not want to be seen on the road in his bathing trunks but there was no traffic and he made the short distance to the Levys' driveway, marked with a PRIVATE PROPERTY sign and a green tube for the *New York Times*. All the doors and windows of the big house were open but there were no signs of life; not even a dog barked. He went around the side of the house to the pool and saw that the Levys had only recently left. Glasses and bottles and dishes of nuts were on a table at the deep end, where there was a bathhouse or gazebo, hung with Japanese lanterns. After swimming the pool he got himself a glass and poured a drink. It was his fourth or fifth drink and he had swum nearly half the length of the Lucinda River. He felt tired, clean, and pleased at that moment to be alone; pleased with everything.

It would storm. The stand of cumulus cloud—that city—had risen and darkened, and while he sat there he heard the percussiveness of thunder again. The de Haviland trainer was still circling overhead and it seemed to Ned that he could almost hear the pilot laugh with pleasure in the afternoon; but when there was another peal of thunder he took off for home. A train whistle blew and he wondered what time it had gotten to be. Four? Five? He thought of the provincial station at that hour, where a waiter, his tuxedo concealed by a raincoat, a dwarf with some flowers wrapped in newspaper, and a woman who had been crying would be waiting for the local. It was suddenly growing dark; it was that moment when the pin-headed birds seemed to organize their song into some acute and knowl-edgeable recognition of the storm's approach. Then there was a fine noise of rushing water from the crown of an oak at his back, as if a spigot there had been turned. Then the noise of fountains came from the crowns of all the tall trees. Why did he love storms, what was the meaning of his excite-ment when the door sprang open and the rain wind fled rudely up the stairs, why had the simple task of shutting the windows of an old house seemed fitting and urgent, why did the first watery notes of a storm wind have for him the unmistakable sound of good news, cheer, glad tidings? Then there was an explosion, a smell of cordite, and rain lashed the Japan-ese lanterns that Mrs. Levy had bought in Kyoto the year before last, or was it the year before that?

He stayed in the Levys' gazebo until the storm had passed. The rain had cooled the air and he shivered. The force of the wind had stripped a maple of its red and yellow leaves and scattered them over the grass and the water. Since it was midsummer the tree must be blighted, and yet he felt a peculiar sadness at this sign of autumn. He braced his shoulders, emptied his glass, and started for the Welchers' pool. This meant crossing the Lind-leys' riding ring and he was surprised to find it overgrown with grass and all the jumps dismantled. He wondered if the Lindleys had sold their hors-es or gone away for the summer and put them out to board. He seemed to remember having heard something about the Lindleys and their horses but the memory was unclear. On he went, barefoot through the wet grass, to the Welchers', where he found their pool was dry.

This breach in his chain of water disappointed him absurdly, and he felt   10
like some explorer who seeks a torrential headwater and finds a dead stream. He was disappointed and mystified. It was common enough to go away for the summer but no one ever drained his pool. The Welchers had definitely gone away. The pool furniture was folded, stacked, and covered with a tarpaulin. The bathhouse was locked. All the windows of the house were shut, and when he went around to the driveway in front he saw a FOR SALE sign nailed to a tree. When had he last heard from the Welchers—when, that is, had he and Lucinda last regretted an invitation to dine with them? It seemed only a week or so ago. Was his memory failing or had he so disciplined it in the repression of unpleas-ant facts that he had damaged his sense of the truth? Then in the distance he heard the sound of a tennis game. This cheered him, cleared away all his appre-hensions and let him regard the overcast sky and the cold air with indifference. This was the day that Neddy Merrill swam across the county. That was the day! He started off then for his most difficult portage.

Had you gone for a Sunday afternoon ride that day you might have seen him, close to naked, standing on the shoulders of Route 424, waiting for a chance to cross. You might have wondered if he was the victim of foul play, had his car broken down, or was he merely a fool. Standing barefoot in the deposits of the highway—beer cans, rags, and blowout patches—exposed to all kinds of ridicule, he seemed pitiful. He had known when he started that this was a part of his journey—it had been on his maps—but confronted with the lines of traffic, worming through the summery light, he found himself unprepared. He was laughed at, jeered at, a beer can was thrown at him, and he had no dignity or humor to bring to the situation. He could have gone back, back to the Westerhazy's, where Lucinda would still be sitting in the sun. He had signed nothing, vowed nothing, pledged nothing, not even to himself. Why, believing as he did, that all human obduracy was susceptible to common sense, was he unable to turn back? Why was he determined to complete his journey even if it meant putting his life in danger? At what point had this prank, this joke, this piece of horseplay become serious? He could not go back, he could not even recall with any clearness the green water at the Westerhazys', the sense of inhaling the day's components, the friendly and relaxed voices saying that they had *drunk* too much. In the space of an hour, more or less, he had covered a distance that made his return impossible.

An old man, tooling down the highway at fifteen miles an hour, let him get to the middle of the road, where there was a grass divider. Here he was exposed to the ridicule of the northbound traffic, but after ten or fifteen minutes he was able to cross. From here he had only a short walk to the Recreation Center at the edge of the village of Lancaster, where there were some handball courts and a public pool.

The effect of the water on voices, the illusion of brilliance and suspense, was the same here as it had been at the Bunkers' but the sounds here were louder, harsher, and more shrill, and as soon as he entered the crowded enclosure he was confronted with regimentation. "ALL SWIMMERS MUST TAKE A SHOWER BEFORE USING THE POOL. ALL SWIMMERS MUST USE THE FOOTBATH. ALL SWIMMERS MUST WEAR THEIR IDENTIFICATION DISKS." He took a shower, washed his feet in a cloudy and bitter solution, and made his way to the edge of the water. It stank of chlorine and looked to him like a sink. A pair of lifeguards in a pair of towers blew police whistles at what seemed to be regular intervals and abused the swimmers through a public address system. Neddy remembered the sapphire water at the Bunkers' with longing and thought that he might contaminate himself—damage his own prosperousness and charm—by swimming in this murk, but he reminded himself that he was an explorer, a pilgrim, and that this was merely a stagnant bend in the Lucinda River. He dove, scowling with distaste, into the chlorine and had to swim with his head above water to avoid collisions, but even so he was bumped into, splashed, and jostled. When he got to the shallow end both lifeguards were shouting at him: "Hey, you, you without the identification disk, get outa the water." He did, but they had no way of pursuing him and he went through the reek of suntan oil and chlorine out through the hurricane fence and passed the handball courts. By crossing the road he entered the wooded part of the Halloran estate. The woods were not cleared and the footing was treacherous and difficult until he reached the lawn and the clipped beech hedge that encircled their pool.

The Hallorans were friends, an elderly couple of enormous wealth who seemed to bask in the suspicion that they might be Communists. They were zealous reformers but they were not Communists, and yet when they were accused, as they sometimes were, of subversion, it seemed to gratify and excite them. Their beech hedge was yellow and he guessed this had been blighted like the Levys' maple. He called hullo, hullo, to warn the

Hallorans of his approach, to palliate his invasion of their privacy. The Hallorans, for reasons that had never been explained to him, did not wear
bathing suits. No explanations were in order, really. Their nakedness was a
detail in their uncompromising zeal for reform and he stepped politely out
of his trunks before he went through the opening in the hedge.

Mrs. Halloran, a stout woman with white hair and a serene face, was   15
reading the *Times*. Mr. Halloran was taking beech leaves out of the water
with a scoop. They seemed not surprised or displeased to see him. Their
pool was perhaps the oldest in the county, a fieldstone rectangle, fed by a
brook. It had no filter or pump and its waters were the opaque gold of the
stream.

"I'm swimming across the county," Ned said.

"Why, I didn't know one could," exclaimed Mrs. Halloran.

"Well, I've made it from the Westerhazys'," Ned said. "That must be
about four miles."

He left his trunks at the deep end, walked to the shallow end, and
swam this stretch. As he was pulling himself out of the water he heard Mrs.
Halloran say, "We've been *terribly* sorry to hear about all your misfortunes,
Neddy."

"My misfortunes?" Ned asked. "I don't know what you mean."   20

"Why we heard that you'd sold the house and that your poor children. . . ."

"I don't recall having sold the house," Ned said, "and the girls are at
home."

"Yes," Mrs. Halloran sighed. "Yes. . . ." Her voice filled the air with an
unseasonable melancholy and Ned spoke briskly. "Thank you for the
swim."

"Well, have a nice trip," said Mrs. Halloran.

Beyond the hedge he pulled on his trunks and fastened them. They   25
were loose and he wondered if, during the space of an afternoon, he could
have lost some weight. He was cold and he was tired and the naked Hallorans and their dark water had depressed him. The swim was too much for
his strength but how could he have guessed this, sliding down the banister
that morning and sitting in the Westerhazys' sun? His arms were lame. His
legs felt rubbery and ached at the joints. The worst of it was the cold in his
bones and the feeling that he might never be warm again. Leaves were
falling down around him and he smelled wood smoke on the wind. Who
would be burning wood at this time of year?

He needed a drink. Whiskey would warm him, pick him up, carry him
through the last of his journey, refresh his feeling that it was original and
valorous to swim across the county. Channel swimmers took brandy. He
needed a stimulant. He crossed the lawn in front of the Hallorans' house
and went down a little path to where they had built a house for their only
daughter, Helen, and her husband, Eric Sachs. The Sachses' pool was small
and he found Helen and her husband there.

"Oh, *Neddy*," Helen said. "Did you lunch at Mother's?"

"Not *really*," Ned said. "I *did* stop to see your parents." This seemed to
be explanation enough. "I'm terribly sorry to break in on you like this but
I've taken a chill and I wonder if you'd give me a drink."

"Why, I'd *love* to," Helen said, "but there hasn't been anything in this
house to drink since Eric's operation. That was three years ago."

Was he losing his memory, had his gift for concealing painful facts let him forget that he had sold his house, that his children were in trouble, and that his friend had been ill? His eyes slipped from Eric's face to his abdomen, where he saw three pale, sutured scars, two of them at least a foot long. Gone was his navel, and what, Neddy thought, would the roving hand, bedchecking one's gifts at 3 A.M., make of a belly with no navel, no link to birth, this breach in the succession?

"I'm sure you can get a drink at the Biswangers'," Helen said. "They're having an enormous do. You can hear it from here. Listen!"

She raised her head and from across the road, the lawns, the gardens, the woods, the fields, he heard again the brilliant noise of voices over water. "Well, I'll get wet," he said, still feeling that he had no freedom of choice about his means of travel. He dove into the Sachses' cold water, and gasping, close to drowning, made his way from one end of the pool to the other. "Lucinda and I want *terribly* to see you," he said over his shoulder, his face set toward the Biswangers'. "We're sorry it's been so long and we'll call you *very* soon."

He crossed some fields to the Biswangers' and the sounds of revelry there. They would be honored to give him a drink, they would be happy to give him a drink. The Biswangers invited him and Lucinda for dinner four times a year, six weeks in advance. They were always rebuffed and yet they continued to send out their invitations, unwilling to comprehend the rigid and undemocratic realities of their society. They were the sort of people who discussed the price of things at cocktails, exchanged market tips during dinner, and after dinner told dirty stories to mixed company. They did not belong to Neddy's set—they were not even on Lucinda's Christmas card list. He went toward their pool with feelings of indifference, charity, and some unease, since it seemed to be getting dark and these were the longest days of the year. The party when he joined it was noisy and large. Grace Biswanger was the kind of hostess who asked the optometrist, the veterinarian, the real-estate dealer, and the dentist. No one was swimming and the twilight, reflected on the water of the pool, had a wintry gleam. There was a bar and he started for this. When Grace Biswanger saw him she came toward him, not affectionately as he had every right to expect, but bellicosely.

"Why, this party has everything," she said loudly, "including a gate crasher."

She could not deal him a social blow—there was no question about this and he did not flinch. "As a gate crasher," he asked politely, "do I rate a drink?"

"Suit yourself," she said. "You don't seem to pay much attention to invitations."

She turned her back on him and joined some guests, and he went to the bar and ordered a whiskey. The bartender served him but he served him rudely. His was a world in which the caterer's men kept the social score, and to be rebuffed by a part-time barkeep meant that he had suffered some loss of social esteem. Or perhaps the man was new and uninformed. Then he heard Grace at his back say: "They went for broke overnight—nothing but income—and he showed up drunk one Sunday and asked us to loan him five thousand dollars. . . ." She was always talking about money. It was worse than eating your peas off a knife. He dove into the pool, swam its length, and went away.

The next pool on his list, the last but two, belonged to his old mistress, Shirley Adams. If he had suffered any injuries at the Biswangers' they would be cured here. Love—sexual roughhouse in fact—was the supreme elixir, the pain killer, the brightly colored pill that would put the spring back into his step, the joy of life in his heart. They had had an affair last week, last month, last year. He couldn't remember. It was he who had broken it off, his was the upper hand, and he stepped through the gate of the wall that surrounded her pool with nothing so considered as self-confidence. It seemed in a way to be his pool, as the lover, particularly the illicit lover, enjoys the possessions of his mistress with an authority unknown to holy matrimony. She was there, her hair the color of brass, but her figure, at the edge of the lighted, cerulean water, excited in him no profound memories. It had been, he thought, a lighthearted affair, although she had wept when he broke it off. She seemed confused to see him and he wondered if she was still wounded. Would she, God forbid, weep again?

"What do you want?" she asked.

"I'm swimming across the county."   40

"Good Christ. Will you ever grow up?"

"What's the matter?"

"If you've come here for money," she said, "I won't give you another cent."

"You could give me a drink."

"I could but I won't. I'm not alone."   45

"Well, I'm on my way."

He dove in and swam the pool, but when he tried to haul himself up onto the curb he found that the strength in his arms and shoulders had gone, and he paddled to the ladder and climbed out. Looking over his shoulder he saw, in the lighted bathhouse, a young man. Going out onto the dark lawn he smelled chrysanthemums or marigolds—some stubborn autumnal fragrance—on the night air, strong as gas. Looking overhead he saw that the stars had come out, but why should he seem to see Andromeda, Cepheus, and Cassiopeia? What had become of the constellations of midsummer? He began to cry.

It was probably the first time in his adult life that he had ever cried, certainly the first time in his life that he had ever felt so miserable, cold, tired, and bewildered. He could not understand the rudeness of the caterer's barkeep or the rudeness of a mistress who had come to him on her knees and showered his trousers with tears. He had swum too long, he had been immersed too long, and his nose and his throat were sore from the water. What he needed then was a drink, some company, and some clean, dry clothes, and while he could have cut directly across the road to his home he went on to the Gilmartins' pool. Here, for the first time in his life, he did not dive but went down the steps into the icy water and swam a hobbled sidestroke that he might have learned as a youth. He staggered with fatigue on his way to the Clydes' and paddled the length of their pool, stopping again and again with his hand on the curb to rest. He climbed up the ladder and wondered if he had the strength to get home. He had done what he wanted, he had swum the county, but he was so stupefied with exhaustion that his triumph seemed vague. Stooped, holding on to the gateposts for support, he turned up the driveway of his own house.

The place was dark. Was it so late that they had all gone to bed? Had Lucinda stayed at the Westerhazys' for supper? Had the girls joined her there or gone someplace else? Hadn't they agreed, as they usually did on Sunday, to regret all their invitations and stay at home? He tried the garage doors to see what cars were in but the doors were locked and rust came off the handles onto his hands. Going toward the house, he saw the force of the thunderstorm had knocked one of the rain gutters loose. It hung down over the front door like an umbrella rib, but it could be fixed in the morning. The house was locked, and he thought that the stupid cook or the stupid maid must have locked the place up until he remembered that it had been some time since they had employed a maid or a cook. He shouted, pounded on the door, tried to force it with his shoulder, and then, looking in at the windows, saw that the place was empty.

[1964]

JOHN CHEEVER (1912–1982)

The Country Husband

To begin at the beginning, the airplane from Minneapolis in which Francis Weed was traveling East ran into heavy weather. The sky had been a hazy blue, with the clouds below the plane lying so close together that nothing could be seen of the earth. Then mist began to form outside the windows, and they flew into a white cloud of such density that it reflected the exhaust fires. The color of the cloud darkened to gray, and the plane began to rock. Francis had been in heavy weather before, but he had never been shaken up so much. The man in the seat beside him pulled a flask out of his pocket and took a drink. Francis smiled at his neighbor, but the man looked away; he wasn't sharing his painkiller with anyone. The plane had begun to drop and flounder wildly. A child was crying. The air in the cabin was overheated and stale, and Francis' left foot went to sleep. He read a little from a paper book that he had bought at the airport, but the violence of the storm divided his attention. It was black outside the ports. The exhaust fires blazed and shed sparks in the dark, and, inside, the shaded lights, the stuffiness, and the window curtains gave the cabin an atmosphere of intense and misplaced domesticity. Then the lights flickered and went out. "You know what I've always wanted to do?" the man beside Francis said suddenly. "I've always wanted to buy a farm in New Hampshire and raise beef cattle." The stewardess announced that they were going to make an emergency landing. All but the child saw in their minds the spreading wings of the Angel of Death. The pilot could be heard singing faintly, "I've got sixpence, jolly, jolly sixpence, I've got Sixpence to last me all my life. . . ." There was no other sound.

The loud groaning of the hydraulic valves swallowed up the pilot's song, and there was a shrieking high in the air, like automobile brakes, and the plane hit flat on its belly in a cornfield and shook them so violently that an old man up forward howled, "Me kidneys! Me kidneys!" The stewardess flung open the door, and someone opened an emergency door at the back, letting in the sweet noise of their continuing mortality—the idle splash and smell of heavy rain. Anxious for their lives, they filed out of the doors and scattered over the cornfield in all directions, praying that the thread would hold. It did. Nothing happened. When it was clear that the plane would not burn or explode, the crew and stewardess gathered the passengers together and led them to the shelter of a barn. They were not far from Philadelphia, and in a little while a string of taxis took them into the city. "It's just like the Marne," someone said, but there was surprisingly little relaxation of that suspiciousness with which many Americans regard their fellow-travelers.

In Philadelphia, Francis Weed got a train to New York. At the end of that journey, he crossed the city and caught, just as it was about to pull out, the commuting train that he took five nights a week to his home in Shady Hill.

He sat with Trace Bearden. "You know, I was in that plane that just crashed outside Philadelphia," he said. "We came down in a field . . ." He had traveled faster than the newspapers or the rain, and the weather in New York was sunny and mild. It was a day in late September, as fragrant and shapely as an apple. Trace listened to the story, but how could he get excited? Francis had no powers that would let him recreate a brush with death—particularly in the atmosphere of a commuting train, journeying through a sunny countryside where already, in the slum gardens, there were signs of harvest. Trace picked up his newspaper, and Francis was left alone with his thoughts. He said good night to Trace on the platform at Shady Hill and drove in his secondhand Volkswagen up to the Blenhollow neighborhood, where he lived.

The Weeds' Dutch Colonial house was larger than it appeared to be   5
from the driveway. The living room was spacious and divided like Gaul into three parts. Around an ell to the left as one entered from the vestibule was the long table, laid for six, with candles and a bowl of fruit in the center. The sounds and smells that came from the open kitchen door were appetizing, for Julia Weed was a good cook. The largest part of the living room centered around a fireplace. On the right were some bookshelves and a piano. The room was polished and tranquil, and from the windows that opened to the west there was some late summer sunlight, brilliant and as clear as water. Nothing here was neglected; nothing had not been burnished. It was not the kind of household where, after prying open a stuck cigarette box, you would find an old shirt button and a tarnished nickel. The hearth was swept, the roses on the piano were reflected in the polish of the broad top, and there was an album of Schubert waltzes on the rack. Louisa Weed, a pretty girl of nine, was looking out the western windows. Her younger brother Henry was standing beside her. Her still younger brother, Toby, was studying the figures of some tonsured monks drinking beer on the polished brass of the wood box. Francis, taking off his hat and putting down his paper, was not consciously pleased with the scene; he was not that reflective. It was his element, his creation, and he returned to it with that sense of lightness and strength with which any creature returns to its home. "Hi, everybody," he said. "The plane from Minneapolis . . ."

Nine times out of ten, Francis would be greeted with affection, but tonight the children are absorbed in their own antagonisms. Francis has not finished his sentence about the plane crash before Henry plants a kick in Louisa's behind. Louisa swings around, saying, "*Damn* you!" Francis makes the mistake of scolding Louisa for bad language before he punishes Henry. Now Louisa turns on her father and accuses him of favoritism. Henry is always right; she is persecuted and lonely; her lot is hopeless. Francis turns to his son, but the boy has justification for the kick—she hit

him first; she hit him on the ear, which is dangerous. Louisa agrees with this
passionately. She hit him on the ear, and she *meant* to hit him on the ear,
because he messed up her china collection. Henry says that this is a lie. Little Toby turns away from the wood box to throw in some evidence for
Louisa. Henry claps his hand over little Toby's mouth. Francis separates the
two boys but accidentally pushes Toby into the wood box. Toby begins to
cry. Louisa is already crying. Just then, Julia Weed comes into that part of
the room where the table is laid. She is a pretty, intelligent woman, and the
white in her hair is premature. She does not seem to notice the fracas.
"Hello, darling," she says serenely to Francis. "Wash your hands, everyone.
Dinner is ready." She strikes a match and lights the six candles in this vale of
tears.

This simple announcement, like the war cries of the Scottish chief-
tains, only refreshes the ferocity of the combatants. Louisa gives Henry a
blow on the shoulder. Henry, although he seldom cries, has pitched nine
innings and is tired. He bursts into tears. Little Toby discovers a splinter in
his hand and begins to howl. Francis says loudly that he has been in a plane
crash and that he is tired. Julia appears again, from the kitchen, and, still
ignoring the chaos, asks Francis to go upstairs and tell Helen that everything is ready. Francis is happy to go; it is like getting back to headquarters
company. He is planning to tell his oldest daughter about the airplane
crash, but Helen is lying on her bed reading a *True Romance* magazine, and
the first thing Francis does is to take the magazine from her hand and
remind Helen that he has forbidden her to buy it. She did not buy it, Helen
replies. It was given to her by her best friend, Bessie Black. Everybody reads
True Romance. Bessie Black's father reads *True Romance*. There isn't a girl
in Helen's class who doesn't read *True Romance*. Francis expresses his
detestation of the magazine and then tells her that dinner is ready—
although from the sounds downstairs it doesn't seem so. Helen follows him
down the stairs. Julia has seated herself in the candlelight and spread a napkin over her lap. Neither Louisa nor Henry has come to the table. Little Toby
is still howling, lying face down on the floor. Francis speaks to him gently.
"Daddy was in a plane crash this afternoon, Toby. Don't you want to hear
about it?" Toby goes on crying. "If you don't come to the table now, Toby,"
Francis says, "I'll have to send you to bed without any supper." The little boy
rises, gives him a cutting look, flies up the stairs to his bedroom, and slams
the door. "Oh dear," Julia says, and starts to go after him. Francis says that she
will spoil him. Julia says that Toby is ten pounds underweight and has to be
encouraged to eat. Winter is coming, and he will spend the cold months in
bed unless he has his dinner. Julia goes upstairs. Francis sits down at the
table with Helen. Helen is suffering from the dismal feeling of having read
too intently on a fine day, and she gives her father and the room a jaded
look. She doesn't understand about the plane crash, because there wasn't a
drop of rain in Shady Hill.

Julia returns with Toby, and they all sit down and are served. "Do I have
to look at that big, fat slob?" Henry says, of Louisa. Everybody but Toby
enters into this skirmish, and it rages up and down the table for five minutes. Toward the end, Henry puts his napkin over his head and, trying to eat
that way, spills spinach all over his shirt. Francis asks Julia if the children
couldn't have their dinner earlier. Julia's guns are loaded for this. She can't
cook two dinners and lay two tables. She paints with lightning strokes that

panorama of drudgery in which her youth, her beauty, and her wit have been lost. Francis says that he must be understood; he was nearly killed in an airplane crash, and he doesn't like to come home every night to a battlefield. Now Julia is deeply committed. Her voice trembles. He doesn't come home every night to a battlefield. The accusation is stupid and mean. Everything was tranquil until he arrived. She stops speaking, puts down her knife and fork, and looks into her plate as if it is a gulf. She begins to cry. "Poor Mummy!" Toby says, and when Julia gets up from the table, drying her tears with a napkin, Toby goes to her side. "Poor Mummy," he says. "Poor Mummy!" And they climb the stairs together. The other children drift away from the battlefield, and Francis goes into the back garden for a cigarette and some air.

It was a pleasant garden, with walks and flower beds and places to sit. The sunset had nearly burned out, but there was still plenty of light. Put into a thoughtful mood by the crash and the battle, Francis listened to the evening sounds of Shady Hill. "Varmints! Rascals!" old Mr. Nixon shouted to the squirrels in his bird-feeding station. "Avaunt and quit my sight!" A door slammed. Someone was playing tennis on the Babcocks' court; someone was cutting grass. Then Donald Goslin, who lived at the corner, began to play the "Moonlight Sonata." He did this nearly every night. He threw the tempo out the window and played it *rubato*—from beginning to end, like an outpouring of tearful petulance, lonesomeness, and self-pity—of everything it was Beethoven's greatness not to know. The music rang up and down the street beneath the trees like an appeal for love, for tenderness, aimed at some lonely housemaid—some freshfaced, homesick girl from Galway, looking at old snapshots in her third-floor room. "Here, Jupiter, here, Jupiter," Francis called to the Mercers' retriever. Jupiter crashed through the tomato vines with the remains of a felt hat in his mouth.

Jupiter was an anomaly. His retrieving instincts and his high spirits were out of place in Shady Hill. He was as black as coal, with a long, alert, intelligent, rake-hell face. His eyes gleamed with mischief, and he held his head high. It was the fierce, heavily collared dog's head that appears in heraldry, in tapestry, and that used to appear on umbrella handles and walking sticks. Jupiter went where he pleased, ransacking wastebaskets, clotheslines, garbage pails, and shoe bags. He broke up garden parties and tennis matches, and got mixed up in the processional at Christ Church on Sunday, barking at the men in red dresses. He crashed through old Mr. Nixon's rose garden two or three times a day, cutting a wide swath through the Condesa de Sastagos, and as soon as Donald Goslin lighted his barbecue fire on Thursday nights, Jupiter would get the scent. Nothing the Goslins did could drive him away. Sticks and stones and rude commands only moved him to the edge of the terrace, where he remained, with his gallant and heraldic muzzle, waiting for Donald Goslin to turn his back and reach for the salt. Then he would spring onto the terrace, lift the steak lightly off the fire, and run away with the Goslins' dinner. Jupiter's days were numbered. The Wrightsons' German gardener or the Farquarsons' cook would soon poison him. Even old Mr. Nixon might put some arsenic in the garbage that Jupiter loved. "Here, Jupiter, Jupiter!" Francis called, but the dog pranced off, shaking the hat in his white teeth. Looking in at the windows of his house, Francis saw that Julia had come down and was blowing out the candles.

Julia and Francis Weed went out a great deal. Julia was well liked and gregarious, and her love of parties sprang from a most natural dread of chaos and loneliness. She went through her morning mail with real anxiety, looking for invitations, and she usually found some, but she was insatiable, and if she had gone out seven nights a week, it would not have cured her of a reflective look—the look of someone who hears distant music—for she would always suppose that there was a more brilliant party somewhere else. Francis limited her to two week-night parties, putting a flexible interpretation on Friday, and rode through the weekend like a dory in a gale. The day after the airplane crash, the Weeds were to have dinner with the Farquarsons.

Francis got home late from town, and Julia got the sitter while he dressed, and then hurried him out of the house. The party was small and pleasant, and Francis settled down to enjoy himself. A new maid passed the drinks. Her hair was dark, and her face was round and pale and seemed familiar to Francis. He had not developed his memory as a sentimental faculty. Wood smoke, lilac, and other such perfumes did not stir him, and his memory was something like his appendix—a vestigial repository. It was not his limitation at all to be unable to escape the past; it was perhaps his limitation that he had escaped it so successfully. He might have seen the maid at other parties, he might have seen her taking a walk on Sunday afternoons, but in either case, he would not be searching his memory now. Her face was, in a wonderful way, a moon face—Norman or Irish—but it was not beautiful enough to account for his feeling that he had seen her before, in circumstances that he ought to be able to remember. He asked Nellie Farquarson who she was. Nellie said that the maid had come through an agency, and that her home was Trénon, in Normandy—a small place with a church and a restaurant that Nellie had once visited. While Nellie talked on about her travels abroad, Francis realized where he had seen the woman before. It had been at the end of the war. He had left a replacement depot with some other men and taken a three-day pass in Trénon. On their second day, they had walked out to a crossroads to see the public chastisement of a young woman who had lived with the German commandant during the Occupation.

It was a cool morning in the fall. The sky was overcast, and poured down onto the dirt crossroads a very discouraging light. They were on high land and could see how like one another the shapes of the clouds and the hills were as they stretched off toward the sea. The prisoner arrived sitting on a three-legged stool in a farm cart. She stood by the cart while the mayor read the accusation and the sentence. Her head was bent and her face was set in that empty half smile behind which the whipped soul is suspended. When the mayor was finished, she undid her hair and let it fall across her back. A little man with a gray mustache cut off her hair with shears and dropped it on the ground. Then, with a bowl of soapy water and a straight razor, he shaved her skull clean. A woman approached and began to undo the fastening of her clothes, but the prisoner pushed her aside and undressed herself. When she pulled her chemise over her head and threw it on the ground, she was naked. The women jeered; the men were still. There was no change in the falseness or the plaintiveness of the prisoner's smile. The cold wind made her white skin rough and hardened the nipples of her breasts. The jeering ended gradually, put down by the recognition of their common humanity. One woman spat on her, but some inviolable grandeur in her nakedness lasted through the ordeal. When the crowd was quiet, she turned—she had begun to cry—and, with nothing on but a pair of worn black shoes and stockings, walked down the dirt road alone away from the village. The round white face had aged a little, but there was no question but that the maid who passed his cocktails and later served Francis his dinner was the woman who had been punished at the crossroads.

The war seemed now so distant and that world where the cost of partisanship had been death or torture so long ago. Francis had lost track of the men who had been with him in Vésey. He could not count on Julia's discretion. He could not tell anyone. And if he had told the story now, at the dinner table, it would have been a social as well as a human error. The people in the Farquarsons' living room seemed united in their tacit claim that there had been no past, no war—that there was no danger or trouble in the world. In the recorded history of human arrangements, this extraordinary meeting would have fallen into place, but the atmosphere of Shady Hill made the memory unseemly and impolite. The prisoner withdrew after passing the coffee, but the encounter left Francis feeling languid; it had opened his memory and his senses, and left them dilated. He and Julia drove home when the party ended, and Julia went into the house. Francis stayed in the car to take the sitter home.

Expecting to see Mrs. Henlein, the old lady who usually stayed with the children, he was surprised when a young girl opened the door and came out onto the lighted stoop. She stayed in the light to count her textbooks. She was frowning and beautiful. Now, the world is full of beautiful young girls, but Francis saw here the difference between beauty and perfection. All those endearing flaws, moles, birthmarks, and healed wounds were missing, and he experienced in his consciousness that moment when music breaks glass, and felt a pang of recognition as strange, deep, and wonderful as anything in his life. It hung from her frown, from an impalpable darkness in her face—a look that impressed him as a direct appeal for love. When she had counted her books, she came down the steps and opened the car door. In the light, he saw that her cheeks were wet. She got in and shut the door.

"You're new," Francis said.

"Yes. Mrs. Henlein is sick; I'm Anne Murchison."

"Did the children give you any trouble?"

"Oh, no, no." She turned and smiled at him unhappily in the dim dashboard light. Her light hair caught on the collar of her jacket, and she shook her head to set it loose.

"You've been crying."

"Yes."

"I hope it was nothing that happened in our house."

"No, no, it was nothing that happened in your house." Her voice was bleak. "It's no secret. Everybody in the village knows. Daddy's an alcoholic, and he just called me from some saloon and gave me a piece of his mind. He thinks I'm immoral. He called just before Mrs. Weed came back."

"I'm sorry."

"Oh, *Lord!*" She gasped and began to cry. She turned toward Francis, and he took her in his arms and let her cry on his shoulder. She shook in his embrace, and this movement accentuated his sense of the fineness of her flesh and bone. The layers of their clothing felt thin, and when her shuddering began to diminish, it was so much like a paroxysm of love that Francis lost his head and pulled her roughly against him. She drew away. "I live on Belleview Avenue," she said. "You go down Lansing Street to the railroad bridge."

"All right." He started the car.

"You turn left at that traffic light. . . . Now you turn right here and go straight on toward the tracks."

The road Francis took brought him out of his own neighborhood, across the tracks, and toward the river, to a street where the near-poor lived, in houses whose peaked gables and trimmings of wooden lace conveyed the purest feelings of pride and romance, although the houses themselves could not have offered much privacy or comfort, they were all so small. The street was dark, and, stirred by the grace and beauty of the troubled girl, he seemed, in turning in to it, to have come to the deepest part of some submerged memory. In the distance, he saw a porch light burning. It was the only one, and she said that the house with the light was where she lived. When he stopped the car, he could see beyond the porch light into a dimly lighted hallway with an old-fashioned clothes tree. "Well, here we are," he said, conscious that a young man would have said something different.

She did not move her hands from the books, where they were folded, and she turned and faced him. There were tears of lust in his eyes. Determinedly—not sadly—he opened the door on his side and walked around to open hers. He took her free hand, letting his fingers in between hers, climbed at her side the two concrete steps, and went up a narrow walk through a front garden where dahlias, marigolds, and roses—things that had withstood the light frosts—still bloomed, and made a bittersweet smell in the night air. At the steps, she freed her hand and then turned and kissed him swiftly. Then she crossed the porch and shut the door. The porch light went out, then the light in the hall. A second later, a light went on upstairs at the side of the house, shining into a tree that was still covered with leaves. It took her only a few minutes to undress and get into bed, and then the house was dark.

Julia was asleep when Francis got home. He opened a second window and got into bed to shut his eyes on that night, but as soon as they were shut—as soon as he had dropped off to sleep—the girl entered his mind, moving with perfect freedom through its shut doors and filling chamber after chamber with her light, her perfume, and the music of her voice. He was crossing the Atlantic with her on the old *Mauritania* and, later, living with her in Paris. When he woke from his dream, he got up and smoked a cigarette at the open window. Getting back into bed, he cast around in his mind for something he desired to do that would injure no one, and he thought of skiing. Up through the dimness in his mind rose the image of a mountain deep in snow. It was late in the day. Wherever his eyes looked, he saw broad and heartening things. Over his shoulder, there was a snow-filled valley, rising into wooded hills where the trees dimmed the whiteness like a sparse coat of hair. The cold deadened all sound but the loud, iron clanking of the lift machinery. The light on the trails was blue, and it was harder than it had been a minute or two earlier to pick the turns, harder to judge—now that the snow was all deep blue—the crust, the ice, the bare spots, and the deep piles of dry powder. Down the mountain he

30

swung, matching his speed against the contours of a slope that had been formed in the first ice age, seeking with ardor some simplicity of feeling and circumstance. Night fell then, and he drank a Martini with some old friend in a dirty country bar.

In the morning, Francis' snow-covered mountain was gone, and he was left with his vivid memories of Paris and the *Mauritania*. He had been bitten gravely. He washed his body, shaved his jaws, drank his coffee, and missed the seven-thirty-one. The train pulled out just as he brought his car to the station, and the longing he felt for the coaches as they drew stubbornly away from him reminded him of the humors of love. He waited for the eight-two, on what was now an empty platform. It was a clear morning; the morning seemed thrown like a gleaming bridge of light over his mixed affairs. His spirits were feverish and high. The image of the girl seemed to put him into relationship to the world that was mysterious and enthralling. Cars were beginning to fill up the parking lot, and he noticed that those that had driven down from the high land above Shady Hill were white with hoarfrost. The first clear sign of autumn thrilled him. An express train—a night train from Buffalo or Albany—came down the tracks between the platforms, and he saw that the roofs of the foremost cars were covered with a skin of ice. Struck by the miraculous physicalness of everything, he smiled at the passengers in the dining car, who could be seen eating eggs and wiping their mouths with napkins as they traveled. The sleeping car compartments, with their soiled bed linen, trailed through the fresh morning like a string of rooming-house windows. Then he saw an extraordinary thing: at one of the bedroom windows sat an unclothed woman of exceptional beauty, combing her golden hair. She passed like an apparition through Shady Hill, combing and combing her hair, and Francis followed her with his eyes until she was out of sight. Then old Mrs. Wrightson joined him on the platform and began to talk.

"Well, I guess you must be surprised to see me here the third morning in a row," she said, "but because of my window curtains I'm becoming a regular commuter. The curtains I bought on Monday, I returned on Tuesday, and the curtains I bought on Tuesday I'm returning today. On Monday, I got exactly what I wanted—it's a wool tapestry with roses and birds—but when I got them home, I found they were the wrong length. Well, I exchanged them yesterday, and when I got them home, I found they were still the wrong length. Now I'm praying to high Heaven that the decorator will have them in the right length, because you know my house, you *know* my living room windows, and you can imagine what a problem they present. I don't know what to do with them."

"I know what to do with them," Francis said.

"What?"

"Paint them black on the inside, and shut up."

There was a gasp from Mrs. Wrightson, and Francis looked down at her to be sure that she knew he meant to be rude. She turned and walked away from him, so damaged in spirit that she limped. A wonderful feeling enveloped him, as if light were being shaken about him, and he thought again of Venus combing and combing her hair as she drifted through the Bronx. The realization of how many years had passed since he had enjoyed being deliberately impolite sobered him. Among his friends and

35

neighbors, there were brilliant and gifted people—he saw that—but many of them, also, were bores and fools, and he had made the mistake of listening to them all with equal attention. He had confused a lack of discrimination with Christian love, and the confusion seemed general and destructive. He was grateful to the girl for this bracing sensation of independence. Birds were singing—cardinals and the last of the robins. The sky shone like enamel. Even the smell of ink from his morning paper honed his appetite for life, and the world that was spread out around him was plainly a paradise.

If Francis had believed in some hierarchy of love—in spirits armed with hunting bows, in the capriciousness of Venus and Eros—or even in magical potions, philters, and stews, in scapulae and quarters of the moon, it might have explained his susceptibility and his feverish high spirits. The autumnal loves of middle age are well publicized, and he guessed that he was face to face with one of these, but there was not a trace of autumn in what he felt. He wanted to sport in the green woods, scratch where he itched, and drink from the same cup.

His secretary, Miss Rainey, was late that morning—she went to a psychiatrist three mornings a week—and when she came in, Francis wondered what advice a psychiatrist would have for him. But the girl promised to bring back into his life something like the sound of music. The realization that this music might lead him straight to a trial for statutory rape at the county courthouse collapsed his happiness. The photograph of his four children laughing into the camera on the beach at Gay Head reproached him. On the letterhead of his firm there was a drawing of the Laocoön, and the figure of the priest and his sons in the coils of the snakes appeared to him to have the deepest meaning.

He had lunch with Pinky Trabert. At a conversational level, the mores of his friends were robust and elastic, but he knew that the moral card house would come down on them all—on Julia and the children as well— if he got caught taking advantage of a babysitter. Looking back over the recent history of Shady Hill for some precedent, he found there was none. There was no turpitude; there had not been a divorce since he lived there; there had not even been a breath of scandal. Things seemed arranged with more propriety even than in the Kingdom of Heaven. After leaving Pinky, Francis went to the jeweler's and bought the girl a bracelet. How happy this clandestine purchase made him, how stuffy and comical the jeweler's clerks seemed, how sweet the woman who passed at his back smelled. On Fifth Avenue, passing Atlas with his shoulders bent under the weight of the world, Francis thought of the strenuousness of containing his physicalness within the patterns he had chosen.

He did not know when he would see the girl next. He had the bracelet   40
in his inside pocket when he got home. Opening the door of his house, he found her in the hall. Her back was to him, and she turned when she heard the door close. Her smile was open and loving. Her perfection stunned him like a fine day—a day after a thunderstorm. He seized her and covered her lips with his, and she struggled but she did not have to struggle for long, because just then little Gertrude Flannery appeared from somewhere and said, "Oh, Mr. Weed . . ."

Gertrude was a stray. She had been born with a taste for exploration, and she did not have it in her to center her life with her affectionate parents.

People who did not know the Flannery's concluded from Gertrude's behavior that she was the child of a bitterly divided family, where drunken quarrels were the rule. This was not true. The fact that little Gertrude's clothing was ragged and thin was her own triumph over her mother's struggle to dress her warmly and neatly. Garrulous, skinny, and unwashed, she drifted from house to house around the Blenhollow neighborhood, forming and breaking alliances based on an attachment to babies, animals, children her own age, adolescents, and sometimes adults. Opening your front door in the morning, you would find Gertrude sitting on your stoop. Going into the bathroom to shave, you would find Gertrude using the toilet. Looking into your son's crib, you would find it empty, and, looking further, you would find that Gertrude had pushed him in his baby carriage into the next village. She was helpful, pervasive, honest, hungry, and loyal. She never went home of her own choice. When the time to go arrived, she was indifferent to all its signs. "Go home, Gertrude," people could be heard saying in one house or another, night after night. "Go home, Gertrude. It's time for you to go home now, Gertrude." "You had better go home and get your supper, Gertrude." "I told you to go home twenty minutes ago, Gertrude." "Your mother will be worrying about your Gertrude." "Go home, Gertrude, go home."

There are times when the lines around the human eye seem like shelves of eroded stone and when the staring eye itself strikes us with such a wilderness of animal feeling that we are at a loss. The look Francis gave the little girl was ugly and queer, and it frightened her. He reached into his pocket—his hands were shaking and took out a quarter. "Go home, Gertrude, go home, and don't tell anyone, Gertrude. Don't—" He choked and ran into the living room as Julia called down to him from upstairs to hurry and dress.

The thought that he would drive Anne Murchison home later that night ran like a golden thread through the events of the party that Francis and Julia went to, and he laughed uproariously at dull jokes, dried a tear when Mabel Mercer told him about the death of her kitten, and stretched, yawned, sighed, and grunted like any other man with a rendezvous at the back of his mind. The bracelet was in his pocket. As he sat talking, the smell of grass was in his nose, and he was wondering where he would park the car. Nobody lived in the old Parker mansion, and the driveway was used as a lovers' lane. Townsend Street was a dead end, and he could park there, beyond the last house. The old lane that used to connect Elm Street to the riverbanks was overgrown, but he had walked there with his children, and he could drive his car deep enough into the brushwoods to be concealed.

The Weeds were the last to leave the party, and their host and hostess spoke of their own married happiness while they all four stood in the hallway saying good night. "She's my girl," their host said, squeezing his wife. "She's my blue sky. After sixteen years, I still bite her shoulders. She makes me feel like Hannibal crossing the Alps."

The Weeds drove home in silence. Francis brought the car up the driveway and sat still, with the motor running. "You can put the car in the garage," Julia said as she got out. "I told the Murchison girl she could leave at eleven. Someone drove her home." She shut the door, and Francis sat in the dark. He would be spared nothing then, it seemed, that a fool was not

45

spared: ravening lewdness, jealousy, this hurt to his feelings that put tears in his eyes, even scorn—for he could see clearly the image he now presented, his arms spread over the steering wheel and his head buried in them for love.

Francis had been a dedicated Boy Scout when he was young, and, remembering the precepts of his youth, he left his office early the next afternoon and played some round robin squash, but, with his body toned up by exercise and a shower, he realized that he might better have stayed at his desk. It was a frosty night when he got home. The air smelled sharply of change. When he stepped into the house, he sensed an unusual stir. The children were in their best clothes, and when Julia came down, she was wearing a lavender dress and her diamond sunburst. She explained the stir. Mr. Hubber was coming at seven to take their photograph for the Christmas card. She had put out Francis' blue suit and a tie with some color in it, because the picture was going to be in color this year. Julia was lighthearted at the thought of being photographed for Christmas. It was the kind of ceremony she enjoyed.

Francis went upstairs to change his clothes. He was tired from the day's work and tired with longing and sitting on the edge of the bed had the effect of deepening his weariness. He thought of Anne Murchison, and the physical need to express himself instead of being restrained by the pink lamps on Julia's dressing table, engulfed him. He went to Julia's desk, took a piece of writing paper, and began to write on it. "Dear Anne, I love you, I love you, I love you . . ." No one would see the letter, and he used no restraint. He used phrases like "heavenly bliss," and "love nest." He salivated, sighed, and trembled. When Julia called him to come down, the abyss between his fantasy and the practical world opened so wide that he felt it affect the muscles of his heart.

Julia and the children were on the stoop, and the photographer and his assistant had set up a double battery of floodlights to show the family and the architectural beauty of the entrance to their house. People who had come home on a late train slowed their cars to see the Weeds being photographed for their Christmas card. A few waved and called to the family. It took half an hour of smiling and wetting their lips before Mr. Hubber was satisfied. The heat of the lights made an unfresh smell in the frosty air, and when they were turned off, they lingered on the retina of Francis' eyes.

Later that night, while Francis and Julia were drinking their coffee in the living room, the doorbell rang. Julia answered the door and let in Clayton Thomas. He had come to pay her for some theater tickets that she had given his mother some time ago, and that Helen Thomas had scrupulously insisted on paying for, though Julia had asked her not to. Julia invited him in to have a cup of coffee. "I won't have any coffee," Clayton said, "but I will come in for a minute." He followed her into the living room, said good evening to Francis, and sat awkwardly in a chair.

Clayton's father had been killed in the war, and the young man's fatherlessness surrounded him like an element. This may have been conspicuous in Shady Hill because the Thomases were the only family that lacked a piece; all the other marriages were intact and productive. Clayton was in his second or third year of college, and he and his mother lived alone in a large house, which she hoped to sell. Clayton had once made some

50

trouble. Years ago, he had stolen some money and run away; he had got to
California before they caught up with him. He was tall and homely, wore
horn-rimmed glasses, and spoke in a deep voice.

"When do you go back to college, Clayton?" Francis asked.

"I'm not going back," Clayton said. "Mother doesn't have the money,
and there's no sense in all this pretense. I'm going to get a job, and if we sell
the house, we'll take an apartment in New York."

"Won't you miss Shady Hill?" Julia asked.

"No," Clayton said. "I don't like it."

"Why not?" Francis asked.   55

"Well, there's a lot here I don't approve of," Clayton said gravely. "Things
like the club dances. Last Saturday night, I looked in toward the end and
saw Mr. Granner trying to put Mrs. Minot into the trophy case. They were
both drunk. I disapprove of so much drinking."

"It was Saturday night," Francis said.

"And all the dovecotes are phony," Clayton said. "And the way people
clutter up their lives. I've thought about it a lot, and what seems to me to be
really wrong with Shady Hill is that it doesn't have any future. So much
energy is spent in perpetuating the place—in keeping out undesirables,
and so forth—that the only idea of the future anyone has is just more and
more commuting trains and more parties. I don't think that's healthy. I think
people ought to be able to dream big dreams about the future. I think people ought to be able to dream great dreams."

"It's too bad you couldn't continue with college," Julia said.

"I wanted to go to divinity school," Clayton said.   60

"What's your church?" Francis asked.

"Unitarian, Theosophist, Transcendentalist, Humanist," Clayton said.

"Wasn't Emerson a transcendentalist?" Julia asked.

"I mean the English transcendentalists," Clayton said. "All the American
transcendentalists were goops."

"What kind of job do you expect to get?" Francis asked.   65

"Well, I'd like to work for a publisher," Clayton said, "but everyone tells
me there's nothing doing. But it's the kind of thing I'm interested in. I'm
writing a long verse play about good and evil. Uncle Charlie might get me
into a bank, and that would be good for me. I need the discipline. I have a
long way to go in forming my character. I have some terrible habits. I talk
too much. I think I ought to take vows of silence. I ought to try not to speak
for a week, and discipline myself. I've thought of making a retreat at one of
the Episcopalian monasteries, but I don't like Trinitarianism."

"Do you have any girl friends?" Francis asked.

"I'm engaged to be married," Clayton said. "Of course, I'm not old
enough or rich enough to have my engagement observed or respected or
anything, but I bought a simulated emerald for Anne Murchison with the
money I made cutting lawns this summer. We're going to be married as
soon as she finishes school."

Francis recoiled at the mention of the girl's name. Then a dingy light
seemed to emanate from his spirit, showing everything—Julia, the boy, the
chairs—in their true colorlessness. It was like a bitter turn of the weather.

"We're going to have a large family," Clayton said. "Her father's a terrible   70
rummy, and I've had my hard times, and we want to have lots of children.
Oh, she's wonderful, Mr. and Mrs. Weed, and we have so much in common.

We like all the same things. We sent out the same Christmas card last year without planning it, and we both have an allergy to tomatos, and our eyebrows grow together in the middle. Well, good night."

Julia went to the door with him. When she returned, Francis said that Clayton was lazy, irresponsible, affected, and smelly. Julia said that Francis seemed to be getting intolerant; the Thomas boy was young and should be given a chance. Julia had noticed other cases where Francis had been short-tempered. "Mrs. Wrightson has asked everyone in Shady Hill to her anniversary party but us," she said.

"I'm sorry, Julia."

"Do you know why they didn't ask us?"

"Why?"

"Because you insulted Mrs. Wrightson."   75

"Then you know about it?"

"June Masterson told me. She was standing behind you."

Julia walked in front of the sofa with a small step that expressed, Francis knew, a feeling of anger.

"I did insult Mrs. Wrightson, Julia, and I meant to. I've never liked her parties, and I'm glad she's dropped us."

"What about Helen?"   80

"How does Helen come into this?"

"Mrs. Wrightson's the one who decides who goes to the assemblies."

"You mean she can keep Helen from going to the dances?"

"Yes."

"I hadn't thought of that."   85

"Oh, I knew you hadn't thought of it," Julia cried, thrusting hilt-deep into this chink of his armor. "And it makes me furious to see this kind of stupid thoughtlessness wreck everyone's happiness."

"I don't think I've wrecked anyone's happiness."

"Mrs. Wrightson runs Shady Hill and has run it for the last forty years. I don't know what makes you think that in a community like this you can indulge every impulse you have to be insulting, vulgar, and offensive."

"I have very good manners," Francis said, trying to give the evening a turn toward the light.

"Damn you, Francis Weed!" Julia cried, and the spit of her words struck   90
him in the face. "I've worked hard for the social position we enjoy in this place, and I won't stand by and see you wreck it. You must have understood when you settled here that you couldn't expect to live like a bear in a cave."

"I've got to express my likes and dislikes."

"You can conceal your dislikes. You don't have to meet everything head on, like a child. Unless you're anxious to be a social leper. It's no accident that we get asked out a great deal. It's no accident that Helen has so many friends. How would you like to spend your Saturday nights at the movies? How would you like to spend your Sundays raking up dead leaves? How would you like it if your daughter spent the assembly nights sitting at her window, listening to the music from the club? How would you like it—" He did something then that was, after all, not so unaccountable, since her words seemed to raise up between them a wall so deadening that he gagged: He struck her full in the face. She staggered and then, a moment later, seemed composed. She went up the stairs to their room. She didn't slam the door. When Francis followed, a few minutes later, he found her packing a suitcase.

"Julia, I'm very sorry."

"It doesn't matter," she said. She was crying.

"Where do you think you're going?"   95

"I don't know. I just looked at a timetable. There's an eleven-sixteen into New York. I'll take that."

"You can't go, Julia."

"I can't stay. I know that."

"I'm sorry about Mrs. Wrightson, Julia, and I'm—"

"It doesn't matter about Mrs. Wrightson. That isn't the trouble."   100

"What is the trouble?"

"You don't love me."

"I do love you, Julia."

"No, you don't."

"Julia, I do love you, and I would like to be as we were—sweet and   105
bawdy and dark—but now there are so many people."

"You hate me."

"I don't hate you, Julia."

"You have no idea of how much you hate me. I think it's subconscious. You don't realize the cruel things you've done."

"What cruel things, Julia?"

"The cruel acts your subconscious drives you to in order to express   110
your hatred of me."

"What, Julia?"

"I've never complained."

"Tell me."

"You don't know what you're doing."

"Tell me."   115

"Your clothes."

"What do you mean?"

"I mean the way you leave your dirty clothes around in order to express your subconscious hatred of me."

"I don't understand."

"I mean your dirty socks and your dirty pajamas and your dirty under-   120
wear and your dirty shirts!" She rose from kneeling by the suitcase and faced him, her eyes blazing and her voice ringing with emotion. "I'm talking about the fact that you've never learned to hang up anything. You just leave your clothes all over the floor where they drop, in order to humiliate me. You do it on purpose!" She fell on the bed, sobbing . . .

"Julia, darling!" he said, but when she felt his hand on her shoulder she got up.

"Leave me alone," she said. "I have to go." She brushed past him to the closet and came back with a dress. "I'm not taking any of the things you've given me," she said. "I'm leaving my pearls and the fur jacket."

"Oh, Julia!" Her figure, so helpless in its self-deceptions, bent over the suitcase made him nearly sick with pity. She did not understand how desolate her life would be without him. She didn't understand the hours that working women have to keep. She didn't understand that most of her friendships existed within the framework of their marriage, and that without this she would find herself alone. She didn't understand about travel, about hotels, about money. "Julia, I can't let you go! What you don't understand, Julia, is that you've come to be dependent on me."

She tossed her head back and covered her face with her hands. "Did you say that *I* was dependent on *you?*" she asked. "Is that what you said? And who is it that tells you what time to get up in the morning and when to go to bed at night? Who is it that prepares your meals and picks up your dirty clothes and invites your friends to dinner? If it weren't for me, your neckties would be greasy and your clothing would be full of moth holes. You were alone when I met you, Francis Weed, and you'll be alone when I leave. When Mother asked you for a list to send out invitations to our wedding, how many names did you have to give her? Fourteen!"

"Cleveland wasn't my home, Julia."   125

"And how many of your friends came to the church? Two!"

"Cleveland wasn't my home, Julia."

"Since I'm not taking the fur jacket," she said quietly, "you'd better put it back into storage. There's an insurance policy on the pearls that comes due in January. The name of the laundry and the maid's telephone number— all those things are in my desk. I hope you won't drink too much, Francis. I hope that nothing bad will happen to you. If you do get into serious trouble, you can call me."

"Oh, my darling, I can't let you go!" Francis said. "I can't let you go, Julia!" He took her in his arms.

"I guess I'd better stay and take care of you for a little while longer," she   130
said.

Riding to work in the morning, Francis saw the girl walk down the aisle of the coach. He was surprised; he hadn't realized that the school she went to was in the city, but she was carrying books, she seemed to be going to school. His surprise delayed his reaction, but then he got up clumsily and stepped into the aisle. Several people had come between them, but he could see her ahead of him, waiting for someone to open the car door, and then, as the train swerved, putting out her hand to support herself as she crossed the platform into the next car. He followed her through that car and halfway through another before calling her name—"Anne! Anne!"— but she didn't turn. He followed her into still another car, and she sat down in an aisle seat. Coming up to her, all his feelings warm and bent in her direction, he put his hand on the back of her seat—even this touch warmed him—and, leaning down to speak to her, he saw that it was not Anne. It was an older woman wearing glasses. He went on deliberately into another car, his face red with embarrassment and the much deeper feeling of having his good sense challenged; for if he couldn't tell one person from another, what evidence was there that his life with Julia and the children had as much reality as his dreams of iniquity in Paris or the litter, the grass smell, and the cave-shaped trees in Lovers' Lane.

Late that afternoon, Julia called to remind Francis that they were going out for dinner. A few minutes later, Trace Bearden called. "Look, fellar," Trace said, "I'm calling for Mrs. Thomas. You know? Clayton, that boy of hers, doesn't seem able to get a job, and I wondered if you could help. If you'd call Charlie Bell—I know he's indebted to you—and say a good word for the kid, I think Charlie would—"

"Trace, I hate to say this," Francis said, "but I don't feel that I can do anything for that boy. The kid's worthless. I know it's a harsh thing to say, but it's a fact. Any kindness done for him would backfire in everybody's face. He's just a worthless kid, Trace, and there's nothing to be done about it. Even if we got him a job, he wouldn't be able to keep it for a week. I know that to be a fact. It's an awful thing, Trace, and I know it is, but instead of recommending that kid, I'd feel obliged to warn people against him— people who knew his father and would naturally want to step in and do something. I'd feel obliged to warn them. He's a thief . . ."

The moment this conversation was finished, Miss Rainey came in and stood by his desk. "I'm not going to be able to work for you any more, Mr. Weed," she said. "I can stay until the seventeenth if you need me, but I've been offered a whirlwind of a job, and I'd like to leave as soon as possible."

She went out leaving him to face alone the wickedness of what he had done to the Thomas boy. His children in their photograph laughed and laughed, glazed with all the bright colors of summer, and he remembered that they had met a bag-piper on the beach that day and he had paid the piper a dollar to play them a battle song of the Black Watch. The girl would be at the house when he got home. He would spend another evening among his kind neighbors, picking and choosing dead-end streets, cart tracks, and the drive-ways of abandoned houses. There was nothing to mitigate his feeling— nothing that laughter or a game of softball with the children would change—and, thinking back over the plane crash, the Farquarsons' new maid; and Anne Murchison's difficulties with her drunken father, he won-dered how he could have avoided arriving at just where he was. He was in trouble. He had been lost once in his life, coming back from a trout stream in the north woods, and he had now the same bleak realization that no amount of cheerfulness or hopefulness or valor or perseverance could help him find, in the gathering dark, the path that he'd lost. He smelled the for-est. The feeling of bleakness was intolerable, and he saw clearly that he had reached the point where he would have to make a choice.

He could go to a psychiatrist, like Miss Rainey; he could go to church and confess his lusts; he could go to a Danish massage parlor in the West Seventies that had been recommended by a salesman; he could rape the girl or trust that he would somehow be prevented from doing this; or he could get drunk. It was his life, his boat, and, like every other man, he was made to be the father of thousands, and what harm could there be in a tryst that would make them both feel more kindly toward the world? This was the wrong train of thought, and he came back to the first, the psychiatrist. He had the telephone number of Miss Rainey's doctor, and he called and asked for an immediate appointment. He was insistent with the doctor's secretary— it was his manner in business—and when she said that the doctor's sched-ule was full for the next few weeks, Francis demanded an appointment that day and was told to come at five.

The psychiatrist's office was in a building that was used mostly by doc-tors and dentists, and the hallways were filled with the candy smell of mouthwash and memories of pain. Francis' character had been formed upon a series of private resolves—resolves about cleanliness, about going off the high diving board or repeating any other feat that challenged his courage, about punctuality, honesty, and virtue. To abdicate the perfect loneliness in which he had made his most vital decisions shattered his con-cept of character and left him now in a condition that felt like shock. He was stupefied. The scene for his *miserere mei Deus* was, like the waiting

135

room of so many doctors' offices, a crude token gesture toward the sweets of domestic bliss: a place arranged with antiques, coffee tables, potted plants, and etchings of snow covered bridges and geese in flight, although there were no children, no marriage bed, no stove, even, in this travesty of a house, where no one had ever spent the night and where the curtained windows looked straight onto a dark air shaft. Francis gave his name and address to a secretary and then saw, at the side of the room, a policeman moving toward him. "Hold it, hold it," the policeman said. "Don't move. Keep your hands where they are."

"I think it's all right, officer," the secretary began. "I think it will be—"

"Let's make sure," the policeman said, and began to slap Francis' clothes, looking for what—pistols, knives, an ice-pick? Finding nothing, he went off, and the secretary began a nervous apology: "When you called on the telephone, Mr. Weed, you seemed very excited, and one of the doctor's patients has been threatening his life, and we have to be careful. If you want to go in now?" Francis pushed open a door connected to an electrical chime, and in the doctor's lair sat down heavily, blew his nose into a handkerchief, searched in his pockets for cigarettes, for matches, for something, and said hoarsely, with tears in his eyes, "I'm in love, Dr. Herzog."

It is a week or ten days later in Shady Hill. The seven-fourteen has come and gone, and here and there dinner is finished and the dishes are in the dishwashing machine. The village hangs, morally and economically, from a thread; but it hangs by its thread in the evening light. Donald Goslin has begun to worry the "Moonlight Sonata" again. *Marcato ma sempre pianissimo!* He seems to be wringing out a wet bath towel, but the housemaid does not heed him. She is writing a letter to Arthur Godfrey. In the cellar of his house, Francis Weed is building a coffee table. Dr. Herzog recommended woodwork as a therapy, and Francis finds some true consolation in the simple arithmetic involved and in the holy smell of new wood. Francis is happy. Upstairs, little Toby is crying, because he is tired. He puts off his cowboy hat, gloves, and fringed jacket, unbuckles the belt studded with gold and rubies, the silver bullets and holsters, slips off his suspenders, his checked shirt, and Levis, and sits on the edge of his bed to pull off his high boots. Leaving this equipment in a heap, he goes to the closet and takes his space suit off a nail. It is a struggle for him to get into the long tights, but he succeeds. He loops the magic cape over his shoulders and, climbing onto the footboard of his bed, he spreads his arms and flies the short distance to the floor, landing with a thump that is audible to everyone in the house but himself.

"Go home, Gertrude, go home," Mrs. Masterson says. "I told you to go home an hour ago, Gertrude. It's way past your suppertime, and your mother will be worried. Go home!" A door on the Babcock's terrace flies open, and out comes Mrs. Babcock without any clothes on, pursued by her naked husband. (Their children are away at boarding school, and their terrace is screened by a hedge.) Over the terrace they go and in at the kitchen door, as passionate and handsome a nymph and satyr, as you will find on any wall in Venice. Cutting the last of the roses in her garden, Julia hears old Mr. Nixon shouting at the squirrels in his bird-feeding station. "Rapscallions! Varmints! Avaunt and quit my sight!" A miserable cat wanders into the garden, sunk in spiritual and physical discomfort. Tied to its head is a small straw hat—a doll's hat—and it is securely buttoned into a doll's dress, from

140

the skirts of which protrudes its long, hairy tail. As it walks, it shakes its feet, as if it had fallen into water.

"Here, pussy, pussy, pussy!" Julia calls.

"Here, pussy, here, poor pussy!" But the cat gives her a skeptical look and stumbles away in its skirts. The last to come is Jupiter. He prances through the tomato vines, holding in his generous mouth the remains of an evening slipper. Then it is dark; it is a night where kings in golden suits ride elephants over the mountains.

[1954]

Questions

1. Do you see evidence in "The Swimmer" and "The Country Husband" that Cheever's fiction is "crypto-autobiography"?

2. In terms of character and theme, what common elements do you see in the Cheever stories (including "Reunion") and Cheever's life?

3. How has Cheever adapted biographical features in his fiction? Are there significant changes? For instance, Anne in "The Country Husband" has a father who seems in significant ways reminiscent of Cheever's own father. Yet there are obvious differences. (Anne is a woman, for starters.) Can you speculate on the motivation for some of these alterations?

4. Are there any similarities in the plots of "Reunion," "Swimmer," and "Country Husband"? Do the plots reflect Cheever's biographical focus?

Suggestions for Writing

What was the best time you've ever had in your life? When were you the most scared? Can you point to a moment when you changed your mind about something important? What's the hardest thing you've ever done?

Answers to questions like these should provide you with stories to tell. Pick one and tell it, but feel free to change what really happened in any way you like, making the story more dramatic, more interesting, more surprising. Feel free also to alter the order of events as you reveal the story: consider how the reader's experience will be changed if you reveal the ending first, or the middle last, or start near the end and flashback a series of scenes as you move toward the conclusion. Just play around, in other words, with the plot. Think also about the character you reveal. Play with that character: how could changing an event, a statement, an action, alter the character?

See if your classmates, when they read your story, can tell what is fictional, and what is autobiographical.

9

Read Drama Thoughtfully: Psychological Criticism

> When a member of my family complains that he or she has bitten his tongue, bruised her finger, and so on, instead of the expected sympathy I put the question, "Why did you do that?"
>
> —Sigmund Freud

Reflection: Someone's Mind

Psychological criticism often seems strange, there is no denying. But just look at what it tries to deal with! In attempting to address the underlying reasons why writers, characters, or readers behave the way they do, psychological criticism focuses on the human mind—and what is more amazing and weird than that? Just think about some of the things your own mind produces—dreams, fantasies, jokes, hunches, even a new recipe—and consider how in the world anyone could explain all that. Take dreams, for instance: Do you control what you dream about? And if you're not in charge of your dreams,

"Leon, do you think it's all psychological?"

© The New Yorker Collection 1991 George Booth from cartoonbank.com. All Rights Reserved.

who or what is? Obviously, there are things going on in our heads that we aren't really aware of. If we control them, it is in some mysterious and unknown way: some "unconscious" way, as Freud taught us to say. Psychology tries to reveal these underground things, and psychological criticism tries to reveal them in the arena of literature.

243

It's doubtful that anyone will seriously question the value of considering how human beings think and behave. Since we all have to deal with human behavior everyday, what could be a more practical subject to think about? But you might well wonder why we should study literary texts—fiction, poetry, drama—rather than case studies, psychology textbooks, or real-life people. There are several reasons to include literature. For one thing, psychologists have always looked to literary texts for insights: Freud, the founder of modern psychology, believed that "the poets and philosophers" had already anticipated everything he learned. Great literary works may allow us access to profound truths about ourselves. For another thing, literary works are generally more pleasurable, more interesting to read than case studies, since we get the added satisfaction (supposedly) of the literary writer's wielding of the language, shaping the material. In other words, the poet, the dramatist, the fiction writer, may have captured human motivation and behavior in a more vivid, more revealing way than any psychological text. Not that you should neglect studying psychology more directly, or that you should think about literature instead of the people around you. On the contrary: the psychological study of literature ought to enrich these other activities, and vice-versa.

Psychological criticism makes use of common sense and careful observation, even though it may sometimes employ theories that admittedly seem strange. This chapter, in its focus on using psychological theories to write about drama (and "dramatic" poetry), will stress these practical and commonsensical aspects. That is one reason why it discusses "psychological criticism" rather than "psychoanalytical criticism," since the latter suggests more specialized, clinically based techniques. Here, we are chiefly concerned with the implications of these two simple assumptions: that people do and say things for reasons they often are not fully aware of; and that these reasons influence our fantasies and fears.

Modern psychology arguably began when Sigmund Freud (1856–1939) started asking people (including his family, as the epigraph indicates) why they did things,

Sigmund Freud (fourth from left) enjoys an elegant meal at home with the rest of his family, including daughter Anna, who will also become a noted psychoanalyst.

suspecting that hidden motivations were at work. Freud seized upon the unconscious (*das Unbewusste, "the unknown"*) in order to explain where these hidden
motivations were coming from. Although both the term "unconscious" and the general idea predated Freud, his theories of the way the unknown mind emerged in
behavior (dreams, slips of the tongue, irrational fears, obsessive actions) revolution-
ized the field. Literary criticism, assuming unconscious motivations that influence
fantasies and fears, attempts to speculate about the psychology of authors, characters, and readers.

Let's consider these assumptions by looking carefully at the following poem.
(We will turn to drama in a moment.)

MICHAEL HAMBURGER (1924–)

A Poet's Progress

Like snooker balls thrown on the table's faded green,
Rare ivory and weighted with his best ambitions,
At first his words are launched: not certain what they mean,
He loves to see them roll, rebound, assume positions
Which—since not he—some power beyond him has assigned.   5

But now the game begins: dead players, living critics
Are watching him—and suddenly one eye goes blind,
The hand that holds the cue shakes like a paralytic's,
Till every thudding, every clinking sound portends
New failure, new defeat. Amazed, he finds that still   10
It is not he who guides his missiles to their ends
But an unkind geometry that mocks his will.

If he persists, for years he'll practise patiently,
Lock all the doors, learn all the tricks, keep noises out,
Though he may pick a ghost or two for company   15
Or pierce the room's inhuman silence with a shout.
More often silence wins; then soon the green felt seems
An evil playground, lawless, lost to time, forsaken,
And he a fool caught in the water-weeds of dreams
Whom only death or frantic effort can awaken.   20

At last, a master player, he can face applause,
Looks for a fit opponent, former friends, emerges;
But no one knows him now. He questions his own cause,
And has forgotten why he yielded to those urges,
Took up a wooden cue to strike a coloured ball.   25
Wise now, he goes on playing; both his house and heart
Unguarded solitudes, hospitable to all
Who can endure the cold intensity of art.

[1950]

Speculation about what is going on in any person's mind, including fictional
persons, is always tricky. In drama, we at least have the advantage (usually) of analyzing the speech of a particular artificial person, who is situated in a particular
time and place. The playwright ordinarily makes the "scene" clear; and an actor and

a director, reading the script, are presumed to be able to determine the motivation for what a character is saying. There may be discussion ("What's my motivation?" asks the actor), but the assumption is that the play should provide enough information about the character and the occasion to allow for a convincing portrayal. Even if you're not actually watching the play, and it is being staged only in your own head, you are still likely to be given much more contextual information than when you read a poem. Fiction also usually provides us with some background information, but with much poetry, the reader is getting nothing but the words of some speaker. We have to figure out who is talking, to whom, in what context, for what purpose.

In the case of "A Poet's Progress," the speaker of the poem has an expansive point of view, looking over the career of "a poet," from a beginning to a point of maturity. At the beginning of his career, the poet's words seem like snooker balls thrown onto the table, randomly rolling around. (Why is the pool table a "faded green" in line one? Because the game of poetry that this new player takes up is a very old one, we might say, with many prior players.) Watching his own words roll out, even the poet himself is "not certain what they mean." He plays the game, we are told, for the pure pleasure of seeing the words "assume positions,/ Which— since not he—some power beyond him has assigned." As he continues the game of writing, the poet realizes he must deal with the historical tradition of poetry (the "dead players") and the current competitive marketplace (the "living critics"); and under this pressure, he falls apart, with one eye going blind, his hand shaking. He finds that he still has not gained control of his words: "Amazed, he finds that still/ It is not he who guides his missiles to their ends/ But an unkind geometry that mocks his will."

Only after years of frustrating practice, described in the third section, does the poet find himself (in the fourth stanza) "a master player," ready to "face applause." But his triumph seems empty, since "no one knows him now." Even more revealing, after acquiring the technical skill he lacked, now "He questions his own cause,/ And has forgotten why he yielded to those urges,/ Took up a wooden cue to strike a coloured ball." Yet he is "Wise now," and "he goes on playing" despite his ignorance and uncertainty, opening "both his house and heart" to all "Who can endure the cold intensity of art." It seems he has set aside, in other words, his concern over controlling his writing, over pursuing his "cause"; and he has embraced "playing"—or rather writing—for its own sake. The game of poetry itself, although it does not respond to his will or desire, has its own "cold intensity," we are told, that the poem indicates is of value to those who can "endure" it. Hamburger's poem thus suggests that the writing of poetry, in the case of this one poet anyway, is a mysterious business, serving unknown forces, a revel without a cause. The poet doesn't have anything to say in the beginning, the middle, or the end. He just goes on playing.

In the Freudian tradition, what seems random and without intention—like a slip of the tongue, an image in a dream—may actually be quite meaningful, as the unconscious mind disguises and displays things we want to express but have blocked and censored. That "power" that directs the poet's words, then, might be seen as the poet's unconscious mind. More recent revisions of traditional psychology would suggest that this unconscious is structured like a language, and thus in a sense language itself controls the poet's words.

Yet Hamburger's poem is such an interesting instance of a poetical investigation of the poet's psychology precisely because it avoids explicitly assigning responsibility to the unconscious or its language. The poet, according to this poem, does not control his words in the first place; later, he "has forgotten why he yielded to those urges" to write in the beginning. He has forgotten, it seems, what he never knew; or, he has forgotten that he wrote simply because he liked watching the words assume positions, if we can call that a "cause." This assertion, however, seems especially strange when we apply it to this poem before us, for doesn't Hamburger clearly have a "cause," a purpose in this poem? Specifically, doesn't the poem powerfully affirm the value of poetry in itself, apart from any meaning or purpose? The wise poet goes on playing simply for the sake of "the cold intensity of art," so the poem tells us. Something, we may suspect, is going on in this poem, something more than what we see on the surface. To get at that something, we might think for a moment about the author. The most obvious question to ask is this one: Is Hamburger talking about himself? And if the "he" in the poem is Hamburger, why does he talk about himself in the third person? Why doesn't he say, in lines four and five, "At first my words were launched: not certain what they meant,/ I loved to see them roll . . ."? What difference does first person (I, me) versus third person (he, him) make? By using third person, Hamburger gives us the sense that the poem's speaker is looking from the outside at the poet being described. There seems to be some objective distance: "I'm talking about him," the poem's voice says.

This kind of turning inside is crucial for much of what we call "psychology": we can guess about other people's minds by examining the way our own works. That necessity is in fact both the great power and the great limitation of psychology: on the power side, we always have right with us an example of the thing we're trying to study. An astronomer can't carry around a star to examine anytime he or she wants; an economist can't bring an economic system into his or her study and watch it work. But anyone can study how the mind works: I've got one, right here, now, working. And so do you. On the limitation side: psychology is using the thing it studies to do the studying. We may pretend, as Hamburger perhaps pretends, to step outside our own minds and look at someone else's, but we never really get "out there." We're always still "in here," imagining someone else's mind within our own.

Thus, the "he" in Hamburger's poem as well as the voice who talks about "him" is unavoidably a reflection in some sense of Hamburger himself. Even if Hamburger were to say, "The poet in this poem is not anything like me," it would still make sense, from a psychological point of view, to think in terms of the mind who created both this "poet" depicted in the poem and the poetic voice of the poem who does the depicting. The poet described may be the opposite of Hamburger himself, or a distortion, or a partial version, or some combination of these, or something else: the crucial point here is that some consciousness—we call it "Michael Hamburger, b. 1924"—created the poem; and as psychological critics, one thing we can do is trace this work back to its creator and his motivations. In this way of thinking through psychological criticism, Shakespeare's *King Lear*, for instance, contains characters who are in a sense different reflections of "Shakespeare," and we can tentatively get back to that creating consciousness through these characters. Hamburger's portrait thus must draw on his own experience, although we cannot know for sure if Hamburger thinks the poet described in the poem is supposed to be himself.

Why, then, would Hamburger create a poet and talk about "his" progress from beginning to maturity? What is there underlying this portrait? In asking this question, which takes us to the heart of psychological criticism, we can see just how acutely this poem reflects the enterprise of psychological criticism itself—because that is the question Hamburger seems to be asking about the poet he creates: What is *underlying* his poetry? The answer that the poem explicitly gives is "nothing." But, as we have seen, this poem clearly seems to have a "cause," contradicting what Hamburger says: that cause is the celebration of poetry itself. Poetry is valuable not for any meaning or purpose, but for "the cold intensity of art," so the poem claims. So why does Hamburger assert at such length that the poet doesn't direct his shots, even though this poem clearly scores points for poetry? Because, we might argue, this contradiction is part of Hamburger's way of defending himself from the devastating implications of admitting that his poetry has no purpose, aside from his own enjoyment.

Thus, looking at "A Poet's Progress" psychologically, we might claim that Hamburger evades the psychologically upsetting sight of his own lack of purpose by insisting on a purposeless purpose—art's cold intensity, which doesn't see anything in particular; it simply sees. The poem says in its conclusion that the poet "has forgotten" why he wrote, yet it seems clear that from the outset he never knew any purpose other than pleasure. He liked to watch the words roll around like snooker balls. Rather than confronting the lack of purpose in his writing, or admitting that his purpose is the self-promotional one of promoting the value of writing poetry, Hamburger instead points strategically to a forgotten purpose. He thereby evades the question: there was a purpose once, he implies; now it's gone; but it doesn't matter because the art itself is the purpose.

We can get this far in our reading of "A Poet's Progress" simply by looking closely at the poem and thinking about the motivations involved. Certainly, we could go farther. Why, for instance, does Hamburger choose to compare poetry to snooker, which the dictionary says is a form of pool? Why "snooker" and not some other game? What fear or fantasy is being disguised and expressed there? As a verb, to "snooker" means "to cheat, to dupe, to fool." Since the poem talks about the struggle to master poetry and control meaning and purpose, the comparison indirectly affirms what the poem itself explicitly denies. The comparison, in other words, suggests that poetry is a kind of cheating, a duping, a snookering, which has no meaning and cannot be controlled—which is precisely what the speaker fears and fights against. In the end the poet says he has mastered his writing only when it actually has become his master, for it is the "cold intensity of art" that he serves, not vice-versa.

We could go even further in thinking about what fears and fantasies are being disclosed in the poem. The poet cannot control his art; later, with others watching, he is unable to perform. Although we might be skeptical of psychological readings that find phallic symbols here, there, and everywhere (sometimes a cigar is just a cigar), it does seem reasonable to find one in this poem, should we want to go beyond common sense and into the realm of fantasy and its symbols. By comparing poetry to a game played with cue sticks and orange-sized, heavy, hard balls, isn't Hamburger at some unconscious level addressing the poet's fears of inadequacy and impotence? If a cue stick resembles a large and powerful pen, it also resembles a penis. With his cue stick, so the poem tells us, the poet has become a "master player," powerful enough to open his "house and heart" to others. His cue stick, a substitute for a more fallible phallus, cannot fail him because now he is in its service, not vice-versa.

Hamburger's poem launches us toward psychological criticism in two ways: it directs our attention to the crucial problem of motivation, trying to explain the underlying reasons why "a poet" writes; and it displays a striking instance of a psychological defense, working to disarm a threatening insight.

Let's turn now to a more explicit consideration of just how to do psychological criticism.

Strategies: Using Psychological Criticism

If you have read any literature at all, it's likely you have read this poem, for it has been reprinted in modern times more than any other. Why is it so popular? One reason, certainly, is that its dramatic quality is so compelling. We imagine these lines being spoken by someone in a particular place. Think of this poem as a scene in a play. In fact, try reading the poem aloud, using your best acting voice.

MATTHEW ARNOLD (1822–1888)

Dover Beach

The sea is calm tonight.
The tide is full, the moon lies fair
Upon the straits;—on the French coast the light
Gleams and is gone; the cliffs of England stand,
Glimmering and vast, out in the tranquil bay.   5
Come to the window, sweet is the night-air!
Only, from the long line of spray
Where the sea meets the moon-blanched land,
Listen! you hear the grating roar
Of pebbles which the waves draw back, and fling,   10
At their return, up the high strand,
Begin, and cease, and then again begin,
With tremulous cadence slow, and bring
The eternal note of sadness in.

Sophocles long ago   15
Heard it on the Aegean, and it brought
Into his mind the turbid ebb and flow
Of human misery; we
Find also in the sound a thought,
Hearing it by this distant northern sea.   20

The Sea of Faith
Was once, too, at the full, and round earth's shore
Lay like the folds of a bright girdle furled.
But now I only hear
Its melancholy, long, withdrawing roar,   25
Retreating, to the breath
Of the night-wind, down the vast edges drear
And naked shingles of the world

Ah, love, let us be true
To one another! for the world, which seems   30
To lie before us like a land of dreams,
So various, so beautiful, so new,
Hath really neither joy, nor love, nor light,
Nor certitude, nor peace, nor help for pain;
And we are here as on a darkling plain   35
Swept with confused alarms of struggle and flight,
Where ignorant armies clash by night.

[1867]

Matthew Arnold lounges on the floor amid a group of literary friends, all posed for an 1857 daguerreotype.

From a New Critical perspective, we might say that this poem is so hugely popular because it holds together and resolves some profound contradictions. Dozens of New Critical readings of this poem have indeed pointed to the way faith and faithlessness, serenity and violence, sight and sound, illusion and reality, sea and land, restfulness and restlessness, and a good many other oppositions are related here. From a reader-response stance, we can talk about how moving the beauty of the opening scene is; and how that beauty heightens our pleasure at the affair of the lovers, which is only hinted at; and how the reader's enjoyment is also enhanced by the contrast of the lovers to the harsh and violent world beyond their immediately peaceful scene.

From a historical vantage point, we might focus on Arnold's reference to the Sea of Faith that is retreating, and therefore talk about the crisis in Christianity in the 1860s, as many believers, primarily under the influence of Darwin and science, drifted away from Christianity. Or, from a political point of view, we might consider why critical commentary on this poem has assumed that the speaker is a man, and the "love" is a woman; or we might think about the political implications of the poem, especially its concluding image. Would we expect this poem, for instance, to be more popular during the Vietnam War era or World War II? And a deconstructive vision of the poem might lead us to unravel the logic of the speaker's request to "be true/ To one another"—by pointing out, for instance, that the speaker cannot hope to live within a world that has no "certitude" and yet be truly "true" to one another. He is safe within a room, looking out on the sea, and yet he compares his location to a "darkling plain." If he cannot even *be* where he is, how can he hope to find certitude in a relationship?

Psychological criticism does something different from these and other approaches: it assumes, for starters, that creative writing represents the fulfillment of a wish or fear. These wishes and fears are not expressed directly, but rather they are revealed in a disguised form. The writer may not even be aware of such wishes and fears; since they are socially or morally unacceptable, they have been repressed—pushed below consciousness. They are "out of sight," but they are only superficially "out of mind," since they continue to exert an influence on one's consciousness.

Inventing

One way to use a psychological stance, then, would be simply to ask ourselves, "What wish or fear is being disguised and expressed here?" Obviously any answers to this question would have to be tentative, but our answers to just about *any* question ought to be tentative. We might further object that we really need to know a very great deal about an author (or a character, or reader) before we make any judgments about such submerged things as unconscious wishes or fears. But every person, although unique in the final analysis, has many formative experiences that are common to other people. And so, it makes sense to assume that we can perhaps identify and understand many disguised wishes and fears precisely because they are common ones, shared by many if not all human beings. In other words, human beings develop (usually) in similar ways, undergoing relatively similar experiences.

For instance, although recently some men have begun to take a more active role in childcare, the primary caregiver for most children is the mother. What is the effect of this common experience of being raised primarily by a female? Girls, as Nancy Chodorow points out, are able to identify with the adult they spend the most time with; but boys, who cannot identify with the mother, must separate and withdraw themselves from the mother (see for example *Feminism and Psychoanalytic Theory*). Girls, according to Chodorow, feel more connected to the world and to their caregiver. Their way of relating to the world is defined by *attachment*, and they are threatened by separation. Boys, who are confronted by a different gender, must define themselves by separation, and they are correspondingly threatened by intimacy. Girls typically engage in *cooperative* play, while boys typically engage in *competitive* play, Chodorow says. Girls think in terms of relationships, and boys think in terms of rules and rights. In a sense, then, Chodorow is doing nothing more than saying what many people already believe about basic differences between the sexes, but she is providing a developmental basis for these differences.

It may seem that we have wandered far from "Dover Beach," but perhaps we are just now arriving there. We might speculate, from a psychological stance, that the poem is so popular because it powerfully expresses some basic wishes or fears. The poem has spoken to so many generations of readers, in other words, because it says something memorably that very many people wish to say. What might that something be?

Here are the notes of one of my students, "Randolph," who is trying to answer this question: What wishes or fears are being expressed?

Lines 1-6: The scene is vast, large. The sea, the moon, the French coast, the cliffs, the bay—all these are enormous. The calmness and the tranquillity of the scene are the result of this scale, I think. Human problems seem very small in this setting, since human beings themselves are very small. I think that is the opening desire of the poem's speaker, to shrink down very small, losing any worries and cares as he contemplates the vast and glimmering sea and coastline. He wants to lose himself in the sea. He wants to look out into the night air, with his companion. When I go to the beach, that's what I feel. The sea is so huge, and I am so small, and it somehow makes my problems seem so little. I think that's why almost everyone likes the ocean.

Lines 6–14:   In these lines he gets pulled back in to his problems. It is interesting that talking to his companion makes him lose his little trance. Instead of seeing the vastness of the ocean, the peacefulness of the bay, he now hears little pebbles getting flung back into the shore. The pebbles are like the things he wants to forget. Even though they are little nothings compared to the sea, they are still what he is thinking about now. The sound of the waves against the pebbles becomes the "eternal note of sadness," as he puts it. He doesn't say exactly what is making him sad, though. I wonder what his little pebbles stand for.

Lines 16–20:   The scale of the poem, which is large in space, also becomes huge in time with these lines. Not only is he looking out over an ocean; now he stretches back to ancient Greece—at least I think Sophocles is ancient Greece. Didn't he write *Oedipus*? Or was he a philosopher? Oh, I think he invented the toga party. (Was it two or three thousand years ago? I'll look this up.) Instead of thinking about his own personal problems, which he was getting away from by looking at the ocean, he turns away to think about all "human misery." This is sure a sad way of thinking. Why would anybody make themselves think about such a big topic? Human misery throughout time? Please. Why would anyone torture themselves so?

Idea: maybe this is like his looking at the ocean, except now he looks at a different kind of largeness to try to lose his own troubles. In the sea of misery, his little pebbles of worry are not so much. I'm not sure this is right.

Lines 21–28:   There are some very weird things in this section. "Girdle" is odd. So is "naked shingles." I don't know which is stranger, thinking of the world as having shingles on it, or thinking of the shingles as "naked." It seems clear that the earth doesn't have a girdle. Women have girdles, or at least they used to. So he is thinking of the earth as a woman, who is naked. But he is also thinking of the earth as a house, isn't he? The only thing I know with shingles is a house (my grandmother had shingles once, but that's the disease, which doesn't fit here, does it?). And he is thinking about the sea as being lovely and calm, until he thinks about the shoreline and the pebbles and the "grating roar."

So, he is talking about the loss of faith, comparing it to a sea moving away or drying up. And he is also talking about the earth as if it were a naked woman. You can't have sex with the earth. But you can think of the earth as our mother—environmentalists talk like that all the time. He wants to be in the earth? One with the earth? He wants to be in the sea?

Lines 29-end: Two things are especially interesting to me now: 1) he likes feeling very tiny; 2) he likes the experience of the sea, removed from the land. Here's another thing: he talks about the earth as a woman. I think he wants to float in the sea like a little baby, which is to say that he wants to return to the womb of his mother? Being in the sea is like being in a womb, floating in salt water. That may be crazy, but he certainly does reject the world in general, for it has no joy or love or light etc. He cannot, to be sure, say "I want to be a fetus again." That would be ridiculous. But he can turn to his companion and say "Let us be true/ to one another," and such a request may reflect his desire for a reunion with his mother: what is a more faithful, more secure relationship (for most people) than the relationship between mother and child?

The ending lines emphasize the contrast between the peaceful world of the sea and the violent conflict of the land. Rather than get involved in the clash and struggle of the world, which seems like ignorant armies fighting at night to him, he longs to withdraw. He says he wants to withdraw with his companion, his love; I have the suspicion that his companion is a substitute for his mother, and the security he says he desires with his lover is just a substitute for the security he really desires with his mother. A grown man can't say that, so he says the other. Dover Beach, I think, is at least partly about the difficulty of leaving the security of one's mother and entering the conflict and competition of the world. In the dog-eat-dog world, it sometimes seems like ignorant armies, I bet.

Shaping

In these notes Randolph hints at some of the same insights Chodorow puts forward. After all, as noted, the claim that boys tend to be competitive and individualistic, and girls tend to be cooperative and relational, is not something most people would find radical or shocking. We might want to stress that Chodorow's point is a generalization, and that these gender traits may not be inevitable. Even so, the thesis for most people is just conventional wisdom.

Randolph's ideas might have been developed without any help from Chodorow or any other psychological theorist; but reading over his notes I pointed out the similarity between his ideas and Chodorow's theories. Since Chodorow had been discussed briefly in class, I suggested that he consider whether this discussion might have stimulated his thinking; and if so, that he cite Chodorow's work. I also directed Randolph to the following discussion of Chodorow's work, which appears in Carol Gilligan's book, *A Different Voice.* You should find this discussion not only fascinating but also very fertile for generating psychological criticism.

Psychological theorists have fallen as innocently as Strunk and White into the same observational bias. Implicitly adopting the male life as the norm, they have tried to fashion women out of a masculine cloth. It all goes back, of course, to Adam and Eve—a story which shows, among other things, that if you make a woman out of a man, you are bound to get into trouble. In the life cycle, as in the Garden of Eden, the woman has been the deviant.

The penchant of developmental theorists to project a masculine image, and one that appears frightening to women, goes back at least to Freud (1905), who built his theory of psychosexual development around the experiences of the male child that culminate in the Oedipus complex. In the 1920s, Freud struggled to resolve the contradictions posed for his theory by the differences in female anatomy and the different configuration of the young girl's early family relationships. After trying to fit women into his masculine conception, seeing them as envying that which they missed, he came instead to acknowledge, in the strength and persistence of women's pre-Oedipal attachments to their mothers, a developmental difference. He considered this difference in women's development to be responsible for what he saw as women's developmental failure.

Having tied the formation of the superego or conscience to castration anxiety, Freud considered women to be deprived by nature of the impetus for a clear-cut Oedipal resolution. Consequently, women's superego—the heir to the Oedipus complex—was compromised: it was never "so inexorable, so impersonal, so independent of its emotional origins as we require it to be in men." From this observation of difference, that "for women the level of what is ethically normal is different from what it is in men," Freud concluded that women "show less sense of justice than men, that they are less ready to submit to the great exigencies of life, that they are more often influenced in their judgements by feelings of affection or hostility" (1925).

Thus a problem in theory became cast as a problem in women's development, and the problem in women's development was located in their experience of relationships. Nancy Chodorow (1974), attempting to account for "the reproduction within each generation of certain general and nearly universal differences that characterize masculine and feminine personality and roles," attributes these differences between the sexes not to anatomy but rather to "the fact that women, universally, are largely responsible for early child care." Because this early social environment differs for and is experienced differently by male and female children, basic sex differences recur in personality development. As a result, "in any given society, feminine personality comes to define itself in relation and connection to other people more than masculine personality does."

In her analysis, Chodorow relies primarily on Robert Stoller's studies which indicate that gender identity, the unchanging core of personality formation, is "with rare exception firmly and irreversibly established for both sexes by the time a child is around three." Given that for both sexes the primary caretaker in the first three years of life is typically female, the interpersonal dynamics of gender identity formation are different for boys and girls. Female identity formation takes place in a context of ongoing relationship since "mothers tend to experience their daughters as more like, and continuous with, themselves." Correspondingly, girls, in identifying themselves as female, experience themselves as like their mothers, thus fusing the experience of attachment with the process of identity formation. In contrast, "mothers experience their sons as a male opposite," and boys, in defining themselves as masculine, separate their mothers from themselves, thus curtailing "their primary love and sense of empathic tie." Consequently, male development entails a "more emphatic individuation and a more defensive firming of experienced ego boundaries." For boys, but not girls, "issues of differentiation have become intertwined with sexual issues."

Writing against the masculine bias of psychoanalytic theory, Chodorow argues that the existence of sex differences in the early experiences of individuation and relationship "does not mean that women have 'weaker' ego boundaries than men or are more prone to psychosis." It means instead that "girls emerge from this period with a basis for 'empathy' built into their primary definition of self in a way that boys do not." Chodorow thus replaces Freud's negative and derivative description of female psychology with a positive and direct account of her own: "Girls emerge with a stronger basis for experiencing another's needs or feelings as one's own (or of thinking that one is so experiencing another's needs and feelings). Furthermore, girls do not define themselves in terms of the denial of preoedipal relational modes to the same extent as do boys. Therefore, regression to these modes tends not to feel as much a basic threat to their ego. From very early, then, because they are parented by a person of the same gender . . . girls come to experience themselves as less differentiated than boys, as more continuous with and related to the external object-world, and as differently oriented to their inner object-world as well."

Consequently, relationships, and particularly issues of dependency, are experienced differently by women and men. For boys and men, separation and individuation are critically tied to gender identity since separation from the mother is essential for the development of masculinity. For girls and women, issues of femininity or feminine identity do not depend on the achievement of separation from the mother or on the progress of individuation. Since masculinity is defined through separation while femininity is defined through attachment, male gender identity is threatened by intimacy while female gender identity is threatened by separation. Thus males tend to have difficulty with relationships, while females tend to have problems with individuation. The quality of embeddedness in social interaction and personal relationships that characterizes women's lives in contrast to men's, however, becomes not only a descriptive difference but also a developmental liability when the milestones of childhood and adolescent development in the psychological literature are markers of increasing separation. Women's failure to separate then becomes by definition a failure to develop.

The sex differences in personality formation that Chodorow describes in early childhood appear during the middle childhood years in studies of children's games. Children's games are considered by George Herbert Mead (1934) and Jean Piaget (1932) as the crucible of social development during the school years. In games, children learn to take the role of the other and come to see themselves through another's eyes. In games, they learn respect for rules and come to understand the ways rules can be made and changed.

Janet Lever (1976), considering the peer group to be the agent of socialization during the elementary school years and play to be a major activity of socialization at that time, set out to discover whether there are sex differences in the games that children play. Studying 181 fifth-grade, white, middle-class children, ages ten and eleven, she observed the organization and structure of their playtime activities. She watched the children as they played at school during recess and in physical education class, and in addition kept diaries of their accounts as to how they spent their out-of-school time. From this study, Lever reports sex differences: boys play out of doors more often than girls do; boys play more often in large and age-heterogeneous groups; they play competitive games more often, and their games last longer than girls' games. The last is in some ways the most interesting finding. Boys games appeared to last longer not only because they required a higher level of skill and were thus less likely to become boring, but also because, when disputes arose in the course of a game, boys were able to resolve the disputes more effectively than girls: "During the course of this study, boys were seen quarrelling all the time, but not once was a game terminated because of a quarrel and no game was interrupted for more than seven minutes. In the gravest debates, the final word was always, to 'repeat the play,' generally followed by a chorus of 'cheater's proof.'" In fact, it seemed that the boys enjoyed the legal debates as much as they did the game itself, and even marginal players of lesser size or skill participated equally in these recurrent squabbles. In contrast, the eruption of disputes among girls tended to end the game.

[1982]

Although Randolph's essay could have been developed successfully without any research, just using his own careful observation and thinking, in this case Randolph did pursue my suggestions. In employing any kind of critical stance, you should find informed help valuable; but psychology itself provides such a rich and vast field that seeking out advice, whenever you can, seems especially wise. (Of course you'll want to give credit in your essay for whatever help you receive.) The more you know about psychology, the more theories you'll have to draw upon. As with every other approach, the more you know, the easier it gets; the more energy and creativity and attentiveness you put into it, the more you'll get out of it.

What does Gilligan's discussion of Chodorow's work do for Randolph's reading of "Dover Beach"? You may want to sketch out some ideas of your own before you read Randolph's notes, which follow:

> I think Chodorow draws my attention more sharply to some
> things in this poem. If men generally have trouble with
> intimacy, because of their development, then it is likely
> that such trouble plays a part in this poem. Right? So where
> is it? Does the speaker, whom I will assume is male, pull
> away from intimacy in the poem? He seems in fact to seek it:
> "Ah, love, let us be true/ To one another!" Maybe that is
> why the poem is so popular, because it allows men to
> experience the seeking of intimacy in a nonthreatening way,
> through the words of a character.
>
>   But I notice that there is really no intimacy given within
> the poem. Further, the man is not quite asking for intimacy,
> is he? He is asking for her to be true. He might have said,
> "Ah, love, let us kiss and hug"; or, "Ah, love, let us hold
> hands and tell each other secrets." Instead, he is in effect

asking her to play by the rules: let's be true to each other. This request is consistent with what Janet Lever found out about the way boys play. Boys are interested in following the rules, in being fair, and in arguing about what's within the rules. This interest in following the rules and being fair is also reflected in the speaker's complaints against the world, I think. The speaker carries on about the world not having this and that which it appears to have. The world does not play fair; it gives false appearances; it cheats. So, the speaker says, let's be sure we conduct ourselves according to the rules, being true to one another. It is not clear that the speaker has any sympathy or empathy for his companion, who supposedly is in the same boat with him.

Drafting

At this point Randolph is ready to write a draft of an essay. By assuming that the poem expresses some disguised wish or fear, and by looking carefully and imaginatively for what might be disguised here, he has arrived at several ideas:

- The speaker's retreat from the world includes the desire to be "true" with his "love," but withdrawing from the world's false promises and senseless violence seems to be much more important than any romantic relationship.
- Instead, the speaker most desires to lose himself in a vast panorama of space and time, making himself small by comparison.
- There are some aspects of the speaker's desire to lose himself that seem like a desire to return to the womb: the sea is like the amniotic fluid; the earth is like a woman.

Here is Randolph's draft, which you'll see is made up mostly of sections from his notes. That is one of the best things about the process of writing as it is explained in this book: using theories to develop your ideas, you'll usually find that your essays are mostly already written by the time you sit down to write them. Imagine, if you've ever struggled to find something to say as a blank sheet of paper stares back at you, how nice it would be to think, "Okay, now I've got to write the essay; oh, wait a minute—it's already almost done!" Randolph's draft is accompanied by some marginal comments he wrote in an attempt to explain what he is doing.

I wrote the title last. I wasn't sure what to call the paper until after I had finished, and then I spent about thirty minutes playing with titles. I like the title I finally came up with.

Randolph
English 102
April 15, 2003

Digging Under "Dover Beach": The Psychology of Matthew Arnold's Speaker

In some ways, Matthew Arnold's "Dover Beach" seems to be a love poem. It deals with two people in an apparently romantic situation, looking out over the English Channel toward the French coast, taking in the "Glimmering and vast" cliffs of

First thing: Quickly orient the reader. What am I talking about? What is my main point? What is the problem I wish to solve? It is, I will say, the problem of a love poem on the surface that has something else underneath it.

England. They are seeing, no doubt, quite a sight, and Arnold effectively suggests the awesome view they have. Throughout the poem the speaker is addressing his lover in an intimate way, opening up his heart and at the same time apparently trying to impress her with his knowledge and his philosophical outlook (I will assume, following most readers, that the speaker is male, the person addressed female). The last section is very moving as the speaker pleads,

First point—it seems like a love poem on the surface.

"Ah, love, let us be true/ To one another!" But there is much about the poem that seems out of place in a love poem, suggesting that something else is going on. There is something that Arnold is not quite telling us, but is nonetheless there, motivating the poem.

But much isn't right for a love poem.

e.g., "grating roar" and "sadness"

For instance, the romantic scene in the opening section is ruined by the speaker's notice of the "grating roar/ Of pebbles which the waves draw back and fling." This image suggests that the sea, which only a few lines before appeared to be tranquil, is actually harboring some mean and violent energy. Yet it is only flinging "pebbles," not crashing into boulders or tossing ships against the cliffs; the sea, which we are told "is calm tonight," is fearsome only on a small scale, from the point of view of a tiny person who hears the "grating roar/ Of *pebbles*" (my emphasis). In this "roar," we find, there is an "eternal note of sadness," and this note further darkens the scene. Although the request to "Come to the window, sweet is the night-air!" may seem in itself to be romantically promising, the speaker undermines any promise of affection with this gloomy turn of his attention.

another example: the focus on human misery

The second and third sections continue to move away from any normal kind of romance and affection. The speaker is drowning himself, or at least his potential love affair, in the "human misery" and atheism that he sees. Of course, these gloomy things are not really in the ocean. Rather, he imposes them on the sea, which seemed very lovely in the opening lines, but then becomes the source of miserable thoughts. In the final section, the speaker appears to return to romance, saying "Ah, love, let us be true/ To one another!" but these lines introduce the most depressing part of the poem, which is just about the opposite of any kind of love poetry. No one is going to feel very affectionate with those metaphorical armies clashing and fighting all night.

Okay, now I've said there is something underneath. What is it? Arnold's troubles make him want to become a baby, even to return to his mother.

The set-up to turn to what is underneath the desire to get away from it all.

So why does Arnold bother to use this particular context to air a complaint about the world's misery, its senseless violence, its ugliness and pain and on and on? Why does Arnold have these lines spoken in a romantic setting by one lover to another? The romantic scene is just the covering, the façade, for the poem's expression of a desire to get away from it all. The sweeping landscape that opens the poem reduces any observer to a very tiny scale. Compared to the sea, the moon, the English channel, the cliffs, the bay, any human is miniscule and insignifiant. In the second section Arnold shifts from space to time, and again the "turbid ebb and flow/ Of human misery" throughout history makes any particular person's misery seem very small.

He wants the Sea of Faith back in.

Thus, although the complaint of Arnold's speaker is about as sad and depressed as you can get, he is able to shrink it down by comparison. Just as the Sea of Faith is retreating, so is the size of his troubles, whatever they are. He finds that the world, which had seemed like a beautiful dream, really has "neither joy, nor love, nor light,/ Nor certitude, nor peace, nor help for pain." In turning to his love, asking that they be "true/ To one another," he is turning away from the disappointing world and its clashing armies, its "struggle and flight." Arnold's speaker wants to shrink and avoid the world, and he also wishes the Sea of Faith could come back in "round earth's shore."

He makes himself and his troubles small.

Two words in this next-to-last section seem especially odd: "girdle" and "naked." Their appearance suggests that the speaker's desire to retreat is a deep and radical wish, and that perhaps his wish for the Sea of Faith to be restored goes beyond any complaint about a decline in religious commitment. This sea lies within a "girdle." It is bounded by nakedness, and this nakedness is an attribute of shingles, which are of course part of a house. The speaker ultimately desires, I would suggest, without being fully aware of it himself, to return to the amniotic fluid of his mother—which is the only "sea" inside a girdle, that is also a "house" surrounded by nakedness.

The sea is in a girdle. The land is a house that is naked.

Obviously, adult men cannot express the desire to "go home to Mommy" in the most literal way. Arnold's poem disguises and really only hints at this profound rejection of the mature world and its miseries and conflicts. But the poem expresses enough of this desire for readers to glimpse, without quite seeing it, this most peaceful

Thus, it is a return-to-the-womb kind of fantasy.

> "tranquil bay" that is desired in the poem. The
> desire is impossible, but it is one all readers
> share to varying degrees. Its presence in the poem
> helps explain the incredible popularity of this
> poem's strange romance.

Randolph's idea, that Arnold's poem disguises and expresses the desire to return to the mother's womb, is only one of many psychological approaches that you could use to think about the poem—common sense and some speculative energy are all you need. Still, just to give you some idea what a more specialized, more theoretical approach might do with Arnold's poem, let's glance for a moment at what Norman Holland, a leading figure in psychological criticism, says about "Dover Beach." Holland focuses more closely on the developmental aspects of the poem, offering a fascinating reading that in some respects supports Randolph's thesis, but certainly goes beyond it (too far, some readers might say). Here is a sample passage, typical of the kind of astonishing conclusions psychological criticism can get to (from *The Dynamics of Literary Response* [Columbia UP, 1989]):

> "Dover Beach" taps the earliest experience of our two major senses. Sight the child comes to first. As early as the third month of life, a baby can recognize a human face as such. By the fourth or fifth month he can distinguish the face of the person who feeds and fondles him from other faces. Sight becomes linked in our minds with being fed, with nurturing mother. Fenichel suggests as a formula, "I want what I see to enter me."
>
> Thus, for example, in "Dover Beach," the strong sight images of the first five lines lead to a demand that a woman come, a taste image ("sweet"), and even, if we identify kinaesthetically with the poet, an inhaling of that sweet night air. In a crude, symbolic way, the cliffs are breasts, "glimmering and vast"; the sea and air are the nurturing fluids, "full," "fair," and "calm." They are seen, for, in infancy, sight becomes associated with a taking in, specifically a taking in from a mother in whom we have faith, whom we expect will give us joy, love, light, certitude, peace, help for pain. Our first disillusionment in life comes as that nurturing figure fails to stand calm, full, fair, vast, tranquil, always there, but instead retreats, withdraws, ebbs and flows. And the poem makes us hear this withdrawal. (119–120)

Let's also look, to give you another sample, at what Holland does with the poem's concluding image, drawing on the voluminous psychological studies dealing with how children think about their parents' sexuality. With the term "primal scene" in this passage, Holland is referring to sexual intercourse between the parents, which children may imagine, or glimpse, or even observe.

> . . . there is a well-nigh universal sexual symbolism in this heard-but-not-seen, naked fighting by night. This is one way Arnold's poem turns our experience of disillusionment or despair into satisfaction, namely, through the covert gratification we get from this final primal scene fantasy. Arnold is talking about hearing a sexual "clash by night," just as children fantasize sex as fight. In fact (it has been suggested to me), the "darkling plain" may evoke in us thoughts of a bed, the "struggle" a man's active role in the sexual

act, and the "flight" a women's more passive situation (perhaps even a wish that she would be in "flight" rather than lying there) . . . .

The conventional explicators have found some logic underlying that final startling image: a logical development from brightness to darkness, from the pebble beach to the darkling plain. Ordinary explication, however, offers little basis for the armies, while psychological explication offers considerable. The poem begins with a world which is very solidly there, a world which is seen, a world which is invested with a faith like a child's trust in the sight of his nurturing mother. The poem moves into sound, to the later, harsher sense and with it the sounds of withdrawal and retreat. Thus, the sound of the ocean shifts from the rhythm of waves to the more permanent, even geological, withdrawal of the "Sea of Faith." The feeling is one of permanent decay, a sense of harsh reality akin to a child's growing an inevitable knowledge that his mother does not exist for him alone. She has an adult life, wishes of her own, which cause her to go away from him and come back, retreat and withdraw.

The final image brings in a still stronger feeling of rhythmic withdrawal, a child's excited but frightened vague awareness. That other, separate adult life has a naked, nighttime, rhythmic sound. It does not lie there like a land of dreams—rather, it is violent, passionate, brutal; the bright girdle is withdrawn and bodies clash by night.

Roughly, we could say that the lovely appearances seen in the poem, the moonlight, the cliffs of England, the stillness, correspond to a faith in a mother. The harsh sounds of withdrawal then heard correspond to the disillusioning knowledge first, of her withdrawal, then of her relationship with the father, he expressed perhaps as Sophocles or, covertly, Thucydides (for Arnold's father did edit Thucydides). In the manner of a dream, the two individuals hidden in the poem, a father and mother, are disguised as two multitudes, "armies" and they, usually all-seeing, all-wise, become in the violent moment of passion, "ignorant."(121–122)

Your own psychological criticism, depending on your knowledge of psychology, may be more or less daring and theoretical than Holland's. The crucial thing, quite simply, is that you think about the mind of the author, the character, or the reader, speculating about what is underlying what you actually see.

✔ Checklist for Psychological Criticism

- ❏ Assume that some wish or fear is being disguised and expressed in the work.
- ❏ Look for clues that suggest what is underlying the work's "surface"—details that don't quite fit or seem unusual.
- ❏ Connect those clues to some common developmental pattern or (if you know the author's or reader's or character's biography) to some trauma or event.

Useful Terms for Psychological Criticism

As you're employing psychological criticism, the following list of commonly used terms may be helpful. The illustrations refer to Shakespeare's *Hamlet* and specifically to the passage discussed below on pages 264–266.

Isolation: Not feeling what one ordinarily would be feeling. Hamlet should be feeling rage, yet his revenge is "dull."

Intellectualization: Explaining away emotions rather than feeling them. Hamlet acknowledges the possibility that he is "thinking too precisely on th' event."

Repression: Submerging an idea or emotion, putting it out of the conscious mind. Hamlet should at least consider the possibility that he is delaying because he fears losing his own life. He doesn't—a major repression.

Projection: Assigning one's own emotions to another person. Hamlet thinks Fortinbras feels the same injury he does, yet Fortinbras takes action. In reality, Hamlet doesn't know what Fortinbras is thinking or feeling.

Displacement: Shifting one's emotions from a threatening target to a less threatening one. Hamlet, rather than getting mad at Claudius, gets mad at himself.

Denial: Refusing to acknowledge what one knows. Hamlet says he doesn't know why he acts, but the answer is right in front of him: he doesn't want to end up like the 20,000 men marching to their meaningless deaths.

Reversal: Turning a situation around; saying the opposite of what is the case. Hamlet says the 20,000 men march to their meaningless deaths to his shame, but isn't the shame really their own?

Elements: Scene, Set, Actor, and Director

Literature, especially drama, has played a key role in the development of psychological theories. As Francoise Meltzer puts it, in *Critical Terms for Literary Study*, "Literature, in the eyes of psychoanalysis, is like a dream, uncovering deep, otherwise invisible workings of unconscious activities" (152). Freud often turned to literature, and he articulated his most famous theory (and perhaps uncovered it) by analyzing Sophocles's great play, *Oedipus Rex*. For Sophocles's original Greek audience, it seems that this play was about the conflict between fate and freedom: Oedipus, according to a prophet, is doomed to murder his father and marry his mother, and all attempts to evade or ignore the prophecy turn out leading to its fulfillment.

For Freud, however, the story of Oedipus represents the desire of all sons to possess their mothers, which requires eliminating the father. Every male child must work through this **Oedipus Complex**, suppressing this desire for the mother and accepting the father's rule, or suffer maladjustment. The son's fear, at its most elemental, is the fear of castration by the father (here, indeed, many people have raised their eyebrows). That deep-seated fear helps to motivate the son to grow up and shift his desires elsewhere. When Oedipus discovers that he has in fact killed his father and married his mother, he tears out his own eyes—certainly an odd reaction, and one that Freud was able to account for by connecting the similarly shaped testes and the eyes: Oedipus is symbolically castrating himself, carrying out the punishment of the father in order to restore justice in the world. (Given the centrality of the Oedipus Complex in his thinking, Freud was never able to account satisfyingly for the development of girls, who are obviously immune to the threat of castration.)

Drama is particularly appealing for psychological analysis because the character is so visibly present (on the stage, or in the theater of our minds), and his or her motivation is often so unarticulated. A fiction writer may employ an omniscient narrator to explain to us why a character is doing something, or we may share in the character's thinking. On the stage, characters do sometimes, usually in an aside to the audience, reveal the contents of their minds, but for the most part the theater simply presents for us what the characters do and say. The audience (or reader) of a play is in a position that is interestingly similar to that of the psychologist: both see a tiny part of someone's life (partly reported, partly witnessed), and both attempt to make sense of the whole. Freud was by no means the first to consider the psychological effects of attempting to recreate and understand a life. **Aristotle** (384–322 BCE) many centuries ago argued that tragic drama had a healthy psychological effect upon audiences because it allowed them to release destructive emotions and cultivate useful ones. The viewers, according to Aristotle, experience pity for the characters who suffer, and fear for themselves, since something similarly awful might happen to them. Aristotle's description of this emotional purging has been so influential that his Greek term is still current: **catharsis**.

Although catharsis, to the extent that it is a real phenomenon, is most often used to talk about drama, there is no intrinsic reason that it cannot be applied to other genres. Indeed, most terms used to analyze fiction and poetry apply just as well to drama. Even so poetic a concept as the sonnet comes in handy when Shakespearean characters speak in that form, as in *Romeo and Juliet*. One of the most popular concepts applied to drama is **Freytag's pyramid**, which points simply to plots that have a **rising action**, a **climax**, and a **falling action** (a sequence that is usually depicted as a pyramid). Short stories, novels, poems, even biographies, perhaps even corporate reports can also be usefully viewed as having this kind of shape, which will be covered in the discussion of "plot." Certainly, what you have learned about character, plot, setting, language, and just about anything else can be usefully applied to drama. But surely there are concepts that are dramatic, and ideas that have to be adapted to talk about plays, aren't there? To see what elements need our attention in reading and writing about drama, let's look at a scene from that play that typifies for many people the pinnacle of theatrical achievement, *Hamlet*.

WILLIAM SHAKESPEARE (1564–1616)

Hamlet Act IV, Scene 4, Lines 32–66

inform against: accuse	How all occasions do inform against me,
	And spur my dull revenge! What is a man,
market: product	If his chief good and market of his time
	Be but to sleep and feed? A beast, no more. 35
discourse: reasoning,	Sure He that made us with such large discourse,
power, language	Looking before and after, gave us not
	That capability and godlike reason
fust: develop mold	To fust in us unus'd. Now, whether it be
craven: cowardly	Bestial oblivion, or some craven scruple 40
event: the result	Of thinking too precisely on th' event—
	A thought which quarter'd hath but one part wisdom
	And ever three parts coward—I do not know
	Why yet I live to say "This thing's to do,"
Sith: since	Sith I have cause, and will, and strength, and means 45
gross: huge, obvious	To do 't. Examples gross as earth exhort me:
	Witness this army of such mass and charge,
	Led by a delicate and tender prince,
	Whose spirit with divine ambition puff'd

Makes mouths:
taunts, scorns

Makes mouths at the invisible event,   50
Exposing what is mortal and unsure
To all that fortune, death, and danger dare,
Even for an egg-shell. Rightly to be great
Is not to stir without great argument,
But greatly to find quarrel in a straw   55
When honor's at the stake. How stand I then,
That have a father kill'd, a mother stain'd,
Excitements of my reason and my blood,
And let all sleep, while to my shame I see
The imminent death of twenty thousand men   60
That for a fantasy and trick of fame
Go to their graves like beds, fight for a plot
Whereon the numbers cannot try the cause,
Which is not tomb enough and continent
To hide the slain? O, from this time forth,   65
My thoughts be bloody, or be nothing worth!

[1600]

Plays are divided conventionally into **acts**, which may be divided into **scenes**. A scene ends when the location of the action before us changes, or perhaps when a character enters or leaves. In a full-length play, when one act ends and another one begins, the playwright often changes the setting, the mood, the characters on stage—whatever. So the end of a scene marks a small unit in a play, and the end of an act is a kind of large punctuation mark, similar to a chapter in a novel, or a section in a long poem. A one-act play often consists of only one scene, with continuous action, but there is no prescribed length for a one-act or a full-length play, anymore than there is a prescribed length for a short story or a novel or a poem. When portions of plays are quoted, whether a long passage or a few words, the act, scene, and line numbers are quoted. You can tell that the preceding scene comes from Act 4, Scene 4, lines 32–66. Five acts, as in *Hamlet*, is a common structure for a full-length classical play; this scene comes well after the midway point in *Hamlet*.

Playwrights often indicate, with explicit directions and with comments by the characters, what sort of **setting** should be created. In this scene, Hamlet has just observed the army of Fortinbras moving to attack a part of Poland. The land the two armies are fighting over is insignificant; Fortinbras's captain says he wouldn't pay "five ducats" to farm it, and yet thousands of ducats and lives will be wasted in the battle. Hearing this, Hamlet makes this speech. Where exactly is Hamlet, and to whom is he speaking? The stage directions, probably not by Shakespeare but reflecting contemporary performances, say simply that the scene is "A plain in Denmark." The director of the play (or film), working with the set designer, thus has lots of creative freedom: it could be raining, and a gust could come up just as Hamlet begins. His observation that "all occasions do inform against me" could then allude to the environment, as if all of nature really is against him. The terrain could be desolate (underscoring the slightness of the prize) or fertile (suggesting that even a small plot of land sparks conflict); There has even been a production set in space in which the "egg-shell" being fought over, not large enough to bury the dead of the battle, is a small hollow asteroid, and the plain of Denmark is the command deck of a space station. If you can't see a play, then you must imagine the setting (or you have the freedom of being the director and set designer, if you prefer looking at it that way).

Hamlet is speaking to no one, according to the **stage directions**, which say "Exe-unt all except Hamlet." This speech then is not a **dialogue**, an interchange between and among characters; it's a **soliloquy**—a speech spoken by a character alone on the stage, allowing the audience access to his or her thoughts. It may seem odd for char-acters to talk to the air, but it is a convention long accepted in the theatre, and it is true that people talk to themselves, sometimes even aloud, especially under stress. Hamlet is certainly agitated in this speech because he is berating himself for not tak-ing revenge against the murderer of his father. As he says, he has "cause, and will, and strength, and means/ To do't," and yet he doesn't act. One aspect of Shakespeare's bril-liance in this play is surely his ability to maintain the **suspense** of the play, even though it is primarily about the main character, the **protagonist,** failing to take action. Hamlet's revenge is "dull" because he has delayed so long, and he compares himself to "a beast" in his inactivity, as if "to sleep and feed" were the only things he's been doing. Hamlet finds himself unable to say why he has hesitated, whether it is "Bestial oblivion, or some craven scruple/ Of thinking too precisely on th' event." Is he living too much in the unconscious, illogical mind, oblivious to revenge and justice, thinking only of his physical desires? Or is he thinking too much, letting his superego overanalyze the rightness of his actions? "I do not know," he says, but he does know that Fortinbras, "a delicate and tender prince," is indirectly putting him to shame by undertaking the battle he is witnessing.

In this respect, Fortinbras acts as a **foil** to Hamlet—a character who contrasts with the protagonist, and thereby helps us understand his or her character better. Fortinbras's actions throughout the play serve as a **subplot**, a line of action that (again) helps us understand the main action better, by means of contrast. Hamlet has, he says, "a father kill'd, a mother stain'd,/ Excitements of my reason and my blood," and yet he still does not take action. Although Hamlet is perplexed by his own inactivity, Freud's Oedipus Complex allows us to explain both his hesitation and his inability to understand his hesitation. Claudius has done what Hamlet him-self wanted to do, at least according to the Oedipus Complex. To take revenge, Hamlet must deal with this repressed desire. The soldiers he sees "Go to their graves like beds," Hamlet says, an odd simile, except that he has just mentioned his "mother stain'd,/ Excitements of my reason and my blood," and he is (if we follow Freud) thinking subconsciously about going to bed. We may notice, in this excerpt's last lines, that he says "My thoughts be bloody, or be nothing worth!" He does not say, yet, "My *actions* be bloody, or be nothing worth!"

There are, to be sure, other specialized terms that may be useful in analyzing drama, but the main thing you need to employ is your own creativity and attentive-ness. The strategies and concepts that work for poetry and fiction will, for the most part, apply to drama as well.

Practice: Brainstorms

Here is a brief one-act that raises interesting psychological questions in a small space.

TERRENCE MCNALLY (1939–)

Terrence McNally is clearly one of the most creative and influential American playwrights. In 1988, when Andre's Mother *first appeared, Terrence McNally was forty-nine years old and already recognized as an important playwright. Born in St. Petersburg, Florida, McNally grew* up primarily in Corpus Christi, Texas, the son of a beer distributor. His first play was produced when he was 25, and The Ritz (1975) was adapted for a successful film in 1976. In 1987, Frankie and Johnny at the Claire de Lune appeared, and McNally soon transformed that play into Frankie and Johnny, a Gary Marshall film starring Al Pacino and Michelle Pfeiffer. In 1990, Andre's Mother was awarded an Emmy (Best Writing in a Miniseries or Special), and throughout the 1990s McNally's body of work and reputation grew exponentially. In 1991, McNally's Lips Together, Teeth Apart told the moving story of two married couples who fear spending a weekend at the home of someone who has just died of AIDS. One of the wives has inherited her brother's summer home on Fire Island, but the couples are afraid to swim in his pool, as McNally exposes widespread irrational fears and prejudices of the time. In the next year, 1992, McNally provided the script for Kiss of the Spider Woman, a haunting musical that examines the unlikely subject of two men imprisoned in a Latin American prison. After Spider Woman won the 1993 Tony for "Best Book of a Musical," McNally continued with Love! Valour! Compassion! (1994), which focuses on eight gay men; Master Class (1995), which deals with Maria Callas, the great opera singer; Ragtime (1997), which transforms E. L. Doctorow's novel into a musical; Corpus Christi (1997), which is clearly McNally's most controversial work, as it reimagines Jesus's life as a gay man, with gay disciples. Corpus Christi brought a storm of protest before it opened, and later a protest against anyone who had seen it—including death threats and even a Fatwa (or death sentence) from a British Muslim group.

    Compared to his most daring work, Andre's Mother may seem quite tame, but it portrays powerfully the effects of a plague and a prejudice that both endure to this day.

Andre's Mother

Characters

Cal, a young man
Arthur, his father
Penny, his sister
Andre's Mother
Time: *Now*
Place: *New York City, Central Park*

> *Four people–Cal, Arthur, Penny, and Andre's Mother—enter. They are nicely dressed and each carries a white helium-filled balloon on a string.*

Cal: You know what's really terrible? I can't think of anything terrific to say. Good-bye. I love you. I'll miss you. And I'm supposed to be so great with words!
Penny: What's that over there?
Arthur: Ask your brother.
Cal: It's a theatre. An outdoor theatre. They do plays there in the summer. Shakespeare's plays. (*To Andre's Mother.*) God, how much he wanted to play Hamlet again. He would have gone to Timbuktu to have another go at that part. The summer he did it in Boston, he was so happy!
Penny: Cal, I don't think she . . . ! It's not the time. Later.
Arthur: Your son was a . . . the Jews have a word for it . . .
Penny (quietly appalled): Oh my God!
Arthur: Mensch, I believe it is, and I think I'm using it right. It means warm, solid, the real thing. Correct me if I'm wrong.

    5

Penny: Fine, Dad, fine. Just quit while you're ahead.   10

Arthur: I won't say he was like a son to me. Even my son isn't always like a son to me. I mean . . . ! In my clumsy way, I'm trying to say how much I liked Andre. And how much he helped me to know my own boy. Cal was always two handsful but Andre and I could talk about anything under the sun. My wife was very fond of him, too.

Penny: Cal, I don't understand about the balloons.

Cal: They represent the soul. When you let go, it means you're letting his soul ascend to Heaven. That you're willing to let go. Breaking the last earthly ties.

Penny: Does the Pope know about this?

Arthur: Penny!   15

Penny: Andre loved my sense of humor. Listen, you can hear him laughing. (*She lets go of her white balloon.*) So long, you glorious, wonderful, I-know-what-Cal-means-about-words . . . *man!* God forgive me for wishing you were straight every time I laid eyes on you. But if any man was going to have you, I'm glad it was my brother! Look how fast it went up. I bet that means something. Something terrific.

Arthur (lets his balloon go): Good-bye. God speed.

Penny: Cal?

Cal: I'm not ready yet.

Penny: Okay. We'll be over there. Come on, Pop, you can buy your little girl   20
a Good Humor.

Arthur: They still make Good Humor?

Penny: Only now they're called Dove Bars and they cost twelve dollars. (*Penny takes Arthur off. Cal and Andre's Mother stand with their balloons.*)

Cal: I wish I knew what you were thinking. I think it would help me. You know almost nothing about me and I only know what Andre told me about you. I'd always had it in my mind that one day we would be friends, you and me. But if you didn't know about Andre and me . . . If this hadn't happened, I wonder if he would have ever told you. When he was sick, if I asked him once I asked him a thousand times, tell her. She's your mother. She won't mind. But he was so afraid of hurting you and of your disapproval. I don't know which was worse. (*No response. He sighs.*) God, how many of us live in this city because we don't want to hurt our mothers and live in mortal terror of their disapproval. We lose ourselves here. Our lives aren't furtive, just our feelings toward people like you are! A city of fugitives from our parents' scorn or heartbreak. Sometimes he'd seem a little down and I'd say, "What's the matter, babe?" and this funny sweet, sad smile would cross his face and he'd say, "Just a little homesick, Cal, just a little bit." I always accused him of being a country boy just playing at being a hotshot, sophisticated New Yorker. (*He sighs.*)

It's bullshit. It's all bullshit. (*Still no response.*)   25

Do you remember the comic strip *Little Lulu*? Her mother had no name, she was so remote, so formidable to all the children. She was just Lulu's mother. "Hello, Lulu's Mother," Lulu's friends would say. She was almost anonymous in her remoteness. You remind me of her. Andre's Mother. Let me answer the questions you can't ask and then I'll leave you alone and you won't ever have to see me again. Andre died of AIDS. I don't know how he got it. I tested negative. He died bravely. You would have been proud of him. The only thing that frightened him was you. I'll have everything that was his sent to you. I'll pay for it. There isn't much. You should have come up the summer he played Hamlet. He was magnificent. Yes, I'm bitter. I'm bitter I've lost him. I'm bitter what's happening. I'm bitter even now, after all this, I can't reach you. I'm beginning to feel your disapproval and it's making me ill. (*He looks at his balloon.*) Sorry, old friend. I blew it. (*He lets go of the balloon.*)

Good night, sweet prince, and flights of angels sing thee to thy rest! (*Beat.*)

Goodbye, Andre's Mother.

(*He goes. Andre's Mother stands alone holding her white balloon. Her lips tremble. She looks on the verge of breaking down. She is about to let go of the balloon when she pulls it down to her. She looks at it awhile before she gently kisses it. She lets go of the balloon. She follows it with her eyes as it rises and rises. The lights are beginning to fade. Andre's Mother's eyes are still on the balloon. The lights fade.*)

Questions

1. This play, titled for Andre's Mother, assigns no lines to her. If you were directing the play, how would you explain the mother's motivation to the actress who plays her? Specifically, why does she not speak? What is she thinking? How should she behave?
2. Explain the mother's action at the end of the play.
3. Andre very much wanted, Cal says, to play Hamlet again. Is this fact significant? How is Cal like Horatio, Hamlet's friend, who is charged by Hamlet at the end of the play to tell his story? How is the mother like Gertrude? In other words, can you expand on the psychological implications of Cal's information? (Notice Cal's last words, before saying goodbye to Andre's Mother.)
4. Cal believes he has failed. Has he?

Suggestion for Writing

Are we always, even when we're alone, "on stage" in some sense? What would it mean to be authentic, honest, perfectly open? Would that be a good idea?

Construct a very brief scene in which a character is acting (that is, putting on a show, pretending to be someone or something that he or she isn't). Feel free to base the scene on your own life, or your imagination, or some combination of the two.

Or, here's another suggestion for constructing a very brief dramatic scene that explores the motivations or one or more characters. You might consider, for instance, bringing the characters in *Andre's Mother* together again at some later date. What might they say to each other later? How might they have changed? Or, create an additional scene for *Andre's Mother* that occurs some months before the scene in the play. You might want to add a scene to some other play, working with characters that are already formed; or you may just want to invent your own characters and events.

Fiction

Fiction

10

Elements of Fiction

The purpose of fiction is still, as it was to Joseph Conrad,
to make the reader see.

—*Peter DeVries*

Engaging the Story

Stories are everywhere. You
already know a lot about stories,
having no doubt told, viewed, listened to, and imagined hundreds,
even thousands of them. You
needn't have read Aristotle's classic *Poetics* (fourth century BCE),
the original handbook to literature, to know that a story ought
to have a beginning, middle, and
end; or that a story ought to have
a point, some central organizing
action that holds all the separate
events together; or that a good
story has a hero in some sense, a
protagonist or main character
who has some redeeming characteristics (he or she can't be all
bad, or we probably won't care

"And what's the story behind the story?"

what happens), and who performs the story's principal action. Even if you've never
read any literary criticism or even any literature at all, you still already know that an
especially *good* story is one that is not worn out by one telling; a really good story just
gets better the second and third and fourth times around.

These assumptions about stories—and a great many more—are part of our
cultural inheritance: you can absorb them simply by hanging around. Every human
culture that has ever existed on this planet appears to have invested considerable

energy in telling tales, preserving their culture's essential truths by means of myth, narrative, fiction. But the conventions for telling a story do vary from culture to culture, sometimes dramatically. In one tribal culture, according to Joseph Grimes's *Thread of Discourse*, it appears that every story ends with a pack of multicolored dogs running off into the distance. This convention, strange as it seems to us, apparently signals to the audience that the story is over. It is as natural in that culture, apparently, as the film credits rolling in our own.

A greater awareness of the conventions of fiction in the culture you inhabit can be useful: for one thing, noticing how a story meets—or sometimes stretches or even violates—certain expectations is often part of the pleasure of appreciating the story. The best way to become familiar with such conventions is, fortunately, simply reading lots of stories. Therefore, this chapter gathers together a variety of excellent short fiction for you to experience. It's also helpful to have some explicit discussion of these elements of fiction, and this chapter will therefore review some basic concepts that are especially relevant for talking about fiction—beginning with the question of what "fiction" is.

Fiction can be true   One common way of distinguishing fiction as a genre is to compare it to history and journalism. Historians and reporters are (supposedly) constrained by the expectation that they will tell us accurately about something that really happened. Works of fiction may be based on history, and sometimes the boundary between fiction and history, or fiction and journalism, may be rather porous. Still, it is possible to distinguish different intentions: while historians and journalists strive to report reality, fiction writers (we assume) strive to create a reality. Historians and journalists try to give us the facts; fiction writers generally try to convey the "real" facts—facts that add up to something, that point us toward some insight, that arrest our thinking and "make the reader see." A novel about Winston Churchill, for instance, might depict a meeting with Albert Einstein that never took place (so far as anyone knows), but the imagined story of this meeting may show us something interesting or valuable about Churchill or Einstein, or about men like them. An imagined event may show us what Churchill and Einstein might have said, had they met. A work of fiction might thereby reveal some "facts" of human nature, more basic and enduring than particular events. (Einstein once said that imagination is more important than knowledge.)

Good fiction can be distinguished by precisely this ability to spark the reader's insight. Much popular fiction is "good" at occupying our attention and passing the time, but it may not alter our vision at all. Romance novels, for example, are notoriously formulaic: experienced readers essentially know what's going to happen and even the way the story is going to be told. Although romance readers enjoy variations and twists on the standard stories of boy meets girl, they generally don't want to be too startled or challenged. The heroine can develop a life-threatening illness, but she shouldn't become permanently disabled; the hero can be attracted to an evil other woman, but he shouldn't run off with her. The hero and heroine can be very passionate and sensual people, but they shouldn't have a history of promiscuity or sadomasochism or heavy drug use. The style can be interesting, but it shouldn't be too complex or demanding, with too many unfamiliar words or complicated sentences.

Formulaic fiction in whatever genre—romance, science fiction, detective fiction, western—is reassuring, providing readers with what they expect, surprising them a little but not too much. And such fiction is often fun to read, especially if you know the conventions of the genre. For those who have mastered the genre and have a gifted imagination, formulaic fiction is relatively easy to write, since a formula already exists. Formulaic fiction is even worth studying, if only because it helps to expose our cultural assumptions. But, examined critically and carefully, formulaic fiction is not likely to be as interesting and rewarding as more "serious" fiction, the kind that occupies most (if not all) of the space in anthologies like this one.

Fiction can be challenging   Most literature courses focus on the kind of "serious" fiction, or "good" fiction, that surprises and enlarges us, and that will repay close and repeated attention. Formulaic fiction is consumed: once the action has been digested, few readers will want to read the story again. Although we may well read good fiction to see what happens, the story isn't used up by being read. Most whodunit detective stories can be pretty much ruined by learning who did it; but good fiction in the detective story genre raises more issues than just the identity and methods of the culprit. As a consequence, those stories that have been noted for their excellence are likely to be more challenging than formulaic fiction, but they are also likely to be more interesting and rewarding, surpassing the conventions of any genre.

No amount of advice can substitute for your own intellectual energy, but there are some suggestions you can follow in reading challenging fiction. Rather than make them in the abstract, let's look at a work of short fiction that is innovative, testing the boundaries of what a short story does.

Let's begin by reading only the first three sentences of the story. It's called "The Hit Man," and it's by T. Coraghessan Boyle (published in 1980).

Early Years

The Hit Man's early years are complicated by the black bag that he wears over his head. Teachers correct his pronunciation, the coach criticizes his attitude, the principal dresses him down for branding preschoolers with a lit cigarette. He is a poor student.

What do you make of this? Have you ever read a short story that began this way? You might take a few moments to jot down a reaction, and then compare it to this student's response:

> I started over several times because I found the first few sentences confusing. I don't understand why he has a black bag over his head. Does that symbolize something? If he is a Hit Man (somebody who kills people for money), then what is he doing in elementary school? He's going to be a Hit Man, I guess. But it sounds as if he is already one. This beginning seemed like a story being told by someone who doesn't know how to tell a story. I must be missing something. I don't like this story.

Another student had this reaction:

> This is a hoot. I'm not really sure what's going on here, but it's funny. The idea of a "hit man" in grade school—I wouldn't have thought of that. The black bag on his head is really weird. What's that about?

The honesty and independence of the first response are appealing: the student isn't going to pretend to like the story's opening just because it's "literature," just because she suspects she's supposed to. She has a point, too. The passage is easy enough to read (the words are common, the sentence structure easy), but what's going on is far from clear. The story doesn't start out like most stories. Except for the present tense, it seems a bit like a news report or a biography or obituary even, especially with the heading, "Early Years." And the black bag is indeed hard to understand. What in the world *is* going on?

Still, the second student clearly is having a better time. The first reader seems to assume that a story should give us the facts clearly and quickly, without confusing or surprising us. Experienced readers of fiction, however, generally are willing to wait for a story to unfold, confident that things will probably clear up shortly— or if they don't, that the obscurity itself will prove significant or interesting. We read fiction not only to find out what happens, but also to see *how* the story is told, and what this telling might mean. It's always possible that you are indeed missing something in reading, as the first student suspects—by all means, look closely; but perhaps you're *supposed* to be missing it, and perhaps the absence is important. Just keep going, willing to experience whatever the story offers.

We've already arrived at the first tips on how to read fiction:

- Read patiently, appreciating not only what happens, but how the story is unfolded.
- Read confidently: don't be discouraged or frustrated if something is unclear to you—it may well be unclear to other readers; it will probably clear up eventually; or perhaps it's supposed to be unclear. Be willing to be pleased, moved, confused—taking whatever the story offers.

Patience, confidence, tolerance for uncertainty—these are qualities of mind cultivated by the study of fiction (and other forms of literature), and they are arguably valuable in any endeavor.

Let's return to Boyle's story, this time reading the whole first paragraph, and then considering a few more responses.

Early Years

The Hit Man's early years are complicated by the black bag that he wears over his head. Teachers correct his pronunciation, the coach criticizes his attitude, the principal dresses him down for branding preschoolers with a lit cigarette. He is a poor student. At lunch he sits alone, feeding bell peppers and salami into the dark slot of his mouth. In the hallways, wiry young athletes snatch at the black hood and slap the back of his head. When he is thirteen he is approached by the captain of the football team, who pins him down and attempts to remove the hood. The Hit Man wastes him. Five years, says the judge.

Now consider this student's reaction to the story so far:

This reminds me of Donnie B., the terror of my third grade. I do not know that he grew up to be a hit man, but

```
he certainly seemed to be headed in that direction.
Although Donnie didn't brand preschoolers with his
cigarettes, he did tie firecrackers to cats. But I don't
remember that he had a black bag over his head! He was so
odd and so distant and so hard to figure out that he might
as well have had a black bag over his head. But he wasn't
quite that weird.
```

This response certainly seems patient, confident, tolerant, but it may also seem a bit like daydreaming. Many students are genuinely relieved to hear that all normal readers have trouble from time to time keeping their attention focused on what's before them. There's nothing wrong with you if you find yourself daydreaming as you read, especially with fiction. In fact, some musing and speculating is likely useful, encouraging a reader-response approach. This student's response compares the character in the story to a character in his life, and such imagining often makes the story itself more vivid, more alive. I encourage you to free-associate, to try to envision, to *see* what you're reading as much as possible. Indeed, try to use all your imaginative senses as you read.

Your imagination can of course become an obstruction to your experience of the text. When you do find yourself truly wandering away, losing your focus rather than enriching it, comparing the story to something in your own life and then going off to think about yourself, leaving the story behind, then you need some strategies for returning your attention to what you're reading. One of the best ways to keep yourself reading attentively is to read *actively*: mark up the text, underline key words and phrases, put comments and questions in the margins.

But don't limit your writing to the small spaces available around the text itself. Many readers keep a reading journal, a "commonplace book" as it is traditionally called, where they record their reactions and impressions. One of the best-known and most enthusiastic keepers of commonplace books was Thomas Jefferson, but such active reading was quite common in his day. There are no rules for such a reading journal, other than you need to write freely and often, concentrating your intelligence, focusing, and enjoying yourself.

You can also become more active by reading aloud, imagining that you are performing the work, in other words, or even by writing out portions of it. Jefferson often copied out sentences or passages ("commonplaces") that he found particularly arresting, storing them up for future use—again, a widespread practice for centuries. The award-winning critic Helen Vendler once said that the key to developing her celebrated readings of Keats's poetry was the act of writing out the poems in her own handwriting. Simply copying a passage can clarify it. It slows the reading process down and forces one to attend to every word.

If problems focusing on the text persist, then you may need to change your environment, take a nap or do some exercise, or take care of something else that will allow you to concentrate.

So, to our first two tips, "read patiently" and "read confidently," we can add two more:

- Read actively, marking up the text, using your imagination.
- Read attentively, returning your focus to the text whenever you catch your mind wandering.

Let's start the story once more, this time reading the first three sections, attempting to practice the tips offered here so far.

Early Years

The Hit Man's early years are complicated by the black bag that he wears over his head. Teachers correct his pronunciation, the coach criticizes his attitude, the principal dresses him down for branding preschoolers with a lit cigarette. He is a poor student. At lunch he sits alone, feeding bell peppers and salami into the dark slot of his mouth. In the hallways, wiry young athletes snatch at the black hood and slap the back of his head. When he is thirteen he is approached by the captain of the football team, who pins him down and attempts to remove the hood. The Hit Man wastes him. Five years, says the judge.

Back on the Street

The Hit Man is back on the street in two months.

First Date

The girl's name is Cynthia. The Hit Man pulls up in front of her apartment in his father's hearse. (The Hit Man's father, whom he loathes and abominates, is a mortician. At breakfast the Hit Man's father had slapped the cornflakes from his son's bowl. The son threatened to waste his father. He did not, restrained no doubt by considerations of filial loyalty and the deep-seated taboos against patricide that permeate the universal unconscious.)

Cynthia's father has silver sideburns and plays tennis. He responds to the Hit Man's knock, expresses surprise at the Hit Man's appearance. The Hit Man takes Cynthia by the elbow, presses a twenty into her father's palm, and disappears into the night.

Consider an entry from another student's reading response:

```
    I expected to find out pretty soon why the hit man wears a
black bag over his head. The story goes on and fails to say
anything about it. Why does he wear a bag? Why is it also
called a "hood"? Which is it? Why does the hit man so strongly
not want anyone to remove the bag? He's like a wrestler on
television, keeping his identity secret. Why is he back on the
street after two months? Is that typical for a five-year
sentence? Or is that supposed to be funny? It is kind of funny
to think about the hit man "feeding bell peppers and salami
into the dark slot of his mouth," or giving twenty dollars to
his date's dad, as if he's paying him. As if he is the
daughter's pimp or something. The hit man doesn't seem like a
real person. Why doesn't he have a name?
```

Good questions are the key to good ideas, as this student seems to know. She is not too concerned at this point with whether she can answer any of these questions, or even with the order in which they appear. Rather, her effort is focused on making connections, moving not only forward through the text, anticipating what will happen, but also backward, observing how her experience has evolved. She is, you may notice, trying out a number of different approaches, moving from gestures toward a reader-response stance ("I expected . . ."), to a deconstructive stance ("The story goes on and fails to say anything . . ."), to a psychological stance ("Why does the hit man so strongly not want anyone to remove . . ."), to a historical stance ("Is that typical for a five-year sentence?"), and so on. The reader here is looking for traction—for a way of thinking about the story that will produce a flow of ideas.

The strategy so far of presenting little snippets of a story, interrupted by comments and analysis, may seem odd—not really a natural reading process. But this procedure is actually only an exaggeration of what good readers do. Just as research has shown that good *writers* frequently reread what they've written as they're composing (and poor writers do not), good readers keep relating what they are reading to what has gone before, noticing how their experience evolves, returning to reread the text as needed.

To become a more insightful reader, however, you'll need to do more than just reread a particular work. Like just about anything else, reading improves with wide-ranging experience and practice. In reading literature, this improvement through experience results in part because so many literary works draw on each other in one way or another. The critic Harold Bloom draws our attention to this interdependence among literary works when he says that every literary work is in its essence a response to some other literary work. It is certainly true that no writer works in a vacuum. A story enters a conversation begun by other stories; or perhaps we should say that a story engages its reader in a conversation that was begun by the reader's engagement with other stories. (To what sort of work is Boyle responding?) The final tip here is to read as much as you can, of as many different kinds of things as you can, but make works recognized for their merit a substantial part of your reading. This tip joins the other six:

Suggestions for Reading Stories

- Read patiently, appreciating not only what happens, but how the story is unfolded.
- Read confidently: don't be discouraged or frustrated if something is unclear to you—it's probably unclear to other readers; it will probably clear up eventually; it's possibly supposed to be unclear.
- Read actively, marking up the text, using your imagination.
- Read attentively, returning your focus to the text whenever you find it wanders away.
- Read forward and backward anticipating what's coming, connecting to what's gone before.
- Read a work and its crucial passages repeatedly.
- Read widely.

Now, armed with these tips, read the entirety of "The Hit Man," trying to use the advice offered here as you read. Pause during and after your reading to write down your reactions, questions, insights.

T. CORAGHESSAN BOYLE (1948–)

T. Coraghessan Boyle began life as Thomas John Boyle, but changed his middle name when he was seventeen. He earned an MFA and a PhD from the University of Iowa in 1977, and he has taught in the English department at the University of California-Santa Barbara since 1978. The author of fourteen books of fiction, his stories have appeared in many American magazines, including The New Yorker, Atlantic Monthly, *and* Playboy. *He lives with his wife and three children near Santa Barbara.*

T. Coraghessan Boyle strikes a pose.

The Hit Man
Early Years

The Hit Man's early years are complicated by the black bag that he wears over his head. Teachers correct his pronunciation, the coach criticizes his attitude, the principal dresses him down for branding preschoolers with a lit cigarette. He is a poor student. At lunch he sits alone, feeding bell peppers and salami into the dark slot of his mouth. In the hallways, wiry young athletes snatch at the black hood and slap the back of his head. When he is thirteen he is approached by the captain of the football team, who pins him down and attempts to remove the hood. The Hit Man wastes him. Five years, says the judge.

Back on the Street

The Hit Man is back on the street in two months.

First Date

The girl's name is Cynthia. The Hit Man pulls up in front of her apartment in his father's hearse. (The Hit Man's father, whom he loathes and abominates, is a mortician. At breakfast the Hit Man's father had slapped the cornflakes from his son's bowl. The son threatened to waste his father. He did not, restrained no doubt by considerations of filial loyalty and the deep-seated taboos against patricide that permeate the universal unconscious.)

Cynthia's father has silver sideburns and plays tennis. He responds to the Hit Man's knock, expresses surprise at the Hit Man's appearance. The Hit Man takes Cynthia by the elbow, presses a twenty into her father's palm, and disappears into the night.

Father's Death

At breakfast the Hit Man slaps the cornflakes from his father's bowl. Then   5
wastes him.

Mother's Death

The Hit Man is in his early twenties. He shoots pool, lifts weights and drinks
milk from the carton. His mother is in the hospital, dying of cancer or heart
disease. The priest wears black. So does the Hit Man.

First Job

Porfirio Buñoz, a Cuban financier, invites the Hit Man to lunch. I hear you're
looking for work, says Buñoz.
    That's right, says the Hit Man.

Peas

The Hit Man does not like peas. They are too difficult to balance on the
fork.

Talk Show

The Hit Man waits in the wings, the white slash of a cigarette scarring   10
the midnight black of his head and upper torso. The makeup girl has
done his mouth and eyes, brushed the nap of his hood. He has been
briefed. The guest who precedes him is a pediatrician. A planetary glow
washes the stage where the host and the pediatrician, separated by a potted palm, cross their legs and discuss the little disturbances of infants
and toddlers.
    After the station break the Hit Man finds himself squeezed into a direc-
tor's chair, white lights in his eyes. The talk-show host is a baby-faced man
in his early forties. He smiles like God and all His Angels. Well, he says. So
you're a hit man. Tell me—I've always wanted to know—what does it feel
like to hit someone?

Death of Mateo Maria Buñoz

The body of Mateo María Buñoz, the cousin and business associate of a
prominent financier, is discovered down by the docks on a hot summer
morning. Mist rises from the water like steam, there is the smell of fish. A
large black bird perches on the dead man's forehead.

Marriage

Cynthia and the Hit Man stand at the altar, side by side. She is wearing a
white satin gown and lace veil. The Hit Man has rented a tuxedo, extra-large,
and a silk-lined black-velvet hood.
    . . . Till death do you part, says the priest.

Moods

The Hit Man is moody, unpredictable. Once, in a luncheonette, the waitress   15
brought him the meatloaf special but forgot to eliminate the peas. There
was a spot of gravy on the Hit Man's hood, about where his chin should be.
He looked up at the waitress, his eyes like pins behind the triangular slots,
and wasted her.

    Another time he went to the track with $25, came back with $1800. He
stopped at a cigar shop. As he stepped out of the shop a wino tugged at his
sleeve and solicited a quarter. The Hit Man reached into his pocket, extracted the $1800 and handed it to the wino. Then wasted him.

First Child

A boy. The Hit Man is delighted. He leans over the edge of the playpen and
molds the tiny fingers around the grip of a nickel-plated derringer. The gun
is loaded with blanks—the Hit Man wants the boy to get used to the noise.
By the time he is four the boy has mastered the rudiments of Tae Kwon Do,
can stick a knife in the wall from a distance of ten feet and shoot a moving
target with either hand. The Hit Man rests his broad palm on the boy's head.
You're going to make the Big Leagues, Tiger, he says.

Work

He flies to Cincinnati. To L.A. To Boston. To London. The stewardesses get to
know him.

Half an Acre and a Garage

The Hit man is raking leaves, amassing great brittle piles of them. He is wearing a black T-shirt, cut off at the shoulders, and a cotton work hood, also
black. Cynthia is edging the flowerbed, his son playing in the grass. The Hit
Man waves to his neighbors as they drive by. The neighbors wave back.

    When he has scoured the lawn to his satisfaction, the Hit Man draws   20
the smaller leaf-hummocks together in a single mound the size of a pickup
truck. Then he bends to ignite it with his lighter. Immediately, flames leap
back from the leaves, cut channels through the pile, engulf it in a ball of fire.
The Hit Man stands back, hands folded beneath the great meaty biceps. At
his side is the three-headed dog. He bends to pat each of the heads, smoke
and sparks raging against the sky.

Stalking the Streets of the City

He is stalking the streets of the city, collar up, brim down. It is late at night.
He stalks past department stores, small businesses, parks, and gas stations.
Past apartments, picket fences, picture windows. Dogs growl in the shad-
ows, then slink away. He could hit any of us.

Retirement

A group of businessman-types—sixtyish, seventyish, portly, diamond rings,
cigars, liver spots—throws him a party. Porfirio Buñoz, now in his eighties,
makes a speech and presents the Hit Man with a gilded scythe. The Hit Man

thanks him, then retires to the lake, where he can be seen in his speedboat, skating out over the blue, hood rippling in the breeze.

Death

He is stricken, shrunken, half his former self. He lies propped against the pillows at Mercy Hospital, a bank of gentians drooping round the bed. Tubes run into the hood at the nostril openings, his eyes are clouded and red, sunk deep behind the triangular slots. The priest wears black. So does the Hit Man.

On the other side of town the Hit Man's son is standing before the   20 mirror of a shop that specializes in Hit Man attire. Trying on his first hood.

[1980]

Boyle's little story defies any easy categorization or translation, and it is in fact this resistance to simplifying, along with Boyle's arresting vividness and imagination, that help make "The Hit Man" so fascinating. Inexperienced readers often assume that good readers understand everything when they finish reading a story; in fact, astute readers often find that their wonderment grows as they move through a story. To emphasize this point, and to encourage you to speculate patiently and creatively on the fiction you read, here are a few more comments on the story. These were written by literature majors as part of a workshop; they responded anonymously, so I cannot attribute their comments. But these reactions were typical in at least this sense: experienced readers, literature majors, graduate students, even teachers, find this story perplexing—and interesting.

Response #1

After reading the story, I've decided he has a black bag on his head because he really is Death, the guy who wears a black robe and a black pointed hood and carries a scythe. Look at the scene when he turns the mound of leaves into "a ball of fire."

At his side is the three-headed dog. He bends to pat each of the heads, smoke and sparks raging against the sky.

Three-headed dogs are more than a little unusual. In fact, I only know of one: Cerberus, the three-headed dog in Greek myth who guards the way to the underworld.

But the problem with saying the Hit Man is Death, however, is that he doesn't quite seem like the supernatural entity who comes to take away everyone sooner or later. The story says, "He could hit any of us," which fits okay with Death (although Death will "hit" all of us eventually), but other things don't seem to fit Death very well. The Hit Man kills only those people he is hired to kill or who offend him. He does yard work and waves to his neighbors. He does not like peas. He has a retirement party and gets a "gilded scythe." He dies. The Hit Man seems to be more than an ordinary person but less than the figure of Death. I think Boyle is saying perhaps that this is what a classical myth comes down to today. Instead of the grand and terrifying myth of the Grim Reaper, we've got "the Hit Man."

Response #2

The story seems physically to be quite organized and clear, like a magazine article perhaps. "Early Years," "Back on the Street," and "First Date" seem like parts of such a familiar biography. This appearance makes for some funny bits because it clearly is not a traditional biography. Take, for instance, the section entitled "Peas": "The Hit Man does not like peas. They are too difficult to balance on the fork." Is this an absurdly trivial detail, presented as if it were important? Or does it actually reveal something important about the Hit Man's impatience, or his clumsiness? Or both? Or something else?

My problem with the peas section is typical. I'm having a hard time trying to figure out how to take everything about the Hit Man. Should I laugh at him? I do think it's funny when the Hit Man hands his date's dad a twenty. It's funny that he has a cotton hood for working in the yard. I also smile, I am embarrassed to say, when the Hit Man wastes the football captain. I almost laugh when he hands the money to the beggar, then kills him, which is pretty sick, I know. Why do I almost laugh? The killing doesn't seem real, I guess. It seems more like a Monty Python skit. Is it wrong to laugh? Even killing his father seems a bit comical. The narrator has just told us that the Hit Man fails to kill his father at breakfast because "of filial loyalty and the deep-seated taboos against patricide that permeate the universal unconscious." The very next section reveals however that the Hit Man does kill his father. He "wastes him," the narrator says. This is so absurd I can't take it seriously. It's like a cartoon character getting clobbered. Who cares?

The Hit Man, although ridiculous, is still also a little pitiful to me. I mean, what kind of life does he have? I think of the weird and sad image of him eating alone and feeding peppers and salami into his dark slot. Somehow he reminds me of a sad terrorist. Maybe it's the bag? I think of how sad a terrorist's life must be. To do such horrible things, terrorists must be angry and miserable. But then I can't feel much pity for the Hit Man or for terrorists because I don't really know them, and they do such awful things. The Hit Man kills a bunch of people.

So that is my problem. I do not know how to take the Hit Man. Laugh at him? Feel sorry? Fear him? How does

Boyle want us to react? Is this uneasiness what Boyle is after?

Response #3

There is some nifty writing in this story. I like the extreme efficiency here. For instance: "Cynthia's father has silver sideburns and plays tennis." Say no more. I can see the guy. Even very little things are sharply drawn: "He is stalking the streets of the city, collar up, brim down." That's an unremarkable sentence, except for the collar and brim. I can see that image. I like this sentence: "A group of business-man types—sixtyish, seventyish, portly, diamond rings, cigars, liver spots—throws him a party." The description of the men is not flashy or spectacular, but it's clear and revealing.

I also like the way certain ideas and phrases reappear: "The Hit Man wastes _____." (Fill in the blank.) The father "slaps" the Hit Man's cornflakes away, and he "slaps" the father's cornflakes away. "The priest wears black. So does the Hit Man." These kind of repeated things help pull the story together. Maybe the most important repetition is the Hit Man's son, who is going to take over.

I also like the way Boyle puts certain things side by side. For example, "Teachers correct his pronunciation, the coach criticizes his attitude, the principal dresses him down for branding preschoolers with a lit cigarette." The first two are ordinary, and they set up the third, which is so horrible by contrast it is amusing. He is younger than thirteen at this point. It's bad enough he smokes. But branding preschoolers!

I love the creative descriptions, like "the white slash of a cigarette scarring the midnight black of his head and upper torso."

All three of these sample responses are attentive and specific, raising some good questions and drawing attention to various aspects of the story. Such responses are the starting points for writing about fiction. These aren't essays, but they are useful material toward essays, and each response would no doubt lead to a very different reading of the story. Notice how different the three respondents' interests are: the first response is concerned with the status of the Hit Man—does he stand for Death, or is he a "real" character? The second response is focused upon the question of how to respond—should we laugh at, pity, or fear the Hit Man? How did Boyle think we would respond? And the third response looks at the story's style—what are the features of Boyle's writing?

Clearly Boyle is playing with the conventions of short stories in "The Hit Man." For the sake of comparison, consider the various elements of fiction as they appear in this gem of a short story.

JANETTE TURNER HOSPITAL (1942–)

Janette Turner Hospital was born in Melbourne, Australia, and grew up in Brisbane. She has lived in India, London, Los Angeles, Boston, Kingston (Ontario), and South Carolina. This story comes from her collection Dislocations, *which won the Fiction Award of the Fellowship of Australian Writers. Her newest novel is* Due Preparations for the Plague, *which is set in seventeenth-century England.*

Morgan Morgan

My grandfather, Morgan Morgan, was a yodeller and a breeder of dahlias. On Collins Street and Bourke Street, I could tug at his hand and plead "Please, Grandpa, please!" and he would throw back his head and do something mysterious in his throat and his yodel would unfurl itself like a silk ribbon. All the trams in Melbourne would come to a standstill, entangled. Bewitched pedestrians stopped and stared. But this was nothing compared with former powers: when he was a young man on the goldfields, handsome and down on his luck, the girls for miles around would come running. Yodel-o-o-o, my grandfather would sing, snaring them, winding them in. The girls would sigh and sway like cobras in the strands of his voice. He was a charmer.

"Get along with you, Morg. You're bad for business," Mrs. Blackburn would say. Flowers bloomed by the bucketful around her. She would lean across roses and carnations, she would catch at his sleeve. "Here's a daisy for the Nipper," and she'd tuck it behind my ear. She didn't want him to move on at all, even I knew that. "Your grandpa," she had said to me often enough, "is a fine figure of a man, they don't make men like him anymore." She'd pull one of her carnations from a bucket and swing the stem in her fingers. "A gentleman is a gentleman," she'd sigh. "Even if he is poor as a church mouse and never found a thimbleful of gold."

It was not entirely true, Grandpa told me, that he'd never struck it rich on the goldfields—the *Kalgoorlie* goldfields, he'd say, with a loving hesitation on the *o's* and *l's*, a rallentando which intimated that music had gone from the language since The Rush petered out.

In those exotic and demented times, men were obsessed with the calibration of luck. Not Morgan Morgan. While other men mapped out their fevers with calipers, measuring the likely run of a seam from existing strikes, Grandpa Morgan simply watched for the aura. Wherever the aura settled, he panned or dug.

"Crazy as a bandicoot," the publican told him. "You've got to have a *system*, mate!"   5

But Morgan Morgan knew that gold was a gift, it never came to men of system, never had. "King David danced before the Lord," he pointed out, "which goes to show; and his goldmines were the richest in the world, I read it somewhere, some archaeologist bloke has proved it." Grandpa had his own methods of fossicking, in scripture or creek bed, it was all the same to him. He found what he wanted, or at any rate learned to want what he found.

He labored at strings of waterholes that were known to be panned out. He was after the Morgan Nugget. This was how it appeared to him in a vision: as big as a man's fist, blackened, gnarled like a prune, cobwebby with the roots of creek ferns. He expected its presence to be announced by an echo of Welsh choirs in the tri-tree and eucalypt scrub. And it was, it was. One day, with the strains of *Cwm Rhondda* all around him, he scratched at a piece of rock with a broken fingernail and the sun caught the gash and almost blinded him.

"Solid gold," he told me. "And big as a man's fist." Not for the first time, he knew himself to be a man of destiny.

"What did you do with it, Grandpa?" I was full of awe. When he spoke of the past, I heard the surf of the delectable world of turbulence that raged beyond our garden wall. We were still at the old place in Ringwood then, across from the railway station. If I buried my face in the box-hedge of golden privet, I could hear the rush of Grandpa's life, the trains careering past to Mitcham and Box Hill and Richmond. He would listen too, leaning into the sound, and I would see his eyes travel on beyond Richmond, beyond Footscray even, out towards the unfenceable Nullarbor Plain and Kalgoorlie.

"What did you do with it, Grandpa?"   10

"With what?" he would ask from far away.

"With the Morgan Nugget?"

"I put it down again," he said, "right back down where I found it, inside the vision. It's still waiting where I put it. Listen," he said, "if you put your ear to the Morgan Dahlia, you can hear it waiting."

I buried my ear in those soft salmon ruchings of petals and heard the deep hush of the past. And then *pop, pop*: he pinched the calix with his fingers. "That's the sound of the Morgan Nugget," he said, "when it gets impatient. It's waiting for one of us to find it again."

"Dad!" Grandma Morgan, with a basket of eggs on her arm, came down   15
the path from the hen house. "Don't confuse the child with your nonsense." She lifted her eyebrows at me. "Always could talk the leg off an iron pot, your Grandpa."

"Pot calling the kettle black, I'd say," he grumbled. He hated to be listened in on; I hated it too. I didn't like the way the Morgan history drooped at the edges when other people were around.

Grandma Morgan was picking mint and tossing the sprigs into her basket. The leaves lay green and vivid against the eggs. "Came to tell you the pension cheques have arrived," she said. "Well, praise be," said Grandpa, mollified. "Praise be. There's corn in Egypt yet. And on top of that," he whispered, as she moved off towards the house, "the Morgan Nugget's still waiting."

"Dad! No more nonsense. That child is never going to know the difference between truth and lies, you mark my words."

"Got eyes in the back of her head," Grandpa grumbled. "And ears in the wind. No flies on her, no siree."

It was one of his favorite sayings: *No flies on so-and-so, no siree.* To me   20
it implied an opposite state, an unsavory kind of person, stupid, sticky, smelling overly sweet in the manner of plums left on the ground beneath our tree for too long. I imagined this person—the person on whom there *were* flies—to be pale and bloated, and to have bad breath and unwashed socks.

There was a man who delivered bonemeal for the dahlia garden on whom I thought there might be flies—if only one could see him at an unguarded moment. His clothes gave off a rich rancid smell. When he laughed it was like looking into the squishy dark mush of fruit I had to collect from the lawn before a mowing. Those few teeth which the bonemeal man still had—they announced themselves like unvanquished sentinels on a crumbling rampart—were given over to a delicate vegetation. I recognized it: it was the same silky green fur that coated the fallen plums over which floated little black parasols of flies.

Yet one day, when I came out to the dahlia garden just as the bonemeal man was leaving, Grandpa Morgan was tossing his fine head of hair in the wind and laughing his fine Welsh laugh. The bonemeal man was laughing too, trundling his barrow down our path, doubled up with mirth between its shafts, his green teeth waving about like banners.

"Grandpa, what is it, what is it? Why are you laughing, Grandpa?"

"Oh," Grandpa gasped, patting me on the head in the way that meant a subject was not for discussing. "No flies on *him*, no siree."

This was the best thing: I could always count on Grandpa Morgan to be out-   25
rageous. That was the word people used: the neighbors, my grandmother, my mother, my uncles. "He's *outrageous*," they would say, shaking their heads and throwing up their hands and smiling.

If I asked him to, he would yodel in the schoolyard when he came to fetch me, and abracadabra, we two were the hub of a circle of awed envy. When I passed the Teachers' Room at morning tea time, I'd hear the older ones whisper and smile: "That's Morgie's granddaughter."

On our walks he would stop and talk to everyone we met, "to *anyone*, anyone at all," Uncle Cyril would groan. He spoke to the butcher, the baker, the lady in the cake shop, to men who did shady undiscussable things, even men who smelled of horses and *took bets*, whatever that was.

"What can you be thinking of?" Grandma would say, "with the child hearing every word? A man *known* to be mixed up with off-course betting."

I knew bets to be deeply evil. I imagined them to be huge and ravenous and almost hidden behind fearful masks. Once upon a time, in Kalgoorlie, Grandpa himself had made bets, but that was before the Lord saved him and showed him the light. Now, he said, he only bet on the Day of Judgement. Still, he couldn't see any harm in talking to people who "knew horses." He would introduce me. "This is Paddy," he would say; "A man who knows horses if ever anyone did." I myself had no interest in knowing horses on account of their large and alarming teeth, but I rather liked those brave horse-knowing men.

Sometimes Grandma, shocked, would call out: "Dad! I want to have a   30
word with you, Dad." From the front window, she would have watched us coming over the bridge from the Ringwood Station. The most *interesting* people came off the trains and walked over that bridge. Grandma would have seen us stop and talk to some gentlemen who wore string, perhaps, for suspenders, and whose shoes were stuffed in an intricate way with newspapers, and who gave off the rank smell of the pubs. "Dad!" she

would say. "What are you *thinking* of, to introduce the child to such strangers?"

"Strangers?" Grandpa would raise his eyebrows in surprise. "That wasn't a stranger. That was Bluey McTavish from back of Geelong. We don't know any strangers."

This was certainly true, though we'd only just met Mr. Bluey McTavish of Geelong, whose life history we would discuss over the sorting of dahlia bulbs. I don't know what it was about Grandpa Morgan, but people told him a great deal about themselves very quickly. "There aren't any such people as strangers," he told me. "Or if there are, I've never met them."

"I don't know what's going to come of that child," Grandma Morgan said, throwing up her hands and trying not to smile. "But one thing's certain: she'll never know the difference between truth and lies."

Grandpa said with ruffled dignity: "One thing she'll know about is dahlias."

The dahlias, the dahlias. They stretched to the edge of the world. When I stood between the rows, I saw nothing but jungle, with great suns of flowers above me, so heavy they nodded on their stalks and shone down through the forests of their own leaves. Such a rainbow of suns: from creamy white to a purple that was almost black. The dahlias believed in excess: they could never have too many petals. The dahlia which could crowd the most pleatings of pure light about its center won a blue ribbon at the Melbourne Show. It was an article of faith with us that some year the Morgan Dahlia would win that ribbon.

Grandpa Morgan did things to the bulbs and the soil. He married broad-petalled pinks to pintucked yellows; he introduced sassy purples to smocked whites with puffed sleeves and lacy hems. He watched over his nurslings, he crooned to them, he prayed. To birds and snails, he issued strong Welsh warnings (the Lord having taken away a certain range of Australian vocabulary). As his flowerlings grew, he murmured endearments; and they gathered themselves up into a delirium of pleats, rank upon rank of petals, tier upon tier, frilled prima donnas. The color of the Morgan dahlia was a salmon that could make judges weep, the salmon of a baby's cheek, the color of a lover's whisper. And it did win yellow ribbons, and red, at the Melbourne Show, but never the coveted blue.

"Is it waiting till we find the Morgan Nugget again?" I asked.

"Very likely," Grandpa said. "Very likely."

The day Grandma came out with the news of Uncle Charlie, we were deep in dahlias.

"Dad," she said. "Charlie's gone."

Grandpa paused in mid-weeding. A clump of clover and crabgrass dangled from between his fingers. He sank down on the ground between the dahlias and rested his head in his hands. "Well," he said, sadly and slowly. "Charlie. So Charlie went first."

"Where's he gone?" I wanted to know.

"Uncle Charlie's gone to heaven," Grandma told me, and Grandpa said: "He's dead." He pushed his trowel into the soil and lifted up a handful of earth. It was alive with ants and worms, we watched it move in the palm of his hand. "I'm next," he sighed, and he smelled the earth and held it for me to smell, and he rubbed it against his cheek as though it were a kitten. "I'm next, I suppose."

"Next for what?"

"Next for dying," he said.   45

"What happens when you die, Grandpa?"

"They put you in a box and they bury you under the ground with the dahlia bulbs."

I stared at him in horror. "Uncle Charlie should run away and hide."

"You can't run away when you're dead," he said.

"Grandpa," I whispered, beginning to shiver, "will they do it to you?"   50

"Yes," he said.

"And to me?"

I crept between his earth-covered arms and he held me tightly and rocked me back and forth between the dahlias. "Yes," he sighed, "one day, yes. That's the way it is. But then we'll be with the Lord."

I didn't want to be with the Lord. I had a brilliant idea. "Grandpa," I said, "we'll run away *before* we die. I know a very good place in the woodshed, they'd never find us."

"Dad!" Grandma's voice steamed over with exasperation. "Now just   55 what have you been telling her this time? How will that child ever know the difference between truth and a lie? Uncle Charlie," she said to me, "has gone straight to heaven, and that is the simple truth."

~

Mr. Peabody knew the truth. Every Sunday it spoke in his bones, it shook him from head to foot.

There must have been some obscure and ancient rule at church. It must have been this rule that forced Mr. Peabody, week after week, to sit directly in front of Grandpa Morgan. Mr. Peabody was a tiny man, elderly, and seemingly frail as a sparrow, though he must have had enormous reserves of stamina on which to draw.

Behind him, sheltering in the leeside of the Spirit of the Lord as it blustered and rushed through Grandpa, my little brother and I kept score. When the spirit moved, Grandpa shouted *hallelujah* in his fine Welsh voice. The shock waves hit Mr. Peabody sharply in the nape of his neck and travelled down his spine with such force that he would rise an inch or two from the pew. Most of his body would go rigid, but his head and his hands would quiver for seconds at a time. *Glory, glory,* he would murmur in terror-stricken prayerful voice.

These seismic interludes infused Sundays with extraordinary interest. And there was also this: from monitoring the passions of Mr. Peabody, my brother and I learned self-control, the ability to tamp down an explosion of mirth and turn it into a mere telegraphed signal of gleaming eyes and a coded numerology of fingers.

But then came the day that a shaft of sunlight fell from a high amber-   60
glass window in the church and placed a crown of gold on Mr. Peabody's
head. "Oh!" I gasped aloud. "*Look!*" And Grandpa shouted *Hallelujah!* and
Mr. Peabody rose up into his corona like a skyrocket and I saw a million
golden doves and the gilded petals of all the dahlias in the world rising up
into the pointed arch above in which God lived.

"It was the Holy Spirit you saw," the pastor told me. "The Holy Spirit
descending as a dove."

"Going *up,*" I corrected. "Lots and lots of them, and dahlias too."

"The Holy Spirit," he said again, less certainly. "In the form of a dove."

"I'm not so sure," my Sunday School teacher said. "She makes things up."

"Out of the mouths of babes," the pastor reminded her.   65

"She makes things up," my Sunday School teacher insisted. "She handles
the truth very carelessly. She believes her own lies."

"Grandpa," I asked, "how can you tell the difference between truth and a lie?"

He was working bonemeal into the soil around his dahlias; over us nodded those heavy salmon suns. He went on kneading the rich black loam,
intent on his labor.

Apprehensively I persisted: "Is the Morgan Nugget true?"

He went on sifting the soil.   70

I thought hopefully: perhaps he made up death.

"The truth," he said at last, "shall make you free. John, chapter 8, verse
32."

"Grandpa," I said, "there were doves with gold wings, and dahlias too.
Mr. Peabody made them fly. I saw them."

"I know you did."

I leaned towards him. "And the Morgan Nugget?" I breathed.   75

"Is true," he said. "Is true."

[1986]

Recognizing Elements: Plot, Character, and Point of View

Let's think first about the plots of "The Hit Man" and "Morgan Morgan." The **plot,**
which we may think of as the sequence of events in a narrative, is fairly simple in
Boyle's story: the plot is structured by the chronology of the Hit Man's life, tracing
his life from his early years to his death. Yet Boyle does play with this structure,
making it more interesting than a straight biography or obituary, by selecting some
unexpected events. "Peas," for instance, is hardly a significant event in his life (is it?),
and other scenes seem to be little unconnected slices from his life. Boyle gives us
enough of what seems to be the story of the Hit Man's life, in what seems to be a
straightforward arrangement, that we try to fit the story's parts into this frame; but
Boyle also gives us enough material that is surreal, comical, and absurd that the
story is unsettling. At the end of "The Hit Man," we're not sure what to think. But
we're thinking.

We begin in Hospital's story with a lucidly orienting sentence: "My grandfather,
Morgan Morgan, was a yodeler and a breeder of dahlias." We know immediately

who's talking, and what is being revealed. Compare Boyle's opening sentence, "The Hit Man's early years are complicated by the black bag that he wears over his head," which is immediately disorienting: Who? What? Huh? And yet Hospital's simple opening sentence is deceptively rich: what sort of a name is "Morgan Morgan"? Is that really his name? Is that a misprint? (Do you know anyone whose first name is the same as the last name?) What we learn about Morgan Morgan is also tantalizingly odd: you just don't meet many yodelers who also breed dahlias. Both Boyle and Hospital are masterfully seducing the reader, drawing us into a more attentive state, arousing our interests: few of us wouldn't want to read beyond these first sentences.

But notice how differently Hospital handles the plot: instead of "this happens, then this, then this, then this," etc., as in "The Hit Man," Hospital's plot swirls around in time. After the orienting first sentence, we are sometime in the past, during the grandchild's life, when Morgan would yodel in her presence in Melbourne. This yodeling, we are told, is "nothing compared with his former powers," when "girls for miles around would come running." This earlier time, when Morgan was "a young man on the goldfields," deepens the sense of legend, of myth, as we imagine these girls running from miles around, as we see these girls "sigh and sway like cobras in the strands of his voice"—a wonderful image. Then the plot jumps back to Melbourne and Mrs. Blackburn, whose comments suggest earlier events in Morgan's life, when he never found "a thimbleful of gold," and yet won the hearts of the ladies, including apparently Mrs. Blackburn.

Hospital's story continues to move about in time—back to the Kalgoorlie goldfields, back further to Morgan's vision of the Morgan Nugget, forward to the granddaughter's questions about the nugget, which lead to another time when Grandma Morgan is chiding Morgan Morgan for confusing the child with his "nonsense." And yet even when it appears that Morgan is finding the Morgan Nugget, and then putting it back, this shift from reality to unreality to reality (as we discover this "event" occurs *inside his vision*) is not difficult for the reader to negotiate. Like the granddaughter, in a sense, the reader momentarily may have trouble telling what is true and what isn't, but we are never lost or confused, as the complicated folds of the story unfurl.

Hospital's plot, in other words, would be very difficult to describe: what is the central action that carries along the story's events? Is it the search for the Morgan Nugget? The granddaughter's quest for what is true? The story of a miraculous vision? What holds the story together, as its title suggests, is not some central action, but the figure of Morgan Morgan. In the biographical genre, the events of Morgan Morgan's life would likely be strung together chronologically—as in "The Hit Man," although it is not a "biography" either. As a superbly accomplished work of fiction, Hospital's story keeps doubling back, twisting around, shape-shifting. In the end, for Morgan Morgan, truth is liberating, allowing for visions that are real. What is the difference between a truth and a lie? Is Charlie dead, buried with the dahlia bulbs, or is he alive, going straight up to heaven? Throughout the story, repetitions echo, like Morgan Morgan's name—the same, but different: "The dahlias, the dahlias." "'Very likely,' Grandpa said. 'Very likely.'" And finally, about the vision of the existence of the Morgan Nugget: "'Is true,' he said. 'Is true.'"

These two works, taken together, suggest in some sense the difference between fiction and biography, fiction and journalism, fiction and memoir, fiction and nonfiction. These apparent opposites would appear to be easy to tell apart, as easy as the difference between a religious vision and a made-up story, between truth and a lie, between being alive and being dead. But fiction often opens up categories of all sorts. Boyle's story uses a chronological structure, a biographical form, and leaves us wondering about the reality of mythical figures—about the difference between a hit man and the grim reaper. Hospital also uses lyrical language and a swirling chronology to open up possibilities, inviting us to ponder differences of all sorts, and the nature of what is true. Biography, journalism, memoir, nonfiction—these seek closure in a way that fiction evades. Boyle creates richness in part by making clear what happened, but blurring the status of the agent; Hospital creates richness in part by blurring what happened, yet revealing so vividly to whom it happened.

The approach to **character** in the two stories is also dramatically different and illustrative. Boyle uses spare details to create a picture that is compelling, and yet he also keeps undermining the reality of that picture, not allowing his reader to take the Hit Man, Cynthia, the beggar, and the others as "real" people. Hospital's Morgan Morgan, Grandma Morgan, Mr. Peabody, even Mrs. Blackburn, are all deftly drawn, with slight details that help make them seem real. (Imagine Mrs. Blackburn, for instance, swinging the stem of a carnation in her fingers.) Yet at the same time, Hospital's characters seem to me to be shrouded in a kind of magical light, as Morgan's yodel snares women, and a gold nugget becomes real in a vision, and he "knows" every stranger he meets, and he prophesies his own death—and so on.

The **point of view** in the stories also points to different possibilities, as Hospital's first-person intimacy contrasts with the elusive point of view of Boyle's storyteller. The reader does follow the Hit Man's awareness, but it would not be easy to retell the story in first person, without completely altering it: "My early years were complicated by the black bag that I wore over my head." The narrator seems to be the implied author, who is mischievously playing with the story and the characters, quite distant from them. The point of view, that is, seems definitively outside the protagonist's consciousness—if the Hit Man can even be called a character. Hospital's storyteller is decidedly within the story.

Boyle actually says a good bit about the **setting** of his story—more than one might realize: there are docks in the town (because a prominent financier is found floating near them); there is a track, a cigar shop, a hospital, a pool room, and so forth. But these places seem generic. The most detailed setting in the story is perhaps the set of the talk show, where an unreal "planetary glow washes the stage," and thus undermines the concreteness of where the story takes place. Boyle has captured an unreality that is eerily engrossing. When we read the following lines, for instance, the scene is vivid—yet it is unclear where this vividness is taking place: "Mist rises from the water like steam, there is the smell of fish. A large black bird perches on the dead man's forehead."

Hospital's story, again, suggests the spectrum available to fiction with regard to setting. Her story is firmly grounded in particular places—Collins and Bourke Street, Melbourne, the Kalgoorlie goldfields, "Mitcham and Box Hill and Richmond," and "beyond Footscray even, out towards the unfenceable Nullarbor Plain and Kalgoorlie." Not that we have much notion *where* these places are (well, other than Australia), but we have the sense that these are real places, on some map, if we had a sufficiently detailed one.

The **style** of Hospital's story is amazing. It seems effortlessly flowing, and yet able to use words like "rallentando" and "*Cwm Rhondda*" and "calix" and "fossicking" and even "cobwebby." We can't say how she does this, but we can point to how dramatically her approach differs from Boyle's, in this story at least. Boyle can also launch into rhapsodic flights, and his style is, to be sure, dazzling in its range. There are fragments ("A boy"), very simple sentences ("The girl's name is Cynthia"), and self-parodying complexity ("He did not, restrained no doubt by considerations of filial loyalty and the deep-seated taboos against patricide that permeate the universal unconscious"). Boyle's plastic style seems appropriate for a story shifting from myth to hard-boiled criminal to comic absurdity. We're never quite sure where we're supposed to stand with Boyle; with Hospital's style, we're not standing at all—we're soaring away.

Literary works do not come with a **theme** tucked inside of them. To articulate the theme of Hospital's or Boyle's story requires some creativity and persuasiveness. A fundamental requirement of a story's theme, of course, is that it should hold the work together, relating to all its parts. In general usage, that's what "theme" means—the idea that holds the thing together. But a theme is something that is not, precisely speaking, in the story. It holds the story together, but it's not in the story. So you can see why readers get to argue over what the theme of a particular story is: it's certainly worthwhile and interesting to talk about what a story "means"— what it adds up to, but it's also certainly implausible to think that all intelligent readers will come up with the same theme for any particular story.

Hospital's story certainly seems to have something to do with the nature of truth and life, inviting us perhaps to see life in death, and truth in lies, and reality in visions. But that sounds too simple and might well horrify the author of "Morgan Morgan." Similarly, the theme of "The Hit Man" also seems elusive. The main problem is that the Hit Man both is and isn't Death. The theme of the story thus can change for you depending on which part of the story you emphasize. At this moment, what is most prominent in my mind is the Hit Man's three-headed dog, as he stands amid the smoke and sparks. Given that focus, I offer this phrasing of the story's theme: "In the modern world, the idea of Death as a supernatural entity is silly, as 'he' becomes something like a rotten guy who wears a black hood and acts like an immature gangster." But you might put it very differently.

As this concept of theme is especially important in distinguishing different kinds of fiction, let's consider briefly some of the various kinds. A **fable**, for example, is defined as a short story designed to convey a moral lesson. Thus, in theory, if the theme of a fable isn't clear, then the fable arguably isn't successful. In practice, even when the moral of a fable is spelled out explicitly, readers may still argue about what the moral, as it's stated, actually means. In order to make the moral both interesting yet obvious, fables often involve magical events and talking animals, as well as relatively brief and patterned plots. The story of the fox and the grapes, one of Aesop's fables, and a discussion of its meaning, appears in Chapter 7.

Parables also are designed to convey a message. Instead of talking animals or other marvels, parables typically deal with familiar human types, everyday situations, realistic events: a son running away from home; a shepherd losing one of his sheep; a man considering where to build his house, a farmer where to sow his seeds. Like fables, parables are usually brief, offering a minimum of characterization and straightforward plots. It seems clear that the story is just a vehicle, pointing beyond itself to some lesson that determines what happens in the story. But if parables are designed to teach a lesson, it's especially interesting to note that Jesus's disciples apparently failed to grasp the meaning of one of his most famous parables. In the fourth chapter of Mark, Jesus tells the story of the sower whose seeds land in four places: on the footpath, on rocky ground, among thistles, and into good soil. When the disciples ask what it means, Jesus responds, "Do you not understand this parable? How then are you to understand any parable?" And he explains that the parable illustrates the different ways that different people will respond to his teachings.

The parable is closely related to another kind of story, the **allegory**. In both parables and allegories, what happens in the story seems to be a vehicle for some other meaning, but the surface details in an allegory relate to an underlying meaning in a more complex and specific way than in a fable or parable. If the fox in Aesop's sour grapes story, for instance, were named "Mr. Society," and if the tree were named a "financial market tree," and if Mr. Society and his friends used a method of jumping taught to them by a red bear named "Karl Communism," then the fable is moving into the realm of allegory. Its theme would accordingly be altered by this symbolic level of meaning: instead of just a fox, who stands in a general way for a kind of person or way of thinking, in this little propagandistic allegory, the fox stands for something more specific—society under the influence of communism. The story then teaches us, perhaps, that communist methods fail, and so they must learn to scorn what they do not have.

Allegories are often easy to spot because the characters, and even places and things, are often given transparent names. The Hit Man's name is pretty evocative, but what does Cynthia stand for? Boyle's story seems not to be an allegory. Other nonallegorical stories may have meaningful names, as in for instance "Revelation" with Mary Grace. But the other elements of the story do not clearly refer to something else.

Some inexperienced readers, having grasped the idea that one thing in a story may stand for something else, may tend to read every work as an allegory, seeing symbols everywhere, even to the point of virtually losing sight of the story itself. Admittedly, it is often hard to know when a seed is just a seed, and when it stands for something else. The very concept of a "theme" assumes that the materials of stories stand for something other than themselves—that there is a meaning written somehow between the lines. If a story truly is an allegory, however, there should be significant clues that a *network* of symbols pervades the story.

Another kind of fiction, the **fairy tale**, is familiar to almost everyone. Fairy tales often begin with a clear cue that we are entering an unrealistic fictional world: "Once upon a time. . . ." Fairy tales do not always have fairies in them, but they take place in the sort of universe in which there *could* be fairies, the world of gingerbread houses, witches who eat children, white ducks that carry children to safety. Although evil forces threaten, in fairy tales the hero and heroine live happily ever after. The prince finds his princess, the little boy slays the giant, the children get out of the forest. Yet what such stories mean is often surprisingly elusive and complex. Here is what William Bennett, in his *Book of Virtues*, says is the meaning of the familiar fairy tale of the emperor's new clothes (the emperor, you recall, is naked, yet no one except a little boy will admit his clothes can't be seen).

> In this classic, we see that it is often harder to be honest than it is to be
> silent, and that trusting ourselves is the best road to the truth. We see the
> pestilence of false flattery, and we find that honesty, unlike new clothes,
> never goes out of fashion.

This kaleidoscope of lessons—Bennett finds no less than four—underscores the complexity of the story's meaning. Bennett's comment also returns us to where this chapter began, with an assertion of the value of reading fiction. Without fiction, we would be hard pressed to make sense of reality. Both Boyle's and Hospital's stories blur, in very different ways, our sense of what is real. They suggest just how impoverished our lives would be if we were limited only to a literal kind of truth.

Stories to Experience

JOHN EDGAR WIDEMAN

(1941–)

John Edgar Wideman was born in Washington, D.C., and attended Peabody High in Pittsburgh, excelling in academics and sports. At the University of Pennsylvania, he was Phi Beta Kappa and All-Ivy League in basketball. He is the first writer to win the PEN/Faulkner Award twice (1984 and 1990), and the second African American to win a Rhodes Scholarship. He has published some fifteen books to critical acclaim. He has taught at Baruch College in New York City, and at the University of Massachusetts. His daughter is a professional basketball player, and his son is a published writer.

Weight

My mother is a weightlifter. You know what I mean. She understands that the best laid plans, the sweetest beginnings have a way of turning to shit. Bad enough when life fattens you up just so it can turn around and gobble you down. Worse for the ones like my mother life keeps skinny, munching on her daily, one cruel, little, needle-toothed bite at a time so the meal lasts and lasts. Mom understands life don't play so spends beaucoup time and energy getting ready for the worst. She lifts weights to stay strong. Not barbells or dumbbells, though most of the folks she deals with, especially her sons, act just that way, like dumbbells. No. The weights she lifts are burdens, her children's, her neighbors', yours. Whatever awful calamities arrive on her doorstep or howl in the news, my mom squeezes her frail body beneath them. Grips, hoists, holds the weight. I swear sometimes I can hear her sinews squeaking and singing under a load of invisible tons.

I ought to know since I'm one of the burdens bowing her shoulders. She loves heavy, hopeless me unconditionally. Before I was born, Mom loved me, forever and ever till death do us part. I'll never be anyone else's darling, darling boy so it's her fault, her doing, isn't it, that neither of us can face the thought of losing the other. How can I resist reciprocating her love. Needing her. Draining her. Feeling her straining underneath me, the pop and cackle of her arthritic joints, her gray hair sizzling with static electricity, the hissing friction, tension and pressure as she lifts more than she can bear. Bears more than she can possibly lift. You have to see it to believe it. Like the flying Wallendas or Houdini's spine-chilling escapes. One of the greatest shows on earth.

My mother believes in a god whose goodness would not permit him to inflict more troubles than a person could handle. A god of mercy and salvation. A sweaty, bleeding god presiding over a fitness class in which his chosen few punish their muscles. She would wear a T-shirt: *God's Gym.*

In spite of a son in prison for life, twin girls born dead, a mind blown son who roams the streets with everything he owns in a shopping cart, a strung out daughter with a crack baby, a good daughter who'd miscarried the only child her dry womb ever produced, in spite of me and the rest of my limp-along, near to normal siblings and their children—my nephews doping and gangbanging, nieces unwed, underage, dropping babies as regularly as the seasons—in spite of breast cancer, sugar diabetes, hypertension, failing kidneys, emphysema, gout, all resident in her body and epidemic in the community, knocking off one by one her girlhood friends, in spite of corrosive poverty and a neighborhood whose streets are no longer safe even for gray, crippled up folks like her, my mom loves her god, thanks him for the blessings he bestows, keeps her faith he would not pile on more troubles than she could bear. Praises his name and prays for strength, prays for more weight so it won't fall on those around her less able to bear up.

You've seen those iron pumping, musclebound brothers fresh out the slam who show up at the playground to hoop and don't get picked on a team cause they can't play a lick, not before they did their bit, and sure not now, back on the set, stiff and stone-handed as Frankenstein, but finally some old head goes on and chooses one on his squad because the brother's so huge and scary looking sitting there with his jaws tight, lip poked out you don't want him freaking out and kicking everybody's ass just because the poor baby's feelings is hurt, you know what I mean, the kind so buff looks like his coiled-up insides about to bust through his skin or his skin's stripped clean off his body so he's a walking anatomy lesson. Well, that's how my mom looks to me sometimes, her skin peeled away, no secrets, every taut nerve string on display.

I can identify the precise moment during a trip with her one afternoon to the supermarket on Walnut Street in Shadyside, a Pittsburgh, Pennsylvania, white community with just a few families of us colored sprinkled at the bottom ends of a couple of streets, when I began to marvel at my mother's prodigious strength. I was very young, young enough not to believe I'd grow old, just bigger. A cashier lady who seemed to be acquainted with my mother asked very loudly, Is this your son, and Mom smiled in reply to the cashier's astonishment saying calmly, Yes, he is, and the doughy white lady in her yellow Kroger's smock with her name on the breast tried to match my mother's smile but only managed a fake grin like she'd just discovered shit stinks but didn't want anybody else to know she knew. Then she blurted, He's a tall one, isn't he.

Not a particularly unusual moment as we unloaded our shopping cart and waited for the bad news to ring up on the register. The three of us understood, in spite of the cashier's quick shuffle, what had seized her attention. In public situations the sight of my pale, caucasian featured mother and her variously colored kids disconcerted strangers. They gulped. Stared. Muttered insults. We were visible proof somebody was sneaking around after dark, breaking the apartheid rule, messy mulatto exceptions to the rule, trailing behind a woman who could be white.

Nothing special about the scene in Krogers. Just an ugly moment temporarily reprieved from turning uglier by the cashier's remark that attributed her surprise to a discrepancy in height not color. But the exchange alerted me to a startling fact—I was taller than my mother. The brown boy, me, could look down at the crown of his light-skinned mother's head. Obsessed by size, like most adolescent boys, size in general and the size of each and every particular part of my body and how mine compared to others, I was always busily measuring and keeping score, but somehow I'd lost track of my mother's size, and mine relative to hers. Maybe because she was beyond size. If someone had asked me my mother's height or weight, I probably would have replied, *Huh.* Ubiquitous I might say now. A tiny, skin-and-bone woman way too huge for size to pin down.

The moment in Krogers is also when I began to marvel at my mother's strength. Unaccountably, unbeknownst to me, my body had grown larger than hers, yes, and the news was great in a way, but more striking and not so comforting was the fact, never mind my advantage in size, I felt hopelessly weak standing there beside my mom in Krogers. A wimpy shadow next to her solid flesh and bones. I couldn't support for one hot minute a fraction of the weight she bore on her shoulders twenty-four hours a day. The weight of the cashier's big-mouthed disbelief. The weight of hating the pudgy white woman forever because she tried to steal my mother from me. The weight of cooking and cleaning and making do with no money, the weight of fighting and loving us iron-headed, ungrateful brats. Would I always feel puny and inadequate when I looked up at the giant fist hovering over our family, the fist of God or the Devil, ready to squash us like bugs if my mother wasn't always on duty, spreading herself thin as an umbrella over our heads, her bones its steel ribs keeping the sky from falling.

Reaching down for the brass handle of this box I must lift to my shoulder, I need the gripping strength of my mother's knobby-knuckled fingers, her superhero power to bear impossible weight.   10

Since I was reading her this story over the phone (I called it a story but Mom knew better), I stopped at the end of the paragraph above you just completed, if you read that far, stopped because the call was long distance, daytime rates, and also because the rest had yet to be written. I could tell by her silence she was not pleased. Her negative reaction didn't surprise me. Plenty in the piece I didn't like either. Raw, stuttering stuff I intended to improve in subsequent drafts, but before revising and trying to complete it, I needed her blessing.

Mom's always been my best critic. I depend on her honesty. She tells the truth yet never affects the holier-than-thou superiority of some people who believe they occupy the high ground and let you know in no uncertain terms that you nor nobody else like you ain't hardly coming close. Huh-uh. My mother smiles as often as she groans or scolds when she hears gossip about somebody behaving badly. *My, my, my* she'll say and nod and smile and gently broom you, the sinner, and herself into the same crowded heap, no one any better than they should be, could be, absolute equals in a mellow sputter of laughter she sometimes can't suppress, hiding it, muffling it with her fist over her mouth, nodding, remembering, how people's badness can be too good to be true, *my, my, my.*

Well, my story didn't tease out a hint of laugh, and forget the 550 miles separating us, I could tell she wasn't smiling either. Why was she holding back the sunshine that could forgive the worst foolishness. Absolve my sins. Retrieve me from the dead end corners into which I paint myself. Mama, please. Please, please, please, don't you weep. And tell ole Martha not to moan. Don't leave me drowning like Willie Boy in the deep blue sea. Smile, Mom. Laugh. Send that healing warmth through the wire and save poor me.

Was it the weightlifting joke, Mom. Maybe you didn't think it was funny.

Sorry. Tell the truth, I didn't see nothing humorous about any of it.   15
God's t-shirt. You know better. Ought to be ashamed of yourself. Taking the Lord's name in vain.

Where do you get such ideas, boy. I think I know my children. God knows I should by now, shouldn't I. How am I not supposed to know youall after all you've put me through beating my brains out to get through to you. *Yes, yes, yes.* Then one youall goes and does something terrible I never would have guessed was in you. Won't say you break my heart. Heart's been broke too many times. In too many little itty-bitty pieces can't break down no more, but youall sure ain't finished with me, are you. Still got some new trick in you to lay on your weary mother before she leaves here.

Guess I ought to be grateful to God an old fool like me's still around to be tricked, Weightlifter. Well, it's different. Nobody ain't called me nothing like weightlifter before. It's different, sure enough.

Now here's where she should have laughed. She'd picked up the stone I'd bull's-eyed right into the middle of her wrinkled brow, between her tender, brown, all-seeing eyes, lifted it and turned it over in her hands like a jeweler with a tiny telescope strapped around his skull inspecting a jewel, testing its heft and brilliance, the marks of god's hands, god's will, the hidden truths sparkling in its depths, multiplied, splintered through mirroring facets. After such a brow scrunching examination, isn't it time to smile. Kiss and make up. Wasn't that Mom's way. Wasn't that how she handled the things that hurt us and hurt her. Didn't she ease the pain of our worst injuries with the balm of her everything's-going-to-be-alright-in-the-morning smile. The smile that takes the weight, every hurtful ounce and forgives, the smile licking our wounds so they scab over, and she can pick them off our skin, stuff their lead weight into the bulging sack of all sorrows slung across her back.

The possibility my wannabe story had actually hurt her dawned on me. Or should I say bopped me upside my head like the Br'er Bear club my middle brother loads in his cart to discourage bandits. I wished I was sitting at the kitchen table across from her so I could check for damage, her first, then check myself in the mirror of those soft, brown, incredibly loving mother's eyes. If I'd hurt her even a teeny-tiny bit, I'd be broken forever unless those eyes repaired me. Yet even as I regretted reading her the clumsy passage and prepared myself to surrender wholly, happily to the hounds of hell if I'd harmed one hair on her tender, gray head, I couldn't deny a sneaky, smarting tingle of satisfaction at the thought that maybe, maybe words I'd written had touched another human being, mama mia or not.

Smile, Mom. It's just a story. Just a start. I know it needs more work. You   20
were supposed to smile at the weightlifting part.

God not something to joke about.

C'mon, mom. How many times have I heard Reverend Fitch cracking you up with his corny God jokes.

Time and a place.

Maybe stories are my time and place, Mom. You know. My time and place to say things I need to say.

No matter how bad it comes out sounding, right. No matter you make   25
a joke of your poor mother . . .

Poor mother's suffering. You were going to say, *Poor mother's suffering,* weren't you.

You heard what I said.

And heard what you didn't say. I hear those words, too. The unsaid ones, Mom. Louder sometimes. Drowning out what gets said, Mom.

Whoa. We gon let it all hang out this morning, ain't we. Son. First that story. Now you accusing me of *your* favorite trick, that muttering under your breath. Testing me this morning, aren't you. What makes you think a sane person would ever pray for more weight. Ain't those the words you put in my mouth. More weight.

And the building shook. The earth rumbled. More weight descended   30
like god's fist on his Hebrew children. Like in Lamentations. The Book in the Bible. The movie based on the Book based on what else, the legend of my mother's long suffering back.

Because she had a point.

People with no children can be cruel. Had I heard it first from Oprah, the diva of suffering my mother could have become if she'd pursued show-biz instead of weightlifting. Or was the damning phrase a line from one of Gwen Brooks's abortion blues. Whatever their source, the words fit and I was ashamed. I do know better. A bachelor and nobody's daddy, but still my words have weight. Like sticks and stones, words can break bones. Metaphors can pull you apart and put you back together all wrong. I know what you mean, Mom. My entire life I've had to listen to people trying to tell me I'm just a white man in a dark skin.

Give me a metaphor long enough and I'll move the earth. Somebody famous said it. Or said something like that. And everybody, famous or not knows words sting. Words change things. Step on a crack, break your mother's back.

On the other hand, Mom, metaphor's just my way of trying to say two things, be in two places at once. Saying goodbye and hello and goodbye. Many things, many places at once. You know, like James Cleveland singing our favorite gospel tune, *Stood on the Bank of Jordan.* Metaphors are very short songs. Mini-mini stories. Rivers between like the Jordan where ships sail on, sail on and you stand and wave goodbye-hello, hello-goodbye.

Weightlifter just a word, just play. I was only teasing, Mom. I didn't   35
mean to upset you. I certainly intended no harm. I'd swallow every stick of dynamite it takes to pay for a Nobel prize before I'd accept one if it cost just one of your soft, curly hairs.

Smile. Let's begin again.

It's snowing in Massachusetts / The ground's white in O-Hi-O. Yes, it's snowing in Massachusetts / And ground's white in O-Hi-O. Shut my eyes, Mr. Weatherman / Can't stand to see my baby go.

When I called you last Thursday evening and didn't get an answer I started worrying. I didn't know why. We'd talked Tuesday and you sounded fine. Better than fine. A lift and lilt in your voice. After I hung up the phone Tuesday said to myself, Mom's in good shape. Frail but her spirit's strong. Said those very words to myself more than once Tuesday. *Frail but her spirit's strong.* The perkiness I sensed in you helped make my Wednesday super. Early rise. Straight to my desk. Two pages before noon and you know me, Mom. Two pages can take a week, a month. I've had two page years. I've had decades dreaming the one perfect page I never got around to writing. Thursday morning reams of routine and no pages but not to worry I told myself. After Wednesday's productivity, wasn't I entitled to some down time. Just sat at my desk, pleased as punch with myself till I got bored feeling so good and started a nice novel, *Call It Sleep*. Dinner at KFC buffet. Must have balled up fifty napkins trying to keep my chin decent. Then home to call you before I snuggled up again with the little jewish boy, his mama and their troubles in old N.Y.C.

Let your phone ring and ring. Too late for you to be out unless you had a special occasion. And you always let me know well ahead of time when something special coming up. I tried calling a half hour later and again twenty minutes after that. By then nearly nine, close to your bedtime. I was getting really worried now. Couldn't figure where you might be. Nine-fifteen and still no answer, no clue what was going on.

Called Sis. Called Aunt Chloe. Nobody knew where you were. Chloe   40
said she'd talked with you earlier just like every other morning. Sis said you called her at work after she got back from lunch. Both of them said you sounded fine. Chloe said you'd probably fallen asleep in your recliner and left the phone in the bedroom or bathroom and your hearing's to the point you can be wide-awake but if the TV's on and the phone's not beside you or the ringer's not turned to high she said sometimes she has to ring and hang up, ring and hang up two, three times before she catches you.

Chloe promised to keep calling every few minutes till she reached you. Said they have a prayer meeting Thursdays in your mother's building and she's been saying she wants to go and I bet she's there, honey. She's alright, honey. Don't worry yourself, O.K. We're old and fuddleheaded now, but we're tough old birds. Your mother's fine. I'll tell her to call you soon's I get through to her. Your mom's okay, baby. God keeps an eye on us.

You know Aunt Chloe. She's your sister. Five hundred miles away and I could hear her squeezing her large self through the telephone line, see her pillow arms reaching for the weight before it comes down on me.

Why would you want to hear any of this. You know what happened. Where you were. You know how it all turned out.

You don't need to listen to my conversation with Sis. Dialing her back after we'd been disconnected. The first time in life I think my sister ever phoned me later than ten o'clock at night. First time a lightning bolt ever disconnected us. Ever disconnected me from anybody ever.

Did you see Eva Wallace first, Mom, coming through your door, or was   45
it the busybody super you've never liked since you moved in. Something about the way she speaks to her granddaughter you said. Little girl's around the building all day because her mother's either in the street or the slam and the father takes the child so rarely he might as well live in Timbuctoo so you know the super doesn't have it easy and on a couple of occasions you've offered to keep the granddaughter when the super needs both hands and her mind free for an hour. You don't hold the way she busies up in everybody's business or the fact the child has to look out for herself too many hours in the day against the super, and you're sure she loves her granddaughter you said but the short way she talks sometimes to a child that young just not right.

Who'd you see first pushing open your door. Eva said you didn't show up after you said you'd stop by for her. She waited awhile she said then phoned you and got no answer and then a friend called her and they got to running their mouths and Eva said she didn't think again about you not showing up when you were supposed to until she hung up the phone. And not right away then. Said as soon as she missed you, soon as she remembered youall had planned on attending the Thursday prayer meeting together she got scared. She knows how dependable you are. Even though it was late, close to your bedtime, she called you anyway and let the phone ring and ring. Way after nine by then. Pulled her coat on over her house- dress, scooted down the hall and knocked on your door cause where else you going to be. No answer so she hustled back to her place and phoned downstairs for the super and they both pounded on your door till the super said we better have a look just in case and unlocked your apartment. Stood there staring after she turned the key, trying to see through the door, then slid it open a little and both of them Eva said tiptoeing in like a couple of fools after all that pounding and hollering in the hall. Said she never thought about it at the time but later, after everything over and she drops down on her couch to have that cigarette she knew she shouldn't have with her lungs rotten as they are and hadn't smoked one for more than a year but sneaks the Camel she'd been saving out its hiding place in a Baggie in the freezer and sinks back in the cushions and lights up, real tired, real shook up and teary she said but couldn't help smiling at herself when she remembered all that hollering and pounding and then tipping in like a thief.

It might have happened that way. Being right or wrong about what happened is less important sometimes than finding a good way to tell it. What's anybody want to hear anyway. Not the truth people want. No-no-no. People want the best told story, the lie that entertains and turns them on. No question about it, is there. What people want. What gets people's attention. What sells soap. Why else do the biggest, most barefaced liars rule the world.

Hard to be a mother, isn't it Mom. I can't pretend to be yours, not even a couple minutes' worth before I go to pieces. I try to imagine a cradle with you lying inside, cute, miniature bedding tucked around the tiny doll of you. I can almost picture you asleep in it, snuggled up, your eyes shut, maybe your thumb in your mouth but then you cry out in the night, you need me to stop whatever I'm doing and rush in and scoop you up and press you to my bosom, lullabye you back to sleep. I couldn't manage it. Not the easy duty I'm imagining, let alone you bucking and wheezing and snot, piss, vomit, shit, blood, you hot and throbbing with fever, steaming in my hands like the heart ripped fresh from some poor soul's chest.

Too much weight. Too much discrepancy in size. As big a boy as I've grown to be, I can't lift you.

Will you forgive me if I cheat, Mom. Dark suited, strong men in somber ties and white shirts will lug you out of the church, down the stone steps, launch your gleaming barge into the black river of the Cadillac's bay. My brothers won't miss me not handling my share of the weight. How much weight could there be. Tiny, scooped out you. The tinny, fake wood shell. The entire affair's symbolic. Heavy with meaning not weight. You know. Like metaphors. Like words interchanged as if they have no weight or too much weight, as if words are never required to bear more than they can stand. As if words, when we're finished mucking with them, go back to just being words.

The word *trouble*. The word *sorrow*. The word *bye-and-bye*.

I was wrong and you were right, as usual, Mom. So smile. Certain situations, yours for instance, being a mother, suffering what mothers suffer,

50

why would anyone want to laugh at that. Who could stand in your shoes a heartbeat—*shoes, shoes, everybody got to have shoes*—bear your burdens one instant and think it's funny. Who ever said it's O.K. to lie and kill as long as it makes a good story.

Smile. Admit you knew from the start it would come to this. Me trembling, needing your strength. It has, Mom, so please, please, a little, bitty grin of satisfaction. They say curiosity kills the cat and satisfaction brings it back. Smiling. Smile Mom. Come back. You know I've always hated spinach but please spoonfeed me a canful so those Popeye muscles pop in my arms. I meant shapeshifter not weightlifter. I meant the point of this round, spinningtop earth must rest somewhere, on something or someone. I meant you are my sunshine. My only sunshine.

The problem never was the word *weightlifter,* was it. If you'd been insulted by my choice of metaphor you would have let me know, not by silence, but nailing me with a quick, funny signifying dig, and then you would have smiled or laughed and we'd have gone on to the next thing. What must have bothered you, stunned you was what I said into the phone before I began reading. Said this is about a man scared he won't survive his mother's passing.

That's what upset you, wasn't it. Saying goodbye to you. Practicing for your death in a story. Trying on for size a world without you. Ignoring like I did when I was a boy, your size. Saying aloud terrible words with no power over us as long as we don't speak them.

So when you heard me let the cat out of the bag, you were shocked, weren't you. Speechless. Smileless. What could you say. The damage had been done. I heard it in your first words after you got back your voice. And me knowing your lifelong, deathly fear of cats. Like the big, furry orange Tom you told me about, how it curled up on the porch just outside your door, trapping you a whole August afternoon inside the hotbox shanty in Washington, D.C., when I lived in your belly.

Why would I write a story that risks your life. Puts our business in the street. I'm the oldest child, supposed to be the man of the family now. No wonder you cried, Oh father. Oh son. Oh holy ghost. Why hath thou forsaken me. I know you didn't cry that. You aren't Miss Oprah. But I sure did mess up, didn't I. Didn't I, Mom. Up to my old tricks. Crawling up inside you. My weight twisting you all out of shape.

I asked you once about the red sailor cap hanging on the wall inside your front door. Knew it was my brother's cap on the nail, but why that particular hat I asked and not another of his countless, fly sombreros on display. Rob, Rob, man of many lids. For twenty years in the old house, now in your apartment, the hat a shrine no one allowed to touch. You never said it but everybody understood the red hat your good luck charm, your mojo for making sure Rob would get out the slam one day and come bopping through the door, pluck the hat from the wall and pull it down over his bean head. Do you remember me asking why the sailor cap. You probably guessed I was fishing. Really didn't matter which cap, did it. Point was you chose the red one and *why* must always be your secret. You could have made up a nice story to explain why the red sailor cap wound up on the nail and I would have listened as I always listened all ears but you knew part of me would be trying to peek through the words at your secret. Always a chance you might slip up and reveal too much. So the hat story and plenty others never told. The old folks had taught you that telling another person your secret wish strips it of its power, a wish's small, small

55

chance, as long as it isn't spoken, to influence what might happen next in the world. You'd never tell anyone the words sheltered in the shadow of your heart. Still, I asked about the red sailor cap because I needed to understand your faith, your weightlifting power, how you can believe a hat, any fucking kind of hat, could bring my baby brother home safe and sound from prison. I needed to spy and pry. Wiretap the telephone in your bosom. Hear the words you would never say to another soul, not even on pain of death.

How would such unsaid words sound, what would they look like on a page. And if you had uttered them, surrendered your stake in them, forfeited their meager, silent claim to work miracles, would it have been worth the risk, even worth the loss, to finally hear the world around you cracking, collapsing, changing as you spoke your little secret tale.

Would you have risen an inch or two from this cold ground. Would you   60
have breathed easier after releasing the heaviness of silent words hoarded so unbearably, unspeakably long. Let go, Mom. Shed the weight just once.

Not possible for you, I know. It would be cheating, I know. The man of unbending faith did not say to the hooded inquisitors piling a crushing load of stones on his chest, *More light, More light*. No. I'm getting my quotes mixed up again. Just at the point the monks thought they'd broken his will, just as spiraling fractures started splintering his bones, he cried, *More bricks. More bricks.*

I was scared, Mom. Scared every cotton picking day of my life I'd lose you. The fear a sing-song taunt like tinnitus ringing in my ear. No wonder I'm a little crazy. But don't get me wrong. Not your fault. I don't blame you for my morbid fears, my unhappiness. It's just that I should have confessed sooner, long, long ago, the size of my fear of losing you. I wish you'd heard me say the words. How fear made me keep my distance, hide how much I depended on your smile. The sunshine of your smiling laughter that could also send me silently screaming out the room in stories I never told you because you'd taught me as you'd been taught, not to say anything aloud I didn't want to come true. Nor say out loud the things I wished to come true. Doesn't leave a hell of a lot to say, does it. No wonder I'm tongue-tied, scared shitless.

But would it be worth the risk, worth failing, if I could find words to tell our story and also keep us covered inside it, work us invisibly into the fret, the warp and woof of the story's design, safe there, connected there as words in perfect poems, the silver apples of the moon, golden apples of the sun, blue guitars. The two of us like those rhyming pairs *never* and *forever, heart* and *part*, in the doo-wop songs I harmonized with the fellas in the alley around the corner from Henderson's barber shop up on Frankstown Avenue, first me then lost brother Sonny and his crew then baby brother Rob and his cut buddy hoodlums rapping and now somebody else black and young and wild and pretty so the song lasts forever and never ever ends even though the voices change back there in the alley where you can hear bones rattling in the men's fists, *fever in the funkhouse looking for a five* and hear wine bottles exploding and hear the rusty shopping cart squeak over the cobblestones of some boy ferrying an old lady's penny-ante groceries home for a nickel once, then a dime, a quarter, four quarters now.

Would it be worth the risk, worth failing.

Shouldn't I try even if I know the strength's not in me. No, you say. Yes.   65
Hold on, let go. Do I hear you saying, Everything's gonna be alright. Saying,

Do what you got to do, baby, smiling as I twist my fingers into the brass handle. As I lift.

[2000]

Questions

1. This story, which won first place in the prestigious O. Henry Awards for 2000, is introduced in the O. Henry collection (*Prize Stories 2000*) by Michael Cunningham, who begins with this sentence: "John Edgar Wideman's 'Weight' does not directly resemble anything I've ever read before, and that is perhaps the highest praise I can offer any work of fiction." In what ways does "Weight" surprise you? How does it play with the conventions of short stories?
2. How does Wideman create tension between the story itself and the telling of the story? How is this tension resolved in the end, if it is resolved?
3. Look closely at the first paragraph and describe the experience of reading it. How does Wideman keep the reader off balance, constantly readjusting to what is being disclosed? How does the style contribute to the experience that the story is being told even as we read it?
4. How does the last paragraph affect your response to the story?
5. How would you describe the relationship between the narrator and his mother, as it is revealed in the story? Is the relationship richly depicted, or is it simple? Is it a healthy relationship? For both mother and son? Have you encountered similar relationships in your reading or your life?
6. Explain why the story is called "Weight." What else might it be called? Is the story really about "Weight"?

ZORA NEALE HURSTON (1891–1960)

Zora Neale Hurston appears to have been born in Eatonville, Florida, in 1891, according to the 1900 census record, but she usually gave her date of birth as 1903 (she also said 1900, 1901, and 1902), and some biographers (including Alice Walker) have listed 1901. Her mother died in 1904, and Zora was shunned by her stepmother. Various relatives raised her until she left home at age fourteen. She completed high school in Baltimore while working as a live-in maid, and enrolled in Howard University in 1918, continuing to work (as a manicurist and maid). Her marriage in 1927 came to "an early, amicable divorce." "Sweat," depicting the death of a marriage, was ironically published a year earlier. Hurston was an important part of the Harlem Renaissance in the 1920s, and in the past few decades

her work has enjoyed a tremendous surge of critical interest and acclaim. She struggled for recognition and financial security almost all of her life, and died in poverty in 1960.

Sweat

It was eleven o'clock of a Spring night in Florida. It was Sunday. Any other night, Delia Jones would have been in bed for two hours by this time. But she was a washwoman, and Monday morning meant a great deal to her. So she collected the soiled clothes on Saturday when she returned the clean things. Sunday night after church, she sorted them and put the white things to soak. It saved her almost a half-day's start. A great hamper in the bedroom held the clothes that she brought home. It was so much neater than a number of bundles lying around.

She squatted on the kitchen floor beside the great pile of clothes, sorting them into small heaps according to color, and humming a song in a mournful key, but wondering through it all where Sykes, her husband, had gone with her horse and buckboard.

Just then something long, round, limp, and black fell upon her shoulders and slithered to the floor beside her. A great terror took hold of her. It softened her knees and dried her mouth so that it was a full minute before she could cry out or move. Then she saw that it was the big bull whip her husband liked to carry when he drove.

She lifted her eyes to the door and saw him standing there bent over with laughter at her fright. She screamed at him.

"Sykes, what you throw dat whip on me like dat? You know it would skeer me—looks just like a snake, an' you knows how skeered Ah is of snakes."   5

"Course Ah knowed it! That's how come Ah done it." He slapped his leg with his hand and almost rolled on the ground in his mirth. "If you such a big fool dat you got to have a fit over a earth worm or a string, Ah don't keer how bad Ah skeer you."

"You ain't got no business doing it. Gawd knows it's a sin. Some day Ah'm gointuh drop dead from some of yo' foolishness. 'Nother thing, where you been wid mah rig? Ah feeds dat pony. He ain't fuh you to be drivin' wid no bull whip."

"You sho' is one aggravatin' nigger woman!" he declared and stepped into the room. She resumed her work and did not answer him at once. "Ah done tole you time and again to keep them white folks' clothes outa dis house."

He picked up the whip and glared at her. Delia went on with her work. She went out into the yard and returned with a galvanized tub and set it on the washbench. She saw that Sykes had kicked all of the clothes together again, and now stood in her way truculently, his whole manner hoping, *praying*, for an argument. But she walked calmly around him and commenced to re-sort the things.

"Next time, Ah'm gointer kick 'em outdoors," he threatened as he struck a match along the leg of his corduroy breeches.   10

Delia never looked up from her work, and her thin, stooped shoulders sagged further.

"Ah ain't for no fuss t'night Sykes. Ah just come from taking sacrament at the church house."

He snorted scornfully. "Yeah, you just come from de church house on a Sunday night, but heah you is gone to work on them clothes. You ain't nothing but a hypocrite. One of them amen-corner Christians—sing, whoop, and shout; then come home and wash white folks' clothes on the Sabbath."

He stepped roughly upon the whitest pile of things, kicking them helter-skelter as he crossed the room. His wife gave a little scream of dismay, and quickly gathered them together again.

"Sykes, you quit grindin' dirt into these clothes! How can Ah git through by Sat'day if Ah don't start on Sunday?"   15

"Ah don't keer if you never git through. Anyhow, Ah done promised Gawd and a couple of other men, Ah ain't gointer have it in mah house. Don't gimme no lip neither, else Ah'll throw'em out and put mah fist up side yo' head to boot."

Delia's habitual meekness seemed to slip from her shoulders like a blown scarf. She was on her feet; her poor little body, her bare knuckly hands bravely defying the strapping hulk before her.

"Looka heah, Sykes, you done gone too fur. Ah been married to you fur fifteen years, and Ah been takin' in washin' fur fifteen years. Sweat, sweat, sweat! Work and sweat, cry and sweat, pray and sweat!"

"What's that got to do with me?" he asked brutally.

"What's it got to do with you, Sykes? Mah tub of suds is filled yo' belly   20
with vittles more times than yo' hands is filled it. Mah sweat is done paid for this house and Ah reckon Ah kin keep on sweatin' in it."

She seized the iron skillet from the stove and struck a defensive pose, which act surprised him greatly, coming from her. It cowed him and he did not strike her as he usually did.

"Naw you won't," she panted, "that ole snaggle-toothed black woman you runnin' with ain't comin' heah to pile up on *mah* sweat and blood. You ain't paid for nothin' on this place, and Ah'm gointer stay right heah till Ah'm toted out foot foremost."

"Well, you better quit gittin' me riled up, else they'll be totin' you out sooner than you expect. Ah'm so tired of you Ah don't know whut to do. Gawd! how Ah hates skinny wimmen!"

A little awed by this new Delia, he sidled out of the door and slammed the back gate after him. He did not say where he had gone, but she knew too well. She knew very well that he would not return until nearly daybreak also. Her work over, she went on to bed but not to sleep at once. Things had come to a pretty pass!

She lay awake, gazing upon the debris that cluttered their matrimonial   25
trail. Not an image left standing along the way. Anything like flowers had long ago been drowned in the salty stream that had been pressed from her heart. Her tears, her sweat, her blood. She had brought love to the union and he had brought a longing after the flesh. Two months after the wedding, he had given her the first brutal beating. She had the memory of his numerous trips to Orlando with all of his wages when he had returned to her penniless, even before the first year had passed. She was young and soft then, but now she thought of her knotty, muscled limbs, her harsh knuckly hands, and drew herself up into an unhappy little ball in the middle of the big feather bed. Too late now to hope for love, even if it were not Bertha it would be someone else. This case differed from the others only in that she

was bolder than the others. Too late for everything except her little home. She had built it for her old days, and planted one by one the trees and flowers there. It was lovely to her, lovely.

Somehow, before sleep came, she found herself saying aloud: "Oh well, whatever goes over the Devil's back, is got to come under his belly. Sometime or ruther, Sykes, like everybody else, is gointer reap his sowing." After that she was able to build a spiritual earthworks against her husband. His shells could no longer reach her. *Amen.* She went to sleep and slept until he announced his presence in bed by kicking her feet and rudely snatching the covers away.

"Gimme some kivah heah, an' git yo' damn foots over on yo' own side! Ah oughter mash you in yo' mouf fuh drawing dat skillet on me."

Delia went clear to the rail without answering him. A triumphant indifference to all that he was or did.

The week was as full of work for Delia as all other weeks, and Saturday found her behind her little pony, collecting and delivering clothes.

It was a hot, hot day near the end of July. The village men on Joe Clarke's porch even chewed cane listlessly. They did not hurl the cane-knots as usual. They let them dribble over the edge of the porch. Even conversation had collapsed under the heat. 30

"Heah come Delia Jones," Jim Merchant said, as the shaggy pony came 'round the bend of the road toward them. The rusty buckboard was heaped with baskets of crisp, clean laundry.

"Yep," Joe Lindsay agreed. "Hot or col', rain or shine, jes' ez reg'lar ez de weeks roll roun' Delia carries 'em an' fetches 'em on Sat'day."

"She better if she wanter eat," said Moss. "Syke Jones ain't wuth de shot an' powder hit would tek tuh kill 'em. Not to *huh* he ain't."

"He sho' ain't," Walter Thomas chimed in. "It's too bad, too, cause she wuz a right pretty li'l trick when he got huh. Ah'd uh mah'ied huh mahself if he hadnter beat me to it."

Delia nodded briefly at the men as she drove past. 35

"Too much knockin' will ruin *any* 'oman. He done beat huh 'nough tuh kill three women, let 'lone change they looks," said Elijah Moseley. "How Syke kin stommuck dat big black greasy Mogul he's layin' roun' wid, gits me. Ah swear dat eight-rock* couldn't kiss a sardine can Ah done thowed out de back do' 'way las' yeah."

"Aw, she's fat, thass how come. He's allus been crazy 'bout fat women," put in Merchant. "He'd a' been tied up wid one long time ago if he could a' found one tuh have him. Did Ah tell yuh 'bout him come sidlin' roun' *mah* wife—bringin' her a basket uh peecans outa his yard fuh a present? Yeah, mah wife! She tol' him tuh take 'em right straight back home, 'cause Delia works so hard ovah dat washtub she reckon everything on de place taste lak sweat an' soapsuds. Ah jus' wisht Ah'd a' caught 'im 'roun' dere! Ah'd a' made his hips ketch on fiah down dat shell road."

"Ah know he done it, too. Ah sees 'im grinnin' at every 'oman dat passes," Walter Thomas said. "But even so, he useter eat some mighty big hunks uh humble pie tuh git dat li'l 'oman he got. She wuz ez pritty ez a speckled

*Eight ball in pool: black.

pup! Dat wuz fifteen yeahs ago. He useter be so skeered uh losin' huh, she could make him do some parts of a husband's duty. Dey never wuz de same in de mind."

"There oughter be a law about him," said Lindsay. "He ain't fit tuh carry guts tuh a bear."

Clarke spoke for the first time. "Tain't no law on earth dat kin make a   40
man be decent if it ain't in 'im. There's plenty men dat takes a wife lak dey do a joint uh sugar-cane. It's round, juicy, an' sweet when dey gits it. But dey squeeze an' grind, squeeze an' grind an' wring tell dey wring every drop uh pleasure dat's in 'em out. When dey's satisfied dat dey is wrung dry, dey treats 'em jes' lak dey do a cane-chew. Dey thows 'em away. Dey knows whut dey is doin' while dey is at it, an' hates theirselves fuh it but they keeps on hangin' after huh tell she's empty. Den dey hates huh fuh bein' a cane-chew an' in de way."

"We oughter take Syke an' dat stray 'oman uh his'n down in Lake Howell swamp an' lay on de rawhide till they cain't say Lawd a' mussy. He allus wuz uh ovahbearin niggah, but since dat white 'oman from up north done teached 'im how to run a automobile, he done got too biggety to live—an' we oughter kill 'im," Old Man Anderson advised.

A grunt of approval went around the porch. But the heat was melting their civic virtue and Elijah Moseley began to bait Joe Clarke.

"Come on, Joe, git a melon outa dere an' slice it up for yo' customers. We'se all sufferin' wid de heat. De bear's done got *me*!"

"Thass right, Joe, a watermelon is jes' whut Ah needs tuh cure de eppizudicks," Walter Thomas joined forces with Moseley. "Come on dere, Joe. We all is steady customers an' you ain't set us up in a long time. Ah chooses dat long, bowlegged Floridy favorite."

"A god, an' be dough. You all gimme twenty cents and slice way," Clarke   45
retorted. "Ah needs a col' slice m'self. Heah, everybody chip in. Ah'll lend y'all mah meat knife."

The money was quickly subscribed and the huge melon brought forth. At that moment, Sykes and Bertha arrived. A determined silence fell on the porch and the melon was put away again.

Merchant snapped down the blade of his jackknife and moved toward the store door.

"Come on in, Joe, an' gimme a slab uh sow belly an' uh pound uh coffee— almost fuhgot 'twas Sat'day. Got to git on home." Most of the men left also.

Just then Delia drove past on her way home, as Sykes was ordering magnificently for Bertha. It pleased him for Delia to see.

"Git whutsoever yo' heart desires, Honey. Wait a minute, Joe. Give huh   50
two bottles uh strawberry soda-water, uh quart parched ground-peas, an' a block uh chewin' gum."

With all this they left the store, with Sykes reminding Bertha that this was his town and she could have it if she wanted it.

The men returned soon after they left, and held their watermelon feast.

"Where did Syke Jones git da 'oman from nohow?" Lindsay asked.

"Ovah Apopka.* Guess dey musta been cleanin' out de town when she lef'. She don't look lak a thing but a hunk uh liver wid hair on it."

---

*A town about ten miles from Eatonville, Florida, Hurston's birthplace.

"Well, she sho' kin squall," Dave Carter contributed. "When she gits   55
ready tuh laff, she jes' opens huh mouf an' latches it back tuh de las' notch.
No ole granpa alligator down in Lake Bell ain't got nothin' on huh."

Bertha had been in town three months now. Sykes was still paying her
room-rent at Della Lewis'—the only house in town that would have taken
her in. Sykes took her frequently to Winter Park to "stomps." He still assured
her that he was the swellest man in the state.

"Sho' you kin have dat li'l ole house soon's Ah kin git dat 'oman outa
dere. Everything b'longs tuh me an' you sho' kin have it. Ah sho' 'bominates
uh skinny 'oman. Lawdy, you sho' is got one portly shape on you! You kin git
anything you wants. Dis is *mah* town an' you sho' kin have it."

Delia's work-worn knees crawled over the earth in Gethsemane and
up the rocks of Calvary many, many times during these months. She avoided the villagers and meeting places in her efforts to be blind and deaf. But
Bertha nullified this to a degree, by coming to Delia's house to call Sykes
out to her at the gate.

Delia and Sykes fought all the time now with no peaceful interludes.
They slept and ate in silence. Two or three times Delia had attempted a
timid friendliness, but she was repulsed each time. It was plain that the
breaches must remain agape.

The sun had burned July to August. The heat streamed down like a mil-   60
lion hot arrows, smiting all things living upon the earth. Grass withered,
leaves browned, snakes went blind in shedding, and men and dogs went
mad. Dog days!

Delia came home one day and found Sykes there before her. She wondered, but started to go on into the house without speaking, even though
he was standing in the kitchen door and she must either stoop under his
arm or ask him to move. He made no room for her. She noticed a soap box
beside the steps, but paid no particular attention to it, knowing that he
must have brought it there. As she was stooping to pass under his outstretched arm, he suddenly pushed her backward, laughingly.

"Look in de box dere Delia, Ah done brung yuh somethin'!"

She nearly fell upon the box in her stumbling, and when she saw what
it held, she all but fainted outright.

"Syke! Syke, mah Gawd! You take dat rattlesnake 'way from heah! You
gottuh. Oh, Jesus, have mussy!"

"Ah ain't got tuh do nuthin' uh de kin'—fact is Ah ain't got tuh do noth-   65
in' but die. Tain't no use uh you puttin' on airs makin' out lak you skeered uh
dat snake—he's gointer stay right heah tell he die. He wouldn't bite me
cause Ah knows how tuh handle 'im. Nohow he wouldn't risk breakin' out
his fangs 'gin *yo'* skinny laigs."

"Naw, now Syke, don't keep dat thing 'roun' tryin' tuh skeer me tuh
death. You knows Ah'm even feared uh earth worms. Thass de biggest snake
Ah evah did see. Kill 'im Syke, please."

"Doan ast me tuh do nothin' fuh yuh. Goin' 'round tryin' tuh be so damn
asterperious. Naw, Ah ain't gonna kill it. Ah think uh damn sight mo' uh him dan
you! Dat's a nice snake an' anybody doan lak 'im kin jes' hit de grit."

The village soon heard that Sykes had the snake, and came to see and
ask questions.

"How de hen-fire did you ketch dat six-foot rattler, Syke?" Thomas asked.

"He's full uh frogs so he cain't hardly move, thass how Ah eased up on 'm. But Ah'm a snake charmer an' knows how tuh handle 'em. Shux, dat ain't nothin'. Ah could ketch one eve'y day if Ah so wanted tuh." 70

"Whut he needs is a heavy hick'ry club leaned real heavy on his head. Dat's de bes' way tuh charm a rattlesnake."

"Naw, Walt, y'all jes' don't understand dese diamon' backs lak Ah do," said Sykes in a superior tone of voice.

The village agreed with Walter, but the snake stayed on. His box remained by the kitchen door with its screen wire covering. Two or three days later it had digested its meal of frogs and literally came to life. It rattled at every movement in the kitchen or the yard. One day as Delia came down the kitchen steps she saw his chalky-white fangs curved like scimitars hung in the wire meshes. This time she did not run away with averted eyes as usual. She stood for a long time in the doorway in a red fury that grew bloodier for every second that she regarded the creature that was her torment.

That night she broached the subject as soon as Sykes sat down to the table.

"Syke, Ah wants you tuh take dat snake 'way fum heah. You done 75 starved me an' Ah put up widcher, you done beat me an Ah took dat, but you done kilt all mah insides bringin' dat varmint heah."

Sykes poured out a saucer full of coffee and drank it deliberately before he answered her.

"A whole lot Ah keer 'bout how you feels inside uh out. Dat snake ain't goin' no damn wheah till Ah gits ready fuh 'im tuh go. So fur as beatin' is concerned, yuh ain't took near all dat you gointer take ef yuh stay 'round *me*."

Delia pushed back her plate and got up from the table. "Ah hates you, Sykes," she said calmly. "Ah hates you tuh de same degree dat Ah useter love yuh. Ah done took an' took till mah belly is full up tuh mah neck. Dat's de reason Ah got mah letter fum de church an' moved mah membership tuh Woodbridge—so Ah don't haftuh take no sacrament wid yuh. Ah don't wantuh see yuh 'round me atall. Lay 'round wid dat 'oman all yuh wants tuh, but gwan 'way fum me an' mah house. Ah hates yuh lak uh suck-egg dog."

Sykes almost let the huge wad of corn bread and collard greens he was chewing fall out of his mouth in amazement. He had a hard time whipping himself up to the proper fury to try to answer Delia.

"Well, Ah'm glad you does hate me. Ah'm sho' tiahed uh you hangin' 80 ontuh me. Ah don't want yuh. Look at yuh stringey ole neck! Yo' rawbony laigs an' arms is enough tuh cut uh man tuh death. You looks jes' lak de devvul's doll-baby tuh *me*. You cain't hate me no worse dan Ah hates you. Ah been hatin' *you* fuh years."

"Yo' ole black hide don't look lak nothin' tuh me, but uh passle uh wrinkled up rubber, wid yo' big ole yeahs flappin' on each side lak uh paih uh buzzard wings. Don't think Ah'm gointuh be run 'way fum mah house neither. Ah'm goin' tuh de white folks 'bout *you*, mah young man, de very nex' time you lay yo' han's on me. Mah cup is done run ovah." Delia said this with no signs of fear and Sykes departed from the house, threatening her, but made not the slightest move to carry out any of them.

That night he did not return at all, and the next day being Sunday, Delia was glad she did not have to quarrel before she hitched up her pony and drove the four miles to Woodbridge.

She stayed to the night service—"love feast"—which was very warm and full of spirit. In the emotional winds her domestic trials were borne far and wide so that she sang as she drove homeward,

> Jurden water, black an' col
> Chills de body, not de soul   85
> An' Ah wantah cross Jurden in uh calm time.

She came from the barn to the kitchen door and stopped.

"Whut's de mattah, ol' Satan, you ain't kickin' up yo' racket?" She addressed the snake's box. Complete silence. She went on into the house with a new hope in its birth struggles. Perhaps her threat to go to the white folks had frightened Sykes! Perhaps he was sorry! Fifteen years of misery and suppression had brought Delia to the place where she would hope *anything* that looked towards a way over or through her wall of inhibitions.

She felt in the match-safe behind the stove at once for a match. There was only one there.

"Dat niggah wouldn't fetch nothin' heah tuh save his rotten neck, but   90
he kin run thew whut Ah brings quick enough. Now he done toted off nigh on tuh haff uh box uh matches. He done had dat 'oman heah in mah house, too."

Nobody but a woman could tell how she knew this even before she struck the match. But she did and it put her into a new fury.

Presently she brought in the tubs to put the white things to soak. This time she decided she need not bring the hamper out of the bedroom; she would go in there and do the sorting. She picked up the pot-bellied lamp and went in. The room was small and the hamper stood hard by the foot of the white iron bed. She could sit and reach through the bedposts—resting as she worked.

"Ah wantah cross Jurden in uh calm time." She was singing again. The mood of the "love feast" had returned. She threw back the lid of the basket almost gaily. Then, moved by both horror and terror, she sprang back toward the door. *There lay the snake in the basket!* He moved sluggishly at first, but even as she turned round and round, jumped up and down in an insanity of fear, he began to stir vigorously. She saw him pouring his awful beauty from the basket upon the bed, then she seized the lamp and ran as fast as she could to the kitchen. The wind from the open door blew out the light and the darkness added to her terror. She sped to the darkness of the yard, slamming the door after her before she thought to set down the lamp. She did not feel safe even on the ground, so she climbed up in the hay barn.

There for an hour or more she lay sprawled upon the hay a gibbering wreck.

Finally she grew quiet, and after that came coherent thought. With this,   95
stalked through her a cold, bloody rage. Hours of this. A period of intro-spection, a space of retrospection, then a mixture of both. Out of this an awful calm.

"Well, Ah done de bes' Ah could. If things ain't right, Gawd knows tain't mah fault."

She went to sleep—a twitch sleep—and woke up to a faint gray sky. There was a loud hollow sound below. She peered out. Sykes was at the wood-pile, demolishing a wire-covered box.

He hurried to the kitchen door, but hung outside there some minutes before he entered, and stood some minutes more inside before he closed it after him.

The gray in the sky was spreading. Delia descended without fear now, and crouched beneath the low bedroom window. The drawn shade shut out the dawn, shut in the night. But the thin walls held back no sound.

"Dat ol' scratch is woke up now!" She mused at the tremendous whirr inside, which every woodsman knows, is one of the sound illusions. The rattler is a ventriloquist. His whirr sounds to the right, to the left, straight ahead, behind, close under foot—everywhere but where it is. Woe to him who guesses wrong unless he is prepared to hold up his end of the argument! Sometimes he strikes without rattling at all.

Inside, Sykes heard nothing until he knocked a pot lid off the stove while trying to reach the match-safe in the dark. He had emptied his pockets at Bertha's.

The snake seemed to wake up under the stove and Sykes made a quick leap into the bedroom. In spite of the gin he had had, his head was clearing now.

"Mah Gawd!" he chattered, "ef Ah could on'y strack uh light!"

The rattling ceased for a moment as he stood paralyzed. He waited. It seemed that the snake waited also.

"Oh, fuh de light! Ah thought he'd be too sick"—Sykes was muttering to himself when the whirr began again, closer, right underfoot this time. Long before this, Sykes' ability to think had been flattened down to primitive instinct and he leaped—onto the bed.

Outside Delia heard a cry that might have come from a maddened chimpanzee, a stricken gorilla. All the terror, all the horror, all the rage that man possibly could express, without a recognizable human sound.

A tremendous stir inside there, another series of animal screams, the intermittent whirr of the reptile. The shade torn violently down from the window, letting in the red dawn, a huge brown hand seizing the window stick, great dull blows upon the wooden floor punctuating the gibberish of sound long after the rattle of the snake had abruptly subsided. All this Delia could see and hear from her place beneath the window, and it made her ill. She crept over to the four o'clocks and stretched herself on the cool earth to recover.

She lay there. "Delia, Delia!" She could hear Sykes calling in a most despairing tone as one who expected no answer. The sun crept on up, and he called. Delia could not move—her legs had gone flabby. She never moved, he called, and the sun kept rising.

"Mah Gawd!" She heard him moan, "Mah Gawd fum Heben!" She heard him stumbling about and got up from her flower-bed. The sun was growing warm. As she approached the door she heard him call out hopefully, "Delia, is dat you Ah heah?"

She saw him on his hands and knees as soon as she reached the door. He crept an inch or two toward her—all that he was able, and she saw his horribly swollen neck and his one open eye shining with hope. A surge of pity too strong to support bore her away from that eye that must, could not, fail to see the tubs. He would see the lamp. Orlando with its doctors was too far. She could scarcely reach the chinaberry tree, where she waited in the growing heat while inside she knew the cold river was creeping up and up to extinguish that eye which must know by now that she knew.

[1926]

Questions

1. In 1973, the novelist Alice Walker placed a gravestone for Hurston, which called her "A Genius of the South." In what ways is "Sweat" a Southern story? Could it have happened elsewhere? How is the storytelling affected by Hurston's "Southern" setting?
2. What does the opening paragraph reveal about Delia, both directly and by implication? Why is this information important at the outset? How does it shape the way we respond to the story? Does the opening paragraph complicate or clarify your response to the rest of the story?
3. How does the dialect contribute to the story? Is there any humor in the story, for instance, and does the dialect affect the humor? Look carefully at Sykes's entrance, when he throws the whip on Delia to frighten her. Is this scene comical? Sykes refers to his wife as "one aggravatin' nigger woman!" Is he being playful, or grossly disrespectful? Why does he use this language if he is himself so sensitive to race relations (he wants the clothes of white people kept out of his house). Has the status of this racist term changed since 1926? How does the presentation of Sykes here prepare the reader for what follows?
4. Explore the significance of Hurston's title. What aspects of the story are *not* indicated by "Sweat"?
5. Is there any ambiguity in the way Hurston prepares readers to respond to the story's conclusion? Can you generate some ambiguity? (At what point do you see the ending coming, and what is your reaction to that perception?)
6. Delia calls the snake "ol' Satan," which alludes to the Expulsion from Eden story in Genesis. Consider how this allusion resonates in the story: that is, think about how "Sweat" might be a retelling or revising or challenge to the story of Adam and Eve. Could Sykes and Delia be a version of Adam and Eve?

11

Charlotte Perkins Gilman and Flannery O'Connor: Two Case Studies

A good short story cannot simply be Lit Lite; it is the successful execution of large truths delivered in tight spaces.

—Barbara Kingsolver

In this chapter you'll find two great stories—classics, influential and celebrated, delivering "large truths" in "tight spaces," as Barbara Kingsolver says. Each story is accompanied by critical and cultural materials that illustrate various approaches and possibilities—materials that should enrich your engagement with these stories. For the most part, these supplementary materials are excerpts, culled from many pages, representing the sort of things that anyone might discover by poking around in a good library. Appendix A offers a guide through the research process to find such materials; this chapter provides the materials such research might uncover, allowing you to practice

"Myrna! Feel sorry for Mrs. DeStefano. She's never read Eudora Welty."

working with background materials and critical resources. This process of developing questions about primary and secondary materials, making connections, and creating relationships is useful in many arenas.

Reading Gilman's "The Yellow Wallpaper"

Since 1973, this story, relatively unknown for much of the twentieth century, has become one of the most widely anthologized and influential stories ever written. It is an amazing story.

CHARLOTTE PERKINS GILMAN (1860–1935)

Charlotte Perkins Gilman in 1896

Shortly after Charlotte Perkins Gilman's birth in Hartford, Connecticut, her father abandoned his family. Frederick Beecher Perkins was a writer, the nephew of two famous abolitionists—Henry Ward Beecher, the minister, and Harriet Beecher Stowe, author of Uncle Tom's Cabin. *His departure meant that Charlotte was raised in poverty, as she and her mother lived with one relative after another. Her formal education was woefully neglected, although she did study at the Rhode Island School of Design in 1878. After marrying in 1884, Gilman fell into a deep depression following the birth of her daughter, and a "rest cure" was prescribed for her. But Gilman soon became a noted public speaker and writer for feminist causes, publishing essays, a book called* Women and Economics, *a science fiction novel called* Herland, *and much more. She married again in 1900, and lived happily until 1934, when George Houghton Gilman died unexpectedly. After discovering that she was suffering from terminal breast cancer, Gilman used chloroform to take her own life.*

The Yellow Wallpaper

It is very seldom that mere ordinary people like John and myself secure ancestral halls for the summer.

A colonial mansion, a hereditary estate, I would say a haunted house and reach the height of romantic felicity—but that would be asking too much of fate!

Still I will proudly declare that there is something queer about it.

Else, why should it be let so cheaply? And why have stood so long untenanted?

John laughs at me, of course, but one expects that.

John is practical in the extreme. He has no patience with faith, an intense horror of superstition, and he scoffs openly at any talk of things not to be felt and seen and put down in figures.

John is a physician, and *perhaps*—(I would not say it to a living soul, of course, but this is dead paper and a great relief to my mind)—*perhaps* that is one reason I do not get well faster.

You see, he does not believe I am sick! And what can one do?

If a physician of high standing, and one's own husband, assures friends and relatives that there is really nothing the matter with one but temporary nervous depression—a slight hysterical tendency—what is one to do?

My brother is also a physician, and also of high standing, and he says the same thing.

So I take phosphates or phosphites—whichever it is—and tonics, and air and exercise, and journeys, and am absolutely forbidden to "work" until I am well again.

Personally, I disagree with their ideas.

Personally, I believe that congenial work, with excitement and change, would do me good.

But what is one to do?

I did write for a while in spite of them; but it *does* exhaust me a good deal—having to be so sly about it, or else meet with heavy opposition.

I sometimes fancy that in my condition, if I had less opposition and more society and stimulus—but John says the very worst thing I can do is to think about my condition, and I confess it always makes me feel bad.

So I will let it alone and talk about the house.

The most beautiful place! It is quite alone, standing well back from the road, quite three miles from the village. It makes me think of English places that you read about, for there are hedges and walls and gates that lock, and lots of separate little houses for the gardeners and people.

There is a *delicious* garden! I never saw such a garden—large and shady, full of box-bordered paths, and lined with long grape-covered arbors with seats under them.

There were greenhouses, but they are all broken now.

There was some legal trouble, I believe, something about the heirs and co-heirs; anyhow, the place has been empty for years.

That spoils my ghostliness, I am afraid, but I don't care—there is something strange about the house—I can feel it.

I even said so to John one moonlight evening, but he said what I felt was a *draught,* and shut the window.

I get unreasonably angry with John sometimes. I'm sure I never used to be so sensitive. I think it is due to this nervous condition.

But John says if I feel so I shall neglect proper self-control; so I take pains to control myself—before him, at least, and that makes me very tired.

I don't like our room a bit. I wanted one downstairs that opened onto the piazza and had roses all over the window, and such pretty old-fashioned chintz hangings! But John would not hear of it.

He said there was only one window and not room for two beds, and no near room for him if he took another.

He is very careful and loving, and hardly lets me stir without special direction.

I have a schedule prescription for each hour in the day; he takes all care from me, and so I feel basely ungrateful not to value it more.

He said he came here solely on my account, that I was to have perfect rest and all the air I could get. "Your exercise depends on your strength, my dear," said he, "and your food somewhat on your appetite; but air you can absorb all the time." So we took the nursery at the top of the house.   30

It is a big, airy room, the whole floor nearly, with windows that look all ways, and air and sunshine galore. It was a nursery first, and then playroom and gymnasium, I should judge, for the windows are barred for little children, and there are rings and things in the walls.

The paint and paper look as if a boys' school had used it. It is stripped off—the paper—in great patches all around the head of my bed, about as far as I can reach, and in a great place on the other side of the room low down. I never saw a worse paper in my life. One of those sprawling, flamboyant patterns committing every artistic sin.

It is dull enough to confuse the eye in following, pronounced enough constantly to irritate and provoke study, and when you follow the lame uncertain curves for a little distance they suddenly commit suicide—plunge off at outrageous angles, destroy themselves in unheard-of contradictions.

The color is repellent, almost revolting: a smouldering unclean yellow, strangely faded by the slow-turning sunlight. It is a dull yet lurid orange in some places, a sickly sulphur tint in others.

No wonder the children hated it! I should hate it myself if I had to live   35
in this room long.

There comes John, and I must put this away—he hates to have me write a word.

We have been here two weeks, and I haven't felt like writing before, since that first day.

I am sitting by the window now, up in this atrocious nursery, and there is nothing to hinder my writing as much as I please, save lack of strength.

John is away all day, and even some nights when his cases are serious.

I am glad my case is not serious!   40

But these nervous troubles are dreadfully depressing.

John does not know how much I really suffer. He knows there is no *reason* to suffer, and that satisfies him.

Of course it is only nervousness. It does weigh on me so not to do my duty in any way!

I meant to be such a help to John, such a real rest and comfort, and here I am a comparative burden already!

Nobody would believe what an effort it is to do what little I am able—   45
to dress and entertain, and order things.

It is fortunate Mary is so good with the baby. Such a dear baby!

And yet I *cannot* be with him, it makes me so nervous.

I suppose John never was nervous in his life. He laughs at me so about this wallpaper!

At first he meant to repaper the room, but afterward he said that I was letting it get the better of me, and that nothing was worse for a nervous patient than to give way to such fancies.

He said that after the wallpaper was changed it would be the heavy bedstead, and then the barred windows, and then that gate at the head of the stairs, and so on.

"You know the place is doing you good," he said, "and really, dear, I don't care to renovate the house just for a three months' rental."

"Then do let us go downstairs," I said. "There are such pretty rooms there."

Then he took me in his arms and called me a blessed little goose, and said he would go down to the cellar, if I wished, and have it whitewashed into the bargain.

But he is right enough about the beds and windows and things.

It is as airy and comfortable a room as anyone need wish, and, of course, I would not be so silly as to make him uncomfortable just for a whim.

I'm really getting quite fond of the big room, all but that horrid paper.

Out of one window I can see the garden—those mysterious deep-shaded arbors, the riotous old-fashioned flowers, and bushes and gnarly trees.

Out of another I get a lovely view of the bay and a little private wharf belonging to the estate. There is a beautiful shaded lane that runs down there from the house. I always fancy I see people walking in these numerous paths and arbors, but John has cautioned me not to give way to fancy in the least. He says that with my imaginative power and habit of story-making, a nervous weakness like mine is sure to lead to all manner of excited fancies, and that I ought to use my will and good sense to check the tendency. So I try.

I think sometimes that if I were only well enough to write a little it would relieve the press of ideas and rest me.

But I find I get pretty tired when I try.

It is so discouraging not to have any advice and companionship about my work. When I get really well, John says we will ask Cousin Henry and Julia down for a long visit; but he says he would as soon put fireworks in my pillow-case as to let me have those stimulating people about now.

I wish I could get well faster.

But I must not think about that. This paper looks to me as if it *knew* what a vicious influence it had!

There is a recurrent spot where the pattern lolls like a broken neck and two bulbous eyes stare at you upside down.

I get positively angry with the impertinence of it and the everlastingness. Up and down and sideways they crawl, and those absurd unblinking eyes are everywhere. There is one place where two breadths didn't match, and the eyes go all up and down the line, one a little higher than the other.

I never saw so much expression in an inanimate thing before, and we all know how much expression they have! I used to lie awake as a child and get more entertainment and terror out of blank walls and plain furniture than most children could find in a toy-store.

I remember what a kindly wink the knobs of our big old bureau used to have, and there was one chair that always seemed like a strong friend.

I used to feel that if any of the other things looked too fierce I could always hop into that chair and be safe.

The furniture in this room is no worse than inharmonious, however, for we had to bring it all from downstairs. I suppose when this was used as a playroom they had to take the nursery things out, and no wonder! I never saw such ravages as the children have made here.

The wallpaper, as I said before, is torn off in spots, and it sticketh closer than a brother—they must have had perseverance as well as hatred.   70

Then the floor is scratched and gouged and splintered, the plaster itself is dug out here and there, and this great heavy bed, which is all we found in the room, looks as if it had been through the wars.

But I don't mind it a bit—only the paper.

There comes John's sister. Such a dear girl as she is, and so careful of me! I must not let her find me writing.

She is a perfect and enthusiastic housekeeper, and hopes for no better profession. I verily believe she thinks it is the writing which made me sick!

But I can write when she is out, and see her a long way off from these   75
windows.

There is one that commands the road, a lovely shaded winding road, and one that just looks off over the country. A lovely country, too, full of great elms and velvet meadows.

This wallpaper has a kind of subpattern in a different shade, a particularly irritating one, for you can only see it in certain lights, and not clearly then.

But in the places where it isn't faded and where the sun is just so—I can see a strange, provoking, formless sort of figure that seems to skulk about behind that silly and conspicuous front design.

There's sister on the stairs!

Well, the Fourth of July is over! The people are all gone, and I am tired   80
out. John thought it might do me good to see a little company, so we just had Mother and Nellie and the children down for a week.

Of course I didn't do a thing. Jennie sees to everything now.

But it tired me all the same.

John says if I don't pick up faster he shall send me to Weir Mitchell in the fall.

But I don't want to go there at all. I had a friend who was in his hands once, and she says he is just like John and my brother, only more so!

Besides, it is such an undertaking to go so far.   85

I don't feel as if it was worthwhile to turn my hand over for anything, and I'm getting dreadfully fretful and querulous.

I cry at nothing, and cry most of the time.

Of course I don't when John is here, or anybody else, but when I am alone.

And I am alone a good deal just now. John is kept in town very often by serious cases, and Jennie is good and lets me alone when I want her to.

So I walk a little in the garden or down that lovely lane, sit on the porch   90
under the roses, and lie down up here a good deal.

I'm getting really fond of the room in spite of the wallpaper. Perhaps *because* of the wallpaper.

It dwells in my mind so!

I lie here on this great immovable bed—it is nailed down, I believe—and follow that pattern about by the hour. It is as good as gymnastics, I assure you. I start, we'll say, at the bottom, down in the corner over there where it has not been touched, and I determine for the thousandth time that I *will* follow that pointless pattern to some sort of a conclusion.

I know a little of the principle of design, and I know this thing was not arranged on any laws of radiation, or alternation, or repetition, or symmetry, or anything else that I ever heard of.

It is repeated, of course, by the breadths, but not otherwise.   95

Looked at in one way, each breadth stands alone; the bloated curves and flourishes—a kind of "debased Romanesque" with *delirium tremens*—go waddling up and down in isolated columns of fatuity.

But, on the other hand, they connect diagonally, and the sprawling outlines run off in great slanting waves of optic horror, like a lot of wallowing sea-weeds in full chase.

The whole thing goes horizontally, too, at least it seems so, and I exhaust myself trying to distinguish the order of its going in that direction.

They have used a horizontal breadth for a frieze, and that adds wonderfully to the confusion.

There is one end of the room where it is almost intact, and there, when   100
the crosslights fade and the low sun shines directly upon it, I can almost fancy radiation after all—the interminable grotesque seems to form around a common center and rush off in headlong plunges of equal distraction.

It makes me tired to follow it. I will take a nap, I guess.

I don't know why I should write this.

I don't want to.

I don't feel able.

And I know John would think it absurd. But I *must* say what I feel and   105
think in some way—it is such a relief!

But the effort is getting to be greater than the relief.

Half the time now I am awfully lazy, and lie down ever so much. John says I mustn't lose my strength, and has me take cod liver oil and lots of tonics and things, to say nothing of ale and wines and rare meat.

Dear John! He loves me very dearly, and hates to have me sick. I tried to have a real earnest reasonable talk with him the other day, and tell him how I wish he would let me go and make a visit to Cousin Henry and Julia.

But he said I wasn't able to go, nor able to stand it after I got there; and I did not make out a very good case for myself, for I was crying before I had finished.

It is getting to be a great effort for me to think straight. Just this nerv-   110
ous weakness, I suppose.

And dear John gathered me up in his arms, and just carried me upstairs and laid me on the bed, and sat by me and read to me till it tired my head.

He said I was his darling and his comfort and all he had, and that I must take care of myself for his sake, and keep well.

He says no one but myself can help me out of it, that I must use my will and self-control and not let any silly fancies run away with me.

There's one comfort—the baby is well and happy, and does not have to occupy this nursery with the horrid wallpaper.

If we had not used it, that blessed child would have! What a fortunate   115
escape! Why, I wouldn't have a child of mine, an impressionable little thing,
live in such a room for worlds.

I never thought of it before, but it is lucky that John kept me here after
all; I can stand it so much easier than a baby, you see.

Of course I never mention it to them any more—I am too wise—but I
keep watch for it all the same.

There are things in the wallpaper that nobody knows about but me, or
ever will.

Behind that outside pattern the dim shapes get clearer every day.

It is always the same shape, only very numerous.   120

And it is like a woman stooping down and creeping about behind that
pattern. I don't like it a bit. I wonder—I begin to think—I wish John would
take me away from here!

It is so hard to talk with John about my case, because he is so wise, and
because he loves me so.

But I tried it last night.

It was moonlight. The moon shines in all around just as the sun does.

I hate to see it sometimes, it creeps so slowly, and always comes in by   125
one window or another.

John was asleep and I hated to waken him, so I kept still and watched
the moonlight on that undulating wallpaper till I felt creepy.

The faint figure behind seemed to shake the pattern, just as if she wanted to get out.

I got up softly and went to feel and see if the paper *did* move, and
when I came back John was awake.

"What is it, little girl?" he said. "Don't go walking about like that—you'll
get cold."

I thought it was a good time to talk, so I told him that I really was not   130
gaining here, and that I wished he would take me away.

"Why, darling!" said he. "Our lease will be up in three weeks, and I can't
see how to leave before.

"The repairs are not done at home, and I cannot possibly leave town
just now. Of course, if you were in any danger, I could and would, but you
really are better, dear, whether you can see it or not. I am a doctor, dear, and
I know. You are gaining flesh and color, your appetite is better, I feel really
much easier about you."

"I don't weigh a bit more," said I, "nor as much; and my appetite may be
better in the evening when you are here but it is worse in the morning
when you are away!"

"Bless her little heart!" said he with a big hug. "She shall be as sick as
she pleases! But now let's improve the shining hours by going to sleep, and
talk about it in the morning!"

"And you won't go away?" I asked gloomily.   135

"Why, how can I, dear? It is only three weeks more and then we will
take a nice little trip for a few days while Jennie is getting the house ready.
Really, dear, you are better!"

"Better in body perhaps—" I began, and stopped short, for he sat up
straight and looked at me with such a stern, reproachful look that I could
not say another word.

"My darling," said he, "I beg you, for my sake and for our child's sake, as well as for your own, that you will never for one instant let that idea enter your mind! There is nothing so dangerous, so fascinating, to a temperament like yours. It is a false and foolish fancy. Can you trust me as a physician when I tell you so?"

So of course I said no more on that score, and we went to sleep before long. He thought I was asleep first, but I wasn't, and lay there for hours trying to decide whether that front pattern and the back pattern really did move together or separately.

On a pattern like this, by daylight, there is a lack of sequence, a defiance of law, that is a constant irritant to a normal mind.   140

The color is hideous enough, and unreliable enough, and infuriating enough, but the pattern is torturing.

You think you have mastered it, but just as you get well under way in following, it turns a back-somersault and there you are. It slaps you in the face, knocks you down, and tramples upon you. It is like a bad dream.

The outside pattern is a florid arabesque, reminding one of a fungus. If you can imagine a toadstool in joints, an interminable string of toadstools, budding and sprouting in endless convolutions—why, that is something like it.

That is, sometimes!

There is one marked peculiarity about this paper, a thing nobody   145
seems to notice but myself, and that is that it changes as the light changes.

When the sun shoots in through the east window—I always watch for that first long, straight ray—it changes so quickly that I never can quite believe it.

That is why I watch it always.

By moonlight—the moon shines in all night when there is a moon—I wouldn't know it was the same paper.

At night in any kind of light, in twilight, candlelight, lamplight, and worst of all by moonlight, it becomes bars! The outside pattern, I mean, and the woman behind it is as plain as can be.

I didn't realize for a long time what the thing was that showed behind,   150
that dim subpattern, but now I am quite sure it is a woman.

By daylight she is subdued, quiet. I fancy it is the pattern that keeps her so still. It is so puzzling. It keeps me quiet by the hour.

I lie down ever so much now. John says it is good for me, and to sleep all I can.

Indeed he started the habit by making me lie down for an hour after each meal.

It is a very bad habit, I am convinced, for you see, I don't sleep.

And that cultivates deceit, for I don't tell them I'm awake—oh, no!   155
The fact is I am getting a little afraid of John.

He seems very queer sometimes, and even Jennie has an inexplicable look.

It strikes me occasionally, just as a scientific hypothesis, that perhaps it is the paper!

I have watched John when he did not know I was looking, and come into the room suddenly on the most innocent excuses, and I've caught him several times *looking at the paper!* And Jennie too. I caught Jennie with her hand on it once.

She didn't know I was in the room, and when I asked her in a quiet, a   160
very quiet voice, with the most restrained manner possible, what she was
doing with the paper, she turned around as if she had been caught stealing,
and looked quite angry—asked me why I should frighten her so!

Then she said that the paper stained everything it touched, that she
had found yellow smooches on all my clothes and John's and she wished
we would be more careful!

Did not that sound innocent? But I know she was studying that pattern, and I am determined that nobody shall find it out but myself!

Life is very much more exciting now than it used to be. You see, I have
something more to expect, to look forward to, to watch. I really do eat better, and am more quiet than I was.

John is so pleased to see me improve! He laughed a little the other day,
and said I seemed to be flourishing in spite of my wallpaper.

I turned it off with a laugh. I had no intention of telling him it was   165
because of the wallpaper—he would make fun of me. He might even want
to take me away.

I don't want to leave now until I have found it out. There is a week
more, and I think that will be enough.

I'm feeling so much better!

I don't sleep much at night, for it is so interesting to watch developments; but I sleep a good deal during the daytime.

In the daytime it is tiresome and perplexing.

There are always new shoots on the fungus, and new shades of yellow   170
all over it. I cannot keep count of them, though I have tried conscientiously.

It is the strangest yellow, that wallpaper! It makes me think of all the
yellow things I ever saw—not beautiful ones like buttercups, but old, foul,
bad yellow things.

But there is something else about that paper—the smell! I noticed it
the moment we came into the room, but with so much air and sun it was
not bad. Now we have had a week of fog and rain, and whether the windows are open or not, the smell is here.

It creeps all over the house.

I find it hovering in the dining-room, skulking in the parlor, hiding in
the hall, lying in wait for me on the stairs.

It gets into my hair.   175

Even when I go to ride, if I turn my head suddenly and surprise it—
there is that smell!

Such a peculiar odor, too! I have spent hours in trying to analyze it, to
find what it smelled like.

It is not bad—at first—and very gentle, but quite the subtlest, most
enduring odor I ever met.

In this damp weather it is awful. I wake up in the night and find it hanging over me.

It used to disturb me at first. I thought seriously of burning the   180
house—to reach the smell.

But now I am used to it. The only thing I can think of that it is like is
the *color* of the paper! A yellow smell.

There is a very funny mark on this wall, low down, near the mopboard.
A streak that runs round the room. It goes behind every piece of furniture,

except the bed, a long, straight, even *smooch,* as if it had been rubbed over and over.

I wonder how it was done and who did it, and what they did it for. Round and round and round—round and round and round—it makes me dizzy!

I really have discovered something at last.

Through watching so much at night, when it changes so, I have finally found out.   185

The front pattern *does* move—and no wonder! The woman behind shakes it!

Sometimes I think there are a great many women behind, and sometimes only one, and she crawls around fast, and her crawling shakes it all over.

Then in the very bright spots she keeps still, and in the very shady spots she just takes hold of the bars and shakes them hard.

And she is all the time trying to climb through. But nobody could climb through that pattern—it strangles so; I think that is why it has so many heads.

They get through and then the pattern strangles them off and turns them upside down, and makes their eyes white!   190

If those heads were covered or taken off it would not be half so bad.

I think that woman gets out in the daytime!

And I'll tell you why—privately—I've seen her!

I can see her out of every one of my windows!

It is the same woman, I know, for she is always creeping, and most women do not creep by daylight.   195

I see her in that long shaded lane, creeping up and down. I see her in those dark grape arbors, creeping all round the garden.

I see her on that long road under the trees, creeping along, and when a carriage comes she hides under the blackberry vines.

I don't blame her a bit. It must be very humiliating to be caught creeping by daylight!

I always lock the door when I creep by daylight. I can't do it at night, for I know John would suspect something at once.

And John is so queer now that I don't want to irritate him. I wish he would take another room! Besides, I don't want anybody to get that woman out at night but myself.   200

I often wonder if I could see her out of all the windows at once.

But, turn as fast as I can, I can only see out of one at one time.

And though I always see her, she *may* be able to creep faster than I can turn! I have watched her sometimes away off in the open country, creeping as fast as a cloud shadow in a wind.

If only that top pattern could be gotten off from the under one! I mean to try it, little by little.

I have found out another funny thing, but I shan't tell it this time! It does not do to trust people too much.   205

There are only two more days to get this paper off, and I believe John is beginning to notice. I don't like the look in his eyes.

And I heard him ask Jennie a lot of professional questions about me. She had a very good report to give.

She said I slept a good deal in the daytime.

John knows I don't sleep very well at night, for all I'm so quiet!

He asked me all sorts of questions too, and pretended to be very loving   210
and kind.

As if I couldn't see through him!

Still, I don't wonder he acts so, sleeping under this paper for three
months.

It only interests me, but I feel sure John and Jennie are affected by it.

Hurrah! This is the last day, but it is enough. John is to stay in town over
night, and won't be out until this evening.

Jennie wanted to sleep with me—the sly thing; but I told her I should   215
undoubtedly rest better for a night all alone.

That was clever, for really I wasn't alone a bit! As soon as it was moonlight and that poor thing began to crawl and shake the pattern, I got up and
ran to help her.

I pulled and she shook. I shook and she pulled, and before morning we
had peeled off yards of that paper.

A strip about as high as my head and half around the room.

And then when the sun came and that awful pattern began to laugh at
me, I declared I would finish it today!

We go away tomorrow, and they are moving all my furniture down   220
again to leave things as they were before.

Jennie looked at the wall in amazement, but I told her merrily that I did
it out of pure spite at the vicious thing.

She laughed and said she wouldn't mind doing it herself, but I must not
get tired.

How she betrayed herself that time!

But I am here, and no person touches this paper but Me—not *alive!*

She tried to get me out of the room—it was too patent! But I said it was   225
so quiet and empty and clean now that I believed I would lie down again
and sleep all I could, and not to wake me even for dinner—I would call
when I woke.

So now she is gone, and the servants are gone, and the things are gone,
and there is nothing left but that great bedstead nailed down, with the canvas mattress we found on it.

We shall sleep downstairs tonight, and take the boat home tomorrow.

I quite enjoy the room, now it is bare again.

How those children did tear about here!

This bedstead is fairly gnawed!   230

But I must get to work.

I have locked the door and thrown the key down into the front path.

I don't want to go out, and I don't want to have anybody come in, till
John comes.

I want to astonish him.

I've got a rope up here that even Jennie did not find. If that woman   235
does get out, and tries to get away, I can tie her!

But I forgot I could not reach far without anything to stand on!

This bed will *not* move!

I tried to lift and push it until I was lame, and then I got so angry I bit
off a little piece at one corner—but it hurt my teeth.

Then I peeled off all the paper I could reach standing on the floor.
It sticks horribly and the pattern just enjoys it! All those strangled

heads and bulbous eyes and waddling fungus growths just shriek with derision!

I am getting angry enough to do something desperate. To jump out of   240
the window would be admirable exercise, but the bars are too strong even
to try.

Besides I wouldn't do it. Of course not. I know well enough that a step
like that is improper and might be misconstrued.

I don't like to *look* out of the windows even—there are so many of
those creeping women, and they creep so fast.

I wonder if they all come out of that wallpaper as I did!

But I am securely fastened now by my well-hidden rope—you don't
get *me* out in the road there!

I suppose I shall have to get back behind the pattern when it comes   245
night, and that is hard!

It is so pleasant to be out in this great room and creep around as I
please!

I don't want to go outside. I won't, even if Jennie asks me to.

For outside you have to creep on the ground, and everything is green
instead of yellow.

But here I can creep smoothly on the floor, and my shoulder just fits in
that long smooch around the wall, so I cannot lose my way.

Why, there's John at the door!   250

It is no use, young man, you can't open it!

How he does call and pound!

Now he's crying to Jennie for an axe.

It would be a shame to break down that beautiful door!

"John, dear!" said I in the gentlest voice. "The key is down by the front   255
steps, under a plantain leaf!"

That silenced him for a few moments.

Then he said, very quietly indeed, "Open the door, my darling!"

"I can't," said I. "The key is down by the front door under a plantain
leaf!" And then I said it again, several times, very gently and slowly, and said
it so often that he had to go and see, and he got it of course, and came in.
He stopped short by the door.

"What is the matter?" he cried. "For God's sake, what are you doing!"

I kept on creeping just the same, but I looked at him over my shoulder.   260

"I've got out at last," said I, "in spite of you and Jane. And I've pulled off
most of the paper, so you can't put me back!"

Now why should that man have fainted? But he did, and right across
my path by the wall, so that I had to creep over him every time!

[1892]

Writing about "The Yellow Wallpaper": Critical Viewpoints

Elaine Hedges: The Initial Appearance and Early Reception

The 1973 Feminist Press edition of Gilman's most famous story, with a long "Afterword" by Elaine Hedges, helped to rescue "The Yellow Wallpaper" from relative
neglect. In this excerpt, Hedges discusses the story's initial appearance and early

reception. (The story's initial title was "The Yellow Wall-Paper," with a hyphen, but Gilman's own usage was inconsistent, and scholars and editors have since conventionally dropped the hyphen.)

It wasn't easy for Charlotte Perkins Gilman to get her story published. She sent it first to William Dean Howells, and he, responding to at least some of its power and authenticity, recommended it to Horace Scudder, editor of *The Atlantic Monthly,* then the most prestigious magazine in the United States. Scudder rejected the story, according to Gilman's account in her autobiography, with a curt note:

> *Dear Madam,*
>
> *Mr. Howells has handed me this story. I could not forgive myself if I made others as miserable as I have made myself!*
>
> *Sincerely yours,*
>
> *H.E. Scudder*

In the 1890s editors, and especially Scudder, still officially adhered to a canon of "moral uplift" in literature, and Gilman's story, with its heroine reduced at the end to the level of a groveling animal, scarcely fitted the prescribed formula. One wonders, however, whether hints of the story's attack on social mores—specifically on the ideal of the submissive wife—came through to Scudder and unsettled him?

The story was finally published, in May 1892, in *The New England Magazine,* where it was greeted with strong but mixed feelings. Gilman was warned that such stories were "perilous stuff," which should not be printed because of the threat they posed to the relatives of such "deranged" persons as the heroine. The implications of such warnings— that women should "stay in their place," that nothing could or should be done except maintain silence or conceal problems—are fairly clear. Those who praised the story, for the accuracy of its portrayal and its delicacy of touch, did so on the grounds that Gilman had captured in literature, from a medical point of view, the most "detailed account of incipient insanity." Howells' admiration for the story, when he reprinted it in 1920 in the *Great Modern American Stories,* limited itself to the story's "chilling" quality. Again, however, no one seems to have made the connection between the insanity and the sex, or sexual role, of the victim, no one explored the story's implications for male-female relationships in the nineteenth century.

From Elaine R. Hedges, "Afterword." In *Charlotte Perkins Gilman, "The Yellow Wallpaper."* Old Westbury, NY: Feminist Press, 1973, pp. 40–41.

Charlotte Perkins Gilman: Autobiographical Insight

Gilman's story is not autobiographical, but it is certainly based on her own experience. Like the story's narrator, she experienced a struggle between her work and marriage. On the one hand, Gilman says she knew it was normal for a woman to be able to have marriage and motherhood. On the other hand, however, Gilman felt she ought to be completely devoted to her work. Gilman debated for two years whether to marry Walter Stetson, and she finally consented after Stetson experienced some "keen personal disappointment," as she puts it. Gilman was perhaps especially sensitive to his disappointment because she spent much of her own life in some state of depression, and she felt that her productivity would have been much greater if she could have avoided her manic-depressive cycles.

Gilman's story was so disturbing, so astonishing to her readers, that many people apparently wondered why she had written such a story. The following passage comes from Gilman's essay explaining "Why I Wrote the Yellow Wallpaper."

For many years I suffered from a severe and continuous nervous breakdown tending to melancholia—and beyond. During about the third year of this trouble I went, in devout faith and some faint stir of hope, to a noted specialist in nervous diseases, the best known in the country. This wise man put me to bed and applied the rest cure, to which a still good physique responded so promptly that he concluded there was nothing much the matter with me, and sent me home with solemn advice to "live as domestic a life as far as possible," to "have but two hours' intellectual life a day," and "never to touch pen, brush or pencil again as long as I lived." This was in 1887.

I went home and obeyed those directions for some three months, and came so near the border line of utter mental ruin that I could see over.

Then, using the remnants of intelligence that remained, and helped by a wise friend, I cast the noted specialist's advice to the winds and went to work again—work, the normal life of every human being; work, in which is joy and growth and service, without which one is a pauper and a parasite; ultimately recovering some measure of power.

Being naturally moved to rejoicing by this narrow escape, I wrote *The Yellow Wallpaper,* with its embellishments and additions to carry out the ideal (I never had hallucinations or objections to my mural decorations) and sent a copy to the physician who so nearly drove me mad. He never acknowledged it.

The little book is valued by alienists [psychiatrists] and as a good specimen of one kind of literature. It has to my knowledge saved one woman from a similar fate—so terrifying her family that they let her out into normal activity and she recovered.

But the best result is this. Many years later I was told that the great specialist had admitted to friends of his that he had altered his treatment of neurasthenia since reading *The Yellow Wallpaper.*

It was not intended to drive people crazy, but to save people from being driven crazy, and it worked.

From the *Forerunner* 4.10 (October 1913): 271.

Barbara Ehrenreich and Deidre English: Historical and Political Stance

The following selection of excerpts is taken from a groundbreaking work of scholarship, Barbara Ehrenreich and Deidre English's *Complaints and Disorders: The Sexual Politics of Sickness* (1973). Ehrenreich and English drew attention to the role of male physicians in shaping women's social roles, self-understanding, and medical treatment and health. The depression and anxiety that Gilman suffered, and that drive the narrator of "The Yellow Wallpaper," appear to have been pervasive. Gilman wrote her story to stop the oppressive therapy of men like Dr. S. Weir Mitchell, who treated her; but his awful approach appears to have been rather mild compared to that of other practitioners.

The boredom and confinement of affluent women fostered a morbid cult of hypochondria—"female invalidism"—that began in the mid-nineteenth century and did not completely fade until the late 1910s. Sickness pervaded upper- and upper-middle-class female culture. Health spas and female specialists sprang up everywhere and became part of the regular circuit of fashionable women. And in the 1850s a steady stream of popular home readers by doctors appeared, all on the subject of female health. Literature aimed at female readers lingered on the romantic pathos of illness and death; popular women's magazines featured such stories as "The Grave of My Friend" and "Song of Dying." Paleness and lassitude (along with filmy white gowns) came into vogue. It was acceptable, even fashionable, to retire to bed with "sick headaches," "nerves," and a host of other mysterious ailments.

In response, feminist writers and female doctors expressed their dismay at the chronic invalidism of affluent women. Dr. Mary Putnam Jacobi, an outstanding woman doctor of the late nineteenth century, wrote in 1985:

> . . . it is considered natural and almost laudable to break down under all conceivable varieties of strain—a winter dissipation, a houseful of servants, a quarrel with a female friend, not to speak of more legitimate reasons. . . . Women who expect to go to bed every menstrual period expect to collapse if by chance they find themselves on their feet for a few hours during such a crisis. Constantly considering their nerves, urged to consider them by well-intentioned but short-sighted advisors, they pretty soon became nothing but a bundle of nerves.

Charlotte Perkins Gilman, the feminist writer and economist, concluded bitterly that American men "have bred a race of women weak enough to be handed about like invalids; or mentally weak enough to pretend they are—and like it." . . .

The association of TB with innate feminine weakness was strengthened by the fact that TB is accompanied by an erratic emotional pattern in which a person may behave sometimes frenetically, sometimes morbidly. The behavior characteristic for the disease fit expectations about woman's personality, and the look of the disease suited—and perhaps helped to create—the prevailing standards of female beauty. The female consumptive did not lose her feminine identity, she embodied it: the bright eyes, translucent skin, and red lips were only an extreme of traditional female beauty. A romantic myth rose up around the figure of the female consumptive and was reflected in portraiture and literature: for example, in the sweet and tragic character of Beth, in *Little Women*. Not only were women seen as sickly—sickness was seen as feminine.

The doctors' views of women as innately sick did not, of course, *make* them sick, or delicate, or idle. But it did provide a powerful rationale against allowing women to act in any other way. Medical arguments were used to explain why women should be barred from medical school (they would faint in anatomy lectures), from higher education altogether, and from voting. For example, a Massachusetts legislator proclaimed:

5

Grant suffrage to women, and you will have to build insane asy-
lums in every county, and establish a divorce court in every
town. Women are too nervous and hysterical to enter into politics.

Medical arguments seemed to take the malice out of sexual oppression:
when you prevented a woman from doing anything active or interesting,
you were only doing this for her own good. . . .

Passivity was the main prescription, along with warm baths, cool baths,
abstinence from animal foods and spices, and indulgence in milk and
puddings, cereals, and "mild sub-acid fruits." Women were to have a nurse—
not a relative—to care for them, to receive no visitors, and as Dr. Dirix
wrote, "all sources of mental excitement should be perseveringly guarded
against." Charlotte Perkins Gilman was prescribed this type of treatment by
Dr. S. Weir Mitchell, who advised her to put away all her pens and books.
Gilman later described the experience in the story "The Yellow Wallpaper,"
in which the heroine, a would-be writer, is ordered by her physician-
husband to "rest":

> *So I take phosphates or phosphites—whichever it is, and*
> *tonics and journeys, and air, and exercise, and am absolutely*
> *forbidden to "work" until I am well again.*
> *Personally, I disagree with their ideas.*
> *Personally, I believe that congenial work, with excitement and*
> *change, would do me good.*
> *But what is one to do?*
> *I did write for a while—in spite of them; but it does exhaust*
> *me a good deal—having to be so sly about it, . . . or else meet*
> *with heavy opposition.*

Slowly Gilman's heroine begins to lose her grip ("It is getting to be a great
effort for me to think straight. Just this nervous weakness, I suppose.") and
finally she frees herself from her prison—into madness, crawling in endless
circles about her room, muttering about the wallpaper.

But it was the field of gynecological surgery that provided the most brutally direct medical treatments of female "personality disorders." And the surgical approach to female psychological problems had what was considered a
solid theoretical basis in the theory of the "psychology of the ovary." After all,
if a woman's entire personality was dominated by her reproductive organs,
then gynecological surgery was the most logical approach to any female psychological problem. Beginning in the late 1860s, doctors began to act on this
principle.

At least one of their treatments probably *was* effective: surgical removal
of the clitoris as a cure for sexual arousal. A medical book of their period
stated: "Unnatural growth of the clitoris . . . is likely to lead to immorality as
well as to serious disease . . . amputation may be necessary." Although many
doctors frowned on the practice of removing the clitoris, they tended to
agree that this might be necessary in cases of "nymphomania." (The last cli-
torectomy we know of in the United States was performed twenty-five years
ago on a child of five, as a cure for masturbation.)

More widely practiced was the surgical removal of the ovaries—
ovariotomy, or "female castration." Thousands of these operations were performed from 1860 to 1890. In his article "The Spermatic Economy," Ben

10

Barker-Benfield describes the invention of the "normal ovariotomy," or removal of ovaries for non-ovarian conditions—in 1872 by Dr. Robert Battey of Rome, Georgia.

> *Among the indications were a troublesomeness, eating like a ploughman, masturbation, attempted suicide, erotic tendencies, persecution mania, simple "cussedness," and dysmenorrhea. Most apparent in the enormous variety of symptoms doctors took to indicate castration was a strong current of sexual appetitiveness on the part of women.*

Patients were often brought in by their husbands, who complained of their unruly behavior. When returned to their husbands, "castrated," they were "tractible, orderly, industrious and cleanly," according to Dr. Battey. (Today ovariotomy, accompanying a hysterectomy, for example, is not known to have these effects on the personality. One can only wonder what, if any, personality changes Dr. Battey's patients really went through.) Whatever the effects, some doctors claimed to have removed from fifteen hundred to two thousand ovaries; in Barker-Benfield's words, they "handed them around at medical society meetings on plates like trophies."

From Barbara Ehrenreich and Deirdre English, *Complaints and Disorders: The Sexual Politics of Sickness.* New York: Feminist Press, 1973.

Loralee MacPike: New Critical, Psychological, Feminist Blend

Shortly after the Feminist Press republished Gilman's classic story in 1973, the pace of critical attention given to it picked up dramatically. Here is an excerpt from a relatively early study (1975) by Loralee MacPike that employs a rather traditional close reading, looking for symbolic unity. But MacPike's essay shows how New Critical strategies might employ psychological terms and be turned to feminist purposes.

The fact that the narrator's prison-room is a nursery indicates her status in society. The woman is legally a child; socially, economically, and philosophically she must be led by an adult—her husband; and therefore the nursery is an appropriate place to house her. The narrator's work threatens to destroy her status as a mere child by gaining her recognition in the adult world; this is reason enough for her husband to forbid her to work. Her work is, as he suggests, dangerous; but its danger is for him, not her, because it removes her from his control. The nursery, then, is an appropriate symbol for the desired state of childlikeness vis-à-vis the adult world that her husband wishes to enforce.

The nursery's windows are barred, making the setting not only a retreat into childhood but a prison. The narrator is to be forever imprisoned in childhood, forbidden to "escape" into adulthood. She instinctively feels that, just as only her work can transport her out of the world of childhood, so too can it alone free her from her dependence upon her husband in particular and the male-created world in general. Emergence from the chrysalis of childhood would also free her in the larger sense, making her a responsible member of society rather than merely a cloistered woman. It could provide for her a physical movement out into an active life, but the bars in the unchosen room of her existence effectively prevent such an emergence.

The bedstead is the third symbol of the narrator's situation. A representation of her sexuality, it is nailed to the floor, ostensibly to prevent the former youthful occupants of the room from pushing it about. As the nursery imprisons her in a state of childhood, so the bedstead prevents her from moving "off center" sensually—not merely sexually—in any sort of physical contact with another human being. Her inability to care for her own child is but another fixity in her life, and the immovable bedstead symbolizes the static nature of both the expression and the product of her sexuality, thus denying her this outlet for her energies just as the bars deny her physical movement and the nursery her adult abilities.

These three items—the nursery, the bars on the windows, and the bedstead—show not only the narrator's mind but the state of the world that formed that mind. Her dilemma is not strictly personal, for the forces that shaped her, cutting off all possibility of personal realization, movement, or sexuality, are the processes that shape many women's lives. Gilman shows, through the normality of the narrator's life, the sources of her frustrations. The apparently unusual circumstances of bars, a nailed-down bed, a nursery for a bedroom are all explained as possible occurrences in a normal household. Although unusual perhaps, they are not extraordinary in the way Hawthorne's settings or Wilkie Collins' plots can be said to be extraordinary. It is not necessary for Gilman to give any background whatever, neither social comment nor history; for her use of the stuff of the narrator's life as symbolic of her state of mind and its causes suffices.

From Loralee MacPike, "Environment as Psychopathological Symbolism in 'The Yellow Wallpaper.'" *American Literary Realism* 8.3 (1975): 286–287.

Jean Kennard: Reader Response and Meta-Criticism

In a brilliant essay in 1981, Jean Kennard stepped back from the emerging feminist celebration of Gilman's story and looked carefully at how critical perceptions of the story had changed. The story hadn't changed, obviously; so why were critics reading it differently? Kennard's essay, called "Convention Coverage or How to Read Your Own Life," explains shifts in the conventions of reading—that is, changes in readers' assumptions, strategies, and goals. In this excerpt, Kennard usefully discusses several different and still famous feminist readings of the story. The self-consciousness of modern criticism (thinking about itself) has made this kind of analysis of other analyses popular.

My suggestion that it is the literary conventions of the 1970s that allowed feminist readings of *The Yellow Wallpaper* does not necessarily imply anything about Gilman's intention. It is essentially irrelevant to my concern here—though in other contexts important—whether or not this meaning was, as Gilbert and Gubar claim, "quite clear to Gilman herself" (p. 91). I am using *The Yellow Wallpaper* as an example, realizing that other works would perhaps be equally fruitful, because of the similarity in the readings which have taken place since 1973 and because of the vast discrepancy between these readings and previous ones. I shall draw on four feminist readings: Elaine Hedges' "Afterword" to the Feminist Press edition of the text; Annette Kolodny's in "A Map for Rereading"; Sandra Gilbert and Susan Gubar's in *The Madwoman in the Attic*; and my own. Although these interpretations emphasize different aspects of the text, they do not conflict with each other.

In its time and until the last eight years, *The Yellow Wallpaper* was read, when it was read at all, "as a Poesque tale of chilling horror," designed "to freeze our blood," praised, when it was praised, for the detail with which it recorded developing insanity. Even as late as 1971 Seon Manley and Godo Lewis included it in a collection entitled *Ladies of Horror: Two Centuries of Supernatural Stories by the Gentle Sex* and introduced it with the following words: "There were new ideas afloat: perhaps some of the horrors were in our own minds, not in the outside world at all. This idea gave birth to the psychological horror story and *The Yellow Wallpaper* by Charlotte Perkins Gilman shows she was a mistress of the art."

No earlier reader saw the story as in any way positive. When Horace Scudder rejected it for publication in *The Atlantic Monthly*, he explained that he did not wish to make his readers as miserable as the story had made him. As Elaine Hedges points out, "No one seems to have made the connection between insanity and the sex, or sexual role of the victim, no one explored the story's implications for male-female relationships in the nineteenth century" (p. 41).

Feminist critics approach *The Yellow Wallpaper* from the point of view of the narrator. "As she tells her story," says Hedges, "the reader has confidence in the reasonableness of her arguments and explanations" (p. 49). The narrator is seen as the victim of an oppressive patriarchal social system which restricts women and prevents their functioning as full human beings. The restrictions on women are symbolized by the narrator's imprisonment in a room with bars on the window, an image the narrator sees echoed in the patterns of the room's yellow wallpaper. "The wallpaper," claims Hedges, symbolizes "the morbid social situation" (p. 52). Gilbert and Gubar talk of "the anxiety-inducing connections between what women writers tend to see as their parallel confinements in texts, houses and maternal female bodies" and describe the wallpaper as "ancient, smoldering, 'unclean' as the oppressive structures of the society in which she finds herself" (p. 90). The women the narrator "sees" in the wallpaper and wants to liberate are perceived to be "creeping." "Women must creep," says Hedges, "the narrator knows this" (p. 53). I see the indoor images of imprisonment echoed in the natural world of the garden with its "walls and gates that lock, and lots of separate little houses for the gardeners and people" (p. 11). Like so many other women in literature, the only access to nature the narrator has is to a carefully cultivated and confined garden. Gilbert and Gubar point out that in contrast the idea of "open country" is the place of freedom (p. 91).

The representative of the repressive patriarchal society is the narrator's husband John, "a censorious and paternalistic physician" (p. 89), as Gilbert and Gubar call him. John has "a doubly authoritative role as both husband and doctor" (p. 457), Kolodny points out. The description of John as rational rather than emotional, as a man who laughs at what cannot be put down in figures, emphasizes his position as representative of a male power which excludes feeling and imagination. Indeed, the first sentence in the story which suggests a feminist reading to me is a comment on John's character: "John laughs at me, of course, but one expects that in marriage" (p. 9).

John's treatment of his wife's mental illness is isolation and the removal of all intellectual stimulation, "a cure worse than the disease" (p. 89), as Gilbert and Gubar call it. Feminist critics see the narrator's being deprived of an opportunity to write, the opportunity for self-expression, as particularly significant. Kolodny (p. 457) and Gilbert and Gubar (p. 89) remind us that the narrator thinks of writing as a relief. Hedges sees the narrator as someone who

15

"wants very much to work." By keeping her underemployed and isolated, John effectively ensures his wife's dependence on him. She must remain the child he treats her as. Hedges draws attention to the fact that he calls her "blessed little goose" and his "little girl" and that the room she stays in was once a nursery (p. 50). For Hedges, John is "an important source of her afflictions" (p. 49).

The narrator experiences her victimization as a conflict between her own personal feelings, perceived by feminist critics as healthy and positive, and the patriarchal society's view of what is proper behavior for women. Since, like so many women up to the present day, she has internalized society's expectations of women, this conflict is felt as a split within herself. Early in the story the words "Personally, I" (p. 10) are twice set against the views of John and her brother. Nevertheless, she also continues to judge her own behavior as John does. "I get unreasonably angry with John sometimes" (p. 11), she explains; "I cry at nothing, and cry most of the time" (p. 19). As Hedges points out, this split is symbolized by the woman behind the wallpaper: "By rejecting that woman, she might free the other imprisoned woman within herself" (p. 35). The narrator's madness is perceived by Hedges and others as a direct result of societally induced confusion over personal identity. If the images of women as child or cripple, as prisoner, even as fungus growth in Gilman's story are "the images men had of women, and hence that women had of themselves," Hedges writes, "it is not surprising that madness and suicide bulk large in the work of late nineteenth-century women writers" (p. 54).

The most radical aspects of the feminist reading of *The Yellow Wallpaper* lies in the interpretation of the narrator's descent into madness as a way to health, as a rejection of and escape from an insane society. Gilbert and Gubar describe her as sinking "more and more deeply into what the world calls madness" (p. 90). They see her "imaginings and creations" as "mirages of health and freedom" (p. 91). Hedges stresses this aspect of the story. She describes the narrator as "ultimately mad and yet, throughout her descent into madness, in many ways more sensible than the people who surround and cripple her" (p. 49). "In her made-sane way she has seen the situation of women for what it is," Hedges continues, and so "madness is her only freedom" (p. 53).

It is the interpretation of madness as a higher form of sanity that allows feminist critics finally to read this story as a woman's quest for her own identity. Deprived of reading material, she begins to read the wallpaper. "Fighting for her identity, for some sense of independent self, she observes the wallpaper" (pp. 50–51), writes Hedges. More sophisticatedly, Kolodny claims the narrator "comes more and more to experience herself as a text which can neither get read nor recorded" (p. 457). Both Kolodny and Gilbert and Gubar emphasize that the narrator creates meaning in the wallpaper in her need to find an image of herself which will affirm the truth of her own situation and hence her identity. Kolodny writes: "Selectively emphasizing one section of the pattern while repressing others, reorganizing and regrouping past impressions into newer, more fully realized configurations—as one might with any formal text—the speaking voice becomes obsessed with her quest for meaning" (p. 458). Gilbert and Gubar describe the narrator's creations of meaning as a reversal of the wallpaper's implications: "Inevitably she studies its suicidal implications—and inevitably, because of her 'imaginative power and habit of story-making,' she revises it, projecting her own passion for escape into its otherwise incomprehensible hieroglyphics" (p. 90). Although the narrator is not seen to emerge either from madness or marriage at the end of the novella, her understanding of her own situation and, by extension, the situation of all women can be read as a sort of triumph. This triumph is symbolized by the overcoming of John, who is last seen fainting on the floor as his wife creeps over him.

In order to read the novel this way, much must be assumed that is not directly stated, much must be ignored that is. There is no overt statement, for example, that invites us to find a socially induced cause for the narrator's madness, to assume that her situation is that of all women. There is perhaps even a certain perversity in claiming that a mentally deranged woman crawling around an attic floor is experiencing some sort of victory. It is also true that if the narrator claims she thinks writing would relieve her mind, she also says it tires her when she tries (p. 16). Since she so often contradicts herself, we are free to believe her only when her comments support our reading. Much is made in the novella of the color yellow; feminist readings do little with this. Despite all these objections, which could probably be continued indefinitely, it is the feminist reading I teach my students and which I believe is the most fruitful. In pointing out the "weaknesses" in my own reading, I am only providing the sort of evidence that could be used to counter any interpretation of the story. I am interested in why we read it as we do, not whether we are correct in doing so.

From Jean Kennard, "Convention Coverage or How to Read Your Own Life." *New Literary History* 13.1 (1981): 74–76.

Judith Fetterley: Reader Response and Feminist Criticism

Judith Fetterley influentially combined reader-response and feminist criticism. This brief excerpt (from an essay on stories by Edgar Allen Poe, Susan Glaspell, and Charlotte Perkins Gilman) suggests the power of Fetterley's notion of the feminist reader as a "resisting" reader. Gilman's story, as Fetterley reminds us, is about writing and reading—and who controls these activities.

Gilman's narrator recognizes that she is in a haunted house, despite the protestations of her John, who is far less up-front than Poe's Roderick. Writing from the point of view of a character trapped in that male text—as if the black cat or Madeline Usher should actually find words and speak— Gilman's narrator shifts the center of attention away from the male mind that has produced the text and directs it instead to the consequences for women's lives of men's control of textuality. For it is precisely at this point that "The Yellow Wallpaper" enters this discussion of the connections between gender and reading. In this text we find the analysis of why who gets to tell the story and what story one is required, allowed, or encouraged to read matter so much, and therefore why in a sexist culture the practice of reading follows the theory proposed by Glaspell. Gilman's story makes clear the connection between male control of textuality and male dominance in other areas, and in it we feel the fact of force behind what is usually passed off as a casual accident of personal preference or justified by invoking "absolute" standards of "universal" value: these are just books I happen to like and I want to share them with you; these are our great texts and you must read them if you want to be literate. As man, husband, and doctor, John controls the narrator's life. That he chooses to make such an issue out of what and how she reads tells us what we need to know about the politics of reading.

In "The Yellow Wallpaper," Gilman argues that male control of textuality constitutes one of the primary causes of women's madness in a patriarchal culture. Forced to read men's texts, women are forced to become characters in those texts. And since the stories men tell assert as fact what women know to be fiction, not only do women lose the power that comes from authoring; more significantly, they are forced to deny their own reality and to commit in effect a kind of psychic suicide. For Gilman works out in considerable detail the position implicit in "A Jury of Her Peers"—namely, that in a sexist culture the interests of men and women are antithetical, and, thus, the stories each has to tell are not simply alternate versions of reality, they are, rather, radically incompatible. The two stories cannot coexist; if one is accepted as true, then the other must be false, and vice versa. Thus, the struggle for control of textuality is nothing less than the struggle for control over the definition of reality and hence over the definition of sanity and madness. The nameless narrator of Gilman's story has two choices. She can accept her husband's definition of reality, the prime component of which is the proposition that for her to write her own text is "madness" and for her to read his text is "sanity"; that is, she can agree to become a character in his text, accept his definition of sanity, which is madness for her, and thus commit psychic suicide, killing herself into his text to serve his interests. Or she can refuse to read his text, refuse to become a character in it, and insist on writing her own, behavior for which John will define and treat her as mad. Though Gilman herself was able to choose a third alternative, that of writing "The Yellow Wallpaper," she implicitly recognizes that her escape from this dilemma is the exception, not the rule. Though the narrator chooses the second alternative, she does as a result go literally mad and, thus, ironically fulfills the script John has written for her. Nevertheless, in the process she manages to expose the fact of John's fiction and the implications of his insistence on asserting his fiction as fact. And she does, however briefly, force him to become a character in her text.

From Judith Fetterley, "Reading About Reading: 'A Jury of Her Peers,' 'The Murders in the Rue Morgue,' and 'The Yellow Wallpaper,'" In Elizabeth Flynn and Patrocino Schweikert, *Gender and Reading: Essays on Readers, Texts, and Contexts.* Baltimore: Johns Hopkins UP, 1986.

John Harvey Kellogg: Historical Materials

Here is an excerpt from John Harvey Kellogg's *The Household Monitor of Health* (1874), which possibly provides some historical context for Gilman's story. Gilman might well have been aware of the contemporary scientific understanding that certain kinds of wallpaper, which contain arsenic, have toxic effects. To what extent does the story open up this possibility? Is our response to Gilman's story affected by this information?

Poisonous Paper. —Many cases of poisoning, some of which were fatal, have been traced to the arsenic contained in several of the colors of wall paper. The most dangerous color is green. It is almost impossible to find a green paper which does not contain arsenic. Green window curtains are especially dangerous. The green dust which can be rubbed off from them is deadly poison. In rolling and unrolling the curtain it is thrown into the air, and is breathed. The same poison is brushed off the surface of arsenical wall paper into the air, by the rubbing of pictures, garments, etc., which come in contact with it.

It is very easy to test papers of this kind before buying, and it would be wise always to take this precaution. Take a piece of the paper, hold it over a saucer, and pour upon it strong aqua ammonia. If there is any arsenic present, this will dissolve it. Collect the liquid in a vial or tube, and drop in a crystal of nitrate of silver. If there is arsenic present, little yellow crystals will make their appearance about the nitrate of silver. Arsenical green, when washed with aqua ammonia, either changes to blue, or fades.

From John Harvey Kellogg, *The Household Monitor of Health*. Battle
   Creek, MI: Good Health Publishing, 1891.

Janet Beer: Psychological Film Criticism

The following excerpts, from Janet Beer's *Kate Chopin, Edith Wharton and Charlotte Perkins Gilman: Studies in Short Fiction* (1997), deal with a ninety-minute adaptation of "The Yellow Wallpaper," which was made for BBC television, and aired in 1992. The screenplay by Maggie Wadey, directed by John Clive, is a bold and revealing interpretation of Gilman's story. The protagonist, for instance, is named "Charlotte" in the film, embracing the notion that the story has autobiographical elements. The story may encourage readers at least to consider the possibility that the house is somehow haunted by a malevolent force (how did those gnawing marks get on the bed?), and that spirits might be trapped behind the paper. The screenplay, on the other hand, makes clear that such supernatural elements are strictly in the protagonist's head. The story's gothic and fantastic hints are reduced to psychopathology. The screenplay is thus, in a sense, a psychological interpretation of Gilman's story.

An event threatened in the story and enacted in the screenplay, which can, additionally, be seen as paradigmatic of the manner in which Wadey expends the drama beyond the limits of the original text, depicts the doctor called in by Charlotte's husband to give a second opinion delivering moral as well as medical advice to his patient:

> Let me repeat what I told you two months ago: I cannot answer
> for your good health, physical or mental, unless you undertake
> to lay aside your writing. Your child, your husband, your home,
> cannot be laid aside and the energy of the human body is finite.
>
> (HE NOW PROCEEDS TO EXAMINE CHARLOTTE'S EYES, PULLING DOWN THE
> LOWER LID WITH HIS THUMB.)
>
> What nature expends in one direction she must economise on in
> another. The young woman who makes too much intellectual
> effort risks decline into a delicate, ailing woman whose future—
> allow me? (HE OPENS HER GOWN)—is more or less suffering. A lesson
> I should not like to see experience teach you, Charlotte.
>
> I see your dressmaker has already begun to help you conceal
> your loss of weight. You must put on flesh, my dear. Surely I can
> appeal to your vanity if nothing else?
>
> (HE CLOSES HER GOWN AGAIN)

But there's nothing gravely wrong with you—we may reassure poor John on that point!

(*HE LIGHTLY TOUCHES ONE OF HER EARRINGS WITH HIS FINGERTIPS*)

Charming earrings, my dear. (pp. 125-6)[1]

Contained within the doctor's pronouncements about the recovery and maintenance of good health are allusions to matters which Gilman considered instrumental in the oppression of women and which are also discussed as significant by Elaine Showalter in the management of female mental illness at the end of the 19th century. With regard to women's capacity for intellectual work Showalter cites manifold pronouncements by male doctors on the limited capacity which women have for study and the deleterious effects which scholarship would have upon their reproductive capacity.[2] In her autobiography Gilman repeats the advice she was given by Silas Weir Mitchell, her physician, "'Live as domestic a life as possible. Have your baby with you all the time. Lie down for an hour after each meal. Have but two hours intellectual life a day. And never touch pen, brush or pencil as long as you live.'"[3] In the dramatisation Wadey actually paraphrases Henry Maudsley, the Victorian psychiatrist, when Dr. Stark invokes the order of the natural world as authority for the physical and cerebral inferiority of women. The example of the natural world, as Charlotte Perkins Gilman constantly tells us, is often used as proof by those eager to establish the lesser status of the female and the selective nature of the evidence thus offered is critiqued throughout her writing by direct reference and also by her own decision to make use of equally selective references to species where the female is dominant.[4] . . .

Ann J. Lane, in her biography of Gilman, talks about the smell which the narrator of 'The Yellow Wallpaper' identifies as emanating from the paper itself: 'It is, she says, "the most enduring odor I ever met," and perhaps it is, even if Gilman did not recognize it, the dreaded smell of sex, a sensual smell, excretion of the night.'[5] The fear of sex which Lane recognises in Gilman's writing, 'I wake up in the night and find it hanging over me,'[6] is made explicit in the dramatic text in a number of forms. When talking to Jennie Charlotte expresses directly one of the reasons why she would want to avoid sexual relations: 'He is such a sweet baby, but—it still makes me so nervous to be with him. I—I worry in case there should be another one, and then—' (p. 75), a fear which Jennie ignores. The distress which is evident in Charlotte's explanation to John of her reasons for needing to leave the house is interpreted by him in the exigencies of his own need, to be a cry for physical attention not the intellectual stimulation she is pleading for:

---

[1] All page references in the text are to the screenplay of "The Yellow Wallpaper" by Maggie Wadey.
[2] *The Female Malady*, p. 126.
[3] *The Living of Charlotte Perkins Gilman*, p. 96.
[4] For example, in the first chapter of *Women and Economics*, 1898, reprinted. Carl N. Degler (New York, Harper Torchbooks, 1966), Gilman argues that 'We are the only animal species in which the female depends upon the male for food, the only animal species in which the sex-relation is also an economic relation.' (p. 4) and goes on to discuss a variety of other species.
[5] Lane, Ann J. *To Herland and Beyond: The Life and Work of Charlotte Perkins Gilman* (New York, Meridian, 1991), p. 129.
[6] "The Yellow Wallpaper," p. 29.

*And you know, when I'm away from you, it's such a joy to
know exactly what you're doing. At one o'clock I can imagine
you lying here in bed.*

(HE TURNS BACK TO CHARLOTTE)

*At three, I know that James has come in to play with you. What
a charming picture that is! At six I can imagine you dressing
for dinner.*

(HE SLIPS THE SLEEVE OF HER DRESS DOWN FROM HER SHOULDER WHICH HE
KISSES)

*But how much better it is to be here beside you. How adorable
you look this evening! Dearest Lotta!*

(CHARLOTTE THROWS AN ARM UP OVER HER EYES TO HIDE HER TEARS)

*Don't hide! You needn't be ashamed with me. There are times I
wish to God I could cry as easily as you do. Tears one moment,
smiles the next. So give me a smile, won't you? Please, my sweet.
That's better. (p. 99)*

Wadey makes plain the connection between Charlotte's helpless despair
and John's desire through both dialogue and action. The timetable of her day,
the control which he exerts over her every movement in his absence, another infantilisation to add to the confining of her within the nursery and forbidding of certain activities, is shown to be an intrinsic part of the way in which
he eroticises her. As he visualises her in the process of following the schedule
he has prescribed so he feels his power; the place in which he confines her is
the place where, as he says, 'I've been looking forward to being alone with you
again. In our nursery. Like another world.' (p. 54). The pressing nature of his
attentions in the film, making love to her on the nailed down bed in a furtive
manner—not undressing or expecting any response but mere compliance—
communicates a powerful sense of the claustrophobia, powerlessness and
physical distress felt by her. The scene where John makes love to Charlotte
does not celebrate or sensationalise sex, it is painful and oppressive, providing
further evidence of a social order in which only one sex is allowed full expression of its desires, whether sexual or professional. When Charlotte reacts to
the final articulation of the spiteful insincerity of John's mother: 'You do John
credit, my dear.' (p. 119) by choking and fainting, tearing at her clothes, she is
making the only effective protest she can against her many constrictions. . . .

Wadey's introduction of the writing and delivery of John's speech to
the Royal Society as another means by which the dramatic action is pro-
pelled is a further substantiation of the dialectic which reigns throughout
the drama between public and private, home and work and men and
women. The gender divide fuels the action and it is expressed in every
scene and motif, reaching a climax as the film cuts between the final stages
of Charlotte's madness and John's delivery of the speech to his fellow
physicians. As John descends to the auditorium, Charlotte wrenches out
the nails which hold the bed to the floor; as he opens his lecture notes
before an audience, she clears surfaces, moves furniture and overturns the
wardrobe; as John holds forth on the beneficial effects of recreation in
reducing instances of ill health amongst the poor, turning the pages of his
lecture, so Charlotte rips the paper from the walls. The camera registers the
attentiveness of John's audience as he delivers his speech whilst the cam-

era in Charlotte's bedroom is positioned so that it looks at her from inside the newly bare wall. As she crawls, demented, around the room in pursuit of a single idea, he receives the congratulations of his peers for the effective expression of his many ideas and theories.

The visual contextualisation of Charlotte's breakdown in the midst of John's professional debut as a public speaker foregrounds the difference between public and private texts as well as lives. John's prominent position in the medical establishment enacts a straightforward contrast between his place in the outside world and Charlotte's obvious isolation from anyone who cares about the stuff of the imagination or the writer's craft. As he becomes more public so she is forced into greater seclusion and internality, as she says in her lament for the loss of her sense of 'community'. The sequence of scenes which show Charlotte writing in her forbidden notebook culminates in her being viewed from outside the bedroom window; the window frames the shot and the visual image is of the writer behind bars, imprisoned for practising her art. A number of exchanges between John and Charlotte in the dramatisation make plain their epistemological divergence, Wadey setting up a dialectic between scientific and poetic truth, between imagination and fact and between varieties of textual authority.

From Janet Beer, *Kate Chopin, Edith Wharton and Charlotte Perkins Gilman: Studies in Short Fiction.* Boston: St. Martin's, 1997.

Richard Feldstein: Deconstruction

Richard Feldstein brings some deconstructive strategies to bear on Gilman's story, exposing the text's ambiguities and celebrating the way Gilman exploits "a play of difference" in her text. The following excerpts suggest the main line of Feldstein's argument. Notice how Feldstein repeatedly exposes uncertainty by identifying binary elements and then challenging the expected reading.

Critics who have written on "The Yellow Wall-Paper" disagree on the most basic issues pertaining to the text. Is it a short story or a novella; should we underline its title or place it in quotations marks? The 1899 edition presents a novella format, but, in fact, "The Yellow Wall-Paper" first appeared as a short story in 1982.[1] There is also disagreement among critics about the writer's name: is it Charlotte Perkins, Charlotte Stetson, Charlotte Perkins Stetson, Charlotte Gilman, Charlotte Perkins Gilman, or Charlotte Perkins Stetson Gilman? Although each name relates to a phase in the writer's life, many commentators have arbitrarily chosen one designation to use normatively when discussing the writer's life and work. Ironically, this confusion over text's and writer's names was in part generated by Charlotte Perkins Gilman herself, who was anything but consistent in the names she used or the way she spelled *wall-paper.* If Gilman had the advantage of our perspective, she might have been pleased by this confusion of textual identity (is *wall-paper* one word or two) and amused by the critics' befuddlement over her name. Even without a historical perspective, however, she might have predicted such bafflement, possibly foresaw the

[1]Charlotte Perkins Gilman, *The Yellow Wall Paper* (Boston: Small, Maynard, 1988); Gilman, "The Yellow Wall-Paper," *New England Magazine* 5 (1891–92), 647–56.

manipulation of the names of the fathers—Perkins, Stetson, Gilman—as a means of destabilizing the process of signification by presenting a proliferation of signifiers that ironically generate a paucity of signifieds.

Meanwhile, Gilman's editors have repeatedly altered the spelling of *wall-paper,* the overdetermined signifier that refers to both the title and the image of protean change featured in the story. The Feminist Press edition would have us believe that Gilman hyphenated the compound in the narrative but gave it in the title of the short story as *Wallpaper.*[2] But the original manuscript presents a different configuration: the use of *wall-paper* shifts arbitrarily, in defiance of any unvarying pattern of logic. The initial five references are *wallpaper, wall paper, wall-paper, wall paper, wall-paper;* its spelling then becomes more ambiguous because *wall-paper* then appears twice, hyphenated at the end of both lines; the final five references construct the indeterminate pattern of *wall-paper, wall paper, wall-paper, paper,* and *wall paper.*[3] Editors of the *New England Magazine,* where the story first appeared, could not abide such "confusion," so they altered the spelling to impose uniformity of textual reference. The title remained "The Yellow Wall-Paper," and the narrative reference still provided the ambiguous alteration of *wall-paper* and *wall paper,* but now there was a perceptible, though random, pattern of word usage: initially, there are three references to *wall-paper;* then, inexplicably, *wallpaper* appears five times before the pattern reverses itself and *wall-paper* is used four times. The next time the story was published, in 1899, Small, Maynard & Company consistently presented the compound as *wall paper.* Today, the version in *The Norton Anthology of Literature by Women* imposes the counterconsistency of *wallpaper.*[4] From Gilman's original manuscript, however, it is apparent that the word(s) *wall(-)paper* were conceived as a shifter calculated to create ambiguity about a referent that resists analysis, even as the narrator resists her husband's diagnosis and prescription for cure.

Despite such confusion, a critical consensus has developed on two issues central to "The Yellow Wall-Paper": John is the story's antagonist and the narrator/protagonist succumbs to a progressive form of madness. . . .

If we read "The Yellow Wall-Paper" ironically and not simply as a case history of one woman's mental derangement, the narrator's madness becomes questionable, and the question of madness itself, an issue raised as a means of problematizing such a reading. Reconfigured, the text becomes an allegorical statement of difference, pitting John, an antagonist and a proponent of realism who condemns his wife as a stricken romantic, against a nameless protagonist whose ironic discourse opposes the empirical gaze of the nineteenth-century American realist to a modern, not romantic, configuration—the wall-paper as gestalt—with its shifting significations born of the intermixture of figure and ground. The wall-paper is given to protean changes of shape from the sun- or moonlight reflecting on it. Combine this mutability with another variable: the wall-paper is a mirroring screen for the protagonist's projections, and the paper becomes an overde-

---

[2]Gilman, *The Yellow Wallpaper* (New York: Feminist Press, 1973). For ease of referral, all subsequent references, unless otherwise noted, are to this edition of the text.

[3]Gilman, "The Yellow Wall-Paper," Schlesinger Library, Radcliffe College, Charlotte Perkins Gilman Collection, Folder 221.

[4]Gilman, *The Yellow Wallpaper,* in *The Norton Anthology of Literature by Women,* ed. Sandra M. Gilbert and Susan Gubar (New York: Norton, 1985), 1148–61.

termined construct destabilizing signification. Like the wall-paper, the text itself shifts, a signifier generating possibilities of interpretation while providing for a metacritique of its textuality. . . .

From this point of view, the conclusion that the narrator of "The Yellow Wall-Paper" has a nervous breakdown, an oft-given answer to the difficulties posed by the text, becomes suspect. Although Gilman herself in *The Living of Charlotte Perkins Gilman* states that "The Yellow Wall-Paper" is a story about a woman's "nervous breakdown," later in her autobiography, she asserts another, more didactic purpose for having written the story: to prevent medical practitioners from prescribing "the rest cure" for "hysterical" patients.[5] In other words, Gilman consciously conceived "The Yellow Wall-Paper" from conflicting impulses; one accepted the narrator as simply "mad" and the other politicized the question of woman's madness and its "cure." Born of this conflict is a feminist text using modernist strategies in opposition to the prevailing literary theory of the period, American realism, which foreclosed examination of the complexities and inconsistencies posed by not only Gilman herself but a multilevel textuality that enunciates ambiguity. From this ironic perspective, to read "The Yellow Wall-Paper" as simply a flat representation of one woman's progressive descent into insanity is to diagnose the protagonist's case by means of the empirical ontology championed by the protagonist's doctor husband John, her doctor brother, and the *sujet supposé savoir,* Doctor Weir Mitchell. . . .

The account the narrator provides is a written transcription inexplicably interrupted and succeeded by a spoken account in which she relates details of her life to a hypothetical audience of confidants. For as the story concludes, we confront yet another contradiction when the narrator asserts she is speaking to us, not writing in her journal, as she had previously explained: "I have found out a funny thing, but I shan't *tell* it this time!" (31, my emphasis). This statement, which equates narrative technique with a verbal recounting of events, is like a question asking how it should be read. It is especially significant because of the protagonist's previously stated concern for being allowed to write, a point of pique in the first half of the story, a mute issue in the second. No matter how we choose to read this contradiction, however, it will remain unassimilable to an interpretation of the text. Whichever reading we choose to affix univocal meaning onto a purposely ambiguous text will impose a thematic reduction that should be resisted, just as Gilman resisted Weir Mitchell's diagnosis and her protagonist resisted John's phallocentric assessment of her situation.

The aim of this essay is to raise a feminist question cast in post-modernist terms: did Charlotte Perkins Gilman, grounding her critique in gender difference, use modernist techniques to form a disjunctive text that plays on the question of identity when emphasizing the narrator/narrated split that presents one entity as two? Could it be possible that Gilman intended the narrator to be both the same as and different from the protagonist, just as she believes the protagonist to be the same as and different from her double(s), the imprisoned other(s) in the wall-paper? From this perspective

[5]Gilman, *The Living of Charlotte Perkins Gilman* (New York: Arno-Hawthorne Books, 1972), 118–21.

one slides into two with the shifting of signification. If we look back to the original manuscript of "The Yellow Wall-Paper," we are reminded that Gilman confused the issue of whether wall-paper was one word, two conjoined by a hyphen, or two separate words, whether this central referent—the paper—already a screen for the protagonist's projections, could become more ambiguous, a lure for transposition by critics and anthologists alike. . . .

Stated another way, "The Yellow Wall-Paper" is more a writerly than a readerly text, which Gilman designed to challenge her readers to pro- duce, not merely consume. Gilman's protagonist, who configures a text from her vision of the wall-paper, illustrates a means of reading that allows for a play of difference, just as her protagonist allows for the play of sun and moon off the wall-paper's surface. This is how Gilman's text presents itself to us, an ambiguous, doubled referent, cast in the interrog- ative mode, a gestalt of changing patterns. Text as question formulates an inconclusiveness that attends enigma generated in part by the hyphen between wall and paper—a sign of difference and reminder of text as Other to which we look for closure, a means of satisfying unsatisfiable desires.

From Richard Feldstein, "Reader, Text, and Ambiguous Referentiality in 'The Yellow Wallpaper.'" Richard Feldstein and Judith Roof, *Feminism and Psychoanalysis*. Ithaca, NY: Cornell UP, 1985.

Douglas Tallack: Deconstructing Feminist Criticism

In this passage, Douglas Tallack pursues an alternative reading of Gilman's feminism, deconstructing the usual stance. When Tallack refers to "O'Connor" in this passage, he is talking about the critic Frank O'Connor and his work on the genre of the short story.

There is little feeling for the female community in Gilman. At home, as Gilman remarks in her autobiography, women work alone "within their four walls" (Gilman 1975: xxiv). And when the work is writing, it is an espe- cially lonely occupation, far removed from the communal and supportive practice of work within a craft economy. Relations with other women gen- erally are not a positive feature of Gilman's writing—as they were for earli- er nineteenth-century middle-class women and as they have become for some twentieth-century feminists who have forged, or have described, pub- lic networks of supportive women. Gilman became more sympathetic towards and reliant upon groups of women later in her life, but Jennie, the "sister of the stairs" (1981: 8) in "The Yellow Wallpaper" is neither a role model nor an aide and confidante. If anything, she is an antagonist, a spy. Mother/daughter relationships are also not common in Gilman's fiction and where they do feature, they are either hostile—in "The Giant Wisteria"— or cursory—in "The Yellow Wallpaper", in which "Mother" visits for a week but the week is not described, and the sex of the narrator's baby is not specified. This does not mean that the role of other women in her fiction is unimportant, because without the similarities and differences between the narrator in "The Yellow Wallpaper" and Jennie, Mary and Mother, her identity would be measured only in relation to John's. But the nature of the relationships indicates the historical situation out of which Gilman was writing.

The loneliness which, initially, we can locate so easily in "The Yellow Wallpaper" differs from that which O'Connor makes central to the short story because the opposition between the heroine and the larger society is much more complex. In Gilman's text gaps, divisions and confusions appear as the narrator tries to cope with the opposition between separate spaces/spheres and related oppositions (inside/outside the wallpaper/the house, writing/not writing, sane/mad). She switches, often alarmingly and contradictorily, from one to the other, deciding that writing is what she must do to get well and then that it makes things worse. Janice Haney-Peritz resists the pressure to merge Gilman and the narrator and percep-tively notes that

> such contradictions not only betray the narrator's dependence
> on the oppressive discursive structure we associate with John
> but also help us to understand why she jumps from one thing
> to another, producing paragraphs that are usually no more
> than a few lines in length. (Haney-Peritz 1989: 98)

The most "unheard-of contradiction" arising from the overall binary structure of the text (and its late nineteenth-century culture, we can now more confidently propose), is that between being mad and sane. If women were absolutely different from men in the nineteenth-century scheme of things, and if John is the epitome of reason, then the implication is that his wife is mad. But this cannot be stated because to be mad is not to be a woman, as such and in women's relations with men:

> "My darling," said he, "I beg of you, for my sake and for our
> child's sake, as well as for your own, that you will never for
> one instant let that idea [of mental illness] enter your mind!
> There is nothing so dangerous, so fascinating, to a tempera-
> ment like yours. It is a false and foolish fancy. Can you not
> trust me as a physician when I tell you so?" (Gilman 1981: 12)

Hence, she is well and ill at the same time, a clear textual indication that the terms of the opposition are implicated, one with the other, in a hierarchical relationship.

From Douglas Tallack, *The Nineteenth-Century American Short Story: Language, Form, and Ideology.* London: Routledge, 1993, pp. 235-237.

Reading O'Connor's "Revelation"

Flannery O'Connor's fiction is disturbing and hilarious, vividly realistic and some-how surreal at the same time. It's powerful. There may be short story writers who are as good in different ways as Flannery O'Connor, but it is unlikely that someone is better. Many readers think "Revelation" is her greatest story.

Readers do not need preparation to appreciate O'Connor's wicked sense of humor and satire that coexist with her sympathy and pity. But a word of warning is perhaps warranted regarding her language—specifically, her use of "nigger," which is

Flannery O'Connor

so outrageous that even using the similar-sounding word "niggard-ly" (which means "stingy," comes from a Scandinavian root word) has caused trouble for some verbally resourceful people. O'Connor was writing in a different era, when white and black people did not consider this reference to be as horrendous as it's considered to be today. With Mark Twain's classic *Huckleberry Finn,* the reader encounters a similar problem with the character who is named "Nigger Jim." Should we stop reading this great book, which powerfully promotes breaking down racial prejudice, because a character has an offensive name? The characters Twain and O'Connor create, living at the times that they did, would certainly have used this word. To omit the word would not be honest or accurate. To avoid this great literature because of it would be a shame.

FLANNERY O'CONNOR (1925–1964)

Revelation

The doctor's waiting room, which was very small, was almost full when the Turpins entered and Mrs. Turpin, who was very large, made it look even smaller by her presence. She stood looming at the head of the magazine table set in the center of it, a living demonstration that the room was inadequate and ridiculous. Her little bright black eyes took in all the patients as she sized up the seating situation. There was one vacant chair and a place on the sofa occupied by a blond child in a dirty blue romper who should have been told to move over and make room for the lady. He was five or six, but Mrs. Turpin saw at once that no one was going to tell him to move over. He was slumped down in the seat, his arms idle at his sides and his eyes idle in his head; his nose ran unchecked.

Mrs. Turpin put a firm hand on Claud's shoulder and said in a voice that included anyone who wanted to listen, "Claud, you sit in that chair there," and gave him a push down into the vacant one. Claud was florid and bald and sturdy, somewhat shorter than Mrs. Turpin, but he sat down as if he were accustomed to doing what she told him to.

Mrs. Turpin remained standing. The only man in the room besides Claud was a lean stringy old fellow with a rusty hand spread out on each knee, whose eyes were closed as if he were asleep or dead or pretending to be so as not to get up and offer her his seat. Her gaze settled agreeably on a well-dressed gray-haired lady whose eyes met hers and whose expression said: if that child belonged to me, he would have some manners and move over—there's plenty of room there for you and him too.

Claud looked up with a sigh and made as if to rise.

"Sit down," Mrs. Turpin said. "You know you're not supposed to stand on that leg. He has an ulcer on his leg," she explained.   5

Claud lifted his foot onto the magazine table and rolled his trouser leg up to reveal a purple swelling on a plump marble-white calf.

"My!" the pleasant lady said. "How did you do that?"

"A cow kicked him," Mrs. Turpin said.

"Goodness!" said the lady.

Claud rolled his trouser leg down.   10

"Maybe the little boy would move over," the lady suggested, but the child did not stir.

"Somebody will be leaving in a minute," Mrs. Turpin said. She could not understand why a doctor—with as much money as they made charging five dollars a day to just stick their head in the hospital door and look at you—couldn't afford a decent-sized waiting room. This one was hardly bigger than a garage. The table was cluttered with limp-looking magazines and at one end of it there was a big green glass ash tray full of cigarette butts and cotton wads with little blood spots on them. If she had had anything to do with the running of the place, that would have been emptied every so often. There were no chairs against the wall at the head of the room. It had a rectangular-shaped panel in it that permitted a view of the office where the nurse came and went and the secretary listened to the radio. A plastic fern in a gold pot sat in the opening and trailed its fronds down almost to the floor. The radio was softly playing gospel music.

Just then the inner door opened and a nurse with the highest stack of yellow hair Mrs. Turpin had ever seen put her face in the crack and called for the next patient. The woman sitting beside Claud grasped the two arms of her chair and hoisted herself up; she pulled her dress free from her legs and lumbered through the door where the nurse had disappeared.

Mrs. Turpin eased into the vacant chair, which held her tight as a corset. "I wish I could reduce," she said, and rolled her eyes and gave a comic sigh.

"Oh, *you* aren't fat," the stylish lady said.

"Ooooo I am too," Mrs. Turpin said. "Claud he eats all he wants to and   15
never weighs over one hundred and seventy-five pounds, but me I just look at something good to eat and I gain some weight," and her stomach and shoulders shook with laughter. "You can eat all you want to, can't you, Claud?" she asked, turning to him.

Claud only grinned.

"Well, as long as you have such a good disposition," the stylish lady said, "I don't think it makes a bit of difference what size you are. You just can't beat a good disposition."

Next to her was a fat girl of eighteen or nineteen, scowling into a thick blue book which Mrs. Turpin saw was entitled *Human Development*. The girl raised her head and directed her scowl at Mrs. Turpin as if she did not like her looks. She appeared annoyed that anyone should speak while she tried to read. The poor girl's face was blue with acne and Mrs. Turpin thought how pitiful it was to have a face like that at that age. She gave the girl a friendly smile but the girl only scowled the harder. Mrs. Turpin herself was fat but she had always had good skin, and though she was forty-seven years old, there was not a wrinkle in her face except around her eyes from laughing too much.

Next to the ugly girl was the child, still in exactly the same position, and next to him was a thin leathery old woman in a cotton print dress. She and Claud had three sacks of chicken feed in their pump house that was in the same print. She had seen from the first that the child belonged with the old woman. She could tell by the way they sat—kind of vacant and white-trashy, as if they would sit there until Doomsday if nobody called and told them to get up. And at right angles but next to the well-dressed pleasant lady was a lank-faced woman who was certainly the child's mother. She had on a yellow sweat shirt and wine-colored slacks, both gritty-looking, and the rims of her lips were stained with snuff. Her dirty yellow hair was tied behind with a little piece of red paper ribbon. Worse than niggers any day, Mrs. Turpin thought.

The gospel hymn playing was, "When I looked up and He looked down," and Mrs. Turpin, who knew it, supplied the last line mentally, "And wona these days I know I'll we-eara crown."

Without appearing to, Mrs. Turpin always noticed people's feet. The well-dressed lady had on red and gray suede shoes to match her dress. Mrs. Turpin had on her good black patent leather pumps. The ugly girl had on Girl Scout shoes and heavy socks. The old woman had on tennis shoes and the white-trashy mother had on what appeared to be bedroom slippers, black straw with gold braid threaded through them—exactly what you would have expected her to have on.

Sometimes at night when she couldn't go to sleep, Mrs. Turpin would occupy herself with the question of who she would have chosen to be if she couldn't have been herself. If Jesus had said to her before he made her, "There's only two places available for you. You can either be a nigger or white-trash," what would she have said? "Please, Jesus, please," she would have said, "just let me wait until there's another place available," and he would have said, "No, you have to go right now and I have only those two places so make up your mind." She would have wiggled and squirmed and begged and plead-ed but it would have been no use and finally she would have said, "All right, make me a nigger then—but that don't mean a trashy one." And he would have made her a neat clean respectable Negro woman, herself but black.

Next to the child's mother was a red-headed youngish woman, reading one of the magazines and working a piece of chewing hum, hell for leather, as Claud would say. Mrs. Turpin could not see the woman's feet. She was not white-trash, just common. Sometimes Mrs. Turpin occupied herself at night naming the classes of people. On the bottom of the heap were most col-ored people, not the kind she would have been if she had been one, but most of them; then next to them—not above, just away from—were the white-trash; then above them were the homeowners, and above them the home-and-land owners, to which she and Claud belonged. Above she and Claud were people with a lot of money and much bigger houses and much more land. But here the complexity of it would begin to bear in on her, for some of the people with a lot of money were common and ought to be below she and Claud and some of the people who had good blood had lost

20

their money and had to rent and then there were colored people who owned their homes and lands as well. There was a colored dentist in town who had two red Lincolns and a swimming pool and a farm with registered white-face cattle on it. Usually by the time she had fallen asleep all the classes of people were moiling and roiling around in her head, and she would dream they were all crammed in together in a box car, being ridden off to be put in a gas oven.

"That's a beautiful clock," she said and nodded to her right. It was a big   25
wall clock, the face encased in a brass sunburst.

"Yes, it's very pretty," the stylish lady said agreeably. "And right on the dot too," she added, glancing at her watch.

The ugly girl beside her cast an eye upward at the clock, smirked, then looked directly at Mrs. Turpin and smirked again. Then she returned her eyes to her book. She was obviously the lady's daughter because, although they didn't look anything alike as to disposition, they both had the same shape of face and the same blue eyes. On the lady they sparkled pleasantly but in the girl's seared face they appeared alternately to smolder and to blaze.

What if Jesus had said, "All right, you can be white-trash or a nigger or ugly"!

Mrs. Turpin felt an awful pity for the girl, though she thought it was one thing to be ugly and another to act ugly.

The woman with the snuff-stained lips turned around in her chair and   30
looked up at the clock. Then she turned back and appeared to look a little to the side of Mrs. Turpin. There was a cast in one of her eyes, "You want to know wher you can get you one of them ther clocks?" she asked in a loud voice.

"No, I already have a nice clock," Mrs. Turpin said. Once somebody like her got a leg in the conversation, she would be all over it.

"You can get you one with green stamps," the woman said. "That's most likely wher he got hisn. Save you up enough, you can get you most anythang. I got me some joo'ry."

Ought to have got you a wash rag and some soap, Mrs. Turpin thought.

"I get contour sheets with mine," the pleasant lady said.

The daughter slammed her book shut. She looked straight in front of   35
her, directly through Mrs. Turpin and on through the yellow curtain and the plate glass window which made the wall behind her. The girl's eyes seemed lit all of a sudden with a peculiar light, an unnatural light like night road signs give. Mrs. Turpin turned her head to see if there was anything going on outside that she should see, but she could not see anything. Figures passing cast only a pale shadow through the curtain. There was no reason the girl should single her out for her ugly looks.

"Miss Finley," the nurse said, cracking the door. The gum-chewing woman got up and passed in front of her and Claud and went into the office. She had on red high-heeled shoes.

Directly across the table, the ugly girl's eyes were fixed on Mrs. Turpin as if she had some very special reason for disliking her.

"This is wonderful weather, isn't it?" the girl's mother said.

"It's good weather for cotton if you can get the niggers to pick it," Mrs. Turpin said, "but niggers don't want to pick cotton any more. You can't get the white folks to pick it and now you can't get the niggers—because they got to be right up there with the white folks."

"They gonna *try* anyways," the white-trash woman said, leaning forward.   40

"Do you have one of the cotton-picking machines?" the pleasant lady asked.

"No," Mrs. Turpin said, "they leave half the cotton in the field. We don't have much cotton anyway. If you want to make it farming now, you have to have a little of everything. We got a couple of acres of cotton and a few hogs and chickens and just enough white-face that Claud can look after them himself."

"One thang I don't want," the white-trash woman said, wiping her mouth with the back of her hand. "Hogs. Nasty stinking things, a-gruntin and a-rootin all over the place."

Mrs. Turpin gave her the merest edge of her attention, "Our hogs are not dirty and they don't stink," she said. "They're cleaner than some children I've seen. Their feet never touch the ground. We have a pig parlor—that's where you raise them on concrete," she explained to the pleasant lady, "and Claud scoots them down with the hose every afternoon and washes off the floor." Cleaner by far than that child right there, she thought. Poor nasty little thing. He had not moved except to put the thumb of his dirty hand into his mouth.

The woman turned her face away from Mrs. Turpin. "I know I wouldn't   45
scoot down no hog with no hose," she said to the wall.

You wouldn't have no hog to scoot down, Mrs. Turpin said to herself.

"A-gruntin and a-rootin and a-groanin," the woman muttered.

"We got a little of everything," Mrs. Turpin said to the pleasant lady. "It's no use in having more than you can handle yourself with help like it is. We found enough niggers to pick our cotton this year but Claud he has to go after them and take them home again in the evening. They can't walk that half a mile. No they can't. I tell you," she said and laughed merrily, "I sure am tired of buttering up niggers, but you got to love em if you want em to work for you. When they come in the morning, I run out and I say, 'Hi yawl this morning?' and when Claud drives them off to the field I just wave to beat the band and they just wave back." And she waved her hand rapidly to illustrate.

"Like you read out of the same book," the lady said, showing she understood perfectly.

"Child, yes," Mrs. Turpin said. "And when they come in from the field, I   50
run out with a bucket of icewater. That's the way it's going to be from now on," she said. "You may as well face it."

"One thang I know," the white-trash woman said. "Two thangs I ain't going to do: love no niggers or scoot down no hog with no hose." And she let out a bark of contempt.

The look that Mrs. Turpin and the pleasant lady exchanged indicated they both understood that you had to *have* certain things before you could *know* certain things. But every time Mrs. Turpin exchanged a look with the lady, she was aware that the ugly girl's peculiar eyes were still on her, and she had trouble bringing her attention back to the conversation.

"When you got something," she said, "you got to look after it." And when you ain't got a thing but breath and britches, she added to herself, you can afford to come to town every morning and just sit on the Court House coping and spit.

A grotesque revolving shadow passed across the curtain behind her and was thrown palely on the opposite wall. Then a bicycle clattered down

against the outside of the building. The door opened and a colored boy glid-
ed in with a tray from the drugstore. It had two large red and white paper
cups on it with tops on them. He was a tall, very black boy in discolored
white pants and a green nylon shirt. He was chewing gum slowly, as if to
music. He set the tray down in the office opening next to the fern and stuck
his head through to look for the secretary. She was not in there. He rested
his arms on the ledge and waited, his narrow bottom stuck out, swaying to
the left and right. He raised a hand over his head and scratched the base of
his skull.

"You see that button there, boy?" Mrs. Turpin said. "You can punch that
and she'll come. She's probably in the back somewhere."

"Is that right?" the boy said agreeably, as if he had never seen the but-   55
ton before. He leaned to the right and put his finger on it. "She sometime
out," he said and twisted around to face his audience, his elbows behind
him on the counter. The nurse appeared and he twisted back again. She
handed him a dollar and he rooted in his pocket and made the change and
counted it out to her. She gave him fifteen cents for a tip and he went out
with the empty tray. The heavy door swung to slowly and closed at length
with the sound of suction. For a moment no one spoke.

"They ought to send all them niggers back to Africa," the white-trash
woman said. "That's where they come from in the first place."

"Oh, I couldn't do without my good colored friends," the pleasant lady
said.

"There's a heap of things worse than a nigger," Mrs. Turpin agreed. "It's
all kinds of them just like it's all kinds of us."

"Yes, and it takes all kinds to make the world go round," the lady said in   60
her musical voice.

As she said it, the raw-complexioned girl snapped her teeth together.
Her lower lip turned downwards and inside out, revealing the pale pink
inside of her mouth. After a second it rolled back up. It was the ugliest face
Mrs. Turpin had ever seen anyone make and for a moment she was certain
that the girl had made it at her. She was looking at her as if she had known
and disliked her all her life—all of Mrs. Turpin's life, it seemed too, not just
all the girl's life. Why, girl, I don't even know you, Mrs. Turpin said silently.

She forced her attention back to the discussion. "It wouldn't be practical to send them back to Africa," she said. "They wouldn't want to go. They
got it too good here."

"Wouldn't be what they wanted—if I had anythang to do with it," the
woman said.

"It wouldn't be a way in the world you could get all the niggers back
over there," Mrs. Turpin said. "They'd be hiding out and lying down and
turning sick on you and wailing and hollering and raring and pitching. It
wouldn't be a way in the world to get them over there."

"They got over here," the trashy woman said. "Get back like they got   65
over."

"It wasn't so many of them then," Mrs. Turpin explained.

The woman looked at Mrs. Turpin as if here was an idiot indeed but
Mrs. Turpin was not bothered by the look, considering where it came from.

"Nooo," she said, "they're going to stay here where they can go to New
York and marry white folks and improve their color. That's what they all
want to do, every one of them, improve their color."

"You know what comes of that, don't you?" Claud asked.

"No, Claud, what?" Mrs. Turpin said.   70

Claud's eyes twinkled. "White-faced niggers," he said with never a smile.

Everybody in the office laughed except the white-trash and the ugly girl. The girl gripped the book in her lap with white fingers. The trashy woman looked around her from face to face as if she thought they were all idiots. The old woman in the feed sack dress continued to gaze expressionless across the floor at the high-top shoes of the man opposite her, the one who had been pretending to be asleep when the Turpins came in. He was laughing heartily, his hands still spread out on his knees. The child had fallen to the side and was lying now almost face down in the old woman's lap.

While they recovered from their laughter, the nasal chorus on the radio kept the room from silence.

"You go to blank blank
And I'll go to mine
But we'll all blank along
To-geth-ther,
And all along the blank
We'll hep each other out
Smile-ling in any kind of
Weath-ther!"

Mrs. Turpin didn't catch every word but she caught enough to agree with the spirit of the song and it turned her thoughts sober. To help anybody out that needed it was her philosophy of life. She never spared herself when she found somebody in need, whether they were white or black, trash or decent. And of all she had to be thankful for, she was most thankful that this was so. If Jesus had said, "You can be high society and have all the money you want and be thin and svelte-like, but you can't be a good woman with it," she would have had to say, "Well don't make me that then. Make me a good woman and it don't matter what else, how fat or how ugly or how poor!" Her heart rose. He had not made her a nigger or white-trash or ugly! He had made her herself and given her a little of everything. Jesus, thank you! she said. Thank you thank you thank you! Whenever she counted her blessings she felt as buoyant as if she weighed one hundred and twenty-five pounds instead of one hundred and eighty.

"What's wrong with your little boy?" the pleasant lady asked the white-   75
trashy woman.

"He has a ulcer," the woman said proudly. "He ain't give me a minute's peace since he was born. Him and her are just alike," she said, nodding at the old woman, who was running her leathery fingers through the child's pale hair. "Look like I can't get nothing down them two but Co' Cola and candy."

That's all you try to get down em, Mrs. Turpin said to herself. Too lazy to light the fire. There was nothing you could tell her about people like them that she didn't know already. And it was not just that they didn't have anything. Because if you gave them everything, in two weeks it would all be broken or filthy or they would have chopped it up for lightwood. She knew all this from her own experience. Help them you must, but help them you couldn't.

All at once the ugly girl turned her lips inside out again. Her eyes fixed like two drills on Mrs. Turpin. This time there was no mistaking that there was something urgent behind them.

Girl, Mrs. Turpin exclaimed silently, I haven't done a thing to you! The girl might be confusing her with somebody else. There was no need to sit by and let herself be intimidated. "You must be in college," she said boldly, looking directly at the girl. "I see you reading a book there."

The girl continued to stare and pointedly did not answer.   80

Her mother blushed at this rudeness. "The lady asked you a question, Mary Grace," she said under her breath.

"I have ears," Mary Grace said.

The poor mother blushed again. "Mary Grace goes to Wellesley College," she explained. She twisted one of the buttons on her dress. "In Massachusetts," she added with a grimace. "And in the summer she just keeps right on studying. Just reads all the time, a real book worm. She's done real well at Wellesley; she's taking English and Math and History and Psychology and Social Studies," she rattled on, "and I think it's too much. I think she ought to get out and have fun."

The girl looked as if she would like to hurl them all through the plate glass window.

"Way up north," Mrs. Turpin murmured and thought, well, it hasn't   85
done much for her manners.

"I'd almost rather to have him sick," the white-trash woman said, wrenching the attention back to herself. "He's so mean when he ain't. Look like some children just take natural to meanness. It's some gets bad when they get sick but he was the opposite. Took sick and turned good. He don't give me no trouble now. It's me waitin to see the doctor," she said.

If I was going to send anybody back to Africa, Mrs. Turpin thought, it would be your kind, woman. "Yes, indeed," she said aloud, but looking up at the ceiling, "it's a heap of things worse than a nigger." And dirtier than a hog, she added to herself.

"I think people with bad dispositions are more to be pitied than anyone on earth," the pleasant lady said in a voice that was decidedly thin.

"I thank the Lord he has blessed me with a good one," Mrs. Turpin said. "The day has never dawned that I couldn't find something to laugh at."

"Not since she married me anyways," Claud said with a comical straight   90
face.

Everybody laughed except the girl and the white-trash.

Mrs. Turpin's stomach shook. "He's such a caution," she said, "that I can't help but laugh at him."

The girl made a loud ugly noise through her teeth.

Her mother's mouth grew thin and tight. "I think the worst thing in the world," she said, "is an ungrateful person. To have everything and not appreciate it. I know a girl," she said, "who has parents who would give her anything, a little brother who loves her dearly, who is getting a good education, who wears the best clothes, but who can never say a kind word to anyone, who never smiles, who just criticizes and complains all day long."

"Is she too old to paddle?" Claud asked.   95

The girl's face was almost purple.

"Yes," the lady said, "I'm afraid there's nothing to do but leave her to her folly. Some day she'll wake up and it'll be too late."

"It never hurt anyone to smile," Mrs. Turpin said. "It just makes you feel better all over."

"Of course," the lady said sadly, "but there are just some people you can't tell anything to. They can't take criticism."

"If it's one thing I am," Mrs. Turpin said with feeling, "it's grateful. When I think who all I could have been besides myself and what all I got, a little of everything, and a good disposition besides, I just feel like shouting, 'Thank you, Jesus, for making everything the way it is!' It could have been different!" For one thing, somebody else could have got Claud. At the thought of this, she was flooded with gratitude and a terrible pang of joy ran through her. "Oh thank you, Jesus, Jesus, thank you!" she cried aloud.

The book struck her directly over her left eye. It struck almost at the same instant that she realized the girl was about to hurl it. Before she could utter a sound, the raw face came crashing across the table toward her, howling. The girl's fingers sank like clamps into the soft flesh of her neck. She heard the mother cry out and Claud shout, "Whoa!" There was an instant when she was certain that she was about to be in an earthquake.

All at once her vision narrowed and she saw everything as if it were happening in a small room far away, or as if she were looking at it through the wrong end of a telescope. Claud's face crumpled and fell out of sight. The nurse ran in, then out, then in again. Then the gangling figure of the doctor rushed out of the inner door. Magazines flew this way and that as the table turned over. The girl fell with a thud and Mrs. Turpin's vision suddenly reversed itself and she saw everything large instead of small. The eyes of the white-trashy woman were staring hugely at the floor. There the girl, held down on one side by the nurse and on the other by her mother, was wrenching and turning in their grasp. The doctor was kneeling astride her, trying to hold her arm down. He managed after a second to sink a long needle into it.

Mrs. Turpin felt entirely hollow except for her heart which swung from side to side as if it were agitated in a great empty drum of flesh.

"Somebody that's not busy call for the ambulance," the doctor said in the off-hand voice young doctors adopt for terrible occasions.

Mrs. Turpin could not have moved a finger. The old man who had been sitting next to her had skipped nimbly into the office and made the call, for the secretary still seemed to be gone.

"Claud!" Mrs. Turpin called.

He was not in his chair. She knew she must jump up and find him but she felt like some one trying to catch a train in a dream, when everything moves in slow motion and the faster you try to run the slower you go.

"Here I am," a suffocated voice, very unlike Claud's, said.

He was doubled up in the corner on the floor, pale as paper, holding his leg. She wanted to get up and go to him but she could not move. Instead, her gaze was drawn slowly downward to the churning face on the floor, which she could see over the doctor's shoulder.

The girl's eyes stopped rolling and focused on her. They seemed a much lighter blue than before, as if a door that had been tightly closed behind them was now open to admit light and air.

100

105

110

Mrs. Turpin's head cleared and her power of motion returned. She leaned forward until she was looking directly into the fierce brilliant eyes. There was no doubt in her mind that the girl did know her, knew her in some intense and personal way, beyond time and place and condition. "What you got to say to me?" she asked hoarsely and held her breath, waiting, as for a revelation.

The girl raised her head. Her gaze locked with Mrs. Turpin's. "Go back to hell where you came from, you old wart hog," she whispered. Her voice was low but clear. Her eyes burned for a moment as if she saw with pleasure that her message had struck its target.

Mrs. Turpin sank back in her chair.

After a moment the girl's eyes closed and she turned her head wearily to the side.

The doctor rose and handed the nurse the empty syringe. He leaned over and put both hands for a moment on the mother's shoulders, which were shaking. She was sitting on the floor, her lips pressed together, holding Mary Grace's hand in her lap. The girl's fingers were gripped like a baby's around her thumb. "Go on to the hospital," he said. "I'll call and make the arrangements."   115

"Now let's see that neck," he said in a jovial voice to Mrs. Turpin. He began to inspect her neck with his first two fingers. Two little moon-shaped lines like pink fish bones were indented over her windpipe. There was the beginning of an angry red swelling above her eye. His fingers passed over this also.

"Lea' me be," she said thickly and shook him off. "See about Claud. She kicked him."

"I'll see about him in a minute," he said and felt her pulse. He was a thin gray-haired man, given to pleasantries. "Go home and have yourself a vacation the rest of the day," he said and patted her on the shoulder.

Quit your pattin me, Mrs. Turpin growled to herself.

"And put an ice pack over that eye," he said. Then he went and squatted down beside Claud and looked at his leg. After a moment he pulled him up and Claud limped after him into the office.   120

Until the ambulance came, the only sounds in the room were the tremulous moans of the girl's mother, who continued to sit on the floor. The white-trash woman did not take her eyes off the girl. Mrs. Turpin looked straight ahead at nothing. Presently the ambulance drew up, a long dark shadow, behind the curtain. The attendants came in and set the stretcher down beside the girl and lifted her expertly onto it and carried her out. The nurse helped the mother gather up her things. The shadow of the ambulance moved silently away and the nurse came back in the office.

"That ther girl is going to be a lunatic, ain't she?" the white-trash woman asked the nurse, but the nurse kept on to the back and never answered her.

"Yes, she's going to be a lunatic," the white-trash woman said to the rest of them.

"Po' critter," the old woman murmured. The child's face was still in her lap. His eyes looked idly out over her knees. He had not moved during the disturbance except to draw one leg up under him.

"I thank Gawd," the white-trash woman said fervently, "I ain't a lunatic."   125
Claud came limping out and the Turpins went home.

As their pick-up truck turned into their own dirt road and made the crest of the hill, Mrs. Turpin gripped the window ledge and looked out suspiciously. The land sloped gracefully down through a field dotted with lavender weeds and at the start of the rise their small yellow frame house, with its little flower beds spread out around it like a fancy apron, sat primly in its accustomed place between two giant hickory trees. She would not have been startled to see a burnt wound between two blackened chimneys.

Neither of them felt like eating so they put on their house clothes and lowered the shade in the bedroom and lay down, Claud with his leg on a pillow and herself with a damp washcloth over her eye. The instant she was flat on her back, the image of a razor-backed hog with warts on its face and horns coming out behind its ears snorted into her head. She moaned, a low quiet moan.

"I am not," she said tearfully, "a wart hog. From hell." But the denial had no force. The girl's eyes and her words, even the tone of her voice, low but clear, directed only to her, brooked no repudiation. She had been singled out for the message, though there was trash in the room to whom it might justly have been applied. The full force of this fact struck her only now. There was a woman there who was neglecting her own child but she had been overlooked. The message had been given to Ruby Turpin, a respectable, hard-working, church-going woman. The tears dried. Her eyes began to burn instead with wrath.

She rose on her elbow and the washcloth fell into her hand. Claud was   130
lying on his back, snoring. She wanted to tell him what the girl had said. At the same time, she did not wish to put the image of herself as a wart hog from hell into his mind.

"Hey, Claud," she muttered and pushed his shoulder.

Claud opened one pale baby blue eye.

She looked into it warily. He did not think about anything. He just went his way.

"Wha, whasit?" he said and closed the eye again.

"Nothing," she said. "Does your leg pain you?"   135

"Hurts like hell," Claud said.

"It'll quit terreckly," she said and lay back down. In a moment Claud was snoring again. For the rest of the afternoon they lay there. Claud slept. She scowled at the ceiling. Occasionally she raised her fist and made a small stabbing motion over her chest as if she was defending her innocence to invisible guests who were like the comforters of Job, reasonable-seeming but wrong.

About five-thirty Claud stirred. "Got to go after those niggers," he sighed, not moving.

She was looking straight up as if there were unintelligible handwriting on the ceiling. The protuberance over her eye had turned a greenish-blue. "Listen here," she said.

"What?"   140

"Kiss me."

Claud leaned over and kissed her loudly on the mouth. He pinched her side and their hands interlocked. Her expression of ferocious concentration did not change. Claud got up, groaning and growling, and limped off. She continued to study the ceiling.

She did not get up until she heard the pick-up truck coming back with the Negroes. Then she rose and thrust her feet in her brown oxfords, which she did not bother to lace, and stumped out onto the back porch and got her red plastic bucket. She emptied a tray of ice cubes into it and filled it half full of water and went out into the back yard. Every afternoon after Claud brought the hands in, one of the boys helped him put out hay and the rest waited in the back of the truck until he was ready to take them home. The truck was parked in the shade under one of the hickory trees.

"Hi yawl this morning?" Mrs. Turpin asked grimly, appearing with the bucket and the dipper. There were three women and a boy in the truck.

"Us doin nicely," the oldest woman said. "Hi you doin?" and her gaze   145
struck immediately on the dark lump on Mrs. Turpin's forehead. "You done fell down, ain't you?" she asked in a solicitous voice. The old woman was dark and almost toothless. She had on an old felt hat of Claud's set back on her head. The other two women were younger and lighter and they both had new bright green sunhats. One of them had hers on her head; the other had taken hers off and the boy was grinning beneath it.

Mrs. Turpin set the bucket down on the floor of the truck. "Yawl hep yourselves," she said. She looked around to make sure Claud had gone. "No, I didn't fall down," she said, folding her arms. "It was something worse than that."

"Ain't nothing bad happen to you!" the old woman said. She said it as if they all knew that Mrs. Turpin was protected in some special way by Divine Providence. "You just had you a little fall."

"We were in town at the doctor's office for where the cow kicked Mr. Turpin," Mrs. Turpin said in a flat tone that indicated they could leave off their foolishness. "And there was this girl there. A big fat girl with her face all broke out. I could look at that girl and tell she was peculiar but I couldn't tell how. And me and her mama was just talking and going along and all of a sudden WHAM! She throws this big book she was reading at me and . . ."

"Naw!" the old woman cried out.

"And then she jumps over the table and commences to choke me."   150

"Naw!" they all exclaimed, "naw!"

"Hi come she do that?" the old woman asked. "What ail her?"

Mrs. Turpin only glared in front of her.

"Somethin ail her," the old woman said.

"They carried her off in an ambulance," Mrs. Turpin continued, "but   155
before she went she was rolling on the floor and they were trying to hold her down to give her a shot and she said something to me." She paused. "You know what she said to me?"

"What she say?" they asked.

"She said," Mrs. Turpin began, and stopped, her face very dark and heavy. The sun was getting whiter and whiter, blanching the sky overhead so that the leaves of the hickory tree were black in the face of it. She could not bring forth the words. "Something real ugly," she muttered.

"She sho shouldn't said nothin ugly to you," the old woman said. "You so sweet. You the sweetest lady I know."

"She pretty too," the one with the hat on said.

"And stout," the other one said. "I never knowed no sweeter white lady."   160

"That's the truth befo' Jesus," the old woman said. "Amen! You des as sweet and pretty as you can be."

Mrs. Turpin knew exactly how much Negro flattery was worth and it added to her rage. "She said," she began again and finished this time with a fierce rush of breath, "that I was an old wart hog from hell."

There was an astounded silence.

"Where she at?" the youngest woman cried in a piercing voice.

"Lemme see her. I'll kill her!"   165

"I'll kill her with you!" the other one cried.

"She b'long in the sylum," the old woman said emphatically. "You the sweetest white lady I know."

"She pretty too," the other two said. "Stout as she can be and sweet. Jesus satisfied with her!"

"Deed he is," the woman declared.

Idiots! Mrs. Turpin growled to herself. You could never say anything   170
intelligent to a nigger. You could talk at them but not with them. "Yawl ain't drunk your water," she said shortly. "Leave the bucket in the truck when you're finished with it. I got more to do than just stand around and pass the time of day," and she moved off and into the house.

She stood for a moment in the middle of the kitchen. The dark protuberance over her eye looked like a miniature tornado cloud which might any moment seep across the horizon of her brow. Her lower lip protruded dangerously. She squared her massive shoulders. Then she marched into the front of the house and out the side door and started down the road to the pig parlor. She had the look of a woman going single-handed, weaponless, into battle.

The sun was deep yellow now like a harvest moon and was riding westward very fast over the far tree line as if it meant to reach the hogs before she did. The road was rutted and she kicked several good-sized stones out of her path as she strode along. The pig parlor was on a little knoll at the end of a lane that ran off from the side of the barn. It was a square of concrete as large as a small room, with a board fence about four feet high around it. The concrete floor sloped slightly so that the hog wash could drain off into a trench where it was carried to the field for fertilizer. Claud was standing on the outside, on the edge of the concrete, hanging onto the top board, hosing down the floor inside. The hose was connected to the faucet of a water trough nearby.

Mrs. Turpin climbed up beside him and glowered down at the hogs inside. There were seven long-snouted bristly shoats in it—tan with liver-colored spots—and an old sow a few weeks off from farrowing. She was lying on her side grunting. The shoats were running about shaking themselves like idiot children, their little slit pig eyes searching the floor for anything left. She had read that pigs were the most intelligent animal. She doubted it. They were supposed to be smarter than dogs. There had even been a pig astronaut. He had performed his assignment perfectly but died of a heart attack afterwards because they left him in his electric suit, sitting upright throughout his examination when naturally a hog should be on all fours.

A-gruntin and a-rootin and a-groanin.

"Gimme that hose," she said, yanking it away from Claud. "Go on and   175
carry them niggers home and then get off that leg."

"You look like you might have swallowed a mad dog," Claud observed, but he got down and limped off. He paid no attention to her humors.

Until he was out of earshot, Mrs. Turpin stood on the side of the pen, holding the hose and pointing the stream of water at the hind quarters of any shoat that looked as if it might try to lie down. When he had had time to get over the hill, she turned her head slightly and her wrathful eyes scanned the path. He was nowhere in sight. She turned back again and seemed to gather herself up. Her shoulders rose and she drew in her breath.

"What do you send me a message like that for?" she said in a low fierce voice, barely above a whisper but with the force of a shout in its concentrated fury. "How am I a hog and me both? How am I saved and from hell too?" Her free fist was knotted and with the other she gripped the hose, blindly pointing the stream of water in and out of the eye of the old sow whose outraged squeal she did not hear.

The pig parlor commanded a view of the back pasture where their twenty beef cows were gathered around the hay-bales Claud and the boy had put out. The freshly cut pasture sloped down to the highway. Across it was their cotton field and beyond that a dark green dusty wood which they owned as well. The sun was behind the wood, very red, looking over the paling of the trees like a farmer inspecting his own hogs.

"Why me?" she rumbled. "It's no trash around here, black or white, that I haven't given to. And break my back to the bone every day working. And do for the church."   180

She appeared to be the right size woman to command the arena before her. "How am I a hog?" she demanded. "Exactly how am I like them?" and she jabbed the stream of water at the shoats. "There was plenty of trash there. It didn't have to be me.

"If you like trash better, go get yourself some trash then," she railed. "You could have made me trash. Or a nigger. If trash is what you wanted why didn't you make me trash?" She shook her fist with the hose in it and a watery snake appeared momentarily in the air. "I could quit working and take it easy and be filthy," she growled. "Lounge about the sidewalks all day drinking root beer. Dip snuff and spit in every puddle and have it all over my face. I could be nasty.

"Or you could have made me a nigger. It's too late for me to be a nigger," she said with deep sarcasm, "but I could act like one. Lay down in the middle of the road and stop traffic. Roll on the ground."

In the deepening light everything was taking on a mysterious hue. The pasture was growing a peculiar glassy green and the streak of highway had turned lavender. She braced herself for a final assault and this time her voice rolled out over the pasture. "Go on," she yelled, "call me a hog! Call me a hog again. From hell. Call me a wart hog from hell. Put that bottom rail on top. There'll still be a top and bottom!"

A garbled echo returned to her.   185

A final surge of fury shook her and she roared, "Who do you think you are?"

The color of everything, field and crimson sky, burned for a moment with a transparent intensity. The question carried over the pasture and across the highway and the cotton field and returned to her clearly like an answer from beyond the wood.

She opened her mouth but no sound came out of it.

A tiny truck, Claud's, appeared on the highway, heading rapidly out of sight. Its gears scraped thinly. It looked like a child's toy. At any moment a bigger truck might smash into it and scatter Claud's and the niggers' brains all over the road.

Mrs. Turpin stood there, her gaze fixed on the highway, all her muscles rigid, until in five or six minutes the truck reappeared, returning. She waited until it had had time to turn into their own road. Then like a monumental statue coming to life, she bent her head slowly and gazed, as if through the very heart of mystery, down into the pig parlor at the hogs. They had settled all in one corner around the old sow who was grunting softly. A red glow suffused them. They appeared to pant with a secret life.

Until the sun slipped finally behind the tree line, Mrs. Turpin remained there with her gaze bent to them as if she were absorbing some abysmal life-giving knowledge. At last she lifted her head. There was only a purple streak in the sky, cutting through a field of crimson and leading, like an extension of the highway, into the descending dusk. She raised her hands from the side of the pen in a gesture hieratic and profound. A visionary light settled in her eyes. She saw the streak as a vast swinging bridge extending upward from the earth through a field of living fire. Upon it a vast horde of souls were rumbling toward heaven. There were whole companies of white-trash, clean for the first time in their lives, and bands of black niggers in white robes, and battalions of freaks and lunatics shouting and clapping and leaping like frogs. And bringing up the end of the procession was a tribe of people whom she recognized at once as those who, like herself and Claud, had always had a little of everything and the God-given wit to use it right. She leaned forward to observe them closer. They were marching behind the others with great dignity, accountable as they had always been for good order and common sense and respectable behavior. They alone were on key. Yet she could see by their shocked and altered faces that even their virtues were being burned away. She lowered her hands and gripped the rail of the hog pen, her eyes small but fixed unblinkingly on what lay ahead. In a moment the vision faded but she remained where she was, immobile.

At length she got down and turned off the faucet and made her slow way on the darkening path to the house. In the woods around her the invisible cricket choruses had struck up, but what she heard were the voices of the souls climbing upward into the starry field and shouting hallelujah.

[1964]

Writing about "Revelation": Critical Viewpoints

C. Ralph Stevens: Biographical Sketch of O'Connor

The moving facts of Flannery O'Connor's life are succinctly told in this excerpt from C. Ralph Stevens's edition of the letters between Brainerd Cheyney, his wife Fannie, and O'Connor. A telling glimpse of her personality is also captured in Stevens's reflection on O'Connor's tone in her letters.

The facts of her early biography are quickly summarized and well known. She was born in Savannah, Georgia, on 25 March 1925, the only child of Regina L. Cline and Edward F. O'Connor, Jr., who was in the real estate business. Both families were Roman Catholic, and O'Connor attended parochial schools. The Clines were a prosperous family, and when Edward O'Connor became fatally ill with disseminated lupus in 1939, the O'Connors moved to Milledgeville to live in the Cline family's antebellum home.

O'Connor graduated from Peabody High School the year after her father died, and enrolled in the Georgia State College for Women in Milledgeville. She majored in sociology and took an active interest in creative writing and cartooning. When she completed her B.A. in 1945, she left Milledgeville for the Writer's Workshop at the University of Iowa, where she won a Rinehart Fellowship for her fiction. She sold her first short story, "The Geranium," to *Accent,* in 1946, and completed her M.F.A. in Literature in 1947. After another year at the University of Iowa, O'Connor was recommended, in part on the strength of work she had already done on *Wise Blood,* to attend Yaddo, a writers retreat in Saratoga Springs, New York. After a few months there, she left, in the spring of 1949, for New York City. She had, in February of that year, become acquainted with Robert and Sally Fitzgerald, with whom she later lived as a friend and boarder when they moved from New York City to a country house in Ridgefield, Connecticut. Late in 1950, as she was finishing the first draft of *Wise Blood,* she was stricken with the disease that had killed her father [lupus erythematosus]. She underwent months of hospital treatment in Atlanta, her life saved and prolonged by an experimental cortisone derivative, ACTH. In the spring of 1951, recovering but too weak to climb the stairs of the house in Milledgeville, she moved with her mother to a nearby family dairy farm, Andalusia, where they lived, Mrs. O'Connor managing the farm and O'Connor writing, until her death on 3 August 1964.

O'Connor's own control of tone—and her ability to "get some distance" on the world around her—is of course a quality readers of her fiction, Cheney early among them, have much valued. And it is one of the chief delights of her letters to the Cheneys. More often than not, the object in focus from O'Connor's "distance" is herself. When *Nashville Tennessean* editor Ralph Morrissey took pictures of O'Connor while she was a guest at the Cheneys' one weekend in 1955, Mrs. Cheney sent O'Connor copies, to which she responded: "That decidedly ain't me except in the picture which looks like an ad for acid indigestion. . . . [Morrissey] sure missed his calling. He ought to work for Photoplay or Snappy Story—to make a divebomb out of the old oaken bucket!!" (Letter 18). And she wrote of other photographs: "The grim pictures arrived. That face over the 'fiery Flannery' caption looked like an old potato the mice had been at" (Letter 15).

When she began to walk on crutches, she wrote the Cheneys that she'd love to visit, "If you are willing to stash me away downstairs and to remove any low altitude vases you have set about" (Letter 21). She wrote them about a talk on "the Wholesome Novel" she was supposed to give to the ladies of the Catholic Parish Council in Macon: "Unfortunately I don't know what a wholesome novel is . . . I am never informed on the subjects I discuss" (Letter 43). "I am now back from being the woman of the hour," she wrote after participating in the 1959 Vanderbilt literary symposium, "to being the woman of the barnyard" (Letter 87). Ten days before she was to give a talk in Savannah, she broke out with hives: "This was perfect timing. The doctor said I could not go. This is what you call anticipatory illness and illustrates psychosomatic disease at its best. I hope that my carcus will bring off another triumph like this the next time it is necessary" (Letter 115). She wrote of another series of speaking engagements: "I am weary of riding upon airyplanes and being the Honored Guest. I think the reason I like chickens is that they don't go to college" (Letter 121).

From C. Ralph Stevens, *The Correspondence of Flannery O'Connor and the Brainard Cheneys.* Jackson: UP of Mississippi, 1986.

Margaret Earley Whitt: The Biographical Context of "Revelation"

This brief description of O'Connor's career, from Margaret Earley Whitt's *Understanding Flannery O'Connor,* provides a useful context for understanding "Revelation."

When Flannery O'Connor's first novel, *Wise Blood,* was published in 1952, Sylvia Stallings of the *New York Herald Tribune Book Review* wondered "where, after an opening performance like this one, she has left herself to go." These words suggested and predicted the puzzling and disturbing effect that O'Connor's writing had and would come to have on her readers. She was a devout Roman Catholic, with a Southern upbringing. Her keen eye for observation and sensitive ear for the dialogue that comes naturally to a story-telling people assisted her in capturing the language and obsessions of a people congenitally "Christ-haunted," as she once explained. Hazel Motes, the fanatical frustrated preacher protagonist of this first novel, becomes a symbolic prototype of the most repeated question in O'Connor's fiction: "What about this Christ? What are we supposed to do with Him?" She readily admitted the importance of Christ's resurrection to her way of seeing the universe.

This Christian orthodoxy was reiterated in her first collection of short stories. Each of the ten stories of *A Good Man Is Hard to Find* (1955), with the exception of "Good Country People," had been previously published in *Sewanee Review, Kenyon Review, Shenandoah,* and *Harper's Bazaar.* By the time of the collection's publication, O'Connor had been included in the 1953 O. Henry Prize anthology for "The Life You Save May Be Your Own," the story of a one-armed tramp who seduces a babbling idiot and her desperate mother in order to get a car that can take him away. The following year, "A Circle in the Fire" won second place in the O. Henry Awards; in this story, three young boys set on fire a farm woman's property for the devilment of it. Contemporary reviewers vacillated on what to do with her writing. The reviewer for *Time* saw her stories as "witheringly sarcastic"; here was a writer who used "a brutal irony, a slambang humor and a style of writing as balefully direct as a death sentence." Something was going on in these stories, but most critics were not sure exactly what to call it, and a representation of orthodox Christianity did not cross their collective minds. "There is brutality in these stories, but since the brutes are as mindless as their victims, all we have, in the end, is a series of tales about creatures who collided and drown, or survive to float passively in the isolated sea of the author's compassion, which accepts them without reflecting anything," suggested a review in the *New Yorker.*

Her stories continued to appear in journals and magazines. In 1960 she published her second novel, *The Violent Bear It Away.* The novel's title comes from Matthew 11:12 of the Rheims-Douay Version of the Bible: "From the days of John the Baptist until now, the kingdom of heaven suffereth violence, and the violent bear it away." The protagonist is fourteen-year-old Francis Marion Tarwater, designated a prophet by his late great-uncle, old Mason Tarwater. Like *Wise Blood*'s Hazel, Tarwater must do everything in his power to run in the opposite direction before finally accepting the call to "GO WARN THE CHILDREN OF GOD OF THE TERRIBLE SPEED OF MERCY." Contemporary reviewers were beginning to understand that something significantly deep—Southern and Catholic—was happening in her work. Although early critics had placed her in the "Southern sunlight Gothic" school, the term was being recast, expanded. Her work was violent, grotesque, and horribly funny, but with a twist. Granville Hicks, after reading *The Violent Bear It Away,* for example, asserted: "From now on there can be no doubt that Miss O'Connor is one of the important American writers."

To affirm her literary reputation, *Esquire*'s fiction editor Rust Hills placed her squarely into "red hot" status in his "The Structure of the American Literary Establishment" chart in July 1963. O'Connor was assigned to "the hot red blob in the middle," which represented "the critics, agents, universities, book publishers, and magazines that habitually work together to establish a literary reputation." By this time, she had won first place in the 1957 O. Henry Prize Collection for "Greenleaf," the story of a farm woman who is gored to death by a scrub bull. She won first place in the contest again in 1963 for "Everything That Rises Must Converge," the story of a young man's response to his mother's eccentricities and her subsequent stroke on a dark street outside her weight-reduction class. And she garnered a third first-place O. Henry Award for "Revelation" in 1965, the story many critics consider her finest.

From Margaret Earley Whitt, *Understanding Flannery O'Connor.* Columbia:
U of South Carolina P, 1995, pp. 1–3.

Flannery O'Connor: On the Genre of the Short Story

In 1959, O'Connor and three other writers were asked "What is a Short Story?" and "What advice do you give to the college student interested in writing—especially the short story?" Here is O'Connor's answer.

1. This is a hellish question inspired by the devil who tempts textbook publishers. I have been writing stories for fifteen years without a definition of one. The best I can do is tell you what a story is not.

    1) It is not a joke.

    2) It is not an anecdote.

3) It is not a lyric rhapsody in prose.

4) It is not a case history.

5) It is not a reported incident.

It is none of these things because it has an extra dimension and I think this extra dimension comes about when the writer puts us in the middle of some human action and shows it as it is illuminated and outlined by mystery. In every story there is some minor revelation which, no matter how funny the story may be, gives us a hint of the unknown, of death.

2. My advice is to start reading and writing and looking and listening. Pay less attention to yourself than to what is outside you and if you must write about yourself, get a good distance away and judge yourself with a stranger's eyes and a stranger's severity.

Remember that reason should always go where the imagination goes. The artist uses his reason to discover an answering reason in everything he sees. For him, to be reasonable is to find in the object, in the situation, in the sequence, the spirit which makes it itself.

The short story writer particularly has to learn to read life in a way that includes the most possibilities—like the medieval commentators on scripture, who found three kinds of meaning in the literal level of the sacred text. If you see things in depth, you will be more liable to write them that way.

From *Esprit* (Winter 1959), published at the University of Scranton.

Margaret Turner: More Biographical Background

In 1960 Margaret Turner wrote an article for *The Atlanta Journal and Constitution* about her visit with Flannery O'Connor at her home in Milledgeville, Georgia. This excerpt comes from that article.

Asked if her characters are drawn from real life, the author said that if she had known too many of the people she writes about she might not be around to write about them.

"The imagination works on what the eye sees, but it molds and directs this to the end of whatever it is making," she explained. "So my characters are both and at the same time drawn from life and entirely imaginary. Not too many people claim to see themselves in them."

She prefers to call her work "grotesque," meaning that she does not write in a naturalistic vein but uses distortion to make what is not readily observable more observable.

Why, we ventured to ask, does a writer of fiction feel that he has to shock to get through to the average reader?

"Not every writer of fiction feels that he has to shock to get through to the average reader," she said. "I believe that the 'average' reader, however, is a good deal below average. People say with considerable satisfaction, 'Oh, I'm an average reader,' when the fact is they never learned to read in the first place, and probably never will.

"You see people who are supposed to be highly educated who don't know trashy fiction from any other kind," she continued. "If you have the values of your time, you can usually write without having to shock anyone to attention; but if you want to show something that the majority don't believe in or wish to see, then you have to get and hold their attention usually by extreme means."

From *The Atlanta Journal and Constitution*, 29 May 1960.

Flannery O'Connor: On Her Motivation

Readers and critics, early in O'Connor's career particularly, were puzzled by her work. What was she trying to do? Why were her characters so freaky? In the two following excerpts from different essays, O'Connor discusses who can understand her work and why she writes.

Whenever I'm asked why Southern writers particularly have a penchant for writing about freaks, I say it is because we are still able to recognize one. To be able to recognize a freak, you have to have some conception of the whole man, and in the South the general conception of man is still, in the main, theological. That is a large statement, and it is dangerous to make it, for almost anything you say about Southern belief can be denied in the next breath with equal propriety. But approaching the subject from the standpoint of the writer, I think it is safe to say that while the South is hardly Christ-centered, it is most certainly Christ-haunted. The Southerner, who isn't convinced of it, is very much afraid that he may have been formed in the image and likeness of God. Ghosts can be very fierce and instructive. They cast strange shadows, particularly in our literature. In any case, it is when the freak can be sensed as a figure for our essential displacement that he attains some depth in literature. . . .

The type of mind that can understand good fiction is not necessarily the educated mind, but it is at all times the kind of mind that is willing to have its sense of mystery deepened by contact with reality, and its sense of reality deepened by contact with mystery. Fiction should be both canny and uncanny. In a good deal of popular criticism, there is the notion operating that all fiction has to be about the Average Man, and has to depict average ordinary everyday life, that every fiction writer must produce what used to be called "a slice of life." But if life, in that sense, satisfied us, there would be no sense in producing literature at all.

Conrad said that his aim as a fiction writer was to render the highest possible justice to the visible universe. That sounds very grand, but it is really very humble. It means that he subjected himself at all times to the limitations that reality imposed, but that reality for him was not simply coextensive with the visible . He was interested in rendering justice to the visible universe because it suggested an invisible one, and he explained his own intentions as a novelist in this way:

> ". . . *and if the [artist's] conscience is clear, his answer to those*
> *who in the fullness of a wisdom which looks for immediate*
> *profit, demand specifically to be edified, consoled, amused;*
> *who demand to be promptly improved, or encouraged, or*

*frightened, or shocked or charmed, must run thus: My task
which I am trying to achieve is, by the power of the written
word, to make you hear, to make you feel—it is, before all, to
make you see. That—and no more, and it is everything. If I
succeed, you shall find there, according to your deserts,
encouragement, consolation, fear, charm, all you demand—
and, perhaps, also that glimpse of truth for which you have
forgotten to ask."*

You may think from all I say that the reason I write is to make the read-   5
er see what I see, and that writing fiction is primarily a missionary activity.
Let me straighten this out.

Last spring I talked here, and one of the girls asked me, "Miss O'Connor, why do you write?" and I said, "Because I'm good at it," and at once I
felt a considerable disapproval in the atmosphere. I felt that this was not
thought by the majority to be a high-minded answer; but it was the only
answer I could give. I had not been asked why I write the way I do, but
why I write at all; and to that question there is only one legitimate
answer.

There is no excuse for anyone to write fiction for public consumption
unless he has been called to do so by the presence of a gift. It is the nature
of fiction not to be good for much unless it is good in itself.

From Flannery O'Connor, *Mystery and Manners: Occasional Prose, Selected
and Edited by Sally and Robert Fitzgerald.* New York: Farrar, 1970.

Anthony Di Renzo: Close Reading

In *American Gargoyles: Flannery O'Connor and the Medieval Grotesque,* Anthony
Di Renzo connects Flannery O'Connor's sensibility to the medieval appreciation for
the grotesquely ugly and monstrous. Di Renzo first made the link, he explains in the
Preface, as he was wandering through the campus bookstore carrying a gargoyle (it
was a prop for a doomed comedy on campus television, a parody of *The Exorcist*),
and happened to open an O'Connor collection to this sentence from "The River":
"[A] huge old man . . . sat like a humped stone on the bumper of a long ancient automobile . . . bent forward with his hands hanging between his knees and his small
eyes half closed." Sounds like a gargoyle, doesn't it? "The monstrosities that adorn—
or is it deface?—the façade of cathedrals," Di Renzo persuasively argues, are like the
comic creations of O'Connor. By transgressing against the ordinary, by comically
shocking us, the gargoyles and monsters of O'Connor are liberating. They serve, Di
Renzo says, a spiritual purpose.

This excerpt focuses on the ending of "Revelation," from the sentence in which
Mrs. Turpin raises her hands "from the side of the pen in a gesture hieratic and pro-
found," to the end. Reread this passage from the story before you work through Di
Renzo's analysis.

This passage is the most glorious in Flannery O'Connor's fiction. It
reminds us of the grotesque processions of the Middle Ages, of the
freaks, floats, and fools of Corpus Christi—not to mention Vachel Lindsay's wonderful poem, "General William Booth Enters Heaven." But the
comic extravagance of this apocalyptic parade creates a problem for the

reader. Mrs. Turpin's vision appears to be a moment of Christian grace, but this moment of grace completely wrecks our conventional understanding of Christianity. We are perplexed by a series of conundrums. Ruby is still an incorrigible bigot—and yet she prophesies. Human beings, supposedly made in the image and likeness of God, are blatantly compared to swine. Angels are compared to crickets—or is it the other way around? The white bourgeoisie, who have been systematically vilified throughout the story, are not exactly damned at the end; but a fire consumes them, burning away what little goodness they have. If there is renewal at the end of "Revelation," it is a renewal through destruction. A holocaust burns that leaves not a rack behind.

Few O'Connor scholars are willing to address these textual ambiguities. Those that do, like Harold Bloom, tend to be overly pessimistic. For Bloom, the fire of "Revelation"—meant to burn away "false or apparent virtues"—"consumes not less than everything" (7). "In O'Connor's mixed realm," he states, "which is neither nature nor grace, Southern reality nor private phantasmagoria, all are necessarily damned" (7). Yet there is another way in interpreting the "mixed realm" of "Revelation," one which has less to do with damnation than with radical indeterminacy. This principle of indeterminacy offers us a new understanding of grace and apocalypse in Flannery O'Connor's fiction and their relationship to the grotesque.

Ruby's vision in "Revelation" unites the saved and the damned in a blaze of fire. It is not good and evil that perish together in these ambiguous flames. Rather, it is the artificial standards of right and wrong, of beauty and ugliness, which mere mortals presumptuously use to divide humankind into two camps: the righteous and the unrighteous. O'Connor's story is a prophetic satire against the external trappings of class and property. It is a judgment against judgment, against all forms of separation. "A social order based on the reality-principle," says Norman O. Brown, "a social order which draws a distinction between the wish and the deed, between the criminal and righteous is still a kingdom of darkness" (152). O'Connor uses the grotesque to undermine pride and materialism. Instead of presenting a vision of a new social order, a utopian *fait accompli,* however, she depicts the flickering fire of transformation, a poetic re-visioning of a world under constant reconstruction. "Truth," Brown says, echoing William Blake, "is error burned up; a light shining in darkness; darkness overcome. The everlasting bonfire. The truth and the life and the joy is in the overcoming. Not in perfection, but in transmutation" (233). To consign all human trappings to the flames is the Last Judgment: "Take but degree away; it is the end of the world. The reality-principle is the importance principle, which commands us to be fooled by appearances, to respect the Emperor's New Clothes. Hierarchy is visible; in the invisible kingdom the first are last. Overthrow the reality-principle: no respect for persons, not to be fooled by masks; no clothes, no emperor. All power is an impostor; a paper tiger, or idol; it is Burnt up the Moment Men cease to behold it" (Brown 235).

O'Connor's carnivalesque treatment of the civil rights movement in *Everything that Rises Must Converge* has symbolic as well as political implications. Segregation and integration become metaphors in her fiction, ways of saying that life is never "black" or "white." Behind the harshness of O'Connor's satire is a burning concern for radical acceptance, for affirming human beings as they are—contradictory and contrary—without resorting to sublimation or to dividing the sheep from the goats. We cannot truly be noble, O'Connor seems to suggest, until we can admit that we are also hoggish. Mrs. Turpin—bawling out God in a pigpen—is forced to confront this paradox in her own nature. "How am I a hog and me both?" she demands. "How am I saved and from hell too?" These questions are essential to our understanding of the grotesque in O'Connor's work. Mrs. Turpin has used hard work and good deeds to disavow her own sowishness. But at this point in "Revelation" O'Connor has gone beyond mere character assassination. There are indications in the story that she has widened her comic vision: her outrageous allusion to Christ as the Good Swineherd; above all, her humorously anthromorphic depiction of the hogs themselves:

> There were seven long-snouted bristly shoats in it [the pen]—
> tan with liver-colored spots—and an old sow a few weeks off
> from farrowing. She was lying on her side grunting. The
> shoats were running about shaking themselves like idiot chil-
> dren, their little slit pig eyes searching the floor for anything
> left. She [Mrs. Turpin] had read that pigs were the most intelli-
> gent animal. She doubted it. They were supposed to be
> smarter than dogs. There had even been a pig astronaut. He
> had performed his assignment perfectly but died of a heart
> attack afterwards because they left him in his electric suit,
> sitting upright throughout his examination when naturally a
> hog should be on all fours.

O'Connor's other fiction contains similar meditations on pigs, particu-   5
larly "The River." She appears to have been fascinated by them. This uneasy affection may have been personal. Pigs, after all, supplied her with the ACTH she needed to combat her lupus. It is more likely, though, that she was aware of the strange role hogs play in Christian art and literature. On the one hand, pigs are the unclean animals of the Bible; in the Gospel of Saint Mark, Christ casts demons into a herd of swine, who then promptly commit suicide by stampeding off a cliff. On the other hand, pigs are talismans against evil, the totemic animals of Saint Anthony of Egypt, who himself was a swineherd. Some paintings of the saint show him resisting a horde of demons with the help of a little sow. Hogs are a puzzling and ambiguous symbol in Christian iconography, neither holy nor unholy. Perhaps they represent the polymorphously perverse side of human nature—that which is beastly, impish, shameless, self-satisfied, incorrigible, and plug-ugly in each of us. Luther's famous Sermon on the Sow addresses this perversity: "For a sow lies in the gutter or on the manure as if on the finest feather bed. She rests safely, snores tenderly, and sleeps sweetly, does not fear king nor master, death nor hell, devil or God's wrath, lives without worry, and does not even think where the clover . . . may be. And if the Turkish Caesar arrived in all his might and anger, the sow would be much too proud to move a single whisker in his honor. . . . And if at last the butcher comes upon her, she thinks maybe a piece of wood is pinching her, or a stone" (qtd. in Erikson 32).

Luther's sermon is a complicated mixture of affections and revulsion, held together by folksy humor and eloquence. The sow's sowishness is criticized, but also accepted, even embraced—a remarkable achievement of rhetoric and tone. The same effect occurs in "Revelation," just before Mrs. Turpin's carnivalesque vision:"She bent her head slowly and gazed, as if through the very heart of mystery, down into the pig parlor at the hogs. They had settled all in one corner around the old sow who was grunting softly. A red glow suffused them. They appeared to pant with a secret life." Ugliness suddenly becomes indistinguishable from beauty. This shift in perception gives Mrs. Turpin an "abysmal life-giving knowledge." It also creates the strange procession of characters—not quite saved, not quite damned—who dance along the horizon. The celebratory ambiguity of the procession and the beautiful ugliness of the pigs are "the very heart of mystery" in O'Connor's grotesque vision. Mrs. Turpin's acceptance of her own sowishness, O'Connor suggests, allows her to accept the Mardi Gras of mortality, where no one is ever only one thing or another. The mystery of the pigpen and the mystery of the parade are the mystery of human indeterminacy. Erik Erikson relates the grotesque tone of Luther's Sermon on the Sow to the paradoxes of Luther's doctrine of Justification by Faith: "We are, Luther proclaimed, totally sinners (*totus homo peccator*) and totally just (*totus homo justus*), always both damned and blessed, both alive and dead. We thus cannot strive, by hook or by crook, to get from one absolute stage into another; we can only use our God-given organs of awareness in the here and now to encompass the paradox of the human condition" (216).

Mrs. Turpin's humiliation and displacement, her self-annihilating confrontation with what is pettiest in her own nature, ironically leads to a broadening of vision, a greater awareness of her true place in the human community. It is a common pattern in O'Connor's fiction: "The self is decentered and then later recentered with a fuller conception of its diversity" (Brinkmeyer 43). What applies to O'Connor's characters, however, also applies to her readers. Our experience as we enter her carnivalesque world is just as disorienting, shocking, and humbling as Mrs. Turpin's. Like Ruby, we take pride in our prejudices. We too feel superior to those who are not as "fortunate" as we—namely O'Connor's unattractive characters. Most of us have been educated to believe that her rednecks and Fundamentalists are either crazy or subhuman. "Confronting us as freaks and cripples who wear their physical and mental deformities like badges," James Cox observes, "they measure a grotesque distance between their religion and the liberal, secular, moral universe" of the majority of O'Connor's readers (783). We are the elect, cleanlimbed, "enlightened" saints, smiling down at gargoyles in overalls and porkpie hats. We feel "blessed" not to be filthy, ignorant, fanatical, bigoted, twisted, petty, or deformed. Despite our blessings, O'Connor's outrageous sense of humor quickly destroys our complacent sense of superiority. The more we laugh at her grotesques, the more the distance closes between us and them, the more we begin to see—*horribile dictu*—how much we resemble each other.

From Anthony Di Renzo, *American Gargoyles: Flannery O'Connor and the Medieval Grotesque*. Carbondale: Southern Illinois UP, 1993, pp. 215–220.

Marshall Bruce Gentry: Close Reading and Textual Evidence

The following excerpt, like the preceding one, is concerned with the ending of "Revelation," but Marshall Bruce Gentry's concerns and conclusions are very different from Di Renzo's. What do you think of Gentry's use of the drafts of the story as evidence in reading the finished version? Who is more convincing— Di Renzo or Gentry?

The precise significance of Mrs. Turpin's vision of hordes on a fiery bridge is not altogether a matter of critical agreement. And O'Connor's letters show her to have been inconsistent in her opinion of "Revelation" while she was writing it. It was the ending of the story that most troubled her, and the sequence of versions shows O'Connor trying to make clear that Ruby is not entirely corrupt. In a letter dated 25 December 1963, O'Connor mentioned that a friend who had read the draft of "Revelation" had called Mrs. Turpin "evil" and had suggested that O'Connor omit the final vision, which the friend considered to be a confirmation of Mrs. Turpin's evilness. O'Connor's reaction was, "I am not going to leave it out. I am going to deepen it so that there'll be no mistaking Ruby is not just an evil Glad Annie." As she finished revising the story, O'Connor made the final vision less obviously of Mrs. Turpin's making. One late draft, for example, contains the statement that the Turpins, "marching behind the others" toward heaven "with great dignity," were "driving them, in fact, ahead of themselves, still responsible as they had always been for good order and common sense and respectable behavior." In the published text, the Turpins are still at the end of the procession, but there is no mention of them "driving" the others on, and they are "accountable" rather than "still responsible." Another significant difference between the draft and the published text is the addition in the final version of the fact that Mrs. Turpin sees that her "virtues" are "being burned away." In both these revisions there is less emphasis on Mrs. Turpin's smug perspective, more emphasis on what shocks her.

The final version makes the vision more clearly redemptive, and one apparent implication of the revisions is that Mrs. Turpin's revelation is supernatural in origin. This implication is misleading, however; there is still much in Mrs. Turpin's vision to suggest that she produces it, and the primary effect of O'Connor's revisions is to make Mrs. Turpin's unconscious more clearly responsible for her vision of entry into a heavenly community. This view may seem peculiar when one considers Mrs. Turpin's bigotry and banality, but one's impression of that bigotry and banality is the result of the narrator's emphasis in describing Mrs. Turpin. The narrator emphasizes the ridiculous aspects of Mrs. Turpin rather than making fully apparent the tracks she has laid to carry herself to the oven in which individuality is renounced and the ideal of heavenly community achieved.

From Marshall Bruce Gentry, *Flannery O'Connor's Religion of the Grotesque.* Jackson: UP of Mississippi, 1986.

Richard Giannone: Historical and Biographical Materials

In *Flannery O'Connor, Hermit Novelist* (2000), Richard Giannone has launched one of the most interesting approaches to O'Connor by taking very seriously a comment she made in a letter to a friend in 1960: "Those desert fathers interest me very much," she wrote, referring to a tradition of ascetic hermits that began about four centuries after Christ. Giannone examines these works of ascetic spirituality, and finds that they often resonate in O'Connor's work, who did say once, "Lord, I'm glad I'm a hermit novelist." In the following excerpt, Giannone meditates on the significance of Mrs. Turpin's Job-like interrogation of God, as she implores, "What do you send me a message like that for?" She even asks God, you will remember, "Who do you think you are?" You may well be surprised by Giannone's assertion that "The story ends as God smiles on Ruby," but he arrives at his insight because he sees Mrs. Turpin's "honest" questions as the path to her humility, which is the path to her salvation. This is, I think, a dazzling critical performance, exemplifying the effective use of historical and biographical sources.

Precisely because Ruby's questions are honest in their barefaced irreverence, O'Connor finds them worthy of an answer. Given Ruby's colossal arrogance before God, one holds one's breath in anticipation over what will happen to Ruby. But always the artist to amaze, O'Connor on this occasion astounds by allowing the reader a sigh of relief, a long deep release of gladness through high jinks. Instead of falling in on Ruby, the sky opens up into a magnificent, carefree procession to heaven. In a fiction noted for violence bearing away the kingdom of God, the spectacle surprises with its restraint and gentleness. Ruby's foolish pride turns not into dust but bursts into horseplay. The merry racket of the enormous throng of human spirits "rumbling toward heaven" graphically answers Ruby's questions about why God sends the message that she is a warthog from hell. Mary Grace's assault is to alert Ruby to the spiritual death, the hell, toward which she was heading and to redirect Ruby's will so that she can take her place among the redeemed—albeit holding up the rear, with her dignified stiffness as something of a drag on the free-spirited cavalcade. The story ends as God smiles on Ruby. O'Connor's theology of pranks is sheer desert humor. When Abba Anthony asks how to deal with demonic attacks, an inspired voice says to him, perhaps with a knowing smile: "'Humility'" (*Sayings,* Anthony the Great 7 [2]). Humility is not only "victorious over the demons," says Amma Theodora (*Sayings,* Theodora 6 [84]); humility "is a great work, and a work of God" (Ward, *Daily Readings* 32).

The great work of God that is humility lays bare the revelation of "Revelation." Besides correcting Ruby's rash heart and her turmoil, humility is God's beaming leniency and quiet forbearance of Ruby in all her laughable sinfulness. Ruby's daredevil anger is not used by God to fuel a corresponding revenge but to elicit a cheerful acceptance of Ruby's weaknesses. On God's side, there is a generosity, a control of violence, that may not rival the humble self-emptying of the Incarnation but does manifest the self-lowering that Ruby needs to incorporate into her life with others. The revelation invites Ruby to share in the divinely human comedy. If she finds the jaunty vision preposterous by her prim notion of decorum, Ruby can also feel the stripping away of her false dignity as enhancing. She will, of course, need to cultivate a sense of humor, which she noticeably lacks, to appreciate the rollicking crowd and accept her starchy self. She who feels ready to give the world "a friendly smile" might turn her amicable expression inward. If she does, then out of her rage would come blessed laughter; and her isolating prejudice would open into the new communal life celebrated in the celestial parade. Out of this life with others will rise Ruby's life with God. The ascetic effect of the vision that exposes Ruby's evil is not to frighten but to encourage her to change.

The ancient hermits have words that speak directly to Ruby's need to change: "Just as one cannot build a ship unless one has some nails," says Amma Syncletica, "so it is impossible to be saved without humility" (*Sayings,* Syncletica 26 [235]). Humility is salvation. The nails of humility will hold Ruby's virtues together and fasten them to God. Moreover, humility will relieve Ruby of the interior humiliations of exerting unrelenting pressure on her spirit. The words of another elder serve to explain Ruby's torment: "We have put the light burden on one side, that is to say, self-accusation, and we have loaded ourselves with a heavy one, that is to say, self-justification" (*Sayings,* John the Dwarf 21 [90]). Unburdened of vindicating herself, Ruby can draw good from her weaknesses, failures, and fears. There is nothing so humbling and democratic, nothing so heartwarming as the sight of all the respectable country landowners, with their faces altered from having their virtues burned away, strutting behind rousing freaks and raving screwballs with unalloyed smiles leading the pack heavenward. Surprised by her sin and shorn of pretenses, Ruby Turpin is saved by God's humor.

From Richard Giannone, *Flannery O'Connor, Hermit Novelist.* Urbana: U of Illinois, 2000, pp. 234–235.

12

More Stories

> The best short stories contain novels. Either they are densely plotted, with each line an insight, or they distill emotions that could easily have spread on for pages, chapters.
>
> —Louise Erdrich

In the United States and Canada, nearly three thousand short stories are published *each year* in magazines and literary journals. The really good short stories from the past century would make a stack as tall as you, or as tall as a house, depending on how you define "really good." Given such an abundance, what stories can you expect to find in a single chapter that provides more short fiction?

The goal here was to include stories that will grab you—stories that had, as Barbara Kingsolver puts it, "large truths delivered in tight spaces." The stories in this chapter should tell you things you didn't know; take you places you've never been; show you life from perspectives you'll probably never otherwise inhabit.

"Once upon a time, they lived happily ever after."

© The New Yorker Collection 1991 Henry Martin from cartoonbank.com. All Rights Reserved.

Also included are stories that will give you some sense of the vast variety of short fiction. You'll find both classic and just-published stories; stories that have appeared in lots of anthologies, and stories never before collected anywhere. These are also stories that should respond most interestingly and revealingly to a variety of critical approaches. The ulterior motive is to have you read more short fiction than you did before this course. You'll be amazed by what you'll find.

Hanan Al-Shaykh (1945–)

Hanan Al-Shaykh, who is considered one of the world's experts on Arab womanhood, was raised in Beirut and educated in Cairo. She worked in Beirut for the Al-Nahar newspaper until 1975, when civil war prompted her to leave and eventually to move to London. The author of six novels and two plays, she saw her first novel banned in several Arab countries for its treatment of female sexuality.

The Keeper of the Virgins

One of the women wondered aloud if he was a dwarf in every way. The other women sitting at the intersection burst out laughing. Even though they prayed to God to forgive them, their laughter grew louder before the dwarf was out of sight.

They had grown used to seeing him every morning shortly after they set to work, bending over the hibiscus bushes to gather the wine-colored blossoms. He would go by with a confident step, heading for the convent, where the pure ones lived, books and magazines tucked under his arm, a cloth bundle containing his food for the day held firmly in his hand. He was content to greet the hibiscus pickers as he passed, although they welcomed him enthusiastically and offered him a glass of tea or some warm bread. He knew it was because he was a dwarf and they felt sorry for him, but he had a great sense of his own importance. Besides keeping up with the politics of his own country and the Arab world in general, he had broadened his interests to take in the whole planet. He studied thoroughly and remembered everything he learned, delved into dictionaries, read novels, both translated and local, and underlined passages in pencil when the subject matter appealed to him or he liked the sound of the words. He wrote poetry and prose, and sent it to newspapers and magazines, even though not a single line of it had ever been published; and he had been going to the convent and waiting by the main gates in its outer wall for a year or more.

He would sit in the generous shade of a sycamore tree or lie on a blanket he had brought with him beneath its spreading branches, staring at the convent walls. He had learned the shape of their dusty red stones by heart; their uneven surfaces and the way they were arranged reminded him of a tray of the vermicelli pastries called *kunafa*. He spent these long stretches of time either reading, sometimes to himself and sometimes out loud, or building a fire with a few sticks to make tea, or waiting for the hoopoe, which appeared out of nowhere from the direction of the trees and the water or from the bare, stony desert. Every now and then he would stare hard at the iron gates of the convent, hearing some kind of commotion on the other side. But he was convinced that it was a figment of his imagination because the place was always calm and still again at once, as if there had been no interruption.

But as the days went by he discovered from one of the men building the nearby tombs, who sat and chatted with him for a while each evening, that the noise he heard was real enough, as the nuns used to sweep the convent yard every now and then. This ruined his concentration for some considerable length of time: he could not read with such enthusiasm, or savor a choice sentence or the hot sweetness of a glass of tea or the food he brought with him. He became entirely focused on the iron gates, as if by staring at them he could melt them and make them collapse before his eyes.

During his first weeks of frequenting the monastery, he had tried to have   5
a conversation with the nuns to persuade them to open the gate, but each
time his request had been refused in dumb silence. He had asked if he could
sweep the yard for nothing, worship in the church, confess, but still he met
with no response from behind the closed gates. Gradually he became convinced that everybody had joined forces to concoct a lie about the existence
of this convent, because he was a dwarf, and he knew very well what people
thought about dwarves. They were all lying to him: the tomb builders, the
hibiscus women, his family, the wind, which must have cooperated with
them by making some noise behind the abandoned gates; Georgette's mother, who had lamented long and loud because her daughter had joined the
pure ones and their door had closed behind her, never to open again.

Georgette's family must be hiding the truth. Georgette must have gone
mad and been locked away, for just before the rumor went around that she
had entered the convent, she would only leave the house to walk over
thorns until her feet bled.

The dwarf became convinced that many people profited from his visits to the convent. His mother regularly rose at dawn to get his food ready,
as if he had a job to go to. His younger brother must have heaved a sigh of
relief at this new routine of his, for however much he might love the dwarf,
he had to be forced to let him participate in his nights out with his friends.
They all used to sit in the dwarf's presence as if they were on eggs, wary of
any joke or chance phrase that might offend him or hurt his feelings. Still,
he couldn't remember his brother ever praising him for his determination
when he saw him preparing to go to the convent, nor even the hibiscus
women, who must have relished the chance to invent hilarious, irreverent
stories about him. And what did the tomb builders think of him? He
couldn't bear to let these thoughts torment him anymore, and hurried res-
olutely to bang on the gates with his giant hands. As usual, he asked for
Georgette. He wanted to see her, to thank her for the affection she had
heaped on him. Time stood still and he felt as if all the power in his body
was in his huge, solid fist with its wide-apart fingers. As he was about to
start hammering on the gates again, he heard a soft voice whispering to him
that Georgette said hello but seeing her was out of the question.

From that moment on he began to have a fixation about the convent.
The iron gates, bolted and barred, had an obsessive hold over him. Georgette's mother had wailed that she would never see her daughter again
even when she died. How did they exist in there for all those years without
being tempted to step over the threshold for a moment?

The gates, unmoved by his devotion to them, had opened a few times
when he was not there; he had discovered their treachery by looking for evidence each morning, and had found tire tracks made by cars, trucks and mule-
drawn carts. He brought his face close to the ground to find out whether the
gates had been opened wide or only on one side, biting his lip in remorse
because he had missed a chance to see the pure ones as they opened the gates
and took the things and paid for them. Where did they get the money from?

As time passed, the dwarf grew ever more obsessed with the convent   10
and its inhabitants. He no longer tried to explain it, and those who saw him
waiting regularly at the gates ceased to worry about him. No doubt they
told themselves that it was something to do with the way dwarves looked
at things, and their different mentality.

Then one night the dwarf failed to return home. His mother wept loudly, blaming herself for not stopping his visits to the convent before. She was
sure that a wild animal had blocked his path and eaten him in one mouth-
ful. His brother suspected that a group of acrobats had kidnapped him and
taken him to the city to train him to work in the circus.

He set off for the convent at high speed. He passed the hibiscus gath-
erers and they directed him to it. One of them winked at him, so he thought
better of asking if they had seen the dwarf. The moment he stood before
the gates he was seized by a violent sense of apprehension. One last grain
of hope had remained, but there was no sign of the dwarf, only the tree and
the blanket that he had hung over a branch and the stone where he used to
sit; a few empty soap-powder cartons, which had been blown up against
the walls; and crushed and broken coffins, some lined with black material
and emblazoned with white crosses. The wind whistled and in the distance
he could see the builders at work on new tombs. He shouted his brother's
name and was answered by silence. He began to blame himself. He had
known that his brother was running away from reality by taking refuge at
the convent, making everyone think that he was strong enough to do the
daily round-trip on foot, about four hours in all, so that he could come
home proud of having had some adventures.

Adventures? The roads were always the same: deserted, except for
stretches of date palms, canals and the sounds of frogs croaking and an
occasional donkey braying.

The brother stumbled hurriedly over the remains of human bones and
crumbling skulls and entered a burial chamber with no roof or doors. He
read on its whitewashed walls, "Remember, O Lord, your obedient servant";
"Remember, O Lord, your erring servant"; "Remember, O Lord, your righteous servant, your repentant servant." Suddenly he burst into tears, mortified
that deep down inside he had blessed his brother's daily visits to the convent. He had not wanted it to be known that he was the dwarf's brother, that
he lived under the same roof as the dwarf. He rushed outside and over to the
tomb builders. One of them was painting a tomb a reddish-brown color and
he asked him if he had seen the dwarf. The man pointed toward the convent. He turned and ran back and pounded on the iron gates, calling out the
dwarf's name. To his astonishment he heard his voice: "Yes?"

"Thank God you're safe," he said, crying tears of joy. "Come on, let's go   15
home, or your mother will do herself mischief."

"Don't worry," replied the dwarf. "Tell her that I've become the nuns'
watchman. I'm happy. Don't worry."

The dwarf had only gained access to the convent by jumping in. Not by
bouncing in off a springy bedstead, an idea he had quickly banished from
his mind, nor by piling the wrecked coffins one on top of another. Instead
he had jumped onto the shoulders of the Lord Bishop, who had come from
the city to pay his annual visit to the convent with several crates of luggage.
The dwarf had planned for this moment for a long time during his vigils by
the gate. He didn't know where he had found the courage, agility and speed
of thought that had enabled him to leap out as soon as he heard the car
engine and alight on the hood before it stopped, like a winged insect, then
jump on the Lord Bishop and relieve him of one of the crates and rush off
with it, his heart beating with almost unbearable ferocity. He hurried disbe-
lievingly through the open gates into the courtyard. To force himself to take
in what was happening, he stood stock-still at the gates once they had been

closed again, seeing them from the inside for the first time. He was certain that they would be opened again shortly and he would be hurled back outside. But things no longer hinged on him. It was as if he had disappeared from sight. The nuns began to gather around in their white habits and crowns of artificial flowers, bowing their heads before the Lord Bishop, who looked like a big black bird, and bending over to kiss his hand.

They were like brides, some of them extremely young and pretty. As they stood in line, their heads drooping bashfully, they resembled a row of beautiful narcissus. For a few moments the dwarf felt embarrassed and scared. He tried to suppress his breathing, which had suddenly become audible. Then he found the Lord Bishop was looking at him. "Is this the one?" he was asking.

One of them, the senior nun, answered him humbly, but with affection, "Yes, My Lord."

Turning back to him the bishop said, "The nuns have told me about you. You have been blessed. You will watch over them."   20

The dwarf felt awkward in the bishop's presence. He didn't know how to answer him. He had been immensely curious to see what was behind the gates; it was like the time he split a battery in two to see what was inside it. And now the bishop was offering him a job as a handyman to the pure ones, and he found himself agreeing to stay in the convent and oversee the cultivation of the fruit and vegetables, without giving the matter more than a moment's thought.

He hadn't imagined the convent would be like this. It bore no relation to its outer walls and to the countryside around it, which was all sand, and the color of sand. The dwarf developed an attachment to the colors in the convent in his early days there. Some of them he was seeing for the first time, sculpted on the walls, or in paintings of animals, bats, angels, flowers, and women holding drums and wearing ornate brocade dresses, flying through the skies or in boats on the sea, with lances and daggers and swords in the background. Then gradually his eyes grew accustomed to the darkness, and he began to see clearly and especially to notice how the nuns lit up the place in their white clothes.

A week went by and the dwarf still hadn't guessed which was Georgette, because they all looked the same. Humbly, they took turns to kneel and pray before the statue of the crucified Christ until their eyes were almost as big as goose eggs. They didn't leave the statue alone day or night, massaging its feet with rose water, putting compresses soaked with oil and perfume on the nails of the crucifix, lighting candles, burning incense, and raising their voices in sweet, sorrowful chanting. They dedicated themselves to their love so wholeheartedly that he once had the feeling that all they did was hover in the air awaiting their turn to cling to the figure on the cross for a few moments before going back to their places. He didn't know why, on a certain day, they brought in a doll and dipped it in water, praying all the time, then rubbed it with colored stones that gave off an enticing fragrance, dried it with an embroidered cloth and dressed it in white baby clothes, which they had taken from a cloth bag studded with precious stones and tied with ropes of pearls.

They were eaten up heart and soul with their love for Christ. This was true love, the like of which he had never found in any novel, translated or otherwise. Never before had he encountered such passion and devotion. Was this what they called sacrifice? The dwarf checked himself. Of course.

They had sacrificed the world and their families for the sake of this love, or for the sake of competing for this love. Closing his eyes, he decided to respond to their love, to help them realize that Christ knew about them and the way they showed their love for him. Moreover, Christ had sent the dwarf as a messenger to them. Wasn't that what the old nun had said? He would help those who were waiting their turn to love Christ by doing their embroidery with them, or by changing the linen in the church. He would snatch the washing out of the boiling water to save them from having to do it. He would have liked to hang it up to dry in the scorching sun, but he wasn't tall enough to reach the washing line. He would light the coals and fan them until they were glowing embers and load them into the flatiron. He would plant flowers and pick them for the garlands they wore on their heads, so that they didn't have to use artificial flowers. He would feed the hens with grain day and night until they were bursting with health and well-being and laid the choicest eggs in the country. He'd polish the nuns' shoes until they could see their faces in them. He'd make their mud-brick beds for them and be close to their sheets—for Christ must smell that they were clean.

At this the dwarf halted his flow of enthusiasm and supressed the leap in his heart, as he did every time he heard the rustle of their bare feet on the coolness of the earth floor. He closed his eyes firmly as if this also closed his ears and steadied his heartbeat, which broke away from its usual rhythm at these unpredictable thoughts. 25

After a few months the dwarf found that he had become quite used to these expectant brides of Christ as they moved around him holding whispered conversations, sighing gently, smiling at him, and not concealing their bad moods in his presence. It was as if he had become one of them, and what was more he had pledged himself to the virgins, swearing that nothing would separate him from them but death. When he died he would put their love to the test. They would either return him to his family or put him in the burial chamber, where he had gone one day with the senior nun to help her sweep the floor. He wouldn't have been able to see anything, but the old woman had lit a little candle and held it up to a casket on a high wooden shelf and raised the lid. He gasped in fright at the sight of a bony frame. The ribs were plainly visible and some flesh still clung around the hands. He heard the old nun's voice whispering, "You shouldn't be frightened. You were sent to us by the Lord."

And so it was. The dwarf only looked at the iron gates occasionally, when he heard his mother's cough and knew that she still had not lost hope. At first this caused him pain, especially when he pictured her sitting on the stone where he had sat. He heard his brother calling him day after day, banging on the gates, urging him to come home. But the dwarf followed instructions, did not reply and turned back to his work. He was growing used to this obligatory link being severed, so that he could concentrate on what he wanted and not let the vibrations from the trivia of the outside world intrude and confuse him. However, when he pictured his mother and his brother taking turns to sit on the stone, he couldn't help thinking of the hoopoe and wondering whether it came to them as it used to come to him, from the direction of the green trees and the canal, or from the barren land, looking for bread crumbs.

Translated from the Arabic by Catherine Cobham [1998]

JAMES BALDWIN (1924–1987)

James Baldwin had an early career as a storefront preacher in Harlem. A Eugene Saxton Fellowship allowed him to write full-time. He received a Rosenwald Fellowship for his book reviews and essays in 1948 and moved to Paris that same year. Baldwin spent the next ten years traveling through Europe before returning to the United States. He was the author of novels, essays, plays, and a collection of poetry. He also received a Guggenheim Fellowship, a Partisan Review fellowship, and a Ford Foundation grant.

Sonny's Blues

I read about it in the paper, in the subway, on my way to work. I read it, and I couldn't believe it, and I read it again. Then perhaps I just stared at it, at the newsprint spelling out his name, spelling out the story. I stared at it in the swinging lights of the subway car, and in the faces and bodies of the people, and in my own face, trapped in the darkness which roared outside.

It was not to be believed and I kept telling myself that, as I walked from the subway station to the high school. And at the same time I couldn't doubt it. I was scared, scared for Sonny. He became real to me again. A great block of ice got settled in my belly and kept melting there slowly all day long, while I taught my classes algebra. It was a special kind of ice. It kept melting, sending trickles of ice water all up and down my veins, but it never got less. Sometimes it hardened and seemed to expand until I felt my guts were going to come spilling out or that I was going to choke or scream. This would always be at a moment when I was remembering some specific thing Sonny had once said or done.

When he was about as old as the boys in my classes his face had been bright and open, there was a lot of copper in it; and he'd had wonderfully direct brown eyes, and great gentleness and privacy. I wondered what he looked like now. He had been picked up, the evening before, in a raid on an apartment downtown, for peddling and using heroin.

I couldn't believe it: but what I mean by that is that I couldn't find any room for it anywhere inside me. I had kept it outside me for a long time. I hadn't wanted to know. I had had suspicions, but I didn't name them, I kept putting them away. I told myself that Sonny was wild, but he wasn't crazy. And he'd always been a good boy, he hadn't ever turned hard or evil or disrespectful, the way kids can, so quick, so quick, especially in Harlem. I didn't want to believe that I'd ever see my brother going down, coming to nothing, all that light in his face gone out, in the condition I'd already seen so many others. Yet it had happened and here I was, talking about algebra to a lot of boys who might, every one of them for all I knew, be popping off needles every time they went to the head. Maybe it did more for them than algebra could.

I was sure that the first time Sonny had ever had horse, he couldn't have been much older than these boys were now. These boys, now, were living as we'd been living then, they were growing up with a rush and their heads bumped abruptly against the low ceiling of their actual possibilities. They were filled with rage. All they really knew were two darknesses, the darkness of their lives, which was now closing in on them, and the darkness of the movies, which had blinded them to that other darkness, and in which they now, vindictively, dreamed, at once more together than they were at any other time, and more alone.

5

When the last bell rang, the last class ended, I let out my breath. It seemed I'd been holding it for all that time. My clothes were wet—I may have looked as though I'd been sitting in a steam bath, all dressed up, all afternoon. I sat alone in the classroom a long time. I listened to the boys outside, downstairs, shouting and cursing and laughing. Their laughter struck me for perhaps the first time. It was not the joyous laughter which—God knows why—one associates with children. It was mocking and insular, its intent was to denigrate. It was disenchanted, and in this, also, lay the authority of their curses. Perhaps I was listening to them because I was thinking about my brother and in them I heard my brother. And myself.

One boy was whistling a tune, at once very complicated and very simple, it seemed to be pouring out of him as though he were a bird, and it sounded very cool and moving through all that harsh, bright air, only just holding its own through all those other sounds.

I stood up and walked over to the window and looked down into the courtyard. It was the beginning of the spring and the sap was rising in the boys. A teacher passed through them every now and again, quickly, as though he or she couldn't wait to get out of that courtyard, to get those boys out of their sight and off their minds. I started collecting my stuff. I thought I'd better get home and talk to Isabel.

The courtyard was almost deserted by the time I got downstairs. I saw this boy standing in the shadow of a doorway, looking just like Sonny. I almost called his name. Then I saw that it wasn't Sonny, but somebody we used to know, a boy from around our block. He'd been Sonny's friend. He'd never been mine, having been too young for me, and, anyway, I'd never liked him. And now, even though he was a grown-up man, he still hung around that block, still spent hours on the street corners, was always high and raggy. I used to run into him from time to time and he'd often work around to asking me for a quarter or fifty cents. He always had some real good excuse, too, and I always gave it to him, I don't know why.

But now, abruptly, I hated him. I couldn't stand the way he looked at   10
me, partly like a dog, partly like a cunning child. I wanted to ask him what the hell he was doing in the school courtyard.

He sort of shuffled over to me, and he said, "I see you got the papers. So you already know about it."

"You mean about Sonny? Yes, I already know about it. How come they didn't get you?"

He grinned. It made him repulsive and it also brought to mind what he'd looked like as a kid. "I wasn't there. I stay away from them people."

"Good for you." I offered him a cigarette and I watched him through the smoke. "You come all the way down here just to tell me about Sonny?"

"That's right." He was sort of shaking his head and his eyes looked   15
strange, as though they were about to cross. The bright sun deadened his damp dark brown skin and it made his eyes look yellow and showed up the dirt in his kinked hair. He smelled funky. I moved a little away from him and I said, "Well, thanks. But I already know about it and I got to get home."

"I'll walk you a little ways," he said. We started walking. There were a couple of kids still loitering in the courtyard and one of them said goodnight to me and looked strangely at the boy beside me.

"What're you going to do?" he asked me. "I mean, about Sonny?"

"Look. I haven't seen Sonny for over a year. I'm not sure I'm going to do anything. Anyway, what the hell *can* I do?"

"That's right," he said quickly, "ain't nothing you can do. Can't much help old Sonny no more, I guess."

It was what I was thinking and so it seemed to me he had no right to say it.   20

"I'm surprised at Sonny, though," he went on—he had a funny way of talking, he looked straight ahead as though he were talking to himself— "I thought Sonny was a smart boy, I thought he was too smart to get hung."

"I guess he thought so too," I said sharply, "and that's how he got hung. And how about you? You're pretty goddamn smart, I bet."

Then he looked directly at me, just for a minute. "I ain't smart," he said. "If I was smart, I'd have reached for a pistol a long time ago."

"Look. Don't tell *me* your sad story, if it was up to me, I'd give you one." Then I felt guilty—guilty, probably, for never having supposed that the poor bastard *had* a story of his own, much less a sad one, and I asked, quickly, "What's going to happen to him now?"

He didn't answer this. He was off by himself some place. "Funny thing,"   25
he said, and from his tone we might have been discussing the quickest way to get to Brooklyn, "when I saw the papers this morning, the first thing I asked myself was if I had anything to do with it. I felt sort of responsible."

I began to listen more carefully. The subway station was on the corner, just before us, and I stopped. He stopped, too. We were in front of a bar and he ducked slightly, peering in, but whoever he was looking for didn't seem to be there. The juke box was blasting away with something black and bouncy and I half watched the barmaid as she danced her way from the juke box to her place behind the bar. And I watched her face as she laughingly responded to something someone said to her, still keeping time to the music. When she smiled one saw the little girl, one sensed the doomed, still-struggling woman beneath the battered face of the semiwhore.

"I never *give* Sonny nothing," the boy said finally, "but a long time ago I come to school high and Sonny asked me how it felt." He paused, I couldn't bear to watch him, I watched the barmaid, and I listened to the music which seemed to be causing the pavement to shake. "I told him it felt great." The music stopped, the barmaid paused and watched the juke box until the music began again. "It did."

All this was carrying me some place I didn't want to go. I certainly didn't want to know how it felt. It filled everything, the people, the houses, the music, the dark, quicksilver barmaid, with menace; and this menace was their reality.

"What's going to happen to him now?" I asked again.

"They'll send him away some place and they'll try to cure him." He   30
shook his head. "Maybe he'll even think he's kicked the habit. Then they'll let him loose"—he gestured, throwing his cigarette into the gutter. "That's all."

"What do you mean, that's *all?*"

But I knew what he meant.

"I *mean,* that's *all.*" He turned his head and looked at me, pulling down the corners of his mouth. "Don't you know what I mean?" he asked, softly.

"How the hell *would* I know what you mean?" I almost whispered it, I don't know why.

"That's right," he said to the air, "how would *he* know what I mean?" He   35
turned toward me again, patient and calm, and yet I somehow felt him shaking, shaking as though he were going to fall apart. I felt that ice in my guts
again, the dread I'd felt all afternoon; and again I watched the barmaid, moving about the bar, washing glasses, and singing. "Listen. They'll let him out
and then it'll just start all over again. That's what I mean."

"You mean—they'll let him out. And then he'll just start working his
way back in again. You mean he'll never kick the habit. Is that what you
mean?"

"That's right," he said, cheerfully. "*You* see what I mean."

"Tell me," I said at last, "why does he want to die? He must want to die,
he's killing himself, why does he want to die?"

He looked at me in surprise. He licked his lips. "He don't want to die.
He wants to live. Don't nobody want to die, ever."

Then I wanted to ask him—too many things. He could not have   40
answered, or if he had, I could not have borne the answers. I started walking. "Well, I guess it's none of my business."

"It's going to be rough on old Sonny," he said. We reached the subway
station. "This is your station?" he asked. I nodded. I took one step down.
"Damn!" he said, suddenly. I looked up at him. He grinned again. "Damn it if
I didn't leave all my money home. You ain't got a dollar on you, have you?
Just for a couple of days, is all."

All at once something inside gave and threatened to come pouring out
of me. I didn't hate him any more. I felt that in another moment I'd start crying like a child.

"Sure," I said. "Don't sweat." I looked in my wallet and didn't have a dollar, I only had a five. "Here," I said. "That hold you?"

He didn't look at it—he didn't want to look at it. A terrible closed look
came over his face, as though he were keeping the number on the bill a
secret from him and me. "Thanks," he said, and now he was dying to see me
go. "Don't worry about Sonny. Maybe I'll write him or something."

"Sure," I said. "You do that. So long."   45

"Be seeing you," he said. I went on down the steps.

And I didn't write Sonny or send him anything for a long time. When I finally did, it was just after my little girl died, he wrote me back a letter which
made me feel like a bastard.

Here's what he said:

Dear brother,

   *You don't know how much I needed to hear from you. I
wanted to write you many a time but I dug how much I must
have hurt you and so I didn't write. But now I feel like a man
who's been trying to climb up out of some deep, real deep and
funky hole and just saw the sun up there, outside. I got to get
outside.*

   *I can't tell you much about how I got here. I mean I don't
know how to tell you. I guess I was afraid of something or I
was trying to escape from something and you know I have
never been very strong in the head (smile). I'm glad Mama
and Daddy are dead and can't see what's happened to their
son and I swear if I'd known what I was doing I would never*

have hurt you so, you and a lot of other fine people who were
nice to me and who believed in me.

I don't want you to think it had anything to do with me
being a musician. It's more than that. Or maybe less than that. I
can't get anything straight in my head down here and I try not
to think about what's going to happen to me when I get out-
side again. Sometimes I think I'm going to flip and never get
outside and sometime I think I'll come straight back. I tell you
one thing, though, I'd rather blow my brains out than go
through this again. But that's what they all say, so they tell me.
If I tell you when I'm coming to New York and if you could
meet me, I sure would appreciate it. Give my love to Isabel and
the kids and I was sure sorry to hear about little Gracie. I wish
I could be like Mama and say the Lord's will be done, but I
don't know it seems to me that trouble is the one thing that
never does get stopped and I don't know what good it does to
blame it on the Lord. But maybe it does some good if you
believe it.

> *Your brother,*
> *Sonny*

Then I kept in constant touch with him and I sent him whatever I
could and I went to meet him when he came back to New York. When I
saw him many things I thought I had forgotten came flooding back to me.
This was because I had begun, finally, to wonder about Sonny, about the life
that Sonny lived inside. This life, whatever it was, had made him older and
thinner and it had deepened the distant stillness in which he had always
moved. He looked very unlike my baby brother. Yet, when he smiled, when
we shook hands, the baby brother I'd never known looked out from the
depths of his private life, like an animal waiting to be coaxed into the light.

"How you been keeping?" he asked me.   50

"All right. And you?"

"Just fine." He was smiling all over his face. "It's good to see you again."

"It's good to see you."

The seven years' difference in our ages lay between us like a chasm: I
wondered if these years would ever operate between us as a bridge. I was
remembering, and it made it hard to catch my breath, that I had been there
when he was born; and I had heard the first words he had ever spoken. When
he started to walk, he walked from our mother straight to me. I caught him
just before he fell when he took the first steps he ever took in this world.

"How's Isabel?"   55

"Just fine. She's dying to see you."

"And the boys?"

"They're fine, too. They're anxious to see their uncle."

"Oh, come on. You know they don't remember me."

"Are you kidding? Of course they remember you."

He grinned again. We got into a taxi. We had a lot to say to each other,   60
far too much to know how to begin.

As the taxi began to move, I asked, "You still want to go to India?"

He laughed. "You still remember that. Hell, no. This place is Indian
enough for me."

"It used to belong to them," I said.

And he laughed again. "They damn sure knew what they were doing   65
when they got rid of it."

Years ago, when he was around fourteen, he'd been all hipped on the
idea of going to India. He read books about people sitting on rocks, naked,
in all kinds of weather, but mostly bad, naturally, and walking barefoot
through hot coals and arriving at wisdom. I used to say that it sounded to
me as though they were getting away from wisdom as fast as they could. I
think he sort of looked down on me for that.

"Do you mind," he asked, "if we have the driver drive alongside the
park? On the west side—I haven't seen the city in so long."

"Of course not," I said. I was afraid that I might sound as though I were
humoring him, but I hoped he wouldn't take it that way.

So we drove along, between the green of the park and the stony, lifeless
elegance of hotels and apartment buildings, toward the vivid, killing streets
of our childhood. These streets hadn't changed, though housing projects
jutted up out of them now like rocks in the middle of a boiling sea. Most of
the houses in which we had grown up had vanished, as had the stores from
which we had stolen, the basements in which we had first tried sex, the
rooftops from which we had hurled tin cans and bricks. But houses exactly
like the houses of our past yet dominated the landscape, boys exactly like
the boys we once had been found themselves smothering in these houses,
came down into the streets for light and air and found themselves encircled
by disaster. Some escaped the trap, most didn't. Those who got out always
left something of themselves behind, as some animals amputate a leg and
leave it in the trap. It might be said, perhaps, that I had escaped, after all, I
was a school teacher; or that Sonny had, he hadn't lived in Harlem for years.
Yet, as the cab moved uptown through streets which seemed, with a rush,
to darken with dark people, and as I covertly studied Sonny's face, it came
to me that what we both were seeking through our separate cab windows
was that part of ourselves which had been left behind. It's always at the
hour of trouble and confrontation that the missing member aches.

We hit 110th Street and started rolling up Lenox Avenue. And I'd   70
known this avenue all my life, but it seemed to me again, as it had seemed
on the day I'd first heard about Sonny's trouble, filled with a hidden menace
which was its very breath of life.

"We almost there," said Sonny.

"Almost." We were both too nervous to say anything more.

We live in a housing project. It hasn't been up long. A few days after it
was up it seemed uninhabitably new, now, of course, it's already rundown.
It looks like a parody of the good, clean, faceless life—God knows the people who live in it do their best to make it a parody. The beat-looking grass
lying around isn't enough to make their lives green, the hedges will never
hold out the streets, and they know it. The big windows fool no one, they
aren't big enough to make space out of no space. They don't bother with
the windows, they watch the TV screen instead. The playground is most
popular with the children who don't play at jacks, or skip rope, or roller
skate, or swing, and they can be found in it after dark. We moved in partly
because it's not too far from where I teach, and partly for the kids; but it's
really just like the houses in which Sonny and I grew up. The same things
happen, they'll have the same things to remember. The moment Sonny and
I started into the house I had the feeling that I was simply bringing him
back into the danger he had almost died trying to escape.

Sonny has never been talkative. So I don't know why I was sure he'd be dying to talk to me when supper was over the first night. Everything went fine, the oldest boy remembered him, and the youngest boy liked him, and Sonny had remembered to bring something for each of them; and Isabel, who is really much nicer than I am, more open and giving, had gone to a lot of trouble about dinner and was genuinely glad to see him. And she's always been able to tease Sonny in a way that I haven't. It was nice to see her face so vivid again and to hear her laugh and watch her make Sonny laugh. She wasn't, or, anyway, she didn't seem to be, at all uneasy or embarrassed. She chatted as though there were no subject which had to be avoided and she got Sonny past his first, faint stiffness. And thank God she was there, for I was filled with that icy dread again. Everything I did seemed awkward to me, and everything I said sounded freighted with hidden meaning. I was trying to remember everything I'd heard about dope addiction and I couldn't help watching Sonny for signs. I wasn't doing it out of malice. I was trying to find out something about my brother. I was dying to hear him tell me he was safe.

"Safe!" my father grunted, whenever Mama suggested trying to move to 75 a neighborhood which might be safer for children. "Safe, hell! Ain't no place safe for kids, nor nobody."

He always went on like this, but he wasn't, ever, really as bad as he sounded, not even on weekends, when he got drunk. As a matter of fact, he was always on the lookout for "something a little better," but he died before he found it. He died suddenly, during a drunken weekend in the middle of the war, when Sonny was fifteen. He and Sonny hadn't ever got on too well. And this was partly because Sonny was the apple of his father's eye. It was because he loved Sonny so much and was frightened for him, that he was always fighting with him. It doesn't do any good to fight with Sonny. Sonny just moves back, inside himself, where he can't be reached. But the principal reason that they never hit it off is that they were so much alike. Daddy was big and rough and loud-talking, just the opposite of Sonny, but they both had—that same privacy.

Mama tried to tell me something about this, just after Daddy died. I was home on leave from the army.

This was the last time I ever saw my mother alive. Just the same, this picture gets all mixed up in my mind with pictures I had of her when she was younger. The way I always see her is the way she used to be on a Sunday afternoon, say, when the old folks were talking after the big Sunday dinner. I always see her wearing pale blue. She'd be sitting on the sofa. And my father would be sitting in the easy chair, not far from her. And the living room would be full of church folks and relatives. There they sit, in chairs all around the living room, and the night is creeping up outside, but nobody knows it yet. You can see the darkness growing against the windowpanes and you hear the street noises every now and again, or maybe the jangling beat of a tambourine from one of the churches close by, but it's real quiet in the room. For a moment nobody's talking, but every face looks darkening, like the sky outside. And my mother rocks a little from the waist, and my father's eyes are closed. Everyone is looking at something a child can't see. For a minute they've forgotten the children. Maybe a kid is lying on the rug, half asleep. Maybe somebody's got a kid in his lap and is absent-mindedly stroking the kid's head. Maybe there's a kid, quiet and big-eyed, curled up in a big chair in the corner. The silence, the darkness coming, and the darkness in the faces frightens the child obscurely. He hopes that the hand which strokes his forehead will never stop—will never die. He hopes that there will never come a time when the old folks won't be sitting around the living room, talking about where they've come from, and what they've seen, and what's happened to them and their kinfolk.

But something deep and watchful in the child knows that this is bound to end, is already ending. In a moment someone will get up and turn on the light. Then the old folks will remember the children and they won't talk any more that day. And when light fills the room, the child is filled with darkness. He knows that everytime this happens he's moved just a little closer to that darkness outside. The darkness outside is what the old folks have been talking about. It's what they've come from. It's what they endure. The child knows that they won't talk any more because if he knows too much about what's happened to *them,* he'll know too much too soon, about what's going to happen to *him.*

The last time I talked to my mother, I remember I was restless. I wanted to get out and see Isabel. We weren't married then and we had a lot to straighten out between us.

There Mama sat, in black, by the window. She was humming an old church song, *Lord, you brought me from a long ways off.* Sonny was out somewhere. Mama kept watching the streets.

"I don't know," she said, "if I'll ever see you again, after you go off from here. But I hope you'll remember the things I tried to teach you."

"Don't talk like that," I said, and smiled. "You'll be here a long time yet."

She smiled, too, but she said nothing. She was quiet for a long time. And I said, "Mama, don't you worry about nothing. I'll be writing all the time, and you be getting the checks. . . ."

"I want to talk to you about your brother," she said, suddenly. "If anything happens to me he ain't going to have nobody to look out for him."

"Mama," I said, "ain't nothing going to happen to you *or* Sonny. Sonny's all right. He's a good boy and he's got good sense."

"It ain't a question of his being a good boy," Mama said, "nor of his having good sense. It ain't only the bad ones, nor yet the dumb ones that gets sucked under." She stopped, looking at me. "Your Daddy once had a brother," she said, and she smiled in a way that made me feel she was in pain. "You didn't never know that, did you?"

"No," I said, "I never knew that," and I watched her face.

"Oh, yes," she said, "your Daddy had a brother." She looked out of the window again. "I know you never saw your Daddy cry. But *I* did—many a time, through all these years."

I asked her, "What happened to his brother? How come nobody's ever talked about him?"

This was the first time I ever saw my mother look old.

"His brother got killed," she said, "when he was just a little younger than you are now. I knew him. He was a fine boy. He was maybe a little full of the devil, but he didn't mean nobody no harm."

Then she stopped and the room was silent, exactly as it had sometimes been on those Sunday afternoons. Mama kept looking out into the streets.

"He used to have a job in the mill," she said, "and, like all young folks, he just liked to perform on Saturday nights. Saturday nights, him and your father would drift around to different places, go to dances and things like that, or just sit around with people they knew, and your father's brother would sing, he had a fine voice, and play along with himself on his guitar. Well, this particular Saturday night, him and your father was coming home from some place, and they were both a little drunk and there was a moon that night, it was bright like day. Your father's brother was feeling kind of good, and he was whistling to himself, and he had his guitar slung over his shoulder. They was coming down a hill and beneath them was a road that turned off from the highway. Well, your father's brother, being always kind of frisky, decided to run down this hill, and he did, with that guitar banging and clanging behind him, and he ran across the road, and he was making water behind a tree. And your father was sort of amused at him and he was still coming down the hill, kind of slow. Then he heard a car motor and that same minute his brother stepped from behind the tree, into the road, in the moonlight. And he started to cross the road. And your father started to run down the hill, he says he don't know why. This car was full of white men. They was all drunk, and when they seen your father's brother they let out a great whoop and holler and they aimed the car straight at him. They was having fun, they just wanted to scare him, the way they do sometimes, you know. But they was drunk. And I guess the boy, being drunk, too, and scared, kind of lost his head. By the time he jumped it was too late. Your father says he heard his brother scream when the car rolled over him, and he heard the wood of that guitar when it give, and he heard them strings go flying, and he heard them white men shouting, and the car kept on a-going and it ain't stopped till this day. And, time your father got down the hill, his brother weren't nothing but blood and pulp."

Tears were gleaming on my mother's face. There wasn't anything I could say.   95

"He never mentioned it," she said, "because I never let him mention it before you children. Your Daddy was like a crazy man that night and for many a night thereafter. He says he never in his life seen anything as dark as that road after the lights of that car had gone away. Weren't nothing, weren't nobody on that road, just your Daddy and his brother and that busted guitar. Oh, yes. Your Daddy never did really get right again. Till the day he died he weren't sure but that every white man he saw was the man that killed his brother."

She stopped and took out her handkerchief and dried her eyes and looked at me.

"I ain't telling you all this," she said, "to make you scared or bitter or to make you hate nobody. I'm telling you this because you got a brother. And the world ain't changed."

I guess I didn't want to believe this. I guess she saw this in my face. She turned away from me, toward the window again, searching those streets.

"But I praise my Redeemer," she said at last, "that He called your Daddy   100 home before me. I ain't saying it to throw no flowers at myself, but, I declare, it keeps me from feeling too cast down to know I helped your father get safely through this world. Your father always acted like he was the roughest, strongest man on earth. And everybody took him to be like that. But if he hadn't had *me* there—to see his tears!"

She was crying again. Still, I couldn't move. I said, "Lord, Lord, Mama, I didn't know it was like that."

"Oh, honey," she said, "there's a lot that you don't know. But you are going to find it out." She stood up from the window and came over to me. "You got to hold on to your brother," she said, "and don't let him fall, no matter what it looks like is happening to him and no matter how evil you gets with him. You going to be evil with him many a time. But don't you forget what I told you, you hear?"

"I won't forget," I said. "Don't you worry, I won't forget. I won't let nothing happen to Sonny."

My mother smiled as though she were amused at something she saw in my face. Then, "You may not be able to stop nothing from happening. But you got to let him know you's *there*."

Two days later I was married, and then I was gone. And I had a lot of things on my mind and I pretty well forgot my promise to Mama until I got shipped home on a special furlough for her funeral.   105

And, after the funeral, with just Sonny and me alone in the empty kitchen, I tried to find out something about him.

"What do you want to do?" I asked him.

"I'm going to be a musician," he said.

For he had graduated, in the time I had been away, from dancing to the juke box to finding out who was playing what, and what they were doing with it, and he had bought himself a set of drums.

"You mean, you want to be a drummer?" I somehow had the feeling   110
that being a drummer might be all right for other people but not for my brother Sonny.

"I don't think," he said, looking at me very gravely, "that I'll ever be a good drummer. But I think I can play a piano."

I frowned. I'd never played the role of the older brother quite so seriously before, had scarcely ever, in fact, *asked* Sonny a damn thing. I sensed myself in the presence of something I didn't really know how to handle, didn't understand. So I made my frown a little deeper as I asked: "What kind of musician do you want to be?"

He grinned. "How many kinds do you think there are?"

"Be *serious*," I said.

He laughed, throwing his head back, and then looked at me. "I *am* seri-   115
ous."

"Well, then, for Christ's sake, stop kidding around and answer a serious question. I mean, do you want to be a concert pianist, you want to play classical music and all that, or—or what?" Long before I finished he was laughing again. "For Christ's *sake*, Sonny!"

He sobered, but with difficulty. "I'm sorry. But you sound so—*scared!*" and he was off again.

"Well, you may think it's funny now, baby, but it's not going to be so funny when you have to make your living at it, let me tell you *that*." I was furious because I knew he was laughing at me and I didn't know why.

"No," he said, very sober now, and afraid, perhaps, that he'd hurt me, "I don't want to be a classical pianist. That isn't what interests me. I mean"— he paused, looking hard at me, as though his eyes would help me to understand, and then gestured helplessly, as though perhaps his hand would help—"I mean, I'll have a lot of studying to do, and I'll have to study *every-*

thing, but, I mean, I want to play *with*—jazz musicians." He stopped. "I want
to play jazz," he said.

Well, the word had never before sounded as heavy, as real, as it sound-   120
ed that afternoon in Sonny's mouth. I just looked at him and I was probably
frowning a real frown by this time. I simply couldn't see why on earth he'd
want to spend his time hanging around nightclubs, clowning around on
bandstands, while people pushed each other around a dance floor. It
seemed—beneath him, somehow. I had never thought about it before, had
never been forced to, but I suppose I had always put jazz musicians in a
class with what Daddy called "good-time people."

"Are you *serious?*"

"Hell, *yes*, I'm serious."

He looked more helpless than ever, and annoyed, and deeply hurt.

I suggested, helpfully: "You mean—like Louis Armstrong?"

His face closed as though I'd struck him. "No. I'm not talking about   125
none of that old-time, down home crap."

"Well, look, Sonny, I'm sorry, don't get mad. I just don't altogether get it,
that's all. Name somebody—you know, a jazz musician you admire."

"Bird."

"Who?"

"Bird! Charlie Parker! Don't they teach you nothing in the goddamn
army?"

I lit a cigarette. I was surprised and then a little amused to discover that   130
I was trembling. "I've been out of touch," I said. "You'll have to be patient
with me. Now. Who's this Parker character?"

"He's just one of the greatest jazz musicians alive," said Sonny, sullenly,
his hands in his pockets, his back to me. "Maybe *the* greatest," he added, bitterly, "that's probably why *you* never heard of him."

"All right," I said, "I'm ignorant. I'm sorry. I'll go out and buy all the cat's
records right away, all right?"

"It don't," said Sonny, with dignity, "make any difference to me. I don't
care what you listen to. Don't do me no favors."

I was beginning to realize that I'd never seen him so upset before.
With another part of my mind I was thinking that this would probably
turn out to be one of those things kids go through and that I shouldn't
make it seem important by pushing it too hard. Still, I didn't think it
would do any harm to ask: "Doesn't all this take a lot of time? Can you
make a living at it?"

He turned back to me and half leaned, half sat, on the kitchen table.   135
"Everything takes time," he said, "and—well, yes, sure, I can make a living at
it. But what I don't seem to be able to make you understand is that it's the
only thing I want to do."

"Well, Sonny," I said, gently, "you know people can't always do exactly
what they *want* to do—"

"*No*, I don't know that," said Sonny, surprising me. "I think people
ought to do what they want to do, what else are they alive for?"

"You getting to be a big boy," I said desperately, "it's time you started
thinking about your future."

"I'm thinking about my future," said Sonny, grimly. "I think about it all
the time."

I gave up. I decided, if he didn't change his mind, that we could always   140
talk about it later. "In the meantime," I said, "you got to finish school." We had
already decided that he'd have to move in with Isabel and her folks. I knew
this wasn't the ideal arrangement because Isabel's folks are inclined to be
dicty and they hadn't especially wanted Isabel to marry me. But I didn't
know what else to do. "And we have to get you fixed up at Isabel's."

There was a long silence. He moved from the kitchen table to the window. "That's a terrible idea. You know it yourself."

"Do you have a *better* idea?"

He just walked up and down the kitchen for a minute. He was as tall as
I was. He had started to shave. I suddenly had the feeling that I didn't know
him at all.

He stopped at the kitchen table and picked up my cigarettes. Looking
at me with a kind of mocking, amused defiance, he put one between his
lips. "You mind?"

"You smoking already?"   145

He lit the cigarette and nodded, watching me through the smoke. "I just
wanted to see if I'd have the courage to smoke in front of you." He grinned
and blew a great cloud of smoke to the ceiling. "It was easy." He looked at
my face. "Come on, now. I bet you was smoking at my age, tell the truth."

I didn't say anything but the truth was on my face, and he laughed. But
now there was something very strained in his laugh. "Sure. And I bet that
ain't all you was doing."

He was frightening me a little. "Cut the crap," I said. "We already decided that you was going to go and live at Isabel's. Now what's got into you all
of a sudden?"

"*You* decided it," he pointed out. "*I* didn't decide nothing." He stopped
in front of me, leaning against the stove, arms loosely folded. "Look, brother.
I don't want to stay in Harlem no more, I really don't." He was very earnest.
He looked at me, then over toward the kitchen window. There was something in his eyes I'd never seen before, some thoughtfulness, some worry all
his own. He rubbed the muscle of one arm. "It's time I was getting out of
here."

"Where do you want to *go*, Sonny?"   150

"I want to join the army. Or the navy, I don't care. If I say I'm old
enough, they'll believe me."

Then I got mad. It was because I was so scared. "You must be crazy. You
goddamn fool, what the hell do you want to go and join the *army* for?"

"I just told you. To get out of Harlem."

"Sonny, you haven't even finished *school*. And if you really want to be
a musician, how do you expect to study if you're in the *army?*"

He looked at me, trapped, and in anguish. "There's ways. I might be able   155
to work out some kind of deal. Anyway, I'll have the G.I. Bill when I come
out."

"*If* you come out." We stared at each other. "Sonny, please. Be reasonable. I know the setup is far from perfect. But we got to do the best we
can."

"I ain't learning nothing in school," he said. "Even when I go." He turned
away from me and opened the window and threw his cigarette out into the
narrow alley. I watched his back. "At least, I ain't learning nothing you'd
want me to learn." He slammed the window so hard I thought the glass

would fly out, and turned back to me. "And I'm sick of the stink of these garbage cans!"

"Sonny," I said, "I know how you feel. But if you don't finish school now, you're going to be sorry later that you didn't." I grabbed him by the shoulders. "And you only got another year. It ain't so bad. And I'll come back and I swear I'll help you do *whatever* you want to do. Just try to put up with it till I come back. Will you please do that? For me?"

He didn't answer and he wouldn't look at me.

"Sonny. You hear me?"   160

He pulled away. "I hear you. But you never hear anything *I* say."

I didn't know what to say to that. He looked out of the window and then back at me. "OK," he said, and sighed. "I'll try."

Then I said, trying to cheer him up a little, "They got a piano at Isabel's. You can practice on it."

And as a matter of fact, it did cheer him up for a minute. "That's right," he said to himself. "I forgot that." His face relaxed a little. But the worry, the thoughtfulness, played on it still, the way shadows play on a face which is staring into the fire.

But I thought I'd never hear the end of that piano. At first, Isabel would   165
write me, saying how nice it was that Sonny was so serious about his music and how, as soon as he came in from school, or wherever he had been when he was supposed to be at school, he went straight to that piano and stayed there until suppertime. And, after supper, he went back to that piano and stayed there until everybody went to bed. He was at the piano all day Saturday and all day Sunday. Then he bought a record player and started playing records. He'd play one record over and over again, all day long sometimes, and he'd improvise along with it on the piano. Or he'd play one section of the record, one chord, one change, one progression, then he'd do it on the piano. Then back to the record. Then back to the piano.

Well, I really don't know how they stood it. Isabel finally confessed that it wasn't like living with a person at all, it was like living with sound. And the sound didn't make any sense to her, didn't make any sense to any of them—naturally. They began, in a way, to be afflicted by this presence that was living in their home. It was as though Sonny were some sort of god, or monster. He moved in an atmosphere which wasn't like theirs at all. They fed him and he ate, he washed himself, he walked in and out of their door; he certainly wasn't nasty or unpleasant or rude, Sonny isn't any of those things; but it was as though he were all wrapped up in some cloud, some fire, some vision all his own; and there wasn't any way to reach him.

At the same time, he wasn't really a man yet, he was still a child, and they had to watch out for him in all kinds of ways. They certainly couldn't throw him out. Neither did they dare to make a great scene about that piano because even they dimly sensed, as I sensed, from so many thousands of miles away, that Sonny was at that piano playing for his life.

But he hadn't been going to school. One day a letter came from the school board and Isabel's mother got it—there had, apparently, been other letters but Sonny had torn them up. This day, when Sonny came in, Isabel's mother showed him the letter and asked where he'd been spending his time. And she finally got it out of him that he'd been down in Greenwich Village, with musicians and other characters, in a white girl's apartment.

And this scared her and she started to scream at him and what came up, once she began—though she denies it to this day—was what sacrifices they were making to give Sonny a decent home and how little he appreciated it.

Sonny didn't play the piano that day. By evening, Isabel's mother had calmed down but then there was the old man to deal with, and Isabel herself. Isabel says she did her best to be calm but she broke down and started crying. She says she just watched Sonny's face. She could tell, by watching him, what was happening with him. And what was happening was that they penetrated his cloud, they had reached him. Even if their fingers had been a thousand times more gentle than human fingers ever are, he could hardly help feeling that they had stripped him naked and were spitting on that nakedness. For he also had to see that his presence, that music, which was life or death to him, had been torture for them and that they had endured it, not at all for his sake, but only for mine. And Sonny couldn't take that. He can take it a little better today than he could then but he's still not very good at it and, frankly, I don't know anybody who is.

The silence of the next few days must have been louder than the sound   170
of all the music ever played since time began. One morning, before she went to work, Isabel was in his room for something and she suddenly realized that all of his records were gone. And she knew for certain that he was gone. And he was. He went as far as the navy would carry him. He finally sent me a postcard from some place in Greece and that was the first I knew that Sonny was still alive. I didn't see him any more until we were both back in New York and the war had long been over.

He was a man by then, of course, but I wasn't willing to see it. He came by the house from time to time, but we fought almost every time we met. I didn't like the way he carried himself, loose and dreamlike all the time, and I didn't like his friends, and his music seemed to be merely an excuse for the life he led. It sounded just that weird and disordered.

Then we had a fight, a pretty awful fight, and I didn't see him for months. By and by I looked him up, where he was living, in a furnished room in the Village, and I tried to make it up. But there were lots of people in the room and Sonny just lay on his bed, and he wouldn't come downstairs with me, and he treated these other people as though they were his family and I weren't. So I got mad and then he got mad, and then I told him that he might just as well be dead as live the way he was living. Then he stood up and he told me not to worry about him any more in life, that he *was* dead as far as I was concerned. Then he pushed me to the door and the other people looked on as though nothing were happening, and he slammed the door behind me. I stood in the hallway, staring at the door. I heard somebody laugh in the room and then the tears came to my eyes. I started down the steps, whistling to keep from crying, I kept whistling to myself, *You going to need me, baby, one of these cold, rainy days.*

I read about Sonny's trouble in the spring. Little Grace died in the fall. She was a beautiful little girl. But she only lived a little over two years. She died of polio and she suffered. She had a slight fever for a couple of days, but it didn't seem like anything and we just kept her in bed. And we would certainly have called the doctor, but the fever dropped, she seemed to be all right. So we thought it had just been a cold. Then, one day, she was up, playing, Isabel was in the kitchen fixing lunch for the two boys when they'd come in from school, and she heard Grace fall down in the living room. When you have a lot of children you don't always start running when one of them falls, unless they start screaming or something. And, this time, Grace was quiet. Yet, Isabel says that when she heard that *thump* and then that silence, something happened in her to make her afraid. And she ran to the living room and there was little Grace on the floor, all twisted up, and the reason she hadn't screamed was that she couldn't get her breath. And when she did scream, it was the worst sound, Isabel says, that she'd ever heard in all her life, and she still hears it sometimes in her dreams. Isabel will sometimes wake me up with a low, moaning, strangled sound and I have to be quick to awaken her and hold her to me and where Isabel is weeping against me seems a mortal wound.

I think I may have written Sonny the very day that little Grace was buried. I was sitting in the living room in the dark, by myself, and I suddenly thought of Sonny. My trouble made his real.

One Saturday afternoon, when Sonny had been living with us, or, anyway, been in our house, for nearly two weeks, I found myself wandering aimlessly about the living room, drinking from a can of beer, and trying to work up the courage to search Sonny's room. He was out, he was usually out whenever I was home, and Isabel had taken the children to see their grandparents. Suddenly I was standing still in front of the living room window, watching Seventh Avenue. The idea of searching Sonny's room made me still. I scarcely dared to admit to myself what I'd be searching for. I didn't know what I'd do if I found it. Or if I didn't.   175

On the sidewalk across from me, near the entrance to a barbecue joint, some people were holding an old-fashioned revival meeting. The barbecue cook, wearing a dirty white apron, his conked hair reddish and metallic in the pale sun, and a cigarette between his lips, stood in the doorway, watching them. Kids and older people paused in their errands and stood there, along with some older men and a couple of very tough-looking women who watched everything that happened on the avenue, as though they owned it, or were maybe owned by it. Well, they were watching this, too. The revival was being carried on by three sisters in black, and a brother. All they had were their voices and their Bibles and a tambourine. The brother was testifying and while he testified two of the sisters stood together, seeming to say, amen, and the third sister walked around with the tambourine outstretched and a couple of people dropped coins into it. Then the brother's testimony ended and the sister who had been taking up the collection dumped the coins into her palm and transferred them to the pocket of her long black robe. Then she raised both hands, striking the tambourine against the air, and then against one hand, and she started to sing. And the two other sisters and the brother joined in.

It was strange, suddenly, to watch, though I had been seeing these street meetings all my life. So, of course, had everybody else down there. Yet, they paused and watched and listened and I stood still at the window. *"Tis the old ship of Zion,"* they sang, and the sister with the tambourine kept a steady, jangling beat, *"it has rescued many a thousand!"* Not a soul under the sound of their voices was hearing this song for the first time, not one of them had been rescued. Nor had they seen much in the way of rescue work being done around them. Neither did they especially believe in the holiness of the three sisters and the brother, they knew too much about them, knew where they lived, and how. The woman with the tambourine, whose voice dominated the air, whose face was bright with joy, was divided by very little from the woman who stood watching her, a cigarette between her heavy, chapped lips, her hair a cuckoo's nest, her face scarred and swollen from many beatings, and her black eyes glittering like coal. Perhaps they both knew this, which was why, when, as rarely, they addressed each other, they addressed each other as Sister. As the singing filled the air the watching, listening faces underwent a change, the eyes focusing on something within; the music seemed to soothe a poison out of them; and time seemed, nearly, to fall away from the sullen, belligerent, battered faces, as though they were fleeing back to their first condition, while dreaming of their last. The barbecue cook half shook his head and smiled, and dropped his cigarette and disappeared into his joint. A man fumbled in his pockets for change and stood holding it in his hand impatiently, as though he had just remembered a pressing appointment further up the avenue. He looked furious. Then I saw Sonny, standing on the edge of the crowd. He was carrying a wide, flat notebook with a green cover, and it made him look, from where I was standing, almost like a schoolboy. The coppery sun brought out the copper in his skin, he was very faintly smiling, standing very still. Then the singing stopped, the tambourine turned into a collection plate again. The furious man dropped in his coins and vanished, so did a couple of the women, and Sonny dropped some change in the plate, looking directly at the woman with a little smile. He started across the avenue, toward the house. He has a slow, loping walk, something like the way Harlem hipsters walk, only he's imposed on this his own half-beat. I had never really noticed it before.

    I stayed at the window, both relieved and apprehensive. As Sonny disappeared from my sight, they began singing again. And they were still singing when his key turned in the lock.

    "Hey," he said.

    "Hey, yourself. You want some beer?"   180

    "No. Well, maybe." But he came up to the window and stood beside me, looking out. "What a warm voice," he said.

    They were singing *If I could only hear my mother pray again!*

    "Yes," I said, "and she can sure beat that tambourine."

    "But what a terrible song," he said, and laughed. He dropped his notebook on the sofa and disappeared into the kitchen. "Where's Isabel and the kids?"

    "I think they went to see their grandparents. You hungry?"   185

    "No." He came back into the living room with his can of beer. "You want to come some place with me tonight?"

    I sensed, I don't know how, that I couldn't possibly say no. "Sure. Where?"

    He sat down on the sofa and picked up his notebook and started leafing through it. "I'm going to sit in with some fellows in a joint in the Village."

    "You mean, you're going to play, tonight?"

    "That's right." He took a swallow of his beer and moved back to the   190 window. He gave me a sidelong look. "If you can stand it."

    "I'll try," I said.

He smiled to himself and we both watched as the meeting across the way broke up. The three sisters and the brother, heads bowed, were singing *God be with you till we meet again.* The faces around them were very quiet. Then the song ended. The small crowd dispersed. We watched the three women and the lone man walk slowly up the avenue.

"When she was singing before," said Sonny, abruptly, "her voice remind-ed me for a minute of what heroin feels like sometimes—when it's in your veins. It makes you feel sort of warm and cool at the same time. And distant. And—and sure." He sipped his beer, very deliberately not looking at me. I watched his face. "It makes you feel—in control. Sometimes you've got to have that feeling."

"Do you?" I sat down slowly in the easy chair.

"Sometimes." He went to the sofa and picked up his notebook again.   195 "Some people do."

"In order," I asked, "to play?" And my voice was very ugly, full of con-tempt and anger.

"Well"—he looked at me with great, troubled eyes, as though, in fact, he hoped his eyes would tell me things he could never otherwise say— "they *think* so. And *if* they think so—!"

"And what do *you* think?" I asked.

He sat on the sofa and put his can of beer on the floor. "I don't know," he said, and I couldn't be sure if he were answering my question or pursu-ing his thoughts. His face didn't tell me. "It's not so much to *play.* It's to *stand* it, to be able to make it at all. On any level." He frowned and smiled: "In order to keep from shaking to pieces."

"But these friends of yours," I said, "they seem to shake themselves to   200 pieces pretty goddamn fast."

"Maybe." He played with the notebook. And something told me that I should curb my tongue, that Sonny was doing his best to talk, that I should listen. "But of course you only know the ones that've gone to pieces. Some don't—or at least they haven't yet and that's just about all *any* of us can say." He paused. "And then there are some who just live, really, in hell, and they know it and they see what's happening and they go right on. I don't know." He sighed, dropped the notebook, folded his arms. "Some guys, you can tell from the way they play, they on something *all* the time. And you can see that, well, it makes something real for them. But of course," he picked up his beer from the floor and sipped it and put the can down again, "they *want* to, too, you've got to see that. Even some of them that say they don't—*some,* not all."

"And what about you?" I asked—I couldn't help it. "What about you? Do *you* want to?"

He stood up and walked to the window and remained silent for a long time. Then he sighed. "Me," he said. Then: "While I was downstairs before, on my way here, listening to that woman sing, it struck me all of a sudden how much suffering she must have had to go through—to sing like that. It's *repulsive* to think you have to suffer that much."

I said: "But there's no way not to suffer—is there, Sonny?"

"I believe not," he said and smiled, "but that's never stopped anyone   205 from trying." He looked at me. "Has it?" I realized, with this mocking look, that there stood between us, forever, beyond the power of time or forgive-ness, the fact that I had held silence—so long!—when he had needed human speech to help him. He turned back to the window. "No, there's no way not to suffer. But you try all kinds of ways to keep from drowning in it, to keep on top of it, and to make it seem—well, like *you*. Like you did something, all right, and now you're suffering for it. You know?" I said nothing. "Well you know," he said, impatiently, "why *do* people suffer? Maybe it's better to do something to give it a reason, *any* reason."

"But we just agreed," I said "that there's no way not to suffer. Isn't it better, then, just to—take it?"

"But nobody just takes it," Sonny cried, "that's what I'm telling you! *Everybody* tries not to. You're just hung up on the *way* some people try—it's not *your* way!"

The hair on my face began to itch, my face felt wet. "That's not true," I said, "that's not true. I don't give a damn what other people do, I don't even care how they suffer. I just care how *you* suffer." And he looked at me. "Please believe me," I said, "I don't want to see you—die—trying not to suffer."

"I won't," he said, flatly, "die trying not to suffer. At least, not any faster than anybody else."

"But there's no need," I said, trying to laugh, "is there? in killing yourself."   210

I wanted to say more, but I couldn't. I wanted to talk about will power and how life could be—well, beautiful. I wanted to say that it was all within; but was it? or, rather, wasn't that exactly the trouble? And I wanted to promise that I would never fail him again. But it would all have sounded—empty words and lies.

So I made the promise to myself and prayed that I would keep it.

"It's terrible sometimes, inside," he said, "that's what's the trouble. You walk these streets, black and funky and cold, and there's not really a living ass to talk to, and there's nothing shaking, and there's no way of getting it out—that storm inside. You can't talk it and you can't make love with it, and when you finally try to get with it and play it, you realize *nobody's* listening. So *you've* got to listen. You got to find a way to listen."

And then he walked away from the window and sat on the sofa again, as though all the wind had suddenly been knocked out of him. "Sometimes you'll do *anything* to play, even cut your mother's throat." He laughed and looked at me. "Or your brother's." Then he sobered. "Or your own." Then: "Don't worry. I'm all right now and I think I'll *be* all right. But I can't forget—where I've been. I don't mean just the physical place I've been, I mean where I've *been*. And *what* I've been."

"What have you been, Sonny?" I asked.   215

He smiled—but sat sideways on the sofa, his elbow resting on the back, his fingers playing with his mouth and chin, not looking at me. "I've been something I didn't recognize, didn't know I could be. Didn't know anybody could be." He stopped, looking inward, looking helplessly young, looking old. "I'm not talking about it now because I feel *guilty* or anything like that—maybe it would be better if I did, I don't know. Anyway, I can't really talk about it. Not to you, not to anybody," and now he turned and faced me. "Sometimes, you know, and it was actually when I was most *out* of the world, I felt that I was in it, that I was *with* it, really, and I could play or I didn't really have to *play*, it just came out of me, it was there. And I don't know how I played, thinking about it now, but I know I did awful things, those times, sometimes, to people. Or it wasn't that I *did* anything to them—it was that they weren't real." He picked up the beer can; it was empty; he rolled it between his palms: "And other times—well, I needed a fix, I needed to find a place to lean, I needed to clear a space to *listen*—and I couldn't find it, and I—went crazy, I did terrible things to *me, I* was terrible *for* me." He began pressing the beer can between his hands, I watched the metal begin to give. It glittered, as he played with it, like a knife, and I was afraid he would cut himself, but I said nothing. "Oh well. I can never tell you. I was all by myself at the bottom of something, stinking and sweating and crying and shaking, and I smelled it, you know? *my* stink, and I thought I'd die if I couldn't get away from it and yet, all the same, I knew that everything I was doing was just locking me in with it. And I didn't know," he paused, still flattening the beer can, "I didn't know, I still *don't* know, something kept telling me that maybe it was good to smell your own stink, but I didn't think that *that* was what I'd been trying to do— and—who can stand it?" and he abruptly dropped the ruined beer can, looking at me with a small, still smile, and then rose, walking to the window as though it were the lodestone rock. I watched his face, he watched the avenue. "I couldn't tell you when Mama died—but the reason I wanted to leave Harlem so bad was to get away from drugs. And then, when I ran away, that's what I was running from—really. When I came back, nothing had changed, *I* hadn't changed, I was just—older." And he stopped, drumming with his fingers on the windowpane. The sun had vanished, soon darkness would fall. I watched his face. "It can come again," he said, almost as though speaking to himself. Then he turned to me. "It can come again," he repeated. "I just want you to know that."

"All right," I said, at last. "So it can come again. All right."

He smiled, but the smile was sorrowful. "I had to try to tell you," he said.

"Yes," I said. "I understand that."

"You're my brother," he said, looking straight at me, and not smiling at all.   220

"Yes," I repeated, "yes. I understand that."

He turned back to the window, looking out. "All that hatred down there," he said, "all that hatred and misery and love. It's a wonder it doesn't blow the avenue apart."

We went to the only nightclub on a short, dark street, downtown. We squeezed through the narrow, chattering, jam-packed bar to the entrance of the big room, where the bandstand was. And we stood there for a moment, for the lights were very dim in this room and we couldn't see. Then, "Hello, boy," said a voice and an enormous black man, much older than Sonny or myself, erupted out of all that atmospheric lighting and put an arm around Sonny's shoulder. "I been sitting right here," he said, "waiting for you."

He had a big voice, too, and heads in the darkness turned toward us.

Sonny grinned and pulled a little away, and said, "Creole, this is my brother. I told you about him."   225

Creole shook my hand. "I'm glad to meet you, son," he said, and it was clear that he was glad to meet me *there,* for Sonny's sake. And he smiled, "You got a real musician in *your* family," and he took his arm from Sonny's shoulder and slapped him, lightly, affectionately, with the back of his hand.

"Well. Now I've heard it all," said a voice behind us. This was another musician, and a friend of Sonny's, a coal-black, cheerful-looking man, built close to the ground. He immediately began confiding to me, at the top of his lungs, the most terrible things about Sonny, his teeth gleaming like a light-house and his laugh coming up out of him like the beginning of an earth-quake. And it turned out that everyone at the bar knew Sonny, or almost everyone; some were musicians, working there, or nearby, or not working, some were simply hangers-on, and some were there to hear Sonny play. I was introduced to all of them and they were all very polite to me. Yet, it was clear that, for them, I was only Sonny's brother. Here, I was in Sonny's world. Or, rather: his kingdom. Here, it was not even a question that his veins bore royal blood.

They were going to play soon and Creole installed me, by myself, at a table in a dark corner. Then I watched them, Creole, and the little black man, and Sonny, and the others, while they horsed around, standing just below the bandstand. The light from the bandstand spilled just a little short of them and, watching them laughing and gesturing and moving about, I had the feeling that they, nevertheless, were being most careful not to step into that circle of light too suddenly: that if they moved into the light too suddenly, without thinking, they would perish in flame. Then, while I watched, one of them, the small, black man, moved into the light and crossed the bandstand and started fooling around with his drums. Then—being funny and being, also, extremely ceremonious—Creole took Sonny by the arm and led him to the piano. A woman's voice called Sonny's name and a few hands started clapping. And Sonny, also being funny and being ceremonious, and so touched, I think, that he could have cried, but neither hiding it nor showing it, riding it like a man, grinned, and put both hands to his heart and bowed from the waist.

Creole then went to the bass fiddle and a lean, very bright-skinned brown man jumped up on the bandstand and picked up his horn. So there they were, and the atmosphere on the bandstand and in the room began to change and tighten. Someone stepped up to the microphone and announced them. Then there were all kinds of murmurs. Some people at the bar shushed others. The waitress ran around, frantically getting in the last orders, guys and chicks got closer to each other, and the lights on the bandstand, on the quartet, turned to a kind of indigo. Then they all looked different there. Creole looked about him for the last time, as though he were making certain that all his chickens were in the coop, and then he—jumped and struck the fiddle. And there they were.

All I know about music is that not many people ever really hear it. And even then, on the rare occasions when something opens within, and the music enters, what we mainly hear, or hear corroborated, are person-al, private, vanishing evocations. But the man who creates the music is hearing something else, is dealing with the roar rising from the void and imposing order on it as it hits the air. What is evoked in him, then, is of another order, more terrible because it has no words, and triumphant, too, for that same reason. And his triumph, when he triumphs, is ours. I just watched Sonny's face. His face was troubled, he was working hard, but he wasn't with it. And I had the feeling that, in a way, everyone on the bandstand was waiting for him, both waiting for him and pushing him along. But as I began to watch Creole, I realized that it was Creole who

230

held them all back. He had them on a short rein. Up there, keeping the beat with his whole body, wailing on the fiddle, with his eyes half closed, he was listening to everything, but he was listening to Sonny. He was having a dialogue with Sonny. He wanted Sonny to leave the shoreline and strike out for the deep water. He was Sonny's witness that deep water and drowning were not the same thing—he had been there, and he knew. And he wanted Sonny to know. He was waiting for Sonny to do the things on the keys which would let Creole know that Sonny was in the water.

And, while Creole listened, Sonny moved, deep within, exactly like someone in torment. I had never before thought of how awful the relationship must be between the musician and his instrument. He has to fill it, this instrument, with the breath of life, his own. He has to make it do what he wants it to do. And a piano is just a piano. It's made out of so much wood and wires and little hammers and big ones, and ivory. While there's only so much you can do with it, the only way to find this out is to try; to try and make it do everything.

And Sonny hadn't been near a piano for over a year. And he wasn't on much better terms with his life, not the life that stretched before him now. He and the piano stammered, started one way, got scared, stopped; started another way, panicked, marked time, started again; then seemed to have found a direction, panicked again, got stuck. And the face I saw on Sonny I'd never seen before. Everything had been burned out of it, and, at the same time, things usually hidden were being burned in, by the fire and fury of the battle which was occurring in him up there.

Yet, watching Creole's face as they neared the end of the first set, I had the feeling that something had happened, something I hadn't heard. Then they finished, there was scattered applause, and then, without an instant's warning, Creole started into something else, it was almost sardonic, it was *Am I Blue.* And, as though he commanded, Sonny began to play. Something began to happen. And Creole let out the reins. The dry, low, black man said something awful on the drums, Creole answered, and the drums talked back. Then the horn insisted, sweet and high, slightly detached perhaps, and Creole listened, commenting now and then, dry, and driving, beautiful and calm and old. Then they all came together again, and Sonny was part of the family again. I could tell this from his face. He seemed to have found, right there beneath his fingers, a damn brand-new piano. It seemed that he couldn't get over it. Then, for awhile, just being happy with Sonny, they seemed to be agreeing with him that brand-new pianos certainly were a gas.

Then Creole stepped forward to remind them that what they were playing was the blues. He hit something in all of them, he hit something in me, myself, and the music tightened and deepened, apprehension began to beat the air. Creole began to tell us what the blues were all about. They were not about anything very new. He and his boys up there were keeping it new, at the risk of ruin, destruction, madness, and death, in order to find new ways to make us listen. For, while the tale of how we suffer, and how we are delighted, and how we may triumph is never new, it always must be heard. There isn't any other tale to tell, it's the only light we've got in all this darkness.

And this tale, according to that face, that body, those strong hands on those strings, has another aspect in every country, and a new depth in every generation. Listen, Creole seemed to be saying, listen. Now these are Sonny's blues. He made the little black man on the drums know it, and the bright,

235

brown man on the horn. Creole wasn't trying any longer to get Sonny in the water. He was wishing him Godspeed. Then he stepped back, very slowly, filling the air with the immense suggestion that Sonny speak for himself.

Then they all gathered around Sonny and Sonny played. Every now and again one of them seemed to say, amen. Sonny's fingers filled the air with life, his life. But that life contained so many others. And Sonny went all the way back, he really began with the spare, flat statement of the opening phrase of the song. Then he began to make it his. It was very beautiful because it wasn't hurried and it was no longer a lament. I seemed to hear with what burning he had made it his, with what burning we had yet to make it ours, how we could cease lamenting. Freedom lurked around us and I understood, at last, that he could help us to be free if we would listen, that he would never be free until we did. Yet, there was no battle in his face now. I heard what he had gone through, and would continue to go through until he came to rest in earth. He had made it his: that long line, of which we knew only Mama and Daddy. And he was giving it back, as everything must be given back, so that, passing through death, it can live forever. I saw my mother's face again, and felt, for the first time, how the stones of the road she had walked on must have bruised her feet. I saw the moon-lit road where my father's brother died. And it brought something else back to me, and carried me past it. I saw my little girl again and felt Isabel's tears again, and I felt my own tears begin to rise. And I was yet aware that this was only a moment, that the world waited outside, as hungry as a tiger, and that trouble stretched above us, longer than the sky.

Then it was over. Creole and Sonny let out their breath, both soaking wet, and grinning. There was a lot of applause and some of it was real. In the dark, the girl came by and I asked her to take drinks to the bandstand. There was a long pause, while they talked up there in the indigo light and after awhile I saw the girl put a Scotch and milk on top of the piano for Sonny. He didn't seem to notice it, but just before they started playing again, he sipped from it and looked toward me, and nodded. Then he put it back on top of the piano. For me, then, as they began to play again, it glowed and shook above my brother's head like the very cup of trembling.

[1957]

Claudia Smith Brinson (1949–)

Claudia Smith Brinson, who won an O. Henry Award for "Einstein's Daughter," has worked at newspapers in Pensacola, Florida, and in Athens, Greece. She is currently a columnist for The State *newspaper in Columbia, South Carolina. Her short stories have been published in such journals as* Iowa Woman, Kalliope, *and* Crescent Review, *as well as the anthology* Life on the Line: Selections on Words and Healing. *She received her MA degree from the University of South Carolina, where she occasionally teaches fiction and nonfiction classes.*

Einstein's Daughter

Like a planarian, I was born with the knowledge of my ancestors and descendants coalescing into one trait, as real as Great-Grandfather Arthur's long nose or Grandmother Reba's red hair. I knew, right from the start, however you want to mark that spot, that you can grow old waiting.

So I drew rocketships, pedalled like mad downhill, ran up escalators. Simple speed was in my bones and blood. And in my head long before I read about it in high school physics, long before I read that tale of twins, one who remains on Earth while the other blasts off at half the speed of light, travels the curve of space-time and returns younger than the twin who stayed on a straight line, who waited.

No wonder women always end up looking older than their men. Starting out even or behind won't save them. Ask Penelope as she sits by her loom; ask Dorothy Parker's character as she sits by her telephone.

My mother did what she could with me. She tried to bring me up right, to train me in the art of waiting. Out of love for her I would practice it even before my time began. The Korean Conflict was over. My father was expected home; I was expected. "Wait," my mother said, rubbing her hands in small circles, pressing her palms against her tight skin. "Don't come just yet, baby. Wait for your father." I obeyed, lingering for a tenth month in that dark ocean of muted sounds, safe in pending arrival.

My mother (a woman who sits patiently, interminably, ankles crossed, hands clasped, head tilted five degrees to the left) says my hair was unnaturally long at birth, reaching to my shoulders, and tiny red scratches covered my cheeks and chest. That she burst into tears at the sight of my flailing arms and legs, the sound of my angry shrieks. An irritable baby, she says, sucking at her breasts so fiercely the milk would stream down my chin, soaking us both. I would wail, she says, when the precisely timed feedings were over, ten minutes at each breast with four firm pats on my back in between. I would wail long enough, loud enough that often I was left in my crib during the day, the door closed to muffle my impatient yowls, the mobile tightly wound to distract me. So I destroyed it, yanking from their strings the stuffed Little Bo Peep, Little Miss Muffet, and Jack Horner.

When I was with her she strapped me into the infant carrier with its smooth plastic seat and edges, its tight white belt. She strapped me into the yellow and white windup swing with its T-shaped cinch. She stored me in the red, white, and blue playpen with its unscalable mesh walls. So I tipped the infant seat over, splitting it and my lip when we tumbled to the floor. I bounced in the swing until it creaked and rattled and shivered in its resistance to my orbit. The mesh I simply gnawed my way through.

My mother would sit with her decaffeinated coffee, staring out the window. She would lean against the stove, slowly stirring the vegetable soup. She would tuck me tightly in the navy blue carriage and languidly walk the three blocks to a friend's house. And the Longine on her fine-boned wrist would tick its way toward five-thirty and dusk, and, some days, the arrival of my pilot father.

But by the time I could reach that watch and all the other clocks, the metal face between the stove dials, the golden face on the den's mantel, the cat face with the shifting eyes in my room, the luminous face humming by my parent's bed, the neon green face on the car's dashboard, I had left my parents to their own time zones.

As she, and sometimes he, sat through half-hour television shows and thirty-second commercials on a direct path to darkness and sleep, I would crawl to the foot of my canopied bed and watch the past before me: my mother on the brick steps of the tin-roofed farmhouse, Reba and Luke rocking behind her; Susannah holding tightly her stillborn Emily, Arthur in exile in the drawing room's twilight, myself to come in their silences. The probabilities would swirl in the corners of my eyes, and if I turned my head quickly, I could catch the future growing behind. Stasis or travel, symmetry or adventure. Why did I never glimpse myself standing there? I found no lines, no planes, nothing flat or straight, nothing simple, nothing set, only arcs of possibilities to enfold myself in.

Sooner or later the door would crack. As light flooded in, I would trav-el back to my bed long before the eyes of a proper parent might see. Go fast enough, and to the watcher the clock stops, mass becomes infinite, meas-urements shrink: disappearance. According to the watcher.   10

"It's all relative," I told my mother, sullenly I admit. This was my her-itage, nothing special, no more than my cowlicked brown hair tinged with red, my green eyes, my slightly crooked nose. So, as the cigarette burned slowly toward her fingers, she told me once she dreamed she could fly. Just once, when she was in love with Danny Blake. She stepped off a balcony, arms out stretched, the air and sun gentle around her, the trees rustling at her passage, her movement finally equal to her soul.

Then, eyes squinting through her trail of smoke, she asked again, "What is it you do?"

I shrugged.

She said, "I saw you once. You were outside, in the back yard by the swing set. Then suddenly, somehow, past the fence and down the block. You were six, but almost gone; still my six year old, but out of my reach."

I looked away, my eyes watering from her smoke.   15

She gripped my wrist, pulled me across the table toward her. "Answer me," she demanded.

"I'm gaining speed," I said.

"You're my daughter," she said, getting up, turning away from me, searching in her pocket for matches. "You're only nine.

"And you're getting fat," she added, and left the room.

She can't help herself; I know that. She believes what people tell her,   20
believes there are immutable rules and consequences. She's been taught it's all cause and effect. Susannah, Reba, her, me. So she thinks she didn't drink enough milk when she was pregnant or my fall down the stairs when I was two really did give me a concussion or my father has not confessed to some crazy aunt locked away in a closet, and that, right there, that's why I am the way I am. That's what she's been taught to think, that we're just floating down the river together, generations caught in the current.

We're always looking ahead into the past, I want to tell her. When you sit on the porch, Mama, and rock and stare, still, struck by starlight, you're looking back millions of years. But at this point I'm a novice, just beginning to catch speed. So I run out the door, letting the screen slam behind me. I dart back and forth, hands cupped, a pocket of air between to cushion the fireflies. Then, with my hands full of light, I whirl and whirl, fling my arms up, casting the light out, away. The sky spins closer as I spiral into its embrace. And my grandfather, not heard from in thirty years, he laughs and whispers in my ear, "Speed up, speed up. See where it will take you."

The past is there; its images linger on the spent light, and that's where I'm going in my childhood: ahead. I rocket into what's already there. I watch my Grandfather Luke pull the soft, heavy carpetbag from under the iron bed. He shakes its folds out then carefully, precisely stacks in it his three white shirts, their stiff collars, his dark bow tie. From the marble top bureau he takes a photograph of Reba, so prim in her pinned-up hair and high-necked wool dress, two of its jet buttons hidden by a cameo. Her slanted, black-inked inscription, "To my dear Luke No finer husband" is fitted so neatly between the two lines of the Hall New Studio stamp.

Luke is leaving Reba, who teaches school, and my mother and her three sisters to travel eighty-eight miles down the road, into Georgia, where his brother Junius will hire him to sell shoes. He will never work again as a cotton broker. He will move from relative to relative, stranger to stranger, sending letters and money, then just money. For eight more years money will appear in the mail every two months, but he will never reappear.

Reba will not forgive him. Her red hair fades, her thin lips sink deeper into her chin, her large eyes grow pale behind rimless glasses. She takes to striking my mother, the oldest of her daughters. She bangs my mother's head into the pump when my mother cries as her hair is scrubbed under cold water. She knocks my mother to the ground when my mother scorches the lace collar of a dress from Mrs. McKinney's stack of ironing. She slaps my mother hard enough to break my mother's nose when she catches her sixteen-year-old daughter climbing out the window to go riding on a summer's night with Danny Blake, who will marry another, have twin sons, die in a hotel fire in Mississippi, but remain to haunt my mother's heart.

My mother tells me the lump on the bridge of her nose comes from a   25
fall from an apple tree. My mother tells me her father died the year he left the family, and her mother sacrificed, slaved. My mother says her father was selfish, fiddled and fished, played gin rummy in the brokerage office and no wonder the business went under. I ask my mother, "Why did Grandmother Reba pull out hair when you dropped the pitcher of milk? You couldn't help it; that fat yellow cat tripped you." My mother looks at me aslant, not at all surprised at my knowledge. She says flatly, "My mother never hurt me. She only punished me when I was in a hurry and did things wrong. She had to teach me to slow down and pay attention."

Fast as I travel I cannot see it all. I see sparks, cataclysms, thunder, conversations, and sighs you can connect this way or that. She sees strands, chains of the foretold woven together into one tight braid. She would say, there, there is the complete description, this past of linear twists knotted together.

Reba, that red-headed tyrant, whispers in my ear, "I loved your mother best of all. She was my firstborn. I had to teach her to be strong. I had to make her see men will love you, leave you. They want only one thing, girl, then they will fly away from you.

"And you, my hurried granddaughter, your mother must make you sit still and listen. She must keep you safe. Put you in high-laced shoes and doubleknot the ties. Plait heavy ribbons in your hair. Starch your skirts, layer you in petticoats. Make you stay clean and fresh.

"Slow down, child, and listen."

She's too late, though. I've seen through her glasses. I can look into   30
those grey eyes turned mean and see her diverted strength playing into my magic. So I move on, to her mother, to Susannah, who rides horses like a man, who attends one of the first women's colleges in the state, who takes to her bed after her eighth child, the third to die within a month of birth. Who practices statics for seventy more years, directing five children, her husband Arthur, servants, and guests from a red horsehair sofa in a front room and a claw-footed, four poster walnut bed in a back room.

She expects Great-Grandfather Arthur and her children to report their lives and the pace of the world, and they will. The younger girls stitch by her bed; the boys recite texts by the sofa; Arthur reads to her late into the night from ledgers, newspapers, books, eventually grandchildren's letters. And three times a day Reba, the eldest, stands by her mother's swaddled feet and nervously rattles the keys of the household. She timidly recites the contents of the larder or describes the soap or butter slowly forming in the sunlight behind the house. Then Reba listens as her mother details the deficits of last night's dinner or this morning's cut flowers. I watch Susannah, so imperious, so definite in her anchoring, so unmindful of Reba's lost childhood. I wonder, if the amount of energy in the universe is constant, is this where my powers began? Did I accrue what she refused to use?

She shakes a long, thin finger at me. "Don't go looking for trouble, young lady, and it won't find you. Your duty is to love people and to serve people, and you can't do that if you're gallivanting around. You give and you do what you can, and you make sure it's good. That's enough for a woman. Love is enough."

But I am not supposed to be visiting Susannah; I am supposed to be vacuuming the den for my mother. The rattle of a trapped paper clip or safety pin spinning in the machine's throat stops me. I sit to unhook its parts and search for the noisemaker, and the silence draws my mother in. She sees me unemployed, exactly what she expected to see. "Not all here again?" she asks impatiently, arms crossed, eyes surveying the room. She lifts a hassock and finds what she expected, the flat fibers of undisturbed carpeting; she lifts the seat cushion of an armchair and finds what she expected, crumbs. I love my mother, and I love her most intensely when I disappoint her. I am rooted then, grounded by her need for a daughter. She wants more than a replication of bones and blood, more than a womanly echo. I don't meet her ironic gaze. I turn the vacuum cleaner back on, attach the crevice tool, invade the crannies of the chair, my back to her.

If I were to succumb entirely, I would draw a direct line from inertia to now, from daughter to daughter. Instead, I turn my attention to my father, to that part-time presence in our family of three. My father has kept flying, moving from the large, death-delivering planes of the war to the sleek, supersonic planes of commerce. I travel his route and watch him in the neon hues of airport bars, follow him to the motel bed, where he plays a harmonica, his back against two pillows, his shoes tossed by the door.

Sometimes there is a woman in the shower or on the other side of the bed, her flight bag open next to his on the long, polished expanse of the dresser. But among his blue shirts and white underwear is always a present for my mother: French perfume, an Irish linen blouse, a Majorcan pearl necklace, a Scandinavian sweater. He leans on one elbow and murmurs, "God knows I love your mother, but. . . ." He sits up, drapes his arms across his knees, stares deep at his dark reflection in the mirror opposite the bed. "But a house and chitchat about the lawn and the PTA, and nights sitting on the couch with the newspaper and the TV? Don't get me wrong. I love you both. But to be honest, kid, not every day, every night. In doses, you know." It is a simple thing to move fast enough to reach the past, so visible, so well preserved, its light established. There you can spend yourself on your choice of revelations. But I tire of the predictable rhythms, of Suzannah's dogged ringing of her silver bell, of Reba's resentful stare into the mailbox, of Arthur eating alone, of Luke staring into a hobo's fire. I grow impatient with my haphazard paths past them. I must set an order to it and chart the consequences.

35

I retreat to my room, crouch on my pink flowered bedspread, graph paper stretching from foot to headboard so I can record the curves of my constant curiosity. If I can write it down, I can understand it; I can rescue myself. If I can design a family tree, put down names and events my travels have revealed, I will know where I must go and the speed and direction I must use to thwart happenstance and fate. I stare through Saturdays and Sundays at the canyon of Luke's leavetaking, the continuous crests of my father's takeoffs and landings. But I cannot draw the picture whole on the green and white plane.

I focus, instead, on a moment from my own past. I have watched the roller derbies on television and am in love with the hefty, blowsy blondes who crouch low, pumping their arms so sternly as their legs carry them past the linked bodies of their competitors. On weekend mornings I practice secretly, racing up and down the block trying to duplicate that fierce, leg-pumping squat. My rhythm is unnatural, though, interrupted by the bumps of tar welding the long stretches of pavement together. I keep my head low, my eyes marking the black breaks in stride.

"Slow down!" my mother shouts. "Stop! You're going to hurt yourself!" I look up to see her frantically waving from the front porch steps, and in that instant, the wheels of my left foot catch, and I am flying forward, the grit of the pavement peeling my skin as my left hand, my right elbow, my knees hit and skid. What did she think as the pavement rasped against my flesh: I told you so, or I'm sorry; it's my fault, or these things wouldn't happen if you'd behave like a normal girl? Or simply: My poor baby. As she wraps her arms around me, dabs at the blood with her apron, I see her terrible secret. She loves me most when I have failed. It is not that she wishes me evil, but that she wishes me needy.

So I choose another route to pleasing her. I slow down. I satisfy my mother with myself in her path. I cannot please her as much as I would like, cannot bear to spend time on painted toenails or hair wrapped around a curling iron, afternoons in a bubble bath, or evenings in a movie theater, one hand free, the other imprisoned by another. But I can bolt myself to a wrought iron chair next to her on the patio and snap beans to her quiet rhythm. I can take each wet white plate she hands me, hold it briefly under the clear running water, wipe away its wetness, stack it in the cabinet to my left.

And at night, when she would wish my lights on past dark to practice girlish rites: writing in a diary, reading slender romances, or experimenting with eye shadow, I tuck my head to protect my neck. I stare into the thick blackness, curve my shoulders, flex my knees, rock from heel to ball of foot and back until I find my center then auger past the tin barrier of space, spinning past time into time. And in the daytime I drive her, only slightly reckless with my learner's permit, to the nearest mall and follow her from linens to china to fragrances to jewelry to junior dresses. "If you would only slow down, get off that bike of yours," she sighs, "and get to know some boys." She pushes me in front of a mirror, yanks my shoulders back until I stand braced in her clutch as a Marine. "Look at you," she says, her mouth puckering. "Hair hacked off with my scissors so you look like a scruffy orphan. Dirt on your neck." She shakes my hand at the image. "Nails bitten to the quick. The elbows of this sweater black and frayed like you scorched it. Worn out jogging shoes."

"I don't have time to worry about such things," I tell her and wait for her to ask what I mean by that.

But she's wandered three racks away to finger thin linens and pastel cottons. I edge toward the jean jackets. Her mother's eye draws me back beside the long-sleeved lace blouses that stain so easily, the silk dresses intended only for dancing and desire, for slow movement toward traditional resolutions. "Yes ma'am," I reply, pretending to take my reflection seriously as she holds aqua then persimmon against me. She lets the dresses float so slowly to the floor. She pulls me to her, squints wistfully, then lifts my calloused, ragged hands, and kisses the fingertips. "Drive me home, darling," she says, "and stop at the red lights."

We creep along, my mother quiet, her seat belt fastened. I stay behind a grey-haired granny in a green finned Chevy, letting her set our pace. I last for three blocks, five, but I want my mother to see that I, unlike her, am not my mother's daughter. I stare ahead at the road, fighting my foot pressing down, my wrist rigid above the stick shift. I say calmly, evenly, "I'm not going to let gravity wreck me. I'm not going to spend my life at home waiting for some man to show back up. The more you try to tie me to you, the faster I'm going to go."

My mother's tone is ironic; her eyes refuse me and the road ahead, looking instead on her tissue-wrapped purchases. "Do you think any daughter wants to be like her mother? I never met one. I swore I'd best mine, and I did. I kept my husband. And she bettered her mother. She worked hard. She never ran from difficulties. That's all you get, one small change." She looks at me now, her eyes fierce, mother's eyes. "You think you can fly? You're my daughter. I'm bred in you."

I pull the car to the side of the street; I put the parking brake on for her,   45
and I leap. I wish I had the flash of Dorothy's red shoes. I can simply spin, but I show her just how fast I can go, just how fast I can disappear. And this time I go where I can't see; I go into uncertainty, into odds, into probabilities.

I have a bicycle, its frame of titanium, its wheels solid to slice the air and ease me into the slipstream. I have a skateboard, its deck maple, rating ninety-seven on the durometer. I have roller skates, speed skates with leather boots, urethane wheels. I have wheels, for circles let you go, spheres of faith and momentum. But right now I have only myself, and in the bombardment of probabilities I spin and twirl and spiral. I circle my mother in the dark of the living room, her cigarette's red the only heat; my mother in bed, her eyes open and dry and patient. But the light is poor, and I cannot find myself in the house.

Pulling my arms tighter, I hug my ribs and increase the spin, and in the keyholes I catch glimpses of myself, a self blurred—by movement or an insistent nearsightedness I cannot guess. Perhaps she is right: perhaps I can't avoid my blood, and the nature of the geography will coax me into their paths: the easiest path between the wind and loss onto the red sofa, the easiest trail between desire and failure into the shoe store, the easiest route between my mother and father into my room. When I slow down, my hands, so red and raw from my trajectory, are speckled with the dust of the possibilities I could not grasp.

"Mamma," I say, "what do you want?"

"From you?" she asks. "From your father?"

"No," I answer and gulp air. "What do you want from you? For you?"   50

"I've got what I want, dear," she says, blowing on her coffee. "You, your father, this house, our health. I wish you didn't run off like you do when you get impatient with me."

She sips her coffee, and I taste despair. To her I am a mystery, a mutation, a miracle unasked for; to me she is mass unconverted, gravity's penalty, my immutable mother. "If you could choose to do anything, without consequences, what would you do? Leave Dad? Go back to school? Travel?"

But she is stubborn. "I have what I always wanted. Security. A husband who loves me and won't ever leave me. A healthy child. I've nothing to wish for, nothing to change. That would be greedy." She puts down the cup and shakes her head, mocks herself. "I'd like to get my daughter to wear a dress once in a while. I'd like her to slow down enough to try out mascara. I'd like to wave goodbye to her as she goes out on the arm of some handsome young man. I want to know I'll have grandchildren some day."

I step toward my mother; I reach out and take her in my arms like a dancing partner. I pull her surprised, resisting body to me and whisper past her pearl earrings, "Come with me just once. There's ceaseless motion. So much to see." I could take off with her right then, rocket right out of there, but she pulls back, her weight opposing me, her hands tight on my arms, her face stern.

"Don't you grow up like your grandfather," she hisses. "Leaving people.   55
Don't you turn selfish like some man."

I take her hand, cold and small, and yank her to the center of the floor and twirl; ease my arms around her waist, lock them behind her back and spin; pull my mother into circumrotation, circumgyrations around the fires in the railroad yard, around the yellow cat, around the ironing board, around her lonely self at the breakfast table. The coffee has finished brewing when our feet touch the floor again.

"I'm your mother," she says gently, turning the coffee machine off, taking a cup from the dish drain and filling it. "I've been there before you. What can you teach me that I don't already know?"

I shrug and go upstairs to my room. Hours later I creep back down and out of the house. I sit on the porch steps, lean back on my elbows, tilt my throat to the sky. This is our summer house on the edge of the beach, and on a winter's night like this, when no one else is on the island, there's no electricity to dim the night. The black is silvered with stars, and I am awash in their white light. I walk to the middle of the sandy yard. I am filled with desire and impatience, determined to lose myself in the space of sky and sea.

Yet I don't. To disentangle is to leave my mother where she is; to leave her standing forever in the damp heavy air of the laundry room, her knees pressed into the warm metal of the still humming dryer. To insist she continue to pull from the frayed plastic basket my father's pale blue shirts, my own faded blue denim and chambray. "Come with me," I tell her. "I waited for you once when you asked. I waited for life for love of you. Now you come for love of me."

She pulls one more shirt from the basket, carefully buttons it onto a   60
hanger. She unlocks the back door, walks onto the stoop, and peers at the sky and at me. Her face is sad. She pulls her wedding band back and forth across her knuckle. "I'll walk with you to the dunes," she says. We climb barefoot in the sand toward the sea. Where the sea oats stop, we stop. "Like all children you ask too much," she says.

We clasp hands and lean back, opposing forces, our heels digging into the dune, our backs angled against the sand, our faces to the stars. We start to circle, feeding off each other. I gain speed, reeling on a path past moon-rise, star-rise. Her hands release me, and I rise. Anabatic I rise, heading toward the only possible destination: now, a now of my own making. She has let go of me as we both knew she should. What will she do without me? I dare not stop to ask.

[1989]

RAYMOND CARVER (1938–1988)

Raymond Carver, poet, author, and dramatist, graduated from Humboldt University and studied at the Iowa Writers' Workshop. He received two grants from the National Endowment for the Arts and a Guggenheim Fellowship, as well as nominations for the National Book Award and Pulitzer Prize. He worked as a night custodian, a textbook editor, and a lecturer at various universities.

Cathedral

This blind man, an old friend of my wife's, he was on his way to spend the night. His wife had died. So he was visiting the dead wife's relatives in Connecticut. He called my wife from his in-laws'. Arrangements were made. He would come by train, a five-hour trip, and my wife would meet him at the station. She hadn't seen him since she worked for him one summer in Seattle ten years ago. But she and the blind man had kept in touch. They made tapes and mailed them back and forth. I wasn't enthusiastic about his visit. He was no one I knew. And his being blind bothered me. My idea of blindness came from the movies. In the movies, the blind moved slowly and never laughed. Sometimes they were led by seeing-eye dogs. A blind man in my house was not something I looked forward to.

That summer in Seattle she had needed a job. She didn't have any money. The man she was going to marry at the end of the summer was in officers' training school. He didn't have any money, either. But she was in love with the guy, and he was in love with her, etc. She'd seen something in the paper: HELP WANTED—*Reading to Blind Man,* and a telephone number. She phoned and went over, was hired on the spot. She'd worked with this blind man all summer. She read stuff to him, case studies, reports, that sort of thing. She helped him organize his little office in the county social-service department. They'd become good friends, my wife and the blind man. How do I know these things? She told me. And she told me something else. On her last day in the office, the blind man asked if he could touch her face. She agreed to this. She told me he touched his fingers to every part of her face, her nose—even her neck! She never forgot it. She even tried to write a poem about it. She was always trying to write a poem. She wrote a poem or two every year, usually after something really important had happened to her.

When we first started going out together, she showed me the poem. In the poem, she recalled his fingers and the way they had moved around over her face. In the poem, she talked about what she had felt at the time, about what went through her mind when the blind man touched her nose and lips. I can remember I didn't think much of the poem. Of course, I didn't tell her that. Maybe I just don't understand poetry. I admit it's not the first thing I reach for when I pick up something to read.

Anyway, this man who'd first enjoyed her favors, the officer-to-be, he'd been her childhood sweetheart. So okay. I'm saying that at the end of the summer she let the blind man run his hands over her face, said good-bye to him, married her childhood etc., who was now a commissioned officer, and she moved away from Seattle. But they'd kept in touch, she and the blind man. She made the first contact after a year or so. She called him up one night from an Air Force base in Alabama. She wanted to talk. They talked. He asked her to send a tape and tell him about her life. She did this. She sent the tape. On the tape, she told the blind man about her husband and about their life together in the military. She told the blind man she loved her husband but she didn't like it where they lived and she didn't like it that he was part of the military-industrial thing. She told the blind man she'd written a poem and he was in it. She told him that she was writing a poem about what it was like to be an Air Force officer's wife. The poem wasn't finished yet. She was still writing it. The blind man made a tape. He sent her the tape. She made a tape. This went on for years. My wife's officer was posted to one base and then another. She sent tapes from Moody AFB, McGuire, McConnell, and finally Travis, near Sacramento, where one night she got to feeling lonely and cut off from people she kept losing in that moving-around life. She got to feeling she couldn't go it another step. She went in and swallowed all the pills and capsules in the medicine chest and washed them down with a bottle of gin. Then she got into a hot bath and passed out.

But instead of dying, she got sick. She threw up. Her officer—why should he have a name? he was the childhood sweetheart, and what more does he want?—came home from somewhere, found her, and called the ambulance. In time, she put it all on a tape and sent the tape to the blind man. Over the years, she put all kinds of stuff on tapes and sent the tapes off lickety-split. Next to writing a poem every year, I think it was her chief means of recreation. On one tape, she told the blind man she'd decided to live away from her officer for a time. On another tape, she told him about her divorce. She and I began going out, and of course she told her blind man about it. She told him everything, or so it seemed to me. Once she asked me if I'd like to hear the latest tape from the blind man. This was a year ago. I was on the tape, she said. So I said okay, I'd listen to it. I got us drinks and we settled down in the living room. We made ready to listen. First she inserted the tape into the player and adjusted a couple of dials. Then she pushed a lever. The tape squeaked and someone began to talk in this loud voice. She lowered the volume. After a few minutes of harmless chitchat, I heard my own name in the mouth of this stranger, this blind man I didn't even know! And then this: "From all you've said about him, I can only conclude—" But we were interrupted, a knock at the door, something, and we didn't ever get back to the tape. Maybe it was just as well. I'd heard all I wanted to.

Now this same blind man was coming to sleep in my house.

5

"Maybe I could take him bowling," I said to my wife. She was at the draining board doing scalloped potatoes. She put down the knife she was using and turned around.

"If you love me," she said, "you can do this for me. If you don't love me, okay. But if you had a friend, any friend, and the friend came to visit, I'd make him feel comfortable." She wiped her hands with the dish towel.

"I don't have any blind friends," I said.

"You don't have *any* friends," she said. "Period. Besides," she said, "god-   10 damn it, his wife's just died! Don't you understand that? The man's lost his wife!"

I didn't answer. She'd told me a little about the blind man's wife. Her name was Beulah. Beulah! That's a name for a colored woman.

"Was his wife a Negro?" I asked.

"Are you crazy?" my wife said. "Have you just flipped or something?" She picked up a potato. I saw it hit the floor, then roll under the stove. "What's wrong with you?" she said. "Are you drunk?"

"I'm just asking," I said.

Right then my wife filled me in with more detail than I cared to know.   15 I made a drink and sat at the kitchen table to listen. Pieces of the story began to fall into place.

Beulah had gone to work for the blind man the summer after my wife had stopped working for him. Pretty soon Beulah and the blind man had themselves a church wedding. It was a little wedding—who'd want to go to such a wedding in the first place?—just the two of them, plus the minister and the minister's wife. But it was a church wedding just the same. It was what Beulah had wanted, he'd said. But even then Beulah must have been carrying the cancer in her glands. After they had been inseparable for eight years—my wife's word, *inseparable*—Beulah's health went into a rapid decline. She died in a Seattle hospital room, the blind man sitting beside the bed and holding on to her hand. They'd married, lived and worked together, slept together—had sex, sure—and then the blind man had to bury her. All this without his having ever seen what the goddamned woman looked like. It was beyond my understanding. Hearing this, I felt sorry for the blind man for a little bit. And then I found myself thinking what a pitiful life this woman must have led. Imagine a woman who could never see herself as she was seen in the eyes of her loved one. A woman who could go on day after day and never receive the smallest compliment from her beloved. A woman whose husband could never read the expression on her face, be it misery or something better. Someone who could wear makeup or not— what difference to him? She could, if she wanted, wear green eye-shadow around one eye, a straight pin in her nostril, yellow slacks, and purple shoes, no matter. And then to slip off into death, the blind man's hand on her hand, his blind eyes streaming tears—I'm imagining now—her last thought maybe this: that he never even knew what she looked like, and she on an express to the grave. Robert was left with a small insurance policy and a half of a twenty-peso Mexican coin. The other half of the coin went into the box with her. Pathetic.

So when the time rolled around, my wife went to the depot to pick him up. With nothing to do but wait—sure, I blamed him for that—I was having a drink and watching the TV when I heard the car pull into the drive. I got up from the sofa with my drink and went to the window to have a look.

I saw my wife laughing as she parked the car. I saw her get out of the car and shut the door. She was still wearing a smile. Just amazing. She went around to the other side of the car to where the blind man was already starting to get out. This blind man, feature this, he was wearing a full beard! A beard on a blind man! Too much, I say. The blind man reached into the backseat and dragged out a suitcase. My wife took his arm, shut the car door, and, talking all the way, moved him down the drive and then up the steps to the front porch. I turned off the TV. I finished my drink, rinsed the glass, dried my hands. Then I went to the door.

My wife said, "I want you to meet Robert. Robert, this is my husband. I've told you all about him." She was beaming. She had this blind man by his coat sleeve.

The blind man let go of his suitcase and up came his hand.   20

I took it. He squeezed hard, held my hand, and then he let it go.

"I feel like we've already met," he boomed.

"Likewise," I said. I didn't know what else to say. Then I said, "Welcome. I've heard a lot about you." We began to move then, a little group, from the porch into the living room, my wife guiding him by the arm. The blind man was carrying his suitcase in his other hand. My wife said things like, "To your left here, Robert. That's right. Now watch it, there's a chair. That's it. Sit down right here. This is the sofa. We just bought this sofa two weeks ago."

I started to say something about the old sofa. I'd liked that old sofa. But I didn't say anything. Then I wanted to say something else, small-talk, about the scenic ride along the Hudson. How going *to* New York, you should sit on the right-hand side of the train, and coming *from* New York, the left-hand side.

"Did you have a good train ride?" I said. "Which side of the train did you   25 sit on, by the way?"

"What a question, which side!" my wife said. "What's it matter which side?" she said.

"I just asked," I said.

"Right side," the blind man said. "I hadn't been on a train in nearly forty years. Not since I was a kid. With my folks. That's been a long time. I'd nearly forgotten the sensation. I have winter in my beard now," he said. "So I've been told, anyway. Do I look distinguished, my dear?" the blind man said to my wife.

"You look distinguished, Robert," she said. "Robert," she said. "Robert, it's just so good to see you."

My wife finally took her eyes off the blind man and looked at me. I had   30 the feeling she didn't like what she saw. I shrugged.

I've never met, or personally known, anyone who was blind. This blind man was late forties, a heavy-set, balding man with stooped shoulders, as if he carried a great weight there. He wore brown slacks, brown shoes, a light-brown shirt, a tie, a sports coat. Spiffy. He also had this full beard. But he didn't use a cane and he didn't wear dark glasses. I'd always thought dark glasses were a must for the blind. Fact was, I wished he had a pair. At first glance, his eyes looked like anyone else's eyes. But if you looked close, there was something different about them. Too much white in the iris, for one thing, and the pupils seemed to move around in the sockets without his knowing it or being able to stop it. Creepy. As I stared at his face, I saw the left pupil turn in toward his nose while the other made an effort to keep in

one place. But it was only an effort, for that eye was on the roam without
his knowing it or wanting it to be.

I said, "Let me get you a drink. What's your pleasure? We have a little of
everything. It's one of our pastimes."

"Bub, I'm a Scotch man myself," he said fast enough in this big voice.

"Right," I said. Bub! "Sure you are. I knew it."

He let his fingers touch his suitcase, which was sitting alongside the   35
sofa. He was taking his bearings. I didn't blame him for that.

"I'll move that up to your room," my wife said.

"No, that's fine," the blind man said loudly. "It can go up when I go up."

"A little water with the Scotch?" I said.

"Very little," he said.

"I knew it," I said.   40

He said, "Just a tad. The Irish actor, Barry Fitzgerald? I'm like that fellow.
When I drink water, Fitzgerald said, I drink water. When I drink whiskey, I
drink whiskey." My wife laughed. The blind man brought his hand up under
his beard. He lifted his beard slowly and let it drop.

I did the drinks, three big glasses of Scotch with a splash of water in
each. Then we made ourselves comfortable and talked about Robert's travels. First the long flight from the West Coast to Connecticut, we covered
that. Then from Connecticut up here by train. We had another drink concerning that leg of the trip.

I remembered having read somewhere that the blind didn't smoke
because, as speculation had it, they couldn't see the smoke they exhaled. I
thought I knew that much and that much only about blind people. But this
blind man smoked his cigarette down to the nubbin and then lit another
one. This blind man filled his ashtray and my wife emptied it.

When we sat down at the table for dinner, we had another drink. My
wife heaped Robert's plate with cube steak, scalloped potatoes, green
beans. I buttered him up two slices of bread. I said, "Here's bread and butter
for you." I swallowed some of my drink. "Now let us pray," I said, and the
blind man lowered his head. My wife looked at me, her mouth agape. "Pray
the phone won't ring and the food doesn't get cold," I said.

We dug in. We ate everything there was to eat on the table. We ate like   45
there was no tomorrow. We didn't talk. We ate. We scarfed. We grazed that
table. We were into serious eating. The blind man had right away located his
foods, he knew just where everything was on his plate. I watched with
admiration as he used his knife and fork on the meat. He'd cut two pieces
of meat, fork the meat into his mouth, and then go all out for the scalloped
potatoes, the beans next, and then he'd tear off a hunk of buttered bread
and eat that. He'd follow this up with a big drink of milk. It didn't seem to
bother him to use his fingers once in a while, either.

We finished everything, including half a strawberry pie. For a few
moments, we sat as if stunned. Sweat beaded on our faces. Finally, we got
up from the table and left the dirty plates. We didn't look back. We took
ourselves into the living room and sank into our places again. Robert and
my wife sat on the sofa. I took the big chair. We had us two or three more
drinks while they talked about the major things that had come to pass for
them in the past ten years. For the most part, I just listened. Now and then
I joined in. I didn't want him to think I'd left the room, and I didn't want
her to think I was feeling left out. They talked of things that had happened
to them—to them!—these past ten years. I waited in vain to hear my name

on my wife's sweet lips: "And then my dear husband came into my life" — something like that. But I heard nothing of the sort. More talk of Robert. Robert had done a little of everything, it seemed, a regular blind jack-of-all-trades. But most recently he and his wife had had an Amway distributorship, from which, I gathered, they'd earned their living, such as it was. The blind man was also a ham radio operator. He talked in his loud voice about conversations he'd had with fellow operators in Guam, in the Philippines, in Alaska, and even in Tahiti. He said he'd have a lot of friends there if he ever wanted to go visit those places. From time to time, he'd turn his blind face toward me, put his hand under his beard, ask me something. How long had I been in my present position? (Three years.) Did I like my work? (I didn't.) Was I going to stay with it? (What were the options?) Finally, when I thought he was beginning to run down, I got up and turned on the TV.

My wife looked at me with irritation. She was heading toward a boil. Then she looked at the blind man and said, "Robert, do you have a TV?"

The blind man said, "My dear, I have two TVs. I have a color set and a black-and-white thing, an old relic. It's funny, but if I turn the TV on, and I'm always turning it on, I turn on the color set. It's funny, don't you think?"

I didn't know what to say to that. I had absolutely nothing to say to that. No opinion. So I watched the news program and tried to listen to what the announcer was saying.

"This is a color TV," the blind man said. "Don't ask me how, but I can tell."   50

"We traded up a while ago," I said.

The blind man had another taste of his drink. He lifted his beard, sniffed it, and let it fall. He leaned forward on the sofa. He positioned his ashtray on the coffee table, then put the lighter to his cigarette. He leaned back on the sofa and crossed his legs at the ankles.

My wife covered her mouth, and then she yawned. She stretched. She said, "I think I'll go upstairs and put on my robe. I think I'll change into something else. Robert, you make yourself comfortable," she said.

"I'm comfortable," the blind man said.

"I want you to feel comfortable in this house," she said.   55

"I am comfortable," the blind man said.

After she'd left the room, he and I listened to the weather report and then to the sports roundup. By that time, she'd been gone so long I didn't know if she was going to come back. I thought she might have gone to bed. I wished she'd come back downstairs. I didn't want to be left alone with a blind man. I asked him if he wanted another drink, and he said sure. Then I asked if he wanted to smoke some dope with me. I said I'd just rolled a number. I hadn't, but I planned to do so in about two shakes.

"I'll try some with you," he said.

"Damn right," I said. "That's the stuff."

I got our drinks and sat down on the sofa with him. Then I rolled us   60
two fat numbers. I lit one and passed it. I brought it to his fingers. He took it and inhaled.

"Hold it as long as you can," I said. I could tell he didn't know the first thing.

My wife came back downstairs wearing her pink robe and her pink slippers.

"What do I smell?" she said.

"We thought we'd have us some cannabis," I said.

My wife gave me a savage look. Then she looked at the blind man and   65
said, "Robert, I didn't know you smoked."

He said, "I do now, my dear. There's a first time for everything. But I
don't feel anything yet."

"This stuff is pretty mellow," I said. "This stuff is mild. It's dope you can
reason with," I said. "It doesn't mess you up."

"Not much it doesn't, bub," he said, and laughed.

My wife sat on the sofa between the blind man and me. I passed her
the number. She took it and toked and then passed it back to me. "Which
way is this going?" she said. Then she said, "I shouldn't be smoking this. I can
hardly keep my eyes open as it is. That dinner did me in. I shouldn't have
eaten so much."

"It was the strawberry pie," the blind man said. "That's what did it," he   70
said, and he laughed his big laugh. Then he shook his head.

"There's more strawberry pie," I said.

"Do you want some more, Robert?" my wife said.

"Maybe in a little while," he said.

We gave our attention to the TV. My wife yawned again. She said, "Your
bed is made up when you feel like going to bed, Robert. I know you must
have had a long day. When you're ready to go to bed, say so." She pulled his
arm. "Robert?"

He came to and said, "I've had a real nice time. This beats tapes, does-   75
n't it?"

I said, "Coming at you," and I put the number between his fingers. He
inhaled, held the smoke, and then let it go. It was like he'd been doing it
since he was nine years old.

"Thanks, bub," he said. "But I think this is all for me. I think I'm beginning to feel it," he said. He held the burning roach out for my wife.

"Same here," she said. "Ditto. Me, too." She took the roach and passed it
to me. "I may just sit here for a while between you two guys with my eyes
closed. But don't let me bother you, okay? Either one of you. If it bothers
you, say so. Otherwise, I may just sit here with my eyes closed until you're
ready to go to bed," she said. "Your bed's made up, Robert, when you're
ready. It's right next to our room at the top of the stairs. We'll show you up
when you're ready. You wake me up now, you guys, if I fall asleep." She said
that and then she closed her eyes and went to sleep.

The news program ended. I got up and changed the channel. I sat back
down on the sofa. I wished my wife hadn't pooped out. Her head lay across
the back of the sofa, her mouth open. She'd turned so that her robe slipped
away from her legs, exposing a juicy thigh. I reached to draw her robe back
over her, and it was then that I glanced at the blind man. What the hell! I
flipped the robe open again.

"You say when you want some strawberry pie," I said.   80

"I will," he said.

I said, "Are you tired? Do you want me to take you up to your bed? Are
you ready to hit the hay?"

"Not yet," he said. "No, I'll stay up with you, bub. If that's all right. I'll stay
up until you're ready to turn in. We haven't had a chance to talk. Know
what I mean? I feel like me and her monopolized the evening." He lifted his
beard and he let it fall. He picked up his cigarettes and his lighter.

"That's all right," I said. Then I said, "I'm glad for the company."

And I guess I was. Every night I smoked dope and stayed up as long as   85
I could before I fell asleep. My wife and I hardly ever went to bed at the
same time. When I did go to sleep, I had these dreams. Sometimes I'd wake
up from one of them, my heart going crazy.

Something about the church and the Middle Ages was on the TV. Not
your run-of-the-mill TV fare. I wanted to watch something else. I turned to
the other channels. But there was nothing on them, either. So I turned back
to the first channel and apologized.

"Bub, it's all right," the blind man said. "It's fine with me. Whatever you
want to watch is okay. I'm always learning something. Learning never ends.
It won't hurt me to learn something tonight. I got ears," he said.

We didn't say anything for a time. He was leaning forward with his head
turned at me, his right ear aimed in the direction of the set. Very discon-
certing. Now and then his eyelids drooped and then they snapped open
again. Now and then he put his fingers into his beard and tugged, like he
was thinking about something he was hearing on the television.

On the screen, a group of men wearing cowls was being set upon and
tormented by men dressed in skeleton costumes and men dressed as devils. The men dressed as devils wore devil masks, horns, and long tails. This
pageant was part of a procession. The Englishman who was narrating the
thing said it took place in Spain once a year. I tried to explain to the blind
man what was happening.

"Skeletons," he said. "I know about skeletons," he said, and he nodded.   90

The TV showed this one cathedral. Then there was a long, slow look at
another one. Finally, the picture switched to the famous one in Paris, with
its flying buttresses and its spires reaching up to the clouds. The camera
pulled away to show the whole of the cathedral rising above the skyline.

There were times when the Englishman who was telling the thing
would shut up, would simply let the camera move around the cathedrals.
Or else the camera would tour the countryside, men in fields walking
behind oxen. I waited as long as I could. Then I felt I had to say something.
I said, "They're showing the outside of this cathedral now. Gargoyles. Little
statues carved to look like monsters. Now I guess they're in Italy. Yeah,
they're in Italy. There's paintings on the walls of this one church."

"Are those fresco paintings, bub?" he asked, and he sipped from his
drink.

I reached for my glass. But it was empty. I tried to remember what I
could remember. "You're asking me are those frescoes?" I said. "That's a
good question. I don't know."

The camera moved to a cathedral outside Lisbon. The differences in the
Portuguese cathedral compared with the French and Italian were not that
great. But they were there. Mostly the interior stuff. Then something occurred
to me, and I said, "Something has occurred to me. Do you have any idea what
a cathedral is? What they look like, that is? Do you follow me? If somebody says
cathedral to you, do you have any notion what they're talking about? Do you
know the difference between that and a Baptist church, say?"

He let the smoke dribble from his mouth. "I know they took hundreds   95
of workers fifty or a hundred years to build," he said. "I just heard the man
say that, of course. I know generations of the same families worked on a
cathedral. I heard him say that, too. The men who began their life's work on

them, they never lived to see the completion of their work. In that wise, bub, they're no different from the rest of us, right?" He laughed. Then his eyelids drooped again. His head nodded. He seemed to be snoozing. Maybe he was imagining himself in Portugal. The TV was showing another cathedral now. This one was in Germany. The Englishman's voice droned on. "Cathedrals," the blind man said. He sat up and rolled his head back and forth. "If you want the truth, bub, that's about all I know. What I just said. What I heard him say. But maybe you could describe one to me? I wish you'd do it. I'd like that. If you want to know, I really don't have a good idea."

I stared hard at the shot of the cathedral on the TV. How could I even begin to describe it? But say my life depended on it. Say my life was being threatened by an insane guy who said I had to do it or else.

I stared some more at the cathedral before the picture flipped off into the countryside. There was no use. I turned to the blind man and said, "To begin with, they're very tall." I was looking around the room for clues. "They reach way up. Up and up. Toward the sky. They're so big, some of them, they have to have these supports. To help hold them up, so to speak. These supports are called buttresses. They remind me of viaducts, for some reason. But maybe you don't know viaducts, either? Sometimes the cathedrals have devils and such carved into the front. Sometimes lords and ladies. Don't ask me why this is," I said.

He was nodding. The whole upper part of his body seemed to be moving back and forth.

"I'm not doing so good, am I?" I said.

He stopped nodding and leaned forward on the edge of the sofa. As he   100
listened to me, he was running his fingers through his beard. I wasn't getting through to him, I could see that. But he waited for me to go on just the same. He nodded, like he was trying to encourage me. I tried to think what else to say. "They're really big," I said. "They're massive. They're built of stone. Marble, too, sometimes. In those olden days, when they built cathedrals, men wanted to be close to God. In those olden days, God was an important part of everyone's life. You could tell this from their cathedral-building. I'm sorry," I said, "but it looks like that's the best I can do for you. I'm just no good at it."

"That's all right, bub," the blind man said. "Hey, listen. I hope you don't mind my asking you. Can I ask you something? Let me ask you a simple question, yes or no. I'm just curious and there's no offense. You're my host. But let me ask if you are in any way religious? You don't mind my asking?"

I shook my head. He couldn't see that, though. A wink is the same as a nod to a blind man. "I guess I don't believe in it. In anything. Sometimes it's hard. You know what I'm saying?"

"Sure, I do," he said.

"Right," I said.

The Englishman was still holding forth. My wife sighed in her sleep.   105
She drew a long breath and went on with her sleeping.

"You'll have to forgive me," I said. "But I can't tell you what a cathedral looks like. It just isn't in me to do it. I can't do any more than I've done."

The blind man sat very still, his head down, as he listened to me.

I said, "The truth is, cathedrals don't mean anything special to me. Nothing. Cathedrals. They're something to look at on late-night TV. That's all they are."

It was then that the blind man cleared his throat. He brought something up. He took a handkerchief from his back pocket. Then he said, "I get it, bub. It's okay. It happens. Don't worry about it," he said. "Hey, listen to me. Will you do me a favor? I got an idea. Why don't you find us some heavy paper? And a pen. We'll do something. We'll draw one together. Get us a pen and some heavy paper. Go on, bub, get the stuff," he said.

So I went upstairs. My legs felt like they didn't have any strength in them.   110
They felt like they did after I'd done some running. In my wife's room, I looked around. I found some ballpoints in a little basket on her table. And then I tried to think where to look for the kind of paper he was talking about.

Downstairs, in the kitchen, I found a shopping bag with onion skins in the bottom of the bag. I emptied the bag and shook it. I brought it into the living room and sat down with it near his legs. I moved some things, smoothed the wrinkles from the bag, spread it out on the coffee table.

The blind man got down from the sofa and sat next to me on the carpet.

He ran his fingers over the paper. He went up and down the sides of the paper. The edges, even the edges. He fingered the corners.

"All right," he said. "All right, let's do her."

He found my hand, the hand with the pen. He closed his hand over my   115
hand. "Go ahead, bub, draw," he said. "Draw. You'll see. I'll follow along with you. It'll be okay. Just begin now like I'm telling you. You'll see. Draw," the blind man said.

So I began. First I drew a box that looked like a house. It could have been the house I lived in. Then I put a roof on it. At either end of the roof, I drew spires. Crazy.

"Swell," he said. "Terrific. You're doing fine," he said. "Never thought anything like this could happen in your lifetime, did you, bub? Well, it's a strange life, we all know that. Go on now. Keep it up."

I put in windows with arches. I drew flying buttresses. I hung great doors. I couldn't stop. The TV station went off the air. I put down the pen and closed and opened my fingers. The blind man felt around over the paper. He moved the tips of his fingers over the paper, all over what I had drawn, and he nodded.

"Doing fine," the blind man said.

I took up the pen again, and he found my hand. I kept at it. I'm no artist.   120
But I kept drawing just the same.

My wife opened up her eyes and gazed at us. She sat up on the sofa, her robe hanging open. She said, "What are you doing? Tell me, I want to know."

I didn't answer her.

The blind man said, "We're drawing a cathedral. Me and him are working on it. Press hard," he said to me. "That's right. That's good," he said. "Sure. You got it, bub, I can tell. You didn't think you could. But you can, can't you? You're cooking with gas now. You know what I'm saying? We're going to really have us something here in a minute. How's the old arm?" he said. "Put some people in there now. What's a cathedral without people?"

My wife said, "What's going on? Robert, what are you doing? What's going on?"

"It's all right," he said to her. "Close your eyes now," the blind man said   125
to me.

I did it. I closed them just like he said.

"Are they closed?" he said. "Don't fudge."

"They're closed," I said.

"Keep them that way," he said. He said, "Don't stop now. Draw."

So we kept on with it. His fingers rode my fingers as my hand went   130
over the paper. It was like nothing else in my life up to now.

Then he said, "I think that's it. I think you got it," he said. "Take a look.
What do you think?"

But I had my eyes closed. I thought I'd keep them that way for a little
longer. I thought it was something I ought to do.

"Well?" he said. "Are you looking?"

My eyes were still closed. I was in my house. I knew that. But I didn't
feel like I was inside anything.

"It's really something," I said.   135

[1983]

KATE CHOPIN (1850–1904)

Kate Chopin was born in St. Louis, but upon the death of her Irish father, she was raised by her mother's family in Louisiana. After a convent education, she married a wealthy cotton broker, Oscar Chopin. She did not start writing seriously until after her thirtieth birthday, when she was widowed and needed to support her family. In the ten years that followed, Chopin published two novels and two collections of short stories. Her final novel, The Awakening, *now recognized as a masterpiece, was initially criticized greatly for its focus on the oppression of women's emotional and sexual needs. As a result, Chopin wrote only a few more short stories during the rest of her life.*

The Storm

I

The leaves were so still that even Bibi thought it was going to rain. Bobinôt, who was accustomed to converse on terms of perfect equality with his little son, called the child's attention to certain somber clouds that were rolling with sinister intention from the west, accompanied by a sullen, threatening roar. They were at Friedheimer's store and decided to remain there till the storm had passed. They sat within the door on two empty kegs. Bibi was four years old and looked very wise.

"Mama'll be 'fraid, yes," he suggested with blinking eyes.

"She'll shut the house. Maybe she got Sylvie helpin' her this evenin'," Bobinôt responded reassuringly.

"No; she ent got Sylvie. Sylvie was helpin' her yistiday," piped Bibi.

Bobinôt arose and going across to the counter purchased a can of   5
shrimps, of which Calixta was very fond. Then he returned to his perch on the keg and sat stolidly holding the can of shrimps while the storm burst. It shook the wooden store and seemed to be ripping great furrows in the distant field. Bibi laid his little hand on his father's knee and was not afraid.

II

Calixta, at home, felt no uneasiness for their safety. She sat at a side window sewing furiously on a sewing machine. She was greatly occupied and did not notice the approaching storm. But she felt very warm and often stopped to mop her face on which the perspiration gathered in beads. She unfastened her white sacque at the throat. It began to grow dark, and suddenly realizing the situation she got up hurriedly and went about closing windows and doors.

Out on the small front gallery she had hung Bobinôt's Sunday clothes to air and she hastened out to gather them before the rain fell. As she stepped outside, Alcée Laballière rode in at the gate. She had not seen him very often since her marriage, and never alone. She stood there with Bobinôt's coat in her hands, and the big rain drops began to fall. Alcée rode his horse under the shelter of a side projection where the chickens had huddled and there were plows and a harrow piled up in the corner.

"May I come and wait on your gallery till the storm is over, Calixta?" he asked.

"Come 'long in, M'sieur Alcée."

His voice and her own startled her as if from a trance, and she seized Bobinôt's vest. Alcée, mounting to the porch, grabbed the trousers and snatched Bibi's braided jacket that was about to be carried away by a sudden gust of wind. He expressed an intention to remain outside, but it was soon apparent that he might as well have been out in the open: the water beat in upon the boards in driving sheets, and he went inside, closing the door after him. It was even necessary to put something beneath the door to keep the water out.   10

"My! what a rain! It's good two years since it rain like that," exclaimed Calixta as she rolled up a piece of bagging and Alcée helped her to thrust it beneath the crack.

She was a little fuller of figure than five years before when she married; but she had lost nothing of her vivacity. Her blue eyes still retained their melting quality; and her yellow hair, dishevelled by the wind and rain, kinked more stubbornly than ever about her ears and temples.

The rain beat upon the low, shingled roof with a force and clatter that threatened to break an entrance and deluge them there. They were in the dining room—the sitting room—the general utility room. Adjoining was her bed room, with Bibi's couch along side her own. The door stood open, and the room with its white, monumental bed, its closed shutters, looked dim and mysterious.

Alcée flung himself into a rocker and Calixta nervously began to gather up from the floor the lengths of a cotton sheet which she had been sewing.

"If this keeps up, *Dieu sait* if the levees goin' to stan' it!" she exclaimed.   15

"What have you got to do with the levees?"

"I got enough to do! An' there's Bobinôt with Bibi out in that storm— if he only didn' left Friedheimer's!"

"Let us hope, Calixta, that Bobinôt's got sense enough to come in out of a cyclone."

She went and stood at the window with a greatly disturbed look on her face. She wiped the frame that was clouded with moisture. It was stiflingly hot. Alcée got up and joined her at the window, looking over her shoulder. The rain was coming down in sheets obscuring the view of far-off cabins and enveloping the distant wood in a gray mist. The playing of the lightning was incessant. A bolt struck a tall chinaberry tree at the edge of the field. It

filled all visible space with a blinding glare and the crash seemed to invade
the very boards they stood upon.

Calixta put her hands to her eyes, and with a cry, staggered backward.   20
Alcée's arm encircled her, and for an instant he drew her close and spas-
modically to him.

"*Bonté!*" she cried, releasing herself from his encircling arm and
retreating from the window, "the house'll go next! If I only knew w'ere Bibi
was!" She would not compose herself; she would not be seated. Alcée
clasped her shoulders and looked into her face. The contact of her warm,
palpitating body when he had unthinkingly drawn her into his arms, had
aroused all the old-time infatuation and desire for her flesh.

"Calixta," he said, "don't be frightened. Nothing can happen. The house
is too low to be struck, with so many tall trees standing about. There! aren't
you going to be quiet? say, aren't you?" He pushed her hair back from her
face that was warm and steaming. Her lips were as red and moist as pome-
granate seed. Her white neck and a glimpse of her full, firm bosom disturbed him powerfully. As she glanced up at him the fear in her liquid blue
eyes had given place to a drowsy gleam that unconsciously betrayed a sensuous desire. He looked down into her eyes and there was nothing for him
to do but gather her lips in a kiss. It reminded him of Assumption.

"Do you remember—in Assumption, Calixta?" he asked in a low voice
broken by passion. Oh! she remembered; for in Assumption he had kissed
her and kissed and kissed her; until his senses would well nigh fail, and to
save her he would resort to a desperate flight. If she was not an immaculate
dove in those days, she was still inviolate; a passionate creature whose very
defenselessness had made her defense, against which his honor forbade
him to prevail. Now—well, now—her lips seemed in a manner free to be
tasted, as well as her round, white throat and her whiter breasts.

They did not heed the crashing torrents, and the roar of the elements
made her laugh as she lay in his arms. She was a revelation in that dim, mysterious chamber; as white as the couch she lay upon. Her firm, elastic flesh that
was knowing for the first time its birthright, was like a creamy lily that the sun
invites to contribute its breath and perfume to the undying life of the world.

The generous abundance of her passion, without guile or trickery, was   25
like a white flame which penetrated and found response in depths of his
own sensuous nature that had never yet been reached.

When he touched her breasts they gave themselves up in quivering
ecstasy, inviting his lips. Her mouth was a fountain of delight. And when he
possessed her, they seemed to swoon together at the very borderland of
life's mystery.

He stayed cushioned upon her, breathless, dazed, enervated, with his
heart beating like a hammer upon her. With one hand she clasped his head,
her lips lightly touching his forehead. The other hand stroked with a sooth-
ing rhythm his muscular shoulders.

The growl of the thunder was distant and passing away. The rain beat
softly upon the shingles, inviting them to drowsiness and sleep. But they
dared not yield.

The rain was over; and the sun was turning the glistening green world
into a palace of gems. Calixta, on the gallery, watched Alcée ride away. He
turned and smiled at her with a beaming face; and she lifted her pretty chin
in the air and laughed aloud.

III

Bobinôt and Bibi, trudging home, stopped without at the cistern to make   30
themselves presentable.

"My! Bibi, w'at will yo' mama say! You ought to be ashame'. You
oughtn' put on those good pants. Look at 'em! An' that mud on yo' collar!
How you got that mud on yo' collar, Bibi? I never saw such a boy!" Bibi was
the picture of pathetic resignation. Bobinôt was the embodiment of serious solicitude as he strove to remove from his own person and his son's
the signs of their tramp over heavy roads and through wet fields. He
scraped the mud off Bibi's bare legs and feet with a stick and carefully
removed all traces from his heavy brogans. Then, prepared for the worst—
the meeting with an overscrupulous housewife, they entered cautiously at
the back door.

Calixta was preparing supper. She had set the table and was dripping
coffee at the hearth. She sprang up as they came in.

"Oh, Bobinôt! You back! My! but I was uneasy. W'ere you been during
the rain? An' Bibi? he ain't wet? he ain't hurt?" She had clasped Bibi and was
kissing him effusively. Bobinôt's explanations and apologies which he had
been composing all along the way, died on his lips as Calixta felt him to see
if he were dry, and seemed to express nothing but satisfaction at their safe
return.

"I brought you some shrimps, Calixta," offered Bobinôt, hauling the can
from his ample side pocket and laying it on the table.

"Shrimps! Oh, Bobinôt! you too good fo' anything!" and she gave him a   35
smacking kiss on the cheek that resounded. "*J'vous réponds,* we'll have
feas' to night! umph-umph!"

Bobinôt and Bibi began to relax and enjoy themselves, and when the
three seated themselves at table they laughed much and so loud that anyone might have heard them as far away as Laballière's.

IV

Alcée Laballière wrote to his wife, Clarisse, that night. It was a loving letter, full
of tender solicitude. He told her not to hurry back, but if she and the babies
liked it at Biloxi, to stay a month longer. He was getting on nicely; and though
he missed them, he was willing to bear the separation a while longer—
realizing that their health and pleasure were the first things to be considered.

V

As for Clarisse, she was charmed upon receiving her husband's letter.
She and the babies were doing well. The society was agreeable; many of
her old friends and acquaintances were at the bay. And the first free
breath since her marriage seemed to restore the pleasant liberty of her
maiden days. Devoted as she was to her husband, their intimate conju-
gal life was something which she was more than willing to forego for a
while.

So the storm passed and everyone was happy.

[1898]

SANDRA CISNEROS (1954–)

Sandra Cisneros grew up in Chicago and Mexico City. She earned her MA degree from the Iowa Writers' Workshop, and returned shortly thereafter to her previous alma mater, Loyola University, to work as a college recruiter. She has published collections of both short stories and poems, as well as books intended for juvenile audiences, and she has taught at high schools and universities. She has received the American Book Award, two National Endowment for the Arts Fellowships, and a MacArthur Fellowship.

One Holy Night

> About the truth, if you give it to a person, then he has power
> over you. And if someone gives it to you, then they have made
> themselves your slave. It is a strong magic. You can never take it
> back.
>
> —*Chaq Uxmal Paloquín*

He said his name was Chaq. Chaq Uxmal Paloquín. That's what he told me. He was of an ancient line of Mayan kings. Here, he said, making a map with the heel of his boot, this is where I come from, the Yucatán, the ancient cities. This is what Boy Baby said.

It's been eighteen weeks since Abuelita chased him away with the broom, and what I'm telling you I never told nobody, except Rachel and Lourdes, who know everything. He said he would love me like a revolution, like a religion. Abuelita burned the pushcart and sent me here, miles from home, in this town of dust, with one wrinkled witch woman who rubs my belly with jade, and sixteen nosy cousins.

I don't know how many girls have gone bad from selling cucumbers. I know I'm not the first. My mother took the crooked walk too, I'm told, and I'm sure my Abuelita has her own story, but it's not my place to ask.

Abuelita says it's Uncle Lalo's fault because he's the man of the family and if he had come home on time like he was supposed to and worked the pushcart on the days he was told to and watched over his goddaughter, who is too foolish to look after herself, nothing would've happened, and I wouldn't have to be sent to Mexico. But Uncle Lalo says if they had never left Mexico in the first place, shame enough would have kept a girl from doing devil things.

I'm not saying I'm not bad. I'm not saying I'm special. But I'm not like   5
the Allport Street girls, who stand in doorways and go with men into alleys.

All I know is I didn't want it like that. Not against the bricks or hunkering in somebody's car. I wanted it come undone like gold thread, like a tent full of birds. The way it's supposed to be, the way I knew it would be when I met Boy Baby.

But you must know, I was no girl back then. And Boy Baby was no boy. Chaq Uxmal Paloquín. Boy Baby was a man. When I asked him how old he was he said he didn't know. The past and the future are the same thing. So he seemed boy and baby and man all at once, and the way he looked at me, how do I explain?

I'd park the pushcart in front of the Jewel food store Saturdays. He bought a mango on a stick the first time. Paid for it with a new twenty. Next

Saturday he was back. Two mangoes, lime juice, and chili powder, keep the change. The third Saturday he asked for a cucumber spear and ate it slow. I didn't see him after that till the day he brought me Kool-Aid in a plastic cup. Then I knew what I felt for him.

Maybe you wouldn't like him. To you he might be a bum. Maybe he looked it. Maybe. He had broken thumbs and burnt fingers. He had thick greasy fingernails he never cut and dusty hair. And all his bones were strong ones like a man's. I waited every Saturday in my same blue dress. I sold all the mango and cucumber, and then Boy Baby would come finally.

What I knew of Chaq was only what he told me, because nobody   10
seemed to know where he came from. Only that he could speak a strange language that no once could understand, said his name translated into boy, or boy-child, and so it was the street people nicknamed him Boy Baby.

I never asked about his past. He said it was all the same and didn't matter, past and the future all the same to his people. But the truth has a strange way of following you, of coming up to you and making you listen to what it has to say.

Night time. Boy Baby brushes my hair and talks to me in his strange language because I like to hear it. What I like to hear him tell is how he is Chaq, Chaq of the people of the sun, Chaq of the temples, and what he says sounds sometimes like broken clay, and at other times like hollow sticks, or like the swish of old feathers crumbling into dust.

He lived behind Esparza & Sons Auto Repair in a little room that used to be a closet—pink plastic curtains on a narrow window, a dirty cot covered with newspapers, and a cardboard box filled with socks and rusty tools. It was there, under one bald bulb, in the back room of the Esparza garage, in the single room with pink curtains, that he showed me the guns—twenty-four in all. Rifles and pistols, one rusty musket, a machine gun, and several tiny weapons with mother-of-pearl handles that looked like toys. So you'll see who I am, he said, laying them all out on the bed of newspapers. So you'll understand. But I didn't want to know.

The stars foretell everything, he said. My birth. My son's. The boy-child who will bring back the grandeur of my people from those who have broken the arrows, from those who have pushed the ancient stones off their pedestals.

Then he told how he had prayed in the Temple of the Magician years   15
ago as a child when his father had made him promise to bring back the ancient ways. Boy Baby had cried in the temple dark that only the bats made holy. Boy Baby who was man and child among the great and dusty guns lay down on the newspaper bed and wept for a thousand years. When I touched him, he looked at me with the sadness of stone.

You must not tell anyone what I am going to do, he said. And what I remember next is how the moon, the pale moon with its one yellow eye, the moon of Tikal, and Tulum, and Chichén, stared through the pink plastic curtains. Then something inside bit me, and I gave out a cry as if the other, the one I wouldn't be anymore, leapt out.

So I was initiated beneath an ancient sky by a great and mighty heir— Chaq Uxmal Paloquín. I, Ixchel, his queen.

The truth is, it wasn't a big deal. It wasn't any deal at all. I put my bloody panties inside my T-shirt and ran home hugging myself. I thought about a lot

of things on the way home. I thought about all the world and how suddenly I became a part of history and wondered if everyone on the street, the
sewing machine lady and the *panadería* saleswomen and the woman with
two kids sitting on the bus bench didn't all know. *Did I look any different?*
Could they tell? We were all the same somehow, laughing behind our
hands, waiting the way all women wait, and when we find out, we wonder
why the world and a million years made such a big deal over nothing.

I know I was supposed to feel ashamed, but I wasn't ashamed. I wanted to stand on top of the highest building, the top-top floor, and yell, *I*
know.

Then I understood why Abuelita didn't let me sleep over at Lourdes's   20
house full of too many brothers, and why the Roman girl in the movies
always runs away from the soldier, and what happens when the scenes in
love stories begin to fade, and why brides blush, and how it is that sex isn't
simply a box you check M or F on in the test we get at school.

I was wise. The corner girls were still jumping into their stupid little
hopscotch squares. I laughed inside and climbed the wooden stairs two by
two to the second floor rear where me and Abuelita and Uncle Lalo live. I
was still laughing when I opened the door and Abuelita asked, Where's the
pushcart?

And then I didn't know what to do.

It's a good thing we live in a bad neighborhood. There are always plenty of
bums to blame for your sins. If it didn't happen the way I told it, it really
could've. We looked and looked all over for the kids who stole my pushcart.
The story wasn't the best, but since I had to make it up right then and there
with Abuelita staring a hole through my heart, it wasn't too bad.

For two weeks I had to stay home. Abuelita was afraid the street kids
who had stolen the cart would be after me again. Then I thought I might go
over to the Esparza garage and take the pushcart out and leave it in some
alley for the police to find, but I was never allowed to leave the house
alone. Bit by bit the truth started to seep out like a dangerous gasoline.

First the nosy woman who lives upstairs from the laundromat told my   25
Abuelita she thought something was fishy, the pushcart wheeled into
Esparza & Sons every Saturday after dark, how a man, the same dark Indian
one, the one who never talks to anybody, walked with me when the sun
went down and pushed the cart into the garage, that one there, and yes we
went inside, there where the fat lady named Concha, whose hair is dyed a
hard black, pointed a fat finger.

I prayed that we would not meet Boy Baby, and since the gods listen
and are mostly good, Esparza said yes, a man like that had lived there but
was gone, had packed a few things and left the pushcart in a corner to pay
for his last week's rent.

We had to pay $20 before he would give us our pushcart back. Then
Abuelita made me tell the real story of how the cart had disappeared, all of
which I told this time, except for that one night, which I would have to tell
anyway, weeks later, when I prayed for the moon of my cycle to come back,
but it would not.

When Abuelita found out I was going to *dar a luz,* she cried until her eyes
were little, and blamed Uncle Lalo, and Uncle Lalo blamed this country, and

Abuelita blamed the infamy of men. That is when she burned the cucumber pushcart and called me a *sinvergüenza* because I *am* without shame.

Then I cried too—Boy Baby was lost from me—until my head was hot with headaches and I fell asleep. When I woke up, the cucumber pushcart was dust and Abuelita was sprinkling holy water on my head.

Abuelita woke up early every day and went to the Esparza garage to see if news about that *demonio* had been found, had Chaq Uxmal Paloquín sent any letters, any, and when the other mechanics heard that name they laughed, and asked if we had made it up, that we could have some letters that had come for Boy Baby, no forwarding address, since he had gone in such a hurry.

There were three. The first, addressed "Occupant," demanded immediate payment for a four-month-old electric bill. The second was one I recognized right away—a brown envelope fat with cake-mix coupons and fabric-softener samples—because we'd gotten one just like it. The third was addressed in a spidery Spanish to a Señor C. Cruz, on paper so thin you could read it unopened by the light of the sky. The return address a convent in Tampico.

This was to whom my Abuelita wrote in hopes of finding the man who could correct my ruined life, to ask if the good nuns might know the whereabouts of a certain Boy Baby—and if they were hiding him it would be of no use because God's eyes see through all souls.

We heard nothing for a long time. Abuelita took me out of school when my uniform got tight around the belly and said it was a shame I wouldn't be able to graduate with the other eighth graders.

Except for Lourdes and Rachel, my grandma and Uncle Lalo, nobody knew about my past. I would sleep in the big bed I share with Abuelita same as always. I could hear Abuelita and Uncle Lalo talking in low voices in the kitchen as if they were praying the rosary, how they were going to send me to Mexico, to San Dionisio de Tlaltepango, where I have cousins and where I was conceived and would've been born had my grandma not thought it wise to send my mother here to the United States so that neighbors in San Dionisio de Tlaltepango wouldn't ask why her belly was suddenly big.

I was happy. I liked staying home. Abuelita was teaching me to crochet the way she had learned in Mexico. And just when I had mastered the tricky rosette stitch, the letter came from the convent which gave the truth about Boy Baby—however much we didn't want to hear.

He was born on a street with no name in a town called Miseria. His father, Eusebio, is a knife sharpener. His mother, Refugia, stacks apricots into pyramids and sells them on a cloth in the market. There are brothers. Sisters too of which I know little. The youngest, a Carmelite, writes me all this and prays for my soul, which is why I know it's all true.

Boy Baby is thirty-seven years old. His name is Chato which means fat-face. There is no Mayan blood.

I don't think they understand how it is to be a girl. I don't think they know how it is to have to wait your whole life. I count the months for the baby to be born, and it's like a ring of water inside me reaching out and out until one day it will tear from me with its own teeth.

Already I can feel the animal inside me stirring in his own uneven sleep. The witch woman says it's the dreams of weasels that make my child sleep the way he sleeps. She makes me eat white bread blessed by the priest, but I know it's the ghost of him inside me that circles and circles, and will not let me rest.

Abuelita said they sent me here just in time, because a little later Boy Baby   40
came back to our house looking for me, and she had to chase him away with the broom. The next thing we hear, he's in the newspaper clippings his sister sends. A picture of him looking very much like stone, police hooked on either arm . . . *on the road to* Las Grutas de Xtacumbilxuna, *the Caves of the Hidden Girl . . . eleven female bodies . . . the last seven years . . .*
   Then I couldn't read but only stare at the little black-and-white dots that make up the face I am in love with.

All my girl cousins here either don't talk to me, or those who do, ask questions they're too young to know *not* to ask. What they want to know really is how it is to have a man, because they're too ashamed to ask their married sisters.
   They don't know what it is to lay so still until his sleep breathing is heavy, for the eyes in the dim dark to look and look without worry at the man-bones and the neck, the man-wrist and man-jaw thick and strong, all the salty dips and hollows, the stiff hair of the brow and sour swirl of sideburns, to lick the fat earlobes that taste of smoke, and stare at how perfect is a man.
   I tell them, "It's a bad joke. When you find out you'll be sorry."

I'm going to have five children. Five. Two girls. Two boys. And one baby.   45
   The girls will be called Lisette and Maritza. The boys I'll name Pablo and Sandro.
   And my baby. My baby will be named Alegre, because life will always be hard.

Rachel says that love is like a big black piano being pushed off the top of a three-story building and you're waiting on the bottom to catch it. But Lourdes says it's not that way at all. It's like a top, like all the colors in the world are spinning so fast they're not colors anymore and all that's left is a white hum.
   There was a man, a crazy who lived upstairs from us when we lived on South Loomis. He couldn't talk, just walked around all day with this harmonica in his mouth. Didn't play it. Just sort of breathed through it, all day long, wheezing, in and out, in and out.
   This is how it is with me. Love I mean.   50

                                                            [1992]

Amanda Davis (1971–)

After graduating from college as a theater major, Amanda Davis worked in public relations for a theatre at the same time she waited tables. Her experience in New York in the corporate world inspired her to return to waiting tables while she focused on her writing. She has also worked in the fiction department at Esquire *magazine. Her first novel was* Wonder When You'll Miss Me; *her first collection of stories,* Circling the Drain, *was published in 1999.*

Louisiana Loses Its Cricket Hum

We who were not there cannot possibly understand how they came like flies: swarming up all of a sudden and buzzing over the horizon, thickening the sky with their heavy shadows. We were playing poker at Jimmy's—beers sweating, fans going round and round, the sound of pool clicking the moments by. Everyone admits it: We all felt the air chill. The dense Louisiana air disappeared and an icy breeze sliced through.

Andy said *Damn,* threw his cards on the table, and headed for the jukebox: full house and James Brown.

I felt it like cold fingers crawling up the back of my neck. *Something is happening all right,* but I just folded quietly and waited to see how the chips lay.

We did not deny that something was happening, but we didn't let it thwart our game. I was down twenty-seven dollars and Jerry was up at least twice that. My gut burned from bar food and the hair on the back of my neck prickled and danced. I wondered who or what we'd invoked, but I didn't see any of it—deep in my liquidy bubble the world warbled on it its usual uneven trajectory, leaning this way and that, odd as ever.

But out there. If you were out there you might have seen it. Luther Binge said he saw the livestock and children proceed single file: the cows and chickens marching in a straight line, the kids frozen in prayer. *Been watching too much television,* I thought, but who was I to say? Of course I wasn't out there. I was swimming in my own inebriated world, muddling things further with the smooth darkness of booze. I was losing at poker, down a hand in life. I was waiting to be swept away by something, but hiding in Jimmy's bar so it couldn't find me if it wanted to.

There was nothing unusual about that night. It started like they always did. We gathered one by one and bought each other drinks. Shots of bourbon and sweaty beer chasers. We swaggered and lurched around until we had enough for cards and then we gathered around the table in the back—like any night—and dealt ourselves a hand, tossing insults like they were the petals of flowers, that loosely, that softly.

I should have been home.

Later Mamie Dixon described them like insects, said she thought the sky was full of giant wasps. I can't imagine a more terrifying sight but she says, *No,* says, *They were beautiful, really.*

But that was the summer of days I closed the restaurant early and came home late, afraid to look Ellie in the eyes if she was up. I wanted nothing to come between me and the inevitable fact of her departure, which I felt lurking on the horizon like the evening's dull hum. I drank until I had buried the soupiness of things—that the elements of my life had remained the same for as long as I could remember, that we made sense only up to a point, that something very wrong was happening all around me, something unnamable and steady. Rolling upon me with the unshakable nature of time and history, streaming generations all coming one after the other like a rush of water, like a flood of humanity.

And like this I was overcome.

At Jimmy's we didn't talk this way. Alan racked and I shot and the sound of me connecting, of me scattering balls to all the corners of that green felt earth was as satisfying as anything I knew. Icy cold beer and music that made our heads nod, our hips swing and grunt in agreement. I never knew then what I needed to know. I never knew that misery leaks like a terrible viscous thing. I never knew the toxins I could spread, nor the stain my unhappiness could create. I never knew what left me lurching toward emptiness, a skeptic looking for proof of abandonment.

I remember coming home after, walking the path to my house. It was dark, all the streetlights blown out, though what worried me was not the blank night sky or the feeling that something had just been there, but the dark of my house. That's what worried me. Each step closer I got, the clench on my stomach tightened until at the porch steps I felt myself shaking and knew if I went in I wouldn't like what I'd find: kitchen light out and Ellie not there.

I slept under pine trees out near Hubert Hall's yard. I always found I moved toward his house when something went wrong. Found his lawn the best place to sleep off a drunk. It seemed to me they led a graced life, Hubert and Betsy and their four perfect children. Their plants flourished, their windows shined. I doubted they had cavities, or rashes, or any other side effects of life, any one of them.

We had no kids. Though Ellie tried fertility tests at one point, what was wrong with us was less nature and more will. How could I bring a baby into a world I felt deteriorating? How could I say I loved someone if I believed that cataclysmic things would find us? Ellie tried to drag me to church with her but I wouldn't go. *I don't believe,* I told her. *What's the point?* She looked away then, out the window or up at the ceiling. *Who you asking for help?* I muttered, but when she asked what I'd said, I mumbled, *Nothing.*

I woke to ants crawling on my face and the peeping whispers of the twin Hall boys, blond and saucer-eyed, poking my legs. I rose and brushed myself free, creaking with the stiffness of a night spent on the ground. The air was light, the day warm. The open sunlight seemed like a redemption of everything, as if to prove something dark couldn't fly to a land as lovely as ours.

Blinking in the light, I made my slow way up the slope to my house. There were brass bands playing in the back of my head and there was Ellie, rocking on the porch. One look at her face told me everything was different, but I chose to ignore that. I smiled like any other day and sat beside her on the swing.

We tossed gently, back and forth, through the cacophony of living things calling to each other. If I could have held the moment in my palm it would have been a shiny bead, precious, carried everywhere for good luck. Off in the distance I saw Len Belton mowing his lawn. Ellie put her head on my shoulder and closed her eyes. We still hadn't spoken. I pushed off a little on the porch and we swung back and forth.

And I knew. Her whole body was tense, anxiety crackled in her like lightning. I could feel it coming off her in waves and it turned everything in me cold.

There's something I have to tell you, Ellie said.

I smiled, a stiff jerk of the lips, but held my breath and couldn't speak. *Something is very very wrong,* she said.

In front of us spread the landscape of our lives: the slope of the hill down our yard to the cul-de-sac. The Halls' house to the left of us, the

15

20

Wintersons' to the right. Off in the distance was the spire of the First Congregational Church of the Lord and beyond that Jimmy's bar. There was a school farther up the road, people, lives. There was the restaurant I managed, the pool we swam in, the library that lent me ideas. There were trees—pine, willow, oak—flowers, honeysuckle, bees. All of it spread from the axis of us into a swirl of life here on earth at that moment. All of it.

I know you know it, she said. *You slept outside, seems like you're aware of something, but we have to* talk *now. Kenny. We have to.*

It's funny how knowing everything is about to up and tumble away from you turns the world rich, nauseating colors. Background sounds rise up and roar at you, sink down and envelop you. I felt it all like a gasp for air.

UFOs, I said. *What happened last night?*

It's not what happened last night, she said. *It's a lot bigger than that.*   25

I still had my arm around her and her head rested on my shoulder. *No,* I whispered and kissed her on the forehead. *We can work it out, El. We always do.*

She sat up and curled herself into a little ball on the other end of the swing, which jerked from side to side.

I don't think so, she said. *Really.*

I couldn't look at her. The sky threatened to fall down. Trees tried to pull up their roots.

You're just confused.   30

I don't want to be your wife anymore, Kenny, she said and undid ten years like they were nothing more than ribbon.

You don't mean that, I said and stood up. The sky had darkened, the wind picked up.

But it tumbled out of her, black and thick: *I don't want to wake up to hear you showering, don't want to find your hairs in the bathroom, your laundry mixed in with mine. I don't want to hear you late-night stumbling drunk or watch you reading book after book and still managing the stupid restaurant.*

I couldn't breathe, but I don't exactly remember what happened next. She was gone when I came to, lying on the porch. She must have stepped over me to leave. I heard the last thing she said, though: *I'm in love with someone else.*

I couldn't quite bear to go inside, so I sat on the steps while the rain threatened to come. Nothing felt like it belonged to me. Jay Winterson came out   35
his back door with a garbage bag. He waved and started up the hill.

Hear about the visitors? he hollered.

I nodded but my throat felt tiny.

Rona says the kids were frozen stiff. She wants them to draw me pictures, he yelled, scratching the place where his hair was thinning. *Wants the kids to draw the whole thing. Keeps saying, show Daddy! Show Daddy what it's all about.*

I didn't see a thing, Jay, I shouted back. My voice cracked.

He laughed and scratched his head again. *Andy phoned earlier. Said*   40
Gloria was all packed and missing when he got up this morning.

He shifted from one foot to the other, took a deep breath before spitting it out. *You think whatever it was is coming back?*

I stared at him as wind began to whip at the trees of our neighborhood.

I'm at a loss here, I told him.

What? he called. It was getting harder to hear over the weather. He was fifteen feet away with a bag of trash hollering to me. I waited for fire to sweep through or the earth to open up like a bottomless cavern and swallow us all, but it just began, gently, to rain.

Ellie's left me, Jay, I called down. *I think I'd better go inside.*   45

I rose unsteadily and reached for the railing. Jay looked uneasy and took a step back.

Aw, Kenny, he said. *Aw,* and he stood there rocking back and forth on his heels, hands stuffed in his pockets like a grade school kid.

Hey listen, you call us if you need anything, he finally shouted and turned to go.

None of it mattered, none of it. I could have been a better this or that, I could have spread myself through the world in a more generous manner. I could have loved Ellie with all of me but she still might have left. The silence of my life was thorough and deafening. I watched him walk away and wished for something in me to erupt.

I was in the wrong place when it happened is all. They had to come   50
back. I wanted them to sweep through our town again and freeze whoever they needed to get to me. I wanted them to shatter everything I knew so I would wake wherever I woke with my world new and pink and fresh. I sat in the dim gray kitchen while the rain beat down and wished, with all the hope and whiskey I had left, for the force of their anger, the size of their hate; for them to come back and land on my house.

I went back out on the porch. The rain had picked up and it blew in sheets now. Trees bent, the sky was the eerie yellow-gray of southern storms. I stood on the steps rocking back and forth. *Return!* I hollered into the whirling wind. *Come back, you cowardly bastards!* I was weeping then, wet and empty. How I must look to them: a small drunk man sobbing on a tiny porch. *You!* I begged with everything I had, as loud as I could. *How can you expect us to pray to you?*

[2001]

RITA DOVE (1952–)

Please see Appendix C for a brief biography of Dove.

The Vibraphone

Christie Phillips was a student in musicology—concentration baroque. Her parents never knew what to make of this—to them, gospel was the only serious music, and whenever she went home to Toledo, they would try to drag her to their AME church to play the organ.

The requirement in college to master at least three instruments had led Christie to the harpsicord—and suddenly she was plunged into the narrow yet measureless world of early music, where embellishment rippled into formata, where time changed to suit one's mood.

When Jerry Murdon had his debut at Carnegie Hall, Christie managed to get a ticket, even though the concert was sold out. Murdon had all the promise of young genius—piano study with the best teachers at Berkeley and then Juilliard, first prize at the National Bach Competition for young performers, several years' experience as a soloist at Spoleto. Half of the female music students at the prominent music schools in the country were in love with him. "There is nothing," the critics were fond of saying, "to keep Murdon from becoming one of the greatest pianists of our time."

At Carnegie Hall he burst onstage, correct and handsome in tails, his reddish afro like an explosion under the spotlight, a tense authority in the jagged face. He seated himself, long curved fingers poised for the Bach Sonata in D Major . . . there was silence. Silence that deepened and chilled the longer he played, for there was something different in this familiar music when he played it—something pepped up, askew. Stunned silence, then, and finally, hissing. Husbands walked out; their wives, some actually in tears, followed more slowly. Jerry Murdon kept on playing; the concert was being recorded and the sound engineers let the tapes run, more from a morbid curiosity than any sense of duty.

Columbia refused to release the tapes; they bought themselves out of the contract, and Murdon used the money to produce his own record. He called his label Lunar Discs—a reference to the fact that Bach had milked his eyes blind copying music by moonlight. The album jacket showed Jerry Murdon at the piano, tails flying and afro exploding, in the far-right corner of a starthick sky a hovering full moon, and the man in the moon was Johann Sebastian Bach. The title spilled across the sky in cobalt script: "Recreation of the Soul. Murdon Plays Bach."   5

Of course Christie bought the album. The record became a hit. It was Bach of the twentieth century—industrialized, anonymous, defiant, the playing technically exquisite. She tried to duplicate certain passages on the conservatory pianos but always came away discouraged. When, on his next LP, Jerry Murdon switched to electric piano, she switched with him.

Five years Jerry Murdon dominated the jazz scene, his Bach interpretations growing more estranged. Then, quite suddenly, there were no more concerts, no more recordings. His rivals claimed he had run out of ideas; gossip columnists predicted yet another victim to drugs. *Billboard* magazine reported seeing him on a beach somewhere in Italy. No confirmations nor contradictions were made in this chaos of wild speculations; Murdon, wherever he was, kept silent and the public, disappointed and just a bit insulted, dropped him. Jerry Murdon, King of Bach, was soon one of the forgotten.

In the meantime Christie had started on the theoretical section of her dissertation, an analysis of her own transfiguration of an obscure seventeenth-century Italian instrumental "opera" for harpsichord, viola da gamba and baroque flute. The composer was very obscure indeed; most of the documents weren't available. She grew tired, discouraged, and humiliated; more from despair than the hope of finding any material, she finally applied for a summer scholarship to conduct research at the musical institute in Florence . . . and was accepted.

Florence was like walking through an oil painting, one of those thronging street scenes radiating with color and the newly-discovered landscape of perspectives. She had more than enough time to decipher those manuscripts waiting for her; September was two weeks gone and the days still warm . . . what better time to take off for a weekend?

That Friday she took a train to Pisa, made the obligatory snapshots of   10
the tower, then caught a local bus to Viareggio. Viareggio was like any Italian resort town—a beach littered with beer cans, tar and seaweed and—
parallel to the beach—the promenade, a broad avenue lined on either side
with expensive jewelry stores and bright boutiques.

It was too windy for swimming; the beach was deserted. She turned back
towards town. Immediately behind the promenade, the city sprouted into a
thicket of smaller, grimier streets where the Italians lived and shopped. She
wandered around, looking for an intimate café, something—when, about two
blocks away, a black man with a dog stepped out into the street—his long
head, the reddish afro, the silhouette so familiar from a distance. . . .

He was gone. She quickened her pace; but the street she thought he
must have turned into was empty. Perplexed, she returned to the corner
and walked slowly to the spot where he had appeared. She was standing in
front of a music store.

The small round man behind the counter looked at her with a patient,
dubious smile. "L'americano?" he repeated, scratching his head.

"Si," she said. "He's a pianist, isn't he?"

"Paese," he replied. He took her to the door and pointed up the street   15
energetically.

Several times she stopped to ask an old woman or a passing school
child the way to Paese, for the street had a maddening habit of dissolving
into spidery alleys. Finally the last stucco house was behind her and the
streets curved upwards sharply, into the vineyards. There she stopped and
put out her thumb.

A cherry red Alfa Romeo pulled over and a middle-aged man in a slinky
shirt rolled down the window: "I'll take you wherever you want, signorina!"
No other car stopped for a good fifteen minutes. Then she got lucky.

A battered, three-wheel pick-up halted, and a young man in baggy
white overalls and paint-splattered boots opened the door. He was
employed at the new villa going up outside the village of Paese, where he
hauled plaster every day and once—about this time of day, three or four—
the Black American with the dog. . . .

The pavement was broken in places, and for a while they rode in
silence, the pick-up slamming hard into the rutted path. Directly outside the
village, they stopped.

"This is as far as I go, signorina."   20

"But—the American?" she stammered.

"This is as far as I took him, signorina. As far as Paese." He hesitated.
"The signorina has been looking for the American for a long time?" His
voice grew dark, solicitous.

"Not really. That is—"

The disappointment in his face surprised her—what had he been
expecting? Then it hit her: in his head an elaborate melodrama, a scenario
in the operatic mode, was brewing. She gasped and swallowed at the same
time, bringing tears to her eyes.

"Signorina!"   25

He held out a hand, checked himself. She buried her face in her hands.

"Signorina, don't cry! Please."

A hand on her arm, patting it as a child pats a doll.

"Don't cry," he repeated, his voice hardening. He put the pick-up in gear. "Don't worry, signorina. We will find him."

Pulling up in front of a crumbling pink church at the village square, he got out and walked over to the neighboring cafe where a group of old men were playing dominoes. The consultation was brief; he returned smiling. The path led through Paese and out the other side, where the road became a dirt trail twisting still higher into the mountains. After another ten minutes of hairpin curves and teeth-jarring potholes, they pulled up behind a rusty Fiat parked at a delapidated gate that seemed to hang in mid-air, suspended by a wilderness of overgrown vegetation.

There was no bell, no mailbox. The gate stood ajar, and beyond it she could just make out the flagstones of a walkway curving through the trees. Christie stepped through the gate. The air was heady with the mixed scents of rosemary and rotting olives. The path swerved to the left.

A bright, clipped lawn, as neat as a starched tablecloth. Rows of flowers, perfectly ordinary daisies and petunias. Dainty white picket fences encasing the plump beds and even a rose arbor.

The house was less spinsterish, two stories high, stone whitewashed to blinding perfection. It was abnormally long and its length was punctuated, from roof to foundation and from pole to pole, with windows.

Then it came, out of nowhere. Music. Sounds wrung from joy and light and squeezed through voltage meters, a whine that twitched like electrocution and sobbed like a maniac; music that robbed the air it rode upon, vibrations that rattled her breath and shoved it back down her throat. It was a sound that made the garden, in its innocent stupidity, glow like a reprimand—a warning from a lost childhood or a lost love, or anything as long as it was lost, lost. . . .

"If it bothers you, I can turn it off."

He looked older than forty—he had grown a beard, which was black, and the reddish afro, his trademark, straggled dully around the mistreated cowl of a speckled gray sweater. The beginnings of a paunch. Hips sunken in, lips full and somehow vulgar in the haggard brown face, dimples cutting along the sides of his cheeks like scars.

He went back inside. A moment later, the terror had stopped.

He reappeared. Wordless, he led her into the house.

The music and the sight of him so suddenly near, so changed, had acted as an anesthetic. She didn't know what to think of the situation, though curiosity and the thrill of adventure helped placate the small anxieties trying to surface.

They entered a large room, airy and bright, an ideal studio. But it was full of reel to reel tape recorders and electronic devices—dubbing machines, splicing decks, amplifiers. Wa-wa pedals littered the floor like poisoned field mice, electrical cords squirming in a maze towards every corner.

Jerry Murdon moved through the room flicking switches, plugging in cords, adjusting tone levels, checking balances. He came to rest at a vibraphone in the center of the room.

"The motif," he said, picking up the mallets. She recognized it as the organ prelude to the fifty-second Cantata: *Falsche Welt, dir trau' ich nicht.*

"—And here it is again."

He flipped a switch and the melodic line, amplified, wailed from massive quadrophonic speakers. He flipped another switch and the same
melody, shaken and broken down nearly beyond recognition, rose from the
floor. Another switch, another—and a roar of sound, grace notes proliferat-
ing like bacteria, chords like a dying train, poured over her . . . and beneath
it all the characteristic undulation of the vibraphone, its relentless throb
taking over her pulse.

"There they are, twenty-four from one. A single source. Can you find   45
the core again?"

"I've—I've lost it."

"But it's there. It's there, you can tell, can't you? Don't try to listen; feel
for it."

She nodded, weakly. He went over to the back wall and pulled a lever.
The music stopped.

"See that hatch?" He pointed to a small square in the ceiling directly
above her. "That's where it all goes. Come on."

He led her upstairs. At first she couldn't make out anything; the shut-   50
ters were drawn. Then she saw a bed, unmade, and an aluminum ladder
hanging from hooks on the wall. She jumped—something growled. Red
eyes glittered from the pillow.

"Quiet, Sebastian!"

The dog grew still. He walked over to the bed, knelt beside it and threw
open the trapdoor. The light from the studio streamed up.

"At night," he said, softly, "I open the hatch and let my latest composition come up. Then I fall asleep and dream the variations." He smiled, his
face suddenly very young.

Christie looked at the blazing hole; it seemed to spread towards her.
"Don't you ever"—she searched for the right word—"get seasick?"

He laughed. "The throbbing, you mean? That's the beauty of it. To float   55
on the lap of the sea, to move with the pitch and reel. To stand up in the
center of things with no point of gravity but your own." He slammed the
hatch shut.

"Would you like some tea?"

This room was much smaller. There was just enough space for a
table—a hexagonal, carved mahogany piece of oriental design, and two tall
leather chairs whose curved backs and armrests were covered with intricate tooling.

"Have a seat—be back in a sec."

She sat down; in the center of the table stood a shallow dish filled with
black candy drops. Licorice. She counted the pieces.

There were exactly twenty-four.   60

Christie looked around, suddenly uneasy. The windows were covered.
Panels of heavy dark red cloth were draped from floor to ceiling to create
an illusion of a six-sided space, like the table. Brocade dragons scaled the
cloth panels.

Jerry Murdon returned, tea things aloft.

"It's not so often I get visitors; I must take advantage of you."

"In what way?" she asked, lightly. She looked over the tray he had
placed between them—smoked oysters skewered with toothpicks, black
olives, sesame rounds, cheese cubes. A bottle of something clear and alcoholic. Cigarettes.

The tea pot exhaled an acrid perfume, Jasmine.   65

"You see," he said, pouring the tea, "I realize you didn't come all the way up here for nothing. Perhaps you came because you're a bored, spoiled little American who thought it would be a blast to see how old Murdon has degenerated. . . ."

"I'm a music student," she said, lamely.

"So," he replied, leaning back, "a music student. Piano, I suppose."

"Harpsichord. I play in a baroque consort."

"More than one way to get at the core," he said, nodding. "Bach, of   70 course, was the purest of them all—but baroque was better than what came afterwards. That maniac Beethoven obscured vision for over a century. Would you like some vodka?"

"No, thank you."

He poured himself a drink. "So why don't you tell me what brings you here."

"I'm studying in Florence." Christie hesitated, "It wasn't easy to find you."

"I can imagine," he countered. "Therefore I won't let you get away unrewarded."

She reached for an oyster, not daring to look him in the eye. He waited,   75 enjoying her discomfort. She thought of her dissertation, in a box in her room in Florence. She thought of the pale sandwiches at the Trattoria. She thought of her first violin, she thought of the first Murdon album with Bach as the man in the moon . . . but none of these thoughts stayed in her mind long enough to count as a full idea. He lifted his shot glass and tossed it off.

"Don't worry," he said, relenting. "You came for my story, didn't you— why I left, how I got here, the whole deal, right?"

She nodded.

"Now then—you might remember, being a fan of mine—" he threw a glance at her, testing—"my keyboard style changed three times during my career. First, of course, there was the classical perfection of Jerry Murdon, the best young pianist of a generation. Then the furor at Carnegie Hall, my real debut in more ways than one. You see, I knew what I wanted; I was just looking for the right break. Colleagues called me an opportunist, critics called me a confidence man. Remember this article?"

He opened one of the table's drawers and extracted a newspaper clipping. "'First he encourages our outrage by his circus antics at Carnegie Hall; now, assured of our attention, he has set out systematically to destroy all that Bach has created. Where, I ask you, in this cacaphony, this parodic bebop, is the spirit of that great man who said he composed "for the glory of God and the recreation of the soul?" What Jerry Murdon is doing amounts to blasphemy.'" He put the clipping away. "Fools," he muttered.

"My second change was in many ways more dramatic than the first. It   80 came a year later, a scant three months after my smashing success at Newport." His dark eyes fixed her like a specimen moth. "My playing became— how shall I describe it?—less agitated, more melodic. One *Downbeat* critic dubbed it 'The Golden Age of Murdon.' The real story begins here. It begins with a woman, naturally.

"She had heard me at Carnegie Hall and was convinced I was a genius. She was tall, attractive, Italian-Jewish descent. She did textile prints for the big ones—Cardin and Blass. Her faith in me was exciting;

indeed, her complete trust spurred me on in more than the musical sphere. I began to see other women, although Elizabeth satisfied me completely. It was an irresistible chain of events; her very submissiveness lured me into more affairs. I was unscrupulous; I wanted her to find out. But she never noticed anything—an intelligent woman, mind you—she chose never to notice anything. I would come home at seven in the morning, stinking of martinis and perfume, with some tale about a new piece I had been working up with the band, and she accepted my story—even if the drummer had phoned the night before to ask where I was.

"I shocked no one except, perhaps, myself. No reproaches, and the thrill fades. Betrayal became time-consuming and, eventually, boring . . . so I stopped. Enter the Golden Age."

He lit a cigarette. "Contrary to the rumors circulated by the press," he added, wryly, "I have never been very highly-sexed."

He pulled the smoke deep into his lungs, leaning back to let it drift down his throat before pushing it out again in a thin gray stream. "When I am making music, I have no time, no room, for anything else. My body disappears. You could call it a by-product of creation. I'm sure, in fact, that if someone investigated the matter, they would find out that God, the supreme artist, has no penis." He smiled. "What is creation after all but a godly act? And what do I need with the pitiful palpitations of human tissues and fluids when my music"—he sprang forward in his seat—"when my music will last forever?"

He leaned back, that youthful look on his face again. Innocent. A fawn.   85

"Cases of sexual disinterest are not so uncommon among artists. Dylan Thomas, for example, neglected his wife—and every other female of the two-legged species—whenever he was engrossed in a poem. And when he had finally written the last line, drunk and freezing in his drafty shack in the Welsh countryside, the rush of creation still glowing, that incredible deranged energy tingling in his groin—do you think he remembered Caitlin, fair and lonely in their farmhouse up the hill? Do you think he thought of a warm bed and the soft words of love?" He paused for effect. "No—he masturbated."

Determined not to give him the satisfaction of showing her shock, Christie held her face impassive. He turned aside abruptly and grimaced. She sipped her tea carefully.

"I finally had what every man or woman of genius needs—a wife."

"So you married her?" she asked, naively. The triumphant look he shot her made her wish she had kept her mouth shut.

"I don't mean marriage contracts and golden rings. I mean wife in all its   90
philosophical implications—that circumstance in which another soul serves as a standard, a foil by which to measure one's progress—or, if you will, one's aberration. I mean the home one turns one's back on, the slippers one kicks aside. The person who believes in you unconditionally. In colloquial terms, a wife."

He paused. "Those were the *cantabile* years. Four years—a perfect quartet. The highest praise"—and he reached in the drawer again, spreading the clippings on the table, articles from *Jazz Monthly, Billboard, Village Voice, Downbeat*—"was written then. When things were almost over. Oh, there were signs. I was dissatisfied. My last record was listless, secondhand,

and I knew it. The third stage flared up—a return to the *prestissimo* of my post-Carnegie days—but my technique had more style than . . . well, brilliance or profundity. I was afraid.

"Then without warning, a woman dies. Elizabeth finds a letter in her mailbox from the attorney in charge of the woman's estate. I didn't think she knew anyone west of the Alleghenies, but there it was, black on white—a sixty-five year old woman dead of asthma complications in Phoenix, Arizona. Elizabeth was an heiress—no considerable fortune but an interesting one nevertheless—namely to all the household and personal possessions of one Mrs. Aaron R. Rosenblatt."

"Her mother?"

He snorted. "Elizabeth was alone in the world. Her parents had died long ago. More tea?"

She shook her head. "I'm ready to try the vodka, please."   95

"Wise decision."

The room was very still. Was it soundproof?

"When I asked her, Elizabeth claimed she had been just an acquaintance, an old neighbor from Brooklyn for whom she bought groceries when she could no longer get around. 'O.K.' I thought, 'I'll go along with that.' It was my turn to believe unconditionally.

"We flew to Arizona. Elizabeth wanted to go alone, but I argued that there were certain business details—liquidating the condominium, for example, or deciding the fate of a six-month old diesel Mercedes—where two heads would be better than one. Besides, I had just finished my fifth record, 'Murdon's Requiem' and I needed a break. 'A little cactus juice will do me good,' I joked. Reluctantly, she agreed.

"I had never been to the Southwest before. It made a very powerful   100
impression on me—a barbarous landscape, raw and beautiful as a baboon's ass."

He looked up, his eyes fierce, bloodshot. "Our great civilization, with its skyscrapers and automobiles"—he was smiling now—"seemed no more than a huge, complicated toy. Mrs. Rosenblatt's condominium complex looked like a battery of cereal boxes hastily set up to ward off a hurricane. We located the correct building, obtained the keys from the manager and let ourselves in. It was an apartment like any other—prefab walls, balcony, built-in shelves, dishwasher and freezer. Color T.V., glass coffee table. At first glance there was little we saw we could use ourselves—maybe the music box from Austria, shaped like a breadbox, with interchangeable melody rolls. Elizabeth discovered a camera with the film still in it. . . .

"We moved on to the kitchen. Spotless formica, stainless steel sinks gleaming like sunken mirrors. A women who kept things up, who would never be caught off guard by unexpected visitors. The kitchen yielded a few odds and ends—a very good old-fashioned meat grinder, like the one my grandmother used, a waffle iron which baked scalloped cakes imprinted with interlocking hearts.

"On to the bedroom, then. A dressing table with the usual assortment of talcs and perfumes, a jewelry box with a ring in it, a diamond in an overladen setting. In the closet, tucked behind polyester pantsuits and cotton sundresses, a very nice mink coat. Elizabeth didn't even want to try it on. 'What's wrong?' I asked, teasing. 'Don't tell me you're superstitious.' I don't like mink,' she snapped, walking out of the room. I had never known her to lose her temper before.

"But I was patient. You see"—he fixed Christie with his bloodshot eyes again—"it was my turn to play wife.

"I decided to explore the rest of the apartment. The bathroom was typ-   105
ical, pink tiles and the smell of bath salts and disinfectant. At the end of the hall a broom closet—nothing to see there—and next to it, opposite the bathroom, another room. The door was shut but the key stood in the lock, so I turned it and pushed the door open.

"The shades were drawn. A single bed, made up like an army cot, stood to the left, the blue blanket folded in a precision envelope and laid at the foot of the mattress. Next to the bed stood a night table, but no lamp. Likewise a bureau against the far wall, devoid of ornaments—no lamp, no knick-knacks, no doilies. The very barrenness of the room, couched in the half light of a day turned dingy by window shades, made me realize how full of life this 'apartment like any other' had been so far. 'Strange,' I thought 'a guest would hardly feel comfortable here'—and that's when I saw it, in a niche in the far right wall. . . ."

His voice trailed off and his gaze, directed towards her but not seeing, was the gaze of the poodle on the bed, a reflected and opaque brilliance.

"The niche," he continued, softly, reverently, "was hidden by a heavy black cloth, with a fluorescent light fastened to the wall above it." His gaze focused briefly, slid away again.

"I went over and lifted the cloth. As with everything Mrs. Rosenblatt owned this, too, was in perfect condition; but there was a difference—for, although the keys' high sheen testified that they had been wiped every day, though the felt damper bar was free of dust, the mallets had not been placed in their holder but lay ready, both pairs, across the keys. As if someone had just left off playing. All this I saw and registered automatically; only much later, in my New York studio, did I put together the entire constellation.

"I found the cord and plugged it in. The discs in the pipes slowly began   110
to turn. I released the damper pedal so that the keys could resonate, picked up the mallets, arranged them to strike perfect fourths. First a C scale—the fourths were nice, and I liked the curious lurching tone of the vibraphone. I was just about to try a few chords when I heard Elizabeth scream in the living room. . . .

"There was a freezing stillness, then the sound of running steps in the hall. She stopped at the door and hung there, holding on to the sides of the doorjamb with both hands. Haunted, face drained of color, she stared at me. Then she fainted.

"By the time she came to, I had carried her into the living room and begun to administer all the first aid one learns from the movies—a cold towel on the forehead, cognac at the lips. She came to and smiled. When she remembered she jumped up, hysterical, and demanded to leave the house. I complied. What else was there to do? We got into the car and drove out of the condominium village, into the desert. The endless vistas of scrubgrass, the wild, magic mountains, seemed to soothe her. I too, was calm, but it was a calmness of despair. I had lost something—I was certain of it—but I couldn't put my finger on what. We drove for nearly an hour. I think we drove in circles; the same adobe ruin loomed up at rhythmic intervals, a caved-in hut with a spot of bright green—a scrap of cloth or a candy wrapper—wedged between two bricks. I said nothing; there was nothing for me to say.

"They had met at a jazz club—one of the countless smoky cellars in Manhattan where young musicians go to try out their wings. He played with a group that did commercial jazz; he was much better than the others. She went up to him afterwards and told him so. They talked. His name was Daniel Rosenblatt."

Christie shifted her position; the chair was very hard. Misreading her restlessness, Jerry Murdon sniffed and laughed shortly.

"I know. It sounds like the typical love affair. In a way, it was. They moved in together after a few months. He took her to meet his mother, who was upset until she learned that Elizabeth was technically Jewish. Then the mother began to hint marriage. She hinted for seven years. Seven years! Finally, they decided to get the license—but first, they said, we'll take the honeymoon. When we come back, we'll tell her. . . .   115

"Where can a young couple go after seven years of blissful shacking up? Somewhere sunny, somewhere south—but not the Bahamas, not Capri, no—a place with a difference. That's when Elizabeth remembered the other half of her blood—peasant blood, her father's, and her grandmother's tales of a life in the mountains, surviving from olives and wine. That's how they decided on Italy."

Tuscany, Christie thought. Paese. *Here.*

"Well, they left Mama in her mink on the airport observation deck, wringing her hands, and to Italy they went—on the beach in the morning, on the mountain paths in the afternoon, and at night in restaurants, wining and dining themselves silly—saltimbocca and fritto misto and canneloni, capuccino in the morning and expresso at night.

"One evening, Daniel decided to have a pear for dessert. There was no reason for either of them to suspect anything; the restaurant, listed with the tourist office, even boasted two stars. The service was swift and polite, the meal impeccable. Who would have suspected that the fruit had been washed too hastily that evening? Who would have thought a simple unwashed pear could breed on its blushing surface such a rare bacillus? Back in their room, Daniel complained of pains in his stomach. An hour later, he couldn't move his legs. . . ."

Murdon lit another cigarette, flung the snuffed match on the floor. "She telephoned an ambulance and rushed him to the hospital. His stomach had   120
stopped hurting; but he was numb up to his nipples. The doctors were helpless. 'A virus,' they said, throwing up their hands. 'Where can we start, there are a million of them in the air . . .' By morning, Daniel Rosenblatt was dead."

Christie watched the cigarette disintegrate, unnoticed, between Murdon's fingers. Was he lying—was the entire story merely invented, a noble allegory of his jumbled ambitions and private doubts? For all the pathos of the story there was also a coldness to it, something structured—as if he had gone over it many times, revising and ornamenting, lying on his bed in the dark with the amplified swell of twenty-four vibraphones frothing below him.

"Now that she had told me," Murdon resumed, the words issuing from his lips almost mechanically, "she felt better, almost cheerful. The energy with which she took charge was baffling. She contacted the lawyer and turned over the management of the remaining personal effects. She decided to keep the Mercedes. As for the vibraphone—Elizabeth's suggestion was to take it to New York with us, where it would bring a better price. I was put in charge of selling it.

"Back in Manhattan, it was as if nothing had happened. She never mentioned Daniel Rosenblatt again, and I never asked. I put an ad in the *Times*, set up the vibraphone in my studio, and waited. But every time I opened the door and saw a prospective buyer's anxious, hopeful face, it was Elizabeth's face I saw, terrified and inscrutable—and I wouldn't sell. When I remembered that face I couldn't practise, either. Instead I sat and looked at the vibraphone, its thirty-six steel plates, those churning columns of sound. What I couldn't understand was why she had never talked about him before. We were an enlightened couple. There was no reason, no reason at all.

"After two weeks had passed, Elizabeth asked me if I had had any luck. I said I had someone coming in in the morning who seemed interested. The next morning I withdrew 3,000 bucks from the bank, gave her the money and told her the customer was satisfied. Then I went to a bar in Soho and got drunk. That night I slept in the studio."

Christie's head was pounding, a dull, wrenching pain to match the thump of her heart, a muffled yelp—but it wasn't her heart at all. It was the poodle, barking at the other end of the hall.   125

"Quiet, Sebastian!" Murdon yelled.

His hand trembled as he reached for the vodka bottle and his voice had an edge to it. "I taught myself to play vibraphone," he said. "I had to play; it was the only way out. I stayed in the studio. When I felt hungry, I heated up a can of soup; when exhaustion overwhelmed me I fell asleep as I was, the mallets in my hands.

"I was asleep when she knocked. I remember it was late afternoon, because the sun slanting through the windows struck the instrument and threw bars of light and shadow on the floor. She demanded an explanation. She began to cry. She said I had to sell it. She begged me to stop playing. 'I can't stop,' I said. I was telling the truth, but she didn't believe me."

Murdon reached for a drawer. A vicious tug sent packets of letters, bound with red string, spilling onto the rug.

"They're all the same," he said, pushing the letters together. "Variations on a theme. She can't leave me alone; but she can't come to me, either. So she writes to me. My fan mail," he whispered, gazing at the heap of envelopes.   130

He stood up abruptly. "If you'll excuse me, I have work to do."

He was kicking her out; shocked, disappointed, Christie picked up her purse and followed him downstairs. He opened the door and stood back to let her by, his face a contemptuous mask.

"They all go in the end, with their tails tucked under," he said. "Don't flatter yourself. You're not the first one to seek Murdon out in the wilds of Tuscany. Every summer someone shows up, sits still and listens."

Christie held out her hand to say goodbye but he stood transfixed, leaning against the door and staring at some point beyond the arbor. "It's the strangest thing," he whispered. "I talk and talk, and you listen. But you never tell anyone else, not a peep"—his face twisted suddenly—"his spell is that strong."

The door closed. Christie turned and began walking slowly down   135
the path. Behind her, the music started up again, that surging, choking wail, a clamor against wasted innocence—she shivered looking over the garden—a search for the contentment lost long ago, without anyone knowing it.

[1985]

LOUISE ERDRICH (1954–)

Louise Erdrich graduated from the first coeducational class at Dartmouth in 1977 with a degree in anthropology. She then worked various jobs (as a waitress and as an attendant weighing trucks on the interstate, for instance) before being awarded a fellowship to attend the writing program at Johns Hopkins in 1979. She has published two collections of poetry, four novels, and two collections of short stories. Her awards include the Academy of American Poets Prize, a Pushcart Prize for Poetry, the O. Henry Prize for short fiction, and a Guggenheim Fellowship.

Wild Geese

Nector Kashpaw

On Friday mornings, I go down to the sloughs with my brother Eli and wait for the birds to land. We have built ourselves a little blind. Eli has second sense and an aim I cannot match, but he is shy and doesn't like to talk. In this way it is a good partnership. Because I got sent to school, I am the one who always walks into town and sells what we shoot. I get the price from the Sisters, who cook for the priests, and then I come home and split the money in half. Eli usually takes his bottle off into the woods, while I go into town, to the fiddle dance, and spark the girls.

So there is a Friday near sundown, the summer I am out of school, that finds me walking up the hill with two geese slung from either wrist, tied with leather bands. Just to set the record clear, I am a good-looking boy, tall and slim, without my father's belly hanging in the way. I can have the pick of girls, is what I'm saying. But that doesn't matter anyhow, because I have already decided that Lulu Nanapush is the one. She is the only one of them I want.

I am thinking of her while I walk—those damn eyes of hers, sharp as ice picks, and the curl of her lips. Her figure is round and plush, yet just at the edge of slim. She is small, yet she will never be an armful or an eyeful because I'll never get a bead on her. I know that even now. She never stops moving long enough for me to see her all in a piece. I catch the gleam on her hair, the flash of her arm, a sly turn of hip. Then she is gone. I think of her little wet tongue and I have to stop then and there, in my tracks, at the taste that floods into my mouth. She is a tart berry full of juice, and I know she is mine. I cannot wait for the night to start. She will be waiting in the bush.

Because I am standing there, lost on the empty road, half drowned in the charms of Lulu, I never see Marie Lazarre barrel down. In fact, I never even hear her until it is too late. She comes straight down like a wagon unbraked, like a damn train. Her eye is on me, glaring under a stained strip of sheet. Her hand is wound tight in a pillowcase like a boxer's fist.

"Whoa," I say, "slow down girl."   5

"Move aside," she says.

She tries to pass. Out of reflex I grab her arm, and then I see the initialed pillowcase. *SHC* is written on it in letters red as wine. Sacred Heart Convent. What is it doing on her arm? They say I am smart as a whip around here, but this time I am too smart for my own good. Marie Lazarre is the youngest daughter of a family of horse-thieving drunks. Stealing sacred linen fits what I know of that blood, so I assume she is running off with the Sisters' pillowcase and other valuables. Who knows? I think a chalice might be hidden beneath her skirt. It occurs to me, next moment, I may get a money bonus if I bring her back.

And so, because I am saving for the French-style wedding band I intend to put on the finger of Lulu Nanapush, I do not let Marie Lazarre go down the hill.

Not that holding on to her is easy.

"Lemme go, you damn Indian," she hisses. Her teeth are strong looking,   10
large and white. "You stink to hell!"

I have to laugh. She is just a skinny white girl from a family so low you cannot even think they are in the same class as Kashpaws. I shake her arm. The dead geese tied to my wrist swing against her hip. I never move her. She is planted solid as a tree. She begins to struggle to get loose, and I look up the hill. No one coming from that direction, or down the road, so I let her try. I am playing with her. Then she kicks me with her hard-sole shoe.

"Little girl," I growl, "don't play with fire!"

Maybe I shouldn't do this, but I twist her arm and screw it up tight. Then I am ashamed of myself because tears come, suddenly, from her eyes and hang bitter and gleaming from her lashes. So I let up for a moment. She moves away from me. But it is just to take aim. Her brown eyes glaze over like a wounded mink's, hurt but still fighting vicious. She launches herself forward and rams her knee in my stomach.

I lose my balance and pitch over. The geese pull me down. Somehow in falling I grip the puffed sleeve of her blouse and tear it from her shoulder.

There I am, on the ground, sprawled and burdened by the geese,   15
clutching that sky-color bit of cloth. I think at first she will do me more damage with her shoes. But she just stands glaring down on me, rail-tough and pale as birch, her face loose and raging beneath the white cloth. I think that now the tears will spurt out. She will sob. But Marie is the kind of tree that doubles back and springs up, whips singing.

She bends over lightly and snatches the sleeve from my grip.

"Lay there you ugly sonofabitch," she says.

I never answer, never say one word, just surge forward, knock her over, and roll on top of her and hold her pinned down underneath my whole length.

"Now we'll talk, skinny white girl, dirty Lazarre!" I yell in her face.

The geese are to my advantage now; their weight on my arms helps pin   20
her; their dead wings flap around us; their necks loll, and their black eyes stare,
frozen. But Marie is not the kind of girl to act frightened of a few dead geese.

She stares into my eyes, furious and silent, her lips clenched white.

"Just give me that pillowcase," I say, "and I'll let you go. I'm gonna bring
that cloth back to the nuns."

She burns up at me with such fierceness, then, that I think she hasn't
understood what a little thing I am asking. Her eyes are tense and wild, animal eyes. My neck chills.

"There now," I say in a more reasonable voice, "quit clutching it and I'll
let you up and go. You shouldn't have stole it."

"Stole it!" she spits. "Stole!"   25

Her mouth drops wide open. If I want I could look all the way down
her throat. Then she makes an odd raspfile noise, cawing like a crow.

She is laughing! It is too much. The Lazarre is laughing in my face!

"Stop that." I put my hand across her mouth. Her slick white teeth
click, harmless, against my palm, but I am not satisfied.

"Lemme up," she mumbles.

"No," I say.   30

She lays still, then goes stiller. I look into her eyes and see the hard tears
have frozen in the corners. She moves her legs. I keep her down. Something
happens. The bones of her hips lock to either side of my hips, and I am held
in a light vise. I stiffen like I am shocked. It hits me then I am lying full length
across a woman, not a girl. Her breasts graze my chest, soft and pointed. I
cannot help but lower myself the slightest bit to feel them better. And then
I am caught. I give way. I cannot help myself, because, to my everlasting wonder, Marie is all tight plush acceptance, graceful movements, little jabs that
lead me underneath her skirt where she is slick, warm, silk.

When I come back, and when I look down on her, I know how badly I
have been weakened. Her tongue flattens against my palm. I know that
when I take my hand away the girl will smile, because somehow I have
been beaten at what I started on this hill. And sure enough, when I take my
hand away she speaks.

"I've had better."

I know that isn't true, that I was just now the first, and I can even hear
the shake in her voice, but that makes no difference. She scares me. I scramble away from her, holding the geese in front. Although she is just a little girl
knocked down in the dirt, she sits up, smooth as you please, fixes the black
skirt over her knees, rearranges the pillowcase tied around her hand.

We are unsheltered by bushes. Anyone could have seen us. I glance   35
around. On the hill, the windows dark in the whitewashed brick seem to
harbor a thousand holy eyes widening and narrowing.

How could I? It is then I panic, mouth hanging open, all but certain.
They saw! I can hardly believe what I have done.

Marie is watching me. She sees me swing blind to the white face of the
convent. She knows exactly what is going through my mind.

"I hope they saw it," she says in the crow's rasp.

I shut my mouth, then open it, then shut my mouth again. Who is this
girl? I feel my breath failing like a stupid fish in the airless space around her.
I lose control.

"I never did!" I shout, breaking my voice. I whirl to her. She is looking   40
at the geese I hold in front to hide my shame. I speak wildly.

"You made me! You forced me!"

"I made you!" She laughs and shakes her hand, letting the pillowcase
drop clear so that I can see the ugly wound.

"I didn't make you do anything," she says.

Her hand looks bad, cut and swollen, and it has not been washed. Even
afraid as I am, I cannot help but feel how bad her hand must hurt and throb.
Thinking this causes a small pain to shoot through my own hand. The girl's
hand must have hurt when I threw her on the ground, and yet she didn't
cry out. Her head, too. I have to wonder what is under the bandage. Did the
nuns catch her and beat her when she tried to steal their linen?

The dead birds feel impossibly heavy. I untie them from my wrists and   45
let them fall in the dirt. I sit down beside her.

"You can take these birds home. You can roast them," I say. "I am giving
them to you."

Her mouth twists. She tosses her head and looks away.

I'm not ashamed, but there are some times this happens: alone in the
woods, checking the trapline, I find a wounded animal that hasn't died well,
or, worse, it's still living, so that I have to put it out of its misery. Sometimes
it's just a big bird I only winged. When I do what I have to do, my throat
swells closed sometimes. I touch the suffering bodies like they were killed
saints I should handle with gentle reverence.

This is how I take Marie's hand. This is how I hold her wounded hand
in my hand.

She never looks at me. I don't think she dares let me see her face. We   50
sit alone. The sun falls down the side of the world and the hill goes dark.
Her hand grows thick and fevered, heavy in my own, and I don't want her,
but I want her, and I cannot let go.

                                                                    [1984]

F. Scott Fitzgerald (1896–1940)

*F. Scott Fitzgerald, despite publishing three novels and one collection of short stories during
his life, did not receive anything approaching the recognition he has today until after his
death. In 1917, Fitzgerald left Princeton University to join the army. After his discharge, he
published his first novel and also began writing short stories for magazines. Fitzgerald was a
frequent contributor to* The Saturday Evening Post; *in his final years, he also worked as
a screenwriter for Metro-Goldwyn-Mayer.*

Babylon Revisited

I

"And where's Mr. Campbell?" Charlie asked.

"Gone to Switzerland. Mr. Campbell's a pretty sick man, Mr. Wales."

"I'm sorry to hear that. And George Hardt?" Charlie inquired.

"Back in America, gone to work."

"And where is the Snow Bird?"   5

"He was in here last week. Anyway, his friend, Mr. Schaeffer, is in Paris."

Two familiar names from the long list of a year and a half ago. Charlie scribbled an address in his notebook and tore out the page.

"If you see Mr. Schaeffer, give him this," He said. "It's my brother-in-law's address. I haven't settled on a hotel yet."

He was not really disappointed to find Paris so empty. But the stillness in the Ritz bar was strange and portentous. It was not an American bar anymore—he felt polite in it, and not as if he owned it. It had gone back into France. He felt the stillness from the moment he got out of the taxi and saw the doorman, usually in a frenzy of activity at this hour, gossiping with a *chasseur* by the servants' entrance.

Passing through the corridor, he heard only a single, bored voice in the once-clamourous women's room. When he turned into the bar he traveled the twenty feet of green carpet with his eyes fixed straight ahead by old habit; and then, with his foot firmly on the rail, he turned and surveyed the room, encountering only a single pair of eyes that fluttered up from a newspaper in the corner. Charlie asked for the head barman, Paul, who in the latter days of the bull market had come to work in his own custom-built car—disembarking, however, with due nicety at the nearest corner. But Paul was at his country house today and Alix giving him information.   10

"No, no more," Charlie said, "I'm going slow these days."

Alix congratulated him: "You were going pretty strong a couple of years ago."

"I'll stick to it all right," Charlie reassured him. "I've stuck to it for over a year and a half now."

"How do you find conditions in America?"

"I haven't been to America for months. I'm in business in Prague, representing a couple of concerns there. They don't know about me down there."   15

Alix smiled.

"Remember the night of George Hardt's bachelor dinner here?" said Charlie. "By the way, what's become of Claude Fessenden?"

Alix lowered his voice confidentially: "He's in Paris, but he doesn't come here any more. Paul doesn't allow it. He ran up a bill of thirty thousand francs, charging all his drinks and his lunches, and usually his dinner, for more than a year. And when Paul finally told him he had to pay, he gave him a bad check."

Alix shook his head sadly.

"I don't understand it, such a dandy fellow. Now he's all bloated up—" He made a plump apple of his hands.   20

Charlie watched a group of strident queens installing themselves in a corner.

"Nothing affects them," he thought. "Stocks rise and fall, people loaf or work, but they go on forever." The place oppressed him. He called for the dice and shook with Alix for the drink.

"Here for long, Mr. Wales?"

"I'm here for four or five days to see my little girl."

"Oh-h! You have a little girl?"   25

Outside, the fire-red, gas-blue, ghost-green signs shone smokily through the tranquil rain. It was late afternoon and the streets were in movement; the *bistros* gleamed. At the corner of the Boulevard des Capucines he took a taxi. The Place de la Concorde moved by in pink majesty; they crossed the logical Seine, and Charlie felt the sudden provincial quality of the Left Bank.

Charlie directed his taxi to the Avenue de l'Opera, which was out of his way. But he wanted to see the blue hour spread over the magnificent façade, and imagine that the cab horns, playing endlessly the first few bars of *La Plus que Lente*, were the trumpets of the Second Empire. They were closing the iron grill in front of Brentano's Book-store, and people were already at dinner behind the trim little bourgeois hedge of Duval's. He had never eaten at a really cheap restaurant in Paris. Five-course dinner, four francs fifty, eighteen cents, wine included. For some odd reason he wished that he had.

As they rolled on to the Left Bank and he felt its sudden provincialism, he thought, "I spoiled this city for myself. I didn't realize it, but the days came along one after another, and then two years were gone, and everything was gone, and I was gone."

He was thirty-five, and good to look at. The Irish mobility of his face was sobered by a deep wrinkle between his eyes. As he rang his brother-in-law's bell in the Rue Palatine, the wrinkle deepened till it pulled down his brows; he felt a cramping sensation in his belly. From behind the maid who opened the door darted a lovely little girl of nine who shrieked "Daddy!" and flew up, struggling like a fish, into his arms. She pulled his head around by one ear and set her cheek against his.

"My old pie," he said.

"Oh, daddy, daddy, daddy, daddy, dads, dads, dads!"

She drew him into the salon, where the family waited, a boy and a girl his daughter's age, his sister-in-law and her husband. He greeted Marion with his voice pitched carefully to avoid either feigned enthusiasm or dislike, but her response was more frankly tepid, though she minimized her expression of unalterable distrust by directing her regard toward his child. The two men clasped hands in a friendly way and Lincoln Peters rested his for a moment on Charlie's shoulder.

The room was warm and comfortably American. The three children moved intimately about, playing through the yellow oblongs that led to the other rooms; the cheer of six o'clock spoke in the eager smacks of the fire and the sounds of French activity in the kitchen. But Charlie did not relax; his heart sat up rigidly in his body and he drew confidence from his daughter, who from time to time came close to him, holding in her arms the doll he had brought.

"Really extremely well," he declared in answer to Lincoln's question. "There's a lot of business there that isn't moving at all, but we're doing even better than ever. In fact, damn well. I'm bringing my sister over from America next month to keep house for me. My income last year was bigger than it was when I had money. You see, the Czechs—"

His boasting was for a specific purpose; but after a moment, seeing a faint restiveness in Lincoln's eye, he changed the subject:

"Those are fine children of yours, well brought up, good manners."

"We think Honoria's a great little girl too."

Marion Peters came back from the kitchen. She was a tall woman with worried eyes, who had once possessed a fresh American loveliness. Charlie had never been sensitive to it and was always surprised when people spoke

30

35

of how pretty she had been. From the first there had been an instinctive antipathy between them.

"Well, how do you find Honoria?" she asked.

"Wonderful. I was astonished how much she's grown in ten months. All the children are looking well."

"We haven't had a doctor for a year. How do you like being back in Paris?"

"It seems very funny to see so few Americans around."

"I'm delighted," Marion said vehemently. "Now at least you can go into a store without their assuming you're a millionaire. We've suffered like everybody, but on the whole it's a good deal pleasanter."

"But it was nice while it lasted," Charlie said. "We were a sort of royalty, almost infallible, with a sort of magic around us. In the bar this afternoon"—he stumbled, seeing his mistake—"there wasn't a man I knew."

She looked at him keenly, "I should think you'd have had enough of bars."

"I only stayed a minute. I take one drink every afternoon, and no more."

"Don't you want a cocktail before dinner?" Lincoln asked.

"I take only one drink every afternoon, and I've had that."

"I hope you keep to it," said Marion.

Her dislike was evident in the coldness with which she spoke, but Charlie only smiled; he had larger plans. Her very aggressiveness gave him an advantage, and he knew enough to wait. He wanted them to initiate the discussion of what they knew had brought him to Paris.

At dinner he couldn't decide whether Honoria was most like him or her mother. Fortunate if she didn't combine the traits of both that had brought them to disaster. A great wave of protectiveness went over him. He thought he knew what to do for her. He believed in character; he wanted to jump back a whole generation and trust in character again as the eternally valuable element. Everything else wore out.

He left soon after dinner, but not to go home. He was curious to see Paris by night with clearer and more judicious eyes than those of other days. He bought a *strapontin* for the Casino and watched Josephine Baker go through her chocolate arabesques.

After an hour he left and strolled toward Montmartre, up the Rue Pigalle into the Place Blanche. The rain had stopped and there were a few people in evening clothes disembarking from taxis in front of cabarets, and *cocottes* prowling singly or in pairs, and many Negroes. He passed a lighted door from which issued music, and stopped with the sense of familiarity; it was Bricktop's, where he had parted with so many hours and so much money. A few doors further on he found another ancient rendezvous and incautiously put his head inside. Immediately an eager orchestra burst into sound, a pair of professional dancers leaped to their feet and a maître d'hôtel swooped toward him, crying, "Crowd just arriving, sir!" But he withdrew quickly.

"You have to be damn drunk," he thought.

Zelli's was closed, the bleak and sinister cheap hotels surrounding it were dark; up in the Rue Blanche there was more light and a local, colloquial French crowd. The Poet's Cave had disappeared, but the two great mouths of the Café of Heaven and the Café of Hell still yawned—even devoured, as he watched, the meager contents of a tourist bus—a German, a Japanese, and an American couple who glanced at him with frightened eyes.

So much for the effort and ingenuity of Montmartre. All the catering to vice and waste was on an utterly childish scale, and he suddenly realized the meaning of the word "dissipate"—to dissipate into thin air; to make nothing out of something. In the little hours of the night every move from place to place was an enormous human jump, an increase of paying for the privilege of slower and slower motion.

He remembered thousand-franc notes given to an orchestra for playing a single number, hundred-franc notes tossed to a doorman for calling a cab.

But it hadn't been given for nothing.

It had been given, even the most wildly squandered sum, as an offering to destiny that he might not remember the things most worth remembering, the things that now he would always remember—his child taken from his control, his wife escaped to a grave in Vermont.

In the glare of a *brasserie* a woman spoke to him. He bought her some eggs and coffee, and then, eluding her encouraging stare, gave her a twenty-franc note and took a taxi to his hotel.   60

II

He woke upon a fine fall day—football weather. The depression of yesterday was gone and he liked the people on the streets. At noon he sat opposite Honoria at Le Grand Vatel, the only restaurant he could think of not reminiscent of champagne dinners and long luncheons that began at two and ended in a blurred and vague twilight.

"Now, how about vegetables? Oughtn't you to have some vegetables?"

"Well, yes."

"Here's *épinards* and *chou-fleur* and carrots and *haricots*."   65

"I'd like *chou-fleur*."

"Wouldn't you like to have two vegetables?"

"I usually only have one at lunch."

The waiter was pretending to be inordinately fond of children. "*Qu'elle est mignonne la petite! Elle parle exactement comme une Française.*"

"How about dessert? Shall we wait and see?"

The waiter disappeared. Honoria looked at her father expectantly.   70

"What are we going to do?"

"First, we're going to that toy store in the Rue Saint-Honoré and buy you anything you like. And then we're going to the vaudeville at the Empire."

She hesitated. "I like it about the vaudeville, but not the toy store."

"Why not?"

"Well, you brought me this doll." She had it with her. "And I've got lots   75
of things. And we're not rich any more, are we?"

"We never were. But today you are to have anything you want."

"All right," she agreed resignedly.

When there had been her mother and a French nurse he had been inclined to be strict; now he extended himself, reached out for a new tolerance; he must be both parents to her and not shut any of her out of communication.

"I want to get to know you," he said gravely. "First let me introduce myself. My name is Charles J. Wales, of Prague."

"Oh, daddy!" her voice cracked with laughter.   80

"And who are you, please?" he persisted, and she accepted a rôle immediately: "Honoria Wales, Rue Palatine, Paris."

"Married or single?"

"No, not married. Single."

He indicated the doll. "But I see you have a child, madame."

Unwilling to disinherit it, she took it to her heart and thought quick-   85
ly: "Yes, I've been married, but I'm not married now. My husband is dead."

He went on quickly, "And the child's name?"

"Simone. That's after my best friend at school."

"I'm very pleased that you're doing so well at school."

"I'm third this month," she boasted. "Elsie"—that was her cousin—"is
only about eighteenth, and Richard is about at the bottom."

"You like Richard and Elsie, don't you?"   90

"Oh, yes. I like Richard quite well and I like her all right."

Cautiously and casually he asked: "And Aunt Marion and Uncle
Lincoln—which do you like best?"

"Oh, Uncle Lincoln, I guess."

He was increasingly aware of her presence. As they came in, a murmur
of ". . . adorable" followed them, and now the people at the next table bent
all their silences upon her, staring as if she were something no more conscious than a flower.

"Why don't I live with you?" she asked suddenly. "Because mamma's   95
dead?"

"You must stay here and learn more French. It would have been hard
for daddy to take care of you so well."

"I don't really need much taking care of any more. I do everything for
myself."

Going out of the restaurant, a man and woman unexpectedly hailed him.

"Well, the old Wales!"

"Hello there, Lorraine. . . . Dunc."   100

Sudden ghosts out of the past: Duncan Schaeffer, a friend from college.
Lorraine Quarrles, a lovely, pale blond of thirty; one of a crowd who had
helped them make months into days in the lavish times of three years ago.

"My husband couldn't come this year," she said, in answer to his question. "We're poor as hell. So he gave me two hundred a month and told me
I could do my worst on that. . . . This your little girl?"

"What about coming back and sitting down?" Duncan asked.

"Can't do it." He was glad for an excuse. As always, he felt Lorraine's
passionate, provocative attraction, but his own rhythm was different now.

"Well, what about dinner?" she asked.   105

"I'm not free. Give me your address and let me call you."

"Charlie, I believe you're sober," she said judicially. "I honestly believe
he's sober, Dunc. Pinch him and see if he's sober."

Charlie indicated Honoria with his head. They both laughed.

"What's your address?" said Duncan skeptically.

He hesitated, unwilling to give the name of his hotel.   110

"I'm not settled yet. I'd better call you. We're going to see the vaudeville at the Empire."

"There! That's what I want to do," Lorraine said. "I want to see some clowns and acrobats and jugglers. That's just what we'll do, Dunc."

"We've got to do an errand first," said Charlie. "Perhaps we'll see you there."

"All right, you snob. . . . Good-by, beautiful little girl."

"Good-by."   115

Honoria bobbed politely.

Somehow, an unwelcome encounter. They liked him because he was functioning, because he was serious; they wanted to see him, because he was stronger than they were now, because they wanted to draw a certain sustenance from his strength.

At the Empire, Honoria proudly refused to sit upon her father's folded coat. She was already an individual with a code of her own, and Charlie was more and more absorbed by the desire of putting a little of himself into her before she crystallized utterly. It was hopeless to try to know her in so short a time.

Between the acts they came upon Duncan and Lorraine in the lobby where the band was playing.

"Have a drink?"   120

"All right, but not up at the bar. We'll take a table."

"The perfect father."

Listening abstractedly to Lorraine, Charlie watched Honoria's eyes leave their table, and he followed them wistfully around the room, wondering what they saw. He met her glance and she smiled.

"I liked that lemonade," she said.

What had she said? What had he expected? Going home in a taxi after-   125
ward, he pulled her over until her head rested against his chest.

"Darling, do you ever think about your mother?"

"Yes, sometimes," she answered vaguely.

"I don't want you to forget her. Have you got a picture of her?"

"Yes, I think so. Anyway, Aunt Marion has. Why don't you want me to forget her?"

"She loved you very much."   130

"I loved her too."

They were silent for a moment.

"Daddy, I want to come and live with you," she said suddenly.

His heart leaped; he had wanted it to come like this.

"Aren't you perfectly happy?"   135

"Yes, but I love you better than anybody. And you love me better than anybody, don't you, now that mummy's dead?"

"Of course I do. But you won't always like me best, honey. You'll grow up and meet somebody your own age and go marry him and forget you ever had a daddy."

"Yes, that's true," she agreed tranquilly.

He didn't go in. He was coming back at nine o'clock and he wanted to keep himself fresh and new for the thing he must say then.

"When you're safe inside, just show yourself in that window."   140

"All right. Good-by, dads, dads, dads, dads."

He waited in the dark street until she appeared, all warm and glowing, in the window above and kissed her fingers out into the night.

III

They were waiting. Marion sat behind the coffee service in a dignified black dinner dress that just faintly suggested mourning. Lincoln was walking up and down with the animation of one who had already been talking. They were as anxious as he was to get into the question. He opened it almost immediately:

"I suppose you know what I want to see you about—why I really came to Paris."

Marion played with the black stars on her necklace and frowned.   145

"I'm awfully anxious to have a home," he continued. "And I'm awfully anxious to have Honoria in it. I appreciate your taking in Honoria for her mother's sake, but things have changed now"—he hesitated and then continued more forcibly—"changed radically with me, and I want to ask you to reconsider the matter. It would be silly for me to deny that about three years ago I was acting badly—"

Marion looked up at him with hard eyes.

"—but all that's over. As I told you, I haven't had more than a drink a day for over a year, and I take that drink deliberately, so that the idea of alcohol won't get too big in my imagination. You see the idea?"

"No," said Marion succinctly.

"It's a sort of stunt I set myself. It keeps the matter in proportion."   150

"I get you," said Lincoln. "You don't want to admit it's got any attraction for you."

"Something like that. Sometimes I forget and don't take it. But I try to take it. Anyhow, I couldn't afford to drink in my position. The people I represent are more than satisfied with what I've done, and I'm bringing my sister over from Burlington to keep house for me, and I want awfully to have Honoria too. You know that even when her mother and I weren't getting along well we never let anything that happened touch Honoria. I know she's fond of me and I know I'm able to take care of her and—well, there you are. How do you feel about it?"

He knew that now he would have to take a beating. It would last an hour or two hours, and it would be difficult, but if he modulated his inevitable resentment to the chastened attitude of the reformed sinner, he might win his point in the end.

Keep your temper, he told himself. You don't want to be justified. You want Honoria.

Lincoln spoke first: "We've been talking it over ever since we got your letter last month. We're happy to have Honoria here. She's a dear little thing, and we're glad to be able to help her, but of course that isn't the question—"   155

Marion interrupted suddenly. "How long are you going to stay sober, Charlie?" she asked.

"Permanently, I hope."

"How can anybody count on that?"

"You know I never did drink heavily until I gave up business and came over here with nothing to do. Then Helen and I began to run around with—"

"Please leave Helen out of it. I can't bear to hear you to talk about her   160
like that."

He stared at her grimly; he had never been certain how fond of each
other the sisters were in life.

"My drinking only lasted about a year and a half—from the time we
came over until I—collapsed."

"It was time enough."

"It was time enough," he agreed.

"My duty is entirely to Helen," she said. "I try to think what she   165
would have wanted me to do. Frankly, from the night you did that terrible
thing you haven't really existed for me. I can't help that. She was my
sister."

"Yes."

"When she was dying she asked me to look out for Honoria. If you had-
n't been in a sanitarium then, it might have helped matters."

He had no answer.

"I'll never in my life be able to forget the morning when Helen
knocked at my door, soaked to the skin and shivering, and said you'd locked
her out."

Charlie gripped the sides of the chair. This was more difficult than he   170
expected; he wanted to launch out into a long expostulation and explanation, but he only said: "The night I locked her out—" and she interrupted, "I
don't feel up to going over that again."

After a moment's silence Lincoln said: "We're getting off the subject.
You want Marion to set aside her legal guardianship and give you Honoria.
I think the main point for her is whether she has confidence in you or not."

"I don't blame Marion," Charlie said slowly, "but I think she can have
entire confidence in me. I had a good record up to three years ago. Of
course, it's within human possibilities I might go wrong at any time. But if
we wait much longer I'll lose Honoria's childhood and my chance for a
home." He shook his head, "I'll simply lose her, don't you see?"

"Yes, I see," said Lincoln.

"Why didn't you think of all this before?" Marion asked.

"I suppose I did, from time to time, but Helen and I were getting   175
along badly. When I consented to the guardianship, I was flat on my back
in a sanitarium and the market had cleaned me out. I knew I'd acted badly,
and I thought if it would bring any peace to Helen, I'd agree to anything.
But now it's different. I'm functioning, I'm behaving damn well, so far
as—"

"Please don't swear at me," Marion said.

He looked at her, startled. With each remark the force of her dislike
became more and more apparent. She had built up all her fear of life into
one wall and faced it toward him. This trivial reproof was possibly the result
of some trouble with the cook several hours before. Charlie became
increasingly alarmed at leaving Honoria in this atmosphere of hostility
against himself; sooner or later it would come out, in a word here, a shake
of the head there, and some of that distrust would be irrevocably implant-
ed in Honoria. But he pulled his temper down out of his face and shut it up
inside him; he had won a point, for Lincoln realized the absurdity of Marion's remark and asked her lightly since when she had objected to the word
"damn."

"Another thing," Charlie said: "I'm able to give her certain advantages now. I'm going to take a French governess to Prague with me. I've got a lease on a new apartment—"

He stopped, realizing that he was blundering. They couldn't be expected to accept with equanimity the fact that his income was again twice as large as their own.

"I suppose you can give her more luxuries than we can," said Marion.   180
"When you were throwing away money we were living along watching every ten francs. . . . I suppose you'll start doing it again."

"Oh, no," he said. "I've learned. I worked hard for ten years, you know— until I got lucky in the market, like so many people. Terribly lucky. It didn't seem any use working any more, so I quit."

There was a long silence. All of them felt their nerves straining, and for the first time in a year Charlie wanted a drink. He was sure now that Lincoln Peters wanted him to have his child.

Marion shuddered suddenly; part of her saw that Charlie's feet were planted on the earth now, and her own maternal feeling recognized the naturalness of his desire; but she had lived for a long time with a prejudice—a prejudice founded on a curious disbelief in her sister's happiness, and which, in the shock of one terrible night, had turned to hatred for him. It had all happened at a point in her life where the discouragement of ill health and adverse circumstances made it necessary for her to believe in tangible villainy and a tangible villain.

"I can't help what I think!" she cried out suddenly. "How much you were responsible for Helen's death, I don't know. It's something you'll have to square with your own conscience."

An electric current of agony surged through him; for a moment he was   185
almost on his feet, an unuttered sound echoing in his throat. He hung on to himself for a moment, another moment.

"Hold on there," said Lincoln uncomfortably. "I never thought you were responsible for that."

"Helen died of heart trouble," Charlie said dully.

"Yes, heart trouble." Marion spoke as if the phrase had another meaning for her.

Then, in the flatness that followed her outburst, she saw him plainly and she knew he had somehow arrived at control over the situation. Glancing at her husband, she found no help from him, and as abruptly as if it were a matter of no importance, she threw up the sponge.

"Do what you like!" she cried, springing up from her chair. "She's your   190
child. I'm not the person to stand in your way. I think if it were my child I'd rather see her—" She managed to check herself. "You two decide it. I can't stand this. I'm sick, I'm going to bed."

She hurried from the room; after a moment Lincoln said:

"This has been a hard day for her. You know how strongly she feels—" His voice was almost apologetic: "When a woman gets an idea in her head."

"Of course."

"It's going to be all right. I think she sees now that you—can provide for the child, and so we can't very well stand in your way or Honoria's way."

"Thank you, Lincoln."   195

"I'd better go along and see how she is."

"I'm going."

He was still trembling when he reached the street, but a walk down the Rue Bonaparte to the *quais* set him up, and as he crossed the Seine, fresh and new by the *quai* lamps, he felt exultant. But back in his room he couldn't sleep. The image of Helen haunted him. Helen whom he had loved so until they had senselessly begun to abuse each other's love, tear it into shreds. On that terrible February night that Marion remembered so vividly, a slow quarrel had gone on for hours. There was a scene at the Florida, and then he attempted to take her home, and then she kissed young Webb at a table; after that there was what she had hysterically said. When he arrived home alone he turned the key in the lock in wild anger. How could he know she would arrive an hour later alone, that there would be a snowstorm in which she wandered about in slippers, too confused to find a taxi? Then the aftermath, her escaping pneumonia by a miracle, and all the attendant horror. They were "reconciled," but that was the beginning of the end, and Marion, who had seen with her own eyes and who imagined it to be one of many scenes from her sister's martyrdom, never forgot.

Going over it again brought Helen nearer, and in the white, soft light that steals upon half sleep near morning he found himself talking to her again. She said that he was perfectly right about Honoria and that she wanted Honoria to be with him. She said she was glad he was being good and doing better. She said a lot of other things—very friendly things—but she was in a swing in a white dress, and swinging faster and faster all the time, so that at the end he could not hear clearly all that she said.

IV

He woke up feeling happy. The door of the world was open again. He made plans, vistas, futures for Honoria and himself, but suddenly he grew sad, remembering all the plans he and Helen had made. She had not planned to die. The present was the thing—work to do and someone to love. But not to love too much, for he knew the injury that a father can do to a daughter or a mother to a son by attaching them too closely; afterward, out in the world, the child would seek in the marriage partner the same blind tenderness and, failing probably to find it, turn against love and life.

It was another bright, crisp day. He called Lincoln Peters at the bank where he worked and asked if he could count on taking Honoria when he left for Prague. Lincoln agreed that there was no reason for delay. One thing—the legal guardianship. Marion wanted to retain that a while longer. She was upset by the whole matter, and it would oil things if she felt that the situation was still in her control for another year. Charlie agreed, wanting only the tangible, visible child.

Then the question of a governess. Charles sat in a gloomy agency and talked to a cross Béarnaise and to a buxom Breton peasant, neither of whom he could have endured. There were others whom he would see tomorrow.

He lunched with Lincoln Peters at Griffons, trying to keep down his exultation.

"There's nothing quite like your own child," Lincoln said. "But you understand how Marion feels too."

200

"She's forgotten how hard I worked for seven years there," Charlie said. "She just remembers one night."

"There's another thing." Lincoln hesitated. "While you and Helen were tearing around Europe throwing money away, we were just getting along. I didn't touch any of the prosperity because I never got ahead enough to carry anything but my insurance. I think Marion felt there was some kind of injustice in it—you not even working toward the end, and getting richer and richer."

"It went just as quick as it came," said Charlie.

"Yes, a lot of it stayed in the hands of *chasseurs* and saxophone players and maîtres d'hôtel—well, the big party's over now. I just said that to explain Marion's feeling about those crazy years. If you drop in about six o'clock tonight before Marion's too tired, we'll settle the details on the spot."

Back at his hotel, Charlie found a *pneumatique* that had been redirected from the Ritz bar where Charlie had left his address for the purpose of finding a certain man.

> *Dear Charlie: You were so strange when we saw you the other day that I wondered if I did something to offend you. If so, I'm not conscious of it. In fact, I have thought about you too much for the last year, and it's always been in the back of my mind that I might see you if I came over here. We did have such good times that crazy spring, like the night you and I stole the butcher's tricycle, and the time we tried to call on the president and you had the old derby rim and the wire cane. Everybody seems so old lately, but I don't feel old a bit. Couldn't we get together some time today for old time's sake? I've got a vile hang-over for the moment, but will be feeling better this afternoon and will look for you about five in the sweatshop at the Ritz.*
>
> > *Always devotedly,*
> > *Lorraine*

His first feeling was one of awe that he had actually, in his mature years, stolen a tricycle and pedaled Lorraine all over the Étoile between the small hours and dawn. In retrospect it was a nightmare. Locking out Helen didn't fit in with any other act of his life, but the tricycle incident did—it was one of many. How many weeks or months of dissipation to arrive at that condition of utter irresponsibility?

He tried to picture how Lorraine had appeared to him then—very attractive; Helen was unhappy about it, though she said nothing. Yesterday, in the restaurant, Lorraine had seemed trite, blurred, worn away. He emphatically did not want to see her, and he was glad Alix had not given away his hotel address. It was a relief to think, instead, of Honoria, to think of Sundays spent with her and of saying good morning to her and knowing she was there in his house at night, drawing her breath in the darkness.

At five he took a taxi and bought presents for all the Peters—a piquant cloth doll, a box of Roman soldiers, flowers for Marion, big linen handkerchiefs for Lincoln.

He saw, when he arrived in the apartment, that Marion had accepted the inevitable. She greeted him now as though he were a recalcitrant member of the family, rather than a menacing outsider. Honoria had been told she was going; Charlie was glad to see that her tact made her conceal her excessive happiness. Only on his lap did she whisper her delight and the question "When?" before she slipped away with the other children.

He and Marion were alone for a minute in the room, and on an impulse he spoke out boldly:

"Family quarrels are bitter things. They don't go according to any rules.   215
They're not like aches or wounds; they're more like splits in the skin that won't heal because there's not enough material. I wish you and I could be on better terms."

"Some things are hard to forget," she answered. "It's a question of confidence." There was no answer to this and presently she asked, "When do you propose to take her?"

"As soon as I can get a governess. I hoped for the day after tomorrow."

"That's impossible. I've got to get her things in shape. Not before Saturday."

He yielded. Coming back into the room, Lincoln offered him a drink.

"I'll take my daily whiskey," he said.   220

It was warm here, it was a home, people together by a fire. The children felt very safe and important; the mother and father were serious, watchful. They had things to do for the children more important than his visit here. A spoonful of medicine was, after all, more important than the strained relations between Marion and himself. They were not dull people, but they were very much in the grip of life and circumstances. He wondered if he couldn't do something to get Lincoln out of his rut at the bank.

A long peal at the door-bell; the *bonne à tout faire* passed through and went down the corridor. The door opened upon another long ring, and then voices, and the three in the salon looked up expectantly; Richard moved to bring the corridor within his range of vision, and Marion rose. Then the maid came back along the corridor, closely followed by the voices, which developed under the light into Duncan Schaeffer and Lorraine Quarrles.

They were gay, they were hilarious, they were roaring with laughter. For a moment Charlie was astounded; unable to understand how they ferreted out the Peters' address.

"Ah-h-h!" Duncan wagged his finger roguishly at Charlie. "Ah-h-h!"

They both slid down another cascade of laughter. Anxious and at a   225
loss, Charlie shook hands with them quickly and presented them to Lincoln and Marion. Marion nodded, scarcely speaking. She had drawn back a step toward the fire; her little girl stood beside her, and Marion put an arm about her shoulder.

With growing annoyance at the intrusion, Charlie waited for them to explain themselves. After some concentration Duncan said:

"We came to invite you out to dinner. Lorraine and I insist that all this chi-chi, cagy business 'bout your address got to stop."

Charlie came closer to them, as if to force them backward down the corridor.

"Sorry, but I can't. Tell me where you'll be and I'll phone you in half an hour."

This made no impression. Lorraine sat down suddenly on the side of a   230
chair, and focusing her eyes on Richard, cried, "Oh, what a nice little boy!

Come here, little boy." Richard glanced at his mother, but did not move. With a perceptible shrug of her shoulders, Lorraine turned back to Charlie:

"Come and dine. Sure your cousins won' mine. See you so sel'om. Or solemn."

"I can't," said Charlie sharply. "You two have dinner and I'll phone you."

Her voice became suddenly unpleasant. "All right, we'll go. But I remember once when you hammered on my door at four A.M. I was enough of a good sport to give you a drink. Come on, Dunc."

Still in slow motion, with blurred, angry faces, with uncertain feet, they retired along the corridor.

"Good night," Charlie said.

"Good night!" responded Lorraine emphatically.   235

When he went back into the salon Marion had not moved, only now her son was standing in the circle of her other arm. Lincoln was still swinging Honoria back and forth like a pendulum from side to side.

"What an outrage!" Charlie broke out. "What an absolute outrage!"

Neither of them answered. Charlie dropped into an armchair, picked up his drink, set it down again and said:

"People I haven't seen for two years having the colossal nerve—"   240

He broke off. Marion had made the sound. "Oh!" in one swift, furious breath, turned her body from him with a jerk and left the room.

Lincoln set down Honoria carefully.

"You children go in and start your soup," he said, and when they obeyed, he said to Charlie:

"Marion's not well and she can't stand shocks. That kind of people make her really physically sick."

"I didn't tell them to come here. They wormed your name out of   245
somebody. They deliberately—"

"Well, it's too bad. It doesn't help matters. Excuse me a minute."

Left alone, Charlie sat tense in his chair. In the next room he could hear the children eating, talking in monosyllables, already oblivious to the scene between their elders. He heard a murmur of conversation from a farther room and then the ticking bell of a telephone receiver picked up, and in a panic he moved to the other side of the room and out of earshot.

In a minute Lincoln came back. "Look here, Charlie. I think we'd better call off dinner tonight. Marion's in bad shape."

"Is she angry with me?"

"Sort of," he said, almost roughly. "She's not strong and—"   250

"You mean she's changed her mind about Honoria?"

"She's pretty bitter right now. I don't know. You phone me at the bank tomorrow."

"I wish you'd explain to her I never dreamed these people would come here. I'm just as sore as you are."

"I couldn't explain anything to her now."

Charlie got up. He took his coat and hat and started down the corridor.   255
Then he opened the door of the dining room and said in a strange voice, "Good night, children."

Honoria rose and ran around the table to hug him.

"Good night, sweetheart," he said vaguely, and then trying to make his voice more tender, trying to conciliate something, "Good night, dear children."

V

Charlie went directly to the Ritz bar with the furious idea of finding Lorraine and Duncan but they were not there, and he realized that in any case there was nothing he could do. He had not touched his drink at the Peters', and now he ordered a whiskey-and-soda. Paul came over to say hello.

"It's a great change," he said sadly. "We do about half the business we did. So many fellows I hear about back in the States lost everything, maybe not in the first crash, but then in the second. Your friend George Hardt lost every cent, I hear. Are you back in the States?"

"No, I'm in business in Prague."   260

"I heard that you lost a lot in the crash."

"I did," and he added grimly, "but I lost everything I wanted in the boom."

"Selling short."

"Something like that."

Again the memory of those days swept over him like a nightmare—the   265
people they had met traveling; then people who couldn't add a row of figures or speak a coherent sentence. The little man Helen had consented to dance with at the ship's party, who had insulted her ten feet from the table; the women and girls carried screaming with drink or drugs out of public places—

—The men who locked their wives out in the snow, because the snow of twenty-nine wasn't real snow. If you didn't want it to be snow, you just paid some money.

He went to the phone and called the Peters' apartment; Lincoln answered.

"I called up because this thing is on my mind. Has Marion said anything definite?"

"Marion's sick," Lincoln answered shortly. "I know this thing isn't altogether your fault, but I can't have her go to pieces about it. I'm afraid we'll have to let it slide for six months; I can't take the chance of working her up to this state again."

"I see."   270

"I'm sorry, Charlie."

He went back to his table. His whiskey glass was empty, but he shook his head when Alix looked at it questioningly. There wasn't much he could do now except send Honoria some things; he would send her a lot of things tomorrow. He thought rather angrily that this was just money—he had given so many people money. . . .

"No, no more," he said to the waiter. "What do I owe you?"

He would come back some day; they couldn't make him pay forever. But he wanted his child, and nothing was much good now, beside that fact. He wasn't young any more, with a lot of nice thoughts and dreams to have by himself. He was absolutely sure Helen wouldn't have wanted him to be so alone.

[1931]

ERNEST GAINES (1933–)

Ernest Gaines is currently the writer-in-residence at the University of Southwestern Louisiana, Lafayette—the area in which he grew up and the setting for most of his fiction. Gaines graduated from San Francisco State University and later won a writing fellowship to Stanford. He has been awarded the National Book Critics Circle Award as well as a MacArthur Foundation grant, a Guggenheim Fellowship, and an award from the National Endowment for the Arts. Gaines is the author of eight books of fiction, including A Lesson Before Dying *and* The Autobiography of Miss Jane Pittman.

Just Like a Tree

I shall not;
    I shall not be moved.
I shall not;
    I shall not be moved.
Just like a tree that's
planted 'side the water.
    Oh, I shall not be moved.

I made my home in glory;
    I shall not be moved.
Made my home in glory;
    I shall not be moved.
Just like a tree that's
planted 'side the water.
    Oh, I shall not be moved.
(from an old Negro spiritual)

Chuckkie

Pa hit him on the back and he jeck in them chains like he pulling, but ever'body in the wagon know he ain't, and Pa hit him on the back again. He jeck again like he pulling, but even Big Red know he ain't doing a thing.

"That's why I'm go'n get a horse," Pa say. "He'll kill that other mule. Get up there, Mr. Bascom."

"Oh, let him alone," Gran'mon say. "How would you like it if you was pulling a wagon in all that mud?"

Pa don't answer Gran'mon; he just hit Mr. Bascom on the back again.

"That's right, kill him," Gran'mon say. "See where you get mo' money to   5 buy another one."

"Get up there, Mr. Bascom," Pa say.

"You hear me talking to you, Emile?" Gran'mon say. "You want me hit you with something?"

"Ma, he ain't pulling," Pa say.

"Leave him alone," Gran'mon say.

Pa shake the lines little bit, but Mr. Bascom don't even feel it, and you   10 can see he letting Big Red do all the pulling again. Pa say something kind o' low to hisself, and I can't make out what it is.

I low' my head little bit, 'cause that wind and fine rain was hitting me in the face, and I can feel Mama pressing close to me to keep me warm. She sitting on one side o' me, and Pa sitting on the other side o' me, and Gran'mon in the back o' me in her setting chair. Pa didn't want bring the setting chair, telling Gran'mon there was two boards in that wagon already and she could sit on one of 'em all by herself if she wanted to, but Gran'mon say she was taking her setting chair with her if Pa liked it or not. She say she didn't ride in no wagon on nobody board, and if Pa liked it or not, that setting chair was going.

"Let her take her setting chair," Mama say. "What's wrong with taking her setting chair."

"Ehhh, Lord," Pa say, and picked up the setting chair and took it out to the wagon. "I guess I'll have to bring it back in the house, too, when we come back from there."

Gran'mon went and clambed in the wagon and moved her setting chair back little bit and sat down and folded her arms, waiting for us to get in, too. I got in and knelt down 'side her, but Mama told me to come up there and sit on the board 'side her and Pa so I could stay warm. Soon 's I sat down, Pa hit Mr. Bascom on the back, saying what a trifling thing Mr. Bascom was, and soon 's he got some mo' money he was getting rid o' Mr. Bascom and getting him a horse.

I raise my head to look see how far we is.   15

"That's it, yonder," I say.

"Stop pointing," Mama say, "and keep your hand in your pocket."

"Where?" Gran'mon say, back there in her setting chair.

"'Cross the ditch, yonder," I say.

"Can't see a thing for this rain," Gran'mon say.   20

"Can't hardly see it," I say. "But you can see the light little bit. That chin-aball tree standing in the way."

"Poor soul," Gran'mon say. "Poor soul."

I know Gran'mon was go'n say "poor soul, poor soul," 'cause she had been saying "poor soul, poor soul," ever since she heard Aunt Fe was go'n leave from back there.

Emile

Darn cane crop to finish getting in and only a mule and a half to do it. If I had my way I'd take that shotgun and a load o' buckshots and—but what's the use.

"Get up, Mr. Bascom—please," I say to that little dried-up, long-eared,   25
tobacco-color thing. "Please, come up. Do your share for God sake—if you don't mind. I know it's hard pulling in all that mud, but if you don't do your share, then Big Red'll have to do his and yours, too. So, please, if it ain't asking you too much to—"

"Oh, Emile, shut up," Leola say.

"I can't hit him," I say, "or Mama back there'll hit me. So I have to talk to him. Please, Mr. Bascom, if you don't mind it. For my sake. No, not for mine; for God sake. No, not even for His'n; for Big Red sake. A fellow mule just like yourself is. Please, come up."

"Now, you hear that boy blaspheming God right in front o' me there," Mama say. "Ehhh, Lord—just keep it up. All this bad weather there like this whole world coming apart—a clap o' thunder come there and knock the fool out you. Just keep it up."

Maybe she right, and I stop. I look at Mr. Bascom there doing nothing, and I jut give up. That mule know long 's Mama's alive he go'n do just what he want to do. He know when Papa was dying he told Mama to look after him, and he know no matter what he do, no matter what he don't do, Mama

ain't go'n never let me do him anything. Sometimes I even feel Mama care
mo' for Mr. Bascom 'an she care for me her own son.

We come up to the grate and I pull back on the lines.   30

"Whoa up, Big Red," I say. "You don't have to stop, Mr. Bascom. You
never started."

I can feel Mama looking at me back there in that setting chair, but she
don't say nothing.

"Here," I say to Chuckkie.

He take the lines and I jump down on the ground to open the old beat-
up gate. I see Etienne's horse in the yard, and I see Chris new red tractor 'side
the house, shining in the rain. When Mama die, I say to myself, Mr. Bascom,
you going. Ever'body getting tractors and horses and I'm still stuck with you.
You going, brother.

"Can you make it through?" I ask Chuckkie. "That gate ain't too wide."   35

"I can do it," he say.

"Be sure to make Mr. Bascom pull," I say.

"Emile, you better get back up here and drive 'em through," Leola say.
"Chuckkie might break up that wagon."

"No, let him stay down there and give orders," Mama say, back there in
that setting chair.

"He can do it," I say. "Come on, Chuckkie boy."   40

"Come up, here, mule," Chuckkie say.

And soon 's he say that, Big Red make a lunge for the yard, and Mr. Bascom don't even move, and 'fore I can bat my eyes I hear *pow-wow; sagg-
sagg; pow-wow.* But above all that noise, Leola up there screaming her head
off. And Mama—not a word; just sitting in that chair, looking at me with her
arms still folded.

"Pull Big Red," I say. "Pull Big Red, Chuckkie."

Poor little Chuckkie up there pulling so hard till one of his little arms
straight out in back; and Big Red throwing his shoulders and ever'thing else
in it, and Mr. Bascom just walking there just 's loose and free, like he's suppose to be there just for his good looks. I move out the way just in time to
let the wagon go by me, pulling half o' the fence in the yard behind it. I
glance up again, and there's Leola still hollering and trying to jump out, but
Mama not saying a word—just sitting there in that setting chair with her
arms still folded.

"Whoa," I hear little Chuckkie saying. "Whoa up, now."   45

Somebody open the door and a bunch o' people come out on the gallery.

"What the world—?" Etienne say. "Thought the whole place was coming to pieces there."

"Chuckkie had a little trouble coming in the yard," I say.

"Goodness," Etienne say. "Anybody hurt?"

Mama just sit there about ten seconds, then she say something to her-   50
self and start clambing out the wagon.

"Let me help you there, Aunt Lou," Etienne say, coming down the steps.

"I can make it," Mama say. When she get on the ground she look up at
Chuckkie. "Hand me my chair there, boy."

Poor little Chuckkie, up there with the lines in one hand, get the chair
and hold it to the side, and Etienne catch it just 'fore it hit the ground. Mama
start looking at me again, and it look like for at least a' hour she stand there

looking at nobody but me. Then she say "Ehhh, Lord," like that again, and go inside with Leola and the rest o' the people.

I look back at half o' the fence laying there in the yard, and I jump back on the wagon and guide the mules to the side o' the house. After unhitching 'em and tying 'em to the wheels, I look at Chris pretty red tractor again, and me and Chuckkie go inside: I make sure he kick all that mud off his shoes 'fore he go in the house.

Leola

Sitting over there by that fireplace, trying to look joyful when ever'body   55
there know she ain't. But she trying, you know; smiling and bowing when people say something to her. How can she be joyful, I ask you; how can she be? Poor thing, she been here all her life—or the most of it, let's say. 'Fore they moved in this house, they lived in one back in the woods 'bout a mile from here. But for the past twenty-five or thirty years, she been right in this one house. I know ever since I been big enough to know people I been seeing her right here.

Aunt Fe, Aunt Fe, Aunt Fe, Aunt Fe; the name's been 'mongst us just like us own family name. Just like the name o' God. Like the name of town—the city. Aunt Fe, Aunt Fe, Aunt Fe, Aunt Fe.

Poor old thing; how many times I done come here and washed clothes for her when she couldn't do it herself. How many times I done hoed in that garden, ironed her clothes, wrung a chicken neck for her. You count the days in the year and you'll be pretty close. And I didn't mind it a bit. No, I didn't mind it a bit. She there trying to pay me. Proud—Lord, talking 'bout pride. "Here." "No, Aunt Fe; no." "Here, here; you got a child there, you can use it." "No, Aunt Fe. No. No. What would Mama think if she knowed I took money from you? Aunt Fe, Mama would never forgive me. No. I love doing these thing for you. I just wish I could do more."

And there, now, trying to make 'tend she don't mind leaving. Ehhh, Lord.

I hear a bunch o' rattling round in the kitchen and I go back there. I see Louise stirring this big pot o' eggnog.

"Louise," I say.   60

"Leola," she say.

We look at each other and she stir the eggnog again. She know what I'm go'n say next, and she can't even look in my face.

"Louise, I wish there was some other way."

"There's no other way," she say.

"Louise, moving her from here's like moving a tree you been used to in   65
your front yard all your life."

"What else can I do?"

"Oh, Louise, Louise."

"Nothing else but that."

"Louise, what people go'n do without her here?"

She stir the eggnog and don't answer.   70

"Louise, us'll take her in with us."

"You all no kin to Auntie. She go with me."

"And us'll never see her again."

She stir the eggnog. Her husband come back in the kitchen and kiss her on the back o' the neck and then look at me and grin. Right from the start I can see I ain't go'n like that nigger.

"Almost ready, honey?" he say.   75

"Almost."

He go to the safe and get one o' them bottles of whiskey he got in there and come back to the stove.

"No," Louise say. "Everybody don't like whiskey in it. Add the whiskey after you've poured it up."

"Okay, hon."

He kiss her on the back o' the neck again. Still don't like that nigger.   80
Something 'bout him ain't right.

"You one o' the family?" he say.

"Same as one," I say. "And you?"

He don't like the way I say it, and I don't care if he like it or not. He look at me there a second, and then he kiss her on the ear.

"Un-unnn," she say, stirring the pot.

"I love your ear, baby," he say.   85

"Go in the front room and talk with the people," she say.

He kiss her on the other ear. A nigger do all that front o' public got something to hide. He leave the kitchen. I look at Louise.

"Ain't nothing else I can do," she say.

"You sure, Louise? You positive?"

"I'm positive," she say.   90

The front door open and Emile and Chuckkie come in. A minute later Washington and Adrieu come in, too. Adrieu come back in the kitchen, and I can see she been crying. Aunt Fe is her godmother, you know.

"How you feel, Adrieu?"

"That weather out there," she say.

"Y'all walked?"

"Yes."   95

"Us here in the wagon. Y'all can go back with us."

"Y'all the one tore the fence down?" she ask.

"Yes, I guess so. That brother-in-law o' yours in there letting Chuckkie drive that wagon."

"Well, I don't guess it'll matter too much. Nobody go'n be here, anyhow."

And she start crying again. I take her in my arms and pat her on the   100
shoulder, and I look at Louise stirring the eggnog.

"What I'm go'n do and my nan-nane gone? I love her so much."

"Ever'body love her."

"Since my mama died, she been like my mama."

"Shhh," I say. "Don't let her hear you. Make her grieve. You don't want her grieving, now, do you?"

She sniffs there 'gainst my dress few times.   105

"Oh, Lord," she say. "Lord, have mercy."

"Shhh," I say. "Shhh. That's what life's 'bout."

"That ain't what life's 'bout," she say. "It ain't fair. This been her home all her life. These the people she know. She don't know them people she going to. It ain't fair."

"Shhh, Adrieu," I say. "Now, you saying things that ain't your business."   110
She cry there some mo'.
"Oh, Lord, Lord," she say.
Louise turn from the stove.
"About ready now," she say, going to the middle door. "James, tell everybody to come back and get some."

James

Let me go on back here and show these country niggers how to have a good time. All they know is talk, talk, talk. Talk so much they make me buggy round here. Damn this weather—wind, rain. Must be a million cracks in this old house.

I go to that old beat-up safe in that corner and get that fifth of Mr. Harp-   115
er (in the South now; got to say Mister), give the seal one swipe, the stopper one jerk, and head back to that old wood stove. (Man, like, these cats are primitive—goodness. You know what I mean? I mean like wood stoves. Don't mention TV, man, these cats here never heard of that.) I start to dump Mr. Harper in the pot and Baby catches my hand again and say not all of them like it. You ever heard of anything like that? I mean a stud's going to drink eggnog, and he's not going to put whiskey in it. I mean he's going to drink it straight. I mean, you ever heard anything like that? Well, I wasn't pressing none of them on Mr. Harper. I mean, me and Mr. Harper get along too well together for me to go around there pressing.

I hold my cup there and let Baby put a few drops of this egg stuff in it; then I jerk my cup back and let Mr. Harper run a while. Couple of these cats come over (some of them aren't so lame) and set their cups, and I let Mr. Harper run for them. Then this cat says he's got 'nough. I let Mr. Harp- er run for this other stud, and pretty soon he says, "Hold it. Good." Coun- try cat, you know. "Hold it. Good." Real country cat. So I raise the cup to see what Mr. Harper's doing. He's just right. I raise the cup again. Just right, Mr. Harper; just right.

I go to the door with Mr. Harper under my arm and the cup in my hand and I look into the front room where they all are. I mean, there's about ninety-nine of them in there. Old ones, young ones, little ones, big ones, yellow ones, black ones, brown ones—you name them, brother, and they were there. And what for? Brother, I'll tell you what for. Just because me and Baby are taking this old chick out of these sticks. Well, I'll tell you where I'd be at this moment if I was one of them. With that weather out there like it is, I'd be under about five blankets with some little warm belly pressing against mine. Brother, you can bet your hat I wouldn't be here. Man, listen to that thing out there. You can hear that rain beating on that old house like grains of rice; and that wind coming through them cracks like it does in those old Charlie Chaplin movies. Man, like you know—like *whooo-ee; whooo-ee.* Man, you talking about some weird cats.

I can feel Mr. Harper starting to massage my wig and I bat my eyes twice and look at the old girl over there. She's still sitting in that funny- looking little old rocking chair, and not saying a word to anybody. Just sit- ting there looking into the fireplace at them two pieces of wood that aren't giving out enough heat to warm a baby, let alone ninety-nine grown people. I mean, you know, like that sleet's falling out there like all get-up-and-go, and them two pieces of wood are lying there just as dead as the rest of these way-out cats.

One of the old cats—I don't know which one he is—Mose, Sam, or something like that—leans over and pokes in the fire a minute; then a little blaze shoots up, and he raises up, too, looking as satisfied as if he'd just sent a rocket into orbit. I mean, these cats are like that. They do these little bitty things, and they feel like they've really done something. Well, back in these sticks, I guess there just isn't nothing big to do.

I feel Mr. Harper touching my skull now—and I notice this little chick   120
passing by me with these two cups of eggnog. She goes over to the fireplace and gives one to each of these old chicks. The one sitting in that setting chair she brought with her from God knows where, and the other cup to the old chick that Baby and I are going to haul from here sometime tomorrow morning. Wait, man, I mean like, you ever heard of anybody going to somebody else's house with a chair? I mean, wouldn't you call that an insult at the basest point? I mean, now, like tell me what you think of that? I mean—dig—here I am at my pad, and in you come with your own stool. I mean, now, like man, you know. I mean that's an insult at the basest point. I mean, you know . . . you know, like way out. . . .

Mr. Harper, what you trying to do, boy?—I mean, *sir.* (Got to watch myself, I'm in the South. Got to keep watching myself.)

This stud touches me on the shoulder and raise his cup and say, "How 'bout a taste?" I know what the stud's talking about, so I let Mr. Harper run for him. But soon 's I let a drop get in, the stud say, "'Nough." I mean I let about two drops get in, and already the stud's got enough. Man, I mean, like you know. I mean these studs are 'way out. I mean like 'way back there.

This stud takes a swig of his eggnog and say, "Ahhh." I mean this real down-home way of saying "Ahhhh." I mean, man, like these studs—I notice this little chick passing by me again, and this time she's crying. I mean weeping, you know. And just because this old ninety-nine-year-old chick's packing up and leaving. I mean, you ever heard of anything like that? I mean, here she is pretty as the day is long and crying because Baby and I are hauling this old chick away. Well, I'd like to make her cry. And I can assure you, brother, it wouldn't be from leaving her.

I turn and look at Baby over there by the stove, pouring eggnog in all these cups. I mean, there're about twenty of these cats lined up there. And I bet you not half of them will take Mr. Harper along. Some way-out cats, man. Some way-out cats.

I go up to Baby and kiss her on the back of the neck and give her a lit-   125
tle pat where she likes for me to pat her when we're in the bed. She say, "Uh-uh," but I know she likes it anyhow.

Ben O

I back under the bed and touch the slop jar, and I pull back my leg and back somewhere else, and then I get me a good sight on it. I spin my aggie couple times and sight again and then I shoot. I hit it right square in the middle and it go flying over the fireplace. I crawl over there to get it and I see 'em all over there drinking they eggnog and they didn't even offer me and Chuckkie none. I find my marble on the bricks, and I go back and tell Chuckkie they over there drinking eggnog.

"You want some?" I say.

"I want shoot marble," Chuckkie say. "Yo' shot. Shoot up."

"I want some eggnog," I say.

"Shoot up, Ben O," he say. "I'm getting cold staying in one place so long.   130
You feel that draft?"

"Coming from that crack under that bed," I say.

"Where?" Chuckkie say, looking for the crack.

"Over by that bedpost over there," I say.

"This sure's a beat-up old house," Chuckkie say.

"I want me some eggnog," I say.   135

"Well, you ain't getting none," Gran'mon say, from the fireplace. "It ain't
good for you."

"I can drink eggnog," I say. "How come it ain't good for me? It ain't
nothing but eggs and milk. I eat chicken, don't I? I eat beef, don't I?"

Gran'mon don't say nothing.

"I want me some eggnog," I say.

Gran'mon still don't say no more. Nobody else don't say nothing, nei-   140
ther.

"I want me some eggnog," I say.

"You go'n get a eggnog," Gran'mon say. "Just keep that noise up."

"I want me some eggnog," I say; "and I 'tend to get me some eggnog
tonight."

Next thing I know, Gran'mon done picked up a chip out o' that corner
and done sailed it back there where me and Chuckkie is. I duck just in time,
and the chip catch old Chuckkie side the head.

"Hey, who that hitting me?" Chuckkie say.   145

"Move, and you won't get hit," Gran'mon say.

I laugh at old Chuckkie over there holding his head, and next thing I
know here's Chuckkie done haul back there and hit me in my side. I jump
up from there and give him two just to show him how it feel, and he jump
up and hit me again. Then we grab each other and start tussling on the
floor.

"You, Ben O," I hear Gran'mon saying. "You, Ben O, cut that out. Y'all cut
that out."

But we don't stop, 'cause neither one o' us want be first. Then I feel
somebody pulling us apart.

"What I ought to do is whip both o' you," Mrs. Leola say. "Is that what   150
y'all want?"

"No'm," I say.

"Then shake hand."

Me and Chuckkie shake hand.

"Kiss," Mrs. Leola say.

"No, ma'am," I say. "I ain't kissing no boy. I ain't that crazy."   155

"Kiss him Chuckkie," she say.

Old Chuckkie kiss me on the jaw.

"Now, kiss him, Ben O."

"I ain't kissing no Chuckkie," I say. "No'm. Uh-uh. You kiss girls."

And the next thing I know, Mama done tipped up back o' me and done   160
whop me on the leg with Daddy belt.

"Kiss Chuckkie," she say.

Chuckkie turn his jaw to me and I kiss him. I almost wipe my mouth. I even feel like spitting.

"Now, come back here and get you some eggnog," Mama say.

"That's right, spoil 'em," Gran'mon say. "Next thing you know, they be drinking from bottles."

"Little eggnog won't hurt 'em, Mama," Mama say.

"That's right, never listen," Gran'mon say. "It's you go'n suffer for it. I be dead and gone, me."

165

Aunt Clo

Be just like wrapping a chain round a tree and jecking and jecking, and then shifting the chain little bit and jecking and jecking some in that direction, and then shifting it some mo' and jecking and jecking in that direction. Jecking and jecking till you get it loose, and then pulling with all your might. Still it might not be loose enough and you have to back the tractor up some and fix the chain round the tree again and start jecking all over. Jeck, jeck, jeck. Then you hear the roots crying, and then you keep on jecking, and then it give, and you jeck some mo', and then it falls. And not till then that you see what you done done. Not till then you see the big hole in the ground and piece of the taproot still way down in it—a piece you won't never get out no matter if you dig till doomsday. Yes, you got the tree—least got it down on the ground, but did you get the taproot? No. No, sir, you didn't get the taproot. You stand there and look down in the hole at it and you grab yo' axe and jump down in it and start chopping at this taproot, but do you get the taproot? No. You don't get the taproot, sir. You never get the taproot. But, sir, I tell you what you do get. You get a big hole in the ground, sir; and you get another big hole in the air where the lovely branches been all these years. Yes, sir, that's what you get. The holes, sir, the holes. Two holes, sir, you can't never fill no matter how hard you try.

So you wrap yo' chain round yo' tree again, sir, and you start dragging it. But the dragging ain't so easy, sir, 'cause she's a heavy old tree—been there a long time, you know—heavy. And you make yo' tractor strain, sir, and the elements work 'gainst you, too, sir, 'cause the elements, they on her side, too, 'cause she part o' the elements, and the elements, they part o' her. So the elements, they do they little share to discourage you—yes, sir, they does. But you will not let the elements stop you. No, sir, you show the elements that they just elements, and man is stronger than elements, and you jeck and jeck on the chain, and soon she start to moving with you, sir, but if you look over yo' shoulder one second you see her leaving a trail—a trail, sir, that can be seen from miles and miles away. You see her trying to hook her little fine branches in different little cracks, in between pickets, round hills o' grass, round anything they might brush 'gainst. But you is a determined man, sir, and you jeck and you jeck and she keep on grabbing and trying to hold, but you stronger, sir—course you the strongest—and you finally get her out on the pave road. But what you don't notice, sir, is just 'fore she get on the pave road she leave couple her little branches to remind the people that it ain't her that want leave, but you, sir, that think she ought to. So you just drag her and drag her, sir, and the folks that live in the houses 'side the pave road, they come out on they gallery and look at her go by, and then they go back in they house and sit by the fire and forget her. So you just go on, sir, and you just go and you go—and for how many days? I don't know. I don't have the least idea. The North to me, sir, is like the elements. It mystify me. But never mind, you finally got there, and then you try to find a place to set her. You look in this corner and you look in that corner, but no corner is good. She kind o' stand in the way no matter where you set her. So finally, sir, you say, "I just stand her up here a little while and see, and if it don't work out, if she keep getting in the way, I guess we'll just have to take her to the dump."

Chris

Just like him, though, standing up there telling them lies when everybody else feeling sad. I don't know what you do without people like him. And, yet, you see him there, he sad just like the rest. But he just got to be funny. Crying on the inside, but still got to be funny.

He didn't steal it, though; didn't steal it a bit. His grandpa was just like   170
him. Mat? Mat Jefferson? Just like that. Mat could make you die laughing. 'Member once at a wake. Who was dead? Yes—Robert Lewis. Robert Lewis laying up in his coffin dead as a door nail. Everybody sad and droopy. Mat look at that and start his lying. Soon, half o' the place laughing. Funniest wake I ever went to, and yet—

Just like now. Look at 'em. Look at 'em laughing. Ten minutes ago you would 'a' thought you was at a funeral. But look at 'em now. Look at her there in that little old chair. How long she had it? Fifty years—a hundred? It ain't a chair no mo', it's a little bit o' her. Just like her arm, just like here leg.

You know, I couldn't believe it. I couldn't. Emile passed the house there the other day, right after the bombing, and I was in my yard digging a water drain to let the water run out in the ditch. Emile, he stopped the wagon there 'fore the door. Little Chuckkie, he in there with him with that little rain cap buckled up over his head. I go out to the gate and I say, "Emile, it's the truth?"

"The truth," he say. And just like that he say it. "The truth."

I look at him there, and he looking up the road to keep from looking back at me. You know, they been pretty close to Aunt Fe ever since they was children coming up. His own mon, Aunt Lou, and Aunt Fe, they been like sisters, there, together.

Me and him, we talk there little while 'bout the cane cutting, then he   175
say he got to get on to the back. He shake the lines and drive on.

Inside me, my heart feel like it done swole up ten times the size it ought to be. Water come in my eyes, and I got to 'mit I cried right there. Yes sir, I cried right there by that front gate.

Louise come in the room and whisper something to Leola, and they go back in the kitchen. I can hear 'em moving things round back there, still getting things together they go'n be taking along. If they offer me anything, I'd like that big iron pot out there in the back yard. Good for boiling water when you killing hog, you know.

You can feel the sadness in the room again. Louise brought it in when she come in and whispered to Leola. Only, she didn't take it out when her and Leola left. Every pan they move, every pot they unhook keep telling you she leaving, she leaving.

Etienne turn over one o' them logs to make the fire pick up some, and I see that boy, Lionel, spreading out his hands over the fire. Watch out, I think to myself, here come another lie. People, he just getting started.

Anne-Marie Duvall

"You're not going?"   180

"I'm not going," he says, turning over the log with the poker. "And if you were in your right mind, you wouldn't go, either."

"You just don't understand, do you?"

"Oh, I understand. She cooked for your daddy. She nursed you when your mama died."

"And I'm trying to pay her back with a seventy-nine-cents scarf. Is that too much?"

He is silent, leaning against the mantel, looking down at the fire. The   185
fire throws strange shadows across the big, old room. Father looks down at me from against the wall. His eyes do not say go nor stay. But I know what he would do.

"Please go with me, Edward."

"You're wasting your breath."

I look at him a long time, then I get the small package from the coffee table.

"You're still going?"

"I am going."   190

"Don't call for me if you get bogged down anywhere back there."

I look at him and go out to the garage. The sky is black. The clouds are moving fast and low. A fine drizzle is falling, and the wind coming from the swamps blows in my face. I cannot recall a worse night in all my life.

I hurry into the car and drive out of the yard. The house stands big and black in back of me. Am I angry with Edward? No, I'm not angry with Edward. He's right. I should not go out into this kind of weather. But what he does not understand is I must. Father definitely would have gone if he were alive. Grandfather definitely would have gone, also. And, therefore, I must. Why? I cannot answer why. Only, I must go.

As soon as I turn down that old muddy road, I begin to pray. Don't let me go into that ditch, I pray. Don't let me go into that ditch. Please, don't let me go into that ditch.

The lights play on the big old trees along the road. Here and there the   195
lights hit a sagging picket fence. But I know I haven't even started yet. She lives far back into the fields. Why? God, why does she have to live so far back? Why couldn't she have lived closer to the front? But the answer to that is as hard for me as is the answer to everything else. It was ordained before I—before father—was born—that she should live back there. So why should I try to understand it now?

The car slides towards the ditch, and I stop it dead and turn the wheel, and then come back into the road again. Thanks, father. I know you're with me. Because it was you who said that I must look after her, didn't you? No, you did not say it directly, father. You said it only with a glance. As grandfather must have said it to you, and as his father must have said it to him.

But now that she's gone, father, now what? I know. I know. Aunt Lou, Ant Clo, and the rest.

The lights shine on the dead, wet grass along the road. There's an old pecan tree, looking dead and all alone. I wish I was a little nigger gal so I could pick pecans and eat them under the big old dead tree.

The car hits a rut, but bounces right out of it. I am frightened for a moment, but then I feel better. The windshield wipers are working well, slapping the water away as fast as it hits the glass. If I make the next half mile all right, the rest of the way will be good. It's not much over a mile now.

That was too bad about that bombing—killing that woman and her two children. That poor woman; poor children. What is the answer? What will happen? What do they want? Do they know what they want? Do they really know what they want? Are they positively sure? Have they any idea? Money to buy a car, is that it? If that is all, I pity them. Oh, how I pity them.

Not much farther. Just around that bend and—there's a water hole. Now what?

I stop the car and just stare out at the water a minute; then I get out to see how deep it is. The cold wind shoots through my body like needles. Lightning comes from towards the swamps and lights up the place. For a split second the night is as bright as day. The next second it is blacker than it has ever been.

I look at the water, and I can see that it's too deep for the car to pass through. I must turn back or I must walk the rest of the way. I stand there a while wondering what to do. Is it worth it all? Can't I simply send the gift by someone tomorrow morning? But will there be someone tomorrow morning? Suppose she leaves without getting it, then what? What then? Father would never forgive me. Neither would grandfather or great-grandfather, either. No, they wouldn't.

The lightning flashes again and I look across the field, and I can see the tree in the yard a quarter of a mile away. I have but one choice: I must walk. I get the package out of the car and stuff it in my coat and start out.

I don't make any progress at first, but then I become a little warmer and I find I like walking. The lightning flashes just in time to show up a puddle of water, and I go around it. But there's no light to show up the second puddle, and I fall flat on my face. For a moment I'm completely blind, then I get slowly to my feet and check the package. It's dry, not harmed. I wash the mud off my raincoat, wash my hands, and I start out again.

The house appears in front of me, and as I come into the yard, I can hear the people laughing and talking. Sometimes I think niggers can laugh and joke even if they see somebody beaten to death. I go up on the porch and knock and an old one opens the door for me. I swear, when he sees me he looks as if he's seen a ghost. His mouth drops open, his eyes bulge—I swear.

I go into the old crowded and smelly room, and every one of them looks at me the same way the first one did. All the joking and laughing has ceased. You would think I was the devil in person.

"Done, Lord," I hear her saying over by the fireplace. They move to the side and I can see her sitting in that little rocking chair I bet you she's had since the beginning of time. "Done, Master," she says. "Child, what you doing in weather like this? Y'all move; let her get to that fire. Y'all move. Move, now. Let her warm herself."

They start scattering everywhere.

"I'm not cold, Aunt Fe," I say. "I just brought you something—something   210
small—because you're leaving us. I'm going right back."

"Done, Master," she says. Fussing over me just like she's done all her life.
"Done, Master. Child, you ain't got no business in a place like this. Get close
to this fire. Get here. Done, Master."

I move closer, and the fire does feel warm and good.

"Done, Lord," she says.

I take out the package and pass it to her. The other niggers gather
around with all kinds of smiles on their faces. Just think of it—a white lady
coming through all of this for one old darky. It is all right for them to come
from all over the plantation, from all over the area, in all kinds of weather:
this is to be expected of them. But a white lady, a white lady. They must
think we white people don't have their kind of feelings.

She unwraps the package, her bony little fingers working slowly and   215
deliberately. When she sees the scarf—the seventy-nine-cents scarf—she
brings it to her mouth and kisses it.

"Y'all look," she says. "Y'all look. Ain't it the prettiest little scarf y'all
ever did see? Y'all look."

They move around her and look at the scarf. Some of them touch it.

"I go'n put it on right now," she says. I go'n put it on right how, my lady."

She unfolds it and ties it round her head and looks up at everybody and
smiles.

"Thank you, my lady," she says. "Thank you, ma'am, from the bottom of   220
my heart."

"Oh, Aunt Fe." I say, kneeling down beside her. "Oh, Aunt Fe."

But I think about the other niggers there looking down at me, and I get
up. But I look into that wrinkled old face again, and I must go back down
again. And I lay my head in that bony old lap, and I cry and I cry—I don't
know how long. And I feel those old fingers, like death itself, passing over
my hair and my neck. I don't know how long I kneel there crying, and when
I stop, I get out of there as fast as I can.

Etíenne

The boy come in, and soon, right off, they get quiet, blaming the boy. If people could look little farther than the tip of they nose—No, they blame the
boy. Not that they ain't behind the boy, what he doing, but they blame him
for what she must do. What they don't know is that the boy didn't start it,
and the people that bombed the house didn't start it, neither. It started a
million years ago. It started when one man envied another man for having
a penny mo' 'an he had, and then the man married a woman to help him
work the field so he could get much 's the other man, but when the other
man saw the man had married a woman to get much 's him, he, himself, he
married a woman, too, so he could still have mo'. Then they start having
children—not from love; but so the children could help 'em work so they
could have mo'. But even with the children one man still had a penny mo'
'an the other, so the other man went and bought him a ox, and the other
man did the same—to keep ahead of the other man. And soon the other
man had bought him a slave to work the ox so he could get ahead of the
other man. But the other man went out and bought him two slaves so he

could stay ahead of the other man, and the other man went out and bought him three slaves. And soon they had a thousand slaves apiece, but they still wasn't satisfied. And one day the slaves all rose and kill the masters, but the masters (knowing slaves was men just like they was, and kind o' expected they might do this) organized theyself a good police force, and the police force, they come out and killed the two thousand slaves.

So it's not this boy you see standing here 'fore you, 'cause it happened a million years ago. And this boy here's just doing something the slaves done a million years ago. Just that this boy here ain't doing it they way. 'Stead of raising arms 'gainst the masters, he bow his head.

No, I say; don't blame the boy 'cause she must go. 'Cause when she's   225
dead, and that won't be long after they get her up there, this boy's work will still be going on. She's not the only one that's go'n die from this boy's work. Many mo' of 'em go'n die 'fore it's over with. The whole place—everything. A big wind is rising, and when a big wind rise, the sea stirs, and the drop o' water you see laying on top the sea this day won't be there tomorrow. 'Cause that's what wind do, and that's what life is. She ain't nothing but one little drop o' water laying on top the sea, and what this boy's doing is called the wind . . . and she must be moved. No, don't blame the boy. Go out and blame the wind. No don't blame him, 'cause tomorrow, what he's doing today, somebody go'n say he ain't done a thing. 'Cause tomorrow will be his time to be turned over just like it's hers today. And after that, be somebody else time to turn over. And it keep going like that till it ain't nothing left to turn—and nobody left to turn it.

"Sure, they bombed the house," he say; "because they want us to stop. But if we stopped today, then what good would we have done? What good? Those who have already died for the cause would have just died in vain."

"Maybe if they had bombed your house you wouldn't be so set on keeping this up."

"If they had killed my mother and my brothers and sisters, I'd press just that much harder. I can see you all point. I can see it very well. But I can't agree with you. You blame me for their being bombed. You blame me for Aunt Fe's leaving. They died for you and for your children. And I love Aunt Fe as much as anybody in here does. Nobody in here loves her more than I do. Not one of you." He looks at her. "Don't you believe me, Aunt Fe?"

She nods—that little white scarf still tied round her head.

"How many times have I eaten in your kitchen, Aunt Fe? A thousand   230
times? How many times have I eaten tea cakes and drank milk on the back steps, Aunt Fe? A thousand times? How many times have I sat at this same fireplace with you, just the two of us, Aunt Fe? Another thousand times— two thousand times? How many times have I chopped wood for you, chopped grass for you, ran to the store for you? Five thousand times? How many times have we walked to church together, Aunt Fe? Gone fishing at the river together—how many times? I've spent as much time in this house as I've spent in my own. I know every crack in the wall. I know every corner. With my eyes shut, I can go anywhere in here without bumping into anything. How many of you can do that? Not many of you." He looks at her. "Aunt Fe?"

She looks at him.

"Do you think I love you, Aunt Fe?"

She nods.

"I love you, Aunt Fe, much as I do my own parents. I'm going to miss you much as I'd miss my own mother if she were to leave me now. I'm goin to miss you, Aunt Fe, but I'm not going to stop what I've started. You told me a story once, Aunt Fe, about my great-grandpa. Remember? Remember how he died?"

She looks in the fire and nods.   235

"Remember how they lynched him—chopped him into pieces?"

She nods.

"Just the two of us were sitting here beside the fire when you told me that. I was so angry I felt like killing. But it was you who told me get killing out of my mind. It was you who told me I would only bring harm to myself and sadness to the others if I killed. Do you remember that, Aunt Fe?"

She nods, still looking in the fire.

"You were right. We cannot raise our arms. Because it would mean   240
death for ourselves, as well as for the others. But we will do something else—and that's what we will do." He looks at the people standing round him. "And if they were to bomb my own mother's house tomorrow, I would still go on."

"I'm not saying for you not to go on," Louise says. "That's up to you. I'm just taking Auntie from here before hers is the next house they bomb."

The boy look at Louise, and then at Aunt Fe. He go up to the chair where she sitting.

"Good-bye, Aunt Fe," he say, picking up her hand. The hand done shriveled up to almost nothing. Look like nothing but loose skin's covering the bones. "I'll miss you," he say.

"Good-bye, Emmanuel," she say. She look at him a long time. "God be with you."

He stand there holding the hand a while longer, then he nods his head,   245
and leaves the house. The people stir round little bit, but nobody say anything.

Aunt Lou

They tell her good-bye, and half of 'em leave the house crying or want cry, but she just sit there 'side the fireplace like she don't mind going at all. When Leola ask me if I'm ready to go, I tell her I'm staying right there till Fe leave that house. I tell her I ain't moving one step till she go out that door. I been knowing her for the past fifty some years now, and I ain't 'bout to leave her on her last night here.

That boy, Chuckkie, want stay with me, but I make him go. He follow his mon and paw out the house and soon I hear that wagon turning round. I hear Emile saying something to Mr. Bascom even 'fore that wagon get out the yard. I tell myself, well, Mr. Bascom, you sure go'n catch it, and me not there to take up for you—and I get up from my chair and go to the door.

"Emile?" I call.

"Whoa," he say.

"You leave that mule 'lone, you hear me?"

"I ain't done Mr. Bascom a thing, Mama," he say.   250

"Well, you just mind you don't," I say. "I'll sure find out."

"Yes'm," he say. "Come up here, Mr. Bascom."

"Now, you hear that boy, Emile?" I say.

"I'm sorry, Mama," he say. "I didn't mean no harm."   255

They go out in the road, and I go back to the fireplace and sit down again. Louise stir round in the kitchen a few minutes, then she come in the front where we at. Everybody else gone. That husband o' hers, there, got drunk long 'fore midnight, and Emile and them had to put him to bed in the other room.

She come there and stand by the fire.

"I'm dead on my feet," she say.

"Why don't you go to bed," I say. "I'm go'n be here."

"You all won't need anything?"   260

"They got wood in that corner?"

"Plenty."

"Then we don't need a thing."

She stand there and warm, and then she say good night and go round the other side.

"Well, Fe?" I say.   265

"I ain't leaving here tomorrow, Lou," she say.

"'Course you is," I say. "Up there ain't that bad."

She shake her head. "No, I ain't going nowhere."

I look at her over in her chair, but I don't say nothing. The fire pops in the fireplace, and I look at the fire again. It's a good little fire—not too big, not too little. Just 'nough there to keep the place warm.

"You want sing, Lou?" she say, after a while. "I feel like singing my 'ter-   270
mination song."

"Sure," I say.

She start singing in that little light voice she got there, and I join with her. We sing two choruses, and then she stop.

"My 'termination for Heaven," she say. "Now—now—"

"What's the matter, Fe?" I say.

"Nothing," she say. "I want get in my bed. My gown hanging over there."   275

I get the gown for her and bring it back to the firehalf. She get out of her dress slowly, like she don't even have 'nough strength to do it. I help her on with her gown, and she kneel down there 'side the bed and say her prayers. I sit in my chair and look at the fire again.

She pray there a long time—half out loud, half to herself. I look at her kneeling down there, little like a little old girl. I see her making some kind o' jecking motion there, but I feel she crying 'cause this her last night here, and 'cause she got to go and leave ever'thing behind. I look at the fire.

She pray there ever so long, and then she start to get up. But she can't make it by herself. I go to help her, and when I put my hand on her shoulder, she say, "Lou? Lou?"

I say, "What's the matter, Fe?"

"Lou?" she say. "Lou?"   280

I feel her shaking in my hand with all her might. Shaking, shaking, shaking—like a person with the chill. Then I hear her take a long breath, longest I ever heard anybody take before. Then she ease back on the bed—calm, calm, calm.

"Sleep on, Fe," I tell her. "When you get up there, tell 'em all I ain't far behind."

                                                                        [1968]

BRENDAN GILL (1914–1997)

Brendan Gill was born in Connecticut and attended Yale University. He worked at The New Yorker *for many years, publishing his first piece there in 1936. His best-selling book* Here at the New Yorker *(1973) chronicles his time at the magazine. An excerpt from that book is the focus of Chapter 2. He published at least a dozen other books on a range of subjects, including novels, poems, essays, and reviews of film, drama, and architecture.*

The Knife

Michael threw himself down, locked his hands over one of his father's knees, and began, in a loud whisper, "'Our Father, who art in heaven, hallowed by thy name, kingdom come, will be done, earth as it is in heaven, give us this day—'"

Carroll folded his newspaper. Michael should have been in bed an hour ago. "Take it easy, kid," he said. "Let's try it again, slow."

Michael repeated distinctly, "'Our Father, who art in heaven, hallowed . . .'" The boy's pajamas, Carroll saw, were dirty at the cuffs; probably he had not brushed his teeth. "'. . . as we forgive them, who trespass against us'—what does 'trespass' mean, Dad?"

"Why, hurting anybody."

"Do I trespass anybody?"   5

"Not much, I guess. Finish it up."

Michael drew a breath. "'And lead us not into temptation, but deliver us from evil. Amen.'"

"Now," his father said, brushing back Michael's tangled hair, "what about a good 'Hail, Mary'?"

"All right," Michael said. "'Hail, Mary, full of grace, the Lord is with thee, blessed art thou among women, and blessed is the fruit of thy womb, Jesus.'" Michael lifted his head to ask if a womb got fruit like a tree, but thought better of it. His father never answered questions seriously, the way his mother used to. Michael decided to wait and ask Mrs. Nolan. "Is Mrs. Nolan coming tomorrow?" he asked.

"She'll be here, all right," Carroll said. "I give you ten seconds to finish   10
the prayer."

Michael grinned at the ultimatum. "I thought you wanted me to go slow. 'Holy Mary, Mother of God, pray for us sinners, now and at the hour of our death. Amen.'" He unlocked his fingers. "Will she?"

"Will she what?"

"Will she now and at the hour of our death, A-men?"

The words of Michael's prayer caught in Carroll's mind and stayed there, a long way beyond his smiling face. "Yes," he said, and set his pipe in the broken dish on the table beside him. He had not emptied the dish of ashes in two days. Mrs. Nolan would give him a piece of her mind tomorrow morning, as she did each week when she came in to give the apartment a general cleaning and to do the laundry.

"What good can she do?" Michael asked.   15

"Climb into bed, young ragamuffin," Carroll said sternly. "It's past nine."

"What *good* can she do?"

"She'll help you get anything you want. I suppose she'll help you climb up into heaven when the time comes. You know all about heaven, don't you?"

Michael felt himself on the defensive. "Of course."

"Well, then, get along with you."   20

But Michael had something difficult to say. "You mean she'll ask God for anything I want and He'll give it to her for me?"

"She's His mother."

Michael stood up and kissed his father carefully on the cheek. Then he walked from the room, and Carroll could hear his bare feet crossing the hall. The bed creaked as Michael lay down on it. Carroll opened the newspaper, read a paragraph, then dropped it in a white heap on the rug. He felt tired; perhaps tonight he might be able to get some sleep. He got up, slipped his suspenders from his shoulders, unknotted his tie, kicked off his shoes. He had learned to undress quickly in the last six months, since his wife had died.

His pajamas were hanging inside out in the bathroom, where he had left them that morning. When he had undressed he felt Michael's toothbrush with his thumb; it was dry. He should have explained to the child what happened to a person's teeth when he forgot to clean them every night and morning.

Carroll stared at his face in the mirror above the basin. He tried smiling.   25
No one could honestly tell what a man was thinking by the way he smiled. Even Michael, who was like a puppy about sensing moods, could not tell. He entered the bedroom on tiptoe. Feeling the sheets bunched at the foot of the mattress, he remembered that he had made the beds in a hurry. The sheets felt fresh and cool only on Saturdays, when Mrs. Nolan changed them.

Michael was not asleep, "Dad?" he whispered.

"Go to sleep."

"I been asking Hail Mary for something."

"Tomorrow."

"No, I been asking her right now."   30

Carroll lay on his back with his hands over his eyes. "What've you been asking her for, Mickey?"

Michael hesitated. "I thought I'd better make it something easy first. To see what happened." He sat up in bed. "A jackknife."

A few blocks away the clock in the Metropolitan Life tower was striking ten. Michael was deep in the noisy middle of a dream. Carroll listened to his breathing. He tried matching his own breath to Michael's, to make sleep come, but it was no use. Every night Carroll pretended to himself he was just at the brink of falling off to sleep, but his eyes always widened with wakefulness in the dark. Now, as the clock stopped striking, Carroll got up and walked into the bathroom and dressed. Then he went into the living room, unlocked the outside door of the apartment, and then locked it again before he walked down the two flights of stairs to the sidewalk. Shops reached out of sight down both sides of Lexington Avenue. Carroll walked uptown as he always did. He stopped in front of each bright shop window, studying its contents for the fifth or sixth time. He knew by now the day on which each window was changed and by whom. Certain plaster models, certain fringed crêpe papers were old friends.

At the top of a long slope Carroll waited for the lights to change. On his left was a bar; on his right, across the street, a drugstore. Carroll waited a moment outside the bar. Between the slats of its cheap orange Venetian blinds he could see the gleaming mahogany counter, the stacked glasses, the barman slicing foam from a mug of beer. A man and a girl were sitting at a table by the window, a foot under Carroll's eyes. They did not seem to be speaking. The man's hands lay halfway across the table and the girl's black dress made her throat look soft and white. Carroll turned away and crossed the street to the drugstore. The owner, Sam Ramatsky, stood sniffing the night air under the painted sign bearing his name.

"Well, Mr. Carroll, nice night for March."   35

"Yes." Carroll wanted only to hear a voice. "How's business?" he asked.

"Can't complain." Sam grinned, shaking his head. "I take that back. It's *lousy.* I got to break myself of this old 'Can't complain.' I got to remember how serious it is. Business is lousy."

Carroll leaned back against Sam's window, which was crammed with hot-water bottles, perfumes, toys, and two cardboard girls in shorts and sandals. The girls had been there for two months. There was dust on their teeth and on their smooth brown legs. "You ought to brush their teeth, Sam," Carroll said, "and run your hand down their legs now and then."

"You walk a lot," Sam said. "I figure on you, ten or eleven, every night."

"I guess I do," Carroll said.   40

Sam patted his hard belly. "Nothing like exercise to keep a man in shape."

Carroll nodded impatiently. It was not Sam's voice he wanted to hear, after all. "Give me a milk shake, Sam."

They walked into the store. Carroll sat down on one of the round stools at the fountain and watched Sam pouring milk into the shaker. "Nothing like milk," Sam said, "keep a man's system clean." Carroll watched the hands of the electric clock above the door. Ten-forty-five. He could not go to bed before twelve. He glanced at the packed counters behind him. "Sell any jackknives, Sam?"

"Sure. I sell everything. That's what keeps me broke. Nothing like keeping a thing in stock to kill demand." Sam lifted a tray of jackknives from a counter, brought it over, and set it down on the fountain. "Beauties," Sam said. "Fifty cents up."

Carroll looked at several of them and finally picked up the biggest and   45
shiniest one. "I'll take this one," he said.

"Such expensive taste! One buck."

Carroll paid for the milk shake and the knife, said "Good night, Sam," and walked out into the street. In another hour and a half he should have walked six miles. By that time his body would be tired enough so that he could sleep. By that time, he hoped, no voice could rouse him.

It was morning when Carroll awoke. He lay with his face on his hands, listening to the sound of the March rain against the windows. He remembered suddenly the absurd song that everyone used to sing: "Though April showers may come your way, they bring the flowers that bloom in May."

March rains brought you nothing. March rains only shut you in your room without any hope of escape.

Michael and Mrs. Nolan were talking together in the kitchen. Michael's voice was high with excitement. "Look at it, Mrs. Nolan, look at it! Isn't it beautiful?"

"It is that," Mrs. Nolan said in her deep voice. Carroll sat up in bed. It   50
was too late to give Mrs. Nolan warning.

"Do you ask for things when you say your prayers, Mrs. Nolan?" Michael demanded.

"I do." A pan clattered to the floor. "I've seen many a nice clean sty I'd swap for this dirty kitchen," Mrs. Nolan said. "You live like a couple of savages from week to week. God love you."

"Do you always get what you ask for?" Michael said.

"It all depends. I sort of try to guess what the good Lord wants to give me, and I ask for that."

"That's how I got this knife," Michael said. "It's got a big blade and a lit-   55
tle blade and a screwdriver and a thing to punch holes in leather with and a file."

"You must have said yourself a fine prayer," Mrs. Nolan said. There was no hint of surprise in her voice.

"It was only a 'Hail, Mary,'" Michael said, "but I did it very slow, the way Dad told me to." Michael was silent for a moment. "But I'm asking for the real thing tonight. The knife was just to see. Someone's going to be here when you come next week."

Mrs. Nolan made a clucking sound in her mouth. "Someone instead of me?"

"She was here with Dad and me before you came," Michael said, his voice thin with its burden, "and she's coming back."

"Michael!" Carroll shouted.   60

Michael ran to the doorway. The knife gleamed in his fist. "Look what I got," he said. "I was showing Mrs. Nolan."

"Come here," Carroll said. When Michael reached the edge of the bed Carroll bent over and fastened his arms behind the child's back. There was only one thing to say, and one way to say it, and that was fast. "I'm glad you like it," he said. "I bought it for you at Ramatsky's last night. The biggest and shiniest one he had."

[1940]

JAMES JOYCE (1882–1941)

James Joyce graduated from University College, Dublin, then studied medicine for a time in Paris before his mother's illness forced him to return to Ireland. After her death, Joyce spent most of his life abroad in Trieste, Switzerland, and France. He worked at various professions—teacher, tweed salesman, journalist, lecturer. In addition to short stories and novels, Joyce also published poetry and a play. He suffered from chronic eye problems and as a result of glaucoma became nearly blind.

Araby

North Richmond Street, being blind, was a quiet street except at the hour when the Christian Brothers' School set the boys free. An uninhabited house of two stories stood at the blind end, detached from its neighbors in a square ground. The other houses of the street, conscious of decent lives within them, gazed at one another with brown imperturbable faces.

The former tenant of our house, a priest, had died in the back drawing-room. Air, musty from having been long enclosed, hung in all the rooms, and the waste room behind the kitchen was littered with old useless papers. Among these I found a few paper-covered books, the pages of which were curled and damp: *The Abbot,* by Walter Scott, *The Devout Communicant* and *The Memoirs of Vidocq.* I liked the last best because its leaves were yellow. The wild garden behind the house contained a central apple-tree and a few straggling bushes under one of which I found the late tenant's rusty bicycle-pump. He had been a very charitable priest; in his will he had left all his money to institutions and the furniture of his house to his sister.

James Joyce with Sylvia Beech, who published the first edition of Joyce's *Ulysses* in 1922.

When the short days of winter came dusk fell before we had well eaten our dinners. When we met in the street the houses had grown somber. The space of sky above us was the color of ever-changing violet and towards it the lamps of the street lifted their feeble lanterns. The cold air stung us and we played till our bodies glowed. Our shouts echoed in the silent street. The career of our play brought us through the dark muddy lanes behind the houses where we ran the gauntlet of the rough tribes from the cottages, to the back doors of the dark dripping gardens where odors arose from the ashpits, to the dark odorous stables where a coachman smoothed and combed the horse or shook music from the buckled harness. When we returned to the street light from the kitchen windows had filled the areas. If my uncle was seen turning the corner we hid in the shadow until we had seen him safely housed. Or if Mangan's sister came out on the doorstep to call her brother in to his tea we watched her from our shadow peer up and down the street. We waited to see whether she would remain or go in and, if she remained, we left our shadow and walked up to Mangan's steps resignedly. She was waiting for us, her figure defined by the light from the half-opened door. Her brother always teased her before he obeyed and I stood by the railings looking at her. Her dress swung as she moved her body and the soft rope of her hair tossed from side to side.

Every morning I lay on the floor in the front parlor watching her door. The blind was pulled down to within an inch of the sash so that I could not be seen. When she came out on the doorstep my heart leaped. I ran to the hall, seized my books and followed her. I kept her brown figure always in my eye and, when we came near the point at which our ways diverged, I

quickened my pace and passed her. This happened morning after morning.
I had never spoken to her, except for a few casual words, and yet her name
was like a summons to all my foolish blood.

Her image accompanied me even in places the most hostile to   5
romance. On Saturday evenings when my aunt went marketing I had to go
to carry some of the parcels. We walked through the flaring streets, jostled
by drunken men and bargaining women, amid the curses of laborers, the
shrill litanies of shop-boys who stood on guard by the barrels of pigs'
cheeks, the nasal chanting of street singers, who sang a *come-all-you* about
O'Donovan Rossa, or a ballad about the troubles in our native land. These
noises converged in a single sensation of life for me: I imagined that I bore
my chalice safely through a throng of foes. Her name sprang to my lips at
moments in strange prayers and praises which I myself did not understand.
My eyes were often full of tears (I could not tell why) and at times a flood
from my heart seemed to pour itself out into my bosom. I thought little of
the future. I did not know whether I would ever speak to her or not or, if I
spoke to her, how I could tell her of my confused adoration. But my body
was like a harp and her words and gestures were like fingers running upon
the wires.

One evening I went into the back drawing-room in which the priest
had died. It was a dark rainy evening and there was no sound in the house.
Through one of the broken panes I heard the rain impinge upon the earth,
the fine incessant needles of water playing in the sodden beds. Some distant lamp or lighted window gleamed below me. I was thankful that I could
see so little. All my senses seemed to desire to veil themselves and, feeling
that I was about to slip from them, I pressed the palms of my hands together until they trembled, murmuring: *"O love! O love!"* many times.

At last she spoke to me. When she addressed the first words to me I
was so confused that I did not know what to answer. She asked me was I
going to *Araby.* I forgot whether I answered yes or no. It would be a splendid bazaar, she said; she would love to go.

"And "why can't you?" I asked.

While she spoke she turned a silver bracelet round and round her
wrist. She could not go, she said, because there would be a retreat that
week in her convent. Her brother and two other boys were fighting for
their caps and I was alone at the railings. She held one of the spikes, bowing her head towards me. The light from the lamp opposite our door caught
the white curve of her neck, lit up her hair that rested there and, falling, lit
up the hand upon the railing. It fell over one side of her dress and caught
the white border of a petticoat, just visible as she stood at ease.

"It's well for you," she said.   10

"If I go," I said, "I will bring you something."

What innumerable follies laid waste my waking and sleeping thoughts
after that evening! I wished to annihilate the tedious intervening days. I
chafed against the work of school. At night in my bedroom and by day in
the classroom her image came between me and the page I strove to read.
The syllables of the word *Araby* were called to me through the silence in
which my soul luxuriated and cast an Eastern enchantment over me. I
asked for leave to go to the bazaar on Saturday night. My aunt was surprised
and hoped it was not some Freemason affair. I answered few questions in
class. I watched my master's face pass from amiability to sternness; he

hoped I was not beginning to idle. I could not call my wandering thoughts together. I had hardly any patience with the serious work of life which, now that it stood between me and my desire, seemed to me child's play, ugly monotonous child's play.

On Saturday morning I reminded my uncle that I wished to go to the bazaar in the evening. He was fussing at the hall-stand, looking for the hat-brush, and answered me curtly:

"Yes, boy, I know."

As he was in the hall I could not go into the front parlor and lie at the   15
window. I left the house in bad humor and walked slowly towards the school. The air was pitilessly raw and already my heart misgave me.

When I came home to dinner my uncle had not yet been home. Still it was early. I sat staring at the clock for some time and, when its ticking began to irritate me, I left the room. I mounted the staircase and gained the upper part of the house. The high cold empty gloomy rooms liberated me and I went from room to room singing. From the front window I saw my companions playing below in the street. Their cries reached me weakened and indistinct and, leaning my forehead against the cool glass, I looked over at the dark house where she lived. I may have stood there for an hour, see-ing nothing but the brown-clad figure cast by my imagination, touched dis-creetly by the lamplight at the curved neck, at the hand upon the railings and at the border below the dress.

When I came downstairs again I found Mrs. Mercer sitting at the fire. She was an old garrulous woman, a pawnbroker's widow, who collected used stamps for some pious purpose. I had to endure the gossip of the tea-table. The meal was prolonged beyond an hour and still my uncle did not come. Mrs. Mercer stood up to go: she was sorry she couldn't wait any longer, but it was after eight o'clock and she did not like to be out late, as the night air was bad for her. When she had gone I began to walk up and down the room, clenching my fists. My aunt said:

"I'm afraid you may put off your bazaar for this night of Our Lord."

At nine o'clock I heard my uncle's latchkey in the halldoor. I heard him talking to himself and heard the hall-stand rocking when it had received the weight of his overcoat. I could interpret these signs. When he was midway through his dinner I asked him to give me the money to go to the bazaar. He had forgotten.

"The people are in bed and after their first sleep now," he said.

I did not smile. My aunt said to him energetically: 20

"Can't you give him the money and let him go? You've kept him late enough as it is."

My uncle said he was very sorry he had forgotten. He said he believed in the old saying: "All work and no play makes Jack a dull boy." He asked me where I was going and, when I had told him a second time he asked me did I know *The Arab's Farewell to His Steed.* When I left the kitchen he was about to recite the opening lines of the piece to my aunt.

I held a florin tightly in my hands as I strode down Buckingham Street towards the station. The sight of the streets thronged with buyers and glar-ing with gas recalled to me the purpose of my journey. I took my seat in a third-class carriage of a deserted train. After an intolerable delay the train moved out of the station slowly. It crept onward among ruinous houses and over the twinkling river. At Westland Row Station a crowd of people

pressed to the carriage doors; but the porters moved them back, saying that
it was a special train for the bazaar. I remained alone in the bare carriage. In
a few minutes the train drew up beside an improvised wooden platform. I
passed out on to the road and saw by the lighted dial of a clock that it was
ten minutes to ten. In front of me was a large building which displayed the
magical name.

    I could not find any sixpenny entrance and, fearing that the bazaar   25
would be closed, I passed in quickly through a turnstile, handing a shilling
to a weary-looking man. I found myself in a big hall girdled at half its height
by a gallery. Nearly all the stalls were closed and the greater part of the hall
was in darkness. I recognized a silence like that which pervades a church
after a service. I walked into the center of the bazaar timidly. A few people
were gathered about the stalls which were still open. Before a curtain, over
which the words *Café Chantant* were written in colored lamps, two men
were counting money on a salver. I listened to the fall of the coins.

    Remembering with difficulty why I had come I went over to one of the
stalls and examined porcelain vases and flowered tea-sets. At the door of
the stall a young lady was talking and laughing with two young gentlemen.
I remarked their English accents and listened vaguely to their conversation.

    "O, I never said such a thing!"

    "O, but you did!"

    "O, but I didn't!"

    "Didn't she say that?"   30

    "She did. I heard her."

    "O, there's a . . . fib!"

    "Observing me the young lady came over and asked me did I wish to
buy anything. The tone of her voice was not encouraging; she seemed to
have spoken to me out of a sense of duty. I looked humbly at the great jars
that stood like eastern guards at either side of the dark entrance to the stall
and murmured:

    "No, thank you."

    The young lady changed the position of one of the vases and went   35
back to the two young men. They began to talk of the same subject. Once
or twice the young lady glanced at me over her shoulder.

    I lingered before her stall, though I knew my stay was useless, to make
my interest in her wares seem the more real. Then I turned away slowly and
walked down the middle of the bazaar. I allowed the two pennies to fall
against the six-pence in my pocket. I heard a voice call from one end of the
gallery that the light was out. The upper part of the hall was now completely dark.

    Gazing up into the darkness I saw myself as a creature driven and
derided by vanity: and my eyes burned with anguish and anger.

                                                  [1914]

GARRISON KEILLOR (1942–)

Garrison Keillor is most famous for his National Public Radio show, The Prairie Home
Companion, *which features news from his fictional "hometown," Lake Woebegone. He
began working for public radio after graduating from the University of Minnesota in 1966.*

The radio show began as a local live variety show, becoming national in 1980. After a two-year break in 1987, Keillor returned to the show and has broadcast ever since. He is also the author of best-selling novels, short story collections, children's books, and various magazine pieces.

Zeus the Lutheran

I. Hera, Fed Up with His Philandering, Hires a Lawyer

Zeus the Father of Heaven, the Father of the Seasons, the Fates, and the Muses, the father of Athena and Apollo and Artemis and Dionysus, plus the father of Hephaestus by Hera, his wife, and of Eros by his daughter Aphrodite, was a guy who didn't take no for an answer. Armed with his thunderbolts, he did exactly as he pleased and followed every amorous impulse of his heart, coupling with nymphs or gods or mortal women as he desired, sometimes changing himself into a swan or a horse or snake or taking the form of a mortal so as to avoid detection. Once, he became a chicken to make it more of a challenge.

His wife Hera was furious and hired a lawyer, Alan, to talk some sense into him. The day before, she had heard that Zeus was involved with a minor deity named Janice, shacked up with her on the island of Patmos, riding around on a Vespa with her clinging to him like a monkey.

"Tail him," she said. "Track down the bastard and nail him to the wall and put the bimbo on a plane to Peru." Hera threw her great bulk into a chair and glared blackly out the temple window. "One of these days, I'll catch him when he has set his thunderbolts aside and I will *trap him!* And then—" she laughed, *ho ho ho ho ho.* "Then we will have the Mother of Heaven. The patriarchy will be put on the shelf once and for all. With Athena, the goddess of wisdom, on my right hand, and Artemis, the goddess of the moon, on my left, I will civilize this universe, this bloody hellhole that men have made. Find Zeus when he is in the throes of desire and we will overthrow him and change the world, Alan."

Alan picked up his briefcase. "Whatever you say. You're the client," he said, and got on a boat to Patmos.

When Alan spotted Zeus, sitting at a table in an outdoor cafe by the harbor, there was no bimbo, only the ageless gentleman himself in a blue T-shirt and white shorts, fragrant with juniper, the Father of Heaven nursing a glass of nectar on the rocks and picking at a spinach salad. Alan introduced himself and sat down. He didn't ask, "How are you?" because he knew the answer: GREAT, ALL-POWERFUL.

"I realize you're omniscient, but let me come right to the point and say what's on my mind," he said. "Enough with the mounting and coupling. Keep it in your pants. What are you trying to prove? You're a god, for Pete's sake. Be a little divine for a change. Knock it off with the fornication, okay? Otherwise, Hera means business, and we're not talking divorce, mister. You should be so lucky. Hera intends to take over the world. She's serious."

"You like magic? You want to see a magic trick?" said Zeus. And right there at the table he turned the young lawyer into a pitcher of vinaigrette dressing and his briefcase into a pine nut and he poured him over the spinach salad and then Zeus waved the waiter over and said, "The spinach

5

is wilted, pal. Take it away, and feed it to the pigs. And bring me a beautiful young woman, passionate but compliant, with small, ripe breasts."

That was his usual way of dealing with opposition: senseless violence followed by easy sex.

Hera was swimming laps in the pool at her summerhouse when she got the tragic news from Victor, Alan's partner. "Alan is gone, eaten by pigs," said Victor. "We found his shoes. They were full of salad dressing." She was hardly surprised; Alan was her six hundredth lawyer in fourteen centuries. Zeus was rough on lawyers. She climbed out of the water, her great alabaster rump rising like Antarctica, and wrapped herself in a vast white towel. "Some god!" she said. "Omniscient except when it comes to himself."

She had always been puzzled by Zeus' lust for mortal women—what   10
did he see in them? they were so shallow, weak, insipid, childish—and once she asked him straight out: *Why fool around with lightweights when you've got me, a real woman?* He told her, "The spirit of love is the cosmic teacher who brings gods and mortals together, lighting the path of beauty, which is both mortal and godly, from each generation to the next. One makes love as a gift and a sacrament so that people in years to come can enjoy music and poetry and feel passion at the sight of flowers."

She said, "You're not that drunk—don't be that stupid."

Now she vowed to redouble her efforts against him, put Victor on the case. But the next day she was in Thebes, being adored, which she loved, and what with all of the flower-strewing and calf-roasting, Hera was out of the loop when a beautiful American woman, Diane, sailed into the harbor at Patmos aboard the S.S. *Bethel* with her husband, Pastor Wes.

II. Bored, He Falls for an American

Wes and Diane were on the second leg of a two-week cruise that the grateful congregation of Zion Lutheran Church in Odense, Pennsylvania, had given them in gratitude for Wes's ten years of ministry. Zeus, who was drinking coffee in the same sidewalk cafe with the passionate, compliant woman and was becoming bored with her breasts, which now seemed to him slightly too small and perhaps a touch overripe, saw Diane standing at the rail high overhead as the *Bethel* tied up. The strawberry-blonde hair and great tan against the blue Mediterranean sky, the healthy American good looks made his heart go boom and he felt the old, familiar itch in the groin—except sharper. He arose. She stood, leaning over the rail, wearing a bright-red windbreaker and blue jeans that showed off her fabulous thighs, and she seemed to be furious at the chubby man in the yellow pants who was laying his big arm on her shoulder, her hubby of sixteen years. She turned, and the arm fell off her. "Please, Diane," he said, and she looked away, up the mountain toward the monastery and the village of white houses.

Zeus paid the check and headed for the gangplank.

The night before, over a standing rib roast and a 1949 Bordeaux that   15
cost enough to feed fifty Ugandan children for a week, Wes and Diane had talked about their good life back in Odense, their four wonderful children, their luck, their kind fellow Lutherans, and had somehow got onto the subject of divine grace, which led into a discussion of pretentious Lutheran

clergy Diane had known, and Wes had to sit and hear her ridicule close friends of his—make fun of their immense reserve, their dopey clothes, their tremendous lack of sex appeal, which led to a bitter argument about their marriage. They leaned across the baklava, quietly yelling things like "How can you say that?" and "I always knew you felt that way!" until diners nearby were studying the ceiling for hairline cracks. In the morning, Diane announced that she wanted a separation. Now Wes gestured at the blue sea, the fishing boats, the mountain, the handsome Greek man in white shorts below who was smiling up at them—"This is the dream trip of a life-time," he said. "We came all this way to Greece to be miserable? We could have done that at home! This is nuts. To go on a vacation trip so you can break up? Give me a break. Why are you so hostile?" And in that moment, as he stood, arms out, palms up, begging for an answer, the god entered his body.

III. In the Heat of Passion, He Converts to Lutheranism

It took three convulsive seconds for Zeus to become Wes, and to the fifty-year-old minister, it felt exactly like a fatal heart attack, the painful tightening in the chest—Oh shit! he thought. Death. And he had quit smoking three years before! All that self-denial and for what? He was going to fall down dead anyway. Tears filled his eyes. Then Zeus took over, and the soul of Wes dropped into an old dog named Spiros, who lived on the docks and suffered from a bad hernia. *Arf*, said Wes, and felt a pain in his crotch. He groaned and leaned down and licked his balls, a strange sensation for a Lutheran.

The transformation shook Zeus up, too. He felt suddenly nauseous and clutched at the rail and nearly vomited; in the last hour, Wes had consumed a shovelful of bacon and fried eggs and many cups of dreadful coffee. The god was filled with disgust, but he touched the woman's porcelain wrist.

"What?" she said.

The god coughed. He tried to focus Wes's watery blue eyes; there was some sort of plastic disc in them. "O Lady whose beauty lights the darkening western skies, your white face flashes when I close my eyes," he said in a rumbly voice.

She stared at him. "*What* did you say?"

The god swallowed. He wanted to talk beautifully, but English sounded raspy and dull to him, an inferior language; it tasted like a cheap cigar.

"A face of such reflection as if carved in stone, and such beauty as only in great paintings shone. O Lady of light, fly no higher, but come into my bed and know eternal fire."

"Where'd you get that? Off a calendar? Is this supposed to be a joke or what?" she said. She told him to be real.

All in all, Zeus thought, *I would rather be a swan*. The dumb mustache, the poofy hair around the bald spot on top, the heavy brass medallion with a fish on it, the sunken chest and wobbly gut and big lunkers of blubber on his hips, the balloon butt, the weak arms and shaky legs, and the poor brain—corroded, stuffed with useless, sad, remorseful thoughts. It was hard for Zeus to keep his mind on love with the brain of Wes thinking of such dumb things to say to her—"I'm sorry you're angry. Let's try to have a nice day together and see the town and write some postcards. Buy some presents for the kids, take some pictures, have lunch, and forget about last

20

night."—Zeus didn't want to write postcards, he wanted to take her below and peel off her clothes and make love so that the *Bethel* rocked in her berth.

Just below, the dog sat on his haunches, a professional theologian cov-   25
ered with filthy, matted fur, and the remains of his breakfast lying before him, the chewed-up hindquarters of a rat, and the rest of the rat in his belly.

"Look. That sweet little dog on the dock," said Diane, who loved dogs.

Zeus cleared his throat. "When you open your thighs, the soft clanging of bells is heard across the valley, O daughter of Harrisburg. Come, glorious woman, and let us waken the day with the music of your clamorous thighs."

"Grow up," she said, and headed down the gangplank, smiling at the dog.

The god's innards rumbled, and a bubble of gas shifted in his belly, a fart as big as a child. He clamped his bowels around it and held it in; he followed her down to the dock, saying: "Dear, dear Lady, O Light of my soul—
the cheerful face of amiable passion in a cold, dry place. To you I offer a thousand tears and lies, an earnest heart longing for the paradise that awaits us in a bed not far away, I trust. Look at me, Lady, or else I turn to dust." His best effort so far. But the language was so flat, and the voice of Wes so pompous.

"I could swear this dog is human," she cried taking its head in her   30
hands, stroking under its chin, scratching its tattered ears.

"Thank you, Diane," said the dog. "I don't know how I became schizo-
phrenic, but I do know I've never loved you more." This came from his mouth as a whine, and then he felt a terrible twinge in the hernia and moaned. The woman knelt and cradled his head in her arms. She crooned, "Oh, honey, precious, baby, sweetness, Mama gonna be so good to you, little darling." She had never said this to him before. He felt small and cozy in her arms.

IV. The Great Lover Tries and Falls Short

The dog, the woman, and the god rode a bus three miles over the mountain to the Sheraton St. John Hotel, the woman holding the dog's head on her lap. She was thinking about the future: she'd leave Wes, take the kids, move to Philadelphia, and go to Bryn Mawr College and study women's studies—the simple glories of the disciplined intellectual life! what a tonic after years of slouching around in a lousy marriage. The god vowed to go without food until she surrendered to him. The dog felt no pain, but he hoped to find a cigarette lying on the floor somewhere, even a cigarette butt, and figure out how to light it.

The hotel room had twin beds, hard as benches, and looked out on a village of white stucco houses with small gardens of tomato plants and beans, where chickens strolled among the vines. Brown goats roamed across the brown hills, their bells clanging softly. Diane undressed in the bathroom, and slid into bed sideways, and lay facing the wall. Zeus sat on the edge of her bed and lightly traced with his finger the neckline of her white negligee. She shrugged. The dog lay at her feet, listening. Zeus held her shoulder strap between his thumb and index finger. It was bewildering, trying to steer his passion through the narrow, twisting mind of Wes. All he wanted was to make love enthusiastically for hours, but dismal Lutheran thoughts sprang up: Go to sleep. Stop making a fool of yourself. You're a grown man. Settle down. Don't be ridiculous. Who do you think you are?

He wished he could change to somebody trim and taut, an athlete, but he could feel the cold, wiggly flesh glued on him and he know that Hera had caught him in the naked moment of metamorphosis and with a well-aimed curse had locked him tight inside the flabby body, this clown sack. A god of grandeur and gallantry living in a dump, wearing a mask of pork. He could hear his fellow gods hooting and cackling up on Olympus. (The Father of Heaven! Turned Down, Given the Heave-Ho! By a Housewife!)

Zeus pulled in his gut and spoke. "Lady, your quiet demeanor mocks the turmoil in my chest, the rage, the foam, the wind blasting love's light ships aground. Surely you see this, Lady, unless you are the cruelest of your race. Surely you hear my heart pound with mounting waves upon your long, passive shore. Miles from your coast, you sit in a placid town, feeling faint reverberations from beneath the floor. It is your lover the sea, who can never rest until you come to him." 35

"I don't know who you're trying to impress, me or yourself," she said. Soon she was snoring.

V. The Husband (the Dog) Takes the Long View

"This is not such a bad deal," said the dog. "For me, this could turn out to be a very positive experience in terms of making an emotional breakthrough in my life, bursting the psychological bonds of pastorhood and Lutheranness, becoming a fully functioning, loving, sensitive, caring human being. Becoming a dog would never have been my choice, but now that I am one, I can see that, as a man, my sense of self always was tied up with power and, in some sense, with being an oppressor, being dominant. In the course of following my maleness, as my culture taught me to think of maleness, I got separated from my beingness, my creaturehood. It is so liberating to see things from down here at floor level. You learn a lot about man's relentlessness."

They spent two sunny days at the Sheraton, during which Zeus worked to seduce Diane and she treated him like a husband. She laughed at him, not at his witty stories but at his ardor. The lines that had worked for him in the past ("Sex is a token of a deeper friendship, an affirmation of mutual humanity, an extension of conversation") made her roll her eyes and snort. She lay on a blue wicker lounge beside the pool—her caramel skin set off by two red bands of bikini, her perfect breasts, her long, tan legs with a pale-golden fuzz. Her slender hands held a book, *The Concrete Shoes of Motherhood*, and she read it as he spoke to her.

"Let's take a shower. They have a sauna. Let me give you a backrub. Let's lie down and take a nap," he said.

"Cheese it," she said. "I'm not interested. Beat it." 40

He lost eighteen pounds. He ran ten miles every morning and swam in the afternoon. He shaved off the mustache. She refused to look at him, but, being a god, he could read her thoughts. She was curious about this sea change in her husband, his new regimen, his amazing discipline. She hiked over the dry brown hills and he walked behind and sang songs to her:

Lady, your shining skin will slide on mine,
Your breasts tremble with gladness.
Your body, naked, be clad in sweet oils,
And rise to the temple of Aphrodite,
Where you will live forever, no more
Lutheran but venerated by mortals. This I pledge.

She pretended not to hear, sweeping the horizon with her binoculars, looking for rare seabirds. Zeus thought, *I should have been a swan. Definitely a swan.* The dog trotted along, his hernia cured by love. She had named him Sweetness. "You go ahead and use my body as long as you like," he said to Zeus. "You're doing wonders for it. I never looked so good until you became me. No kidding. But when it comes to lyrics, you're no Cole Porter, pal."

VI. The Great Lover Tries Again

She wouldn't let him touch her until they got on the plane back to America and they had eaten the lasagna and watched the movie and were almost over Newfoundland. The *Fasten Seat Belts* signs flashed on and the pilot announced that they would be passing through a turbulent period and suddenly the plane bucked and shuddered in the boiling clouds, and Diane reached over and grabbed him as the plane tipped and plunged and rattled, and people shrieked and children cried. "If this is our time to die, then I want you to know that they were good years, really they were," Diane said, kissing him. "I love you, Wes. I'm crazy about you." Her kisses were hot and excited, and soon she was grabbing him and groping under his sportcoat, digging her sharp tongue into the corners of his mouth and writhing in his arms and groaning and saying his name, but Zeus was unable to respond somehow. His divine penis was as limp as an empty balloon. He tried to encourage it by thinking of smokestacks, pistols, pedestals, pole vaults, peninsulas, but nothing worked. Her hands reached for his zipper but he fought her off. "Not here, people are watching," he muttered, and then the plane hit the concrete at Kennedy and bounced and touched down and rolled to a stop, and Diane shuddered and said, "I can't wait to get you home, big boy."

In the terminal, Zeus felt so weak, he could not carry their bags through customs. They fetched the dog, who emerged from the baggage room dopey and confused and out of sorts. He bit Zeus on the hand. Zeus limped to the curb and collapsed into the back seat of a van driven by a burly man named Paul, who, Zeus gathered, was his brother. Paul and Diane sat in front, Zeus and the dog in back. "Wes is pretty jet-lagged," Diane said, but the man yammered on and on about some football team that Zeus gathered he was supposedly interested in. "Hope you had a great time," said Paul. Yes, they said, they had. "Always wanted to go over there myself," he said. "But things come up. You know." He talked for many miles about what he had done instead of going to Greece: resodding, finishing the attic, adding on a bedroom, taking the kids to Yellowstone.

Do we have kids? Zeus wondered. "Four," said the dog, beaming. "Great kids. I can't wait for you to meet them, mister." Then he dropped his chin on the seat and groaned. "The littlest guy is murder on animals. One look at me,

45

he'll have me in a headlock until my eyeballs pop." He groaned again. "I forgot about Mojo. Our black Lab." His big brown eyes filled with tears. "I've
come home in disgrace to die like a dog," he said. "I feed Mojo for ten years
and now he's going to go for my throat. It's too hard." The god told him to
buck up, but the dog was gloomy all the way home.

VII. The Husband Disappears

When Paul pulled up to the double garage behind the green frame house
and Diane climbed out, the dog squeezed out the door behind her and tore
off down the street and across a playground and disappeared. *"Sweetness!"*
she screeched.

Paul and Zeus cruised the streets for half an hour searching for the
mutt, Zeus with gathering apprehension, even panic. Without Wes to
resume being Wes, he now realized, he couldn't get out of Wes and back
into Zeus. There was, however, no way to explain this to Paul.

"You seem a little—I don't know—distant," said Paul.

"Just tired," said Zeus.

They circled the blocks, peering into the bushes whistling for the dog,   50
calling his name, and then Paul went home for a warm jacket (he said, but Zeus
guessed he was tired and would find some reason not to come back). The god
strode across yards, through hedges, crying, "Sweetness! Sweetness!" The yards
were cluttered with machines, which he threw aside. Sweetness!

The dog was huddled by an incinerator behind the school. He had
coached boys' hockey here for ten years. "I'm so ashamed," he wept. The god
held him tightly in his arms. "To be a dog in a foreign place is one thing, but
to come home and have to crawl around your own neighborhood—" He was
a small dog, but he sobbed like a man—deep, convulsive sobs.

Zeus was about to say, "Oh, it's not all that bad," and then he felt a feathery hand on his shoulder. Actually, a wing. It was Victor, Hera's lawyer, in a
blue pin-striped suit and two transparent wings like a locust's.

VIII. The Lover's Feet Held to the Fire

Zeus tried to turn him into a kumquat, but the lawyer only chuckled. "Heh,
heh, heh. Don't waste my time. You wanna know how come you feel a little limp? Lemme tell ya. Hera is extremely upset, Mr. Z. Frankly, I don't know
if godhood is something you're ever going to experience again. It wouldn't
surprise me that much if you spent the rest of recorded time as a frozen
meatball."

"What does she want?"

"She wants what's right. Justice. She wants half your power. No more,   55
no less."

"Divide power? Impossible. It wouldn't be power if I gave it up."

"Okay. Then see how you like these potatoes." And Victor snatched up
the dog, and his wings buzzed as he zoomed up and over the pleasant
rooftops of Odense.

"Wait!" the god cried. "Forty-five percent!" But his voice was thin and
whispery. On the way home, he swayed, his knees caved in, he had to hang
on to a mailbox.

IX. Trapped

For three days, Zeus was flat on his back, stunned by monogamy: what a cruel fate for a great man! The dog Mojo barked and barked at him, Diane waited on him hand and foot, bringing him bad food and despicable wine; wretched little children hung around, onlookers at the site of a disaster, children who he had to pretend were his own. They clung to him on the couch, fighting over the choice locations, whining, weeping, pounding each other. They stank of sugar and yet he had to embrace them. He could not get their names straight. Melissa and Donnie (or Sean or Jon), or Melinda and Randy, and the fat one was Penny, and the little one's name began with an *H*. He called him Hector, and the little boy cried. "Go away," the god snapped at them. "You are vile and disgusting. I'm sorry but it's the truth. I'm dying. Let me die in peace. Bug off." The older boy wept: something about a promise, a trip to see a team play a game, a purchase—Zeus couldn't understand him. "Speak up!" he said, but the boy blubbered and bawled, his soft lemurlike face slimy with tears and mucus. The god swung down his legs and sat up on the couch and raised his voice: "I am trapped here, a divine being fallen from a very high estate indeed—you have no idea—and what I see around me I do not want."

Everybody felt lousy, except Diane. "It's only jet lag!" she cried, bringing in a tray of cold, greasy, repulsive food, which he could see from her smile was considered a real treat here. He ate a nugget of cheese and gagged.   60

"You'll feel better tomorrow," she said.

From outside came a burst of fierce barks and a brief dogfight and then yelping, and Diane tore out the door and returned a moment later with her husband, wounded, weeping, in her arms. "Oh, Sweetness, Sweetness," she murmured, kissing him on the snout, "we'll make it up to you somehow."

Later, Penny, the fat girl, asked Zeus if Greece was as dirty as they said. She asked if he and Mom had had a big fight. She asked why he felt trapped. She wanted to hear all the bad news.

"I felt crazy the moment we landed in America. The air is full of piercing voices, thousands of perfectly normal, handsome, tall people talk-talk-talk-talk-talking away like chickadees, and I can hear each one of them all the time, and they make me insane. You're used to this, I'm not. What do you people have against silence? Your country is so beautiful, and it is in the grip of invincible stupidity. Your politicians are habitual liars and toadies, and the writers are arrogant hacks," he said. "The country is inflamed with debt and swollen with blight and trash and sworn to flaming idiocy, and there is no civility left except among drunks and cab-drivers."

"How can you say that, Dad?"   65

"Because I'm omniscient."

"You are?"

"I know everything. It's a fact." She looked at him with a level gaze, not smirking, not pouting, an intelligent child. The only one prepared to understand him.

"Do my homework," she whispered. So he did. He whipped off dozens of geometry exercises, algebra, trigonometry, in a flash. He identified the nations of Africa, the law of averages, the use of the dative. "You are so smart," she said.

X. The Wife Courts the Lover While the Husband Watches

Diane packed the kids off to bed. "Now," she said, "where's that guy I rode   70
home with on the plane?"

How could she understand? Passion isn't an arrangement, it's an accident, and Zeus was worn out. Nonetheless, he allowed himself to be undressed and helped into bed, and then Diane slowly undressed, letting her white silk slip slide to the floor, unhooking her garter belt and stripping the nylons slowly from her magnificent golden legs, unsnapping the brassiere and tossing it over her right shoulder, and stepping out of her silver panties. Then, naked, she stood a moment for his admiration, and turned and went into the bathroom.

"Relax, she'll be in there fifteen minutes if I know Diane," said the dog, sitting in the doorway. "She likes to do her nails before making love, I don't know why. Anyway, let me give you a few pointers about making love to her. She comes out of the gate pretty fast and gets excited and you think you're on the straightaway stretch, but you're not—she slows you down at that point, and she doesn't mount you until you're practically clawing at the walls."

"She mounts *me?*" asked Zeus.

"Yes," the dog said. "She's always on top."

When Diane emerged from the bathroom, she found Zeus in the living   75
room, fully dressed, trying to make a long-distance call to Greece. She wanted him to see a therapist, but Zeus knew he was going back to Olympus. He just had to talk Hera down a little.

XI. Last Chance

The next morning, Zeus drove to the church, with Penny snuggled at his side. The town lay in a river valley, the avenues of homes extending up and over the hills like branches laden with fruit. The church stood on a hill, a red brick hangar with a weathervane for a steeple, a sanctuary done up with fake beams and mosaics, and a plump secretary with piano legs, named Tammy. She cornered him, hugged him, and fawned like a house afire. "Oh, Pastor Wes, we missed you so much! I've been reading your sermons over and over—they're so spirit-filled! We've got to publish them in a book!" she squealed.

"Go home," said Zeus. "Put your head under cold water." He escaped from the sanctuary into the study and slammed the door. The dog sat in the big leather chair behind the long desk. He cleared his throat. "I'd be glad to help with the sermon for tomorrow," he said. "I think your topic has got to be change—the life-affirming nature of change—how it teaches us not to confuse being with having—the Christian's willingness to accept and nurture change . . . I'll work up an outline for you."

"That's a lot of balloon juice," said Zeus. "If I weren't going home tomorrow, I'd give a sermon and tell them to go home and hump like bunnies." He caught a look at himself in a long mirror: a powerful, handsome, tanned fellow in a white collar. Not bad.

"You sure you want to leave tomorrow?" asked the dog.

"That's the deal I made with Victor. Didn't he tell you?"   80

"You couldn't stay until Monday? This town needs shaking up. I always wanted to do it and didn't know how, and now you could preach on Sunday and it'd be a wonderful experience for all of us."

"You're a fool," Zeus said. "This is not a long-term problem, and the answer to it is not the willingness to accept change. You need heart, but you're Lutherans, and you go along with things. We know this from history. You're in danger and months will pass and it'll get worse, but you won't change your minds. You'll sit and wait. Lutherans are fifteen percent faith and eight-five percent loyalty. They are nobody to lead a revolt. Your country is coming apart."

The dog looked up at the god with tears in his brown eyes. "Please tell my people," he whispered.

"Tell them yourself."

"They won't believe me."   85

"Good for them. Neither do I."

"Love me," Diane told Zeus that night in bed. "Forget yourself. Forget that we're Lutheran. Hurl your body off the cliff into the dark abyss of wild, mindless, passionate love." But he was too tired. He couldn't find the cliff. He seemed to be on a prairie.

XII. The Lover Leaves, the Husband Returns

In the morning, he hauled himself out of bed and dressed in a brown suit and white shirt. He peered into the closet. "These your only ties?" he asked the dog. The dog nodded.

Zeus glanced out the bedroom window to the east, to a beech tree by the garage, where a figure with waxen wings was sitting on a low limb. He said, silently, "Be with you in one minute." He limped into the kitchen and found Diane in the breakfast nook, eating bran flakes and reading an article in the Sunday paper about a couple who are able to spend four days a week in the country home now that they have a fax machine. He brushed her cheek with his lips and whispered, "O you woman, farewell, you sweet, sexy Lutheran love of my life," and jumped out of Wes and into the dog, loped out the back door, and climbed into Victor's car.

"She'll be glad to hear you're coming," said Victor. "She misses you. I'm   90 sorry you'll have to make the return flight in a small cage, doped on a heavy depressant, and be quarantined for sixty days in Athens, both July and August, but after that, things should start to get better for you."

XIII. How the Husband Saw It

At eleven o'clock, having spent the previous two hours tangled in the sheet with his amazing wife, Wes stood in the pulpit and grinned. The church was almost half full, not bad for July, and the congregation seemed glad to see him. "First of all, Diane and I want to thank you for the magnificent gift of the trip to Greece, which will be a permanent memory, a token of your generosity and love," he said. "A tremendous thing happened on the trip that I want to share with you this morning. For the past week, I have lived in the body of a dog while an ancient god lived with Diane and tried to seduce her."

He didn't expect the congregation to welcome this news, but he was unprepared for their stony looks: they glared at him as if he were a criminal. They cried out, "Get down out of that pulpit, you filth, you!"

"Why are you so hostile?" he said.

Why are you so hostile? The lamp swayed as the ship rolled, and Diane said, "Why so hostile? Why? You want to know why I'm hostile? Is that what you're asking? About hostility? My hostility to you? Okay. I'll answer your question. Why I'm hostile—right? Me. Hostile. I'll tell you why. Why are you smiling?"

He was smiling, of course, because it was a week ago—and they were   95
still in Greece, the big fight was still on, and God had kindly allowed him one more try. He could remember exactly the horrible words he'd said for the first time, and this time he did not have to say them and become a dog. He was able to swallow the 1949 wine, and think, and say, "The sight of you fills me with tender affection and a sweet longing to be flat on my back in a dark, locked room with you naked, lying on top, kissing me, and me naked, too."

So they did, and in the morning the boat docked at Patmos, and they went up to the monastery and walked through the narrow twisting streets of the village, looking for a restaurant someone had told them about that served great lamb.

XIV. What the Lover Learned

The lawyer and the dog rode to the airport in the limousine, and somewhere along the way Zeus signed a document that gave Hera half his power and promised absolute fidelity. "Absolute?" he woofed. "You mean 'total' in the sense of bottom line, right? A sort of basic faithfulness? Fidelity in principle? Isn't that what you mean here? The spirit of fidelity?"

"I mean pure," the lawyer said.

Zeus signed. The lawyer tossed him a small, dry biscuit. Zeus wolfed it down and barked. In the back of his mind, he thought maybe he'd find a brilliant lawyer to argue that the paw print wasn't a valid signature. He thought about a twenty-four-ounce T-bone steak, and he wasn't sure he'd get that either.

[1993]

DORIS LESSING (1919–)

Doris Lessing was born in Persia (now Iran) and moved to Rhodesia (now Zimbabwe) when she was six. Lessing left school at age fourteen. She joined the Communist Party for several years while she was in her twenties; in her thirties she moved to London, where she continues to live. Her political writing about South Africa caused the country to ban her books for thirty years. In addition to fiction, Lessing has written nonfiction books and librettos and has been appointed a Companion of Honour in the United Kingdom.

A Woman on a Roof

It was during the week of hot sun, that June.

Three men were at work on the roof, where the leads got so hot they had the idea of throwing water on to cool them. But the water steamed, then sizzled; and they made jokes about getting an egg from some woman in the flats under them to poach it for their dinner. By two it was not possible to touch the guttering they were replacing, and they speculated about what workmen did in regularly hot countries. Perhaps they should borrow kitchen gloves with the egg? They were all a bit dizzy, not used to the heat; and they shed their coats and stood side by side squeezing themselves into a foot-wide patch of shade against a chimney, careful to keep their feet in the thick socks and boots out of the sun. There was a fine view across several acres of roofs. Not far off a man sat in a deck chair reading the newspapers. Then they saw her, between chimneys, about fifty yards away. She lay face down on a brown blanket. They could see the top part of her; black hair, a flushed solid back, arms spread out.

"She's stark naked," said Stanley, sounding annoyed.

Harry, the oldest, a man of about forty-five, said: "Looks like it."

Young Tom, seventeen, said nothing, but he was excited and grinning.   5

Stanley said: "Someone'll report her if she doesn't watch out."

"She thinks no one can see," said Tom, craning his head all ways to see more.

At this point the woman, still lying prone, brought her two hands up behind her shoulders with the ends of a scarf in them, tied it behind her back, and sat up. She wore a red scarf tied around her breasts and brief red bikini pants. This being the first day of the sun she was white, flushing red. She sat smoking, and did not look up when Stanley let out a wolf whistle. Harry said: "Small things amuse small minds," leading the way back to their part of the roof, but it was scorching. Harry said: "Wait, I'm going to dig up some shade," and disappeared down the skylight into the building. Now that he'd gone, Stanley and Tom went to the farthest point they could to peer at the woman. She had moved, and all they could see were two pink legs stretched on the blanket. They whistled and shouted but the legs did not move. Harry came back with a blanket and shouted: "Come on, then." He sounded irritated with them. They clambered back to him and he said to Stanley: "What about your missus?" Stanley was newly married, about three months. Stanley said, jeering: "What about my missus?"—preserving his independence. Tom said nothing, but his mind was full of the nearly naked woman. Harry slung the blanket, which he had borrowed from a friendly woman downstairs, from the stem of a television aerial to a row of chimney-pots. This shade fell across the piece of gutter they had to replace. But the shade kept moving, they had to adjust the blanket, and not much progress was made. At last some of the heat left the roof, and they worked fast, making up for lost time. First Stanley, then Tom, made a trip to the end of the roof to see the woman. "She's on her back," Stanley said, adding a jest which made Tom snicker, and the older man smile tolerantly. Tom's report was that she hadn't moved, but it was a lie. He wanted to keep what he had seen to himself: he had caught her in the act of rolling down the little red pants over her hips, till they were no more than a small triangle. She was on her back, fully visible, glistening with oil.

Next morning, as soon as they came up, they went to look. She was already there, face down, arms spread out, naked except for the little red pants. She had turned brown in the night. Yesterday she was a scarlet-and-white woman, today she was a brown woman. Stanley let out a whistle. She lifted her head, startled, as if she'd been asleep, and looked straight over at him. The sun was in her eyes, she blinked and stared, then she dropped her head again. At this gesture of indifference, they all three, Stanley, Tom and old Harry, let out whistles and yells. Harry was doing it in parody of the younger men, making fun of them, but he was also angry. They were all angry because of her utter indifference to the three men watching her.

"Bitch," said Stanley.

"She should ask us over," said Tom, snickering.

Harry recovered himself and reminded Stanley: "If she's married, her old man wouldn't like that."

"Christ," said Stanley virtuously, "if my wife lay about like that, for everyone to see, I'd soon stop her."

Harry said smiling: "How do you know, perhaps she's sunning herself at this very moment?"

"Not a chance, not on our roof." The safety of his wife put Stanley into a good humor, and they went to work. But today it was hotter than yesterday; and several times one or the other suggested they should tell Matthew, the foreman, and ask to leave the roof until the heat wave was over. But they didn't. There was work to be done in the basement of the big block of flats, but up here they felt free, on a different level from ordinary humanity shut in the streets or the buildings. A lot more people came out on the roofs that day, for an hour at midday. Some married couples sat side by side in deck chairs, the women's legs stockingless and scarlet, the men in vests with reddening shoulders.

The woman stayed on her blanket, turning herself over and over. She ignored them, no matter what they did. When Harry went off to fetch more screws, Stanley said: "Come on." Her roof belonged to a different system of roofs, separated from theirs at one point by about twenty feet. It meant a scrambling climb from one level to another, edging along parapets, clinging to chimneys, while their big boots slipped and slithered, but at last they stood on a small square projecting roof looking straight down at her, close. She sat smoking, reading a book. Tom thought she looked like a poster, or a magazine cover, with the blue sky behind her and her legs stretched out. Behind her a great crane at work on a new building in Oxford Street swung its black arm across roofs in a great arc. Tom imagined himself at work on the crane, adjusting the arm to swing over and pick her up and swing her back across the sky to drop her near him.

They whistled. She looked up at them, cool and remote, then went on reading. Again, they were furious. Or, rather, Stanley was. His sun-heated face was screwed into a rage as he whistled again and again, trying to make her look up. Young Tom stopped whistling. He stood beside Stanley, excited, grinning; but he felt as if he were saying to the woman: Don't associate me with *him,* for his grin was apologetic. Last night he had thought of the unknown woman before he slept, and she had been tender with him. This tenderness he was remembering as he shifted his feet by the jeering, whistling Stanley, and watched the indifferent, healthy brown woman a few feet off, with the gap that plunged to the street between them. Tom thought it was romantic, it was like being high on two hilltops. But there was a shout from Harry, and they clambered back. Stanley's face was hard, really angry. The boy kept looking at him and wondered why he hated the woman so much, for by now he loved her.

They played their little games with the blanket, trying to trap shade to work under; but again it was not until nearly four that they could work seriously, and they were exhausted, all three of them. They were grumbling about the weather by now. Stanley was in a thoroughly bad humor. When

they made their routine trip to see the woman before they packed up for
the day, she was apparently asleep, face down, her back all naked save for
the scarlet triangle on her buttocks. "I've got a mind to report her to the
police," said Stanley, and Harry said: "What's eating you? What harm's she
doing?"

"I tell you, if she was my wife!"

"But she isn't is she?" Tom knew that Harry, like himself, was uneasy at   20
Stanley's reaction. He was normally a sharp young man, quick at his work,
making a lot of jokes, good company.

"Perhaps it will be cooler tomorrow," said Harry.

But it wasn't; it was hotter, if anything, and the weather forecast said
the good weather would last. As soon as they were on the roof, Harry went
over to see if the woman was there, and Tom knew it was to prevent Stanley going, to put off his bad humor. Harry had grownup children, a boy the
same age as Tom, and the youth trusted and looked up to him.

Harry came back and said: "She's not there."

"I bet her old man has put his foot down," said Stanley, and Harry and
Tom caught each other's eyes and smiled behind the young married man's
back.

Harry suggested they should get permission to work in the basement,   25
and they did, that day. But before packing up Stanley said: "Let's have a
breath of fresh air." Again Harry and Tom smiled at each other as they followed Stanley up to the roof, Tom in the devout conviction that he was
there to protect the woman from Stanley. It was about five-thirty, and a
calm, full sunlight lay over the roofs. The great crane still swung its black
arm from Oxford Street to above their heads. She was not there. Then there
was a flutter of white from behind a parapet, and she stood up, in a belted,
white dressing-gown. She had been there all day, probably, but on a different patch of roof, to hide from them. Stanley did not whistle; he said nothing, but watched the woman bend to collect papers, books, cigarettes, then
fold the blanket over her arm. Tom was thinking: If they weren't here, I'd go
over and say . . . what? But he knew from his nightly dreams of her that she
was kind and friendly. Perhaps she would ask him down to her flat? Perhaps . . . He stood watching her disappear down the skylight. As she went,
Stanley let out a shrill derisive yell: she started, and it seemed as if she nearly fell. She clutched to save herself, they could hear things falling. She
looked straight at them, angry. Harry said, facetiously: "Better be careful on
those slippery ladders, love." Tom knew he said it to save her from Stanley,
but she could not know it. She vanished, frowning. Tom was full of a secret
delight, because he knew her anger was for the others, not for him.

"Roll on some rain," said Stanley, bitter, looking at the blue evening sky.

Next day was cloudless, and they decided to finish the work in the
basement. They felt excluded, shut in the grey cement basement fitting
pipes, from the holiday atmosphere in London in a heat wave. At lunchtime
they came up for some air, but while the married couples, and the men in
shirt-sleeves or vests, were there, she was not there, either on her usual
patch of roof or where she had been yesterday. They all, even Harry, clambered about, between chimney-pots, over parapets, the hot leads stinging
their fingers. There was not a sign of her. They took off their shirts and vests
and exposed their chests, feeling their feet sweaty and hot. They did not

mention the woman. But Tom felt alone again. Last night she had him into her flat: it was big and had fitted white carpets and a bed with a padded white leather headboard. She wore a black filmy negligée and her kindness to Tom thickened his throat as he remembered it. He felt she had betrayed him by not being there.

And again after work they climbed up, but still there was nothing to be seen of her. Stanley kept repeating that if it was as hot as this tomorrow he wasn't going to work and that's all there was to it. But they were all there next day. By ten the temperature was in the middle seventies, and it was eighty long before noon. Harry went to the foreman to say it was impossible to work on the leads in that heat; but the foreman said there was nothing else he could put them on, and they'd have to. At midday they stood, silent, watching the skylight on her roof open, and then she slowly emerged in her white gown, holding a bundle of blanket. She looked at them, gravely, then went to the part of the roof where she was hidden from them. Tom was pleased. He felt she was more his when the other men couldn't see her. They had taken off their shirts and vests, but now they put them back again, for they felt the sun bruising their flesh. "She must have the hide of a rhino," said Stanley, tugging at guttering and swearing. They stopped work, and sat in the shade, moving around behind chimney stacks. A woman came to water a yellow window box opposite them. She was middle-aged, wearing a flowered summer dress. Stanley said to her: "We need a drink more than them." She smiled and said: "Better drop down to the pub quick, it'll be closing in a minute." They exchanged pleasantries, and she left them with a smile and a wave.

"Not like Lady Godiva," said Stanley. "She can give us a bit of a chat and a smile."

"You didn't whistle at *her*," said Tom, reproving.

"Listen to him," said Stanley, "you didn't whistle, then?"   30

But the boy felt as if he hadn't whistled, as if only Harry and Stanley had. He was making plans, when it was time to knock off work, to get left behind and somehow make his way over to the woman. The weather report said the hot spell was due to break, so he had to move quickly. But there was no chance of being left.

The other two decided to knock off work at four, because they were exhausted. As they went down, Tom quickly climbed a parapet and hoisted himself higher by pulling his weight up a chimney. He caught a glimpse of her lying on her back, her knees up, eyes closed, a brown woman lolling in the sun. He slipped and clattered down, as Stanley looked for information: "She's gone down," he said. He felt as if he had protected her from Stanley, and that she must be grateful to him. He could feel the bond between the woman and himself.

Next day, they stood around on the landing below the roof, reluctant to climb up into the heat. The woman who had lent Harry the blanket came out and offered them a cup of tea. They accepted gratefully, and sat around Mrs. Pritchett's kitchen an hour or so, chatting. She was married to an airline pilot. A smart blonde, of about thirty, she had an eye for the handsome sharp-eyed Stanley; and the two teased each other while Harry sat in a corner, watching, indulgent, though his expression reminded Stanley that he was married. And young Tom felt envious of Stanley's ease in badinage; felt, too, that Stanley's getting off with Mrs. Pritchett left his romance with the woman on the roof safe and intact.

"I thought they said the heat wave'd break," said Stanley, sullen, as the time approached when they really would have to climb up into the sunlight. 35

"You don't like it, then?" asked Mrs. Pritchett.

"All right for some," said Stanley. "Nothing to do but lie about as if it was a beach up there. Do you ever go up?"

"Went up once," said Mrs. Pritchett. "But it's a dirty place up there, and it's too hot."

"Quite right too," said Stanley.

Then they went up, leaving the cool neat little flat and the friendly Mrs. Pritchett. 40

As soon as they were up they saw her. The three men looked at her, resentful at her ease in this punishing sun. Then Harry said, because of the expression on Stanley's face: "Come on, we've got to pretend to work, at least."

They had to wrench another length of guttering that ran beside a parapet out of its bed, so that they could replace it. Stanley took it in his two hands, tugged, swore, stood up. "Fuck it," he said, and sat down under a chimney. He lit a cigarette. "Fuck them," he said. "What do they think we are, lizards? I've got blisters all over my hands." Then he jumped up and climbed over the roofs and stood with his back to them. He put his fingers either side of his mouth and let out a shrill whistle. Tom and Harry squatted, not looking at each other, watching him. They could just see the woman's head, the beginnings of her brown shoulders. Stanley whistled again. Then he began stamping with his feet, and whistled and yelled and screamed at the woman, his face getting scarlet. He seemed quite mad, as he stamped and whistled, while the woman did not move, she did not move a muscle.

"Barmy," said Tom.

"Yes," said Harry, disapproving.

Suddenly the older man came to a decision. It was, Tom knew, to save some sort of scandal or real trouble over the woman. Harry stood up and began packing tools into a length of oily cloth. "Stanley," he said, commanding. At first Stanley took no notice, but Harry said: "Stanley, we're packing it in, I'll tell Matthew." 45

Stanley came back, cheeks mottled, eyes glaring.

"Can't go on like this," said Harry. "It'll break in a day or so. I'm going to tell Matthew we've got sunstroke, and if he doesn't like it, it's too bad." Even Harry sounded aggrieved, Tom noted. The small, competent man, the family man with his grey hair, who was never at a loss, sounded really off balance. "Come on," he said, angry. He fitted himself into the open square in the roof, and went down, watching his feet on the ladder. Then Stanley went, with not a glance at the woman. Then Tom, who, his throat beating with excitement, silently promised her on a backward glance: Wait for me, wait, I'm coming.

On the pavement Stanley said, "I'm going home." He looked white now, so perhaps he really did have sunstroke. Harry went off to find the foreman, who was at work on the plumbing of some flats down the street. Tom slipped back, not into the building they had been working on, but the building on whose roof the woman lay. He went straight up, no one stopping him. The skylight stood open, with an iron ladder leading up. He emerged on to the roof a couple of yards from her. She sat up, pushing back her black hair with both hands. The scarf across her breasts bound them tight, and brown flesh bulged around it. Her legs were brown and smooth. She stared at him in silence. The boy stood grinning, foolish, claiming the tenderness he expected from her.

"What do you want?" she asked.

"I . . . I came to . . . make your acquaintance," he stammered, grinning,   50
pleading with her.

They looked at each other, the slight, scarlet-faced excited boy, and the serious, nearly naked woman. Then, without a word, she lay down on her brown blanket, ignoring him.

"You like the sun, do you?" he enquired of her glistening back.

Not a word. He felt panic, thinking of how she had held him in her arms, stroked his hair, brought him where he sat, lordly, in her bed, a glass of some exhilarating liquor he had never tasted in life. He felt that if he knelt down, stroked her shoulders, her hair, she would turn and clasp him in her arms.

He said: "The sun's all right for you, isn't it?"

She raised her head, set her chin on two small fists: "Go away," she said.   55
He did not move. "Listen," she said, in a slow reasonable voice, where anger was kept in check, though with difficulty; looking at him, her face weary with anger, "if you get a kick out of seeing women in bikinis, why don't you take a sixpenny bus ride to the Lido? You'd see dozens of them, without all this mountaineering."

She hadn't understood him. He felt her unfairness pale him. He stammered: "But I like you, I've been watching you and . . ."

"Thanks," she said, and dropped her face again, turned away from him.

She lay there. He stood there. She said nothing. She had simply shut him out. He stood, saying nothing at all, for some minutes. He thought: She'll have to say something if I stay. But the minutes went past, with no sign of them in her, except in the tension of her back, her thighs, her arms—the tension of waiting for him to go.

He looked up at the sky, where the sun seemed to spin in heat; and over the roofs where he and his mates had been earlier. He could see the heat quivering where they had worked. And they expect us to work in these conditions! he thought, filled with righteous indignation. The woman hadn't moved. A bit of hot wind blew her black hair softly; it shone, and was iridescent. He remembered how he had stroked it last night.

Resentment of her at last moved him off and away down the ladder,   60
through the building, into the street. He got drunk then, in hatred of her.

Next day when he woke the sky was grey. He looked at the wet grey and thought, vicious: Well, that's fixed you, hasn't it now? That's fixed you good and proper.

The three men were at work early on the cool leads, surrounded by damp drizzling roofs where no one came to sun themselves, black roofs, slimy with rain. Because it was cool now, they would finish the job that day, if they hurried.

[1963]

ALICE MUNRO (1931–)

Alice Munro was in her teens when she published her first short story. At the time, she lived in southwestern Ontario, which is the setting for most of her fiction. After two years of college, Munro moved to Vancouver, where she helped to set up a bookstore. Twenty years later, she returned to Ontario and now lives there on a farm. Her fiction has won Canada's most prestigious award, the Governor General's Award, three times and has also been shortlisted for the Booker Prize. Munro was the first-ever recipient of the Marian Engel Award for women authors and has received the Special Award for Continuing Achievement from the O. Henry Awards.

How I Met My Husband

We heard the plane come over at noon, roaring through the radio news, and we were sure it was going to hit the house, so we all ran out into the yard. We saw it come in over the treetops, all red and silver, the first close-up plane I ever saw. Mrs. Peebles screamed.

"Crash landing," their little boy said. Joey was his name.

"It's okay," said Dr. Peebles. "He knows what he's doing." Dr. Peebles was only an animal doctor, but had a calming way of talking, like any doctor.

This was my first job—working for Dr. and Mrs. Peebles, who had bought an old house out on the Fifth Line, about five miles out of town. It was just when the trend was starting of town people buying up old farms, not to work them but to live on them.

We watched the plane land across the road, where the fairgrounds   5 used to be. It did make a good landing field, nice and level for the old race track, and the barns and display sheds torn down now for scrap lumber so there was nothing in the way. Even the old grandstand bays had burned.

"All right," said Mrs. Peebles, snappy as she always was when she got over her nerves. "Let's go back in the house. Let's not stand here gawking like a set of farmers."

She didn't say that to hurt my feelings. It never occurred to her.

I was just setting the dessert down when Loretta Bird arrived, out of breath, at the screen door.

"I thought it was going to crash into the house and kill youse all!"

She lived on the next place and the Peebleses thought she was a   10 country-woman, they didn't know the difference. She and her husband didn't farm, he worked on the roads and had a bad name for drinking. They had seven children and couldn't get credit at the HiWay Grocery. The Peebleses made her welcome, not knowing any better, as I say, and offered her dessert.

Dessert was never anything to write home about, at their place. A dish of Jell-O or sliced bananas or fruit out of a tin. "Have a house without a pie, be ashamed until you die," my mother used to say, but Mrs. Peebles operated differently.

Loretta Bird saw me getting the can of peaches.

"Oh, never mind," she said. "I haven't got the right kind of a stomach to trust what comes out of those tins, I can only eat home canning."

I could have slapped her. I bet she never put down fruit in her life.

"I know what he's landed here for," she said. "He's got permission to use   15 the fairgrounds and take people up for rides. It costs a dollar. It's the same fellow who was over at Palmerston last week and was up the lakeshore before that. I wouldn't go up, if you paid me."

"I'd jump at the chance," Dr. Peebles said. "I'd like to see this neighborhood from the air."

Mrs. Peebles said she would just as soon see it from the ground. Joey said he wanted to go and Heather did, too. Joey was nine and Heather was seven.

"Would you, Edie?" Heather said.

I said I didn't know. I was scared, but I never admitted that, especially in front of children I was taking care of.

"People are going to be coming out here in their cars raising dust and trampling your property, if I was you I would complain," Loretta said. She hooked her legs around the chair rung and I knew we were in for a lengthy visit. After Dr. Peebles went back to his office or out on his next call and Mrs. Peebles went for her nap, she would hang around me while I was trying to do the dishes. She would pass remarks about the Peebleses in their own house.

"She wouldn't find time to lay down in the middle of the day, if she had seven kids like I got."

She asked me did they fight and did they keep things in the dresser drawer not to have babies with. She said it was a sin if they did. I pretended I didn't know what she was talking about.

I was fifteen and away from home for the first time. My parents had made the effort and sent me to high school for a year, but I didn't like it. I was shy of strangers and the work was hard, they didn't make it nice for you or explain the way they do now. At the end of the year the averages were published in the paper, and mine came out at the very bottom, 37 percent. My father said that's enough and I didn't blame him. The last thing I wanted, anyway, was to go on and end up teaching school. It happened the very day the paper came out with my disgrace in it, Dr. Peebles was staying at our place for dinner, having just helped one of the cows have twins, and he said I looked smart to him and his wife was looking for a girl to help. He said she felt tied down, with the two children, out in the country. I guess she would, my mother said, being polite, though I could tell from her face she was wondering what on earth it would be like to have only two children and no barn work, and then to be complaining.

When I went home I would describe to them the work I had to do, and it made everybody laugh. Mrs. Peebles had an automatic washer and dryer, the first I ever saw. I have had those in my own home for such a long time now it's hard to remember how much of a miracle it was to me, not having to struggle with the wringer and hang up and haul down. Let alone not having to heat water. Then there was practically no baking. Mrs. Peebles said she couldn't make pie crust, the most amazing thing I ever heard a woman admit. I could, of course, and I could make light biscuits and a white cake and dark cake, but they didn't want it, she said they watched their figures. The only thing I didn't like about working there, in fact, was feeling half hungry a lot of the time. I used to bring back a box of doughnuts made out at home, and hide them under my bed. The children found out, and I didn't mind sharing, but I thought I better bind them to secrecy.

The day after the plane landed Mrs. Peebles put both children in the car and drove over to Chesley, to get their hair cut. There was a good woman then at Chesley for doing hair. She got hers done at the same place, Mrs. Peebles did, and that meant they would be gone a good while. She had

20

25

to pick a day Dr. Peebles wasn't going out into the country, she didn't have her own car. Cars were still in short supply then, after the war.

I loved being left in the house alone, to do my work at leisure. The kitchen was all white and bright yellow, with fluorescent lights. That was before they ever thought of making the appliances all different colors and doing the cupboards like dark old wood and hiding the lighting. I loved light. I loved the double sink. So would anybody new-come from washing dishes in a dishpan with a rag-plugged hole on an oilcloth-covered table by light of a coal-oil lamp. I kept everything shining.

The bathroom too. I had a bath in there once a week. They wouldn't have minded if I took one oftener, but to me it seemed like asking too much, or maybe risking making it less wonderful. The basin and the tub and the toilet were all pink, and there were glass doors with flamingoes painted on them, to shut off the tub. The light had a rosy cast and the mat sank under your feet like snow, except that it was warm. The mirror was three-way. With the mirror all steamed up and the air like a perfume cloud, from things I was allowed to use, I stood up on the side of the tub and admired myself naked, from three directions. Sometimes I thought about the way we lived out at home and the way we lived here and how one way was so hard to imagine when you were living the other way. But I thought it was still a lot easier, living the way we lived at home, to picture something like this, the painted flamingoes and the warmth and the soft mat, than it was anybody knowing only things like this to picture how it was the other way. And why was that?

I was through my jobs in no time, and had the vegetables peeled for supper and sitting in cold water besides. Then I went into Mrs. Peebles' bedroom. I had been in there plenty of times, cleaning, and I always took a good look in her closet, at the clothes she had hanging there. I wouldn't have looked in her drawers, but a closet is open to anybody. That's a lie. I would have looked in drawers, but I would have felt worse doing it and been more scared she could tell.

Some clothes in her closet she wore all the time, I was quite familiar with them. Others she never put on, they were pushed to the back. I was disappointed to see no wedding dress. But there was one long dress I could just see the skirt of, and I was hungering to see the rest. Now I took note of where it hung and lifted it out. It was satin, a lovely weight on my arm, light bluish-green in color, almost silvery. It had a fitted, pointed waist and a full skirt and an off-the-shoulder fold hiding the little sleeves.

Next thing was easy. I got out of my own things and slipped it on. I was   30
slimmer at fifteen than anybody would believe who knows me now and the fit was beautiful. I didn't, of course, have a strapless bra on, which was what it needed, I just had to slide my straps down my arms under the material. Then I tried pinning up my hair, to get the effect. One thing led to another. I put on rouge and lipstick and eyebrow pencil from her dresser. The heat of the day and the weight of the satin and all the excitement made me thirsty, and I went out to the kitchen, got-up as I was, to get a glass of ginger ale with ice cubes from the refrigerator. The Peebleses drank ginger ale, or fruit drinks, all day, like water, and I was getting so I did too. Also there was no limit on ice cubes, which I was so fond of I would even put them in a glass of milk.

I turned from putting the ice tray back and saw a man watching me through the screen. It was the luckiest thing in the world I didn't spill the ginger ale down the front of me then and there.

"I never meant to scare you. I knocked but you were getting the ice out, you didn't hear me."

I couldn't see what he looked like, he was dark the way somebody is pressed up against a screen door with the bright daylight behind them. I only knew he wasn't from around here.

"I'm from the plane over there. My name is Chris Watters and what I was wondering was if I could use that pump."

There was a pump in the yard. That was the way the people used to get their water. Now I noticed he was carrying a pail.

"You're welcome," I said. "I can get it from the tap and save you pumping." I guess I wanted him to know we had piped water, didn't pump ourselves.

"I don't mind the exercise." He didn't move, though, and finally he said, "Were you going to a dance?"

Seeing a stranger there had made me entirely forget how I was dressed.

"Or is that the way ladies around here generally get dressed up in the afternoon?"

I didn't know how to joke back then. I was too embarrassed.

"You live here? Are you the lady of the house?"

"I'm the hired girl."

Some people change when they find that out, their whole way of looking at you and speaking to you changes, but his didn't.

"Well, I just wanted to tell you you look very nice. I was so surprised when I looked in the door and saw you. Just because you looked so nice and beautiful."

I wasn't even old enough then to realize how out of the common it is, for a man to say something like that to a woman, or somebody he is treating like a woman. For a man to say a word like *beautiful.* I wasn't old enough to realize or to say anything back, or in fact to do anything but wish he would go away. Not that I didn't like him, but just that it upset me so, having him look at me, and me trying to think of something to say.

He must have understood. He said good-bye, and thanked me, and went and started filling his pail from the pump. I stood behind the Venetian blinds in the dining room, watching him. When he had gone, I went into the bedroom and took the dress off and put it back in the same place. I dressed in my own clothes and took my hair down and washed my face, wiping it on Kleenex, which I threw in the wastebasket.

The Peebleses asked me what kind of man he was. Young, middle-aged, short, tall? I couldn't say.

"Good-looking?" Dr. Peebles teased me.

I couldn't think a thing but that he would be coming to get his water again, he would be talking to Dr. or Mrs. Peebles, making friends with them, and he would mention seeing me that first afternoon, dressed up. Why not mention it? He would think it was funny. And no idea of the trouble it would get me into.

After supper the Peebleses drove into town to go to a movie. She wanted to go somewhere with her hair fresh done. I sat in my bright kitchen wondering what to do, knowing I would never sleep. Mrs. Peebles might not fire me, when she found out, but it would give her a different feeling about me altogether. This was the first place I ever worked but I already had picked up things about the way people feel when you are working for them. They like to think you aren't curious. Not just that you aren't dishonest, that isn't enough. They like to feel you don't notice things, that you don't think or wonder about anything but what they liked to eat and how they liked things ironed, and so on. I don't mean they weren't kind to me, because they were. They had me eat my meals with them (to tell the truth I expected to, I didn't know there were families who don't) and sometimes they took me along in the car. But all the same.

I went up and checked on the children being asleep and then I went out. I had to do it. I crossed the road and went in the old fairgrounds gate. The plane looked unnatural sitting there, and shining with the moon. Off at the far side of the fairgrounds where the bush was taking over, I saw his tent.

He was sitting outside it smoking a cigarette. He saw me coming.

"Hello, were you looking for a plane ride? I don't start taking people up till tomorrow." Then he looked again and said, "Oh, it's you. I didn't know you without your long dress on."

My heart was knocking away, my tongue was dried up. I had to say something. But I couldn't. My throat was closed and I was like a deaf-and-dumb.

"Did you want a ride? Sit down. Have a cigarette."   55

I couldn't even shake my head to say no, so he gave me one.

"Put it in your mouth or I can't light it. It's a good thing I'm used to shy ladies."

I did. It wasn't the first time I had smoked a cigarette, actually. My girlfriend out home, Muriel Lowe, used to steal them from her brother.

"Look at your hand shaking. Did you just want to have a chat, or what?"

In one burst I said, "I wisht you wouldn't say anything about that dress."   60

"What dress? Oh, the long dress."

"It's Mrs. Peebles'."

"Whose? Oh, the lady you work for? She wasn't home so you got dressed up in her dress, eh? You got dressed up and played queen. I don't blame you. You're not smoking the cigarette right. Don't just puff. Draw it in. Did anybody ever show you how to inhale? Are you scared I'll tell on you? Is that it?"

I was so ashamed at having to ask him to connive this way I couldn't nod. I just looked at him and he saw *yes*.

"Well I won't. I won't in the slightest way mention it or embarrass you.   65
I give you my word of honor."

Then he changed the subject, to help me out, seeing I couldn't even thank him.

"What do you think of this sign?"

It was a board sign lying practically at my feet.

SEE THE WORLD FROM THE SKY. ADULTS $1.00, CHILDREN 50¢. QUALIFIED PILOT.

"My old sign was getting pretty beat up, I thought I'd make a new one.   70
That's what I've been doing with my time today."

The lettering wasn't all that handsome, I thought. I could have done a better one in half an hour.

"I'm not an expert at sign making."

"It's very good," I said.

"I don't need it for publicity, word of mouth is usually enough. I turned away two carloads tonight. I felt like taking it easy. I didn't tell them ladies were dropping in to visit me."

Now I remembered the children and I was scared again, in case one of   75
them had waked up and called me and I wasn't there.

"Do you have to go so soon?"

I remembered some manners. "Thank you for the cigarette."

"Don't forget. You have my word of honor."

I tore off across the fairgrounds, scared I'd see the car heading home
from town. My sense of time was mixed up, I didn't know how long I'd
been out of the house. But it was all right, it wasn't late, the children were
asleep. I got in my bed myself and lay thinking what a lucky end to the day,
after all, and among things to be grateful for I could be grateful Loretta Bird
hadn't been the one who caught me.

The yard and borders didn't get trampled, it wasn't as bad as that. All   80
the same it seemed very public, around the house. The sign was on the fairgrounds gate. People came mostly after supper but a good many in the
afternoon, too. The Bird children all came without fifty cents between
them and hung on the gate. We got used to the excitement of the plane
coming in and taking off, it wasn't excitement anymore. I never went over,
after that one time, but would see him when he came to get his water. I
would be out on the steps doing sitting-down work, like preparing vegetables, if I could.

"Why don't you come over? I'll take you up in my plane."

"I'm saving my money," I said, because I couldn't think of anything else.

"For what? For getting married?"

I shook my head.

"I'll take you up for free if you come sometime when it's slack. I   85
thought you would come, and have another cigarette."

I made a face to hush him, because you never could tell when the children would be sneaking around the porch, or Mrs. Peebles herself listening
in the house. Sometimes she came out and had a conversation with him. He
told her things he hadn't bothered to tell me. But then I hadn't thought to
ask. He told her he had been in the war, that was where he learned to fly a
plane, and how he couldn't settle down to ordinary life, this was what he
liked. She said she couldn't imagine anybody liking such a thing. Though
sometimes, she said, she was almost bored enough to try anything herself,
she wasn't brought up to living in the country. It's all my husband's idea,
she said. This was news to me.

"Maybe you ought to give flying lessons," she said.

"Would you take them?"

She just laughed.

Sunday was a busy flying day in spite of it being preached against from two   90
pulpits. We were all sitting out watching. Joey and Heather were over on
the fence with the Bird kids. Their father had said they could go, after their
mother saying all week they couldn't.

A car came down the road past the parked cars and pulled up right in
the drive. It was Loretta Bird who got out, all importance, and on the driver's
side another woman got out, more sedately. She was wearing sunglasses.

"This is a lady looking for the man that flies the plane," Loretta Bird
said. "I heard her inquire in the hotel coffee shop where I was having a
Coke and I brought her out."

"I'm sorry to bother you," the lady said. "I'm Alice Kelling, Mr. Watters'
fiancée."

This Alice Kelling had on a pair of brown and white checked slacks and a yellow top. Her bust looked to me rather low and bumpy. She had a worried face. Her hair had had a permanent, but had grown out, and she wore a yellow band to keep it off her face. Nothing in the least pretty or even young-looking about her. But you could tell from how she talked she was from the city, or educated, or both.

Dr. Peebles stood up and introduced himself and his wife and me and   95
asked her to be seated.

"He's up in the air right now, but you're welcome to sit and wait. He gets his water here and he hasn't been yet. He'll probably take his break about five."

"That is him, then?" said Alice Kelling, wrinkling and straining at the sky.

"He's not in the habit of running out on you, taking a different name?" Dr. Peebles laughed. He was the one, not his wife, to offer iced tea. Then she sent me into the kitchen to fix it. She smiled. She was wearing sunglasses too.

"He never mentioned his fiancée," she said.

I loved fixing iced tea with lots of ice and slices of lemon in tall glass-   100
es. I ought to have mentioned before, Dr. Peebles was an abstainer, at least around the house, or I wouldn't have been allowed to take the place. I had to fix a glass for Loretta Bird too, though it galled me, and when I went out she had settled in my lawn chair, leaving me the steps.

"I knew you was a nurse when I first heard you in that coffee shop."

"How would you know a thing like that?"

"I get my hunches about people. Was that how you met him, nursing?"

"Chris? Well yes. Yes, it was."

"Oh, were you overseas?" said Mrs. Peebles.   105

"No, it was before he went overseas. I nursed him when he was sta-tioned at Centralia and had a ruptured appendix. We got engaged and then he went overseas. My, this is refreshing, after a long drive."

"He'll be glad to see you," Dr. Peebles said. "It's a rackety kind of life, isn't it, not staying one place long enough to really make friends."

"Youse've had a long engagement," Loretta Bird said.

Alice Kelling passed that over. "I was going to get a room at the hotel, but when I was offered directions I came on out. Do you think I could phone them?"

"No need," Dr. Peebles said. "You're five miles away from him if you stay   110
at the hotel. Here, you're right across the road. Stay with us. We've got rooms on rooms, look at this big house."

Asking people to stay, just like that, is certainly a country thing, and maybe seemed natural to him now, but not to Mrs. Peebles, from the way she said, oh yes, we have plenty of room. Or to Alice Kelling, who kept protesting, but let herself be worn down. I got the feeling it was a tempta-tion to her, to be that close. I was trying for a look at her ring. Her nails were painted red, her fingers were freckled and wrinkled. It was a tiny stone. Muriel Lowe's cousin had one twice as big.

Chris came to get his water, late in the afternoon just as Dr. Peebles had predicted. He must have recognized the car from a way off. He came smiling.

"Here I am chasing after you to see what you're up to," called Alice Kelling. She got up and went to meet him and they kissed, just touched, in front of us.

"You're going to spend a lot on gas that way," Chris said.

Dr. Peebles invited Chris to stay for supper, since he had already put   115
up the sign that said: NO MORE RIDES TILL 7 P.M. Mrs. Peebles wanted it served
in the yard, in spite of the bugs. One thing strange to anybody from the
country is this eating outside. I had made a potato salad earlier and she had
made a jellied salad, that was one thing she could do, so it was just a matter of getting those out, and some sliced meat and cucumbers and fresh
leaf lettuce. Loretta Bird hung around for some time saying, "Oh, well, I
guess I better get home to those yappers," and, "It's so nice just sitting here,
I sure hate to get up," but nobody invited her, I was relieved to see, and
finally she had to go.

That night after rides were finished Alice Kelling and Chris went
off somewhere in her car. I lay awake till they got back. When I saw the
car lights sweep my ceiling I got up to look down on them through the
slats of my blind. I don't know what I thought I was going to see. Muriel
Lowe and I used to sleep on her front veranda and watch her sister and
her sister's boy friend saying good night. Afterward we couldn't get to
sleep, for longing for somebody to kiss us and rub against us and we
would talk about suppose you were out in a boat with a boy and he
wouldn't bring you in to shore unless you did it, or what if somebody
got you trapped in a barn, you would have to, wouldn't you, it wouldn't
be your fault. Muriel said her two girl cousins used to try with a toilet
paper roll that one of them was a boy. We wouldn't do anything like
that; just lay and wondered.

All that happened was that Chris got out of the car on one side and she
got out on the other and they walked off separately—him toward the fairgrounds and her toward the house. I got back in bed and imagined about
me coming home with him, not like that.

Next morning Alice Kelling got up late and I fixed a grapefruit for her
the way I had learned and Mrs. Peebles sat down with her to visit and have
another cup of coffee. Mrs. Peebles seemed pleased enough now, having
company. Alice Kelling said she guessed she better get used to putting in a
day just watching Chris take off and come down, and Mrs. Peebles said she
didn't know if she should suggest it because Alice Kelling was the one with
the car, but the lake was only twenty-five miles away and what a good day for
a picnic.

Alice Kelling took her up on the idea and by eleven o'clock they were
in the car, with Joey and Heather and a sandwich lunch I had made. The
only thing was that Chris hadn't come down, and she wanted to tell him
where they were going.

"Edie'll go over and tell him," Mrs. Peebles said. "There's no problem."   120
Alice Kelling wrinkled her face and agreed.

"Be sure and tell him we'll be back by five!"

I didn't see that he would be concerned about knowing this right
away, and I thought of him eating whatever he ate over there, alone, cooking on his camp stove, so I got to work and mixed up a crumb cake and
baked it, in between the other work I had to do; then, when it was a bit
cooled, wrapped it in a tea towel. I didn't do anything to myself but take off
my apron and comb my hair. I would like to have put some makeup on, but
I was too afraid it would remind him of the way he first saw me, and that
would humiliate me all over again.

He had come and put another sign on the gate: NO RIDES THIS P.M. APOLO-
GIES. I worried that he wasn't feeling well. No sign of him outside and the
tent flap was down. I knocked on the pole.

"Come in," he said, in a voice that would just as soon have said *Stay out*.   125
I lifted the flap.

"Oh, it's you. I'm sorry. I didn't know it was you."

He had been just sitting on the side of the bed, smoking. Why not at
least sit and smoke in the fresh air?

"I brought a cake and hope you're not sick," I said.

"Why would I be sick? Oh—that sign. That's all right. I'm just tired of   130
talking to people. I don't mean you. Have a seat." He pinned back the tent
flap. "Get some fresh air in here."

I sat on the edge of the bed, there was no place else. It was one of those
foldup cots, really: I remembered and gave him his fiancée's message.

He ate some of the cake. "Good."

"Put the rest away for when you're hungry later."

"I'll tell you a secret. I won't be around here much longer."

"Are you getting married?"   135

"Ha ha. What time did you say they'd be back?"

"Five o'clock."

"Well, by that time this place will have seen the last of me. A plane can
get further than a car." He unwrapped the cake and ate another piece of it,
absentmindedly.

"Now you'll be thirsty."

"There's some water in the pail."   140

"It won't be very cold. I could bring some fresh. I could bring some ice
from the refrigerator."

"No," he said. "I don't want you to go. I want a nice long time of saying
good-bye to you."

He put the cake away carefully and sat beside me and started those
little kisses, so soft, I can't ever let myself think about them, such kindness in his face and lovely kisses, all over my eyelids and neck and ears,
all over, then me kissing back as well as I could (I had only kissed a boy
on a dare before, and kissed my own arms for practice) and we lay back
on the cot and pressed together, just gently, and he did some other
things, not bad things or not in a bad way. It was lovely in the tent, that
smell of grass and hot tent cloth with the sun beating down on it, and he
said, "I wouldn't do you any harm for the world." Once, when he had
rolled on top of me and we were sort of rocking together on the cot, he
said softly, "Oh, no," and freed himself and jumped up and got the water
pail. He splashed some of it on his neck and face, and the little bit left, on
me lying there.

"That's to cool us off, miss."

When we said good-bye I wasn't at all sad, because he held my face and   145
said, "I'm going to write you a letter. I'll tell you where I am and maybe you
can come and see me. Would you like that? Okay then. You wait." I was really glad I think to get away from him, it was like he was piling presents on
me I couldn't get the pleasure of till I considered them alone.

No consternation at first about the plane being gone. They thought he
had taken somebody up, and I didn't enlighten them. Dr. Peebles had

phoned he had to go to the country, so there was just us having supper, and then Loretta Bird thrusting her head in the door and saying, "I see he's took off."

"What?" said Alice Kelling, and pushed back her chair.

"The kids come and told me this afternoon he was taking down his tent. Did he think he'd run through all the business there was around here? He didn't take off without letting you know, did he?"

"He'll send me word," Alice Kelling said. "He'll probably phone tonight. He's terribly restless, since the war."

"Edie, he didn't mention to you, did he?" Mrs. Peebles said. "When you took over the message?"   150

"Yes," I said. So far so true.

"Well why didn't you say?" All of them were looking at me. "Did he say where he was going?"

"He said he might try Bayfield," I said. What made me tell such a lie? I didn't intend it.

"Bayfield, how far is that?" said Alice Kelling.

Mrs. Peebles said, "Thirty, thirty-five miles."   155

"That's not far. Oh, well, that's really not far at all. It's on the lake, isn't it?"

You'd think I'd be ashamed of myself, setting her on the wrong track. I did it to give him more time, whatever time he needed. I lied for him, and also, I have to admit, for me. Women should stick together and not do things like that. I see that now, but didn't then. I never thought of myself as being in any way like her, or coming to the same troubles, ever.

She hadn't taken her eyes off me. I thought she suspected my lie.

"When did he mention this to you?"

"Earlier."   160

"When you were over at the plane?"

"Yes."

"You must've stayed and had a chat." She smiled at me, not a nice smile. "You must've stayed and had a little visit with him."

"I took a cake," I said, thinking that telling some truth would spare me telling the rest.

"We didn't have a cake," said Mrs. Peebles rather sharply.   165

"I baked one."

Alice Kelling said, "That was very friendly of you."

"Did you get permission," said Loretta Bird. "You never know what these girls'll do next," she said. "It's not they mean harm so much, as they're ignorant."

"The cake is neither here nor there," Mrs. Peebles broke in. "Edie, I wasn't aware you knew Chris that well."

I didn't know what to say.

"I'm not surprised," Alice Kelling said in a high voice. "I knew by the look   170 of her as soon as I saw her. We get them at the hospital all the time." She looked hard at me with her stretched smile. "Having their babies. We have to put them in a special ward because of their diseases. Little country tramps. Fourteen and fifteen years old. You should see the babies they have, too."

"There was a bad woman here in town had a baby that pus was running out of its eyes," Loretta Bird put in.

"Wait a minute," said Mrs. Peebles. "What is this talk? Edie. What about you and Mr. Watters? Were you intimate with him?"

"Yes," I said. I was thinking of us lying on the cot and kissing, wasn't that intimate? And I would never deny it.

They were all one minute quiet, even Loretta Bird.   175

"Well," said Mrs. Peebles. "I am surprised. I think I need a cigarette. This is the first of any such tendencies I've seen in her," she said, speaking to Alice Kelling, but Alice Kelling was looking at me.

"Loose little bitch." Tears ran down her face. "Loose little bitch, aren't you? I knew as soon as I saw you. Men despise girls like you. He just made use of you and went off, you know that, don't you? Girls like you are just nothing, they're just public conveniences, just filthy little rags!"

"Oh, now," said Mrs. Peebles.

"Filthy," Alice Kelling sobbed. "Filthy little rags!"

"Don't get yourself upset," Loretta Bird said. She was swollen up with   180 pleasure at being in on this scene. "Men are all the same."

"Edie, I'm very surprised," Mrs. Pebbles said. "I thought your parents were so strict. You don't want to have a baby, do you?"

I'm still ashamed of what happened next. I lost control, just like a six-year-old, I started howling. "You don't get a baby from just doing that!"

"You see. Some of them are that ignorant," Loretta Bird said.

But Mrs. Peebles jumped up and caught my arms and shook me.

"Calm down. Don't get hysterical. Calm down. Stop crying. Listen to   185 me. Listen I'm wondering, if you know what being intimate means. Now tell me. What did you think it meant?"

"Kissing," I howled.

She let go. "Oh, Edie. Stop it. Don't be silly. It's all right. It's all a misunderstanding. Being intimate means a lot more than that. Oh, I *wondered*."

"She's trying to cover up, now," said Alice Kelling. "Yes. She's not so stupid. She sees she got herself in trouble."

"I believe her," Mrs. Peebles said. "This is an awful scene."

"Well there is one way to find out," said Alice Kelling, getting up. "After   190 all, I am a nurse."

Mrs. Peebles drew a breath and said, "No. No. Go to your room, Edie. And stop that noise. This is too disgusting."

I heard the car start in a little while. I tried to stop crying, pulling back each wave as it started over me. Finally I succeeded, and lay heaving on the bed.

Mrs. Peebles came and stood in the doorway.

"She's gone," she said. "That Bird woman too. Of course, you know you should never have gone near that man and that is the cause of all this trouble. I have a headache. As soon as you can, go and wash your face in cold water and get at the dishes and we will not say any more about this."

Nor we didn't. I didn't figure out till years later the extent of what I had   195 been saved from. Mrs. Peebles was not very friendly to me afterward, but she was fair. Not very friendly is the wrong way of describing what she was. She had never been very friendly. It was just that now she had to see me all the time and it got on her nerves, a little.

As for me, I put it all out of my mind like a bad dream and concentrated on waiting for my letter. The mail came every day except Sunday, between one-thirty and two in the afternoon, a good time for me because Mrs. Peebles was always having her nap. I would get the kitchen all cleaned and then go up to the mailbox and sit in the grass, waiting. I was perfectly happy, waiting. I forgot all about Alice Kelling and her misery and awful talk and Mrs. Peebles and her chilliness and the embarrassment of whether she told Dr. Peebles and the face of Loretta Bird, getting her fill of other people's troubles. I was always smiling when the mailman got there, and continued smiling even after he gave me the mail and I saw today wasn't the day. The mailman was a Carmichael. I knew by his face because there are a lot of Carmichaels living out by us and so many of them have a sort of sticking-out top lip. So I asked his name (he was a young man, shy, but good-humored, anybody could ask him anything) and then I said, "I knew by your face!" He was pleased by that and always glad to see me and got a little less shy. "You've got the smile I've been waiting for all day!" he used to holler out the car window.

It never crossed my mind for a long time a letter might not come. I believed in it coming just like I believed the sun would rise in the morning. I just put off my hope from day to day, and there was the goldenrod out around the mailbox and the children gone back to school, and the leaves turning, and I was wearing a sweater when I went to wait. One day walking back with the hydro bill stuck in my hand, that was all, looking across at the fairgrounds with the full-blown milkweed and dark teasels, so much like fall, it just struck me: *No letter was ever going to come.* It was an impossible idea to get used to. No, not impossible. If I thought about Chris's face when he said he was going to write me, it was impossible, but if I forgot that and thought about the actual tin mailbox, empty, it was plain and true. I kept on going to meet the mail, but my heart was heavy now like a lump of lead. I only smiled because I thought of the mailman counting on it, and he didn't have an easy life, with the winter driving ahead.

Till it came to me one day there were women doing this with their lives, all over. There were women just waiting and waiting by mailboxes for one letter or another. I imagined me making this journey day after day and year after year, and my hair starting to get gray, and I thought, I was never made to go on like that. So I stopped meeting the mail. If there were women all through life waiting, and women busy and not waiting, I knew which I had to be. Even though there might be things the second kind of women have to pass up and never know about, it still is better.

I was surprised when the mailman phoned the Peebleses' place in the evening and asked for me. He said he missed me. He asked if I would like to go to Goderich, where some well-known movie was on, I forget now what. So I said yes, and I went out with him for two years and he asked me to marry him, and we were engaged a year more while I got my things together, and then we did marry. He always tells the children the story of how I went after him by sitting by the mailbox every day, and naturally I laugh and let him, because I like for people to think what pleases them and makes them happy.

[1974]

LESLIE NORRIS (1921–)

Leslie Norris was born in Merthyr Tydfil in Wales, and educated at Coventry College and Southampton University. After serving in the Royal Air Force, he worked as a government officer, schoolteacher, and university lecturer. He has published two collections of short stories and many books of poetry. Among other honors, he has been named a Fellow of the Royal Society of Literature.

Blackberries

Mr. Frensham opened his shop at eight-thirty, but it was past nine when the woman and the child went in. The shop was empty and there were no footmarks on the fresh sawdust shaken onto the floor. The child listened to the melancholy sound of the bell as the door closed behind him and he scuffed his feet in the yellow sawdust. Underneath, the boards were brown and worn, and dark knots stood up in them. He had never been in this shop before. He was going to have his hair cut for the first time in his life, except for the times when his mother had trimmed it gently behind his neck.

Mr. Frensham was sitting in a large chair, reading a newspaper. He could make the chair turn around, and he spun twice about in it before he put down his paper, smiled, and said, "Good morning."

He was an old man, thin, with flat white hair. He wore a white coat.

"One gentleman," he said, "to have his locks shorn."

He put a board across the two arms of his chair, lifted the child, and sat him on it.   5

"How are you, my dear? And your father, is he well?" he said to the child's mother.

He took a sheet from the cupboard on the wall and wrapped it about the child's neck, tucking it into his collar. The sheet covered the child completely and hung almost to the floor. Cautiously the boy moved his hidden feet. He could see the bumps they made in the cloth. He moved his finger against the inner surface of the sheet and made a six with it, and then as eight. He liked those shapes.

"Snip, snip," said Mr. Frensham, "and how much does the gentlemen want off? All of it? All his lovely curls? I think not."

"Just an ordinary cut, please, Mr. Frensham," said the child's mother, "not too much off. I, my husband and I, we thought it was time for him to look like a little boy. His hair grows so quickly."

Mr. Frensham's hands were very cold. His hard fingers turned the boy's   10
head first to one side and then to the other and the boy could hear the long scissors snapping away behind him, and above his ears. He was quite frightened, but he liked watching the small tufts of his hair drop lightly on the sheet which covered him, and then roll an inch or two before they stopped. Some of the hair fell to the floor and by moving his hand surreptitiously he could make nearly all of it fall down. The hair fell without a sound. Tilting his head slightly, he could see little bunches on the floor, not belonging to him any more.

"Easy to see who this boy is," Mr. Frensham said to the child's mother. "I won't get redder hair in the shop today. Your father had hair like this when he was young, very much this color. I've cut your father's hair for fifty years. He's keeping well, you say? There, I think that's enough. We don't want him to dislike coming to see me."

He took the sheet off the child and flourished it hard before folding it and putting it on a shelf. He swept the back of the child's neck with a small brush. Nodding his own old head in admiration, he looked at the child's hair for flaws in the cutting.

"Very handsome," he said.

The child saw his face in a mirror. It looked pale and large, but also much the same as always. When he felt the back of his neck, the new short hairs stood up sharp against his hand.

"We're off to do some shopping," his mother said to Mr. Frensham as she handed him the money.

They were going to buy the boy a cap, a round cap with a little button on top and a peak over his eyes, like his cousin Harry's cap. The boy want-ed the cap very much. He walked seriously behind his mother and he was not impatient even when she met Mrs. Lewis and talked to her, and then took a long time at the fruiterer's buying apples and potatoes.

"This is the smallest size we have," the man in the clothes shop said. "It may be too large for him."

"He's just had his hair cut, "said his mother. "That should make a difference."

The man put the cap on the boy's head and stood back to look. It was a beautiful cap. The badge in front was shaped like a shield and it was red and blue. It was not too big, although the man could put two fingers under it, at the side of the boy's head.

"On the other hand, we don't want it too tight," the man said. "We want something he can grow into, something that will last him a long time."

"Oh, I hope so," his mother said, "It's expensive enough."

The boy carried the cap himself, in a brown paper bag that had "Price, Clothiers, High Street" on it. He could read it all except "Clothiers" and his mother told him that. They put his cap, still in its bag, in a drawer when they got home.

His father came home late in the afternoon. The boy heard the firm clap of the closing door and he father's long step down the hall. He leaned against his father's knee while the man ate his dinner. The meal had been keeping warm in the oven and the plate was very hot. A small steam was rising from the potatoes, and the gravy had dried to a thin crust where it was shallow at the side of the plate. The man lifted the dry gravy with his knife and fed it to his son, very carefully lifting it into the boy's mouth, as if he were feeding a small bird. The boy loved this. He loved the hot savor of his father's dinner, the way his father cut away small delicacies for him and fed them to him slowly. He leaned drowsily against his father's leg.

Afterwards he put on his cap and stood before his father, certain of the man's approval. The man put his hand on the boy's head and looked at him without smiling.

"On Sunday," he said, "we'll go for a walk. Just you and I. We'll be men together."

Although it was late in September, the sun was warm and the paths dry. The man and his boy walked beside the disused canal and powdery white dust covered their shoes. The boy thought of the days before he had been born, when the canal had been busy. He thought of the long boats pulled by solid horses, gliding through the water. In his head he listened to the hushed, wet noises they would have made, the soft waves slapping the banks, and green tench looking up as the barges moved above them, their water suddenly darkened. His grandfather had told him about that. But now the channel was filled with mud and tall reeds. Bullrush and watergrass grew in the damp passages. He borrowed his father's walking stick and knocked the heads off a company of seeding dandelions, watching the tiny parachutes carry away their minute dark burdens.

"There they go," he said to himself. "There they go, sailing away to China."

"Come on," said his father, "or we'll never reach Fletcher's Woods."

The boy hurried after his father. He had never been to Fletcher's Woods. Once his father had heard a nightingale there. It had been in the summer, long ago, and his father had gone with his friends, to hear the singing bird. They had stood under a tree and listened. Then the moon went down and his father, stumbling home, had fallen into a blackberry bush.

"Will there be blackberries?" he asked.   30

"There should be," his father said. "I'll pick some for you."

In Fletcher's Woods there was shade beneath the trees, and sunlight, thrown in yellow patches on to the grass, seemed to grow out of the ground rather than come from the sky. The boy stepped from sunlight to sunlight, in and out of shadow. His father showed him a tangle of bramble, hard with thorns, its leaves just beginning to color into autumn, its long runners dry and brittle on the grass. Clusters of purple fruit hung in the branches. His father reached up and chose a blackberry for him. Its skin was plump and shining, each of its purple globes held a point of reflected light.

"You can eat it," his father said.

The boy put the blackberry in his mouth. He rolled it with his tongue, feeling its irregularity, and crushed it against the roof of his mouth. Released juice, sweet and warm as summer, ran down his throat, hard seeds cracked between his teeth. When he laughed his father saw that his mouth was deeply stained. Together they picked and ate the dark berries, until their lips were purple and their hands marked and scratched.

"We should take some for your mother," the man said.   35

He reached with his stick and pulled down high canes where the choicest berries grew, picking them to take home. They had nothing to carry them in, so the boy put his new cap on the grass and they filled its hollow with berries. He held the cap by its edges and they went home.

"It was a stupid thing to do," his mother said, "utterly stupid. What were you thinking of?"

The young man did not answer.

"If we had the money, it would be different," his mother said, "Where do you think the money comes from?"

"I know where the money comes from," his father said. "I work hard   40
enough for it."

"His new cap," his mother said. "How am I to get him another?"

The cap lay on the table and by standing on tiptoe the boy could see it. Inside it was wet with the sticky juice of blackberries. Small pieces of blackberry skins were stuck to it. The stains were dark and irregular.

"It will probably dry out all right," his father said.

His mother's face was red and distorted, her voice shrill.

"If you had anything like a job," she shouted, "and could buy caps by   45
the dozen, then—"

She stopped and shook her head. His father turned away, his mouth hard.

"I do what I can," he said.

"That's not much!" his mother said. She was tight with scorn. "You don't do much!"

Appalled, the child watched the quarrel mount and spread. He began to cry quietly, to himself, knowing that it was a different weeping to any he had experienced before, that he was crying for a different pain. And the child began to understand that they were different people; his father, his mother, himself, and that he must learn sometimes to be alone.

[1988]

JOYCE CAROL OATES (1938–)

Joyce Carol Oates graduated as valedictorian from Syracuse University and then received her Master's from the University of Wisconsin. She began teaching in 1968 at the University of Windsor in Canada and has taught at Princeton University since 1978. A prolific author, Oates has published forty-four novels and novellas, in addition to collections of short stories, poetry, drama, and critical works. She has received the National Book Award, the O. Henry Prize for Continued Achievement in the Short Story, a Guggenheim Fellowship, and has been a finalist for the Pulitzer Prize three times.

Nairobi

Early Saturday afternoon the man who had introduced himself as Oliver took Ginny to several shops on Madison Avenue above 70th Street to buy her what he called an appropriate outfit. For an hour and forty-five minutes she modeled clothes, watching with critical interest her image in the three-way mirrors, unable to decide if this was one of her really good days or only a mediocre day. Judging by Oliver's expression she looked all right, but it was difficult to tell. The salesclerk saw too many beautiful young women to be impressed, though one told Ginny she envied her her hair—not just that shade of chestnut red but the thickness too. In the changing room she told Ginny that her own hair was "coming out in hand-fuls" but Ginny told her it didn't show. It will begin to show one of these days, the salesgirl said.

Ginny modeled a green velvet jumpsuit with a brass zipper and over-sized buckles, and an Italian knit dress with bunchy sleeves in a zigzag pattern of beige, brown, and cream, and a ruffled organdy "tea dress" in pale orange, and a navy-blue blazer made of Irish linen, with a pleated white linen skirt and a pale blue silk blouse. Assuming she could only have one costume, which seemed to be the case, she would have preferred the jumpsuit, not just because it was the most expensive outfit (the price tag read $475) but because the green velvet reflected in her eyes. Oliver decided on the Irish linen blazer and skirt and blouse, however, and told the salesclerk to remove the tags and to pack up Ginny's own clothes, since she intended to wear the new outfit.

Strolling uptown, he told her that with her hair down like that, and her bangs combed low on her forehead, she looked like a "convent schoolgirl." In theory, that was. Tangentially.

It was a balmy, windy day in early April. Everyone was out. Ginny kept seeing people she almost knew, Oliver waved hello to several acquaintances. There were baby buggies, dogs being walked, sports cars with their tops down. In shop windows—particularly in the broad window of galleries—Ginny's reflection in the navy-blue blazer struck her as unfamiliar and quirky but not bad: the blazer with its built-up shoulders and wide lapels was more stylish than she'd thought at first. Oliver too was pleased. He had slipped on steel-frame tinted glasses. He said they had plenty of time. A pair of good shoes—really good shoes—might be an idea.

But first they went into a jewelry boutique at 76th Street, where Oliver   5
bought her four narrow silver bracelets, engraved in bird and animal heads, and a pair of conch-shaped silver earrings from Mexico. Ginny slipped her gold studs out and put on the new earrings as Oliver watched. Doesn't it hurt to force those wire through your flesh? He was standing rather close.

No, Ginny said. My earlobes are numb, I don't feel a thing. It's easy.

When did you get your ears pierced? Oliver asked.

Ginny felt her cheeks color slightly—as if he were asking a favor of her and her instinct wasn't clear enough, whether to acquiesce or draw away just perceptibly. She drew away, still adjusting the earrings, but said: I don't have any idea, maybe I was thirteen, maybe twelve, it was a long time ago. We all went out and had our ears pierced.

In a salon called Michel's she exchanged her chunky-heeled red shoes for a pair of kidskin sandals that might have been the most beautiful shoes she'd ever seen. Oliver laughed quizzically over them: they were hardly anything but a few straps and a price tag, he told the salesman, but they looked like the real thing, they were what he wanted. The salesman told Oliver that his taste was "unerring."

Do you want to keep your old shoes? Oliver asked Ginny.   10

Of course, Ginny said, slightly hurt, but as the salesman was packing them she changed her mind. No, the hell with them, she said. They're too much trouble to take along.—Which she might regret afterward: but it was the right thing to say at that particular moment.

In the cab headed west and then north along the park, Oliver gave her instructions in a low, casual voice. The main thing was that she should say very little. She shouldn't smile unless it was absolutely necessary. While he and his friends spoke—if they spoke at any length, he couldn't predict Marguerite's attitude—Ginny might even drift away, pick up a magazine and leaf through it if something appropriate was available, not nervously, just idly, for something to do, as if she were bored; better yet, she might look out the window or even step out on the terrace, since the afternoon was so warm. Don't even look at me, Oliver said. Don't give the impression that anything I say—anything the three of us say—matters very much to you.

Yes, said Ginny.

The important thing, Oliver said, squeezing her hand and releasing it, is that you're basically not concerned. I mean with the three of us. With Marguerite. With anyone. Do you understand?

Yes, said Ginny. She was studying her new shoes. Kidskin in a shade   15
called "vanilla," eight straps on each shoe, certainly the most beautiful shoes she'd ever owned. The price had taken her breath away too. She hadn't any questions to ask Oliver.

When Ginny had been much younger—which is to say, a few years ago, when she was new to the city—she might have had some questions to ask. In fact she had had a number of questions to ask, then. But the answers had invariably disappointed. The answers had contained so much less substance than her own questions, she had learned, by degrees, not to ask.

So she told Oliver a second time, to assure *him:* Of course I understand.

The apartment building they entered at Fifth and 88th was older than Ginny might have guessed from the outside—the mosaic murals in the lobby were in a quaint ethereal style unknown to her. Perhaps they were meant to be amusing, but she didn't think so. It was impressive that the uniformed doorman knew Oliver, whom he called "Mr. Leahy," and that he was so gracious about keeping their package for them while they visited upstairs; it was impressive that the black elevator operator nodded and murmured hello in a certain tone. Smiles were measured and respectful all around, but Ginny didn't trouble to smile; she knew it wasn't expected of her.

In the elevator—which was almost uncomfortably small—Oliver looked at Ginny critically, standing back to examine her from her toes upward and finding nothing wrong except a strand of hair or two out of place. The Irish lined blazer was an excellent choice, he said. The earrings too. The bracelets. The shoes. He spoke with assurance though Ginny had the idea he was nervous, or excited. He turned to study his own reflection in the bronze-frosted mirror on the elevator wall, facing it with a queer childlike squint. This was his "mirror face," Ginny supposed, the way he had of confronting himself in the mirror so that it wasn't *really* himself but a certain habitual expression that protected him. Ginny hadn't any mirror face herself. She had gone beyond that, she knew better, those childish frowns and half-smiles and narrowed eyes and heads turned coyly or hopefully to one side—ways of protecting her from seeing "Ginny" when the truth of "Ginny" was that she required being seen head-on. But it would have been difficult for her to explain to another person.

Oliver adjusted his handsome blue-striped cotton tie and ran his finger deftly through his hair. It was pale, fine, airily colorless hair, blond perhaps, shading into premature silver, rather thin, Ginny thought, for a man his age. (She estimated his age at thirty-four, which seemed "old" to her in certain respects, but she knew it was reasonably "young" in others.) Oliver's skin was slightly coarse; his nose wide at the bridge, and the nostrils disfigured by a few dark hairs that should have been snipped off; his lower jaw was somewhat heavy. But he was a handsome man. In his steel-rimmed blue-tinted glasses he was a handsome man, and Ginny saw for the first time that they made an attractive couple.

20

Don't trouble to answer any questions they might ask, Oliver said. In any case the questions won't be serious—just conversation.

I understand, Ginny said.

A Hispanic maid answered the door. The elevator and the corridor had been so dimly lit, Ginny wasn't prepared for the flood of sunlight in the apartment. They were on the eighteenth floor overlooking the park and the day was still cloudless.

Oliver introduced Ginny to his friends Marguerite and Herbert—the last name sounded like Crews—and Ginny shook hands with them unhesitatingly, as if it were a customary gesture with her. The first exchanges were about the weather. Marguerite was vehement in her gratitude since the past winter, January in particular, had been uncommonly long and dark and depressing. Ginny assented without actually agreeing. For the first minute or two she felt thrown off balance, she couldn't have said why, by the fact the Marguerite Crews was so tall a woman—taller even than Ginny. And she was, or had been, a very beautiful woman as well, with a pale olive-dark complexion and severely black hair parted in the center of her head and fixed in a careless knot at the nape of her neck.

Oliver was explaining apologetically that they couldn't stay. Not even   25
for a drink, really: they were in fact already late for another engagement in the Village. Both the Crewses expressed disappointment. And Oliver's plans for the weekend had been altered as well, unavoidably. At this announce- ment the disappointment was keener, and Ginny looked away before Mar- guerite's eyes could lock with hers.

But Oliver was working too hard, Marguerite protested.

But he *must* come out to the Point as they'd planned, Herbert said, and bring his friend along.

Ginny eased discreetly away. She was aloof, indifferent, just slightly bored, but unfailingly courteous: a mark of good breeding. And the Irish linen blazer and skirt were just right.

After a brief while Herbert Crews came over to comment on the view and Ginny thought it wouldn't be an error to agree: the view of Central Park was, after all, something quite real. He told her they'd lived here for eleven years "off and on." They traveled a good deal, he was required to travel almost more than he liked, being associated with an organization Ginny might have heard of—the Zieboldt Foundation. He had just returned from Nairobi, he said. Two days ago. And still feeling the strain—the fatigue. Ginny thought his affable talkative "social" manner showed not the least hint of fatigue but did not make this observation to Herbert Crews.

She felt a small pinprick of pity for the way Marguerite Crew's collar-   30
bones showed through her filmy muslin Indian blouse, and for the extreme thinness of her waist (cinched tight with a belt of silver coins or medallions), and for the faint scolding voice—so conspicuously a "voice"—with which she was speaking to Oliver. She saw that Oliver, though smiling nervously, and standing in a self-conscious pose with the thumb of his right hand hooked in his sports coat pocket, was enjoying the episode very much—she noted for the first time something vehement and cruel though at the same time unmistakably boyish in his face. Herbert Crews was telling her about Nairobi but she couldn't concentrate on his words. She was wondering if it might be proper to ask where Nairobi was—she assumed it was a country somewhere in Africa—but Herbert Crews continued, speaking now with zest of the wild animals, including great herds of "the most exquisitely beautiful gazelles," in the Kenya pre- serves. Had she ever been there, he asked. No, Ginny said. Well, said Her- bert, nodding vigorously, it really *is* worth it. Next time Marguerite promised to come along.

Ginny heard Oliver explain again that they were already late for an appointment in the Village, unfortunately they couldn't stay for a drink, yes, it was a pity but he hoped they might do it another time: with which Mar- guerite warmly agreed. Though it was clearly all right for Oliver and Ginny to leave now, Herbert Crews was telling her about the various animals he'd seen—elands, giraffes, gnus, hippopotami, crocodiles, zebras, "feathered monkeys," impalas—he had actually eaten impala and found it fairly good. But the trip was fatiguing and his business in Nairobi disagreeable. He'd discovered—as in the fact the Foundation had known from certain clumsily fudged reports—that the microbiological research being subsidized there had not only come to virtually nothing, but that vast sums of money had "disappeared" into nowhere. Ginny professed to feel some sympathy though at the same time, as she said, she wasn't surprised. Well, she said, easing away from Herbert Crew's side, that seems to be human nature, doesn't it. All around the world.

Americans and Swedes this time, Herbert Crews said—equally taken in.

It couldn't be avoided that Herbert told Oliver what he'd been saying— Oliver in fact seemed to be interested, he might have had some indirect connection with the Foundation himself—but, unfortunately they were late for their engagement downtown, and within five minutes they were out of the apartment and back in the elevator going down.

Oliver withdrew a handkerchief from his breast pocket, unfolded it, and carefully wiped his forehead. Ginny was studying her reflection in the mirror and felt a pinprick of disappointment—her eyes looked shadowed and tired, and her hair wasn't really all that wonderful, falling straight to her shoulders. Though she'd shampooed it only that morning, it was already getting dirty—the wind had been so strong on their walk up Madison.

On Fifth Avenue, in the gusty sunlight, they walked together for several blocks. Ginny slid her arm through Oliver's as if they were being watched, but at an intersection they were forced to walk at different paces and her arm slipped free. It was time in any case to say good-bye: she sensed that he wasn't going to ask her, even out of courtesy, to have a drink with him: and she had made up her mind not to feel even tangentially insulted. After all, she hadn't been insulted.   35

He signaled a cab for her. He handed over the pink cardboard box with her denim jumper and sweater in it and shook her hand vigorously. You were lovely up there, Oliver said—just perfect. Look, I'll call you, all right?

She felt the weight, the subtle dizzying blow, of the "were." But she thanked him just the same. And got into the cab. And wasn't so stricken by a sudden fleeting sense of loss—of loss tinged with a queer cold sickish knowledge—that, as the cab pulled away into the traffic stream, she couldn't give him a final languid wave of her hand, and even shape her mouth into a puckish kiss. All she had really lost, in a sense, was her own pair of shoes.

[1984]

FRANK O'CONNOR (1903–1966)

Frank O'Connor, the pen name of Michael Donovan, served in the Irish Republican Army (IRA) during Ireland's Civil War over the 1922 treaty with Great Britain. Although the IRA lost, O'Connor kept his faith, writing a biography about the rebellion's leader, Michael Collins. He also published plays and hundreds of short stories, in addition to his translations of Gaelic poems into English. O'Connor served as the director of the Abbey Theatre in Dublin during his thirties and later lectured at Harvard University, Northwestern University, and Trinity College, Dublin.

My Oedipus Complex

Father was in the army all through the war—the first war, I mean—so, up to the age of five, I never saw much of him, and what I saw did not worry me. Sometimes I woke and there was a big figure in khaki peering down at me in the candlelight. Sometimes in the early morning I heard the slamming of the front door and the clatter of nailed boots down the cobbles of the lane. These were Father's entrances and exits. Like Santa Claus he came and went mysteriously.

In fact, I rather liked his visits, though it was an uncomfortable squeeze between Mother and him when I got into the big bed in the early morning. He smoked, which gave him a pleasant musty smell, and shaved, an operation of astounding interest. Each time he left a trail of souvenirs—model tanks and Gurkha knives with handles made of bullet cases, and German helmets and cap badges and buttonsticks, and all sorts of military equipment—carefully stowed away in a long box on top of the wardrobe, in case they ever came in handy. There was a bit of the magpie about Father; he expected everything to come in handy. When his back was turned, Mother let me get a chair and rummage through his treasures. She didn't seem to think so highly of them as he did.

The war was the most peaceful period of my life. The window of my attic faced southeast. My mother had curtained it, but that had small effect. I always woke with the first light and, with all the responsibilities of the previous day melted, feeling myself rather like the sun, ready to illumine and rejoice. Life never seemed so simple and clear and full of possibilities as then. I put my feet out from under the clothes—I called them Mrs. Left and Mrs. Right—and invented dramatic situations for them in which they discussed the problems of the day. At least Mrs. Right did; she was very demonstrative, but I hadn't the same control of Mrs. Left, so she mostly contented herself with nodding agreement.

They discussed what Mother and I should do during the day, what Santa Claus should give a fellow for Christmas, and what steps should be taken to brighten the home. There was that little matter of the baby, for instance. Mother and I could never agree about that. Ours was the only house in the terrace without a new baby, and Mother said we couldn't afford one till Father came back from the war because they cost seventeen and six. That showed how simple she was. The Geneys up the road had a baby, and everyone knew they couldn't afford seventeen and six. It was probably a cheap baby, and Mother wanted something really good, but I felt she was too exclusive. The Geneys' baby would have done us fine.

Having settled my plans for the day, I got up, put a chair under the attic window, and lifted the frame high enough to stick out my head. The window overlooked the front gardens of the terrace behind ours, and beyond these it looked over a deep valley to the tall, red-brick houses terraced up the opposite hillside, which were all still in shadow, while those at our side of the valley were all lit up, though with long strange shadows that made them seem unfamiliar; rigid and painted.

After that I went into Mother's room and climbed into the big bed. She woke and I began to tell her of my schemes. By this time, though I never seem to have noticed it, I was petrified in my nightshirt, and I thawed as I talked until, the last frost melted, I fell asleep beside her and woke again only when I heard her below in the kitchen, making the breakfast.

After breakfast we went into town; heard Mass at St. Augustine's and said a prayer for Father, and did the shopping. If the afternoon was fine we either went for a walk in the country or a visit to Mother's great friend in the convent, Mother St. Dominic. Mother had them all praying for Father, and every night, going to bed, I asked God to send him back safe from the war to us. Little, indeed, did I know what I was praying for!

One morning, I got into the big bed, and there, sure enough, was Father in his usual Santa Claus manner, but later, instead of uniform, he put on his best blue suit, and Mother was as pleased as anything. I saw nothing to be pleased about, because, out of uniform, Father was altogether less interesting, but she only beamed, and explained that our prayers had been answered, and off we went to Mass to thank God for having brought Father safely home.

The irony of it! That very day when he came in to dinner he took off his boots and put on his slippers, donned the dirty old cap he wore about the house to save him from colds, crossed his legs, and began to talk gravely to Mother, who looked anxious. Naturally, I disliked her looking anxious, because it destroyed her good looks, so I interrupted him.

"Just a moment, Larry!" she said gently.   10

This was only what she said when we had boring visitors, so I attached no importance to it and went on talking.

"Do be quiet, Larry!" she said impatiently. "Don't you hear me talking to Daddy?"

This was the first time I had heard those ominous words, "talking to Daddy," and I couldn't help feeling that if this was how God answered prayers, he couldn't listen to them very attentively.

"Why are you talking to Daddy?" I asked with as great a show of indifference as I could muster.

"Because Daddy and I have business to discuss. Now, don't interrupt   15 again!"

In the afternoon, at Mother's request, Father took me for a walk. This time we went into town instead of out the country, and I thought at first, in my usual optimistic way, that it might be an improvement. It was nothing of the sort. Father and I had quite different notions of a walk in town. He had no proper interest in trams, ships, and horses, and the only thing that seemed to divert him was talking to fellows as old as himself. When I wanted to stop he simply went on, dragging me behind him by the hand; when he wanted to stop I had no alternative but to do the same. I noticed that it seemed to be a sign that he wanted to stop for a long time whenever he leaned against a wall. The second time I saw him do it I got wild. He seemed to be settling himself forever. I pulled him by the coat and trousers, but, unlike Mother who, if you were too persistent, got into a wax and said: "Larry, if you don't behave yourself, I'll give you a good slap," Father had an extraordinary capacity for amiable inattention. I sized him up and wondered would I cry, but he seemed to be too remote to be annoyed even by that. Really, it was like going for a walk with a mountain! He either ignored the wrenching and pummelling entirely, or else glanced down with a grin of amusement from his peak. I had never met anyone so absorbed in himself as he seemed.

At teatime, "talking to Daddy" began again, complicated this time by the fact that he had an evening paper, and every few minutes he put it down and told Mother something new out of it. I felt this was foul play. Man for man, I was prepared to compete with him anytime for Mother's attention, but when he had it all made up for him by other people it left me no chance. Several times I tried to change the subject without success.

"You must be quiet while Daddy is reading, Larry," Mother said impatiently.

It was clear that she either genuinely liked talking to Father better than talking to me, or else that he had some terrible hold on her which made her afraid to admit the truth.

"Mummy," I said that night when she was tucking me up, "do you think   20
if I prayed hard God would send Daddy back to the war?"

She seemed to think about that for a moment.

"No, dear," she said with a smile. "I don't think he would."

"Why wouldn't he, Mummy?"

"Because there isn't a war any longer, dear."

"But, Mummy, couldn't God make another war, if He liked?"   25

"He wouldn't like to, dear. It's not God who makes wars, but bad people."

"Oh!" I said.

I was disappointed about that. I began to think that God wasn't quite what he was cracked up to be.

Next morning I woke at my usual hour, feeling like a bottle of champagne. I put out my feet and invented a long conversation in which Mrs. Right talked of the trouble she had with her own father till she put him in the Home. I didn't quite know what the Home was but it sounded the right place for Father. Then I got my chair and stuck my head out of the attic window. Dawn was just breaking, with a guilty air that made me feel I had caught it in the act. My head bursting with stories and schemes, I stumbled in next door, and in the half-darkness scrambled into the big bed. There was no room at Mother's side so I had to get between her and Father. For the time being I had forgotten about him, and for several minutes I sat bolt upright, racking my brains to know what I could do with him. He was taking up more than his fair share of the bed, and I couldn't get comfortable, so I gave him several kicks that made him grunt and stretch. He made room all right, though. Mother waked and felt for me. I settled back comfortably in the warmth of the bed with my thumb in my mouth.

"Mummy!" I hummed, loudly and contentedly. "Sssh! dear," she whis-   30
pered. "Don't wake Daddy!"

This was a new development, which threatened to be even more serious than "talking to Daddy." Life without my early-morning conferences was unthinkable.

"Why?" I asked severely.

"Because poor Daddy is tired."

This seemed to me a quite inadequate reason, and I was sickened by the sentimentality of her "poor Daddy." I never liked that sort of gush; it always struck me as insincere.

"Oh!" I said lightly. Then in my most winning tone: "Do you know   35
where I want to go with you today, Mummy?"

"No, dear," she sighed.

"I want to go down the Glen and fish for thornybacks with my new net, and then I want to go out to the Fox and Hounds, and—"

"Don't-wake-daddy!" she hissed angrily, clapping her hand across my mouth.

But it was too late. He was awake, or nearly so. He grunted and reached for the matches. Then he stared incredulously at his watch.

"Like a cup of tea, dear?" asked Mother in a meek, hushed voice I had never heard her use before. It sounded almost as though she were afraid.   40

"Tea?" he exclaimed indignantly. "Do you know what the time is?"

"And after that I want to go up the Rathcooney Road," I said loudly, afraid I'd forget something in all those interruptions.

"Go to sleep at once, Larry!" she said sharply.

I began to snivel. I couldn't concentrate, the way that pair went on, and smothering my early-morning schemes was like burying a family from the cradle.

Father said nothing, but lit his pipe and sucked it, looking out into the   45
shadows without minding Mother or me. I knew he was mad. Every time I made a remark Mother hushed me irritably. I was mortified. I felt it wasn't fair; there was even something sinister in it. Every time I had pointed out to her the waste of making two beds when we could both sleep in one, she had told me it was healthier like that, and now here was this man, this stranger, sleeping with her without the least regard for her health!

He got up early and made tea, but though he brought Mother a cup he brought none for me.

"Mummy," I shouted, "I want a cup of tea, too."

"Yes, dear," she said patiently. "You can drink from Mummy's saucer."

That settled it. Either Father or I would have to leave the house. I didn't want to drink from Mother's saucer; I wanted to be treated as an equal in my own home, so, just to spite her, I drank it all and left none for her. She took that quietly, too.

But that night when she was putting me to bed she said gently: 50

"Larry, I want you to promise me something."

"What is it?" I asked.

"Not to come in and disturb poor Daddy in the morning. Promise?"

"Poor Daddy" again! I was becoming suspicious of everything involving that quite impossible man.

"Why?" I asked.   55

"Because poor Daddy is worried and tired and he doesn't sleep well."

"Why doesn't he, Mummy?"

"Well, you know, don't you, that while he was at the war Mummy got the pennies from the Post Office?"

"From Miss MacCarthy?"

"That's right. But now, you see, Miss MacCarthy hasn't any more   60
pennies, so Daddy must go out and find us some. You know what would happen if he couldn't?"

"No," I said, "tell us."

"Well, I think we might have to go out and beg for them like the poor old woman on Fridays. We wouldn't like that, would we?"

"No," I agreed. "We wouldn't."

"So you'll promise not to come in and wake him?"

"Promise." 65

Mind you, I meant that. I knew pennies were a serious matter, and I was all against having to go out and beg like the old woman on Fridays. Mother laid out all my toys in a complete ring around the bed so that, whatever way I got out, I was bound to fall over one of them.

When I woke I remembered my promise all right. I got up and sat on the floor and played—for hours, it seemed to me. Then I got my chair and looked out the attic window for more hours. I wished it was time for Father to wake; I wished someone would make me a cup of tea. I didn't feel in the least like the sun; instead, I was bored and so very, very cold! I simply longed for the warmth and depth of the big featherbed.

At last I could stand it no longer. I went into the next room. As there was still no room at Mother's side I climbed over her and she woke with a start.

"Larry," she whispered, gripping my arm very tightly, "what did you promise?"

"But I did Mummy," I wailed, caught in the very act. "I was quiet for ever 70
so long."

"Oh, dear, and you're perished!" she said sadly, feeling me all over. "Now, if I let you stay will you promise not to talk?"

"But I want to talk, Mummy," I wailed.

"That has nothing to do with it," she said with a firmness that was new to me. "Daddy wants to sleep. Now, do you understand that?"

I understood it only too well. I wanted to talk, he wanted to sleep—whose house was it, anyway?

"Mummy," I said with equal firmness, "I think it would be healthier for 75
Daddy to sleep in his own bed."

That seemed to stagger her, because she said nothing for a while.

"Now, once for all," she went on, "you're to be perfectly quiet or go back to your own bed. Which is it to be?"

The injustice of it got me down. I had convicted her out of her own mouth of inconsistency and unreasonableness, and she hadn't even attempted to reply. Full of spite, I gave Father a kick, which she didn't notice but which made him grunt and open his eyes in alarm.

"What time is it?" he asked in a panic-stricken voice, not looking at Mother but at the door, as if he saw someone there.

"It's early yet," she replied soothingly. "It's only the child. Go to sleep 80
again. . . . Now, Larry," she added, getting out of bed, "you've wakened Daddy and you must go back."

This time, for all her quiet air, I knew she meant it, and knew that my principal rights and privileges were as good as lost unless I asserted them at once. As she lifted me, I gave a screech, enough to wake the dead, not to mind Father. He groaned.

"That damn child! Doesn't he ever sleep?"

"It's only a habit, dear," she said quietly, though I could see she was vexed.

"Well, it's time he got out of it," shouted Father, beginning to heave in the bed. He suddenly gathered all the bedclothes about him, turned to the wall, and then looked back over his shoulder with nothing showing only two small, spiteful, dark eyes. The man looked very wicked.

To open the bedroom door, Mother had to let me down, and I broke free 85
and dashed for the farthest corner, screeching. Father sat bolt upright in bed.

"Shut up, you little puppy!" he said in a choking voice.

I was so astonished that I stopped screeching. Never, never had any-one spoken to me in that tone before. I looked at him incredulously and saw his face convulsed with rage. It was only then that I fully realized how God had codded me, listening to my prayers for the safe return of this monster.

"Shut up, you!" I bawled, beside myself.

"What's that you said?" shouted Father, making a wild leap out of the bed.

"Mick, Mick!" cried Mother. "Don't you see the child isn't used to you?"   90

"I see he's better fed than taught," snarled Father, waving his arms wild-ly. "He wants his bottom smacked."

All his previous shouting was as nothing to these obscene words refer-ring to my person. They really made my blood boil.

"Smack your own!" I screamed hysterically. "Smack your own! Shut up! Shut up!"

At this he lost his patience and let fly at me. He did it with the lack of conviction you'd expect of a man under Mother's horrified eyes, and it ended up as a mere tap, but the sheer indignity of being struck at all by a stranger, a total stranger who had cajoled his way back from the war into our big bed as a result of my innocent intercession, made me completely dotty. I shrieked and shrieked, and danced in my bare feet, and Father, look-ing awkward and hairy in nothing but a short gray army shirt, glared down at me like a mountain out for murder. I think it must have been then that I realized he was jealous too. And there stood Mother in her nightdress, look-ing as if her heart was broken between us. I hoped she felt as she looked. It seemed to me that she deserved it all.

From that morning out my life was a hell. Father and I were enemies,   95 open and avowed. We conducted a series of skirmishes against one anoth-er, he trying to steal my time with Mother and I his. When she was sitting on my bed, telling me a story, he took to looking for some pair of old boots which he alleged he had left behind him at the beginning of the war. While he talked to Mother I played loudly with my toys to show my total lack of concern. He created a terrible scene one evening when he came in from work and found me at his box, playing with his regimental badges, Gurkha knives and buttonsticks. Mother got up and took the box from me.

"You mustn't play with Daddy's toys unless he lets you, Larry," she said severely. "Daddy doesn't play with yours."

For some reason Father looked at her as if she had struck him and then turned away with a scowl.

"Those are not toys," he growled, taking down the box again to see had I lifted anything. "Some of those curios are very rare and valuable."

But as time went on I saw more and more how he managed to alienate Mother and me. What made it worse was that I couldn't grasp his method or see what attraction he had for Mother. In every possible way he was less winning than I. He had a common accent and made noises at his tea. I thought for a while that it might be the newspapers she was interested in, so I made up bits of news on my own to read to her. Then I thought it might be the smoking, which I personally thought attractive, and took his pipes and went round the house dribbling into them till he caught me. I even made noises at my tea, but Mother only told me I was disgusting. It all seemed to hinge round that unhealthy habit of sleeping together, so I made a point of dropping into their bedroom and nosing round, talking to myself,

so that they wouldn't know I was watching them, but they were never up
to anything that I could see. In the end it beat me. It seemed to depend on
being grown-up and giving people rings, and I realized I'd have to wait.

But at the same time I wanted him to see that I was only waiting, not   100
giving up the fight. One evening when he was being particularly obnox-
ious, chattering away well above my head, I let him have it.

"Mummy," I said, "do you know what I'm going to do when I grow up?"

"No, dear," she replied. "What?"

"I'm going to marry you," I said quietly.

Father gave a great guffaw out of him, but he didn't take me in. I knew
it must only be pretense. And Mother, in spite of everything, was pleased. I
felt she was probably relieved to know that one day Father's hold on her
would be broken.

"Won't that be nice?" she said with a smile.   105

"It'll be very nice," I said confidently. "Because we're going to have lots
and lots of babies."

"That's right, dear," she said placidly. "I think we'll have one soon, and
then you'll have plenty of company."

I was no end pleased about that because it showed that in spite of the
way she gave in to Father she still considered my wishes. Besides, it would
put the Geneys in their place.

It didn't turn out like that, though. To begin with, she was very
preoccupied—I supposed about where she would get the seventeen and six—
and though Father took to staying out late in the evenings it did me no particular good. She stopped taking me for walks, became as touchy as blazes, and
smacked me for nothing at all. Sometimes I wished I'd never mentioned the
confounded baby—I seemed to have a genius for bringing calamity on myself.

And calamity it was! Sonny arrived in the most appalling hullabaloo—   110
even that much he couldn't do without a fuss—and from the first moment I
disliked him. He was a difficult child—so far as I was concerned he was
always difficult—and demanded far too much attention. Mother was simply
silly about him, and couldn't see when he was only showing off. As company
he was worse than useless. He slept all day, and I had to go round the house
on tiptoe to avoid waking him. It wasn't any longer a question of not waking
Father. The slogan now was "Don't-wake-Sonny!" I couldn't understand why
the child wouldn't sleep at the proper time, so whenever Mother's back was
turned I woke him. Sometimes to keep him awake I pinched him as well.
Mother caught me at it one day and gave me a most unmerciful flaking.

One evening, when Father was coming in from work, I was playing
trains in the front garden. I let on not to notice him; instead, I pretended to
be talking to myself, and said in a loud voice: "If another bloody baby comes
into this house, I'm going out."

Father stopped dead and looked at me over his shoulder.

"What's that you said?" he asked sternly.

"I was only talking to myself," I replied, trying to conceal my panic. "It's
private."

He turned and went in without a word. Mind you, I intended it as a   115
solemn warning, but its effect was quite different. Father started being quite
nice to me. I could understand that, of course. Mother was quite sickening
about Sonny. Even at mealtimes she'd get up and gawk at him in the cradle
with an idiotic smile, and tell Father to do the same. He was always polite
about it, but he looked so puzzled you could see he didn't know what she was

talking about. He complained of the way Sonny cried at night, but she only got cross and said that Sonny never cried except when there was something up with him—which was a flaming lie, because Sonny never had anything up with him, and only cried for attention. It was really painful to see how simple-minded she was. Father wasn't attractive, but he had a fine intelligence. He saw through Sonny, and now he knew that I saw through him as well.

One night I woke with a start. There was someone beside me in the bed. For one wild moment I felt sure it must be Mother, having come to her senses and left Father for good, but then I heard Sonny in convulsions in the next room, and Mother saying: "There! There! There!" and I knew it wasn't she. It was Father. He was lying beside me, wide awake, breathing hard and apparently as mad as hell.

After awhile it came to me what he was mad about. It was his turn now. After turning me out of the big bed, he had been turned out himself. Mother had no consideration now for anyone but that poisonous pup, Sonny. I couldn't help feeling sorry for Father. I had been through it all myself, and even at that age I was magnanimous. I began to stroke him down and say: "There! There!" He wasn't exactly responsive.

"Aren't you asleep either?" he snarled.

"Ah, come on and put your arm around us, can't you?" I said, and he did, in a sort of way. Gingerly, I suppose, is how you'd describe it. He was very bony but better than nothing.

At Christmas he went out of his way to buy me a really nice model   120
railway.

[1950]

CYNTHIA OZICK (1928–)

Cynthia Ozick, author of short stories, plays, and novellas, was born in New York City and graduated with a B.A. from New York University and an M.A. from Ohio State University. She has received several O. Henry Awards for fiction, fellowships from both the Guggenheim and the National Endowment for the Arts, and the prestigious Mildred and Harold Strauss Living Award. Her work has often dealt with Jewish themes, including the Holocaust.

The Shawl

Stella, cold, cold, the coldness of hell. How they walked on the roads together, Rosa with Magda curled up between sore breasts, Magda wound up in the shawl. Sometimes Stella carried Magda. But she was jealous of Magda. A thin girl of fourteen, too small, with thin breasts of her own, Stella wanted to be wrapped in a shawl, hidden away, asleep, rocked by the march, a baby, a round infant in arms. Magda took Rosa's nipple, and Rosa never stopped walking, a walking cradle.

There was not enough milk; sometimes Magda sucked air; then she screamed. Stella was ravenous. Her knees were tumors on sticks, her elbows chicken bones.

Rosa did not feel hunger; she felt light, not like someone walking but like someone in a faint, in trance, arrested in a fit, someone who is already a floating angel, alert and seeing everything, but in the air, not there, not touching the road. As if teetering on the tips of her fingernails. She looked into Magda's face through a gap in the shawl: a squirrel in a nest, safe, no one could reach her inside the little house of the shawl's windpings. The face, very round, a pocket mirror of a face: but it was not Rosa's bleak complexion, dark like cholera, it was another kind of face altogether, eyes blue as air, smooth feathers of hair nearly as yellow as the Star sewn into Rosa's coat. You could think she was one of *their* babies.

Rosa, floating, dreamed of giving Magda away in one of the villages. She could leave the line for a minute and push Magda into the hands of any woman on the side of the road. But if she moved out of line they might shoot. And even if she fled the line for half a second and pushed the shawl-bundle at a stranger, would the woman take it? She might be surprised, or afraid; she might drop the shawl, and Magda would fall out and strike her dead and die. The little round head. Such a good child, she gave up screaming, and sucked now only for the taste of the drying nipple itself. The neat grip of the tiny gums. One mite of a tooth tip sticking up in the bottom gum, how shining, an elfin tombstone of white marble gleaming there. Without complaining, Magda relinquished Rosa's teats, first the left, then the right; both were cracked, not a sniff of milk. The duct-crevice extinct, a dead volcano, blind eye, chill hole, so Magda took the corner of the shawl and milked it instead. She sucked and sucked, flooding the threads with wetness. The shawl's good flavor, milk of linen.

It was a magic shawl, it could nourish an infant for three days and three nights. Magda did not die, she stayed alive, although very quiet. A peculiar smell, of cinnamon and almonds, lifted out of her mouth. She held her eyes open every moment, forgetting how to blink or nap, and Rosa and sometimes Stella studied their blueness. On the road they raised one burden of a leg after another and studied Magda's face. "Aryan," Stella said, in a voice grown as thin as a string; and Rosa thought how Stella gazed at Magda like a young cannibal. And the time that Stella said "Aryan," it sounded to Rosa as if Stella had really said "Let us devour her."

But Magda lived to walk. She lived that long, but she did not walk very well, partly because she was only fifteen months old, and partly because the spindles of her legs could not hold up her fat belly. It was fat with air, full and round. Rosa gave almost all her food to Magda, Stella gave nothing; Stella was ravenous, a growing child herself, but not growing much. Stella did not menstruate. Rosa did not menstruate. Rosa was ravenous, but also not; she learned from Magda how to drink the taste of a finger in one's mouth. They were in a place without pity, all pity was annihilated in Rosa, she looked at Stella's bones without pity. She was sure that Stella was waiting for Magda to die so she could put her teeth into the little thighs.

Rosa knew Magda was going to die very soon; she should have been dead already, but she had been buried away deep inside the magic shawl, mistaken there for the shivering mound of Rosa's breasts; Rosa clung to the shawl as if it covered only herself. No one took it away from her. Magda was

5

mute. She never cried. Rosa hid her in the barracks, under the shawl, but she knew that one day someone would inform; or one day someone, not even Stella, would steal Magda to eat her. When Magda began to walk, Rosa knew that Magda was going to die very soon, something would happen. She was afraid to fall asleep; she slept with the weight of her thigh on Magda's body; she was afraid she would smother Magda under her thigh. The weight of Rosa was becoming less and less; Rosa and Stella were slowly turning into air.

Magda was quiet, but her eyes were horribly alive, like blue tigers. She watched. Sometimes she laughed—it seemed a laugh, but how could it be? Magda had never seen anyone laugh. Still, Magda laughed at her shawl when the wind blew its corners, the bad wind with pieces of black in it, that made Stella's and Rosa's eyes tear. Magda's eyes were always clear and tearless. She watched like a tiger. She guarded her shawl. No one could touch it; only Rosa could touch it. Stella was not allowed. The shawl was Magda's own baby, her pet, her little sister. She tangled herself up in it and sucked on one of the corners when she wanted to be very still.

Then Stella took the shawl away and made Magda die.

Afterward Stella said: "I was cold."

And afterward she was always cold, always. The cold went into her heart: Rosa saw that Stella's heart was cold. Magda flopped onward with her little pencil legs scribbling this way and that, in search of the shawl; the pencils faltered at the barracks opening, where the light began. Rosa saw and pursued. But already Magda was in the square outside the barracks, in the jolly light. It was the roll-call arena. Every morning Rosa had to conceal Magda under the shawl against a wall of the barracks and go out and stand in the arena with Stella and hundreds of others, sometimes for hours, and Magda, deserted, was quiet under the shawl, sucking on her corner. Every day Magda was silent, and so she did not die. Rosa saw that today Magda was going to die, and at the same time a fearful joy ran in Rosa's two palms, her fingers were on fire, she was astonished, febrile: Magda, in the sunlight, swaying on her pencil legs, was howling. Ever since the drying up of Rosa's nipples, ever since Magda's last scream on the road, Magda had been devoid of any syllable; Magda was a mute. Rosa believed that something had gone wrong with her vocal cords, with her windpipe, with the cave of her larynx; Magda was defective, without a voice; perhaps she was deaf; there might be something amiss with her intelligence; Magda was dumb. Even the laugh that came when the ash-stippled wind made a clown out of Magda's shawl was only the air-blown showing of her teeth. Even when the lice, head lice and body lice, crazed her so that she became as wild as one of the big rats that plundered the barracks at daybreak looking for carrion, she rubbed and scratched and kicked and bit and rolled without a whimper. But now Magda's mouth was spilling a long viscous rope of clamor.

"Maaaa—"

It was the first noise Magda had ever sent out from her throat since the drying up of Rosa's nipples.

"Maaaa . . . aaa!"

Again! Magda was wavering in the perilous sunlight of the arena, scribbling on such pitiful little bent shins. Rosa saw. She saw that Magda was grieving for the loss of her shawl, she saw that Magda was going to die. A tide of commands hammered in Rosa's nipples: Fetch, get, bring! But she

10

did not know which to go after first, Magda or the shawl. If she jumped out into the arena to snatch Magda up, the howling would not stop, because Magda would still not have the shawl; but if she ran back into the barracks to find the shawl, and if she found it, and if she came after Magda holding it and shaking it, then she would get Magda back, Magda would put the shawl in her mouth and turn dumb again.

Rosa entered the dark. It was easy to discover the shawl. Stella was heaped under it, asleep in her thin bones. Rosa tore the shawl free and flew—she could fly, she was only air—into the arena. The sunheat murmured of another life, of butterflies in summer. The light was placid, mellow. On the other side of the steel fence, far away, there were green meadows speckled with dandelions and deep-colored violets; beyond them, even farther, innocent tiger lilies, tall, lifting their orange bonnets. In the barracks they spoke of "flowers," of "rain": excrement, thick turd-braids, and the slow stinking maroon waterfall that slunk down from the upper bunks, the stink mixed with a bitter fatty floating smoke that greased Rosa's skin. She stood for an instant at the margin of the arena. Sometimes the electricity inside the fence would seem to hum; even Stella said it was only an imagining, but Rosa heard real sounds in the wire: grainy sad voices. The farther she was from the fence, the more clearly the voices crowded at her. The lamenting voices strummed so convincingly, so passionately, it was impossible to suspect them of being phantoms. The voices told her to hold up the shawl, high; the voices told her to shake it, to whip with it, to unfurl it like a flag. Rosa lifted, shook, whipped, unfurled. Far off, very far, Magda leaned across her air-fed belly, reaching out with the rods of her arms. She was high up, elevated, riding someone's shoulder. But the shoulder that carried Magda was not coming toward Rosa and the shawl, it was drifting away, the speck of Magda was moving more and more into the smoky distance. Above the shoulder a helmet glinted. The light tapped the helmet and sparkled it into a goblet. Below the helmet a black body like a domino and a pair of black boots hurled themselves in the direction of the electrified fence. The electric voices began to chatter wildly. "Maamaa, maaamaaa," they all hummed together. How far Magda was from Rosa now, across the whole square, past a dozen barracks, all the way on the other side! She was no bigger than a moth.

All at once Magda was swimming through the air. The whole of Magda traveled through loftiness. She looked like a butterfly touching a silver vine. And the moment Magda's feathered round head and her pencil legs and balloonish belly and zigzag arms splashed against the fence, the steel voices went mad in their growling, urging Rosa to run and run to the spot where Magda had fallen from her flight against the electrified fence; but of course Rosa did not obey them. She only stood, because if she ran they would shoot, and if she tried to pick up the sticks of Magda's body they would shoot, and if she let the wolf's screech ascending now through the ladder of her skeleton break out, they would shoot; so she took Magda's shawl and filled her own mouth with it, stuffed it in and stuffed it in, until she was swallowing up the wolf's screech and tasting the cinnamon and almond depth of Magda's saliva; and Rosa drank Magda's shawl until it dried.

[1981]

GRACE PALEY (1922–)

Grace Paley who was born in the Bronx, became the first official New York State Author by an act of state legislature in 1988. After studying at New York University, Paley taught at Columbia University and Syracuse University, and currently teaches at both City College of New York and Sarah Lawrence College. She has also dedicated herself to political activism, founding the Greenwich Village Peace Center in 1961 and later becoming founding chair of Women's WORLD. She has published three collections of short stories and three collections of poetry.

A Conversation with My Father

My father is eighty-six years old and in bed. His heart, that bloody motor, is equally old and will not do certain jobs any more. It still floods his head with brainy light. But it won't let his legs carry the weight of his body around the house. Despite my metaphors, this muscle failure is not due to his old heart, he says, but to a potassium shortage. Sitting on one pillow, leaning on three, he offers last-minute advice and makes a request.

"I would like you to write a simple story just once more," he says, "the kind de Maupassant wrote, or Chekhov, the kind you used to write. Just recognizable people and then write down what happened to them next."

I say, "Yes, why not? That's possible." I want to please him, though I don't remember writing that way. I *would* like to try to tell such a story, if he means the kind that begins: "There was a woman . . . " followed by plot, the absolute line between two points which I've always despised. Not for literary reasons, but because it takes all hope away. Everyone, real or invented, deserves the open destiny of life.

Finally I thought of a story that had been happening for a couple of years right across the street. I wrote it down and read it aloud. "Pa," I said, "how about this? Do you mean something like this?"

> *Once in my time there was a woman and she had a son. They lived nicely, in a small apartment in Manhattan. This boy at about fifteen became a junkie, which is not unusual in our neighborhood. In order to maintain her close friendship with him, she became a junkie too. She said it was part of the youth culture, with which she felt very much at home. After a while, for a number of reasons, the boy gave it all up and left the city and his mother in disgust. Hopeless and alone, she grieved. We all visit her.*

"O.K., Pa, that's it," I said, "an unadorned and miserable tale."   5

"But that's not what I mean," my father said. "You misunderstood me on purpose. You know there's a lot more to it. You know that. You left everything out. Turgenev wouldn't do that. Chekhov wouldn't do that. There are in fact Russian writers you never heard of, you don't have an inkling of, as good as anyone, who can write a plain ordinary story, who would not leave out what you have left out. I object not to facts but to people sitting in trees talking senselessly, voices from who knows where . . ."

"Forget that one, Pa, what have I left out now? In this one?"

"Her looks, for instance."

"Oh. Quite handsome, I think. Yes."

"Her hair?"   10

"Dark, with heavy braids, as though she were a girl or a foreigner."

"What were her parents like, her stock? That she became such a person. It's interesting, you know."

"From out of town. Professional people. The first to be divorced in their county. How's that? Enough?" I asked.

"With you, it's all a joke," he said. "What about the boy's father? Why didn't you mention him? Who was he? Or was the boy born out of wedlock?"

"Yes," I said. "He was born out of wedlock."   15

"For Godsakes, doesn't anyone in your stories get married? Doesn't anyone have the time to run down to City Hall before they jump into bed?"

"No," I said. "In real life, yes. But in my stories, no."

"Why do you answer me like that?"

"Oh, Pa, this is a simple story about a smart woman who came to N.Y.C. full of interest love trust excitement very up to date, and about her son, what a hard time she had in this world. Married or not, it's of small consequence."

"It is of great consequence," he said.   20

"O.K.," I said.

"O.K. O.K. yourself," he said, "but listen. I believe you that she's good-looking, but I don't think she was so smart."

"That's true," I said. "Actually that's the trouble with stories. People start out fantastic. You think they're extraordinary, but it turns out as the work goes along, they're just average with a good education. Sometimes the other way around, the person's a kind of dumb innocent, but he outwits you and you can't even think of an ending good enough."

"What do you do then?" he asked. He had been a doctor for a couple of decades and then an artist for a couple of decades and he was still interested in details, craft, technique.

"Well, you just have to let the story lie around till some agreement can   25
be reached between you and the stubborn hero."

"Aren't you talking silly, now?" he asked. "Start again," he said. "It so happens I'm not going out this evening. Tell the story again. See what you can do this time."

"O.K.," I said. "But it's not a five-minute job." Second attempt:

Once, across the street from us, there was a fine handsome woman, our neighbor. She had a son whom she loved because she'd known him since birth (in helpless chubby infancy, and in the wrestling, hugging ages, seven to ten, as well as earlier and later). This boy, when he fell into the fist of adolescence, became a junkie. He was not a hopeless one. He was in fact hopeful, an ideologue and successful converter. With his busy brilliance, he wrote persuasive articles for his high-school newspaper. Seeking a wider audience, using important connections, he drummed into Lower Manhattan newsstand distribution a periodical called Oh! Golden Horse!

In order to keep him from feeling guilty (because guilt is the stony heart of nine tenths of all clinically diagnosed cancers in America today, she said), and because she had always believed in giving bad habits room at home where one could

*keep an eye on them, she too became a junkie. Her kitchen was
famous for a while—a center for intellectual addicts who
knew what they were doing. A few felt artistic like Coleridge
and others were scientific and revolutionary like Leary.
Although she was often high herself, certain good mothering
reflexes remained, and she saw to it that there was lots of
orange juice around and honey and milk and vitamin pills.
However, she never cooked anything but chili, and that no
more than once a week. She explained, when we talked to her,
seriously, with neighborly concern, that it was her part in the
youth culture and she would rather be with the young, it was
an honor, than with her own generation.*

    *One week, while nodding through an Antonioni film, this
boy was severely jabbed by the elbow of a stern and proselytiz-
ing girl, sitting beside him. She offered immediate apricots and
nuts for his sugar level, spoke to him sharply, and took him
home.*

    *She had heard of him and his work and she herself pub-
lished, edited, and wrote a competitive journal called* Man Does
Live By Bread Alone. *In the organic heat of her continuous presence he could not help but become interested once more in his
muscles, his arteries, and nerve connections. In fact he began to
love them, treasure them, praise them with funny little songs in*
Man Does Live . . .

*the fingers of my flesh transcend
my transcendental soul
the tightness in my shoulders end
my teeth have made me whole*

    *To the mouth of his head (that glory of will and determina-
tion) he brought hard apples, nuts, wheat germ, and soybean
oil. He said to his old friends, From now on, I guess I'll keep my
wits about me. I'm going on the natch. He said he was about to
begin a spiritual deep-breathing journey. How about you too,
Mom? he asked kindly.*

    *His conversion was so radiant, splendid, that neighbor-
hood kids his age began to say that he had never been a real
addict at all, only a journalist along for the smell of the story.
The mother tried several times to give up what had become
without her son and his friends a lonely habit. This effort only
brought it to supportable levels. The boy and his girl took their
electronic mimeograph and moved to the bushy edge of another borough. They were very strict. They said they would not see
her again until she had been off drugs for sixty days.*

    *At home alone in the evening, weeping, the mother read
and reread the seven issues of* Oh! Golden Horse! *They seemed
to her as truthful as ever. We often crossed the street to visit and
console. But if we mentioned any of our children who were at
college or in the hospital or dropouts at home, she would cry
out, My baby! My baby! and burst into terrible, face-scarring,
time-consuming tears. The End.*

First my father was silent, then he said, "Number One: You have a nice sense of humor. Number Two: I see you can't tell a plain story. So don't waste time." Then he said sadly, "Number Three: I suppose that means she was alone, she was left like that, his mother. Alone. Probably sick?"

I said, "Yes."

"Poor woman. Poor girl, to be born in a time of fools, to live among 30 fools. The end. The end. You were right to put that down. The end."

I didn't want to argue, but I had to say, "Well, it is not necessarily the end, Pa."

"Yes," he said, "what a tragedy. The end of a person."

"No, Pa," I begged him. "It doesn't have to be. She's only about forty. She could be a hundred different things in this world as time goes on. A teacher or a social worker. An ex-junkie! Sometimes it's better than having a master's in education."

"Jokes," he said. "As a writer that's your main trouble. You don't want to recognize it. Tragedy! Plain tragedy! Historical tragedy! No hope. The end."

"Oh, Pa," I said. "She could change." 35

"In your own life, too, you have to look it in the face." He took a couple of nitroglycerin. "Turn to five," he said, pointing to the dial on the oxygen tank. He inserted the tubes into his nostrils and breathed deep. He closed his eyes and said, "No."

I had promised the family to always let him have the last word when arguing, but in this case I had a different responsibility. That woman lives across the street. She's my knowledge and my invention. I'm sorry for her. I'm not going to leave her there in that house crying. (Actually neither would Life, which unlike me has no pity.)

Therefore: She did change. Of course her son never came home again. But right now, she's the receptionist in the storefront community clinic in the East Village. Most of the customers are young people, some old friends. The head doctor has said to her, "If we only had three people in this clinic with your experiences . . ."

"The doctor said that?" My father took the oxygen tubes out of his nostrils and said, "Jokes. Jokes again."

"No, Pa, it could really happen that way, it's a funny world nowadays." 40

"No," he said. "Truth first. She will slide back. A person must have character. She does not."

"No, Pa," I said. "That's it. She's got a job. Forget it. She's in the storefront working."

"How long will it be?" he asked. "Tragedy! You too. When will you look it in the face?"

[1974]

KATHERINE ANNE PORTER (1890–1980)

Born in Indian Creek, Texas, Katherine Anne Porter ended her formal education at the age of sixteen when she ran away from home to get married. After separating from her first husband, Porter began a life of travel. She moved to Chicago and Denver where she worked as a journalist and later moved to New York City. She received a Guggenheim Fellowship that allowed her to travel to Mexico and Europe. Porter remarried at least twice during her lifetime. In 1965, she received a Pulitzer Prize and a National Book Award for her Collected Stories.

Wearing her elegant and ever-present hat, Katherine
Anne Porter sits on her terrace.

The Jilting of Granny Weatherall

She flicked her wrist neatly out of Doctor Harry's pudgy careful fingers
and pulled the sheet up to her chin. The brat ought to be in knee breeches. Doctoring around the country with spectacles on his nose! "Get along
now, take your schoolbooks and go. There's nothing wrong with me."

Doctor Harry spread a warm paw like a cushion on her forehead where
the forked green vein danced and made her eyelids twitch. "Now, now, be a
good girl, and we'll have you up in no time."

"That's no way to speak to a woman nearly eighty years old just
because she's down. I'd have you respect your elders, young man."

"Well, Missy, excuse me." Doctor Harry patted her cheek. "But I've got
to warn you, haven't I? You're a marvel, but you must be careful or you're
going to be good and sorry."

"Don't tell me what I'm going to be. I'm on my feet now, morally speak-   5
ing. It's Cornelia. I had to go to bed to get rid of her."

Her bones felt loose, and floated around in her skin, and Doctor Harry
floated like a balloon around the foot of the bed. He floated and pulled
down his waistcoat and swung his glasses on a cord. "Well, stay where you
are, it certainly can't hurt you."

"Get along and doctor your sick," said Granny Weatherall. "Leave a well
woman alone. I'll call for you when I want you. . . . Where were you forty
years ago when I pulled through milk-leg and double pneumonia? You
weren't even born. Don't let Cornelia lead you on," she shouted, because
Doctor Harry appeared to float up to the ceiling and out. "I pay my own
bills, and I don't throw my money away on nonsense!"

She meant to wave good-by, but it was too much trouble. Her eyes
closed of themselves, it was like a dark curtain drawn around the bed. The
pillow rose and floated under her, pleasant as a hammock in a light wind.
She listened to the leaves rustling outside the window. No, somebody was
swishing newspapers: no, Cornelia and Doctor Harry were whispering
together. She leaped broad awake, thinking they whispered in her ear.

"She was never like this, *never* like this!" "Well, what can we expect?"
"Yes, eighty years old. . . ."

Well, and what if she was? She still had ears. It was like Cornelia to   10
whisper around doors. She always kept things secret in such a public way.
She was always being tactful and kind. Cornelia was dutiful; that was the
trouble with her. Dutiful and good: "So good and dutiful," said Granny, "that
I'd like to spank her." She saw herself spanking Cornelia and making a fine
job of it.

"What'd you say, Mother?"

Granny felt her face tying up in hard knots.

"Can't a body think, I'd like to know?"

"I thought you might want something."

"I do. I want a lot of things. First off, go away and don't whisper."   15

She lay and drowsed, hoping in her sleep that the children would keep
out and let her rest a minute. It had been a long day. Not that she was tired.
It was always pleasant to snatch a minute now and then. There was always
so much to be done, let me see: tomorrow.

Tomorrow was far away and there was nothing to trouble about. Things
were finished somehow when the time came; thank God there was always a
little margin over for peace: then a person could spread out the plan of life
and tuck in the edges orderly. It was good to have everything clean and
folded away, with the hair brushes and tonic bottles sitting straight on the
white embroidered linen: the day started without fuss and the pantry
shelves laid out with rows of jelly glasses and brown jugs and white
stone-china jars with blue whirligigs and words painted on them: coffee,
tea, sugar, ginger, cinnamon, allspice: and the bronze clock with the lion
on top nicely dusted off. The dust that lion could collect in twenty-four
hours! The box in the attic with all those letters tied up, well, she'd have
to go through that tomorrow. All those letters—George's letters and
John's letters and her letters to them both—lying around for the children
to find afterwards made her uneasy. Yes, that would be tomorrow's business. No use to let them know how silly she had been once.

While she was rummaging around she found death in her mind and it
felt clammy and unfamiliar. She had spent so much time preparing for death
there was no need for bringing it up again. Let it take care of itself now.
When she was sixty she had felt very old, finished, and went around making farewell trips to see her children and grandchildren, with a secret in her
mind: This is the very last of your mother, children! Then she made her will
and came down with a long fever. That was all just a notion like a lot of
other things, but it was lucky too, for she had once for all got over the idea
of dying for a long time. Now she couldn't be worried. She hoped she had
better sense now. Her father had lived to be one hundred and two years old
and had drunk a noggin of strong hot toddy on his last birthday. He told the
reporters it was his daily habit, and he owed his long life to it. He had made
quite a scandal and was very pleased about it. She believed she'd just plague
Cornelia a little.

"Cornelia! Cornelia!" No footsteps, but a sudden hand on her cheek.
"Bless you, where have you been?"

"Here, Mother."   20

"Well, Cornelia, I want a noggin of hot toddy."

"Are you cold, darling?"

"I'm chilly, Cornelia. Lying in bed stops the circulation. I must have told
you that a thousand times."

Well, she could just hear Cornelia telling her husband that Mother was
getting a little childish and they'd have to humor her. The thing that most
annoyed her was that Cornelia thought she was deaf, dumb, and blind. Little hasty glances and tiny gestures tossed around her and over her head saying, "Don't cross her, let her have her way, she's eighty years old," and she
sitting there as if she lived in a thin glass cage. Sometimes Granny almost
made up her mind to pack up and move back to her own house where
nobody could remind her every minute that she was old. Wait, wait, Cornelia, till your own children whisper behind your back!

In her day she had kept a better house and had got more work done.   25
She wasn't too old yet for Lydia to be driving eighty miles for advice when
one of the children jumped the track, and Jimmy still dropped in and talked
things over: "Now, Mammy, you've a good business head, I want to know
what you think of this? . . ." Old. Cornelia couldn't change the furniture
around without asking. Little things, little things! They had been so sweet
when they were little. Granny wished the old days were back again with
the children young and everything to be done over. It had been a hard pull,
but not too much for her. When she thought of all the food she had cooked,
and all the clothes she had cut and sewed, and all the gardens she had
made—well, the children showed it. There they were, made out of her, and
they couldn't get away from that. Sometimes she wanted to see John again
and point to them and say, Well, I didn't do so badly, did I? But that would
have to wait. That was for tomorrow. She used to think of him as a man, but
now all the children were older than their father, and he would be a child
beside her if she saw him now. It seemed strange and there was something
wrong in the idea. Why, he couldn't possibly recognize her. She had fenced
in a hundred acres once, digging the post holes herself and clamping the
wires with just a negro boy to help. That changed a woman. John would be
looking for a young woman with the peaked Spanish comb in her hair and
the painted fan. Digging post holes changed a woman. Riding country roads
in the winter when women had their babies was another thing: sitting up
nights with sick horses and sick negroes and sick children and hardly ever
losing one. John, I hardly ever lost one of them! John would see that in a
minute, that would be something he could understand, she wouldn't have
to explain anything!

It made her feel like rolling up her sleeves and putting the whole place
to rights again. No matter if Cornelia was determined to be everywhere at
once, there were a great many things left undone on this place. She would
start tomorrow and do them. It was good to be strong enough for everything, even if all you made melted and changed and slipped under your
hands, so that by the time you finished you almost forgot what you were
working for. What was it I set out to do? she asked herself intently, but she
could not remember. A fog rose over the valley, she saw it marching across
the creek swallowing the trees and moving up the hill like an army of
ghosts. Soon it would be at the near edge of the orchard, and then it was
time to go in and light the lamps. Come in, children, don't stay out in the
night air.

Lighting the lamps had been beautiful. The children huddled up to her
and breathed like little calves waiting at the bars in the twilight. Their eyes
followed the match and watched the flame rise and settle in a blue curve,
then they moved away from her. The lamp was lit, they didn't have to be

scared and hang on to mother any more. Never, never, never more. God, for all my life I thank Thee. Without Thee, my God, I could never have done it. Hail, Mary, full of grace.

I want you to pick all the fruit this year and see that nothing is wasted. There's always someone who can use it. Don't let good things rot for want of using. You waste life when you waste good food. Don't let things get lost. It's bitter to lose things. Now, don't let me get to thinking, not when I am tired and taking a little nap before supper. . . .

The pillow rose about her shoulders and pressed against her heart and the memory was being squeezed out of it: oh, push down the pillow, some-body: it would smother her if she tried to hold it. Such a fresh breeze blow-ing and such a green day with no threats in it. But he had not come, just the same. What does a woman do when she has put on the white veil and set out the white cake for a man and he doesn't come? She tried to remember. No, I swear he never harmed me but in that. He never harmed me but in that . . . and what if he did? There was the day, the day, but a whirl of dark smoke rose and covered it, crept up and over into the bright field where everything was planted so carefully in orderly rows. That was hell, she knew hell when she saw it. For sixty years she had prayed against remembering him and against losing her soul in the deep pit of hell, and now the two things were mingled in one and the thought of him was a smoky cloud from hell that moved and crept in her head when she had just got rid of Doctor Harry and was trying to rest a minute. Wounded vanity, Ellen, said a sharp voice in the top of her mind. Don't let your wounded vanity get the upper hand of you. Plenty of girls get jilted. You were jilted, weren't you? Then stand up to it. Her eyelids wavered and let in streamers of blue-gray light like tissue paper over her eyes. She must get up and pull the shades down or she'd never sleep. She was in bed again and the shades were not down. How could that happen? Better turn over, hide from the light, sleeping in the light gave you nightmares. "Mother, how do you feel now?" and a stinging wetness on her forehead. But I don't like having my face washed in cold water!

Hapsy? George? Lydia? Jimmy? No, Cornelia, and her features were   30
swollen and full of little puddles. "They're coming, darling, they'll all be here soon." Go wash your face, child, you look funny.

Instead of obeying, Cornelia knelt down and put her head on the pil-low. She seemed to be talking but there was no sound. "Well, are you tongue-tied? Whose birthday is it? Are you going to give a party?"

Cornelia's mouth moved urgently in strange shapes. "Don't do that, you bother me, daughter."

"Oh, no, Mother. Oh, no. . . ."

Nonsense. It was strange about children. They disputed your every word. "No what, Cornelia?"

"Here's Doctor Harry."   35

"I won't see that boy again. He just left three minutes ago."

"That was this morning, Mother. It's night now. Here's the nurse."

"This is Doctor Harry, Mrs. Weatherall. I never saw you look so young and happy!"

"Ah, I'll never be young again—but I'd be happy if they'd let me lie in peace and get rested."

She thought she spoke up loudly, but no one answered. A warm weight on her forehead, a warm bracelet on her wrist, and a breeze went on

whispering, trying to tell her something. A shuffle of leaves in the everlast-   40
ing hand of God. He blew on them and they danced and rattled. "Mother,
don't mind, we're going to give you a little hypodermic." "Look here, daughter, how do ants get in this bed? I saw sugar ants yesterday." Did you send for
Hapsy too?

It was Hapsy she really wanted. She had to go a long way back through
a great many rooms to find Hapsy standing with a baby on her arm. She
seemed to herself to be Hapsy also, and the baby on Hapsy's arm was Hapsy
and himself and herself, all at once, and there was no surprise in the meeting. Then Hapsy melted from within and turned flimsy as gray gauze and
the baby was a gauzy shadow, and Hapsy came up close and said, "I thought
you'd never come," and looked at her very searchingly and said, "You
haven't changed a bit!" They leaned forward to kiss, when Cornelia began
whispering from a long way off, "Oh, is there anything you want to tell me?
Is there anything I can do for you?"

Yes, she had changed her mind after sixty years and she would like to
see George. I want you to find George. Find him and be sure to tell him I forgot him. I want him to know I had my husband just the same and my children and my house like any other woman. A good house too and a good
husband that I loved and fine children out of him. Better than I hoped for
even. Tell him I was given back everything he took away and more. Oh, no,
oh, God, no, there was something else besides the house and the man and
the children. Oh, surely they were not all? What was it? Something not
given back . . . Her breath crowded down under her ribs and grew into a
monstrous frightening shape with cutting edges; it bored up into her head,
and the agony was unbelievable: Yes, John, get the Doctor now, no more
talk, my time has come.

When this one was born it should be the last. The last. It should have
been born first, for it was the one she had truly wanted. Everything came in
good time. Nothing left out, left over. She was strong, in three days she
would be as well as ever. Better. A woman needed milk in her to have her
full health.

"Mother, do you hear me?"

"I've been telling you—"   45

"Mother, Father Connolly's here."

"I went to Holy Communion only last week. Tell him I'm not so sinful
as all that."

"Father just wants to speak to you."

He could speak as much as he pleased. It was like him to drop in and
inquire about her soul as if it were a teething baby, and then stay on for a
cup of tea and a round of cards and gossip. He always had a funny story of
some sort, usually about an Irishman who made his little mistakes and confessed them, and the point lay in some absurd thing he would blurt out in
the confessional showing his struggles between native piety and original
sin. Granny felt easy about her soul. Cornelia, where are your manners? Give
Father Connolly a chair. She had her secret comfortable understanding with
a few favorite saints who cleared a straight road to God for her. All as surely
signed and sealed as the papers for the new Forty Acres. Forever . . . heirs
and assigns forever. Since the day the wedding cake was not cut, but
thrown out and wasted. The whole bottom dropped out of the world, and
there she was blind and sweating with nothing under her feet and the walls

falling away. His hand had caught her under the breast, she had not fallen, there was the freshly polished floor with the green rug on it, just as before. He had cursed like a sailor's parrot and said, "I'll kill him for you." Don't lay a hand on him, for my sake leave something to God. "Now, Ellen, you must believe what I tell you. . . ."

So there was nothing, nothing to worry about any more, except some- 50 times in the night one of the children screamed in a nightmare, and they both hustled out shaking and hunting for the matches and calling, "There, wait a minute, here we are!" John, get the doctor now, Hapsy's time has come. But there was Hapsy standing by the bed in a white cap. "Cornelia, tell Hapsy to take off her cap. I can't see her plain."

Her eyes opened very wide and the room stood out like a picture she had seen somewhere. Dark colors with the shadows rising towards the ceiling in long angles. The tall black dresser gleamed with nothing on it but John's picture, enlarged from a little one, with John's eyes very black when they should have been blue. You never saw him, so how do you know how he looked? But the man insisted the copy was perfect, it was very rich and handsome. For a picture, yes, but it's not my husband. The table by the bed had a linen cover and a candle and a crucifix. The light was blue from Cornelia's silk lampshades. No sort of light at all, just frippery. You had to live forty years with kerosene lamps to appreciate honest electricity. She felt very strong and she saw Doctor Harry with a rosy nimbus around him.

"You look like a saint, Doctor Harry, and I vow that's as near as you'll ever come to it."

"She's saying something."

"I heard you, Cornelia. What's all this carrying-on?"

"Father Connolly's saying—" 55

Cornelia's voice staggered and bumped like a cart in a bad road. It rounded corners and turned back again and arrived nowhere. Granny stepped up in the cart very lightly and reached for the reins, but a man sat beside her and she knew him by his hands, driving the cart. She did not look in his face, for she knew without seeing, but looked instead down the road where the trees leaned over and bowed to each other and a thousand birds were singing a Mass. She felt like singing too, but she put her hand in the bosom of her dress and pulled out a rosary, and Father Connolly murmured Latin in a very solemn voice and tickled her feet. My God, will you stop that nonsense? I'm a married woman. What if he did run away and leave me to face the priest by myself? I found another a whole world better. I wouldn't have exchanged my husband for anybody except St. Michael himself, and you may tell him that for me with a thank you in the bargain.

Light flashed on her closed eyelids, and a deep roaring shook her. Cornelia, is that lightning? I hear thunder. There's going to be a storm. Close all the windows. Call the children in. . . . "Mother, here we are, all of us." "Is that you, Hapsy?" "Oh, no, I'm Lydia. We drove as fast as we could." Their faces drifted above her, drifted away. The rosary fell out of her hands and Lydia put it back. Jimmy tried to help, their hands fumbled together, and Granny closed two fingers around Jimmy's thumb. Beads wouldn't do, it must be something alive. She was so amazed her thoughts ran round and round. So, my dear Lord, this is my death and I wasn't even thinking about it. My children have come to see me die. But I can't, it's not time. Oh, I always hated surprises. I wanted to give Cornelia the amethyst set—

Cornelia, you're to have the amethyst set, but Hapsy's to wear it when she wants, and, Doctor Harry, do shut up. Nobody sent for you. Oh, my dear Lord, do wait a minute. I meant to do something about the Forty Acres, Jimmy doesn't need it and Lydia will later on, with that worthless husband of hers. I meant to finish the altar cloth and send six bottles of wine to Sister Borgia for her dyspepsia. I want to send six bottles of wine to Sister Borgia, Father Connolly, now don't let me forget.

Cornelia's voice made short turns and tilted over and crashed, "Oh, Mother, oh, Mother, oh, Mother. . . ."

"I'm not going, Cornelia. I'm taken by surprise. I can't go."

You'll see Hapsy again. What about her? "I thought you'd never come." Granny made a long journey outward, looking for Hapsy. What if I don't find her? What then? Her heart sank down and down, there was no bottom to death, she couldn't come to the end of it. The blue light from Cornelia's lampshade drew into a tiny point in the center of her brain, it flickered and winked like an eye, quietly it fluttered and dwindled. Granny lay curled down within herself, amazed and watchful, staring at the point of light that was herself; her body was now only a deeper mass of shadow in an endless darkness and this darkness would curl around the light and swallow it up. God, give a sign!

For the second time there was no sign. Again no bridegroom and the priest in the house. She could not remember any other sorrow because this grief wiped them all away. Oh, no, there's nothing more cruel than this—I'll never forgive it. She stretched herself with a deep breath and blew out the light.

60

[1930]

JOHN STEINBECK (1902–1968)

Born in Salinas, California, John Steinbeck left his studies at Stanford University to pursue a writing career. His first three novels received very little attention; but Tortilla Flat *(1935) and* The Grapes of Wrath *(1939) brought success and acclaim, including the Pulitzer Prize. He worked as a war correspondent during World War II, and in 1962 he won the Nobel Prize for Literature.*

The Chrysanthemums

The high grey-flannel fog of winter closed off the Salinas Valley from the sky and from all the rest of the world. On every side it sat like a lid on the mountains and made of the great valley a closed pot. On the broad, level land floor the gang plows bit deep and left the black earth shining like metal where the shares had cut. On the foothill ranches across the Salinas River, the yellow stubble fields seemed to be bathed in pale cold sunshine, but there was no sunshine in the valley now in December. The thick willow scrub along the river flamed with sharp and positive yellow leaves.

It was a time of quiet and of waiting. The air was cold and tender. A light wind blew up from the southwest so that the farmers were mildly hopeful of a good rain before long; but fog and rain do not go together.

Across the river, on Henry Allen's foothill ranch there was little work to be done, for the hay was cut and stored and the orchards were plowed up to receive the rain deeply when it should come. The cattle on the higher slopes were becoming shaggy and rough-coated.

Elisa Allen, working in her flower garden, looked down across the yard and saw Henry, her husband, talking to two men in business suits. The three of them stood by the tractor shed, each man with one foot on the side of the little Fordson. They smoked cigarettes and studied the machine as they talked.

Elisa watched them for a moment and then went back to her work. She   5
was thirty-five. Her face was lean and strong and her eyes were as clear as water. Her figure looked blocked and heavy in her gardening costume, a man's black hat pulled low down over her eyes, clod-hopper shoes, a figured print dress almost completely covered by a big corduroy apron with four big pockets to hold the snips, the trowel and scratcher, the seeds and the knife she worked with. She wore heavy leather gloves to protect her hands while she worked.

She was cutting down the old year's chrysanthemum stalks with a pair of short and powerful scissors. She looked down toward the men by the tractor shed now and then. Her face was eager and mature and handsome; even her work with the scissors was over-eager, over-powerful. The chrysanthemum stems seemed too small and easy for her energy.

She brushed a cloud of hair out of her eyes with the back of her glove, and left a smudge of earth on her cheek in doing it. Behind her stood the neat white farm house with red geraniums close-banked around it as high as the windows. It was a hard-swept looking little house with hard-polished windows, and a clean mud-mat on the front steps.

Elisa cast another glance toward the tractor shed. The strangers were getting into their Ford coupe. She took off a glove and put her strong fingers down into the forest of new green chrysanthemum sprouts that were growing around the old roots. She spread the leaves and looked down among the close-growing stems. No aphids were there, no sowbugs or snails or cutworms. Her terrier fingers destroyed such pests before they could get started.

Elisa started at the sound of her husband's voice. He had come near quietly, and he leaned over the wire fence that protected her flower garden from cattle and dogs and chickens.

"At it again," he said. "You've got a strong new crop coming."   10

Elisa straightened her back and pulled on the gardening glove again. "Yes. They'll be strong this coming year." In her tone and on her face there was a little smugness.

"You've got a gift with things," Henry observed. "Some of those yellow chrysanthemums you had this year were ten inches across. I wish you'd work out in the orchard and raise some apples that big."

Her eyes sharpened. "Maybe I could do it, too. I've a gift with things, all right. My mother had it. She could stick anything in the ground and make it grow. She said it was having planters' hands that knew how to do it."

"Well, it sure works with flowers," he said.

"Henry, who were those men you were talking to?"   15

"Why, sure, that's what I came to tell you. They were from the Western Meat Company. I sold those thirty head of three-year-old steers. Got nearly my own price, too."

"Good," she said. "Good for you."

"And I thought," he continued, "I thought how it's Saturday afternoon, and we might go into Salinas for dinner at a restaurant, and then to a picture show—to celebrate, you see."

"Good," she repeated. "Oh, yes. That will be good."

Henry put on his joking tone. "There's fights tonight. How'd you like to go to the fights?"   20

"Oh, no," she said breathlessly. "No, I wouldn't like fights."

"Just fooling, Elisa. We'll go to a movie. Let's see. It's two now. I'm going to take Scotty and bring down those steers from the hill. It'll take us maybe two hours. We'll go in town about five and have dinner at the Cominos Hotel. Like that?"

"Of course I'll like it. It's good to eat away from home."

"All right, then. I'll go get up a couple of horses."

She said, "I'll have plenty of time to transplant some of these sets, I guess."   25

She heard her husband calling Scotty down by the barn. And a little later she saw the two men ride up the pale yellow hillside in search of the steers.

There was a little square sandy bed kept for rooting the chrysanthemums. With her trowel she turned the soil over and over, and smoothed it and patted it firm. Then she dug ten parallel trenches to receive the sets. Back at the chrysanthemum bed she pulled out the little crisp shoots, trimmed off the leaves of each one with her scissors and laid it on a small orderly pile.

A squeak of wheels and plod of hoofs came from the road. Elisa looked up. The country road ran along the dense bank of willows and cotton-woods that bordered the river, and up this road came a curious vehicle, curiously drawn. It was an old spring-wagon, with a round canvas top on it like the cover of a prairie schooner. It was drawn by an old bay horse and a little grey-and-white burro. A big stubble-bearded man sat between the cover flaps and drove the crawling team. Underneath the wagon, between the hind wheels, a lean and rangy mongrel dog walked sedately. Words were painted on the canvas, in clumsy, crooked letters. "Pots, pans, knives, sisors, lawn mores, Fixed." Two rows of articles, and the triumphantly definitive "Fixed" below. The black paint had run down in little sharp points beneath each letter.

Elisa, squatting on the ground, watched to see the crazy, loose-jointed wagon pass by. But it didn't pass. It turned into the farm road in front of her house, crooked old wheels skirling and squeaking. The rangy dog darted from between the wheels and ran ahead. Instantly the two ranch shepherds flew out at him. Then all three stopped, and with stiff and quivering tails, with taut straight legs, with ambassadorial dignity, they slowly circled, sniffing daintily. The caravan pulled up to Elisa's wire fence and stopped. Now the newcomer dog, feeling out-numbered, lowered his tail and retired under the wagon with raised hackles and bared teeth.

The man on the wagon seat called out, "That's a bad dog in a fight when he gets started."   30

Elisa laughed. "I see he is. How soon does he generally get started?"

The man caught up her laughter and echoed it heartily. "Sometimes not for weeks and weeks," he said. He climbed stiffly down, over the wheel. The horse and the donkey drooped like unwatered flowers.

Elisa saw that he was a very big man. Although his hair and beard were greying, he did not look old. His worn black suit was wrinkled and spotted with grease. The laughter had disappeared from his face and eyes the moment his laughing voice ceased. His eyes were dark, and they were full of the brooding that gets in the eyes of teamsters and of sailors. The calloused hands he rested on the wire fence were cracked, and every crack was a black line. He took off his battered hat.

"I'm off my general road, ma'am," he said. "Does this dirt road cut over across the river to the Los Angeles highway?"

Elisa stood up and shoved the thick scissors in her apron pocket. "Well, yes, it does, but it winds around and then fords the river. I don't think your team could pull through the sand."   35

He replied with some asperity. "It might surprise you what them beasts can pull through."

"When they get started?" she asked.

He smiled for a second. "Yes. When they get started."

"Well," said Elisa, "I think you'll save time if you go back to the Salinas road and pick up the highway there."

He drew a big finger down the chicken wire and made it sing. "I ain't   40
in any hurry, ma'am. I go from Seattle to San Diego and back every year. Takes all my time. About six months each way. I aim to follow nice weather."

Elisa took off her gloves and stuffed them in the apron pocket with the scissors. She touched the under edge of her man's hat, searching for fugitive hairs. "That sounds like a nice kind of a way to live," she said.

He leaned confidentially over the fence. "Maybe you noticed the writing on my wagon. I mend pots and sharpen knives and scissors. You got any of them things to do?"

"Oh, no," she said quickly. "Nothing like that." Her eyes hardened with resistance.

"Scissors is the worst thing," he explained. "Most people just ruin scissors trying to sharpen 'em, but I know how. I got a special tool. It's a little bobbit kind of thing, and patented. But it sure does the trick."

"No. My scissors are all sharp."   45

"All right, then. Take a pot," he continued earnestly, "a bent pot, or a pot with a hole. I can make it like new so you don't have to buy no new ones. That's a saving for you."

"No," she said shortly. "I tell you I have nothing like that for you to do."

His face fell to an exaggerated sadness. His voice took on a whining undertone. "I ain't had a thing to do today. Maybe I won't have no supper tonight. You see I'm off my regular road. I know folks on the highway clear from Seattle to San Diego. They save their things for me to sharpen up because they know I do it so good and save them money."

"I'm sorry," Elisa said irritably. "I haven't anything for you to do."

His eyes left her face and fell to searching the ground. They roamed   50
about until they came to the chrysanthemum bed where she had been working. "What's them plants, ma'am?"

The irritation and resistance melted from Elisa's face. "Oh, those are chrysanthemums, giant whites and yellows. I raise them every year, bigger than anybody around here."

"Kind of a long-stemmed flower? Looks like a quick puff of colored smoke?" he asked.

"That's it. What a nice way to describe them."

"They smell kind of nasty till you get used to them," he said.

"It's a good bitter smell," she retorted, "not nasty at all."   55

He changed his tone quickly. "I like the smell myself."

"I had ten-inch blooms this year," she said.

The man leaned farther over the fence. "Look. I know a lady down the road a piece, has got the nicest garden you ever seen. Got nearly every kind of flower but no chrysanthemums. Last time I was mending a copper-bottom washtub for her (that's a hard job but I do it good), she said to me, 'If you ever run acrost some nice chrysanthemums I wish you'd try to get me a few seeds.' That's what she told me."

Elisa's eyes grew alert and eager. "She couldn't have known much about chrysanthemums. You *can* raise them from seed, but it's much easier to root the little sprouts you see there."

"Oh," he said. "I s'pose I can't take none to her, then."   60

"Why yes you can," Elisa cried. "I can put some in damp sand, and you can carry them right along with you. They'll take root in the pot if you keep them damp. And then she can transplant them."

"She's sure like to have some, ma'am. You say they're nice ones?"

"Beautiful," she said. "Oh, beautiful." Her eyes shone. She tore off the battered hat and shook out her dark pretty hair. "I'll put them in a flower pot, and you can take them right with you. Come into the yard."

While the man came through the picket gate Elisa ran excitedly along the geranium-bordered path to the back of the house. And she returned carrying a big red flower pot. The gloves were forgotten now. She kneeled on the ground by the starting bed and dug up the sandy soil with her fingers and scooped it into the bright new flower pot. Then she picked up the little pile of shoots she had prepared. With her strong fingers she pressed them in the sand and tamped around them with her knuckles. The man stood over her. "I'll tell you what to do," she said. "You remember so you can tell the lady."

"Yes, I'll try to remember."   65

"Well, look. These will take root in about a month. Then she must set them out, about a foot apart in good rich earth like this, see?" She lifted a handful of dark soil for him to look at. "They'll grow fast and tall. Now remember this: In July tell her to cut them down, about eight inches from the ground."

"Before they bloom?" he asked.

"Yes, before they bloom." Her face was tight with eagerness. "They'll grow right up again. About the last of September the buds will start."

She stopped and seemed perplexed. "It's the budding that takes the most care," she said hesitantly. "I don't know how to tell you." She looked deep into his eyes, searchingly. Her mouth opened a little, and she seemed to be listening. "I'll try to tell you," she said, "Did you ever hear of planting hands?"

"Can't say I have, ma'am."   70

"Well, I can only tell you what it feels like. It's when you're picking off the buds you don't want. Everything goes right down into your fingertips. You watch your fingers work. They do it themselves. You can feel how it is. They pick and pick the buds. They never make a mistake. They're with the plant. Do you see? Your fingers and the plant. You can feel that, right up your arm. They know. They never make a mistake. You can feel it. When you're like that you can't do anything wrong. Do you see that? Can you understand that?"

She was kneeling on the ground looking up at him. Her breast swelled passionately.

The man's eyes narrowed. He looked away self-consciously. "Maybe I know," he said. "Sometimes in the night in the wagon there—"

Elisa's voice grew husky. She broke in on him, "I've never lived as you do, but I know what you mean. When the night is dark—why, the stars are sharp-pointed, and there's quiet. Why, you rise up and up! Every pointed star gets driven into your body. It's like that. Hot and sharp and—lovely."

Kneeling there, her hand went out toward his legs in the greasy black   75
trousers. Her hesitant fingers almost touched the cloth. Then her hand dropped to the ground. She crouched low like a fawning dog.

He said, "It's nice, just like you say. Only when you don't have no dinner, it ain't."

She stood up then, very straight, and her face was ashamed. She held the flower pot out to him and placed it gently in his arms. "Here. Put it in your wagon, on the seat, where you can watch it. Maybe I can find something for you to do."

At the back of the house she dug in the can pile and found two old and battered aluminum saucepans. She carried them back and gave them to him. "Here, maybe you can fix these."

His manner changed. He became professional. "Good as new I can fix them." At the back of his wagon he set a little anvil, and out of an oily tool box dug a small machine hammer. Elisa came through the gate to watch him while he pounded out the dents in the kettles. His mouth grew sure and knowing. At a difficult part of the work he sucked in his under-lip.

"You sleep right in the wagon?" Elisa asked.   80

"Right in the wagon, ma'am. Rain or shine I'm dry as a cow in there."

"It must be nice," she said. "It must be very nice. I wish women could do such things."

"It ain't the right kind of life for a woman."

Her upper lip raised a little, showing her teeth. "How do you know? How can you tell?" she said.

"I don't know, ma'am," he protested. "Of course I don't know. Now   85
here's your kettles, done. You don't have to buy no new ones."

"How much?"

"Oh, fifty cents'll do. I keep my prices down and my work good. That's why I have all them satisfied customers up and down the highway."

Elisa brought him a fifty-cent piece from the house and dropped it in his hand. "You might be surprised to have a rival some time. I can sharpen scissors, too. And I can beat the dents out of little pots. I could show you what a woman might do."

He put his hammer back in the oily box and shoved the little anvil out of sight. "It would be a lonely life for a woman, ma'am, and a scary life, too, with animals creeping under the wagon all night." He climbed over the singletree, steadying himself with a hand on the burro's white rump. He settled himself in the seat, picked up the lines. "Thank you kindly, ma'am," he said. "I'll do like you told me; I'll go back and catch the Salinas road."

"Mind," she called, "if you're long in getting there, keep the sand damp."   90

"Sand, ma'am? . . . Sand? Oh, sure. You mean around the chrysanthemums. Sure I will." He clucked his tongue. The beasts leaned luxuriously into their collars. The mongrel dog took his place between the back wheels. The wagon turned and crawled out the entrance road and back the way it had come, along the river.

Elisa stood in front of her wire fence watching the slow progress of the caravan. Her shoulders were straight, her head thrown back, her eyes half-closed, so that the scene came vaguely into them. Her lips moved silently, forming the words "Good-bye—good-bye." Then she whispered, "That's a bright direction. There's a glowing there." The sound of her whisper startled her. She shook herself free and looked about to see whether anyone had been listening. Only the dogs had heard. They lifted their heads toward her from their sleeping in the dust, and then stretched out their chins and settled asleep again. Elisa turned and ran hurriedly into the house.

In the kitchen she reached behind the stove and felt the water tank. It was full of hot water from the noonday cooking. In the bathroom she tore off her soiled clothes and flung them into the corner. And then she scrubbed herself with a little block of pumice, legs and thighs, loins and chest and arms, until her skin was scratched and red. When she had dried herself she stood in front of a mirror in her bedroom and looked at her body. She tightened her stomach and threw out her chest. She turned and looked over her shoulder at her back.

After a while she began to dress, slowly. She put on her newest under-clothing and her nicest stockings and the dress which was the symbol of her prettiness. She worked carefully on her hair, penciled her eyebrows and rouged her lips.

Before she was finished she heard the little thunder of hoofs and the shouts of Henry and his helper as they drove the red steers into the corral. She heard the gate bang shut and set herself for Henry's arrival.   95

His step sounded on the porch. He entered the house calling, "Elisa, where are you?"

"In my room, dressing. I'm not ready. There's hot water for your bath. Hurry up. It's getting late."

When she heard him splashing in the tub, Elisa laid his dark suit on the bed, and shirt and socks and tie beside it. She stood his polished shoes on the floor beside the bed. Then she went to the porch and sat primly and stiffly down. She looked toward the river road where the willow-line was still yellow with frosted leaves so that under the high grey fog they seemed a thin band of sunshine. This was the only color in the grey afternoon. She sat unmoving for a long time. Her eyes blinked rarely.

Henry came banging out of the door, shoving his tie inside his vest as he came. Elisa stiffened and her face grew tight. Henry stopped short and looked at her. "Why—why, Elisa. You look so nice!"

"Nice? You think I look nice? What do you mean by 'nice'?"   100

Henry blundered on. "I don't know. I mean you look different, strong and happy."

"I am strong? Yes, strong. What do you mean 'strong'?"

He looked bewildered. "You're playing some kind of a game," he said helplessly. "It's a kind of a play. You look strong enough to break a calf over your knee, happy enough to eat it like a watermelon."

For a second she lost her rigidity. "Henry! Don't talk like that. You didn't know what you said." She grew complete again. "I'm strong," she boasted. "I never knew before how strong."

Henry looked down toward the tractor shed, and when he brought his   105
eyes back to her, they were his own again. "I'll get out the car. You can put
on your coat while I'm starting."

Elisa went into the house. She heard him drive to the gate and idle
down his motor, and then she took a long time to put on her hat. She pulled
it here and pressed it there. When Henry turned the motor off she slipped
into her coat and went out.

The little roadster bounced along on the dirt road by the river, raising
the birds and driving the rabbits into the brush. Two cranes flapped heavily over the willow-line and dropped into the river-bed.

Far ahead on the road Elisa saw a dark speck. She knew.

She tried not to look as they passed it, but her eyes would not obey. She
whispered to herself sadly, "He might have thrown them off the road. That
wouldn't have been much trouble, not very much. But he kept the pot," she
explained. "He had to keep the pot. That's why he couldn't get them off the
road."

The roadster turned a bend and she saw the caravan ahead. She swung   110
full around toward her husband so she could not see the little covered
wagon and the mismatched team as the car passed them.

In a moment it was over. The thing was done. She did not look back.

She said loudly, to be heard above the motor, "It will be good, tonight, a
good dinner."

"Now you're changed again," Henry complained. He took one hand
from the wheel and patted her knee. "I ought to take you to dinner oftener.
It would be good for both of us. We get so heavy out on the ranch."

"Henry," she asked, "could we have wine at dinner?"

"Sure we could. Say! That will be fine."   115

She was silent for a while; then she said, "Henry, at those prize fights, do
the men hurt each other very much?"

"Sometimes a little, not often. Why?"

"Well, I've read how they break noses, and blood runs down their
chests. I've read how the fighting gloves get heavy and soggy with blood."

He looked around at her. "What's the matter, Elisa? I didn't know you
read things like that." He brought the car to a stop, then turned to the right
over the Salinas River bridge.

"Do any women ever go to the fights?" she asked.   120

"Oh, sure, some. What's the matter, Elisa? Do you want to go? I don't
think you'd like it, but I'll take you if you really want to go."

She relaxed limply in the seat. "Oh, no. No. I don't want to go. I'm sure
I don't." Her face was turned away from him. "It will be enough if we can
have wine. It will be plenty." She turned up her coat collar so he could not
see that she was crying weakly—like an old woman.

[1936]

AMY TAN (1952–)

*Amy Tan was born in Oakland, California, a few years after her parents immigrated from
China. After graduating from high school in Switzerland, she received her M.A. in linguistics
from San Jose State University. She made her living as a business writer and began writing the
stories that would become her first novel,* The Joy Luck Club, *which won the National Book*

Award and the L.A. Times Book Award in 1989. She has published three novels and two books for children.

Two Kinds

My mother believed you could be anything you wanted to be in America. You could open a restaurant. You could work for the government and get good retirement. You could buy a house with almost no money down. You could become rich. You could become instantly famous.

"Of course you can be prodigy, too," my mother told me when I was nine. "You can be best anything. What does Auntie Lindo know? Her daughter, she is only best tricky."

America was where all my mother's hopes lay. She had come here in 1949 after losing everything in China: her mother and father, her family home, her first husband, and two daughters, twin baby girls. But she never looked back with regret. There were so many ways for things to get better.

We didn't immediately pick the right kind of prodigy. At first my mother thought I could be a Chinese Shirley Temple. We'd watch Shirley's old movies on TV as though they were training films. My mother would poke my arm and say, "*Ni kan.*" —You watch. And I would see Shirley tapping her feet, or singing a sailor song, or pursing her lips into a very round O while saying "Oh, my goodness."

"*Ni kan*," said my mother as Shirley's eyes flooded with tears. "You already know how. Don't need talent for crying!"   5

Soon after my mother got this idea about Shirley Temple, she took me to a beauty training school in the Mission district and put me in the hands of a student who could barely hold the scissors without shaking. Instead of getting big fat curls, I emerged with an uneven mass of crinkly black fuzz. My mother dragged me off to the bathroom and tried to wet down my hair.

"You look like Negro Chinese," she lamented, as if I had done this on purpose.

The instructor of the beauty training school had to lop off these soggy clumps to make my hair even again. "Peter Pan is very popular these days," the instructor assured my mother. I now had hair the length of a boy's, with straight-across bangs that hung at a slant two inches above my eyebrows. I liked the haircut and it made me actually look forward to my future fame.

In fact, in the beginning, I was just as excited as my mother, maybe even more so. I pictured this prodigy part of me as many different images, trying each one on for size. I was a dainty ballerina girl standing by the curtains, waiting to hear the music that would send me floating on my tiptoes. I was like the Christ child lifted out of the straw manger, crying with holy indignity. I was Cinderella stepping from her pumpkin carriage with sparkly cartoon music filling the air.

In all of my imaginings, I was filled with a sense that I would soon   10
become *perfect.* My mother and father would adore me. I would be beyond reproach. I would never feel the need to sulk for anything.

But sometimes the prodigy in me became impatient. "If you don't hurry up and get me out of here, I'm disappearing for good," it warned. "And then you'll always be nothing."

Every night after dinner, my mother and I would sit at the Formica kitchen table. She would present new tests, taking her examples from stories of amazing children she had read in *Ripley's Believe It or Not,* or *Good House-keeping, Reader's Digest,* and a dozen other magazines she kept in a pile in our bathroom. My mother got these magazines from people whose houses she cleaned. And since she cleaned many houses each week, we had a great assortment. She would look through them all, searching for stories about remarkable children.

The first night she brought out a story about a three-year-old boy who knew the capitals of all the states and even most of the European countries. A teacher was quoted as saying the little boy could also pronounce the names of the foreign cities correctly.

"What's the capital of Finland?" my mother asked me, looking at the magazine story.

All I knew was the capital of California, because Sacramento was the name of the street we lived on in Chinatown. "Nairobi!" I guessed, saying the most foreign word I could think of. She checked to see if that was possibly one way to pronounce "Helsinki" before showing me the answer.

The tests got harder—multiplying numbers in my head, finding the queen of hearts in a deck of cards, trying to stand on my head without using my hands, predicting the daily temperatures in Los Angeles, New York, and London.

One night I had to look at a page from the Bible for three minutes and then report everything I could remember. "Now Jehoshaphat had riches and honor in abundance and . . . that's all I remember, Ma," I said.

And after seeing my mother's disappointed face once again, something inside of me began to die. I hated the tests, the raised hopes and failed expectations. Before going to bed that night, I looked in the mirror above the bathroom sink and when I saw only my face staring back—and that it would always be this ordinary face—I began to cry. Such a sad, ugly girl! I made high-pitched noises like a crazed animal, trying to scratch out the face in the mirror.

And then I saw what seemed to be the prodigy side of me—because I had never seen that face before. I looked at my reflection, blinking so I could see more clearly. The girl staring back at me was angry, powerful. This girl and I were the same. I had new thoughts, willful thoughts, or rather thoughts filled with lots of won'ts. I won't let her change me, I promised myself. I won't be what I'm not.

So now on nights when my mother presented her tests, I performed listlessly, my head propped on one arm. I pretended to be bored. And I was. I got so bored I started counting the bellows of the foghorns out on the bay while my mother drilled me in other areas. The sound was comforting and reminded me of the cow jumping over the moon. And the next day, I played a game with myself, seeing if my mother would give up on me before eight bellows. After a while I usually counted only one, maybe two bellows at most. At last she was beginning to give up hope.

Two or three months had gone by without any mention of my being a prodigy again. And then one day my mother was watching *The Ed Sullivan Show* on TV. The TV was old and the sound kept shorting out. Every time my mother got halfway up from the sofa to adjust the set, the sound would

15

20

go back on and Ed would be talking. As soon as she sat down, Ed would go silent again. She got up, the TV broke into loud piano music. She sat down. Silence. Up and down, back and forth, quiet and loud. It was like a stiff embraceless dance between her and the TV set. Finally she stood by the set with her hand on the sound dial.

She seemed entranced by the music, a little frenzied piano piece with this mesmerizing quality, sort of quick passages and then teasing lilting ones before it returned to the quick playful parts.

"*Ni kan,*" my mother said, calling me over with hurried hand gestures, "Look here."

I could see why my mother was fascinated by the music. It was being pounded out by a little Chinese girl, about nine years old, with a Peter Pan haircut. The girl had the sauciness of a Shirley Temple. She was proudly modest like a proper Chinese child. And she also did this fancy sweep of a curtsy, so that the fluffy skirt of her white dress cascaded slowly to the floor like the petals of a large carnation.

In spite of these warning signs, I wasn't worried. Our family had no   25 piano and we couldn't afford to buy one, let alone reams of sheet music and piano lessons. So I could be generous in my comments when my mother bad-mouthed the little girl on TV.

"Play note right, but doesn't sound good! No singing sound," my mother complained.

"What are you picking on her for?" I said carelessly. "She's pretty good. Maybe she's not the best, but she's trying hard." I knew almost immediately I would be sorry I said that.

"Just like you," she said. "Not the best. Because you not trying." She gave a little huff as she let go of the sound dial and sat down on the sofa.

The little Chinese girl sat down also to play an encore of "Anitra's Dance," by Grieg. I remember the song, because later on I had to learn how to play it.

Three days after watching *The Ed Sullivan Show,* my mother told me what   30 my schedule would be for piano lessons and piano practice. She had talked to Mr. Chong, who lived on the first floor of our apartment building. Mr. Chong was a retired piano teacher and my mother had traded housecleaning services for weekly lessons and a piano for me to practice on every day, two hours a day, from four until six.

When my mother told me this, I felt as though I had been sent to hell. I whined and then kicked my foot a little when I couldn't stand it anymore.

"Why don't you like me the way I am? I'm *not* a genius! I can't play the piano. And even if I could, I wouldn't go on TV if you paid me a million dollars!" I cried.

My mother slapped me. "Who ask you be genius?" she shouted. "Only ask you be your best. For you sake. You think I want you be genius? Hnnh! What for! Who ask you!"

"So ungrateful," I heard her mutter in Chinese. "If she had as much talent as she has temper, she would be famous now."

Mr. Chong, whom I secretly nicknamed Old Chong, was very strange,   35 always tapping his fingers to the silent music of an invisible orchestra. He looked ancient in my eyes. He had lost most of the hair on top of his head and he wore thick glasses and had eyes that always looked tired and sleepy.

But he must have been younger than I thought, since he lived with his mother and was not yet married.

I met Old Lady Chong once and that was enough. She had this peculiar smell like a baby that had done something in its pants. And her fingers felt like a dead person's, like an old peach I once found in the back of the refrigerator; the skin just slid off the meat when I picked it up.

I soon found out why Old Chong had retired from teaching piano. He was deaf. "Like Beethoven!" he shouted to me. "We're both listening only in our head!" And he would start to conduct his frantic silent sonatas.

Our lessons went like this. He would open the book and point to different things, explaining their purpose: "Key! Treble! Bass! No sharps or flats! So this is C major! Listen now and play after me!"

And then he would play the C scale a few times, a simple chord, and then, as if inspired by an old, unreachable itch, he gradually added more notes and running trills and a pounding bass until the music was really something quite grand.

I would play after him, the simple scale, the simple chord, and then I just played some nonsense that sounded like a cat running up and down on top of garbage cans. Old Chong smiled and applauded and then said, "Very good! But now you must learn to keep time!"

So that's how I discovered that Old Chong's eyes were too slow to keep up with the wrong notes I was playing. He went through the motions in half-time. To help me keep rhythm, he stood behind me, pushing down on my right shoulder for every beat. He balanced pennies on top of my wrists so I would keep them still as I slowly played scales and arpeggios. He had me curve my hand around an apple and keep that shape when playing chords. He marched stiffly to show me how to make each finger dance up and down, staccato like an obedient little soldier.

He taught me all these things, and that was how I also learned I could be lazy and get away with mistakes, lots of mistakes. If I hit the wrong notes because I hadn't practiced enough, I never corrected myself. I just kept playing in rhythm. And Old Chong kept conducting his own private reverie.

So maybe I never really gave myself a fair chance. I did pick up the basics pretty quickly, and I might have become a good pianist at that young age. But I was so determined not to try, not to be anybody different that I learned to play only the most ear-splitting preludes, the most discordant hymns.

Over the next year I practiced like this, dutifully in my own way. And then one day I heard my mother and her friend Lindo Jong both talking in a loud bragging tone of voice so others could hear. It was after church, and I was leaning against the brick wall wearing a dress with stiff white petticoats. Auntie Lindo's daughter, Waverly, who was about my age, was standing farther down the wall about five feet away. We had grown up together and shared all the closeness of two sisters squabbling over crayons and dolls. In other words, for the most part, we hated each other. I thought she was snotty. Waverly Jong had gained a certain amount of fame as "Chinatown's Littlest Chinese Chess Champion."

"She bring home too many trophy," lamented Auntie Lindo that Sunday. "All day she play chess. All day I have no time do nothing but dust off her winnings." She threw a scolding look at Waverly, who pretended not to see her.

"You lucky you don't have this problem," said Auntie Lindo with a sigh to my mother.

And my mother squared her shoulders and bragged: "Our problem worser than yours. If we ask Jing-mei wash dish, she hear nothing but music. It's like you can't stop this natural talent."

And right then, I was determined to put a stop to her foolish pride.

A few weeks later, Old Chong and my mother conspired to have me play in a talent show which would be held in the church hall. By then, my parents had saved up enough to buy me a secondhand piano, a black Wurlitzer spinet with a scarred bench. It was the showpiece of our living room.

For the talent show, I was to play a piece called "Pleading Child" from   50
Schumann's *Scenes from Childhood.* It was a simple, moody piece that sounded more difficult than it was. I was supposed to memorize the whole thing, playing the repeat parts twice to make the piece sound longer. But I dawdled over it, playing a few bars and then cheating, looking up to see what notes followed. I never really listened to what I was playing. I day-dreamed about being somewhere else, about being someone else.

The part I liked to practice best was the fancy curtsy: right foot out, touch the rose on the carpet with a pointed foot, sweep to the side, left leg bends, look up and smile.

My parents invited all the couples from the Joy Luck Club to witness my debut. Auntie Lindo and Uncle Tin were there. Waverly and her two older brothers had also come. The first two rows were filled with chil-dren both younger and older than I was. The littlest ones got to go first. They recited simple nursery rhymes, squawked out tunes on miniature violins, twirled Hula Hoops, pranced in pink ballet tutus, and when they bowed or curtsied, the audience would sigh in unison, "Awww," and then clap enthusiastically.

When my turn came, I was very confident. I remember my childish excitement. It was as if I knew, without a doubt, that the prodigy side of me really did exist. I had no fear whatsoever, no nervousness. I remember think-ing to myself, This is it! This is it! I looked out over the audience, at my mother's blank face, my father's yawn, Auntie Lindo's stiff-lipped smile, Waverly's sulky expression. I had on a white dress layered with sheets of lace, and a pink bow in my Peter Pan haircut. As I sat down I envisioned people jumping to their feet and Ed Sullivan rushing up to introduce me to everyone on TV.

And I started to play. It was so beautiful. I was so caught up in how love-ly I looked that at first I didn't worry how I would sound. So it was a surprise to me when I hit the first wrong note and I realized something didn't sound quite right. And then I hit another and another followed that. A chill start-ed at the top of my head and began to trickle down. Yet I couldn't stop play-ing, as though my hands were bewitched. I kept thinking my fingers would adjust themselves back, like a train switching to the right track. I played this strange jumble through two repeats, the sour notes staying with me all the way to the end.

When I stood up, I discovered my legs were shaking. Maybe I had just   55
been nervous and the audience, like Old Chong, had seen me go through the right motions and had not heard anything wrong at all. I swept my right foot out, went down on my knee, looked up and smiled. The room was quiet,

except for Old Chong, who was beaming and shouting, "Bravo! Bravo! Well done!" But then I saw my mother's face, her stricken face. The audience clapped weakly, and as I walked back to my chair, with my whole face quivering as I tried not to cry, I heard a little boy whisper loudly to his mother, "That was awful," and the mother whispered back, "Well, she certainly tried."

And now I realized how many people were in the audience, the whole world it seemed. I was aware of eyes burning into my back. I felt the shame of my mother and father as they sat stiffly throughout the rest of the show.

We could have escaped during intermission. Pride and some strange sense of honor must have anchored my parents to their chairs. And so we watched it all: the eighteen-year-old boy with a fake moustache who did a magic show and juggled flaming hoops while riding a unicycle. The breasted girl with white makeup who sang from *Madame Butterfly* and got honorable mention. And the eleven-year-old boy who won first prize playing a tricky violin song that sounded like a busy bee.

After the show, the Hsus, the Jongs, and the St. Clairs from the Joy Luck Club, came up to my mother and father.

"Lots of talented kids," Auntie Lindo said vaguely, smiling broadly.

"That was somethin' else," said my father, and I wondered if he was referring to me in a humorous way, or whether he even remembered what I had done.

Waverly looked at me and shrugged her shoulders. "You aren't a genius like me," she said matter-of-factly. And if I hadn't felt so bad, I would have pulled her braids and punched her stomach.

But my mother's expression was what devastated me: a quiet, blank look that said she had lost everything. I felt the same way, and it seemed as if everybody were now coming up, like gawkers at the scene of an accident, to see what parts were actually missing. When we got on the bus to go home, my father was humming the busy-bee tune and my mother was silent. I kept thinking she wanted to wait until we got home before shouting at me. But when my father unlocked the door to our apartment, my mother walked in and then went to the back, into the bedroom. No accusations. No blame. And in a way, I felt disappointed. I had been waiting for her to start shouting, so I could shout back and cry and blame her for all my misery.

I assumed my talent-show fiasco meant I never had to play the piano again. But two days later, after school, my mother came out of the kitchen and saw me watching TV.

"Four clock," she reminded me as if it were any other day. I was stunned, as though she were asking me to go through the talent-show torture again. I wedged myself more tightly in front of the TV.

"Turn off TV," she called from the kitchen five minutes later.

I didn't budge. And then I decided. I didn't have to do what my mother said anymore. I wasn't her slave. This wasn't China. I had listened to her before and look what happened. She was the stupid one.

She came out from the kitchen and stood in the arched entryway of the living room. "Four clock," she said once again, louder.

"I'm not going to play anymore," I said nonchalantly. "Why should I? I'm not a genius."

She walked over and stood in front of the TV. I saw her chest was heaving up and down in an angry way.

60

65

"No!" I said, and I now felt stronger, as if my true self had finally   70
emerged. So this was what had been inside me all along.

"No! I won't!" I screamed.

She yanked me by the arm, pulled me off the floor, snapped off the TV.
She was frighteningly strong, half pulling, half carrying me toward the
piano as I kicked the throw rugs under my feet. She lifted me up and onto
the hard bench. I was sobbing by now, looking at her bitterly. Her chest was
heaving even more and her mouth was open, smiling crazily as if she were
pleased I was crying.

"You want me to be someone that I'm not!" I sobbed. "I'll never be the
kind of daughter you want me to be!"

"Only two kinds of daughters," she shouted in Chinese. "Those who are
obedient and those who follow their own mind! Only one kind of daughter
can live in this house. Obedient daughter!"

"Then I wish I wasn't your daughter. I wish you weren't my mother," I   75
shouted. As I said these things I got scared. It felt like worms and toads and
slimy things crawling out of my chest, but it also felt good, as if this awful
side of me had surfaced, at last.

"Too late change this," said my mother shrilly.

And I could sense her anger rising to its breaking point. I wanted to see
it spill over. And that's when I remembered the babies she had lost in
China, the ones we never talked about. "Then I wish I'd never been born!"
I shouted. "I wish I were dead! Like them."

It was as if I had said the magic words. Alakazam!—and her face went
blank, her mouth closed, her arms went slack, and she backed out of the
room, stunned, as if she were blowing away like a small brown leaf, thin,
brittle, lifeless.

It was not the only disappointment my mother felt in me. In the years that
followed, I failed her so many times, each time asserting my own will, my
right to fall short of expectations. I didn't get straight As. I didn't become
class president. I didn't get into Stanford. I dropped out of college.

For unlike my mother, I did not believe I could be anything I wanted to   80
be. I could only be me.

And for all those years, we never talked about the disaster at the recital
or my terrible accusations afterward at the piano bench. All of that
remained unchecked, like a betrayal that was now unspeakable. So I never
found a way to ask her why she had hoped for something so large that failure was inevitable.

And even worse, I never asked her what frightened me the most: Why
had she given up hope?

For after our struggle at the piano, she never mentioned my playing
again. The lessons stopped. The lid to the piano was closed, shutting out the
dust, my misery, and her dreams.

So she surprised me. A few years ago, she offered to give me the piano,
for my thirtieth birthday. I had not played in all those years. I saw the offer
as a sign of forgiveness, a tremendous burden removed.

"Are you sure?" I asked shyly. "I mean, won't you and Dad miss it?"   85

"No, this your piano," she said firmly. "Always your piano. You only one
can play."

"Well, I probably can't play anymore," I said. "It's been years."

"You pick up fast," said my mother, as if she knew this was certain. "You have natural talent. You could been genius if you want to."

"No I couldn't."

"You just not trying," said my mother. And she was neither angry nor   90
sad. She said it as if to announce a fact that could never be disproved. "Take it," she said.

But I didn't at first. It was enough that she had offered it to me. And after that, every time I saw it in my parents' living room, standing in front of the bay windows, it made me feel proud, as if it were a shiny trophy I had won back.

Last week I sent a tuner over to my parents' apartment and had the piano reconditioned, for purely sentimental reasons. My mother had died a few months before and I had been getting things in order for my father, a little bit at a time. I put the jewelry in special silk pouches. The sweaters she had knitted in yellow, pink, bright orange—all the colors I hated—I put those in moth-proof boxes. I found some old Chinese silk dresses, the kind with little slits up the sides. I rubbed the old silk against my skin, then wrapped them in tissue and decided to take them home with me.

After I had the piano tuned, I opened the lid and touched the keys. It sounded even richer than I remembered. Really, it was a very good piano. Inside the bench were the same exercise notes with handwritten scales, the same secondhand music books with their covers held together with yellow tape.

I opened up the Schumann book to the dark little piece I had played at the recital. It was on the left-hand side of the page, "Pleading Child." It looked more difficult than I remembered. I played a few bars, surprised at how easily the notes came back to me.

And for the first time, or so it seemed, I noticed the piece on the right-   95
hand side. It was called "Perfectly Contented." I tried to play this one as well. It had a lighter melody but the same flowing rhythm and turned out to be quite easy. "Pleading Child" was shorter but slower; "Perfectly Contented" was longer, but faster. And after I played them both a few times, I realized they were two halves of the same song.

[1989]

James Thurber (1894–1961)

James Thurber was raised in Columbus, Ohio, the source for much of his fiction. He studied at Ohio State University, where he worked on the school newspaper. He then made his living as a journalist in Columbus, Paris, and the Riviera. Thurber later moved to New York City where he became managing editor of The New Yorker, *also publishing thousands of cartoons there. Despite being legally blind for most of his adult life, Thurber published over thirty books, two children's books, a play, and three memoirs.*

The Catbird Seat

Mr. Martin bought the pack of Camels on Monday night in the most crowded cigar store on Broadway. It was theater time and seven or eight men were buying cigarettes. The clerk didn't even glance at Mr. Martin, who put the pack in his overcoat pocket and went out. If any of the staff at F & S had seen him buy the cigarettes, they would have been astonished, for it was generally known that Mr. Martin did not smoke, and never had. No one saw him.

It was just a week to the day since Mr. Martin had decided to rub out Mrs. Ulgine Barrows. The term "rub out" pleased him because it suggested nothing more than the correction of an error—in this case an error of Mr. Fitweiler. Mr. Martin had spent each night of the past week working out his plan and examining it. As he walked home now he went over it again. For the hundredth time he resented the element of imprecision, the margin of guesswork that entered into the business. The project as he had worked it out was casual and bold, the risks were considerable. Something might go wrong anywhere along the line. And therein lay the cunning of his scheme. No one would ever see in it the cautious, painstaking hand of Erwin Martin, head of the filing department at F & S, of whom Mr. Fitweiler had once said "Man is fallible but Martin isn't." No one would see his hand, that is, unless it were caught in the act.

Sitting in his apartment, drinking a glass of milk, Mr. Martin reviewed his case against Mrs. Ulgine Barrows, as he had every night for seven nights. He began at the beginning. Her quacking voice and braying laugh had first profaned the halls of F & S on March 7, 1941 (Mr. Martin had a head for dates). Old Roberts, the personnel chief, had introduced her as the newly appointed special adviser to the president of the firm, Mr. Fitweiler. The woman had appalled Mr. Martin instantly, but he hadn't shown it. He had given her his dry hand, a look of studious concentration, and a faint smile. "Well," she had said, looking at the papers on his desk, "are you lifting the oxcart out of the ditch?" As Mr. Martin recalled that moment, over his milk, he squirmed slightly. He must keep his mind on her crimes as a special adviser, not on her peccadillos as a personality. This he found difficult to do, in spite of entering an objection and sustaining it. The faults of the woman as a woman kept chattering on in his mind like an unruly witness. She had, for almost two years now, baited him. In the halls, in the elevator, even in his own office, into which she romped now and then like a circus horse, she was constantly shouting these silly questions as him. "Are you lifting the oxcart out of the ditch? Are you tearing up the pea patch? Are you hollering down the rain barrel? Are you scraping around the bottom of the pickle barrel? Are you sitting in the catbird seat?"

It was Joey Hart, one of Mr. Martin's two assistants, who explained what the gibberish meant. "She must be a Dodger fan," he had said. "Red Barber announces the Dodger games over the radio and he uses those expressions—picked 'em up down South." Joey had gone on to explain one or two. "Tearing up the pea patch" meant going on a rampage; "sitting in the catbird seat" meant sitting pretty, like a batter with three balls and no strikes on him. Mr. Martin dismissed all this with an effort. It had been annoying, it had driven him near to distraction, but he was too solid a man to be moved to murder by anything so childish. It was fortunate, he reflected as he passed on to the important charges against Mr. Barrows, that he had stood up under it so well. He had maintained always an outward appearance of polite tolerance. "Why, I even believe you like the woman," Miss Paird, his other assistant, had once said to him. He had simply smiled.

A gavel rapped in Mr. Martin's mind and the case proper was resumed.   5
Mrs. Ulgine Barrows stood charged with willful, blatant, and persistent
attempts to destroy the efficiency and system of F & S. It was competent,
material, and relevant to review her advent and rise to power. Mr. Martin
had got the story from Miss Paird, who seemed always able to find things
out. According to her, Mrs. Barrows had met Mr. Fitweiler at a party, where
she had rescued him from the embraces of a powerfully built drunken man
who had mistaken the president of F & S for a famous retired Middle Western football coach. She had led him to a sofa and somehow worked upon
him a monstrous magic. The aging gentleman had jumped to the conclusion there and then that this was a woman of singular attainments,
equipped to bring out the best in him and in the firm. A week later he had
introduced her into F & S as his special adviser. On that day confusion got its
foot in the door. After Miss Tyson, Mr. Brundage, and Mr. Bartlett had been
fired and Mr. Munson had taken his hat and stalked out, mailing in his resignation later, old Roberts had been emboldened to speak to Mr. Fitweiler. He
mentioned that Mr. Munson's department had been "a little disrupted" and
hadn't they perhaps better resume the old system there? Mr. Fitweiler had
said certainly not. He had the greatest faith in Mrs. Barrow's ideas. "They
require a little seasoning, a little seasoning, is all," he had added. Mr. Roberts
had given it up. Mr. Martin reviewed in detail all the changes wrought by Mrs.
Barrows. She had begun chipping at the cornices of the firm's edifice and
now she was swinging at the foundation stones with a pickaxe.

Mr. Martin came now, in his summing up, to the afternoon of Monday,
November 2, 1942—just one week ago. On that day, at 3 P.M., Mrs. Barrows
had bounced into his office. "Boo!" she had yelled. "Are you scraping around
the bottom of the pickle barrel?" Mr. Martin had looked at her from under
his green eyeshade, saying nothing. She had begun to wander about the
office, taking it in with her great, popping eyes. "Do you really need *all*
these filing cabinets?" she had demanded suddenly. Mr. Martin's heart had
jumped. "Each of these files," he had said, keeping his voice even, "plays an
indispensable part in the system of F & S." She had brayed at him, "Well,
don't tear up the pea patch!" and gone to the door. From there she had
brawled, "But you sure have got a lot of fine scrap in here!" Mr. Martin could
no longer doubt that the finger was on his beloved department. Her pickaxe was on the upswing, poised for the first blow. It had not come yet; he
had received no blue memo from the enchanted Mr. Fitweiler bearing nonsensical instructions deriving from the obscene woman. But there was no
doubt in Mr. Martin's mind that one would be forthcoming. He must act
quickly. Already a precious week had gone by. Mr. Martin stood up in his living room, still holding his milk glass. "Gentlemen of the jury," he said to himself, "I demand the death penalty for this horrible person."

The next day Mr. Martin followed his routine, as usual. He polished his glasses more often and once sharpened an already sharp pencil, but not even
Miss Paird noticed. Only once did he catch sight of his victim; she swept
past him in the hall with a patronizing "Hi!" At five-thirty he walked home,
as usual, and had a glass of milk, as usual. He had never drunk anything
stronger in his life—unless you could count ginger ale. The late Sam
Schlosser, the S of F & S, had praised Mr. Martin at a staff meeting several

years before for his temperate habits. "Our most efficient worker neither drinks nor smokes," he had said. "The results speak for themselves." Mr. Fitweiler had sat by, nodding approval.

Mr. Martin was still thinking about the red-letter day as he walked over to the Schrafft's on Fifth Avenue near Forty-sixth Street. He got there, as he always did, at eight o'clock. He finished his dinner and the financial page of the *Sun* at a quarter to nine, as he always did. It was his custom after dinner to take a walk. This time he walked down Fifth Avenue at a casual pace. His gloved hands felt moist and warm, his forehead cold. He transferred the Camels from his overcoat to a jacket pocket. He wondered, as he did so, if they did not represent an unnecessary note of strain. Mrs. Barrows smoked only Luckies. It was his idea to puff a few puffs on a Camel (after the rubbing-out), stub it out in the ashtray holding her lipstick-stained Luckies, and thus drag a small red herring across the trail. Perhaps it was not a good idea. It would take time. He might even choke, too loudly.

Mr. Martin had never seen the house on West Twelfth Street where Mrs. Barrows lived, but he had a clear enough picture of it. Fortunately, she had bragged to everybody about her ducky first-floor apartment in the perfectly darling three-story red-brick. There would be no doorman or other attendants; just the tenants of the second and third floors. As he walked along, Mr. Martin realized that he would get there before nine-thirty. He had considered walking north on Fifth Avenue from Schrafft's to a point from which it would take him until ten o'clock to reach the house. At that hour people were less likely to be coming in or going out. But the procedure would have made an awkward loop in the straight thread of his casualness, and he had abandoned it. It was impossible to figure when people would be entering or leaving the house, anyway. There was a great risk at any hour. If he ran into anybody, he would simply have to place the rubbing-out of Ulgine Barrows in the inactive file forever. The same thing would hold true if there were someone in her apartment. In that case he would just say that he had been passing by, recognized her charming house and thought to drop in.

It was eighteen minutes after nine when Mr. Martin turned into   10
Twelfth Street. A man passed him, and a man and a woman talking. There was no one within fifty paces when he came to the house, halfway down the block. He was up the steps and in the small vestibule in no time, pressing the bell under the card that said "Mrs. Ulgine Barrows." When the clinking in the lock started, he jumped forward against the door. He got inside fast, closing the door behind him. A bulb in a lantern hung from the hall ceiling on a chain seemed to give a monstrously bright light. There was nobody on the stair, which went up ahead of him along the left wall. A door opened down the hall in the wall on the right. He went toward it swiftly, on tiptoe.

"Well, for God's sake, look who's here!" bawled Mrs. Barrows, and her braying laugh rang out like the report of a shotgun. He rushed past her like a football tackle, bumping her. "Hey, quit shoving!" she said, closing the door behind them. They were in her living room, which seemed to Mr. Martin to be lighted by a hundred lamps. "What's after you?" she said. "You're as jumpy as a goat." He found he was unable to speak. His heart was wheezing in his throat. "I—yes," he finally brought out. She was jabbering and laughing as she started to help him off with his coat. "No, no" he said. "I'll put it here."

He took it off and put it on a chair near the door. "Your hat and gloves, too," she said. "You're in a lady's house." He put his hat on top of the coat. Mrs. Barrows seemed larger than he had thought. He kept his gloves on. "I was passing by," he said. "I recognized—is there anyone here?" She laughed louder than ever. "No," she said, "we're all alone. You're as white as a sheet, you funny man. Whatever *has* come over you? I'll mix you a toddy." She started toward a door across the room. "Scotch-and-soda be all right? But say, you don't drink, do you?" She turned and gave him her amused look. Mr. Martin pulled himself together. "Scotch-and-soda will be all right," he heard himself say. He could hear her laughing in the kitchen.

Mr. Martin looked quickly around the living room for the weapon. He had counted on finding one there. There were andirons and a poker and something in the corner that looked like an Indian club. None of them would do. It couldn't be that way. He began to pace around. He came to a desk. On it lay a metal paper knife with an ornate handle. Would it be sharp enough? He reached for it and knocked over a small brass jar. Stamps spilled out of it and it fell to the floor with a clatter. "Hey," Mrs. Barrows yelled from the kitchen, "are you tearing up the pea patch?" Mr. Martin gave a strange laugh. Picking up the knife, he tried its point against his left wrist. It was blunt. It wouldn't do.

When Mrs. Barrows reappeared, carrying two highballs, Mr. Martin, standing there with his gloves on, became acutely conscious of the fantasy he had wrought. Cigarettes in his pocket, a drink prepared for him—it was all too grossly improbable. It was more than that; it was impossible. Somewhere in the back of his mind a vague idea stirred, sprouted. "For heaven's sake, take off those gloves," said Mrs. Barrows. "I always wear them in the house," said Mr. Martin. The idea began to bloom, strange and wonderful. She put the glasses on a coffee table in front of a sofa and sat on the sofa. "Come over here, you odd little man," she said. Mr. Martin went over and sat beside her. It was difficult getting a cigarette out of the pack of Camels, but he managed it. She held a match for him, laughing. "Well," she said, handing him his drink, "this is perfectly marvelous. You with a drink and a cigarette."

Mr. Martin puffed, not too awkwardly, and took a gulp of the highball. "I drink and smoke all the time," he said. He clinked his glass against hers. "Here's nuts to that old windbag, Fitweiler," he said, and gulped again. The stuff tasted awful, but he made no grimace. "Really, Mr. Martin," she said, her voice and posture changing, "you are insulting our employer." Mrs. Barrows was now all special adviser to the president. "I am preparing a bomb," said Mr. Martin, "which will blow the old goat higher than hell." He had only had a little of the drink, which was not strong. It couldn't be that. "Do you take dope or something?" Mrs. Barrows asked coldly. "Heroin," said Mr. Martin. "I'll be coked to the gills when I bump that old buzzard off." "Mr. Martin!" she shouted, getting to her feet. "That will be all of that. You must go at once." Mr. Martin took another swallow of his drink. He tapped his cigarette out in the ashtray and put the pack of Camels on the coffee table. Then he got up. She stood glaring at him. He walked over and put on his hat and coat. "Not a word about this," he said, and laid an index finger against his lips. All Mrs. Barrows could bring out was "Really!" Mr. Martin put his hand on the doorknob. "I'm sitting in the catbird seat," he said. He stuck his tongue out at her and left. Nobody saw him go.

Mr. Martin got to his apartment, walking, well before eleven. No one   15
saw him go in. He had two glasses of milk after brushing his teeth, and he
felt elated. It wasn't tipsiness, because he hadn't been tipsy. Anyway, the
walk had worn off all effects of the whisky. He got in bed and read a magazine for a while. He was asleep before midnight.

Mr. Martin got to the office at eight-thirty the next morning, as usual. At a
quarter to nine, Ulgine Barrows, who had never before arrived at work
before ten, swept into his office. "I'm reporting to Mr. Fitweiler now!" she
shouted. "If he turns you over to the police, it's no more than you deserve!"
Mr. Martin gave her a look of shocked surprise. "I beg your pardon?" he said.
Mrs. Barrows snorted and bounced out of the room, leaving Miss Paird and
Joey Hart staring after her. "What's the matter with that old devil now?"
asked Miss Paird. "I have no idea," said Mr. Martin, resuming his work. The
other two looked at him and then at each other. Miss Paird got up and went
out. She walked slowly past the closed door of Mr. Fitweiler's office. Mrs.
Barrows was yelling inside, but she was not braying. Miss Paird could not
hear what the woman was saying. She went back to her desk.

Forty-five minutes later, Mrs. Barrows left the president's office and went
into her own, shutting the door. It wasn't until half an hour later that Mr.
Fitweiler sent for Mr. Martin. The head of the filing department, neat, quiet,
attentive, stood in front of the old man's desk. Mr. Fitweiler was pale and nervous. He took his glasses off and twiddled them. He made a small, bruffing
sound in his throat. "Martin," he said "you have been with us more than twenty years." "Twenty-two, sir," said Mr. Martin. "In that time," pursued the president, "your work and your—uh—manner have been exemplary." "I trust so,
sir," said Mr. Martin. "I have understood, Martin," said Mr. Fitweiler, "that you
have never taken a drink or smoked." "That is correct, sir," said Mr. Martin. "Ah,
yes." Mr. Fitweiler polished his glasses. "You may describe what you did after
leaving the office yesterday, Martin," he said. Mr. Martin allowed less than a
second for his bewildered pause. "Certainly, sir," he said. "I walked home.
Then I went to Schrafft's for dinner. Afterward I walked home again. I went
to bed early, sir, and read a magazine for a while. I was asleep before eleven."
"Ah, yes," said Mr. Fitweiler again. He was silent for a moment, searching for
the proper words to say to the head of the filing department. "Mrs. Barrows,"
he said finally, "Mrs. Barrows has worked hard, Martin, very hard. It grieves
me to report that she has suffered a severe breakdown. It has taken the
form of a persecution complex accompanied by distressing hallucinations." "I am very sorry, sir," said Mr. Martin. "Mrs. Barrows is under the delu-
sion," continued Mr. Fitweiler, "that you visited her last evening and behaved
yourself in an—uh—unseemly manner." He raised his hand to silence Mr. Martin's little pained outcry. "It is the nature of these psychological diseases," Mr.
Fitweiler said, "to fix upon the least likely and most innocent party as the—
uh—source of persecution. These matters are not for the lay mind to grasp,
Martin. I've just had my psychiatrist, Dr. Fitch, on the phone. He would not, of
course, commit himself, but he had enough generalizations to substantiate
my suspicions. I suggested to Mrs. Barrows when she had completed her—
uh—story to me this morning that she visit Dr. Fitch, for I suspected a condition at once. She flew, I regret to say, into a rage, and demanded—
uh—requested that I call you on the carpet. You may not know, Martin, but
Mrs. Barrows had planned a reorganization of your department—subject to

my approval, of course, subject to my approval. This brought you, rather than anyone else, to her mind—but again that is a phenomenon for Dr. Fitch and not for us. So, Martin, I am afraid Mrs. Barrows' usefulness here is at an end." "I am dreadfully sorry, sir," said Mr. Martin.

It was at this point that the door to the office blew open with the suddenness of a gas-main explosion and Mrs. Barrows catapulted through it. "Is the little rat denying it?" she screamed. "He can't get away with that!" Mr. Martin got up and moved discreetly to a point beside Mr. Fitweiler's chair. "You drank and smoked at my apartment," she bawled at Mr. Martin, "and you know it! You called Mr. Fitweiler an old windbag and said you were going to blow him up when you got coked to the gills on your heroin!" She stopped yelling to catch her breath and a new glint came into her popping eyes. "If you weren't such a drab, ordinary little man," she said, "I'd think you'd planned it all. Sticking your tongue out at me, saying you were sitting in the catbird seat, because you thought no one would believe me when I told it! My God, it's really too perfect!" She brayed loudly and hysterically, and the fury was on her again. She glared at Mr. Fitweiler. "Can't you see how he has tricked us, you old fool? Can't you see his little game?" But Mr. Fitweiler had been surreptitiously pressing all the buttons under the top of his desk and employees of F & S began pouring into the room. "Stockton," said Mr. Fitweiler, "you and Fishbein will take Mrs. Barrows to her home. Mrs. Powell, you will go with them." Stockton, who had played football in high school, blocked Mrs. Barrows as she made for Mr. Martin. It took him and Fishbein together to force her out of the door into the hall, crowded with stenographers and office boys. She was still screaming imprecations at Mr. Martin, tangled and contradictory imprecations. The hubbub finally died out down the corridor.

"I regret that this has happened," said Mr. Fitweiler. "I shall ask you to dismiss it from your mind, Martin." "Yes, sir," said Mr. Martin, anticipating his chief's "That will be all" by moving to the door. "I will dismiss it." He went out and shut the door, and his step was light and quick in the hall. When he entered his department he had slowed down to his customary gait, and he walked quietly across the room to the W20 file, wearing a look of studious concentration.

[1943]

JOHN UPDIKE (1932–)

For a brief biography of Updike, please see Appendix C.

Deaths of Distant Friends

Though I was between marriages for several years, in a disarray that preoccupied me completely, other people continued to live and die. Len, an old golf partner, overnight in the hospital for what they said was a routine examination, dropped dead in the lavatory, having just placed a telephone call to his hardware store saying he would be back behind the counter in the morning. He owned the store and could take sunny afternoons off on short notice. His swing was too quick, and he kept his weight back on his right foot, and the ball often squirted off to the left without getting into the air at all, but he sank some gorgeous putts in his day, and he always dressed with a nattiness that seemed to betoken high hopes for his game. In buttercup-yellow slacks, sky-blue turtleneck, and tangerine cashmere cardigan he would wave from the practice green as, having driven out from Boston through clouds of grief and sleeplessness and moral confusion, I would drag my cart across the asphalt parking lot, my cleats scraping, like a monster's claws, at every step.

Though Len had known and liked Julia, the wife I had left, he never spoke of my personal condition or of the fact that I drove an hour out from Boston to meet him instead of, as formerly, ten minutes down the road. Golf in that interim was a great haven; as soon as I stepped off the first tee in pursuit of my drive, I felt enclosed in a luminous wide bubble, safe from women, stricken children, solemn lawyers, disapproving old acquaintances—the entire offended social order. Golf had its own order, and its own love, as the three or four of us staggered and shouted our way toward each hole, laughing at misfortune and applauding the rare strokes of relative brilliance. Sometimes the summer sky would darken and a storm arise, and we would cluster in an abandoned equipment shed or beneath a tree that seemed less tall than its brothers. Our natural nervousness and our impatience at having the excitements of golf interrupted would in this space of shelter focus into an almost amorous heat—the breaths and sweats of middle-aged men packed together in the pattering rain like cattle in a boxcar. Len's face bore a number of spots of actinic keratosis; he was going to have them surgically removed before they turned into skin cancer. Who would have thought that the lightning bolt of a coronary would fall across his plans and clean remove him from my tangled life? Never again (no two snowflakes or fingerprints, no two heartbeats traced on the oscilloscope, and no two golf swings are exactly alike) would I exultantly see his so hopefully addressed drive ("Hello dere, ball," he would joke, going into his waggle and squat) squirt off low to the left in that unique way of his, and hear him exclaim in angry frustration (he was a born-again Baptist, and had developed a personal language of avoided curses), "Ya dirty ricka-fric!"

I drove out to Len's funeral and tried to tell his son, "Your father was a great guy," but the words fell flat in that cold bare Baptist church. Len's gaudy colors, his Christian effervescence, his game and futile swing, our crowing back and forth, our fellowship within the artificial universe composed of variously resistant lengths and types of grass, were tints of life too delicate to capture, and had flown.

A time later, I read in the paper that Miss Amy Merrymount, ninety-one, had at last passed away, as a dry leaf passes into leaf mold. She had always seemed ancient; she was one of those New Englanders, one of the last, who spoke of Henry James as if he had just left the room. She possessed letters, folded and unfolded almost into pieces, from James to her parents, in which she was mentioned, not only as a little girl but as a young lady "coming into her 'own,' into a liveliness fully rounded." She lived in a few rooms, crowded with antiques, of a great inherited country house of which she was constrained to rent out the larger portion. Why she had never married was a mystery that sat upon her lightly in old age; the slender smooth beauty that sepia photographs remembered, the breeding and intelligence and,

in a spiritual sense, ardor she still possessed must have intimidated as many
suitors as they attracted and given her, in her own eyes, in an age when the
word *inviolate* still had force and renunciation, a certain prestige, a value
whose winged moment of squandering never quite arose. Also, she had a
sardonic dryness to her voice and something restless and dismissive in her
manner. She was a keen self-educator; she kept up with new developments
in art and science, took up organic foods and political outrage when they
became fashionable, and liked to have young people about her. When Julia
and I moved to town with our babies and fresh faces, we became part of
her tea circle, and in an atmosphere of tepid but mutual enchantment maintained acquaintance for twenty years.

Perhaps not so tepid: now I think Miss Merrymount loved us, or at least   5
loved Julia, who always took on a courteous brightness, a soft daughterly
shine, in those chill window-lit rooms crowded with spindly, feathery heir-
looms once spread through the four floors of a Back Bay town house. In
memory the glow of my former wife's firm chin and exposed throat and
shoulders merges with the ghostly smoothness of those old framed studio
photos of the Merrymount sisters—three, of whom two died sadly young,
as if bequeathing their allotment of years to the third, the survivor sitting
with us in her gold-brocaded wing chair. Her face had become unforesee-
ably brown with age, and totally wrinkled, like an Indian's, with something
in her dark eyes of glittering Indian cruelty. "I found her rather disappointing," she might say of an absent mutual acquaintance, or, of one who had
been quite dropped from her circle, "She wasn't absolutely first-rate."

The search for the first-rate had been a pastime of her generation. I cannot think, now, of whom she utterly approved, except Father Daniel Berrigan
and Sir Kenneth Clark. She saw them both on television. Her eyes with their
opaque glitter were failing, and for her cherished afternoons of reading while
the light died outside her windows and a little fire of birch logs in the brass-
skirted fireplace warmed her ankles were substituted scheduled hours tuned
in to educational radio and television. In those last years, Julia would go and
read to her—Austen, *Middlemarch,* Joan Didion, some Proust and Mauriac in
French, when Miss Merrymount decided that Julia's accent passed muster.
Julia would practice a little on me, and , watching her lips push forward and
go small and tense around the French sounds like the lips of an African mask
of ivory, I almost fell in love with her again. Affection between women is a
touching, painful, exciting thing for a man, and in my vision of it—tea yielding to sherry in those cluttered rooms where twilight thickened until the
pages being slowly turned and the patient melody of Julia's voice were the
sole signs of life—love was what was happening between this gradually
dying old lady and my wife, who had gradually become middle-aged, our children grown into absent adults, her voice nowhere else harkened to as it was
here. No doubt there were confidences, too, between the pages. Julia always
returned from Miss Merrymount's, to make my late dinner, looking younger
and even blithe, somehow emboldened.

In that awkward postmarital phase when old friends still feel obliged
to extend invitations and one doesn't yet have the wit or courage to
decline, I found myself at a large gathering at which Miss Merrymount was
present. She was not quite blind and invariably accompanied by a young person, a round-faced girl hired as companion and guide. The fragile old lady, dis-

played like peacock feathers under a glass bell, had been established in a chair in a corner of the room beyond the punch bowl. At my approach, she sensed a body coming near and held out her withered hand, but when she heard my voice her hand dropped. "You have done a dreadful thing," she said, all on one long intake of breath, like a draft rippling a piece of crinkly cellophane. Her face turned away, showing her hawk-nosed profile, as though I had offended her sight. The face of her young companion, round as a radar dish, registered slight shock; but I smiled, in truth not displeased. There is a relief at judgment, even adverse. It is good to know that somewhere a seismograph records our quakes and slippages. I imagine Miss Merrymount's death, not too many months after this, as a final serenely flat line on the hospital monitor attached to her. Something sardonic in that flat line, too—of unviolated rectitude, of magnificent patience with a world that for over ninety years failed to prove itself other than disappointing. By this time, Julia and I were at last divorced.

Everything of the abandoned home is lost, of course—the paintings on the walls, the way shadows and light contended in this or that corner, the gracious warmth from the radiators. The pets. Canute was a male golden retriever we had acquired as a puppy when the children were still a tumbling, pre-teen pack. Endlessly amiable, as his breed tends to be, he suffered all, including castration, as if life were a steady hail of blessings. Curiously, not long before he died, my youngest child, who sings in a female punk group that has just started up, brought Canute to the house where now I live with Jenny as my wife. He sniffed around politely and expressed with only a worried angle of his ears the wonder of his old master reconstituted in this strange-smelling home; then he collapsed with a heavy sigh onto the kitchen floor. He looked fat and seemed lethargic. My daughter, whose hair is cut short and dyed mauve in patches, said that the dog roamed at night and got into the neighbor's garbage, and even into one neighbor's horse feed. This sounded like mismanagement to me; Julia's new boyfriend is a middle-aged former Dartmouth quarterback, a golf and tennis and backpack freak, and she is hardly ever home, so busy is she keeping up with him and trying to learn new games. The house and lawn are neglected; the children drift in and out with their friends and once in a while clean out the rotten food in the refrigerator. Jenny, sensing my suppressed emotions, said something tactful and bent down to scratch Canute behind one ear. Since the ear was infected and sensitive, he feebly snapped at her, then thumped the kitchen floor with his tail in apology.

Like me when snubbed by Miss Merrymount, my wife seemed more pleased than not, encountering a touch of resistance, her position in the world as it were confirmed. She discussed dog antibiotics with my daughter, and at a glance one could not have been sure who was the older, though it was clear who had the odder hair. It is true, as the cliché runs, that Jenny is young enough to be my daughter. But now that I am fifty everybody under thirty-five is young enough to be my daughter. Most of the people in the world are young enough to be my daughter.

A few days after his visit, Canute disappeared, and a few days later he was found far out on the mashes near my old house, his body bloated. The dog officer's diagnosis was a heart attack. Can that happen, I wondered, to

10

four-footed creatures? The thunderbolt had hit my former pet by moonlight, his heart full of marshy joy and his stomach fat with garbage, and he had lain for days with ruffling fur while the tides went in and out. The image makes me happy, like the sight of a sail popping full of wind and tugging its boat swiftly out from shore. In truth—how terrible to acknowledge—all three of these deaths make me happy, in a way. Witnesses to my disgrace are being removed. The world is growing lighter. Eventually there will be none to remember me as I was in those embarrassing, disarrayed years while I scuttled without a shell, between houses and wives, a snake between skins, a monster of selfishness, my grotesque needs naked and pink, my social presence beggarly and vulnerable. The deaths of others carry us off bit by bit, until there will be nothing left; and this too will be, in a way, a mercy.

[1983]

Poetry

Poetry

13

Elements of Poetry

The way to develop good taste in literature is to read poetry. . . . For, being the supreme form of human locution, poetry is not only the most concise, the most condensed way of conveying the human experience; it also offers the highest possible standards for any linguistic operation—especially one on paper. The more one reads poetry, the less tolerant one becomes of any sort of verbosity, be that in political or philosophical discourse, be that in history, social studies, or the art of fiction.

—Joseph Brodsky, from "How to Read a Book"

Dealing with Difficulty

In 1999, at the Poetry International Festival in Rotterdam, Orhan Kocak assessed poetry's current fortunes in this way: "hypertrophy of supply, atrophy of demand." But poetry, particularly in the United States, is actually enjoying a resurgence of interest. One indication is the popularity of poetry "slams," which are competitive poetry readings, a bit like the World Wrestling Federation crossed with a spelling bee. Creative writing programs seem to be thriving. Poetry-writing workshops quickly fill up. Poetry may be as old as language; it will

likely last as long. It is, as Joseph Brodsky says in the epigraph, "the supreme form of human locution."

But poetry is also, many students will say, a challenge. So let's begin this focus on poetry with a poem about its difficulty.

WILLIAM MERIDETH (1919–)

See Appendix C for biographies of poets.

A Major Work

Poems are hard to read
Pictures are hard to see
Music is hard to hear   5
And people are hard to love

But whether from brute need
Or divine energy
At last mind eye and ear
And the great sloth heart will move.

[1958]

William Merideth's "A Major Work" emphasizes for us why someone might want to undertake the hard work of reading poems—or viewing pictures, listening to music, loving another person. These efforts, Merideth indicates, "move" us; and his reference to "the great sloth heart" suggests that such moving is not easy. Sloths, as you may know, are such slow-moving, lazy creatures, spending so much of their time just hanging upside-down in trees, that their name has come to mean "laziness" and "indolence." You should read poetry, in other words, to avoid sleepwalking through life, to become more fully alive.

No doubt there is a pearl of wisdom here, that good things require effort, but don't you ever wonder what sort of world we live in, in which it seems that every-thing that tastes especially good is bad for you, that the most beautiful places are the hardest to get to, and that all the joggers getting into shape have these terrible gri-maces on their faces as they exercise? Why is this a "no pain, no gain" world—even when it comes to poetry? So we'll appreciate what we earn?

Actually, it's not at all that simple. For one thing, while poems certainly are some-times "hard to read," and you should expect to put forth some effort studying them, it is also true that poems are often easy and even fun to read—especially if you have some idea of what you're doing. Merideth's little poem isn't that hard to read, is it? Some punctuation we'd normally expect to see is missing, but that hardly causes great confusion. The reader also has to notice that the four items in the last two lines that "will move"—"mind eye and ear/ And the great sloth heart"—are parallel to the difficult actions in the first four lines: "mind" goes with reading, of course; "eye" with pictures; "ear" with music; "heart" with love. But this connection is pretty easy to make. We may also want to ponder the question Merideth raises but doesn't answer, whether this moving comes from "brute need/ Or divine energy," but we don't have to resolve this problem to appreciate the poem.

If, however, this little poem is in fact rather easy to read, then it undermines its own assertion: it says that poems are hard to read, but this one isn't. If we think about it a bit more, the poem also seems to be betrayed by its own title: surely it is not real-ly "A Major Work," is it?

And at this point, perhaps this little poem *is* getting confusing, becoming harder to read the more we look at it. Does it in fact make sense? Let's consider the title further. To me, the title seems amusing, like a rusted-out, near-death Ford Pinto with "Indy Pace Car" written on the side. Also, while a critic might pronounce some poem to be "a major work," we don't expect an author to apply such a description to his own productions (imagine a novelist who calls her work "A Great Novel," especially if it's only five pages long; or a director who calls his movie "A Cinematic Milestone," when it's actually a ten-minute training film for fast-food employees). Beyond this humor of incongruence, what significance does the title have?

Perhaps the title doesn't actually name the poem itself, but rather its subject. In that sense, then, "A Major Work" is about what happens when you encounter "a major work." The poem thus presents the act of loving someone as an accomplishment on the order of other artistic achievements—difficult but vitally rewarding. Such acts of reading, seeing, hearing, loving, are thus themselves "major works." So, we might say the title functions in at least three ways: as an ironic joke, deconstructing the poem it names; as a reference to great works—poems, art, music, and loves; and as a reference to the acts of appreciating such "works."

This poem, we find, is easy to read in one sense, but it is also more stimulating and even challenging as we examine it further. In the same way, it is easy enough to look at a picture without seeing much, or to sit quietly and doze while music is playing, or to say casually to someone "I love you." But to really see a picture, noticing every detail, every relationship, every play of light and shadow—that's hard; to hear all the notes of a piece of music, all the silences, and the relationships of the notes and silences—that's hard; and to make yourself profoundly vulnerable to another person, to link your own happiness to another person's well-being—that's hard. The more deeply we engage in these efforts, the more we put into them, the more deeply rewarding we tend to find them.

This insight, in fact, takes us very close to the question of what poetry is. Let's revisit that question, briefly discussed in Chapter 4.

The Nature of Poetry

If you think poetry consists of lines that rhyme, then our poetry anthologies have lots of things in them that aren't poems, and your local greeting-card shop is crammed with poetry. Most scholars and critics want to distinguish *verse* (which adorns most greeting cards) from *poetry* (an arrangement of words that is somehow better, more profound, than greeting-card verse). Obviously, something other than rhyme, or rhythm, or even a certain arrangement on the page is required of poetry. But what is that something? In such matters of definition, Louis Armstrong's famous reply to the question "What is jazz?" is often quoted: "Man, if you gotta ask," Mr. Armstrong said, "you'll never know." And Robert Frost's similar response to a question about the nature of poetry is also often cited: "Poetry," Frost said, "is the sort of thing poets write."

Such answers would seem strange in most other contexts. Can you imagine a tennis pro explaining "tennis" as "the sort of game tennis players play"? Or a physicist, being asked to define "physics," replying "if you have to ask, you are hopelessly stupid"? Why then are Frost's and Armstrong's replies considered to be profound and memorable and not merely ridiculous? In large part, I think, because their evasiveness is based on genuine insight: Poetry (like jazz) really isn't a thing. Poetry (like jazz) is an activity, engaged in by writers and readers (or musicians and listeners) and the nature of that activity is hard to pin down because it changes, from person to person, from time to time, from place to place. At a particular moment, reading a particular poem, you may very well have a clear idea of "poetry"—until, that is, you read another poem that isn't quite what you expected. However we try to define and limit the kind of thing pointed to as "Poetry," poets will find a way to escape that container.

Indeed, one of the qualities we might assign to poetry (or jazz), if we were to attempt a definition, would be its tendency to surprise us, to go beyond or around or under our expectations, to do things with language (or music) that we hadn't quite counted on. Poetry and jazz really don't have clear rules and boundaries. Part of their essence and appeal lies in the way they break down, violate, and expand what we expect music and words to do. Although some kinds of poems, to be sure, do follow rather strict rules (a sonnet has fourteen lines and a certain rhyme scheme, for instance), simply following those rules won't guarantee you'll produce poetry. To know what poetry (or jazz) is, you do in a sense have to experience it: any definition of "poetry" would just be an invitation to write a poem that defies the definition.

Here for instance is a way of looking at poetry *as a thing* that I bet you haven't considered before.

MARK STRAND (1934–)

Eating Poetry

Ink runs from the corners of my mouth.
There is no happiness like mine.
I have been eating poetry.

The librarian does not believe what she sees.
Her eyes are sad   5
and she walks with her hands in her dress.

The poems are gone.
The light is dim.
The dogs are on the basement stairs and coming up.

Their eyeballs roll,   10
their blond legs burn like brush.
The poor librarian begins to stamp her feet and weep.

She does not understand.
When I get on my knees and lick her hand, she screams.

I am a new man.   15
I snarl at her and bark.
I romp with joy in the bookish dark.

[1979]

What you have just read, most everyone would agree, is a poem, an instance of poetry. But what the speaker in the poem says he has been eating, I would argue, isn't poetry, at least not in the same sense. One could, it seems clear, eat the paper and ink that record a poem, that save it for the reader's *intellectual* consumption, but would one really be eating "poetry," eating "the poem"? There is something funny about the idea of "poetry" as something we can point to, grasp, describe, pin down, even eat, as Strand's vividly liberated imagination suggests.

But if "poetry" is an open category, a label used to refer to all sorts of arrangements of words (and even nonwords sometimes), how will we ever know if we are in fact reading (or even eating) poetry? If poetry is the kind of things poets write, and Robert Frost is a poet, then is a note that Frost left on a friend's refrigerator, apologizing for eating his fruit—is *that* poetry? Surely not everything a poet writes is "poetry". But how do we know?

Another example may help us here.

Liechtenstein

For a moment we look back
at the sunlit plain
lying green and fruitful
amidst the towering mountains.

Silently we bid farewell   5
to the land without soldiers,
the land without hunger—the valley of peace.
Then we get into the car
and drive slowly away.

[1990]

This text, written by (so far as I know) the only native of Liechtenstein I've ever taught, announces itself as poetry: the title and the spacing of the lines indicate "this is a poem."

But wait. The student "wrote" this poem as part of a class exercise by copying and re-arranging the closing sentences out of Barbara Greene's book, *Liechtenstein: A History.* In Greene's book, the "poem" appeared this way, as prose:

> For a moment we look back at the sunlit plain lying green and fruitful amidst the towering mountains. Silently we bid farewell to the land without soldiers, the land without hunger—the valley of peace.
>
> Then we get into the car and drive slowly away.

If you first looked at "Leaving Liechtenstein" as a poem, do you now, knowing its origin, remove it from that category? Surely Greene's words are not poetry as they appear in her book. Does merely arranging them on the page transform them into a poem? And if so, who is the author of this poem?

You will have to decide whether this poem is one. With every poem, in fact, you will have to decide what is special about it, what distinguishes it (if anything) from prose. This point is supported by Stanley Fish's famous experiment in which he asked his students to interpret a poem already written on the board as they arrived for class. After a lengthy and stimulating discussion of this interesting work, Fish revealed to his students that the poem actually originated as a list of names he found left on the board from the previous class. This experiment, Fish believed, tells us something important about the nature of texts in general and "poetry" in particular. Namely, that a poem is made by the perception of poetry. A poem is whatever we read as a poem. And how do we read a poem? Simply as a place to start, let's consider three qualities that experienced readers bring to poems:

- *A special intensity.* We read poems more carefully than prose, generally speaking, because we assume that poetry is more carefully constructed.

When we give to some text the status of "a poem," we are assuming that it represents in some way a particularly rich, intense, clever, or revealing use of language.

- *A special awareness of the language itself.* We assume that poems offer us more than just the meaning: we expect that rhythms, sounds, spacings, patterns, have been constructed for our pleasure.
- *A special creativity.* We assume that poems respond to imaginative reading: we may have to fill in some facts or ideas, or extend the implications beyond what is actually said.

If we view a particular text as a poem, then we are saying it deserves the sort of attention readers bring to poems. That attention, of course, can be brought to any text—a prose passage, a list of names on a blackboard, or an arrangement of fourteen rhyming lines. So when Frost says that a poem is "the sort of thing poets write," he is only partly right. A poem is also the sort of thing that readers of poetry read.

The following two poems may help illuminate further what it means to write or read a text *as poetry.* One of them is very famous, appearing in many introduction-to-literature anthologies. It appears in fact in this one, and you may have seen it already. Pretend that you haven't. It's by William Carlos Williams (1883–1963), a physician who was also a major twentieth-century poet, and it appeared in 1934. The other work is not quite so famous. In fact, since being written in 1991, it's never been previously published. It's by a student, Stacy Bochis, who was consciously attempting to write something that would be like a poem, but wasn't: a fake poem. Can you tell which is which?

This Is Just to Say

I have eaten
the plums
that were in
the icebox
and which   5
you were probably
saving
for breakfast

Forgive me
they were delicious   10
so sweet
and so cold

Poetry

Gazing upon the roast
that is sliced
    and laid out
across the plate

I spoon the juices   5
of carrot
    and onion

I am sorry to have eaten
    your lunch.

If we accept either or both of these texts as poems, then we bring to them a certain attention and thoughtfulness, and we are thereby encouraged to think about the ordinary act of leaving a note of apology. "Sorry I ate your food" becomes something potentially more significant. In its startling simplicity, the first poem freezes a nice moment, allowing us to participate in the speaker's confession. Although the speaker says "Forgive me," his apology seems to be overshadowed by his joy in the plums' deliciousness.

In the second poem, the speaker's apology is more direct and less ambiguous. There is perhaps some hint in the word "gazing" that the speaker likes the food, but that is unclear. Is the speaker really sorry to have eaten someone else's lunch? It's hard to say based on the poem. The first poem's speaker does seem less sincere: he says "Forgive me," not "I'm sorry," and you may well suspect he isn't really sorry since "Forgive me" is a bit excessive for the act involved. The exaggeration suggests that he'd probably eat them again, given the chance. And yet the first poem's confession is probably more effective than the second's, simply because the speaker's joy in eating the plums is such that few people would begrudge him such a delight.

But the second poem does give us something to think about with its title. "Poetry"? In what way is poetry like a roast that belongs to one person and is eaten by another? Perhaps the author owns the poem, and the reader eats it? In that case, what do the carrots and onions stand for?

And now do you know which one is the famous poem? Yes, although I said, discussing Mark Strand's poem, that a note on a refrigerator about eating someone's food wouldn't be a poem, the first one is a poem by Williams. But the second text might be a poem also, especially if you can think of a way to make it mean more. It doesn't seem, at this point however, to be the sort of thing that poets write, or readers of poetry read and think about.

So, if you decide that a certain text falls into the category of poetry—and usually this is a relatively easy decision—then you are agreeing that the text deserves a certain attentiveness, a commitment to look more carefully and patiently at everything about it: to see whatever there is. Since poets count on this close attention, they may employ any resource language offers: rhythm, rhyme, spacing, repetition, metaphor, allusion—whatever. Over time certain forms or patterns have been used again and again (the sonnet, the limerick, the haiku, for instance), so that the form itself can create certain expectations and meanings for the experienced reader. Not everyone can supply the energy and intelligence any particular poem calls for; but you will find, as your experience and ability grow, that more and more poems richly repay the effort you put into them. So don't worry if you don't "get" a particular poem, or even if you don't see why a particular poem is called one in the first place. Just keep reading. You'll soon find poems that speak to you. And when you do, you'll understand why poetry really is one of life's greatest pleasures. And you'll know, better than any definition, what poetry is.

How to Read a Poem

If poetry calls for an intense and creative attention, then this kind of reading will unavoidably strengthen your problem-solving skills and your imagination—and it's hard to see how you can have too much of either of those. So, maybe you are ready to admit that poetry is one of those things that you ought to struggle through because it's good for you. No pain, no gain—remember?

But wait. Things are even better than you may have thought. There are in fact tons of things that are good for you and that are also delicious (ever had tree-ripened

South Carolina peaches? Silver Queen corn? Freshly squeezed orange juice? Just-caught salmon grilled under the moon?).And it really isn't true that all the beautiful places are hard to get to; you are probably only minutes away from something spectacular, if you just take the time to look. And those joggers with pained expressions on their faces are actually experiencing, or are on the verge of experiencing, a wonderful feeling, a natural endorphin-produced high. That's not a grimace; that's the verge of a socially acceptable ecstasy.

Words

Although sometimes confusion is fun, as a general rule poems are much more enjoyable if they make sense. Making them make sense, as we've noted, may require some energy and patience. It may also require a dictionary, as you likely already know. What you may not have considered is that sometimes it's not just *unfamiliar* words that you need to look up; even words familiar to you may have special or meanings essential to the poem. With this warning, read the following poem and discussion.

EMILY DICKINSON (1830–1886)

The Soul Selects Her Own Society

The Soul selects her own Society—
Then—shuts the Door—
To her divine Majority—
Present no more—

Unmoved—she notes the Chariots—pausing—   5
At her low Gate—
Unmoved—an Emperor be kneeling
Upon her Mat—

I've known her—from an ample nation—
Choose One—   10
Then—close the Valves of her attention—
Like Stone—

[About 1862]

This poem does not appear to be made of difficult or obscure words. Some readers may want to look up "ample" ("fully sufficient," "plentiful," "copious") or some other word, but the vocabulary seems familiar enough to most students. Also, although Dickinson's odd punctuation slows us down, it is not that hard to figure out how to translate all those dashes, which do seem to create emphasis, drama, and strangeness: we just have to work out the structure of the sentences.

So why is this poem hard to understand, even though the individual words seem easy enough? It's a good idea whenever you're puzzled to try to pinpoint exactly where things get murky. This much of the poem seems pretty clear:

The Soul selects her own Society, then shuts the Door.

But we get into trouble with the very next statement. At first, the poem may seem to go this way:

The Soul selects her own Society, then shuts the Door to her divine Majority.

But what does "her divine Majority" mean? You may know what a "majority" is, but can you see how "the larger part" fits in here? Perhaps it is the name of a place. What kind of a place might it be? Did the Society come out of the divine Majority and then close the door, or did it go into the divine Majority with the Soul, and close the door?

The best thing to do, when you're puzzled with a poem, is to keep on reading, and oftentimes things clear up shortly. But the fourth line does not immediately clarify things, does it? Does it say that the divine Majority, whatever it is, is not there anymore—it is "Present no more"? That still doesn't seem to make sense, so we press on further. The next four lines present images of the Soul ignoring—"Unmoved" by—a succession of chariots and even an Emperor. And the last four lines underscore the Soul's elite status with the image of her choosing only one from an entire nation.

So, what do we do now? Clearly we need to return to the third and fourth lines and think some more. To make sense of these lines, we at some point will have to consider the possibility that the first sentence ends with "Door," and that the third and fourth lines stand alone: in other words, that "Present" is a verb, not an adjective. (You may have seen it this way from the start.) Thus, the sentence tells us to present—that is to offer, to deliver—no more candidates to her divine Majority: the Soul's Society is full, and you might as well forget about it. People in chariots, Emperors, former Presidents—it doesn't matter: no one else in fact can get in.

But the sentence is still not entirely clear, is it? What does "Majority" mean in this sentence? What does it mean to present no other candidates to her "divine Majority"? Even though "majority" is a familiar word, perhaps this would be a good time to check a dictionary. And in *Webster's College Dictionary,* we find this information under the fourth definition of "majority": "the state or time of being of full legal age: *to attain one's majority."* The Soul's "Majority," it now seems clear, is the state of being able to choose for herself. When the Soul attains maturity, arriving at her "full legal age," in charge of herself, she will select "her own Society." After that, the poem tells us, don't expect to get in.

Are there still other parts of the poem that are puzzling to you? What about the last two lines? What does "close the Valves of her attention—/ Like Stone—" mean? Again, "valve" is a common word, familiar to anyone with a minimal understanding of kitchen faucets or car engines. But it seems a bit strange to talk about such valves of the Soul's attention. It is hard to see how a valve relates to attention. Again, consulting the same dictionary reveals these two definitions, numbers five and eight: "one of two or more separate pieces composing certain shells: *the valves of a clamshell"*; and "*Archaic:* one of the leaves of a double or folding door."

This information suggests the possibility that the Soul's attention is like a clam or oyster, the two halves of the shell closing together "Like stone," or that the Soul's attention is closed off behind a double door made of stone. In fact, we aren't limited to one or the other meaning of "Valves." The various definitions all enrich this closing image of the poem: the idea of a mechanical valve suggests the coldness and efficiency of the Soul's closure; the idea of an oyster or mussel conveys the image of the Soul's attention snapping shut, with shells hard as stone; and the idea of the valves as a double door reinforces the picture of a house in the earlier lines—with a door, a gate, a mat.

Here then is the simple but important tip: not only do you need to look up any words you don't know; you also may need to look up some words that seem familiar in order to make the most sense of a poem.

Sentences

Almost always, poems are written in sentences. Making sense of a poem thus requires that you understand both the words and how they fit together. If you think about it, making sense of any sentence is a kind of miracle: it would appear that we can't understand what a particular word means until we understand how it fits into the sentence as a whole; but we can't understand the sentence as a whole until we understand all the individual words. So how do we understand anything? The best theory seems to be that we proceed to construct the meaning of statements by a series of lightning-fast guesses and revisions. The process is a little like the swimming pool game called "Marco Polo." In the game, one player, who has his or her eyes closed, tries to locate and touch some other player. The sightless player gets clues as to where the other players are by saying "Marco," to which the other players are obliged to respond "Polo." The "Marco" player's job is tough because the "Polo" players can move around; but by guessing and revising, the chasing player usually can pin down an evading player.

Good readers are continually guessing how sentences are structured and what they mean—yelling out "Marco" in other words. But they also keep testing their guesses, revising them as the words unfold, as they understand the speaker's (or even their own) situation better—as they see how the sentence's "Polo" fits their guesses. Writing about literature or discussing it with other readers allows us another level of testing, evolving, and perhaps modifying our readings. We develop meaning.

But reading would appear to differ from "Marco Polo" in a crucial way: the game is based on locating what is attempting to slip away, while reading is based on finding something that is attempting to be found—isn't it? Don't writers want us to find their meanings? Don't all writers try to speak as directly and clearly as possible? You may be smiling, because we all know the answer: not always, and not entirely. No doubt you can think of many instances in which a partial or confusing disclosure is in the writer's interest. Therefore, reading between the lines and untangling obscurities are extremely valuable abilities, even if you don't plan to attend law school or work for the Internal Revenue Service.

Poets, however, generally have more noble goals than preparing us for government work. Why do poems not always speak clearly and directly? Why do we sometimes have to unravel the syntax (or sentence structure) of their sentences? The following poem offers some ideas.

ROBERT FRANCIS (1901-1987)

Catch

Two boys uncoached are tossing a poem together,
Overhand, underhand, backhand, sleight of hand, every hand,
Teasing with attitudes, latitudes, interludes, altitudes,
High, make him fly off the ground for it, low, make him stoop,
Make him scoop it up, make him as-almost-as-possible miss it,   5
Fast, let him sting from it, now, now fool him slowly,
Anything, everything tricky, risky, nonchalant,
Anything under the sun to outwit the prosy,
Over the tree and the long sweet cadence down,

Over his head, make him scramble to pick up the meaning,   10
And now, like a posy, a pretty one plump in his hands.

[1950]

According to Francis's speaker, poets trick us sometimes, in various ways, in order "to outwit the prosy." Who are "the prosy"? Those who are unpoetical, who lean toward prose, who can't appreciate poetry and its verbal games ("prosaic" means of course "commonplace or dull"). When readers do get the meaning, it lands in their hands like a flower, a "posy," which is an interesting word—"prosy" without one letter. But "posy" is also very close to "poesy," an old word for "a poem" or "poetry" in general (check your dictionary). There is, it seems, a thin line between prose and poetry (or poesy).

That difference is surely central to Francis's point. The poet makes us "as-almost-as-possible miss it" for the same reason that one boy, pitching to another, might create the opportunity for his friend to make a spectacular catch. The poet creates the conditions for the reader to do something marvelous. The poet keeps tripping us up, firing the meaning in hard and fast, then fooling us with a slow curve, in part just for the fun of it—but also in order to be poetic: to indicate that he is doing something special with language, something beyond ordinary and commonplace prose.

Here's one more way to think about it: The boys aren't trying to accomplish anything in particular by tossing the poem. They are tossing the poem for the joy of doing it. Whenever you wish a poet had just come straight out and said whatever he or she meant to say, think about this poem. How would it be different if the two boys were "tossing the instructions for how to put together a barbecue grill"? Poetry isn't just the art of throwing out a meaning; it's the art of expanding meaning, and making possible the marvelous catching of expanding meaning.

Experience, in the final analysis, will give you the best notions about how to make sense of difficult poems. The second tip: be patient and take your time. Don't expect a poem to land "plump" in your hands all at once. Play with a poem. Toss it around. Work through it slowly, catching its parts and reading it repeatedly. Don't impatiently lunge for the meaning.

A Sonnet Unfolded

To give you some better idea of how patient attention will let you make sense of challenging poems, consider the following discussion of a Shakespearean sonnet, "So shall I live." First read through the poem a few times, then try to write down what you think it says. Then read the following discussion and compare your reading to the one discussed here. Although making sense of the poem unavoidably involves me in an interpretation of it, the goal here is just to show you how to figure out what it says. The explination may be overly explicit, explaining too much, but it should give you a good idea of what's involved in making sense of a difficult poem.

WILLIAM SHAKESPEARE (1564–1616)

Sonnet 93

So shall I live, supposing thou art true,
Like a deceivéd husband; so love's face
May still seem love to me, though altered new;

Thy looks with me, thy heart in other place:
For there can live no hatred in thine eye,   5
Therefore in that I cannot know thy change.
In many's looks, the false heart's history
Is writ in moods, and frowns, and wrinkles strange,
But heaven in thy creation did decree
That in thy face sweet love should ever dwell;   10
Whate'er thy thoughts or thy heart's workings be,
Thy looks should nothing thence but sweetness tell.
     How like Eve's apple doth thy beauty grow,
     If thy sweet virtue answer not thy show!

If the poem you're reading lacks punctuation, supplying some is likely to be helpful: to make sense of the poem, you will have to figure out where the sentences begin and end, where the subjects and verbs are, which words modify which other words. Readers aren't always aware that they're making such decisions, but such sentence structure work is essential to understanding. Keep in mind that your first guesses about how the words go together may be wrong; stay flexible. Such misdirection may in fact have motivated the poem's lack of punctuation.

If the poem *has* punctuation, then pay close attention to it, identifying the parts and the boundaries of the sentences. If your punctuation knowledge is shaky, consult the punctuation section of a reliable grammar handbook. (Your teacher can suggest one.) You may find it helpful to mark up a copy of the poem as you figure out its structure.

After you've identified the sentence structures, then you can move through the poem one sentence or complete thought at a time, paraphrasing or reorganizing until the lines make sense to you.

Let's look at Shakespeare's first sentence:

So shall I live, supposing thou art true,
Like a deceivéd husband.

What would that be in ordinary speech? We probably would say "So, I shall live" rather than "So shall I live." Live how? I shall live "supposing thou art true," the speaker says. Maybe the person addressed is true (faithful, honest); maybe not. We don't know, at least at this point, but the issue has been raised. All we know is that the speaker is going to *pretend*, or *assume* (big difference!), that the person addressed is true.

And how does "Like a deceivéd husband" fit in? There are at least two possibilities: (1) I'm going to suppose you are true in the same way that a deceived husband is true; (2) I'm going to live like a deceived husband and suppose you are true. Although the phrase is placed in the sentence closer to "thou," it seems to make more sense modifying "I," doesn't it? (In what way would a deceived husband be true? Perhaps he would be "true" by cheating also? That seems a bit of a stretch, and so I favor the second possibility.) The rest of the poem, as it turns out, seems to confirm that the speaker is resolving to play the role of the deceived husband. (To simplify things, let's assume for the moment that the speaker is male, and the person addressed female—although the genders aren't specified, and you may well want to consider what happens if you assume otherwise.)

Another main clause follows the first semicolon:

so love's face
May still seem love to me, though altered new.

In other words, by supposing she is true, the speaker believes she will still appear to love him: her face will still seem like the face of love. Again, we need to decide the relationship of a phrase: what does "though altered new" modify? Shakespeare places it next to "me," and one could argue that the speaker is "altered new"; but the sense of the sentence ties "though altered new" to "love's face," doesn't it? Thus, a paraphrase of the poem so far:

> *I am going to suppose you are true to me, living my life as if I were a deceived husband. Therefore, your face, even if it has changed, will still look like the face of love to me.*

Continuing with this process of making sense: The colon in line 3 links what follows it to the preceding idea:

> Thy looks with me, thy heart in another place.

This idea seems clear enough to me. The speaker is just explaining how she has changed or been "altered." Her face will still be there, looking the same way; but inside, she'll be different, with her heart somewhere else.

Here's the next sentence:

> For there can live no hatred in thine eye,
> Therefore in that I cannot know thy change.

How does this sentence relate to the preceding part of the poem? The "For" and "Therefore" indicate that the speaker is explaining his line of reasoning, restating and elaborating on his conclusion. In my words:

> *Since your eye cannot show any hatred, it will be impossible for me to tell if you have changed—if your heart really does belong to someone else.*

The next sentence expands further upon this notion, comparing her to other people:

> In many's looks the false heart's history
> Is writ in moods and frowns and wrinkles strange,
> But heaven in thy creation did decree
> That in thy face sweet love should ever dwell;

In other people's looks, the speaker says, one can see evidence of their cheating and deception: their moods, frowns, and revealing wrinkles show up on their faces. But his love's face is so loving and lovely, so free of moods, frowns, and distorting wrinkles, that she looks like love itself. God created her that way. And the next main clause reiterates this idea yet again:

> Whate'er thy thoughts or thy heart's workings be,
> Thy looks should nothing thence but sweetness tell.

No matter what she is thinking or feeling, the speaker says she will appear to be thinking and feeling sweet and loving thoughts.

How do the last two lines bring the poem to a close?

> How like Eve's apple doth thy beauty grow,
> If thy sweet virtue answer not thy show!

"Eve's apple" refers no doubt to the Genesis story of Adam and Eve and their temptation. The Serpent offers the forbidden fruit to Eve, who then gives it to Adam, getting them both kicked out of Paradise. Eve's apple is a symbol of deceit and treachery. It was no doubt a temptingly beautiful fruit, but it led to disaster. Shakespeare's speaker tells his beloved that her beauty, like Eve's apple, will grow into something terrible if she is not truly virtuous.

Here now is a paraphrase of the entire poem:

I am going to suppose you are true to me, living my life as if I were a deceived husband. Therefore, your face, even if it has changed, will still look like the face of love to me. If you do love another, then your looks will be here with me, but your heart will be somewhere else.

Since your eyes cannot show any hatred, it will be impossible for me to tell if your heart really does belong to someone else. In other people's looks, evidence of their cheating and deception is readily apparent: their moods, frowns, and revealing wrinkles show up on their faces. But your face is so loving and lovely, so free of moods, frowns, and distorting wrinkles, that you look like love itself. God created you so that no matter what you are thinking or feeling, you appear to be thinking and feeling sweet and loving thoughts.

Your beauty will be very much like Eve's apple if you are not truly virtuous: it will grow into something terrible.

Obviously there is a vast difference between the paraphrase and the poem. The poem says much more in fewer words, and what the poem says is different from what the paraphrase says. For instance, the paraphrase says her beauty will be like Eve's apple, but the poem actually notes "How like Eve's apple doth thy beauty grow." The poem also has patterns of sound and structure the paraphrase misses. In the opening lines, the repetition of "so" at the beginning of the first two clauses creates a parallel structure. The ending phrases of these parallel sentences, "Like a deceivéd husband" and "though altered new," both expose her possible treachery: the balancing main clauses both deteriorate from a positive assertion ("So shall I live . . ." and "so love's face/ May still . . ."), to an ominous posture ("supposing thou art true" and "seem love to me"), to a tragedy ("Like a deceived husband" and "though altered new"). The sixth line, just to pick one other example, begins with an inversion of the fifth line, as "For there" is turned around into "Therefore," just as her lack of the appearance of hatred is turned around into possible hatred.

The purpose here, however, is not to do a thorough analysis of this very rich sonnet, but rather to show you how to make sense of it. Once you've understood what Shakespeare is saying, patiently constructing the poem's literal meaning, then you can begin to ask the interpretive questions—such as what the speaker might hope to accomplish by making such a declaration to his love, or whether the speaker's jealousy has doomed the relationship even if the lover happened to this point to be completely in love with him.

Recognizing Kinds

We all know that there are all kinds of houses: ranch, modern, Georgian, Victorian, Tudor, and many others. Although every house is unique, homebuilders and home-buyers find such categories useful. Recognizing the various kinds of poems is likewise helpful as such awareness can help you appreciate how the poem fulfills certain conventions and how it modifies or departs from them. You can see how one poem compares to or draws on other poems. Although the suggestion that a particular poem is ultimately always "about" another poem may seem extreme, it is certainly true that we unavoidably read any poem in the context of other poems we know. This idea is nicely expressed in one of Robert Frost's notebook entries:

The way to read a poem in prose or verse is in the light of all the other poems ever written. We may begin anywhere. We duff into our first. We

read that imperfectly (thoroughness with it would be fatal), but the bet-
ter to read the second. We read the second the better to read the third, the
third better to read the fourth, the fourth better to read the fifth, the fifth
better to read the first again, or the second if it so happens.

If you see, as Frost says, that the first poem has something in the common with the
third, then you're a bit closer to appreciating them both. This section quickly covers
some of the more important conventions (but by no means all) that link various
poems together.

Stances

Stance indicates the attitude or situation of the speaker of the poem. Some of the
most common and important stances used in poetry are described here.

Apostrophe   If the speaker in a poem addresses his dead mother, or a house, or
an imaginary dolphin, then the speech is said to be an **apostrophe**. The punctuation mark we call an apostrophe is used to indicate the omission of a letter or
letters: in "she's" for "she is," the apostrophe takes the place of the missing "i." In
the case of a poetic apostrophe, the speaker is addressing something that isn't
there or that isn't ordinarily spoken to. That's how an apostrophe differs from regular dialogue: the thing or person being addressed is not going to respond. In
"Down, Wanton, Down" (see page 591), Robert Graves addresses a part of his own
body. The poem is an apostrophe: the part he's talking to is not going to respond—
at least not verbally!

Aubade   An **aubade** is a song or poem associated with the dawn or the morning—specifically, with lovers who must part at the dawn. The form is immortalized
in Shakespeare's *Romeo and Juliet* when Romeo has to leave Juliet's room at
dawn. Richard Wilbur's "A Late Aubade" (see page 592) offers a twist on this type
of poem.

Carpe Diem   *Carpe diem* is Latin for "seize the day." In *carpe diem* poems, the
speaker usually encourages someone else to take advantage of the present moment.
In other words, the poems say "Don't wait until later, when you may be dead; seize
the opportunity today." When the speaker in Wilbur's "A Late Aubade" says, "Time flies,
and I need not rehearse/ The rosebuds-theme of centuries of verse," he is alluding to
centuries of *carpe diem* poems, which often stress how time flies, and how one
should gather rosebuds (that is, take advantage of life) before they wilt and die
(before you get too old).

Elegy   In the narrowest sense, an **elegy** is a poem of mourning, reacting to someone's death. But elegy has also been used to refer to any formal poem that employs
a somber and reflective stance. In Shakespeare's day, some love poems were called
elegies if they involved a sad complaint. But by the eighteenth century, the elegy
was associated with lamenting a death; so, an elegiac tone is serious, mournful,
meditative.

Ode   The **ode** is an ancient form, going back at least to Pindar (522–442? BC), whose
odes were chanted by a moving chorus. Pindar's odes had three parts: in the first part,
the *strophe,* the chorus moved in one direction; in the second part, the *antistrophe,* the
chorus moved in the opposite direction, repeating the rhythms of the *strophe;* and in
the third part, the *epode,* the chorus stayed in one place. Imported into English, this

form was particularly challenging, since the complex rhyme and rhythm of each part had to be repeated in subsequent parts. Many English poets employed less restrictive forms of the ode, the Horatian and even the "irregular," but these forms still called for challenging and complex repetitions of rhyme and meter. The forms of odes have come to vary so much, however, that the stance of an ode is more important than any technical feature. What you need to know about this stance is that the emotions, the imagination, and the language are all elevated. Odes thus usually deal with important occasions or lofty topics; readers expect a poetic voice that is inspired, concentrated, exalted even. Thus, the ode combines a demanding form together with powerful passion—a combination that is difficult to pull off, and easy in more cynical times to parody.

Pastoral   Think of the **pastoral** as the "pastural"—that is, a poem having to do with pastures, grazing fields, and, more specifically, shepherds. (The Latin term for "shepherd" is "pastor.") The shepherds in the typical pastoral poem are articulate, learned, poetical, musical, romantic. While there are in all likelihood real shepherds with these qualities somewhere, experienced readers of pastoral poetry understand that the shepherds are conventional: pastoral poems are a means, as William Empson argues, of putting complex ideas into a simplified context. The pastoral stance in fact does not require shepherds: in modern critical terms, any work may be termed "pastoral" if it suggests the idealized rural qualities of the conventional pastoral poem. In Shakespeare's "When daisies pied and violets blue," the song that concludes *Love's Labor's Lost*, the references to the shepherds piping upon "oaten straws," and to the ploughmen using "the merry larks" as clocks, both create a pastoral atmosphere.

Forms

This section briefly presents some other useful terms. These deal with the forms of poems.

Narrative, Lyric, and Dramatic Poetry   A poem may explicitly tell a story, tracing in some way a sequence of events. Such poems are called **narrative** poetry. A **romance** offers a fanciful tale, freed from strict realism. An **epic** tells a heroic story on a grand scale. A **ballad** usually deals in a simplified way with ordinary people, but the supernatural may also figure in the story.

In **lyric poetry**, a speaker expresses the ideas and emotions of a particular moment. Lyric poetry can be difficult because the reader needs to create a context, a background, in order to appreciate the expression of the moment. A lyric poem offers us only the words of someone speaking, as if everything has been erased from a cartoon drawing except the little balloon with the speaker's words inside. The previous scenes are missing, and even the current scene is not explicated fully. Instead, the reader is given a brief, expressive, often musical statement. Many poems, obviously, fit the very loose category of lyric poetry.

A third term, **dramatic poetry**, may be used to refer to poems that more explicitly present a character or characters speaking. In a lyric poem, someone is speaking, but the reader must determine who it is; in dramatic poetry, characters are more developed. The poetry depicts, in other words, a dramatic situation, one that we can imagine being acted out. But as T. S. Eliot asked in his "Dialogue on Dramatic Poetry," "What great poetry is not dramatic?"

Rhyme and Rhythm   Have you ever wondered why so many children learn the alphabet by singing the "ABC" song? It is of course the way it sounds that makes this information easier to remember: the melody, the rhymes at the end of every line, the repeated basic rhythm with its little variations—these all make the sense (in this case, a sequence of letters) memorable. Even adults, perhaps standing in front of a filing cabinet late in the day, will sometimes run through this little song to figure out if *this* comes before *that*. And you probably know the similar verses to help us remember how to spell "receive" ("i" before "e," except after "c") and lots of other things.

Poems use **rhyme** and **rhythm** in part for the same reason the alphabet song uses them: to make their statements memorable. In ancient times before writing, storytellers relied on various verbal formulas to help them remember what to say. But the patterns also helped make their statements more striking, distinguishing the words of the storyteller from ordinary language. In Homer's great *Iliad*, an oral poem that survived into the age of print, there is a rather long list of some of the hometowns the Greek warriors left behind in their journey to the Trojan War. The list, surprisingly, is not at all boring—is in fact interesting—to most people because the rhythms and textures of the names are so appealing.

There is something particularly pleasing to us about the repetition of rhythms and sounds. We like to drum on the kitchen table, or swing our legs like pendulums. Our bodies stay alive by means of patterns and rhythms, as we breathe in and out, our hearts pumping and pulsating, our minds waking and sleeping, and so on. Poems try to appeal to us on this visceral, bodily level. You don't need to know the names of various kinds of rhymes and rhythms in order to hear and enjoy them, although this chapter and the glossary will cover the most common terms.

Closed Versus Open Form

Before the 1960s, most people danced by following certain prescribed steps (the swing, waltz, tango, square dance, fox-trot, etc.). Even though each person added his or her own individual styling, the basic pattern for each kind of dance was the same. If both partners knew the basic steps, strangers could dance together. In the 1960s many people largely stopped doing dances that called for particular steps and instead began contorting their bodies and moving around rhythmically (in theory) in whatever fashion they desired. In the 1990s, anything was possible on the dance floor, from highly choreographed line dances, to the traditionally structured partner dances, to the violent anarchy of head-bangers.

The different forms that poets use are like different kinds of dances. In a certain place and time, various patterns of poems (and dances) have been popular. A poet today can choose from all sorts of forms, ranging from very strict and time-honored ones—poetic line dances—to those that seem to be made up as the poem goes along. When a poet is dancing to a certain pattern, we say she or he is employing a **closed form.** And if the poet is making up the pattern, inventing the music of the lines for a particular occasion, then we say he or she is using an **open form.** In an open-form poem, in other words, the words are arranged in whatever way the poet chooses. The length of each line, the amount of white space between words and lines, the number of lines, the rhythm of each line, whether sounds are repeated or varied—these things are all "open" to the poet's artistry.

Although open form, which is also called **free verse,** can be traced in English back to the eighteenth century, its popularity really dates from the early part of the twentieth century. And the rapid expansion of free verse, interestingly, seems to have occurred at the same time that rules for dancing opened up; since the 1960s, the open form has been used most often by poets. Like free-form dancing, free verse may seem to some to be just another sign of the disappearance of discipline and the decay of civilization. Robert Frost's comment is probably the most famous disapproval of open-form poetry: "For my pleasure I had as soon write free verse as play tennis with the net down."

Dancing without steps, playing tennis without a net, writing poems without a pattern—these all might well seem at first to be much easier than the traditional alternative. Certainly, after the '60s, anyone can now get up and dance in just about any fashion; but anyone who has recently been to a high school reunion from that era can tell you, it often isn't a pretty sight. To dance well without any guidelines may require more ability and imagination than carrying out the prescribed moves of a traditional dance, even with personal variations on the pattern. Likewise, playing tennis without a net would be easier if the goal were simply to hit the ball into the other court. But to make tennis without a net interesting, allowing the other player to keep the ball in play (think of Robert Francis's boys playing "catch"), would probably require two excellent players and reimagining the game itself, and perhaps a new set of rules. Free verse may *seem* easier to write since there are no rules—but it's not necessarily easier to write free verse that holds an audience's interest, that stands up to repeated readings over time.

Open Form   Consider in the following poem how Denise Levertov, a master of free verse, uses line breaks, white spaces, rhythms, and sounds to capture and hold her readers.

DENISE LEVERTOV (1923–)

Advent 1966

Because in Vietnam the vision of a Burning Babe
is multiplied, multiplied,
                                       the flesh on fire
not Christ's, as Southwell saw it, prefiguring
the Passion upon the Eve of Christmas,   5

but wholly human and repeated, repeated,
infant after infant, their names forgotten,
their sex unknown in the ashes, set alight, flaming but not vanishing,
not vanishing as his vision but lingering,

cinders upon the earth or living on   10
moaning and stinking in hospitals three abed;

because of this my strong sight,
my clear caressive sight, my poet's sight I was given
that it might stir me to song,
is blurred.   15
                    There is a cataract filming over
my inner eyes. Or else a monstrous insect
has entered my head, and looks out
from my sockets with multiple vision,

seeing not the unique Holy Infant   20
burning sublimely, an imagination of redemption,
furnace in which souls are wrought into new life,
but, as off a beltline, more, more senseless figures aflame.

And this insect (who is not there—
it is my own eyes do my seeing, the insect   25
is not there, what I see is there)
will not permit me to look elsewhere,

or if I look, to see except dulled and unfocused
the delicate, firm, whole flesh of the still unburned.

[1967]

This poem does not have regular stanzas or rhyme scheme, but its language is clearly different from what one might encounter in a newspaper article or chemistry textbook. Read the first five lines again aloud and see what you notice. What seems "poetic" about Levertov's opening words?

Because in Vietnam the vision of a Burning Babe
is multiplied, multiplied,

                                the flesh on fire
not Christ's, as Southwell saw it, prefiguring
the Passion upon the Eve of Christmas, . . .

Obviously, the words are arranged on the page in a way that is not designed to be efficient or conserve paper. Most poetry, just by its spacing, indicates its status as poetry, and implicitly suggests we should weigh the words carefully. But why does Levertov arrange the words in this poem in this particular way? How is she using the freedom of not having a particular pattern to follow? For starters, consider the space at the end of the second line and the beginning of the third. What does it do? The white space, I think most readers would agree, creates a dramatic pause, emphasizing "the flesh on fire," an image that is central to the poem. After the fifth line, Levertov skips a line, thus creating a separate section, and this section is divided into two parts. Before "the flesh on fire," the poem focuses on the burning children in Vietnam: "Because in Vietnam the vision of a Burning Babe/ is multiplied, multiplied." But what happens in the second part of the first section or stanza, after "the flesh on fire"?

The second part would be very difficult if not impossible to understand without some familiarity with a poem by Robert Southwell, a sixteenth-century poet. Levertov assumes her readers know this very famous poem, called "The Burning Babe." In Southwell's poem, the speaker sees a vision of a burning infant, floating in the air, and realizes at the end of the poem "That it was Christmas Day." Levertov's vision takes place, according to the title, in the time leading up to Christmas, at "Advent 1966." So the last part of the first stanza begins the contrast that continues throughout the poem, a contrast between Levertov's and Southwell's Christmas-time visions: "not Christ's, as Southwell saw it, prefiguring/ the Passion upon the Eve of Christmas, . . ." In Southwell's poem, the burning babe is clearly Christ, and the speaker perceives the fire as an indication of the way Christ eradicates sin. Levertov thus uses Southwell's inspiring vision as a striking counterpoint to her own shocking vision; and the spacing of the first stanza helps convey that contrast.

What else can we say about the "poetic" nature of the opening lines? Aside from the spacing, perhaps the most obvious feature of these lines is their repetition of initial sounds (alliteration): "Vietnam" and "vision," "Burning" and "Babe," "flesh" and "fire," "Southwell" and "saw," "prefiguring" and "Passion." But there is also the repetitiveness of "multiplied, multiplied," which appears again in the next section in "repeated, repeated" and "not vanishing,/ not vanishing." Why would such a pattern of repeated sounds and words seem particularly effective in this poem? Because it is about the speaker's growing horror at the repeated burning of "infant after infant," an image that returns throughout the poem, an image the speaker (who may be seen as Levertov) cannot look away from. (During the Vietnam war, as you probably know, American soldiers often found themselves being attacked by enemy fighters who were hidden and sometimes disguised in villages; they were also attacked by villagers themselves.

By burning large patches of forest with napalm, and by setting whole villages on fire, the soldiers were, in theory, trying to fight back and defend themselves. But innocent children, including infants, were sometimes caught in the flames.)

We have looked at only two aspects of only the first five lines of this poem, but I think you can see how a poet can use an open form thoughtfully and creatively.

Closed Form   Writing in a closed form, poets fit what they have to say to some sort of preexisting pattern. This pattern sets up, in a sense, the rules of the verbal game the poet is playing. Such restrictions, although they might seem at first sight to hamper poets, putting a limit on what they can say, in practice poets often find that the form serves to inspire them. In basketball, the restrictions on movement in the lane and the limitations set by the shot clock (just to pick two examples) may well force a player to make a spectacular shot. Likewise, the necessity for a certain rhyme or sentence structure may well force a writer to come up with a remarkable word or idea that otherwise never would have appeared.

For instance, if the poet is writing a **sonnet**, then he or she knows that the poem will have a total of fourteen lines, and that these lines will follow a certain rhyming scheme. The most popular rhyming patterns for sonnets are the Shakespearean and the Italian. The Shakespearean sonnet we discussed, "So shall I live," features the following line endings: true, face, new, place, eye, change, history, strange, decree, dwell, be, tell, grow, show. Following the conventional practice of representing rhyming words by the same letter, the sonnet's rhymes take this form (in Elizabethan English, "eye" and "history" rhymed):

a, b, a, b, c, d, c, d, e, f, e, f, g, g

As you can see, this pattern breaks down into four groups of lines, three **quatrains** (or four-line units) and one **couplet** (two-line unit).

a b a b
c d c d
e f e f
g g

This grouping of lines in Shakespearean sonnets naturally encourages poets to employ a shift in meaning or focus after one or more of the quatrains. Also, oftentimes the couplet offers a reversal or surprise.

The Italian sonnet, which is the earliest form of the sonnet, was perfected by Petrarch, writing love sonnets to his Laura. Sometimes called the Petrarchan sonnet, its rhyming form goes like this:

a b b a
a b b a
c d c d c d

The first eight lines of a Petrarchan sonnet are called the *octave,* and the last six the *sestet.* This kind of sonnet also tends to break into two parts, often displaying a turn or shift of ideas between the octave and sestet.

The sonnet is only the most famous closed form; many others have been invented and adapted, creating traditions of poems in a particular form. It would be foolish to attempt an exhaustive survey here, as entire books have been written just to do that. To give you some sense, however, of the way a particular closed form gives shape and meaning to a poem, let's look at the Robert Southwell poem referred to in Levertov's poem. Since it somehow adds to the charm of Southwell's poem, I have not modernized the spelling, which was more flexible and creative four hundred years ago.

ROBERT SOUTHWELL (1561–1595)

The Burning Babe

As I in hoary winter's night stood shivering in the snow,
Surpris'd I was with sudden heat which made my heart to glow;
And lifting up a fearful eye to view what fire was near,
A pretty Babe all burning bright did in the air appear;
Who, scorched with excessive heat, such floods of tears did shed   5
As though his floods should quench his flames which with his tears
    were fed.
"Alas!" quoth he, "but newly born, in fiery heats I fry,
Yet none approach to warm their hearts or feel my fire but I!
My faultless breast the furnace is, the fuel wounding thorns,
Love is the fire, and sighs the smoke, the ashes shame and scorns;   10
The fuel Justice layeth on, and Mercy blows the coals,
The metal in this furnace wrought are men's defiled souls,
For which, as now on fire I am to work them to their good,
So will I melt into a bath to wash them in my blood."
With this he vanish'd out of sight and swiftly shrunk away,   15
And straight I called unto mind that it was Christmas day.

[1602]

We might notice first how many of Southwell's lines are punctuated at the end: only lines 1, 5, and 7 flow on to the next line; the others end with a comma, semicolon, or period at the end. Although this arrangement may seem quite natural, it's actually not that easy because each line has to be a certain length. Try chanting out the first two lines and you'll find that some syllables are stressed and some aren't. As I hear it, the first line looks like this, with "X" standing for a stressed syllable, and "x" an unstressed syllable:

   x X x X x X x   X
   As I in hoarie Winters night

Obviously this looks like a pattern: unstressed, then stressed, times four: xX xX xX xX. The second line, using the same notation system, looks like this:

   x   X   x X x X
   Stood shivering in the snow,

Or, unstressed, then stressed, times three: xX xX xX. In fact, looking at the first four lines, it's easy to see the rhythmic pattern, which is called "iambic" (for the names of other patterns, see the glossary under "meter"):

   xX xX xX xX
   xX xX xX
   xX xX xX xX
   xX xX xX

What do these patterned features—these rules—do for the poem?

    Sing a few bars of your favorite song, and consider the same question: what does the rhythmical pattern, the rhyme scheme, and the punctuation (with pauses and longer notes at the ends of ideas)—what do these things do for the song? For one thing, they make it more memorable. The rhymes also create little expectations that are fulfilled (satisfyingly) when we hear the rhyme completed. The pauses ending most lines indicate how to process the words—telling us that an idea ends *here*, and another one (to be related to the first one) begins *here*. Plus, the rhyming words receive additional emphasis: not only are they at the end of the line, where the emphasis typically falls in spoken English; they are followed by a pause, usually; and they are linked to the rhyming word. Southwell uses the rhyming line (lines 4, 8, 12, etc.) to complete a thought. Notice how these lines end in a semicolon, colon, or period—punctuation marks that signal the end of an idea, and thus divide the poem into four-line bits.

Southwell exploits this sectioning very effectively: notice how the first four lines begin with the winter night, the cold, the snow; then suddenly heat appears; and then, most dramatically, placed at the end in the most dramatic position, we see (rather amazingly) the speaker's heart begin "to glow." Likewise, the next four lines build up to the image of a "prettie Babe" on fire, which is striking enough. But the most astonishing detail is saved, again, for the most emphatic position—at the end: the burning baby just appears in the air. Throughout the poem, in fact, Southwell uses the last line of these four-line units to introduce the most dramatic information. In the next unit, lines 9–12, we find first that the infant is shedding so many tears that he appears to be attempting to put out the flames by crying. That's a pretty weird image, but the last line of this unit twists the strangeness up another notch, revealing that these tears, which appear to be an effort to quench the flames, are actually their source: the flames "were bred" by the tears.

We're only beginning to approach an "interpretation" of Southwell's poem (your teacher may invite you to pursue this task), but it should be clear already how an awareness of a poem's form can help us appreciate its meaning. Form and meaning, in fact, are inseparable. Whether a poet uses an open or closed form, we cannot really see what the poem is saying unless we also see *how* it is saying. An explanation of a poem, or any carefully crafted work, cannot stand for (that is, substitute for) the work itself—whether the explanation is the woefully inadequate summary by some "notes" or "guides" series, or the most sophisticated study by the most celebrated brainiac critic. We need the experience of the poem itself. Still, even though writing about a poem cannot take the place of the poem, it is the act of writing (and talking) about literature that allows us to experience it most deeply and actively.

Now it's time to turn to some reading. The following poems provide opportunities to apply and expand upon the points this chapter has made.

Poems for Making Sense

WILLIAM SHAKESPEARE (1564–1616)

Sonnet 138

When my love swears that she is made of truth,
I do believe her, though I know she lies,
That she might think me some untutor'd youth,
Unlearned in the world's false subtleties.
Thus vainly thinking that she thinks me young,   5
Although she knows my days are past the best,

Simply I credit her false-speaking tongue:
On both sides thus is simple truth suppress'd.
But wherefore says she not she is unjust?
And wherefore say not I that I am old?   10
O, love's best habit is in seeming trust,
And age in love loves not t' have years told:
    Therefore I lie with her, and she with me,
    And in our faults by lies we flattered be.

[1609]

WILLIAM CARLOS WILLIAMS (1883–1963)

The Red Wheelbarrow

so much depends
upon

a red wheel
barrow

glazed with rain   5
water

beside the white
chickens.

[1923]

ROBERT GRAVES (1895–1985)

Down, Wanton, Down!

Down, wanton, down! Have you no shame
That at the whisper of Love's name,
Or Beauty's, presto! up you raise
Your angry head and stand at gaze?

Poor bombard-captain, sworn to reach   5
The ravelin and effect a breach—
Indifferent what you storm or why,
So be that in the breach you die!

Love may be blind, but Love at least
Knows what is man and what mere beast;   10
Or Beauty wayward, but requires
More delicacy from her squires.

Tell me, my witless, whose one boast
Could be your staunchness at the post,
When were you made a man of parts   15
To think fine and profess the arts?

Will many-gifted Beauty come
Bowing to your bald rule of thumb,
Or Love swear loyalty to your crown?
Be gone, have done! Down, wanton, down!

[1933]

GARY SNYDER (1930–)

Some Good Things to Be Said for the Iron Age

A ringing tire iron
    dropped on the pavement
Whang of a saw
brusht on limbs
the taste   5
of rust

[1970]

Gary Snyder (left) and Allen Ginsberg—American
poets of the Beat Generation—take part in a
1965 protest.

RICHARD WILBUR (1921-)

A Late Aubade

You could be sitting now in a carrel
Turning some liver-spotted page,
Or rising in an elevator-cage
Toward Ladies' Apparel.

You could be planting a raucous bed   5
Of salvia, in rubber gloves,
Or lunching through a screed of someone's loves
With pitying head,

Or making some unhappy setter
Heel, or listening to a bleak   10
Lecture on Schoenberg's serial technique.

Isn't this better?

Think of all the time you are not
Wasting, and would not care to waste,
Such things, thank God, not being to your taste.   15
Think what a lot

Of time, by woman's reckoning,
You've saved, and so may spend on this,
You who had rather lie in bed and kiss
Than anything.   20

It's almost noon, you say? If so,
Time flies, and I need not rehearse
The rosebuds-theme of centuries of verse.
If you *must* go,

Wait for a while, then slip downstairs   25
And bring us up some chilled white wine,
And some blue cheese, and crackers, and some fine
Ruddy-skinned pears.

[1968]

14

Poetic Conversations

It is a classic instance of the maxim that literary works
are made out of other literary works.

—Donald Howard, on Coleridge's "Kubla Kahn"

This chapter highlights the usefulness of thinking of literature and literary study as a conversation—an ongoing, incredibly complex, constantly shifting discussion. This idea helps to clarify at least three fundamental issues:

1. Why published literary criticism is often so hard to understand, and how to make it easier;
2. Why literary works are often so hard to understand, and how to make them easier;
3. Why some works are part of an accepted canon, appearing on lots of readings lists and syllabi, while other works are rarely or never read.

"I just love your poetry!"

1. Literary critics often are writing to other literary critics: it's a conversation within a community of specialists. Literary criticism is a specialized genre, in other words. Publications in anthropology or medicine or any field would be hard to understand without an awareness of the theories and concepts underlying the field. This basic knowledge in any discipline is ordinarily taken for granted: when people

are conversing, they usually don't constantly fill in the background of what they're talking about. In any field, including literary criticism, some writers try to expand the conversation, addressing a more general audience. Although you may not be able to understand the articles published in *The Journal of the American Association of Dermatology*, your chances increase as you encounter the same research in *Scientific American* (which assumes a general but scientifically astute audience), or *Discover* (which assumes a general audience with some interest in science), or *Newsweek* (which tries to reach just about everyone). This textbook tries to expose what adept readers take for granted, and may not even know that they know.

Once you understand the basics of a particular knowledge community, however, you may still have difficulty figuring out what's going on. If you encounter a group of your friends intently discussing "Susan's horse," and you've never heard of Susan, and you didn't know your friends had any interest in horses, you might well be baffled. You could ask someone, "What are you guys talking about?" Or you could listen for a while, tolerating your confusion, and eventually figure out that "Susan's Horse" is the name of a painting that your art-major friends are interested in. Literary criticism is like that: there are conversations ongoing, some of them for hundreds of years. To catch up, you need information, patience, and the energy to explore what has been said; and it's helpful to be able to ask someone (which is where your teacher can be especially valuable!).

Thus, when you do research on literary criticism, you're not looking for ideas you can use in your paper. You're looking for ideas that will spark your own ideas; you're trying to figure out what the conversation is about so you can contribute to it, or shift it, or enlarge it, or something else. You wouldn't want to contribute to a conversation by simply repeating what someone else has already said; that would be weird. You've got to come up with your own ideas.

Literary criticism is often hard simply because you're relatively new in town, but it will become easier as you experience more of it, and get a better sense of what people are talking about, what they assume, and what they're trying to accomplish.

This insight may be both comforting (there's nothing wrong with you if reading and writing literary criticism seems difficult) and dismaying (there's no magic wand that will make writing and reading literary criticism easy). And you may wonder if you really want to put forth the effort to join the conversation about literature. The answer is that you do, for the simple reason that literary study is essential to modern culture. Not only is the literature you're studying a valuable resource for understanding all the intersecting conversations in your world, but the tools used in literary analysis are applicable in every aspect of your life. We're all involved in noticing ambiguities while at the same time trying to make things fit together; in describing vividly and interestingly our experiences; in detecting unstated assumptions and unacknowledged contradictions and exposing them; in analyzing unspoken desires and fears that motivate other people; in becoming politically connected and active; in relating people's lives and times to what they say and do; and so forth.

There are good reasons to learn the theories and concepts of dermatology (or anthropology, geology, biology, law, etc.), but you probably will have to choose some areas and not others. Literary study, however, is a specialty that affects just about everyone because literature (in some sense) affects just about everyone. That's one reason why almost all schools require some kind of literary study.

2. The idea of literature itself as a conversation illuminates its difficulty. Just as literary critics are talking to each other, so also are writers responding to other writers. (Some of those writers may be literary critics!) According to Harold Bloom, one

of the last century's most interesting and prolific literary critics, a poem is always a response to some other poem. This response, as Bloom sees it, is anxious and competitive, as writers try to overcome the work of prior writers. Bloom's idea that a great poet is always struggling with previous poets, trying to be "strong" by somehow outdoing, or redoing some prior work, may be an exaggeration. For some writers (and critics), to be sure, publishing may be a kind of contest, with winners and losers, as successive writers attempt to play "king of the hill." There may not be a game called "queen of the hill," and it may be that writers sometimes have motivations that are not as competitive as Bloom thinks. But it certainly makes sense to think of a poet as always writing with some awareness of previous poems.

A writer, in a sense, is then engaging in a conversation with other writers, other works. The reader who is unaware of this conversation, who doesn't know the prior work that is being invoked, is obviously operating at a severe disadvantage. When students feel uncomfortable reading a literary work, the issue often isn't intelligence—it's just knowledge and experience. This chapter thus provides opportunities for you to see how certain works are responding to the other works. In the case of the first pairing here, for instance, Robert Frost in "Choose Something Like a Star" refers explicitly to John Keats's earlier poem, "Bright Star." No matter how smart you are, you really can't understand the allusion in Frost's poem unless you know Keats's poem. An editor of Frost's poem might provide an explanatory note, which would help, but the two poems offer very different ways of looking at life: each poem illuminates the other by contrast. A note really wouldn't be a good substitute for reading the other poem. Likewise, in the "Shepherds in Love" section, John Donne's "The Bait" is obviously a response to the preceding poems in the sequence. Although "The Bait" has been anthologized without these earlier poems, the point of Donne's poem would be impossible to see without the context given. If some works are baffling because we don't perceive the conversation that work is joining, the solution is clear enough: more reading, more experience within the genre.

3. Although some poems, like Frost's and Donne's, are clearly written as responses, in other cases the conversation between and among literary works may be unimagined by the authors. Although we shouldn't, for instance, assume that James Dickey was thinking of the shepherd poems collected here when he was writing "The Sheep Child," it's mischievously fun to read Dickey's poem in this pastoral context, creating a relationship. The "First Couple" poems, gathered in this section, create a conversation because they all address a cultural nexus, the story of Adam and Eve and the Forbidden Fruit; they may not be responding to each other as much as they are responding to a common tradition. Speaking of forbidden fruit—the poems in the "Bowl of Plums for Wordsworth" are related most obviously because they have something to do with plums. There may be deeper interconnections, of course, but those will be created by readers. Likewise, the "Swine Songs" might well seem to be a purely whimsical collection, but pigs in fact have a richly evocative cultural history, ranging from the demons that Jesus cast into a herd of swine, to the many stories in which a person is turned into a pig (from *Harry Potter* to Homer's *Odyssey*), to the growing genre of films starring pigs.

My point here is that readers not only *observe* the conversations of literature, but they also *create* them, by bringing works—sometimes unexpectedly—together in impromptu genres. Those works that respond to various conjunctions, that seem to speak to us and to each other in a variety of contexts, are the works we read again and again. Such often-read works are said to make up the **canon**, which is an imaginary list of the most-valued works. Different readers would make up different lists of

"The Works That Everyone Should Know," and these lists would unavoidably be subject to each reader's taste, politics, age, education—everything. Hence, "the canon" is an imaginary list. One might say that "the canon" is the name we use to point to the ongoing struggle over what we ought to read and value.

While the canon is always evolving, as certain works and writers get more or less attention in the conversation, in the past few decades works by women and minorities have increasingly been included on reading lists, in literature anthologies (including this one), and in scholarly discussions. Such shifts in the canon reflect changes in the community of readers, as people seek to turn the conversation to new topics, or to frame old topics in new ways. It's possible—and this is an exciting idea—for one person to influence the conversation, by discovering an unknown or neglected writer, by reviving interest in an established writer, by raising a new set of issues, or by simply bringing different works together. As you talk with your classmates and teacher about the poems in this chapter, you should find it's rewarding, as in any conversation, to discover and create connections and meanings.

The meaningful connections we see and create are not limited to those between and among poems. To indicate the kinds of connections that can be made, one set includes a painting and poems related to it. Sometimes, if we are lucky enough to have an earlier version of a poem, we might see how a poem is in a sense a response to an earlier version of itself; thus this chapter also offers three poems in draft and published versions—including in one case comments by the great American poet James Dickey upon a draft by his student, Pat Armstrong; and in another case, comments by the author upon her own draft.

Two Stars

Compare the dramatically different views of stars and life in these two poems

---

JOHN KEATS (1795–1821)

Bright star! would I were steadfast as thou art

Bright star! would I were steadfast as thou art—
   Not in lone splendor hung aloft the night,
And watching, with eternal lids apart,
   Like nature's patient, sleepless Eremite
The moving waters at their priest-like task   5
   Of pure ablution round earth's human shores,
Or gazing on the new soft-fallen mask
   Of snow upon the mountains and the moors—
No—yet still steadfast, still unchangeable,
   Pillowed upon my fair love's ripening breast,   10
To feel for ever its soft fall and swell,
   Awake for ever in a sweet unrest,
Still, still to hear her tender-taken breath,
And so live ever—or else swoon to death.

[1819]

ROBERT FROST (1874–1963)

Choose Something Like a Star

O Star (the fairest one in sight),
We grant your loftiness the right
To some obscurity of cloud—
It will not do to say of night,
Since dark is what brings out your light.   5
Some mystery becomes the proud.
But to be wholly taciturn
In your reserve is not allowed.
Say something to us we can learn
By heart and when alone repeat.   10
Say something! And it says, 'I burn.'
But say with what degree of heat.
Talk Fahrenheit, talk Centigrade.
Use language we can comprehend.
Tell us what elements you blend.   15
It gives us strangely little aid,
But does tell something in the end.
And steadfast as Keats' Eremite,
Not even stooping from its sphere,
It asks a little of us here.   20
It asks of us a certain height,
So when at times the mob is swayed
To carry praise or blame too far,
We may choose something like a star
To stay our minds on and be staid.

[1949]

Questions: Two Stars

1. Keats's poem may be difficult to decipher until you understand the sentence
    structure. Notice how the dash at the end of the first line interrupts the sen-
    tence, and how the dash following "No" in line 9 closes that interruption.
    Notice also how the comparisons extend Keats's ideas: it's easy enough to
    get lost in the comparisons and forget what is being talked about. Can you
    translate Keats's lines into your own words, giving you a clear sense of what
    is being said?
2. What is the form of Keats's poem? (How many lines does it have? What kind
    of poem has that number of lines?) Is that form an interesting one for this
    poem? Is there a turn or shift of meaning in the poem? Where?
3. How reasonable is what Keats's speaker desires? That is, can he get what he
    wants (assuming the speaker is a "he")? Explain.
4. How does "or else swoon to death" (in the final line) alter the poem? Why is
    the dash used nicely there? (One way to judge the effect of something, is to
    imagine the poem without it. How would the poem be different without
    that phrase?)

5. How is Frost's poem similar to Keats's? How is it different?
6. How does Frost use Keats's poem? That is, what does the explicit reference to Keats's poem do for Frost's poem? (Is Frost advocating a different approach to life?)
7. Elaborate on Frost's last line. What is its significance? How does Frost's title help to distinguish his poem from Keats's poem?

An Odd Couple?

What is appealing? Neatness, disorder, or something else?

BEN JONSON (1573–1637)

Still To Be Neat

Still to be neat, still to be dressed,
As you were going to a feast;
Still to be powdered, still perfumed:
Lady, it is to be presumed,
Though art's hid causes are not found,   5
All is not sweet, all is not sound.

Give me a look, give me a face,
That makes simplicity a grace;
Robes loosely flowing, hair as free:
Such sweet neglect more taketh me   10
Than all the adulteries of art;
They strike mine eyes, but not my heart.

[1609]

ROBERT HERRICK (1591–1674)

Delight in Disorder

A sweet disorder in the dress
Kindles in clothes a wantonness:
A lawn about the shoulders thrown
Into a fine distraction;
An erring lace, which here and there   5
Enthralls the crimson stomacher;

A cuff neglectful, and thereby
Ribbons to flow confusedly:
A winning wave, deserving note,
In the tempestuous petticoat;   10
A carelesse shoestring, in whose tie
I see a wild civility:
Do more bewitch me, than when art
Is too precise in every part.

[1648]

Questions: An Odd Couple?

1. Do Herrick and Jonson agree or disagree?
2. What is your position on this issue? (What is the issue?) Can you add to the
   examples that the two poets use to support your stance?

The First Couple

Here is one version of how it all began, and what it means—and a sampling of poets'
efforts to make sense of this beginning, to apply its signficance, to move beyond it,
to reinvent it.

Genesis 1:26–28, 2:7–10, 2:15–3:24
(from The King James Version)

Chapter 1

26 ¶And God said, let us make man in our image, after our likeness: and let
   them have dominion over the fish of the sea, and over the fowl of the
   air, and over the cattle, and over all the earth, and over every creeping
   thing that creepeth upon the earth.
27 So God created man in his *own* image, in the image of God created he
   him; male and female created he them.
28 And God blessed them, and God said unto them, Be fruitful, and
   multiply, and replenish the earth, and subdue it: and have dominion
   over the fish of the sea, and over the fowl of the air, and over every
   living thing that moveth upon the earth. . . .

Chapter 2

7 And the LORD God formed man *of* the dust of the ground, and breathed
   into his nostrils the breath of life; and man became a living soul.
8 ¶And the LORD God planted a garden eastward in Eden; and there he put   5
   the man whom he had formed.
9 And out of the ground made the LORD God to grow every tree that is
   pleasant to the sight, and good for food; the tree of life also in the
   midst of the garden, and the tree of knowledge of good and evil.
10 And a river went out of Eden to water the garden; and from thence it
   was parted, and became into four heads. . . .
15 And the LORD God took the man, and put him into the garden of Eden
   to dress it and to keep it.

16 And the Lord God commanded the man saying, Of every tree of the
    garden thou mayest freely eat:

17 But of the tree of the knowledge of good and evil, thou shalt not eat of   10
    it: for in the day that thou eatest thereof thou shalt surely die.

18 ¶And the Lord God said, *It is* not good that the man should be alone; I
    will make him an help meet for him.

19 And out of the ground the Lord God formed every beast of the field,
    and every fowl of the air; and brought *them* unto Adam to see what
    he would call them: and whatsoever Adam called every living
    creature, that *was* the name thereof.

20 And Adam gave names to all cattle, and to the fowl of the air, and to
    every beast of the field; but for Adam there was not found an help
    meet for him.

21 And the Lord God caused a deep sleep to fall upon Adam, and he slept:
    and he took one of his ribs, and closed up the flesh instead thereof;

22 And the rib, which the Lord God had taken from man, made he a   15
    woman, and brought her unto the man.

23 And Adam said, This *is* now bone of my bones, and flesh of my flesh:
    she shall be called Woman, because she was taken out of Man.

24 Therefore shall a man leave his father and his mother, and shall cleave
    unto his wife: and they shall be one flesh.

25 And they were both naked, the man and his wife, and were not ashamed.

Chapter 3

Now the serpent was more subtil than any beast of the field which the
    Lord God had made. And he said unto the woman, Yea, hath God said,
    Ye shall not eat of every tree of the garden?

2 And the woman said unto the serpent, We may eat of the fruit of the   20
    trees of the garden:

3 But of the fruit of the tree which *is* in the midst of the garden, God hath
    said, Ye shall not eat of it, neither shall ye touch it, lest ye die.

4 And the serpent said unto the woman, Ye shall not surely die:

5 For God doth know that in the day ye eat thereof, then your eyes shall
    be opened, and ye shall be as gods, knowing good and evil.

6 And when the woman saw that the tree *was* good for food, and that it
    was pleasant to the eyes, and a tree to be desired to make *one* wise,
    she took of the fruit thereof, and did eat, and gave also unto her
    husband with her; and he did eat.

7 And the eyes of them both were opened, and they knew that they *were*   25
    naked; and they sewed fig leaves together, and made themselves aprons.

8 And they heard the voice of the Lord God walking in the garden in the
    cool of the day: and Adam and his wife hid themselves from the
    presence of the Lord God amongst the trees of the garden.

9 And the Lord God called unto Adam, and said unto him, Where *art* thou?

10 And he said, I heard thy voice in the garden, and I was afraid, because I
    was naked; and I hid myself.

11 And he said, Who told thee that thou *wast* naked? Hast thou eaten of
    the tree, whereof I commanded thee that thou shouldest not eat?

12 And the man said, The woman who thou gavest *to be* with me, she gave   30
    me of the tree, and I did eat.

13 And the Lord God said unto the woman, What *is* this *that* thou hast

done? And the woman said, The serpent beguiled me, and I did eat.

14 And the LORD God said unto the serpent, Because thou hast done this,
thou *art* cursed above all cattle, and above every beast of the field;
upon thy belly shalt thou go, and dust shalt thou eat all the days of thy
life:

15 And I will put enmity between thee and the woman, and between thy
seed and her seed; it shall bruise thy head, and thou shalt bruise his heel.

16 Unto the woman he said, I will greatly multiply thy sorrow and thy
conception; in sorrow thou shalt bring forth children; and thy desire
shall be to thy husband, and he shall rule over thee.

17 And unto Adam he said, Because thou hast hearkened unto the voice of   35
thy wife, and hast eaten of the tree, of which I commanded thee,
saying, Thou shalt not eat of it: cursed *is* the ground for thy sake; in
sorrow shalt thou eat *of* it all the days of thy life;

18 Thorns also and thistles shall it bring forth to thee; and thou shalt eat
the herb of the field;

19 In the sweat of thy face shalt thou eat bread, till thou return unto the
ground; for out of it wast thou taken: for dust thou *art*, and unto dust
shalt thou return.

20 And Adam called his wife's name Eve; because she was the mother of
all living.

21 Unto Adam also and to his wife did the LORD God make coats of skins,
and clothed them.

22 ¶And the LORD God said, Behold, the man is become as one of us, to   40
know good and evil: and now, lest he put forth his hand, and take also
of the tree of life, and eat, and live for ever:

23 Therefore the LORD God sent him forth from the garden of Eden, to till
the ground from whence he was taken.

24 So he drove out the man; and he placed at the east of the garden of
Eden Cherubims, and a flaming sword, which turned every way, to
keep the way of the tree of life.

WILLIAM BUTLER YEATS (1865–1939)

Adam's Curse

We sat together at one summer's end
That beautiful mild woman your close friend
And you and I, and talked of poetry.
I said, "A line will take us hours maybe,
Yet if it does not seem a moment's thought   5
Our stitching and unstitching has been naught.
Better go down upon your marrow bones
And scrub a kitchen pavement, or break stones
Like an old pauper in all kinds of weather;
For to articulate sweet sounds together   10
Is to work harder than all these and yet
Be thought an idler by the noisy set
Of bankers, schoolmasters, and clergymen
The martyrs call the world."

                              That woman then   15

Murmured with her young voice, for whose mild sake
There's many a one shall find out all heartache
In finding that it's young and mild and low.
"There is one thing that all we women know
Although we never heard of it at school.   20
That we must labour to be beautiful."

I said, "It's certain there is no fine thing
Since Adam's fall but needs much labouring.
There have been lovers who thought love should be
So much compounded of high courtesy   25
That they would sigh and quote with learned looks
Precedents out of beautiful old books;
Yet now it seems an idle trade enough."

We sat grown quiet at the name of love.
We saw the last embers of daylight die   30
And in the trembling blue-green of the sky
A moon, worn as if it had been a shell
Washed by time's waters as they rose and fell
About the stars and broke in days and years.

I had a thought for no one's but your ears;   35
That you were beautiful and that I strove
To love you in the old high way of love;
That it had all seemed happy, and yet we'd grown
As weary hearted as that hollow moon.

[1903]

STEVIE SMITH (1902–1971)

How Cruel Is the Story of Eve

How cruel is the story of Eve
What responsibility
It has in history
For cruelty.

Touch, where the feeling is most vulnerable,   5
Unblameworthy—ah reckless—desiring children,
Touch there with a touch of pain?
Abominable.

Ah what cruelty,
In history   10
What misery.

Put up to barter
The tender feelings
Buy her a husband to rule her
Fool her to marry a master   15
She must or rue it
The Lord said it.

And man, poor man,
Is he fit to rule,

Pushed to it?   20
How can he carry it, the governance,
And not suffer for it
Insuffisance?
He must make woman lower then

So he can be higher then.   25
Oh what cruelty,
In history what misery.

Soon woman grows cunning
Masks her wisdom,
How otherwise will he   30
Bring food and shelter, kill enemies?
If he did not feel superior
It would be worse for her
And for the tender children
Worse for them.   35

Oh what cruelty,
In history what misery
Of falsity.

It is only a legend
You say? But what   40
Is the meaning of the legend
If not
To give blame to women most
And most punishment?

This is the meaning of a legend that colours   45
All human thought; it is not found among animals.

How cruel is the story of Eve,
What responsibility it has
In history
For misery.   50

Yet there is this to be said still:
Life would be over long ago
If men and women had not loved each other
Naturally, naturally,
Forgetting their mythology   55
They would have died of it else
Long ago, long ago,
And all would be emptiness now
And silence.

Oh dread Nature, for your purpose,   60
To have made them love so.

                                                    [1972]

TED HUGHES (1930–1998)

Theology

No, the serpent did not

Seduce Eve to the apple.
All that's simply
Corruption of the facts.

Adam ate the apple.   5
Eve ate Adam.
The serpent ate Eve.
This is the dark intestine.

The serpent, meanwhile,
Sleeps his meals off in Paradise—   10
Smiling to hear

God's querulous calling.

                                                                    [1967]

EDNA ST. VINCENT MILLAY (1892–1950)

Never May the Fruit Be Plucked

Never, never may the fruit be plucked from the bough
And gathered into barrels.
He that would eat of love must eat it where it hangs.
Though the branches bend like reeds,
Though the ripe fruit splash in the grass or wrinkle on the tree,   5
He that would eat of love may bear away with him
Only what his belly can hold,
Nothing in the apron,
Nothing in the pockets.
Never, never may the fruit be gathered from the bough   10

Edna St. Vincent Millay

And harvested in barrels.
The winter of love is a cellar of empty bins,
In an orchard soft with rot.

[1923]

LOUISE GLÜCK (1943–)

The Apple Trees

Your son presses against me
his small intelligent body.

I stand beside his crib
as in another dream
you stood among trees hung   5
with bitten apples
holding out your arms.
I did not move
but saw the air dividing
into panes of color—at the very last   10
I raised him to the window saying
See what you have made
and counted out the whittled ribs,
the heart on its blue stalk
as from among the trees   15
the darkness issued:

In the dark room your son sleeps.
The walls are green, the walls
are spruce and silence.
I wait to see how he will leave me.   20
Already on his hand the map appears
as though you carved it there,
the dead fields, women rooted to the river.

[1975]

THOMAS CAMPION (1567–1620)

There Is a Garden in Her Face

There is a garden in her face
Where roses and white lilies grow;
A heav'nly paradise is that place
Wherein all pleasant fruits do flow.
There cherries grow which none may buy   5
Till "Cherry-ripe" themselves do cry.

Those cherries fairly do enclose
Of orient pearl a double row,
Which when her lovely laughter shows,
They look like rose-buds filled with snow;   10
Yet them nor peer nor prince can buy,
Till "Cherry-ripe" themselves do cry.

Her eyes like angels watch them still;
Her brows like bended bows do stand,
   Threat'ning with piercing frowns to kill
All that attempt, with eye or hand   15
   Those sacred cherries come nigh
   Till "Cherry-ripe" themselves do cry.

[1617]

JOHN MILTON (1608–1674)

Paradise Lost, Book IV: [Eve Tells Adam about Her First Awareness]

That day I oft remember, when from sleep
I first awak'r, and found myself repos'd
Under a shade on flow'rs, much wond'ring where
And what I was, whence thither brought, and how.
Not distant far from thence a murmuring sound   5
Of waters issu'd from a Cave and spread
Into a liquid Plain, then stood unmov'd
Pure as th' expanse of Heav'n; I thither went
With unexperience't thought, and laid me down
On the green bank, to look into the clear   10
Smooth Lake, that to me seem'd another Sky-
As I bent down to look, just opposite,
A Shape within the war'ry gleam appear'd,
Bending to look on me, I started back,
It started back, but pleas'd I soon return'd,   15
Pleas'd it return'd as soon with answering looks
Of sympathy and love; there I had fixt
Mine eyes till now, and pin'd with vain desire,
What there thou seest fair Creature is thyself,
With thee it came and goes; but follow me,   20
And I will bring thee where no shadow stays
Thy coming, and they soft imbraces, hee
Whose image thou art, him though shalt enjoy
Inseperably thine, to him shalt hear
Multitudes like thyself, and thence be call'd   25
Mother of human Race ... what could I do,
But follow straight, invisibly thus led?
Till I espi'd thee, fair indeed and tall,
Under a Platan, yet methought less fair,
Less winning soft, less amiably mild,   30
Than that smooth wat'ry image.

[1667]

Questions: The First Couple

1. What is surprising about the Genesis story? Many people are familiar with the story, but haven't read the Bible version, or read it carefully, in many years. What do you see there that you didn't expect to see?

2. Some of these poems are related more directly to the Eden story than others. How does reading these poems in the context of each other, and in the context of the Genesis story, affect your experience of them?
3. Do any of the poems highlight problems (in logic, in ethics, in motivation, etc.) in the Genesis story? Do any of the poems help explain or illuminate the Genesis story? Explain.
4. Can you write a poem, or imagine a poem, in which Eve is the hero of this story? Can you imagine a different ending? What might that be?

Swine Songs

Explore the surprisingly rich significance of poems about pigs and pig-relations.

GALWAY KINNELL (1927–)

Saint Francis and the Sow

The bud
stands for all things,
even for those things that don't flower,
for everything flowers, from within, of self-blessing:
though sometimes it is necessary   5
to reteach a thing its loveliness,
to put a hand on its brow
of the flower
and retell it in words and in touch
it is lovely   10
until it flowers again from within, of self-blessing:
as Saint Francis
put his hand on the creased forehead
of the sow, and told her in words and in touch
blessings of earth on the sow, and the sow   15
began remembering all down her thick length,
from the earthen snout all the way
through the fodder and slops to the spiritual curl of the tail,
from the hard spininess spiked out from the spine
down through the great broken heart   20
to the sheer blue milken dreaminess spurting and shuddering
from the fourteen teats into the fourteen mouths sucking and blowing
    beneath them:
the long, perfect loveliness of sow.

[1980]

SYLVIA PLATH (1932–1963)

Sow

God knows how our neighbor managed to breed
His great sow:
Whatever his shrewd secret, he kept it hid

In the same way
He kept the sow—impounded from public stare,   5
Prize ribbon and pig show.

But one dusk our questions commended us to a tour
Through his lantern-lit
Maze of barns to the lintel of the sunk sty door

To gape at it: 10
This was no rose-and-larkspurred china suckling
With a penny slot

For thrift children, nor dolt pig ripe for heckling,
About to be
Glorified for prime flesh and golden crackling   15

In a parsley halo;
Nor even one of the common barnyard sows,
Mire-smirched, blowzy,

Maunching thistle and knotweed on her snout-
cruise—   20
Bloat tun of milk
On the move, hedged by a litter of feat-foot ninnies

Shrilling her hulk
To half for a swig at the pink teats. No. This vast
Brobdingnag bulk   25

Of a sow lounged belly-bedded on that black
compost,
Fat-rutted eyes
Dream-filmed. What a vision of ancient hoghood
must   30

Thus wholly engross
The great grandam!—our marvel blazoned a knight,
Helmed, in cuirass,

Unhorsed and shredded in the grove of combat
By a grisly-bristled   35
Boar, fabulous enough to straddle that sow's heat.

But our farmer whistled,
Then, with a jocular fist thwacked the barrel nape,
And the green-copse-castled

Pig hove, letting legend like dried mud drop,   40
Slowly, grunt
On grunt, up in the flickering light to shape

A monument
Prodigious in gluttonies as that hog whose want
Made lean Lent   45

Of kitchen slops and, stomaching no constraint,
Proceeded to swill
The seven troughed seas and every earthquaking
continent.

[1957]

THOM GUNN (1929–)

Moly

Nightmare of beasthood, snorting, how to wake.
I woke. What beasthood skin she made me take?

Leathery toad that ruts for days on end,
Or cringing dribbling dog, man's servile friend,

Or cat that prettily pounces on its meat,   5
Tortures it hours, then does not care to eat:

Parrot, moth, shark, wolf, crocodile, ass, flea.
What germs, what jostling mobs there were in me.

   These seem like bristles, and the hide is tough.
No claw or web here: each foot ends in hoof.   10

Into what bulk has method disappeared?
Like ham, streaked. I am gross—grey, gross, flap-eared.

The pale-lashed eyes my only human feature.
My teeth tear, tear. I am the snouted creature

That bites through anything, root, wire, or can.   15
If I was not afraid I'd eat a man.

Oh a man's flesh already is in mine.
Hand and foot poised for risk. Buried in swine.

   I root and root, you think that it is greed,
It is, but I seek out a plant I need.   20

Direct me gods, whose changes are all holy,
To where it flickers deep in grass, the moly:

Cool flesh of magic in each leaf and shoot,
From milky flower to the black forked root.

From this fat dungeon I could rise to skin   25
And human title, putting pig within.

I push my big grey wet snout through the green,
Dreaming the flower I have never seen.

                    [1971]

WILLIAM COWPER (1731–1800)

The Love of the World Reproved: or, Hypocrisy Detected

Thus says the prophet of the Turk,
Good Mussulman, abstain from pork;
There is a part in every swine
No friend of follower of mine
May taste, whate'er his inclination,   5
On pain of excommunication.

Such Mahomet's mysterious charge,
And thus he left the point at large.
Had he the sinful part express'd,
They might with safety eat the rest;   10
But for one piece they thought it hard
From the whole hog to be debarr'd;
And set their wit at work to find
What joint the prophet had in mind.   15
Much controversy straight arose,
These choose the back, the belly those;
By some 'tis confidently said
He meant not to forbid the head;
While others at that doctrine rail,   20
And piously prefer the tail.
Thus, conscience freed from every clog,
Mahometans eat up the hog.
You laugh-'tis well-the tale applied
May make you laugh on t'other side.   25
Renounce the world-the preacher cries.
We do-a multitude replies.
While one as innocent regards
A snug and friendly game at cards;
And one, whatever you may say,   30
Can see no evil in a play;
Some love a concert, or a race;
And others shooting, and the chase.

                                          [1985]

CHARLES TOMLINSON (1927–)

On a Pig's Head

Once it had gorged itself
to a pitch of succulence, they slew it:
it was the stare in the eyes
the butcher hated, and so removed
with a quick knife,   5
transforming the thing
to a still life, hacked
and halved, cross-cutting it
into angles with ears.
It bled no more,   10
though the black pearls
still lurked on its rawness
The ears were streaked with wax,
the teeth stained near the roots
like an inveterate smoker's.   15
It was the nose looked freshest—

a rubbery, soft pink.
With a spill of paper, I cleaned
the orifice of each ear,
and played water into the nostrils.   20
The brain was a mere thimble of a brain,
and the tongue, smaller than a sheep's
sliced neatly. The severed ears
seemed delicate on their plate
with their maze of veins.   25
When we submerged it in brine
to change it to brawn and galantine,
it wouldn't fit the bowls:
evidently, it had been conceived
for a more capacious age.   30
Divided, it remained massive
leaving no room for reflection
save the peppercorns, cloves
of garlic, bay-leaves and wine
would be necessary for its transformation.   35
When set to boil, it required
a rock, a great
red one
from Macuilxochitl
to keep it down.

[1981]

RICHARD EBERHART (1904–)

The Groundhog

In June, amid the golden fields,
I saw a groundhog lying dead.
Dead lay he; my sense shook,
And mind outshot our naked frailty.
There lowly in the vigorous summer   5
His form began its senseless change,
And made my senses waver dim
Seeing nature ferocious in him.
Inspecting close his maggots' might
And seething cauldron of his being,   10
Half with loathing, half with strange love,
I poked him with an angry stick.
The fever arose, became a flame
And Vigour circumscribed the skies,
Immense energy in the sun,   15
And through my flame a sunless trembling.
My stick had done nor good nor harm.
Then stood I silent in the day
Watching the object, as before;
And kept my reverence for knowledge
Trying for control, to be still,   20

To quell the passion of the blood;
Until I had bent down on my knees
Praying for joy in the sight of decay.
And so I left; and I returned   25
In Autumn strict of eye, to see
The sap gone out of the groundhog,
But the bony sodden hulk remained.
But the year had lost its meaning,
And in intellectual chains   30
I lost both love and loathing,
Mured up in the wall of wisdom.
Another summer took the fields again
Massive and burning, full of life,
But when I chanced upon the spot   35
There was only a little hair left,
And bones bleaching in the sunlight
Beautiful as architecture;
I watched them like a geometer,
And cut a walking stick from a birch.   40
It has been three years, now.
There is no sign of the groundhog.
I stood there in the whirling summer,
My hand capped a withered heart,
And thought of China and of Greece,   45
Of Alexander in his tent;
Of Montaigne in his tower,
Of Saint Theresa in her wild lament.

[1936]

PAUL MULDOON (1951–)

Hedgehog

The snail moves like a
Hovercraft, held up by a
Rubber cushion of itself,
Sharing its secret

With the hedgehog. The hedgehog   5
Shares its secret with no one.
We say, Hedgehog, come out
Of yourself and we will love you.

We mean no harm. We want
Only to listen to what   10
You have to say. We want
Your answers to our questions.

The hedgehog gives nothing
Away, keeping itself to itself.
We wonder what a hedgehog   15
Has to hide, why it so distrusts.

We forget the god
Under this crown of thorns.
We forget that never again
Will a god trust in the world.   20

                                                      [1973]

Questions: Swine Songs

1. Which of these poems is most difficult? What makes it difficult? Which is the
   easiest? Why? Does the difficult poem "earn" its difficulty? That is, is there some
   reward for the reader's effort? In particular, think about the imagery in one of
   these poems. How does the imagery contribute to the poem's theme?
2. Compare the imagery in any two of these poems. Compare how the two
   poems "work"—in the way that the poem advances its argument or thesis
   (supposedly, the imagery plays some role in that thesis).
3. For each of these poems, select the most important word or phrase. Also,
   select the most interesting word or phrase.
4. Discuss the tone in one or two of these poems. Is the poem what you would
   expect, given the subject matter? What is the purpose of the tone?

A Bowl of Plums for Wordsworth

Once you have experienced the forlornness of Wordsworth's "The World Is Too
Much with Us," consider how William Carlos Williams' "This is just to say" (see page
574) might be seen as one kind of antidote to Wordsworth's complaint. How do
the other poems here (by Koch, Chasin, Levertov, and Clampitt) extend or complicate Williams' sensual indulgence? What sense do the other poems make as
responses to Wordsworth's alienation?

WILLIAM WORDSWORTH (1770–1850)

The World Is Too Much with Us

The world is too much with us; late and soon,
Getting and spending, we lay waste our powers;
Little we see in Nature that is ours;
We have given our hearts away, a sordid boon!
This Sea that bares her bosom to the moon;   5
The winds that will be howling at all hours,
And are up-gathered now like sleeping flowers;
For this, for everything, we are out of tune;
It moves us not. –Great God! I'd rather be
A Pagan suckled in a creed outworn;   10
So might I, standing on this pleasant lea,
Have glimpses that would make me less forlorn;
Have sight of Proteus rising from the sea;
Or hear old Triton blow his wreathèd horn.

                                                      [1807]

KENNETH KOCH (1925–2002)

Variations on a Theme by William Carlos Williams

1

I chopped down the house that you had been saving to live in next summer.
I am sorry, but it was morning, and I had nothing to do
and its wooden beams were so inviting.

2

We laughed at the hollyhocks together
and then I sprayed them with lye.   5
Forgive me. I simply do not know what I am doing.

3

I gave away the money that you had been saving to live on for the next
    ten years.
The man who asked for it was shabby
and the firm March wind on the porch was so juicy and cold.

4

Last evening we went dancing and I broke your leg.   10
Forgive me. I was clumsy and
I wanted you here in the wards, where I am a doctor!

[1962]

HELEN CHASIN (1938–)

The Word Plum

The word *plum* is delicious

pout and push, luxury of
self-love, and savoring murmur

full in the mouth and falling
like fruit   5

taut skin
pierced, bitten, provoked into
juice, and tart flesh

question
and reply, lip and tongue   10
of pleasure.

[1986]

DENISE LEVERTOV (1923–1997)

O Taste and See

The world is
not with us enough

O taste and see

the subway Bible poster said,
meaning The Lord, meaning   5
if anything all that lives
to the imagination's tongue,

grief, mercy, language,
tangerine, weather, to
breathe them, bite   10
savor, chew, swallow, transform

into our flesh our
deaths, crossing the streets, plum, quince,
living in the orchard and being

hungry, and plucking   15
the fruit.

                                                                        [1962]

AMY CLAMPITT (1923–1994)

Nothing Stays Put

The strange and wonderful are too much with us.
The protea of the antipodes—a great,
globed, blazing honeybee of a bloom—
for sale in the supermarket! We are in
our decadence, we are not entitled.   5
What have we done to deserve
all the produce of the tropics—
this fiery trove, the largesse of it
heaped up like cannonballs, these pineapples, bossed
and crested, standing like troops at attention,   10
these tiers, these balconies of green, festoons
grown sumptuous with stoop labor?

The exotic is everywhere, It comes to us
before there is a yen or a need for it. The green-
grocers, uptown and down, are from South Korea.   15
Orchids, opulence by the pailful, just slightly
fatigued by the plane trip from Hawaii, are
disposed on the sidewalks; alstroemerias, freesias
fattened a bit in translation from overseas; gladioli
likewise estranged from their piercing ancestral crimson;   20
as well as, less altered from the original blue cornflower
of the roadsides and railway embankments of Europe, these
bachelor's buttons. But it isn't the railway embankments
their featherweight wheels of cobalt remind me of—it's
a row of them among prim colonnades of cosmos,   25
snapdragon, nasturtium, bloodsilk red poppies
in my grandmother's garden; a prairie childhood,
the grassland shorn, overlaid with a grid,
unsealed, furrowed, harrowed, and sown with immigrant grasses,

their massive corduroy, their wavering feltings embroidered   30
here and there by the scarlet shoulder patch of cannas
on a courthouse lawn, by a love know, a cross-stitch
of living matter, sown and tended by women,
nurturers everywhere of the strange and wonderful,
beneath whose hands what had been alien begins,   35
as it alters, to grow as though it were indigenous.

But at this remove what I think of as
strange and wonderful—strolling the side streets of Manhattan
on an April afternoon, seeing hybrid pear trees in blossom,
a tossing, vertiginous colonnade of foam up above—   40
is the white petalfall, the warm snowdrift
of the indigenous wild plum of my childhood.
Nothing stays put. The world is a wheel.
All that we know, that we're
made of, is motion.   45

[1989]

Questions: A Bowl of Plums for Wordsworth

1. Are these poems about sensual indulgence? Which ones (if any) are about
   that? Which ones aren't? What else (if anything) are they about?
2. How are these poems related? For some, the relationship is obvious; for others, you will have to be creative. Here is the challenge: explain this grouping,
   and how each poem is somehow made more interesting (richer, deeper, fun-
   nier, something) by being placed in the company of the others.

God?

These poems all shed some light, or "darkness visible" as Milton put it, on the ultimate question(s).

WILLIAM WORDSWORTH (1770–1850)

Afterthought

I THOUGHT of Thee, my partner and my guide,
As being past away.—Vain sympathies!
For, backward, Duddon! as I cast my eyes,
I see what was, and is, and will abide;
Still glides the Stream, and shall for ever glide;   5
The Form remains, the Function never dies;
While we, the brave, the mighty, and the wise,
We Men, who in our morn of youth defied
The elements, must vanish;—be it so!
Enough, if something from our hands have power   10
To live, and act, and serve the future hour;
And if, as toward the silent tomb we go,

Through love, through hope, and faith's transcendent dower,
We feel that we are greater than we know.

[1820]

STEPHEN CRANE (1871–1900)

A Man Said to the Universe

A man said to the universe:
"Sir, I exist!"
"However," replied the universe,
"The fact has not created in me
A sense of obligation."   5

[1899]

THEODORE ROETHKE (1908–1963)

Root Cellar

Nothing would sleep in that cellar, dank as a ditch,
Bulbs broke out of boxes hunting for chinks in the dark,
Shoots dangled and drooped,
Lolling obscenely from mildewed crates,
Hung down long yellow evil necks, like tropical snakes.   5
And what a congress of stinks!—
Roots ripe as old bait,
Pulpy stems, rank, silo-rich,
Leaf-mold, manure, lime, piled against slippery planks.
Nothing would give up life: 10
Even the dirt kept breathing a small breath.

[1948]

PERCY BYSSHE SHELLEY (1792–1822)

Ozymandias

I met a traveler from an antique land
Who said: Two vast and trunkless legs of stone
Stand in the desert. Near them, on the sand,
Half sunk, a shattered visage lies, whose frown,
And wrinkled lip, and sneer of cold command,   5
Tell that its sculptor well those passions read
Which yet survive, stamped on these lifeless things,
The hand that mocked them and the heart that fed;
And on the pedestal these words appear:
"My name is Ozymandias, king of kings: 10
Look on my works, ye Mighty, and despair!"
Nothing beside remains. Round the decay

Of that colossal wreck, boundless and bare
The lone and level sands stretch far away.

[1818]

JAMES FENTON (1949–)

God, A Poem

A nasty surprise in a sandwich
A drawing-pin caught in your sock,
The limpest of shakes from a hand which
You'd thought would be firm as a rock,

A serious mistake in a nightie,   5
A grave disappointment all round
Is all that you'll get from th'Almighty,
Is all that you'll get underground.

Oh he *said*: 'If you lay off the crumpet
I'll see you alright in the end.   10
Just hang on until the last trumpet.
Have faith in me, chum — I'm your friend.'

But if you remind him, he'll tell you :
'I'm sorry, I must have been pissed —
Though your name rings a sort of a bell. You   15
Should have guessed that I do not exist.

'I didn't exist at Creation,
I didn't exist at the Flood,
And I won't be around for Salvation
To sort out the sheep from the cud —   20

'Or whatever the phrase is. The fact is
In soteriological terms
I'm a crude existential malpractice
And you are a diet of worms.

'You're a nasty surprise in a sandwich.   25
You're a drawing-pin caught in my sock.
You're the limpest of shakes from a hand which
I'd have thought would be firm as a rock,

'You're a serious mistake in a nightie,
You're a grave disappointment all round —   30
That's all that you are,' says th'Almighty,
'And that's all that you'll be underground.'

[1983]

THOMAS HARDY (1840–1928)

The Oxen

Christmas Eve, and twelve of the clock.
  "Now they are all on their knees,"

An elder said as we sat in a flock
   By the embers in hearthside ease.

We pictured the meek mild creatures where   5
   They dwelt in their strawy pen,
Nor did it occur to one of us there
   To doubt they were kneeling then.

So fair a fancy few would weave
   In these years! Yet, I feel,   10
If someone said on Christmas Eve,
   "Come; see the oxen kneel

"In the lonely barton[1] by yonder coomb[2]
   Our childhood used to know,"
I should go with him in the gloom,   15
   Hoping it might be so.

[1915]

[1]farmyard   [2]narrow valley

WALLACE STEVENS (1879–1955)

Anecdote of the Jar

I placed a jar in Tennessee,
And round it was, upon a hill.
It made the slovenly wilderness
Surround that hill.

The wilderness rose up to it,   5
And sprawled around, no longer wild.
The jar was round upon the ground
And tall and of a port in air.

It took dominion everywhere.
The jar was gray and bare.   10
It did not give of bird or bush,
Like nothing else in Tennessee.

[1923]

MARK STRAND (1934–)

Keeping Things Whole

In a field
I am the absence
of field.
This is
always the case.   5
Wherever I am
I am what is missing.

When I walk
I part the air

and always
the air moves in
to fill the spaces
where my body's been.   10

We all have reasons
for moving.   15
I move
to keep things whole.

[1969]

GERARD MANLEY HOPKINS (1844–1889)

God's Grandeur

The world is charged with the grandeur of God.
  It will flame out, like shining from shook foil;
  It gathers to a greatness, like the ooze of oil
Crushed. Why do men then now not reck his rod?
Generations have trod, have trod, have trod;   5
  And all is seared with trade; bleared, smeared with toil;
  And wears man's smudge and shares man's smell: the soil
Is bare now, nor can foot feel, being shod.

And for all this, nature is never spent;
  There lives the dearest freshness deep down things;   10
And though the last lights off the black West went
  Oh, morning, at the brown brink eastward, springs—
Because the Holy Ghost over the bent
  World broods with warm breast and with ah! bright wings.

[1877]

AMY CLAMPITT (1923–1994)

Lindenbloom

Before midsummer density
opaques with shade the checker-
tables underneath, in daylight
unleafing lindens burn
green-gold a day or two,   5
no more, with intimations
of an essence I saw once,
in what had been the pleasure-
garden of the popes
at Avignon, dishevel   10

into half (or possibly three-
quarters of) a million
hanging, intricately
tactile, blond bell-pulls

of bloom, the in-mid-air   15
resort of honeybees'
hirsute cotillion
teasing by the milligram
out of those necklaced
nectaries, aromas   20

so intensely subtle,
strollers passing under
looked up confused,
as though they'd just
heard voices, or   25
inhaled the ghost
of derelict splendor
and/or of seraphs shaken
into pollen dust
no transubstantiating   30
pope or antipope could sift
or quite precisely ponder.

                                                                    [1987]

Questions: God

1. Which one of these poems speaks most deeply to your own views regarding God? Try a reader-response approach on that poem.
2. Which poem seems to you most wrong-headed in this group? Try a reader-response approach on it.
3. Compare the two poems you identified in the first two questions.
4. See if you can imitate Hopkins's amazing style. How do you react to this poem? How is the meaning of Hopkins's poem tied up with the way he puts his meaning? Are there other poems here in which the sound and sense seem intimately linked?
5. See if you can add one line to any of these poems and totally alter its effect. (Try the Strand poem first.)

Shorelines

The following poems respond to—or can be related to—"Dover Beach," which appears on page 249.

Anthony Hecht (1923–)

The Dover Bitch

A Criticism of Life

For Andrews Wanning

So there stood Matthew Arnold and this girl
With the cliffs of England crumbling away behind them,
And he said to her, "Try to be true to me,

And I'll do the same for you, for things are bad
All over, etc., etc."   5
Well now, I knew this girl. It's true she had read
Sophocles in a fairly good translation
And caught that bitter allusion to the sea,
But all the time he was talking she had in mind
The notion of what his whiskers would feel like   10
On the back of her neck. She told me later on
That after a while she got to looking out
At the lights across the channel, and really felt sad,
Thinking of all the wine and enormous beds
And blandishments in French and the perfumes.   15
And then she got really angry. To have been brought
All the way down from London, and then be addressed
As sort of a mournful cosmic last resort
Is really tough on a girl, and she was pretty,
Anyway, she watched him pace the room
And finger his watch-chain and seem to sweat a bit,   20
And then she said one or two unprintable things.
But you mustn't judge her by that. What I mean to say is,
She's really all right. I still see her once in a while
And she always treats me right.
We have a drink   25
And I give her a good time, and perhaps it's a year
Before I see her again, but there she is.
Running to fat, but dependable as they come.
And sometimes I bring her a bottle of *Nuit d'Amour*.

                                                               [1967]

JOHN BREHM (1954–)

Sea of Faith

Once when I was teaching "Dover Beach"
to a class of freshman, a young woman
raised her hand and said, "I'm confused
about this 'Sea of Faith.'" "Well," I said,
"let's talk about it. We probably need   5
to talk a bit about figurative language.
What confuses you about it?"
"I mean, is it a real sea?" she asked.
"You mean, is it a real body of water
that you could point to on a map   10
or visit on a vacation?"
"Yes," she said. "Is it a real sea?"
Oh Christ, I thought, is this where we are?
Next year I'll be teaching them the alphabet
and how to sound words out.   15
I'll have to teach them geography, apparently,
before we can move on to poetry.
I'll have to teach them history, too—

a few weeks on the Dark Ages might be instructive.
"Yes," I wanted to say, "it is.   20
It is a real sea. In fact it flows
right into the Sea of Ignorance
IN WHICH YOU ARE DROWNING.
Let me throw you a Rope of Salvation
before the Sharks of Desire gobble you up.   25
Let me hoist you back up onto this Ship of Fools
so that we might continue our search
for the Fountain of Youth. Here, take a drink
of this. It's fresh from the River of Forgetfulness."
But of course I didn't say any of that.   30
I tried to explain in such a way
as to protect her from humiliation,
tried to explain that poets
often speak of things that don't exist.
It was only much later that I wished   35
I could have answered differently,
only after I'd betrayed myself
and been betrayed that I wished
it was true, wished there really was a Sea of Faith
that you could wade into,   40
dive under its blue and magic waters,
hold your breath, swim like a fish
down to the bottom, and then emerge again
able to believe in everything, faithful
and unafraid to ask even the simplest of questions,   45
happy to have them simply answered.

                                                        [1999]

FRED DINGS

Chains of Change

In drought the mind clouds with humid visions,
and in cold seas we sail for the islands of summer
where pink roses of pleasure petal open

and fall in fleshy halos on the grass. Serenity   5
waits for us in the green silence after
love, in the aftertaste of wine, in the heaven

where we imagine we could linger forever
But desire gathers on the boundaries of difference
like droplets on a cold grass in warm air,   10

and when the sparkling moment eventually warms
to the general mood, the dew steams back
to its former self, driftin toward some

new island in time. Aren't we like that?
Wouldn't the long incarcerations in happiness
leave us longing for sadness, praying for a few   15

flames to singe our ease, for archipelagos
of pain to erupt in our seas of content reasons
for sailing, as the indepensable linkage of our lives.   20

[1999]

CATHY SONG (1955–)

Waterwings

The mornings are his,
blue and white
like the tablecloth at breakfast.
He's happy in the house,
a sweep of the spoon   5
brings the birds under his chair.
He sings and the dishes disappear.

Or holding a crayon like a candle,
he draws a circle.
It is his hundredth dragonfly,   10
Calling for more paper,
this one is red-winged
and like the others,
he wills it to fly, simply
by the unformed curve of his signature.   15

Waterwings he call them,
the floats I strap to his arms.
I wear an apron of concern,
sweep the morning of birds.
To the water he returns,   20
plunging where it's cold,
moving and squealing into sunlight.
The water from here seems flecked with gold.

I watch the circles
his small body makes   25
fan and ripple,
disperse like an echo
into the sum of water, light and air,
His imprint on the water
has but a brief lifespan,   30
the flicker of a dragonfly's delicate wing.

This is sadness, I tell myself,
the morning he chooses to leave his wings behind,
because he will not remember
that he and beauty were aligned,   35
skimming across the water, nearly airborne,
on his first solo flight.
I'll write "how he could not
contain his delight."
At the other end,   40

in another time frame,
he waits for me—
having already outdistanced this body,
the one that slipped from me like a fish,
floating, free of itself.

[1988]

WILLIAM SHAKESPEARE (1564–1616)

Sonnet 60

Like as the waves make towards the pebbled shore,
So do our minutes hasten to their end;
Each changing place with that which goes before,
In sequent toil all forwards do contend.
Nativity, once in the main of light,   5
Crawls to maturity, wherewith being crowned,
Crookèd eclipses 'gainst his glory fight,
And Time that gave doth now his gift confound.
Time doth transfix the flourish set on youth
And delves the parallels in beauty's brow,   10
Feeds on the rarities of nature's truth,
And nothing stands but for his scythe to mow.
   And yet to times in hope my verse shall stand,
   Praising thy worth, despite his cruel hand.

[1609]

ALFRED, LORD TENNYSON (1809–1892)

Ulysses

It little profits that an idle king,
By this still hearth, among these barren crags,
Matched with an agèd wife, I mete and dole
Unequal laws unto a savage race
That hoard, and sleep, and feed, and know not me.   5
I cannot rest from travel; I will drink
Life to the lees. All times I have enjoyed
Greatly, have suffered greatly, both with those
That loved me, and alone; on shore, and when
Through scudding drifts the rainy Hyades   10
Vexed the dim sea. I am become a name;
For always roaming with a hungry heart
Much have I seen and known—cities of men
And manners, climates, councils, governments,
Myself not least, but honored of them all—   15
And drunk delight of battle with my peers,
Far on the ringing plains of windy Troy.
I am a part of all that I have met;
Yet all experience is an arch wherethrough

Gleams that untraveled world whose margin fades   20
Forever and forever when I move.
How dull it is to pause, to make an end,
To rust unburnished, not to shine in use!
As though to breathe were life! Life piled on life
Were all too little, and of one to me   25
Little remains; but every hour is saved
From that eternal silence, something more,
A bringer of new things; and vile it were
For some three suns to store and hoard myself,
And this grey spirit yearning in desire   30
To follow knowledge like a sinking star,
Beyond the utmost bound of human thought.
    This is my son, mine own Telemachus,
To whom I leave the scepter and the isle—
Well-loved of me, discerning to fulfill   35
This labor, by slow prudence to make mild
A rugged people, and through soft degrees
Subdue them to the useful and the good.
Most blameless is he, centered in the sphere
Of common duties, decent not to fail   40
In offices of tenderness, and pay
Meet adoration to my household gods,
When I am gone. He works his work, I mine.
    There lies the port; the vessel puffs her sail;
There gloom the dark, broad seas. My mariners,   45
Souls that have toiled, and wrought, and thought with me—
That ever with a frolic welcome took
The thunder and the sunshine, and opposed
Free hearts, free foreheads—you and I are old;
Old age hath yet his honor and his toil.   50
Death closes all; but something ere the end,
Some work of noble note, may yet be done,
Not unbecoming men that strove with Gods.
The lights begin to twinkle from the rocks;
The long day wanes; the low moon climbs; the deep   55
Moans round with many voices. Come, my friends,
'Tis not too late to seek a newer world.
Push off, and sitting well in order smite
The sounding furrows; for my purpose holds
To sail beyond the sunset, and the baths   60
Of all the western stars, until I die.
It may be that the gulfs will wash us down;
It may be we shall touch the Happy Isles,
And see the great Achilles, whom we knew.
Though much is taken, much abides; and though   65
We are not now that strength which in old days
Moved earth and heaven, that which we are, we are—
One equal temper of heroic hearts,
Made weak by time and fate, but strong in will
To strive, to seek, to find, and not to yield.

[1833]

Questions: Shorelines

1. Thinking of these poems as a group, see if you can come up with a single word that relates to all of them. Explain.
2. These poems have something to do with people who are on the edge of something. Support or deny this assertion.
3. Is Sting's song a version, in a sense, of Arnold's poem? Explain your answer.
4. How many different kinds of faith and faithfulness can you find in these poems?

Love among the Sheep

Love—seeking, resisting, refining—is always an act of imagination.

CHRISTOPHER MARLOWE (1564–1593)

The Passionate Shepherd to His Love

Come live with me and be my love
And we will all the pleasures prove
That valleys, groves, hills, and fields
Woods, or steepy mountain yields.

And we will sit upon the rocks,   5
Seeing the shepherds feed their flocks,
By shallow rivers to whose falls
Melodious birds sing madrigals.

And I will make thee beds of roses
And a thousand fragrant posies,   10
A cap of flowers, and a kirtle
Embroidered all with leaves of myrtle;

A gown made of the finest wool
Which from our pretty lambs we pull;
Fair lined slippers for the cold,   15
With buckles of the purest gold;

A belt of straw and ivy buds,
With coral clasps and amber studs:
And if these pleasures may thee move
Come live with me, and be my love.   20

The shepherds' swains shall dance and sing
For thy delight each May morning:
If these delights thy mind may move,
Then live with me and be my love.

[1600]

WALTER RALEIGH (1552–1618)

The Nymph's Reply to the Shepherd

If all the world and love were young,
And truth in every shepherd's tongue,
These pretty pleasures might me move

To live with thee and be thy love.

Time drives the flocks from field to fold   5
When rivers rage and rocks grow cold,
And Philomel becometh dumb;
The rest complain of cares to come.

The flowers do fade, and wanton fields
To wayward winter reckoning yields;   10
A honey tongue, a heart of gall,
Is fancy's spring, but sorrow's fall.

Thy gowns, thy shoes, thy beds of roses,
Thy cap, thy kirtle, and thy posies
Soon break, soon wither, soon forgotten–   15
In folly ripe, in reason rotten.

Thy belt of straw and ivy buds,
Thy coral clasps and amber studs,
All these in me no means can move
To come to thee and be thy love.   20

But could youth last and love still breed,
Had joys no date nor age no need,
Then these delights my mind might move
To live with thee and be thy love.

[1600]

JOHN DONNE (1572–1631)

The Bait

Come live with me, and be my love,
And we will some new pleasures prove
Of golden sands, and crystal brooks,
With silken lines, and silver hooks.

There will the river whispering run   5
Warmed by thy eyes, more than the sun.
And there the enamored fish will stay,
Begging themselves they may betray.

When thou wilt swim in that live bath,
Each fish, which every channel hath,   10
Will amorously to thee swim,
Gladder to catch thee, than thou him.

If thou, to be so seen, be'st loath,
By sun or moon, thou darkenest both,
And if myself have leave to see,
I need not their light, having thee.   15

Let others freeze with angling reeds,
And cut their legs with shells and weeds,
Or treacherously poor fish beset,
With strangling snare, or windowy net: 20

Let coarse bold hands from slimy nest

The bedded fish in banks out-wrest,
Or curious traitors, sleave-silk flies
Bewitch poor fishes' wandering eyes.

For thee, thou need'st no such deceit,   25
For thou thyself are thine own bait;
That fish, that is not catched thereby,
Alas, is wiser far than I.

                                                    [1633]

ROBERT HERRICK (1591–1674)

To Phillis *to love, and live with him*

Live, live with me, and thou shalt see
The pleasures I'll prepare for thee:
What sweets the Country can afford
Shall blesse thy Bed, and blesse thy Board.
The soft sweet Mosse shall be thy bed,   5
With crawling Woodbine over-spread:
By which the silver-shedding streames
Shall gently melt thee into dreames.
Thy clothing next, shall be a Gowne
Made of the Fleeces purest Downe.   10
The tongues of Kids shall be thy meate;
Their Milke thy drinke; and thou shalt eate
The Paste of Filberts for thy bread
With Cream of Cowslips buttered:
Thy Feasting-Tables shall be Hills   15
With *Daisies* spread, and *Daffadils*;
Where thou shalt sit, and *Red-brest* by,
For meat, shall give thee melody.
I'll give thee Chaines and Carkanets
Of *Primroses* and *Violets*.   20
A Bag and Bottle thou shalt have;
That richly wrought, and This as brave;
So that as either shall expresse
The Wearer's no meane Shepheardesse.
At Sheering-times, and yearly Wakes,   25
When *Tbemilis* his pastime makes,
There thou shalt be; and be the wit,
Nay more, the Feast, and grace of it.
On Holy-dayes, when Virgins meet
To dance the Heyes with nimble feet;   30
Thou shalt come forth, and then appeare
The *Queen of Roses* for that yeere.
And having danc't ('bove all the best)
Carry the Garland from the rest.
In Wicker-baskets Maids shall bring   35
To thee, (my dearest Shephardling)
The blushing Apple, bashfull Peare,

And shame-fac't Plum, (all simp'ring there).
Walk in the Groves, and thou shalt find
The name of *Phillis* in the Rind
Of every straight, and smooth-skin tree;   40
Where kissing that, I'll twice kisse thee.
To thee a Sheep-hook I will send,
Be-pranckt with Ribbands, to this end,
This, this alluring Hook might be
Lesse for to catch a sheep, then me.   45
Thou shalt have Possets, Wassails fine,
Not made of Ale, but spiced Wine;
To make thy Maids and selfe free mirth,
All sitting neer the glitt'ring Hearth.   50
Thou sha't have Ribbands, Roses, Rings,
Gloves, Garters, Stockings, Shooes, and Strings
Of winning Colours, that shall move
Others to Lust, but me to Love.
These (nay) and more, thine own shall be,   55
If thou wilt love, and live with me.

[1648]

C. DAY LEWIS (1904–1972)

Song

Come, live with me and be my love,
And we will all the pleasures prove
Of peace and plenty, bed and board
That chance employment may afford.

I'll handle dainties on the docks   5
And thou shalt read of summer frocks:
At evening by the sour canals
We'll hope to hear some madrigals.

Care on thy maiden brow shall put
A wreath of wrinkles, and thy foot   10
Be shod with pain: not silken dress
But toil shall tire thy loveliness.

Hunger shall make thy modest zone
And cheat fond death of all but bone —
If these delights thy mind may move,   15
Then live with me and be my love.

[1935]

WILLIAM CARLOS WILLIAMS (1883–1963)

Raleigh Was Right

We cannot go to the country
for the country will bring us no peace

What can the small violets tell us
that grow on furry stems in
the long grass among lance shaped leaves?

Though you praise us
and call to mind the poets
who sung of our loveliness
it was long ago!
long ago! when country people
would plow and sow with
flowering minds and pockets at ease —
if ever this were true.

Not now. Love itself a flower
with roots in a parched ground.
Empty pockets make empty heads.
Cure it if you can but
do not believe that we can live
today in the country
for the country will bring us no peace.

                                                5

                                               10

                                               15

[1941]

JAMES DICKEY (1923–1997)

The Sheep Child

Farm boys wild to couple
With anything   with soft-wooded trees
With mounds of earth   mounds
Of pinestraw   will keep themselves off
Animals by legends of their own:
In the hay-tunnel dark
And dung of barns, they will
Say   I have heard tell

That in a museum in Atlanta
Way back in a corner somewhere
There's this thing that's only half
Sheep   like a woolly baby
Pickled in alcohol   because
Those things can't live   his eyes
Are open   but you can't stand to look
I heard from someone who . . .

But this is now almost all
Gone. The boys have taken
Their own true wives in the city.
The sheep are safe in the west hill
Pasture   but we who were born there
Still are not sure. Are we,
Because we remember, remembered
In the terrible dust of museums?

Merely with his eyes, the sheep-child may

Be saying   saying

                                                5

                                               10

                                               15

                                               20

                                               25

I am here, in my father's house.
I who am half of your world, came deeply
To my mother in the long grass
Of the west pasture, where she stood like moonlight 30
Listening for foxes. It was something like love
From another world that seized her
From behind, and she gave, not lifting her head
Out of dew, without ever looking, her best
Self to that great need. Turned loose, she dipped her face 35
Farther into the chill of the earth, and in a sound
Of sobbing   of something stumbling
Away, began, as she must do
To carry me. I woke, dying.

In the summer sun of the hillside, with my eyes 40
Far more than human. I saw for a blazing moment
The great grassy world from both sides,
Man and beast in the round of their need,
And the hill wind stirred in my wool,
My hoof and my hand clasped each other, 45
I ate my one meal
Of milk, and died
Staring. From dark grass I came straight

To my father's house, whose dust
Whirls up in the hall's for no reason 50
When no one comes   piling deep in a hellish mild corner,
And, through my immortal waters,
I meet the sun's grains eye
To eye, and they fail at my closet of glass.
Dead, I am most surely living 55
In the minds of farm boys: I am he who drives
Them like wolves from the hound bitch and calf
And from the chaste ewe in the wind.
They go into woods   into bean fields   they go
Deep into their known right hands. Dreaming of me, 60
They groan   they wait   they suffer
Themselves, they marry, they raise their kind.

[1967]

CARYN CRABB

Caryn Crabb was the author's student at Florida Southern College.

The Passionate Businessman to a Foxy Chick

Come live with me and be my love,
And we will all the pleasures prove,
And we for better, not for worse,
Shall prove the pleasures of the purse.

A diamond here, a sapphire there, 5
Upon your dainty finger wear,

And if the ring your hand weigh down,
These jewels shall grace your royal crown.

Lobster boiled and escargot,
My gourmet taste shall surely show;   10
Your slightest wish shall be the cause
Of chilled champagne and vichyssoise.

Exotic pleasure is not hard
With crispy bill and credit card;
I've got the bucks with which to please 'ya,   15
Take my wallet, use my Visa.

Swimming pool at mansion tall
With foreign maid to sweep the hall,
Your lady servant makes the bed
With satin pillows for your head.   20

With silver coins and paper green
A truer man you've never seen;
If these desires your mind may move,
Come live with me and be my love.

[1990]

Questions: Love among the Sheep

1. Imagine that you have written Raleigh's poem in response to someone who
   wrote Marlowe's. How would you react to Donne's? What sort of poem
   would be possible next? Explain.
2. Dickey's poem is clearly out of place here, isn't it? How is it a "pastoral"
   poem? What happens to the other poems when Dickey's poem comes after
   them? What happens to Dickey's poem in this grouping?
3. Is Marlowe's poem vivid? Does it have precisely described details? What is
   Marlowe trying to do? Is the offer plausible?
4. What does Raleigh's speaker think is the trouble with the offer? Which lines
   point to that problem? Elaborate on those lines.
5. How plausible is the offer made by Herrick's speaker? Compare the invitation in this poem to the other invitations.
6. What's funny in these poems? What purpose does the humor serve?

Revisions

DIANE WOOD MIDDLEBROOK (1942–)

February Afternoon, In a Boat on the Seine

Leah's eyes: aura of riverwater;
Of island willows trailing early green;
Of the moss-garnished stone where water shatters,
Sunspray rushing in the rapid stream.

[1980]

When my daughter, Leah, was four years old, we spent the winter traveling together in Europe. She always needed distraction at dinnertime in restaurants: drawing pictures, or making up stories and rhymes. One afternoon in Paris while we were taking a boat ride, I noticed that the gray-green of her eyes matched colors in the water and the young leaves budding on the willows of the Ile de la Cité. I wrote out a few lines for that evening's entertainment:

> Leah's eyes—the color of riverwater,
> Of willow withes dividing winter light;
> Of the moss-garnished stone where water shatters;
> Of the moted bright.

Later, only one line and the rhyme pairing "water" with "shatters" seemed worth saving in their first form. Because I had chosen to write in meter, I had to negotiate the claims of both sound and sense. I wanted to make a poem that would integrate my impressions of the many resemblances between my daughter's eyes and the river in that weather. At the same time, I wanted to compose a flowing, falling, rushing rhythm evoking the sound of water. The last line represented a desperate settlement of the need for rhyme: a hackneyed "bright" to close up with "light." And many of the other words seemed either too self-conscious and arty—"willow withes dividing"; "moted"—or too flat: "color of riverwater."

In the final version, two changes please me very much. "Color" became "aura"—a word not only precise but also suggestive of many things I discovered I wanted to say once I had found that word. "Aura" means "a distinctive highly individualized atmosphere surrounding or attributed to a given source." It also means "a luminous radiation." In the context of the poem, the use of "aura" conveys something about the power of eyes. It was the sight of my daughter's eyes, so essential a link between herself and the world, that set the poem going in my mind. Not only the color of her eyes but their quickness and brightness were what I wanted to capture; I was seeing the world through them, and under their influence: Leah's aura.

"Rapid" also pleases me as good addition to the poem, a word in which sound collaborates with sense to convey energy. Its sound pattern (trochaic) echoes that of many other two-syllable words in the poem: "Léah," "aúra," "ís´land," "wí´llows," "tráiling," "eárly," "gárnished," "wáter," "shátters," "súnspray," "rúshing." Adjectives are always spots in a line that need watching, like soft spots in fruit: the poem can go bad there. My early choice of "moted" is a good example: too decorative. "Rapid" not only filled out the rhythm as needed on the way to the closing rhyme; it also added information essential to the precision of the image.

PATRICK ARMSTRONG (1972–)

How I Wrote "Kitty Hawk"

Last March, I happened to visit the place where the Wright Brothers made their historic flight. It was a windy, overcast afternoon, and the field, which stretched out green and wind-combed for a half-mile in all directions, suggested pure, unadulterated freedom—childhood freedom—kite-flying and cart-wheeling freedom: if I'd been a dog, I would have been gone, running and barking down the grassy slopes. I thought *yes, this is the place where we would learn to fly*, and I imagined the Wright Brothers arrogantly soaring through the air.

But the museum tells a different story. The glass cases are filled with gears and wheels, braces, and bicycle parts. There are sketches of ailerons and propellers, and there are columns—hundreds of columns—chronicling the most minute mathematical observations. In a back room, there is a copy of the original airplane *painstakingly* reproduced; it's a very complicated machine, more like an enormous watch than a kite or glider.

By the time I'd finished looking at the displays, the weather had gotten pretty bad. I walked out into a cold drizzle. In the middle of the field I came across the cabin where the Wright Brothers had lived; it had been reconstructed and furnished with a crude wooden table and straight-back chairs, a dented tea kettle and a make-shift wood stove. I guess the cabin was supposed to look cozy and human, but it looked very governmental instead; in fact, with the entrance roped off, and the various photographs of the Wright family tacked against the wall, it looked like a crime scene being investigated by the F.B.I. Just past this cabin, I found the stone pillars that marked the take off and landing spots of the first flight. There was only about a hundred feet or so between them, and the field stretched out to the edge of my sight. *So little, for so much effort*, I thought. And I wrote this draft of a poem.

Kitty Hawk [draft]

A man might have jumped
from here to there.
wine tucked under one arm,
hands flapping and the world,
round at each corner,   5
sloping off beneath his feet.

And as the wind
rises and sweeps and dips
across this immense field,
so might he have soared,   10
laughing like a boy
up at the sun's simple face.

But we know
how such legends go:
we've seen the fossils   15
flashed into stone.

And when we learned to fly
it was not with a gusty leap
and it was not accompanied
by a sharp and desperate soprano;   20

it was when,
after picking through the bones
we found the ones we would rather wear:
and yes they are hideous,
        but they fly.

For me, this poem was both more successful and more "finished" than most. Looking back on it now, I can see how the conditions at Kitty Hawk—not even excluding the weather—probably played a role in the outcome of the poem. Also, I was reading a lot of Wallace Stevens and W. H. Auden at the time, and I can see how their voices entered the poem (especially in the first three stanzas, the section of the poem Rilké would call "the mastered emotion" part).

I call the poem successful because it gave me satisfaction: it is a whole thing, a tree with a trunk, roots, and leaves. And the tree metaphor is apt, for, like a successful tree, a successful poem must begin in the ground, roots first (to complete the metaphor, consider the initial image, thought, or inspiration to be the seed). In the case of "Kitty Hawk," I didn't begin by discussing Flight or Science or some other abstraction, but by discussing that one flight, that one place, that single, specific event. Goethe says "it makes a great difference whether the poet seeks the particular in relation to the universal or contemplates the universal in the particular." And in the latter, the move from the particular to the universal, that works in poetry: induction, not deduction.

Several weeks after writing this poem (which I considered finished), I gave it to my teacher, the poet James Dickey. I suppose I had hoped he'd say something like "this is excellent, don't change a word," because there is something within poets—at least beginning poets—that is very fragile. The poem becomes precious, like children; but, like children, they must not be held too close if they are to grow.

This is the same draft of "Kitty Hawk" with his comments and suggestions written in. [See page 638.]

The suggestions Mr. Dickey made concerning the first few stanzas of the poem can be characterized as mostly grammatical: comma changes, line breaks and deletions—mainly deletions. The importance of these changes, however, should not be underestimated, for the poet, like the athlete, musician, mathematician—like all people engaged in a task, must be concerned with the details; as a mountain is made up of stones, a poem is made up of words. And for a poem, there is one grammatical consideration more important than all others: the choosing of the right word.

While Mr. Dickey wrote notes on my poem, he also talked about elements of revision, of how to "take the good and make it great, take the great and make it better." He spoke of ways to get back into the poem, he spoke of revision as an enjoyable, creative endeavor. "Revision," he said, "is a discovering of possibilities."

And he also, several times, said the words "flying lizard." I know the idea of a flying lizard is somewhat ridiculous, and yet there have been, and in fact still are, such strange creatures. The two images—that of a flying lizard and that of the Wright Brothers' flight—began to circle around each other in my mind. I started to reconsider the poem, to think about how we had come to fly, about how old the dream actually was. The images began to merge. I was right there, in the place where what you see is not the product of your thoughts: inspiration, imagination—call it what you will—it is that connection, that glimpse that lasts only an instant, as brief as the Wright Brothers' first flight, and yet is worth all the effort.

The flying lizard gave me a way to reenter the poem consciously, to try to improve my unconscious flight:

Kitty Hawk

A man might have jumped
from here to there,
wine tucked under one arm, ~~hands flapping and~~ the world,
~~round at each corner,~~
sloping off ~~beneath~~ his feet.
        under

And as the wind
rises and sweeps and dips
across this immense field, . . .
~~so might he have soared,~~
~~laughing like a boy~~
~~up at the sun's simple face.~~

But listen: ~~But we know~~ *we are those . . . .*
how such legends go:
we've seen the ~~fossils~~   *Flying lizards*
flashed into stone.

And when we learned to fly
it was not with a gusty leap
and it was not accompanied
by a sharp and desperate soprano;

it was when,
after picking through the bones
we found the ones we would rather wear:
and yes they are hideous,
                but they fly.

Kitty Hawk [final]

A man might have jumped
from here to there,
wine tucked under one arm,
the world
sloping under his feet.

And as the wind
rises and sweeps and dips
across the immense field . . .

but listen: we are those
who have searched
under rocks for flight,

who have sludged through the old swamp,
who have picked through the boneyard,
who have plundered the lizard's tomb.

5

10

Here is a feather, small as a finger,   15
here is a bone, and here another bone;
lean, step by step, forward, run

into the wind, the beam across your back;
we have seen them soar above us,
we have found their fossils flashed into stone.   20
God of bird and flying lizard,
of bat and wing-borne lightning bug,
we wear these bones, these feathers,
to fly up to you,
who will not come down to us.

[1995]

ROBERT FROST (1874–1963)

In White [draft]

A dented spider like a snow drop white
On a white Heal-all, holding up a moth
Like a white piece of lifeless satin cloth—
Saw ever curious eye so strange a sight?—
Portent in little, assorted death and blight   5
Like ingredients of a witches' broth?—
The beady spider, the flower like a froth,
And the moth carried like a paper kite.

What had that flower to do with being white,
The blue prunella every child's delight.   10
What brought the kindred spider to that height?
(Make we no thesis of the miller's plight.)
What but design of darkness and of night?
Design, design! Do I use the word aright?

Design [final]

I found a dimpled spider, fat and white,
On a white heal-all, holding up a moth
Like a white piece of rigid satin cloth—
Assorted characters of death and blight
Mixed ready to begin the morning right,   5
Like the ingredients of a witches' broth—
A snow-drop spider, a flower like a froth,
And dead wings carried like a paper kite.

What had that flower to do with being white,
The wayside blue and innocent heal-all?   10
What brought the kindred spider to that height,
Then steered the white moth thither in the night?
What but design of darkness to appall?—
If design govern in a thing so small.

W. H. Auden (1907–1973)

Musée des Beaux Arts

About suffering they were never wrong,
The Old Masters: how well they understood
Its human position; how it takes place
While someone else is eating or opening a window or just walking dully
    along;
How, when the aged are reverently, passionately waiting   5
For the miraculous birth, there always must be
Children who did not specially want it to happen, skating
On a pond at the edge of the wood:
They never forgot
That even the dreadful martyrdom must run its course   10
Anyhow in a corner, some untidy spot
Where the dogs go on with their doggy life and the torturer's horse
Scratches its innocent behind on a tree.

In Brueghel's *Icarus*, for instance: how everything turns away
Quite leisurely from the disaster; the ploughman may   15
Have heard the splash, the forsaken cry,
But for him it was not an important failure; the sun shone
As it had to on the white legs disappearing into the green
Water; and the expensive delicate ship that must have seen
Something amazing, a boy falling out of the sky,   20
Had somewhere to get to and sailed calmly on.

               [1940]

Dannie Abse (1923–)

Brueghel in Naples

> *'About suffering they were never wrong, The Old Masters . . .'*
> —W. H. Auden

Ovid would never have guessed how far
and Father's notion about wax melting, bah!
It's ice up there. Freezing.
Soaring and swooping over solitary altitudes
I was breezing along (a record I should think)   5
when my wings began to moult not melt.
These days, workmanship, I ask you.
Appalling.
There's a mountain down there on fire
and I'm falling, falling away from it.   10
Phew, the sun's on the horizon
or am I upside down?
Great Bacchus, the sea is rearing

Landscape with the Fall of Icarus by Pieter Breughel the Elder, 16th century. Musée d'Art Ancien, Musée Royaux des Beaux-Arts, Belgium. Photo: Scala / Art Resource, NY.

up. Will I drown? My white legs
the last to disappear? (I have no trousers on.)   15
A little to the left the ploughman,
a little to the right a galleon,
a sailor climbing the rigging,
a fisherman casting his line,
and now I hear a shepherd's dog barking.   20
I'm that near.

Lest I leave no trace
but a few scattered feathers on the water
show me your face, sailor,
look up, fisherman,   25
look this way, shepherd,
turn around, ploughman.
Raise the alarm! Launch a boat!

My luck. I'm seen
only by a jackass of an artist   30
interested in composition, in the green
tinge of the sea, in the aesthetics
of disaster—not in me.
I drown, bubble by bubble,
(Help! Save me!)   35
while he stands ruthlessly
before the canvas, busy busy,
intent on becoming an Old Master.

[1991]

ALAN DEVENISH (1948–)

Icarus Again

You'd think we'd have enough of falling
since that sunny day high off the coast of Crete. Air disasters
appalling and impersonal. The bomber's hate
made potent with a bit of plastic and some altitude. Spacecrafts
with schoolteachers aboard—exploding over and over
again. The parents aghast at the pure Icarian sky of Florida
suddenly emptied of their child.

What is myth if not an early version of what's been happening
all along? (The arrogance of flight brought down
by faulty gaskets).

As Auden would have it: the way we plow through life
head bent to the furrow while tragedy falls from the sky.

Bruegel shows only the legs—flailing and white—scissoring
into a pitiless green sea.

Williams treats a distant casualty in his clinical
little sketch. (Did the astronauts feel their fall
or breathe instantly the killing fumes?)

Matisse plays it another way. It's color—Icarus' love
for color and who can blame him? His poor heart
waxing red as he falls through blue and what might be
a scatter of sunbursts or a vision of war—the enemy
aces sighting Icarus in their crosshairs over France.

In Ovid the line that never fails to move me is
   And he saw the wings on the waves . . .
The way it comes to the father. His lofty design reduced to this
little detritus as he hovers in the left-hand corner of the myth
grieving wingbeats wrinkling the surface of the sea.

Even in bad prints of the Bruegel I can't help feeling sorry
for this kid. And dismay at our constant clumsiness. Our light
heart pulling us down. Love itself believing against all gravity
that what we say is what is bound to happen. How foolish to trust
our waxen wings and how foolish not to.

[1999]

Questions: Revisions

1. Discuss the changes made by Middlebrook, Armstrong, and Frost. Do you agree that the revisions are improvements? Explain.
2. Why is the Icarus myth so resonant? Why have painters and writers returned to it so often? What clues to the fascination of this story can you find in these works?
3. What details from the painting are picked up in the various poems? Why?
4. How do these poems affect each other? How do they affect your experience of the painting?

15

Robert Frost and Gwendolyn Brooks: Two Case Studies

I don't trust folk who don't re-read. . . . What you've got to teach people is to read slowly.

—Robert Frost, quoted by Octavio Paz in *Poets and Others*

This chapter presents in some depth the poetry of two celebrated modern American poets, Robert Frost and Gwendolyn Brooks. The chapter also provides you with a sampling of the literary criticism on these two poets, along with excerpts from other documents you should find both interesting and useful.

ROBERT FROST

(1874–1963)

Although he was born in San Francisco, Robert Frost and his mother moved to New England in 1885, after the

"*Is there any Robert Frost in the house?*"

death of his father. He graduated from high school in Lawrence, Massachusetts, in 1892, and married Eleanor White, who attended the same school, in 1895. Frost spent time at Dartmouth and Harvard, and he worked at a variety of jobs, but he was most determined to become a poet. In 1901 he moved to a farm in Derry, New

Hampshire, supporting his family (a son and three daughters) by teaching school. In 1912, Frost sold his farm and moved to England, where he found his publishing breakthrough with *A Boy's Will* in 1913 and *North of Boston* in 1914. When Frost returned to New Hampshire in 1915, he found plentiful lecture, reading, and teaching opportunities. He taught at the University of Michigan, Amherst (1926–1938), Harvard (1939–1943), and Dartmouth (1943–1949), then settled at Amherst permanently in 1949. Frost won the Pulitzer Prize in 1924, 1931, 1937, and 1943.

This sketch of his life, with its triumphant accomplishments, doesn't suggest the difficulties he encountered. Consider this paragraph from Peter Davison's excellent brief biography of Frost (from the *Atlantic Brief Lives*):

> His was the poetry of experience, and it came hard and late. His maturing years were dogged by poverty and his mature years by disaster. His wife at first refused to marry him; she yielded to the strength of his will (see "The Subverted Flower"), and for the forty years of their marriage she continued to submit and to resent. Of their six children, two died in infancy, one by suicide, one after giving birth, and at least one was plagued (like Frost's only sister) by mental illness. From his marriage until he was over seventy, Frost was seldom at any far remove from personal disaster and sorrow (see "Home Burial" and "The Hill Wife"), yet these disasters are never directly, and only infrequently, touched on in the poetry. (287)

The following poems have been selected to provide some sense of Frost's accomplishment, which is marked by his ability to convey deeply provocative ideas in relatively simple language and appealing imagery. Although, as Davison says, his personal woes are infrequently and indirectly "touched on in the poetry," a troubling undercurrent of potential doom nevertheless runs through even Frost's most charming poetry. In some poems, the dark side is deeply buried; in others, it's obvious. Frost's vision is an optimistic one, but it is not innocent. His clear-sighted wisdom is deceptively complex.

Frost's poems are among the best-known and most-beloved poems in the English language, and many of those that follow may well be familiar to you. That's good: as Frost himself says in the epigraph, the trick is to "read slowly." If there are poems here that you already know well, don't skip them: read them more slowly, enjoying things you might have missed, looking more carefully for nuances and layers of suggested meaning you hadn't realized. Frost's relatively simple poems are simply amazing for the way they reward rereading (and slow reading).

Reading Robert Frost

Mending Wall

Something there is that doesn't love a wall,
That sends the frozen-ground-swell under it,
And spills the upper boulders in the sun;
And makes gaps even two can pass abreast.   5
The work of hunters is another thing:
I have come after them and made repair
Where they have left not one stone on a stone,
But they would have the rabbit out of hiding,
To please the yelping dogs. The gaps I mean,   10
No one has seen them made or heard them made,
But at spring mending-time we find them there.
I let my neighbor know beyond the hill;
And on a day we meet to walk the line
And set the wall between us once again.   15
We keep the wall between us as we go.
To each the boulders that have fallen to each.
And some are loaves and some so nearly balls
We have to use a spell to make them balance:
"Stay where you are until our backs are turned!"   20
We wear our fingers rough with handling them.
Oh, just another kind of outdoor game,
One on a side. It comes to little more:
There where it is we do not need the wall:
He is all pine and I am apple orchard.   25
My apple trees will never get across
And eat the cones under his pines, I tell him.
He only says, "Good fences make good neighbors."
Spring is the mischief in me, and I wonder
If I could put a notion in his head: 30
"*Why* do they make good neighbors? Isn't it
Where there are cows? But here there are no cows.
Before I built a wall I'd ask to know
What I was walling in or walling out,
And to whom I was like to give offence.   35
Something there is that doesn't love a wall,
That wants it down." I could say "Elves" to him,
But it's not elves exactly, and I'd rather
He said it for himself. I see him there
Bringing a stone grasped firmly by the top   40
In each hand, like an old-stone savage armed.
He moves in darkness as it seems to me,
Not of woods only and the shade of trees.
He will not go behind his father's saying,

And he likes having thought of it so well
He says again, "Good fences make good neighbors."   45

[1914]

The Road Not Taken

Two roads diverged in a yellow wood,
And sorry I could not travel both
And be one traveler, long I stood
And looked down one as far as I could
To where it bent in the undergrowth;   5

Then took the other, as just as fair,
And having perhaps the better claim,
Because it was grassy and wanted wear;
Though as for that the passing there
Had worn them really about the same,   10

And both that morning equally lay
In leaves no step had trodden black.
Oh, I kept the first for another day!
Yet knowing how way leads on to way,
I doubted if I should ever come back.   15

I shall be telling this with a sigh
Somewhere ages and ages hence:
Two roads diverged in a wood, and I—
I took the one less traveled by,
And that has made all the difference.   20

[1916]

After Apple-Picking

My long two-pointed ladder's sticking through a tree
Toward heaven still,
And there's a barrel that I didn't fill
Beside it, and there may be two or three
Apples I didn't pick upon some bough.   5
But I am done with apple-picking now.
Essence of winter sleep is on the night,
The scent of apples: I am drowsing off.
I cannot rub the strangeness from my sight
I got from looking through a pane of glass   10
I skimmed this morning from the drinking trough
And held against the world of hoary grass.
It melted, and I let it fall and break.
But I was well
Upon my way to sleep before it fell,   15
And I could tell
What form my dreaming was about to take.
Magnified apples appear and disappear,
Stem end and blossom end,
And every fleck of russet showing clear.   20
My instep arch not only keeps the ache,
It keeps the pressure of a ladder-round.

I feel the ladder sway as the boughs bend.
And I keep hearing from the cellar bin
The rumbling sound
Of load on load of apples coming in.   25
For I have had too much
Of apple-picking: I am overtired
Of the great harvest I myself desired.
There were ten thousand thousand fruit to touch,   30
Cherish in hand, lift down, and not let fall.
For all
That struck the earth,
No matter if not bruised or spiked with stubble,
Went surely to the cider-apple heap   35
As of no worth.
One can see what will trouble
This sleep of mine, whatever sleep it is.
Were he not gone,
The woodchuck could say whether it's like his   40
Long sleep, as I describe its coming on,
Or just some human sleep.

                                                        [1916]

Birches

When I see birches bend to left and right
Across the lines of straighter darker trees,
I like to think some boy's been swinging them.
But swinging doesn't bend them down to stay
As ice storms do. Often you must have seen them   5
Loaded with ice a sunny winter morning
After a rain. They click upon themselves
As the breeze rises, and turn many-colored
As the stir cracks and crazes their enamel.
Soon the sun's warmth makes them shed crystal shells   10
Shattering and avalanching on the snow crust—
Such heaps of broken glass to sweep away
You'd think the inner dome of heaven had fallen.
They are dragged to the withered bracken by the load,
And they seem not to break; though once they are bowed   15
So low for long, they never right themselves:
You may see their trunks arching in the woods
Years afterwards, trailing their leaves on the ground
Like girls on hands and knees that throw their hair
Before them over their heads to dry in the sun.   20
But I was going to say when Truth broke in
With all her matter of fact about the ice storm
I should prefer to have some boy bend them
As he went out and in to fetch the cows—
Some boy too far from town to learn baseball,   25
Whose only play was what he found himself,
Summer or winter, and could play alone.
One by one he subdued his father's trees

By riding them down over and over again
Until he took the stiffness out of them,   30
And not one but hung limp, not one was left
For him to conquer. He learned all there was
To learn about not launching out too soon
And so not carrying the tree away
Clear to the ground. He always kept his poise   35
To the top branches, climbing carefully
With the same pains you use to fill a cup
Up to the brim, and even above the brim.
Then he flung outward, feet first, with a swish,
Kicking his way down through the air to the ground.   40
So was I once myself a swinger of birches.
And so I dream of going back to be.
It's when I'm weary of considerations,
And life is too much like a pathless wood
Where your face burns and tickles with the cobwebs   45
Broken across it, and one eye is weeping
From a twig's having lashed across it open.
I'd like to get away from earth awhile
And then come back to it and begin over.
May no fate willfully misunderstand me   50
And half grant what I wish and snatch me away
Not to return. Earth's the right place for love:
I don't know where it's likely to go better.
I'd like to go by climbing a birch tree,
And climb black branches up a snow-white trunk   55
Toward heaven, till the tree could bear no more,
But dipped its top and set me down again.
That would be good both going and coming back.
One could do worse than be a swinger of birches.

                                                                   [1916]

"Out, Out—"

The buzz-saw snarled and rattled in the yard
And made dust and dropped stove-length sticks of wood,
Sweet-scented stuff when the breeze drew across it.
And from there those that lifted eyes could count
Five mountain ranges one behind the other   5
Under the sunset far into Vermont.
And the saw snarled and rattled, snarled and rattled,
As it ran light, or had to bear a load.
And nothing happened: day was all but done.
Call it a day, I wish they might have said   10
To please the boy by giving him the half hour
That a boy counts so much when saved from work.
His sister stood beside them in her apron
To tell them "Supper." At the word, the saw,
As if to prove saws knew what supper meant,   15
Leaped out at the boy's hand, or seemed to leap—
He must have given the hand. However it was,

Neither refused the meeting. But the hand!
The boy's first outcry was a rueful laugh,
As he swung toward them holding up the hand
Half in appeal, but half as if to keep
The life from spilling. Then the boy saw all—   20
Since he was old enough to know, big boy
Doing a man's work, though a child at heart—
He saw all spoiled. "Don't let him cut my hand off—
The doctor, when he comes. Don't let him, sister!"
So. But the hand was gone already.   25
The doctor put him in the dark of ether.
He lay and puffed his lips out with his breath.
And then—the watcher at his pulse took fright.
No one believed. They listened at his heart.
Little—less—nothing!—and that ended it.   30
No more to build on there. And they, since they
Were not the one dead, turned to their affairs.

[1916]

Fire and Ice

Some say the world will end in fire,
Some say in ice.
From what I've tasted of desire
I hold with those who favor fire.
But if it had to perish twice,   5
I think I know enough of hate
To say that for destruction ice
Is also great
And would suffice.

[1923]

Stopping by Woods on a Snowy Evening

Whose woods these are I think I know.
His house is in the village though;
He will not see me stopping here
To watch his woods fill up with snow.

My little horse must think it queer   5
To stop without a farmhouse near
Between the woods and frozen lake
The darkest evening of the year.

He gives his harness bells a shake
To ask if there is some mistake.   10
The only other sound's the sweep
Of easy wind and downy flake.

The woods are lovely, dark and deep,
But I have promises to keep,
And miles to go before I sleep,   15
And miles to go before I sleep.

[1923]

Desert Places

Snow falling and night falling fast, oh, fast
In a field I looked into going past,
And the ground almost covered smooth in snow,
But a few weeds and stubble showing last.

The woods around it have it—it is theirs.   5
All animals are smothered in their lairs,
I am too absent-spirited to count;
The loneliness includes me unawares.

And lonely as it is, that loneliness
Will be more lonely ere it will be less—   10
A blanker whiteness of benighted snow
With no expression, nothing to express.

They cannot scare me with their empty spaces
Between stars—on stars where no human race is.
I have it in me so much nearer home   15
To scare myself with my own desert places.

[1936]

Neither Out Far Nor In Deep

The people along the sand
All turn and look one way.
They turn their back on the land.
They look at the sea all day.

As long as it takes to pass   5
A ship keeps raising its hull;
The wetter ground like glass
Reflects a standing gull.

The land may vary more;
But wherever the truth may be—   10
The water comes ashore,
And the people look at the sea.

They cannot look out far.
They cannot look in deep.
But when was that ever a bar   15
To any watch they keep?

[1933]

Provide, Provide

The witch that came (the withered hag)
To wash the steps with pail and rag,
Was once the beauty Abishag,

The picture pride of Hollywood.
Too many fall from great and good   5
For you to doubt the likelihood.

Die early and avoid the fate.

Or if predestined to die late,
Make up your mind to die in state.

Make the whole stock exchange your own!   10
If need be occupy a throne,
Where nobody can call *you* crone.

Some have relied on what they knew;
Others on being simply true.
What worked for them might work for you.   15

No memory of having starred
Atones for later disregard,
Or keeps the end from being hard.

Better to go down dignified
With boughten friendship at your side   20
Than none at all. Provide, provide!

[1933]

Nothing Gold Can Stay

Nature's first green is gold,
Her hardest hue to hold.
Her early leaf's a flower;
But only so an hour.
Then leaf subsides to leaf.   5
So Eden sank to grief,
So dawn goes down to day.
Nothing gold can stay.

[1923]

The Need of Being Versed in Country Things

The house had gone to bring again
To the midnight sky a sunset glow.
Now the chimney was all of the house that stood,
Like a pistil after the petals go.

The barn opposed across the way,   5
That would have joined the house in flame
Had it been the will of the wind, was left
To bear forsaken the place's name.

No more it opened with all one end
For teams that came by the stony road   10
To drum on the floor with scurrying hoofs
And brush the mow with the summer load.

The birds that came to it through the air
At broken windows flew out and in,
Their murmur more like the sigh we sigh   15
From too much dwelling on what has been.

Yet for them the lilac renewed its leaf,
And the aged elm, though touched with fire;
And the dry pump flung up an awkward arm;

And the fence post carried a strand of wire.   20

For them there was really nothing sad.
But though they rejoiced in the nest they kept,
One had to be versed in country things
Not to believe the phoebes wept.

[1923]

Sitting by a Bush in Broad Sunlight

When I spread out my hand here today,
I catch no more than a ray
To feel of between thumb and fingers;
No lasting effect of it lingers.

There was one time and only the one   5
When dust really took in the sun;
And from that one intake of fire
All creatures still warmly suspire.

And if men have watched a long time
And never seen sun-smitten slime   10
Again come to life and crawl off,
We must not be too ready to scoff.

God once declared he was true
And then took the veil and withdrew,
And remember how final a hush   15
Then descended of old on the bush.

God once spoke to people by name.
The sun once imparted its flame.
One impulse persists as our breath;   20
The other persists as our faith.

[1928]

Once by the Pacific

The shattered water made a misty din.
Great waves looked over others coming in,
And thought of doing something to the shore
That water never did to land before.
The clouds were low and hairy in the skies,   5
Like locks blown forward in the gleam of eyes.
You could not tell, and yet it looked as if
The shore was lucky in being backed by cliff,
The cliff in being backed by continent;
It looked as if a night of dark intent   10
Was coming, and not only a night, an age.
Someone had better be prepared for rage.
There would be more than ocean-water broken
Before God's last *Put out the Light* was spoken.

[1928]

The Most of It

He thought he kept the universe alone;
For all the voice in answer he could wake
Was but the mocking echo of his own
From some tree-hidden cliff across the lake.
Some morning from the boulder-broken beach   5
He would cry out on life, that what it wants
Is not its own love back in copy speech,
But counter-love, original response.
And nothing ever came of what he cried
Unless it was the embodiment that crashed   10
In the cliff's talus on the other side,
And then in the far distant water splashed,
But after a time allowed for it to swim,
Instead of proving human when it neared
And someone else additional to him,   15
As a great buck it powerfully appeared,
Pushing the crumpled water up ahead,
And landed pouring like a waterfall,
And stumbled through the rocks with horny tread,
And forced the underbrush—and that was all.   20

[1942]

Writing about Robert Frost: Critical Viewpoints

In the following excerpts, you'll find some useful and interesting materials to advance your understanding of Frost. You'll see a variety of different interests and approaches; as you're learning more about Frost, also pay some attention to the different critics' assumptions: what is important to a particular critic? What motivates the critic to convey this piece of information, or this opinion? The goal here, ultimately, is to allow you to develop your own insights into Frost.

Donald Greiner on Frost's Critical Reception

This excerpt from Greiner's survey of Frost criticism up to the 1970s discusses the early encouragement that Frost failed to receive, his temperament, and his pose of being uninterested in the comments of critics.

Like most creative artists, Robert Frost claimed to be both unaware of and uninterested in the criticism of his work. Part of his public mask was that of a gentle farmer-poet who somehow remained above such pedestrian matters as literary gossip and critical debate. But Frost's professed immunity to commentary about his poetry may have had more meaningful causes than the typical aversion of the artist or the demands of the public pose.

His publicized dismissal of reviews and of critical evaluations may have covered his private determination to succeed as a poet in spite of the discouraging opinions of friends and associates. For Frost was nearly forty years old before he found a publishing house willing to print his first book: in 1913 David Nutt of London published *A Boy's Will*. Before 1913 he experienced more than twenty years of unrecognized creative effort which he feared would go for naught. Between his schoolboy poetry of the early 1890s and the appearance of *A Boy's Will* in 1913, Frost found publication for only a few of his poems. Conservative editors of prestigious journals like *Atlantic Monthly* rejected his work, and an uninformed reading public seemed satisfied with the dormant state of American poetry in the first years of this century. Typical of the discouragement he encountered was the comment by Maurice Thompson that Frost should give up writing because the life of a poet was too hard. In 1939 Frost recalled his frustration when he noted that too often the genuine poet must rely solely upon self-appraisal: "For twenty years the world neglected him; then for twen-

Time Magazine honors the poet Robert Frost on its October 9, 1950, cover.

ty years it entreated him kindly. He has to take the responsibility of deciding when the world was wrong" (see "Remarks Accepting the Gold Medal of the National Institute of Arts and Letters," *National Institute News Bulletin*, 1939).

Frost's determination to be a poet despite two decades of neglect suggests that he knew the world was wrong about him. But his frustration went beyond the fairly common story of the youthful artist seeking a public hearing. In addition to the editors and critics who had to be won over, Frost believed that his family and even his future wife, Elinor White, looked askance at his writing. In 1894 he privately printed two copies of *Twilight*, a booklet of five poems, which he hoped would illustrate his potential achievement with poetry. Giving one to his fiancée Elinor, he soon destroyed his own copy when he decided that she failed to recognize and appreciate his talent. Several years later, following marriage to Elinor, he convinced himself, in spite of facts to the contrary, that his grandfather would rather keep him starving on a poor New England farm than support him while he tried to secure his name as a poet.

The point is that Frost's professed unawareness of the criticism of his work was a stance he had to assume publicly, for in his desire to gain recognition he was forced to decide that the public dismissal of his work was unwarranted. Even during the 1912–15 sojourn in England, those years when he found fame with the publication of *A Boy's Will* and *North of Boston*, Frost broke with Ezra Pound, his first influential supporter, over questions of how he should write. Understandably, then, when he found himself lionized as a major author of the New Poetry, he claimed not to care about reviews and criticism. Since the editors and reviewers, and even his family, had been wrong earlier about his chances of succeeding, they would probably be just as mistaken about his art now that he had proved his worth. Frost's lack of concern was a mask which enabled him to hide his lack of confidence. It may also have helped to endear him to a public ready to believe in the myth of Frost, the farmer-poet, but it did not prevent him from privately expressing disappointment, fear, and rage when he disagreed with published evaluations of his poetry. His letters are full of complaints about conservative editors and ignorant critics, and some of his comments amount to tirades against the supposed injustices of unfavorable reviews. For Robert Frost was a poet who could not tolerate criticism. Louis Untermeyer reports that one negative remark, no matter how insignificant, in an otherwise favorable essay could set off Frost's vindictive temper. Perhaps this is why he cultivated the influential critics of his day: Untermeyer, Lascelles Abercrombie, Edward Thomas, W.S. Braithwaite, Amy Lowell, Sidney Cox, Bernard De Voto, and all of the others who published consistently appreciative remarks about his work.

From Donald Greiner, *Robert Frost: The Poet and His Critics*. (Chicago: American Library Association, 1974), pp. ix–xi.

Malcolm Cowley: New Critical Analysis

Malcolm Cowley, a noted editor and critic, commented in 1944 that "Robert Frost has been heaped with more official and academic honors than any other American poet, living or dead" (312). Cowley says that "Frost deserves all these honors," but he also objected to Frost being used by his "zealous admirers . . . as a sort of banner for their own moral or political crusades." And Cowley also, as the following excerpt indicates, attempted to moderate the praise of Frost. In this essentially New Critical analysis of the image of the woods in Frost's poetry, Cowley compares Frost's use of this metaphor for "the uncharted country within ourselves" to its use in other American writers. It's a beautiful piece of writing. Is he right?

The woods play a curious part in Frost's poems; they seem to be his symbol for the uncharted country within ourselves, full of possible beauty, but also full of horror. From the woods at dusk, you might hear the hidden music of the brook, "a slender, tinkling fall"; or you might see wood creatures, a buck and a doe, looking at you over the stone fence that marks the limit of the pasture lot. But you don't cross the fence, except in dreams; and then, instead of brook or deer, you are likely to meet a strange Demon rising "from his wallow to laugh." And so, for fear of the Demon, and also because of your moral obligations, you merely stand at the edge of the woods to listen:

Far in the pillared dark
Thrush music went—
Almost like a call to come in
To the dark and lament.

But no, I was out for stars:
I would not come in.
I meant, not even if asked,
And I hadn't been.

But Hawthorne before him, timid and thin and conventional as he was in many of his tales, still plucked up his courage and ventured into the inner wilderness; and Conrad Aiken's poems (to mention one example of New England work today) are written almost wholly from within that haunted mid-region. To explore the real horrors of the mind is a long tradition in American letters, one that goes back to our first professional novelist, Charles Brockden Brown. He said in one of his letters, quoted in a footnote by Van Wyck Brooks, "You, you tell me, are one of those who would rather travel into the mind of a plowman than into the interior of Africa. I confess myself of your way of thinking." The same tendency was continued by Poe and Melville and Henry James, and extends in an almost unbroken line into the late work of Hemingway and Faulkner. But Frost, even in his finest lyrics, is content to stop outside the woods, either in the thrush-haunted dusk or on a snowy evening:

The woods are lovely, dark and deep.
But I have promises to keep,
And miles to go before I sleep,
And miles to go before I sleep.

If he does not strike far inward, neither does he follow the other great American tradition (extending from Whitman through Dos Passos) of standing on a height to observe the panorama of nature and society. Let us say that he is a poet neither of the mountains nor of the woods, although he lives among both, but rather of the hill pastures, the intervales, the dooryard in autumn with the leaves swirling, the closed house shaking in the winter storms (and who else has described these scenes more accurately, in more lasting colors?). In the same way, he is not the poet of New England in its great days, or in its late-nineteenth-century decline (except in some of his earlier poems); he is rather a poet who celebrates the diminished but prosperous and self-respecting New England of the tourist home and the antique shop in the abandoned gristmill. And the praise heaped on Frost in recent years is somehow connected in one's mind with the search for ancestors and authentic old furniture. You imagine a saltbox cottage restored to its original lines; outside it a wellsweep preserved for its picturesque quality, even though there is also an electric pump; at the doorway a coach lamp wired and polished; inside the house a set of Hitchcock chairs, a Salem rocker, willow-ware plates and Sandwich glass; and, on the tip-top table, carefully dusted, a first edition of Robert Frost.

From Malcolm Cowley, "Frost: A Dissenting Opinion." *New Republic,* September 11, 1944, and September 18, 1944, pp. 312–313 and 345–347.

H. A. Maxson: Survey of Various Approaches to Frost

The following discussion, published in 1997, is particularly useful because it surveys lucidly various readings of a famous poem. H. A. Maxson, writing about Frost's sonnets (the only "fixed" form that Frost used—37 times, according to Maxson), examines interpretations by Randall Jarrell, Richard Poirier, Frank Lentricchia, Elizabeth Isaacs, Elaine Barry, and George Montiero. This kind of summary is not only helpful in understanding a work, showing us how other people have read it, and using a variety of critical approaches, but it is also useful in generating one's own reading. It's usually not the case that reading criticism obstructs an original approach; instead, it usually sparks it. For that reason, this sort of summary of different views of a work is a common writing assignment. Even when you offer your own interpretation, it's often helpful to frame your own reading in terms of what other people have said. (The poem "Design," in draft and revised form, can be found on page 639.)

"Design"

> *The first known copy of the poem was sent to Susan Hayes Ward in a letter dated January 15, 1912. It was then titled "[A Study] In White." It was first published in* American Poetry 1922, A Miscellany *as "Design." Reprinted in* A Further Range, *1936 and in* Complete Poems of Robert Frost, *1968.*

Like "Acquainted with the Night," "Design" has drawn an immense amount of commentary, from Randall Jarrell's enthusiastic appreciation in "To the Labdiceans," to George Montiero's "Robert Frost's Metaphysical Sonnet," a very useful line-by-line comparison to the original "In White," to Richard Poirier's extended discussion of the poem in *Robert Frost: The Work of Knowing*. As with "Acquainted . . . " it seems unnecessary to add yet another voice to an already remarkably harmonious chorus. A Look at the major responses to this poem seems to be the most instructive strategy.

Jarrell's is a brief but intense discussion that begins: "This is the Argument from Design with a vengeance . . . " and continues: " . . . this little albino catastrophe is too whitely catastrophic to be accidental, too impossibly unlikely ever to be coincidence: accident, chance, statistics, natural selection are helpless to account for such designed terror and heartbreak, such an awful symbolic perversion of the innocent being of the world" (46). Jarrell must be given credit for admiring this poem into the place of prominence it enjoys today.

Following a line-by-line, image-by-image reading and commentary, he goes on to say: "What had that flower to do with being white,/ The wayside blue and innocent heal-all?' expresses as well as anything ever has the arbitrariness of our guilt, the fact that Original Sin is only Original accident. . . . [T]he name 'heal-all' comes to a sad, ironic, literal life: it healed all, [but] itself it could not heal" (48). After a nod to the poem's literary forefathers— including Emerson, Bryant, Melville and the Puritan preachers—Jarrell concludes by saying: "This poem, I think most people will admit, makes Pascal's 'eternal silence of those infinite spaces' seem the hush between the movements of a cantata" (49).

The opening of Richard Poirier's discussion also seeks the influences on "design." He, however, finds the major influence in William James' *Psychology*. After a long quotation from that source, he quoted both the early "In White" and the revised version, "Design." Unlike Montiero, Poirier does not do a line-by-line comparison/contrast. What he does do is examine the independence from the source, the maturity and self-assurance displayed in the 1922 rewrite. He says that " 'Design' is a rather playful poem, much closer to the charmingly confident willingness in James to allow for alternate or conflicting possibilities" (250). As we have seen, this penchant for holding conflicting thoughts in the mind simultaneously is a hallmark of some of Frost's finest poems.

Poirier's analysis next looks very closely at the language of the poem 5 and most specifically at the word "appall," which he reads as 1) close to pale, 2) as in "impaled" (the spider holding the moth) and 3) pale as in fence slat. He concludes this reading with, "Thus, an extended and potentially self-canceling reading of the line would be 'What but design of darkness to . . . design'" (251).

His analysis runs to over fifteen pages and is worthwhile to anyone wishing to see the poem from the multiple critical standpoints that are extended and wide ranging.

Also taken up by Poirier are the subjects of why Frost "found" the poem to be a sonnet, even in its earliest form; where the poems are situated in *A Further Range;* the five poems that follow "Design," forming a smaller design within the design of the volume; why it is a "political" poem and "social commentary." This later discussion is especially helpful in understanding the advertising language and rhythms that appear in the octave. As summary, one paragraph deserves an extended quotation:

> *It might seem as if Frost's attitude toward design is at odds with his earlier confidence in the virtues of form, but no contradiction emerges if it is kept in mind that from the beginning he demonstrated a habitual suspicion of any form or "design" or "provision" that does not find itself by almost lucky accident. Form, like the act of love, induces a sense of pleasure and security which fortunately cannot be permanent. If it were, the form would be without the efficacy and pleasure that comes from the act of discovery and shaping it, time after time. (258)*

Although Frank Lentricchia's comments are very brief, they do serve to hold the poem differently to the light. He writes: "[T]he 'design of darkness' . . . is first, and perhaps last, a metaphorical projection of the brooding, philosophical mind, not necessarily a reflection in poetry of ontological fact" (99). He goes on to support this: "Frost counterpoints a mechanical, nursery rhyme iambic rhythm against a scene of Natural horror. The effect of such counterpointing is two-fold: first, it heightens the macabre quality of the scene imaged; second, it implies the pressure of a self-conscious poetic craftsman . . . . [T]he poet's self-consciousness saves him; it allows the pressure of a difficult situation to be released" (99).

The sonnet may have been the "strictest form" Frost "behaved in," and   10 he may have done so by "pretending it wasn't a sonnet." But if Lentricchia is correct, and there is no reason to doubt that he is, there is good reason to believe that Frost was probably extremely grateful for a poetic design historically fecund and readily available in those moments when doubt loomed large. I would not call it hubris, exactly, but control in the shape of "form" must have been very welcomed, a "momentary stay" of proportions beyond the sonnet's meager size.

Although most of the critics writing on this poem speak of the persona more as a philosopher, plumbing the depths and distances of man's thought, Elizabeth Isaacs sees the "scientist-poet" of the octave becoming the "philosopher-poet" in the sestet. First there is the observation of "weird combinations of existence" (115), the horrified wondering at how these elements, all grotesquely obvious in their whiteness, could come together at this moment, in this place before the "eye's microscope." It is, Isaacs asserts, "one of the best examples of Frost's existential poetry" (115).

After discussing the whiteness of the scene, and what the lack of color symbolizes in Frost—"snow, isolation and death"—she returns to the coincidence of these three coming together:

> *The almost-but-not-quite possibility of this luminous trio, brought together out of the huge gloom of a dark universe and spot-lighted before the wary eye of the poet, magnifies the coincidence from microscopic to macroscopic terror in his mind. . . . If this incident can possibly have been planned and de-signed, then it is impossibly terrifying. . . . If it is unplanned, then life is utterly desolate in connotation; and thinking man must re-ject this idea if he will live with sanity and die with faith. (116)*

The language of the questions in the sestet—"steered," "brought" and "thither to that height"—says Isaacs, all suggest a designer, a system con-trolled. And the direction in which we are steered by such language serves to intensify the "casual" "If" of the final line to the terrible size that it assumes.

Isaac's is a solid, straightforward formalist reading of the poem. She is deadly accurate in pointing out the shift of language and focus that occurs simultaneously with the turn of the sonnet. Hers is a very useful discussion for any student of the poem or of Frost in general. Her apt analysis lays bare the very essence of Frost's poetry long missed by earlier critics.

Elaine Barry's discussion of "Design" in *Robert Frost* is valuable for its   15 no-nonsense approach. But it breaks virtually no new ground. She makes it a point to note the double design of the poem—sonnet and "traditional sequence of logical debate" (89). She also points out the irony of this too-white world finally being summed up in "design of darkness." Barry's brief comparison of "Design" to "In White" offers a nice introduction to the method of George Montiero's "Robert Frost's Metaphysical Sonnet." How-ever, the latter essay is much more illuminating.

Prefacing his line-by-line comparison of the two versions of the poem (1912, 1922) Montiero writes:

> *In paradigm, "Design" expresses those perplexing fears spawned and scattered by evidence which indicates that (1) human exis-tence continues without supportive design and ultimate purpose, or (2) human existence is subject to a design of unmitigated nat-ural evil. The details of the poem appear to sustain these comple-mentary readings without choosing between them. . . . It is one of those rare poems achetypal to the entire ouvre of a poet, which in brief compass offers a valuable key to a poet's richness and reach. (333)*

Montiero makes essentially ten major points about the differences between the two versions of the poem, concluding that the revisions show maturity, and constant faithfulness to the sonnet form and deepening belief on Frost's part in the irony of both the argument and his poem.

The first point Montiero makes is that "Design" is more narrative than "In White," thus making the incident more mysterious and shifting the focus onto the spider. Secondly, he claims, and rightly so, that little of the original manuscript is left after the revision, and the changes make clear the genius of the poet and the poem.

Point number three concerns the shift in language in the revision toward more charged words—"dimpled," "fat," and "white" replace the more neutral "dented," for example. His fourth point addresses the omission of the "limp, lifeless" fourth line of "In White" and the improvement of the poem because of it. Points five and six are discussions of "kitchen domesticity" and the advertising language that is intertwined with it.

The change from "beady" to "snowdrop," and from "moth" to "dead   20
wings" is Montiero's seventh point. Both changes, he points out, underscore the "childlike" description of line one. Point number eight echoes Jarrell's observation that the repetition of "heal-all" magnifies the irony that it can heal all, but it cannot heal itself.

"And of night," the end of line thirteen in "In White," is merely repetitive, Montiero observes. However, the resonant "to appall" in "Design" refortifies the power of bringing "design" and "darkness" together in such close proximity.

Montiero's final comments concern the closing line and the cumulative effect that "govern" offers because of its close relationship to "steered" and "brought." The comments are all insightful and instructive. The running commentary also serves to illuminate the achievement of each revision and the depth and enrichment each brought to the poem.

On the sonnetness of the poem he writes "That the poem was conceived in the form of a sonnet, I would propose, is the poet's final irony, for the strict formal design which characterizes the sonnet apes and mimes the internal argument of the poem" (338).

That "Design" is almost universally admired needs only the quotations, summaries and paraphrases above for proof. I have not discovered any disparaging words or even any hints that "Design" is not first-class poetry. As Thompson points out, the poem was first published in the same year as Eliot's "The Waste Land." "Design" is as modern, as richly dark, as "The Waste Land." It is a poem not only representative of a good deal of Frost's work, but it also stands quite clearly as a beacon for an entire age and all of the doubt, fear, loneliness and uncertainty it reflected upon. As Borges has written: "I think Frost is a finer poet than Eliot. I mean a finer *poet*. But I suppose Eliot was a far more intelligent man; however, intelligence has little to do with poetry. Poetry springs from something deeper; it's beyond intelligence. It may not even be linked with wisdom. It's a thing of its own; it has a nature of its own. Undefinable."

From H. A. Maxson, *On the Sonnets of Robert Frost: A Critical Examination of the 37 Poems.* Jefferson, NC: McFarland, 1997, pp. 89–94.

Karen Kilcup: Feminist View of Frost

It's an understatement to say that Frost's poetry is well known, that he is a popular poet. In magazines like *Reader's Digest* and *Saturday Evening Post,* more than three hundred articles on Frost appeared between 1915 and 1980. A similarly voluminous commentary has appeared in scholarly publications. So we think we know Frost well. But we know his work, Karen Kilcup has recently argued, only within a masculine literary tradition. The achievement of Kilcup's *Robert Frost and Feminine Literary Tradition* (1998) is that she convincingly argues for a different approach: what happens when the feminine and sentimental elements in Frost's poetry are not suppressed or ignored, but noticed? Here is Kilcup's discussion of the famous "Stopping by Woods on a Snowy Evening," reorienting the conventional way of reading this poem.

In this context we might consider "Stopping by Woods on a Snowy Evening," which intimates the affiliations in Frost's "better" poetry with the nineteenth-century feminine poetic tradition. I will cite only its conclusion, which focuses first on the speaker's "little horse":

He gives his harness bells a shake
To ask if there is some mistake.
The only other sound's the sweep
Of easy wind and downy flake.

The woods are lovely, dark and deep,
But I have promises to keep,
And miles to go before I sleep,
And miles to go before I sleep.

The poem as a whole, of course, encodes many of the tensions between popular and elite poetry. For example, it appears in an anthology of children's writing alongside Amy Lowell's "Crescent Moon," Joyce Kilmer's "Trees," and Edward Lear's "Owl and the Pussy-Cat." Pritchard situates it among a number of poems that "have . . . repelled or embarrassed more highbrow sensibilities," which suggests the question: "haven't these poems ['The Pasture', 'Stopping by Woods . . . ,' 'Birches,' 'Mending Wall'] been so much exclaimed over by people whose poetic taste is dubious or hardly existent, that on these grounds alone Frost is to be distrusted?" The views represented—and the representations of the poem itself, affiliated with the work of Dickinson, Longfellow, Dante, and the Romantics—range from emphasis on its gentility to its modernist ambiguity. Nevertheless, more than one critic underscores its threat to individualism, its "dangerous prospect of boundarilessness," which suggests the masculine conception of poetic selfhood with which the poem is commonly framed.

    In apparent harmony with these views the poem appears almost entirely restrained in its emotion; we are given only glimpses: "the darkest evening of the year," "the woods are lovely, dark and deep." It is not from the poem's language—or, for that matter, structure, which is as predictable as Thaxter's "Alone"—that the stream of emotion flows. Rather, as in "My November Guest," the season and the elegiac tone provide the link with Frost's antecedents. Walker observes of nineteenth-century women writers that "at mid-century the seasons were especially popular with Indian Summer a particular favorite, perhaps because its juxtaposition of different seasonal moods liberated a poet to illustrate her mixed feelings about so much in her life and culture." Seasons were a conventional means to illustrate feelings, as in Helen Hunt Jackson's "'Down to Sleep'":

November woods are bare and still;
    November days are clear and bright;
Each noon burns up the morning's chill;
    The morning's snow is gone by night;
    Each day my steps grow slow, grow light,
As through the woods I reverent creep,
Watching all things lie "down to sleep."
I never knew before what beds,

Fragrant to smell, and soft to touch,
The forest sifts and shapes and spreads;
    I never knew before how much
    Of human sound there is in such
Low tones as through the forest sweep
When all wild things lie "down to sleep."

Each day I find new coverlids
    Tucked in and more sweet eyes shut tight;
Sometimes the viewless mother bids
    Her ferns kneel down full in my sight;
    I hear their chorus of "good night,"
And half I smile, and half I weep,
Listening while they lie "down to sleep."

November woods are bare and still;
    November days are bright and good;
Life's noon burns up life's morning chill;
    Life's night rests feet which long have stood;
    Some warm soft bed, in field or wood,
The mother will not fail to keep,
Where we can "lay us down to sleep."

Jackson's poem relies on the associations with the mother as well as the seasonal metaphor to make its point, making explicit what Frost's intimates: his speaker's desire to merge with the lovely, snow-clad woods suggests a desire to merge with the mother (Mother Nature) as strong as Jackson's. Having removed the traces of religiosity encoded in the refrain "down to sleep," a child's nighttime prayer to God, Frost's speaker nevertheless evinces his prayerful attitude in "the woods are lovely, dark and deep," as well as in the hymnlike regularity of the stanzas. And, in the affectionate reference to "my little horse" reminiscent of the cow-calf image in "The Pasture," he suggests the connection between human and animal parallel to Jackson's explicit observation: "I never knew before how much / Of human sound there is in such / Low tones as through the forest sweep / When all wild things lie 'down to sleep.'" "Sweep," of course, recurs in Frost's quiet poem: "The only other sound's the sweep / Of easy wind and downy flake." Though probably accidental, Frost's echoing of sweep-sleep rhyme indicates some of the emotional resonances and connections, especially with "weep," itself embedded in "sweep," that are explicit in Jackson. Finally, Jackson's narrator acknowledges only slightly more directly the movement toward age and death that Frost's suggests: "Each day my steps grow slow, grow light / As through the woods I reverent creep." The subjectivity of both Frost's and Jackson's poems is simultaneously individual and representative, suggesting that "Stopping by Woods on a Snowy Evening" is a feminine poem with close connections to its popular antecedents.

    Once again we can trace the emotional resonance of Frost's poem   5
back to the concrete situation that helped engender it. Shortly before Christmas of 1905, Frost had made an unsuccessful trip into town to sell eggs in order to raise money for his children's Christmas presents. "Alone in the driving snow, the memory of his years of hopeful but frustrated strug-

gle welled up, and he let his long-pent feelings out in tears." The intensity of this tearful moment translates into the affective content that permeates but never overwhelms "Stopping by Woods on a Snowy Evening." The fact that the poem would be written seventeen years after the moment that it reflected testifies to the deep suffering that this experience engendered; too painful to be dwelt upon, it would be only with time and distance that the emotions of that awful moment could be balanced, in a "momentary stay against confusion," by the comforting restraint of formal expression.

"Stopping by Woods" provides a doorway into an understanding of the poet's great popularity with "ordinary" readers. Jarrell observes, "ordinary readers think Frost the greatest poet alive, and love some of his best poems almost as much as they love some of his worst ones. He seems to them a sensible, tender, humorous poet who knows all about trees and farms and folks in New England." This view clashes with that of "intellectuals," who have "neglected or depreciated" him: "the reader of Eliot or Auden usually dismisses Frost as something inconsequentially good that *he* knew all about long ago." Slightly later poems like "The Onset" and "Evening in a Sugar Orchard" would do nothing to alleviate this polarization. Put plainly, professional and nonprofessional readers admire poems like "Stopping by Woods" in different ways and for different reasons. Let me digress here briefly to reemphasize that, as my occasional interpolations discussing my own responses to individual poems suggest, this distinction is not a secure one; in fact, it is wholly created by a professional elite that requires for its survival the perception that readers need special knowledge to read poetry. Though they frequently left no written record, I suspect that Frosts's contemporary "amateur" readers responded less to his irony, playfulness, and modernist ambiguity and sophistication than they did to his accessibility and appeal to domestic, familiar, and emotional values reiterated from mainstream nineteenth-century poetry.

The implication of Frosts's popularity (and his image as the Poet) in these values is as evident today as it was during his lifetime. As a lecturer for New England Humanities Councils, I have given a variety of public talks on Frost, but the one that leaps to mind I gave at the Frost Farm in Derry, New Hampshire, a number of years ago. I was discussing early portions of this work, focusing on the female voices in the early dramatic poems, and at one point I lingered on the subtextual violence in "Home Burial," mentioning the famous (and contested) episode described by Thompson in which Frost, brandishing a gun, dragged a sleepy Lesley out of bed and ordered her to choose between himself and her mother. Listeners in the audience, many of whom knew Frosts's poetry as well as I did, were uncomfortable, even dismayed, with this story. The reason: it cast a shadow on their reverent image of the poet as kindly, avuncular storyteller-sage whose poetry confirmed some of their deeply cherished values not only about Frost but also about the family, New England, and the United States. I could see from the faces of more than one or two in the audience that they doubted my veracity—didn't I, perhaps, have it wrong?

I tell this story not to cast aspersions on popular readers—for, as I have suggested, everyone, myself included, is to a degree such a reader—but, rather, to underscore the continuing fissure between academic and nonprofessional readers. We can trace this split, perhaps, to Lionel Trilling's description of Frost as "a terrifying poet," an observation he made, to the shock of many listeners (including the poet's own), at Frost's eighty-fifth birthday party.

From Karen Kilcup, *Robert Frost and Feminine Literary Tradition.* Ann
    Arbor: University of Michigan Press, 1998, pp. 45–48.

Mordecai Marcus: Biographical versus Formal Readings of Two Poems

Frost's poems often appeared in volumes, and the ideal way to read a particular poem might be in the midst of the other poems. Or, perhaps the biographical context of a poem might be more important. In the first excerpt here, Mordecai Marcus considers these strategies and ultimately relies upon a close reading of the text itself. Marcus's explications of "The Road Not Taken" and "Stopping by Woods," two of Frost's most popular poems, are particularly useful because they include references to other critics.

In the original edition "The Road Not Taken" and the last poem, "The Sound of Trees," were set in italics, implying introduction and farewell. Frost seems to have been willing to use this initial poem with meanings not supported by its autobiographical context, for he had sent it to his close friend Edward Thomas, who was notorious for indecisiveness (but who did not see Frost's point). Some critics think the poem represents Thomas's voice, but Frost could hardly have expected his readers to recognize that, and during his frequent public readings of the poem he often warned that it was tricky and shouldn't be interpreted hastily. The poem's popularity seems to be based on the mistaken notion that it celebrates the triumph of independent choices—most likely Frost's choices as artist and man. Frost's warning showed that he hoped readers could come to see its satirical intention, which he evidently never cared to explain. But the poem's seemingly genial celebration of a fortunate choice remains seductive, even to those who perceive a satirical intention.

Yellow wood and leaves not yet trodden black place the scene in the nostalgic autumn season. The speaker's desire to take two different ways and yet remain "one traveler" is gently stated. As the first stanza ends, the future is undecipherable. In the second stanza, although the speaker chooses the less-traveled road as if he were doing it a favor, four vivid lines insist that the differences between the two roads in terms of wear as well as attractiveness are negligible. The speaker's hopes to return to the road not chosen and his reflection on such an unlikelihood seem casual. His thought that "way leads on to way" implies a symbolic choice, but his having "kept the first [road] for another day" suggests that rather than having chosen a way of life, he has made just a partial choice. As he looks far ahead and sees himself looking back to this moment and making a declaration about it, he makes a crucial change in point of view. Then—not now—he will declare that his having taken the less-traveled road made all the difference, and so the last line is part of what he will say in the future, not part of what he now declares. The core idea seems to be that he will have succeeded in fooling himself about the importance of a choice. It will have made all the difference in his imagination, not in reality. The poem may raise the question of how our casual choices affect our destinies, but if these choices are casual, they are more matters of whim and chance than matters of character and determination. Frost believes in such forces, but he also sees that the fatality of whim can be overestimated. Still, readers continue to insist on symbolic depths here. Robert McPhillips argues, perhaps with excessive sophistication, that Frost's being as concerned with the road not taken as the one taken connects to the taken road as a horizontal way and the road not taken as the vertical way, counterposing the earthly and spiritual, which must somewhere converge. Thus, Frost implies that the road of transcendence has been take in the imagination. John Evangelist Walsh argues that the voice in the poem is a combination of Thomas's and Frost's, and that Frost's final point is that the ability to make choices, especially when they are difficult, is a triumph over circumstances.

    . . . "Stopping by Woods on a Snowy Evening" is Frost's most popular poem, and the poet himself was very fond of it. Despite its apparent simplicity, it has inspired numerous detailed analyses. Its vivid scene combines contrasts between white snow and dark woods, and adds other sensuous appeals in the sound of harness bells, the sweeping wind, and the snow's softness. The time is the winter solstice, "the darkest evening of the year" (usually December 21). The speaker is alone but sets up relationships with his horse, the absent owner of the woods he has stopped to contemplate, and the people to whom he has "promises to keep." He has been riding home on a horse-driven sleigh, and he delights in his feeling of contemplative possession of a snow-filled field that is really owned by a man in the village, as he also enjoys his momentary isolation. The horse's fancied questioning of their stopping reinforces the sense of his nonpractical delight in the pause and in what he sees. The absence of farmhouses increases the pleasure of his isolation, and the time of year adds a gentle note of ease about the darkness and the coming winter. The horse's questioning emphasizes that there has been no mistake, and perhaps its shaken bells make more vivid the quietly appealing sounds of wind and snowflake. The appealing softness of the snow gracefully increases the speaker's feeling of deep and comforting beauty in the snow-filled woods, which seem so inviting. Many critics have debated whether the speaker is tempted to yield to death, and his attraction to the snowy woods has often been referred to as a death wish, in correspondence to Freudian ideas of a death instinct. Frost was angry at such suggestions, perhaps because he didn't understand them. Surely, the transition from the picture of the appealing woods to the speaker's thoughts of the promises he must keep and the miles he must travel before sleep represents a desire not to give up, or at least not to yield to passivity in the face of duty. As Theodore Morrison argues, however, it is important not to let this interpretation dim the fact that the poem is primarily oriented towards the pleasures of the scene and the responsibility of life, and that sleep is a restorative as well as a metaphor for that end which, in this poem, looks a long way off. Interpretations of possible symbolisms in the traveler, the owner, the horse, the woods, and the goal will doubtless continue to proliferate.

From Mordecai Marcus, *The Poems of Robert Frost: An Explication.*
    Boston: Hall, 1991, pp. 64–65, 105–106.

Robert Frost: On Poetic Creativity

Frost notoriously did not like prose very much—writing it or reading it. "If I wrote myself up," he wrote to John Freeman around 1925, "it would have to be in verse since I write no prose and am scared blue at any demand on me for prose." The following excerpt is from Frost's favorite, and perhaps his best-known piece of prose, and one could argue that its lyrical qualities carry it near to being a prose poem. It is included here because Frost's description of poetic creativity is especially interesting and famous.

From "The Figure A Poem Makes"

. . . Granted no one but a humanist much cares how sound a poem is if it is only *a* sound The sound is the gold in the ore. Then we will have the sound out alone and dispense with the inessential. We do till we make the discovery that the object in writing poetry is to make all poems sound as different as possible from each other, and the resources for that of vowels, consonants, punctuation, syntax, words, sentences, meter are not enough. We need the help of context—meaning—subject matter. That is the greatest help towards variety. All that can be done with words is soon told. So also with meters—particularly in our language where there are virtually but two, strict iambic and loose iambic. The ancients with many were still poor if they depended on meters for all tune. It is painful to watch our sprung-rhythmists straining at the point of omitting one short from a foot for relief from monotony. The possibilities for tune from the dramatic tones of meaning struck across the rigidity of a limited meter are endless. And we are back in poetry as merely one more art of having something to say, sound or unsound. Probably better if sound, because deeper and from wider experience.

Then there is this wildness whereof it is spoken. Granted again that it has an equal claim with sound to being a poem's better half. If it is a wild tune, it is a poem. Our problem then is, as modern abstractionists, to have the wildness pure; to be wild with nothing to be wild about. We bring up as aberrationists, giving way to undirected associations and kicking ourselves from one chance suggestion to another in all directions as of a hot afternoon in the life of a grasshopper. Theme alone can steady us down. Just as the first mystery was how a poem could have a tune in such a straightness as meter, so the second mystery is how a poem can have wildness and at the same time a subject that shall be fulfilled.

It should be of the pleasure of a poem itself to tell how it can. The figure a poem makes. It begins in delight and ends in wisdom. The figure is the same as for love. No one can really hold that the ecstasy should be static and stand still in one place. It begins in delight, it inclines to the impulse, it assumes direction with the first line laid down, it runs a course of lucky events, and ends in a clarification of life—not necessarily a great clarification, such as sects and cults are founded on, but in a momentary stay against confusion. It has denouement. It has an outcome that though unforeseen was predestined from the first image of the original mood—and indeed from the very mood. It is but a trick poem and no poem at all if the best of it was thought of first and saved for the last. It finds its own name as it goes and discovers the best waiting for it in some final phrase at once wise and sad—the happy-sad blend of the drinking song.

No tears in the writer, no tears in the reader. No surprise for the writer, no surprise for the reader. For me the initial delight is in the surprise of remembering something I didn't know I knew. I am in a place, in a situation, as if I had materialized from cloud or risen out of the ground. There is a glad recognition of the long lost and the rest follows. Step by step the wonder of unexpected supply keeps growing.

From *The Selected Prose of Robert Frost*, eds. Hyde Cox and Edward Connery Lathan. New York: Holt, 1939.

GWENDOLYN BROOKS (1917–2000)

Like Robert Frost, Gwendolyn Brooks is a poet who is identified with a locality: Frost, although born in San Francisco, is a rural New England poet, writing about snowy woods, birch trees, stone walls, "country things"; Brooks, although born in Topeka, Kansas, is a Chicago poet, writing about ordinary but unforgettable African American lives in the city's South Side. Brooks attended three high schools: the foremost white school in Chicago, Hyde Park; the entirely black school, Wendell Phillips; and then an integrated school, Englewood. One might argue that this progression suggests the shape of her poetic career: she was early on encouraged to study Ezra Pound, T. S. Eliot, and e.e. cummings, and it is possible to see evidence in her work of these three "white" writers, as she adopted established forms and styles. Success in the traditional publishing world came early and dramatically for Brooks. Her first book, *A Street in Bronzeville,* was immediately applauded by critics in 1945, and she won a prestigious Guggenheim Award. By 1950, Brooks had published her third book and become the first African American to win the Pulitzer Prize. In 1962, President Kennedy (who had tapped Frost to read at his inauguration in 1961) asked Brooks to read at the Library of Congress.

Brooks's success within a predominantly white literary establishment gave way in the late 1960s to a conscious decision to involve herself in the Black Arts movement. A determining moment in her career was Brooks's participation in 1967 in Fisk University's Second Black Writers' Conference. She began to publish her work with small black presses, rather than the foremost publishers of her early career. A more emotional involvement with social issues, with the plight of poor urban blacks, began to dominate her work, even as she also began to experiment with the form of her work, drawing on the rhythms of jazz and the blues. Her mature work has demonstrated that she is a poet of broad appeal, however focused her subjects may be. Among the many awards of her career, one of the most telling is being named the 1994 Jefferson Lecturer, which is the greatest honor given in the humanities by the United States.

Reading Gwendolyn Brooks

Sadie and Maud

Maud went to college.
Sadie stayed at home.
Sadie scraped life
With a fine-tooth comb.

She didn't leave a tangle in.   5
Her comb found every strand.
Sadie was one of the livingest chits
In all the land.

Sadie bore two babies
Under her maiden name.   10
Maud and Ma and Papa
Nearly died of shame.
Every one but Sadie
Nearly died of shame.

When Sadie said her last so-long   15
Her girls struck out from home.
(Sadie had left as heritage
Her fine-tooth comb.)

Maud, who went to college,
Is a thin brown mouse.   20
She is living all alone
In this old house.

[1945]

the ballad of chocolate Mabbie

It was Mabbie without the grammar school gates.
And Mabbie was all of seven.
And Mabbie was cut from a chocolate bar.
And Mabbie thought life was heaven.

The grammar school gates were the pearly gates,   5
For Willie Boone went to school.
When she sat by him in history class
Was only her eyes were cool.

It was Mabbie without the grammar school gates
Waiting for Willie Boone.   10
Half hour after the closing bell!
He would surely be coming soon.

Oh, warm is the waiting for joys, my dears!
And it cannot be too long.

Oh, pity the little poor chocolate lips   15
That carry the bubble of song!

Out came the saucily bold Willie Boone.
It was woe for our Mabbie now.
He wore like a jewel a lemon-hued lynx
With sand-waves loving her brow.   20

It was Mabbie alone by the grammar school gates.
Yet chocolate companions had she:
Mabbie on Mabbie with hush in the heart.
Mabbie on Mabbie to be.

                                                [1945]

the preacher: ruminates behind the sermon

I think it must be lonely to be God.
Nobody loves a master. No. Despite
The bright hosannas, bright dear-Lords, and bright
Determined reverence of Sunday eyes.

Picture Jehovah striding through the hall   5
Of His importance, creatures running out
From servant-corners to acclaim, to shout
Appreciation of His merit's glare.

But who walks with Him?—dares to take His arm,
To slap Him on the shoulder, tweak His ear,   10
Buy Him a Coca-Cola or a beer,
Pooh-pooh His politics, call Him a fool?

Perhaps—who knows?—He tires of looking down.
Those eyes are never lifted. Never straight.
Perhaps sometime He tires of being great   15
In solitude. Without a hand to hold.

                                                [1945]

A Bronzeville Mother Loiters in Mississippi. Meanwhile, a Mississippi Mother Burns Bacon

From the first it had been like a
Ballad. It had the beat inevitable. It had the blood.
A wildness cut up, and tied in little bunches,
Like the four-line stanzas of the ballads she had never quite
Understood—the ballads they had set her to, in school.   5

Herself: the milk-white maid, the "maid mild"
Of the ballad. Pursued
By the Dark Villain. Rescued by the Fine Prince.
The Happiness-Ever-After.
That was worth anything.   10
It was good to be a "maid mild."
That made the breath go fast.

Her bacon burned. She
Hastened to hide it in the step-on can, and

Drew more strips from the meat case. The eggs and sour-milk biscuits   15
Did well. She set out a jar
Of her new quince preserve.

. . . But there was something about the matter of the Dark Villain.
He should have been older, perhaps.
The hacking down of a villain was more fun to think about   20
When his menace possessed undisputed breadth, undisputed height,
And a harsh kind of vice.
And best of all, when his history was cluttered
With the bones of many eaten knights and princesses.

The fun was disturbed, then all but nullified   25
When the Dark Villain was a blackish child
Of fourteen, with eyes still too young to be dirty,
And a mouth too young to have lost every reminder
Of its infant softness.

That boy must have been surprised! For   30
These were grown-ups. Grown-ups were supposed to be wise.
And the Fine Prince—and that other—so tall, so broad, so
Grown! Perhaps the boy had never guessed
That the trouble with grown-ups was that under the magnificent shell of
     adulthood, just under,
Waited the baby full of tantrums.   35
It occurred to her that there may have been something
Ridiculous in the picture of the Fine Prince
Rushing (rich with the breadth and height and
Mature solidness whose lack, in the Dark Villain, was impressing her,
Confronting her more and more as this first day after the trial   40
And acquittal wore on) rushing
With his heavy companion to hack down (unhorsed)
That little foe.
So much had happened, she could not remember now what that foe had
     done
Against her, or if anything had been done.   45
The one thing in the world that she did know and knew
With terrifying clarity was that her composition
Had disintegrated. That, although the pattern prevailed,
The breaks were everywhere. That she could think
Of no thread capable of the necessary   50
Sew-work.

She made the babies sit in their places at the table.
Then, before calling Him, she hurried
To the mirror with her comb and lipstick. It was necessary
To be more beautiful than ever.   55
The beautiful wife.
For sometimes she fancied he looked at her as though
Measuring her. As if he considered, Had she been worth It?
Had *she* been worth the blood, the cramped cries, the little stuttering
     bravado,
The gradual dulling of those Negro eyes,   60
The sudden, overwhelming *little-boyness* in that barn?

Whatever she might feel or half-feel, the lipstick necessity was something
    apart. He must never conclude
That she had not been worth It.

He sat down, the Fine Prince, and
Began buttering a biscuit. He looked at his hands.   65
He twisted in his chair, he scratched his nose.
He glanced again, almost secretly, at his hands.
More papers were in from the North, he mumbled. More meddling
    headlines.
With their pepper-words, "bestiality," and "barbarism," and
"Shocking."   70
The half-sneers he had mastered for the trial worked across
His sweet and pretty face.

What he'd like to do, he explained, was kill them all.
The time lost. The unwanted fame.
Still, it had been fun to show those intruders   75
A thing or two. To show that snappy-eyed mother,
That sassy, Northern, brown-black—

Nothing could stop Mississippi.
He knew that. Big Fella
Knew that.   80
And, what was so good, Mississippi knew that.
Nothing and nothing could stop Mississippi.
They could send in their petitions, and scar
Their newspapers with bleeding headlines. Their governors
Could appeal to Washington. . . .   85

"What I want," the older baby said, "is 'lasses on my jam."
Whereupon the younger baby
Picked up the molasses pitcher and threw
The molasses in his brother's face. Instantly
The Fine Prince leaned across the table and slapped   90
The small and smiling criminal.

She did not speak. When the Hand
Came down and away, and she could look at her child,
At her baby-child,
She could think only of blood.   95
Surely her baby's cheek
Had disappeared, and in its place, surely,
Hung a heaviness, a lengthening red, a red that had no end.
She shook her head. It was not true, of course.
It was not true at all. The   100
Child's face was as always, the
Color of the paste in her paste-jar.

She left the table, to the tune of the children's lamentations, which were
    shriller
Than ever. She
Looked out of a window. She said not a word. *That*   105
Was one of the new Somethings—
The fear,

Tying her as with iron.

Suddenly she felt his hands upon her. He had followed her
To the window. The children were whimpering now.   110
Such bits of tots. And she, their mother,
Could not protect them. She looked at her shoulders, still
Gripped in the claim of his hands. She tried, but could not resist the idea
That a red ooze was seeping, spreading darkly, thickly, slowly,
Over her white shoulders, her own shoulders,   115
And over all of Earth and Mars.

He whispered something to her, did the Fine Prince, something
About love, something about love and night and intention.

She heard no hoof-beat of the horse and saw no flash of the shining steel.

He pulled her face around to meet   120
His, and there it was, close close,
For the first time in all those days and nights.
His mouth, wet and red,
So very, very, very red,
Closed over hers.   125

Then a sickness heaved within her. The courtroom Coca-Cola,
The courtroom beer and hate and sweat and drone,
Pushed like a wall against her. She wanted to bear it.
But his mouth would not go away and neither would the
Decapitated exclamation points in that Other Woman's eyes.   130

She did not scream.
She stood there.
But a hatred of him burst into glorious flower,
And its perfume enclasped them—big,
Bigger than all magnolias.   135

The last bleak news of the ballad.
The rest of the rugged music.
The last quatrain.

                                                        [1960]

The Chicago Defender Sends a Man to Little Rock
Fall, 1957

In Little Rock the people bear
Babes, and comb and part their hair
And watch the want ads, put repair
To roof and latch. While wheat toast burns
A woman waters multiferns.   5

Time upholds or overturns
The many, tight, and small concerns.

In Little Rock the people sing
Sunday hymns like anything,
Through Sunday pomp and polishing.   10

And after testament and tunes,

Some soften Sunday afternoons
With lemon tea and Lorna Doones.

I forecast
And I believe   15
Come Christmas Little Rock will cleave
To Christmas tree and trifle, weave,
From laugh and tinsel, texture fast.

In Little Rock is baseball; Barcarolle.
That hotness in July . . . the uniformed figures raw and implacable   20
And not intellectual,
Batting the hotness or clawing the suffering dust.
The Open Air Concert, on the special twilight green . . .
When Beethoven is brutal or whispers to lady-like air.
Blanket-sitters are solemn, as Johann troubles to lean   25
To tell them what to mean. . . .

There is love, too, in Little Rock. Soft women softly
Opening themselves in kindness
Or, pitying one's blindness,
Awaiting one's pleasure   30
In azure
Glory with anguished rose at the root. . . .
To wash away old semi-discomfitures.
They re-teach purple and unsullen blue.
The wispy soils go. And uncertain   35
Half-havings have they clarified to sures.

In Little Rock they know
Not answering the telephone is a way of rejecting life,
That it is our business to be bothered, is our business
To cherish bores or boredom, be polite   40
To lies and love and many-faceted fuzziness.

I scratch my head, massage the hate-I-had.
I blink across my prim and pencilled pad.
The saga I was sent for is not down.
Because there is a puzzle in this town.   45
The biggest News I do not dare
Telegraph to the Editor's chair:
"They are like people everywhere."

The angry Editor would reply
In hundred harryings of Why.   50

And true, they are hurling spittle, rock,
Garbage and fruit in Little Rock.
And I saw coiling storm a-writhe
On bright madonnas. And a scythe
Of men harassing brownish girls.   55
(The bows and barrettes in the curls
And braids declined away from joy.)

I saw a bleeding brownish boy. . . .

The lariat lynch-wish I deplored.
The loveliest lynchee was our Lord.   60

[1960]

Langston Hughes

        is merry glory.
Is saltatory.
Yet grips his right of twisting free.

Has a long reach,
Strong speech,   5
Remedial fears.
Muscular tears.

Holds horticulture
In the eye of the vulture

Infirm profession.   10
In the Compression—
In mud and blood and sudden death—
In the breath
Of the holocaust he
Is helmsman, hatchet, headlight.   15
See
One restless in the exotic time! and ever,
Till the air is cured of its fever.

[1963]

The Sundays of Satin-Legs Smith

Inamoratas, with an approbation,
Bestowed his title. Blessed his inclination.

He wakes, unwinds, elaborately: a cat
Tawny, reluctant, royal. He is fat
And fine this morning. Definite. Reimbursed.   5

He waits a moment, he designs his reign,
That no performance may be plain or vain.
Then rises in a clear delirium.

He sheds, with his pajamas, shabby days.
And his desertedness, his intricate fear, the   10
Postponed resentments and the prim precautions.

Now, at his bath, would you deny him lavender
Or take away the power of his pine?
What smelly substitute, heady as wine,
Would you provide? life must be aromatic.   15
There must be scent, somehow there must be some.
Would you have flowers in his life? suggest
Asters? a Really Good geranium?
A white carnation? would you prescribe a Show
With the cold lilies, formal chrysanthemum   20
Magnificence, poinsettias, and emphatic
Red of prize roses? might his happiest
Alternative (you muse) be, after all,
A bit of gentle garden in the best
Of taste and straight tradition? Maybe so.   25
But you forget, or did you ever know,
His heritage of cabbage and pigtails,
Old intimacy with alleys, garbage pails,
Down in the deep (but always beautiful) South
Where roses blush their blithest (it is said)   30
And sweet magnolias put Chanel to shame.

No! He has not a flower to his name.
Except a feather one, for his lapel.
Apart from that, if he should think of flowers
It is in terms of dandelions or death.   35
Ah, there is little hope. You might as well—

Unless you care to set the world a-boil
And do a lot of equalizing things,
Remove a little ermine, say, from kings,
Shake hands with paupers and appoint them men,   40
For instance—certainly you might as well
Leave him his lotion, lavender and oil.

Let us proceed. Let us inspect, together
With his meticulous and serious love,
The innards of this closet. Which is a vault   45
Whose glory is not diamonds, not pearls,
Not silver plate with just enough dull shine.
But wonder-suits in yellow and in wine,
Sarcastic green and zebra-striped cobalt.
All drapes. With shoulder padding that is wide   50
And cocky and determined as his pride;
Ballooning pants that taper off to ends
Scheduled to choke precisely.
                              Here are hats
Like bright umbrellas; and hysterical ties   55
Like narrow banners for some gathering war.

People are so in need, in need of help.
People want so much that they do not know.

Below the tinkling trade of little coins
The gold impulse not possible to show   60
Or spend. Promise piled over and betrayed.

These kneaded limbs receive the kiss of silk.
Then they receive the brave and beautiful
Embrace of some of that equivocal wool.
He looks into his mirror, loves himself—   65
The neat curve here; the angularity
That is appropriate at just its place;
The technique of a variegated grace.

Here is all his sculpture and his art
And all his architectural design.   70
Perhaps you would prefer to this a fine
Value of marble, complicated stone.
Would have him think with horror of baroque,
Rococo. You forget and you forget.

He dances down the hotel steps that keep   75
Remnants of last night's high life and distress.
As spat-out purchased kisses and spilled beer.
He swallows sunshine with a secret yelp.

Passes to coffee and a roll or two.
Has breakfasted.   80
                    Out. Sounds about him smear,
Become a unit. He hears and does not hear
The alarm clock meddling in somebody's sleep;
Children's governed Sunday happiness;
The dry tone of a plane; a woman's oath;   85
Consumption's spiritless expectoration;

An indignant robin's resolute donation
Pinching a track through apathy and din;
Restaurant vendors weeping; and the L
That comes on like a slightly horrible thought.   90

Pictures, too, as usual, are blurred.
He sees and does not see the broken windows
Hiding their shame with newsprint; little girl
With ribbons decking wornness, little boy
Wearing the trousers with the decentest patch,   95
To honor Sunday; women on their way
From "service," temperate holiness arranged
Ably on asking faces; men estranged
From music and from wonder and from joy
But far familiar with the guide awe   100
Of foodlessness.
                    He loiters.
                        Restaurant vendors
Weep, or out of them rolls a restless glee.
The Lonesome Blues, the Long-lost Blues, I Want A
Big Fat Mama. Down these sore avenues   105
Comes no Saint-Saëns, no piquant elusive Grieg,
And not Tschaikovsky's wayward eloquence
And not the shapely tender drift of Brahms.
But could he love them? Since a man must bring   110
To music what his mother spanked him for
When he was two: bits of forgotten hate,
Devotion: whether or not his mattress hurts:
The little dream his father humored: the thing
His sister did for money: what he ate   115
For breakfast—and for dinner twenty years
Ago last autumn: all his skipped desserts.

The pasts of his ancestors lean against
Him. Crowd him. Fog out his identity.
Hundreds of hungers mingle with his own,   120
Hundreds of voices advise so dexterously
He quite considers his reactions his,
Judges he walks most powerfully alone,
That everything is—simply what it is.

But movie-time approaches, time to boo   125
The hero's kiss, and boo the heroine
Whose ivory and yellow it is sin
For his eye to eat of. The Mickey Mouse,
However, is for everyone in the house.

Squires his lady to dinner at Joe's Eats.   130
His lady alters as to leg and eye,
Thickness and height, such minor points as these,
From Sunday to Sunday. But no matter what
Her name or body positively she's
In Queen Lace stockings with ambitious heels   135
That strain to kiss the calves, and vivid shoes
Frontless and backless, Chinese fingernails,

Earrings, three layers of lipstick, intense hat
Dripping with the most voluble of veils.
Her affable extremes are like sweet bombs   140
About him, whom no middle grace or good
Could gratify. He had no education
In quiet arts of compromise. He would
Not understand your counsels on control, nor
Thank you for your late trouble.   145

                    At Joe's Eats
You get your fish or chicken on meat platters.
With coleslaw, macaroni, candied sweets,
Coffee and apple pie. You go out full.
(The end is—isn't it?—all that really matters.)   150

    And even and intrepid come
    The tender boots of night to home.

    Her body is like new brown bread
    Under the Woolworth mignonette.
    Her body is a honey bowl   155
    Whose waiting honey is deep and hot.
    Her body is like summer earth,
    Receptive, soft and absolute . . .

                                                    [1945]

gay chaps at the bar

    . . . and guys I knew in the States, young officers, return from
    the front crying and trembling. Gay chaps at the bar in Los
    Angeles, Chicago, New York. . . .

                                        Lieutenant William Couch
                                        in the South Pacific

We knew how to order. Just the dash
Necessary. The length of gaiety in good taste.
Whether the raillery should be slightly iced
And given green, or served up hot and lush.
And we knew beautifully how to give to women   5
The summer spread, the tropics, of our love.
When to persist, or hold a hunger off.
Knew white speech. How to make a look an omen.
But nothing ever taught us to be islands.
And smart, athletic language for this hour   10
Was not in the curriculum. No stout
Lesson showed how to chat with death. We brought
No brass fortissimo, among our talents,
To holler down the lions in this air.

                                                    [1945]

"God works in a mysterious way"

But often now the youthful eye cuts down its
Own dainty veiling. Or submits to winds.

And many an eye that all its age had drawn its
Beam from a Book endures the impudence
Of modern glare that never heard of tact   5
Or timeliness, or Mystery that shrouds
Immortal joy: it merely can direct
Chancing feet across dissembling clods.
Out from Thy shadows, from Thy pleasant meadows,
Quickly, in undiluted light. Be glad, whose   10
Mansions are bright, to right Thy children's air.
If Thou be more than hate or atmosphere
Step forth in splendor, mortify our wolves.
Or we assume a sovereignty ourselves.

[1945]

"do not be afraid of no"

"Do not be afraid of no,
Who has so far so very far to go":

New caution to occur
To one whose inner scream set her to cede, for softer lap-
        ping and smooth fur!

Whose esoteric need   5
Was merely to avoid the nettle, to not-bleed.

Stupid, like a street
That beats into a dead end and dies there, with nothing
        left to reprimand or meet.

And like a candle fixed
Against dismay and countershine of mixed   10

Wild moon and sun. And like
A flying furniture, or bird with lattice wing; or gaunt thing,
        a-stammer down a nightmare neon peopled with con-
        dor, hawk and shrike.

To say yes is to die
A lot or a little. The dead wear capably their wry

Enameled emblems. They smell.   15
But that and that they do not altogether yell is all that we
        know well.

It is brave to be involved,
To be not fearful to be unresolved.

Her new wish was to smile
When answers took no airships, walked a while.

[1949]

The Bean Eaters

They eat beans mostly, this old yellow pair.
Dinner is a casual affair.
Plain chipware on a plain and creaking wood,

Tin flatware.

Two who are Mostly Good.   5
Two who have lived their day,
But keep on putting on their clothes
And putting things away.

And remembering . . .
Remembering, with tinklings and twinges,   10
As they lean over the beans in their rented back room that
    is full of beads and receipts and dolls and cloths,
    tobacco crumbs, vases and fringes.

                                                            [1960]

We Real Cool

The Pool Players.
Seven at the Golden Shovel.

We real cool. We
Left school. We

Lurk late. We
Strike straight. We

Sing sin. We   5
Thin gin. We

Jazz June. We
Die soon.

                                                            [1960]

The following three poems come from the volume *Annie Allen,* published in 1949.
Fifteen of the volume's poems are gathered together under the title "The Womanhood." These three poems comprise Sections 2, 3, and 4 of "the children of the poor,"
which is part of "The Womanhood." These numbered poems, in other words, are
poems within a poem within a poem. Although these poems stand nicely alone, they
(perhaps like any poem that is conceived as part of a volume) should ideally be seen
as part of a larger whole.

2

What shall I give my children? who are poor,
Who are adjudged the leastwise of the land,
Who are my sweetest lepers, who demand
No velvet and no velvety velour;
But who have begged me for a brisk contour,   5
Crying that they are quasi, contraband
Because unfinished, graven by a hand
Less than angelic, admirable or sure.
My hand is stuffed with mode, design, device.
But I lack access to my proper stone.   10
And plenitude of plan shall not suffice
Nor grief nor love shall be enough alone

To ratify my little halves who bear
Across an autumn freezing everywhere.

3

And shall I prime my children, pray, to pray?
Mites, come invade most frugal vestibules
Spectered with crusts of penitents' renewals
And all hysterics arrogant for a day.
Instruct yourselves here is no devil to pay.   5
Children, confine your lights in jellied rules;
Resemble graves; be metaphysical mules;
Learn Lord will not distort nor leave the fray.
Behind the scurryings of your neat motif
I shall wait, if you wish: revise the psalm   10
If that should frighten you: sew up belief
If that should tear: turn, singularly calm
At forehead and at fingers rather wise,
Holding the bandage ready for your eyes.

4

First fight. Then fiddle. Ply the slipping string
With feathery sorcery; muzzle the note
With hurting love; the music that they wrote
Bewitch, bewilder. Qualify to sing
Threadwise. Devise no salt, no hempen thing   5
For the dear instrument to bear. Devote
The bow to silks and honey. Be remote
A while from malice and from murdering.
But first to arms, to armor. Carry hate
In front of you and harmony behind.   10
Be deaf to music and to beauty blind.
Win war. Rise bloody, maybe not too late
For having first to civilize a space
Wherein to play your violin with grace.

Writing about Gwendolyn Brooks: Critical Viewpoints

Paul Engle: New Critical and Biographical Stances

Here is a review from 1945, taking note of the "exceptional event" that was the publication of Gwendolyn Brooks' *A Street in Bronzeville*. Although much in the review reminds us of how much things have changed, the issue of Brooks' relationship to her racial status would persist as critics attempted to come to terms with her work. Notice how the critic works to combine New Critical and biographical stances into a coherent review.

The publication of *A Street in Bronzeville* is an exceptional event in the literary life of Chicago, for it is the first book of a solidly Chicago person. Miss Brooks attended Englewood High School and Wilson Junior College. I hope they know it and are proud. But it is also an event of national importance, for Miss Brooks is the first Negro poet to write wholly out of a deep and imaginative talent, without relying on the fact of color to draw sympathy and interest. Her poems would be finely lyrical and delightfully witty without the fact of color ever being mentioned. This is a remarkable thing which must be praised.

But the poems must be praised too, and in their own right. Here is the story of a day on the south side; it has the marvelous title of "The Sundays of Satin-Legs Smith," itself a poem. In it Miss Brooks shows that she has a vigorous mind of her own, and she uses it cunningly and with slow concentration of word. There are many poems about people, and they are all accurate, human, alert, moving. Miss Brooks goes through Chicago with her eyes wide open and the poems are wide open too, taking you right inside the reality observed. There are keen notes on our mortal frailty, such as the amorous gentleman who, seeing an attractive woman, "wonders as his stomach breaks up into fire and lights":

> How long it will be
> Before he can, with reasonably slight risk of rebuke,
> put his hand on her knee.

There are poems which bear the immediate sense of the personal life strongly lived out:

> It was quite a time for loving. It was midnight. It was May.
> But in the crowding darkness not a word did they say.

There is the quick observation of the shame and sorrow behind the gay performance, as in "Queen of the Blues":

> Mame was singing
> At the Midnight club.
> And the place was red
> With blues.
> She could shake her body
> Across the floor.
> For what did she have
> To lose?

The biggest piece in the book is a sequence of poems about the soldier, called "Gay Chaps at the Bar." They are the most controlled, the most   5
intense poems in the book. And finest of all, they can be read for what they are and not, as the publishers want us to believe, as Negro poems. For they should no more be called Negro poetry than the poems of Robert Frost should be called white poetry. They are handsome and real and genuine poems by a civilized American citizen. They are poems for all men who left warmth and a softness and quick hand and slow voice. They come out of the pages of the book, as Miss Brooks says in another connection, "like the tender struggle of a fan."

I hope that the people of Chicago, who generously support genuine midwestern writing, will find in Miss Brooks exactly the kind of young but permanent talent they are looking for. The finest praise that can be given the book is that it would be a superb volume of poetry in any year by any person of any color. This is the kind of writing we need in this time. I want to show you a final example from a poem in which a hunchback girl thinks of heaven:

My Father, it is surely a blue place
And straight. Right. Regular . . .
. . . .
I shall walk straightly through most proper halls
Proper myself, princess of properness.

This is the real thing. So is Miss Brooks.

From Paul Engle, "Chicago Can Take Pride in New, Young Voice in Poetry."
In Stephen Caldwell Wright, ed. *On Gwendolyn Brooks: Reliant Contemplation.* Ann Arbor: University of Michigan Press, 1999.

Harvey Webster: Political Criticism

In 1962, less than two decades after Paul Engle's 1945 review, this review by Harvey Curtis Webster appeared. Webster helps suggest how Brooks' work was interpreted in terms of the political context of the reader. The "troubled times" that Webster refers to concern what he calls "the Negro dilemma": should blacks be segregated from whites? Should they be integrated? Should the two races live apart or together? Were they, and should they be, equal? Although prejudice and oppression certainly still exist today, it is easy to forget their viciousness in the not-so-distant past.

Pity the Giants

In times as troubled as ours what sensitive writer can avoid a certain obsession with contemporary ills that may be temporary? Gwendolyn Brooks, from her very good *A Street in Bronzeville,* through her nearly as good *Annie Allen,* to her better *The Bean Eaters,* has never denied her engagement in the contemporary situation or been overobsessed by it. In her engagement she resembles Langston Hughes, Countee Cullen, and Margaret Walker, to name the other Negro poets I know best. In her ability to see through the temporal, she equals Richard Wright, James Baldwin and Ralph Ellison, writers of fiction who accept Negro-ness as prizeable differentiation and a dilemma [and] include it to transcend it. Of course she writes of Emmett Till, of Little Rock, of Dorie Miller, of a white maid disgusted to see her child embrace the Negro maid. Of course, she uses (less frequently and less successfully than Langston Hughes) blues rhythms, writes of the blessing-curse, the accident of color. Like all good writers, she acknowledges Now by vivifying it, accepts it, accepts herself and the distinguishing background that is part of her distinction. But she refuses to let Negro-ness limit her humanity. She does not "marvel at this curious thing: / to make a poet black, and bid him sing." Gwendolyn Brooks accepts to transcend.

To me, now, her poems about the Negro dilemma today seem her best because they help me and others to identify as we must. Excluding the trivial verse that emphasizes Now or color too much ("patent leather" and "the battle" in her first volume; "downtown vaudeville" and "old laughter" in

Annie Allen; "My Little 'Bout-town Gal" and "For Clarice . . ." in *The Bean Eaters*), her bitter and sympathetic poems make the Negro a problem in the heart of every American. Her best social poems yet are in *The Bean Eaters.* "A Bronzeville Mother Loiters in Mississippi. Meanwhile, a Mississippi Mother Burns Bacon" is notable because it is written from the point of view of the white woman married to a man who thinks with pride of the killing of Emmett Till. "Mrs. Smith," serious light verse about Mrs. Small's spilling of coffee on the white insurance collector, is as good. So are "The *Chicago Defender* Sends a Man to Little Rock," "The Ballad of Rudolph Reed" (perhaps her best in the mode) and "Bronzeville Woman in a Red Hat."

Yet these poems, necessary for Gwendolyn Brooks to write and for us to read, are not really the best. Negro-ness, the contemporary situation, Miss Brooks's individuality, mastered craft, and foreverness coalesce in her best poems. "Race" is then an accident; the contemporary situation a source of detail; craft the skilled accomplice of matter; Miss Brooks every-woman differentiated. Increasingly, in each of her books these poems have appeared.

From Harvey Curtis Webster, Review of *The Bean Eaters, Annie Allen,*
        and *A Street in Bronzeville.* In *The Nation,* September 1, 1962.

Kenny Jackson Williams: Historical Influences

In this brief excerpt, Kenny Jackson Williams reflects on the literary influences Brooks has absorbed.

Trying to determine clear lines of influence from the work of earlier writers to later ones is always a risky business; however, knowing some identifiable poetic traditions can aid in understanding the work of Gwendolyn Brooks. On one level there is the English metaphysical tradition perhaps best exemplified by John Donne. From nineteenth-century American poetry one can detect elements of Walt Whitman, Emily Dickinson, and Paul Laurence Dunbar. From twentieth-century American poetry there are many strains, most notably the compact style of T S. Eliot, the frequent use of the lower-case for titles in the manner of e. e. cummings, and the racial consciousness of the Harlem Renaissance, especially as found in the work of Countee Cullen and Langston Hughes; but, of perhaps greater importance, she seems to be a direct descendant of the urban commitment and attitude of the "Chicago School" of writing. For Brooks, setting goes beyond the Midwest with a focus on Chicago and concentrates on a small neglected corner of the city. Consequently, in the final analysis, she is not a carbon copy of any of the Chicago writers.

From Kenny Jackson Williams, *The Oxford Companion to African-
        American Literature.* Oxford: Oxford University Press, 1997.

Gertrude Reif Hughes: Feminist Criticism

This brief section comes from an essay by Gertrude Reif Hughes, who argues that Gwendolyn Brooks and Hildo Doolittle embody "the Feminist Potential of

Modern Poetry." Not only does Hughes offer some sense of a feminist approach to Brooks, but she also clarifies what it would mean to read Brooks as a "modernist" poet.

The midcentury poems of Doolittle and Brooks offer excellent examples of modernism's feminist potential. Written between 1945 and 1968, before the second wave of feminism and during its beginnings, these poems take as their theme the oppressions of otherness that Simone de Beauvior's *The Second Sex* described in 1952. Otherness, said de Beauvoir, "is the lot assigned to woman in the patriarchate, but it is in no way a vocation, any more than slavery is the vocation of the slave."

Both Brooks and Doolittle used the high modernist devices and anti-heroic perspectives of Pound, Eliot, Joyce, and Williams to explore women's assigned alterity and to challenge the priority of the first sex. Imagistic, synchronistic, and hard to read, Gwendolyn Brooks's "The Anniad," the heart of her Pulitzer Prize-winning poem sequence, *Annie Allen* (149), exposed the misogyny of romance conventions by making a woman's struggle to disentangle herself from them the measure, and the menace, of her maturity. In similarly difficult modernist poetry, Doolittle made Helen of Troy, Western culture's most famous sex object, the protagonist, instead of the pawn, in her "epic of consciousness," *Helen in Egypt,* written from 1952 to 1956 and published just before Doolittle died in 1961. In their hands, the conservative and often misogynistic modernism of Pound and Eliot turned out to have surprisingly liberating uses.

Doolittle and Brooks adapted four poetic elements of masculinist modernism. I call them modernist elements rather than techniques, devices, conventions, or the like, because the word "element" can refer to both the more attitudinal and technical ones, while at the same time suggesting the intrinsic modernness of all four: (1) merging subjects with objects—particularly as in imagist poetry; (2) the deflating attitudes of an anti-heroic sensibility; (3) synchronicity, the creation of strange compounds by radically juxtaposing or compressing what is temporally or spatially far apart; and (4) the characteristic attribute of modernist texts—the infamous obscurity that resists, or seems to resist, interpretation.

At first, these poetic elements seem like naturals for evoking the themes of alienation, fragmentation, and decadence that are associated with high modernism. By collapsing subjects and objects, for example, the poet can evoke a world order in which predicates disappear and the intensity of one individual's impression overwhelms the sense of shared experience. Anti-heroism also perceives community feeling as a lost blessing. Nostalgically, anti-heroism mourns the days when the values of a given society were supposedly so unanimous that a single, recognized representative could champion them. Similarly, synchronicity can promote nostalgia by matching classical subjects with their latter-day counterparts to demonstrate a supposed social and cultural decline. Finally, textual obscurity seems to represent the world as intrinsically baffling and to undermine the hope that understanding can be achieved. Though classical modernist negations often make a gloomy and conservative world picture seem inevitable, modernism also has more progressive uses.

The poetry of Brooks and Doolittle exemplifies these progressive uses   5
of modernism. Rarely considered together, the two poets are extremely dis-
similar. Not only do Brooks and Doolittle belong to two different generations, races, and classes—with all the contrasts in experience and interest
that such differences suggest—but the resonances of their poetry—one
urban and local, the other classical and remote—do not harmonize or correspond. Because these two poets' lives and styles contrast so sharply, it is
all the more interesting and suggestive that both should concur in using the
elements of modernist negation for creating modernist affirmations of
political and spiritual possibility. Different as they are, both Brooks and
Doolittle turn the ordinarily conservative and negative features of modernist poetry to radical and hopeful ends.

From Gertrude Reif Hughes, "Making It *Really* New: Hilda Doolittle, Gwen-
    dolyn Brooks, and the Feminist Potential of Modern Poetry." *American
    Quarterly* 42.3 (September 1990): 375–401.

Brooke Kenton Horvath: New Criticism

In the first excerpt following, Brooke Kenton Horvath sets up some questions
that you may well wish to weigh in on: Is Brooks difficult to read? Is she unnecessarily difficult? Is there a "white" style at war with a "black" content in her work?
The second excerpt is a snippet out of Horvath's answer, considering the complexity of "do not be afraid of no." Horvath's critical stance is evident from the
strategy he pursues: Brooks is a worthy poet because she is complex in a way that
is "satisfying."

Gwendolyn Brooks has been both praised and condemned for her often
mandarin style. Thus David Littlejohn, writing in 1966, could acknowledge her craft—"she exercises, customarily," he wrote, "a greater degree of
artistic control than any other American Negro writer"—but not, finally, the
results of that craftsmanship. "In many of her early poems," Littlejohn felt,

> *Mrs. Brooks appears only to pretend to talk of things and of
> people; her real love is words. The inlay work of words, the
> précieux sonics, the lapidary insets of jeweled images (like
> those of Gerard Manley Hopkins) can, in excess, squeeze out life
> and impact altogether, and all but give the lie to the passions
> professed in the verbs.*

For other critics, the real bone of contention has been the fact that,
despite her efforts to forge a black aesthetic, Brooks has practiced a poetics
indebted as much to T. S. Eliot as to Langston Hughes (though brought to
bear on black subject matter). This white style/black content debate can be
heard clearly in Houston A. Baker's *Singers of Daybreak:* "Mrs. Brooks," says
Baker, "writes tense, complex, rhythmic verse that contains the metaphysical complexities of John Donne and the word magic of Apollinaire, Pound,
and Eliot." Yet this style is employed "to explicate the condition of the black
American trapped behind a veil that separates him from the white world.
What one seems to have is 'white' style and 'black' content—two warring
ideals in one dark body." . . .

Her poetry may not seem imagistic, because it is more mimetic, less stylized, than that of classical imagists like Pound, Doolittle, and Williams, but Brooks's poems, like the more classical imagistic ones, use precise evocations to convey, not merely what things look like, but "the reciprocity of inner and outer realities." A generation after the founding of imagism, Brooks, too, strives "for a penetrating kind of seeing which makes sight insight." Moreover, her poems show that the imagistic techniques and aims of making subject experience and object status interpenetrate need not conflict with historicity. Indeed, as Doolittle found in a different way, where subjectivity historically has been denied to a group of human beings so that they are thought of only as objects in someone else's "outer reality," the process of finding their own subjectivities become a political as well as psychological struggle, and understanding "reciprocity" among various "inner and outer realities" becomes an adventure in cognition that the fusings and relocations of imagism can register effectively.

To align "inner and outer realities," Brooks frequently embeds distinctly unromantic situations in romancelike or balladlike poems. Take, for example, her emphatic allusions to romance and ballads in her anti-ballad, "A Bronzeville Mother Loiters in Mississippi. Meanwhile, a Mississippi Mother Burns Bacon." This poem narrates the aftermath of the real-life lynching of Emmet Till in the daily lives of some of its perpetrators and survivors. Yet it works imagistically in several ways.

. . . The celebrated textual obscurity of modernism may be considered masculinist insofar as it invokes this self-indulgent alibi, flattering "laziness and vanity at once" by projecting its own ignorance as an irresolvable perplexity in what is to be known. "How can we know the dancer from the dance?" Yeats asked rhetorically. And, "Did she put on his knowledge with his power?" Such questions stop us cold, which is what they're supposed to do. Like the infamous obscurity of modern texts in general, such baffling questions are designed to make us admit how little we know, and they imply that we must learn to accept limits to what can be considered knowable.

At first glance epistemological concerns may seem to have little to do with sexual or racial politics. But when limiting the knowable is the privilege of men, whose gender has them play knower to women's unknowable, the political dimension of textual obscurity starts to emerge. The otherness assigned to women in patriarchy traditionally makes women a mystery in the sense of something irritatingly, or perhaps beguilingly, elusive. Of course, "mystery" also refers to that which always can be known more fully, rather than something that can never be known.

Keeping that more dynamic sense of "mystery" in mind, the assumption that there must be limits to knowledge begins to sound expedient, potentially oppressive, and, therefore, as much an ethical and political matter as an epistemological one. That is, someone who gets thought of as an enigma (What do women want?) or who has been assigned membership among the inscrutable exotics may prefer not to dismiss difficult mysteries as muddles or marvels. Such a person may be more inclined to try to develop new capacities for knowing than to accept principled limits to what can be known. The antipatriarchal potential of modernism extends even to how an artist construes obscurity.

5

Doolittle and Brooks clearly knew that a sense of being entitled to evade discomfiting knowledge operates underneath all the forms of racial and sexual arrogance they challenged. The white women of the Ladies' Betterment League in Brooks's "Lovers of the Poor," for instance, recoil from the presence of those they have come to help. Overwhelmed by guilt and disgust, they decide to look for some less disturbing place to bestow their "loathe-love largesse" (*Bean Eaters*). Their counterparts, the white tourists slumming in Bronzeville restaurants, "love those little booths at Benvenuti's," because, "Boothed-in, one can detect,/Dissect" (*Annie Allen*). Insulated by arrogance, neither group knows that it fears and despises blackness, so they either run away like the do-gooders, or feel unaccountably rejected, like the tourists who don't find the exotic behaviors they've come to ogle. In both cases, "It is the innocence that constitutes the crime."

. . . The complexity of "'do not be afraid of no'" is, then, aesthetically justified because the poem teaches at every level of itself the need to remain actively engaged (as one must be involved with it) yet wary of reaching closure (as one must be when confronted by a poem that refuses too quickly to relinquish its meaning). No image easily elicits the reader's consent, which must anyway await one's understanding of each part in relation to the whole, just as one must assess any extratexual consent in relation to its effect on one's life as a whole. Similarly, the poem's terribly precise vagueness is likewise justified insofar as it leaves the poem open to speak to anyone confronted by any situation where a preemptive assent seems the path of least resistance (a message as intensely relevant for blacks in 1949 as it ever was before or after this date). Just as does Brooks's famous sonnet "First fight. Then fiddle," "'do not be afraid of no'" places stylistic resistance at the center of her message concerning the need for resistance at the social/political level. And if "'do not be afraid of no'" is still worlds away from the directness of, say, "We Real Cool," Brooks might be seen in this early poem to be considering already that stylistic maneuver Park discovers in the much later "In the Mecca" (1968), wherein the critic finds Brooks "los[ing] faith in the kind of music she had loved and was so well qualified to sing" but which "blacks now found unusable." 10

At the poem's end, as I have noted, whatever it was—social issue, personal concern, aesthetic challenge—that planted the seed of the poem in Brooks's mind ("set her to cede") remains as indefinite as it was when we began. We can ask, Does she wish to urge "no" upon blacks too willing to accept token adjustments of the status quo? Or does she desire to tell women not to surrender their dreams too easily? Or to tell readers not to dismiss her work too quickly? Does she wish to say "no" to a poetic style already proving itself unsatisfactory? All would be provocative messages— and Brooks allows us to entertain each of them—but I see no special textual support for any of them.

"'Do not be afraid of no'" works hard at keeping the reader involved with it by making her feel she has not yet fully gotten into it, leaving open a multiplicity of interpretive possibilities by neither sanctioning nor precluding any of them. And if this assessment is accurate, the poem reveals as well the wisdom of Brooks's strategy as the vehicle for black (social/political) content, for she knows, as do we all, that America will, alas, always provide situations demanding rejection but tempting us to acquiesce either because we grow exhausted and resigned or because the carrot on the stick is lusciously attractive.

From Brooke Kenton Horvath, "The Satisfactions of What's Difficult in Gwendolyn Brooks's Poetry." In *American Literature* 62 (December 1990): 606–616.

R. Baxter Miller: Reader-Response

In this excerpt, from R. Baxter Miller's extended analysis of "The Sundays of Satin-Legs," you can observe a critic moving carefully through a poem, indicating how the poem educates the reader as it unfolds. Miller is especially interested in how the reader experiences a unified imagery and style, thus providing a responsive reading that is informed by New Critical values.

"Satin-Legs" posed early the existential question that was to concern Brooks for more than thirty years. As with later poems, such as number XV in *Annie Allen* and "Second Sermon on the Warpland" in *Mecca,* it sets style and imagination against a deterministic reality and asks if they can prevail. In *Annie* the answer is maybe; in "Second Sermon," a presupposed yes; in "Satin-Legs," no. "Satin-Legs" can be conveniently divided into three parts. The first (lines 1–42) describes a folk character who rises from bed and gets dressed one morning in black Chicago. Some sweet scents ironically suggest his royalty and contrast sharply with his impoverished environment. The resulting tensions indirectly show the relative beauty of roses, dandelions, and garbage. The second part (lines 43–74) illustrates a common journey by narrator and reader into Satin-Legs's closet, a metaphor of man. Here the wide shoulder padding representing Satin-Legs's sculpture and art contrasts with the baroque and rococo styles, European forms of the seventeenth and eighteenth centuries. In the third part (lines 75–158), ear and eye imagery reveal Satin-Legs's unawareness of the world about him, as clothing helps to suggest human deprivation. The narrative movement leads first from the speaker's original antagonism toward her listener ("you") to a light epic concerning Satin-Legs's wardrobe. Following the disappearance of "you" from the poem, the narrator finally views Satin-Legs from a lonely detachment. Ironically this last section juxtaposes blues with the European classics of the late nineteenth century and simultaneously shows that cultural values are relative. In a final irony, Satin-Legs ends each Sunday sleeping with a different prostitute.

The human dimension in the first part, more narrowly confined, first depends upon animal imagery (Satin-Legs, the elaborate cat), then upon the metaphor of life's drama (getting dressed), and last upon the irony characterizing social code ("prim precautions"). An oxymoron communicates Satin-Legs's confusion ("clear delirium"), yet the phrase clarifies a double consciousness working in the poem where the narrator's thinking occasionally merges with that of Satin-Legs. Whereas his perspective is generally muddled, hers is usually clear. Applying some theories of Noam Chomsky, Lévi-Strauss, and Jacques Derrida stimulates two questions. First, what unifies Satin-Legs with his narrator? Second, what does the narrator share with the listener, whom George Kent (in his essay) calls white? Unconsciously Satin-Legs wants to re-search his limited life and his deferred human potential in order to redefine life's meaning. At first he temporarily succeeds when the narrator's words reveal his consciousness: "life must be aromatic./There must be scent, somehow there must be some." His clothing style and cologne merely translate beauty into different kinds of imagery, either visual or olfactory. Conceptions of art, ideal in nature, are universal; but their manifestations, their concrete realities, differ. With a playful tone, the narrator begins her journey, which leads through aloofness and sarcasm to sympathetic judgment. En route she ironically opposes the cultural transformations of humanity to humanity itself.

The final two stanzas in the first part firmly establish the opposition. Would the "you," the narrator questions, "deny" Satin-Legs his scent of lavender and pine? What substitute would the listener provide? In a recent article on Brooks's *In the Mecca,* I observe that Brooks alludes to the Biblical passage in which God speaks to his afflicted servant Job out of the whirlwind. The observation pertains here because the same chapter ends with God's inquiring, "Who provideth for the raven his food?" (Job 38:41). Whereas in "Satin-Legs" the narrator asks the listener if he or she can be God, the speaker in "Second Sermon" secularizes God's command: "Live and go out./Define and/medicate the whirlwind." An overall difference separates Satin-Legs, who needs an external definition for his life, from the speaker who in "Second Sermon" both demonstrates and demands self-definition.

Coming after 1967, "Second Sermon" characterized a later period when Brooks's concern for a white audience lessened, and her voice became more definite. "Satin-Legs," in contrast, shows a more introspective and questioning tone. Should Smith have flowers, the speaker asks, good geraniums, formal chrysanthemums, magnificent poinsettias and beautiful roses "in the best/Of taste and straight tradition?" While bolstering the narrator's sensitivity, the images prepare for the inquiry as to whether a common humanity can exist: "But you forget, or did you ever know,/His heritage of cabbage and pigtails. . . ." Here the poem implies some questions. Is oppression both synchronic and diachronic? When does one's perception shift from momentary to universal time? How do race and class transform the perception? For the speaker such unstated queries are secondary because the listener's desire for knowledge must precede their being asked. After the narrator describes Smith as being flowerless, except for a feather in his lapel, she relates dandelions to death. But for whom?

> *You [the reader] might as well—*
> *Unless you care to set the world a-boil*
> *And do a lot of equalizing things,*
> *Remove a little ermine, say, from kings,*
> *Shake hands with paupers and appoint them men,*
> *For instance—certainly you might as well*
> *Leave him [Smith] his lotion, lavender and oil.*

For Brooks's narrator and the reader, to "shake hands with paupers and appoint them men" is to perceive that worth and happiness are human rights, not social privileges. And the poem's listener must accept the responsibility required by the understanding in order to participate fully in the aesthetic experience.

The second part of "Satin Legs" educates the reader by representing Smith as humanity's icon and its need to create art. Form, as a motif, unifies Smith's clothes style as described in the first part with the literary styles of the sixteenth and seventeenth centuries, as well as with the architectural styles of the seventeenth and eighteenth centuries. "Let us" signals the simultaneous entry by the narrator and the reader into the "innards" of Smith's closet, a journey not into his wardrobe alone but into the human heart. His closet, a vault, lacks those diamonds, pearls, and silver plate that characterize the modern upper class. When addressed earlier to a speaker's coy mistress, Andrew Marvell's lines imply a more genteel tone: "Thy beauty shall no more be found,/Nor, in thy marble vault, small sound/My echoing song. . . ." Brooks subtly parodies Anglo-American poetry, for to transpose "vault" from the pastoral world to the urban one is to retrace Anglo-American and African literature to their anthropomorphic center. In her only direct intrusion, the narrator interrupts: "People are so in need, in need of help./People want so much that they do not know." By their directness, the lines bridge the aesthetic distance that separates Satin-Legs from his speaker. Yet the closure accentuates human time, the rupture between the flawed medium of language and the mythic ideal which evokes language. Language can only signify myth, and the discrepancy between the two represents the difference between the real and the ideal. Paradoxically the poem becomes a linguistic object that divides Smith from his narrator; its language separates its reader from both, even while simultaneously involving the reader. The aesthetic experience becomes grotesque for the same reason Smith's wardrobe finally does. The weakness of all art forms and styles lies in their absolute objectification, because only humanness can invest art with meaning.

From R. Baxter Miller, "'Does Man Love Art?': The Humanistic Aesthetic of
   Gwendolyn Brooks." In *Black American Literature and Humanism.*
   Ed. R. Baxter Miller. Lexington: UP of Kentucky, 1981.

Joanne Gabbin: Political Criticism

In these excerpts, you can see Joanne Gabbin dealing with the charge that Brooks has undergone a radical change: from poetry that was unemotional and unconcerned with black issues, but technically adept, to poetry that is more stridently political and passionate. Gabbin's reading of "the mother" contributes to her argument.

From the earliest publication of *A Street in Bronzeville*, Brook's poetry has had strength of conviction. The themes of mothering, nurture without neglect; loving, the tentative encounters of first love or the comfortable meanderings of mature love; the pain of betrayal and loss; the heroism of simply "being" are uncompromised in her writing. Brooks is unsentimental in her portrayal of Jessie Mitchell's mother, who confronts her illness and impending death by finding solace in the notion that her "shabby" dark-skinned daughter's youth will never compare to her "exquisite yellow"

one. In "A Bronzeville Mother Loiters in Mississippi, Meanwhile a Mississippi Mother Burns Bacon," Brooks is clear-eyed as she looks at the Emmett
Till murder through the eyes of the white woman on whose account the
boy of fourteen was slain. Brooks avoids the hysteria of protest and special
pleading by skillfully registering the encroaching revulsion the woman
feels as she becomes convicted of her husband's guilt. The "Ballad of Pearl
May Lee" also reveals a poet whose tone ranges from mild irony to derisive
sarcasm as she exposes the outrage of a black woman who has been
spurned by her black lover who preferred "a taste of pink and white
honey."

     This poem is her treatment of the black woman—black man—white
woman triad of revenge, pain, and death that is played out in a scenario
made illicit by the ethics of a racist and chauvinistic society. The speaker is
not the black man who is torn between forbidden desire and fear of violence. The speaker is not a chorus of Sirens warning of the dangerous lust
for white flesh. On the contrary, the speaker is a forlorn, enraged black
woman whose voice had rarely been heard in American literature. "Though
never was a poor gal lorner," she has urged her despair and personal rejection into a private vengeance. As he had cut her passion cold, she coldly
views his fate.

> *You paid for your dinner, Sammy boy,*
> *And you didn't pay with money.*
> *You paid with your hide and my heart, Sammy boy,*
> *For your taste of pink and white honey,*
> > *Honey,*
> > *Honey,*
> *For your taste of pink and white honey. (63)*

Admitting that this woman's rage was not foreign to her sensibility, Brooks
says in an interview with Claudia Tate in *Black Women Writers at Work*, "I
hope you sense some real rage in the 'Ballad of Pearl May Lee' [*A Street in
Bronzeville*]. The speaker is a very enraged person. I know because I consulted myself on how I have felt." . . .

     Some critics, however, have attempted to assert that Brooks's poetry
made a radical departure in 1967 from what she had created previously.
With too great simplicity, they have declined to see the political assertive-
ness and protest in her earlier poems. In the above-mentioned interview in
Black Women Writers at Work, Claudia Tate says, "Your earlier works, *A
Street in Bronzeville* and *Annie Allen*, don't seem to focus directly on
heightened political awareness. Do your more recent works tend to deal
directly with this concern?" After proffering the examples "of DeWitt
Williams on his way to Lincoln Cemetery" and "The Sundays of Satin-legs
Smith," Brooks says,

> *Many of the poems, in my new and old books, are "politically
> aware"; I suggest you reread them. You know, when you say
> "political," you really have to be exhaustive. You aren't always
> to think of Andy Young and his comments on Africa, for ex-
> ample. I try to picture in "The Sundays of Satin-Legs Smith" a
> young man who didn't even know he was a tool of the estab-*

lishment, who didn't know his life was being run for him from birth straight to death, and even before birth. As I say in that poem:"Here are hats/Like bright umbrellas; and hysterical ties/Like narrow banners for some gathering war." Now this book was published in '45 and even then I could sense, although not brilliantly, not in great detail, that what was happening to us was going to make us erupt at some later time.

. . . It is with this same depth of understanding that she explores   5
motherhood and children. No other major American poet has given such consistent treatment to these themes. In her often-quoted poem "The Mother," appearing in *A Street in Bronzeville,* Brooks introduces a mother whose decision to abort her children seems to defy the boundaries that are predestined for their lives. Writing about the poem in her autobiography, Brooks says, "Hardly your crowned and praised and 'customary' Mother; but a Mother not unfamiliar, who decided that *she,* rather than her World, will kill her children. The decision is not nice, not simple, and the emotional consequences are neither nice nor simple." Interestingly, Brooks's description of this mother could well fit the woman that Toni Morrison immortalizes in her novel *Beloved.* Determined to kill her children before she will see them dragged back into slavery, Morrison's Sethe succeeds in cutting her daughter's throat before the slave catchers stop her. Though the circumstances appear dramatically different, the urgency and the anguish associated with the choices are similar.

However, Brooks insists that this poem is not so much about abortions as it is about mothering and refuses to allow any group whether pro-choice or pro-life to use it to promote its cause. In the opening ten lines of the poem, the speaker achieves a relative distance from the subject of abortions. Addressing an indefinite "you," the mother attempts to shield herself from the remorse and guilt she feels.

> *Abortions will not let you forget.*
> *You remember the children you got that you did not get,*
> *The damp small pulps with a little or with no hair,*
> *The singers and workers that never handled the air.*
> *You will never neglect or beat*
> *Them, or silence or buy with a sweet.*
> *You will never wind up the sucking-thumb*
> *Or scuttle off ghosts that come.*
> *You will never leave them, controlling your luscious sigh,*
> *Return for a snack of them, with gobbling mother-eye.*

In evoking the unfinished lives of the unborn, Brooks registers significant poignancy; however, the corresponding loss of the mother, forever tied emotionally to her "dim killed children," is overwhelming. The artificial distance erected in the opening lines must be abandoned and we find the mother confessing and accepting her portion of responsibility. Brooks powerfully suggests the tyranny choices exercise in the life of this woman. Written in irregularly metered couplets, her monologue is faltering and strained, and the tone is wistful and deeply remorseful.

When the choice is made to bear children and seek to ensure their survival within the context of life's inexorable limitations, great courage is needed. In poem 2 of "the children of the poor," the narrator, who has now become a mother, asks,

> *What shall I give my children? who are poor,*
> *Who are adjudged the leastwise of the land,*
> *Who are my sweetest lepers, who demand*
> *No velvet and no velvety velour. (116)*

When one of these limitations is racism that defines and separates, that makes them feel "quasi," "contraband," the mother is helpless "to ratify [her] little halves."

From Joanne Gabbin, "Blooming in the Whirlwind: The Early Poetry of Gwendolyn Brooks." In *The Furious Flowering of African American Poetry.* Ed. Joanne Gabbin. Charlottesville: UP of Virginia, 1999.

16

More Poems

"Reading poetry is an adventure in renewal, a creative act, a perpetual beginning, a rebirth of wonder."

—Edward Hirsch

In the preface to his recent and acclaimed book *How to Read a Poem,* Edward Hirsch quotes Matsuo Basho, the seventeenth-century Japanese poet: "Learn about pines from the pine, and about bamboo from the bamboo." Obviously Hirsch thinks it's helpful to have someone tell you about botany (and poetry), but textbooks and teachers can only go so far: you've got to get out into the woods and look around for yourself. In this chapter, you'll find a small forest of poems to explore. It is, to be sure, a relatively cultivated woodland—some important kinds of poems and poets are slightly represented or entirely neglected. To pick only one example, you won't find T. S. Eliot represented here; not "The Love Song of J. Alfred Prufrock," not *The Wasteland,* not even "Sweeney Among the Nightingales." Eliot, who is discussed in the chapter on New Criticism, is an important modern poet (and critic). But obviously this book can't hold everything, and perhaps Eliot is an intellectual challenge that should come after a thorough grounding in poetry. What you will find here is a wide range of poems—by men and

"Here as on a darkling plain swept with confused alarms of struggle and flight, where ignorant armies clash by night, Matthew Arnold, Fox News, Channel Five."

women, American and Other, modern and not, gay and straight, funny and disturbing, teasingly difficult and refreshingly simple, well known (mostly) and obscure (some) and unknown (a few). You probably won't like all of these poems, but I'm confident that you'll like many of them. And you'll find that all of them have something to offer you— an insight, a phrase, a way of thinking about something, perhaps only a word.

Your teacher will provide some guiding questions, but at some point you'll want to practice generating your own lines of inquiry. That is, after all, the idea behind the preceding theory chapters, which aim to show you how to invent ideas. Sometimes, as you read and reread and think, a poem may seem to call for a certain fundamental approach, be it New Critical, deconstructive, psychological, or reader-response. You will, of course, draw on your own unique insights, perhaps blending and combining different approaches, creating your own.

At other times, a poem may seem at first inscrutable, needing no critical approach because it has nothing to say, or what it has to say is so transparent, there's nothing to say to someone else who's read the poem. In such cases, when you don't know what to do, it's helpful to imagine *your* reader, and to consider what *you* might say to some real person who has the poem (or poems) you're discussing. Unless you are writing about some truly obscure work, that is precisely the reader you want to imagine: someone who is familiar with the work, and who is willing to consider what you have to say, provided it seems worthwhile. You do not want to imagine someone who needs you to summarize the poem (unless it's not clear what goes on), or who is forced to read whatever you say, no matter how obvious or boring, or who is interested *only* in whether your writing is grammatically correct. Your reader doesn't want to be distracted by poorly written prose, to be sure, but that's not the main point. The main point is—what can you, as the uniquely situated person that you are, tell your reader about this work, that will help your reader enjoy and appreciate it more?

To determine what you can tell us, if the poem itself doesn't guide you (or if you choose to look beyond its guiding), you may simply try different critical stances. As you read through the poems in this section, you may find the thumbnail sketches of critical approaches (on the inside front cover) helpful, reminding you of the absolute basics of each approach, and prompting you to try various approaches on whatever you're reading. In addition, offered here are some generic questions that may be useful for any poem from a variety of viewpoints. Each question (or cluster of questions) is also analyzed a bit, to give you a better sense of how the question would work within various sets of assumptions. This isn't a complete list of prompting questions, by any means; they're just a few, designed to stretch your imagination and help you feel more comfortable exploring on your own.

Suggestions for Reading Poetry

1. *What is the most important word or phrase in the poem? Explain.*

This question may promote a New Critical reading that unifies the poem, as you discover that the word or phrase is most important because it ties the poem together. Or, you may find yourself moving toward a deconstructive reading, as the word or phrase is most important because it undermines what appears to be the thrust of the poem, calling its apparent position into question. Or, you may find a reader-response piece emerging, as the word or phrase is most important for the way that it shapes your evolving reaction to the poem. Or, is the word or phrase bio-

graphically, or historically, or culturally most significant, or psychologically or politically revealing? It is just a trick, of course, to get you to focus on details.

> 2. *What would happen if you changed a particular word or phrase in the poem? Change a few and explain what happens.*

This question often leads to a clearer vision of what various words and phrases are doing in the poem by seeing what happens if they aren't there to do it anymore. If you're working with the poet's drafts and revisions (a kind of biographical criti-cism), then you're able to oversee the poet, in a sense, seeing what happens as dif-ferent words and phrases are tried. Occasionally, a poet has published different versions of a poem, which may suggest some interesting questions from several per-spectives: taking the New Critic's sort of organic view of the work, you may wonder if a poem with two versions is the same poem, or two poems. A biographical critic, to take another instance, might wonder if the changes are motivated entirely by artis-tic considerations, or if some personal event or awakening is involved.

> 3. *Is the title important? How?*

For most poems, the title is crucially important and carefully considered. (Or, at least, readers can make this assumption and often find interesting and meaningful things to say.) For the reader-response critic, the title creates the initial (and power-ful) impression that the experience of the work may amplify, contradict, or clarify. For a New Critic, of course, the title most likely provides essential insight into the work's unifying theme. A title may be a key allusion, to another work or historical event, that must be understood for the poem to work.

> 4. *What is the poem's shape, and what difference does that shape make?*

In other words, how would you divide the poem into parts? Does the poem have an obvious structure? If so, is this obvious structure the only way to divide the poem into parts?

Again, this cluster may take you in various directions: the poem's parts may inform shifts in the reader's experience, or conflicts that are (or are not) resolved, or some pattern that is psychologically significant. At the most basic level, thinking about structure, breaking the poem into parts, can be very helpful in making sense. I remember vividly the first time I understood John Keat's "Bright Star!"—which was the result of diagramming the poem's parts.

> 5. *How does the poem end? Why does it end that way?*

"Life is the journey, not the arrival." "It's not who wins or loses, but how you play the game." We say such things perhaps to try to keep ourselves from becoming so goal-oriented, so teleological, that we overlook the traveling and the playing. But endings are usually very important, and a poem in which the ending is not important is unusual: indeed, such a poem *has* an important ending in its departure from the norm.

Certain poems are open-ended, or appear to be open-ended, and part of their power is the shock of violating a norm. Such an apparently open-ended poem may well invoke deconstructive kinds of insights, about how the poem is calling some-thing we take for granted into question. For a New Critical reading, the ending typi-cally resolves the poem's tensions; for a reader-response critic, the ending is the experience that the poem has been preparing us for—if we assume that the poem is a prepared experience.

> 6. *Who is speaking in the poem? In what circumstances?*

If the poem doesn't reveal this information, then use your imagination: under what conditions might someone say what this poem says?

It's useful to think about these basic matters just to make sense of the poem, no matter what approach emerges. But many readers surprisingly give little or not thought to who is speaking, to whom, under what conditions. If someone thinks of a poem as always being the expression of the poet's own personal emotion, then such questions are perhaps limited, since the answers are always, "The poet is speaking, to whomever he or she was thinking about, regarding whatever was going on in his or her life." Yet even this restricted biographical focus demands considerable imagination, not to mention research; and our answers can only be tentative. It's often helpful, in trying to imagine the poem as an event, to read it aloud. Try reading it aloud, in fact, several times, in different ways. You'll likely find that the voices you adopt help suggest the sort of speaker and situation allowed for by the poem.

> 7. *Imagine that the poem is a response to this demand: "Say something that will make me want to change my life." Does the poem work as a response to such a command? Explain how it does.*

This final suggestion points the way to a broader range of questions that try to create an attentiveness and imaginativeness in you as you work with the poem. You can ask just about any question with regard to the poem: If the poem had a color, what would it be? If the poem had another line, what would it say? If you wanted to ruin this poem, how could you do it with the least effort? If you had written this poem, how would it be different? And so forth. Such questions may spark some ideas; maybe not.

Any particular question is just a probe. If you ask enough questions, you're bound to hit paydirt sooner or later, producing ideas you can shape, evolving one approach or another. Ideas about poems are certainly a renewable resource: there's no way you can run out of them. You just have to be willing to explore.

Diane Ackerman (1948–)

Driving through Farm Country at Sunset

As I drive through farm country,
a damp reek brewing by the roadway
hits me. Manure, cut grass, honeysuckle,
spearmint. The air feels light as rusk.
And I want to lie down in the newly turned   5
earth, amid the wheat-chaff and the chicory,
while sunlight creeps up a mountainside

off in the distant whelm of color.
Each cemetery, flanked by poplars, looks ready
to play as a chess set. A dozen washloads   10
blow on the line, sock lanterns ablaze,
towels bellied like a schooner's rigging.
In a dogwood's petaled salon, bees leave
their pollen footprints as calling cards.

The occasional samba of a dragonfly   15
tightens the puffy-lidded dusk.
Clouds begin to curdle overhead. And I want
to lie down with you in this boggy dirt,
our legs rubbing like locusts'.

I want you here with the scallions   20
sweet in the night air, to lie down with you
heavy in my arms, and take root.

[1997]

MAYA ANGELOU (1928–)

My Arkansas

There is a deep brooding
in Arkansas.
Old crimes like moss pend
from poplar trees.
The sullen earth
is much too   5
red for comfort.

Sunrise seems to hesitate
and in that second
lose its
incandescent aim, and   10
dusk no more shadows
than the noon.
The past is brighter yet.

Old hates and
ante-bellum lace are rent   15
but not discarded.
Today is yet to come
in Arkansas.
It writhes. It writhes in awful
waves of brooding.   20

[1978]

MARGARET ATWOOD (1939–)

Siren Song

This is the one song everyone
would like to learn: the song
that is irresistible:

the song that forces men
to leap overboard in squadrons   5
even though they see the beached skulls

the song nobody knows
because anyone who has heard it
is dead, and the others can't remember.

Shall I tell you the secret
and if I do, will you get me   10
out of this bird suit?

I don't enjoy it here

squatting on this island
looking picturesque and mythical   15

with these two feathery maniacs,
I don't enjoy singing
this trio, fatal and valuable.

I will tell the secret to you,
to you, only to you.   20
Come closer. This song

is a cry for help: Help me!
Only you, only you can,
you are unique

at last. Alas   25
it is a boring song
but it works every time.

[1974]

Variation on the Word Sleep

I would like to watch you sleeping,
which may not happen.
I would like to watch you,
sleeping. I would like to sleep
with you, to enter   5
your sleep as its smooth dark wave
slides over my head

and walk with you through that lucent
wavering forest of bluegreen leaves
with its watery sun & three moons   10
towards the cave where you must descend,
towards your worst fear

I would like to give you the silver
branch, the small white flower, the one
word that will protect you   15
from the grief at the center
of your dream, from the grief
at the center. I would like to follow
you up the long stairway
again & become   20
the boat that would row you back
carefully, a flame
in two cupped hands
to where your body lies
beside me, and you enter   25
it as easily as breathing in

I would like to be the air
that inhabits you for a moment
only. I would like to be that unnoticed
& that necessary.   30

[1987]

W. H. AUDEN (1907–1973)

In Memory of W. B. Yeats

(d. January 1939)

1

He disappeared in the dead of winter:
The brooks were frozen, the air-ports almost deserted,
And snow disfigured the public statues;
The mercury sank in the mouth of the dying day.
O all the instruments agree   5
The day of his death was a dark cold day.

Far from his illness
The wolves ran on through the evergreen forests,
The peasant river was untempted by the fashionable quays;
By mourning tongues   10
The death of the poet was kept from his poems.

But for him it was his last afternoon as himself,
An afternoon of nurses and rumours;
The provinces of his body revolted,
The squares of his mind were empty,   15
Silence invaded the suburbs,
The current of his feeling failed; he became his admirers.

Now he is scattered among a hundred cities
And wholly given over to unfamiliar affections;
To find his happiness in another kind of wood   20
And be punished under a foreign code of conscience.
The words of a dead man
Are modified in the guts of the living.

But in the importance and noise of to-morrow
When the brokers are roaring like beasts on the floor of the Bourse,   25
And the poor have the sufferings to which they are fairly accustomed,
And each in the cell of himself is almost convinced of his freedom,
A few thousand will think of this day
As one thinks of a day when one did something slightly unusual.

O all the instruments agree   30
The day of his death was a dark cold day.

2

You were silly like us: your gift survived it all;
The parish of rich women, physical decay,
Yourself; mad Ireland hurt you into poetry.
Now Ireland has her madness and her weather still,   35
For poetry makes nothing happen: it survives
In the valley of its saying where executives
Would never want to tamper; it flows south
From ranches of isolation and the busy griefs,
Raw towns that we believe and die in; it survives,   40
A way of happening, a mouth.

3

Earth, receive an honoured guest;
William Yeats is laid to rest:
Let the Irish vessel lie
Emptied of its poetry.   45

Time that is intolerant
Of the brave and innocent,
And indifferent in a week
To a beautiful physique,

Worships language and forgives   50
Everyone by whom it lives;
Pardons cowardice, conceit,
Lays its honours at their feet.

Time that with this strange excuse
Pardoned Kipling and his views,   55
And will pardon Paul Claudel,
Pardons him for writing well.

In the nightmare of the dark
All the dogs of Europe bark,
And the living nations wait,   60
Each sequestered in its hate;

Intellectual disgrace
Stares from every human face,
And the seas of pity lie
Locked and frozen in each eye.   65

Follow, poet, follow right
To the bottom of the night,
With your unconstraining voice
Still persuade us to rejoice;

With the farming of a verse   70
Make a vineyard of the curse,
Sing of human unsuccess
In a rapture of distress;

In the deserts of the heart
Let the healing fountain start,   75
In the prison of his days
Teach the free man how to praise.

                                                    [1940]

IMAMU AMIRI BARAKA (LEROI JONES) (1934–)

Preface to a Twenty Volume Suicide Note

Lately, I've become accustomed to the way
The ground opens up and envelops me
Each time I go out to walk the dog.
Or the broad edged silly music the wind
Makes when I run for a bus—   5

Things have come to that.

And now, each night I count the stars,
And each night I get the same number.
And when they will not come to be counted
I count the holes they leave.   10

Nobody sings anymore.

And then last night, I tiptoed up
To my daughter's room and heard her
Talking to someone, and when I opened
The door, there was no one there . . .   15
Only she on her knees,
Peeking into her own clasped hands.

[1964]

APHRA BEHN (c. 1640–1689)

Song: Love Armed[1]

Love in fantastic triumph[2] sate,
    Whilst bleeding hearts around him flowed,
For whom fresh pains he did create,
    And strange tyrannic power he showed:
From thy bright eyes he took his fire,   5
    Which round about in sport he hurled;
But 'twas from mine he took desire,
    Enough to undo the amorous world.

From me he took his sighs and tears:
    From thee, his pride and cruelty;   10
From me, his languishments and fears;
    And every killing dart[3] from thee.
Thus thou and I the god have armed
    And set him up a deity;
But my poor heart alone is harmed,   15
    Whilst thine the victor is, and free.

[1676]

Aphra Behn was not only England's first professional female writer, but she was also an English spy, code-named "Astrea" or "Agent 160."

LOUISE BOGAN (1897–1970)

Women

Women have no wilderness in them,
They are provident instead,
Content in the tight hot cell of their hearts
To eat dusty bread.

---

[1]This poem is a song in a Behn play. *Abdelazer; or, The Moor's Revenge.* "Love" here is Cupid, who is armed with bow and arrows.
[2]A "triumph" can be a celebration, a kind of parade in honor of a success.
[3]The "dart" here may refer to Cupid's darts, or arrows. "Killing" may not be literal.

They do not see cattle cropping red winter grass,   5
They do not hear
Snow water going down under culverts
Shallow and clear.

They wait, when they should turn to journeys,
They stiffen, when they should bend.   10
They use against themselves that benevolence
To which no man is friend.

They cannot think of so many crops to a field
Or of clean wood cleft by an axe.
Their love is an eager meaninglessness   15
Too tense, or too lax.

They hear in every whisper that speaks to them
A shout and a cry.
As like as not, when they take life over their door-sills
They should let it go by.   20

                                                              [1923]

ANNE BRADSTREET (1612?–1672)

The Author to Her Book[1]

Thou ill-formed offspring of my feeble brain,
Who after birth did'st by my side remain,
Till snatched from thence by friends, less wise than true,
Who thee abroad exposed to public view;
Made thee in rags, halting, to the press to trudge,   5
Where errors were not lessened, all may judge.
At thy return my blushing was not small,
My rambling brat (in print) should mother call;
I cast thee by as one unfit for light,
Thy visage was so irksome in my sight;   10
Yet being mine own, at length affection would
Thy blemishes amend, if so I could:
I washed thy face, but more defects I saw,
And rubbing off a spot, still made a flaw.
I stretched thy joints to make thee even feet,[2]   15
Yet still thou run'st more hobbling than is meet;[3]
In better dress to trim thee was my mind,
But nought save homespun cloth in the house I find.
In this array, 'mongst vulgars[4] may'st thou roam;
In critics' hands beware thou dost not come;   20
And take thy way where yet thou are not known.

---

[1]In 1650, Bradstreet's *The Tenth Muse*, a collection of poems, was published without her knowledge or approval. This poem relates to the second edition of this volume, which Bradstreet revised and published.
[2]"Feet" in a poem refer to the meter. Bradstreet is saying that she has made the poem more correct, improving the meter.
[3]"Meet" here means "proper," "correct," "appropriate."
[4]"Vulgars" here refers to the common people.

If for thy Father asked, say thou had'st none;
And for thy Mother, she alas is poor,
Which caused her thus to send thee out of door.

[1678]

WILLIAM CULLEN BRYANT (1798–1878)

To a Waterfowl

Whither, midst falling dew,
    While glow the heavens with the last steps of day,
Far, through their rosy depths, dost thou pursue
    Thy solitary way?

    Vainly the fowler's eye   5
Might mark thy distant flight to do thee wrong,
As, darkly painted on the crimson sky,
    Thy figure floats along.

    Seek'st thou the plashy brink
Of weedy lake, or marge of river wide,   10
Or where the rocking billows rise and sink
    On the chafed ocean-side?

    There is a Power whose care
Teaches thy way along that pathless coast—
The desert and illimitable air—   15
    Lone wandering, but not lost.

    All day thy wings have fanned,
At that far height, the cold, thin atmosphere,
Yet stoop not, weary, to the welcome land,
    Though the dark night is near.   20

    And soon that toil shall end;
Soon shalt thou find a summer home, and rest,
And scream among thy fellows; reeds shall bend,
    Soon, o'er thy sheltered nest.

    Thou'rt gone, the abyss of heaven   25
Hath swallowed up thy form; yet, on my heart
Deeply hath sunk the lesson thou hast given,
    And shall not soon depart.

    He who, from zone to zone,
Guides through the boundless sky thy certain flight,   30
In the long way that I must tread alone,
    Will lead my steps aright.

[1818]

ROBERT BURNS (1759–1796)

Oh, my love is like a red, red rose

Oh, my love is like a red, red rose
    That's newly sprung in June;

My love is like the melody
    That's sweetly played in tune.

So fair art thou, my bonny lass,   5
    So deep in love am I;
And I will love thee still, my dear,
    Till a' the seas gang dry.

Till a' the seas gang dry, my dear,
    And the rocks melt wi' the sun;   10
And I will love thee still, my dear,
    While the sands o' life shall run.

And fare thee weel, my only love!
    And fare thee weel awhile!
And I will come again, my love   15
    Though it were ten thousand mile.

[about 1788]

COUNTEE CULLEN (1903–1946)

Incident

Once riding in old Baltimore,
    Heart-filled, head-filled with glee,
I saw a Baltimorean
    Keep looking straight at me.

Now I was eight and very small,   5
    And he was no whit bigger,
And so I smiled, but he poked out
    His tongue, and called me, "Nigger."

I saw the whole of Baltimore
    From May until December: 10
Of all the things that happened there
    That's all that I remember.

[1925]

---

e.e. cummings (1894–1962)

anyone lived in a pretty how town

anyone lived in a pretty how town
(with up so floating many bells down)
spring summer autumn winter
he sang his didn't he danced his did.

Women and men(both little and small)   5
cared for anyone not at all
they sowed their isn't they reaped their same
sun moon stars rain

children guessed(but only a few

and down they forgot as up they grew   10
autumn winter spring summer)
that noone loved him more by more

when by now and tree by leaf
she laughed his joy she cried his grief
bird by snow and stir by still   15
anyone's any was all to her

someones married their everyones
laughed their cryings and did their dance
(sleep wake hope and then)they
said their nevers they slept their dream   20

stars rain sun moon
(and only the snow can begin to explain
how children are apt to forget to remember
with up so floating many bells down)

one day anyone died i guess   25
(and noone stooped to kiss his face)
busy folk buried them side by side
little by little and was by was

all by all and deep by deep
and more by more they dream their sleep   30
noone and anyone earth by april
wish by spirit and if by yes.

Women and men(both dong and ding)
summer autumn winter spring
reaped their sowing and went their came   35
sun moon stars rain

[1940]

KWAME DAWES (1963–)

Umpire at the Portrait Gallery

At the Portrait Gallery near Trafalgar Square
I am searched by an ancient umpire
who mumbles his request with marbles or loose
dentures in his mouth. I see my first
portrait: the blotched bony fingers, the warts,   5
the clumsy overlarge gold ring loosely turning
like it will when he is entombed for good;
that look of boredom around the eyes
he masks with considered politeness
like a drunk man's careful compensations   10
and this self-important thinning of lips;
the nose, the greenish veins, the cliché
of a mole on his brow. It is too dark here
to study him well, besides he has found nothing
and the natives are restless at my back.   15

I am looking for the faces of this country;
the rustic, the jaundiced, the worn,
sharp tight snaps so close the pores talk;
faces caught in unaware blankness,
the rituals of rocking to numb silence   5
on the trains; dirty light, the thin
mist of darkness in the underground
making the faces collectors' bits,
keepables of a post-nuclear tribe.
I find only the posed stateliness   10
of another time—the courtly manners,
the clean colors staring from the palette
masking the stench and filth of older ways—
nothing to write about, really, nothing.
I am back in the lobby staring at the native,   15
his Adam's apple bobbing, his fingers,
the thick blackened nails, the stale suit,
the cap, the poem he is—the simple grammar
of another time—the years of the bombs
falling; he must have seen broken bodies   20
too. Now he fingers my underthings
searching for what I may have taken.
He finds nothing, nods me along.
Still, the globular ring keeps me
from forgetting him altogether,   25
that and the absence of stories to tell.
It is brilliant outside. A black-faced
Bobby points me the way to the Southern
Bank where the river reeks of history
and word weavers converge in snotty halls   30
to flaunt their musings to the world.
Here we are in the carcass of empire
searching in vain for sweetest honey.

                                    [2001]

EMILY DICKINSON (1830–1886)

Because I could not stop for Death

Because I could not stop for Death—
He kindly stopped for me—
The Carriage held but just Ourselves—
And Immortality.

We slowly drove—He knew no haste   5
And I had put away
My labor and my leisure too,
For His Civility—

We passed the School, where Children strove
At Recess—in the Ring—   10

We passed the Fields of Gazing Grain—
We passed the Setting Sun—

Or rather—He passed Us—
The Dews drew quivering and chill—
For only Gossamer, my Gown—
My Tippet[1]—only Tulle—

We passed before a House that seemed
A Swelling of the Ground—
The Roof was scarcely visible—
The Cornice—in the Ground—

Since then—'tis Centuries—and yet
Feels shorter than the Day
I first surmised the Horses Heads
Were toward Eternity—

[about 1863]

"Faith" is a fine invention

"Faith" is a fine invention
When Gentlemen can *see*—
But *Microscopes* are prudent
In an Emergency.

[1851]

I heard a Fly buzz—When I Died

I heard a Fly buzz—when I died—
The Stillness in the Room
Was like the Stillness in the Air—
Between the Heaves of Storm—

The Eyes around—had wrung them dry—   5
And Breaths were gathering firm
For that last Onset—when the King
Be witnessed—in the Room—

I willed my Keepsakes—Signed away
What portion of me be   10
Assignable—and then it was
There interposed a Fly—

With Blue—uncertain stumbling Buzz—
Between the light—and me—
And then the Windows failed—and then   15
I could not see to see—

[about 1862]

Amherst College Archives and Special
Collections

I like to see it lap the Miles

I like to see it lap the Miles—
And lick the Valleys up—

[1]cape

And stop to feed itself at Tanks—
And then—prodigious step

Around a Pile of Mountains—   5
And supercilious peer
In Shanties—by the sides of Roads—
And then a Quarry pare

To fit its Ribs
And crawl between   10
Complaining all the while
In horrid—hooting stanza—
Then chase itself down Hill—

And neigh like Boanerges—
Then—punctual as a Star   15
Stop—docile and omnipotent
At its own stable door—

[about 1862]

FRED DINGS (1962–)

The Divers

This pool, though only chlorine-pure, is much preferred
to the rock ledge and bile-green water of the quarry outside town
with its algal rafts and snakes and submerged logs
which can dislodge and rise at any time.
So, on these cloud-fluffed summer days,   5
they commune here for relief from the heat and to master
the dive, to practice springing from the boards to the air
so they may fall in their own way to the sky-blue box
of water waiting beneath. The children train to plunge
head-first, making a steeple of their arms so their bodies   10
slide painlessly in. They learn it's all about style,
this entering the water. Miss your angle and you will sting
at the change in density; miss your time and you may slap
flat on your back as if stunned on concrete. But beyond that,
what draws them up these ladders is greater than fear: 15
it's a certain joy in perfecting the body's expression
on its way to total immersion: watch the time-defying
somersaults and twists crammed into split seconds,
watch the arched cross of the swan as it lunges face-first
into space, watch the quick click of the jack knife as it opens   20
and slips through the slit it cuts in the water's skin,
watch even the graceless cannonball, that anarchic favorite
of the young, which requires a certain skill to rise high
above the earth in a tight fetal curl and plummet so hard
you pock the pool like a meteor and douse the self-annointing   25
chaise-lounge crowd with a crater-edge of spray.
Ah, dear divers, these are good days and may they stay with you,
may they soak so thoroughly in that when you stand someday

on that jagged ledge above the pit of dark water, you will open
your arms to embrace it all or steeple yourself into hope   30
or roll yourself into a ball of experience, a world, globed,
and ready to lodge in that denser sphere of what is.

[2002]

JOHN DONNE (1572–1631)

The Canonization

For God's sake hold your tongue, and let me love,
    Or chide my palsy, or my gout,
My five gray hairs, or ruined fortune flout,
    With wealth your state, your mind with arts improve,
        Take you a course, get you a place,   5
    Observe his Honor, or his Grace,
Or the King's real, or his stampèd face
    Contemplate, what you will, approve,
    So you will let me love.

Alas, alas, who's injured by my love?   10
    What merchant's ships have my sighs drowned?
Who says my tears have overflowed his ground?
    When did my colds a forward spring remove?
        When did the heats which my veins fill
        Add one more to the plaguy bill?   15
Soldiers find wars, and lawyers find out still
    Litigious men, which quarrels move
    Though she and I do love.

Call us what you will, we are made such by love;
    Call her one, me another fly,   20
We are tapers too, and at our own cost die,
    And we in us find the eagle and the dove.
        The phoenix riddle hath more wit
    By us; we two being one, are it.
So to one neutral thing both sexes fit,   25
    We die and rise the same, and prove
    Mysterious by this love.

We can die by it, if not live by love,
    And if unfit for tombs and hearse
Our legend be, it will be fit for verse;   30
    And if no piece of chronicle we prove,
        We'll build in sonnets pretty rooms;
        As well a well wrought urn becomes
The greatest ashes, as half-acre tombs,
    And by these hymns, all shall approve   35
    Us canonized for love:

And thus invoke us: You whom reverend love
    Made one another's hermitage;
You, to whom love was peace, that now is rage;

Who did the whole world's soul contract, and drove   40
  Into the glasses of your eyes
    (So made such mirrors, and such spies,
That they did all to you epitomize)
    Countries, towns, courts: beg from above
    A pattern of your love!   45

[1633]

RITA DOVE (1952–)

Motherhood

She dreams the baby's so small she keeps
misplacing it—it rolls from the hutch
and the mouse carries it home, it disappears
with his shirt in the wash.
Then she drops it and it explodes   5
like a watermelon, eyes spitting.

Finally they get to the countryside;
Thomas has it in a sling.
He's strewing rice along the road
while the trees chitter with tiny birds.   10
In the meadow to their right three men
are playing rough with a white wolf. She calls

warning but the wolf breaks free
and she runs, the rattle
rolls into the gully, then she's   15
there and tossing the baby behind her,
listening for its cry as she straddles
the wolf and circles its throat, counting
until her thumbs push through to the earth.
White fur seeps red. She is hardly breathing.   20
The small wild eyes
go opaque with confusion and shame, like a child's.

[1986]

JOHN DRYDEN (1631–1700)

To the Memory of Mr. Oldham[1]

Farewell, too little and too lately known,
Whom I began to think and call my own;
For sure our souls were near allied, and thine
Cast in the same poetic mold with mine.
One common note on either lyre did strike,   5
And knaves and fools we both abhorred alike.
To the same goal did both our studies drive:

[1]John Oldham was a poet who died at the age of thirty.

The last set out the soonest did arrive.
Thus Nissus fell upon the slippery place,
While his young friend performed and won the race.[2]   10
O early ripe! to thy abundant store
What could advancing age have added more?
It might (what Nature never gives the young)
Have taught the numbers of thy native tongue.
But satire needs not those, and wit will shine   15
Through the harsh cadence of a rugged line.
A noble error, and but seldom made,
When poets are by too much force betrayed.
Thy gen'rous fruits, though gathered ere their prime,
Still showed a quickness; and maturing time   20
But mellows what we write to the dull sweets of rhyme.
Once more, hail, and farewell! farewell, thou young
But ah! too short, Marcellus[3] of our tongue!
Thy brows with ivy and with laurels bound;
But fate and gloomy night encompass thee around.[4]   25

[1684]

RICHARD EBERHART (1904–)

The Fury of Aerial Bombardment[5]

You would think the fury of aerial bombardment
Would rouse God to relent; the infinite spaces
Are still silent. He looks on shock-pried faces.
History, even, does not know what is meant.

You would feel that after so many centuries   5
God would give man to repent; yet he can kill
As Cain could, but with multitudinous will,
No farther advanced than in his ancient furies.

Was man made stupid to see his own stupidity?
Is God by definition indifferent, beyond us all?   10
Is the eternal truth man's fighting soul
Wherein the Beast ravens in its own avidity?

Of Van Wettering I speak, and Averill,
Names on a list, whose faces I do not recall

---

[2]In Virgil's *Aeneid*, two friends raced for the prize of an olive crown; as the poem says, Nissus slipped, allowing his friend to win.

[3]Marcellus would have followed the Roman Emperor Augustus, had he not died at age twenty. Dryden's age was especially interested in drawing modern parallels to classical events, and in employing classical literary references.

[4]In Virgil's *Aeneid* (Book 6, line 886), Marcellus is said to be followed by a cloud of doom.

[5]Eberhart was a Naval Reserve officer during World War II. He taught, according to his own estimate, "tens of thousands" of men to shoot machine guns from aircraft. Depressingly often, Eberhart said later, the names of the young men he trained would show up on the lists of those killed in action.

But they are gone to early death, who late in school   15
Distinguished the belt feed lever from the belt holding pawl.

[1947]

ROBERT FRANCIS (1901–1987)

Pitcher

His art is eccentricity, his aim
How not to hit the mark he seems to aim at,

His passion how to avoid the obvious,
His technique how to vary the avoidance.

The others throw to be comprehended. He   5
Throws to be a moment misunderstood.

Yet not too much. Not errant, arrant, wild,
But every seeming aberration willed.

Not to, yet still, still to communicate
Making the batter understand too late.   10

[1960]

MICHAEL HARPER (1938–)

Dear John, Dear Coltrane[1]

a love supreme, a love supreme
a love supreme, a love supreme[2]

Sex fingers toes
in the marketplace
near your father's church
in Hamlet, North Carolina—
witness to this love   5
in this calm fallow
of these minds,
there is no substitute for pain:
genitals gone or going,
seed burned out,   10
you tuck the roots in the earth,
turn back, and move
by river through the swamps,
singing: *a love supreme, a love supreme;*
what does it all mean?   15
Loss, so great each black
woman expects your failure
in mute change, the seed gone.
You plod up into the electric city—

---

[1] John Coltrane was an American jazz composer and saxophonist (1926–1967).
[2] Coltrane performed a song, "A Love Supreme," that contained these lines.

your song now crystal and   20
the blues. You pick up the horn
with some will and blow
into the freezing night:
a love supreme, a love supreme—

Dawn comes and you cook   25
up the thick sin 'tween
impotence and death, fuel
the tenor sax cannibal
heart, genitals and sweat
that makes you clean—   30
a love supreme, a love supreme—

Why you so black?
cause I am
why you so funky?
cause I am   35
why you so black?
cause I am
why you so sweet?
cause I am
why you so black?   40
cause I am
a love supreme, a love supreme:

So sick
you couldn't play *Naima*,[3]
so flat we ached   45
for song you'd concealed
with your own blood,
your diseased liver gave
out its purity,
the inflated heart   50
pumps out, the tenor[4] kiss,
tenor love:
a love supreme, a love supreme—
a love supreme, a love supreme—

[1970]

ROBERT HERRICK (1591–1674)

To the Virgins, to Make Much of Time

Gather ye rose-buds while ye may,
   Old Time is still a-flying;
And this same flower that smiles today,
   Tomorrow will be dying.

The glorious lamp of heaven, the sun,   5
   The higher he's a-getting,

[3]Coltrane performed a song by this name.
[4]Coltrane played a tenor saxophone.

The sooner will his race be run,
　　And nearer he's to setting.

That age is best which is the first,
　　When youth and blood are warmer;
But being spent, the worse, and worst   10
　　Times still succeed the former.

Then be not coy, but use your time,
　　And while ye may, go marry;
For having lost but once your prime,   15
　　You may for ever tarry.

[1648]

A.E. HOUSMAN (1859–1936)

Loveliest of Trees, the Cherry Now

Loveliest of trees, the cherry now
Is hung with bloom along the bough,
And stands about the woodland ride
Wearing white for Eastertide.

Now, of my threescore years and ten,   5
Twenty will not come again,
And take from seventy springs a score,
It only leaves me fifty more.

And since to look at things in bloom
Fifty springs are little room,   10
About the woodlands I will go
To see the cherry hung with snow.

[1896]

LANGSTON HUGHES (1902–1967)

The Negro Speaks of Rivers

I've known rivers:
I've known rivers ancient as the world and older than the flow of
　　human blood in human veins.

My soul has grown deep like the rivers.

I bathed in the Euphrates when dawns were young.
I built my hut near the Congo and it lulled me to sleep.   5
I looked upon the Nile and raised the pyramids above it.
I heard the singing of the Mississippi when Abe Lincoln went down to
　　New Orleans, and I've seen its muddy bosom turn all golden in the
　　sunset.

I've known rivers:
Ancient, dusky rivers.

My soul has grown deep like the rivers.   10

[1926]

The Weary Blues

Droning a drowsy syncopated tune,
Rocking back and forth to a mellow croon,
   I heard a Negro play.
Down on Lenox Avenue the other night
By the pale dull pallor of an old gas light   5
   He did a lazy sway. . . .
   He did a lazy sway. . . .
To the tune o' those Weary Blues.
With his ebony hands on each ivory key
He made that poor piano moan with melody.   10
   O Blues!
Swaying to and fro on his rickety stool
He played that sad raggy tune like a musical fool.
   Sweet Blues!
Coming from a black man's soul.   15
   O Blues!
In a deep song voice with a melancholy tone
I heard that Negro sing, that old piano moan—
   "Ain't got nobody in all this world,
    Ain't got nobody but ma self.
   I's gwine to quit ma frownin'   20
   And put ma troubles on the shelf."

Thump, thump, thump, went his foot on the floor.
He played a few chords then he sang some more—
   "I got the Weary Blues
   And I can't be satisfied.   25
   Got the Weary Blues
   And can't be satisfied—
   I ain't happy no mo'
   And I wish that I had died."
And far into the night he crooned that tune.   30
The stars went out and so did the moon.
The singer stopped playing and went to bed
While the Weary Blues echoed through his head.
He slept like a rock or a man that's dead.

[1926]

Theme for English B

The instructor said,

   Go home and write
   a page tonight.
   And let that page come out of you—
   Then, it will be true.   5

I wonder if it's that simple?
I am twenty-two, colored, born in Winston-Salem.
I went to school there, then Durham, then here
to this college on the hill above Harlem.
I am the only colored student in my class.   10

The steps from the hill lead down into Harlem,
through a park, then I cross St. Nicholas,
Eighth Avenue, Seventh, and I come to the Y,
the Harlem Branch Y, where I take the elevator
up to my room, sit down, and write this page: 15

It's not easy to know what is true for you and me
at twenty-two, my age. But I guess I'm what
I feel and see and hear, Harlem, I hear you:
hear you, hear me—we two—you, me, talk on this page.
(I hear New York, too.) Me—who?   20
Well, I like to eat, sleep, drink, and be in love.
I like to work, read, learn, and understand life.
I like a pipe for a Christmas present,
or records—Bessie, bop, or Bach.
I guess being colored doesn't make me not like   25
the same things other folks like who are other races.
So will my page be colored that I write?
Being me, it will not be white.

But it will be
a part of you, instructor.   30
You are white—
yet a part of me, as I am a part of you.
That's American.
Sometimes perhaps you don't want to be a part of me.
Nor do I often want to be a part of you.   35
But we are, that's true!
As I learn from you,
I guess you learn from me—
although you're older—and white—
and somewhat more free.   40

This is my page for English B.

                                                      [1951]

LUISA IGLORIA (1961–)

Dinakdakan

For Mama Tet

This could be
the supermarket of your dreams,
the shelves slick and
showy with fruit, wide-   5
mouthed mason jars of herring,
rice grains longer
than your fingernail.

Our shopping cart would quickly swell
with breads whose names till now   10
were fable: rye, stone-ground
wheat, poppyseed buns;

the brie and Camembert
longed for at Christmas time
instead of the yearly *queso
de bola;* the Spam and corned
beef worth a whole week's pay.   15

And then I think of you
as on a trip to market long ago:
the marvel was not merely
how the wind lifted our hair,
knifed raw the flesh of our mouths,   20
wrist, cheeks—how our rubber
boots were worthless in steady rain
and slippery mud.

It was you, plunging a bare
arm into a pail of still-breathing milkfish,   25
certain which had the sweetest belly;
knowing where to find
tamarind pods cracking
out of their rinds for ripeness,   30
the lemon grass for boiling
with white rice, the river snails
to steep into a heady broth.
(We extricated these with safety
pins, smacking lips, fingers.)   35

Among the rows of plastic-sealed,
aseptically packaged food,
I stare and stare, imagining flat,
dried, salted fish-shapes pressed
between the cereal boxes,   40
fresh blood and entrails forming
a dark pool on the white linoleum.

(Above the click and hum
of computerized cash registers
I hear your singing knife   45
slice pigs' ears paper-thin,
your fork twirl thick
with clouds of boiled brain and minced
shallots for the evening meal.

[1994]

GALWAY KINNELL (1927–)

The Bear

1

In late winter
I sometimes glimpse bits of steam
coming up from
some fault in the old snow

and bend close and see it is lung-colored
and put down my nose   5
and know
the chilly, enduring odor of bear.

      2

I take a wolf's rib and whittle
it sharp at both ends   10
and coil it up
and freeze it in blubber and place it out
on the fairway of the bears.

And when it has vanished
I move out on the bear tracks,   15
roaming in circles
until I come to the first, tentative, dark
splash on the earth.

And I set out
running, following the splashes   20
of blood wandering over the world.
At the cut, gashed resting places
I stop and rest,
at the crawl-marks
where he lay out on his belly   25
to overpass some stretch of bauchy ice
I lie out
dragging myself forward with bear-knives in my fists.

      3

On the third day I begin to starve,
at nightfall I bend down as I knew I would   30
at a turd sopped in blood,
and hesitate, and pick it up,
and thrust it in my mouth, and gnash it down,
and rise
and go on running.   35

      4

On the seventh day,
living by now on bear blood alone,
I can see his upturned carcass far out ahead, a scraggled,
steamy hulk,
the heavy fur riffling in the wind.   40

I come up to him
and stare at the narrow-spaced, petty eyes,
the dismayed
face laid back on the shoulder, the nostrils
flared, catching   45
perhaps the first taint of me as he
died.

I hack
a ravine in his thigh, and eat and drink,   50

and tear him down his whole length
and open him and climb in
and close him up after me, against the wind,
and sleep.

5

And dream
of lumbering flatfooted
over the tundra,
stabbed twice from within,
splattering a trail behind me,
splattering it out no matter which way I lurch,
no matter which parabola of bear-transcendence,
which dance of solitude I attempt,
which gravity-clutched leap,
which trudge, which groan.

6

Until one day I totter and fall—
fall on this
stomach that has tried so hard to keep up,
to digest the blood as it leaked in,
to break up
and digest the bone itself: and now the breeze
blows over me, blows off
the hideous belches of ill-digested bear blood
and rotted stomach
and the ordinary, wretched odor of bear,

blows across
my sore, lolled tongue a song
or screech, until I think I must rise up
and dance. And I lie still.

7

I awaken I think. Marshlights
reappear, geese
come trailing again up the flyway.
In her ravine under the snow the dam-bear
lies, licking
lumps of smeared fur
and drizzly eyes into shapes
with her tongue. And one
hairy-soled trudge stuck out before me,
the next,
the next,
the rest of my days I spend
wandering: wondering
what, anyway,
was the sticky infusion, that rank flavor of blood, that poetry by which
        I lived?

[1993]

PHILIP LARKIN (1922–1985)

A Study of Reading Habits

When getting my nose in a book
Cured most things short of school,
It was worth ruining my eyes
To know I could still keep cool,
And deal out the old right hook   5
To dirty dogs twice my size.

Later, with inch-thick specs,
Evil was just my lark:
Me and my cloak and fangs
Had ripping times in the dark.   10
The women I clubbed with sex!
I broke them up like meringues.

Don't read much now: the dude
Who lets the girl down before
The hero arrives, the chap   15
Who's yellow and keeps the store,
Seem far too familiar. Get stewed:
Books are a load of crap.

[1964]

LI-YOUNG LEE (1957–)

Persimmons

In sixth grade Mrs. Walker
slapped the back of my head
and made me stand in the corner
for not knowing the difference
between *persimmon* and *precision*.   5
How to choose

persimmons. This is precision.
Ripe ones are soft and brown-spotted.
Sniff the bottoms. The sweet one
will be fragrant. How to eat: 10
put the knife away, lay down newspaper.
Peel the skin tenderly, not to tear the meat.
Chew the skin, suck it,
and swallow. Now, eat
the meat of the fruit,   15
so sweet
all of it, to the heart.

Donna undresses, her stomach is white.
In the yard, dewy and shivering
with crickets, we lie naked,   20

face-up, face-down,
I teach her Chinese.
Crickets: *chiu chiu.* Dew: I've forgotten.
Naked: I've forgotten.
Ni, wo: you and me.   25
I part her legs,
remember to tell her
she is beautiful as the moon.

Other words
that got me into trouble were   30
fight and *fright, wren* and *yarn.*
Fight was what I did when I was frightened,
fright was what I felt when I was fighting.
Wrens are small, plain birds,
yarn is what one knits with.   35
Wrens are soft as yarn.
My mother made birds out of yarn.
I loved to watch her tie the stuff;
a bird, a rabbit, a wee man.

Mrs. Walker brought a persimmon to class   40
and cut it up
so everyone could taste
a *Chinese apple.* Knowing
it wasn't ripe or sweet, I didn't eat
but watched the other faces.   45

My mother said every persimmon has a sun
inside, something golden, glowing,
warm as my face.

Once, in the cellar, I found two wrapped in newspaper,
forgotten and not yet ripe.   50
I took them and set both on my bedroom windowsill,
where each morning a cardinal
sang, *The sun, the sun.*

Finally understanding
he was going blind,   55
my father sat up all one night
waiting for a song, a ghost.
I gave him the persimmons,
swelled, heavy as sadness,
and sweet as love.   60

This year, in the muddy lighting
of my parents' cellar, I rummage, looking
for something I lost.
My father sits on the tired, wooden stairs,
black cane between his knees,   65
hand over hand, gripping the handle.

He's so happy that I've come home.
I ask how his eyes are, a stupid question.
All gone, he answers.

Under some blankets, I find a box.   70
Inside the box I find three scrolls.
I sit beside him and untie
three paintings by my father:
Hibiscus leaf and a white flower.
Two cats preening.   75
Two persimmons, so full they want to drop from the cloth.

He raises both hands to touch the cloth,
asks, *Which is this?*
This is persimmons, Father.

Oh, the feel of the wolftail on the silk,   80
the strength, the tense
precision in the wrist.
I painted them hundreds of times
eyes closed. These I painted blind.
Some things never leave a person: 85
scent of the hair of one you love,
the texture of persimmons,
in your palm, the ripe weight.

                                                                                [1986]

DENISE LEVERTOV (1923–1997)

Pleasures

I like to find
what's not found
at once, but lies

within something of another nature,
in repose, distinct.   5
Gull feathers of glass, hidden

in white pulp: the bones of squid
which I pull out and lay
blade by blade on the draining board—

    tapered as if for swiftness, to pierce   10
    the heart, but fragile, substance
    belying design.   Or a fruit, *mamey,*

cased in rough brown peel, the flesh
rose-amber, and the seed:
the seed a stone of wood, carved and   15

polished, walnut-colored, formed
like a brazilnut, but large,
large enough to fill
the hungry palm of a hand.

I like the juicy stem of grass that grows   20
within the coarser leaf folded round,
and the butteryellow glow

in the narrow flute from which the morning-glory
opens blue and cool on a hot morning.

[1959]

RICHARD LOVELACE (1618–1658)

To Amarantha, That She Would Dishevel Her Hair

Amarantha sweet and fair,
Ah, braid no more that shining hair!
As my curious hand or eye
Hovering round thee, let it fly!

Let it fly as unconfined   5
As its calm ravisher the wind,
Who hath left his darling, th' East,
To wanton o'er that spicy nest.

Every tress must be confest,
But neatly tangled at the best;   10
Like a clew of golden thread
Most excellently ravellèd.

Do not then wind up that light
In ribbands, and o'ercloud in night,
Like the Sun in 's early ray;   15
But shake your head, and scatter day!

See, 'tis broke! Within this grove,
The bower and the walks of love,
Weary lie we down and rest
And fan each other's panting breast.   20

Here we'll strip and cool our fire
In cream below, in milk-baths higher;
And when all wells are drawn dry,
I'll drink a tear out of thine eye,

Which our very joys shall leave,   25
That sorrows thus we can deceive;
Or our very sorrows weep,
That joys so ripe so little keep.

[1649]

AMY LOWELL (1874–1925)

Patterns

I walk down the garden-paths,
And all the daffodils
Are blowing, and the bright blue squills.
I walk down the patterned garden-paths
In my stiff, brocaded gown.   5
With my powdered hair and jewelled fan,

I too am a rare
Pattern. As I wander down
The garden paths.

My dress is richly figured,   10
And the train
Makes a pink and silver stain
On the gravel, and the thrift
Of the borders.
Just a plate of current fashion,   15
Tripping by in high-heeled, ribboned shoes.
Not a softness anywhere about me,
Only whalebone and brocade.
And I sink on a seat in the shade
Of a lime tree. For my passion   20
Wars against the stiff brocade.
The daffodils and squills
Flutter in the breeze
As they please.
And I weep;   25
For the lime-tree is in blossom
And one small flower has dropped upon my bosom.
And the plashing of waterdrops
In the marble fountain
Comes down the garden paths.   30
The dripping never stops.
Underneath my stiffened gown
Is the softness of a woman bathing in a marble basin,
A basin in the midst of hedges grown
So thick, she cannot see her lover hiding,   35
But she guesses he is near,
And the sliding of the water
Seems the stroking of a dear
Hand upon her.
What is Summer in a fine brocaded gown!   40
I should like to see it lying in a heap upon the ground.
All the pink and silver crumpled up on the ground.

I would be the pink and silver as I ran along the paths,
And he would stumble after,
Bewildered by my laughter.   45
I should see the sun flashing from his sword-hilt and the buckles on his shoes.
I would choose
To lead him in a maze along the patterned paths,
A bright and laughing maze for my heavy-booted lover.
Till he caught me in the shade,   50
And the buttons of his waistcoat bruised my body as he clasped me,
Aching, melting, unafraid.
With the shadows of the leaves and the sundrops,
And the plopping of the waterdrops,
All about us in the open afternoon—   55
I am very like to swoon
With the weight of this brocade,

For the sun sifts through the shade.

Underneath the fallen blossom
In my bosom   60
Is a letter I have hid.
It was brought to me this morning by a rider from the Duke.
'Madam, we regret to inform you that Lord Hartwell
Died in action Thursday se'ennight.'
As I read it in the white, morning sunlight,   65
The letters squirmed like snakes.
'Any answer, Madam,' said my footman.
'No,' I told him.
'See that the messenger takes some refreshment.
No, no answer.'   70
And I walked into the garden,
Up and down the patterned paths,
In my stiff, correct brocade.
The blue and yellow flowers stood up proudly in the sun,
Each one.   75
I stood upright too,
Held rigid to the pattern
By the stiffness of my gown;
Up and down I walked,
Up and down.   80

In a month he would have been my husband.
In a month, here, underneath this lime,
We would have broke the pattern;
He for me, and I for him,
He as Colonel, I as Lady,   85
On this shady seat.
He had a whim
That sunlight carried blessing.
And I answered, 'It shall be as you have said.'
Now he is dead.   90

In Summer and in Winter I shall walk
Up and down
The patterned garden paths
In my stiff, brocaded gown.
The squills and daffodils   95
Will give place to pillared roses, and to asters, and to snow.
I shall go
Up and down,
In my gown.
Gorgeously arrayed,   100
Boned and stayed.
And the softness of my body will be guarded from embrace
By each button, hook, and lace.
For the man who should loose me is dead,
Fighting with the Duke in Flanders,   105
In a pattern called a war.
Christ! What are patterns for?

                                                                        [1915]

CLAUDE MCKAY (1890–1948)

If We Must Die

If we must die, let it not be like hogs
Hunted and penned in an inglorious spot,
While round us bark the mad and hungry dogs,
Making their mock at our accursed lot.
If we must die, O let us nobly die,   5
So that our precious blood may not be shed
In vain; then even the monsters we defy
Shall be constrained to honor us though dead!
O kinsmen! we must meet the common foe!
Though far outnumbered let us show us brave,   10
And for their thousand blows deal one deathblow!
What though before us lies the open grave?
Like men we'll face the murderous, cowardly pack,
Pressed to the wall, dying, but fighting back!

                                                        [1922]

America

Although she feeds me bread of bitterness,
And sinks into my throat her tiger's tooth,
Stealing my breath of life, I will confess
I love this cultured hell that tests my youth.
Her vigor flows like tides into my blood,   5
Giving me strength erect against her hate,
Her bigness sweeps my being like a flood.
Yet, as a rebel fronts a king in state,
I stand within her walls with not a shred
Of terror, malice, not a word of jeer.   10
Darkly I gaze into the days ahead,
And see her might and granite wonders there,
Beneath the touch of Time's unerring hand,
Like priceless treasures sinking in the sand.

                                                        [1922]

W. S. MERWIN (1927–)

For the Anniversary of My Death

Every year without knowing it I have passed the day
When the last fires will wave to me
And the silence will set out
Tireless traveler
Like the beam of a lightless star   5

Then I will no longer
Find myself in life as in a strange garment

Surprised at the earth
And the love of one woman
And the shamelessness of men   10
As today writing after three days of rain
Hearing the wren sing and the falling cease
And bowing not knowing to what

                                                                  [1967]

Leviathan[1]

This is the black sea-brute bulling through wave-wrack,
Ancient as ocean's shifting hills, who in sea-toils
Travelling, who furrowing the salt acres
Heavily, his wake hoary behind him,[2]
Shoulders spouting, the fist of his forehead   5
Over wastes gray-green crashing, among horses unbroken
From bellowing fields, past bone-wreck of vessels,
Tide-ruin, wash of lost bodies bobbing
No longer sought for, and islands of ice gleaming,
Who ravening the rank flood, wave-marshalling,   10
Overmastering the dark sea-marches, finds home
And harvest. Frightening to foolhardiest
Mariners, his size were difficult to describe:
The hulk of him is like hills heaving,
Dark, yet as crags of drift-ice, crowns cracking in thunder,   15
Like land's self by night black-looming, surf churning and trailing
Along his shores' rushing, shoal-water boding
About the dark of his jaws; and who should moor at his edge
And fare on afoot would find gates of no gardens,
But the hill of dark underfoot diving,   20
Closing overhead, the cold deep, and drowning.
He is called Leviathan, and named for rolling,
First created he was of all creatures,[3]
He has held Jonah three days and nights,
He is that curling serpent that in ocean is,[4]   25
Sea-fright he is, and the shadow under the earth.
Days there are, nonetheless, when he lies
Like an angel, although a lost angel
On the waste's unease, no eye of man moving,
Bird hovering, fish flashing, creature whatever   30
Who after him came to herit earth's emptiness.
Froth at flanks seething soothes to stillness,

[1]A "leviathan" is usually thought of as a whale, but the word comes from the Hebrew word for "great sea creature."

[2]The word "hoary" means ancient, or gray (or white) with age. In the Bible book of Job, Job is confronted with his ignorance of how one might make so grand a creature as the leviathan, whose "wake" is said to be "hoary" in the King James version.

[3]According to Genesis 1:21, the leviathan was created first.

[4]As a "curling serpent," a leviathan is perhaps better thought of as a giant sea monster, a sea serpent, rather than a whale.

Waits; with one eye he watches
Dark of night sinking last, with one eye dayrise
As at first over foaming pastures. He makes no cry   35
Though that light is a breath. The sea curling,
Star-climbed, wind-combed, cumbered with itself still
As at first it was, is the hand not yet contented
Of the Creator. And he waits for the world to begin.

[1956]

EDNA ST. VINCENT MILLAY (1892–1950)

Love Is Not All

Love is not all; it is not meat nor drink
Nor slumber nor a roof against the rain;
Nor yet a floating spar to men that sink
And rise and sink and rise and sink again;
Love cannot fill the thickened lung with breath,   15
Nor clean the blood, nor set the fractured bone;
Yet many a man is making friends with death
Even as I speak, for lack of love alone.
It well may be that in a difficult hour,
Pinned down by pain and moaning for release   10
Or nagged by want past resolution's power,
I might be driven to sell your love for peace,
Or trade the memory of this night for food.
It well may be. I do not think I would.

[1931]

HOWARD NEMEROV (1920–1991)

The Goose Fish

On the long shore, lit by the moon
To show them properly alone,
Two lovers suddenly embraced
So that their shadows were as one.
The ordinary night was graced   5
For them by the swift tide of blood
That silently they took at flood,
And for a little time they prized
    Themselves emparadised.

Then, as if shaken by stage-fright   10
Beneath the hard moon's bony light,
They stood together on the sand—
Embarrassed in each other's sight
But still conspiring hand in hand,
Until they saw, there underfoot,
As though the world had found them out,   15
The goose fish turning up, though dead,

His hugely grinning head.
There in the china light he lay,
Most ancient and corrupt and grey.   20
They hesitated at his smile,
Wondering what it seemed to say
To lovers who a little while
Before had thought to understand,
By violence upon the sand,   25
The only way that could be known
   To make a world their own.

It was a wide and moony grin
Together peaceful and obscene;
They knew not what he would express,   30
So finished a comedian
He might mean failure or success,
But took it for an emblem of
Their sudden, new and guilty love
To be observed by, when they kissed,   35
   That rigid optimist.

So he became their patriarch,
Dreadfully mild in the half-dark.
His throat that the sand seemed to choke,
His picket teeth, these left their mark   40
But never did explain the joke
That so amused him, lying there
While the moon went down to disappear
Along the still and tilted track
   That bears the zodiac.   45

                   [1955]

WILFRED OWEN (1893–1918)

Dulce et Decorum Est[1]

Bent double, like old beggars under sacks,
Knock-kneed, coughing like hags, we cursed through sludge,
Till on the haunting flares we turned our backs
And towards our distant rest began to trudge.
Men marched asleep. Many had lost their boots   5
But limped on, blood-shod. All went lame; all blind;
Drunk with fatigue; deaf even to the hoots
Of tired, outstripped Five-Nines[2] that dropped behind.

Gas! Gas! Quick, boys!—An ecstasy of fumbling,
Fitting the clumsy helmets just in time;   10
But someone still was yelling out and stumbling

---

[1]Latin for "It is sweet and proper," the line is excerpted from Horace's *Ode* (3.2.13): "It is sweet
and proper to die for one's country."
[2]"Five-Nines" refers to 5.9-inch caliber shells.

And flound'ring like a man in fire or lime . . .
Dim, through the misty panes[3] and thick green light,
As under a green sea, I saw him drowning.

In all my dreams, before my helpless sight,   15
He plunges at me, guttering, choking, drowning.

If in some smothering dreams you too could pace
Behind the wagon that we flung him in,
And watch the white eyes writhing in his face,
His hanging face, like a devil's sick of sin;   20
If you could hear, at every jolt, the blood
Come gargling from the froth-corrupted lungs,
Obscene as cancer, bitter as the cud
Of vile, incurable sores on innocent tongues,—
My friend,[4] you would not tell with such high zest   25
To children ardent for some desperate glory,
The old Lie: Dulce et decorum est
Pro patria mori.

[c. 1917]

Wilfred Owen with his son, shortly before the poet's death in 1918.

DOROTHY PARKER (1893–1967)

Résumé

Razors pain you;
Rivers are damp;

---

[3]Gas masks, used during World War I, would fog up, producing "misty panes."
[4]Owen's friend, Jessie Pope, wrote *Jessie Pope's War Poems* (1915). The poem was originally dedicated to Pope.

Acids stain you;
And drugs cause cramp.
Guns aren't lawful;
Nooses give;   5
Gas smells awful;
You might as well live.

[1926]

SYLVIA PLATH (1932–1963)

Metaphors

I'm a riddle in nine syllables,
An elephant, a ponderous house,
A melon strolling on two tendrils.
O red fruit, ivory, fine timbers!
This loaf's big with its yeasty rising.   5
Money's new-minted in this fat purse.
I'm a means, a stage, a cow in calf.
I've eaten a bag of green apples,
Boarded the train there's no getting off.

[1960]

DUDLEY RANDALL (1914–2000)

Ballad of Birmingham

*(On the Bombing of a Church in
Birmingham, Alabama, 1963)*

"Mother dear, may I go downtown
Instead of out to play,
And march the streets of Birmingham
In a Freedom March today?"

"No, baby, no, you may not go,   5
For the dogs are fierce and wild,
And clubs and hoses, guns and jail
Aren't good for a little child."

"But, mother, I won't be alone.
Other children will go with me,   10
And march the streets of Birmingham
To make our country free."

"No, baby, no, you may not go,
For I fear those guns will fire.
But you may go to church instead   15
And sing in the children's choir."

She has combed and brushed her night-dark hair,
And bathed rose petal sweet,

And drawn white gloves on her small brown hands,
And white shoes on her feet.   20

The mother smiled to know her child
Was in the sacred place,
But that smile was the last smile
To come upon her face.

For when she heard the explosion,   25
Her eyes grew wet and wild.
She raced through the streets of Birmingham
Calling for her child.

She clawed through bits of glass and brick,
Then lifted out a shoe.   30
"O here's the shoe my baby wore,
But, baby, where are you?"

[1966]

JOHN CROWE RANSOM (1888–1974)

Bells for John Whiteside's Daughter

There was such speed in her little body,
And such lightness in her footfall,
It is no wonder her brown study
Astonishes us all.

Her wars were bruited in our high window.   5
We looked among orchard trees and beyond
Where she took arms against her shadow,
Or harried unto the pond

The lazy geese, like a snow cloud
Dripping their snow on the green grass,   10
Tricking and stopping, sleepy and proud,
Who cried in goose, Alas,

For the tireless heart within the little
Lady with rod that made them rise
From their noon apple-dreams and scuttle   15
Goose-fashion under the skies!

But now go the bells, and we are ready,
In one house we are sternly stopped
To say we are vexed at her brown study,
Lying so primly propped.   20

[1924]

HENRY REED (1914–1986)

Naming of Parts

Today we have naming of parts. Yesterday,
We had daily cleaning. And tomorrow morning,

We shall have what to do after firing. But today,
Today we have naming of parts. Japonica
Glistens like coral in all of the neighboring gardens,   5
    And today we have naming of parts.

This is the lower sling swivel. And this
Is the upper sling swivel, whose use you will see,
When you are given your slings. And this is the piling swivel,
Which in your case you have not got. The branches   10
Hold in the gardens their silent, eloquent gestures,
    Which in our case we have not got.

This is the safety-catch, which is always released
With an easy flick of the thumb. And please do not let me
See anyone using his finger. You can do it quite easy   15
If you have any strength in your thumb. The blossoms
Are fragile and motionless, never letting anyone see
    Any of them using their finger.

And this you can see is the bolt. The purpose of this
Is to open the breech, as you see. We can slide it   20
Rapidly backwards and forwards: we call this
Easing the spring. And rapidly backwards and forwards
The early bees are assaulting and fumbling the flowers:
    They call it easing the Spring.

They call it easing the Spring: it is perfectly easy   25
If you have any strength in your thumb: like the bolt,
And the breech, and the cocking-piece, and the point of balance,
Which in our case we have not got; and the almond-blossom
Silent in all of the gardens and the bees going backwards and forwards,
    For today we have naming of parts.

                                                        [1946]

ADRIENNE RICH (1929–)

Aunt Jennifer's Tigers

Aunt Jennifer's tigers prance across a screen,
Bright topaz denizens of a world of green.
They do not fear the men beneath the tree;
They pace in sleek chivalric certainty.

Aunt Jennifer's fingers fluttering through her wool   5
Find even the ivory needle hard to pull.
The massive weight of Uncle's wedding band
Sits heavily upon Aunt Jennifer's hand.

When Aunt is dead, her terrified hands will lie
Still ringed with ordeals she was mastered by.   10
The tigers in the panel that she made
Will go on prancing, proud and unafraid.

                                                        [1954]

WILLIAM SHAKESPEARE (1564–1616)

When, in Disgrace with Fortune and Men's Eyes (Sonnet 29)

When, in disgrace with Fortune and men's eyes,
I all alone beweep my outcast state,
And trouble deaf heaven with my bootless cries,
And look upon myself and curse my fate,
Wishing me like to one more rich in hope,
Featured like him, like him with friends possessed,   5
Desiring this man's art, and that man's scope,
With what I most enjoy contented least,
Yet in these thoughts myself almost despising,
Haply I think on thee, and then my state,
Like to the lark at break of day arising   10
From sullen earth, sings hymns at heaven's gate;
    For thy sweet love rememb'red such wealth brings
    That then I scorn to change my state with kings.

[1609]

Thy Bosom is Endeared with All Hearts (Sonnet 31)

Thy bosom is endearèd with all hearts,
Which I by lacking have supposèd dead,
And there reigns love and all love's loving parts,
And all those friends which I thought burièd.
How many a holy and obsequious tear
Hath dear religious love stol'n from mine eye
As interest of the dead, which now appear
But things removed that hidden in thee lie!   5
Thou art the grave where buried love doth live,
Hung with the trophies of my lovers gone,
Who all their parts of me to thee did give;
That due of many now is thine alone.   10
    Their images I loved I view in thee,
    And thou, all they, hast all the all of me.

[1609]

STEVIE SMITH (1902–1971)

Not Waving but Drowning

Nobody heard him, the dead man,
But still he lay moaning:
I was much further out than you thought
And not waving but drowning.

Poor chap, he always loved larking
And now he's dead   5

It must have been too cold for him his heart gave way,
They said.

Oh, no no no, it was too cold always
(Still the dead one lay moaning)   10
I was much too far out all my life
And not waving but drowning.

[1959]

WILLIAM STAFFORD (1914–1993)

Traveling Through the Dark

Traveling through the dark I found a deer
dead on the edge of the Wilson River road.
It is usually best to roll them into the canyon:
that road is narrow; to swerve might make more dead.

By glow of the tail-light I stumbled back of the car   5
and stood by the heap, a doe, a recent killing;
she had stiffened already, almost cold.
I dragged her off; she was large in the belly.

My fingers touching her side brought me the reason—
her side was warm; her fawn lay there waiting,   10
alive, still, never to be born.
Beside that mountain road I hesitated.

The car aimed ahead its lowered parking lights;
under the hood purred the steady engine.
I stood in the glare of the warm exhaust turning red;   15
around our group I could hear the wilderness listen.

I thought hard for us all—my only swerving—
then pushed her over the edge into the river.

[1962]

JONATHAN SWIFT (1667–1745)

A Description of the Morning

Now hardly here and there an hackney-coach,
Appearing, showed the ruddy morn's approach.
Now Betty from her master's bed had flown
And softly stole to discompose her own.
The slipshod 'prentice from his master's door   5
Had pared the dirt, and sprinkled round the floor.
Now Moll had whirled her mop with dextrous airs,
Prepared to scrub the entry and the stairs.
The youth with broomy stumps began to trace
The kennel-edge, where wheels had worn the place.   10

The small-coal man was heard with cadence deep
Till drowned in shriller notes of chimneysweep,
Duns at his lordship's gate began to meet,
And Brickdust Moll had screamed through half the street.
The turnkey now his flock returning sees,   15
Duly let out a-nights to steal for fees;
The watchful bailiffs take their silent stands;
And schoolboys lag with satchels in their hands.

                                                                    [1711]

DYLAN THOMAS (1914–1953)

Do Not Go Gentle into That Good Night

Do not go gentle into that good night,
Old age should burn and rave at close of day;
Rage, rage against the dying of the light.

Though wise men at their end know dark is right,
Because their words had forked no lightning they   5
Do not go gentle into that good night.

Good men, the last wave by, crying how bright
Their frail deeds might have danced in a green bay,
Rage, rage against the dying of the light.

Wild men who caught and sang the sun in flight,   10
And learn, too late, they grieved it on its way,
Do not go gentle into that good night.

Grave men, near death, who see with blinding sight
Blind eyes could blaze like meteors and be gay,
Rage, rage against the dying of the light.   15

And you, my father, there on the sad height,
Curse, bless, me now with your fierce tears, I pray.
Do not go gentle into that good night.
Rage, rage against the dying of the light.

                                                                    [1952]

Fern Hill

Now as I was young and easy under the apple boughs
About the lilting house and happy as the grass was green,
   The night above the dingle[1] starry,
     Time let me hail and climb
     Golden in the heydeys of his eyes,   5
And honoured among wagons I was prince of the apple towns
And once below a time I lordly had the trees and leaves
     Trail with daisies and barley

[1]valley.

Down the rivers of the windfall light.
And as I was green and carefree, famous among the barns   10
About the happy yard and singing as the farm was home,
   In the sun that is young once only,
      Time let me play and be
   Golden in the mercy of his means,
And green and golden I was huntsman and herdsman, the calves   15
Sang to my horn, the foxes on the hills barked clear and cold,
      And the sabbath rang slowly
   In the pebbles of the holy streams.

All the sun long it was running, it was lovely, the hay
Fields high as the house, the tunes from the chimneys, it was air   20
   And playing, lovely and watery
      And fire green as grass.
   And nightly under the simple stars
As I rode to sleep the owls were bearing the farm away,
All the moon long I heard, blessed among stables, the nightjars   25
   Flying with the ricks,[2] and the horses
      Flashing into the dark.

And then to awake, and the farm, like a wanderer white
With the dew, come back, the cock on his shoulder: it was all
   Shining, it was Adam and maiden,   30
      The sky gathered again
   And the sun grew round that very day.
So it must have been after the birth of the simple light
In the first, spinning place, the spellbound horses walking warm
   Out of the whinnying green stable   35
      On to the fields of praise.

And honoured among foxes and pheasants by the gay house
Under the new made clouds and happy as the heart was long,
   In the sun born over and over,
      I ran my heedless ways,   40
   My wishes raced through the house high hay
And nothing I cared, at my sky blue trades, that time allows
In all his tuneful turning so few and such morning songs
   Before the children green and golden
      Follow him out of grace,   45

Nothing I cared, in the lamb white days, that time would take me
Up to the swallow thronged loft by the shadow of my hand,
   In the moon that is always rising,
      Nor that riding to sleep
   I should hear him fly with the high fields   50
And wake to the farm forever fled from the childless land.
Oh as I was young and easy in the mercy of his means,
      Time held me green and dying
   Though I sang in my chains like the sea.

                        [1946]

[2]haystacks.

JOHN UPDIKE (1932–)

Ex-Basketball Player

Pearl Avenue runs past the high-school lot,
Bends with the trolley tracks, and stops, cut off
Before it has a chance to go two blocks,
At Colonel McComsky Plaza. Berth's Garage
Is on the corner facing west, and there,   5
Most days, you'll find Flick Webb, who helps Berth out.

Flick stands tall among the idiot pumps—
Five on a side, the old bubble-head style,
Their rubber elbows hanging loose and low.
One's nostrils are two S's, and his eyes   10
An E and O. And one is squat, without
A head at all—more of a football type.

Once Flick played for the high-school team, the Wizards.
He was good: in fact, the best. In '46
He bucketed three hundred ninety points,   15
A county record still. The ball loved Flick.
I saw him rack up thirty-eight or forty
In one home game. His hands were like wild birds.

He never learned a trade, he just sells gas,
Checks oil, and changes flats. Once in a while,   20
As a gag, he dribbles an inner tube,
But most of us remember anyway.
His hands are fine and nervous on the lug wrench.
It makes no difference to the lug wrench, though.

Off work, he hangs around Mae's luncheonette.   25
Grease-gray and kind of coiled, he plays pinball,
Smokes those thin cigars, nurses lemon phosphates.
Flick seldom says a word to Mae, just nods
Beyond her face toward bright applauding tiers
Of Necco Wafers, Nibs, and Juju Beads.

[1958]

WALT WHITMAN (1819–1892)

O Captain! My Captain!

O Captain! my Captain! our fearful trip is done,
The ship has weather'd every rack, the prize we sought is won,
The port is near, the bells I hear, the people all exulting,
While follow eyes the steady keel, the vessel grim and daring;
    But O heart! heart! heart!   5
      O the bleeding drops of red,
        Where on the deck my Captain lies,
          Fallen cold and dead.

O Captain! my Captain! rise up and hear the bells;

Rise up—for you the flag is flung—for you the bugle trills,   10
For you bouquets and ribbon'd wreaths—for you the shores a-crowding,
For you they call, the swaying mass, their eager faces turning;
   Here Captain! dear father!
     This arm beneath your head!
       It is some dream that on the deck,   15
        You've fallen cold and dead.

My Captain does not answer, his lips are pale and still,
My father does not feel my arm, he has no pulse nor will,
The ship is anchor'd safe and sound, its voyage closed and done,
From fearful trip the victor ship comes in with object won;   20
   Exult O shores, and ring O bells!
     But I with mournful tread,
       Walk the deck my Captain lies,
        Fallen cold and dead.

                                 [1865]

RICHARD WILBUR (1921–)

The Death of a Toad

   A toad the power mower caught
Chewed and clipped of a leg, with a hobbling hop has got
   To the garden verge, and sanctuaried him
   Under the cineraria leaves, in the shade
     Of the ashen heartshaped leaves, in a dim,   5
      Low, and a final glade.

   The rare original heartsblood goes,
Spends on the earthen hide, in the folds and wizenings, flows
   In the gutters of the banked and staring eyes. He lies
   As still as if he would return to stone,   10
     And soundlessly attending, dies
      Toward some deep monotone,

   Toward misted and ebullient seas
And cooling shores, toward lost Amphibia's emperies.
   Day dwindles, drowning, and at length is gone   15
   In the wide and antique eyes, which still appear
     To watch, across the castrate lawn,
      The haggard daylight steer.

                                 [1950]

WILLIAM CARLOS WILLIAMS (1883–1965)

Spring and All

By the road to the contagious hospital
under the surge of the blue
mottled clouds driven from the
northeast—a cold wind. Beyond, the
waste of broad, muddy fields   5

brown with dried weeds, standing and fallen

patches of standing water
the scattering of tall trees
All along the road the reddish
purplish, forked, upstanding, twiggy   10
stuff of bushes and small trees
with dead, brown leaves under them
leafless vines—

Lifeless in appearance, sluggish
dazed spring approaches—   15

They enter the new world naked,
cold, uncertain of all
save that they enter. All about them
the cold, familiar wind—

Now the grass, tomorrow   20
the stiff curl of wildcarrot leaf
One by one objects are defined—
It quickens: clarity, outline of leaf

But now the stark dignity of
entrance—Still, the profound change   25
has come upon them: rooted, they
grip down and begin to awaken

                                                    [1923]

The Dance

In Breughel's great picture, The Kermess,
the dancers go round, they go round and
around, the squeal and the blare and the

Flemish Kermess (Peasants' Dance) by Pieter Breughel the Elder
1568. Oil on oakwood, 114 x 164 cm. Kunsthistorisches Museum,
Vienna. Photo: (c)Erich Lessing / Art Resource, NY

tweedle of bagpipes, a bugle and fiddles   5
tipping their bellies (round as the thick-
sided glasses whose wash they impound)
their hips and their bellies off balance
to turn them. Kicking and rolling about
the Fair Grounds, swinging their butts, those   10
shanks must be sound to bear up under such
rollicking measures, prance as they dance
in Breughel's great picture, The Kermess.

                                                              [1944]

JAMES WRIGHT (1927–1980)

A Blessing

Just off the highway to Rochester, Minnesota,
Twilight bounds softly forth on the grass.
And the eyes of those two Indian ponies
Darken with kindness.
They have come gladly out of the willows   5
To welcome my friend and me.
We step over the barbed wire into the pasture
Where they have been grazing all day, alone.
They ripple tensely, they can hardly contain their happiness
That we have come.   10
They bow shyly as wet swans. They love each other.
There is no loneliness like theirs.
At home once more,
They begin munching the young tufts of spring in the darkness.
I would like to hold the slenderer one in my arms,   15
For she has walked over to me
And nuzzled my left hand.
She is black and white,
Her mane falls wild on her forehead,
And the light breeze moves me to caress her long ear   20
That is delicate as the skin over a girl's wrist.
Suddenly I realize
That if I stepped out of my body I would break
Into blossom.

                                                              [1961]

WILLIAM BUTLER YEATS (1865–1939)

The Second Coming

Turning and turning in the widening gyre
The falcon cannot hear the falconer;
Things fall apart; the center cannot hold;
Mere anarchy is loosed upon the world,

The blood-dimmed tide is loosed, and everywhere   5
The ceremony of innocence is drowned;
The best lack all conviction, while the worst
Are full of passionate intensity.

Surely some revelation is at hand;
Surely the Second Coming is at hand;   10
The Second Coming! Hardly are those words out
When a vast image out of *Spiritus Mundi*
Troubles my sight: somewhere in sands of the desert
A shape with lion body and the head of a man,
A gaze blank and pitiless as the sun,   15
Is moving its slow thighs, while all about it
Reel shadows of the indignant desert birds.
The darkness drops again; but now I know
That twenty centuries of stony sleep
Were vexed to nightmare by a rocking cradle,   20
And what rough beast, its hour come round at last,
Slouches towards Bethlehem to be born?

                                                    [1921]

Drama

17

Elements of Drama

> The stage is not merely the meeting place of all the arts,
> but is also the return of art to life.
>
> —Oscar Wilde

The World's a Stage

The meanings of the word **"drama"** reveal something about the type of literature explored in this section. Our word "drama" comes from the ancient Greek word *drâma*, which means either "an action with consequences" or "an action in a play." Thus the Greeks, who provided much of the foundation for Western civilization, used the same word for theatrical actions and for real ones—if the real actions were consequential. For the Greeks, and for us, this verbal link between real life and drama teaches us how to see one in terms of the other. We say, for instance, that a recent debate in Congress was "dra-

"I don't mind if something's Shakespearean, just as long as it's not Shakespeare."

matic," meaning that it had the sort of intense, engaging, vivid, and consequential quality we find in theatrical events. Like the Greeks, we value those dramatic productions that show us aspects of our reality we have not previously or fully envisioned. A play can attempt to reenact a real event or use historical events as the frame for its action, or interpret or even rewrite history.

With a screenplay, it is even possible to insert actors into documentary footage, as seen for instance in *Forrest Gump*, when it appears that Tom Hanks's

747

character is meeting President Kennedy. Although there are certainly important differences between plays and films, their kinship is obvious, as we see plays and musicals turned into movies, and actors often moving from one form to the other. The critical strategies this text encourages you to practice can be applied effectively to plays, films, television—anything. The focus in what follows is generally on drama (on plays written to be performed for a live audience), but the terms and concepts used to analyze theatre have a broad applicability.

In plays, films, or life, when we call a series of events a "drama," or say they are "dramatic," we also mean they involve some kind of **conflict.** We say the Cuban missile crisis for instance was a real-life drama, as the world waited to see whether Kennedy or Castro would blink, and whether the world would plunge into war. A theatrical drama also depicts a conflict; even in comedies, there are opposing forces that struggle toward some **resolution,** who "act" and react toward some end point.

"**Act**"—a major section of a play— is another of the many everyday terms that are also theatrical terms and it is thus another indication of the extent to which we tend to see life in terms of movies and the theatre, and vice-versa. Around the world, one of the most common reactions to the terrorist attack of September 11, 2001, was that the planes striking the towers of the World Trade Center seemed unreal, like a scene in a movie. Most of us witnessed these horrible events on small screens. Visually, the tragedy was indistinguishable from a spectacular special effect in a movie. Ironically, the explosion of the White House by aliens in *Independence Day* was a vividly realistic scene—in some ways (sound, visual detail), especially on a large theatre screen, more compellingly "realistic" than the collapse of the Twin Towers.

This crossing of real-life and drama can also be seen in another common term, "**play**": in life, play is the opposite of work; in drama, a work (paradoxically) is a "play." We realize that the people on stage are playing: it's not for real; they're pretending. (The method of some actors is to pretend so intently that they strive to "become" their characters.) If a play works at all (if it is a "work," that is), we still care about what happens, even though we know it isn't real. Conversely, if our real-world work goes really well, it seems most like play. As Shakespeare so memorably put it, "all the world's a stage," and we are all always in some sense "acting," making believe, believing. We act; we put on a show, even if the audience is only ourselves. What such words reveal, in other words, is that our sense of life is profoundly theatrical.

In fact, you may not realize it, but you are a playwright. On many a night you stage a whole festival of dramatic performances in your mind. These plays often have intricate plots, with surprising twists and turns; they have any number of characters, many of them with speaking roles. The lighting is often creatively done, shifting perhaps from black and white to color, from deep shadows to blazing sunlight, and the special effects are often dazzling, featuring slow-motion scenes, sudden appearances and disappearances, and amazing stunts that sometimes defy all possibility and logic. Although scientists are still studying the purpose of these plays—which are, of course, our dreams—they do seem to be essential to our mental health. Dreams are a powerful testimony to humankind's need to tell stories, even to ourselves, to explore our hopes and fears by creating scenes, characters, dialogue.

Some playwrights also work when they're awake, although they no doubt draw on their night job for inspiration, and the word "drama" in fact also refers to the script of a play, a text. But notice this: to be considered a true drama, the work has to be intended to be staged. Indeed, the Greek root of *drâma* is *drân*, which means "to do." If we don't assume that the author intended for actors "to do" the text, to transform it into action, then we don't consider it a true drama. (A **"closet drama"** is a play that cannot easily or practically be performed, except in the reader's head.) So these waking dreamers we call playwrights write plays because they want to express themselves, and because we apparently crave drama: how else can one explain the amazing number of television dramas and comedies and mysteries, not to mention movies, that are available on any given day? Even commercials often take the form of micro-plays, carefully staged to suggest characters and plots and to capture our imagination and desire. A drama therefore, strictly speaking, is a performance, at least in intention and potential.

Finally, the term "drama" also refers to the form itself, the whole body of plays (that are works), in which consequential actions (that are make-believe) are designed to be lived out (on a stage).

Since our appetite for drama, for seeing and hearing others' lives played out, seems virtually insatiable, it is not surprising that some dramatic works have been so stimulating and fulfilling that human beings have preserved them, wanting to experience them again and again. A few plays have become so precious to our culture that we continue to act them out, hundreds, even thousands of years after they were first performed. Such plays might be seen, in part, as the awakened collective dreaming of our culture, not only making visible our deepest questions and insights, but also helping to create and maintain our common bonds.

Why do we value those plays that we treasure enough to perform, to save, to perform again and again? They make us laugh, cry, ponder, understand, and much more—but that's just the beginning. The reasons are no doubt many and various. Consider this chapter your invitation to explore the pleasures and meanings of drama.

Getting the Play off the Page

Although you have just been invited to explore the plays collected here and everywhere, we could argue that in a sense there aren't any plays in print for you to study. From a certain perspective, there are in fact only *the texts* of various plays, because a play in the strictest sense is a performance, not just words on a page. Who would read the scripts of *Jurassic Park* or *Star Wars* and claim to have experienced the movies? From this perspective, the book you are holding—even though it is pretty big—could not possibly have any plays in it; it only has a few scripts.

In another sense, however, we could argue that a play also can't be limited to a particular production of it. Some fifteen years ago at the University of Texas, I saw a production of Shakespeare's *Merchant of Venice* that was set in space, with Venice as a planet, and the Merchant an intergalactic trader. Years later, at the University of South Carolina, I saw the same play as a production in which the actors were dressed in 1920s gangster outfits, and at about the same time I saw a very traditional production at the Folger Shakespeare Library, with everyone wearing Elizabethan costumes from Shakespeare's day. Which of these versions was "the play"? Perhaps, all of them and none of them. They're all versions of the play, but none of them is *the* play.

You can already see that drama is different from poetry and fiction: fiction and poetry are written to be read; plays are written to be performed. But they do have to be read in order to be performed. In the study of drama, one could argue it is imperative that you see the plays you are reading.

And that would be great, except for two things. First, even if you lived in New York or London, or even if you traveled all the time, you would not be able to see all the major plays you'd want to see in order to understand the Western tradition. Some important and interesting plays are rarely performed, so you'd need to hire your own acting company, which not many of us can do; and besides, you probably couldn't get that many good actors, because who would want to perform for such a limited audience? And, second, when you see a play in performance, as we've already noted, you see only one *version* of that play. Even that version will change from performance to performance, as the actors react to the audience and to each other. There is, in other words, some advantage to *reading* a play, provided that you're able to envision it as a play. A text is, after all, what directors and actors begin with; when you read a play's text, you are dealing with the potential plays that might be brought off the page. You are staging your own production, exercising your own creativity.

Most of us, however, aren't directors or actors, and our theatres of the mind might well be limited. So what should you as a student of drama do? Enjoy the resources you have. Read as many plays as you can, with as much imagination as you can. Go to see as many plays as possible. Supplement live theatre with the wealth of plays that are available now on video. With major plays, especially with Shakespeare, there are likely several productions available at a good video rental store. Some plays on video attempt to re-create the theatre-going experience; others take advantage of the resources of movies. You can enhance your study of drama, and your critical awareness as well, by thinking of the movies and television shows you watch as dramatic works—thereby becoming a more discriminating and insightful consumer of all kinds of drama.

Suggestions for Reading Plays

Here, then, are three commonsense tips:

1. The first time through a play, either reading or viewing it, the most important consideration should be to enjoy it, to be engaged by it, to experience it. Let your imagination go, and don't be frustrated by anything you don't understand. Just keep going and assume you'll understand eventually.
2. As you read a play, keep in mind that it is meant to be a performance; try to imagine how the various scenes might be played. If you can see a production, even on video, it is well worth your effort.
3. As you view a play (or film), keep in mind that it is an interpretation of a script, one embodiment out of infinite possibility; try to assess and appreciate the choices the director and the actors have made.

In drama, as well as film criticism, as in any other field, it's useful to know the terms and conventions. Perhaps it would be possible to build a house or perform brain surgery successfully without knowing any construction or medical terminology, but it would be very awkward. ("Nurse, hand me one of those little shiny things—no, the other shiny thing—no, the sharper one—no, no, not that one—the other one.") This is not to say that an informed and experienced playgoer sits in the theatre and says, "Ah, I see now an instance of foreshadowing" or "Here is a soliloquy"—anymore than an experienced builder or surgeon thinks "Yes, there's an eave" or "Aha, I see the cerebrum." Basic terms and information become most useful when we don't have to think about them—when they have become simply part of what we know.

Toward that goal of making the basic terms and conventions of drama something that you know, let's review and expand upon the treatment of drama in Chapter 9 by looking at the initial episode in Douglas Adams's hugely successful radio series, *The Hitch-Hiker's Guide to the Galaxy*. This text also represents an interesting compromise between viewing a play and reading a text, since a radio script is fully realized only in the audience's head. In reading Adams's drama, you will have to imagine what is going on—but so, to a certain extent, did the original audience, who could only hear voices and sound effects. Sit back and try to hear Adams's voices and imagine the action. (The radio drama is widely available; you should check it out also.)

DOUGLAS ADAMS (1952–2001)

Born in Cambridge, England, Douglas Adams was educated in Essex and St. John's College, Cambridge. His relatively unsuccessful attempts to write comedy were supported by various jobs, including security guard for an extremely wealthy Arab family. Then Adams wrote The Hitch-Hiker's Guide to the Galaxy, *which was first a wildly popular BBC radio series in 1978, and then in 1979 a novel that with its four sequels has sold over fifteen million copies. Adams also wrote two comical detective novels and coauthored a book about endangered species.* The Hitch-Hiker's Guide *is currently in development as a Disney film. Adams died suddenly in 2001 of a heart attack.*

The cast for the original BBC production of *The Hitch-Hiker's Guide*

Fit the First (from *The Hitch-Hiker's Guide to the Galaxy*)

In which the Earth is unexpectedly destroyed and the great Hitch-Hike begins.

Narrator: (Over music. Matter of fact, characterless voice)
This is the story of *The Hitch-Hiker's Guide to the Galaxy*, perhaps the most remarkable, certainly the most successful book ever to come out of the great publishing corporations of Ursa Minor—more popular than the *Celestial Home Care Omnibus*, better selling than *53 More*

Things To Do In Zero Gravity, and more controversial than Oolon Coluphid's trilogy of philosophical blockbusters: *Where God Went Wrong, Some More of God's Greatest Mistakes* and *Who is This God Person Anyway?*

And in many of the more relaxed civilizations on the outer Eastern rim of the Galaxy, the Hitch-Hiker's Guide has already supplanted the great Encyclopaedia Galactica as the standard repository of all knowledge and wisdom, because although it has many omissions, contains much that is apocryphal, or at least wildly inaccurate, it scores over the older, more pedestrian work in two important ways. First, it is slightly cheaper, and second it has the words 'DON'T PANIC' inscribed in large, friendly letters on the cover.

To tell the story of the book, it is best to tell the story of some of the minds behind it. A human from the planet Earth was one of them, though as our story opens he no more knows his destiny than a tea leaf knows the history of the East India Company. His name is Arthur Dent, he is a six foot tall ape descendant, and someone is trying to drive a bypass through his home.

F/X: GENERAL ROAD BUILDING NOISES, BULLDOZERS, PNEUMATIC DRILLS, ETC.

(The following conversation is carried out over this noise. The man from the Council, Mr. Prosser, is being dictatorial through a megaphone, and Arthur is shouting his answers rather faintly in the distance.)

Prosser: Come off it Mr. Dent, you can't win you know. There's no point in lying down in the path of progress.
Arthur: I've gone off the idea of progress. It's overrated.   5
Prosser: But you must realize that you can't lie in front of the bulldozers indefinitely.
Arthur: I'm game, we'll see who rusts first.
Prosser: I'm afraid you're going to have to accept it. This bypass has got to be built, and it's going to be built. Nothing you can say or do . . .
Arthur: Why's it got to be built?
Prosser: What do you mean, why's it got to be built? It's a bypass, you've got   10
to build bypasses.
Arthur: Didn't anyone consider the alternatives?
Prosser: There aren't any alternatives. Look, you were quite entitled to make any suggestions or protests at the appropriate time.
Arthur: Appropriate time? The first I knew about it was when a workman arrived at the door yesterday. I asked him if he'd come to clean the windows and he said he'd come to demolish the house. He didn't tell me straight away of course. No, first he wiped a couple of windows and charged me a fiver. Then he told me.
Prosser: *(Ordinary voice, but he is still clearly audible. In other words, he was standing next to Arthur anyway.)*

But Mr Dent, the plans have been available in the planning office for the last nine months.

Arthur: Yes. I went round to find them yesterday afternoon. You hadn't   15
   exactly gone out of your way to call much attention to them had you?
   I mean, like actually telling anybody or anything.

Prosser: The plans were on display.

Arthur: And how many average members of the public are in the habit of
   causally dropping round at the local planning office of an evening? It's
   not exactly a noted social venue is it? And even if you had popped in
   on the off-chance that some raving bureaucrat wanted to knock your
   house down, the plans weren't immediately obvious to the eye, were
   they?

Prosser: That depends where you were looking.

Arthur: I eventually had to go down to the cellar . . .

Prosser: That's the display department.   20

Arthur: . . . with a torch.

Prosser: Ah, the lights had probably gone.

Arthur: So had the stairs.

Prosser: But you found the notice didn't you?

Arthur: Yes. It was on display in the bottom of a locked filing cabinet stuck   25
   in a disused lavatory with a sign on the door saying 'Beware of the
   Leopard'. Ever thought of going into advertising?

Prosser: It's not as if it's a particularly nice house anyway.

Arthur: I happen rather to like it.

Prosser: Mr Dent!

Arthur: Hello? Yes?

Prosser: Have you any idea how much damage that bulldozer would suffer   30
   if I just let it roll straight over you?

Arthur: How much?

Prosser: None at all.

GRAMS: NARRATOR BACKGROUND

Narrator: By a strange coincidence, 'None at all' is exactly how much
   suspicion the ape descendant Arthur Dent had that one of his closest friends was not descended from an ape, but was in fact from a
   small planet somewhere in the vicinity of Betelgeuse. Arthur Dent's
   failure to suspect this reflects the care with which his friend blend-
   ed himself into human society after a fairly shaky start. When he first
   arrived fifteen years ago the minimal research he had done suggested to him that the name Ford Prefect would be nicely inconspicu-
   ous. He will enter our story in 35 seconds and say 'Hello Arthur'. The
   ape descendant will greet him in return, but in deference to a million years of evolution he will not attempt to pick fleas off him.
   Earthmen are not proud of their ancestors and never invite them
   round to dinner.

Ford: *(Arriving)* Hello Arthur.

Arthur: Ford, hi, how are you?   35

Ford: Fine, look, are you busy?

Arthur: Well, I've just got this bulldozer to lie in front of, otherwise no, not
   especially.

Ford: There's a pub down the road. Let's have a drink and we can talk.

Arthur: Look, don't you understand?

Prosser: Mr Dent, we're waiting.   40

Arthur: Ford, that man wants to knock my house down!

Ford: Well, he can do it whilst you're away can't he?

Arthur: But I don't want him to!

Ford: Well just ask him to wait till you get back.

Arthur: Ford . . .   45

Ford: Arthur! Will you please just listen to me, I'm not fooling. I have got to
       tell you the most important thing you've ever heard, I've got to tell you
       now, and I've got to tell you in that pub there.

Arthur: Why?

Ford: Because you're going to need a very stiff drink. Now, just trust me.

Arthur: *(Reluctantly)* I'll see what I can do. It'd better be good. *(Calls)*
       Hello! Mr Prosser!

Prosser: Yes Mr Dent? Have you come to your senses yet?   50

Arthur: Can we just for a moment assume for the moment that I haven't?

Prosser: Well?

Arthur: And that I'm going to be staying put here till you go away?

Prosser: So?

Arthur: So you're going to be standing around all day doing nothing.   55

Prosser: Could be.

Arthur: Well, if you're resigned to standing around doing nothing all day
       you don't actually need me here all the time do you?

Prosser: Er, no. Not as such.

Arthur: So if you can just take it as read that I am actually here, I could just
       slip off down to the pub for half an hour. How does that sound?

Prosser: Er . . . that sounds . . . very er, reasonable I think Mr Dent. I'm sure   60
       we don't actually need you there for the *whole* time. We can just hold
       up our end of the confrontation.

Arthur: And if you want to pop off for a bit later on I can always cover for
       you in return.

Prosser: Oh, thank you. Yes. That'll be fine Mr Dent. Very kind.

Arthur: And of course it goes without saying that you don't try and knock
       my house over whilst I'm away.

Prosser: What? Good Lord no Mr Dent. *The mere thought hadn't even
       begun to speculate about the merest possibility of crossing my mind.*

Arthur: Do you think we can trust him?   65

Ford: Myself, I'd trust him to the end of the Earth.

Arthur: Yes, but how far's that?

Ford: About twelve minutes away. Come on, I need a drink.

GRAMS: NARRATOR BACKGROUND

Narrator: By drink Ford Prefect meant alcohol. The *Encyclopaedia
       Galactica* describes alcohol as a colourless, volatile liquid formed by
       the fermentation of sugars, and also notes its intoxicating effect on
       certain carbon-based life forms. *The Hitch-Hiker's Guide to the
       Galaxy* also mentions alcohol. It says that the best drink in exis-
       tence is the Pan Galactic Gargle Blaster, the effect of which is like
       having your brains smashed out with a slice of lemon wrapped
       round a large gold brick. The *Guide* also tells you on which planets
       the best Pan Galactic Gargle Blasters are mixed, how much you can
       expect to pay for one, and what voluntary organizations exist to
       help you rehabilitate.

The man who invented this mind-pummelling drink also invented the wisest remark ever made, which was this: 'Never drink more than two Pan Galactic Gargle Blasters unless you are a thirty ton elephant with bronchial pneumonia.' His name is Zaphod Beeblebrox and we shall learn more of his wisdom later.

F/X: PUB INTERIOR. GENERAL CONVERSATION CHATTER, CLINK OF GLASSES, JUKEBOX, ETC.

Ford: Six pints of bitter. And quickly please, the world's about to end.   70

Barman: Oh yes, sir? Nice weather for it. Going to watch the match this afternoon sir?

Ford: No. No point.

Barman: Foregone conclusion that, you reckon sir? Arsenal without a chance?

Ford: No, it's just that the world's going to end.

Barman: Oh yes, sir, so you said. Lucky escape for Arsenal if it did.   75

Ford: No, not really.

Barman: There you are sir, six pints.

F/X: DRINKS BEING PUT ON BAR. RUSTLE OF BANK NOTES

Ford: Keep the change.

Barman: What, from a fiver? Thank you, sir.

Ford: You've got ten minutes left to spend it.   80

Arthur: Ford, would you please tell me what the hell is going on? *I think I'm beginning to lose my grip on the day.*

Ford: Drink up, you've got three pints to get through.

Arthur: Three? At lunchtime?

Ford: Time is an illusion. Lunchtime doubly so.

Arthur: Very deep. You should send that in to the *Reader's Digest*. They've   85
got a page for people like you.

Ford: Drink up.

Arthur: Why three pints?

Ford: Muscle relaxant. You'll need it.

Arthur: Did I do something wrong today, or has the world always been like this and I've been too wrapped up in myself to notice?

Ford: All right. I'll try to explain. How long have we known each other   90
Arthur?

Arthur: Er . . . five years, maybe six. Most of it seemed to make some kind of sense at the time.

Ford: All right. How would you react if I said that I'm not from Guildford after all, but from a small planet somewhere in the vicinity of Betelgeuse?

Arthur: *(Really baffled now)* I don't know. Why, do you think it's the sort of thing you feel you're likely to say?

Ford: Drink up, the world's about to end.

Arthur: This must be Thursday. I never could get the hang of Thursdays.   95

F/X GRAMS: NARRATOR BACKGROUND

Narrator: On this particular Thursday, something was moving quietly through the ionosphere miles above the surface of the planet. But few people on the surface of the planet were aware of it. One of the six thousand million people who hadn't glanced into the ionosphere recently was called Lady Cynthia Fitzmelton. She was at that moment standing in front of Arthur Dent's house in Cottington. Many of those listening to her speech would probably have experienced great satisfaction to know that in four minutes time she would evaporate into a whiff of hydrogen, ozone and carbon monoxide. However, when the moment came they would hardly notice because they would be too busy evaporating themselves.

(Lady Cynthia Fitzmelton is a sort of Margaret Thatcher, Penelope Keith character, who delivers this speech with dignity and utter conviction through a barrage of enraged boos and catcalls.)

Lady Cynthia: I have been asked to come here to say a few words to mark the beginning of work on the very splendid and worthwhile new Bevingford bypass. And I must say immediately what a great honour and a great privilege I think it must be for you, the people of Cottington, to have this gleaming new motorway going through your cruddy little village . . . I'm sorry, your little country village of cruddy Cottington. *(Shouts from annoyed crowd)* I know how proud you must feel at this moment to know that your obscure and unsung hamlet will now arise reborn as the very splendid and worthwhile Cottington Service Station, providing welcome refreshment and sanitary relief for every weary traveller on his way.

Voice 1: Why don't you push off, you crud-faced old bat?

Voice 2: What about our bloody homes?

Lady Cynthia: And for myself, it gives me great pleasure to take this bottle   100
of very splendid and worthwhile champagne and break it against the noble prow of this very splendid and worthwhile yellow bulldozer.

F/X: BOTTLE SMASHING AGAINST BULLDOZER, WHICH BEGINS TO RUMBLE FORWARD

F/X: *CAST* LOUD JEERS AND ALSO A PERFUNCTORY RIPPLE OF APPLAUSE FROM ONE OR TWO HIRED LACKEYS

F/X: SWITCH BACK TO THE PUB INTERIOR ATMOS. THE MUFFLED SOUND OF THE HOUSE BEING KNOCKED DOWN FILTERS THROUGH

Arthur: What's that?

Ford: Don't worry, they haven't started yet.

Arthur: Oh good.

Ford: It's probably just your house being knocked down.

Arthur: What?   105

Ford: It hardly makes any difference at this stage.

Arthur: My God it is! What the hell are they doing? We had an agreement!

Ford: Let 'em have their fun.

Arthur: Damn you and your fairy stories, they're smashing up my home!

F/X: HE RUNS OUT OF THE PUB

Arthur: *(Shouting)* Stop you vandals! You home wreckers! You half-crazed   110
visigoths, stop will you!

Ford: Arthur! Come back. It's pointless! Hell, I'd better go after him. Barman, quickly, can you just give me four packets of peanuts?

Barman: Certainly, sir. There you are, twenty eight pence.

F/X: NOTE SLAPPED ON TABLE

Ford: Keep the change.

Barman: Are you serious sir? I mean, do you really think the world's going
    to end this afternoon?

Ford: Yes, in just over one minute and thirty five seconds.   115

Barman: Well, isn't there anything we can do?

Ford: No, nothing.

Barman: I always thought we were meant to lie down or put a paper bag
    over our head or something.

Ford: If you like, yes.

Barman: Will that help?   120

Ford: No. Excuse me, I've got to find my friend. *(Goes)*

Barman: Oh well then, last orders please!

F/X: OUTSIDE ATMOS.

Arthur: *(Yelling)* You pinstriped barbarians! I'll sue the council for every
    penny it's got! I'll have you hung, drawn and quartered, and whipped
    and boiled, and then I'll chop you up into little bits until . . .
    until . . . until you've had enough!

Ford: Arthur, don't bother, there isn't time, get over here, there's only ten
    seconds left!

Arthur: *(Oblivious)* And then I'll do it some more! And when I've finished   125
    I will take all the little bits . . . and I will *jump* on them! And I will
    carry on jumping on them until I get blisters or I can think of some-
    thing even more unpleasant to do, and then I'll . . . WHAT THE HELL'S
    THAT????

F/X: AN UNEARTHLY SCREAM OF JETS THUNDERS ACROSS THE SKY.
    MASS PANDEMONIUM BREAKS OUT, WITH PEOPLE SHOUTING, RUN-
    NING IN EVERY DIRECTION

Ford: Arthur! Quick, over here!

Arthur: What the hell is it?

Ford: It's a fleet of flying saucers, what do you think it is? Quick, you've got
    to get hold of this rod!

Arthur: What do you mean, flying saucers?

Ford: Just that, it's a Vogon constructor fleet.   130

Arthur: A what?

Ford: A Vogon constructor fleet, I picked up news of their arrival a few
    hours ago on my sub-ether radio.

Arthur: *(Still yelling to be heard over din)* Ford, I don't think I can cope
    with any more of this. I think I'll just go and have a little lie down
    somewhere.

Ford: No! Just stay here! Keep calm . . . and just take hold of . . . *(lost
    in din)*.

F/X: CLICK OF A P.A. CHANNEL OPENING. ALIEN VOICE REVERBERATES
    ACROSS THE LAND:-

Alien: People of Earth, your attention please. This is Prostetnic Vogon Jeltz   135
    of the Galactic Hyperspace Planning Council. As you will no doubt be
    aware, the plans for the development of the outlying regions of the

Western Spiral arm of the Galaxy require the building of a hyperspace express route through your star system and, regrettably, your planet is one of those scheduled for demolition. The process will take slightly less than two of your Earth minutes. Thank you very much.

F/X: CLICK OF CHANNEL TURNING OFF. WILD HUBBUB OF PROTEST AS PANIC BREAKS OUT. CLICK AS CHANNEL OPENS AGAIN

Alien: There's no point in acting all surprised about it. All the planning charts and demolition orders have been on display at your local planning department in Alpha Centauri for fifty of your Earth years, so you've had plenty of time to lodge any formal complaints, and it's far too late to start making a fuss about it now.

F/X: MORE PROTESTING HUBBUB

Alien: What do you mean you've never been to Alpha Centauri? Oh, for heaven's sake mankind it's only four light years away you know. I'm sorry, but if you can't be bothered to take an interest in local affairs that's your own lookout. Energize the demolition beams. *(To himself)* God, I don't know, apathetic bloody planet, I've no sympathy at all . . .

F/X: A LOW THROBBING HUM WHICH BUILDS QUICKLY IN INTENSITY AND PITCH. WIND & THUNDER, RENDING, GRINDING CRASHES. ALL THE NIGGLING LITTLE FRUSTRATIONS THAT THE BBC SOUND EFFECTS ENGINEERS HAVE EVER HAD CAN ALL COME OUT IN A FINAL DEVASTATING EXPLOSION WHICH THEN DIES AWAY INTO SILENCE

(Longish pause. Then:)

A FAINT BUT CLEAR BACKGROUND HUM STARTS UP. VARIOUS QUIET ELECTRONIC MECHANISMS. A FEW VAGUE RUSTLES OF MOVEMENT. SOME SOFTLY PADDING FOOTSTEPS

(A pause—just long enough to build up the suspense, then:)

Ford: I bought some peanuts.
Arthur: Whhhrrr?

(This conversation mostly in hushed tones)

Ford: If you've never been through a matter transference beam before   140
you've probably lost some salt and protein. The beer you had should have cushioned your system a bit. How are you feeling?
Arthur: Like a military academy—bits of me keep on passing out. If I asked you where the hell we were would I regret it?
Ford: We're safe.
Arthur: Good.
Ford: We're in a small galley cabin in one of the spaceships of the Vogon Constructor Fleet.
Arthur: Ah, this is obviously some strange usage of the word safe that I   145
wasn't previously aware of.
Ford: I'll have to look for the light.
Arthur: All right. How did we get here?
Ford: We hitched a lift.
Arthur: Excuse me, are you trying to tell me that we just stuck out our thumbs and some bug-eyed monster stuck his head out and said 'Hi, fellas, hop right in, I can take you as far as the Basingstoke roundabout'?

Ford: Well, the thumb's an electronic sub-ether device, the roundabout's at   150
    Barnard's Star six light years away, but otherwise that's more or less right.
Arthur: And the bug-eyed monster?
Ford: Is green, yes.
Arthur: Fine. When can I go home?
Ford: You can't. Ah, I've found the light.

F/X: THE SOUND OF LIGHT GOING ON IN A VOGON SPACESHIP

Arthur: (*Wonderment*) Good grief! Is this really the interior of a flying   155
    saucer?
Ford: It certainly is. What do you think?
Arthur: It's a bit squalid, isn't it?
Ford: What did you expect?
Arthur: Well I don't know. Gleaming control panels, flashing lights, com-
    puter screens. Not old mattresses.
Ford: These are the Dentrassi sleeping quarters.   160
Arthur: I thought you said they were called Vogons or something.
Ford: The Vogons run the ship. The Dentrassi are the cooks. They let us on
    board.
Arthur: I'm confused.
Ford: Here, have a look at this.
Arthur: What is it?   165
Ford: *The Hitch-Hiker's Guide to the Galaxy*. It's a sort of electronic book.
    It'll tell you everything you want to know. That's its job.
Arthur: I like the cover. 'DON'T PANIC.' It's the first helpful or intelligible
    thing anybody's said to me all day.
Ford: That's why it sells so well. Here, press this button and the screen will
    give you the index, several million entries, fast wind through the index
    to 'V.' There you are, Vogon Constructor Fleets. Enter that code on the
    tabulator and read what it says.
Narrator: Vogon Constructor Fleets.
    Here is what to do if you want to get a lift from a Vogon: Forget it. They
    are one of the most unpleasant races in the Galaxy—not actually evil,
    but bad-tempered, bureaucratic, officious and callous. They wouldn't
    even lift a finger to save their own grandmothers from the Ravenous
    Bugblatter Beast of Traal without orders signed in triplicate, sent in,
    sent back, queried, lost, found, subjected to public inquiry, lost again,
    and finally buried in soft peat for three months and recycled as fire
    lighters. The best way to get a drink out of a Vogon is stick your finger
    down his throat, and the best way to irritate him is to feed his grand-
    mother to the Ravenous Bugblatter Beast of Traal.
Arthur: What a strange book. How did we get a lift then?   170
Ford: That's the point, it's out of date now. I'm doing the field research for
    the new revised edition of the *Guide*. So, for instance, I will have to
    include a revision pointing out that since the Vogons have made so
    much money being professionally unpleasant, they can now afford to
    employ Dentrassi cooks. Which gives us a rather useful little loophole.
Arthur: Who are the Dentrassi?
Ford: The best cooks and the best drinks mixers, and they don't give a wet
    slap about anything else. And they will always help hitch-hikers on
    board, partly because they like the company, but mostly because it
    annoys the Vogons. Which is exactly the sort of thing you need to

know if you're an impoverished hitch-hiker trying to see the marvels of
the Galaxy for less than thirty Altarian dollars a day. And that's my job.
Fun, isn't it?

Arthur: It's amazing.

Ford: Unfortunately I got stuck on the Earth for rather longer than I intend-   175
ed. I came for a week and was stranded for fifteen years.

Arthur: But how did you get there in the first place?

Ford: Easy, I got a lift with a teaser. You don't know what a teaser is, I'll tell you.
Teasers are usually rich kids with nothing to do. They cruise around looking for planets which haven't made interstellar contact yet, and buzz them.

Arthur: Buzz them?

Ford: Yes. They find some isolated spot with very few people around, then
land right by some poor unsuspecting soul whom no one's ever going to
believe and then strut up and down in front of him wearing silly anten-
nae on their head and making beep beep noises. Rather childish really.

Arthur: Ford, I don't know if this sounds like a silly question, but what am   180
I doing here?

Ford: Well, you know that. I rescued you from the Earth.

Arthur: And what happened to the Earth?

Ford: It's been disintegrated.

Arthur: Has it?

Ford: Yes, it just boiled away into space.   185

Arthur: Look. I'm a bit upset about that.

Ford: Yes, I can understand.

Arthur: So what do I do?

Ford: You come along with me and enjoy yourself. You'll need to have this
fish in your ear.

Arthur: I beg your pardon?   190

F/X: A RATHER EXTRAORDINARY NOISE STARTS UP. IT SOUNDS LIKE A
COMBINATION OF GARGLING, HOWLING, SNIFFING AND FIGHT-
ING OFF A PACK OF WOLVES

Arthur: What's the devil's that?

Ford: Listen, it might be important.

Arthur: What?

Ford: It's the Vogon Captain making an announcement on the PA.

Arthur: But I can't speak Vogon!   195

Ford: You don't need to. Just put the fish in your ear, come on, it's only a
little one.

Arthur: Uuuuuuuuggh!

F/X: THE CACOPHONOUS AND HIGHLY IMAGINATIVE SOUNDS
DESCRIBED ABOVE ABRUPTLY TRANSFORM INTO THE VOICE OF
THE ALIEN WHO ADDRESSED THE EARTH

Alien: . . . should have a good time. Message repeat. This is your Captain
speaking so stop whatever you're doing and pay attention. First of all I
see from our instruments that we have a couple of hitch-hikers aboard
our ship. Hello wherever you are, I just want to make it totally clear
that you are not at all welcome. I worked hard to get where I am today,
and I didn't become Captain of a Vogon Constructor ship simply so
that I could turn it into a taxi service for degenerate freeloaders. I have
sent out a search party, and as soon as they find you I will put you off
the ship. If you're very lucky I might read you some of my poetry first.

Secondly, we are about to jump into hyperspace for the journey to Barnard's Star. On arrival we will stay in dock for a seventy two hour refit, and no-one's to leave the ship during that time. I repeat, all planet leave is cancelled. I've just had an unhappy love affair, so I don't see why anyone else should have a good time. Message ends.

Arthur: Charming these Vogons. I wish I had a daughter so I could forbid her to marry one.

Ford: You wouldn't need to. They've got as much sex appeal as a road acci-   200
dent. And you'd better be prepared for the jump into hyperspace. It's unpleasantly like being drunk.

Arthur: Well what's so unpleasant about being drunk?

Ford: You ask a glass of water.

Arthur: Ford.

Ford: Yes?

Arthur: What's this fish doing in my ear?   205

Ford: Translating for you. Look under Babel Fish in the book.

F/X: BOOK MOTIF, INTERRUPTED BY A SUDDEN SWELLING SOUND OF FANTASTIC ACCELERATION . . .

Arthur: *(A slurring distort)* What's happening?

Ford: *(A slurring distort)* We're going into hyperspace.

Arthur: Ugggh! I'll never be cruel to a gin and tonic again.

F/X: SOUND DISTORTS TOTALLY. THE NARRATOR'S VOICE CUTS ACROSS IT

GRAMS: NARRATOR BACKGROUND

Narrator: The Babel Fish is small, yellow, leechlike, and probably the odd-   210
est thing in the Universe. It feeds on brainwave energy, absorbing all unconscious frequencies and then excreting telepathically a matrix formed from the conscious frequencies and nerve signals picked up from the speech centres of the brain; the practical upshot of which is that if you stick one in your ear you can instantly understand anything said to you in any form of language—the speech you hear decodes the brainwave matrix. Now it is such a bizarrely improbable coincidence that anything so mindbogglingly useful could evolve purely by chance that some thinkers have chosen to see it as a final clinching proof of the non-existence of God.

The argument goes something like this:
'I refuse to prove that I exist' says God, 'for proof denies faith, and without faith I am nothing'. 'But', says Man, 'the Babel Fish is a dead giveaway isn't it? It proves you exist, and so therefore you don't. QED'. 'Oh dear', says God, 'I hadn't thought of that' and promptly vanishes in a puff of logic. 'Oh, that was easy' says Man, and for an encore he proves that black is white and gets killed on the next zebra crossing.

Most leading theologians claim that this argument is a load of dingo's kidneys, but that didn't stop Oolon Colluphid making a small fortune when he used it as the central theme of his best-selling book *Well, That About Wraps It Up For God.*

Meanwhile, the poor Babel Fish, by effectively removing all barriers to communication between different cultures and races, has caused more and bloodier wars than anything else in the history of creation.

Arthur: What an extraordinary book.

Ford: Help me write the new edition.

Arthur: No, I want to go back to Earth again I'm afraid. Or its nearest
    equivalent.

Ford: You're turning down a hundred billion new worlds to explore.

Arthur: Did you get much useful material on Earth?   215

Ford: I was able to extend the entry, yes.

Arthur: Oh, let's see what it says in this edition then.

Ford: OK.

Arthur: Lets see. E . . . Earth . . . tap out the code (F/X BOOK
    MOTIF) . . . there's the page. Oh, it doesn't seem to have an entry.

Ford: Yes it does. See, right there at the bottom of the screen. Just under   220
    Eccentrica Gallumbits, the triple-breasted whore of Eroticon VI.

Arthur: What, there? Oh yes.

Book: Harmless.

Arthur: Is that all it's got to say? One word? Harmless? What the hell's that
    supposed to mean?

Ford: Well, there are a hundred billion stars in the Galaxy and a limited
    amount of space in the book. And no one knew much about the Earth
    of course.

Arthur: Well I hope you've managed to rectify that a little.   225

Ford: Yes, I transmitted a new entry off to the Editor. He had to trim it a bit,
    but it's still an improvement.

Arthur: What does it say now?

Ford: 'Mostly harmless.'

Arthur: *Mostly* harmless?

Ford: That's the way it is. We're on a different scale now.   230

Arthur: OK Ford, I'm with you. I'm bloody well coming with you. Where
    are we now?

Ford: Not far from Barnard's Star. It's a beautiful place, and a sort of hyper-
    space junction. You can get virtually anywhere from there.

F/X: MARCHING FEET OUTSIDE

Ford: That is, assuming that we actually get there.

F/X: BANGING ON THE STEEL DOOR

Arthur: What's that?

Ford: Well, if we're lucky it's just the Vogons come to throw us into space.   235

Arthur: And if we're unlucky?

Ford: If we're unlucky the Captain might want to read us some of his poet-
    ry first.

Narrator: Vogon poetry is, of course, the third worst in the Universe. The
    second worst is that of the Azgoths of Kria. During a recitation by their
    Poet Master Grunthos the Flatulent of his poem 'Ode to a Small Lump of
    Green Putty I found in My Armpit One Midsummer Morning' four of his
    audience died of internal haemorrhaging, and the President of the Mid-
    Galactic Arts Nobbling Council survived by gnawing one of his own
    legs off. Grunthos is reported to have been 'disappointed' by the poem's
    reception, and was about to embark on a reading of his twelve book
    epic entitled 'My Favourite Bathtime Gurgles' when his own major intes-
    tine, in a desperate attempt to save humanity, leapt straight up through
    his neck and throttled his brain. The very worst poetry of all perished
    along with its creator, Paula Nancy Millstone Jennings of Greenbridge in
    the destruction of the Planet Earth. Vogon poetry is mild by compari-

son, and when the Vogon Captain began to read it provoked this reaction from Ford Prefect . . .

Ford: Aaaaaaaaaaaarrrrrrrggggghhhh!!!

Narrator: And this from Arthur Dent.

Arthur: Nnnnnnnyyyyyyuuuuuurrrrrggghhh!!! *(Continues ad lib)*

Vogon: Oh freddled gruntbuggly! Thy micturations are to me
  As plurdled gabbletlotchits in a lurgid bee.
  Groop I implore thee my foonting turlingdromes,
  And hooptiously drangle me with crinkly bindle werdles,
  For otherwise I will rend thee in the gobberwarts with
  My blurglecruncheon see if I don't.

So Earthlings. I present you with a simple choice. I was going to throw
you straight out into the empty blackness of space to die horribly and
slowly. But there is one way, one simple way in which you may save
yourselves. Think very carefully, for you hold your very lives in your
hands. Now choose! Either die in the vacuum of space or . . .

GRAMS: DRAMATIC CHORD

Vogon: . . . tell me how good you thought my poem was.

Narrator: Will our heroes survive this terrible ordeal? Can they win
  through with their integrity unscathed? Can they escape without completely compromising their honour and artistic judgement?
  Tune in next week for the next exciting installment of 'The Hitch-
  Hiker's Guide to the Galaxy.'

[1978]

Footnotes (By Geoffrey Perkins)

The first series of six programmes was transmitted for the first time starting
on 8 March 1978. . .

The pilot of *Hitch-Hiker's*, which subsequently became the first programme, was commissioned by the BBC Radio Light Entertainment Department on 1 March 1977 and produced by Simon Brett on 28 June with the
assistance of Paddy Kingsland at the Radiophonic Workshop and a small furry
creature from the Crab Nebula.

Probably the script was commissioned in the first place not out of a
burning desire to do a sci-fi comedy but because the Chief Producer at the
time was rather taken with a sketch Douglas had written for *The Burkiss
Way* about a Kamikaze pilot being briefed for his nineteenth mission.

Simon has very kindly looked up his diary for this vital time of creative
gestation and it seems to consist chiefly of sitting down with Douglas over
an inordinately large number of meals (mostly Japanese). In this respect
Douglas' working method has remained unchanged over the years.

The go ahead for the series was given on 31 August and was celebrated in the traditional way with a large meal (Greek this time).

Simon remembers that right from the start Douglas knew exactly what
he wanted. For instance, he spent some time looking for a signature tune
which had to be electronic but which also had a banjo in it. Quite why he
was so keen on a banjo is a bit of a mystery (he says he thought it would
help give an 'on the road, hitch-hiking feel' to the whole thing), but there is
no doubt that the choice of *Journey of the Sorcerer* from the Eagles album

One of These Nights was inspired. Interestingly many of the people who wrote in asking what it was were surprised to find that they already had it. It just seemed to be one of those album tracks that nobody had noticed until it was taken out of context.

Peter Jones was not the first person approached to play the Book, but curiously from the start there had been a desire to cast someone with a 'Peter Jonesy sort of voice'. After three or four people (including Michael Palin) had turned it down the search for the Peter Jonesy sort of voice narrowed in on Peter Jones. His calmly reassuring tone as the Earth and the Universe disintegrated around him was a great comfort for those people who were somewhat bewildered by the whole thing, and his performance perhaps took much of its strength from the fact that Peter himself was somewhat bewildered by the whole thing.

Douglas claims to have based many of the characteristics of Arthur Dent on the actor who played him, Simon Jones (who contrary to several people's belief is not in fact Peter Jones' son) though Simon himself is wary of being seen as a role model for a character he describes as "whingeing around the Universe trying to find a cup of tea'. An early thought was to call the character Aleric B., but the name Arthur Dent was chosen as being distinctive without being peculiar. (Peculiarly enough quite a few people have already come across an Arthur Dent who in 1601 had published a Puritan tract called 'The Plaine Man's Pathway to Heaven'. Douglas claims never to have heard of this, despite being hard pressed about it over several large meals.)

Ford Prefect (whose original name is sadly only pronounceable in an obscure Betelgeusian dialect) was played by the estimable Geoffrey McGivern, star of several Footlights revues. He was virtually typecast as the disreputable alien, Ford Prefect. Fit the First also featured David Gooderson as the barman, Jo Kendall (who had featured in *I'm Sorry I'll Read that Again* and *The Burkiss Way*) as Lady Cynthia Fizmelton and Bill Wallis (who literally came in on the day to replace another actor who had gone sick), memorably doubled up as Prossor and Prostetnic Vogon Jeltz.

Many people have been interested in the recipe for a Pan Galactic Gargle Blaster. It must be said that it is in fact impossible to mix a Pan Galactic Gargle Blaster under Earth's atmospheric conditions, but readers will be delighted to know that all profits from this book will go towards purchasing a ticket on a future space shuttle to see if it is possible to mix one in low orbit. (This is in fact a piece of complete nonsense, thought up over several large lunches, which have already, in fact, absorbed all possible profits from the book.)

As Paddy Kingsland points out the effect of the Earth's destruction . . . is an amalgam of very ordinary sounds . . . thunderclaps, explosions, old train crashes and so on. In fact, all it would have needed was a heartbeat to have the complete set of radio sound effects clichés. Despite that it's all mixed together in a way that makes it the technical highlight of the first show.

The Vogon space ship background, with its distinctive little pings, was inspired by *Star Trek,* and (rather more obscurely) the Book Motif was inspired by Tom and Jerry and made up from lots of little bits of tape that had been left lying around on the floor in the Radiophonic Workshop.

The Babel fish is a brilliant device for getting round a basic problem which most Sci-Fi series seem to ignore, namely, why is it that all aliens seem to be able to speak English? Although it is never actually mentioned again it is safe to assume that Arthur has it firmly in his ear over the next eleven episodes.

The extraordinary noise of gargling, howling, sniffing and so on . . . was the first of many effects that were made perfectly satisfactorily by completely ignoring the convoluted directions in the script. In fact, it was made quite simply by reversing the speech.

Mildly interested *Hitch-Hiker's* devotees will note that Paula Nancy Millstone Jennings . . . is a pretty strange name. Real fanatics will know that it has been changed from the name that actually appeared on the programme. This is for legal reasons, and is not in fact a typing error made after a particularly arduous lunch.

Absolutely tonto *Hitch-Hiker's* fans will also be interested to know that in a recent edition of the fanzine *Playbeing* the line 'I never could get the hang of Thursdays' was voted the most popular line of the series, shortly ahead of 'Life? Don't talk to me about life.' (About which see the note on the second episode.)

Recognizing Elements:
Conflict, Resolution, Act, and Play

Plot, like many of the terms used to talk about drama, is also used to talk about fiction and poetry. The arrangement of events in any sort of creative story is called the "plot." A plot can move straight through time, or it may move back and forth, or even jump around. This episode from the *Guide* moves chronologically, but Adams could have included, for instance, some scenes from the Vogon captain's unhappy love affair. Those scenes would constitute a **flashback,** which is a scene from the past that explains or illuminates what is going on in the plot's "present."

If the plot seemed to focus on the Vogon captain's fortunes, as well as Arthur Dent's, then we could say the play had a **double plot.** Usually, however, as in this episode, one plot is central; and if there is another plot, it is a **subplot,** a secondary story that somehow reflects on the primary plot. In a traditional play, all the incidents or parts of the plot can be related significantly to the main plot, and we then may say that a plot displays **unity of action.** In this episode from Adams's comedy series, the audience stays right with Arthur Dent, effectively following one line of development, although potential subplots are opened up with other characters.

There is no term for the opposite of a flashback. A flash forward? But plays and films are often structured so that an event in some way **foreshadows** (that is, points toward) something that will happen later. For instance, to make way for a bypass, Arthur's house is being demolished by a bulldozer that is directed by an imbecilic and apparently pointless bureaucracy. This event clearly foreshadows the demolition of Arthur's entire home planet to clear the space for an intergalactic freeway. The first event becomes a **type** of what is to come only when we encounter the second event and, thinking back (or rereading), see the parallels. Foreshadowing can be used, as in Adams's script, for comic effect, when the parallels are absurd. Strangely enough, it seems funny to consider the notion that the entire earth can be destroyed just as easily as one person's house, if the planet or house stands in the way of traffic. We laugh at the absurdity, however, only because we do not take the tragedy entirely seriously.

In fact, one way of thinking about the difference between the two main dramatic genres, **tragedy** and **comedy,** is that in comedy, we do not take misfortunes seriously; in tragedy, we do. When Bugs Bunny tricks Elmer Fudd into stepping in front of a truck, we don't think about how much that would hurt, or whether Elmer will survive; we know that Elmer will be fine. It's comic. When Shakespeare's Othello threatens and then murders Desdemona, however, we do care. We know, if we are at all familiar with the conventions of each genre, that a tragedy will end sadly, and that we should feel **fear and pity;** and we know that everything will be fine in a comedy, and that we should laugh. The comic brilliance of Adams' work is thus evident in part in the way the destruction of the entire earth affects us: it's funny.

For many works, however, readers and viewers understand **genre** in a complex way. Some works are best described as a **tragicomedy,** combining thoroughly laughter and tears. In a **romantic comedy,** we're expected to laugh, but at the same time to take the characters and the action seriously enough to care whether (or when) the protagonists are finally able to discover and share their love for each other. In film, the **horror** genre, which has been particularly popular in the past two decades, seems to have some interesting similarities to comedy, as characters behave in a mechanical fashion, and audiences are not emotionally troubled by the demise of various characters. Whatever the genre—science fiction, fantasy, detective story, martial arts—experienced audiences have certain expectations based on the kind of thing they perceive themselves to be viewing.

In whatever way a plot moves through time, and whatever our involvement in its action, the events in a play are driven, as noted, by **conflict.** Without conflict of some sort, it is hard to imagine how there could be a plot. This conflict creates some kind of problem that the play (ordinarily) moves toward solving. This problem is sometimes called the **dramatic question,** and in Adams's drama we have a series of dramatic questions—Will Arthur's house be destroyed? Will Arthur and his planet be destroyed?—which conclude with those amusing dramatic questions offered by the author: "Will our heroes survive this terrible ordeal? Can they win through with their integrity unscathed? Can they escape without completely compromising their honour and artistic judgment?"

If the conflict is between two major characters, it is often useful to think of a central or leading character, a **protagonist,** who is pitted against a significant opponent, an **antagonist.** In the *Guide* episode, Arthur Dent is our hero, and he comes into conflict with Prosser and the Vogon captain, comic villains. Ford Prefect is a **supporting character,** it seems—a companion or **sidekick** for Arthur.

The typical shape of a plot is often described in the terms used by Gustav Freytag in *Technique of the Drama* in 1863. Freytag noted that many plays have a **rising action,** in which suspense builds and things get more complicated; a **climax,** or crisis, in which the suspense reaches a peak and a turning point or resolution begins; and a **falling action,** in which the complications and problems are worked out and the action moves toward its conclusion. Freytag's typical plot structure is often called **Freytag's Pyramid** because it is usually diagrammed like this:

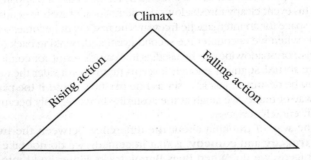

Climax

Rising action

Falling action

Adams's episode, which is only a slender part of the work, doesn't quite fit this model, but the terms are still useful: the plot in this case begins in the middle of things, or *in medias res* (to use the Latin term), with our hero facing a bulldozer. That crisis is resolved, in a sense, only to be displaced by a second more serious crisis, the arrival of the Vogon demolition fleet. The hero is saved rather miraculously, in a fashion that might well be called, to use another well-known Latin term, a *deus ex machina* resolution: literally, *deus ex machina* means "a god from a machine," which refers to the practice of solving a play's crisis by having a divine being swoop in and save the day. In the ancient theatre, Apollo or Zeus or some other deity would usually be lowered down onto the stage by some machinery—hence, "a god from a machine."

Needless to say, such a **resolution** is usually not considered to be the most artful kind of plot in a serious drama. Adams's episode does resolve one crisis by having the main characters miraculously transported off the Earth just as it is being destroyed, but in the comic absurdity of the *Hitch-Hiker's Guide,* such an improbable rescue just adds to the fun. But the episode's falling action is not completed, as their rescue immediately delivers the heroes into another mess. In an episode, of course, we would not expect an ending that resolves all the problems—Adams wants us to tune in next time, and so the ending leaves us in suspense (just like a **soap opera** installment, an **episodic drama**). In a regular play, we would expect the play's problems to be solved and the suspense to be cleared away; this phase of a play, which is missing in Adams's episode, is often called a *denoument* (French for "unknotting").

Whether a play has a subplot, a double plot, or just single plot, we conventionally assume that a play is one thing: audiences expect a play to have some kind of **unity.** Whatever events occur, we assume that they can be related to each other in some way. In addition to this unity of action, there is also another kind of **dramatic unity** that refers to the place and time of the events in a play. In a play that observes the **unities of time and space,** the action we see on stage in front of us takes up the same amount of time as our watching of the play: in other words, in such a play, the first scene doesn't occur in Atlanta in 1930 and the second scene in New York in 1935. Rather, the action stays in one place and time elapses on stage as it does for the audience.

While such unities were once considered essential to a well-crafted play, Samuel Johnson and other critics convinced many people in the eighteenth century that such restrictions as the unities impose on our imaginations were unnecessary and unreasonable. If we can imagine that we are watching people speaking to each other in Atlanta in 1930, even though we know we are actually sitting in a theatre many years later, then we can also imagine, a few minutes after the first imagining, that we are watching people in New York in 1935. Adams's script actually has fun with this convention of a unity of time: when Arthur and Ford are carried to the Vogon Captain, for instance, the time needed for Arthur and Ford to move from the galley cabin to the Captain's location is taken up by the narrator's discussion of Vogon poetry. Thus, the play seems to evolve without skipping over any time. Part of the craft of playmaking is convincing an audience, when one needs to, that time in the world of the play has elapsed (even though it is only minutes or seconds later for us). Shakespeare is especially good at creating this illusion.

The action of the plot is moved forward in Adams's script primarily by **dialogue**—that is, by characters speaking to each other. What they say to each other allows the reader or listener to imagine what is going on without being able to see it. We know that Arthur Dent is lying in front of a bulldozer because Prosser says to him, "But you must realize that you can't lie in front of the bulldozers indefinitely." The term **exposition** is commonly used to refer to those parts of a text that do not so much move the action forward as provide background information needed to understand the action.

In addition to dialogue, a character may speak alone; and in Adams's radio drama, much information—and comedy—is provided by the narrator and by the *Hitch-Hiker's Guide* itself, who both speak directly to the audience. The convention of having a character speak to himself or herself (or itself) is called **soliloquy.** By speaking in soliloquy, characters can reveal their thoughts and their motivations to the audience, perhaps saying something that they would not say to another character. Usually "soliloquy" is used to refer to significant comments characters make to themselves; technically, when Arthur runs out of the pub to try to stop the bulldozer, Ford speaks in soliloquy, saying "Hell, I'd better go after him"—although the comment is so insignificant it might not be noted as a separate speech.

In addition to being overheard by the audience in a soliloquy, a character may also speak directly to the audience in an **aside.** Such comments would ordinarily be audible to the other characters, but by convention an aside is not heard by them. In an aside, the character often actually turns to the audience, turning "aside" from the other characters on the stage, thereby indicating visually that only the audience knows what the character is thinking. In film, such internal monologues can be rendered very effectively simply by having the character's voice heard when his or her lips are not moving. Audiences understand by this convention that they are hearing the character's thoughts. Soliloquies and asides often provide important information about what is conventionally called a play's **subtext**—the underlying meanings and motivations of a play.

For instance, Adams nowhere tells us explicitly that his play is designed to expose the absurdity of the way governments and organizations wield power, but that is pretty clearly part of the play's subtext. Thus, the actor who plays Lady Cynthia Fitzmelton should understand that despite her "dignity and utter conviction," Lady Fitzmelton is not an admirable character. She is inept, but moreover she is ridiculous because she does not realize her ineptness. The play's subtext makes clear that Adams's comparison of her to "a sort of Margaret Thatcher, Penelope Keith character" is not meant to be entirely complimentary. The actor (who might personally find Margaret Thatcher totally admirable) thus knows from the subtext that she should be sure to play Lady Fitzmelton with enough exaggerated seriousness to make her comical.

A play's subtext, as it is construed, not only helps the actors and director know how to play a scene; it can also help the audience to grasp the significance of what happens. Such significance is often conveyed in literary works by a **symbol**—which stands for something other than itself. The bypass, on both the local and galactic levels, might be thought of as a symbol for mindlessly destructive development, oblivious to what is lost for the sake of "progress."

We derive clues about how to decipher a play's subtext and symbols from more than just the words of the characters (including, in Adams's case, the narrator and the book as characters). Films often begin with a text that may simply tell us the time and place of the action ("London. April 1601"), or the text may supply a significant amount of context, as for example in the first *Star Wars* movie, in which the text famously appeared to flow away from the audience, out into space, providing the necessary background. A script usually contains **instructions to the director and the actors,** telling them (with varying degrees of explicitness) what is going on, helping them know how to play a particular scene or speak particular lines. These **stage directions** (which are themselves often quite funny in Adams's hands) let us know for instance that the narrator at the very outset of the play should speak in a "Matter of fact, characterless voice," and that Prosser should sound "dictatorial" and speak "through a megaphone." Adams also describes the special effects he wants used, indicating these by "F/X," which is a conventional shorthand for "effects." Such effects are often referred to as **stage business**—the road-building noises at the play's outset, for instance.

In Adams's script, the stage business is all auditory; but in a play intended to be viewed, the stage business could include visual effects as well—characters pouring tea, running behind a curtain: anything that isn't part of the spoken script but that should be noticed by the audience could be considered stage business. In its radio production, the *Hitch-Hiker's Guide* was particularly rich in sound effects, as Adams was able to create various settings by means of sounds—settings that might be quite difficult to convey on stage. (On stage, it might be hard to convince us a bulldozer is about to run over Arthur, or that a Vogon constructor fleet is flying overhead. Although there have been efforts to stage the *Hitch-Hiker's Guide,* these have not been successful despite some creative publicity stunts, which included throwing a whale—a fake one—off the top of a building.)

Although there are many other technical terms for talking about drama, the aim of this chapter has been simply to add to what was covered in Chapter 9, giving you more tools to work on drama. As a way of reviewing the material covered in this chapter, see if you can explain the following elements of drama (each is covered in this chapter, in the listed order): plot, flashback, double plot, subplot, incident, unity of action, tragedy, comedy, dramatic question, protagonist, antagonist, rising action, climax, falling action, Freytag's Pyramid, *in medias res, deus ex machina,* suspense, *denoument,* dramatic unities, dialogue, soliloquy, aside, subtext, symbol, stage directions, special effects, stage business.

Writing about Drama

This section illustrates how various critical approaches can help you write and think about drama more insightfully and persuasively. Specifically, as this textbook has expressed throughout, but especially in Part II, by understanding the various critical stances available, you'll have a better notion of what kinds of questions to ask, and you'll be better able to generate ideas and support. The broader your understanding of the kinds of critical approaches, the richer your possibilities in engaging with a play—or any other kind of literature.

Writing about drama is not essentially different from writing about anything else. There are, as we've just seen, some terms that are especially pervasive in writing about drama, and other terms that are especially useful in talking about films. The camera angle (the point of view from which the audience sees what is displayed on the screen) can be crucial. A director may choose to have an attacker come straight at the camera, as if the audience is in the place of the person being attacked. Or, the director may pull back from the fight, showing the audience the entire setting. Or, more likely, a scene may involve numerous camera angles, each one shaping the audience's reaction. Playgoers and moviegoers are very familiar with many conventions: if the stage darkens and the scenery has changed when the lights come up, audiences know that the action is now set somewhere else. Likewise, movies often present a momentary black screen to indicate a shift of the action or the passing of time.

In any genre, using any terms, you still must proceed from certain assumptions, using certain techniques, making assertions and backing them up. Even if you are not consciously aware of your reading and writing strategies, they are nonetheless at work if you're able to say anything about a play or film or anything. The goal here, and throughout this text, is to help you become more aware of your options as a reader and writer.

Toward that goal of clarifying your options, let's take a specific example, a one-act play that has become so popular, so respected, that it almost always appears in any introduction-to-literature anthology. It's a great play. Read it carefully, and then we'll consider the kinds of options you have in thinking and writing about it, as you watch an essay being evolved.

SUSAN GLASPELL (1882–1948)

Susan Glaspell, after growing up in Iowa, attending Drake University, and working as journalist in Des Moines, moved to New York's Greenwich Village. She founded the Provincetown Players with her husband in 1915. She wrote successful plays (Allison's House won the Pulitzer in 1930), as well as ten novels. Glaspell rewrote Trifles *as a short story, "A Jury of Her Peers," shortly after she finished the play.*

Trifles

Characters

George Henderson, county attorney
Henry Peters, sheriff
Lewis Hale, a neighboring farmer
Mrs. Peters
Mrs. Hale

> Scene: *The kitchen in the now abandoned farmhouse of John Wright, a gloomy kitchen, and left without having been put in order— unwashed pans under the sink, a loaf of bread outside the breadbox, a dish towel on the table—other signs of incompleted work. At the rear the outer door opens and the Sheriff comes in followed by the County Attorney and Hale. The Sheriff and Hale are men in middle life, the County Attorney is a young man; all are much bundled up and go at once to the stove. They are followed by two women—the Sheriff's wife first; she is a slight wiry woman, a thin nervous face. Mrs. Hale is larger and would ordinarily be called more comfortable looking, but she is disturbed now and looks fearfully about as she enters. The women have come in slowly, and stand close together near the door.*

County Attorney: [*Rubbing his hands.*] This feels good. Come up to the fire, ladies.

Mrs. Peters: [*After taking a step forward.*] I'm not—cold.

Sheriff: [*Unbuttoning his overcoat and stepping away from the stove as if to mark the beginning of official business.*] Now, Mr. Hale, before we move things about, you explain to Mr. Henderson just what you saw when you came here yesterday morning.

County Attorney: By the way, has anything been moved? Are things just as you left them yesterday?

Sheriff: [*Looking about.*] It's just the same. When it dropped below zero last night I thought I'd better send Frank out this morning to make a   5 fire for us—no use getting pneumonia with a big case on, but I told him not to touch anything except the stove—and you know Frank.

County Attorney: Somebody should have been left here yesterday.

Sheriff: Oh—yesterday. When I had to send Frank to Morris Center for that man who went crazy—I want you to know I had my hands full yesterday, I knew you could get back from Omaha by today and as long as I went over everything here myself—

County Attorney: Well, Mr. Hale, tell just what happened when you came here yesterday morning.

Hale: Harry and I had started to town with a load of potatoes. We came along the road from my place and as I got here I said, "I'm going to see if I can't get John Wright to go in with me on a party telephone." I spoke to Wright about it once before and he put me off, saying folks talked too much anyway, and all he asked was peace and quiet—I guess you know about how much he talked himself; but I thought maybe if I went to the house and talked about it before his wife, though I said to Harry that I didn't know as what his wife wanted made much difference to John—

County Attorney: Let's talk about that later, Mr. Hale. I do want to talk about   10
that, but tell now just what happened when you got to the house.

Hale: I didn't hear or see anything; I knocked at the door, and still it was all quiet inside. I knew they must be up, it was past eight o'clock. So I knocked again, and I thought I heard somebody say, "Come in." I wasn't sure, I'm not sure yet, but I opened the door—this door [*Indicating the door by which the two women are still standing*] and there in that rocker—[*Pointing to it*] sat Mrs. Wright.

[*They all look at the rocker.*]

County Attorney: What—was she doing?

Hale: She was rockin' back and forth. She had her apron in her hand and was kind of—pleating it.

County Attorney: And how did she—look?

Hale: Well, she looked queer.   15

County Attorney: How do you mean—queer?

Hale: Well, as if she didn't know what she was going to do next. And kind of done up.

County Attorney: How did she seem to feel about your coming?

Hale: Why, I don't think she minded—one way or other. She didn't pay much attention. I said, "How do, Mrs. Wright, it's cold, ain't it?" And she said, "Is it?"—and went on kind of pleating at her apron. Well, I was surprised; she didn't ask me to come up to the stove, or to set down, but just sat there, not even looking at me, so I said, "I want to see John." And then she—laughed. I guess you would call it a laugh. I thought of Harry and the team outside, so I said a little sharp: "Can't I see John?" "No," she says, kind o' dull like. "Ain't he home?" says I. "Yes," says she, "he's home." "Then why can't I see him?" I asked her, out of patience. "'Cause he's dead," says she. *"Dead?"* says I. She just nodded her head, not getting a bit excited, but rockin' back and forth. "Why—where is he?" says I, not knowing what to say. She just pointed upstairs—like that [*Himself pointing to the room above.*] I got up, with the idea of going up there. I walked from there to here—then I says, "Why, what did he die of?" "He died of a rope round his neck," says she, and just went on pleatin' at her apron. Well, I went out and called Harry. I thought I might—need help. We went upstairs and there he was lyin'—

County Attorney: I think I'd rather have you go into that upstairs, where   20
you can point it all out. Just go on now with the rest of the story.

Hale: Well, my first thought was to get that rope off. It looked . . . [*Stops, his face twitches*] . . . but Harry, he went up to him, and he said, "No, he's dead all right, and we'd better not touch anything." So we went back down stairs. She was still sitting that same way. "Has anybody been notified?" I asked. "No," says she, unconcerned. "Who did this, Mrs. Wright?" said Harry. He said it businesslike—and she stopped pleatin' of her apron. "I don't know," she says. "You don't *know*?" says Harry. "No," says she. "Weren't you sleepin' in the bed with him?" says Harry. "Yes," says she, "but I was on the inside." "Somebody slipped a rope round his neck and strangled him and you didn't wake up?" says Harry. "I didn't wake up," she said after him. We must 'a looked as if we didn't see how that could be, for after a minute she said, "I sleep sound." Harry was going to ask her more questions but I said maybe we ought to let her tell her story first to the coroner, or the sheriff, so Harry went fast as he could to Rivers' place, where there's a telephone.

County Attorney: And what did Mrs. Wright do when she knew that you had gone for the coroner?

Hale: She moved from that chair to this one over here [*Pointing to a small chair in the corner*] and just sat there with her hands held together and looking down. I got a feeling that I ought to make some conversation, so I said I had come in to see if John wanted to put in a telephone, and at that she started to laugh, and then she stopped and looked at me—scared. [*The County Attorney, who has had his notebook out, makes a note.*] I dunno, maybe it wasn't scared. I wouldn't like to say it was. Soon Harry got back, and then Dr. Lloyd came, and you, Mr. Peters, and so I guess that's all I know that you don't.

County Attorney: [*Looking around.*] I guess we'll go upstairs first—and then out to the barn and around there. [*To the Sheriff*] You're convinced that there was nothing important here—nothing that would point to any motive.

Sheriff: Nothing here but kitchen things.   25

[*The County Attorney, after again looking around the kitchen, opens the door of a cupboard closet. He gets up on a chair and looks on a shelf. Pulls his hand away, sticky.*]

County Attorney: Here's a nice mess.

[*The women draw nearer.*]

Mrs. Peters: [*To the other woman.*] Oh, her fruit; it did freeze. [*To the County Attorney*] She worried about that when it turned so cold. She said the fire'd go out and her jars would break.

Sheriff: Well, can you beat the women! Held for murder and worryin' about her preserves.

County Attorney: I guess before we're through she may have something more serious than preserves to worry about.

Hale: Well, women are used to worrying over trifles.   30

[*The two women move a little closer together.*]

County Attorney: [*With the gallantry of a young politician.*] And yet, for all their worries, what would we do without the ladies? [*The women do not unbend. He goes to the sink, takes a dipperful of water from the pail and pouring it into a basin, washes his hands. Starts to wipe them on the roller towel, turns it for a cleaner place.*] Dirty towels! [*Kicks his foot against the pans under the sink.*] Not much of a housekeeper, would you say, ladies?

Mrs. Hale: [*Stiffly.*] There's a great deal of work to be done on a farm.

County Attorney: To be sure. And yet [*With a little bow to her*] I know there are some Dickson county farmhouses which do not have such roller towels.

[*He gives it a pull to expose its full length again.*]

Mrs. Hale: Those towels get dirty awful quick. Men's hands aren't always as clean as they might be.

County Attorney: Ah, loyal to your sex, I see. But you and Mrs. Wright were   35
neighbors. I suppose you were friends, too.

Mrs. Hale: [*Shaking her head.*] I've not seen much of her of late years. I've not been in this house—it's more than a year.

County Attorney: And why was that? You didn't like her?

Mrs. Hale: I liked her all well enough. Farmers' wives have their hands full, Mr. Henderson. And then—

County Attorney: Yes—?

Mrs. Hale: [*Looking about.*] It never seemed a very cheerful place.   40

County Attorney: No—it's not cheerful. I shouldn't say she had the home-making instinct.

Mrs. Hale: Well, I don't know as Wright had, either.

County Attorney: You mean that they didn't get on very well?

Mrs. Hale: No, I don't mean anything. But I don't think a place'd be any cheerfuller for John Wright's being in it.

County Attorney: I'd like to talk more of that a little later. I want to get the   45
lay of things upstairs now.

[*He goes to the left, where three steps lead to a stair door.*]

Sheriff: I suppose anything Mrs. Peters does'll be all right. She was to take in some clothes for her, you know, and a few little things. We left in such a hurry yesterday.

County Attorney: Yes, but I would like to see what you take, Mrs. Peters, and keep an eye out for anything that might be of use to us.

Mrs. Peters: Yes, Mr. Henderson.

[*The women listen to the men's steps on the stairs, then look about the kitchen.*]

Mrs. Hale: I'd hate to have men coming into my kitchen, snooping around and criticizing.

[*She arranges the pans under sink which the County Attorney had shoved out of place.*]

Mrs. Peters: Of course it's no more than their duty.   50

Mrs. Hale: Duty's all right, but I guess that deputy sheriff that came out to make the fire might have got a little of this on. [*Gives the roller towel a pull.*] Wish I'd thought of that sooner. Seems mean to talk about her for not having things slicked up when she had to come away in such a hurry.

Mrs. Peters: [*Who has gone to a small table in the left rear corner of the room, and lifted one end of a towel that covers a pan.*] She had bread set.

[*Stands still.*]

Mrs. Hale: [*Eyes fixed on a loaf of bread beside the breadbox, which is on a low shelf at the other side of the room. Moves slowly toward it.*] She was going to put this in there. [*Picks up loaf, then abruptly drops it. In a manner of returning to familiar things.*] It's a shame about her fruit. I wonder if it's all gone. [*Gets up on the chair and looks.*] I think there's some here that's all right, Mrs. Peters. Yes—here; [*Holding it toward the window*] this is cherries, too. [*Looking again.*] I declare I believe that's the only one. [*Gets down, bottle in her hand. Goes to the sink and wipes it off on the outside.*] She'll feel awful bad after all her hard work in the hot weather. I remember the afternoon I put up my cherries last summer.

[*She puts the bottle on the big kitchen table, center of the room. With a sigh, is about to sit down in the rocking-chair. Before she is seated realizes what chair it is; with a slow look at it, steps back. The chair which she has touched rocks back and forth.*]

Mrs. Peters: Well, I must get those things from the front room closet. [*She goes to the door at the right, but after looking into the other room, steps back.*] You coming with me, Mrs. Hale? You could help me carry them.

[*They go in the other room; reappear, Mrs. Peters carrying a dress and skirt, Mrs. Hale following with a pair of shoes.*]

Mrs. Peters: My, it's cold in there.   55

[*She puts the clothes on the big table, and hurries to the stove.*]

Mrs. Hale: [*Examining her skirt.*] Wright was close. I think maybe that's why she kept so much to herself. She didn't even belong to the Ladies Aid. I suppose she felt she couldn't do her part, and then you don't enjoy things when you feel shabby. She used to wear pretty clothes and be lively, when she was Minnie Foster, one of the town girls singing in the choir. But that—oh, that was thirty years ago. This all you was to take in?

Mrs. Peters: She said she wanted an apron. Funny thing to want, for there isn't much to get you dirty in jail, goodness knows. But I suppose just to make her feel more natural. She said they was in the top drawer in this cupboard. Yes, here. And then her little shawl that always hung behind the door. [*Opens stair door and looks.*] Yes, here it is.

[*Quickly shuts door leading upstairs.*]

Mrs. Hale: [*Abruptly moving toward her.*] Mrs. Peters?

Mrs. Peters: Yes, Mrs. Hale?

Mrs. Hale: Do you think she did it?   60

Mrs. Peters: [*In a frightened voice.*] Oh, I don't know.

Mrs. Hale: Well, I don't think she did. Asking for an apron and her little shawl. Worrying about her fruit.

Mrs. Peters: [*Starts to speak, glances up, where footsteps are heard in the room above. In a low voice.*] Mr. Peters says it looks bad for her. Mr.

Henderson is awful sarcastic in a speech and he'll make fun of her sayin' she didn't wake up.

Mrs. Hale: Well, I guess John Wright didn't wake when they was slipping that rope under his neck.

Mrs. Peters: No, it's strange. It must have been done awful crafty and still. They say it was such a—funny way to kill a man, rigging it all up like that.   65

Mrs. Hale: That's just what Mr. Hale said. There was a gun in the house. He says that's what he can't understand.

Mrs. Peters: Mr. Henderson said coming out that what was needed for the case was a motive; something to show anger, or—sudden feeling.

Mrs. Hale: [*Who is standing by the table.*] Well, I don't see any signs of anger around here. [*She puts her hand on the dish towel which lies on the table, stands looking down at table, one half of which is clean, the other half messy.*] It's wiped to here. [*Makes a move as if to finish work, then turns and looks at loaf of bread outside the breadbox. Drops towel. In that voice of coming back to familiar things.*] Wonder how they are finding things upstairs. I hope she had it a little more red-up up there. You know, it seems kind of *sneaking*. Locking her up in town and then coming out here and trying to get her own house to turn against her!

Mrs. Peters: But Mrs. Hale, the law is the law.

Mrs. Hale: I s'pose 'tis. [*Unbuttoning her coat.*] Better loosen up your things, Mrs. Peters. You won't feel them when you go out.   70

[*Mrs. Peters takes off her fur tippet, goes to hang it on hook at back of room, stands looking at the under part of the small corner table.*]

Mrs. Peters: She was piecing a quilt.

[*She brings the large sewing basket and they look at the bright pieces.*]

Mrs. Hale: It's a log cabin pattern. Pretty, isn't it? I wonder if she was goin' to quilt it or just knot it?

[*Footsteps have been heard coming down the stairs. The Sheriff enters followed by Hale and the County Attorney.*]

Sheriff: They wonder if she was going to quilt it or just knot it!

[*The men laugh; the women look abashed.*]

County Attorney: [*Rubbing his hands over the stove.*] Frank's fire didn't do much up there, did it? Well, let's go out to the barn and get that cleared up.

[*The men go outside.*]

Mrs. Hale: [*Resentfully.*] I don't know as there's anything so strange, our takin' up our time with little things while we're waiting for them to get the evidence. [*She sits down at the big table smoothing out a block with decision.*] I don't see as it's anything to laugh about.   75

Mrs. Peters: [*Apologetically.*] Of course they've got awful important things on their minds.

[*Pulls up a chair and joins Mrs. Hale at the table.*]

Mrs. Hale: [*Examining another block.*] Mrs. Peters, look at this one. Here, this is the one she was working on, and look at the sewing! All the rest

of it has been so nice and even. And look at this! It's all over the place!
Why, it looks as if she didn't know what she was about!

[*After she has said this they look at each, then start to glance back at
the door. After an instant Mrs. Hale has pulled at a knot and ripped
the sewing.*]

Mrs. Peters: Oh, what are you doing, Mrs. Hale?

Mrs. Hale: [*Mildly.*] Just pulling out a stitch or two that's not sewed very
good. [*Threading a needle.*] Bad sewing always made me fidgety.

Mrs. Peters: [*Nervously.*] I don't think we ought to touch things.   80

Mrs. Hale: I'll just finish up this end. [*Suddenly stopping and leaning forward.*] Mrs. Peters?

Mrs. Peters: Yes, Mrs. Hale?

Mrs. Hale: What do you suppose she was so nervous about?

Mrs. Peters: Oh—I don't know. I don't know as she was nervous. I sometimes sew awful queer when I'm just tired. [*Mrs. Hale starts to say
something, looks at Mrs. Peters, then goes on sewing.*] Well, I must get
these things wrapped up. They may be through sooner than we think.
[*Putting apron and other things together.*] I wonder where I can find
a piece of paper, and string.

Mrs. Hale: In that cupboard, maybe.   85

Mrs. Peters: [*Looking in cupboard.*] Why, here's a birdcage. [*Holds it up.*]
Did she have a bird, Mrs. Hale?

Mrs. Hale: Why, I don't know whether she did or not—I've not been here
for so long. There was a man around last year selling canaries cheap,
but I don't know as she took one; maybe she did. She used to sing real
pretty herself.

Mrs. Peters: [*Glancing around.*] Seems funny to think of a bird here. But
she must have had one, or why would she have a cage? I wonder what
happened to it.

Mrs. Hale: I s'pose maybe the cat got it.

Mrs. Peters: No, she didn't have a cat. She's got that feeling some people   90
have about cats—being afraid of them. My cat got in her room and she
was real upset and asked me to take it out.

Mrs. Hale: My sister Bessie was like that. Queer, ain't it?

Mrs. Peters: [*Examining the cage.*] Why, look at this door. It's broke. One
hinge is pulled apart.

Mrs. Hale: [*Looking too.*] Looks as if someone must have been rough with it.

Mrs. Peters: Why, yes.

[*She brings the cage forward and puts it on the table.*]

Mrs. Hale: I wish if they're going to find any evidence they'd be about it. I   95
don't like this place.

Mrs. Peters: But I'm awful glad you came with me, Mrs. Hale. It would be
lonesome for me sitting here alone.

Mrs. Hale: It would, wouldn't it? [*Dropping her sewing.*] But I tell you what
I do wish, Mrs. Peters. I wish I had come over sometimes when *she* was
here. I—[*Looking around the room.*]—wish I had.

Mrs. Peters: But of course you were awful busy, Mrs. Hale—your house and
your children.

Mrs. Hale: I could've come. I stayed away because it weren't cheerful—and
that's why I ought to have come. I—I've never liked this place. Maybe
because it's down in a hollow and you don't see the road. I dunno what

it is but it's a lonesome place and always was. I wish I had come over to see Minnie Foster sometimes. I can see now—

[*Shakes her head.*]

Mrs. Peters: Well, you mustn't reproach yourself, Mrs. Hale. Somehow we   100
just don't see how it is with other folks until—something comes up.

Mrs. Hale: Not having children makes less work—but it makes a quiet house, and Wright out to work all day, and no company when he did come in. Did you know John Wright, Mrs. Peters?

Mrs. Peters: Not to know him; I've seen him in town. They say he was a good man.

Mrs. Hale: Yes—good; he didn't drink, and kept his word as well as most, I guess, and paid his debts. But he was a hard man, Mrs. Peters. Just to pass the time of day with him—[*Shivers.*] Like a raw wind that gets to the bone. [*Pauses, her eye falling on the cage.*] I should think she would'a wanted a bird. But what do you suppose went with it?

Mrs. Peters: I don't know, unless it got sick and died.

[*She reaches over and swings the broken door, swings it again. Both women watch it.*]

Mrs. Hale: You weren't raised round here, were you? [*Mrs. Peters shakes*   105
her head.] You didn't know—her?

Mrs. Peters: Not till they brought her yesterday.

Mrs. Hale: She—come to think of it, she was kind of like a bird herself—real sweet and pretty, but kind of timid and—fluttery. How—she—did—change. [*Silence; then as if struck by a happy thought and relieved to get back to everyday things.*] Tell you what, Mrs. Peters, why don't you take the quilt in with you? It might take up her mind.

Mrs. Peters: Why, I think that's a real nice idea, Mrs. Hale. There couldn't possibly be any objection to it, could there? Now, just what would I take? I wonder if her patches are in here—and her things.

[*They look in the sewing basket.*]

Mrs. Hale: Here's some red. I expect this has got sewing things in it. [*Brings out a fancy box.*] What a pretty box. Looks like something somebody would give you. Maybe her scissors are in here. [*Opens box. Suddenly puts her hand to her nose.*] Why—[*Mrs. Peters bends nearer, then turns her face away.*] There's something wrapped up in this piece of silk.

Mrs. Peters: Why, this isn't her scissors.   110

Mrs. Hale: [*Lifting the silk.*] Oh, Mrs. Peters—it's—

[*Mrs. Peters bends closer.*]

Mrs. Peters: It's the bird.

Mrs. Hale: [*Jumping up.*] But, Mrs. Peters—look at it! Its neck! Look at its neck! It's all—other side *too.*

Mrs. Peters: Somebody—wrung—its—neck.

[*Their eyes meet. A look of growing comprehension, of horror. Steps are heard outside. Mrs. Hale slips box under quilt pieces, and sinks into her chair. Enter Sheriff and County Attorney. Mrs. Peters rises.*]

County Attorney: [*As one turning from serious things to little pleas-*   115
antries.] Well, ladies, have you decided whether she was going to quilt it or knot it?

Mrs. Peters: We think she was going to—knot it.

County Attorney: Well, that's interesting, I'm sure. [*Seeing the birdcage.*] Has the bird flown?

Mrs. Hale: [*Putting more quilt pieces over the box.*] We think the—cat got it.

County Attorney: [*Preoccupied.*] Is there a cat?

[*Mrs. Hale glances in a quick covert way at Mrs. Peters.*]

Mrs. Peters: Well, not *now*. They're superstitious, you know. They leave.   120

County Attorney: [*To Sheriff Peters, continuing an interrupted conversation.*] No sign at all of anyone having come from the outside. Their own rope. Now let's go up again and go over it piece by piece. [*They start upstairs.*] It would have to have been someone who knew just the—

[*Mrs. Peters sits down. The two women sit there not looking at one another, but as if peering into something and at the same time holding back. When they talk now it is in the manner of feeling their way over strange ground, as if afraid of what they are saying, but as if they cannot help saying it.*]

Mrs. Hale: She liked the bird. She was going to bury it in that pretty box.

Mrs. Peters: [*In a whisper.*] When I was a girl—my kitten—there was a boy took a hatchet, and before my eyes—and before I could get there—[*Covers her face an instant.*] If they hadn't held me back I would have—[*Catches herself, looks upstairs where steps are heard, falters weakly*]—hurt him.

Mrs. Hale: [*With a slow look around her.*] I wonder how it would seem never to have had any children around. [*Pause.*] No, Wright wouldn't like the bird—a thing that sang. She used to sing. He killed that, too.

Mrs. Peters: [*Moving uneasily.*] We don't know who killed the bird.   125

Mrs. Hale: I knew John Wright.

Mrs. Peters: It was an awful thing was done in this house that night, Mrs. Hale. Killing a man while he slept, slipping a rope around his neck that choked the life out of him.

Mrs. Hale: His neck. Choked the life out of him.

[*Her hand goes out and rests on the birdcage.*]

Mrs. Peters: [*With rising voice.*] We don't know who killed him. We don't know.

Mrs. Hale: [*Her own feeling not interrupted.*] If there'd been years and   130
years of nothing, then a bird to sing to you, it would be awful—still, after the bird was still.

Mrs. Peters: [*Something within her speaking.*] I know what stillness is. When we homesteaded in Dakota, and my first baby died—after he was two years old, and me with no other then—

Mrs. Hale: [*Moving.*] How soon do you suppose they'll be through looking for the evidence?

Mrs. Peters: I know what stillness is. [*Pulling herself back.*] The law has got to punish crime, Mrs. Hale.

Mrs. Hale: [*Not as if answering that.*] I wish you'd seen Minnie Foster when she wore a white dress with blue ribbons and stood up there in the choir and sang. [*A look around the room.*] Oh, I *wish* I'd come over here once in a while! That was a crime! That was a crime! Who's going to punish that?

Mrs. Peters: [*Looking upstairs.*] We mustn't—take on.   135

Mrs. Hale: I might have known she needed help! I know how things can be—for women. I tell you, it's queer, Mrs. Peters. We live close together and we live far apart. We all go through the same things—it's all just a different kind of the same thing. [*Brushes her eyes; noticing the bottle of fruit, reaches out for it.*] If I was you I wouldn't tell her her fruit was gone. Tell her it *ain't*. Tell her it's all right. Take this in to prove it to her. She—she may never know whether it was broke or not.

Mrs. Peters: [*Takes the bottle, looks about for something to wrap it in; takes petticoat from the clothes brought from the other room, very nervously begins winding this around the bottle. In a false voice.*] My, it's a good thing the men couldn't hear us. Wouldn't they just laugh! Getting all stirred up over a little thing like a—dead canary. As if that could have anything to do with—with—wouldn't they *laugh*!

[*The men are heard coming down stairs.*]

Mrs. Hale: [*Under her breath.*] Maybe they would—maybe they wouldn't.

County Attorney: No, Peters, it's all perfectly clear except a reason for doing it. But you know juries when it comes to women. If there was some definite thing. Something to show—something to make a story about—a thing that would connect up with this strange way of doing it—

[*The women's eyes meet for an instant. Enter Hale from outer door.*]

Hale: Well, I've got the team around. Pretty cold out there.   140

County Attorney: I'm going to stay here a while by myself. [*To the Sheriff.*] You can send Frank out for me, can't you? I want to go over everything. I'm not satisfied that we can't do better.

Sheriff: Do you want to see what Mrs. Peters is going to take in?

[*The County Attorney goes to the table, picks up the apron, laughs.*]

County Attorney: Oh, I guess they're not very dangerous things the ladies have picked out. [*Moves a few things about, disturbing the quilt pieces which cover the box. Steps back.*] No, Mrs. Peters doesn't need supervising. For that matter, a sheriff's wife is married to the law. Ever think of it that way, Mrs. Peters?

Mrs. Peters: Not—just that way.

Sheriff: [*Chuckling.*] Married to the law. [*Moves toward the other room.*] I   145 just want you to come in here a minute, George. We ought to take a look at these windows.

County Attorney: [*Scoffingly.*] Oh, windows!

Sheriff: We'll be right out, Mr. Hale.

[*Hale goes outside. The Sheriff follows the County Attorney into the other room. Then Mrs. Hale rises, hands tight together, looking intensely at Mrs. Peters, whose eyes make a slow turn, finally meeting Mrs. Hale's. A moment Mrs. Hale holds her, then her own eyes point the way to where the box is concealed. Suddenly Mrs. Peters throws back quilt pieces and tries to put the box in the bag she is wearing. It is too big. She opens box, starts to take bird out, cannot touch it, goes to pieces, stands there helpless. Sound of a knob turning in the other*] *room. Mrs. Hale snatches the box and puts it in the pocket of her big coat. Enter County Attorney and Sheriff.*]

County Attorney: [*Facetiously.*] Well, Henry, at least we found out that she was not going to quilt it. She was going to—what is it you call it, ladies?

Mrs. Hale: [*Her hand against her pocket.*] We call it—knot it, Mr. Henderson.

CURTAIN

[1916]

Understanding the Play

Now that you've read the play, how would you get started writing a paper about it? If you've been given an assignment, then there may be some theoretical stance already laid out for you. You might be asked, for instance, to explain how a particular passage contributes to the play's theme—an assignment that most logically calls for New Critical strategies because it assumes, for starters, that the play has a unifying theme, and that the details of the passage somehow contribute to this theme. Or you might be asked to discuss your response to a play, or some part of it, which suggests that reader-response strategies are in order. You might be asked to write about the way men and women are depicted in the play, which would seem to invoke the concerns of political criticism. And so forth.

Outside the classroom (and sometimes inside), critics usually aren't given a specific assignment from someone else; they're free to evolve whatever ideas they think the text will support. A critic may decide to employ a particular approach, or the approach may simply seem to be what is called for, by the critic or even by the text itself. Whatever critical orientation is being adopted, you still need to understand what happens in a play in order to develop an interpretation of it.

First, with any play, you want to make sure you understand the setting: what are we told about where the action is taking place? How is that information significant? In the case of *Trifles,* the setting is obviously crucial. It is the scene of a crime, and the scene reveals very different things to the different people on stage. Glaspell offers a detailed description of the setting; as a reader, you would certainly want to visualize the setting of the scene before reading how the County Attorney opens the play. You would want to consider questions such as:

- What mood do you think should be created by the setting? How is this mood created?
- What details in the setting become more significant the second time you read the play? What is their significance?

You also want to make sure that you understand the characters in a play. In *Trifles*, think about Mr. Hale, for instance. In the opening of the play, he reveals something of what has happened, but as he tells his story he is also unavoidably revealing something of his own character, and the character of others through his eyes. You should be able to answer questions such as:

- What might Mr. Hale be thinking but not saying? How do we know?
- What do we learn about John Wright, and how do we get this information?
- What do we find out about his wife? At one point Mrs. Hale says, for example, that she doesn't think that Minnie Wright killed her husband. Her reasoning is that in jail Minnie asks for an apron and a shawl and worries about her fruit preserves. What do we learn here about Mrs. Hale?

- And what does Minnie's request suggest about her? How would you explain this behavior? In other words, why, in your opinion, does Minnie Wright ask about these things?
- Also, what do we learn about the Wrights' marriage? What information are we given, and what inferences should we draw?

In addition to questions about setting and character, you should also understand the plot. You'll want to understand not only what happens, but how the dramatist unfolds to us an awareness of what happens. In *Trifles,* the plot involves the piecing together of another story, one that is never entirely told to us, but only suggested. Here are some sample questions about the plot:

- How is the investigation conducted? Are the official investigators careful and efficient?
- What evidence is crucial? What's the significance of Mr. Hale's remark, "Well, women are used to worrying over trifles"?
- Why does Mrs. Hale rework some of the stitches in the one block of the quilt that "looks as if she didn't know what she was about"? Mrs. Peters even says, "I don't think we ought to touch things," but Mrs. Hale proceeds anyway. Why?
- What clues do the women follow in order to determine that the bird's neck has been "wrung"? What information do they provide that makes the bird's death especially significant?
- How important is the evidence that the women decide to hide? Do the women realize that importance? How does their decision evolve?

One of the best activities to deepen your understanding of the setting, the characters, and the plot, is simply to write about the play. Notice how this student's journal entry clarifies what she is reading, as she first takes notes and then tries to articulate what she understands:

Journal Entry: Student Example

    Scene, described in italics. "Gloomy" kitchen. The men
enter first; women don't approach the fire. Huddle together
near door—seem frightened.
    Older men deferring to younger man because of his rank.
    County Attorney doesn't want to hear about whether John
Wright had much interest in what his wife wanted.
    Testimonial of a witness—Mr. Henderson. Or is it Mr. Hale?
    The opening scene of "Trifles" deals with the testimony
of a man who has discovered a murder. Mr. Hale relates to
the Sheriff and the County Attorney how he discovered that
his neighbor John Wright was murdered. The scene takes place
the day after the murder and at the Wright's house. The
Sheriff's wife and Mrs. Henderson have accompanied the men
to the house but they stand silently on stage for a long
time before speaking. The County Attorney, although he is a
younger man, is clearly the authority figure in the scene,
as he reprimands the sheriff and directs Mr. Hale's
testimony. He appears to consider himself to be logical—a
just-the-facts kind of guy. This is seen when he cuts off

Mr. Hale's comment that he "didn't know as what his wife
wanted made much difference to John." However, later in the
questioning, he shows that he trusts Mr. Hale's impressions
of Mrs. Wright's state of mind enough to make a note of his
comment that she seemed "scared."

Such questions about setting, character, and plot do not lead you to consider everything you'd ever want to know about *Trifles*. There are many more questions you could ask. But these questions should give you some idea of the kind of basic facts and inferences required to write about a play. It is unlikely that such questions will lead you directly to an interesting essay topic: they are more likely in fact to lead you to a plot summary—which is rarely an assignment, and usually something teachers want you to avoid. It's often helpful, to be sure, to write out for yourself a summary of what you have observed, as this student did, but such an understanding is only the starting point for a critical essay. If you find yourself retelling the story of a play, rather than supporting an arguable assertion, then you're probably engaging in a plot summary, and you need to reconsider your essay's plan.

With Glaspell's play, it is certainly important to recognize, for instance, that the crucial evidence consists of what might be considered trifles, and that Mr. Hale's comment that "women are used to worrying over trifles" is ironic. But you couldn't write an essay arguing that the women's attention to "trifles" is more revealing than the men's attention to what they consider "important"; for anyone who understands what happens in the play, there's no argument about that.

A Writing Plan: Critical Strategies

When you are satisfied that you're familiar with what happens in the play, and you're ready to start writing, to start generating ideas for an argument, then you'll be ready to make use of critical strategies. Although it's always risky to generalize about something as individual as the process of writing, most students will find it useful to think about the writing process in terms of the following steps—even though any particular writing experience is likely to vary from these:

A Sample Writing Plan

1. Generate some questions; try to answer them.
2. Look for energy, insight, surprise in your questions and answers.
3. Focusing on those aspects of the questions and answers that seem promising, generate more questions and answers until you're ready to formulate a tentative thesis (that is, an arguable, supportable, and revealing assertion).
4. Develop an argument supporting this tentative thesis; if you bog down, return to the previous steps until you're ready to go forward again.
5. Once you've arrived at a viable thesis and sketched out an argument in its support, then craft an introduction and a conclusion.
6. Revise the whole thing, returning to any previous steps as needed.

Given this very general outline, let's look now at how various theories can help guide your writing process.

Reader-Response Strategies

To illustrate how reader-response criticism can help you write about a play, let's go to the first step of the Writing Plan:

1. Generate some questions; try to answer them.

From a reader-response stance, you are trying to generate certain kinds of questions—namely, questions which assume that it matters how readers respond. You're looking at the play itself as a process, an experience—and not an artistic object, or a political action, or a biographical document, or a psychological product, or anything else. From this perspective, the play equals the response to it.

Thus, one obvious way to proceed in developing a reader-response essay would be simply to ask yourself questions about how particular features of the play—a passage, a statement, a phrase, even a word—affect an attentive audience. You may think of that "attentive audience" as including all sensible readers or just all readers who respond the way you do. In any event, by moving through the play and articulating a response, you'll be able to create, in a sense, a kind of slow-motion version of the reading experience. (In describing this experience for your reader, you may want to be selective and suggestive, rather than exhaustive.) You're looking for questions, then, that help you develop and express a response.

Here are some sample questions generated by adopting a reader-response stance. These are not the only questions to ask, or maybe even the best ones for you; but they suggest the kinds of questions you can ask when you work from a reader-response orientation:

Reader-Response Questions

1. How do you respond to Lewis Hale's telling of the story of how he found John Wright's dead body? What do you think Glaspell wants the audience to think of him?
2. What do you think of the way the Sheriff and the Attorney handle the investigation? How well, for instance, has the Sheriff secured the crime scene? How thoroughly does the Attorney look for clues? What do you think Glaspell wants the audience to think of these men? What is your first impression, and is it confirmed or altered?
3. Is Glaspell's choice of a songbird as Mrs. Wright's pet a good one? Is your response to the discovery of the songbird similar to Mrs. Hale's and Mrs. Peters's response?
4. When the audience learns how John Wright died, how do you think Glaspell wants them to respond? How does learning about the bird's fate affect this response?
5. At crucial points in the play, Mrs. Peters and Mrs. Hale interrupt what they're saying with a pause, which is indicated in the script by a dash. How do these hesitations affect you? How would your reaction be different if the hesitations were removed?
6. Do you like Mrs. Peters and Mrs. Hale? What is your first impression of them? How does Glaspell shape your response? How do you feel about Mrs. Wright, and how are those feelings generated?
7. What is your response to the final lines? How does the ending affect your response to the play as a whole? What if the Attorney had found the bird, or if Mrs. Hale had broken down and confessed what the ladies suspected? Would your response to the play change significantly?

To answer the questions you raise, you might assume the posture of that famous sculpture of "The Thinker," and proceed to cogitate. Usually a better strategy, however, would be to write down any ideas you have, and to talk to someone else, or both. For example, here is a journal entry responding to the last question, about the play's ending.

Journal Entry: Student Example

I had to laugh when I read the ending to Glaspell's "Trifles." The County Attorney and the other men think it is funny that the women have discussed the way Mrs. Wright intended to sew her quilt. As Glaspell's direction says, the County Attorney at the end asks "facetiously" what the ladies call her method. He is laughing at her. But in my eyes, the men are ridiculous since they have entirely missed the little clues that tell the story. Glaspell makes it even more comical with the stage direction telling Mrs. Hale to hold her hand against her pocket. We know that is where she has placed the bird. Mrs. Wright had the last laugh on her husband, and Mrs. Hale and Mrs. Peters have the last laugh on the County Attorney and the Sheriff. They make fun of the ladies, but we can see how silly they are and laugh at them.

Is there any potential for developing an essay in this journal entry? Let's look again at the second step in the writing plan:

2. Look for energy, insight, surprise in your questions and answers.

Is there anything surprising, interesting, insightful in the student response? It's surprising to find, at the end of such a tense and gloomy play, that someone is laughing. Is this reaction eccentric, or is it based on something in Glaspell's text? Does this laughter, in other words, reveal anything about how an audience reasonably responds to *Trifles?*

To see if an essay can be developed from this hint, the student could go to the next step in our writing plan:

3. Focusing on those aspects of the questions and answers that seem promising, generate more questions and answers until you're ready to formulate a tentative thesis (that is, an arguable, supportable, and revealing assertion).

This step would involve simply going back through the play looking for other instances of humor, asking questions, considering how the play's darkly comic ending is prepared for, and noting whatever else seemed interesting. The student's goal thus might be to describe the role of humor in response to Glaspell's sombre play. This idea might not work out; there are no guarantees.

Here are some questions and answers from this rereading of the play:

More Questions and Answers

Q: The women are invited to come over to the stove, but they don't. Why not?

A: Mrs. Peters says "I'm not—cold." That seems silly because it was below zero the night before, and everyone is bundled up. The pause indicated by the dash maybe suggests she doesn't want to come over to the fire for some other reason. She says "I'm not" and then decides not to finish her statement.

She even takes a step forward, then stops. Why doesn't the County Attorney say, "Oh my, surely you ladies are cold? Please come on over." They aren't very thoughtful.

Q: Is there anything funny about the Sheriff? Is he bumbling the investigation?

A: The Sheriff sent Frank out to make the fire and to Morris Center for the man who went crazy. Frank seems to do all the work, but the Sheriff said he had his hands full. The attorney implies that the Sheriff is incompetent. What if the stove contained crucial evidence? Frank has burned it up. As the attorney says, "Somebody should have been left here yesterday." Maybe this isn't really funny, but the Sheriff seems a little silly. Barney Fife?

Q: Is Mr. Hale's telling of what happened the previous day comical?

A: Well, he does seem to wander about. He first explains about a load of potatoes, as if that somehow were relevant. He talks about discussing the telephone installation with Mr. Wright, which also seems irrelevant, but actually provides important insight into the story, because Wright said "all he asked was peace and quiet." OOOOh, that's a big clue, a foreshadowing I guess. I didn't see that the first time through.

Q: Does anyone laugh in the play?

A: Hale says Mrs. Wright laughed when he asked if he could see Mr. Wright. "I guess you would call it a laugh," he says. Hale wants to know why he can't see Wright if he's home, and she says, "'Cause he's dead." Hale asks what he died of, and she says "He died of a rope around his neck." Mrs. Wright is wisecracking, it seems.

—Mrs. Wright laughs again when Hale feels he ought to "make some conversation" and explains why he has come over. Here she is with her husband dead upstairs, strangled in the bed with her, so she says, and he's making conversation about putting in a phone.

—Also, the Attorney laughs when the Sheriff asks if he wants to see what Mrs. Peters is removing from the house. Here the Sheriff is actually being careful, and it is the Attorney who looks foolish. When he asks Mrs. Peters if she thinks of herself as being "married to the law," she says "Not—just that way." That is amusing because we have just seen her defy the law and her husband.

Q: What about when Mrs. Wright maintains she did not wake up when someone strangled her husband?

A: Her excuse, that she was "on the inside" and sleeps "sound," is laughable. It would be funny if someone were not dead.

Q: Is the Attorney comical in any way?

A: He goes upstairs first and then to the barn, ignoring the kitchen. He asks the Sheriff to assure him that there is "nothing that would point to any motive" in the kitchen. But the Sheriff has already bungled the investigation. He may not be comical, but he seems really dumb.

Q: How much did Mrs. Wright laugh before her husband's death?
A: Mrs. Hale says she stayed away "because it weren't cheerful." Mrs. Wright had brought some cheer to the place, the ladies will assume, by buying a canary.
Q: Is Mrs. Wright's laughter really laughter?
A: Mrs. Wright's laughter is nervous, overwhelmed laughter. When we hear about her laughing, we feel sorry for her. When we see the men laughing, we laugh at them.
Q: Is the ending really funny?
A: I'm not sure the ending is funny "ha-ha," but it is satisfying to see Mrs. Hale and Mrs. Peters cover-up the crime. Glaspell makes the audience want Mrs. Wright to get away with the murder. The investigators are made ridiculous, and Mr. Wright is made dispicable. That really is my point, isn't it? Glaspell makes the audience happy that Mrs. Peters decides to hide the crucial evidence.

As you can see, the student is moving toward a thesis here: namely, that Glaspell crafts the experience of the play so that the audience feels for Mrs. Wright, and not Mr. Wright. The evidence persuasively incriminates Mrs. Wright in a murder, yet the audience is likely to be pulling for her to get away with it. We sympathize with Mrs. Wright so much that we may, like the student, celebrate when Mrs. Hale puts the bird in her pocket. How does Glaspell manage to bring about this effect? Answering this question takes us to the fourth step in the sample writing plan:

4. Attempt to develop an argument supporting this tentative thesis; if you bog down, return to the previous steps until you're ready to go forward again.

With any luck, by the time you get to this step, you will have lots of material to work with. In looking through the play again, as you can see, the student did not find very much that was all that funny. He did find things that were ridiculous and absurd, but nothing really hilarious. He found that the characters' laughter was revealing, but not amusing. He came to see his own laughter at the end of the play as a response to the entire play.

Here then is the first draft of his thesis:

Although there are little flashes of humor, the play as a whole isn't funny, even though the reader laughs at the end.

And here is his assessment of this thesis:

I don't like my thesis yet. It seems vague and negative. It says more about what the play isn't, than what it is. I need to zero in on the response at the end, and how my reaction at the end is the product of what has gone before.

Here is the revised thesis, with the supporting points (taken from the notes provided):

Thesis: Glaspell crafts the experience of *Trifles* so that the audience is pleased, and even amused, by the concluding decision of Mrs. Hale and Mrs. Peters to cover up important evidence.

Support:

A. The Attorney and Sheriff seem arrogant and thoughtless. We do not want them to succeed.

- The first hint of their attitude: They crowd around the fire, leaving the women to stand apart.
- Both the Sheriff and Attorney make blunders: leaving no one at the crime scene, dismissing any possible evidence in the kitchen.
- They ignore any contribution the women could make to the investigation; in fact, they ridicule the women for their interest in Mrs. Wright's sewing and other activities.
- The men come and go, but the audience stays with the women on stage. The audience gets their point of view.

B. By the end of the play, Mrs. Wright's apparent murder of her husband seems understandable, maybe even justified.

- We hear statements indicating that Mr. Wright was a cold person.
- We see how the ladies understand Mrs. Wright's loneliness, and Mrs. Hale even begins to blame herself: "I could've come. I stayed away because it weren't cheerful—and that's why I ought to have come."
- We see how much the bird might have meant to Mrs. Wright, and how cruel Mr. Wright must have been to murder the bird.
- Mrs. Wright's crime seems even more understandable when Mrs. Peters says that she once would have sought revenge for such a similar cruelty: "When I was a girl—my kitten—there was a boy took a hatchet, and before my eyes—and before I could get there—[*Covers her face an instant.*] If they hadn't held me back I would have—[*Catches herself, looks upstairs where steps are heard, falters weakly.*]—hurt him."
- Mrs. Wright seems harmless and out of touch with things. She laughs when Mr. Hale asks about her husband, and says "He died of a rope around his neck." Glaspell thus uses some dark humor to lighten the seriousness of the crime.
- Her excuse of sleeping soundly and being on the other side of the bed is so ludicrous the audience has to laugh.
- The dead bird is seen on stage; Mr. Wright isn't.
- The crime itself seems unreal: how could you slip a rope around a man's neck and strangle him?
- Mrs. Hale and Mrs. Peters work toward their decision in front of us, showing the audience that they do struggle with the morality of obstructing the investigation.

The next step in the writing process:

5. Once you've arrived at a viable thesis and sketched out an argument and its support, then craft an introduction, a conclusion, and a title.

A good introduction says "hello," engaging the reader and moving energetically toward arguing the case. One way to engage the reader is simply to lay out clearly what the problem is that you're trying to solve. A good conclusion says "goodbye," giving the reader some kind of perspective on what has been covered. A good title gives the reader some idea of the essay's contents, and also entices them to read it.

Once you have the whole draft, feedback from readers (if your teacher allows it) can be very valuable. Readers can tell you if the title draws them in, if the introduction hooks them, if the argument is persuasive, if the conclusion is satisfying. If you don't have other readers, then you'll want to try to read your own work with fresh eyes, playing the role of an "objective" reader, looking for guidance in the final step:

6. Revise the whole thing, returning to any previous steps as needed. Use the proper format, and proofread.

Here is our student's final product:

Walton Brock
Professor Schimpf
English 101-059

"And Then She—Laughed": Glaspell's *Trifles* and the Reader's Response

A crime has been committed in a rural farmhouse. It appears that a woman has murdered her husband while he was sleeping in his bed. She has slipped a rope around his neck and coldly strangled him. Perhaps she drugged him beforehand, so he would not be able to struggle out of the noose. Or maybe she tied him up. Or perhaps she had an assistant. We do not know. All we do know is that the woman appears to have had a motive: her pet bird was strangled, presumably by this husband. We know also that the woman claims, unbelievably, that her husband was strangled in his bed while she slept beside him. While strangling a pet bird is very unkind, it is also very different from murdering your husband. Surely no reasonable person could approve of such a murder.

Yet somehow, in *Trifles*, Susan Glaspell manages to convince her audience that the bird's death is the greater crime. At the end of the play, when Mrs. Hale and Mrs. Peters decide to remove the bird's body, thus covering up crucial evidence, the audience is not horrified at this miscarriage of justice. Instead, we are relieved. Even more, we are amused. Why does the audience feel good at the end, even though we reasonably believe that Mrs. Wright will get

away with a terrible crime? The audience's experience, as
Glaspell constructs it, undermines sympathy for Mr. Wright
and the men who investigate his murder; and the experience
of the play develops sympathy and understanding for
Mrs. Wright and the women who cover up her crime.

From the beginning of the play, the men seem arrogant and
thoughtless. We do not want them to succeed. The first hint
of their attitude appears when they crowd around the fire,
leaving the women to stand in the cold. The women are feebly
encouraged to join them, but the men really pay little
attention to Mrs. Peters and Mrs. Hale. They ignore any
contribution the women could make to the investigation; in
fact, they ridicule the women for their interest in
Mrs. Wright's sewing and other activities. But the Sheriff
and Attorney are in no position to make fun of anyone, since
they make significant blunders in the investigation, leaving
no one at the crime scene overnight, and in effect dismissing
the possibility of important evidence in the kitchen.

One reason why the audience sees things from the point of
view of Mrs. Peters and Mrs. Hale is simply that the women
stay on stage. The men come and go, but the audience always
sees and hears Mrs. Peters and Mrs. Hale. Mrs. Hale and
Mrs. Peters work toward their decision in front of us,
revealing that they do struggle with the morality of
obstructing the investigation. They arrive at their
decision, and take the audience along with them, for a
variety of reasons. Mr. Wright apparently was a cold person,
and we see how the ladies understand Mrs. Wright's
loneliness. Mrs. Hale even blames herself for not providing
companionship: "I could've come. I stayed away because it
weren't cheerful—and that's why I ought to have come."

Given such a gloomy and lonely setting, the audience can
see how much the bird might have meant to Mrs. Wright, and
how cruel Mr. Wright must have been to murder the bird.

Also, the murdered bird is seen on stage; Mr. Wright is not. The bird is depicted as a source of joy; Mr. Wright is not. Mrs. Wright's crime seems even more understandable when Mrs. Peters says that she once would have sought revenge for such a similar cruelty:

"When I was a girl—my kitten—there was a boy took a hatchet, and before my eyes—and before I could get there—[Covers her face an instant.] If they hadn't held me back I would have—[Catches herself, looks upstairs where steps are heard, falters weakly.]—hurt him."

Although Mrs. Wright does not appear on stage, she hardly seems mean or vicious in Mr. Hale's report. In fact, she seems harmless and out of touch with things. She laughs when Mr. Hale asks about her husband, and says "He died of a rope around his neck." Her excuse, that she was sleeping soundly on the other side of the bed, is so ludicrous it approaches being amusing. The crime itself seems unreal: how could one slip a rope around a man's neck and strangle him?

The legal penalty for killing a bird is slight compared to the penalty for murder. It appears that Mrs. Wright is not going to be held accountable by the law, and she is not going to be held accountable by Glaspell's audience either. Glaspell carefully shapes the audience's response to Mrs. Wright's apparent action so that by the end of play, the audience is pulling for her to get away with it. Glaspell has the play end not with the decision by the ladies to obstruct justice, but with the facetious question by the Attorney. Thus, our final impression is of the way these men dismiss Mrs. Hale and Mrs. Peters, which underscores our sense of the way Mrs. Wright must have suffered. Mr. Wright certainly must have been worse than these men. He did an awful thing.

Political Strategies

Like reader-response criticism, the varieties of political criticism endorse the idea that different readers make meaning differently. From this perspective, it matters who is reading the work (or writing it), and for what purpose; thus, feminist criticism, which is one variety of political criticism, emphasizes that in the making of meaning, gender is especially important. Of course, individual readers can hardly be reduced to their sexuality (which is biological) or their gender (which is social). It is in fact possible to emphasize (or privilege) economic issues, or racial issues, or geographical issues—or any feature, in fact, of the writer, the reader, or the work. Since Glaspell's play clearly raises issues of gender, the questions here will try to suggest how you might gather ideas for a feminist reading.

The process of answering these questions and developing an essay won't be worked through here, since the reader-response example provided has already gone into such detail, and since it would likely be most useful for you to work through the process yourself.

Political Strategy Questions

1. The opening scene includes the positioning of the characters on the stage, and so you would want to consider the significance of where they are standing. Where are the women standing, and where are the men standing?
2. Toward the end of the play, Mrs. Hale urges Mrs. Peters to tell Minnie Wright that her preserves are not gone. She even suggests taking in the surviving jar as proof. What leads up to this decision? What are Mrs. Hale's reasons for suggesting this duplicity?
3. Consider the play's title. What is its significance? Who talks about "trifles" in the play? When Glaspell rewrote this play as a short story, she called it "A Jury of Her Peers." How do these two titles point to somewhat different aspects of the story? Which title do you prefer?
4. In what ways, particularly early in the play, do Mrs. Hale and Mrs. Peters reinforce the stereotype of women at the time of the play? Do they ever depart from that stereotype? Explain.
5. How do the men also represent a stereotype? Is this play critical of men? Does Glaspell have a political agenda, or is this simply a good story?
6. How might the investigation have gone differently if the County Attorney or Sheriff had been a woman? What if all the evidence remained the same except that Mr. Hale had discovered John Wright sitting in the rocking chair, with Minnie Wright upstairs in bed with a rope around her neck? Would the women have reacted differently?
7. Why do the men miss so many clues? Why do the women see them?

New Critical Strategies

Unlike reader-response and political criticism, which focus on a work's readers, New Criticism focuses on the work itself. Why does New Criticism focus on the work? The purpose is twofold and paradoxical: to show how the work is unified, and at the same time, to show how it is complex. You can locate the complexity in a work by looking for contradictions, paradoxes, tensions, levels of meaning, patterns of imagery—whatever gives the work richness. You can discover unity by considering what idea holds the work's various elements together, as if the work were an organic whole, a single entity composed of disparate elements. This central unifying idea, sometimes called the work's "theme," should be evident throughout the work, so close analysis of any particular scene or passage ought to reveal material you can use.

Here are some questions to illustrate a New Critical stance:

New Critical Strategy Questions

1. The women discover a number of items in the kitchen that can be seen as symbols. What are they? How do these images help make the story into more than just a crime story?

2. New Criticism especially values works that have no extraneous parts—or, to put it another way, that have an "organic" unity. Look at Mr. Hale's first speech and explain its contribution to the play. Why, for instance, is it significant that he has come to talk with John Wright about sharing the expense of a "party telephone"? Indeed, how many important facts are alluded to in this speech?

3. Mrs. Peters, as the wife of a sheriff, is in a particularly tricky position, being pulled in two directions. For New Criticism, such opposition and tension make a work richer. Identify those places in the play where Mrs. Peters feels the weight of her obligation to be a sheriff's wife.

4. Assuming that Minnie Wright has murdered her husband, what is the moral ambiguity of that action? Is the ambiguity resolved in the end? What happens to the opposition between right and wrong at the end of the play? Explain.

5. How are Minnie Wright and the strangled bird explicitly related? How does this connection contribute to the play's unity?

Deconstructive Strategies

A New Critical reading focuses on the work itself, assuming that the play is unified. A deconstructive reading also focuses on the work itself but makes the alternative assumption—that the work, if looked at closely and creatively enough, ultimately starts to unravel and divide. Oftentimes, this unraveling is sufficiently suggested by showing how the opposite of what seems obvious is actually plausible. It seems obvious, for instance, that we are supposed to feel sympathy for Minnie Wright, revulsion for John Wright, and agree with the ladies' decision to suppress evidence. A deconstructive stance might suggest, however, the shallowness of such an assumption.

Deconstructive Strategy Questions

1. How certain is the assumption that John Wright killed Minnie Wright's bird? Who else might have killed the bird? (That is, who else had access to the bird?) If we assume that someone other than John Wright may have killed the bird, how does our view of the murder of Wright change?

2. The women see things that the men either overlook or misunderstand. We may tend to think, then, that the women see everything clearly. What, in fact, do the women finally overlook in deciding to remove important evidence? In what way are they blinded? What do the men, for all their errors, see clearly?

3. Could there be a pun in Mrs. Hale's final comment, "knot it"? How could this pun be extended to other parts of the play, thus undermining inferences that seem secure? Are there other possible puns in the play?

4. Mrs. Peters says, "We don't know who killed him. We don't *know*." Would the evidence that the women have be enough to convince a jury beyond a rea-

sonable doubt that Mrs. Wright killed her husband? How many different theories (however outrageous) can you imagine that would explain all the evidence? Here is an obvious one you can pursue to get started: Mr. Wright, seeking revenge and an end to pain, framed Mrs. Wright. You explain how.

5. Assume the contrary of what seems obvious: Mrs. Wright is actually being truthful when she says she doesn't know who killed her husband. Explain.

6. When Hale says that "women are used to worrying over trifles," he is referring to the ladies' concern for Mrs. Wright's preserves. What if his statement is applied to the act that the ladies come to believe Mrs. Wright committed? Did Minnie Wright worry over a trifle? What if his statement is applied also to the County Attorney's remark immediately following? His question, "What would we do without the ladies?", is no doubt meant to be rhetorical (that is, he doesn't really expect an answer), but what if he is taken literally? How would the investigation have developed without the ladies?

Psychological Strategies

Deconstruction tries to unsettle what may seem settled, causing us to think again, think otherwise. Psychological criticism, while it does not set out to be unsettling, nonetheless often involves us in speculations and insights that *are* disturbing. Psychological criticism seeks, for instance, to expose those motivations and urges that would ordinarily be disguised and suppressed. Glaspell's play, in a sense, is about the motivations of the different characters. Here are some questions that will help you think in psychological terms about the play.

Psychological Strategy Questions

1. Mrs. Peters and Mrs. Hale have different personalities, different backgrounds. Compare and contrast their characters.

2. Mrs. Peters and Mrs. Hale apparently come to believe that Mrs. Wright did murder her husband—although they never say this to anyone, not even each other. They piece together, it seems, an understanding of Mrs. Wright's motivation. This understanding extends beyond just the fate of her bird, although that is crucial. What is it that Mrs. Peters and Mrs. Hale determine about Mrs. Wright's psychology? What is the evidence, and what do they make of it?

3. Mr. Wright, even though he is apparently murdered, gets little or no sympathy from most readers. Use the clues that the text provides and construct as sympathetic a psychological profile (or history) of him as you can. You will have to make up all sorts of things to provide an explanation for what we do know about him from the play. Help us to understand Mr. Wright sympathetically.

4. Same as Number 3, except create an *unsympathetic* profile. Write a psychological history that explains how and why Mr. Wright is a monster.

5. Consider how much of the story can be explained in terms of a desire to exert control. In other words, look at the actions of each character and ask, "How is this person trying to exercise control over others?"

Biographical, Historical, and New Historical Strategies

Criticism that incorporates a biographical, historical, or new historical stance requires you to do some research, applying whatever you can learn about the author's life to the play (biographical), or whatever you can learn about the author's time, or perhaps the work's time, to the play (historical), or whatever you can learn about systems of thinking to the play (new historical). Here are some questions that illustrate the kinds of things you can do historically.

Biographical, Historical, and New Historical Strategy Questions

1. Given only the few facts in the biographical note on Susan Glaspell, which appears right before the play (page 770), speculate on how Glaspell's life might have influenced *Trifles*.

2. In this play, we learn why one wife has murdered her husband (it seems), and we see another wife decide to hide crucial evidence from her husband, obstructing his work and the legal system. To most readers and viewers, these decisions seem defensible, even justified. Find a magazine from 1915 or 1916 (most libraries have collections of major magazines that go that far back; in some cases you may have to work with microfilm) and see what you can infer about the relationship between men and women at this time. How are men depicted? How are women depicted? How is their relationship depicted? Can you find any evidence that Glaspell's play is reflecting some underlying tension or frustration between the sexes?

3. Related to the previous question: in the history of women's struggle for equality, what is going on in the years preceding this play? (In addition to general historical surveys, such as you will find in an American history course, your librarian can also direct you to other appropriate historical works.) Does this play contribute anything to that struggle? Explain.

4. Investigate the case of Leo M. Frank, who was lynched in August of 1915. The reference book *What Happened When,* published by HarperPerennial, has a brief recounting in the entry for 1915 (see Section IV). How does the structure of that case compare to the structure of *Trifles?* How might Frank's case influence Glaspell's ideas about making sense of crime evidence?

18

Sophocles and Shakespeare: Three Case Studies

Everything is determined, the beginning as well as the end, by forces over which we have no control. It is determined for the insect as well as for the star. Human beings, vegetables, or cosmic dust, we all dance to a mysterious tune, intoned in the distance by an invisible piper.

—*Albert Einstein*

In this chapter, you'll find three classic plays: a Greek tragedy, a Shakespearean tragedy, and a Shakespearean comic romance. You'll also find a sampling—a tiny sliver—of the critical attention they have generated. These plays have fascinated audiences for centuries, and they continue to exert an influence on theatre in particular and culture in general. Actors aspire to be in them; directors want to direct them; filmmakers want their shot at them. You may well have read them yourself. They are plays that amply reward multiple encounters.

"*I never realized they had feelings.*"

Oedipus the King

Oedipus is the story of the guy who scored four touchdowns in his first varsity football game and then the next year fumbled away the game-winning touchdown at the goal line. It is the story of the cardiologist who made a singularly brilliant diagnosis early in her career, saving the lives of many children; and then years later made an error in judgment in a similar case, resulting in the patient's death, and her own eventual ruin. It is the story of a college president who immediately after taking office launches the most successful fund-raising campaign in the school's history, transforming the quality of life for hundreds of faculty and thousands of students; and then years later somehow finds himself indicted for tax evasion and misman-agement of funds, leading ultimately to his resignation and imprisonment.

Oedipus and the Rest of Us

Oedipus is far more than the very ancient story of a man who saved an entire city from disaster by solving a mysterious riddle; and then years later could not decipher the mystery of his own identity. For many generations Sophocles' most famous play has seemed to be a model for all our stories in which the same person who achieves stupendous success goes on eventually to just as stupendous disaster. It is a para-digm of human life, suggesting how unexpectedly and totally human fortunes can change. Sophocles' *Oedipus* is also, for Aristotle and many other readers for many hundreds of years, the preeminent model of tragedy as a literary genre.

For Freud, however, the story of Oedipus is a different kind of paradigm: it points to the son's desire to possess his mother—a desire that must be overcome to achieve a more mature psychological outlook. Freud's theory, even his supporters would agree, is very strange; but so is the story of Oedipus—which Freud did not invent. Freud (among other motivations) is trying to explain the enduring appeal of Sophocles' work. It cer-tainly is uncanny that Oedipus's strange story would speak to us at all, much less be taken as a paradigm for anything. It is, we cannot deny, a strange story.

The story itself would have already been very familiar to Sophocles' audience. Their interest in the play would not be in finding out *what* happened, but in seeing how Sophocles tells the story of what happened. Much of the play's energy depends on the audience's knowing more than the characters: when Oedipus vows, for instance, to bring vengeance upon the murderer of Laius, the audience knows that he is in fact dooming himself, since he will shortly realize that he is that murderer. Such irony, which runs throughout the play, is called "**tragic irony**," or "**dramatic irony**"—when a character does not realize the full implications of what he or she is saying. To see this kind of irony today, we need obviously to know the story, which goes something like this:

> In a prophecy, Laius and Jocasta, king and queen of Thebes, are told by an oracle that their son will kill his father and marry his mother. To avert this fate, they decide to get rid of the infant by leaving him on a moun-tainside with a metal pin stuck through his feet. The servant who was supposed to leave him has pity on him instead, and gives him to a shep-herd. The shepherd takes him to the king and queen of Corinth, who raise him as their own son. His name is "Oedipus," which means "swollen foot" ("OIDi" = swollen; "POUS" = foot).
>
> Oedipus later learns from another oracle that he is destined to kill his father and marry his mother. In horror, he flees Corinth, thinking to keep his parents safe. He meets an entourage at a crossroads, and in a fit of rage Oedipus kills them all.
>
> He then travels on to Thebes, a city that is being ravaged by the Sphinx, a flying monster with a lion's body and a woman's head. Oedipus cor-

rectly answers the Sphinx's riddle, which causes the Sphinx to kill herself. The riddle: "What travels on four feet in the morning, two feet at noon, and three feet in the afternoon?" The answer: "Man"—because he crawls as a baby, walks as an adult, and uses a cane as an old man. In Greek, "Oedipus" also suggests "He who knows [OIDe] the foot [POUS]"—fittingly enough, since he solves a riddle about feet.

For saving the Thebans from the Sphinx, Oedipus is rewarded with the throne and the Queen, Jocasta. Oedipus and Jocasta have children, and everything is fine until Oedipus, by a series of events depicted in Sophocles' play, relentlessly pursues the truth about his parentage, and finally comes to the conclusion that the man he killed was his father, and the woman he has married is his mother. He has thus fulfilled the prophecy he and his parents were trying to evade. He reveals his insight and is banished, calling into play yet another pun on his name: "He who is known to everyone" (PASI).

Aristotle and Tragedy

As Cedric Whitman puts it, "The *Oedipus Rex* passes almost universally for the greatest extant Greek play—an assumption based, no doubt, on Aristotle's preference" (*Sophocles: A Study of Heroic Humanism*, p. 123). Frederick Ahl agrees, saying that Aristotle "has formed our judgment" (*Sophocles's Oedipus: Evidence and Self-Conviction*, p. 16). Because Aristotle's critical ideas, which are significantly based on Sophocles' *Oedipus*, have had such an impact on the Western tradition's understanding of drama in general and tragedy in particular, it will be worthwhile to look at Aristotle's most important ideas. Indeed, some of Aristotle's terms have been so popular through the ages that they are still in use, as we shall see.

In his *Poetics* (fourth century BCE), Aristotle conceived of tragedy as involving a great man or woman who suffers a terrible fate, falling from the heights of power and prestige and accomplishment, to the depths of misery and despair. If the main character (or protagonist) is a bad or insignificant person, as Aristotle saw it, then their fall is not nearly so shocking as the wreck of a good and important person. Although the tragic hero should not seem to deserve what happens, at the same time he or she should not appear entirely innocent. Consider: If the disaster is completely undeserved, then it seems simply accidental, random, without any real meaning: stuff happens.

What is most tragic and moving to an audience, Aristotle argued, is the fall of a great character who is in between—who has some virtues, but also has a **tragic flaw,** or a *hamartia* to use Aristotle's still-current term. Although the character is in no sense simply reducible to his or her *harmatia*, this flaw is likely to be intimately bound up with the character's greatness: the flaw may even be an excess of a virtue, or a virtue in another situation, or it may just be an error of judgment rather than character. Oftentimes tragic heroes are guilty of pride, which many people would argue is a healthy emotion, up to a point (even though pride is one of the Seven Deadly Sins in the Christian tradition). The Greek term for excessive pride, which is sometimes called "overweening pride," is *hubris.* The football player, the physician, the administrator, or the riddle solver who naively believes on the basis of a past success that any future difficulties will be conquered, and who charges in with a blind confidence, may well be displaying *hubris*, and setting the stage for a reversal.

It is toward such a **reversal,** or *peripeteia* in Aristotle's terms, that a tragedy moves. At such a defining moment in the play, the hero's fortunes turn, changing direction, as the heroic becomes tragic. At some point the tragic hero experiences an *anagnorisis*—a recognition of what has happened, a courageous perception of his or her fate. The effect upon the audience of this undeserved suffering and insight explains, for Aristotle anyway, the popularity and utility of tragedy. After all, why in the world would any normal person want to endure the spectacle of a good man or woman suffering more than he or she deserves? Aristotle's explanation is that the audience experiences a *catharsis*—a releasing or venting of certain emotions that is both healthy and invigorating. This *catharsis* (or *katharsis*) is usually described in English as "the purgation of pity and fear." While scholars have argued over whether Aristotle means that tragedy somehow *eliminates* the audience's pity and fear, arousing and then exhausting these feelings completely, or that tragedy *refines* our fear and pity, controlling and balancing them, it seems clear in any event that experiencing tragedy is good for the audience, as Aristotle sees it.

Thus, for Aristotle the benefits of tragedy are psychological or even physiological: *catharsis* in fact is taken by Aristotle from ancient medical terminology. Other theorists at various times have argued for other benefits and purposes of tragedy: for instance, deterring the audience from similar errors of judgment; emphasizing the fragility of life, as even the greatest can meet disaster; preparing the audience to accept suffering; and even inspiring the audience, as the hero confronts his fate with nobility and courage.

For instance, if you were to decide to write a tragedy about Richard Nixon, you might point to the way he used his presidency to open up relations with China, thus establishing his stature. You would also want to reveal his *harmatia*, which might be seen as his desire to win no matter what, including covering up a break-in. Nixon, one could argue, displayed *hubris* in deciding to tape his conversations in the White House, thinking perhaps that history would be interested in how his great accomplishments were fashioned. Such pride in his private dealings created the Watergate tapes, which led ultimately to his downfall. The discovery of the Watergate tapes might be seen as the *peripeteia* of the Nixon plot, and the moment when Nixon decided that he must resign as the *anagnorisis*. Whether this play on Nixon would purge, inspire, deter, or enlighten the audience would depend both on the play and the audience. But, in any event, this modern tragedy would be quite different from the performance of an ancient Greek tragedy over 2,400 years ago. To understand *Oedipus* better, let's look briefly at the ancient Greek theatre.

The Greek Theatre

The word **tragedy** in Greek means literally "goat-song," which is obviously a very strange term for the plays we have inherited. There are no goats, singing or otherwise, in Sophocles' *Oedipus* or in the other major tragedies. The term points rather to the origins of Greek drama, which scholars' best guesses relate to very ancient religious rituals in honor of Dionysus, god of fertility and wine. It appears that these primitive rituals, performed in hopes of fertility and productive vines, included dismembering a goat and scattering its parts across the countryside as an offering to the god. The ceremony included, historians think, singing songs and dancing; and at some point someone apparently realized that a perfectly good goat was being destroyed, and that Dionysus would probably be just as pleased with the singing and dancing alone—and then the goat could be given as a prize for the best song. According to the great classical scholar, C. M. Bowra, "The songs told of heroic or mythical events, and in due course a speaker would stand out from the other singers and dramatize some incident in the story, and from this tragedy was born" (*The Greek Experience*, p. 129).

The poet Thespis is credited with adding the speaker to the singers, and the monumental importance of this step is indicated by the fact that even today another term for actors is "thespians." Curiously enough, the Greeks never used more than four actors; in *Oedipus*, we are told, Sophocles uses only three actors and a chorus. Since more than a dozen characters actually appear in *Oedipus*, one may certainly wonder how Sophocles' cast could be limited to three actors. The answer is that no more than three characters were on stage at any time, thus allowing an actor to play more than one role. By wearing masks, the actors were able to indicate when they changed from one character to another: they simply changed the mask—and, we would assume, their voices. There were, it appears, no women actors; female roles were played by men dressed up as women.

From our perspective, a mask would appear to be a considerable handicap for an actor, considering the importance of an actor's facial expressions. But the ancient Greek plays were acted outdoors in huge amphitheatres, holding perhaps 14,000 spectators—which tells us something important about the popularity of these plays. Much of the audience would be too far away to see an actor's facial expressions, and the masks, which were large and dramatically painted, helped the audience keep the characters straight. We might consider too how many characters even today have been effectively portrayed in some sort of mask—Batman, Spiderman, the Lone Ranger, Darth Vader, and others. In fact, masks are still associated with the theatre, which is often symbolized by two masks, one happy and the other sad.

The actors also wore padded costumes and extremely high-heeled shoes, making themselves larger than life; and their masks appear to have had mouthpieces to help the actors project their voices, sort of like small megaphones. Indeed, in the design of their outdoor theatres, the Greeks seem to have understood acoustics very well, making it possible for a huge crowd to hear distinctly one person speaking.

At the back of an elevated stage, the Greeks placed a building, the *skene*, which they used as a changing room and stage prop: the wall of the *skene* could be painted to suggest a particular setting; the roof could serve as a mountaintop, or gods could be lowered from it (the practice of lowering a god to extricate a character from some impossible situation came to be known, as previously noted, as *deus ex machina*, or "god from the machine"). In addition, by using the *skene's* wall as a backdrop, the Greeks helped to direct the actors' voices outward. Standing on a stage in front of the *skene*, the actors projected their voices out over a flat open surface, the *orchestra*—which is acoustically the ideal setup. In addition to reflecting sound, the orchestra was also used by the fifteen or so members of the chorus, who danced across the orchestra, moving together rhythmically in one direction for part of a chant or song (the *strophe*); then moving back across the orchestra in the other direction for the second part (the *antistrophe*). The chorus was often used to provide background information or to serve as townspeople. Beyond the orchestra the audience sat in tiered seats, again the perfect design. Thus, by placing the actors at the bottom of a kind of bowl, the Greeks ensured that the sound was not muffled by the front rows, and would carry nicely over the lower rows out to the farthest spectators.

Understanding the physical setting of Greek drama helps clarify a number of things about the plays themselves. For one thing, the plays depended on language rather than on-stage action. A play typically would be set in one place, indicated by the backdrop; events that occurred elsewhere would be reported on by (and to) the characters on stage. Hence, violence typically was not depicted for the audience, but was reported to them. While this arrangement might seem relatively ineffective, a mere accommodation to the conditions of the theatre, in reality what we imagine is often more horrible and affecting than what we actually see and hear.

It must have been a magnificent spectacle: thousands of people gathered around the masked, costumed, larger-than-life actors and the chanting, dancing chorus, their

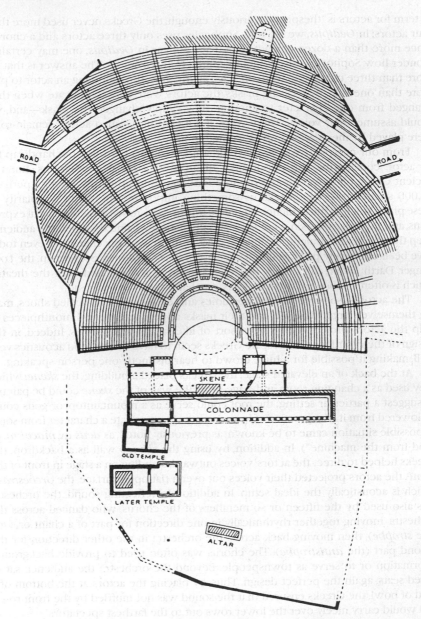

A modern reconstruction of the Athens theater of Sophocles' time.
From R.C. Flickinger, *The Greek Theatre and Its Drama* (1918).

voices booming out, filling the space, grabbing the audience. Although it has been suggested that Greek drama, with its poetic speeches alternating with singing and choreographed movement, might seem a lot like modern opera, it was probably in truth unlike anything we have today. Reading it on the page is undoubtedly a faint reflection of the real thing, but what we do have available is powerful and quite precious: of the thousands of that were performed, a few dozen plays survive, including only seven plays by Sophocles.

The remains of the Greek amphitheater at Epidauros. The design created excellent acoustics, allowing spectators on the top rows to hear distinctly.

Indeed, for more than five hundred years, Greeks came to the Dionysian festivals to see these dramatic performances. As the celebration evolved, various playwrights would compete against each other, with each competing author entering three major plays and one minor entertainment. The year that Sophocles' greatest play, *Oedipus the King*, was in the competition, sometime (most scholars agree) between 429 and 425 BCE, the first prize was won by Philocles, who has otherwise vanished from history. Perhaps we should not assume, in Philocles' absence, that the judges made an error, but many generations of readers have found it difficult to imagine a play better than Sophocles' masterpiece. (Sophocles, by the way, did win in some of the other years.)

The Play Itself

Sophocles not only lived a long life, about ninety years (496?–406 BCE), but he also lived a very full one, serving as treasurer, ambassador, musician, priest—and successful playwright. His most famous Oedipus play, originally titled *Oedipus Tyrannos*, first appeared when he was well over sixty. At the time, Athenians were just recovering from (or were in the midst of) an outbreak of the plague (430–428 BCE); and the play opens with Thebes undergoing a plague, a detail that Sophocles appears to have invented, thus connecting his audience immediately with the situation in the play. He wrote another play about Oedipus near the end of his life, *Oedipus at Colonus*, which portrays Oedipus at the end of *his* life.

Although *Oedipus Tyrannos* is usually translated as *Oedipus the King* or *Oedipus Rex* ("rex" is Latin for "king"), the Greek title is not really equal to "Oedipus the King." The term "tyrannos" was used to indicate rule by one person that was not inherited. At best, "tyrannos" is a neutral term, usually indicating that the ruler has seized absolute power; and the usage of most Greek writers, as classical scholars have shown, supports translating "tyrannos" as "tyrant." Oedipus, however, has not seized power; he has been given the throne of Thebes as a reward for saving the city from the Sphinx. Why then is he called "tyrannos" in Sophocles' title? It is not as if he has murdered the previous ruler and taken his place. In fact, however, as Sophocles' audience well knew, that is precisely what Oedipus has done, although he himself did not know what he was doing at the time. Sophocles' title is thus the play's first irony, reminding the audience of something they know that the characters do not know as the play begins. Oedipus will learn, as the plot unfolds, how he is "tyrannos," an absolute ruler or tyrant who has taken the throne by force.

SOPHOCLES (496?–406 BCE)

Oedipus the King

Translated by Dudley Fitts and Robert Fitzgerald

Characters

Oedipus	Messenger
A Priest	Shepherd of Laïos
Creon	Second Messenger
Teiresias	Chorus of Theban Elders
Iocastê	

Scene: Before the palace of Oedipus, King of Thebes. A central door and two lateral doors open onto a platform which runs the length of the façade. On the platform, right and left, are altars; and three steps lead down into the "orchestra," or chorus-ground. At the beginning of the action these steps are crowded by suppliants who have brought branches and chaplets of olive leaves and who lie in various attitudes of despair. Oedipus enters.

Prologue

Oedipus: My children, generations of the living
    In the line of Kadmos*, nursed at his ancient hearth:
    Why have you strewn yourself before these altars
    In supplication, with your boughs and garlands?
    The breath of incense rises from the city   5
    With a sound of prayer and lamentation.

                  Children,

2 *Kadmos* founder of Thebes

I would not have you speak through messengers,
And therefore I have come myself to hear you—
I, Oedipus, who bear the famous name.
(To a Priest.) You, there, since you are eldest in the company,   10
Speak for them all, tell me what preys upon you,
Whether you come in dread, or crave some blessing:
Tell me, and never doubt that I will help you
In every way I can; I should be heartless
Were I not moved to find you suppliant here.   15
Priest: Great Oedipus, O powerful King of Thebes!
You see how all the ages of our people
Cling to your altar steps: here are boys
Who can barely stand alone, and here are priests
By weight of age, as I am a priest of God,   20
And young men chosen from those yet unmarried;
As for the others, all that multitude,
They wait with olive chaplets in the squares,
At the two shrines of Pallas, and where Apollo
Speaks in the glowing embers.
                                    Your own eyes   25
Must tell you: Thebes is tossed on a murdering sea
And can not lift her head from the death surge.
A rust consumes the buds and fruits of the earth;
The herds are sick; children die unborn,
And labor is vain. The god of plague and pyre   30
Raids like detestable lightning through the city,
And all the house of Kadmos is laid waste,
All emptied, and all darkened: Death alone
Battens upon the misery of Thebes.

You are not one of the immortal gods, we know;   35
Yet we have come to you to make our prayer
As to the man surest in mortal ways
And wisest in the ways of God. You saved us
From the Sphinx, that flinty singer, and the tribute
We paid to her so long; yet you were never   40
Better informed than we, nor could we teach you:
It was some god breathed in you to set us free.

Therefore, O mighty King, we turn to you:
Find us our safety, find us a remedy,
Whether by counsel of the gods or men.   45
A king of wisdom tested in the past
Can act in a time of troubles, and act well.
Noblest of men, restore
Life to your city! Think how all men call you
Liberator for your triumph long ago;   50
Ah, when your years of kingship are remembered,
Let them not say *We rose, but later fell*—
Keep the State from going down in the storm!
Once, years ago, with happy augury,
You brought us fortune; be the same again!   55

No man questions your power to rule the land:
But rule over men, not over a dead city!
Ships are only hulls, citadels are nothing,
When no life moves in the empty passageways.

Oedipus: Poor children! You may be sure I know   60
All that you longed for in your coming here.
I know that you are deathly sick; and yet,
Sick as you are, not one is as sick as I.
Each of you suffers in himself alone
His anguish, not another's; but my spirit   65
Groans for the city, for myself, for you.

I was not sleeping, you are not waking me.
No, I have been in tears for a long while
And in my restless thought walked many ways.
In all my search, I found one helpful course,   70
And that I have taken: I have sent Creon,
Son of Menoikeus, brother of the Queen,
To Delphi, Apollo's place of revelation,
To learn there, if he can,
What act or pledge of mine may save the city.   75
I have counted the days, and now, this very day,
I am troubled, for he has overstayed his time.
What is he doing? He has been gone too long.
Yet whenever he comes back, I should do ill
To scant whatever duty God reveals.   80

Priest: It is a timely promise. At this instant
    They tell me Creon is here.

Oedipus: O Lord Apollo!
    May his news be fair as his face is radiant!

Priest: It could not be otherwise: he is crowned with bay,
    The chaplet is thick with berries.

Oedipus: We shall soon know;   85
    He is near enough to hear us now.

    Enter Creon.
    O Prince:
    Brother: son of Menoikeus:
    What answer do you bring us from the god?

Creon: A strong one. I can tell you, great afflictions
    Will turn out well, if they are taken well.   90

Oedipus: What was the oracle? These vague words
    Leave me still hanging between hope and fear.

Creon: Is it your pleasure to hear me with all these
    Gathered around us? I am prepared to speak,
    But should we not go in?

Oedipus: Let them all hear it.   95
    It is for them I suffer, more than for myself.

Creon: Then I will tell you what I heard at Delphi.

    In plain words
    The god commands us to expel from the land of Thebes
    An old defilement we are sheltering.   100

It is a deathly thing, beyond cure.
We must not let it feed upon us longer.
Oedipus: What defilement? How shall we rid ourselves of it?
Creon: By exile or death, blood for blood. It was
    Murder that brought the plague-wind on the city.   105
Oedipus: Murder of whom? Surely the god has named him?
Creon: My lord: long ago Laïos was our king,
    Before you came to govern us.
Oedipus: I know;
    I learned of him from others; I never saw him.
Creon: He was murdered; and Apollo commands us now   110
    To take revenge upon whoever killed him.
Oedipus: Upon whom? Where are they? Where shall we find a clue
    To solve that crime, after so many years?
Creon: Here in this land, he said.
                    If we make enquiry,
    We may touch things that otherwise escape us.   115
Oedipus: Tell me: Was Laïos murdered in his house,
    Or in the fields, or in some foreign country?
Creon: He said he planned to make a pilgrimage.
    He did not come home again.
Oedipus: And was there no one,
    No witness, no companion, to tell what happened?   120
Creon: They were all killed but one, and he got away
    So frightened that he could remember one thing only.
Oedipus: What was that one thing? One may be the key
    To everything, if we resolve to use it.
Creon: He said that a band of highwaymen attacked them,   125
    Outnumbered them, and overwhelmed the King.
Oedipus: Strange, that a highwayman should be so daring—
    Unless some faction here bribed him to do it.
Creon: We thought of that. But after Laïos' death
    New troubles arose and we had no avenger.   130
Oedipus: What troubles could prevent your hunting down the killers?
Creon: The riddling Sphinx's song
    Made us deaf to all mysteries but her own.
Oedipus: Then once more I must bring what is dark to light.
    It is most fitting that Apollo shows,   135
    As you do, this compunction for the dead.
    You shall see how I stand by you, as I should,
    To avenge the city and the city's god,
    And not as though it were for some distant friend,
    But for my own sake, to be rid of evil.   140
    Whoever killed King Laïos might—who knows?—
    Decide at any moment to kill me as well.
    By avenging the murdered king I protect myself.

    Come, then, my children: leave the altar steps,
    Lift up your olive boughs!
                 One of you go   145
    And summon the people of Kadmos to gather here.
    I will do all that I can; you may tell them that.

Exit a Page.

So, with the help of God,
We shall be saved—or else indeed we are lost.
Priest: Let us rise, children. It was for this we came,   150
And now the King has promised it himself.
Phoibos* has sent us an oracle; may he descend
Himself to save us and drive out the plague.

*Exeunt Oedipus and Creon into the palace by the central door. The
Priest and the Suppliants disperse right and left. After a short pause
the Chorus enters the orchestra from the Párados.*

Párodos

Strophe 1

Chorus: What is God singing in his profound
Delphi of gold and shadow?
What oracle for Thebes, the sunwhipped city?

Fear unjoints me, the roots of my heart tremble.

Now I remember, O Healer, your power, and wonder: 5
Will you send doom like a sudden cloud, or weave it
Like nightfall of the past?

Speak, speak to us, issue of holy sound:
Dearest to our expectancy: be tender!

Antistrophe 1

Let me pray to Athenê, the immortal daughter of Zeus,   10
And to Artemis her sister
Who keeps her famous throne in the market ring,
And to Apollo, bowman at the far butts of heaven—

O gods, descend! Like three streams leap against
The fires of our grief, the fires of darkness;   15
Be swift to bring us rest!

As in the old time from the brilliant house
Of air you stepped to save us, come again!

Strophe 2

Now our afflictions have no end,
Now all our stricken host lies down   20
And no man fights off death with his mind;

The noble plowland bears no grain,
And groaning mothers can not bear—

See, how our lives like birds take wing,
Like sparks that fly when a fire soars,   25
To the shore of the god of evening.

Antistrophe 2

The plague burns on, it is pitiless,
Though pallid children laden with death
Lie unwept in the stony ways,

152 *Phoibos* Apollo

And old gray women by every path   30
Flock to the strand about the altars

There to strike their breasts and cry
Worship of Phoibos in wailing prayers:
Be kind, God's golden child!

                                                        Strophe 3

There are no swords in this attack by fire,   35
No shields, but we are ringed with cries.
Send the besieger plunging from our homes
Into the vast sea-room of the Atlantic
Or into the waves that foam eastward of Thrace—
For the day ravages what the night spares—   40

Destroy our enemy, lord of the thunder!
Let him be riven by lightning from heaven!

                                                    Antistrophe 3

Phoibos Apollo, stretch the sun's bowstring,
That golden cord, until it sing for us,
Flashing arrows in heaven!
                        Artemis*, Huntress,   45
Race with flaring lights upon our mountains!
O scarlet god, O golden-banded brow,
O Theban Bacchos* in a storm of Maenads*,

Enter Oedipus, center.

Whirl upon Death, that all the Undying hate!
Come with blinding torches, come in joy!   50

Scene I

Oedipus: Is this your prayer? It may be answered. Come,
        Listen to me, act as the crisis demands,
        And you shall have relief from all these evils.

        Until now I was a stranger to this tale,
        As I had been a stranger to the crime.   5
        Could I track down the murderer without a clue?
        But now, friends,
        As one who became a citizen after the murder,
        I make this proclamation to all Thebans:
        If any man knows by whose hand Laïos, son of Labdakos,   10
        Met his death, I direct that man to tell me everything,
        No matter what he fears for having so long withheld it.
        Let it stand as promised that no further trouble
        Will come to him, but he may leave the land in safety.

        Moreover: If anyone knows the murderer to be foreign,   15
        Let him not keep silent: he shall have his reward from me.
        However, if he does conceal it; if any man
        Fearing for his friend or for himself disobeys this edict,
        Hear what I propose to do:

45 *Artemis* goddess of hunting   48 *Bacchos* god of wine   *Maenads* female attendants

I solemnly forbid the people of this country,   20
Where power and throne are mine, ever to receive that man
Or speak to him, no matter who he is, or let him
Join in sacrifice, lustration, or in prayer.
I decree that he be driven from every house,
Being, as he is, corruption itself to us: the Delphic   25
Voice of Zeus has pronounced this revelation.
Thus I associate myself with the oracle
And take the side of the murdered king.

As for the criminal, I pray to God—
Whether it be a lurking thief, or one of a number—   30
I pray that that man's life be consumed in evil and wretchedness.
And as for me, this curse applies no less
If it should turn out that the culprit is my guest here,
Sharing my hearth.
                    You have heard the penalty.
I lay it on you now to attend to this   35
For my sake, for Apollo's, for the sick
Sterile city that heaven has abandoned.
Suppose the oracle had given you no command:
Should this defilement go uncleansed for ever?
You should have found the murderer: your king,   40
A noble king, had been destroyed!
                    Now I,
Having the power that he held before me,
Having his bed, begetting children there
Upon his wife, as he would have, had he lived—
Their son would have been my children's brother,   45
If Laïos had had luck in fatherhood!
(But surely ill luck rushed upon his reign)—
I say I take the son's part, just as though
I were his son, to press the fight for him
And see it won! I'll find the hand that brought   50
Death to Labdakos' and Polydoros' child,
Heir of Kadmos' and Agenor's line.
And as for those who fail me,
May the gods deny them the fruit of the earth,
Fruit of the womb, and may they rot utterly!   55
Let them be wretched as we are wretched, and worse!

For you, for loyal Thebans, and for all
Who find my actions right, I pray the favor
Of justice, and of all the immortal gods.
Choragos: Since I am under oath, my lord, I swear   60
    I did not do the murder, I can not name
    The murderer. Might not the oracle
    That has ordained the search tell where to find him?
Oedipus: An honest question. But no man in the world
    Can make the gods do more than the gods will.   65
Choragos: There is one last expedient—
Oedipus: Tell me what it is.

Though it seem slight, you must not hold it back.
Choragos: A lord clairvoyant to the lord Apollo,
    As we all know, is the skilled Teiresias.
    One might learn much about this from him, Oedipus.   70
Oedipus: I am not wasting time:
    Creon spoke of this, and I have sent for him—
    Twice, in fact; it is strange that he is not here.
Choragos: The other matter—that old report—seems useless.
Oedipus: Tell me. I am interested in all reports.   75
Choragos: The King was said to have been killed by highwaymen.
Oedipus: I know. But we have no witnesses to that.
Choragos: If the killer can feel a particle of dread,
    Your curse will bring him out of hiding!
Oedipus: No.
    The man who dared that act will fear no curse.   80

Enter the blind seer Teiresias, led by a Page.

Choragos: But there is one man who may detect the criminal.
    This is Teiresias, this is the holy prophet
    In whom, alone of all men, truth was born.
Oedipus: Teiresias: seer: student of mysteries,
    Of all that's taught and all that no man tells,   85
    Secrets of Heaven and secrets of the earth:
    Blind though you are, you know the city lies
    Sick with plague; and from this plague, my lord,
    We find that you alone can guard or save us.

    Possibly you did not hear the messengers?   90
    Apollo, when we sent to him,
    Sent us back word that this great pestilence
    Would lift, but only if we established clearly
    The identity of those who murdered Laïos.
    They must be killed or exiled.
                            Can you use   95
    Birdflight or any art of divination
    To purify yourself, and Thebes, and me
    From this contagion? We are in your hands.
    There is no fairer duty
    Than that of helping others in distress.   100
Teiresias: How dreadful knowledge of the truth can be
    When there's no help in truth! I knew this well,
    But made myself forget. I should not have come.
Oedipus: What is troubling you? Why are your eyes so cold?
Teiresias: Let me go home. Bear your own fate, and I'll   105
    Bear mine. It is better so: trust what I say.
Oedipus: What you say is ungracious and unhelpful
    To your native country. Do not refuse to speak.
Teiresias: When it comes to speech, your own is neither temperate
    Nor opportune. I wish to be more prudent.   110
Oedipus: In God's name, we all beg you—
Teiresias: You are all ignorant.

No; I will never tell you what I know.
Now it is my misery; then, it would be yours.
Oedipus: What! You do know something, and will not tell us?
You would betray us all and wreck the State?   115
Teiresias: I do not intend to torture myself, or you.
Why persist in asking? You will not persuade me.
Oedipus: What a wicked old man you are! You'd try a stone's
Patience! Out with it! Have you no feeling at all?
Teiresias: You call me unfeeling. If you could only see   120
The nature of your own feelings . . .
Oedipus: Why,
Who would not feel as I do? Who could endure
Your arrogance toward the city?
Teiresias: What does it matter!
Whether I speak or not; it is bound to come.
Oedipus: Then, if "it" is bound to come, you are bound to tell me.   125
Teiresias: No, I will not go on. Rage as you please.
Oedipus: Rage? Why not!
                            And I'll tell you what I think:
You planned it, you had it done, you all but
Killed him with your own hands: if you had eyes,
I'd say the crime was yours, and yours alone.   130
Teiresias: So? I charge you, then,
Abide by the proclamation you have made:
From this day forth
Never speak again to these men or to me;
You yourself are the pollution of this country.   135
Oedipus: You dare say that! Can you possibly think you have
Some way of going free, after such insolence?
Teiresias: I have gone free. It is the truth sustains me.
Oedipus: Who taught you shamelessness? It was not your craft.
Teiresias: You did. You made me speak. I did not want to.   140
Oedipus: Speak what? Let me hear it again more clearly.
Teiresias: Was it not clear before? Are you tempting me?
Oedipus: I did not understand it. Say it again.
Teiresias: I say that you are the murderer whom you seek.
Oedipus: Now twice you have spat out infamy. You'll pay for it!   145
Teiresias: Would you care for more? Do you wish to be really angry?
Oedipus: Say what you will. Whatever you say is worthless.
Teiresias: I say you live in hideous shame with those
Most dear to you. You can not see the evil.
Oedipus: It seems you can go on mouthing like this for ever.   150
Teiresias: I can, if there is power in truth.
Oedipus: There is:
But not for you, not for you,
You sightless, witless, senseless, mad old man!
Teiresias: You are the madman. There is no one here
Who will not curse you soon, as you curse me.   155
Oedipus: You child of endless night! You can not hurt me
Or any other man who sees the sun.
Teiresias: True: it is not from me your fate will come.
That lies within Apollo's competence,

As it is his concern.

Oedipus: Tell me: 160
    Are you speaking for Creon, or for yourself?

Teiresias: Creon is no threat. You weave your own doom.

Oedipus: Wealth, power, craft of statesmanship!
    Kingly position, everywhere admired!
    What savage envy is stored up against these,   165
    If Creon, whom I trusted, Creon my friend,
    For this great office which the city once
    Put in my hands unsought—if for this power
    Creon desires in secret to destroy me!

    He has brought this decrepit fortune-teller, this   170
    Collector of dirty pennies, this prophet fraud—
    Why, he is no more clairvoyant than I am!

                    Tell us:
    Has your mystic mummery ever approached the truth?
    When that hellcat the Sphinx was performing here,
    What help were you to these people?   175
    Her magic was not for the first man who came along:
    It demanded a real exorcist. Your birds—
    What good were they? or the gods, for the matter of that?
    But I came by,
    Oedipus, the simple man, who knows nothing—   180
    I thought it out for myself, no birds helped me!
    And this is the man you think you can destroy,
    That you may be close to Creon when he's king!
    Well, you and your friend Creon, it seems to me,
    Will suffer most. If you were not an old man,   185
    You would have paid already for your plot.

Choragos: We can not see that his words or yours
    Have been spoken except in anger, Oedipus,
    And of anger we have no need. How can God's will
    Be accomplished best? That is what most concerns us.   190

Teiresias: You are a king. But where argument's concerned
    I am your man, as much a king as you.
    I am not your servant, but Apollo's.
    I have no need of Creon to speak for me.

    Listen to me. You mock my blindness, do you?   195
    But I say that you, with both your eyes, are blind:
    You can not see the wretchedness of your life,
    Nor in whose house you live, no, nor with whom.
    Who are your father and mother? Can you tell me?
    You do not even know the blind wrongs   200
    That you have done them, on earth and in the world below.
    But the double lash of your parents' curse will whip you
    Out of this land some day, with only night
    Upon your precious eyes.
    Your cries then—where will they not be heard?   205
    What fastness of Kithairon* will not echo them?

206 *Kithairon* where Oedipus was abandoned

And that bridal-descant of yours—you'll know it then,
The song they sang when you came here to Thebes
And found your misguided berthing.
All this, and more, that you can not guess at now,   210
Will bring you to yourself among your children.

Be angry, then. Curse Creon. Curse my words.
I tell you, no man that walks upon the earth
Shall be rooted out more horribly than you.
Oedipus: Am I to bear this from him?—Damnation   215
    Take you! Out of this place! Out of my sight!
Teiresias: I would not have come at all if you had not asked me.
Oedipus: Could I have told that you'd talk nonsense, that
    You'd come here to make a fool of yourself, and of me?
Teiresias: A fool? Your parents thought me sane enough.   220
Oedipus: My parents again!—Wait: who were my parents?
Teiresias: This day will give you a father, and break your heart.
Oedipus: Your infantile riddles! Your damned abracadabra!
Teiresias: You were a great man once at solving riddles.
Oedipus: Mock me with that if you like; you will find it true.   225
Teiresias: It was true enough. It brought about your ruin.
Oedipus: But if it saved this town?
Teiresias (to the Page):   Boy, give me your hand.
Oedipus: Yes, boy; lead him away.
                    —While you are here
    We can do nothing. Go; leave us in peace.
Teiresias: I will go when I have said what I have to say.   230
    How can you hurt me? And I tell you again:
    The man you have been looking for all this time,
    The damned man, the murderer of Laïos,
    That man is in Thebes. To your mind he is foreignborn,
    But it will soon be shown that he is a Theban,   235
    A revelation that will fail to please.

                        A blind man,
    Who has his eyes now; a penniless man, who is rich now;
    And he will go tapping the strange earth with his staff;
    To the children with whom he lives now he will be
    Brother and father—the very same; to her   240
    Who bore him, son and husband—the very same
    Who came to his father's bed, wet with his father's blood.

    Enough. Go think that over.
    If later you find error in what I have said,
    You may say that I have no skill in prophecy.   245

Exit Teiresias, led by his Page. Oedipus goes into the palace.

Ode I

Strophe 1

Chorus: The Delphic stone of prophecies
        Remembers ancient regicide
        And a still bloody hand.

That killer's hour of flight has come.
He must be stronger than riderless   5
Coursers of untiring wind,
For the son of Zeus armed with his father's thunder
Leaps in lightning after him;
And the Furies follow him, the sad Furies.

Antistrophe 1

Holy Parnassos' peak of snow   10
Flashes and blinds that secret man,
That all shall hunt him down:
Though he may roam the forest shade
Like a bull gone wild from pasture
To rage through glooms of stone.   15
Doom comes down on him; flight will not avail him;
For the world's heart calls him desolate,
And the immortal Furies follow, for ever follow.

Strophe 2

But now a wilder thing is heard
From the old man skilled at hearing Fate in the wingbeat of a bird.   20
Bewildered as a blown bird, my soul hovers and can not find
Foothold in this debate, or any reason or rest of mind.
But no man ever brought—none can bring
Proof of strife between Thebes' royal house,
Labdakos' line, and the son of Polybos*;   25
And never until now has any man brought word
Of Laïos' dark death staining Oedipus the King.

Antistrophe 2

Divine Zeus and Apollo hold
Perfect intelligence alone of all tales ever told;
And well though this diviner works, he works in his own night;   30
No man can judge that rough unknown or trust in second sight,
For wisdom changes hands among the wise.
Shall I believe my great lord criminal
At a raging word that a blind old man let fall?
I saw him, when the carrion woman faced him of old,   35
Prove his heroic mind! These evil words are lies.

Scene II

Creon: Men of Thebes:
    I am told that heavy accusations
    Have been brought against me by King Oedipus.

I am not the kind of man to bear this tamely.

If in these present difficulties   5
He holds me accountable for any harm to him
Through anything I have said or done—why, then,
I do not value life in this dishonor.

It is not as though this rumor touched upon
Some private indiscretion. The matter is grave.   10
The fact is that I am being called disloyal

25 *Polybos* Oedipus's foster father

To the State, to my fellow citizens, to my friends.

Choragos: He may have spoken in anger, not from his mind.

Creon: But did you not hear him say I was the one

    Who seduced the old prophet into lying?   15

Choragos: The thing was said; I do not know how seriously.

Creon: But you were watching him! Were his eyes steady?

    Did he look like a man in his right mind?

Choragos: I do not know.

    I can not judge the behavior of great men.

    But here is the King himself.

    Enter Oedipus.

Oedipus: So you dared come back.   20

    Why? How brazen of you to come to my house,

    You murderer!

               Do you think I do not know

    That you plotted to kill me, plotted to steal my throne?

    Tell me, in God's name: am I coward, a fool,

    That you should dream you could accomplish this?   25

    A fool who could not see your slippery game?

    A coward, not to fight back when I saw it?

    You are the fool, Creon, are you not? hoping

    Without support or friends to get a throne?

    Thrones may be won or bought: you could do neither.   30

Creon: Now listen to me. You have talked; let me talk, too.

    You can not judge unless you know the facts.

Oedipus: You speak well: there is one fact; but I find it hard

    To learn from the deadliest enemy I have.

Creon: That above all I must dispute with you.   35

Oedipus: That above all I will not hear you deny.

Creon: If you think there is anything good in being stubborn

    Against all reason, then I say you are wrong.

Oedipus: If you think a man can sin against his own kind

    And not be punished for it, I say you are mad.   40

Creon: I agree. But tell me: what have I done to you?

Oedipus: You advised me to send for that wizard, did you not?

Creon: I did. I should do it again.

Oedipus: Very well. Now tell me:

    How long has it been since Laïos—

Creon: What of Laïos?

Oedipus: Since he vanished in that onset by the road?   45

Creon: It was long ago, a long time.

Oedipus: And this prophet,

    Was he practicing here then?

Creon: He was; and with honor, as now.

Oedipus: Did he speak of me at that time?

Creon: He never did;

    At least, not when I was present.

Oedipus: But . . . the enquiry?

    I suppose you held one?

Creon: We did, but we learned nothing.   50

Oedipus: Why did the prophet not speak against me then?
Creon: I do not know; and I am the kind of man
    Who holds his tongue when he has no facts to go on.
Oedipus: There's one fact that you know, and you could tell it.
Creon: What fact is that? If I know it, you shall have it.   55
Oedipus: If he were not involved with you, he could not say
    That it was I who murdered Laïos.
Creon: If he says that, you are the one that knows it!—
    But now it is my turn to question you.
Oedipus: Put your questions. I am no murderer.   60
Creon: First then: You married my sister?
Oedipus: I married your sister.
Creon: And you rule the kingdom equally with her?
Oedipus: Everything that she wants she has from me.
Creon: And I am the third, equal to both of you?
Oedipus: That is why I call you a bad friend.   65
Creon: No. Reason it out, as I have done.
    Think of this first: Would any sane man prefer
    Power, with all a king's anxieties,
    To that same power and the grace of sleep?
    Certainly not I.   70
    I have never longed for the king's power—only his rights.
    Would any wise man differ from me in this?
    As matters stand, I have my way in everything
    With your consent, and no responsibilities.
    If I were king, I should be a slave to policy.   75

    How could I desire a scepter more
    Than what is now mine—untroubled influence?
    No, I have not gone mad; I need no honors,
    Except those with the perquisites I have now.
    I am welcome everywhere; every man salutes me,   80
    And those who want your favor seek my ear,
    Since I know how to manage what they ask.
    Should I exchange this ease for that anxiety?
    Besides, no sober mind is treasonable.
    I hate anarchy   85
    And never would deal with any man who likes it.

    Test what I have said. Go to the priestess
    At Delphi, ask if I quoted her correctly.
    And as for this other thing: if I am found
    Guilty of treason with Teiresias,   90
    Then sentence me to death! You have my word
    It is a sentence I should cast my vote for—
    But not without evidence!
                 You do wrong
    When you take good men for bad, bad men for good.
    A true friend thrown aside—why, life itself   95
    Is not more precious!
             In time you will know this well:
    For time, and time alone, will show the just man,

Though scoundrels are discovered in a day.
Choragos: This is well said, and a prudent man would ponder it.
    Judgments too quickly formed are dangerous.   100
Oedipus: But is he not quick in his duplicity?
    And shall I not be quick to parry him?
    Would you have me stand still, hold my peace, and let
    This man win everything, through my inaction?
Creon: And you want—what is it, then? To banish me?   105
Oedipus: No, not exile. It is your death I want,
    So that all the world may see what treason means.
Creon: You will persist, then? You will not believe me?
Oedipus: How can I believe you?
Creon: Then you are a fool.
Oedipus: To save myself?
Creon: In justice, think of me.   110
Oedipus: You are evil incarnate.
Creon: But suppose that you are wrong?
Oedipus: Still I must rule.
Creon: But not if you rule badly.
Oedipus: O city, city!
Creon: It is my city, too!
Choragos: Now, my lords, be still. I see the Queen,
    Iocastê, coming from her palace chambers;   115
    And it is time she came, for the sake of you both.
    This dreadful quarrel can be resolved through her.

    Enter Iocastê.

Iocastê: Poor foolish men, what wicked din is this?
    With Thebes sick to death, is it not shameful
    That you should rake some private quarrel up?   120
    (*To Oedipus.*) Come into the house.
                      —And you, Creon, go now:
    Let us have no more of this tumult over nothing.
Creon: Nothing? No, sister: what your husband plans for me
    Is one of two great evils: exile or death.
Oedipus: He is right.
            Why, woman, I have caught him squarely   125
    Plotting against my life.
Creon: No! Let me die
    Accurst if ever I have wished you harm!
Iocastê: Ah, believe it, Oedipus!
    In the name of the gods, respect this oath of his
    For my sake, for the sake of these people here!   130
                                 Strophe 1
Choragos: Open your mind to her, my lord. Be ruled by her, I beg you!
Oedipus: What would you have me do?
Choragos: Respect Creon's word. He has never spoken like a fool,
    And now he has sworn an oath.
Oedipus: You know what you ask?
Choragos: I do.
Oedipus: Speak on, then.

Choragos: A friend so sworn should not be baited so,   135
  In blind malice, and without final proof.
Oedipus: You are aware, I hope, that what you say
  Means death for me, or exile at the least.

Strophe 2

Choragos: No, I swear by Helios, first in Heaven!
  May I die friendless and accurst,   140
  The worst of deaths, if ever I meant that!
    It is the withering fields
      That hurt my sick heart:
    Must we bear all these ills,
      And now your bad blood as well?   145
Oedipus: Then let him go. And let me die, if I must,
  Or be driven by him in shame from the land of Thebes.
  It is your unhappiness, and not his talk,
  That touches me.
            As for him—
  Wherever he goes, hatred will follow him.   150
Creon: Ugly in yielding, as you were ugly in rage!
  Natures like yours chiefly torment themselves.
Oedipus: Can you not go? Can you not leave me?
Creon: I can.
  You do not know me; but the city knows me,
  And in its eyes I am just, if not in yours.   155

  Exit Creon.

Antistrophe 1

Choragos: Lady Iocastê, did you not ask the King to go to his chambers?
Iocastê: First tell me what has happened.
Choragos: There was suspicion without evidence; yet it rankled
  As even false charges will.
Iocastê: On both sides?
Choragos: On both.
Iocastê: But what was said?
Choragos: Oh let it rest, let it be done with! Have we not suffered enough?   160
Oedipus: You see to what your decency has brought you:
  You have made difficulties where my heart saw none.

Antistrophe 2

Choragos: Oedipus, it is not once only I have told you—
  You must know I should count myself unwise   165
  To the point of madness, should I now forsake you—
  You, under whose hand,
    In the storm of another time,
  Our dear land sailed out free.
    But now stand fast at the helm!   170
Iocastê: In God's name, Oedipus, inform your wife as well:
  Why are you so set in this hard anger?
Oedipus: I will tell you, for none of these men deserves
  My confidence as you do. It is Creon's work,
  His treachery, his plotting against me.   175

Iocastê: Go on, if you can make this clear to me.
Oedipus: He charges me with the murder of Laïos.
Iocastê: Has he some knowledge? Or does he speak from hearsay?
Oedipus: He would not commit himself to such a charge,
    But he has brought in that damnable soothsayer   180
    To tell his story.
Iocastê: Set your mind at rest.
    If it is a question of soothsayers, I tell you
    That you will find no man whose craft gives knowledge
    Of the unknowable.
                  Here is my proof:

    An oracle was reported to Laïos once   185
    (I will not say from Phoibos himself, but from
    His appointed ministers, at any rate)
    That his doom would be death at the hands of his own son—
    His son, born of his flesh and of mine!

    Now, you remember the story: Laïos was killed   190
    By marauding strangers where three highways meet;
    But his child had not been three days in this world
    Before the King had pierced the baby's ankles
    And left him to die on a lonely mountainside.

    Thus, Apollo never caused that child   195
    To kill his father, and it was not Laïos' fate
    To die at the hands of his son, as he had feared.
    This is what prophets and prophecies are worth!
    Have no dread of them.
                  It is God himself
    Who can show us what he wills, in his own way.   200
Oedipus: How strange a shadowy memory crossed my mind,
    Just now while you were speaking; it chilled my heart.
Iocastê: What do you mean? What memory do you speak of?
Oedipus: If I understand you, Laïos was killed
    At a place where three roads meet.
Iocastê: So it was said;   205
    We have no later story.
Oedipus: Where did it happen?
Iocastê: Phokis, it is called: at a place where the Theban Way
    Divides into the roads toward Delphi and Daulia.
Oedipus: When?
Iocastê: We had the news not long before you came
    And proved the right to your succession here.   210
Oedipus: Ah, what net has God been weaving for me?
Iocastê: Oedipus! Why does this trouble you?
Oedipus: Do not ask me yet.
    First, tell me how Laïos looked, and tell me
    How old he was.
Iocastê: He was tall, his hair just touched
    With white; his form was not unlike your own.   215
Oedipus: I think that I myself may be accurst
    By my own ignorant edict.

Iocastê: You speak strangely.
  It makes me tremble to look at you, my King.
Oedipus: I am not sure that the blind man can not see.
  But I should know better if you were to tell me—   220
Iocastê: Anything—though I dread to hear you ask it.
Oedipus: Was the King lightly escorted, or did he ride
  With a large company, as a ruler should?
Iocastê: There were five men with him in all: one was a herald,
  And a single chariot, which he was driving.   225
Oedipus: Alas, that makes it plain enough!

                                      But who—
  Who told you how it happened?
Iocastê: A household servant,
  The only one to escape.
Oedipus: And is he still
  A servant of ours?
Iocastê: No; for when he came back at last
  And found you enthroned in the place of the dead king,   230
  He came to me, touched my hand with his, and begged
  That I would send him away to the frontier district
  Where only the shepherds go—
  As far away from the city as I could send him.
  I granted his prayer; for although the man was a slave,   235
  He had earned more than this favor at my hands.
Oedipus: Can he be called back quickly?
Iocastê: Easily.
  But why?
Oedipus: I have taken too much upon myself
  Without enquiry; therefore I wish to consult him.
Iocastê: Then he shall come.

                          But am I not one also   240
  To whom you might confide these fears of yours?
Oedipus: That is your right; it will not be denied you,
  Now least of all; for I have reached a pitch
  Of wild foreboding. Is there anyone
  To whom I should sooner speak?   245

  Polybos of Corinth is my father.
  My mother is a Dorian: Meropê.
  I grew up chief among the men of Corinth
  Until a strange thing happened—
  Not worth my passion, it may be, but strange.   250

  At a feast, a drunken man maundering in his cups
  Cries out that I am not my father's son!

  I contained myself that night, though I felt anger
  And a sinking heart. The next day I visited
  My father and mother, and questioned them. They stormed,   255
  Calling it all the slanderous rant of a fool;
  And this relieved me. Yet the suspicion
  Remained always aching in my mind;
  I knew there was talk; I could not rest;
  And finally, saying nothing to my parents,   260

I went to the shrine at Delphi.
The god dismissed my question without reply;
He spoke of other things.
      Some were clear,
Full of wretchedness, dreadful, unbearable:
As, that I should lie with my own mother, breed   265
Children from whom all men would turn their eyes;
And that I should be my father's murderer.

I heard all this, and fled. And from that day
Corinth to me was only in the stars
Descending in that quarter of the sky,   270
As I wandered farther and farther on my way
To a land where I should never see the evil
Sung by the oracle. And I came to this country
Where, so you say, King Laïos was killed.

I will tell you all that happened there, my lady.   275

There were three highways
Coming together at a place I passed;
And there a herald came towards me, and a chariot
Drawn by horses, with a man such as you describe
Seated in it. The groom leading the horses   280
Forced me off the road at his lord's command;
But as this charioteer lurched over towards me
I struck him in my rage. The old man saw me
And brought his double goad down upon my head
As I came abreast.
      He was paid back, and more!   285
Swinging my club in this right hand I knocked him
Out of his car, and he rolled on the ground.
          I killed him.

I killed them all.
Now if that stranger and Laïos were—kin,
Where is a man more miserable than I?   290
More hated by the gods? Citizen and alien alike
Must never shelter me or speak to me—
I must be shunned by all.
       And I myself
Pronounced this malediction upon myself!

Think of it: I have touched you with these hands,   295
These hands that killed your husband. What defilement!

Am I all evil, then? It must be so,
Since I must flee from Thebes, yet never again
See my own countrymen, my own country,
For fear of joining my mother in marriage   300
And killing Polybos, my father.
      Ah,
If I was created so, born to this fate,

Who could deny the savagery of God?

O holy majesty of heavenly powers!
May I never see that day! Never!   305
Rather let me vanish from the race of men
Than know the abomination destined me!
Choragos: We too, my lord, have felt dismay at this.
But there is hope: you have yet to hear the shepherd.
Oedipus: Indeed, I fear no other hope is left me.   310
Iocastê: What do you hope from him when he comes?
Oedipus: This much:
If his account of the murder tallies with yours,
Then I am cleared.
Iocastê: What was it that I said
Of such importance?
Oedipus: Why, "marauders," you said,
Killed the King, according to this man's story.   315
If he maintains that still, if there were several,
Clearly the guilt is not mine: I was alone.
But if he says one man, singlehanded, did it,
Then the evidence all points to me.
Iocastê: You may be sure that he said there were several;   320
And can he call back that story now? He can not.
The whole city heard it as plainly as I.
But suppose he alters some detail of it:
He can not ever show that Laïos' death
Fulfilled the oracle: for Apollo said
My child was doomed to kill him; and my child—   325
Poor baby!—it was my child that died first.

No. From now on, where oracles are concerned,
I would not waste a second thought on any.
Oedipus: You may be right.
                             But come: let someone go   330
For the shepherd at once. This matter must be settled.
Iocastê: I will send for him.
I would not wish to cross you in anything,
And surely not in this.—Let us go in.

Exeunt into the palace.

Ode II

Chorus: Let me be reverent in the ways of right,   *Strophe 1*
Lowly the paths I journey on;
Let all my words and actions keep
The laws of the pure universe
From highest Heaven handed down.   5
For Heaven is their bright nurse,
Those generations of the realms of light;
Ah, never of mortal kind were they begot,

Nor are they slaves of memory, lost in sleep:
Their Father is greater than Time, and ages not.   10

Antistrophe 1

The tyrant is a child of Pride
Who drinks from his great sickening cup
Recklessness and vanity,
Until from his high crest headlong
He plummets to the dust of hope.   15
That strong man is not strong.
But let no fair ambition be denied;
May God protect the wrestler for the State
In government, in comely policy,
Who will fear God, and on His ordinance wait.   20

Strophe 2

Haughtiness and the high hand of disdain
Tempt and outrage God's holy law;
And any mortal who dares hold
No immortal Power in awe
Will be caught up in a net of pain: 25
The price for which his levity is sold.
Let each man take due earnings, then,
And keep his hands from holy things,
And from blasphemy stand apart—
Else the crackling blast of heaven   30
Blows on his head, and on his desperate heart;
Though fools will honor impious men,
In their cities no tragic poet sings.

Antistrophe 2

Shall we lose faith in Delphi's obscurities,
We who have heard the world's core   35
Discredited, and the sacred wood
Of Zeus at Elis praised no more?
The deeds and the strange prophecies
Must make a pattern yet to be understood.
Zeus, if indeed you are lord of all,   40
Throned in light over night and day,
Mirror this in your endless mind:
Our masters call the oracle
Words on the wind, and the Delphic vision blind!
Their hearts no longer know Apollo,   45
And reverence for the gods has died away.

Scene III

Enter Iocastê.

Iocastê: Princes of Thebes, it has occurred to me
   To visit the altars of the gods, bearing
   These branches as a suppliant, and this incense.
   Our King is not himself: his noble soul
   Is overwrought with fantasies of dread,   5

Else he would consider
The new prophecies in the light of the old.
He will listen to any voice that speaks disaster,
And my advice goes for nothing.

She approaches the altar, right.

                              To you, then, Apollo,
Lycean lord, since you are nearest, I turn in prayer.   10
Receive these offerings, and grant us deliverance
From defilement. Our hearts are heavy with fear
When we see our leader distracted, as helpless sailors
Are terrified by the confusion of their helmsman.

Enter Messenger.

Messenger: Friends, no doubt you can direct me: 15
    Where shall I find the house of Oedipus,
    Or, better still, where is the King himself?
Choragos: It is this very place, stranger; he is inside.
    This is his wife and mother of his children.
Messenger: I wish her happiness in a happy house,   20
    Blest in all the fulfillment of her marriage.
Iocastê: I wish as much for you: your courtesy
    Deserves a like good fortune. But now, tell me:
    Why have you come? What have you to say to us?
Messenger: Good news, my lady, for your house and your husband.   25
Iocastê: What news? Who sent you here?
Messenger: I am from Corinth.
    The news I bring ought to mean joy for you,
    Though it may be you will find some grief in it.
Iocastê: What is it? How can it touch us in both ways?
Messenger: The word is that the people of the Isthmus   30
    Intend to call Oedipus to be their king.
Iocastê: But old King Polybos—is he not reigning still?
Messenger: No. Death holds him in his sepulchre.
Iocastê: What are you saying? Polybos is dead?
Messenger: If I am not telling the truth, may I die myself.   35
Iocastê (to a Maidservant): Go in, go quickly; tell this to your master.

    O riddlers of God's will, where are you now!
    This was the man whom Oedipus, long ago,
    Feared so, fled so, in dread of destroying him—
    But it was another fate by which he died.   40

    Enter Oedipus, center.

Oedipus: Dearest Iocastê, why have you sent for me?
Iocastê: Listen to what this man says, and then tell me
    What has become of the solemn prophecies.
Oedipus: Who is this man? What is his news for me?
Iocastê: He has come from Corinth to announce your father's death!   45
Oedipus: Is it true, stranger? Tell me in your own words.

Messenger: I can not say it more clearly: the King is dead.
Oedipus: Was it by treason? Or by an attack of illness?
Messenger: A little thing brings old men to their rest.
Oedipus: It was sickness, then?
Messenger: Yes, and his many years.   50
Oedipus: Ah!
     Why should a man respect the Pythian hearth*, or
     Give heed to the birds that jangle above his head?
     They prophesied that I should kill Polybos,
     Kill my own father; but he is dead and buried,   55
     And I am here—I never touched him, never,
     Unless he died of grief for my departure,
     And thus, in a sense, through me. No. Polybos
     Has packed the oracles off with him underground.
     They are empty words.
Iocastê: Had I not told you so?   60
Oedipus: You had; it was my faint heart that betrayed me.
Iocastê: From now on never think of those things again.
Oedipus: And yet—must I not fear my mother's bed?
Iocastê: Why should anyone in this world be afraid,
     Since Fate rules us and nothing can be foreseen?   65
     A man should live only for the present day.

     Have no more fear of sleeping with your mother:
     How many men, in dreams, have lain with their mothers!
     No reasonable man is troubled by such things.
Oedipus: That is true; only—   70
     If only my mother were not still alive!
     But she is alive. I can not help my dread.
Iocastê: Yet this news of your father's death is wonderful.
Oedipus: Wonderful. But I fear the living woman.
Messenger: Tell me, who is this woman that you fear?   75
Oedipus: It is Meropê, man; the wife of King Polybos.
Messenger: Meropê? Why should you be afraid of her?
Oedipus: An oracle of the gods, a dreadful saying.
Messenger: Can you tell me about it or are you sworn to silence?
Oedipus: I can tell you, and I will.   80
     Apollo said through his prophet that I was the man
     Who should marry his own mother, shed his father's blood
     With his own hands. And so, for all these years
     I have kept clear of Corinth, and no harm has come—
     Though it would have been sweet to see my parents again.   85
Messenger: And is this the fear that drove you out of Corinth?
Oedipus: Would you have me kill my father?
Messenger: As for that
     You must be reassured by the news I gave you.
Oedipus: If you could reassure me, I would reward you.
Messenger: I had that in mind, I will confess: I thought   90
     I could count on you when you returned to Corinth.
Oedipus: No: I will never go near my parents again.

52 *Pythian hearth* another name for Delphi

Messenger: Ah, son, you still do not know what you are doing—
Oedipus: What do you mean? In the name of God tell me!
Messenger: —If these are your reasons for not going home.   95
Oedipus: I tell you, I fear the oracle may come true.
Messenger: And guilt may come upon you through your parents?
Oedipus: That is the dread that is always in my heart.
Messenger: Can you not see that all your fears are groundless?
Oedipus: How can you say that? They are my parents, surely?   100
Messenger: Polybos was not your father.
Oedipus: Not my father?
Messenger: No more your father than the man speaking to you.
Oedipus: But you are nothing to me!
Messenger: Neither was he.
Oedipus: Then why did he call me son?
Messenger: I will tell you:
    Long ago he had you from my hands, as a gift.   105
Oedipus: Then how could he love me so, if I was not his?
Messenger: He had no children, and his heart turned to you.
Oedipus: What of you? Did you buy me? Did you find me by chance?
Messenger: I came upon you in the crooked pass of Kithairon.
Oedipus: And what were you doing there?
Messenger: Tending my flocks.   110
Oedipus: A wandering shepherd?
Messenger: But your savior, son, that day.
Oedipus: From what did you save me?
Messenger: Your ankles should tell you that.
Oedipus: Ah, stranger, why do you speak of that childhood pain?
Messenger: I cut the bonds that tied your ankles together.
Oedipus: I have had the mark as long as I can remember.   115
Messenger: That was why you were given the name you bear.*
Oedipus: God! Was it my father or my mother who did it?
    Tell me!
Messenger: I do not know. The man who gave you to me
    Can tell you better than I.   120
Oedipus: It was not you that found me, but another?
Messenger: It was another shepherd gave you to me.
Oedipus: Who was he? Can you tell me who he was?
Messenger: I think he was said to be one of Laïos' people.
Oedipus: You mean the Laïos who was king here years ago?   125
Messenger: Yes; King Laïos; and the man was one of his herdsmen.
Oedipus: Is he still alive? Can I see him?
Messenger: These men here
    Know best about such things.
Oedipus: Does anyone here
    Know this shepherd that he is talking about?
    Have you seen him in the fields, or in the town?   130
    If you have, tell me. It is time things were made plain.
Choragos: I think the man he means is that same shepherd
    You have already asked to see. Iocastê perhaps
    Could tell you something.

116 *name you bear* "Oedipus" or "swollen foot"

Oedipus: Do you know anything
    About him, Lady? Is he the man we have summoned?   135
    Is that the man this shepherd means?
Iocastê: Why think of him?
    Forget this herdsman. Forget it all.
    This talk is a waste of time.
Oedipus: How can you say that,
    When the clues to my true birth are in my hands?
Iocastê: For God's love, let us have no more questioning!   140
    Is your life nothing to you?
    My own is pain enough for me to bear.
Oedipus: You need not worry. Suppose my mother a slave,
    And born of slaves: no baseness can touch you.
Iocastê: Listen to me, I beg you: do not do this thing!   145
Oedipus: I will not listen; the truth must be made known.
Iocastê: Everything that I say is for your own good!
Oedipus: My own good
    Snaps my patience, then; I want none of it.
Iocastê: You are fatally wrong! May you never learn who you are!
Oedipus: Go, one of you, and bring the shepherd here.   150
    Let us leave this woman to brag of her royal name.
Iocastê: Ah, miserable!
    That is the only word I have for you now.
    That is the only word I can ever have.

    Exit into the palace.

Choragos: Why has she left us, Oedipus? Why has she gone   155
    In such a passion of sorrow? I fear this silence:
    Something dreadful may come of it.
Oedipus: Let it come!
    However base my birth, I must know about it.
    The Queen, like a woman, is perhaps ashamed
    To think of my low origin. But I   160
    Am a child of Luck; I can not be dishonored.
    Luck is my mother; the passing months, my brothers,
    Have seen me rich and poor.
            If this is so,
    How could I wish that I were someone else?
    How could I not be glad to know my birth?   165

Ode III

                                             Strophe

Chorus: If ever the coming time were known
    To my heart's pondering,
    Kithairon, now by Heaven I see the torches
    At the festival of the next full moon,
    And see the dance, and hear the choir sing   5
    A grace to your gentle shade:
    Mountain where Oedipus was found,
    O mountain guard of a noble race!

May the god who heals us lend his aid,
And let that glory come to pass   10
For our king's cradling-ground.

Antistrophe

Of the nymphs that flower beyond the years,
Who bore you, royal child,
To Pan of the hills or the timberline Apollo,
Cold in delight where the upland clears,   15
Or Hermês for whom Kyllenê's heights* are piled?
Or flushed as evening cloud,
Great Dionysos*, roamer of mountains,
He—was it he who found you there,
And caught you up in his own proud   20
Arms from the sweet god-ravisher
Who laughed by the Muses' fountains?

Scene IV

Oedipus: Sirs: though I do not know the man,
    I think I see him coming, this shepherd we want:
    He is old, like our friend here, and the men
    Bringing him seem to be servants of my house.
    But you can tell, if you have ever seen him.   5

    Enter Shepherd escorted by servants.

Choragos: I know him, he was Laïos' man. You can trust him.
Oedipus: Tell me first, you from Corinth: is this the shepherd
    We were discussing?
Messenger: This is the very man.
Oedipus (to Shepherd): Come here. No, look at me. You must answer
    Everything I ask.—You belonged to Laïos?   10
Shepherd: Yes: born his slave, brought up in his house.
Oedipus: Tell me: what kind of work did you do for him?
Shepherd: I was a shepherd of his, most of my life.
Oedipus: Where mainly did you go for pasturage?
Shepherd: Sometimes Kithairon, sometimes the hills near-by.   15
Oedipus: Do you remember ever seeing this man out there?
Shepherd: What would he be doing there? This man?
Oedipus: This man standing here. Have you ever seen him before?
Shepherd: No. At least, not to my recollection.
Messenger: And that is not strange, my lord. But I'll refresh   20
    His memory: he must remember when we two
    Spent three whole seasons together, March to September,
    On Kithairon or thereabouts. He had two flocks;
    I had one. Each autumn I'd drive mine home
    And he would go back with his to Laïos' sheepfold.—   25
    Is this not true, just as I have described it?
Shepherd: True, yes; but it was all so long ago.
Messenger: Well, then: do you remember, back in those days
    That you gave me a baby boy to bring up as my own?
Shepherd: What if I did? What are you trying to say?   30

16 *Kyllenê's heights* birthplace of Hermes   18 *Dionysos* god of wine; also called Bacchos

Messenger: King Oedipus was once that little child.

Shepherd: Damn you, hold your tongue!

Oedipus: No more of that!

    It is your tongue needs watching, not this man's.

Shepherd: My King, my Master, what is it I have done wrong?

Oedipus: You have not answered his question about the boy.   35

Shepherd: He does not know . . . He is only making trouble . . .

Oedipus: Come, speak plainly, or it will go hard with you.

Shepherd: In God's name, do not torture an old man!

Oedipus: Come here, one of you; bind his arms behind him.

Shepherd: Unhappy king! What more do you wish to learn?   40

Oedipus: Did you give this man the child he speaks of?

Shepherd: I did.

    And I would to God I had died that very day.

Oedipus: You will die now unless you speak the truth.

Shepherd: Yet if I speak the truth, I am worse than dead.

Oedipus: Very well; since you insist upon delaying—   45

Shepherd: No! I have told you already that I gave him the boy.

Oedipus: Where did you get him? From your house? From somewhere else?

Shepherd: Not from mine, no. A man gave him to me.

Oedipus: Is that man here? Do you know whose slave he was?

Shepherd: For God's love, my King, do not ask me any more!   50

Oedipus: You are a dead man if I have to ask you again.

Shepherd: Then . . . Then the child was from the palace of Laïos.

Oedipus: A slave child? or a child of his own line?

Shepherd: Ah, I am on the brink of dreadful speech!

Oedipus: And I of dreadful hearing. Yet I must hear.   55

Shepherd: If you must be told, then . . .

                  They said it was Laïos' child;

    But it is your wife who can tell you about that.

Oedipus: My wife!—Did she give it to you?

Shepherd: My lord, she did.

Oedipus: Do you know why?

Shepherd: I was told to get rid of it.

Oedipus: An unspeakable mother!

Shepherd: There had been prophecies . . .   60

Oedipus: Tell me.

Shepherd: It was said that the boy would kill his own father.

Oedipus: Then why did you give him over to this old man?

Shepherd: I pitied the baby, my King,

    And I thought that this man would take him far away   65

    To his own country.

              He saved him—but for what a fate!

    For if you are what this man says you are,

    No man living is more wretched than Oedipus.

Oedipus: Ah God!

    It was true!

        All the prophecies!

              —Now,   70

    O Light, may I look on you for the last time!

I, Oedipus,
Oedipus, damned in his birth, in his marriage damned,
Damned in the blood he shed with his own hand!

He rushes into the palace.

Ode IV

Chorus: Alas for the seed of men.

Strophe 1

What measure shall I give these generations
That breathe on the void and are void
And exist and do not exist?

Who bears more weight of joy   5
Than mass of sunlight shifting in images,
Or who shall make his thought stay on
That down time drifts away?

Your splendor is all fallen.

O naked brow of wrath and tears,   10
O change of Oedipus!
I who saw your days call no man blest—
Your great days like ghosts gone.

Antistrophe 1

That mind was a strong bow.

Deep, how deep you drew it then, hard archer,   15
At a dim fearful range,
And brought dear glory down!

You overcame the stranger—
The virgin with her hooking lion claws—
And though death sang, stood like a tower   20
To make pale Thebes take heart.

Fortress against our sorrow!

True king, giver of laws,
Majestic Oedipus!
No prince in Thebes had ever such renown,   25
No prince won such grace of power.

Strophe 2

And now of all men ever known
Most pitiful is this man's story:
His fortunes are most changed, his state
Fallen to a low slave's   30
Ground under bitter fate.

O Oedipus, most royal one!
The great door that expelled you to the light
Gave at night—ah, gave night to your glory:
As to the father, to the fathering son.

All understood too late.   35

How could that queen whom Laïos won,
The garden that he harrowed at his height,
Be silent when that act was done?

Antistrophe 2

But all eyes fail before time's eye,   40
All actions come to justice there.
Though never willed, though far down the deep past,
Your bed, your dread sirings,
Are brought to book at last.

Child by Laïos doomed to die,   45
Then doomed to lose that fortunate little death,
Would God you never took breath in this air
That with my wailing lips I take to cry:

For I weep the world's outcast.
I was blind, and now I can tell why: 50
Asleep, for you had given ease of breath
To Thebes, while the false years went by.

Éxodos

Enter, from the palace, Second Messenger.

Second Messenger: Elders of Thebes, most honored in this land,
    What horrors are yours to see and hear, what weight
    Of sorrow to be endured, if, true to your birth,
    You venerate the line of Labdakos!
    I think neither Istros nor Phasis, those great rivers,   5
    Could purify this place of the corruption
    It shelters now, or soon must bring to light—
    Evil not done unconsciously, but willed.

    The greatest griefs are those we cause ourselves.
Choragos: Surely, friend, we have grief enough already;   10
    What new sorrow do you mean?
Second Messenger: The Queen is dead.
Choragos: Iocastê? Dead? But at whose hand?
Second Messenger: Her own.
    The full horror of what happened, you can not know,
    For you did not see it; but I, who did, will tell you
    As clearly as I can how she met her death.   15

    When she had left us,
    In passionate silence, passing through the court,
    She ran to her apartment in the house,
    Her hair clutched by the fingers of both hands.
    She closed the doors behind her; then, by that bed   20
    Where long ago the fatal son was conceived—
    That son who should bring about his father's death—
    We heard her call upon Laïos, dead so many years,
    And heard her wail for the double fruit of her marriage,
    A husband by her husband, children by her child.   25

Exactly how she died I do not know:
For Oedipus burst in moaning and would not let us
Keep vigil to the end: it was by him
As he stormed about the room that our eyes were caught.
From one to another of us he went, begging a sword,   30
Cursing the wife who was not his wife, the mother
Whose womb had carried his own children and himself.
I do not know: it was none of us aided him,
But surely one of the gods was in control!
For with a dreadful cry   35
He hurled his weight, as though wrenched out of himself,
At the twin doors: the bolts gave, and he rushed in.
And there we saw her hanging, her body swaying
From the cruel cord she had noosed about her neck.
A great sob broke from him, heartbreaking to hear,   40
As he loosed the rope and lowered her to the ground.

I would blot out from my mind what happened next!
For the King ripped from her gown the golden brooches
That were her ornament, and raised them, and plunged them down
Straight into his own eyeballs, crying, "No more,   45
No more shall you look on the misery about me,
The horrors of my own doing! Too long you have known
The faces of those whom I should never have seen,
Too long been blind to those for whom I was searching!
From this hour, go in darkness!" And as he spoke,   50
He struck at his eyes—not once, but many times;
And the blood spattered his beard,
Bursting from his ruined sockets like red hail.

So from the unhappiness of two this evil has sprung,
A curse on the man and woman alike. The old   55
Happiness of the house of Labdakos
Was happiness enough: where is it today?
It is all wailing and ruin, disgrace, death—all
The misery of mankind that has a name—
And it is wholly and for ever theirs.   60
Choragos: Is he in agony still? Is there no rest for him?
Second Messenger: He is calling for someone to lead him to the gates
So that all the children of Kadmos may look upon
His father's murderer, his mother's—no,
I can not say it!
                And then he will leave Thebes,   65
Self-exiled, in order that the curse
Which he himself pronounced may depart from the house.
He is weak, and there is none to lead him,
So terrible is his suffering.
                But you will see:
Look, the doors are opening; in a moment   70
You will see a thing that would crush a heart of stone.

The central door is opened; Oedipus, blinded, is led in.

Choragos: Dreadful indeed for men to see.
    Never have my own eyes
    Looked on a sight so full of fear.
    Oedipus!   75
    What madness came upon you, what daemon
    Leaped on your life with heavier
    Punishment than a mortal man can bear?
    No: I can not even
    Look at you, poor ruined one.   80
    And I would speak, question, ponder,
    If I were able. No.
    You make me shudder.

Oedipus: God. God.
    Is there a sorrow greater?   85
    Where shall I find harbor in this world?
    My voice is hurled far on a dark wind.
    What has God done to me?

Choragos: Too terrible to think of, or to see.

                            Strophe 1

Oedipus: O cloud of night,   90
    Never to be turned away: night coming on,
    I can not tell how: night like a shroud!

    My fair winds brought me here.
                    Oh God. Again
    The pain of the spikes where I had sight,
    The flooding pain   95
    Of memory, never to be gouged out.

Choragos: This is not strange.
    You suffer it all twice over, remorse in pain,
    Pain in remorse.

                          Antistrophe 1

Oedipus: Ah dear friend   100
    Are you faithful even yet, you alone?
    Are you still standing near me, will you stay here,
    Patient, to care for the blind?
                  The blind man!
    Yet even blind I know who it is attends me,
    By the voice's tone—   105
    Though my new darkness hide the comforter.

Choragos: Oh fearful act!
    What god was it drove you to rake black
    Night across your eyes?

                          Strophe 2

Oedipus: Apollo. Apollo. Dear   110
    Children, the god was Apollo.
    He brought my sick, sick fate upon me.
    But the blinding hand was my own!
    How could I bear to see
    When all my sight was horror everywhere?   115

Choragus: Everywhere; that is true.
Oedipus: And now what is left?
    Images? Love? A greeting even,
    Sweet to the senses? Is there anything?
    Ah, no, friends: lead me away.   120
    Lead me away from Thebes.
                    Lead the great wreck
    And hell of Oedipus, whom the gods hate.
Choragos: Your fate is clear, you are not blind to that.
    Would God you had never found it out!

                                   Antistrophe 2

Oedipus: Death take the man who unbound   125
    My feet on that hillside
    And delivered me from death to life! What life?
    If only I had died,
    This weight of monstrous doom
    Could not have dragged me and my darlings down.   130
Choragos: I would have wished the same.
Oedipus: Oh never to have come here
    With my father's blood upon me! Never
    To have been the man they call his mother's husband!
    Oh accurst! Oh child of evil,   135
    To have entered that wretched bed—
                    the selfsame one!
    More primal than sin itself, this fell to me.
Choragos: I do not know how I can answer you.
    You were better dead than alive and blind.
Oedipus: Do not counsel me any more. This punishment   140
    That I have laid upon myself is just.
    If I had eyes,
    I do not know how I could bear the sight
    Of my father, when I came to the house of Death,
    Or my mother: for I have sinned against them both   145
    So vilely that I could not make my peace
    By strangling my own life.
                  Or do you think my children,
    Born as they were born, would be sweet to my eyes?
    Ah never, never! Nor this town with its high walls,
    Nor the holy images of the gods.
               For I,   150
    Thrice miserable!—Oedipus, noblest of all the line
    Of Kadmos, have condemned myself to enjoy
    These things no more, by my own malediction
    Expelling that man whom the gods declared
    To be a defilement in the house of Laïos.   155
    After exposing the rankness of my own guilt,
    How could I look men frankly in the eyes?
    No, I swear it,
    If I could have stifled my hearing at its source,
    I would have done it and made all this body   160

A tight cell of misery, blank to light and sound:
So I should have been safe in a dark agony
Beyond all recollection.
                        Ah Kithairon!
Why did you shelter me? When I was cast upon you,
Why did I not die? Then I should never   165
Have shown the world my execrable birth.

Ah Polybos! Corinth, city that I believed
The ancient seat of my ancestors: how fair
I seemed, your child! And all the while this evil
Was cancerous within me!
                        For I am sick   170
In my daily life, sick in my origin.

O three roads, dark ravine, woodland and way
Where three roads met: you, drinking my father's blood,
My own blood, spilled by my own hand: can you remember
The unspeakable things I did there, and the things   175
I went on from there to do?
                        O marriage, marriage!
The act that engendered me, and again the act
Performed by the son in the same bed—
                        Ah, the net
Of incest, mingling fathers, brothers, sons,
With brides, wives, mothers: the last evil   180
That can be known by men: no tongue can say
How evil!
            No. For the love of God, conceal me
Somewhere far from Thebes; or kill me; or hurl me
Into the sea, away from men's eyes for ever.

Come, lead me. You need not fear to touch me.   185
Of all men, I alone can bear this guilt.

Enter Creon.

Choragos: We are not the ones to decide; but Creon here
        May fitly judge of what you ask. He only
        Is left to protect the city in your place.
Oedipus: Alas, how can I speak to him? What right have I   190
        To beg his courtesy whom I have deeply wronged?
Creon: I have not come to mock you, Oedipus,
        Or to reproach you, either.
        (To Attendants.)   —You, standing there:
        If you have lost all respect for man's dignity,
        At least respect the flame of Lord Helios: 195
        Do not allow this pollution to show itself
        Openly here, an affront to the earth
        And Heaven's rain and the light of day. No, take him
        Into the house as quickly as you can.
        For it is proper   200
        That only the close kindred see his grief.

Oedipus: I pray you in God's name, since your courtesy
    Ignores my dark expectation, visiting
    With mercy this man of all men most execrable:
    Give me what I ask—for your good, not for mine.   205
Creon: And what is it that you would have me do?
Oedipus: Drive me out of this country as quickly as may be
    To a place where no human voice can ever greet me.
Creon: I should have done that before now—only,
    God's will had not been wholly revealed to me.   210
Oedipus: But his command is plain: the parricide
    Must be destroyed. I am that evil man.
Creon: That is the sense of it, yes; but as things are,
    We had best discover clearly what is to be done.
Oedipus: You would learn more about a man like me?   215
Creon: You are ready now to listen to the god.
Oedipus: I will listen. But it is to you
    That I must turn for help. I beg you, hear me.

    The woman in there—
    Give her whatever funeral you think proper: 220
    She is your sister.
                —But let me go, Creon!
    Let me purge my father's Thebes of the pollution
    Of my living here, and go out to the wild hills,
    To Kithairon, that has won such fame with me,
    The tomb my mother and father appointed for me,   225
    And let me die there, as they willed I should.
    And yet I know
    Death will not ever come to me through sickness
    Or in any natural way: I have been preserved
    For some unthinkable fate. But let that be.   230

    As for my sons, you need not care for them.
    They are men, they will find some way to live.
    But my poor daughters, who have shared my table,
    Who never before have been parted from their father—
    Take care of them, Creon; do this for me.   235
    And will you let me touch them with my hands
    A last time, and let us weep together?
    Be kind, my lord,
    Great prince, be kind!
                Could I but touch them,
    They would be mine again, as when I had my eyes.   240

Enter Antigonê and Ismene, attended.

    Ah, God!
    Is it my dearest children I hear weeping?
    Has Creon pitied me and sent my daughters?
Creon: Yes, Oedipus: I knew that they were dear to you
    In the old days, and know you must love them still.   245
Oedipus: May God bless you for this—and be a friendlier
    Guardian to you than he has been to me!

Children, where are you?
Come quickly to my hands: they are your brother's—
Hands that have brought your father's once clear eyes   250
To this way of seeing—
      Ah dearest ones,
I had neither sight nor knowledge then, your father
By the woman who was the source of his own life!
And I weep for you—having no strength to see you—,
I weep for you when I think of the bitterness   255
That men will visit upon you all your lives.
What homes, what festivals can you attend
Without being forced to depart again in tears?
And when you come to marriageable age,
Where is the man, my daughters, who would dare   260
Risk the bane that lies on all my children?
Is there any evil wanting? Your father killed
His father; sowed the womb of her who bore him;
Engendered you at the fount of his own existence!
That is what they will say of you.
        Then, whom   265
Can you ever marry? There are no bridegrooms for you,
And your lives must wither away in sterile dreaming.

O Creon, son of Menoikeus!
You are the only father my daughters have,
Since we, their parents, are both of us gone for ever.   270
They are your own blood: you will not let them
Fall into beggary and loneliness;
You will keep them from the miseries that are mine!
Take pity on them; see, they are only children,
Friendless except for you. Promise me this,   275
Great Prince, and give me your hand in token of it.

Creon clasps his right hand.

Children:
I could say much, if you could understand me,
But as it is, I have only this prayer for you:
Live where you can, be as happy as you can—   280
Happier, please God, than God has made your father!
Creon: Enough. You have wept enough. Now go within.
Oedipus: I must; but it is hard.
Creon: Time eases all things.
Oedipus: But you must promise—
Creon: Say what you desire.
Oedipus: Send me from Thebes!
Creon: God grant that I may!   285
Oedipus: But since God hates me . . .
Creon: No, he will grant your wish.
Oedipus: You promise?
Creon: I can not speak beyond my knowledge.
Oedipus: Then lead me in.
Creon: Come now, and leave your children.

Oedipus: No! Do not take them from me!

Creon: Think no longer

> That you are in command here, but rather think   290
> How, when you were, you served your own destruction.

*Exeunt into the house all but the Chorus; the Choragos chants direct-
ly to the audience.*

Choragos: Men of Thebes: look upon Oedipus.

> This is the king who solved the famous riddle
> And towered up, most powerful of men.
> No mortal eyes but looked on him with envy,   295
> Yet in the end ruin swept over him.

> Let every man in mankind's frailty
> Consider his last day; and let none
> Presume on his good fortune until he find
> Life, at his death, a memory without pain.   300

                                                            [425 BCE]

Questions

1. How is the setting of the play communicated to the audience?
2. How does Oedipus contribute to his own ruin? How is his character flawed? How is he admirable? Does he seem noble or foolish, or both, for pursuing the truth so relentlessly?
3. What is Oedipus's relationship to the people he rules? How does this relationship figure into the overall action and effect of the play?
4. Why does Oedipus blind himself? Why does Jocasta kill herself? (Note that Jocasta's death does not occur in some other treatments of the myth—Seneca's for instance.) How do these acts of self-harm affect your view of the characters? How would your idea of Oedipus or Jocasta change if they had decided to forgive themselves?
5. What is the significance of blindness in the play? In what sense is Oedipus blind at the beginning of the play?
6. Is Oedipus a symbol? What indications in the play suggest that he might be considered a symbol?
7. What part does fate play in Oedipus's life? Would you argue that everything that happens to him is caused by his fate? Is Oedipus a helpless victim? How is he different from Job in the Old Testament?
8. In what ways is the play like a detective story? In what ways is it different? Would Oedipus be convicted today in a court of law of murdering Laius? Is the discrepancy regarding whether one person or many killed Laius ever resolved? As his lawyer, how would you defend Oedipus?

Critical Viewpoints

This section contains excerpts from a variety of critical viewpoints.

James C. Hogan: Historical and Cultural Criticism

In this fascinating excerpt, Hogan discusses the mythic materials that Sophocles inherited, and the cultural values of his audience, comparing the sequel, Oedipus at Colonus, *to this play.*

What particularly fascinates us about Oedipus in the *Colonus* is his attitude toward his crimes. In the *Oedipus the King* the discovery brings violent guilt: he would kill Jocasta if she were not quicker, and his self-blinding is followed by a demand that he be cast from the city, self-cursed and loathsome to himself, his countrymen and his family. Thus in the earlier play the full force of polluting murder and incest is acknowledged as both personal and social. The child of Fortune has proven to be both blessing and curse to himself and his city. The murder of king and father cancels the triumph over the Sphinx. Sophocles obviously knew his Aeschylus very well, and he could have had Oedipus undergo those formal rites of absolution and expiation that purify Orestes and other similar victims in Greek myth. But Sophocles wanted a more personal—and more problematic—story. On three occasions in the *Colonus*, Oedipus defends his innocence, and yet both he and the chorus of Athenians remain profoundly sensitive to the pollution that still clings. Oedipus rationalizes the murder: it was an accident; he did not know the man; he was provoked. A court of law would be sympathetic. Still, the stain remains: he recoils from embracing Theseus, afraid of harming his generous host. His rationalized and intuitive sense of his own innocence cannot deny the social and religious opprobrium. What is dramatized is more than a personal odyssey; it is as much the edge of cultural change, where irrevocable sin meets rational introspection and personal accountability. The fundamental mystery of his fate so carefully charted in the *Oedipus the King* will be, for some, resolved by the final heroization, and Theseus' ready hospitality may seem to vouch for a socially acceptable purification. Yet he has not convinced himself. No confession of sin, no rationalization of circumstance, no years in the desert, have washed away the sense of guilt and shame. Perhaps his terrible and vindictive curse on his sons confirms, at least psychologically, the necessity of his personal alienation. We may think of Lear. Unlike Lear, Oedipus never achieves peace, is never fully reconciled, and must die alone amid thunder and lightning, closer to the daimons of the earth than to humanity.

From James C. Hogan, *A Commentary on the Plays of Sophocles.*
    Carbondale: Southern Illinois UP, 1991, pp. 19–21.

Bernard Knox: New Critical Reading

In the following excerpt, Bernard Knox displays his interest in revealing the play's theme. Oedipus's one freedom, the freedom to pursue the truth, Knox asserts, is "the key to the play's tragic theme," and hence its unity. Knox's analysis of Oedipus's character assumes that these stable qualities are accessible in the text. Knox, in making the case for Oedipus's greatness, is creating a complex and paradoxical view of his character: an incestuous murderer, Oedipus is nonetheless heroic.

Oedipus did have one freedom: he was free to find out or not find out the truth. This was the element of Sophoclean sleight-of-hand that enabled him to make a drama out of the situation which the philosophers used as the classic demonstration of man's subjection to fate. But it is more than a solution to an apparently insoluble dramatic problem; it is the key to the play's tragic theme and the protagonist's heroic stature. One freedom is allowed him: the freedom to search for the truth, the truth about the prophecies, about the gods, about himself. And of this freedom he makes full use. Against the advice and appeals of others, he pushes on, searching for the truth, the whole truth, and nothing but the truth. And in this search he shows all those great qualities that we admire in him—courage, intelligence, perseverance, the qualities that make human beings great. This freedom to search, and the heroic way in which Oedipus uses it, makes the play not a picture of man's utter feebleness caught in the toils of fate, but on the contrary, a heroic example of man's dedication to the search for truth, the truth about himself. This is perhaps the only human freedom, the play seems to say, but there could be none more noble.

From Bernard M. W. Knox, *Oedipus at Thebes*. New Haven, CN:
    Yale UP, 1957, pp. 19–21.

Sigmund Freud: Psychological Criticism

In this excerpt from the classic Interpretation of Dreams, *Freud uses Sophocles to develop his famous Oedipal theory.*

If *Oedipus Rex* moves a modern audience no less than it did the contemporary Greek one, the explanation can only be that its effect does not lie in the contrast between destiny and human will, but is to be looked for in the particular nature of the material on which that contrast is exemplified. There must be something which makes a voice within us ready to recognize the compelling force of destiny in the *Oedipus,* while we can dismiss as merely arbitrary such dispositions as are laid down in [Grillparzer's] *Die Ahnfrau* or other modern tragedies of destiny. And a factor of this kind is in fact involved in the story of King Oedipus. His destiny moves us only because it might have been ours—because the oracle laid the same curse upon us before our birth as upon him. It is the fate of all of us, perhaps, to direct our first sexual impulse toward our mother and our first hatred and our first murderous wish against our father. Our dreams convince us that that is so. King Oedipus, who slew his father Laius and married his mother Jocasta, merely shows us the fulfillment of our own childhood wishes. But, more fortunate than he, we have meanwhile succeeded, in so far as we have not become psychoneurotics, in detaching our sexual impulses from our mothers and in forgetting our jealousy of our fathers. Here is one in whom these primeval wishes of our childhood have been fulfilled, and we shrink back from him with the whole force of the repression by which those wishes have since that time been held down within us.

. . . There is an unmistakable indication in the text of Sophocles' tragedy itself that the legend of Oedipus sprang from some primeval dream material which had as its content the distressing disturbance of a child's relation to his parents owing to the first stirrings of sexuality. At a point when Oedipus, though he is not yet enlightened, has begun to feel troubled by his recollection of the oracle, Jocasta consoles him by referring to a dream which many people dream, though, as she thinks, it has no meaning:

> Many a man ere now in dreams hath lain
> With her who bare him. He hath least annoy
> Who with such omens troubleth not his mind.

Today, just as then, many men dream of having sexual relations with their mothers, and speak of the fact with indignation and astonishment. It is clearly the key to the tragedy and the complement to the dream of the dreamer's father being dead. The story of Oedipus is the reaction of the imagination to these two typical dreams. And just as these dreams, when dreamt by adults, are accompanied by feelings of repulsion, so too the legend must include horror and self-punishment.

From Sigmund Freud, *The Interpretation of Dreams*. New York: Modern Library, 1950, pp. 161–62.

Adrian Poole: A Comment on Freud

Here is an interesting angle on Freud's reading.

The most significant thing that Freud has to say about Sophocles' Oedipus is to do with the form and structure of the play rather than its hidden content: "The action of the play consists in nothing other than the process of revelation, with cunning delays and ever mounting excitement—a process that can be likened to the work of a psychoanalysis—that Oedipus himself is the murderer of Laius." "The work of a psychoanalysis": that is, the specific confrontation and intercourse between analyst and patient. This suggests that a psychoanalysis is constructed like a tragedy, or at least like this tragedy, and that what a psychoanalysis and a tragedy have in common is something to do with their work of discovery. In each case we are moved by the products of revelation only in so far as we are moved by the process of revelation.

When we consider the importance of Oedipus for Freud, we should therefore recall not only the image of a man who acts out our (supposedly) deepest fantasies, but also the action of the play through which Oedipus must discover the truth. If there is a "compulsion" in Sophocles' play, it is much less obviously the compulsion to act out infantile fantasies than the compulsion to know the truth. Sophocles' Oedipus and Shakespeare's Hamlet are the two characters in tragic drama most actively engaged in analysis and interpretation. Their importance for Freud is more to do with a passion for knowledge than with an occult or repressed guilt.

From Adrian Poole, *Tragedy: Shakespeare and the Greek Example*. Oxford: Blackwell, 1989, p. 182.

Suggestions for Writing

You can always adopt any theoretical stance and focus on any passage, or set of passages, using the questions generated by that stance (see the inside covers) to evolve an essay. Here are a few other suggestions.

1. The critical excerpts on *Oedipus* employ a variety of critical approaches. Write an essay in which you explain what one (or two or three) of the critics is trying to do. What are his or her assumptions? What counts as evidence for this critic? Which approach, or approaches, do you see being used?

2. Write an essay that is a reaction to one or more of the critics excerpted here. You might agree, disagree, or some of both, perhaps drawing on the other critics for additional support. You may want to focus on a particular point, or what you perceive to be a main idea.

3. Use one of the questions on page 837 as the starting point for an essay. The eighth question in particular offers some room for creativity.

4. Is any reader or viewer likely to identify with Oedipus's circumstances? Or is Oedipus's predicament so bizarre that modern audiences cannot empathize with him? Why does any reader or viewer care what happens to Oedipus? Or does any reader or viewer care?

5. Many critics have talked about Oedipus's heroic efforts to find out the truth about himself. Do you agree with this assessment? Aristotle certainly seems to have seen Oedipus as heroic, and Aristotle's opinion has been influential. But is Oedipus really admirable? Have we been misled by Aristotle's venerable opinion? In what sense might Oedipus not be one of us at our best?

6. What could possibly happen after the devastating ending of *Oedipus Tyrannos*? Sophocles did write a sequel, *Oedipus at Colonus*, and you might consult that play and discuss its relationship with the earlier play, or how it surprises you, or how it contains what you expected. Alternately, without consulting Sophocles' sequel, you might sketch out the plot for your own sequel. Or, here's another creative opportunity: could the play be set in the present? How would it be changed?

Hamlet

Suppression and sublimation alike are devices by which we endeavor to avoid issues which might bewilder us. The essence of Tragedy is that it forces us to live for a moment without them.

—*I. A. Richards*

The Weight of Hamlet

Hamlet has a ghost who prowls the night; it has a dastardly villain who has poisoned his brother in a horrible manner, by pouring an evil potion into his ear; it has a beautiful young heroine who is spurned, goes mad, and tragically kills herself. It has spies and intrigue, with subplots and counterplots; it has a hero who is clever and enigmatic, and bent on revenge, and who talks to a human skull. And at its end it has a dramatic swordfight, and more poisons, and dead bodies all over the place. Why shouldn't it be one of the most popular, most often staged, most discussed plays in history?

If you've read the play before, you might well be thinking that this murder-and-mayhem description doesn't quite seem like the play you read. And in a sense, it isn't, because Shakespeare's remarkable tragedy of revenge features an avenger who delays, who puts off his vengeance, who thinks and meditates and doubts and muses and wonders, until he finally is forced to act, or perhaps we should say react. It is a play that focuses on the hero's inactivity in the face of a powerful, but possibly ambiguous, command to act. It is easy enough to write a play with ghosts and revenge and poison and intrigue and swordplay; and so many of Shakespeare's contemporaries did write such a play that we can recognize *Hamlet* as a type of what is called "the revenge tragedy." While those other revenge tragedies have been all but forgotten or lost, *Hamlet* continues to fascinate us. Why?

To answer that question would require writing a book, and then probably another book, and then another, because *Hamlet* has proved to be so endlessly engaging to readers and viewers that it would be very difficult, if not impossible, to try to explain fully why it has moved and interested us so, and how Shakespeare has transformed his story of revenge into something profoundly meaningful. Let us consider here, in a very small way, just how richly this play rewards its readers and viewers by seemingly adapting itself to our different perspectives and interests.

During the play's dramatic climax, Hamlet's fencing match with Laertes, Hamlet's mother remarks that her son is "fat, and scant of breath." Most readers and viewers probably don't pause to consider Gertrude's comment, especially since it comes in the middle of a tense scene: Laertes is using a sword with a poisoned tip. The audience knows Laertes is trying to kill Hamlet, who thinks they are only playing.

But Gertrude's comment may well be puzzling, if we do stop to consider it, especially if we should be watching the classic film starring an athletic Laurence Olivier, or the more recent version starring Mel Gibson, or any number of other stagings. Hamlet has been played by all sorts of actors, including even women, but it is not a role that traditionally has been played by anyone overweight. And yet there is Gertrude's remark: "He's fat."

Editors have always felt obliged to explain this comment—or rather, explain it away. Early editors suggested it was a smiling reference to the weight gained by Richard Burbage, the actor who first played Hamlet. Later editors have generally dismissed the idea that the comment refers to the actor and not the character, and they argue that Gertrude means merely that Hamlet is "not physically fit; out of training" (as Kittredge's edition puts it) and not that he is really fat.

"Well," you may be thinking, "who cares whether Hamlet was supposed to be skinny or obese, whether he ate a strictly macrobiotic diet or wore an Elvis girdle and scarfed down ten Big Macs a day?" Certainly, one might read the play for years without pausing over Hamlet's girth; lots of brilliant readers have. But *Hamlet* is one of the richest of Shakespeare's plays, which is to say that it is one of the most rewarding and thought-provoking plays ever written in any language. Not since the great Greek tragedies, some two thousand years earlier, had there been such a dramatic masterwork. The first of Shakespeare's four greatest tragedies, *Hamlet* has been repaying its readers' attention to all sorts of details, from all sorts of approaches, for almost five hundred years.

So what happens if we decide to focus on this apparently minor detail that generations of readers and viewers have ignored, explained, or set aside?

Here, for an example, is what Hamlet says right after promising the ghost of his father that he will seek revenge against his father's murderer, and after swearing his companions to secrecy:

> Rest, rest, perturbed spirit! So, gentlemen,
> With all my love I do commend me to you;
> And what so poor a man as Hamlet is may do,
> T' express his love and friending to you,
> God willing, shall not lack. Let us go in together,
> And still your fingers on your lips, I pray.
> The time is out of joint. O cursed spite,
> That ever I was born to set it right!

Imagine first these lines being spoken by a youthful and athletic Hamlet, Mel Gibson or Kevin Kline, say, to pick two recent Hamlets. Now imagine these lines delivered by an overweight or even fat Hamlet, say John Goodman or Dan Akroyd. On the one (skinny) hand, we see a modest ("what so poor a man as Hamlet is"), determined ("I was born to set it right!") young man resolving to do what he can ("God willing"). On the other (weightier) hand, we see a man being asked to do something for which he is really not suited. We learn that Hamlet has been at school, at Wittenburg University, and his speeches as the play unfolds reveal that he is indeed a student, a scholar, a thinker. He is not used to *doing* things; he is not a man of action. He is used to sitting around, reading, contemplating. Like many students, suddenly becoming largely sedentary, sitting in front of their books, Hamlet has put on some weight— and now he's being asked to take up arms and fight for revenge.

He's not a kid anymore either. Although readers and viewers may tend to think of Hamlet as a young man, since he is a student, and he is the *Prince* of Denmark, Shakespeare does reveal indirectly (in the graveyard scene with Osric) that Hamlet is thirty years old. He is of course not decrepit, although thirty in Shakespeare's day may be considered relatively older than in our time. Even many athletes today are past their physical prime at thirty.

When this sedentary, mature, out-of-shape Hamlet says he will do whatever he can, while referring at the same time to "what so poor a man as Hamlet is," one of the central problems of the play comes into a different light. Shelves of books have considered the question of why Hamlet delays, why he keeps on talking when revenge has been called for. The Ghost in fact relates fat to delay when he tells Hamlet, "duller shouldst thou be than the fat weed/ That roots itself in ease on Lethe wharf" if he does not "sweep" to his revenge. Since Lethe is the river of forgetfulness in Hades, wiping clean the memories of anyone who passes over it, a fat weed growing next to that river would be about as oblivious and useless as anything one could imagine. With a "fat" Hamlet, the answers to the question of why Hamlet delays must include "he's lethargic and slow" and "he doesn't think he can do it."

There is then a different, and in a way a sadder and more poignant emphasis on these lines if Hamlet appears physically unable to do what needs to be done:

> The time is out of joint. O cursed spite,
>   That ever I was born to set it right!

Someone else, this larger Hamlet is saying, should have been born to be given this task, someone more agile and athletic. But he vows nonetheless to do whatever he can. And as we see in the fencing scene, he does remarkably well, despite the weight that Shakespeare is careful to draw to our attention with Gertrude's remark. But Hamlet succeeds in his revenge after all, at a tremendous price however; and the more there is of him, the weightier his achievement, in a sense.

This focus on Hamlet's weight is, admittedly, unusual if not eccentric; it seems unlikely that anyone has ever thought seriously about *Hamlet* in terms of the stereotypes and self-perceptions of "fat." The point here is that this play, even though it has been read by millions of people for generations—even though you may have read it before—*Hamlet* still has new possibilities, new things to say to us. You might, for instance, think about Hamlet's pleasure when he meets the actors, and the intimate knowledge of the theatre that he displays; and this focus might lead you to think about Hamlet as an actor, as he puts on different masks in different scenes. Or, you might focus more on Hamlet as a scholar: how does his intellect and education influence the way he pursues and worries over revenge? Or, you might focus on Hamlet's status as a grieving son, or notice his pleasure in wordplay and his skill in swordplay, or any number of other aspects of his character. These suggestions are generally limited to psychological views of one character; obviously there are many other critical approaches and many other aspects of the play for you to explore. And they are worth exploring because *Hamlet*,

like all great tragedies, focuses our attention on things that we find troubling, things that
we ought to think about but would rather not, as I. A. Richards says in the epigraph to
this chapter: how, for instance, one should deal with a responsibility that seems beyond
our capabilities, and that may be questionable in the first place.

But before you turn to the play itself, it may be helpful to think a bit about
Shakespeare, his theatre, and the plot of the play.

The Author, the Theatre, the Play

Although scholars often lament that so little is known about William Shakespeare,
the truth is that we do know a great deal, thanks to diligent and imaginative
research. Here's a quick profile of the world's greatest playwright:

- Born: April 1564; died April 1616.
- Parents: His father was a glovemaker who thought of himself as a gentleman.
- Education: Although some readers have speculated, given the vast learning
  in his plays, that Shakespeare must have had a university education, no evidence supports it. A few readers have even speculated that someone else
  must have written the plays, but that claim seems silly to most people.
  Somehow Shakespeare acquired a familiarity with the law, science, medicine, geography, myth, history, and so forth, of his day. His grammar school
  education, assuming it was typical, would have stressed eloquence in Latin,
  cultivating a pleasure in words.
- Marriage: to Anne Hathaway, who was 26, when he was 18. Three children,
  including twins, Judith and Hamnet, his only son, who died at age 11.
- Early career: Began as a poet, but when he failed to secure a patron to support him financially, Shakespeare turned to the theatre.
- First success: English history plays, which London audiences craved.
- Mature work: successful tragedies, comedies, and romances (at the end),
  adding up to some 37 plays. Although he did not seem interested in preserving his plays for posterity, Shakespeare was apparently a superb business-
  man, receiving a portion of the ticket sales, payment for his acting work
  (minor roles), and especially payment as the playwright. He made shrewd
  investments in property and retired a wealthy man.

When Shakespeare was born, acting was a disreputable and even illegal profession. In the 1570s, English law made acting legal. Although with some people it
never quite became reputable, the theatre certainly was popular in Shakespeare's
London. Shakespeare—some students have trouble believing this—was a very successful playwright, appealing to all sorts of people, who paid the equivalent of about
$10 for admission to his plays. An admission ticket would allow a playgoer to stand
on the ground, which was about five feet below the level of the stage. For another
"penny" (again, about $10), playgoers could have a seat in an upper gallery. Amaz-
ingly enough, many frugal or poor playgoers were very happy to watch standing
up—"groundlings," they were called.

The stage itself was about forty feet by twenty-five feet and featured few
props. Playgoers were accustomed to using the actors' words and their imaginations in order to create the play's settings. From our perspective, it appears that
in one respect their imaginations must have been especially fertile: no women
were allowed on stage, and so the female parts were played by men or boys.
Ophelia in this play, for instance, or Juliet in *Romeo and Juliet*, would have been
played by a boy.

The general plot of *Hamlet* can be quickly summarized: the ghost of the former King of Denmark appears and reveals to his son, Prince Hamlet, that he was murdered by his brother, Claudius, who has taken his crown and his wife, Gertrude. Hamlet is sworn to seek revenge, but he fails to act immediately. Instead, he feigns madness, or possibly is mad; he worries that the ghost may be an evil spirit who is lying to him; he is repulsed by the act of murdering Claudius; he contemplates death; he upbraids his mother for incestuously marrying her husband's brother; and he foils plots by Claudius against him—but he does not carry out his revenge.

Finally, to determine Claudius's guilt and the ghost's reliability, he arranges for a play that depicts the poisoning of a king; and by observing Claudius's reaction to this play, he satisfies himself of Claudius's guilt. But still he does not act until Claudius plots to use Laertes to kill Hamlet in a fencing match. The plot is exposed, and Hamlet finally kills Claudius, but Laertes, Gertrude, and Hamlet himself are also dead by the end of the play.

The Swan Playhouse, as copied from Johannes De Witt's sixteenth-century drawing. This is the only extant drawing of a public theater made in Shakespeare's day.

The genius of *Hamlet* is not in its plot, but in the psychological depth of its characters, especially Hamlet, and in the brilliance of its language.

WILLIAM SHAKESPEARE (1564–1616)

Hamlet, Prince of Denmark*

Edited by David Bevington

[Dramatis Personae

Ghost of Hamlet, the former King of Denmark
Claudius, King of Denmark, the former King's brother
Gertrude, Queen of Denmark, widow of the former King and now wife of
   Claudius
Hamlet, Prince of Denmark, son of the late King and of Gertrude
Polonius, councillor to the King
Laertes, his son
Ophelia, his daughter

NOTE ON THE TEXT: This text is based primarily on the Second Quarto of 1604–1605.

Reynaldo, his servant
Horatio, Hamlet's friend and fellow student
Voltimand,
Cornelius,
Rosencrantz,
Guildenstern, } members of the Danish court
Osric,
A Gentleman,
A Lord,
Bernardo,
Francisco, } officers and soldiers on watch
Marcellus,
Fortinbras, Prince of Norway
Captain in his army
Three or Four Players, taking the roles of *Prologue, Player King, Player
    Queen,* and *Lucianus*
Two Messengers
First Sailor
Two Clowns, a gravedigger and his companion
Priest
First Ambassador from England
*Lords, Soldiers, Attendants, Guards, other Players, Followers of Laertes,
    other Sailors, another Ambassador or Ambassadors from England*

Scene: *Denmark*]

Act I

Scene I [*Elsinore Castle. A Guard Platform.*]

   Enter Bernardo and Francisco, two sentinels, [*meeting*].

Bernardo: Who's there?
Francisco: Nay, answer me.* Stand and unfold yourself.*
Bernardo: Long live the King!
Francisco: Bernardo?
Bernardo: He.   5
Francisco: You come most carefully upon your hour.
Bernardo: 'Tis now struck twelve. Get thee to bed, Francisco.
Francisco: For this relief much thanks. 'Tis bitter cold,
    And I am sick at heart.
Bernardo: Have you had quiet guard?   10
Francisco: Not a mouse stirring.
Bernardo: Well, good night.
    If you do meet Horatio and Marcellus,
    The rivals* of my watch, bid them make haste.

   Enter Horatio and Marcellus.

2 *me* (Francisco emphasizes that *he* is the sentry currently on watch.)   *unfold yourself* reveal your
identity   14 *rivals* partners

Francisco: I think I hear them.—Stand, ho! Who is there?   15
Horatio: Friends to this ground.*
Marcellus: And liegemen to the Dane.*
Francisco: Give* you good night.
Marcellus: O, farewell, honest soldier. Who hath relieved you?
Francisco: Bernardo hath my place. Give you good night.   20

                                            Exit Francisco.

Marcellus: Holla! Bernardo!
Bernardo: Say, what, is Horatio there?
Horatio: A piece of him.
Bernardo: Welcome, Horatio. Welcome, good Marcellus.
Horatio: What, has this thing appeared again tonight?   25
Bernardo: I have seen nothing.
Marcellus: Horatio says 'tis but our fantasy,*
    And will not let belief take hold of him
    Touching this dreaded sight twice seen of us.
    Therefore I have entreated him along*   30
    With us to watch* the minutes of this night,
    That if again this apparition come
    He may approve* our eyes and speak to it.
Horatio: Tush, tush, 'twill not appear.
Bernardo: Sit down awhile,
    And let us once again assail your ears,   35
    That are so fortified against our story,
    What* we have two nights seen.
Horatio: Well, sit we down,
    And let us hear Bernardo speak of this.
Bernardo: Last night of all,*
    When yond same star that's westward from the pole*   40
    Had made his* course t' illume* that part of heaven
    Where now it burns, Marcellus and myself,
    The bell then beating one—

    Enter Ghost.

Marcellus: Peace, break thee off! Look where it comes again!
Bernardo: In the same figure like the King that's dead.   45
Marcellus: Thou art a scholar.* Speak to it, Horatio.
Bernardo: Looks 'a* not like the King? Mark it, Horatio.
Horatio: Most like. It harrows me with fear and wonder.
Bernardo: It would be spoke to.*
Marcellus: Speak to it, Horatio.
Horatio: What are thou that usurp'st* this time of night,   50
    Together with that fair and warlike form

---

16 *ground* country, land   17 *liegemen to the Dane* men sworn to serve the Danish king   18 *Give* i.e., may God give   27 *fantasy* imagination   30 *along* to come along   31 *watch* keep watch during   33 *approve* corroborate   37 *What* with what   39 *Last . . . all* i.e., this *very* last night (Emphatic.)   40 *pole* polestar, north star   41 *his* its.   *illume* illuminate   46 *scholar* one learned enough to know how to question a ghost properly   47 *'a* he   49 *It . . . to* (It was commonly believed that a ghost could not speak until spoken to.)   50 *usurp'st* wrongfully takes over

      In which the majesty of buried Denmark*
      Did sometime* march? By heaven, I charge thee, speak!
Marcellus: It is offended.
Bernardo: See, it stalks away.
Horatio: Stay! Speak, speak! I charge thee, speak!   *Exit Ghost.*   55
Marcellus: 'Tis gone and will not answer.
Bernardo: How now, Horatio? You tremble and look pale.
      Is not this something more than fantasy?
      What think you on 't?*
Horatio: Before my God, I might not this believe   60
      Without the sensible* and true avouch*
      Of mine own eyes.
Marcellus: Is it not like the King?
Horatio: As thou art to thyself.
      Such was the very armor he had on
      When he the ambitious Norway* combated.   65
      So frowned he once when, in an angry parle,*
      He smote the sledded* Polacks* on the ice.
      'Tis strange.
Marcellus: Thus twice before, and jump* at this dead hour,
      With martial stalk* hath he gone by our watch.   70
Horatio: In what particular thought to work* I know not,
      But in the gross and scope* of mine opinion
      This bodes some strange eruption to our state.
Marcellus: Good now,* sit down, and tell me, he that knows,
      Why this same strict and most observant watch   75
      So nightly toils* the subject* of the land,
      And why such daily cast* of brazen cannon
      And foreign mart* for implements of war,
      Why such impress* of shipwrights, whose sore task
      Does not divide the Sunday from the week.   80
      What might be toward,* that this sweaty haste
      Doth make the night joint-laborer with the day?
      Who is 't that can inform me?
Horatio: That can I;
      At least, the whisper goes so. Our last king,
      Whose image even but now appeared to us,   85
      Was, as you know, by Fortinbras of Norway,
      Thereto* pricked* on by a most emulate* pride,
      Dared to the combat; in which our valiant Hamlet—
      For so this side of our known world* esteemed him—

52 *buried Denmark* the buried King of Denmark   53 *sometime* formerly   59 *on 't* of it
61 *sensible* confirmed by the senses.   *avouch* warrant, evidence   65 *Norway* King of Norway
66 *parle* parley   67 *sledded* traveling on sleds.   *Polacks* Poles   69 *jump* exactly   70 *stalk* stride
71 *to work* i.e., to collect my thoughts and try to understand this   72 *gross and scope* general drift
74 *Good now* (An expression denoting entreaty or expostulation.)   76 *toils* causes to toil.   *subject*
subjects   77 *cast* casting   78 *mart* buying and selling   79 *impress* impressment, conscription
81 *toward* in preparation   87 *Thereto . . . pride* (Refers to old Fortinbras, not the Danish King.)
pricked on incited.   *emulate* emulous, ambitious   89 *this . . . world* i.e., all Europe, the Western
world

Did slay this Fortinbras; who by a sealed* compact   90
Well ratified by law and heraldry
Did forfeit, with his life, all those his lands
Which he stood seized* of, to the conqueror;
Against the* which a moiety competent*
Was gagèd* by our king, which had returned*   95
To the inheritance *of Fortinbras
Had he been vanquisher, as, by the same cov'nant*
And carriage of the article designed,*
His fell to Hamlet. Now, sir, young Fortinbras,
Of unimprovèd mettle* hot and full,   100
Hath in the skirts* of Norway here and there
Sharked up* a list* of lawless resolutes*
For food and diet* to some enterprise
That hath a stomach* in 't, which is no other—
As it doth well appear unto our state—   105
But to recover of us, by strong hand
And terms compulsatory, those foresaid lands
So by his father lost. And this, I take it,
Is the main motive of our preparations,
The source of this our watch, and the chief head*   110
Of this posthaste and rummage* in the land.
Bernardo: I think it be no other but e'en so.
Well may it sort* that this portentous figure
Comes armèd through our watch so like the King
That was and is the question* of these wars.   115
Horatio: A mote* it is to trouble the mind's eye.
In the most high and palmy* state of Rome,
A little ere the mightiest Julius fell,
The graves stood tenantless, and the sheeted* dead
Did squeak and gibber in the Roman streets;   120
As* stars with trains* of fire and dews of blood,
Disasters* in the sun; and the moist star*
Upon whose influence Neptune's* empire stands*
Was sick almost to doomsday* with eclipse.
And even the like precurse* of feared events,   125

90 *sealed* certified, confirmed   93 *seized* possessed   94 *Against the* in return for.
moiety competent corresponding portion   95 *gagèd* engaged, pledged.   *had returned* would have
passed   96 *inheritance* possession   97 *cov'nant* i.e., the *sealed compact* of line 90
98 *carriage. . . designed* carrying out of the article or clause drawn up to cover the point
100 *unimprovèd mettle* untried, undisciplined spirits   101 *skirts* outlying regions, outskirts
102 *Sharked up* gathered up, as a shark takes fish.   *list* i.e., troop.   *resolutes* desperadoes
103 *For food and diet* i.e., they are to serve as *food*, or "means," *to some enterprise*; also they
serve in return for the rations they get   104 *stomach* (1) a spirit of daring (2) an appetite that is
fed by the *lawless resolutes*   110 *head* source   111 *rummage* bustle, commotion   113 *sort* suit
115 *question* focus of contention   116 *mote* speck of dust   117 *palmy* flourishing
119 *sheeted* shrouded   121 *As* (This abrupt transition suggests that matter is possibly omitted
between lines 120 and 121.)   *trains* trails   122 *Disasters* unfavorable signs or aspects.
moist star i.e., moon, governing tides   123 *Neptune* god of the sea.   *stands* depends
124 *sick. . . doomsday* (See Matthew 24:29 and Revelation 6:12.)   125 *precurse* heralding,
foreshadowing

As harbingers* preceding still* the fates
And prologue to the omen* coming on,
Have heaven and earth together demonstrated
Unto our climatures* and countrymen.

Enter Ghost.

But soft,* behold! Lo, where it comes again!   130
I'll cross* it, though it blast* me. (*It spreads his* arms.*) Stay, illusion!
If thou hast any sound or use of voice,
Speak to me!
If there be any good thing to be done
That may to thee do ease and grace to me,   135
Speak to me!
If thou art privy to* thy country's fate,
Which, happily,* foreknowing may avoid,
O, speak!
Or if thou hast uphoarded in thy life   140
Extorted treasure in the womb of earth,
For which, they say, you spirits oft walk in death,
Speak of it! (*The cock crows.*) Stay and speak!—Stop it, Marcellus.

Marcellus: Shall I strike at it with my partisan?*
Horatio: Do, if it will not stand.   [*They strike at it.*]   145
Bernardo: 'Tis here!
Horatio: 'Tis here!   [*Exit Ghost.*]
Marcellus: 'Tis gone.
We do it wrong, being so majestical,
To offer it the show of violence,   150
For it is as the air invulnerable,
And our vain blows malicious mockery.
Bernardo: It was about to speak when the cock crew.
Horatio: And then it started like a guilty thing
Upon a fearful summons. I have heard   155
The cock, that is the trumpet* to the morn,
Doth with his lofty and shrill-sounding throat
Awake the god of day, and at his warning,
Whether in sea or fire, in earth or air,
Th' extravagant and erring* spirit hies*   160
To his confine; and of the truth herein
This present object made probation.*
Marcellus: It faded on the crowing of the cock.
Some say that ever 'gainst* that season comes
Wherein our Savior's birth is celebrated,   165
This bird of dawning singeth all night long,
And then, they say, no spirit dare stir abroad;
The nights are wholesome, then no planets strike,*

126 *harbingers* forerunners. *still* continually   127 *omen* calamitous event   129 *climatures*
regions   130 *soft* i.e., enough, break off   131 *cross* stand in its path, confront. *blast* wither,
strike with a curse. *stage direction: his* its   137 *privy to* in on the secret of   13 *happily* haply,
perchance   144 *partisan* long-handled spear   156 *trumpet* trumpeter   160 *extravagant and*
erring wandering beyond bounds. (The words have similar meaning.) *hies* hastens
162 *probation* proof   164 *'gainst* just before   168 *strike* destroy by evil influence

No fairy takes,* nor witch hath power to charm,
So hallowed and so gracious* is that time.   170
Horatio: So have I heard and do in part believe it.
But, look, the morn in russet mantle clad
Walks o'er the dew of yon high eastward hill.
Break we our watch up, and by my advice
Let us impart what we have seen tonight   175
Unto young Hamlet; for upon my life,
This spirit, dumb to us, will speak to him.
Do you consent we shall acquaint him with it,
As needful in our loves, fitting our duty?
Marcellus: Let's do 't, I pray, and I this morning know   180
Where we shall find him most conveniently.

Exeunt.

Scene II [*The Castle.*]

*Flourish. Enter Claudius, King of Denmark, Gertrude the Queen,
[the] Council, as* Polonius and his son Laertes, Hamlet, cum aliis**
[including Voltimand and Cornelius].

King: Though yet of Hamlet our* dear brother's death
The memory be green, and that it us befitted
To bear our hearts in grief and our whole kingdom
To be contracted in one brow of woe,
Yet so far hath discretion fought with nature   5
That we with wisest sorrow think on him
Together with remembrance of ourselves.
Therefore our sometime* sister, now our queen,
Th' imperial jointress* to this warlike state,
Have we, as 'twere with a defeated joy—   10
With an auspicious and a dropping eye,*
With mirth in funeral and with dirge in marriage,
In equal scale weighing delight and dole*—
Taken to wife. Nor have we herein barred
Your better wisdoms, which have freely gone   15
With this affair along. For all, our thanks.
Now follows that you know* young Fortinbras,
Holding a weak supposal* of our worth,
Or thinking by our late dear brother's death
Our state to be disjoint and out of frame,   20
Co-leaguèd with* this dream of his advantage,*
He hath not failed to pester us with message
Importing* the surrender of those lands

169 *takes* bewitches   170 *gracious* full of grace   *stage direction: as* i.e., such as, including.   *cum
aliis* with others   1 *our* my. (The royal "we"; also in the following lines.)   8 *sometime* former
9 *jointress* woman possessing property with her husband   11 *With . . . eye* with one eye smiling and
the other weeping   13 *dole* grief   17 *that you know* what you know already, that; or, that you be
informed as follows   18 *weak supposal* low estimate   21 *Co-leaguèd with* joined to, allied with.
dream. . . advantage illusory hope of having the advantage. (His only ally is this hope.)
23 *Importing* pertaining to

Lost by his father, with all bonds* of law,
To our most valiant brother. So much for him.   25
Now for ourself and for this time of meeting.
Thus much the business is: we have here writ
To Norway, uncle of young Fortinbras—
Who, impotent* and bed-rid, scarcely hears
Of this his nephew's purpose—to suppress   30
His* further gait* herein, in that the levies,
The lists, and full proportions are all made
Out of his subject;* and we here dispatch
You, good Cornelius, and you, Voltimand,
For bearers of this greeting to old Norway,   35
Giving to you no further personal power
To business with the King more than the scope
Of these dilated* articles allow.   [*He gives a paper.*]
Farewell, and let your haste commend your duty.*

Cornelius, Voltimand: In that, and all things, will we show our duty.   40
King: We doubt it nothing.* Heartily farewell.

                          [*Exeunt Voltimand and Cornelius.*]

And now, Laertes, what's the news with you?
You told us of some suit; what is 't, Laertes?
You cannot speak of reason to the Dane*
And lose your voice.* What wouldst thou beg, Laertes,   45
That shall not be my offer, not thy asking?
The head is not more native* to the heart,
The hand more instrumental* to the mouth,
Than is the throne of Denmark to thy father.
What wouldst thou have, Laertes?

Laertes: My dread lord,   50
Your leave and favor* to return to France,
From whence though willingly I came to Denmark
To show my duty in your coronation,
Yet now I must confess, that duty done,
My thoughts and wishes bend again toward France   55
And bow them to your gracious leave and pardon.*

King: Have you your father's leave? What says Polonius?
Polonius: H'ath,* my lord, wrung from me my slow leave
By laborsome petition, and at last
Upon his will I sealed* my hard* consent.   60
I do beseech you, give him leave to go.
King: Take thy fair hour,* Laertes. Time be thine,

---

24 *bonds* contracts   29 *impotent* helpless   31 *His* i.e., Fortinbras'.   *gait* proceeding
31–33 *in that. . . subject* since the levying of troops and supplies is drawn entirely from the King of
Norway's own subjects   38 *dilated* set out at length   39 *let. . . duty* let your swift obeying of
orders, rather than mere words, express your dutifulness   41 *nothing* not at all   44 *the Dane* the
Danish king   45 *lose your voice* waste your speech   47 *native* closely connected, related
48 *instrumental* serviceable   51 *leave and favor* kind permission   56 *bow. . . pardon* entreatingly
make a deep bow, asking your permission to depart   58 *H'ath* he has   60 *sealed* (as if sealing a
legal document).   *hard* reluctant   62 *Take thy fair hour* enjoy your time of youth

And thy best graces spend it at thy will!*
But now, my cousin* Hamlet, and my son—
Hamlet: A little more than kin, and less than kind.* 65
King: How is it that the clouds still hang on you?
Hamlet: Not so, my lord. I am too much in the sun.*
Queen: Good Hamlet, cast thy nighted color* off,
  And let thine eye look like a friend on Denmark.*
  Do not forever with thy vailèd lids* 70
  Seek for thy noble father in the dust.
  Thou know'st 'tis common,* all that lives must die,
  Passing through nature to eternity.
Hamlet: Ay, madam, it is common.
Queen: If it be,
  Why seems it so particular* with thee? 75
Hamlet: Seems, madam? Nay, it is. I know not "seems."
  'Tis not alone my inky cloak, good Mother,
  Nor customary* suits of solemn black,
  Nor windy suspiration* of forced breath,
  No, nor the fruitful* river in the eye, 80
  Nor the dejected havior* of the visage,
  Together with all forms, moods,* shapes of grief,
  That can denote me truly. These indeed seem,
  For they are actions that a man might play.
  But I have that within which passes show; 85
  These but the trappings and the suits of woe.
King: 'Tis sweet and commendable in your nature, Hamlet,
  To give these mourning duties to your father.
  But you must know your father lost a father,
  That father lost, lost his, and the survivor bound 90
  In filial obligation for some term
  To do obsequious* sorrow. But to persever*
  In obstinate condolement* is a course
  Of impious stubbornness. 'Tis unmanly grief.
  It shows a will most incorrect to heaven, 95
  A heart unfortified,* a mind impatient,
  An understanding simple* and unschooled.
  For what we know must be and is as common
  As any the most vulgar thing to sense,*

63 *And . . . will* and may your finest qualities guide the way you choose to spend your time
64 *cousin* any kin not of the immediate family   65 *A little . . . kind* i.e., closer than an ordinary
nephew (since I am stepson), and yet more separated in natural feeling (with pun on *kind* meaning
"affectionate" and "natural," "lawful." This line is often read as an aside, but it need not be. The
King chooses perhaps not to respond to Hamlet's cryptic and bitter remark.)   67 *the sun* i.e., the
sunshine of the King's royal favor (with pun on *son*)   68 *nighted color* (1) mourning garments of
black (2) dark melancholy   69 *Denmark* the King of Denmark   70 *vailèd lids* lowered eyes
72 *common* of universal occurrence. (But Hamlet plays on the sense of "vulgar" in line 74.)
75 *particular* personal   78 *customary* (1) socially conventional (2) habitual with me
79 *suspiration* sighing   80 *fruitful* abundant   81 *havior* expression   82 *moods* outward
expression of feeling   92 *obsequious* suited to obsequies or funerals.   *persever* persevere
93 *condolement* sorrowing   96 *unfortified* i.e., against adversity   97 *simple* ignorant
99 *As . . . sense* as the most ordinary experience

Why should we in our peevish opposition　　　　　100
Take it to heart? Fie, 'tis a fault to heaven,
A fault against the dead, a fault to nature,
To reason most absurd, whose common theme
Is death of fathers, and who still* hath cried,
From the first corpse* till he that died today,　　105
"This must be so." We pray you, throw to earth
This unprevailing* woe and think of us
As of a father; for let the world take note,
You are the most immediate* to our throne,
And with no less nobility of love　　　　　　　110
Than that which dearest father bears his son
Do I impart toward* you. For* your intent
In going back to school* in Wittenberg,*
It is most retrograde* to our desire,
And we beseech you bend you* to remain　　　115
Here in the cheer and comfort of our eye,
Our chiefest courtier, cousin, and our son.
Queen: Let not thy mother lose her prayers, Hamlet.
I pray thee, stay with us, go not to Wittenberg.
Hamlet: I shall in all my best* obey you, madam.　　120
King: Why, 'tis a loving and a fair reply.
Be as ourself in Denmark. Madam, come.
This gentle and unforced accord of Hamlet
Sits smiling to* my heart, in grace* whereof
No jocund* health that Denmark drinks today　125
But the great cannon to the clouds shall tell,
And the King's rouse* the heaven shall bruit again,*
Respeaking earthly thunder.* Come away.

Flourish. Exeunt all but Hamlet.

Hamlet: O, that this too too sullied* flesh would melt,
Thaw, and resolve itself into a dew!　　　　　130
Or that the Everlasting had not fixed
His canon* 'gainst self-slaughter! O God, God,
How weary, stale, flat, and unprofitable
Seem to me all the uses* of this world!
Fie on 't, ah fie! 'Tis an unweeded garden　　135
That grows to seed. Things rank and gross in nature
Possess it merely.* That it should come to this!
But two months dead—nay, not so much, not two.
So excellent a king, that was to* this

---

104 *still* always　105 *the first corpse* (Abel's)　107 *unprevailing* unavailing, useless
109 *most immediate* next in succession　112 *impart toward* i.e., bestow my affection on.　*For as
for*　113 *to school* i.e., to your studies.　*Wittenberg* famous German university founded in 1502
114 *retrograde* contrary　115 *bend you* incline yourself　120 *in all my best* to the best of my
ability　124 *to* i.e., at.　*grace* thanksgiving　125 *jocund* merry　127 *rouse* drinking of a draft of
liquor.　*bruit again* loudly echo　128 *thunder* i.e., of trumpet and kettledrum, sounded when the
King drinks; see 1.4.8–12　129 *sullied* defiled. (The early quartos read *sallied*; the Folio, *solid.*)
132 *canon* law　134 *all the uses* the whole routine　137 *merely* completely　139 *to* in
comparison to

Hyperion* to a satyr,* so loving to my mother   140
That he might not beteem* the winds of heaven
Visit her face too roughly. Heaven and earth,
Must I remember? Why, she would hang on him
As if increase of appetite had grown
By what it fed on, and yet within a month—   145
Let me not think on 't; frailty, thy name is woman!—
A little month, or ere* those shoes were old
With which she followed my poor father's body,
Like Niobe,* all tears, why she, even she—
O God, a beast, that wants discourse of reason,*   150
Would have mourned longer—married with my uncle,
My father's brother, but no more like my father
Than I to Hercules. Within a month,
Ere yet the salt of most unrighteous tears
Had left the flushing in her gallèd* eyes,   155
She married. O, most wicked speed, to post*
With such dexterity to incestuous* sheets!
It is not, nor it cannot come to good.
But break, my heart, for I must hold my tongue.

Enter Horatio, Marcellus, and Bernardo.

Horatio: Hail to your lordship!
Hamlet: I am glad to see you well.   160
     Horatio!—or I do forget myself.
Horatio: The same, my lord, and your poor servant ever.
Hamlet: Sir, my good friend; I'll change that name* with you.
     And what make you from* Wittenberg, Horatio?
     Marcellus.   165
Marcellus: My good lord.
Hamlet: I am very glad to see you. [*To Bernardo.*] Good even, sir.—
     But what in faith make you from Wittenberg?
Horatio: A truant disposition, good my lord.
Hamlet: I would not hear your enemy say so,   170
     Nor shall you do my ear that violence
     To make it truster of your own report
     Against yourself. I know you are no truant.
     But what is your affair in Elsinore?
     We'll teach you to drink deep ere you depart.   175
Horatio: My lord, I came to see your father's funeral.
Hamlet: I prithee, do not mock me, fellow student;
     I think it was to see my mother's wedding.

140 *Hyperion* Titan sun-god, father of Helios.   *satyr* a lecherous creature of classical mythology,
half-human but with a goat's legs, tail, ears, and horns   141 *beteem* allow   147 *or ere* even before
149 *Niobe* Tantalus' daughter, Queen of Thebes, who boasted that she had more sons and
daughters than Leto; for this, Apollo and Artemis, children of Leto, slew her fourteen children.
She was turned by Zeus into a stone that continually dropped tears.   150 *wants. . . reason* lacks
the faculty of reason   155 *gallèd* irritated, inflamed   156 *post* hasten   157 *incestuous* (In
Shakespeare's day, the marriage of a man like Claudius to his deceased brother's wife was
considered incestuous.)   163 *change that name* i.e., give and receive reciprocally the name of
"friend" (rather than talk of "servant")   164 *make you from* are you doing away from

Horatio: Indeed, my lord, it followed hard* upon.

Hamlet: Thrift, thrift, Horatio! The funeral baked meats*   180
    Did coldly* furnish forth the marriage tables.
    Would I had met my dearest* foe in heaven
    Or ever* I had seen that day, Horatio!
    My father!—Methinks I see my father.

Horatio: Where, my lord?

Hamlet: In my mind's eye, Horatio.   185

Horatio: I saw him once. 'A* was a goodly king.

Hamlet: 'A was a man. Take him for all in all,
    I shall not look upon his like again.

Horatio: My lord, I think I saw him yesternight.

Hamlet: Saw? Who?   190

Horatio: My lord, the King your father.

Hamlet: The King my father?

Horatio: Season your admiration* for a while
    With an attent* ear till I may deliver,
    Upon the witness of these gentlemen,   195
    This marvel to you.

Hamlet: For God's love, let me hear!

Horatio: Two nights together had these gentlemen,
    Marcellus and Bernardo, on their watch,
    In the dead waste* and middle of the night,
    Been thus encountered. A figure like your father,   200
    Armèd at point* exactly, cap-à-pie,*
    Appears before them, and with solemn march
    Goes slow and stately by them. Thrice he walked
    By their oppressed and fear-surprisèd eyes
    Within his truncheon's* length, whilst they, distilled*   205
    Almost to jelly with the act* of fear,
    Stand dumb and speak not to him. This to me
    In dreadful* secrecy impart they did,
    And I with them the third night kept the watch,
    Where, as they had delivered, both in time,   210
    Form of the thing, each word made true and good,
    The apparition comes. I knew your father;
    These hands are not more like.

Hamlet: But where was this?

Marcellus: My lord, upon the platform where we watch.

Hamlet: Did you not speak to it?

Horatio: My lord, I did,   215
    But answer made it none. Yet once methought
    It lifted up its head and did address
    Itself to motion, like as it would speak;*

---

179 *hard* close   180 *baked meats* meat pies   181 *coldly* i.e., as cold leftovers   182 *dearest* closest
(and therefore deadliest)   183 *Or ever* before   186 *'A* he   193 *Season your admiration* restrain
your astonishment   194 *attent* attentive   199 *dead waste* desolate stillness   201 *at point*
correctly in every detail.   *cap-à-pie* from head to foot   205 *truncheon* officer's staff.   *distilled*
dissolved   206 *act* action, operation   208 *dreadful* full of dread   217–218 *did. . . speak* began to
move as though it were about to speak

But even then* the morning cock crew loud,
And at the sound it shrunk in haste away   220
And vanished from our sight.
Hamlet: 'Tis very strange.
Horatio: As I do live, my honored lord, 'tis true,
And we did think it writ down in our duty
To let you know of it.
Hamlet: Indeed, indeed, sirs. But this troubles me.   225
Hold you the watch tonight?
All: We do, my lord.
Hamlet: Armed, say you?
All: Armed, my lord.
Hamlet: From top to toe?
All: My lord, from head to foot.   230
Hamlet: Then saw you not his face?
Horatio: O, yes, my lord, he wore his beaver* up.
Hamlet: What* looked he, frowningly?
Horatio: A countenance more in sorrow than in anger.
Hamlet: Pale or red?   235
Horatio: Nay, very pale.
Hamlet: And fixed his eyes upon you?
Horatio: Most constantly.
Hamlet: I would I had been there.
Horatio: It would have much amazed you.   240
Hamlet: Very like, very like. Stayed it long?
Horatio: While one with moderate haste might tell* a hundred.
Marcellus, Bernardo: Longer, longer.
Horatio: Not when I saw 't.
Hamlet: His beard was grizzled*—no?   245
Horatio: It was, as I have seen it in his life,
A sable silvered.*
Hamlet: I will watch tonight.
Perchance 'twill walk again.
Horatio: I warrant* it will.
Hamlet: If it assume my noble father's person,
I'll speak to it though hell itself should gape   250
And bid me hold my peace. I pray you all,
If you have hitherto concealed this sight,
Let it be tenable* in your silence still,
And whatsoever else shall hap tonight,
Give it an understanding but no tongue.   255
I will requite your loves. So, fare you well.
Upon the platform twixt eleven and twelve
I'll visit you.
All: Our duty to your honor.
Hamlet: Your loves, as mine to you. Farewell.

Exeunt [all but Hamlet].

219 *even then* at that very instant   232 *beaver* visor on the helmet   233 *What* how   242 *tell* count
245 *grizzled* gray   247 *sable silvered* black mixed with white   248 *warrant* assure you
253 *tenable* held

My father's spirit in arms! All is not well.   260
I doubt* some foul play. Would the night were come!
Till then sit still, my soul. Foul deeds will rise,
Though all the earth o'erwhelm them, to men's eyes.

Exit.

Scene III [*Polonius' Chambers.*]

Enter Laertes and Ophelia, his sister.

Laertes: My necessaries are embarked. Farewell.
      And, sister, as the winds give benefit
      And convoy is assistant,* do not sleep
      But let me hear from you.
Ophelia: Do you doubt that?
Laertes: For Hamlet, and the trifling of his favor,   5
      Hold it a fashion and a toy in blood,*
      A violet in the youth of primy* nature,
      Forward,* not permanent, sweet, not lasting,
      The perfume and suppliance* of a minute—
      No more.
Ophelia: No more but so?
Laertes: Think it no more.   10
      For nature crescent* does not grow alone
      In thews* and bulk, but as this temple* waxes
      The inward service of the mind and soul
      Grows wide withal.* Perhaps he loves you now,
      And now no soil* nor cautel* doth besmirch   15
      The virtue of his will;* but you must fear,
      His greatness weighed,* his will is not his own.
      For he himself is subject to his birth.
      He may not, as unvalued persons do,
      Carve* for himself, for on his choice depends   20
      The safety and health of this whole state,
      And therefore must his choice be circumscribed
      Unto the voice and yielding* of that body
      Whereof he is the head. Then if he says he loves you,
      It fits your wisdom so far to believe it   25
      As he in his particular act and place*
      May give his saying deed, which is no further
      Than the main voice* of Denmark goes withal.*
      Then weigh what loss your honor may sustain
      If with too credent* ear you list* his songs,   30
      Or lose your heart, or your chaste treasure open

---

261 *doubt* suspect   3 *convoy is assistant* means of conveyance are available   6 *toy in blood*
passing amorous fancy   7 *primy* in its prime, springtime   8 *Forward* precocious   9 *suppliance*
supply, filler   11 *crescent* growing, waxing   12 *thews* bodily strength.   *temple* i.e., body
14 *Grows wide withal* grows along with it   15 *soil* blemish.   *cautel* deceit   16 *will* desire
17 *His greatness weighed* if you take into account his high position   20 *Carve* i.e., choose
23 *voice and yielding* assent, approval   26 *in. . . place* in his particular restricted circumstances
28 *main voice* general assent.   *withal* along with   30 *credent* credulous.   *list* listen to

To his unmastered importunity.
Fear it, Ophelia, fear it, my dear sister,
And keep you in the rear of your affection,*
Out of the shot and danger of desire.   35
The chariest* maid is prodigal enough
If she unmask* her beauty to the moon.*
Virtue itself scapes not calumnious strokes.
The canker galls* the infants of the spring
Too oft before their buttons* be disclosed,*   40
And in the morn and liquid dew* of youth
Contagious blastments* are most imminent.
Be wary then; best safety lies in fear.
Youth* to itself rebels, though none else near.

Ophelia: I shall the effect of this good lesson keep   45
As watchman to my heart. But, good my brother,
Do not, as some ungracious* pastors do,
Show me the steep and thorny way to heaven,
Whiles like a puffed* and reckless libertine
Himself the primrose path of dalliance treads,   50
And recks* not his own rede.*

Enter Polonius.

Laertes: O, fear me not.*
I stay too long. But here my father comes.
A double* blessing is a double grace;
Occasion smiles upon a second leave.*

Polonius: Yet here, Laertes? Aboard, aboard, for shame!   55
The wind sits in the shoulder of your sail,
And you are stayed for. There—my blessing with thee!
And these few precepts in thy memory
Look* thou character.* Give thy thoughts no tongue,
Nor any unproportioned* thought his* act.   60
Be thou familiar,* but by no means vulgar.*
Those friends thou hast, and their adoption tried,*
Grapple them unto thy soul with hoops of steel,
But do not dull thy palm* with entertainment
Of each new-hatched, unfledged courage.* Beware   65
Of entrance to a quarrel, but being in,
Bear 't that* th' opposèd may beware of thee.

---

34 *keep . . . affection* don't advance as far as your affection might lead you. (A military metaphor.)
36 *chariest* most scrupulously modest   37 *If she unmask* if she does no more than show her
beauty.   *moon* (Symbol of chastity.)   39 *canker galls* cankerworm destroys   40 *buttons* buds.
disclosed opened   41 *liquid dew* i.e., time when dew is fresh and bright   42 *blastments* blights
44 *Youth . . . rebels* youth is inherently rebellious   47 *ungracious* ungodly   49 *puffed* bloated, or
swollen with pride   51 *recks* heeds.   *rede* counsel.   51 *fear me not* don't worry on my account
53 *double* (Laertes has already bid his father good-bye.)   54 *Occasion . . . leave* happy is the
circumstance that provides a second leave-taking. The goddess Occasion, or Opportunity, smiles.)
59 *Look* be sure that.   *character* inscribe   60 *unproportioned* badly calculated, intemperate.
his its   61 *familiar* sociable.   *vulgar* common   62 *and their adoption tried* and also their
suitability for adoption as friends having been tested   64 *dull thy palm* i.e., shake hands so often as
to make the gesture meaningless   65 *courage* young man of spirit   67 *Bear 't that* manage it so that

Give every man thy ear, but few thy voice;
Take each man's censure,* but reserve thy judgment.
Costly thy habit* as thy purse can buy,   70
But not expressed in fancy;* rich, not gaudy,
For the apparel oft proclaims the man,
And they in France of the best rank and station
Are of a most select and generous chief in that.*
Neither a borrower nor a lender be,   75
For loan oft loses both itself and friend,
And borrowing dulleth edge of husbandry.*
This above all: to thine own self be true,
And it must follow, as the night the day,
Thou canst not then be false to any man.   80
Farewell. My blessing season* this in thee!
Laertes: Most humbly do I take my leave, my lord.
Polonius: The time invests* you. Go, your servants tend.*
Laertes: Farewell, Ophelia, and remember well
      What I have said to you.   85
Ophelia: 'Tis in my memory locked,
      And you yourself shall keep the key of it.
Laertes: Farewell.   *Exit Laertes.*
Polonius: What is 't, Ophelia, he hath said to you?
Ophelia: So please you, something touching the Lord Hamlet.   90
Polonius: Marry,* well bethought.
      'Tis told me he hath very oft of late
      Given private time to you, and you yourself
      Have of your audience been most free and bounteous.
      If it be so—as so 'tis put on* me,   95
      And that in way of caution—I must tell you
      You do not understand yourself so clearly
      As it behooves* my daughter and your honor.
      What is between you? Give me up the truth.
Ophelia: He hath, my lord, of late made many tenders*   100
      Of his affection to me.
Polonius: Affection? Pooh! You speak like a green girl,
      Unsifted* in such perilous circumstance.
      Do you believe his tenders, as you call them?
Ophelia: I do not know, my lord, what I should think.   105
Polonius: Marry, I will teach you. Think yourself a baby
      That you have ta'en these tenders for true pay
      Which are not sterling.* Tender* yourself more dearly,
      Or—not to crack the wind* of the poor phrase,
      Running it thus—you'll tender me a fool.*   110

---

69 *censure* opinion, judgment   70 *habit* clothing   71 *fancy* excessive ornament, decadent fashion
74 *Are. . . that* are of a most refined and well-bred preeminence in choosing what to wear
77 *husbandry* thrift   81 *season* mature   83 *invests* besieges, presses upon.   *tend* attend, wait
91 *Marry* i.e., by the Virgin Mary. (A mild oath.)   95 *put on* impressed on, told to   98 *behooves*
befits   100 *tenders* offers   103 *Unsifted* i.e., untried   108 *sterling* legal currency.   *Tender* hold,
look after, offer   109 *crack the wind* i.e., run it until it is broken-winded   110 *tender me a fool*
(1) show yourself to me as a fool (2) show me up as a fool (3) present me with a grand-child. (*Fool*
was a term of endearment for a child.)

Ophelia: My lord, he hath importuned me with love
    In honorable fashion.*
Polonius: Ay, fashion you may call it. Go to,* go to.
Ophelia: And hath given countenance* to his speech, my lord,
    With almost all the holy vows of heaven.   115
Polonius: Ay, springes* to catch woodcocks.* I do know,
    When the blood burns, how prodigal* the soul
    Lends the tongue vows. These blazes, daughter,
    Giving more light than heat, extinct in both
    Even in their promise as it* is a-making,   120
    You must not take for fire. From this time
    Be something* scanter of your maiden presence.
    Set your entreatments* at a higher rate
    Than a command to parle.* For Lord Hamlet,
    Believe so much in him* that he is young,   125
    And with a larger tether may he walk
    Than may be given you. In few,* Ophelia,
    Do not believe his vows, for they are brokers,*
    Not of that dye* which their investments* show,
    But mere implorators* of unholy suits,   130
    Breathing* like sanctified and pious bawds,
    The better to beguile. This is for all:*
    I would not, in plain terms, from this time forth
    Have you so slander* any moment* leisure
    As to give words or talk with the Lord Hamlet.   135
    Look to 't, I charge you. Come your ways.*
Ophelia: I shall obey, my lord.   *Exeunt.*

Scene IV [The Guard Platform.]

Enter Hamlet, Horatio, and Marcellus.

Hamlet: The air bites shrewdly;* it is very cold.
Horatio: It is a nipping and an eager* air.
Hamlet: What hour now?
Horatio: I think it lacks of* twelve.
Marcellus: No, it is struck.
Horatio: Indeed? I heard it not.
    It then draws near the season*   5
    Wherein the spirit held his wont* to walk.

---

113 *fashion* mere form, pretense.   *Go to* (An expression of impatience.)   114 *countenance* credit,
confirmation   116 *springes* snares.   *woodcocks* birds easily caught; here used to connote
gullibility.   117 *prodigal* prodigally   120 *it* i.e., the promise   122 *something* somewhat
123 *entreatments* negotiations for surrender. (A military term.)   124 *parle* discuss terms with the
enemy. (Polonius urges his daughter, in the metaphor of military language, not to meet with
Hamlet and consider giving in to him merely because he requests an interview.)   125 *so. . . him*
this much concerning him   127 *In few* briefly   128 *brokers* go-between, procurers   129 *dye* color
or sort.   *investments* clothes. (The vows are not what they seem.)   130 *mere implorators* out and
out solicitors   131 *Breathing* speaking   132 *for all* once for all, in sum   134 *slander* abuse,
misuse.   *moment* moment's   136 *Come your ways* come along   1 *shrewdly* keenly, sharply
2 *eager* biting   5 *lacks of* is just short of   5 *season* time   6 *held his wont* was accustomed.

A flourish of trumpets, and two pieces* go off [within].

What does this mean, my lord?

Hamlet: The King doth wake* tonight and takes his rouse,*
Keeps wassail,* and the swaggering upspring* reels;*
And as he drains his drafts of Rhenish* down,   10
The kettledrum and trumpet thus bray out
The triumph of his pledge.*

Horatio: Is it a custom?

Hamlet: Ay, marry, is 't,
But to my mind, though I am native here
And to the manner* born, it is a custom   15
More honored in the breach than the observance.*
This heavy-headed revel east and west*
Makes us traduced and taxed of* other nations.
They clepe* us drunkards, and with swinish phrase*
Soil our addition;* and indeed it takes   20
From our achievements, though performed at height,*
The pith and marrow of our attribute.*
So, oft it chances in particular men,
That for* some vicious mole of nature* in them,
As in their birth—wherein they are not guilty,   25
Since nature cannot choose his* origin—
By their o'ergrowth of some complexion,*
Oft breaking down the pales* and forts of reason,
Or by some habit that too much o'erleavens*
The form of plausive* manners, that these men,   30
Carrying, I say, the stamp of one defect,
Being nature's livery* or fortune's star,*
His virtues else,* be they as pure as grace,
As infinite as man may undergo,*
Shall in the general censure* take corruption   35
From that particular fault. The dram of evil
Doth all the noble substance often dout
To his own scandal.*

Enter Ghost.

---

stage direction: *pieces* i.e., of ordnance, cannon   8 *wake* stay awake and hold revel.   *takes his rouse* carouses   9 *wassail* carousal.   *upspring* wild German dance.   *reels* dances   10 *Rhenish* Rhine wine   12 *The triumph. . . pledge* i.e., his feat in draining the wine in a single draft   15 *manner* custom (of drinking)   16 *More. . . observance* better neglected than followed   17 *east and west* i.e., everywhere   18 *taxed of* censured by   19 *clepe* call.   *with swinish phrase* i.e., by calling us swine   20 *addition* reputation   21 *at height* outstandingly   22 *The pith. . . attribute* the essence of the reputation that others attribute to us   24 *for* on account of.   *mole of nature* natural blemish in one's constitution   26 *his* its   27 *their o'ergrowth. . . complexion* the excessive growth in individuals of some natural trait   28 *pales* palings, fences (as of a fortification)   29 *o'erleavens* induces a change throughout (as yeast works in dough)   30 *plausive* pleasing   32 *nature's livery* sign of one's servitude to nature.   *fortune's star* the destiny that chance brings   33 *His virtues else* i.e., the other qualities of *these men* (line 30)   34 *may undergo* can sustain   35 *general censure* general opinion that people have of him   36–38 *The dram. . . scandal* i.e., the small drop of evil blots out or works against the noble substance of the whole and brings it into disrepute. To *dout* is to blot out. (A famous crux.)

Horatio: Look, my lord, it comes!
Hamlet: Angels and ministers of grace* defend us!
    Be thou* a spirit of health* or goblin damned,   40
    Bring* with thee airs from heaven or blasts from hell,
    Be thy intents* wicked or charitable,
    Thou com'st in such a questionable* shape
    That I will speak to thee. I'll call thee Hamlet,
    King, father, royal Dane. O, answer me!   45
    Let me not burst in ignorance, but tell
    Why thy canonized* bones, hearsèd* in death,
    Have burst their cerements;* why the sepulcher
    Wherein we saw thee quietly inurned*
    Hath oped his ponderous and marble jaws   50
    To cast thee up again. What may this mean,
    That thou, dead corpse, again in complete steel,*
    Revisits thus the glimpses of the moon,*
    Making night hideous, and we fools of nature*
    So horridly to shake our disposition*   55
    With thoughts beyond the reaches of our souls?
    Say, why is this? Wherefore? What should we do?

                    [*The Ghost*] *beckons* [*Hamlet*].

Horatio: It beckons you to go away with it,
    As if it some impartment* did desire
    To you alone.
Marcellus: Look with what courteous action   60
    It wafts you to a more removèd ground.
    But do not go with it.
Horatio: No, by no means.
Hamlet: It will not speak. Then I will follow it.
Horatio: Do not, my lord!
Hamlet: Why, what should be the fear?
    I do not set my life at a pin's fee,*   65
    And for my soul, what can it do to that,
    Being a thing immortal as itself?
    It waves me forth again. I'll follow it.
Horatio: What if it tempt you toward the flood,* my lord,
    Or to the dreadful summit of the cliff   70
    That beetles o'er* his base into the sea,
    And there assume some other horrible form
    Which might deprive your sovereignty* of reason*
    And draw you into madness? Think of it.

---

39 *ministers of grace* messengers of God   40 *Be thou* whether you are.   *spirit of health* good angel
41 *Bring* whether you bring   42 *Be thy intents* whether your intentions are   43 *questionable* inviting
question   47 *cannonized* buried according to the canons of the church. *hearsèd* coffined
48 *cerements* grave clothes   49 *inurned* entombed   52 *complete steel* full armor   53 *glimpses of the
moon* pale and uncertain moonlight   54 *fools of nature* mere men, limited to natural knowledge and
subject to nature   55 *So . . . disposition* to distress our mental composure so violently
59 *impartment* communication   65 *fee* value   69 *flood* sea   71 *beetles o'er* overhangs threateningly
(like bushy eyebrows.)   73 *deprive . . . reason* take away the rule of reason over your mind

The very place puts toys of desperation,*   75
Without more motive, into every brain
That looks so many fathoms to the sea
And hears it roar beneath.
Hamlet: It wafts me still.—Go on, I'll follow thee.
Marcellus: You shall not go, my lord.   [*They try to stop him.*]
Hamlet: Hold off your hands!   80
Horatio: Be ruled. You shall not go.
Hamlet: My fate cries out,*
And makes each petty* artery* in this body
As hardy as the Nemean lion's* nerve.*
Still am I called. Unhand me, gentlemen.
By heaven, I'll make a ghost of him that lets* me!   85
I say, away!—Go on, I'll follow thee.

                                              Exeunt Ghost and Hamlet.

Horatio: He waxes desperate with imagination.
Marcellus: Let's follow. 'Tis not fit thus to obey him.
Horatio: Have after.* To what issue* will this come?
Marcellus: Something is rotten in the state of Denmark.   90
Horatio: Heaven will direct it.*
Marcellus: Nay, let's follow him.   *Exeunt.*

Scene V [The Battlements of the Castle.]

   Enter Ghost and Hamlet.

Hamlet: Whither wilt thou lead me? Speak. I'll go no further.
Ghost: Mark me.
Hamlet: I will.
Ghost: My hour is almost come,
When I to sulfurous and tormenting flames
Must render up myself.
Hamlet: Alas, poor ghost!
Ghost: Pity me not, but lend thy serious hearing   5
To what I shall unfold.
Hamlet: Speak. I am bound* to hear.
Ghost: So art thou to revenge, when thou shalt hear.
Hamlet: What?
Ghost: I am thy father's spirit,   10
Doomed for a certain term to walk the night,
And for the day confined to fast* in fires,
Till the foul crimes* done in my days of nature*
Are burnt and purged away. But that* I am forbid

---

75 *toys of desperation* fancies of desperate acts, i.e., suicide   81 *My fate cries out* my destiny
summons me   82 *petty* weak.   *artery* (through which the vital spirits were thought to have been
conveyed)   83 *Nemean lion* one of the monsters slain by Hercules in his twelve labors.
nerve sinew   85 *lets* hinders   89 *Have after* let's go after him.   *issue* outcome   91 *it* i.e., the
outcome   7 *bound* (1) ready (2) obligated by duty and fate. (The Ghost, in line 8, answers in the
second sense.)   12 *fast* do penance by fasting   13 *crimes* sins.   *of nature* as a mortal   14 *But
that* were it not that

To tell the secrets of my prison house,   15
I could a tale unfold whose lightest word
Would harrow up* thy soul, freeze thy young blood,
Make thy two eyes like stars start from their spheres,*
Thy knotted and combinèd locks* to part,
And each particular hair to stand on end   20
Like quills upon the fretful porcupine.
But this eternal blazon* must not be
To ears of flesh and blood. List, list, O, list!
If thou didst ever thy dear father love—

Hamlet: O God!   25
Ghost: Revenge his foul and most unnatural murder.
Hamlet: Murder?
Ghost: Murder most foul, as in the best* it is,
But this most foul, strange, and unnatural.
Hamlet: Haste me to know 't, that I, with wings as swift   30
As meditation or the thoughts of love,
May sweep to my revenge.
Ghost: I find thee apt;
And duller shouldst thou be* than the fat* weed
That roots itself in ease on Lethe* wharf,
Wouldst thou not stir in this. Now, Hamlet, hear.   35
'Tis given out that, sleeping in my orchard,*
A serpent stung me. So the whole ear of Denmark
Is by a forgèd process* of my death
Rankly abused.* But know, thou noble youth,
The serpent that did sting thy father's life   40
Now wears his crown.
Hamlet: O, my prophetic soul! My uncle!
Ghost: Ay, that incestuous, that adulterate* beast,
With witchcraft of his wit, with traitorous gifts*—
O wicked wit and gifts, that have the power   45
So to seduce!—won to his shameful lust
The will of my most seeming-virtuous queen.
O Hamlet, what a falling off was there!
From me, whose love was of that dignity
That it went hand in hand even with the vow*   50
I made to her in marriage, and to decline
Upon a wretch whose natural gifts were poor
To* those of mine!
But virtue, as it* never will be moved,
Though lewdness court it in a shape of heaven,*   55
So lust, though to a radiant angel linked,

---

17 *harrow up* lacerate, tear   18 *spheres* i.e., eye-sockets, here compared to the orbits or transparent
revolving spheres in which, according to Ptolemaic astronomy, the heavenly bodies were fixed
19 *knotted. . . locks* hair neatly arranged and confined   22 *eternal blazon* revelation of the secrets of
eternity   28 *in the best* even at best   33 *shouldst thou be* you would have to be.   *fat* torpid, lethargic
34 *Lethe* the river of forgetfulness in Hades   36 *orchard* garden   38 *forgèd process* falsified account
39 *abused* deceived   43 *adulterate* adulterous   44 *gifts* (1) talents (2) presents   50 *even with the vow*
with the very vow   53 *To* compared to   54 *virtue, as it* as virtue   55 *shape of heaven* heavenly form

Will sate itself in a celestial bed*
And prey on garbage.
But soft, methinks I scent the morning air.
Brief let me be. Sleeping within my orchard,   60
My custom always of the afternoon,
Upon my secure* hour thy uncle stole,
With juice of cursèd hebona* in a vial,
And in the porches of my ears* did pour
The leprous distillment,* whose effect   65
Holds such an enmity with blood of man
That swift as quicksilver it courses through
The natural gates and alleys of the body,
And with a sudden vigor it doth posset*
And curd, like eager* droppings into milk,   70
The thin and wholesome blood. So did it mine,
And a most instant tetter* barked* about,
Most lazar-like,* with vile and loathsome crust,
All my smooth body.
Thus was I, sleeping, by a brother's hand   75
Of life, of crown, of queen at once dispatched,*
Cut off even in the blossom of my sin,
Unhouseled,* disappointed,* unaneled,*
No reckoning* made, but sent to my account
With all my imperfections on my head.   80
O, horrible! O, horrible, most horrible!
If thou hast nature* in thee, bear it not.
Let not the royal bed of Denmark be
A couch for luxury* and damnèd incest.
But, howsoever thou pursues this act,   85
Taint not thy mind nor let thy soul contrive
Against thy mother aught. Leave her to heaven
And to those thorns that in her bosom lodge,
To prick and sting her. Fare thee well at once.
The glowworm shows the matin* to be near,   90
And 'gins to pale his* uneffectual fire.
Adieu, adieu, adieu! Remember me.   [*Exit.*]
Hamlet: O all you host of heaven! O earth! What else?
And shall I couple* hell? O, fie! Hold,* hold, my heart,
And you, my sinews, grow not instant* old,   95
But bear me stiffly up. Remember thee?

---

57 *sate. . . bed* cease to find sexual pleasure in a virtuously lawful marriage   62 *secure* confident,
unsuspicious   63 *hebona* a poison. (The word seems to be a form of *ebony*, though it is thought
perhaps to be related to *henbane*, a poison, or to *ebenus*, "yew.")   64 *porches of my ears* ears
as a porch or entrance of the body   65 *leprous distillment* distillation causing leprosylike
disfigurement   69 *posset* coagulate, curdle   70 *eager* sour, acid   72 *tetter* eruption of scabs.
barked covered with a rough covering, like bark of a tree   73 *lazar-like* leperlike   76 *dispatched*
suddenly deprived   78 *Unhouseled* without having received the Sacrament.   *disappointed*
unready (spiritually) for the last journey.   *unaneled* without having received extreme unction
79 *reckoning* settling of accounts   82 *nature* i.e., the promptings of a son   84 *luxury* lechery
90 *matin* morning   91 *his* its   94 *couple* add.   *Hold* hold together   95 *instant* instantly

Ay, thou poor ghost, whiles memory holds a seat
In this distracted globe.* Remember thee?
Yea, from the table* of my memory
I'll wipe away all trivial fond* records,   100
All saws* of books, all forms,* all pressures* past
That youth and observation copied there,
And thy commandment all alone shall live
Within the book and volume of my brain,
Unmixed with baser matter. Yes, by heaven!   105
O most pernicious woman!
O villain, villain, smiling, damnèd villain!
My tables*—meet it is* I set it down
That one may smile, and smile, and be a villain.
At least I am sure it may be so in Denmark.   110

                                                              [*Writing.*]

So, uncle, there you are.* Now to my word:
It is "Adieu, adieu! Remember me."
I have sworn 't.

Enter Horatio and Marcellus.

Horatio: My lord, my lord!
Marcellus: Lord Hamlet!   115
Horatio: Heavens secure him!*
Hamlet: So be it.
Marcellus: Hilo, ho, ho, my lord!
Hamlet: Hillo, ho, ho, boy! Come, bird, come.*
Marcellus: How is 't, my noble lord?   120
Horatio: What news, my lord?
Hamlet: O, wonderful!
Horatio: Good my lord, tell it.
Hamlet: No, you will reveal it.
Horatio: Not I, my lord, by heaven.   125
Marcellus: Nor I, my lord.
Hamlet: How say you, then, would heart of man once* think it?
    But you'll be secret?
Horatio, Marcellus: Ay, by heaven, my lord.
Hamlet: There's never a villain dwelling in all Denmark
    But he's an arrant* knave.   130
Horatio: There needs no ghost, my lord, come from the grave
    To tell us this.
Hamlet: Why, right, you are in the right.
    And so, without more circumstance* at all,
    I hold it fit that we shake hands and part,

---

98 *globe* (1) head (2) world   99 *table* tablet, slate   100 *fond* foolish   101 *saws* wise sayings.
forms shapes or images copied onto the slate; general ideas.   *pressures* impressions stamped
108 *tables* writing tablets.   *meet it is* it is fitting   111 *there you are* i.e., there, I've written that
down against you   116 *secure him* keep him safe   119 *Hillo. . . come* (A falconer's call to a hawk
in air. Hamlet mocks the hallooing as though it were a part of hawking.)   127 *once* ever
130 *arrant* thoroughgoing   133 *circumstance* ceremony, elaboration

You as your business and desire shall point you—　　　　135
For every man hath business and desire,
Such as it is—and for my own poor part,
Look you, I'll go pray.
Horatio: These are but wild and whirling words, my lord.
Hamlet: I am sorry they offend you, heartily;　　　　140
Yes, faith, heartily.
Horatio:　　　　　　　There's no offense, my lord.
Hamlet: Yes, by Saint Patrick,* but there is, Horatio,
And much offense* too. Touching this vision here,
It is an honest ghost,* that let me tell you.
For your desire to know what is between us,　　　　145
O'ermaster 't as you may. And now, good friends,
As you are friends, scholars, and soldiers,
Give me one poor request.
Horatio: What is 't, my lord? We will.
Hamlet: Never make known what you have seen tonight.　　　　150
Horatio, Marcellus: My lord, we will not.
Hamlet: Nay, but swear 't.
Horatio: In faith, my lord, not I.*
Marcellus: Nor I, my lord, in faith.
Hamlet: Upon my sword.*　　　　　　　　　[*He holds out his sword.*]　　155
Marcellus: We have sworn, my lord, already.*
Hamlet: Indeed, upon my sword, indeed.
Ghost (cries under the stage): Swear.
Hamlet: Ha, ha, boy, sayst thou so? Art thou there, truepenny?*
Come on, you hear this fellow in the cellarage.　　　　160
Consent to swear.
Horatio:　　　　　　　Propose the oath, my lord.
Hamlet: Never to speak of this that you have seen,
Swear by my sword.
Ghost [beneath]: Swear.
Hamlet: Hic et ubique?* Then we'll shift our ground.　　　[*They swear.*]*　　165

[*He moves to another spot.*]

Come hither, gentlemen,
And lay your hands again upon my sword.
Swear by my sword
Never to speak of this that you have heard.
Ghost [beneath]: Swear by his sword.　　　　　　　[*They swear.*]　　170
Hamlet: Well said, old mole. Canst work i' th' earth so fast?
A worthy pioner!*—Once more remove, good friends.

142 *Saint Patrick* (The keeper of Purgatory and patron saint of all blunders and confusion.)
143 *offense* (Hamlet deliberately changes Horatio's "no offense taken" to "an offense against all
decency.")　144 *an honest ghost* i.e., a real ghost and not an evil spirit　153 *In faith*. . . *I* i.e., I swear
not to tell what I have seen. (Horatio is not refusing to swear.)　155 *sword* i.e., the hilt in the form of a
cross　156 *We*. . . *already* i.e., we swore in faith　159 *truepenny* honest old fellow　164 *stage
direction: They swear* (Seemingly they swear here, and at lines 170 and 190, as they lay their hands on
Hamlet's sword. Triple oaths would have particular force; these three oaths deal with what they have
seen, what they have heard, and what they promise about Hamlet's *antic disposition*.)　165 *Hic et
ubique* here and everywhere. (Latin.)　172 *pioner* foot soldier assigned to dig tunnels and excavations

[*He moves again.*]

Horatio: O day and night, but this is wondrous strange!

Hamlet: And therefore as a stranger* give it welcome.

There are more things in heaven and earth, Horatio,   175
Than are dreamt of in your philosophy.*
But come;
Here, as before, never, so help you mercy,*
How strange or odd soe'er I bear myself—
As I perchance hereafter shall think meet   180
To put an antic* disposition on—
That you, at such times seeing me, never shall,
With arms encumbered* thus, or this headshake,
Or by pronouncing of some doubtful phrase
As "Well, we know," or "We could, an if* we would,"   185
Or "If we list* to speak," or "There be, an if they might,"*
Or such ambiguous giving out,* to note*
That you know aught* of me—this do swear,
So grace and mercy at your most need help you.

Ghost [*beneath*]: Swear.   [*They swear.*]   190

Hamlet: Rest, rest, perturbèd spirit! So, gentlemen,
With all my love I do commend me to you;*
And what so poor a man as Hamlet is
May do t' express his love and friending* to you,
God willing, shall not lack.* Let us go in together,   195
And still* your fingers on your lips, I pray.
The time* is out of joint. O cursèd spite*
That ever I was born to set it right!

[*They wait for him to leave first.*]

Nay, come, let's go together.*   *Exeunt.*

Act II

Scene I [*Polonius' Chambers.*]

Enter Old Polonius With His Man [*Reynaldo*].

Polonius: Give him this money and these notes, Reynaldo.

[*He gives money and papers.*]

Reynaldo: I will, my lord.

---

174 *as a stranger* i.e., needing your hospitality   176 *your philosophy* this subject called "natural philosophy" or "science" that people talk about   178 *so help you mercy* as you hope for God's mercy when you are judged   181 *antic* fantastic   183 *encumbered* folded   185 *an if* if   186 *list* wished.   *There . . . might* i.e., there are people here (we, in fact) who could tell news if we were at liberty to do so   187 *giving out* intimation.   *note* draw attention to the fact   188 *aught* i.e., something secret   192 *do . . . you* entrust myself to you   194 *friending* friendliness   195 *lack* be lacking   196 *still* always   197 *The time* the state of affairs.   *spite* i.e., the spite of Fortune 199 *let's go together* (Probably they wait for him to leave first, but he refuses this ceremoniousness.)

Polonius: You shall do marvelous* wisely, good Reynaldo,
>   Before you visit him, to make inquire*
>   Of his behavior.
Reynaldo: My lord, I did intend it.   5
Polonius: Marry, well said, very well said. Look you, sir,
>   Inquire me first what Danskers* are in Paris,
>   And how, and who, what means,* and where they keep,*
>   What company, at what expense; and finding
>   By this encompassment* and drift* of question   10
>   That they do know my son, come you more nearer
>   Than your particular demands will touch it.*
>   Take you,* as 'twere, some distant knowledge of him,
>   As thus, "I know his father and his friends,
>   And in part him." Do you mark this, Reynaldo?   15
Reynaldo: Ay, very well, my lord.
Polonius: "And in part him, but," you may say, "not well.
>   But if 't be he I mean, he's very wild,
>   Addicted so and so," and there put on* him
>   What forgeries* you please—marry, none so rank*   20
>   As may dishonor him, take heed of that,
>   But, sir, such wanton,* wild, and usual slips
>   As are companions noted and most known
>   To youth and liberty.
Reynaldo: As gaming, my lord.   25
Polonius: Ay, or drinking, fencing, swearing,
>   Quarreling, drabbing*—you may go so far.
Reynaldo: My lord, that would dishonor him.
Polonius: Faith, no, as you may season* it in the charge.
>   You must not put another scandal on him   30
>   That he is open to incontinency;*
>   That's not my meaning. But breathe his faults so quaintly*
>   That they may seem the taints of liberty,*
>   The flash and outbreak of a fiery mind,
>   A savageness in unreclaimèd blood,   35
>   Of general assault.*
Reynaldo: But, my good lord—
Polonius: Wherefore should you do this?
Reynaldo: Ay, my lord, I would know that.
Polonius: Marry, sir, here's my drift,   40
>   And I believe it is a fetch of warrant.*
>   You laying these slight sullies on my son,

---

3 *marvelous* marvelously   4 *inquire* inquiry   7 *Danskers* Danes   8 *what means* what wealth
(they have).   *keep* dwell   10 *encompassment* roundabout talking.   *drift* gradual approach or
course   11–12 *come. . . it* you will find out more this way than by asking pointed questions
(*particular demands*)   13 *Take you* assume, pretend   19 *put on* impute to   20 *forgeries* invented
tales.   *rank* gross   22 *wanton* sportive, unrestrained   27 *drabbing* whoring   29 *season* temper,
soften   31 *incontinency* habitual sexual excess   32 *quaintly* artfully, subtly   33 *taints of liberty*
faults resulting from free living   35–36 *A savageness. . . assault* a wildness in untamed youth that
assails all indiscriminately   41 *fetch of warrant* legitimate trick

As 'twere a thing a little soiled wi' the working,*
Mark you,
Your party in converse,* him you would sound,*   45
Having ever* seen in the prenominate crimes*
The youth you breathe* of guilty, be assured
He closes with you in this consequence:*
"Good sir," or so, or "friend," or "gentleman,"
According to the phrase or the addition*   50
Of man and country.
Reynaldo: Very good, my lord.
Polonius: And then, sir, does 'a this—'a does—
  what was I about to say? By the Mass, I was
  about to say something. Where did I leave?
Reynaldo: At "closes in the consequence."   55
Polonius: At "closes in the consequence," ay, marry.
  He closes thus: "I know the gentleman,
  I saw him yesterday," or "th' other day,"
  Or then, or then, with such or such, "and as you say,
  There was 'a gaming," "there o'ertook in 's rouse,"*   60
  "There falling out* at tennis," or perchance
  "I saw him enter such a house of sale,"
  Videlicet* a brothel, or so forth. See you now,
  Your bait of falsehood takes this carp* of truth;
  And thus do we of wisdom and of reach,*   65
  With windlasses* and with assays of bias,*
  By indirections find directions* out.
  So by my former lecture and advice
  Shall you my son. You have* me, have you not?
Reynaldo: My lord, I have.
Polonius: God b' wi'* ye; fare ye well.   70
Reynaldo: Good my lord.
Polonius: Observe his inclination in yourself.*
Reynaldo: I shall, my lord.
Polonius: And let him ply his music.
Reynaldo: Well, my lord.   75
Polonius: Farewell.   Exit Reynaldo.

  Enter Ophelia.

          How now, Ophelia, what's the matter?

---

43 *soiled wi' the working* soiled by handling while it is being made, i.e., by involvement in the ways
of the world   45 *converse* conversation.   *sound* i.e., sound out   46 *Having ever* if he has ever.
prenominate crimes before-mentioned offenses   47 *breathe* speak   48 *closes. . . consequence*
takes you into his confidence in some fashion, as follows   50 *addition* title   60 *o'ertook in 's rouse*
overcome by drink   61 *falling out* quarreling   63 *Videlicet* namely   64 *carp* a fish   65 *reach*
capacity, ability   66 *windlasses* i.e., circuitous paths. (Literally, circuits made to head off the
game in hunting.)   *assays of bias* attempts through indirection (like the curving path of the
bowling ball, which is biased or weighted to one side)   67 *directions* i.e., the way things really
are   69 *have* understand   70 *b' wi'* be with   72 *in yourself* in your own person (as well as by
asking questions)

Ophelia: O my lord, my lord, I have been so affrighted!
Polonius: With what, i' the name of God?
Ophelia: My lord, as I was sewing in my closet,*
 Lord Hamlet, with his doublet* all unbraced,*   80
 No hat upon his head, his stockings fouled,
 Ungartered, and down-gyvèd* to his ankle,
 Pale as his shirt, his knees knocking each other,
 And with a look so piteous in purport*
 As if he had been loosèd out of hell   85
 To speak of horrors—he comes before me.
Polonius: Mad for thy love?
Ophelia: My lord, I do not know,
 But truly I do fear it.
Polonius: What said he?
Ophelia: He took me by the wrist and held me hard.
 Then goes he to the length of all his arm,   90
 And, with his other hand thus o'er his brow
 He falls to such perusal of my face
 As* 'a would draw it. Long stayed he so.
 At last, a little shaking of mine arm
 And thrice his head thus waving up and down,   95
 He raised a sigh so piteous and profound
 As it did seem to shatter all his bulk*
 And end his being. That done, he lets me go,
 And with his head over his shoulder turned
 He seemed to find his way without his eyes,   100
 For out o' doors he went without their helps,
 And to the last bended their light on me.
Polonius: Come, go with me. I will go seek the King.
 This is the very ecstasy* of love,
 Whose violent property* fordoes* itself   105
 And leads the will to desperate undertakings
 As oft as any passion under heaven
 That does afflict our natures. I am sorry.
 What, have you given him any hard words of late?
Ophelia: No, my good lord, but as you did command   110
 I did repel his letters and denied
 His access to me.
Polonius: That hath made him mad.
 I am sorry that with better heed and judgment
 I had not quoted* him. I feared he did but trifle
 And meant to wrack* thee. But beshrew my jealousy!* 115
 By heaven, it is as proper to our age*
 To cast beyond* ourselves in our opinions

---

79 *closet* private chamber   80 *doublet* close-fitting jacket.   *unbraced* unfastened   82 *down-gyvèd* fallen to the ankles (like gyves or fetters)   84 *in purport* in what it expressed   93 *As* as if (also in line 97)   97 *bulk* body   104 *ecstasy* madness   105 *property* nature.   *fordoes* destroys   114 *quoted* observed   115 *wrack* ruin, seduce.   *beshrew my jealousy* a plague upon my suspicious nature   116 *proper. . . . age* characteristic of us (old) men   117 *cast beyond* overshoot, miscalculate. (A metaphor from hunting.)

As it is common for the younger sort
To lack discretion. Come, go we to the King.
This must be known,* which, being kept close,* might move   120
More grief to hide than hate to utter love.*
Come.   *Exeunt.*

Scene II [*The Castle.*]

*Flourish. Enter King and Queen, Rosencrantz, and Guildenstern
[with others].*

King: Welcome, dear Rosencrantz and Guildenstern.
    Moreover that* we much did long to see you,
    The need we have to use you did provoke
    Our hasty sending. Something have you heard
    Of Hamlet's transformation—so call it,   5
    Sith nor* th' exterior nor the inward man
    Resembles that* it was. What it should be,
    More than his father's death, that thus hath put him
    So much from th' understanding of himself,
    I cannot dream of. I entreat you both   10
    That, being of so young days* brought up with him,
    And sith so neighbored to* his youth and havior,*
    That you vouchsafe your rest* here in our court
    Some little time, so by your companies
    To draw him on to pleasures, and to gather   15
    So much as from occasion* you may glean,
    Whether aught to us unknown afflicts him thus
    That, opened,* lies within our remedy.
Queen: Good gentlemen, he hath much talked of you,
    And sure I am two men there is not living   20
    To whom he more adheres. If it will please you
    To show us so much gentry* and good will
    As to expend your time with us awhile
    For the supply and profit of our hope,*
    Your visitation shall receive such thanks   25
    As fits a king's remembrance.*
Rosencrantz: Both Your Majesties
    Might, by the sovereign power you have of* us,
    Put your dread* pleasures more into command
    Than to entreaty.

120 *known* made known (to the King).   *close* secret   120–121 *might. . . love* i.e., might cause
more grief (because of what Hamlet might do) by hiding the knowledge of Hamlet's strange
behavior to Ophelia than unpleasantness by telling it   2 *Moreover that* besides the fact that
6 *Sith nor* since neither   7 *that* what   11 *of. . . days* from such early youth   12 *And sith so
neighbored to* and since you are (or, and since that time you are) intimately acquainted with.
havior demeanor   13 *vouchsafe your rest* please to stay   16 *occasion* opportunity   18 *opened*
being revealed   22 *gentry* courtesy   24 *supply. . . hope* aid and furtherance of what we hope for
26 *As fits. . . remembrance* as would be a fitting gift of a king who rewards true service   27 *of* over
28 *dread* inspiring awe

Guildenstern: But we both obey,
     And here give up ourselves in the full bent*   30
     To lay our service freely at your feet,
     To be commanded.
King: Thanks, Rosencrantz and gentle Guildenstern.
Queen: Thanks, Guildenstern and gentle Rosencrantz.
     And I beseech you instantly to visit   35
     My too much changèd son. Go, some of you,
     And bring these gentlemen where Hamlet is.
Guildenstern: Heavens make our presence and our practices*
     Pleasant and helpful to him!
Queen: Ay, amen!

         Exeunt Rosencrantz and Guildenstern [with some attendants].

     Enter Polonius.

Polonius: Th' ambassadors from Norway, my good lord,   40
     Are joyfully returned.
King: Thou still* hast been the father of good news.
Polonius: Have I, my lord? I assure my good liege
     I hold* my duty, as* I hold my soul,
     Both to my God and to my gracious king;   45
     And I do think, or else this brain of mine
     Hunts not the trail of policy* so sure
     As it hath used to do, that I have found
     The very cause of Hamlet's lunacy.
King: O, speak of that! That do I long to hear.   50
Polonius: Give first admittance to th' ambassadors.
     My news shall be the fruit* to that great feast.
King: Thyself do grace* to them and bring them in.

                                                [Exit Polonius.]

     He tells me, my dear Gertrude, he hath found
     The head and source of all your son's distemper.   55
Queen: I doubt* it is no other but the main,*
     His father's death and our o'erhasty marriage.

     Enter Ambassadors [Voltimand and Cornelius, with Polonius].

King: Well, we shall sift him.*—Welcome, my good friends!
     Say, Voltimand, what from our brother* Norway?
Voltimand: Most fair return of greetings and desires.*   60
     Upon our first,* he sent out to suppress
     His nephew's levies, which to him appeared
     To be a preparation 'gainst the Polack,
     But, better looked into, he truly found
     It was against Your Highness. Whereat grieved   65
     That so his sickness, age, and impotence*

---

30 *in. . . bent* to the utmost degree of our capacity. (An archery metaphor.)   38 *practices* doings
425 *still* always   44 *hold* maintain.   *as* as firmly as   47 *policy* sagacity   52 *fruit* dessert   53 *grace*
honor (punning on *grace* said before a *feast*, line 52)   56 *doubt* fear, suspect.   *main* chief point,
principal concern   58 *sift him* question Polonius closely   59 *brother* fellow king   60 *desires* good
wishes   61 *Upon our first* at our first words on the business   66 *impotence* helplessness

Was falsely borne in hand,* sends out arrests*
On Fortinbras, which he, in brief, obeys,
Receives rebuke from Norway, and in fine*
Makes vow before his uncle never more   70
To give th' assay* of arms against Your Majesty.
Whereon old Norway, overcome with joy,
Gives him three thousand crowns in annual fee
And his commission to employ those soldiers,
So levied as before, against the Polack,   75
With an entreaty, herein further shown,

                                    [giving a paper]

That it might please you to give quiet pass
Through your dominions for this enterprise
On such regards of safety and allowance*
As therein are set down.
King: It likes* us well,   80
And at our more considered* time we'll read,
Answer, and think upon this business.
Meantime we thank you for your well-took labor.
Go to your rest; at night we'll feast together.
Most welcome home!   *Exeunt Ambassadors.*
Polonius: This business is well ended.   85
My liege, and madam, to expostulate*
What majesty should be, what duty is,
Why day is day, night night, and time is time,
Were nothing but to waste night, day, and time.
Therefore, since brevity is the soul of wit,*   90
And tediousness the limbs and outward flourishes,
I will be brief. Your noble son is mad.
Mad call I it, for, to define true madness,
What is 't but to be nothing else but mad?
But let that go.
Queen: More matter, with less art.   95
Polonius: Madam, I swear I use no art at all.
That he's mad, 'tis true; 'tis true 'tis pity,
And pity 'tis 'tis true—a foolish figure,*
But farewell it, for I will use no art.
Mad let us grant him, then, and now remains   100
That we find out the cause of this effect,
Or rather say, the cause of this defect,
For this effect defective comes by cause.*
Thus it remains, and the remainder thus.
Perpend.*   105

67 *borne in hand* deluded, taken advantage of. *arrests* orders to desist 69 *in fine* in conclusion
71 *give th' assay* make trial of strength, challenge 79 *On. . . allowance* i.e., with such
considerations for the safety of Denmark and permission for Fortinbras 80 *likes* pleases
81 *considered* suitable for deliberation 86 *expostulate* expound, inquire into 90 *wit* sense or
judgment 98 *figure* figure of speech 103 *For. . . cause* i.e., for this defective behavior, this
madness, has a cause 105 *Perpend* consider

I have a daughter—have while she is mine—
Who, in her duty and obedience, mark,
Hath given me this. Now gather and surmise.*
[*He reads the letter.*] "To the celestial and my soul's idol, the most beautified
Ophelia"—That's an ill phrase, a vile phrase; "beautified" is a vile phrase.   110
But you shall hear. Thus:

                                          [*He reads.*]

       "In her excellent white bosom,* these,* etc."
Queen: Came this from Hamlet to her?
Polonius: Good madam, stay* awhile, I will be faithful.*

                                          [*He reads.*]

       "Doubt thou the stars are fire,   115
            Doubt that the sun doth move,
       Doubt truth to be a liar,
            But never doubt I love.*

       O dear Ophelia, I am ill at these numbers.* I have not art to reckon* my
       groans. But that I love thee best, O most best, believe it. Adieu.   120
       Thine evermore, most dear lady, whilst this machine* is to him, Hamlet."
       This in obedience hath my daughter shown me,
       And, more above,* hath his solicitings,
       As they fell out* by* time, by means, and place,
       All given to mine ear.*
King: But how hath she   125
       Received his love?
Polonius: What do you think of me?
King: As of a man faithful and honorable.
Polonius: I would fain* prove so. But what might you think,
       When I had seen this hot love on the wing—
       As I perceived it, I must tell you that,   130
       Before my daughter told me—what might you,
       Or my dear Majesty your queen here, think,
       If I had played the desk or table book,*
       Or given my heart a winking,* mute and dumb,
       Or looked upon this love with idle sight?*   135
       What might you think? No, I went round* to work,
       And my young mistress thus I did bespeak:*
       "Lord Hamlet is a prince out of thy star;*
       This must not be." And then I prescripts* gave her,
       That she should lock herself from his resort,*   140
       Admit no messengers, receive no tokens.

---

108 *gather and surmise* draw your own conclusions   112 *In. . . . bosom* (The letter is poetically
addressed to her heart.)   *these* i.e., the letter   114 *stay* wait.   *faithful* i.e., in reading the letter
accurately   115 *Doubt* suspect   119 *ill. . . numbers* unskilled at writing verses.   *reckon* (1) count
(2) number metrically, scan   121 *machine* i.e., body   123 *more above* moreover   124 *fell out*
occurred.   *by* according to   125 *given . . . ear* i.e., told me about   128 *fain* gladly
133 *played. . . table book* i.e., remained shut up, concealing the information   134 *given. . . winking*
closed the eyes of my heart to this   135 *with idle sight* complacently or incomprehendingly
136 *round* roundly, plainly   137 *bespeak* address   138 *out of thy star* above your sphere,
position   139 *prescripts* orders   140 *his resort* his visits

Which done, she took the fruits of my advice;
And he, repellèd—a short tale to make—
Fell into a sadness, then into a fast,
Thence to a watch,* thence into a weakness,   145
Thence to a lightness,* and by this declension*
Into the madness wherein now he raves,
And all we* mourn for.
King [*to the Queen*]:   Do you think 'tis this?
Queen: It may be, very like.
Polonius: Hath there been such a time—I would fain know that—   150
    That I have positively said "'Tis so,"
    When it proved otherwise?
King: Not that I know.
Polonius: Take this from this,* if this be otherwise.
    If circumstances lead me, I will find
    Where truth is hid, though it were hid indeed   155
    Within the center.*
King: How may we try* it further?
Polonius: You know sometimes he walks four hours together
    Here in the lobby.
Queen: So he does indeed.
Polonius: At such a time I'll loose* my daughter to him.
    Be you and I behind an arras* then.   160
    Mark the encounter. If he love her not
    And be not from his reason fall'n thereon,*
    Let me be no assistant for a state,
    But keep a farm and carters.*
King: We will try it.

    Enter Hamlet [*reading on a book*].

Queen: But look where sadly* the poor wretch comes reading.   165
Polonius: Away, I do beseech you both, away.
    I'll board* him presently.* O, give me leave.*

        Exeunt King and Queen [*with attendants*].

    How does my good Lord Hamlet?
Hamlet: Well, God-a-mercy.*
Polonius: Do you know me, my lord?   170
Hamlet: Excellent well. You are a fishmonger.*
Polonius: Not I, my lord.
Hamlet: Then I would you were so honest a man.

---

145 *watch* state of sleeplessness   146 *lightness* lightheadedness.   *declension* decline, deterioration
(with a pun on the grammatical sense)   148 *all we* all of us, or, into everything that we   153 *Take
this from this* (The actor probably gestures, indicating that he means his head from his shoulders,
or his staff of office or chain from his hands or neck, or something similar.)   156 *center* middle
point of the earth (which is also the center of the Ptolemaic universe).   *try* test, judge
159 *loose* (as one might release an animal that is being mated)   160 *arras* hanging, tapestry
162 *thereon* on that account   164 *carters* wagon drivers   165 *sadly* seriously   167 *board* accost.
presently at once.   *give me leave* i.e., excuse me, leave me alone. (Said to those he hurries
offstage, including the King and Queen.)   169 *God-a-mercy* God have mercy, i.e., thank you
171 *fishmonger* fish merchant

Polonius: Honest, my lord?

Hamlet: Ay, sir. To be honest, as this world goes, is to be one man picked out   175
of ten thousand.

Polonius: That's very true, my lord.

Hamlet: For if the sun breed maggots in a dead dog, being a good kissing
carrion*—Have you a daughter?

Polonius: I have, my lord.   180

Hamlet: Let her not walk i' the sun.* Conception* is a blessing, but as your
daughter may conceive, friend, look to 't.

Polonius [aside]: How say you by that? Still harping on my daughter. Yet he
knew me not at first; 'a* said I was a fishmonger. 'A is far gone. And truly
in my youth I suffered much extremity for love, very near this. I'll speak   185
to him again.—What do you read, my lord?

Hamlet: Words, words, words.

Polonius: What is the matter,* my lord?

Hamlet: Between who?

Polonius: I mean, the matter that you read, my lord.   190

Hamlet: Slanders, sir; for the satirical rogue says here that old men have gray
beards, that their faces are wrinkled, their eyes purging* thick amber* and
plum-tree gum, and that they have a plentiful lack of wit,* together with
most weak hams. All which, sir, though I most powerfully and potently
believe, yet I hold it not honesty* to have it thus set down, for yourself, sir,   195
shall grow old* as I am, if like a crab you could go backward.

Polonius [aside]: Though this be madness, yet there is method in 't.—Will
you walk out of the air,* my lord?

Hamlet: Into my grave.

Polonius: Indeed, that's out of the air. [*Aside.*] How pregnant* sometimes his   200
replies are! A happiness* that often madness hits on, which reason and
sanity could not so prosperously* be delivered of. I will leave him and suddenly* contrive the means of meeting between him and my daughter.—
My honorable lord, I will most humbly take my leave of you.

Hamlet: You cannot, sir, take from me anything that I will more willingly   205
part withal*—except my life, except my life, except my life.

Enter Guildenstern and Rosencrantz.

Polonius: Fare you well, my lord.

Hamlet: These tedious old fools!*

Polonius: You go to seek the Lord Hamlet. There he is.

Rosencrantz [to Polonius]: God save you, sir!   210

[*Exit Polonius.*]

Guildenstern: My honored lord!

178–179 *a good kissing carrion* i.e., a good piece of flesh for kissing, or for the sun to kiss
181 *i' the sun* in public (with additional implication of the sunshine of princely favors).
Conception (1) understanding (2) pregnancy   184 *'a* he   188 *matter* substance. (But Hamlet
plays on the sense of "basis for a dispute.")   192 *purging* discharging.   *amber* i.e., resin, like
the resinous *plum-tree gum*   193 *wit* understanding   195 *honesty* decency, decorum   196 *old* as
old   198 *out of the air* (The open air was considered dangerous for sick people.)   200 *pregnant*
quick-witted, full of meaning   201 *happiness* felicity of expression   202 *prosperously*
successfully   203 *suddenly* immediately   206 *withal* with   208 *old fools* i.e., old men like
Polonius

Rosencrantz: My most dear lord!

Hamlet: My excellent good friends! How dost thou, Guildenstern? Ah, Rosencrantz! Good lads, how do you both?

Rosencrantz: As the indifferent* children of the earth.   215

Guildenstern: Happy in that we are not overhappy.
    On Fortune's cap we are not the very button.

Hamlet: Nor the soles of her shoe?

Rosencrantz: Neither, my lord.

Hamlet: Then you live about her waist, or in the middle of her favors?*   220

Guildenstern: Faith, her privates we.*

Hamlet: In the secret parts of Fortune? O, most true, she is a strumpet.* What news?

Rosencrantz: None, my lord, but the world's grown honest.

Hamlet: Then is doomsday near. But your news is not true. Let me question   225
    more in particular. What have you, my good friends, deserved at the
    hands of fortune that she sends you to prison hither?

Guildenstern: Prison, my lord?

Hamlet: Denmark's a prison.

Rosencrantz: Then is the world one.   230

Hamlet: A goodly one, in which there are many confines,* wards,* and dun-
    geons, Denmark being one o' the worst.

Rosencrantz: We think not so, my lord.

Hamlet: Why then 'tis none to you, for there is nothing either good or bad
    but thinking makes it so. To me it is a prison.   235

Rosencrantz: Why then, your ambition makes it one. 'Tis too narrow for
    your mind.

Hamlet: O God, I could be bounded in a nutshell and count myself a king of
    infinite space, were it not that I have bad dreams.

Guildenstern: Which dreams indeed are ambition, for the very substance of   240
    the ambitious* is merely the shadow of a dream.

Hamlet: A dream itself is but a shadow.

Rosencrantz: Truly, and I hold ambition of so airy and light a quality that it
    is but a shadow's shadow.

Hamlet: Then are our beggars bodies,* and our monarchs and outstretched*   245
    heroes the beggars' shadows. Shall we to the court? For, by my fay,* I
    cannot reason.

Rosencrantz, Guildenstern: We'll wait upon* you.

Hamlet: No such matter. I will not sort* you with the rest of my servants,
    for, to speak to you like an honest man, I am most dreadfully attended.*
    But, in the beaten way* of friendship, what make* you at Elsinore?   250

---

215 *indifferent* ordinary, at neither extreme of fortune or misfortune   220 *favors* i.e., sexual favors   221 *her privates we* i.e., (1) we are sexually intimate with Fortune, the fickle goddess who bestows her favors indiscriminately (2) we are her private citizens   222 *strumpet* prostitute. (A common epithet for indiscriminate Fortune; see line 430.)   231 *confines* places of confinement. *wards* cells   240–241 *the very. . . ambitious* that seemingly very substantial thing that the ambitious pursue   245 *bodies* i.e., solid substances rather than shadows (since beggars are not ambitious).   *outstretched* (1) far-reaching in their ambition (2) elongated as shadows   246 *fay* faith   247 *wait upon* accompany, attend. (But Hamlet uses the phrase in the sense of providing menial service.)   248 *sort* class, categorize   249 *dreadfully attended* waited upon in slovenly fashion   250 *beaten way* familiar path, tried-and-true course.   *make* do

Rosencrantz: To visit you, my lord, no other occasion.

Hamlet: Beggar that I am, I am even poor in thanks; but I thank you, and
    sure, dear friends, my thanks are too dear a halfpenny.* Were you not
    sent for? Is it your own inclining? Is it a free* visitation? Come, come,
    deal justly with me. Come, come. Nay, speak.   255

Guildenstern: What should we say, my lord?

Hamlet: Anything but to the purpose.* You were sent for, and there is a
    kind of confession in your looks which your modesties* have not craft
    enough to color.* I know the good King and Queen have sent for you.

Rosencrantz: To what end, my lord?   260

Hamlet: That you must teach me. But let me conjure* you, by the rights of our
    fellowship, by the consonancy of our youth,* by the obligation of our ever-
    preserved love, and by what more dear a better* prosper could charge*
    you withal, be even* and direct with me whether you were sent for or no.

Rosencrantz [aside to Guildenstern]: What say you?   265

Hamlet [aside]: Nay, then, I have an eye of* you.—If you love me, hold not off.*

Guildenstern: My lord, we were sent for.

Hamlet: I will tell you why; so shall my anticipation prevent your discovery,*
    and your secrecy to the King and Queen molt no feather.* I have of late—
    but wherefore I know not—lost all my mirth, forgone all custom of exer-   270
    cises; and indeed it goes so heavily with my disposition that this goodly
    frame, the earth, seems to me a sterile promontory; this most excellent
    canopy, the air, look you, this brave* o'erhanging firmament, this majesti-
    cal roof fretted* with golden fire, why, it appeareth nothing to me but a
    foul and pestilent congregation* of vapors. What a piece of work* is a   275
    man! How noble in reason, how infinite in faculties, in form and moving
    how express* and admirable, in action how like an angel, in apprehen-
    sion* how like a god! The beauty of the world, the paragon of animals!
    And yet, to me, what is this quintessence* of dust? Man delights not me—
    no, nor woman neither, though by your smiling you seem to say so.   280

Rosencrantz: My lord, there was no such stuff in my thoughts.

Hamlet: Why did you laugh, then, when I said man delights not me?

Rosencrantz: To think, my lord, if you delight not in man, what Lenten
    entertainment* the players shall receive from you. We coted* them on
    the way, and hither are they coming to offer you service.   285

Hamlet: He that plays the king shall be welcome; His Majesty shall have trib-
    ute* of* me. The adventurous knight shall use his foil and target,* the lover

253 *too dear a halfpenny* (1) too expensive at even a halfpenny, i.e., of little worth (2) too
expensive *by* a halfpenny in return for worthless kindness   254 *free* voluntary   257 *Anything but
to the purpose* anything except a straightforward answer. (Said ironically.)   258 *modesties* sense
of shame   259 *color* disguise   261 *conjure* adjure, entreat   262 *the consonancy of our youth* our
closeness in our younger days   263 *better* more skillful.   *charge* urge   264 *even* straight, honest
266 *of* on.   *hold not off* don't hold back   268 *so. . . discovery* in that way my saying it first will
spare you from revealing the truth   269 *molt no feather* i.e., not diminish in the least   273 *brave*
splendid   274 *fretted* adorned (with fretwork, as in a vaulted ceiling)   275 *congregation* mass.
piece of work masterpiece   276 *express* well-framed, exact, expressive   277 *apprehension* power
of comprehending   279 *quintessence* the fifth essence of ancient philosophy, beyond earth, water,
air, and fire, supposed to be the substance of the heavenly bodies and to be latent in all things
283–284 *Lenten entertainment* meager reception (appropriate to Lent)   284 *coted* overtook and
passed by   287 *tribute* (1) applause (2) homage paid in money.   *of* from.   *foil and target* sword
and shield

shall not sigh gratis,* the humorous man* shall end his part in peace,*
the clown shall make those laugh whose lungs are tickle o' the sear,*
and the lady shall say her mind freely, or the blank verse shall halt* for 't.   290
What players are they?

Rosencrantz: Even those you were wont to take such delight in, the tragedians*
of the city.

Hamlet: How chances it they travel? Their residence,* both in reputation
and profit, was better both ways.   295

Rosencrantz: I think their inhibition* comes by the means of the late*
innovation.*

Hamlet: Do they hold the same estimation they did when I was in the city?
Are they so followed?

Rosencrantz: No, indeed are they not.

Hamlet: How* comes it? Do they grow rusty?   300

Rosencrantz: Nay, their endeavor keeps* in the wonted* pace. But there is, sir,
an aerie* of children, little eyases,* that cry out on the top of question*
and are most tyrannically* clapped for 't. These are now the fashion, and
so berattle* the common stages*—so they call them—that many wearing
rapiers* are afraid of goose quills* and dare scarce come thither.   305

Hamlet: What, are they children? Who maintains 'em? How are they escoted?* Will they pursue the quality* no longer than they can sing?* Will
they not say afterwards, if they should grow themselves to common*
players—as it is most like,* if their means are no better*—their writers
do them wrong to make them exclaim against their own succession?*   310

Rosencrantz: Faith, there has been much to-do* on both sides, and the
nation holds it no sin to tar* them to controversy. There was for a while
no money bid for argument unless the poet and the player went to
cuffs in the question.*

Hamlet: Is 't possible?

Guildenstern: O, there has been much throwing about of brains.   315

Hamlet: Do the boys carry it away?*

---

288 *gratis* for nothing.   *humorous man* eccentric character, dominated by one trait or
"humor."   *in peace* i.e., with full license   289 *tickle o' the sear* easy on the trigger, ready to
laugh easily. (A *sear* is part of a gunlock.)   290 *halt* limp   292 *tragedians* actors
294 *residence* remaining in their usual place, i.e., in the city   296 *inhibition* formal prohibition
(from acting plays in the city).   *late* recent.   *innovation* i.e., the new fashion in satirical plays
performed by boy actors in the "private" theaters; or possibly a political uprising; or the strict
limitations set on the theaters in London in 1600   300–317 *How. . . load too* (The passage,
omitted from the early quartos, alludes to the so-called War of the Theaters, 1599–1602, the
rivalry between the children's companies and the adult actors.)   301 *keeps* continues.
wonted usual   302 *aerie* nest.   *eyases* young hawks.   *cry. . . question* speak shrilly,
dominating the controversy (in decrying the public theaters)   303 *tyrannically* outrageously
304 *berattle* berate, clamor against.   *common stages* public theaters. *many wearing rapiers*
i.e., many men of fashion, afraid to patronize the common players for fear of being satirized by
the poets writing for the boy actors   305 *goose quills* i.e., pens of satirists   306 *escoted*
maintained   307 *quality* (acting) profession.   *no longer . . . sing* i.e., only until their voices
change   308 *common* regular, adult   309 *like* likely.   *if. . . better* if they find no better way to
support themselves   310 *succession* i.e., future careers   311 *to-do* ado   312 *tar* set on (as
dogs)   312–313 *There. . . question* i.e., for a while, no money was offered by the acting
companies to playwrights for the plot to a play unless the satirical poets who wrote for the boys
and the adult actors came to blows in the play itself   316 *carry it away* i.e., win the day

Rosencrantz: Ay, that they do, my lord—Hercules and his load* too.

Hamlet: It is not very strange; for my uncle is King of Denmark, and those that
would make mouths* at him while my father lived give twenty, forty, fifty,
a hundred ducats* apiece for his picture in little.* 'Sblood,* there is some-   320
thing in this more than natural, if philosophy* could find it out.

A flourish [of trumpets within].

Guildenstern: There are the players.

Hamlet [to Rosenkrantz and Guildenstern]: Gentlemen, you are welcome to
Elsinore. Your hands, come then. Th' appurtenance* of welcome is fashion
and ceremony. Let me comply* with you in this garb,* lest my extent* to   325
the players, which, I tell you, must show fairly outwards,* should more
appear like entertainment* than yours. You are welcome. But my uncle-
father and aunt-mother are deceived.

Guildenstern: In what, my dear lord?

Hamlet: I am but mad north-north-west.* When the wind is southerly I   330
know a hawk* from a handsaw.

Enter Polonius.

Polonius: Well be with you, gentlemen!

Hamlet: Hark you, Guildenstern, and you too; at each ear a hearer. That
great baby you see there is not yet out of his swaddling clouts.*

Rosencrantz: Haply* he is the second time come to them, for they say an   335
old man is twice a child.

Hamlet: I will prophesy he comes to tell me of the players. Mark it.—You
say right, sir, o' Monday morning, 'twas then indeed.

Polonius: My lord, I have news to tell you.

Hamlet: My lord, I have news to tell you. When Roscius* was an actor in   340
Rome—

Polonius: The actors are come hither, my lord.

Hamlet: Buzz,* buzz!

Polonius: Upon my honor—

Hamlet: Then came each actor on his ass.

Polonius: The best actors in the world, either for tragedy, comedy, history, pas-   345
toral, pastoral-comical, historical-pastoral, tragical-historical, tragical-
comical-historical-pastoral, scene individable,* or poem unlimited.* Seneca*

---

317 *Hercules. . . load* (Thought to be an allusion to the sign of the Globe Theatre, which was
Hercules bearing the world on his shoulders.)   319 *mouths* faces   320 *ducats* gold coins.   *in
little* in miniature.   *'Sblood* by God's (Christ's) blood   321 *philosophy* i.e., scientific inquiry
324 *appurtenance* proper accompaniment   325 *comply* observe the formalities of courtesy.
garb i.e., manner.   *my extent* that which I extend, i.e., my polite behavior   326–327 *show
fairly outwards* show every evidence of cordiality   327 *entertainment* a (warm) reception
330 *north-north-west* just off true north, only partly   331 *hawk, handsaw* i.e., two very
different things, though also perhaps meaning a mattock (or *hack*) and a carpenter's cutting
tool, respectively; also birds, with a play on *hernshaw*, or heron   334 *swaddling clouts* cloths
in which to wrap a newborn baby   335 *Haply* perhaps   340 *Roscius* a famous Roman actor
who died in 62 B.C.   342 *Buzz* (An interjection used to denote stale news.)   347 *scene
individable* a play observing the unity of place; or perhaps one that is unclassifiable, or
performed without intermission.   *poem unlimited* a play disregarding the unities of time and
place; one that is all-inclusive.   *Seneca* writer of Latin tragedies

cannot be too heavy, nor Plautus* too light. For the law of writ and the
liberty,* these* are the only men.

Hamlet: O Jephthah, judge of Israel,* what a treasure hadst thou!   350

Polonius: What a treasure had he, my lord?

Hamlet: Why,

> *"One fair daughter, and no more,*
> *The which he lovèd passing* well."*

Polonius [aside]: Still on my daughter.   355

Hamlet: Am I not i' the right, old Jephthah?

Polonius: If you call me Jephthah, my lord, I have a daughter that I love
passing well.

Hamlet: Nay, that follows not.

Polonius: What follows then, my lord?   360

Hamlet: Why,

> *"As by lot,* God wot,"**
> *and then, you know,*
> *"It came to pass, as most like* it was"*—

the first row* of the pious chanson* will show you more, for look   365
where my abridgement* comes.

Enter the Players.

You are welcome, masters; welcome, all. I am glad to see thee well. Welcome, good friends. O, old friend! Why, thy face is valanced* since I saw
thee last. Com'st thou to beard* me in Denmark? What, my young lady*
and mistress! By 'r Lady,* your ladyship is nearer to heaven than when I   370
saw you last, by the altitude of a chopine.* Pray God your voice, like a
piece of uncurrent* gold, be not cracked within the ring.* Masters, you
are all welcome. We'll e'en to 't* like French falconers, fly at anything we
see. We'll have a speech straight.* Come, give us a taste of your quality.*
Come, a passionate speech.   375

First Player: What speech, my good lord?

Hamlet: I heard thee speak me a speech once, but it was never acted, or if it
was, not above once, for the play, I remember, pleased not the million; 'twas
caviar to the general.* But it was—as I received it, and others, whose judgments in such matters cried in the top of* mine—an excellent play, well   380
digested* in the scenes, set down with as much modesty* as cunning.* I

---

348 *Plautus* writer of Latin comedy   348–349 *law. . . liberty* dramatic composition both
according to the rules and disregarding the rules   349 *these* i.e., the actors
350 *Jephthah. . . Israel* (Jephthah had to sacrifice his daughter; see Judges 11. Hamlet goes on to
quote from a ballad on the theme.)   354 *passing* surpassingly   362 *lot* chance.   *wot* knows
364 *like* likely, probable   365 *row* stanza.   *chanson* ballad, song   365–366 *my abridgment*
something that cuts short my conversation; also, a diversion   368 *valanced* fringed (with a beard)
369 *beard* confront, challenge (with obvious pun).   *young lady* i.e., boy playing women's parts
370 *By 'r Lady* by Our Lady   371 *chopine* thick-soled shoe of Italian fashion   371–372 *uncurrent*
not passable as lawful coinage.   *cracked. . . ring* i.e., changed from adolescent to male voice, no
longer suitable for women's roles. (Coins featured rings enclosing the sovereign's head; if the coin
was cracked within this ring, it was unfit for currency.)   373 *e'en to 't* go at it   374 *straight* at
once.   *quality* professional skill   379 *caviar to the general* caviar to the multitude, i.e., a choice
dish too elegant for coarse tastes   380 *cried in the top of* i.e., spoke with greater authority than
381 *digested* arranged, ordered.   *modesty* moderation, restraint.   *cunning* skill

remember one said there were no sallets* in the lines to make the matter
savory, nor no matter in the phrase that might indict* the author of affec-
tation, but called it an honest method, as wholesome as sweet, and by very
much more handsome* than fine.* One speech in 't I chiefly loved: 'twas   385
Aeneas' tale to Dido, and there-about of it especially when he speaks of
Priam's slaughter.* If it live in your memory, begin at this line: let me see, let
me see—
"The rugged Pyrrhus,* like th' Hyrcanian beast"—
'Tis not so. It begins with Pyrrhus:
"The rugged* Pyrrhus, he whose sable* arms,   390
Black as his purpose, did the night resemble
When he lay couchèd* in the ominous horse,*
Hath now this dread and black complexion smeared
With heraldry more dismal.* Head to foot
Now is he total gules,* horridly tricked*   395
With blood of fathers, mothers, daughters, sons,
Baked and impasted* with the parching streets,*
That lend a tyrannous* and a damnèd light
To their lord's* murder. Roasted in wrath and fire,
And thus o'ersizèd* with coagulate gore,   400
With eyes like carbuncles,* the hellish Pyrrhus
Old grandsire Priam seeks."
So proceed you.
Polonius: 'Fore God, my lord, well spoken, with good
    accent and good discretion.
First Player: "Anon he finds him   405
    Striking too short at Greeks. His antique* sword,
    Rebellious to his arm, lies where it falls,
    Repugnant* to command. Unequal matched,
    Pyrrhus at Priam drives, in rage strikes wide,
    But with the whiff and wind of his fell* sword   410
    Th' unnervèd* father falls. Then senseless Ilium,*
    Seeming to feel this blow, with flaming top
    Stoops to his* base, and with a hideous crash
    Takes prisoner Pyrrhus' ear. For, lo! His sword,

---

382 *sallets* i.e., something savory, spicy improprieties   383 *indict* convict
385 *handsome* well-proportioned.   *fine* elaborately ornamented, showy   386 *Priam's slaughter*
the slaying of the ruler of Troy, when the Greeks finally took the city   388 *Pyrrhus* a Greek hero
in the Trojan War, also known as Neoptolemus, son of Achilles—another avenging son. *Hyrcanian
beast* i.e., tiger. (On the death of Priam, see Virgil, Aeneid, 2.506 ff.; compare the whole speech
with Marlowe's *Dido Queen of Carthage*, 2.1.214 ff. On the *Hyrcanian* tiger, see *Aeneid*,
4.466–467. Hyrcania is on the Caspian Sea.)   390 *rugged* shaggy, savage.   *sable* black (for
reasons of camouflage during the episode of the Trojan horse)   392 *couchèd* concealed.
ominous horse fateful Trojan horse, by which the Greeks gained access to Troy   394 *dismal* ill-
omened   395 *total gules* entirely red. (A heraldic term.)   *tricked* spotted and smeared.
(Heraldic.)   397 *impasted* crusted, like a thick paste.   *with. . . streets* by the parching heat of the
streets (because of the fires everywhere)   398 *tyrannous* cruel   399 *their lord's* i.e., Priam's
400 *o'ersizèd* covered as with size or glue   401 *carbuncles* large fiery-red precious stones
thought to emit their own light   406 *antique* ancient, long-used   408 *Repugnant* disobedient,
resistant   410 *fell* cruel   411 *unnervèd* strengthless.   *senseless Ilium* inanimate citadel of Troy
413 *his* its

Which was declining* on the milky* head   415
Of reverend Priam, seemed i' th' air to stick.
So as a painted* tyrant Pyrrhus stood,
And, like a neutral to his will and matter,*
Did nothing.
But as we often see against* some storm   420
A silence in the heavens, the rack* stand still,
The bold winds speechless, and the orb* below
As hush as death, anon the dreadful thunder
Doth rend the region,* so, after Pyrrhus' pause,
A rousèd vengeance sets him new a-work,   425
And never did the Cyclops'* hammers fall
On Mars's armor forged for proof eterne*
With less remorse* than Pyrrhus' bleeding sword
Now falls on Priam.
Out, out, thou strumpet Fortune! All you gods   430
In general synod* take away her power!
Break all the spokes and fellies* from her wheel,
And bowl the round nave* down the hill of heaven*
As low as to the fiends!"
Polonius: This is too long.   435
Hamlet: It shall to the barber's with your beard.—Prithee, say on. He's for a
jig* or a tale of bawdry, or he sleeps. Say on; come to Hecuba.*
First Player: "But who, ah woe! had* seen the moblèd* queen"—
Hamlet: "The moblèd queen?"
Polonius: That's good. "Moblèd queen" is good.   440
First Player: "Run barefoot up and down, threat'ning the flames*
With bisson rheum,* a clout* upon that head
Where late* the diadem stood, and, for a robe,
About her lank and all o'erteemèd* loins
A blanket, in the alarm of fear caught up—   445
Who this had seen, with tongue in venom steeped,
'Gainst Fortune's state* would treason have pronounced.*
But if the gods themselves did see her then
When she saw Pyrrhus make malicious sport
In mincing with his sword her husband's limbs,   450
The instant burst of clamor that she made,
Unless things mortal move them not at all,
Would have made milch* the burning eyes of heaven,*
And passion* in the gods."

---

415 *declining* descending.   *milky* white-haired   417 *painted* i.e., painted in a picture
418 *like . . . matter* i.e., as though suspended between his intention and its fulfillment
420 *against* just before   421 *rack* mass of clouds   422 *orb* globe, earth   424 *region* sky
426 *Cyclops* giant armor makers in the smithy of Vulcan   427 *proof eterne* eternal resistance to
assault   428 *remorse* pity   431 *synod* assembly   432 *fellies* pieces of wood forming the rim of a wheel
433 *nave* hub.   *hill of heaven* Mount Olympus   437 *jig* comic song and dance often given at the end
of a play.   *Hecuba* wife of Priam   438 *who. . . had* anyone who had (also in line 446).   *moblèd*
muffled   441 *threat'ning the flames* i.e., weeping hard enough to dampen the flames
442 *bisson rheum* blinding tears.   *clout* cloth   443 *late* lately   444 *all o'erteemèd* utterly worn out
with bearing children   447 *state* rule, managing.   *pronounced* proclaimed   453 *milch* milky, moist
with tears.   *burning eyes of heaven* i.e., heavenly bodies   454 *passion* overpowering emotion

Polonius: Look whe'er* he has not turned his color and has tears in 's eyes.   455
    Prithee, no more.
Hamlet: 'Tis well; I'll have thee speak out the rest of this soon.—Good my
    lord, will you see the players well bestowed?* Do you hear, let them be
    well used, for they are the abstract* and brief chronicles of the time.
    After your death you were better have a bad epitaph than their ill
    report while you live.   460
Polonius: My lord, I will use them according to their desert.
Hamlet: God's bodikin,* man, much better. Use every man after* his desert,
    and who shall scape whipping? Use them after your own honor and
    dignity. The less they deserve, the more merit is in your bounty. Take
    them in.
Polonius: Come, sirs.   [*Exit.*]   465
Hamlet: Follow him, friends. We'll hear a play tomorrow. [*As they start to
    leave, Hamlet detains the First Player.*] Dost thou hear me, old friend?
    Can you play *The Murder of Gonzago?*
First Player: Ay, my lord.
Hamlet: We'll ha 't* tomorrow night. You could, for a need, study* a speech   470
    of some dozen or sixteen lines which I would set down and insert in
    't, could you not?
First Player: Ay, my lord.
Hamlet: Very well. Follow that lord, and look you mock him not.

                         (*Exeunt Players.*)

    My good friends, I'll leave you till night. You are welcome to Elsinore.
Rosencrantz: Good my lord!   475

           Exeunt [Rosencrantz and Guildenstern].

Hamlet: Ay, so, goodbye to you.—Now I am alone.
    O, what a rogue and peasant slave am I!
    Is it not monstrous that this player here,
    But* in a fiction, in a dream of passion,
    Could force his soul so to his own conceit*   480
    That from her working* all his visage wanned,*
    Tears in his eyes, distraction in his aspect,*
    A broken voice, and his whole function suiting
    With forms to his conceit?* And all for nothing!
    For Hecuba!   485
    What's Hecuba to him, or he to Hecuba,
    That he should weep for her? What would he do
    Had he the motive and the cue for passion
    That I have? He would drown the stage with tears
    And cleave the general ear* with horrid* speech,   490

---

455 *whe'er* whether   458 *bestowed* lodged   459 *abstract* summary account   462 *God's bodikin* by
God's (Christ's) little body, *bodykin.* (Not to be confused with *bodkin,* "dagger."). *after*
according to   470 *ha 't* have it. *study* memorize   479 *But* merely   480 *force . . . conceit* bring
his innermost being so entirely into accord with his conception (of the role)   481 *from her working*
as a result of, or in response to, his soul's activity. *wanned* grew pale   482 *aspect* look, glance
483–484 *his whole . . . conceit* all his bodily powers responding with actions to suit his thought
490 *the general ear* everyone's ear. *horrid* horrible

Make mad the guilty and appall* the free,*
Confound the ignorant,* and amaze* indeed
The very faculties of eyes and ears. Yet I,
A dull and muddy-mettled* rascal, peak*
Like John-a-dreams,* unpregnant* of my cause,   495
And can say nothing—no, not for a king
Upon whose property* and most dear life
A damned defeat* was made. Am I a coward?
Who calls me villain? Breaks my pate* across?
Plucks off my beard and blows it in my face?   500
Tweaks me by the nose? Gives me the lie i' the throat*
As deep as to the lungs? Who does me this?
Ha, 'swounds,* I should take it; for it cannot be
But I am pigeon-livered* and lack gall
To make oppression bitter,* or ere this   505
I should ha' fatted all the region kites*
With this slave's offal.* Bloody, bawdy villain!
Remorseless,* treacherous, lecherous, kindless* villain!
O, vengeance!
Why, what an ass am I! This is most brave,*   510
That I, the son of a dear father murdered,
Prompted to my revenge by heaven and hell,
Must like a whore unpack my heart with words
And fall a-cursing, like a very drab,*
A scullion!* Fie upon 't, foh! About,* my brains!   515
Hum, I have heard
That guilty creatures sitting at a play
Have by the very cunning* of the scene*
Been struck so to the soul that presently*
They have proclaimed their malefactions;   520
For murder, though it have no tongue, will speak
With most miraculous organ. I'll have these players
Play something like the murder of my father
Before mine uncle. I'll observe his looks;
I'll tent* him to the quick.* If 'a do blench,*   525
I know my course. The spirit that I have seen
May be the devil, and the devil hath power
T' assume a pleasing shape; yea, and perhaps,

491 *appall* (Literally, make pale.) *free* innocent   492 *Confound the ignorant* i.e., dumbfound
those who know nothing of the crime that has been committed. *amaze* stun   494 *muddy-mettled*
dull-spirited. *peak* mope, pine   495 *John-a-dreams* a sleepy, dreaming idler. *unpregnant of*
not quickened by   497 *property* i.e., the crown; also character, quality   498 *damned defeat*
damnable act of destruction   499 *pate* head   501 *Gives . . . throat* calls me an out-and-out liar
503 *'swounds* by his (Christ's) wounds   504 *pigeon-livered* (The pigeon or dove was popularly
supposed to be mild because it secreted no gall.)   505 *bitter* i.e., bitter to me   506 *region kites*
kites (birds of prey) of the air   507 *offal* entrails   508 *Remorseless* pitiless. *kindless* unnatural
510 *brave* fine, admirable. (Said ironically.)   514 *drab* whore   515 *scullion* menial kitchen
servant (apt to be foul-mouthed). *About* about it, to work   518 *cunning* art, skill. *scene*
dramatic presentation   519 *presently* at once   525 *tent* probe. *the quick* the tender part of a
wound, the core. *blench* quail, flinch

Out of my weakness and my melancholy,
As he is very potent with such spirits,*   530
Abuses* me to damn me. I'll have grounds
More relative* than this. The play's the thing
Wherein I'll catch the conscience of the King.   *Exit.*

Act III

Scene I [The Castle.]

*Enter King, Queen, Polonius, Ophelia, Rosencrantz, Guildenstern,
    lords.*

King: And can you by no drift of conference*
      Get from him why he puts on this confusion,
      Grating so harshly all his days of quiet
      With turbulent and dangerous lunacy?
Rosencrantz: He does confess he feels himself distracted,   5
      But from what cause 'a will by no means speak.
Guildenstern: Nor do we find him forward* to be sounded,*
      But with a crafty madness keeps aloof
      When we would bring him on to some confession
      Of his true state.
Queen: Did he receive you well?   10
Rosencrantz: Most like a gentleman.
Guildenstern: But with much forcing of his disposition.*
Rosencrantz: Niggard* of question,* but of our demands
      Most free in his reply.
Queen: Did you assay* him   15
      To any pastime?
Rosencrantz: Madam, it so fell out that certain players
      We o'erraught* on the way. Of these we told him,
      And there did seem in him a kind of joy
      To hear of it. They are here about the court,
      And, as I think, they have already order   20
      This night to play before him.
Polonius: 'Tis most true,
      And he beseeched me to entreat Your Majesties
      To hear and see the matter.
King: With all my heart, and it doth much content me
      To hear him so inclined.   25
      Good gentlemen, give him a further edge*
      And drive his purpose into these delights.
Rosencrantz: We shall, my lord.

                              Exeunt Rosencrantz and Guildenstern.

King: Sweet Gertrude, leave us too,

530 *spirits* humors (of melancholy)   531 *Abuses* deludes   532 *relative* cogent, pertinent
1 *drift of conference* directing of conversation   7 *forward* willing.   *sounded* questioned
12 *disposition* inclination   13 *Niggard* stingy.   *question* conversation   14 *assay* try to win
17 *o'erraught* overtook   26 *edge* incitement

For we have closely* sent for Hamlet hither,
That he, as 'twere by accident, may here   30
Affront* Ophelia.
    Her father and myself, lawful espials,*
Will so bestow ourselves that seeing, unseen,
We may of their encounter frankly judge,
And gather by him, as he is behaved,   35
If 't be th' affliction of his love or no
That thus he suffers for.
Queen: I shall obey you.
    And for your part, Ophelia, I do wish
That your good beauties be the happy cause
Of Hamlet's wildness. So shall I hope your virtues   40
Will bring him to his wonted* way again,
To both your honors.
Ophelia: Madam, I wish it may.

                                              [Exit Queen.]

Polonius: Ophelia, walk you here.—Gracious,* so please you,
    We will bestow* ourselves. [To Ophelia.] Read on this book,
    [giving her a book]
    That show of such an exercise* may color*   45
    Your loneliness.* We are oft to blame in this—
    'Tis too much proved*—that with devotion's visage
    And pious action we do sugar o'er
    The devil himself.
King [aside]: O, 'tis too true!   50
    How smart a lash that speech doth give my conscience!
    The harlot's cheek, beautied with plastering art,
    Is not more ugly to* the thing* that helps it
    Than is my deed to my most painted word.
    O heavy burden!   55
Polonius: I hear him coming. Let's withdraw, my lord.

                          [The King and Polonius withdraw.*]
    Enter Hamlet. [Ophelia pretends to read a book.]

Hamlet: To be, or not to be, that is the question:
    Whether 'tis nobler in the mind to suffer
    The slings* and arrows of outrageous fortune,
    Or to take arms against a sea of troubles
    And by opposing end them. To die, to sleep—   60
    No more—and by a sleep to say we end
    The heartache and the thousand natural shocks
    That flesh is heir to. 'Tis a consummation
    Devoutly to be wished. To die, to sleep;   65

29 closely privately   31 Affront confront, meet   32 espials spies   41 wonted accustomed
43 Gracious Your Grace (i.e., the King)   44 bestow conceal   45 exercise religious exercise. (The
book she reads is one of devotion.)   color give a plausible appearance to   46 loneliness being alone
47 too much proved too often shown to be true, too often practiced   53 to compared to.   the thing
i.e., the cosmetic   56 stage direction: withdraw (The King and Polonius may retire behind an arras.
The stage direction:s specify that they "enter" again near the end of the scene.)   59 slings missiles

To sleep, perchance to dream. Ay, there's the rub,*
For in that sleep of death what dreams may come,
When we have shuffled* off this mortal coil,*
Must give us pause. There's the respect*
That makes calamity of so long life.*   70
For who would bear the whips and scorns of time,
Th' oppressor's wrong, the proud man's contumely,*
The pangs of disprized* love, the law's delay,
The insolence of office,* and the spurns*
That patient merit of th' unworthy takes,*   75
When he himself might his quietus* make
With a bare bodkin?* Who would fardels* bear,
To grunt and sweat under a weary life,
But that the dread of something after death,
The undiscovered country from whose bourn*   80
No traveler returns, puzzles the will,
And makes us rather bear those ills we have
Than fly to others that we know not of?
Thus conscience does make cowards of us all;
And thus the native hue* of resolution   85
Is sicklied o'er with the pale cast* of thought,
And enterprises of great pitch* and moment*
With this regard* their currents* turn awry
And lose the name of action.—Soft you* now,
The fair Ophelia. Nymph, in thy orisons*   90
Be all my sins remembered.
Ophelia: Good my lord,
    How does your honor for this many a day?
Hamlet: I humbly thank you; well, well, well.
Ophelia: My lord, I have remembrances of yours,
    That I have longèd long to redeliver.   95
    I pray you, now receive them.   [*She offers tokens.*]
Hamlet: No, not I, I never gave you aught.
Ophelia: My honored lord, you know right well you did,
    And with them words of so sweet breath composed
    As made the things more rich. Their perfume lost,   100
    Take these again, for to the noble mind
    Rich gifts wax poor when givers prove unkind.
    There, my lord.   [*She gives tokens.*]
Hamlet: Ha, ha! Are you honest?*
Ophelia: My lord?   105
Hamlet: Are you fair?*

---

66 *rub* (Literally, an obstacle in the game of bowls.)   68 *shuffled* sloughed, cast.   *coil* turmoil
69 *respect* consideration   70 *of. . . life* so long-lived, something we willingly endure for so long
(also suggesting that long life is itself a calamity)   72 *contumely* insolent abuse   73 *disprized*
unvalued   74 *office* officialdom.   *spurns* insults   75 *of. . . takes* receives from unworthy persons
76 *quietus* acquitance; here, death   77 *a bare bodkin* a mere dagger, unsheathed.
fardels burdens   80 *bourn* frontier, boundary   85 *native hue* natural color, complexion
86 *cast* tinge, shade of color   87 *pitch* height (as of a falcon's flight).   *moment* importance
88 *regard* respect, consideration.   *currents* courses   89 *Soft you* i.e., wait a minute, gently
90 *orisons* prayers   104 *honest* (1) truthful (2) chaste   106 *fair* (1) beautiful (2) just, honorable

Ophelia: What means your lordship?

Hamlet: That if you be honest and fair, your honesty* should admit no discourse to* your beauty.

Ophelia: Could beauty, my lord, have better commerce* than with honesty?   110

Hamlet: Ay, truly, for the power of beauty will sooner transform honesty
from what it is to a bawd than the force of honesty can translate beauty into his* likeness. This was sometime* a paradox,* but now the time*
gives it proof. I did love you once.

Ophelia: Indeed, my lord, you made me believe so.   115

Hamlet: You should not have believed me, for virtue cannot so inoculate*
our old stock but we shall relish of it.* I loved you not.

Ophelia: I was the more deceived.

Hamlet: Get thee to a nunnery.* Why wouldst thou be a breeder of sinners?
I am myself indifferent honest,* but yet I could accuse me of such   120
things that it were better my mother had not borne me: I am very
proud, revengeful, ambitious, with more offenses at my beck* than I
have thoughts to put them in, imagination to give them shape, or time
to act them in. What should such fellows as I do crawling between
earth and heaven? We are arrant knaves all; believe none of us. Go thy
ways to a nunnery. Where's your father?   125

Ophelia: At home, my lord.

Hamlet: Let the doors be shut upon him, that he may play the fool nowhere
but in 's own house. Farewell.

Ophelia: O, help him, you sweet heavens!

Hamlet: If thou dost marry, I'll give thee this plague for thy dowry: be thou   130
as chaste as ice, as pure as snow, thou shalt not escape calumny. Get
thee to a nunnery, farewell. Or, if thou wilt needs marry, marry a fool,
for wise men know well enough what monsters* you* make of them.
To a nunnery, go, and quickly too. Farewell.

Ophelia: Heavenly powers, restore him!   135

Hamlet: I have heard of your paintings too, well enough. God hath given
you one face, and you make yourselves another. You jig,* you amble,*
and you lisp, you nickname God's creatures,* and make your wantonness your ignorance.* Go to, I'll no more on 't;* it hath made me mad. I
say we will have no more marriage. Those that are married already—all   140
but one—shall live. The rest shall keep as they are. To a nunnery, go.

Exit.

Ophelia: O, what a noble mind is here o'erthrown!
The courtier's, soldier's, scholar's, eye, tongue, sword,
Th' expectancy* and rose* of the fair state,
The glass of fashion and the mold of form,*   145

---

108 *your honesty* your chastity   109 *discourse to* familiar dealings with   110 *commerce* dealings,
intercourse   112 *his* its   113 *sometime* formerly.   u *paradox* a view opposite to commonly held
opinion.   *the time* the present age   116 *inoculate* graft, be engrafted to   117 *but . . . it* that we do
not still have about us a taste of the old stock, i.e., retain our sinfulness   119 *nunnery* convent
(with possibly an awareness that the word was also used derisively to denote a brothel)
120 *indifferent honest* reasonably virtuous   122 *beck* command   133 *monsters* (An illusion to the
horns of a cuckold.)   *you* i.e., you women   137 *jig* dance.   *amble* move coyly   137–138 *you
nickname. . . creatures* i.e., you give trendy names to things in place of their God-given names
138 *make. . . ignorance* i.e., excuse your affectation on the grounds of pretended ignorance
139 *on 't* of it   144 *expectancy* hope.   *rose* ornament   145 *The glass. . . form* the mirror of true
self-fashioning and the pattern of courtly behavior

Th' observed of all observers,* quite, quite down!
And I, of ladies most deject and wretched,
That sucked the honey of his music* vows,
Now see that noble and most sovereign reason
Like sweet bells jangled out of tune and harsh,   150
That unmatched form and feature of blown* youth
Blasted* with ecstasy.* O, woe is me,
T' have seen what I have seen, see what I see!

Enter King and Polonius.

King: Love? His affections* do not that way tend;
Nor what he spake, though it lacked form a little,   155
Was not like madness. There's something in his soul
O'er which his melancholy sits on brood,*
And I do doubt* the hatch and the disclose*
Will be some danger; which for to prevent,
I have in quick determination   160
Thus set it down:* he shall with speed to England
For the demand of* our neglected tribute.
Haply the seas and countries different
With variable objects* shall expel
This something-settled matter in his heart,*   165
Whereon his brains still* beating puts him thus
From fashion of himself.* What think you on 't?
Polonius: It shall do well. But yet do I believe
The origin and commencement of his grief
Sprung from neglected love.—How now, Ophelia?   170
You need not tell us what Lord Hamlet said;
We heard it all.—My lord, do as you please,
But, if you hold it fit, after the play
Let his queen-mother* all alone entreat him
To show his grief. Let her be round* with him;   175
And I'll be placed, so please you, in the ear
Of all their conference. If she find him not,*
To England send him, or confine him where
Your wisdom best shall think.
King: It shall be so.
Madness in great ones must not unwatched go.   180

                                                    Exeunt.

Scene II [The Castle.]

Enter Hamlet and three of the Players.

146 Th' observed . . . observers i.e., the center of attention and honor in the court   148 *music*
musical, sweetly uttered   151 *blown* blooming   152 *Blasted* withered. *ecstasy* madness
154 *affections* emotions, feelings   157 *sits on brood* sits like a bird on a nest, about to *hatch*
mischief (line 158)   158 *doubt* fear. *disclose* disclosure, hatching   161 *set it down* resolved
162 *For . . . of* to demand   164 *variable objects* various sights and surroundings to divert him
165 *This something . . . heart* the strange matter settled in his heart   166 *still* continually
167 *From . . . himself* out of his natural manner   174 *queen-mother* queen and mother
175 *round* blunt   177 *find him not* fails to discover what is troubling him

Hamlet: Speak the speech, I pray you, as I pronounced it to you, trippingly
on the tongue. But if you mouth it, as many of our players* do, I had as
lief* the town crier spoke my lines. Nor do not saw the air too much
with your hand, thus, but use all gently; for in the very torrent, tempest,
and, as I may say, whirlwind of your passion, you must acquire and   5
beget a temperance that may give it smoothness. O, it offends me to the
soul to hear a robustious* periwig-pated* fellow tear a passion to tatters, to very rags, to split the ears of the groundlings,* who for the most
part are capable of* nothing but inexplicable dumb shows* and noise.
I would have such a fellow whipped for o'erdoing Termagant.* It out-
Herods Herod.* Pray you, avoid it.   10
First Player: I warrant your honor.
Hamlet: Be not too tame neither, but let your own discretion be your tutor.
Suit the action to the word, the word to the action, with this special
observance, that you o'erstep not the modesty* of nature. For anything
so o'erdone is from* the purpose of playing, whose end, both at the   15
first and now, was and is to hold as 't were the mirror up to nature, to
show virtue her feature, scorn* her own image, and the very age and
body of the time* his* form and pressure.* Now this overdone or come
tardy off,* though it makes the unskillful* laugh, cannot but make the
judicious grieve, the censure of the which one* must in your allowance*   20
o'erweigh a whole theater of others. O, there be players that I have
seen play, and heard others praise, and that highly, not to speak it profanely,* that, neither having th' accent of Christians* nor the gait of
Christian, pagan, nor man,* have so strutted and bellowed that I have
thought some of nature's journeymen* had made men and not made
them well, they imitated humanity so abominably.*   25
First Player: I hope we have reformed that indifferently* with us, sir.
Hamlet: O, reform it altogether. And let those that play your clowns speak
no more than is set down for them; for there be of them* that will
themselves laugh, to set on some quantity of barren* spectators to
laugh too, though in the meantime some necessary question of the   30
play be then to be considered. That's villainous, and shows a most pitiful ambition in the fool that uses it. Go make you ready.

[Exeunt Players.]

2 *our players* players nowadays.   *I had as lief* I would just as soon   6 *robustious* violent,
boisterous   7 *periwig-pated* wearing a wig   8 *groundlings* spectators who paid least and stood in
the yard of the theater.   *capable of* able to understand   9 *dumb shows* mimed performances,
often used before Shakespeare's time to precede a play or each act   10 *Termagant* a supposed
deity of the Mohammedans, not found in any English medieval play but elsewhere portrayed as
violent and blustering.   *Herod* Herod of Jewry. (A character in *The Slaughter of the Innocents*
and other cycle plays. The part was played with great noise and fury.)   14 *modesty* restraint,
moderation   15 *from* contrary to   17 *scorn* i.e., something foolish and deserving of scorn.
the very. . . time i.e., the present state of affairs.   *his* its   18 *pressure* stamp, impressed
character.   *come tardy off* inadequately done   18–19 *the unskillful* those lacking in judgment
19–20 *the censure. . . one* the judgment of even one of whom   20 *your allowance* your scale of
values   22 *not. . . profanely* (Hamlet anticipates his idea in lines 24–25 that some men were not
made by God at all.)   22–23 *Christians* i.e., ordinary decent folk   23 *nor man* i.e., nor any
human being at all   24 *journeymen* laborers who are not yet masters in their trade
25 *abominably* (Shakespeare's usual spelling, abhominably, suggests a literal though etymologically
incorrect meaning, "removed from human nature.")   26 *indifferently* tolerably   28 *of them* some
among them   29 *barren* i.e., of wit

Enter Polonius, Guildenstern, and Rosencrantz.

How now, my lord, will the King hear this piece of work?
Polonius: And the Queen too, and that presently.*
Hamlet: Bid the players make haste.   [*Exit Polonius.*]   35
    Will you two help to hasten them?
Rosencrantz: Ay, my lord.   *Exeunt they two.*
Hamlet: What ho, Horatio!

    Enter Horatio.

Horatio: Here, sweet lord, at your service.
Hamlet: Horatio, thou art e'en as just a man
    As e'er my conversation coped withal.*   40
Horatio: O, my dear lord—
Hamlet: Nay, do not think I flatter,
    For what advancement may I hope from thee
    That no revenue hast but thy good spirits
    To feed and clothe thee? Why should the poor be flattered?
    No, let the candied* tongue lick absurd pomp,   45
    And crook the pregnant* hinges of the knee
    Where thrift* may follow fawning. Dost thou hear?
    Since my dear soul was mistress of her choice
    And could of men distinguish her election,*
    Sh' hath sealed thee* for herself, for thou hast been   50
    As one, in suffering all, that suffers nothing,
    A man that Fortune's buffets and rewards
    Hast ta'en with equal thanks; and blest are those
    Whose blood* and judgment are so well commeddled*
    That they are not a pipe for Fortune's finger   55
    To sound what stop* she please. Give me that man
    That is not passion's slave, and I will wear him
    In my heart's core, ay, in my heart of heart,
    As I do thee.—Something too much of this.—
    There is a play tonight before the King.   60
    One scene of it comes near the circumstance
    Which I have told thee of my father's death.
    I prithee, when thou seest that act afoot,
    Even with the very comment of thy soul*
    Observe my uncle. If his occulted* guilt   65
    Do not itself unkennel* in one speech,
    It is a damnèd* ghost that we have seen,
    And my imaginations are as foul
    As Vulcan's stithy.* Give him heedful note,
    For I mine eyes will rivet to his face,   70
    And after we will both our judgments join

34 *presently* at once   40 *my. . . withal* my dealings encountered   45 *candied* sugared, flattering
46 *pregnant* compliant   47 *thrift* profit   49 *could. . . election* could make distinguishing choices
among persons   50 *sealed thee* (Literally, as one would seal a legal document to mark possession.)
54 *blood* passion.   *commeddled* commingled   56 *stop* hole in a wind instrument for controlling the
sound   64 *very. . . soul* your most penetrating observation and consideration   65 *occulted* hidden
66 *unkennel* (As one would say of a fox driven from its lair.)   67 *damnèd* in league with Satan
69 *stithy* smithy, place of stiths (anvils)

In censure of his seeming.*

Horatio: Well, my lord.
If 'a steal aught* the whilst this play is playing
And scape detecting, I will pay the theft.

[*Flourish.*] *Enter trumpets and kettledrums, King,*

Queen, Polonius, Ophelia, [Rosencrantz, Guildenstern, and other lords, with guards carrying torches].

Hamlet: They are coming to the play. I must be idle.* Get you a place.   75

[*The King, Queen, and courtiers sit.*]

King: How fares our cousin* Hamlet?

Hamlet: Excellent, i' faith, of the chameleon's dish:* I eat the air, promise-crammed. You cannot feed capons* so.

King: I have nothing with* this answer, Hamlet. These words are not mine.*

Hamlet: No, nor mine now.* [*To Polonius.*] My lord, you played once i' th'   80
university, you say?

Polonius: That did I, my lord, and was accounted a good actor.

Hamlet: What did you enact?

Polonius: I did enact Julius Caesar. I was killed i' the Capitol; Brutus killed me.

Hamlet: It was a brute* part* of him to kill so capital a calf* there.—Be the   85
players ready?

Rosencrantz: Ay, my lord. They stay upon* your patience.

Queen: Come hither, my dear Hamlet, sit by me.

Hamlet: No, good Mother, here's metal* more attractive.

Polonius [*to the King*]: O, ho, do you mark that?   90

Hamlet: Lady, shall I lie in your lap?

[*Lying down at Ophelia's feet.*]

Ophelia: No, my lord.

Hamlet: I mean, my head upon your lap?

Ophelia: Ay, my lord.

Hamlet: Do you think I meant country matters?*   95

Ophelia: I think nothing, my lord.

Hamlet: That's a fair thought to lie between maids' legs.

Ophelia: What is, my lord?

Hamlet: Nothing.*

Ophelia: You are merry, my lord.   100

72 *censure of his* seeming judgment of his appearance or behavior   73 *If 'a steal aught* if he gets away with anything   75 *idle* (1) unoccupied (2) mad   76 *cousin* i.e., close relative   77 *chameleon's dish* (Chameleons were supposed to feed on air. Hamlet deliberately misinterprets the King's *fares* as "feeds." By his phrase *eat the air*, he also plays on the idea of feeding himself with the promise of succession, of being the *heir*.)   78 *capons* roosters castrated and *crammed* with feed to make them succulent   79 *have . . . with* make nothing of, or gain nothing from.   *are not mine* do not respond to what I asked   80 *nor mine now* (Once spoken, words are proverbially no longer the speaker's own—and hence should be uttered warily.)   85 *brute* (The Latin meaning of *brutus*, "stupid," was often used punningly with the name Brutus.)   *part* (1) deed (2) role.   *calf* fool   87 *stay upon* await   89 *metal* substance that is *attractive*, i.e., magnetic, but with suggestion also of *mettle*, "disposition"   95 *country matters* sexual intercourse (making a bawdy pun on the first syllable of *country*)   99 *Nothing* the figure zero or naught, suggesting the female sexual anatomy. (*Thing* not infrequently has a bawdy connotation of male or female anatomy, and the reference here could be male.)

Hamlet: Who, I?

Ophelia: Ay, my lord.

Hamlet: O God, your only jig maker.* What should a man do but be merry?
   For look you how cheerfully my mother looks, and my father died
   within 's* two hours.   105

Ophelia: Nay, 'tis twice two months, my lord.

Hamlet: So long? Nay then, let the devil wear black, for I'll have a suit of
   sables.* O heavens! Die two months ago, and not forgotten yet? Then
   there's hope a great man's memory may outlive his life half a year. But,
   by'r Lady, 'a must build churches, then, or else shall 'a suffer not thinking on,* with the hobbyhorse, whose epitaph is "For O, for O, the hob-   110
   byhorse is forgot."*

The trumpets sound. Dumb show follows.

*Enter a King and a Queen [very lovingly]; the Queen embracing
him, and he her. [She kneels, and makes show of protestation unto
him.] He takes her up, and declines his head upon her neck. He lies
him down upon a bank of flowers. She, seeing him asleep, leaves
him. Anon comes in another man, takes off his crown, kisses it,
pours poison in the sleeper's ears, and leaves him. The Queen returns, finds the King dead, makes passionate action. The Poisoner
with some three or four come in again, seem to condole with her.
The dead body is carried away. The Poisoner woos the Queen with
gifts; she seems harsh awhile, but in the end accepts love.*

                                                        [*Exeunt players.*]

Ophelia: What means this, my lord?

Hamlet: Marry, this' miching mallico;* it means mischief.

Ophelia: Belike* this show imports the argument* of the play.

   Enter Prologue.

Hamlet: We shall know by this fellow. The players cannot keep counsel;*   115
   they'll tell all.

Ophelia: Will 'a tell us what this show meant?

Hamlet: Ay, or any show that you will show him. Be not you* ashamed to
   show, he'll not shame to tell you what it means.

Ophelia: You are naught, you are naught.* I'll mark the play.   120

Prologue: For us, and for our tragedy,
   Here stooping* to your clemency,
   We beg your hearing patiently.   [*Exit.*]

---

103 *only jig maker* very best composer of jigs, i.e., pointless merriment. (Hamlet replies
sardonically to Ophelia's observation that he is merry by saying, "If you're looking for someone
who is really merry, you've come to the right person.")   104 *within 's* within this (i.e., these)
107 *suit of sables* garments trimmed with the fur of the sable and hence suited for a wealthy person,
not a mourner (but with a pun on *sable,* "black," ironically suggesting mourning once again)
110 *suffer. . . on* undergo oblivion   111 *For. . .forgot* (Verse of a song occurring also in *Love's
Labor's Lost,* 3.1.27–28. The hobbyhorse was a character made up to resemble a horse and rider,
appearing in the morris dance and such May-game sports. This song laments the disappearance of
such customs under pressure from the Puritans.)   113 *this' miching mallico* this is sneaking
mischief   114 *Belike* probably.   *argument* plot   115 *counsel* secret   118 *Be not you* provided
you are not   120 *naught* indecent. (Ophelia is reacting to Hamlet's pointed remarks about not
being ashamed to show all.)   122 *stooping* bowing

Hamlet: Is this a prologue, or the posy of a ring?*
Ophelia: 'Tis brief, my lord.   125
Hamlet: As woman's love.

    Enter [two Players as] King and Queen.

Player King: Full thirty times hath Phoebus' cart* gone round
    Neptune's salt wash* and Tellus'* orbèd ground,
    And thirty dozen moons with borrowed* sheen
    About the world have times twelve thirties been,
    Since love our hearts and Hymen* did our hands   130
    Unite commutual* in most sacred bands.*
Player Queen: So many journeys may the sun and moon
    Make us again count o'er ere love be done!
    But, woe is me, you are so sick of late,
    So far from cheer and from your former state,   135
    That I distrust* you. Yet, though I distrust,
    Discomfort* you, my lord, it nothing* must.
    For women's fear and love hold quantity;*
    In neither aught, or in extremity.*
    Now, what my love is, proof* hath made you know,   140
    And as my love is sized,* my fear is so.
    Where love is great, the littlest doubts are fear;
    Where little fears grow great, great love grows there.
Player King: Faith, I must leave thee, love, and shortly too;   145
    My operant powers* their functions leave to do.*
    And thou shalt live in this fair world behind,*
    Honored, beloved; and haply one as kind
    For husband shalt thou—
Player Queen: O, confound the rest!
    Such love must needs be treason in my breast.   150
    In second husband let me be accurst!
    None* wed the second but who* killed the first.
Hamlet: Wormwood,* wormwood.
Player Queen: The instances* that second marriage move*
    Are base respects of thrift,* but none of love.   155
    A second time I kill my husband dead
    When second husband kisses me in bed.
Player King: I do believe you think what now you speak,
    But what we do determine oft we break.
    Purpose is but the slave to memory,*   160

---

124 *posy . . . ring* brief motto in verse inscribed in a ring   127 *Phoebus' cart* the sun-god's chariot,
making its yearly cycle   128 *salt wash* the sea.   *Tellus* goddess of the earth, of the *orbèd ground*
129 *borrowed* i.e., reflected   131 *Hymen* god of matrimony   132 *commutual* mutually.
bands bonds   137 *distrust* am anxious about   138 *Discomfort* distress.   *nothing* not at all
139 *hold quantity* keep proportion with one another   140 *In . . . extremity* i.e., women fear and
love either too little or too much, but the two, fear and love, are equal in either case   141 *proof*
experience   142 *sized* in size   146 *operant powers* vital functions.   *leave to do* cease to perform
147 *behind* after I have gone   152 *None* i.e., let no woman.   *but who* except the one who
153 *Wormwood* i.e., how bitter. (Literally, a bitter-tasting plant.)   154 *instances* motives.
move motivate   155 *base . . . thrift* ignoble considerations of material prosperity   160 *Purpose . . .
memory* our good intentions are subject to forgetfulness

Of violent birth, but poor validity,*
Which* now, like fruit unripe, sticks on the tree,
But fall unshaken when they mellow be.
Most necessary 'tis that we forget
To pay ourselves what to ourselves is debt.*   165
What to ourselves in passion we purpose,
The passion ending, doth the purpose lose.
The violence of either grief or joy
Their own enactures* with themselves destroy.
Where joy most revels, grief doth most lament;   170
Grief joys, joy grieves, on slender accident.*
This world is not for aye,* nor 'tis not strange
That even our loves should with our fortunes change;
For 'tis a question left us yet to prove,
Whether love lead fortune, or else fortune love.   175
The great man down,* you mark his favorite flies;
The poor advanced makes friends of enemies.*
And hitherto* doth love on fortune tend;*
For who not needs* shall never lack a friend,
And who in want* a hollow friend doth try*   180
Directly seasons him* his enemy.
But, orderly to end where I begun,
Our wills and fates do so contrary run*
That our devices still* are overthrown;
Our thoughts are ours, their ends* none of our own.   185
So think thou wilt no second husband wed,
But die thy thoughts when thy first lord is dead.
Player Queen: Nor* earth to me give food, nor heaven light,
Sport and repose lock from me day and night,*
To desperation turn my trust and hope,   190
An anchor's cheer* in prison be my scope!*
Each* opposite that blanks* the face of joy
Meet what I would have well and it destroy!
Both here and hence* pursue me lasting strife
If, once a widow, ever I be wife!   195
Hamlet: If she should break it now!
Player King: 'Tis deeply sworn. Sweet, leave me here awhile;

161 *validity* strength, durability   162 *Which* i.e., purpose   164–165 *Most. . . debt* it's inevitable
that in time we forget the obligations we have imposed on ourselves   169 *enactures* fulfillments
170–171 *Where. . . accident* the capacity for extreme joy and grief go together, and often one
extreme is instantly changed into its opposite on the slightest provocation   172 *aye* ever
176 *down* fallen in fortune   177 *The poor. . . enemies* when one of humble station is promoted,
you see his enemies suddenly becoming his friends   178 *hitherto* up to this point in the argument,
or, to this extent.   *tend* attend   179 *who not needs* he who is not in need (of wealth)   180 *who in
want* he who, being in need.   *try* test (his generosity)   181 *seasons him* ripens him into
183 *Our. . . run* what we want and what we get go so contrarily   184 *devices still* intentions
continually   185 *ends* results   188 *Nor* let neither   189 *Sport. . . night* may day deny me its
pastimes and night its repose   191 *anchor's cheer* anchorite's or hermit's fare.   *my scope* the
extent of my happiness   192–193 *Each. . . destroy* may every adverse thing that causes the face of
joy to turn pale meet and destroy everything that I desire to see prosper.   192 *blanks* causes to
blanch or grow pale   194 *hence* in the life hereafter

My spirits* grow dull, and fain I would beguile
The tedious day with sleep.
Player Queen: Sleep rock thy brain,
And never come mischance between us twain!   200

[*He sleeps.*] *Exit* [*Player Queen*].

Hamlet: Madam, how like you this play?
Queen: The lady doth protest too much,* methinks.
Hamlet: O, but she'll keep her word.
King: Have you heard the argument?* Is there no offense* in 't?
Hamlet: No, no, they do but jest,* poison in jest. No offense i' the world.   205
King: What do you call the play?
Hamlet: The Mousetrap. Marry, how? Tropically.* This play is the image of
a murder done in Vienna. Gonzago is the Duke's* name, his wife, Bap-
tista. You shall see anon. 'Tis a knavish piece of work, but what of that?
Your Majesty, and we that have free* souls, it touches us not. Let the   210
galled jade* wince, our withers* are unwrung.*

Enter Lucianus.

This is one Lucianus, nephew to the King.
Ophelia: You are as good as a chorus,* my lord.
Hamlet: I could interpret* between you and your love, if I could see the
puppets dallying.*   215
Ophelia: You are keen, my lord, you are keen.*
Hamlet: It would cost you a groaning to take off mine edge.
Ophelia: Still better, and worse.*
Hamlet: So* you mis-take* your husbands. Begin, murderer; leave thy damnable
faces and begin. Come, the croaking raven doth bellow for revenge.   220
Lucianus: Thoughts black, hands apt, drugs fit, and time agreeing,
Confederate season,* else* no creature seeing,*
Thou mixture rank, of midnight weeds collected,
With Hecate's ban* thrice blasted, thrice infected,
Thy natural magic and dire property*   225

198 *spirits* vital spirits   202 *doth. . . much* makes too many promises and protestations
204 *argument* plot   204–205 *offense. . . offense* cause for objection. . . actual injury, crime
205 *jest* make believe   207 *Tropically* figuratively. (The First Quarto reading, *trapically*, suggests
a pun on *trap* in *Mousetrap*.)   208 *Duke's* i.e., King's. (A slip that may be due to Shakespeare's
possible source, the alleged murder of the Duke of Urbino by Luigi Gonzaga in 1538.)
210 *free* guiltless.   *galled jade* horse whose hide is rubbed by saddle or harness.   211 *withers* the
part between the horse's shoulder blades   *unwrung* not rubbed sore   213 *chorus* (In many
Elizabethan plays, the forthcoming action was explained by an actor known as the "chorus"; at a
puppet show, the actor who spoke the dialogue was known as an "interpreter," as indicated by the
lines following.)   214 *interpret* (1) ventriloquize the dialogue, as in puppet show (2) act as pander
214–215 *puppets dallying* (With suggestion of sexual play, continued in lines 216–218:
keen, "sexually aroused," *groaning,* "moaning in pregnancy," and *edge,* "sexual desire" or
"impetuosity.")   216 *keen* sharp, bitter   218 *Still. . . worse* more keen, always *bettering* what
other people say with witty wordplay, but at the same time more offensive   219 *So* even thus (in
marriage).   *mis-take* take falseheartedly and cheat on. (The marriage vows say "for better, for
worse.")   222 *Confederate season* the time and occasion conspiring (to assist the murderer).   *else*
otherwise.   *seeing* seeing me   224 *Hecate's ban* the curse of Hecate, the goddess of witchcraft
225 *dire property* baleful quality

On wholesome life usurp immediately.

[He pours the poison into the sleeper's ear.]

Hamlet: 'A poison him i' the garden for his estate.* His* name's Gonzago.
The story is extant, and written in very choice Italian. You shall see
anon how the murderer gets the love of Gonzago's wife.

[Claudius rises.]

Ophelia: The King rises.   230
Hamlet: What, frighted with false fire?*
Queen: How fares my lord?
Polonius: Give o'er the play.
King: Give me some light. Away!
Polonius: Lights, lights, lights!   235

Exeunt all but Hamlet and Horatio.

Hamlet: *"Why,* let the strucken deer go weep,
            The hart ungallèd play.*
            For some must watch, while some must sleep;*
            *Thus runs the world away."**

Would not this,* sir, and a forest of feathers*—if the rest of my fortunes   240
turn Turk with* me—with two Provincial roses* on my razed* shoes,
get me a fellowship* in a cry* of players?

Horatio: Half a share.
Hamlet: A whole one, I.
            "For thou dost know, O Damon dear,*   245
            This realm dismantled* was*
            Of Jove himself, and now reigns here
            A very, very—pajock."

Horatio: You might have rhymed.
Hamlet: O good Horatio, I'll take the ghost's word for a thousand pound.   250
Didst perceive?
Horatio: Very well, my lord.
Hamlet: Upon the talk of the poisoning?
Horatio: I did very well note him.

Enter Rosencrantz and Guildenstern.

---

227 *estate* i.e., the kingship.   *His* i.e., the King's   231 *false fire* the blank discharge of a gun
loaded with powder but no shot   236–239 *Why. . . away* (Probably from an old ballad, with
allusion to the popular belief that a wounded deer retires to weep and die; compare with *As You
Like It*, Act II, Scene i, lines 33–66.)   237 *ungallèd* unafflicted   238 *watch* remain awake
239 *Thus. . . away* thus the world goes   240 *this* i.e., the play.   *feathers* (Allusion to the plumes
that Elizabethan actors were fond of wearing.)   240–241 *turn Turk with* turn renegade against, go
back on   241 *Provincial roses* rosettes of ribbon, named for roses grown in a part of France.
razed with ornamental slashing.   241–242 *fellowship. . . players* partnership in a theatrical
company.   242 *cry* pack (of hounds)   245 *Damon* the friend of Pythias, as Horatio is friend of
Hamlet; or, a traditional pastoral name   246–248 *This realm. . . pajock* i.e., Jove, representing
divine authority and justice, has abandoned this realm to its own devices, leaving in his stead only a
peacock or vain pretender to virtue (though the rhyme-word expected in place of *pajock* or "peacock"
suggests that the realm is now ruled over by an "ass").   246 *dismantled* stripped, divested

Hamlet: Aha! Come, some music! Come, the recorders.*   255
    "For if the King like not the comedy,
        Why then, belike, he likes it not, perdy."*
    Come, some music.
Guildenstern: Good my lord, vouchsafe me a word with you.
Hamlet: Sir, a whole history.   260
Guildenstern: The King, sir—
Hamlet: Ay, sir, what of him?
Guildenstern: Is in his retirement* marvelous distempered.*
Hamlet: With drink, sir?
Guildenstern: No, my lord, with choler.   265
Hamlet: Your wisdom should show itself more richer to signify this to the
    doctor, for for me to put him to his purgation* would perhaps plunge
    him into more choler.*
Guildenstern: Good my lord, put your discourse into some frame* and
    start* not so wildly from my affair.   270
Hamlet: I am tame, sir. Pronounce.
Guildenstern: The Queen, your mother, in most great affliction of spirit,
    hath sent me to you.
Hamlet: You are welcome.
Guildenstern: Nay, good my lord, this courtesy is not of the right breed.* If   275
    it shall please you to make me a wholesome answer, I will do your
    mother's commandment; if not, your pardon* and my return shall be
    the end of my business.
Hamlet: Sir, I cannot.   280
Rosencrantz: What, my lord?
Hamlet: Make you a wholesome answer; my wit's diseased. But, sir, such
    answer as I can make, you shall command, or rather, as you say, my
    mother. Therefore no more, but to the matter. My mother, you say—
Rosencrantz: Then thus she says: your behavior hath struck her into
    amazement and admiration.*   285
Hamlet: O wonderful son, that can so stonish a mother! But is there no
    sequel at the heels of this mother's admiration? Impart.
Rosencrantz: She desires to speak with you in her closet* ere you go to bed.
Hamlet: We shall obey, were she ten times our mother. Have you any fur-
    ther trade with us?   290
Rosencrantz: My lord, you once did love me.
Hamlet: And do still, by these pickers and stealers.*
Rosencrantz: Good my lord, what is your cause of distemper? You do surely bar
    the door upon your own liberty* if you deny* your griefs to your friend.

255 *recorders* wind instruments of the flute kind   257 *perdy* (A corruption of the French *par dieu*, "by God.")   263 *retirement* withdrawal to his chambers.   *distempered* out of humor. (But Hamlet deliberately plays on the wider application to any illness of mind or body, especially to drunkenness.)   267 *purgation* (Hamlet hints at something going beyond medical treatment to blood-letting and the extraction of confession.)   268 *choler* anger. (But Hamlet takes the word in its more basic humoral sense of "bilious disorder.")   269 *frame* order.   *start* shy or jump away (like a horse; the opposite of *tame* in line 271)   275 *breed* (1) kind (2) breeding, manners   277 *pardon* permission to depart   285 *admiration* bewilderment   288 *closet* private chamber   292 *pickers and stealers* i.e., hands. (So called from the catechism, "to keep my hands from picking and stealing.")   294 *liberty* i.e., being freed from *distemper*, line 293; but perhaps with a veiled threat as well.   *deny* refuse to share

Hamlet: Sir, I lack advancement. 295
Rosencrantz: How can that be, when you have the voice of the King himself for your succession in Denmark?
Hamlet: Ay, sir, but "While the grass grows"*—the proverb is something* musty.

    Enter the Players with recorders.*

    O, the recorders. Let me see one. [*He takes a recorder.*] To withdraw*
    with you: why do you go about to recover the wind* of me, as if you 300
    would drive me into a toil?*
Guildenstern: O, my lord, if my duty be too bold, my love is too unmannerly.*
Hamlet: I do not well understand that.* Will you play upon this pipe?
Guildenstern: My lord, I cannot.
Hamlet: I pray you. 305
Guildenstern: Believe me, I cannot.
Hamlet: I do beseech you.
Guildenstern: I know no touch of it, my lord.
Hamlet: It is as easy as lying. Govern these ventages* with your fingers and
    thumb, give it breath with your mouth, and it will discourse most elo- 310
    quent music. Look you, these are the stops.
Guildenstern: But these cannot I command to any utterance of harmony. I
    have not the skill.
Hamlet: Why, look you now, how unworthy a thing you make of me! You
    would play upon me, you would seem to know my stops, you would 315
    pluck out the heart of my mystery, you would sound* me from my low-
    est note to the top of my compass,* and there is much music, excellent
    voice, in this little organ,* yet cannot you make it speak. 'Sblood, do you
    think I am easier to be played on than a pipe? Call me what instrument
    you will, though you can fret* me, you cannot play upon me. 320

    Enter Polonius.

    God bless you, sir!
Polonius: My lord, the Queen would speak with you, and presently.*
Hamlet: Do you see yonder cloud that's almost in shape of a camel?
Polonius: By the Mass and 'tis, like a camel indeed.
Hamlet: Methinks it is like a weasel. 325
Polonius: It is backed like a weasel.
Hamlet: Or like a whale.
Polonius: Very like a whale
Hamlet: Then I will come to my mother by and by.* [*Aside.*] They fool me*
    to the top of my bent.*—I will come by and by. 330

---

298 *While. . . grows* (The rest of the proverb is "the silly horse starves"; Hamlet may not live
long enough to succeed to the kingdom.)   *something* somewhat.   *stage direction: Players* actors
299 *withdraw* speak privately   300 *recover the wind* get to the windward side (thus driving the
game into the *toil*, or "net")   301 *toil* snare   302 *if. . . unmannerly* if I am using an
unmannerly boldness, it is my love that occasions it   303 *I . . . that* i.e., I don't understand
how genuine love can be unmannerly   309 *ventages* finger-holes or *stops* (line 315) of the
recorder   316 *sound* (1) fathom (2) produce sound in   317 *compass* range (of voice).
organ musical instrument   319 *fret* irritate (with a quibble on *fret*, meaning the piece of wood,
gut, or metal that regulates the fingering on an instrument)   322 *presently* at once
329 *by and by* quite soon.   *fool me* trifle with me, humor my fooling   330 *top of my bent* limit
of my ability or endurance. (Literally, the extent to which a bow may be bent.)

Polonius: I will say so.   [*Exit.*]
Hamlet: "By and by" is easily said. Leave me, friends.

                                             [*Exeunt all but Hamlet.*]

    'Tis now the very witching time* of night,
    When churchyards yawn and hell itself breathes out
    Contagion to this world. Now could I drink hot blood   335
    And do such bitter business as the day
    Would quake to look on. Soft, now to my mother.
    O heart, lose not thy nature!* Let not ever
    The soul of Nero* enter this firm bosom.
    Let me be cruel, not unnatural;   340
    I will speak daggers to her, but use none.
    My tongue and soul in this be hypocrites:
    How in my words soever* she be shent,*
    To give them seals* never my soul consent!   *Exit.*

Scene III [*The Castle.*]

    Enter King, Rosencrantz, and Guildenstern.

King: I like him* not, nor stands it safe with us
    To let his madness range. Therefore prepare you.
    I your commission will forthwith dispatch,*
    And he to England shall along with you.
    The terms of our estate* may not endure   5
    Hazard so near 's as doth hourly grow
    Out of his brows.*
Guildenstern: We will ourselves provide.
    Most holy and religious fear* it is
    To keep those many many bodies safe
    That live and feed upon Your Majesty.   10
Rosencrantz: The single and peculiar* life is bound
    With all the strength and armor of the mind
    To keep itself from noyance,* but much more
    That spirit upon whose weal depends and rests
    The lives of many. The cess* of majesty   15
    Dies not alone, but like a gulf* doth draw
    What's near it with it; or it is a massy* wheel
    Fixed on the summit of the highest mount,
    To whose huge spokes ten thousand lesser things
    Are mortised* and adjoined, which, when it falls,*   20

---

333 *witching time* time when spells are cast and evil is abroad   338 *nature* natural feeling
339 *Nero* murderer of his mother, Agrippina   343 *How. . . soever* however much by my words.
shent rebuked   344 *give them seals* i.e., confirm them with deeds   1 *him* i.e., his behavior
3 *dispatch* prepare, cause to be drawn up   5 *terms of our estate* circumstances of my royal
position   7 *Out of his brows* i.e., from his brain, in the form of plots and threats
8 *religious fear* sacred concern   11 *single and peculiar* individual and private   13 *noyance* harm
15 *cess* decrease, cessation   16 *gulf* whirlpool   17 *massy* massive   20 *mortised* fastened (as with
a fitted joint).   *when it falls* i.e., when it descends, like the wheel of Fortune, bringing a king
down with it

Each small annexment, petty consequence,*
Attends* the boisterous ruin. Never alone
Did the King sigh, but with a general groan.
King: Arm* you, I pray you, to this speedy voyage,
    For we will fetters put about this fear,   25
    Which now goes too free-footed.
Rosencrantz: We will haste us.

          Exeunt gentlemen [Rosencrantz and Guildenstern].

   Enter Polonius.

Polonius: My lord, he's going to his mother's closet.
    Behind the arras* I'll convey myself
    To hear the process.* I'll warrant she'll tax him home,*
    And, as you said—and wisely was it said—   30
    'Tis meet* that some more audience than a mother,
    Since nature makes them partial, should o'erhear
    The speech, of vantage.* Fare you well, my liege.
    I'll call upon you ere you go to bed
    And tell you what I know.
King: Thanks, dear my lord.   35

                       Exit [Polonius].

O, my offense is rank! It smells to heaven.
It hath the primal eldest curse* upon 't,
A brother's murder. Pray can I not,
Though inclination be as sharp as will;*
My stronger guilt defeats my strong intent,   40
And like a man to double business bound*
I stand in pause where I shall first begin,
And both neglect. What if this cursèd hand
Were thicker than itself with brother's blood,
Is there not rain enough in the sweet heavens   45
To wash it white as snow? Whereto serves mercy
But to confront the visage of offense?*
And what's in prayer but this twofold force,
To be forestallèd* ere we come to fall,
Or pardoned being down? Then I'll look up.   50
My fault is past. But O, what form of prayer
Can serve my turn? "Forgive me my foul murder"?
That cannot be, since I am still possessed
Of those effects for which I did the murder:
My crown, mine own ambition, and my queen.   55

---

21 *Each. . . consequence* i.e., every hanger-on and unimportant person or thing connected with the
King 22 *Attends* participates in 24 *Arm* prepare 28 *arras* screen of tapestry placed around the
walls of household apartments. (On the Elizabethan stage, the arras was presumably over a door or
discovery space in the tiring-house facade.) 29 *process* proceedings. *tax him home* reprove him
severely 31 *meet* fitting 33 *of vantage* from an advantageous place, or, in addition 37 *the primal
eldest curse* the curse of Cain, the first murderer; he killed his brother Abel 39 *Though. . . will*
though my desire is as strong as my determination 41 *bound* (1) destined (2) obliged. (The King
wants to repent and still enjoy what he has gained.) 46–47 *Whereto. . . offense* what function does
mercy serve other than to meet sin face to face? 49 *forestallèd* prevented (from sinning)

May one be pardoned and retain th' offense?*
In the corrupted currents* of this world
Offense's gilded hand* may shove* by justice,
And oft 'tis seen the wicked prize* itself
Buys out the law. But 'tis not so above.   60
There* is no shuffling,* there the action lies*
In his* true nature, and we ourselves compelled,
Even to the teeth and forehead* of our faults,
To give in* evidence. What then? What rests?*
Try what repentance can. What can it not?   65
Yet what can it, when one cannot repent?
O wretched state, O bosom black as death,
O limèd* soul that, struggling to be free,
Art more engaged!* Help, angels! Make assay.*
Bow, stubborn knees, and heart with strings of steel,   70
Be soft as sinews of the newborn babe!
All may be well.   [He kneels.]

Enter Hamlet.

Hamlet: Now might I do it pat,* now 'a is a-praying;
   And now I'll do 't. [*He draws his sword.*] And so 'a goes to heaven,
   And so am I revenged. That would be scanned:*   75
   A villain kills my father, and for that,
   I, his sole son, do this same villain send
   To heaven.
   Why, this is hire and salary, not revenge.
   'A took my father grossly, full of bread,*   80
   With all his crimes broad blown,* as flush* as May;
   And how his audit* stands who knows save* heaven?
   But in our circumstance and course of thought*
   'Tis heavy with him. And am I then revenged,
   To take him in the purging of his soul,   85
   When he is fit and seasoned* for his passage?
   No!
   Up, sword, and know* thou a more horrid hent.*

                                         [*He puts up his sword.*]

   When he is drunk asleep, or in his rage,*
   Or in th' incestuous pleasure of his bed,   90
   At game,* a-swearing, or about some act

56 *th' offense* the thing for which one offended   57 *currents* courses   58 *gilded hand* hand
offering gold as a bribe.   *shove by* thrust aside   59 *wicked prize* prize won by wickedness
61 *There* i.e., in heaven.   *shuffling* escape by trickery.   *the action lies* the accusation is made
manifest. (A legal metaphor.)   62 *his* its   63 *to the teeth and forehead* face to face, concealing
nothing   64 *give in* provide.   *rests* remains   68 *limèd* caught as with birdlime, a sticky substance
used to ensnare birds   69 *engaged* entangled.   *assay* trial. (Said to himself.)   73 *pat*
opportunely   75 *would be scanned* needs to be looked into, or, would be interpreted as follows
80 *grossly, full of bread* i.e., enjoying his worldly pleasures rather than fasting. (See Ezekiel
16:49.)   81 *crimes broad blown* sins in full bloom.   *flush* vigorous   82 *audit* account.   *save*
except for   83 *in . . . thought* as we see it from our mortal perspective   86 *seasoned* matured,
readied   88 *know . . . hent* await to be grasped by me on a more horrid occasion.   *hent* act of
seizing   89 *drunk . . . rage* dead drunk, or in a fit of sexual passion   91 *game* gambling

That has no relish* of salvation in 't—
Then trip him, that his heels may kick at heaven,
And that his soul may be as damned and black
As hell, whereto it goes. My mother stays.*   95
This physic* but prolongs thy sickly days.   *Exit.*
King: My words fly up, my thoughts remain below.
Words without thoughts never to heaven go.   *Exit.*

Scene IV [The Queen's Private Chamber.]

Enter [Queen] Gertrude and Polonius.

Polonius: 'A will come straight. Look you lay home* to him.
Tell him his pranks have been too broad* to bear with,
And that Your Grace hath screened and stood between
Much heat* and him. I'll shroud* me even here.
Pray you, be round* with him.   5
Hamlet (within): Mother, Mother, Mother!
Queen: I'll warrant you, fear me not.
Withdraw, I hear him coming.

[*Polonius hides behind the arras.*]
Enter Hamlet.

Hamlet: Now, Mother, what's the matter?
Queen: Hamlet, thou hast thy father* much offended.   10
Hamlet: Mother, you have my father much offended.
Queen: Come, come, you answer with an idle* tongue.
Hamlet: Go, go, you question with a wicked tongue.
Queen: Why, how now, Hamlet?
Hamlet: What's the matter now?
Queen: Have you forgot me?*
Hamlet: No, by the rood,* not so: 15
You are the Queen, your husband's brother's wife,
And—would it were not so!—you are my mother.
Queen: Nay, then, I'll set those to you that can speak.*
Hamlet: Come, come, and sit you down; you shall not budge.
You go not till I set you up a glass   20
Where you may see the inmost part of you.
Queen: What wilt thou do? Thou wilt not murder me?
Help, ho!
Polonius [behind the arras]: What ho! Help!
Hamlet [drawing]: How now? A rat? Dead for a ducat,* dead!   25

[*He thrusts his rapier through the arras.*]

Polonius [behind the arras]: O, I am slain!   [*He falls and dies.*]

92 *relish* trace, savor   95 *stays* awaits (me)   96 *physic* purging (by prayer), or, Hamlet's
postponement of the killing   1 *lay home* thrust to the heart, reprove him soundly   2 *broad*
unrestrained   4 *Much heat* i.e., the King's anger.   *shroud* conceal (with ironic fitness to
Polonius' imminent death. The word is only in the First Quarto; the Second Quarto and the Folio
read "silence.")   5 *round* blunt   10 *thy father* i.e., your stepfather, Claudius   12 *idle* foolish
15 *forgot me* i.e., forgotten that I am your mother.   *rood* cross of Christ   18 *speak* i.e., to
someone so rude   25 *Dead for a ducat* i.e., I bet a ducat he's dead; or, a ducat is his life's fee

Queen: O me, what has thou done?
Hamlet: Nay, I know not. Is it the King?
Queen: O, what a rash and bloody deed is this!
Hamlet: A bloody deed—almost as bad, good Mother,
     As kill a king, and marry with his brother.   30
Queen: As kill a king!
Hamlet: Ay, lady, it was my word.

                  [*He parts the arras and discovers Polonius.*]
     Thou wretched, rash, intruding fool, farewell!
     I took thee for thy better. Take thy fortune.
     Thou find'st to be too busy* is some danger.—
     Leave wringing of your hands. Peace, sit you down,   35
     And let me wring your heart, for so I shall,
     If it be made of penetrable stuff,
     If damnèd custom* have not brazed* it so
     That it be proof* and bulwark against sense.*
Queen: What have I done, that thou dar'st wag thy tongue   40
     In noise so rude against me?
Hamlet: Such an act
     That blurs the grace and blush of modesty,
     Calls virtue hypocrite, takes off the rose
     From the fair forehead of an innocent love
     And sets a blister* there, makes marriage vows   45
     As false as dicers' oaths. O, such a deed
     As from the body of contraction* plucks
     The very soul, and sweet religion makes*
     A rhapsody* of words. Heaven's face does glow
     O'er this solidity and compound mass   50
     With tristful visage, as against the doom,
     Is thought-sick at the act.*
Queen: Ay me, what act,
     That roars so loud and thunders in the index?*
Hamlet [*showing her two likenesses*]: Look here upon this picture, and on
     this,
     The counterfeit presentment* of two brothers.   55
     See what a grace was seated on this brow:
     Hyperion's* curls, the front* of Jove himself,
     An eye like Mars* to threaten and command,
     A station* like the herald Mercury*
     New-lighted* on a heaven-kissing hill—   60
     A combination and a form indeed

---

34 *busy* nosey   38 *damnèd custom* habitual wickedness.   *brazed* brazened, hardened   39 *proof*
armor.   *sense* feeling   45 *sets a blister* i.e., brands as a harlot   47 *contraction* the marriage
contract   48 *sweet religion makes* i.e., makes marriage vows   49 *rhapsody* senseless string
49–52 *Heaven's. . . act* heaven's face blushes at this solid world compounded of the various
elements, with sorrowful face as though the day of doom were near, and is sick with horror at the
deed (i.e., Gertrude's marriage)   53 *index* table of contents, prelude or preface   55 *counterfeit
presentment* portrayed representation   57 *Hyperion's* the sun-god's.   *front* brow   58 *Mars* god
of war   59 *station* manner of standing.   *Mercury* winged messenger of the gods   60 *New-lighted*
newly alighted

Where every god did seem to set his seal*
To give the world assurance of a man.
This was your husband. Look you now what follows:
Here is your husband, like a mildewed ear,*   65
Blasting* his wholesome brother. Have you eyes?
Could you on this fair mountain leave* to feed
And batten* on this moor?* Ha, have you eyes?
You cannot call it love, for at your age
The heyday* in the blood* is tame, it's humble,   70
And waits upon the judgment, and what judgment
Would step from this to this? Sense,* sure, you have,
Else could you not have motion, but sure that sense
Is apoplexed,* for madness would not err,*
Nor sense to ecstasy was ne'er so thralled,   75
But* it reserved some quantity of choice
To serve in such a difference.* What devil was 't
That thus hath cozened* you at hoodman-blind?*
Eyes without feeling, feeling without sight,
Ears without hands or eyes, smelling sans* all,   80
Or but a sickly part of one true sense
Could not so mope.* O shame, where is thy blush?
Rebellious hell,
If thou canst mutine* in a matron's bones,
To flaming youth let virtue be as wax   85
And melt in her own fire.* Proclaim no shame
When the compulsive ardor gives the charge,
Since frost itself as actively doth burn,
And reason panders will.*
Queen: O Hamlet, speak no more!   90
Thou turn'st mine eyes into my very soul,
And there I see such black and grainèd* spots
As will not leave their tinct.*
Hamlet: Nay, but to live
In the rank sweat of an enseamèd* bed,
Stewed* in corruption, honeying and making love   95

62 *set his seal* i.e., affix his approval   65 *ear* i.e., of grain   66 *Blasting* blighting   67 *leave* cease
68 *batten* gorge.   *moor* barren or marshy ground (suggesting also "dark-skinned")   70 *heyday* state
of excitement.   *blood* passion   72 *Sense* perception through the five senses (the functions of the
middle or sensible soul)   74 *apoplexed* paralyzed. (Hamlet goes on to explain that, without such a
paralysis of will, mere madness would not so err, nor would the five senses so enthrall themselves to
ecstasy or lunacy; even such deranged states of mind would be able to make the obvious choice
between Hamlet Senior and Claudius.)   *err* so err   76 *But* but that   77 *To. . . difference* to help in
making a choice between two such men   78 *cozened* cheated.   *hoodman-blind* blindman's buff. (In
this game, says Hamlet, the devil must have pushed Claudius toward Gertrude while she was
blindfolded.)   80 *sans* without   82 *mope* be dazed, act aimlessly   84 *mutine* incite mutiny
85–86 *be as wax. . . fire* melt like a candle or stick of sealing wax held over the candle flame
86–89 *Proclaim. . . will* call it no shameful business when the compelling ardor of youth delivers the
attack, i.e., commits lechery, since the *frost* of advanced age burns with as active a fire of lust and
reason perverts itself by fomenting lust rather than restraining it   92 *grainèd* dyed in grain, indelible
93 *leave their tinct* surrender their color   94 *enseamèd* saturated in the grease and filth of passionate
lovemaking   95 *Stewed* soaked, bathed (with a suggestion of "stew," brothel)

Over the nasty sty!

Queen: O, speak to me no more!
These words like daggers enter in my ears.
No more, sweet Hamlet!

Hamlet: A murderer and a villain,
A slave that is not twentieth part the tithe*   100
Of your precedent lord,* a vice* of kings,
A cutpurse of the empire and the rule,
That from a shelf the precious diadem stole
And put it in his pocket!

Queen: No more!   105

Enter Ghost.

Hamlet: A king of shreds and patches*—
Save me, and hover o'er me with your wings,
You heavenly guards! What would your gracious figure?

Queen: Alas, he's mad!

Hamlet: Do you not come your tardy son to chide,   110
That, lapsed* in time and passion, lets go by
Th' important* acting of your dread command?
O, say!

Ghost: Do not forget. This visitation
Is but to whet thy almost blunted purpose.   115
But look, amazement* on thy mother sits.
O, step between her and her fighting soul!
Conceit* in weakest bodies strongest works.
Speak to her, Hamlet.

Hamlet: How is it with you, lady?

Queen: Alas, how is 't with you,   120
That you do bend your eye on vacancy,
And with th' incorporal* air do hold discourse?
Forth at your eyes your spirits wildly peep,
And, as the sleeping soldiers in th' alarm,*
Your bedded* hair, like life in excrements,*   125
Start up and stand on end. O gentle son,
Upon the heat and flame of thy distemper*
Sprinkle cool patience. Whereon do you look?

Hamlet: On him, on him! Look you how pale he glares!
His form and cause conjoined,* preaching to stones,   130
Would make them capable.*—Do not look upon me,
Lest with this piteous action you convert
My stern effects.* Then what I have to do

100 *tithe* tenth part   101 *precedent lord* former husband.   *vice* buffoon. (A reference to the Vice
of the morality plays.)   106 *shreds and patches* i.e., motley, the traditional costume of the clown
or fool   111 *lapsed* delaying   112 *important* importunate, urgent   116 *amazement* distraction
118 *Conceit* imagination   122 *incorporal* immaterial   124 *as. . . alarm* like soldiers called out of
sleep by an alarm   125 *bedded* laid flat.   *like life in excrements* i.e., as though hair, an outgrowth
of the body, had a life of its own. (Hair was thought to be lifeless because it lacks sensation, and so
its standing on end would be unnatural and ominous.)   127 *distemper* disorder
130 *His. . . conjoined* his appearance joined to his cause for speaking   131 *capable* receptive
132–133 *convert. . . effects* divert me from my stern duty

Will want true color—tears perchance for blood.*
Queen: To whom do you speak this?   135
Hamlet: Do you see nothing there?
Queen: Nothing at all, yet all that is I see.
Hamlet: Nor did you nothing hear?
Queen: No, nothing but ourselves.
Hamlet: Why, look you there, look how it steals away!   140
  My father, in his habit* as* he lived!
  Look where he goes even now out at the portal!

                                                            Exit Ghost.

Queen: This is the very* coinage of your brain.
  This bodiless creation ecstasy
  Is very cunning in.*   145
Hamlet: Ecstasy?
  My pulse as yours doth temperately keep time,
  And makes as healthful music. It is not madness
  That I have uttered. Bring me to the test,
  And I the matter will reword,* which madness   150
  Would gambol* from. Mother, for love of grace,
  Lay not that flattering unction* to your soul
  That not your trespass but my madness speaks.
  It will but skin* and film the ulcerous place,
  Whiles rank corruption, mining* all within,   155
  Infects unseen. Confess yourself to heaven,
  Repent what's past, avoid what is to come,
  And do not spread the compost* on the weeds
  To make them ranker. Forgive me this my virtue;*
  For in the fatness* of these pursy* times   160
  Virtue itself of vice must pardon beg,
  Yea, curb* and woo for leave* to do him good.
Queen: O Hamlet, thou hast cleft my heart in twain.
Hamlet: O, throw away the worser part of it,
  And live the purer with the other half.   165
  Good night. But go not to my uncle's bed;
  Assume a virtue, if you have it not.
  That monster, custom, who all sense doth eat,*
  Of habits devil,* is angel yet in this,
  That to the use of actions fair and good   170
  He likewise gives a frock or livery*
  That aptly* is put on. Refrain tonight,
  And that shall lend a kind of easiness

134 *want . . . blood* lack plausibility so that (with a play on the normal sense of *color*) I shall shed
colorless tears instead of blood   141 *habit* clothes.   *as* as when   143 *very* mere   144–145 *This . . . in*
madness is skillful in creating this kind of hallucination   150 *reword* repeat word for word
151 *gambol* skip away   152 *unction* ointment   154 *skin* grow a skin for   155 *mining* working
under the surface   158 *compost* manure   159 *this my virtue* my virtuous talk in reproving you
160 *fatness* grossness.   *pursy* flabby, out of shape   162 *curb* bow, bend the knee.   *leave*
permission   168 *who . . . eat* which consumes all proper or natural feeling, all sensibility
169 *Of habits devil* devil-like in prompting evil habits   171 *livery* an outer appearance, a
customary garb (and hence a predisposition easily assumed in time of stress)   172 *aptly* readily

To the next abstinence; the next more easy;
For use* almost can change the stamp of nature,*   175
And either*. . . the devil, or throw him out
With wondrous potency. Once more, good night;
And when you are desirous to be blest,
I'll blessing beg of you.* For this same lord,

[*pointing to Polonius*]

I do repent; but heaven hath pleased it so   180
To punish me with this, and this with me,
That I must be their scourge and minister.*
I will bestow* him, and will answer* well
The death I gave him. So, again, good night.
I must be cruel only to be kind.   185
This* bad begins, and worse remains behind.*
One word more, good lady.
Queen: What shall I do?
Hamlet: Not this by no means that I bid you do:
Let the bloat* king tempt you again to bed,
Pinch wanton* on your cheek, call you his mouse,   190
And let him, for a pair of reechy* kisses,
Or paddling* in your neck with his damned fingers,
Make you to ravel all this matter out*
That I essentially am not in madness,
But mad in craft.* 'Twere good* you let him know,   195
For who that's but a queen, fair, sober, wise,
Would from a paddock,* from a bat, a gib,*
Such dear concernings* hide? Who would do so?
No, in despite of sense and secrecy,*
Unpeg the basket* on the house's top,   200
Let the birds fly, and like the famous ape,*
To try conclusions,* in the basket creep
And break your own neck down.*
Queen: Be thou assured, if words be made of breath,
And breath of life, I have no life to breathe   205
What thou hast said to me.
Hamlet: I must to England. You know that?

---

175 *use* habit.   *the stamp of nature* our inborn traits   176 *And either* (A defective line, usually
emended by inserting the word *master* after *either*, following the Fourth Quarto and early editors.)
178–179 *when. . . you* i.e., when you are ready to be penitent and seek God's blessing, I will ask
your blessing as a dutiful son should   182 *their scourge and minister* i.e., agent of heavenly
retribution. (By *scourge*, Hamlet also suggests that he himself will eventually suffer punishment in
the process of fulfilling heaven's will.)   183 *bestow* stow, dispose of.   *answer* account or pay for
186 *This* i.e., the killing of Polonius.   *behind* to come   189 *bloat* bloated   190 *Pinch wanton* i.e.,
leave his love pinches on your cheeks, branding you as wanton   191 *reechy* dirty, filthy
192 *paddling* fingering amorously   193 *ravel. . . out* unravel, disclose   195 *in craft* by cunning.
good (Said sarcastically; also the following eight lines.)   197 *paddock* toad.   *gib* tomcat
198 *dear concernings* important affairs   199 *sense and secrecy* secrecy that common sense
requires   200 *Unpeg the basket* open the cage, i.e., let out the secret   201 *famous ape* (In a story
now lost.)   202 *try conclusions* test the outcome (in which the ape apparently enters a cage from
which birds have been released and then tries to fly out of the cage as they have done, falling to its
death)   203 *down* in the fall: utterly

Queen: Alack,
    I had forgot. 'Tis so concluded on.
Hamlet: There's letters sealed, and my two schoolfellows,
        Whom I will trust as I will adders fanged,   210
        They bear the mandate; they must sweep my way
        And marshal me to knavery.* Let it work.*
        For 'tis the sport to have the enginer*
        Hoist with* his own petard,* and 't shall go hard
        But I will* delve one yard below their mines*   215
        And blow them at the moon. O, 'tis most sweet
        When in one line* two crafts* directly meet.
        This man shall set me packing.*
        I'll lug the guts into the neighbor room.
        Mother, good night indeed. This counselor   220
        Is now most still, most secret, and most grave,
        Who was in life a foolish prating knave.—
        Come, sir, to draw toward an end* with you.—
        Good night, Mother.
                    Exeunt [separately, Hamlet dragging in Polonius].

Act IV

Scene I [The Castle.]

Enter King and Queen, with Rosencrantz and Guildenstern.*

King: There's matter* in these sighs, these profound heaves.*
        You must translate; 'tis fit we understand them.
        Where is your son?
Queen: Bestow this place on us a little while.
                        [Exeunt Rosencrantz and Guildenstern.]
        Ah, mine own lord, what have I seen tonight!   5
King: What, Gertrude? How does Hamlet?
Queen: Mad as the sea and wind when both contend
        Which is the mightier. In his lawless fit,
        Behind the arras hearing something stir,
        Whips out his rapier, cries, "A rat, a rat!"   10
        And in this brainish apprehension* kills
        The unseen good old man.

211–212 *sweep. . . knavery* sweep a path before me and conduct me to some *knavery* or treachery
prepared for me   212 *work* proceed   213 *enginer* maker of military contrivances   214 *Hoist
with* blown up by.   *petard* an explosive used to blow in a door or make a breach   214–215 *'t
shall. . . will* unless luck is against me, I will   215 *mines* tunnels used in warfare to undermine the
enemy's emplacements: Hamlet will countermine by going under their mines   217 *in one line* i.e.,
mines and countermines on a collision course, or the countermines directly below the mines.
crafts acts of guile, plots   218 *set me packing* set me to making schemes, and set me to lugging
(him), and, also, send me off in a hurry   223 *draw. . . end* finish up (with a pun on *draw*, "pull")
stage direction: Enter. . . Queen (Some editors argue that Gertrude never exits in Act III, Scene iv, and
that the scene is continuous here, as suggested in the Folio, but the Second Quarto marks an entrance
for her and at line 35 Claudius speaks of Gertrude's *closet* as though it were elsewhere. A short
time has elapsed, during which the King has become aware of her highly wrought emotional state.)
1 *matter* significance.   *heaves* heavy sighs   11 *brainish apprehension* headstrong conception

King: O heavy* deed!
It had been so with us,* had we been there.
His liberty is full of threats to all—
To you yourself, to us, to everyone.   15
Alas, how shall this bloody deed be answered?*
It will be laid to us, whose providence*
Should have kept short,* restrained, and out of haunt*
This mad young man. But so much was our love,
We would not understand what was most fit,   20
But, like the owner of a foul disease,
To keep it from divulging,* let it feed
Even on the pith of life. Where is he gone?
Queen: To draw apart the body he hath killed,
O'er whom his very madness, like some ore*   25
Among a mineral* of metals base,
Shows itself pure: 'a weeps for what is done.
King: O Gertrude, come away!
The sun no sooner shall the mountains touch
But we will ship him hence, and this vile deed   30
We must with all our majesty and skill
Both countenance* and excuse.—Ho, Guildenstern!

Enter Rosencrantz and Guildenstern.

Friends both, go join you with some further aid.
Hamlet in madness hath Polonius slain,
And from his mother's closet hath he dragged him.   35
Go seek him out, speak fair, and bring the body
Into the chapel. I pray you, haste in this.

            [*Exeunt Rosencrantz and Guildenstern.*]

Come, Gertrude, we'll call up our wisest friends
And let them know both what we mean to do
And what's untimely done. . . . . . .*   40
Whose whisper o'er the world's diameter,*
As level* as the cannon to his blank,*
Transports his poisoned shot, may miss our name
And hit the woundless* air. O, come away!
My soul is full of discord and dismay.   *Exeunt.*   45

Scene II [*The Castle.*]

        Enter Hamlet.
Hamlet: Safely stowed.
Rosencrantz, Guildenstern (within): Hamlet! Lord Hamlet!

12 *heavy* grievous   13 *us* i.e., me. (The royal "we"; also in line 15.)   16 *answered* explained
17 *providence* foresight   18 *short* i.e., on a short tether.   *out of haunt* ecluded   22 *divulging*
becoming evident   25 *ore* vein of gold   26 *mineral* mine   32 *countenance* put the best face on
40 *And. . . done* (A defective line: conjectures as to the missing words include *So, haply, slander*
[Capell and others]; *For, haply, slander* [Theobald and others]; and *So envious slander*
[Jenkins].)   41 *diameter* extent from side to side   42 *As level* with as direct aim.   *his blank* its
target at point-blank range   44 *woundless* invulnerable

Hamlet: But soft, what noise? Who calls on Hamlet? O, here they come.

    Enter Rosencrantz and Guildenstern.

Rosencrantz: What have you done, my lord, with the dead body?

Hamlet: Compounded it with dust, whereto 'tis kin.   5

Rosencrantz: Tell us where 'tis, that we may take it thence
    And bear it to the chapel.

Hamlet: Do not believe it.

Rosencrantz: Believe what?

Hamlet: That I can keep your counsel and not mine own.* Besides, to be   10
    demanded of* a sponge, what replication* should be made by the son
    of a king?

Rosencrantz: Take you me for a sponge, my lord?

Hamlet: Ay, sir, that soaks up the King's countenance,* his rewards, his
    authorities.* But such officers do the King best service in the end. He
    keeps them, like an ape, an apple, in the corner of his jaw, first mouthed   15
    to be last swallowed. When he needs what you have gleaned, it is but
    squeezing you, and, sponge, you shall be dry again.

Rosencrantz: I understand you not, my lord.

Hamlet: I am glad of it. A knavish speech sleeps in* a foolish ear.

Rosencrantz: My lord, you must tell us where the body is and go with us to   20
    the King.

Hamlet: The body is with the King, but the King is not with the body.* The
    King is a thing—

Guildenstern: A thing, my lord?

Hamlet: Of nothing.* Bring me to him. Hide fox, and all after!*   25

                                                Exeunt [running].

Scene III [The Castle.]

    Enter King, and two or three.

King: I have sent to seek him, and to find the body.
    How dangerous is it that this man goes loose!
    Yet must not we put the strong law on him.
    He's loved of* the distracted* multitude,
    Who like not in their judgment, but their eyes,*   5
    And where 'tis so, th' offender's scourge* is weighed,*
    But never the offense. To bear all smooth and even,*

---

10 *That . . . own* i.e., that I can follow your advice (by telling where the body is) and still keep my
own secret   10–11 *demanded of* questioned by   11 *replication* reply   13 *countenance* favor.
13–14 *authorities* delegated power, influence   19 *sleeps in* has no meaning to   22 *The . . . body*
(Perhaps alludes to the legal commonplace of "the king's two bodies," which drew a distinction
between the sacred office of kingship and the particular mortal who possessed it at any given time.
Hence, although Claudius' body is necessarily a part of him, true kingship is not contained in it.
Similarly, Claudius will have Polonius' body when it is found, but there is no kingship in this
business either.)   25 *Of nothing* (1) of no account (2) lacking the essence of kingship, as in line 22
and note.   *Hide . . . after* (An old signal cry in the game of hide-and-seek, suggesting that Hamlet
now runs away from them.)   4 *of* by. *distracted* fickle, unstable 5 *Who . . . eyes* who choose not
by judgment but by appearance 6 *scourge* punishment. (Literally, blow with a whip.) *weighed*
sympathetically considered 7 *To . . . even* to manage the business in an unprovocative way

This sudden sending him away must seem
Deliberate pause.* Diseases desperate grown
By desperate appliance* are relieved,   10
Or not at all.

Enter Rosencrantz, [Guildenstern,] and all the rest.

              How now, what hath befall'n?
Rosencrantz: Where the dead body is bestowed, my lord,
    We cannot get from him.
King: But where is he?
Rosencrantz: Without, my lord; guarded, to know your pleasure.
King: Bring him before us.
Rosencrantz: Ho! Bring in the lord.   15

    They enter [with Hamlet].

King: Now, Hamlet, where's Polonius?
Hamlet: At supper.
King: At supper? Where?
Hamlet: Not where he eats, but where 'a is eaten. A certain convocation of
    politic worms* are e'en* at him. Your worm* is your only emperor for diet.*   20
    We fat all creatures else to fat us, and we fat ourselves for maggots. Your fat
    king and your lean beggar is but variable service*—two dishes, but to one
    table. That's the end.
King: Alas, alas!
Hamlet: A man may fish with the worm that hath eat* of a king, and eat of   25
    the fish that hath fed of that worm.
King: What dost thou mean by this?
Hamlet: Nothing but to show you how a king may go a progress* through
    the guts of a beggar.
King: Where is Polonius?   30
Hamlet: In heaven. Send thither to see. If your messenger find him not
    there, seek him i' th' other place yourself. But if indeed you find him not
    within this month, you shall nose him as you go up the stairs into the
    lobby.
King [to some attendants]: Go seek him there.
Hamlet: 'A will stay till you come.   [*Exeunt attendants.*]   35
King: Hamlet, this deed, for thine especial safety—
    Which we do tender,* as we dearly* grieve
    For that which thou hast done—must send thee hence
    With fiery quickness. Therefore prepare thyself.
    The bark* is ready, and the wind at help,   40
    Th' associates tend,* and everything is bent*
    For England.
Hamlet: For England!

---

9 *Deliberate pause* carefully considered action   10 *appliance* remedies   20 *politic worms* crafty
worms (suited to a master spy like Polonius).   *e'en* even now.   *Your worm* your average worm
(Compare *your fat king* and *your lean beggar* in lines 21–22)   *diet* food, eating (with a punning
reference to the Diet of Worms, a famous *convocation* held in 1521)   22 *variable service* different
courses of a single meal   25 *eat* eaten. (Pronounced *et.*)   28 *progress* royal journey of state
37 *tender* regard, hold dear.   *dearly* intensely   40 *bark* sailing vessel   41 *tend* wait.   *bent* in
readiness

King: Ay, Hamlet.
Hamlet: Good.   45
King: So is it, if thou knew'st our purposes.
Hamlet: I see a cherub* that sees them. But come, for England! Farewell,
     dear mother.
King: Thy loving father, Hamlet.
Hamlet: My mother. Father and mother is man and wife, man and wife is   50
     one flesh, and so, my mother. Come, for England!   *Exit.*
King: Follow him at foot;* tempt him with speed aboard.
     Delay it not. I'll have him hence tonight.
     Away! For everything is sealed and done
     That else leans on* th' affair. Pray you, make haste.   55

                              [*Exeunt all but the King.*]

     And, England,* if my love thou hold'st at aught—*
     As my great power thereof may give thee sense,*
     Since yet thy cicatrice* looks raw and red
     After the Danish sword, and thy free awe*
     Pays homage to us—thou mayst not coldly set*   60
     Our sovereign process,* which imports at full,*
     By letters congruing* to that effect,
     The present* death of Hamlet. Do it, England,
     For like the hectic* in my blood he rages,
     And thou must cure me. Till I know 'tis done,   65
     Howe'er my haps,* my joys were ne'er begun.   *Exit.*

Scene IV [The Coast of Denmark.]

     Enter Fortinbras with his army over the stage.

Fortinbras: Go, Captain, from me greet the Danish king.
     Tell him that by his license* Fortinbras
     Craves the conveyance of* a promised march
     Over his kingdom. You know the rendezvous.
     If that His Majesty would aught with us,   5
     We shall express our duty* in his eye;*
     And let him know so.
Captain: I will do 't, my lord.
Fortinbras: Go softly* on. [*Exeunt all but the Captain.*]

     Enter Hamlet, Rosencrantz, [Guildenstern,] etc.

Hamlet: Good sir, whose powers* are these?   10
Captain: They are of Norway, sir.
Hamlet: How purposed, sir, I pray you?

---

47 *cherub* (Cherubim are angels of knowledge. Hamlet hints that both he and heaven are onto
Claudius' tricks.)   52 *at foot* close behind, at heel   55 *leans on* bears upon, is related to
56 *England* i.e., King of England.   *at aught* at any value   57 *As. . . sense* for so my great power
may give you a just appreciation of the importance of valuing my love   58 *cicatrice* scar
59 *free awe* voluntary show of respect   60 *coldly set* regard with indifference   61 *process* command.
imports at full conveys specific directions for   62 *congruing* agreeing   63 *present* immediate
64 *hectic* persistent fever   66 *haps* fortunes   2 *license* permission   3 *the conveyance of* escort during
6 *duty* respect.   *eye* presence   9 *softly* slowly, circumspectly   10 *powers* forces

Captain: Against some part of Poland.
Hamlet: Who commands them, sir?
Captain: The nephew to old Norway, Fortinbras.   15
Hamlet: Goes it against the main* of Poland, sir,
 Or for some frontier?
Captain: Truly to speak, and with no addition,*
 We go to gain a little patch of ground
 That hath in it no profit but the name.   20
 To pay* five ducats, five, I would not farm it;*
 Nor will it yield to Norway or the Pole
 A ranker* rate, should it be sold in fee.*
Hamlet: Why, then the Polack never will defend it.
Captain: Yes, it is already garrisoned.   25
Hamlet: Two thousand souls and twenty thousand ducats
 Will not debate the question of this straw.*
 This is th' impostume* of much wealth and peace,
 That inward breaks, and shows no cause without
 Why the man dies. I humbly thank you, sir.   30
Captain: God b' wi' you, sir.   [*Exit.*]
Rosencrantz: Will 't please you go, my lord?
Hamlet: I'll be with you straight. Go a little before.

           [*Exeunt all except Hamlet.*]

 How all occasions do inform against* me
 And spur my dull revenge! What is a man,
 If his chief good and market of* his time   35
 Be but to sleep and feed? A beast, no more.
 Sure he that made us with such large discourse,*
 Looking before and after,* gave us not
 That capability and godlike reason
 To fust* in us unused. Now, whether it be   40
 Bestial oblivion,* or some craven* scruple
 Of thinking too precisely* on th' event—*
 A thought which, quartered, hath but one part wisdom
 And ever three parts coward—I do not know
 Why yet I live to say "This thing's to do,"   45
 Sith* I have cause, and will, and strength, and means
 To do 't. Examples gross* as earth exhort me:
 Witness this army of such mass and charge,*
 Led by a delicate and tender* prince,
 Whose spirit with divine ambition puffed   50
 Makes mouths* at the invisible event,*
 Exposing what is mortal and unsure

16 *main* main part   18 *addition* exaggeration   21 *To pay* i.e., for a yearly rental of.   *farm it* take
a lease of it   23 *ranker* higher.   *in fee* fee simple, outright   27 *debate. . . straw* settle this trifling
matter   28 *impostume* abscess   33 *inform against* denounce, betray: take shape against
35 *market of* profit of, compensation for   37 *discourse* power of reasoning   38 *Looking before
and after* able to review past events and anticipate the future   40 *fust* grow moldy   41 *oblivion*
forgetfulness.   *craven* cowardly   42 *precisely* scrupulously.   *event* outcome   46 *Sith* since
47 *gross* obvious   48 *charge* expense   49 *delicate and tender* of fine and youthful qualities
51 *Makes mouths* makes scornful faces.   *invisible event* unforeseeable outcome

To all that fortune, death, and danger dare,*
Even for an eggshell. Rightly* to be great
Is not to stir without great argument,   55
But greatly to find quarrel in a straw
When honor's at the stake.* How stand I, then,
That have a father killed, a mother stained,
Excitements of* my reason and my blood,
And let all sleep, while to my shame I see   60
The imminent death of twenty thousand men
That for a fantasy* and trick* of fame
Go to their graves like beds, fight for a plot*
Whereon the numbers cannot try the cause,*
Which is not tomb enough and continent*   65
To hide the slain? O, from this time forth
My thoughts be bloody or be nothing worth!   *Exit.*

Scene V [The Castle.]

Enter Horatio, [Queen] Gertrude, and a Gentleman.

Queen: I will not speak with her.
Gentleman: She is importunate,
   Indeed distract.* Her mood will needs be pitied.
Queen: What would she have?
Gentleman: She speaks much of her father, says she hears
   There's tricks* i' the world, and hems,* and beats her heart,*   5
   Spurns enviously at straws,* speaks things in doubt*
   That carry but half sense. Her speech is nothing,
   Yet the unshapèd use* of it doth move
   The hearers to collection;* they yawn* at it,
   And botch* the words up fit to their own thoughts,   10
   Which,* as her winks and nods and gestures yield* them,
   Indeed would make one think there might be thought,*
   Though nothing sure, yet much unhappily.*
Horatio: 'Twere good she were spoken with, for she may strew
   Dangerous conjectures in ill-breeding* minds.   15
Queen: Let her come in.   [*Exit Gentleman.*]
   [*Aside.*] To my sick soul, as sin's true nature is,
   Each toy* seems prologue to some great amiss.*
   So full of artless jealousy is guilt,
   It spills itself in fearing to be spilt.*   20

---

53 *dare* could do (to him)   54–57 *Rightly. . . stake* true greatness does not normally consist of rushing
into action over some trivial provocation: however, when one's honor is involved, even a trifling insult
requires that one respond greatly (?)   *at the stake* (A metaphor from gambling or bear-baiting.)
59 *Excitements of* promptings by   62 *fantasy* fanciful caprice, illusion.   *trick* trifle, deceit   63 *plot*
plot of ground   64 *Whereon. . . cause* on which there is insufficient room for the soldiers needed to
engage in a military contest   65 *continent* receptacle, container   2 *distract* distracted   5 *tricks*
deceptions.   *hems* makes "hmm" sounds.   *heart* i.e., breast   6 *Spurns. . . straws* kicks spitefully,
takes offense at trifles.   *in doubt* obscurely   8 *unshapèd use* incoherent manner   9 *collection*
inference, a guess at some sort of meaning.   *yawn* gape, wonder; grasp. (The Folio reading, *aim*, is
possible.)   10 *botch* patch   11 *Which* which words.   *yield* deliver, represent   12 *thought* intended
13 *unhappily* unpleasantly near the truth, shrewdly   15 *ill-breeding* prone to suspect the worst and to
make mischief   18 *toy* trifle.   *amiss* calamity

Enter Ophelia [*distracted*].

Ophelia: Where is the beauteous majesty of Denmark?

Queen: How now, Ophelia?

Ophelia (she sings):

> *"How should I your true love know*
> *From another one?*   25
> *By his cockle hat* and staff,*
> *And his sandal shoon.*"*

Queen: Alas, sweet lady, what imports this song?

Ophelia:

> *Say you? Nay, pray you, mark.*
> *"He is dead and gone, lady,*   (*Song.*)
> *He is dead and gone;*   30
> *At his head a grass-green turf,*
> *At his heels a stone."*

O, ho!

Queen: Nay, but Ophelia—

Ophelia: Pray you, mark. [*Sings.*]   35

> *"White his shroud as the mountain snow"*—

Enter King.

Queen: Alas, look here, my lord.

Ophelia:

> *"Larded* with sweet flowers;*   (*Song.*)
> *Which bewept to the ground did not go*
> *With true-love showers.*"*   40

King: How do you, pretty lady?

Ophelia: Well, God 'ild* you! They say the owl* was a baker's daughter.
Lord, we know what we are, but know not what we may be. God be at
your table!

King: Conceit* upon her father.

Ophelia: Pray let's have no words of this; but when they ask you what it   45
means, say you this:

> *"Tomorrow is Saint Valentine's day,*   (*Song.*)
> *All in the morning betime,**
> *And I a maid at your window,*
> *To be your Valentine.*   50
> *Then up he rose, and donned his clothes,*
> *And dupped* the chamber door,*
> *Let in the maid, that out a maid*
> *Never departed more."*

King: Pretty Ophelia—   55

Ophelia: Indeed, la, without an oath, I'll make an end on 't:

> *"By Gis* and by Saint Charity,*

19–20 *So. . . split* guilt is so full of suspicion that it unskillfully betrays itself in fearing betrayal
20 *stage direction: Enter Ophelia* (In the First Quarto, Ophelia enters, "playing on a lute, and her
hair down, singing.")   25 *cockle hat* hat with cockleshell stuck in it as a sign that the wearer had
been a pilgrim to the shrine of Saint James of Compostella in Spain   26 *shoon* shoes   38 *Larded*
decorated   40 *showers* i.e., tears   42 *God 'ild* God yield or reward.   *owl* (Refers to a legend about
a baker's daughter who was turned into an owl for being ungenerous when Jesus begged a loaf of
bread.)   44 *Conceit* brooding   48 *betime* early   52 *dupped* did up, opened   57 *Gis* Jesus

> *Alack, and he for shame!*
> *Young men will do 't, if they come to 't;*
> *By Cock,* they are to blame.* 60
> *Quoth she, 'Before you tumbled me,*
> *You promised me to wed.'"*

He answers:

> *"'So would I ha' done, by yonder sun,*
> *An* thou hadst not come to my bed.'"* 65

King: How long hath she been thus?

Ophelia: I hope all will be well. We must be patient, but I cannot choose but weep to think they would lay him i' the cold ground. My brother shall know of it. And so I thank you for your good counsel. Come, my coach! Good night, ladies, good night, sweet ladies, good night, good night.   *[Exit.]* 70

King [to Horatio]: Follow her close. Give her good watch, I pray you.

                                                    [Exit Horatio.]

> O, this is the poison of deep grief; it springs
> All from her father's death—and now behold!
> O Gertrude, Gertrude,
> When sorrows come, they come not single spies,* 75
> But in battalions. First, her father slain;
> Next, your son gone, and he most violent author
> Of his own just remove;* the people muddied,*
> Thick and unwholesome in their thoughts and whispers
> For good Polonius' death—and we have done but greenly,* 80
> In hugger-mugger* to inter him; poor Ophelia
> Divided from herself and her fair judgment,
> Without the which we are pictures or mere beasts;
> Last, and as much containing* as all these,
> Her brother is in secret come from France, 85
> Feeds on this wonder, keeps himself in clouds*,
> And wants* not buzzers* to infect his ear
> With pestilent speeches of his father's death,
> Wherein necessity,* of matter beggared,*
> Will nothing stick our person to arraign 90
> In ear and ear.* O my dear Gertrude, this,
> Like to a murdering piece,* in many places
> Gives me superfluous death.*   *A noise within.*

Queen: Alack, what noise is this?

King: Attend!* 95

> Where is my Switzers?* Let them guard the door.

60 *Cock* (A perversion of "God" in oaths; here also with a quibble on the slang word for penis.)
65 *An* if   75 *spies* scouts sent in advance of the main force   78 *remove* removal.   *muddied* stirred up, confused   80 *greenly* in an inexperienced way, foolishly   81 *hugger-mugger* secret haste   84 *as much containing* as full of serious matter   86 *Feeds. . . clouds* feeds his resentment or shocked grievance, holds himself inscrutable and aloof amid all this rumor   87 *wants* lacks. *buzzers* gossipers, informers   89 *necessity* i.e., the need to invent some plausible explanation. *of matter beggared* unprovided with facts   90–91 *Will. . . ear* will not hesitate to accuse my (royal) person in everybody's ears   92 *murdering piece* cannon loaded so as to scatter its shot   93 *Gives. . . death* kills me over and over   95 *Attend* i.e., guard me   96 *Switzers* Swiss guards, mercenaries

Enter a Messenger.

What is the matter?

Messenger: Save yourself, my lord!
   The ocean, overpeering of his list,*
   Eats not the flats* with more impetuous* haste
   Than young Laertes, in a riotous head,*   100
   O'erbears your officers. The rabble call him lord,
   And, as* the world were now but to begin,
   Antiquity forgot, custom not known,
   The ratifiers and props of every word,*
   They cry, "Choose we! Laertes shall be king!"   105
   Caps,* hands, and tongues applaud it to the clouds,
   "Laertes shall be king, Laertes king!"

Queen: How cheerfully on the false trail they cry!   *A noise within.*
   O, this is counter,* you false Danish dogs!

Enter Laertes with others.

King: The doors are broke.   110
Laertes: Where is this King?—Sirs, stand you all without.
All: No, let's come in.
Laertes: I pray you, give me leave.
All: We will, we will.
Laertes: I thank you. Keep the door.   [*Exeunt followers.*]
                              O thou vile king, Give me my father!   115
Queen [*restraining him*]: Calmly, good Laertes.
Laertes: That drop of blood that's calm proclaims me bastard,
   Cries cuckold to my father, brands the harlot
   Even here, between* the chaste unsmirchèd brow
   Of my true mother.
King: What is the cause, Laertes,   120
   That thy rebellion looks so giantlike?
   Let him go, Gertrude. Do not fear our* person.
   There's such divinity doth hedge* a king
   That treason can but peep to what it would,*
   Acts little of his will.* Tell me, Laertes,   125
   Why thou art thus incensed. Let him go, Gertrude.
   Speak, man.
Laertes: Where is my father?
King: Dead.
Queen: But not by him.
King: Let him demand his fill.
Laertes: How came he dead? I'll not be juggled with.*

98 *overpeering of his list* overflowing its shore, boundary   99 *flats* i.e., flatlands near shore.
impetuous violent (perhaps also with the meaning of impiteous [*impitious, Second Quarto*],
"pitiless")   100 *head* insurrection   102 *as* as if   104 *The ratifiers. . . word* i.e., *antiquity* (or
tradition) and *custom* ought to confirm (*ratify*) and underprop our every word or promise
106 *Caps* (The caps are thrown in the air.)   109 *counter* (A hunting term, meaning to follow the
trail in a direction opposite to that which the game has taken.)   119 *between* in the middle of
122 *fear our* fear for my   123 *hedge* protect, as with a surrounding barrier   124 *can. . . would*
can only peep furtively, as through a barrier at what it would intend   125 *Acts. . . will* (but)
performs little of what it intends   129 *juggled with* cheated, deceived

> To hell, allegiance! Vows, to the blackest devil!   130
> Conscience and grace, to the profoundest pit!
> I dare damnation. To this point I stand,*
> That both the worlds I give to negligence,*
> Let come what comes, only I'll be revenged
> Most throughly* for my father.   135

King: Who shall stay you?

Laertes: My will, not all the world's.*
> And for* my means, I'll husband them so well
> They shall go far with little.

King: Good Laertes,
> If you desire to know the certainty   140
> Of your dear father, is 't writ in your revenge
> That, swoopstake,* you will draw both friend and foe,
> Winner and loser?

Laertes: None but his enemies.

King: Will you know them, then?   145

Laertes: To his good friends thus wide I'll ope my arms,
> And like the kind life-rendering pelican*
> Repast* them with my blood.

King: Why, now you speak
> Like a good child and a true gentleman.
> That I am guiltless of your father's death,   150
> And am most sensibly* in grief for it,
> It shall as level* to your judgment 'pear
> As day does to your eye.   *A noise within.*

Laertes: How now, what noise is that?

> *Enter Ophelia.*

King: Let her come in.

Laertes: O heat, dry up my brains! Tears seven times salt   155
> Burn out the sense and virtue* of mine eye!
> By heaven, thy madness shall be paid with weight*
> Till our scale turn the beam.* O rose of May!
> Dear maid, kind sister, sweet Ophelia!
> O heavens, is 't possible a young maid's wits   160
> Should be as mortal as an old man's life?
> Nature is fine in* love, and where 'tis fine
> It sends some precious instance* of itself
> After the thing it loves.*

Ophelia:

> "They bore him barefaced on the bier,   (Song.)   165
> Hey non nonny, nonny, hey nonny,
> And in his grave rained many a tear—"

132 *To. . . stand* I am resolved in this   133 *both. . . negligence* i.e., both this world and the next are of no consequence to me   135 *throughly* thoroughly   137 *My will. . . world's* I'll stop (*stay*) when my will is accomplished, not for anyone else's.   138 *for* as for   142 *swoopstake* i.e., indiscriminately. (Literally taking all stakes on the gambling table at once. *Draw* is also a gambling term meaning "take from.")   147 *pelican* (Refers to the belief that the female pelican fed its young with its own blood.) 148 *Repast* feed   151 *sensibly* feelingly   152 *level* plain   156 *virtue* faculty, power   157 *paid with weight* repaid, avenged equally or more   158 *beam* crossbar of a balance   162 *fine in* refined by 163 *instance* token   164 *After. . . loves* i.e., into the grave, along with Polonius

Fare you well, my dove!

Laertes: Hadst thou thy wits and didst persuade* revenge,
It could not move thus.   170

Ophelia: You must sing "A-down a-down," and you "call him a-down-a.*" O,
how the wheel* becomes it! It is the false steward* that stole his master's daughter.

Laertes: This nothing's more than matter.*

Ophelia: There's rosemary,* that's for remembrance; pray you, love, remember. And there is pansies;* that's for thoughts.   175

Laertes: A document* in madness, thoughts and remembrance fitted.

Ophelia: There's fennel* for you, and columbines.* There's rue* for you, and
here's some for me; we may call it herb of grace o' Sundays. You must
wear your rue with a difference.* There's a daisy.* I would give you
some violets,* but they withered all when my father died. They say 'a
made a good end—   180

[*Sings.*]

        "For bonny sweet Robin is all my joy."

Laertes: Thought* and affliction, passion,* hell itself,
She turns to favor* and to prettiness.

Ophelia:

        "And will 'a not come again?   (*Song.*)
        And will 'a not come again?   185
        No, no, he is dead.
        Go to thy deathbed,
        He never will come again.
        "His beard was as white as snow,
        All flaxen was his poll.*   190
        He is gone, he is gone,
        And we cast away moan.
        God ha' mercy on his soul!"

And of all Christian souls, I pray God. God b' wi' you.

                    [*Exit, followed by Gertrude.*]

Laertes: Do you see this, O God?   195

King: Laertes, I must commune with your grief,
Or you deny me right. Go but apart,
Make choice of whom* your wisest friends you will,
And they shall hear and judge twixt you and me.
If by direct or by collateral hand*   200

---

169 *persuade* argue cogently for   171 *You. . . a-down a* (Ophelia assigns the singing of refrains,
like her own "Hey non nonny," to others present.)   172 *wheel* spinning wheel as accompaniment
to the song, or refrain.   *false steward* (The story is unknown.)   173 *This. . . matter* this seeming
nonsense is more eloquent than sane utterance   174 *rosemary* (Used as a symbol of remembrance
both at weddings and at funerals.)   175 *pansies* (Emblems of love and courtship; perhaps from
French *pensées,* "thoughts.")   176 *document* instruction, lesson   177 *fennel* (Emblem of flattery.)
columbines (Emblems of unchastity or ingratitude.)   *rue* (Emblem of repentance—a signification
that is evident in its popular name, *herb of grace.*)   179 *with a difference* (A device used in
heraldry to distinguish one family from another on the coat of arms, here suggesting that Ophelia
and the others have different causes of sorrow and repentance; perhaps with a play on *rue* in the
sense of "ruth," "pity.")   *daisy* (Emblem of dissembling, faithlessness.)   *violets* (Emblems of
faithfulness.)   182 *Thought* melancholy.   *passion* suffering   183 *favor* grace, beauty
190 *poll* head   198 *whom* whichever of   200 *collateral hand* indirect agency

They find us touched,* we will our kingdom give,
Our crown, our life, and all that we call ours
To you in satisfaction; but if not,
Be you content to lend your patience to us,
And we shall jointly labor with your soul   205
To give it due content.

Laertes: Let this be so.
His means of death, his obscure funeral—
No trophy,* sword, nor hatchment* o'er his bones,
No noble rite, nor formal ostentation*—
Cry to be heard, as 'twere from heaven to earth,   210
That* I must call 't in question.*

King: So you shall,
And where th' offense is, let the great ax fall.
I pray you, go with me.   *Exeunt.*

Scene VI [The Castle.]

Enter Horatio and others.

Horatio: What are they that would speak with me?
Gentleman: Seafaring men, sir. They say they have letters for you.
Horatio: Let them come in.   [*Exit Gentleman.*]
     I do not know from what part of the world
     I should be greeted, if not from Lord Hamlet.   5

Enter Sailors.

First Sailor: God bless you, sir.
Horatio: Let him bless thee too.
First Sailor: 'A shall, sir, an 't* please him. There's a letter for you, sir—it
     came from th' ambassador* that was bound for England—if your name
     be Horatio, as I am let to know it is.   [*He gives a letter.*] 10
Horatio [*reads*]: "Horatio, when thou shalt have overlooked* this, give
     these fellows some means* to the King; they have letters for him. Ere
     we were two days old at sea, a pirate of very warlike appointment*
     gave us chase. Finding ourselves too slow of sail, we put on a com-
     pelled valor, and in the grapple I boarded them. On the instant they got 15
     clear of our ship, so I alone became their prisoner. They have dealt
     with me like thieves of mercy,* but they knew what they did: I am to
     do a good turn for them. Let the King have the letters I have sent, and
     repair* thou to me with as much speed as thou wouldest fly death. I
     have words to speak in thine ear will make thee dumb, yet are they
     much too light for the bore* of the matter. These good fellows will   20
     bring thee where I am. Rosencrantz and Guildenstern hold their
     course for England. Of them I have much to tell thee. Farewell.
                         He that thou knowest thine, Hamlet."

---

201 *us touched* be implicated   208 *trophy* memorial.   *hatchment* tablet displaying the armorial
bearings of a deceased person   209 *ostentation* ceremony   211 *That* so that.   *call 't in question*
demand an explanation   8 *an 't* if it   9 *th' ambassador* (Evidently Hamlet. The sailor is being
circumspect.)   11 *overlooked* looked over   12 *means* means of access   13 *appointment* equipage
16 *thieves of mercy* merciful thieves   18 *repair* come   20 *bore* caliber, i.e., importance

Come, I will give you way* for these your letters,
And do 't the speedier that you may direct me   25
To him from whom you brought them.   *Exeunt.*

Scene VII [*The Castle.*]

Enter King and Laertes.

King: Now must your conscience my acquittance seal,*
     And you must put me in your heart for friend,
     Sith* you have heard, and with a knowing ear,
     That he which hath your noble father slain
     Pursued my life.
Laertes: It well appears. But tell me   5
     Why you proceeded not against these feats*
     So crimeful and so capital* in nature,
     As by your safety, greatness, wisdom, all things else,
     You mainly* were stirred up.
King: O, for two special reasons,   10
     Which may to you perhaps seem much unsinewed,*
     But yet to me they're strong. The Queen his mother
     Lives almost by his looks, and for myself—
     My virtue or my plague, be it either which—
     She is so conjunctive* to my life and soul   15
     That, as the star moves not but in his* sphere,*
     I could not but by her. The other motive
     Why to a public count* I might not go
     Is the great love the general gender* bear him,
     Who, dipping all his faults in their affection,   20
     Work* like the spring* that turneth wood to stone,
     Convert his gyves* to graces, so that my arrows,
     Too slightly timbered* for so loud* a wind,
     Would have reverted* to my bow again
     But not where I had aimed them.   25
Laertes: And so have I a noble father lost,
     A sister driven into desperate terms,*
     Whose worth, if praises may go back* again,
     Stood challenger on mount* of all the age
     For her perfections. But my revenge will come.   30
King: Break not your sleeps for that. You must not think
     That we are made of stuff so flat and dull
     That we can let our beard be shook with danger

---

24 *way* means of access   1 *my acquittance seal* confirm or acknowledge my innocence
3 *Sith* since   6 *feats* acts   7 *capital* punishable by death   9 *mainly* greatly   11 *unsinewed* weak
15 *conjunctive* closely united. (An astronomical metaphor.)   16 *his* its.   *sphere* one of the hollow
spheres in which, according to Ptolemaic astronomy, the planets were supposed to move
18 *count* account, reckoning, indictment   19 *general gender* common people   21 *Work* operate,
act.   *spring* i.e., a spring with such a concentration of lime that it coats a piece of wood with
limestone, in effect gilding and petrifying it   22 *gyves* fetters (which, gilded by the people's praise,
would look like badges of honor)   23 *slightly timbered* light.   *loud* (suggesting public outcry on
Hamlet's behalf)   24 *reverted* returned   27 *terms* state, condition   28 *go back* i.e., recall what
she was   29 *on mount* set up on high

And think it pastime. You shortly shall hear more.
I loved your father, and we love ourself;   35
And that, I hope, will teach you to imagine—

Enter a Messenger with letters.

How now? What news?

Messenger: Letters, my lord, from Hamlet:
This to Your Majesty, this to the Queen.

                                                   [*He gives letters.*]

King: From Hamlet? Who brought them?
Messenger: Sailors, my lord, they say. I saw them not.   40
They were given me by Claudio. He received them
Of him that brought them.
King: Laertes, you shall hear them.—
Leave us.   [*Exit Messenger.*]
[*He reads.*] "High and mighty, you shall know I am set naked* on your
kingdom. Tomorrow shall I beg leave to see your kingly eyes, when I   45
shall, first asking your pardon,* thereunto recount the occasion of my
sudden and more strange return.   Hamlet."
What should this mean? Are all the rest come back? Or is it some
abuse,* and no such thing?*
Laertes: Know you the hand?
King: 'Tis Hamlet's character.* "Naked!"   50
And in a postscript here he says "alone."
Can you devise* me?
Laertes: I am lost in it, my lord. But let him come.
It warms the very sickness in my heart
That I shall live and tell him to his teeth,   55
"Thus didst thou.*"
King: If it be so, Laertes—
As how should it be so? How otherwise?*—
Will you be ruled by me?
Laertes: Ay, my lord,
So* you will not o'errule me to a peace.
King: To thine own peace. If he be now returned,   60
As checking at* his voyage, and that* he means
No more to undertake it, I will work him
To an exploit, now ripe in my device,*
Under the which he shall not choose but fall;
And for his death no wind of blame shall breathe,   65
But even his mother shall uncharge the practice*
And call it accident.
Laertes: My lord, I will be ruled,

44 *naked* destitute, unarmed, without following   46 *pardon* permission   49 *abuse* deceit.
no such thing not what it appears   50 *character* handwriting   52 *devise* explain to   56 *Thus
didst thou* i.e., here's for what you did to my father   57 *As . . . otherwise* how can this (Hamlet's
return) be true? Yet how otherwise than true (since we have the evidence of his letter)?
59 *So* provided that   61 *checking at* i.e., turning aside from (like a falcon leaving the quarry to fly
at a chance bird).   *that* if   63 *device* devising, invention   66 *uncharge the practice* acquit the
stratagem of being a plot

The rather if you could devise it so
That I might be the organ.*
King: It falls right.
You have been talked of since your travel much,   70
And that in Hamlet's hearing, for a quality
Wherein they say you shine. Your sum of parts*
Did not together pluck such envy from him
As did that one, and that, in my regard,
Of the unworthiest siege.*   75
Laertes: What part is that, my lord?
King: A very ribbon in the cap of youth,
Yet needful too, for youth no less becomes*
The light and careless livery that it wears
Than settled age his sables* and his weeds*   80
Importing health and graveness.* Two months since
Here was a gentleman of Normandy.
I have seen myself, and served against, the French,
And they can well* on horseback, but this gallant
Had witchcraft in 't; he grew unto his seat,   85
And to such wondrous doing brought his horse
As had he been incorpsed and demi-natured*
With the brave beast. So far he topped* my thought
That I in forgery* of shapes and tricks
Come short of what he did.
Laertes: A Norman was 't?   90
King: A Norman.
Laertes: Upon my life, Lamord.
King: The very same.
Laertes: I know him well. He is the brooch* indeed
And gem of all the nation.
King: He made confession* of you.   95
And gave you such a masterly report
For art and exercise in your defense,*
And for your rapier most especial,
That he cried out 'twould be a sight indeed
If one could match you. Th' escrimers* of their nation,   100
He swore, had neither motion, guard, nor eye
If you opposed them. Sir, this report of his
Did Hamlet so envenom with his envy
That he could nothing do but wish and beg
Your sudden* coming o'er, to play* with you.   105
Now, out of this—
Laertes: What out of this, my lord?

69 *organ* agent, instrument   72 *Your. . . parts* i.e., all your other virtues   75 *unworthiest siege*
least important rank   78 *no less becomes* is no less suited by   80 *his sables* its rich robes furred
with sable.   *weeds* garments   81 *Importing. . . graveness* signifying a concern for health and
dignified prosperity; also, giving an impression of comfortable prosperity   84 *can well* are skilled
87 *As. . . demi-natured* as if he had been of one body and nearly of one nature (like the centaur)
88 *topped* surpassed   89 *forgery* imagining   93 *brooch* ornament   95 *confession* testimonial,
admission of superiority   97 *For. . . defense* with respect to your skill and practice with your
weapon   100 *escrimers* fencers   105 *sudden* immediate.   *play* fence

King: Laertes, was your father dear to you?
    Or are you like the painting of a sorrow,
    A face without a heart?
Laertes: Why ask you this?
King: Not that I think you did not love your father,   110
    But that I know love is begun by time,*
    And that I see, in passages of proof,*
    Time qualifies* the spark and fire of it.
    There lives within the very flame of love
    A kind of wick or snuff* that will abate it,   115
    And nothing* is at a like goodness still,
    For goodness, growing to a pleurisy,*
    Dies in his own too much.* That* we would do,
    We should do when we would; for this "would" changes
    And hath abatements* and delays as many   120
    As there are tongues, are hands, are accidents,*
    And then this "should" is like a spendthrift sigh,*
    That hurts by easing.* But, to the quick o' th' ulcer:*
    Hamlet comes back. What would you undertake
    To show yourself in deed your father's son   125
    More than in words?
Laertes: To cut his throat i' the church.
King: No place, indeed, should murder sanctuarize;*
    Revenge should have no bounds. But good Laertes,
    Will you do this,* keep close within your chamber.
    Hamlet returned shall know you are come home.   130
    We'll put on those shall* praise your excellence
    And set a double varnish on the fame
    The Frenchman gave you, bring you in fine* together,
    And wager on your heads. He, being remiss,*
    Most generous,* and free from all contriving,   135
    Will not peruse the foils, so that with ease,
    Or with a little shuffling, you may choose
    A sword unbated,* and in a pass of practice*
    Requite him for your father.
Laertes: I will do 't,
    And for that purpose I'll anoint my sword.   140
    I bought an unction* of a mountebank*

---

111 *begun by time* i.e., created by the right circumstance and hence subject to change
112 *passages of proof* actual instances that prove it   113 *qualifies* weakens, moderates   115 *snuff* the
charred part of a candlewick   116 *nothing. . . still* nothing remains at a constant level of perfection
117 *pleurisy* excess, plethora. (Literally, a chest inflammation.)   118 *in. . . much* of its own excess.
That that which   120 *abatements* diminutions   121 *As. . . accidents* as there are tongues to dissuade,
hands to prevent, and chance events to intervene   122 *spendthrift sigh* (An allusion to the belief that
sighs draw blood from the heart.)   123 *hurts by easing* i.e., costs the heart blood and wastes precious
opportunity even while it affords emotional relief   *quick o' th' ulcer* i.e., heart of the matter
127 *sanctuarize* protect from punishment. (Alludes to the right of sanctuary with which certain
religious places were invested.)   129 *Will you do this* if you wish to do this   131 *put on those shall*
arrange for some to   133 *in fine* finally   134 *remiss* negligently unsuspicious   135 *generous* noble-
minded   138 *unbated* not blunted, having no button.   *pass of practice* treacherous thrust
141 *unction* ointment.   *mountebank* quack doctor

So mortal that, but dip a knife in it,
Where it draws blood no cataplasm* so rare,
Collected from all simples* that have virtue*
Under the moon,* can save the thing from death   145
That is but scratched withal. I'll touch my point
With this contagion, that if I gall* him slightly,
It may be death.

King: Let's further think of this,
Weigh what convenience both of time and means
May fit us to our shape.* If this should fail,   150
And that our drift look through our bad performance,*
'Twere better not assayed. Therefore this project
Should have a back or second, that might hold
If this did blast in proof.* Soft, let me see.
We'll make a solemn wager on your cunnings*—   155
I ha 't!
When in your motion you are hot and dry—
As* make your bouts more violent to that end—
And that he calls for drink, I'll have prepared him
A chalice for the nonce,* whereon but sipping,   160
If he by chance escape your venomed stuck,*
Our purpose may hold there. [*A cry within.*] But stay, what noise?

Enter Queen.

Queen: One woe doth tread upon another's heel,
So fast they follow. Your sister's drowned, Laertes.
Laertes: Drowned! O, where?   165
Queen: There is a willow grows askant* the brook,
That shows his hoar leaves* in the glassy stream;
Therewith fantastic garlands did she make
Of crowflowers, nettles, daisies, and long purples,*
That liberal* shepherds give a grosser name,*   170
But our cold* maids do dead men's fingers call them.
There on the pendent* boughs her crownet* weeds
Clamb'ring to hang, an envious sliver* broke,
When down her weedy* trophies and herself
Fell in the weeping brook. Her clothes spread wide,   175
And mermaidlike awhile they bore her up,
Which time she chanted snatches of old lauds,*
As one incapable of* her own distress,

143 *cataplasm* plaster or poultice   144 *simples* herbs.   *virtue* potency   145 *Under the moon* i.e.,
anywhere (with reference perhaps to the belief that herbs gathered at night had a special power)
147 *gall* graze, wound   150 *shape* part we propose to act   151 *drift . . . performance* intention
should be made visible by our bungling   154 *blast in proof* burst in the test (like a cannon)
155 *cunnings* respective skills   158 *As* i.e., and you should   160 *nonce* occasion   161 *stuck*
thrust. (From *stoccado*; a fencing term.)   166 *askant* aslant   167 *hoar leaves* white or gray
undersides of the leaves   169 *long purples* early purple orchids   170 *liberal* free-spoken.
a grosser name (The testicle-resembling tubers of the orchid, which also in some cases resemble *dead
men's fingers*, have earned various slang names like "dogstones" and "cullions.")   171 *cold* chaste
172 *pendent* overhanging.   *crownet* made into a chaplet or coronet   173 *envious sliver* malicious
branch   174 *weedy* i.e., of plants   177 *lauds* hymns   178 *incapable of* lacking capacity to
apprehend

Or like a creature native and endued*
Unto that element. But long it could not be   180
Till that her garments, heavy with their drink,
Pulled the poor wretch from her melodious lay
To muddy death.

Laertes: Alas, then she is drowned?

Queen: Drowned, drowned.

Laertes: Too much of water hast thou, poor Ophelia,   185
And therefore I forbid my tears. But yet
It is our trick;* nature her custom holds.
Let shame say what it will. [*He weeps.*] When these are gone,
The woman will be out.* Adieu, my lord.
I have a speech of fire that fain would blaze,   190
But that this folly douts* it.   *Exit.*

King: Let's follow, Gertrude.
How much I had to do to calm his rage!
Now fear I this will give it start again;
Therefore let's follow.   *Exeunt.*

Act V

Scene I [*A Churchyard.*]

Enter two Clowns [*with spades and mattocks*].*

First Clown: Is she to be buried in Christian burial, when she willfully seeks
her own salvation?*

Second Clown: I tell thee she is; therefore make her grave straight.* The
crowner* hath sat on her,* and finds it* Christian burial.

First Clown: How can that be, unless she drowned herself in her own
defense?   5

Second Clown: Why, 'tis found so.*

First Clown: It must be *se offendendo,** it cannot be else. For here lies the
point: if I drown myself wittingly, it argues an act, and an act hath three
branches—it is to act, to do, and to perform. Argal,* she drowned herself wittingly.   10

Second Clown: Nay, but hear you, goodman* delver—

First Clown: Give me leave. Here lies the water; good. Here stands the man;
good. If the man go to this water and drown himself, it is, will he, nill he,*
he goes, mark you that. But if the water come to him and drown him,
he drowns not himself. Argal, he that is not guilty of his own death   15
shortens not his own life.

---

179 *endued* adapted by nature   187 *It is our trick* i.e., weeping is our natural way (when sad)
188–189 *When. . . out* when my tears are all shed, the woman in me will be expended, satisfied
191 *douts* extinguishes. (The Second Quarto reads "drowns.")   *stage direction: Clowns* rustics
2 *salvation* (A blunder for "damnation," or perhaps a suggestion that Ophelia was taking her own
shortcut to heaven.)   3 *straight* straightway, immediately. (But with a pun on *strait*, "narrow.")
4 *crowner* coroner.   *sat on her* conducted an inquest on her case.   *finds it* gives his official
verdict that her means of death was consistent with   6 *found so* determined so in the coroner's
verdict   7 *se offendendo* (A comic mistake for *se defendendo*, a term used in verdicts of justifiable
homicide.)   9 *Argal* (Corruption of *ergo*, "therefore.")   11 *goodman* (An honorific title often
used with the name of a profession or craft.)   13 *will he, nill he* whether he will or no, willy-nilly

Second Clown: But is this law?

First Clown: Ay, marry, is 't—crowner's quest law.

Second Clown: Will you ha' the truth on 't? If this had not been a gentle-
woman, she should have been buried out o' Christian burial.   20

First Clown: Why, there thou sayst.* And the more pity that great folk should
have countenance* in this world to drown or hang themselves, more than
their even-Christian.* Come, my spade. There is no ancient* gentlemen but
gardeners, ditchers, and grave makers. They hold up* Adam's profession.

Second Clown: Was he a gentleman?   25

First Clown: 'A was the first that ever bore arms.*

Second Clown: Why, he had none.

First Clown: What, art a heathen? How dost thou understand the Scripture?
The Scripture says Adam digged. Could he dig without arms?* I'll put
another question to thee. If thou answerest me not to the purpose, con-   30
fess thyself*—

Second Clown: Go to.

First Clown: What is he that builds stronger than either the mason, the shipwright, or the carpenter?

Second Clown: The gallows maker, for that frame* outlives a thousand tenants.   35

First Clown: I like thy wit well, in good faith. The gallows does well.* But
how does it well? It does well to those that do ill. Now thou dost ill to
say the gallows is built stronger than the church. Argal, the gallows may
do well to thee. To 't again, come.

Second Clown: "Who builds stronger than a mason, a shipwright, or a   40
carpenter?"

First Clown: Ay, tell me that, and unyoke.*

Second Clown: Marry, now I can tell.

First Clown: To 't.

Second Clown: Mass,* I cannot tell.   45

Enter Hamlet and Horatio [at a distance].

First Clown: Cudgel thy brains no more about it, for your dull ass will not
mend his pace with beating; and when you are asked this question
next, say "a grave maker." The houses he makes lasts till doomsday. Go
get thee in and fetch me a stoup* of liquor.

> [*Exit Second Clown. First Clown digs.*]
>
> *Song.*

> "In youth, when I did love, did love,*   50
> Methought it was very sweet,

---

21 *there thou sayst,* i.e., that's right   22 *countenance* privilege   23 *even-Christian* fellow
Christians.   *ancient* going back to ancient times   24 *hold up* maintain   26 *bore arms* (To be
entitled to bear a coat of arms would make Adam a gentleman, but as one who bore a spade, our
common ancestor was an ordinary delver in the earth.)   29 *arms* i.e., the arms of the body
30–31 *confess thyself* (The saying continues, "and be hanged.")   35 *frame* (1) gallows (2) structure
36 *does well* (1) is an apt answer (2) does a good turn   42 *unyoke* i.e., after this great effort, you
may unharness the team of your wits   45 *Mass* by the Mass   49 *stoup* two-quart measure
50 *In. . . love* (This and the two following stanzas, with nonsensical variations, are from a poem
attributed to Lord Vaux and printed in *Tottel's Miscellany,* 1557. The *O* and *a* [*for* "ah"] seemingly
are the grunts of the digger.)

> *To contract—O—the time for—a—my behove,**
> *O, methought there—a—was nothing—a—meet.**

Hamlet: Has this fellow no feeling of his business, 'a* sings in grave-making?

Horatio: Custom hath made it in him a property of easiness.*   55

Hamlet: 'Tis e'en so. The hand of little employment hath the daintier sense.*

First Clown: *Song.*

> *"But age with his stealing steps*
> *Hath clawed me in his clutch,*
> *And hath shipped me into the land,**
> *As if I had never been such."*   60

[He throws up a skull.]

Hamlet: That skull had a tongue in it and could sing once. How the knave
   jowls* it to the ground, as if 'twere Cain's jawbone, that did the first
   murder! This might be the pate of a politician,* which this ass now
   o'erreaches,* one that would circumvent God, might it not?

Horatio: It might, my lord.   65

Hamlet: Or of a courtier, which could say, "Good morrow, sweet lord! How
   dost thou, sweet lord?" This might be my Lord Such-a-one, that praised
   my Lord Such-a-one's horse when 'a meant to beg it, might it not?

Horatio: Ay, my lord.

Hamlet: Why, e'en so, and now my Lady Worm's, chapless,* and knocked   70
   about the mazard* with a sexton's spade. Here's fine revolution,* an*
   we had the trick to see* 't. Did these bones cost no more the breeding
   but* to play at loggets* with them? Mine ache to think on 't.

First Clown: *Song.*

> *"A pickax and a spade, a spade,*
> *For and* a shrouding sheet;*   75
> *O, a pit of clay for to be made*
> *For such a guest is meet."*

[He throws up another skull.]

Hamlet: There's another. Why may not that be the skull of a lawyer? Where be
   his quiddities* now, his quillities,* his cases, his tenures,* and his tricks?
   Why does he suffer this mad knave now to knock him about the sconce*   80
   with a dirty shovel, and will not tell him of his action of battery?* Hum,
   this fellow might be in 's time a great buyer of land, with his statutes, his

---

52 *To contract. . . behove* i.e., to shorten the time for my own advantage. (Perhaps he means to
prolong it.)   53 *meet* suitable, i.e., more suitable   54 *'a* that he   55 *property of easiness*
something he can do easily and indifferently   56 *daintier sense* more delicate sense of feeling
59 *into the land* i.e., toward my grave (?) (But note the lack of rhyme in *steps, land.*)
62 *jowls* dashes (with a pun on *jowl*, "jawbone")   63 *politician* schemer, plotter.
o'erreaches circumvents, gets the better of (with a quibble on the literal sense)
70 *chapless* having no lower jaw.   71 *mazard* i.e., head. (Literally, a drinking vessel.)
revolution turn of Fortune's wheel, change.   *an* if   72 *trick to see* knack of seeing.
cost . . . but involve so little expense and care in upbringing that we may.   73 *loggets* a game in
which pieces of hard wood shaped like Indian clubs or bowling pins are thrown to lie as near as
possible to a stake   75 *For and* and moreover   79 *quiddities* subtleties, quibbles. (From Latin
quid, "a thing.")   *quillities* verbal niceties, subtle distinctions. (Variation of *quiddities.*)
tenures the holding of a piece of property or office, or the conditions or period of such holding
80 *sconce* head   81 *action of battery* lawsuit about physical assault

recognizances,* his fines,* his double* vouchers* his recoveries.* Is this
the fine of his fines and the recovery of his recoveries, to have his fine
pate full of fine dirt?* Will his vouchers vouch him no more of his pur-   85
chases, and double ones too, than the length and breadth of a pair of
indentures?* The very conveyances* of his lands will scarcely lie in this
box,* and must th' inheritor* himself have no more, ha?

Horatio: Not a jot more, my lord.

Hamlet: Is not parchment made of sheepskins?   90

Horatio: Ay, my lord, and of calves' skins too.

Hamlet: They are sheep and calves which seek out assurance in that.* I will
    speak to this fellow.—Whose grave's this, sirrah?*

First Clown: Mine, sir. [*Sings.*]

> "O, pit of clay for to be made   95
> For such a guest is meet."

Hamlet: I think it be thine, indeed, for thou liest in 't.

First Clown: You lie out on 't, sir, and therefore 'tis not yours. For my part, I
    do not lie in 't, yet it is mine.

Hamlet: Thou dost lie in 't, to be in 't and say it is thine. 'Tis for the dead,   100
    not for the quick;* therefore thou liest.

First Clown: 'Tis a quick lie, sir; 'twill away again from me to you.

Hamlet: What man dost thou dig it for?

First Clown: For no man, sir.

Hamlet: What woman, then?   105

First Clown: For none, neither.

Hamlet: Who is to be buried in 't?

First Clown: One that was a woman, sir, but, rest her soul, she's dead.

Hamlet: How absolute* the knave is! We must speak by the card,* or equiv-
    ocation* will undo us. By the Lord, Horatio, this three years I have took*   110
    note of it: the age is grown so picked* that the toe of the peasant comes
    so near the heel of the courtier, he galls his kibe.*—How long hast thou
    been grave maker?

First Clown: Of all the days i' the year, I came to 't that day that our last king
    Hamlet overcame Fortinbras.   115

Hamlet: How long is that since?

First Clown: Cannot you tell that? Every fool can tell that. It was that
    very day that young Hamlet was born—he that is mad and sent into
    England.

Hamlet: Ay, marry, why was he sent into England?

82–83 *statutes, his recognizances* legal documents guaranteeing a debt by attaching land and
property   83 *fines, recoveries* ways of converting entailed estates into "fee simple" or freehold.
double signed by two signatories.   *vouchers* guarantees of the legality of a title to real estate
83–85 *fine of his fines. . . fine pate. . . fine dirt* end of his legal maneuvers. . . elegant
head. . . minutely sifted dirt   86 *pair of indentures* legal document drawn up in duplicate on a
single sheet and then cut apart on a zigzag line so that each pair was uniquely matched. (Hamlet
may refer to two rows of teeth or dentures.)   87 *conveyances* deeds.   *box* (1) deed box (2) coffin.
("Skull" has been suggested.)   88 *inheritor* possessor, owner   92 *assurance in that* safety in legal
parchments   93 *sirrah* (A term of address to inferiors.)   101 *quick* living   109 *absolute* strict,
precise.   *by the card* i.e., with precision. (Literally, by the mariner's compass-card, on which the
points of the compass were marked.)   109–110 *equivocation* ambiguity in the use of terms   110
took taken   111 *picked* refined, fastidious   112 *galls his kibe* chafes the courtier's chilblain

First Clown: Why, because 'a was mad. 'A shall recover his wits there, or if   120
    'a do not, 'tis no great matter there.
Hamlet: Why?
First Clown: 'Twill not be seen in him there. There the men are as mad as
    he.
Hamlet: How came he mad?
First Clown: Very strangely, they say.   125
Hamlet: How strangely?
First Clown: Faith, e'en with losing his wits.
Hamlet: Upon what ground?*
First Clown: Why, here in Denmark. I have been sexton here, man and boy,
    thirty years.   130
Hamlet: How long will a man lie i' th' earth ere he rot?
First Clown: Faith, if 'a be not rotten before 'a die—as we have many pocky*
    corpses nowadays, that will scarce hold the laying in*—'a will last you*
    some eight year or nine year. A tanner will last you nine year.
Hamlet: Why he more than another?   135
First Clown: Why, sir, his hide is so tanned with his trade that 'a will keep
    out water a great while, and your water is a sore* decaver of your
    whoreson* dead body. [*He picks up a skull.*] Here's a skull now hath
    lien you* i' th' earth three-and-twenty years.
Hamlet: Whose was it?   140
First Clown: A whoreson mad fellow's it was. Whose do you think it was?
Hamlet: Nay, I know not.
First Clown: A pestilence on him for a mad rogue! 'A poured a flagon of
    Rhenish* on my head once. This same skull, sir, was, sir, Yorick's skull,
    the King's jester.   145
Hamlet: This?
First Clown: E'en that.
Hamlet: Let me see. [*He takes the skull.*] Alas, poor Yorick! I knew him,
    Horatio, a fellow of infinite jest, of most excellent fancy. He hath bore*
    me on his back a thousand times, and now how abhorred in my imagi-   150
    nation it is! My gorge rises* at it. Here hung those lips that I have kissed
    I know not how oft. Where be your gibes now? Your gambols, your
    songs, your flashes of merriment that were wont* to set the table on a
    roar? Not one now, to mock your own grinning?* Quite chopfallen?*
    Now get you to my lady's chamber and tell her, let her paint an inch
    thick, to this favor* she must come. Make her laugh at that. Prithee, Hor-   155
    atio, tell me one thing.
Horatio: What's that, my lord?
Hamlet: Dost thou think Alexander looked o' this fashion i' th' earth?

---

128 *ground* cause. (But, in the next line, the gravedigger takes the word in the sense of "land,"
"country.")   132 *pocky* rotten, diseased. (Literally, with the pox, or syphilis.)
133 *hold the laying in* hold together long enough to be interred.   *last you* last. (*You* is used
colloquially here and in the following lines.)   137 *sore* i.e., terrible, great.   *whoreson* i.e., vile,
scurvy   138 *lien you* lain. (See the note at line 133.)   144 *Rhenish* Rhine wine   149 *bore* borne
150–151 *My gorge rises* i.e., I feel nauseated   153 *were wont* used   153–154 *mock your own
grinning* mock at the way your skull seems to be grinning (just as you used to mock at yourself and
those who grinned at you)   154 *chopfallen* (1) lacking the lower jaw (2) dejected
155 *favor* aspect, appearance

Horatio: E'en so.

Hamlet: And smelt so? Pah! [*He throws down the skull.*]   160

Horatio: E'en so, my lord.

Hamlet: To what base uses we may return, Horatio! Why may not imagination trace the noble dust of Alexander till 'a find it stopping a
bunghole?*

Horatio: 'Twere to consider too curiously* to consider so.

Hamlet: No, faith, not a jot, but to follow him thither with modesty*   165
enough, and likelihood to lead it. As thus: Alexander died, Alexander
was buried, Alexander returneth to dust, the dust is earth, of earth we
make loam,* and why of that loam whereto he was converted might
they not stop a beer barrel?

> Imperious* Caesar, dead and turned to clay,   170
> Might stop a hole to keep the wind away.
> O, that that earth which kept the world in awe
> Should patch a wall t' expel the winter's flaw!*

*Enter King, Queen, Laertes, and the corpse [of Ophelia, in proces-
sion, with Priest, lords, etc.].*

> But soft,* but soft awhile! Here comes the King,
> The Queen, the courtiers. Who is this they follow?   175
> And with such maimèd* rites? This doth betoken
> The corpse they follow did with desperate hand
> Fordo* its own life. 'Twas of some estate.*
> Couch we* awhile and mark.

[*He and Horatio conceal themselves. Ophelia's body is taken to
the grave.*]

Laertes: What ceremony else?   180

Hamlet [*to Horatio*]: That is Laertes, a very noble youth. Mark.

Laertes: What ceremony else?

Priest: Her obsequies have been as far enlarged
As we have warranty.* Her death was doubtful,
And but that great command o'ersways the order*   185
She should in ground unsanctified been lodged*
Till the last trumpet. For* charitable prayers,
Shards,* flints, and pebbles should be thrown on her.
Yet here she is allowed her virgin crants,*
Her maiden strewments,* and the bringing home   190
Of bell and burial.*

Laertes: Must there no more be done?

Priest: No more be done.
We should profane the service of the dead

---

163 *bunghole* hole for filling or emptying a cask   164 *curiously* minutely   165 *modesty* plausible
moderation   167 *loam* mortar consisting chiefly of moistened clay and straw   170 *Imperious* imperial
173 *flaw* gust of wind   174 *soft* i.e., wait, be careful   176 *maimèd* mutilated, incomplete
178 *Fordo* destroy.   *estate* rank   179 *Couch we* let's hide, lie low   184 *warranty* i.e., ecclesiastical
authority   185 *great. . . order* orders from on high overrule the prescribed procedures
186 *She should. . . lodged* she should have been buried in unsanctified ground   187 *For* in place of
188 *Shards* broken bits of pottery   189 *crants* garlands betokening maidenhood
190 *strewments* flowers strewn on a coffin   190–191 *bringing. . . burial* laying the body to rest, to the
sound of the bell

To sing a requiem and such rest* to her
As to peace-parted souls.*

Laertes: Lay her i' th' earth,   195
And from her fair and unpolluted flesh
May violets spring! I tell thee, churlish priest,
A ministering angel shall my sister be
When thou liest howling.*

Hamlet [to Horatio]:   What, the fair Ophelia!

Queen [scattering flowers]: Sweets to the sweet! Farewell.   200
I hoped thou shouldst have been my Hamlet's wife.
I thought thy bride-bed to have decked, sweet maid,
And not t' have strewed thy grave.

Laertes: O, treble woe
Fall ten times treble on that cursèd head
Whose wicked deed thy most ingenious sense*   205
Deprived thee of! Hold off the earth awhile,
Till I have caught her once more in mine arms.

[*He leaps into the grave and embraces Ophelia.*]

Now pile your dust upon the quick and dead,
Till of this flat a mountain you have made
T' o'ertop old Pelion or the skyish head   210
Of blue Olympus.*

Hamlet [coming forward]: What is he whose grief
Bears such an emphasis,* whose phrase of sorrow
Conjures the wandering stars* and makes them stand
Like wonder-wounded* hearers? This is I,
Hamlet the Dane.*   215

Laertes [grappling with him]:* The devil take thy soul!

Hamlet: Thou pray'st not well.
I prithee, take thy fingers from my throat,
For though I am not splenitive* and rash,
Yet have I in me something dangerous,   220
Which let thy wisdom fear. Hold off thy hand.

King: Pluck them asunder.

Queen: Hamlet, Hamlet!

All: Gentlemen!

Horatio: Good my lord, be quiet.   225

[*Hamlet and Laertes are parted.*]

Hamlet: Why, I will fight with him upon this theme

194 *such rest* i.e., to pray for such rest   195 *peace-parted souls* those who have died at peace with
God   199 *howling* i.e., in hell   205 *ingenious sense* a mind that is quick, alert, of fine qualities
210–211 *Pelion, Olympus* sacred mountains in the north of Thessaly   212 *emphasis* i.e.,
rhetorical and florid emphasis. (*Phrase* has a similar rhetorical connotation.)   213 *wandering
stars* planets   214 *wonder-wounded* struck with amazement   215 *the Dane* (This title normally
signifies the King; see Act I, Scene i, line 17 and note.)   216 *stage direction: grappling with him*
The testimony of the First Quarto that "*Hamlet leaps in after Laertes*" and the "*Elegy on
Burbage*" ("Oft have I seen him leap into the grave") seem to indicate one way in which this fight
was staged; however, the difficulty of fitting two contenders and Ophelia's body into a confined
space (probably the trapdoor) suggests to many editors the alternative, that Laertes jumps out of
the grave to attack Hamlet.)   219 *splenitive* quick-tempered

Until my eyelids will no longer wag.*

Queen: O my son, what theme?

Hamlet: I loved Ophelia. Forty thousand brothers
    Could not with all their quantity of love   230
    Make up my sum. What wilt thou do for her?

King: O, he is mad, Laertes.

Queen: For love of God, forbear him.*

Hamlet: 'Swounds,* show me what thou'lt do.
    Woo't* weep? Woo't fight? Woo't fast? Woo't tear thyself?   235
    Woo't drink up* eisel?* Eat a crocodile?*
    I'll do 't. Dost come here to whine?
    To outface me with leaping in her grave?
    Be buried quick* with her, and so will I.
    And if thou prate of mountains, let them throw   240
    Millions of acres on us, till our ground,
    Singeing his pate* against the burning zone,*
    Make Ossa* like a wart! Nay, an* thou'lt mouth,*
    I'll rant as well as thou.

Queen: This is mere* madness,
    And thus awhile the fit will work on him;   245
    Anon, as patient as the female dove
    When that her golden couplets* are disclosed,*
    His silence will sit drooping.

Hamlet: Hear you, sir.
    What is the reason that you use me thus?
    I loved you ever. But it is no matter.   250
    Let Hercules himself do what he may,
    The cat will mew, and dog will have his day.*

                            Exit Hamlet.

King: I pray thee, good Horatio, wait upon him.

                            [*Exit*] *Horatio.*

[*To Laertes.*] Strengthen your patience in* our last night's speech;
    We'll put the matter to the present push.*—   255
    Good Gertrude, set some watch over your son.—
    This grave shall have a living* monument.
    An hour of quiet* shortly shall we see;
    Till then, in patience our proceeding be.   *Exeunt.*

---

227 *wag* move. (A fluttering eyelid is a conventional sign that life has not yet gone.)
233 *forbear him* leave him alone   234 *'Swounds* by His (Christ's) wounds   235 *Woo't* wilt thou
236 *drink up* drink deeply.   *eisel* vinegar.   *crocodile* (Crocodiles were tough and dangerous, and
were supposed to shed hypocritical tears.)   239 *quick* alive   242 *his pate* its head, i.e., top.
burning zone zone in the celestial sphere containing the sun's orbit, between the tropics of Cancer and
Capricorn   243 *Ossa* another mountain in Thessaly. (In their war against the Olympian gods, the
giants attempted to heap Ossa on Pelion to scale Olympus.)   *an* if.   *mouth* i.e., rant
244 *mere* utter   247 *golden couplets* two baby pigeons, covered with yellow down.   *disclosed* hatched
251–252 *Let. . . . day* i.e., (1) even Hercules couldn't stop Laertes' theatrical rant (2) I, too, will have
my turn; i.e., despite any blustering attempts at interference, every person will sooner or later do
what he or she must do   254 *in* i.e., by recalling   255 *present push* immediate test
257 *living* lasting. (For Laertes' private understanding, Claudius also hints that Hamlet's death will
serve as such a monument.)   258 *hour of quiet* time free of conflict

Scene II [*The Castle.*]

Enter Hamlet and Horatio.

Hamlet: So much for this, sir; now shall you see the other.*
 You do remember all the circumstance?
Horatio: Remember it, my lord!
Hamlet: Sir, in my heart there was a kind of fighting
 That would not let me sleep. Methought I lay   5
 Worse than the mutines* in the bilboes.* Rashly,*
 And praised be rashness for it—let us know*
 Our indiscretion* sometimes serves us well
 When our deep plots do pall,* and that should learn* us
 There's a divinity that shapes our ends,   10
 Rough-hew* them how we will—
Horatio: That is most certain.
Hamlet: Up from my cabin,
 My sea-gown* scarfed* about me, in the dark
 Groped I to find out them,* had my desire,
 Fingered* their packet, and in fine* withdrew   15
 To mine own room again, making so bold,
 My fears forgetting manners, to unseal
 Their grand commission; where I found, Horatio—
 Ah, royal knavery!—an exact command,
 Larded* with many several* sorts of reasons   20
 Importing* Denmark's health and England's too,
 With, ho! such bugs* and goblins in my life,*
 That on the supervise,* no leisure bated,*
 No, not to stay* the grinding of the ax,
 My head should be struck off.
Horatio: Is 't possible?   25
Hamlet [*giving a document*]: Here's the commission. Read it at more
 leisure.
 But wilt thou hear now how I did proceed?
Horatio: I beseech you.
Hamlet: Being thus benetted round with villainies—
 Ere I could make a prologue to my brains,   30
 They had begun the play*—I sat me down,
 Devised a new commission, wrote it fair.*
 I once did hold it, as our statists* do,
 A baseness* to write fair, and labored much
 How to forget that learning, but, sir, now   35

1 *see the other* hear the other news   6 *mutines* mutineers.   *bilboes* shackles.   *Rashly* on impulse.
(This adverb goes with lines 12 ff.)   7 *know* acknowledge   8 *indiscretion* lack of foresight and
judgment (not an indiscreet act)   9 *pall* fail, falter, go stale.   *learn* teach   11 *Rough-hew* shape
roughly   13 *sea-gown* seaman's coat.   *scarfed* loosely wrapped   14 *them* i.e., Rosencrantz and
Guildenstern   15 *Fingered* pilfered, pinched.   *in fine* finally, in conclusion   20 *Larded*
garnished.   *several* different   21 *Importing* relating to   22 *bugs* bugbears, hobgoblins.   *in my
life* i.e., to be feared if I were allowed to live   23 *supervise* reading.   *leisure bated* delay
allowed   24 *stay* await   30–31 *Ere . . . play* before I could consciously turn my brain to the
matter, it had started working on a plan   32 *fair* in a clear hand   33 *statists* statesmen
34 *baseness* i.e., lower-class trait

It did me yeoman's* service. Wilt thou know
 Th' effect* of what I wrote?
Horatio: Ay, good my lord.
Hamlet: An earnest conjuration* from the King,
 As England was his faithful tributary,   40
 As love between them like the palm* might flourish,
 As peace should still* her wheaten garland* wear
 And stand a comma* 'tween their amities,
 And many suchlike "as"es* of great charge,*
 That on the view and knowing of these contents,
 Without debatement further more or less,   45
 He should those bearers put to sudden death,
 Not shriving time* allowed.
Horatio: How was this sealed?
Hamlet: Why, even in that was heaven ordinant.*
 I had my father's signet* in my purse,
 Which was the model* of that Danish seal;   50
 Folded the writ* up in the form of th' other,
 Subscribed* it, gave 't th' impression,* placed it safely,
 The changeling* never known. Now, the next day
 Was our sea fight, and what to this was sequent*
 Thou knowest already.   55
Horatio: So Guildenstern and Rosencrantz go to 't.
Hamlet: Why, man, they did make love to this employment.
 They are not near my conscience. Their defeat*
 Does by their own insinuation* grow.
 'Tis dangerous when the baser* nature comes   60
 Between the pass* and fell* incensed points
 Of mighty opposites.*
Horatio: Why, what a king is this!
Hamlet: Does it not, think thee, stand me now upon*—
 He that hath killed my king and whored my mother,
 Popped in between th' election* and my hopes,   65
 Thrown out his angle* for my proper* life,
 And with such cozenage*—is 't not perfect conscience
 To quit* him with this arm? And is 't not to be damned
 To let this canker* of our nature come
 In* further evil?   70

36 *yeoman's* i.e., substantial, faithful, loyal 37 *effect* purport 38 *conjuration* entreaty
40 *palm* (An image of health; see Psalm 92:12.) 41 *still* always. *wheaten garland* (Symbolic of
fruitful agriculture, of peace and plenty.) 42 *comma* (Indicating continuity, link.) 43 *"as"es*
(1) the "whereases" of a formal document (2) asses. *charge* (1) import (2) burden (appropriate to
asses) 47 *shriving time* time for confession and absolution 48 *ordinant* directing
49 *signet* small seal 50 *model* replica 51 *writ* writing 52 *Subscribed* signed (with forged
signature). *impression* i.e., with a wax seal 53 *changeling* i.e., substituted letter. (Literally, a
fairy child substituted for a human one.) 54 *was sequent* followed 58 *defeat* destruction
59 *insinuation* intrusive intervention, sticking their noses in my business 60 *baser* of lower social
station 61 *pass* thrust. *fell* fierce 62 *opposites* antagonists 63 *stand me now upon* become
incumbent on me now 65 *election* (The Danish monarch was "elected" by a small number of high-
ranking electors.) 66 *angle* fishhook. *proper* very 67 *cozenage* trickery 68 *quit* requite, pay
back 69 *canker* ulcer 69–70 *come in* grow into

Horatio: It must be shortly known to him from England
    What is the issue of the business there.
Hamlet: It will be short. The interim is mine.
    And a man's life's no more than to say "one."*
    But I am very sorry, good Horatio,   75
    That to Laertes I forgot myself.
    For by the image of my cause I see
    The portraiture of his. I'll court his favors.
    But, sure, the bravery* of his grief did put me
    Into a tow'ring passion.
Horatio: Peace, who comes here?   80

    Enter a Courtier [Osric].

Osric: Your lordship is right welcome back to Denmark.
Hamlet: I humbly thank you, sir. [*To Horatio.*] Dost know this water fly?
Horatio: No, my good lord.
Hamlet: Thy state is the more gracious, for 'tis a vice to know him. He hath
    much land, and fertile. Let a beast be lord of beasts, and his crib* shall   85
    stand at the King's mess*. 'Tis a chuff,* but, as I say, spacious in the pos-
    session of dirt.
Osric: Sweet lord, if your lordship were at leisure, I should impart a thing to
    you from His Majesty.
Hamlet: I will receive it, sir, with all diligence of spirit.
    Put your bonnet* to his* right use; 'tis for the head.   90
Osric: I thank your lordship, it is very hot.
Hamlet: No, believe me, 'tis very cold. The wind is northerly.
Osric: It is indifferent* cold, my lord, indeed.
Hamlet: But yet methinks it is very sultry and hot for my complexion.*
Osric: Exceedingly, my lord. It is very sultry, as 'twere—I cannot tell how. My   95
    lord, His Majesty bade me signify to you that 'a has laid a great wager
    on your head. Sir, this is the matter—
Hamlet: I beseech you, remember.

    [*Hamlet moves him to put on his hat.*]

Osric: Nay, good my lord; for my ease,* in good faith. Sir, here is newly
    come to court Laertes—believe me, an absolute* gentleman, full of   100
    most excellent differences,* of very soft society* and great showing.*
    Indeed, to speak feelingly* of him, he is the card* or calendar* of gentry,*
    for you shall find in him the continent of what part a gentleman would
    see.*

---

74 *a man's. . . "one"* one's whole life occupies such a short time, only as long as it takes to
count to 1   79 *bravery* bravado   85–86 *Let. . . mess* i.e., if a man, no matter how beastlike, is as
rich in livestock and possessions as Osric, he may eat at the King's table   85 *crib* manger
86 *chuff* boor, churl. (The Second Quarto spelling, *chough*, is a variant spelling that also suggests
the meaning here of "chattering jackdaw.")   90 *bonnet* any kind of cap or hat.   *his* its
93 *indifferent* somewhat   94 *complexion* temperament   99 *for my ease* (A conventional reply
declining the invitation to put his hat back on.)   100 *absolute* perfect   101 *differences* special
qualities.   *soft society* agreeable manners.   *great showing* distinguished appearance
101–102 *feelingly* with just perception   102 *card* chart, map.   *calendar* guide.   *gentry* good
breeding   103 *the continent. . . see* one who contains in him all the qualities a gentleman would
like to see. (A *continent* is that which contains.)

Hamlet: Sir, his definement* suffers no perdition* in you,* though I know to
    divide him inventorially* would dozy* th' arithmetic of memory, and   105
    yet but yaw* neither* in respect of* his quick sail. But, in the verity of
    extolment,* I take him to be a soul of great article,* and his infusion* of
    such dearth and rareness* as, to make true diction* of him, his sem-
    blable* is his mirror and who else would trace* him his umbrage,*
    nothing more.
Osric: Your lordship speaks most infallibly of him.   110
Hamlet: The concernancy,* sir? Why do we wrap the gentleman in our
    more rawer breath?*
Osric: Sir?
Horatio: Is 't not possible to understand in another tongue?* You will do 't,*
    sir, really.   115
Hamlet: What imports the nomination of this gentleman?
Osric: Of Laertes?
Horatio [to Hamlet]: His purse is empty already; all 's golden words are
    spent.
Hamlet: Of him, sir.   120
Osric: I know you are not ignorant—
Hamlet: I would you did, sir. Yet in faith if you did, it would not much
    approve* me. Well, sir?
Osric: You are not ignorant of what excellence Laertes is—
Hamlet: I dare not confess that, lest I should compare with him in excel-
    lence. But to know a man well were to know himself.*   125
Osric: I mean, sir, for* his weapon; but in the imputation laid on him by
    them,* in his meed* he's unfellowed.*
Hamlet: What's his weapon?
Osric: Rapier and dagger.
Hamlet: That's two of his weapons—but well.*   130
Osric: The King, sir, hath wagered with him six Barbary horses, against the
    which he* has impawned,* as I take it, six French rapiers and
    poniards,* with their assigns,* as girdle, hangers,* and so.* Three of the

---

104 *definement* definition. (Hamlet proceeds to mock Osric by throwing his lofty diction back at
him.)   *perdition* loss, diminution.   *you* your description   104–105 *divide him inventorially*
enumerate his graces.   *dozy* dizzy.   106 *yaw* swing unsteadily off course. (Said of a ship.)
neither for all that.   *in respect of* in comparison with.   *in . . . extolment* in true praise (of him)
107 *of great article* one with many articles in his inventory.   *infusion* essence, character infused
into him by nature   107–108 *dearth and rareness* rarity   *make true diction* speak truly.
semblable only true likeness   109 *who . . . trace* any other person who would wish to follow.
umbrage shadow   111 *concernancy* import, relevance   112 *rawer breath* unrefined speech that
can only come short in praising him   114 *to understand . . . tongue* i.e., for you, Osric, to
understand when someone else speaks your language. (Horatio twits Osric for not being able to
understand the kind of flowery speech he himself uses, when Hamlet speaks in such a vein.
Alternatively, all this could be said to Hamlet.)   *You will do 't* i.e., you can if you try, or, you may
well have to try (to speak plainly)   121 *approve* commend   124–125 *I dare . . . himself* I dare not
boast of knowing Laertes' excellence lest I seem to imply a comparable excellence in myself.
Certainly to know another person well, one must know oneself   126 *for* i.e., with.
imputation . . . them reputation given him by others   127 *meed* merit.   *unfellowed* unmatched
130 *but well* but never mind   132 *he* i.e., Laertes.   *impawned* staked, wagered.   *poniards*
daggers   133 *assigns* appurtenances.   *hangers* straps on the sword belt (*girdle*), from which the
sword hung.   *and so* and so on.

carriages,* in faith, are very dear to fancy,* very responsive* to the hilts,
most delicate* carriages, and of very liberal conceit.*   135

Hamlet: What call you the carriages?

Horatio [to Hamlet]: I knew you must be edified by the margent* ere you
had done.

Osric: The carriages, sir, are the hangers.

Hamlet: The phrase would be more germane to the matter if we could
carry a cannon by our sides; I would it might be hangers till then. But,   140
on: six Barbary horses against six French swords, their assigns, and
three liberal—conceited carriages; that's the French bet against the
Danish. Why is this impawned, as you call it?

Osric: The King, sir, hath laid,* sir, that in a dozen passes* between yourself
and him, he shall not exceed you three hits. He hath laid on twelve for   145
nine, and it would come to immediate trial, if your lordship would
vouchsafe the answer.*

Hamlet: How if I answer no?

Osric: I mean, my lord, the opposition of your person in trial.

Hamlet: Sir, I will walk here in the hall. If it please His Majesty, it is the   150
breathing time* of day with me. Let* the foils be brought, the gentleman willing, and the King hold his purpose, I will win for him an I can;
if not, I will gain nothing but my shame and the odd hits.

Osric: Shall I deliver you* so?

Hamlet: To this effect, sir—after what flourish your nature will.   155

Osric: I commend* my duty to your lordship.

Hamlet: Yours, yours. [*Exit Osric.*] 'A does well to commend it himself;
there are no tongues else for 's turn.*

Horatio: This lapwing* runs away with the shell on his head.

Hamlet: 'A did comply with his dug* before 'a sucked it. Thus has he—and   160
many more of the same breed that I know the drossy* age dotes on—
only got the tune* of the time and, out of an habit of encounter,* a kind
of yeasty* collection,* which carries them through and through the
most fanned and winnowed opinions;* and do* but blow them to their
trial, the bubbles are out.*

134 *carriages* (An affected way of saying *hangers;* literally, gun carriages.)   *dear to fancy* delightful
to the fancy.   *responsive* corresponding closely, matching or well-adjusted.   *delicate* (i.e., in
workmanship)   135 *liberal conceit* elaborate design   137 *margent* margin of a book, place for
explanatory notes   144 *laid* wagered.   *passes* bouts. (The odds of the betting are hard to explain.
Possibly the King bets that Hamlet will win at least five out of twelve, at which point Laertes raises the
odds against himself by betting he will win nine.)   146–147 *vouchsafe the answer* be so good as to
accept the challenge. (Hamlet deliberately takes the phrase in its literal sense of replying.)
151 *breathing time* exercise period.   *Let* i.e., if   154 *deliver you* report what you say
156 *commend* commit to your favor. (A conventional salutation, but Hamlet wryly uses a more literal
meaning, "recommend," "praise," in line 157.)   158 *for 's turn* for his purposes, i.e., to do it for him
159 *lapwing* (A proverbial type of youthful forwardness. Also, a bird that draws intruders away from
its nest and was thought to run about with its head in the shell when newly hatched; a seeming reference to Osric's hat.)   160 *comply. . . dug* observe ceremonious formality toward his nurse's or mother's teat   161 *drossy* laden with scum and impurities, frivolous   162 *tune* temper, mood, manner of
speech.   *an habit of encounter* a demeanor in conversing (with courtiers of his own kind).   *yeasty*
frothy   162–163 *collection* i.e., of current phrases   163–164 *carries. . . opinions* sustains them right
through the scrutiny of persons whose opinions are select and refined. (Literally, like grain separated
from its chaff. Osric is both the chaff and the bubbly froth on the surface of the liquor that is soon
blown away.)   164 *and do* yet do.   *blow. . . out* test them by merely blowing on them, and their
bubbles burst

Enter a Lord.

Lord: My lord, His Majesty commended him to you by young Osric, who   165
   brings back to him that you attend him in the hall. He sends to know if
   your pleasure hold to play with Laertes, or that you will take longer
   time.

Hamlet: I am constant to my purposes; they follow the King's pleasure. If
   his fitness speaks, mine is ready;* now or whensoever, provided I be so
   able as now.   170

Lord: The King and Queen and all are coming down.

Hamlet: In happy time.*

Lord: The Queen desires you to use some gentle entertainment* to Laertes
   before you fall to play.

Hamlet: She well instructs me.   [*Exit Lord.*]   175

Horatio: You will lose, my lord.

Hamlet: I do not think so. Since he went into France, I have been in continual practice; I shall win at the odds. But thou wouldst not think how
   ill all's here about my heart; but it is no matter.

Horatio: Nay, good my lord—   180

Hamlet: It is but foolery, but it is such a kind of gaingiving* as would perhaps trouble a woman.

Horatio: If your mind dislike anything, obey it. I will forestall their repair*
   hither and say you are not fit.

Hamlet: Not a whit, we defy augury. There is special providence in the fall   185
   of a sparrow. If it be now, 'tis not to come; if it be not to come, it will be
   now; if it be not now; yet it will come. The readiness is all. Since no man
   of aught he leaves knows, what is 't to leave betimes? Let be.*

   A table prepared. [*Enter*] *trumpets, drums, and officers with cush-*
   ions; King, Queen, [*Osric,*] *and all the state; foils, daggers,* [*and wine*
   borne in;] *and Laertes.*

King: Come, Hamlet, come and take this hand from me.

               [*The King puts Laertes' hand into Hamlet's.*]

Hamlet [*to Laertes*]*:* Give me your pardon, sir. I have done you wrong,   190
   But pardon 't as you are a gentleman.
   This presence* knows,
   And you must needs have heard, how I am punished*
   With a sore distraction. What I have done
   That might your nature, honor, and exception*   195
   Roughly awake, I here proclaim was madness.
   Was 't Hamlet wronged Laertes? Never Hamlet.
   If Hamlet from himself be ta'en away,
   And when he's not himself does wrong Laertes,
   Then Hamlet does it not, Hamlet denies it.   200
   Who does it, then? His madness. If 't be so,
   Hamlet is of the faction* that is wronged;

168–169 *If. . . ready* if he declares his readiness, my convenience waits on his
172 *In happy time* (A phrase of courtesy indicating that the time is convenient.)
173 *entertainment* greeting   181 *gaingiving* misgiving   183 *repair* coming
187–188 *Since. . . Let be* since no one has knowledge of what he is leaving behind, what does an
early death matter after all? Enough; don't struggle against it.   192 *presence* royal assembly
193 *punished* afflicted   195 *exception* disapproval   202 *faction* party

His madness is poor Hamlet's enemy.
Sir, in this audience
Let my disclaiming from a purposed evil   205
Free me so far in your most generous thoughts
That I have* shot my arrow o'er the house
And hurt my brother.

Laertes: I am satisfied in nature,*
Whose motive* in this case should stir me most
To my revenge. But in my terms of honor   210
I stand aloof, and will no reconcilement
Till by some elder masters of known honor
I have a voice* and precedent of peace*
To keep my name ungored.* But till that time
I do receive your offered love like love,   215
And will not wrong it.

Hamlet: I embrace it freely,
And will this brother's wager frankly* play.—
Give us the foils. Come on.

Laertes: Come, one for me.

Hamlet: I'll be your foil,* Laertes. In mine ignorance
Your skill shall, like a star i' the darkest night,   220
Stick fiery off* indeed.

Laertes: You mock me, sir.

Hamlet: No, by this hand.

King: Give them the foils, young Osric. Cousin Hamlet,
You know the wager?

Hamlet: Very well, my lord.
Your Grace has laid the odds o'* the weaker side.   225

King: I do not fear it; I have seen you both.
But since he is bettered,* we have therefore odds.

Laertes: This is too heavy. Let me see another.

[*He exchanges his foil for another.*]

Hamlet: This likes me* well. These foils have all a length?

[*They prepare to play.*]

Osric: Ay, my good lord.   230

King: Set me the stoups of wine upon that table.
If Hamlet give the first or second hit,
Or quit in answer of the third exchange,*
Let all the battlements their ordnance fire.
The King shall drink to Hamlet's better breath,*   235
And in the cup an union* shall he throw

---

207 *That I have* as if I had   208 *in nature* i.e., as to my personal feelings   209 *motive* prompting
213 *voice* authoritative pronouncement.   *of peace* for reconciliation   214 *name ungored*
reputation unwounded   217 *frankly* without ill feeling or the burden of rancor   219 *foil* thin
metal background that sets a jewel off (with pun on the blunted rapier for fencing)   221 *Stick*
fiery off stand out brilliantly   225 *laid the odds o'* bet on, backed   227 *is bettered* has improved;
is the odds-on favorite. (Laertes' handicap is the "three hits" specified in line 145.)   229 *likes me*
pleases me   233 *Or . . . exchange* i.e., or requites Laertes in the third bout for having won the first
two   235 *better breath* improved vigor   236 *union* pearl. (So called, according to Pliny's *Natural*
History, 9, because pearls are *unique*, never identical.)

Richer than that which four successive kings
In Denmark's crown have worn. Give me the cups,
And let the kettle* to the trumpet speak,
The trumpet to the cannoneer without,   240
The cannons to the heavens, the heaven to earth,
"Now the King drinks to Hamlet." Come, begin.

Trumpets the while.

And you, the judges, bear a wary eye.
Hamlet: Come on, sir.
Laertes: Come, my lord. [*They play. Hamlet scores a hit.*]   245
Hamlet: One.
Laertes: No.
Hamlet: Judgment.
Osric: A hit, a very palpable hit.

Drum, trumpets, and shot. Flourish.
A piece goes off.

Laertes: Well, again.
King: Stay, give me drink. Hamlet, this pearl is thine.   250

[*He drinks, and throws a pearl in Hamlet's cup.*]

Here's to thy health. Give him the cup.
Hamlet: I'll play this bout first. Set it by awhile.
Come. [*They play.*] Another hit; what say you?
Laertes: A touch, a touch, I do confess 't.
King: Our son shall win.
Queen: He's fat* and scant of breath.   255
Here, Hamlet, take my napkin,* rub thy brows.
The Queen carouses* to thy fortune, Hamlet.
Hamlet: Good madam!
King: Gertrude, do not drink.
Queen: I will, my lord, I pray you pardon me.   [*She drinks.*] 260
King [aside]: It is the poisoned cup. It is too late.
Hamlet: I dare not drink yet, madam; by and by.
Queen: Come, let me wipe thy face.
Laertes [to King]: My lord, I'll hit him now.
King: I do not think 't.
Laertes [aside]: And yet it is almost against my conscience.   265
Hamlet: Come, for the third, Laertes. You do but dally.
I pray you, pass* with your best violence;
I am afeard you make a wanton of me.*
Laertes: Say you so? Come on.   [*They play.*]
Osric: Nothing neither way.   270
Laertes: Have at you now!

[*Laertes wounds Hamlet; then, in scuffling, they change rapiers,*
and Hamlet wounds Laertes.]

239 *kettle* kettledrum   255 *fat* not physically fit, out of training   256 *napkin* handkerchief
257 *carouses* drinks a toast   267 *pass* thrust   268 *make. . . me* i.e., treat me like a spoiled child,
trifle with me   271 *stage direction: in scuffling, they change rapiers* (This stage direction occurs
in the Folio. According to a widespread stage tradition, Hamlet receives a scratch, realizes that
Laertes' sword is unbated, and accordingly forces an exchange.)

King: Part them! They are incensed.
Hamlet: Nay, come, again.   *[The Queen falls.]*
Osric: Look to the Queen there, ho!
Horatio: They bleed on both sides. How is it, my lord?
Osric: How is 't, Laertes?
Laertes: Why, as a woodcock* to mine own springe,* Osric;   275
     I am justly killed with mine own treachery.
Hamlet: How does the Queen?
King: She swoons to see them bleed.
Queen: No, no, the drink, the drink—O my dear Hamlet—
     The drink, the drink! I am poisoned.   *[She dies.]*
Hamlet: O villainy! Ho, let the door be locked!   280
     Treachery! Seek it out.   *[Laertes falls. Exit Osric.]*
Laertes: It is here, Hamlet. Hamlet, thou art slain.
     No med'cine in the world can do thee good;
     In thee there is not half an hour's life.
     The treacherous instrument is in thy hand,   285
     Unbated* and envenomed. The foul practice*
     Hath turned itself on me. Lo, here I lie,
     Never to rise again. Thy mother's poisoned.
     I can no more. The King, the King's to blame.
Hamlet: The point envenomed too? Then, venom, to thy work.   290
                                        [He stabs the King.]

All: Treason! Treason!
King: O, yet defend me, friends! I am but hurt.
Hamlet [forcing the King to drink]:
     Here, thou incestuous, murderous, damnèd Dane,
     Drink off this potion. Is thy union* here?
     Follow my mother.   *[The King dies.]*
Laertes: He is justly served.   295
     It is a poison tempered* by himself.
     Exchange forgiveness with me, noble Hamlet.
     Mine and my father's death come not upon thee,
     Nor thine on me!   *[He dies.]*
Hamlet: Heaven make thee free of it! I follow thee.   300
     I am dead, Horatio. Wretched Queen, adieu!
     You that look pale and tremble at this chance,*
     That are but mutes* or audience to this act,
     Had I but time—as this fell* sergeant,* Death,
     Is strict* in his arrest*—O, I could tell you—   305
     But let it be. Horatio, I am dead;
     Thou livest. Report me and my cause aright
     To the unsatisfied.
Horatio: Never believe it.

---

275 *woodcock* a bird, a type of stupidity or as a decoy. *springe* trap, snare   286 *Unbated* not
blunted with a button.   *practice* plot   294 *union* pearl. (See line 236; with grim puns on the
word's other meanings: marriage, shared death.)   296 *tempered* mixed   302 *chance* mischance
303 *mutes* silent observers. (Literally, actors with nonspeaking parts.)   304 *fell* cruel.
sergeant sheriff's officer   305 *strict* (1) severely just (2) unavoidable.   *arrest* (1) taking into
custody (2) stopping my speech

I am more an antique Roman* than a Dane.
Here's yet some liquor left.

[*He attempts to drink from the poisoned cup. Hamlet prevents him.*]

Hamlet: As thou'rt a man,   310
Give me the cup! Let go! By heaven, I'll ha 't.
O God, Horatio, what a wounded name,
Things standing thus unknown, shall I leave behind me!
If thou didst ever hold me in thy heart,
Absent thee from felicity awhile,   315
And in this harsh world draw thy breath in pain
To tell my story. *A march afar off* [*and a volley within*]. What warlike
noise is this?

Enter Osric.

Osric: Young Fortinbras, with conquest come from Poland,
To th' ambassadors of England gives
This warlike volley.
Hamlet: O, I die, Horatio!   320
The potent poison quite o'ercrows* my spirit.
I cannot live to hear the news from England,
But I do prophesy th' election lights
On Fortinbras. He has my dying voice.*
So tell him, with th' occurrents* more and less   325
Which have solicited*—the rest is silence.   [*He dies.*]
Horatio: Now cracks a noble heart. Good night, sweet prince,
And flights of angels sing thee to thy rest!

[*March within.*]

Why does the drum come hither?

Enter Fortinbras, with the [*English*] *Ambassadors* [*with drum, colors, and attendants*].

Fortinbras: Where is this sight?
Horatio: What is it you would see?   330
If aught of woe or wonder, cease your search.
Fortinbras: This quarry* cries on havoc.* O proud Death,
What feast* is toward* in thine eternal cell,
That thou so many princes at a shot
So bloodily hast struck?
First Ambassador: The sight is dismal,   335
And our affairs from England come too late.
The ears are senseless that should give us hearing,
To tell him his commandment is fulfilled,
That Rosencrantz and Guildenstern are dead.
Where should we have our thanks?

---

309 *Roman* (Suicide was an honorable choice for many Romans as an alternative to a dishonorable
life.)   321 *o'ercrows* triumphs over (like the winner in a cockfight)   324 *voice* vote
325 *occurrents* events, incidents   326 *solicited* moved, urged. (Hamlet doesn't finish saying what
the events have prompted—presumably, his acts of vengeance, or his reporting of those events to
Fortinbras.)   332 *quarry* heap of dead.   *cries on havoc* proclaims a general slaughter
333 *feast* i.e., Death feasting on those who have fallen.   *toward* in preparation

Horatio: Not from his* mouth,   340
    Had it th' ability of life to thank you.
    He never gave commandment for their death.
    But since, so jump* upon this bloody question,*
    You from the Polack wars, and you from England,
    Are here arrived, give order that these bodies   345
    High on a stage* be placèd to the view,
    And let me speak to th' yet unknowing world
    How these things came about. So shall you hear
    Of carnal, bloody, and unnatural acts,
    Of accidental judgments,* casual* slaughters,   350
    Of deaths put on* by cunning and forced cause,*
    And, in this upshot, purposes mistook
    Fall'n on th' inventors' heads. All this can I
    Truly deliver.
Fortinbras: Let us haste to hear it,
    And call the noblest to the audience.   355
    For me, with sorrow I embrace my fortune.
    I have some rights of memory* in this kingdom,
    Which now to claim my vantage* doth invite me.
Horatio: Of that I shall have also cause to speak,
    And from his mouth whose voice will draw on more.*   360
    But let this same be presently* performed,
    Even while men's minds are wild, lest more mischance
    On* plots and errors happen.
Fortinbras: Let four captains
    Bear Hamlet, like a soldier, to the stage,
    For he was likely, had he been put on,*   365
    To have proved most royal; and for his passage,*
    The soldiers' music and the rite of war
    Speak* loudly for him.
    Take up the bodies. Such a sight as this
    Becomes the field,* but here shows much amiss.   370
    Go bid the soldiers shoot.

    Exeunt [marching, bearing off the dead bodies; a peal of ordnance
    is shot off].

                               [about 1600]

Questions

Act I

    1. Everybody seems a little jumpy in act I, right from the very beginning. What reasons do the various characters have for being nervous?

340 *his* i.e., Claudius'   343 *jump* precisely, immediately.   *question* dispute, affair   346 *stage* platform   350 *judgments* retributions.   *casual* occurring by chance   351 *put on* instigated.   *forced cause* contrivance   357 *of memory* traditional, remembered, unforgotten   358 *vantage* favorable opportunity   360 *voice. . . more* vote will influence still others   361 *presently* immediately   363 *On* on the basis of; on top of   365 *put on* i.e., invested in royal office and so put to the test   366 *passage* i.e., from life to death   368 *Speak* (let them) speak   370 *Becomes the field* suits the field of battle

2. What is troubling Hamlet *before* he talks with the ghost? What do you think is on his mind immediately after talking with the ghost?

3. Is the ghost real? How do you know? How does Hamlet know the ghost is who (or what) he says he is?

4. Before he speaks to the ghost, what is Hamlet's relationship to his mother and stepfather? What does he say about them outside their presence, and why doesn't he say it to their faces?

5. How much is Hamlet surprised by what the ghost has to say? In what ways does his encounter with the ghost affect him?

6. Why are the officers standing guard?

Act II

1. What kind of person is Polonius? Cite specific examples for your conclusions.

2. What does Polonius mean when he says of Hamlet's behavior, "Though this be madness, yet there is method in't"? Do you agree with Polonius?

3. How does Hamlet intend to use the acting troupe, and why does he find it necessary to use them?

4. Why does Hamlet immediately seem to cheer up in the presence of the troupe?

5. What sort of people are Rosencrantz and Guildenstern? What seems to be important to them?

Act III

1. Immediately after hearing what Hamlet has to say to Ophelia, the King decides to send Hamlet to England. Why?

2. How firmly (at this point) does Hamlet believe in the reality of the ghost and what the ghost has to say? Citing specific statements and events as evidence, explain why Hamlet does or does not have sufficient reason to seek revenge for his father's death.

3. At the end of act III, Hamlet says he will trust Rosencrantz and Guildenstern "as I will adders fang'd." Why doesn't he trust his old friends?

4. What exactly does Hamlet hold against his mother?

5. What evidence is there that Hamlet's treatment of Ophelia is connected to his attitude toward his mother?

Act IV

1. In scene IV of this act, Hamlet considers himself a coward for not acting more like a soldier. Is the argument he presents in this scene convincing? Why or why not?

2. Why is the King so sure that Hamlet will want to fence Laertes? If you were Hamlet, would you have done anything differently?

3. Why doesn't the King have Hamlet arrested for the murder of Polonius?

4. Compare Hamlet's "madness" to Ophelia's.

Act V

1. Compare the Clown's attitude toward death to Hamlet's. Cite instances where Hamlet jokes about death. How does his joking relate to his more serious thinking on the subject?

2. What happened to Rosencrantz and Guildenstern? What do you think about their fate?
3. Why does Hamlet jump into Ophelia's grave with Laertes?
4. What is Laertes's attitude toward Hamlet in the final scene?
5. Why is it important to Hamlet that Horatio tell the world his story?

Critical Viewpoints

The following excerpts represent a sampling of the vast critical commentary on *Hamlet,* illustrating a variety of approaches and interests.

H. D. F. Kitto: Historical Criticism

In this excerpt, H. D. F. Kitto draws some interesting parallels between Hamlet *and* Oedipus, *arguing that* Hamlet *should be seen, like* Oedipus, *against the backdrop "of Nature and Heaven." The play, in other words, is not simply the story of Hamlet, but rather gives Hamlet's story cosmic proportions.*

Hamlet and Oedipus

The *Oedipus Tryannus* begins by describing twice, once in dialogue and once in lyrics, the plague which is afflicting Thebes. The cause of the plague is the presence in the city of a man who has done two things foul and unnatural above all others: he has killed his own father, and he is living incestuously with his own mother. The details of the plague are so described that we can see how its nature is strictly proportioned to its cause: to death is added sterility; the soil of Thebes, the animals, and the human kind are all barren. The meaning is obvious—unless we make it invisible by reducing the play to the stature of Tragedy of Character: what Oedipus has done is an affront to what we should call Nature, to what Sophocles calls Dikê; and since it is the first law of Nature, or Dikê, that she cannot indefinitely tolerate what is contrary to Nature, she rises at last against these unpurged affronts. The plague of sterility is the outcome of the unnatural things which Oedipus has done to his parents.

Hamlet begins in the same way. The two soldiers Marcellus and Bernardo, and Horatio, who is both a soldier and a scholar, are almost terrified out of their wits by something so clean contrary to the natural order that

> I might not this believe
> Without the sensible and true avouch
> Of mine own eyes.

Professor Dover Wilson, learned in sixteenth-century demonology, has explained that the eschatology of Horatio and Hamlet is Protestant, that the Ghost is a Catholic ghost, and that Bernardo and Marcellus are plain untheological Elizabethans. On this it would be impertinent for an ignoramus to express an opinion, but it does seem that if the "statists" in Shakespeare's audience, and scholars from the Inns of Court, saw and savoured theological *expertise* in this scene, they would be in danger of missing the main point: that the repeated appearances of the Ghost are something quite outside ordinary experience. Horatio the scholar has heard of something similar, in ancient history, "a little ere the mightiest Julius fell." So perhaps this present unnatural terror "bodes some strange eruption to our state"; or—a less disturbing thought—perhaps the ghost is concerned for some uphoarded treasure hidden in the womb of the Earth.

But at this point Shakespeare decides to write some poetry—and he is never so dangerous as when he is writing poetry:

> It faded on the crowing of the cock.
> Some say that ever 'gainst that season comes
> Wherein our Saviour's birth is celebrated,
> The bird of dawning singeth all night long:
> And then, they say, no spirit dare stir abroad,
> The nights are wholesome; then no planets strike,
> No fairy takes, nor witch hath power to charm,
> So hallowed and so gracious is the time.

Pretty good, for a simple soldier. The intense and solemn beauty of these verses lifts us, and was designed to lift us, high above the level of Horatio's conjectures. The night "wherein our Saviour's birth is celebrated" is holy and pure beyond all others; therefore these nights which the Ghost makes hideous by rising so incredibly from the grave, are impure beyond most. Unless Greek Tragedy has bemused me, this passage does more than "give a religious background to the supernatural happenings" of the scene; they give the "background," that is, the logical and dynamic centre, of the whole play. We are in the presence of evil. Hamlet's own prophetic soul recognises this as soon as he hears of the Ghost:

> Foul deeds will rise,
> Though all the earth o'erwhelm them, to men's eyes.

If we may assume that Shakespeare had not read Sophocles—and that Hamlet had not read him, at Wittenberg, behind Shakespeare's back—the parallel with the *Oedipus* becomes the more interesting; for when Oedipus has at last discovered the truth the Chorus observes:

> Time sees all, and it has found you out, in your own despite. It exacts
> Dikê from you for that unnatural marriage that united mother with son.

"Foul deeds will rise": there are evils so great that Nature will not allow them to lie unpurged. So, returning to the battlements with Hamlet, and enquiring with him

> Why thy canonized bones, hearsed in death,
> Have burst their cerements; why the sepulchre
> Wherein we saw thee quietly inurned
> Hath o'ped his ponderous and marble jaws
> To cast thee up again—

we learn the cause: fratricide, incest, "Murder most foul, strange and unnatural."

Here, most emphatically stated, are the very foundations and framework of the tragedy. We can, of course, neglect these, and erect a framework of our own which we find more interesting or more congenial to us. We can say, with Dr. Gregg, that the Ghost is all my eye; or, with Professor Dover Wilson, that the first act, "a little play of itself," is "an epitome of the ghost-lore of the age"—in which case it becomes something of a learned Prologue to the real play; or, like Dr. de Madariaga, we can neglect this encircling presence of evil, and substitute what we know of sixteenth-century Court manners; or, again without constant reference to the background which Shakespeare himself erected, we can subtly anatomise the soul and mind of Hamlet, on the assumption that Hamlet is the whole play. But if we do these things, let us not then complain that Shakespeare attempted a task too difficult for him, or conclude that the play is an ineffable mystery. Turning it into "secular" tragedy we shall be using the wrong focus. The correct focus is one which will set the whole action against a background of Nature and Heaven; for this is the background which the dramatist himself has provided.

From H.D.F. Kitto, *Form and Meaning in Drama*. New York: Methuen, 1956.

Eleanor Prosser: Historical Criticism

In this excerpt from a classic example of historical criticism, Eleanor Prosser relies on historical research into Elizabethan ideas about ghosts. We have misunderstood the play, Prosser argues, because we do not share the assumptions of Shakespeare's audience. In this brief excerpt from her careful reading, Prosser looks at the first appearance of the ghost in a historical context.

The study of Elizabethan ghost lore does not contradict our intuitive response to the first scene of *Hamlet*. It indicates that modern uneasiness may closely approximate the response of Shakespeare's audience. The play frankly invited both Protestants and Catholics to test the Ghost according to their religious beliefs and then presented them with recognizable warnings of danger.

No one in the first scene gives any indication of believing the Ghost to be the true soul of the dead King. The point of view is Protestant. Horatio, Marcellus, and Bernardo all consistently refer to the apparition as "it": not as the soul of the King himself, but as a spirit whose identity is in doubt. When Marcellus asks if this "thing" has appeared, his diction suggests not contemptuous levity but the cautious Protestant's awareness that the Ghost cannot be the actual King. It is an unknown, the nature of which is still to be determined. Similarly, Horatio's "Stay, illusion" is not an echo of his earlier skepticism but the correct response of a wary Protestant. The Ghost is, indeed, an "illusion." The point at issue is what kind of illusion.

In its first minute on stage, the Ghost reveals that something is seriously wrong. What is the purpose of its first appearance? It merely enters and leaves. Little is established that could not be included in the second appearance. The usual explanation is that its first entrance is a shrewd bit of theatrical trickery intended to catch the audience's attention. The episode does much more than that. It firmly establishes one point: this Ghost is forced to leave when Heaven is invoked. Horatio follows the warnings of religion. He charges the Ghost in the name of Heaven to identify itself, and it took no pious scholar to know that only demons would be "chased" by the invocation of God. The first episode reaches its climax as the Ghost is "offended" and stalks away, leaving Horatio pale and trembling.

A minor detail in this episode may also be a hint that this is a demon who usurps the form of the dead King. The Ghost "would be spoke to," and Horatio, as a scholar, is urged to question it. In my judgment, this fact has been faultily glossed. It is generally held that ghosts could not speak until they were spoken to, although the only corroborating evidence seems to be a remark about Samuel Johnson in the eighteenth century. The Elizabethan belief appears to have been specifically related to the problem of identifying an evil spirit. A false spirit might speak first, in which case one should be even more cautious. The informed Christian would speak before being spoken to, conjuring the spirit in the name of God to reveal its nature: if good, by speaking; if bad, by leaving. In other words, the fact that "it would be spoke to" does not prove that Bernardo believes it is a true ghost. Moreover, the fact that a scholar is urged to address it may mean that Marcellus fears it is a demon. Since Francis Douce, editors have repeated his assertion that ghosts had to be addressed in Latin. On the contrary, the evidence most frequently cited indicates something quite different. In Fletcher's *The Night-Walker,* Coachman Toby says:

> *Let's call the butler up, for he speaks Latine,*
> *And that will daunt the devil.*   *(II.i)*

Exactly. Latin was the language used in the rite of exorcism. No writer claimed that good spirits must be so addressed. If Marcellus is appealing to Horatio to use Latin, he is fearful that the Ghost may be a demon. More probably, however, Marcellus simply believes that a scholar is better equipped to address a doubtful spirit with safety. He is terrified, and with good reason.

The physical appearance of the Ghost may also suggest that it is suspect. As Catholics believed and Protestants had heard, Purgatory souls and good spirits both were "of sweet and amiable aspect," moved only by grace and charity. This ghost frowns as did the dead King once when he was angry with the Polacks. Moreover, Purgatory souls and good spirits are both spirits of peace. Many have noted the curious fact that the Ghost is in arms, bearing a truncheon as it moves with martial stalk. This is surely not the typical stage ghost described in the Induction to *A Warning for Fair Women* as "Lapt in some foul sheet or a leather pilch." It is conceivable that the costume is intended to lend awe, or to create a figure acceptable to a man of Hamlet's intelligence, or to portend some danger to the State. But it is also possible that Shakespeare's audience believed that armed spirits were demonic. Virgil had explained such apparitions as souls who still embraced the goods and appetites that had dominated them in life, but Le Loyer disagreed. Military garb proved that they were not souls but "devils who took the clothes and even the arms" of the men whose form they assumed. I have found no indication that this belief was widespread, but it does suggest a possible association.

From Eleanor Prosser, *Hamlet and Revenge,* 2nd ed. Palo Alto, CA: Stanford University Press, 1971, pp. 118-19.

5

Maynard Mack: Close Reading

Maynard Mack was one of the twentieth century's most influential and prolific critics. In the following excerpt, he explores what he calls "the interrogative mood" of Hamlet, *which begins with questions and is suffused throughout with mysteries.*

Hamlet's world is preeminently in the interrogative mood. It reverberates with questions, anguished, meditative, alarmed. There are questions that in this play, to an extent I think unparalleled in any other, mark the phases and even the nuances of the action, helping to establish its peculiar baffled tone. There are other questions whose interrogations, innocent at first glance, are subsequently seen to have reached beyond their contexts and to point toward some pervasive inscrutability in Hamlet's world as a whole. Such is that tense series of challenges with which the tragedy begins: Bernardo's of Francisco, "Who's there?" Francisco's of Horatio and Marcellus, "Who is there?" Horatio's of the ghost, "What art thou. . . ?"

And then there are the famous questions. In them the interrogations seem to point not only beyond the context but beyond the play, out of Hamlet's predicaments into everyone's: "What a piece of work is a man! . . . And yet to me what is this quintessence of dust?" (Act 2. Scene 2). "To be, or not to be—that is the question" (3.1.). "Get thee to a nunnery. Why wouldst thou be a breeder of sinners?" (3.1.). "I am very proud, revengeful, ambitious, with more offenses at my beck than I have thoughts to put them in, imagination to give them shape, or time to act them in. What should such fellows as I do crawling between earth and heaven?" (3.1.). "Dost thou think Alexander looked o' this fashion i' th' earth? . . . And smelt so?" (5.1.).

Further, Hamlet's world is a world of riddles. The hero's own language is often riddling, as the critics have pointed out. When he puns, his puns have receding depths in them, like the one which constitutes his first speech: "A little more than kin, and less than kind!" (1.2.). His utterances in madness, even if wild and whirling, are simultaneously, as Polonius discovers, pregnant: "Do you know me, my lord?" "Excellent well. You are a fishmonger" (2.2.). Even the madness itself is riddling: How much is real? How much is feigned? What does it mean?

Sane or mad, Hamlet's mind plays restlessly about his world, turning up one riddle upon another. The riddle of character, for example, and how it is that in a man whose virtues else are "pure as grace," some vicious mole of nature, some "dram of evil," can "all the noble substance [oft adulter]" (1.4.). Or the riddle of the player's art, and how a man can so project himself into a fiction, a dream of passion, that he can weep for Hecuba (2.2.). Or the riddle of action: how we may think too little—"What to ourselves in passion we propose," says the player-king, "The passion ending, doth the purpose lose" (3.2.); and again, how we may think too much: "Thus conscience does make cowards of us all,/And thus the native hue of resolution/Is sicklied o'er with the pale cast of thought" (3.1.).

There are also more immediate riddles. His mother—how could she "on this fair mountain leave to feed, And batten on this moor" (3.4.)? The ghost —which may be a devil, for "the devil hath power T' assume a pleasing shape" (2.2.). Ophelia—what does her behavior to him mean? Surprising her in her closet, he falls to such perusal of her face as he would draw it (2.1.). Even the king at his prayers is a riddle. Will a revenge that takes him

5

in the purging of his soul be vengeance, or hire and salary (3.3.)? As for himself, Hamlet realizes, he is the greatest riddle of all—a mystery, he warns Rosencrantz and Guildenstern from which he will not have the heart plucked out. He cannot tell why he has of late lost all his mirth, forgone all custom of exercises. Still less can he tell why he delays: "I do not know Why yet I live to say, 'This thing's to do,'/Sith I have cause, and will, and strength, and means/To do't" (4.4.).

Thus the mysteriousness of Hamlet's world is of a piece. It is not simply a matter of missing motivations, to be expunged if only we could find the perfect clue. It is built in. It is evidently an important part of what the play wishes to say to us. And it is certainly an element that the play thrusts upon us from the opening word. Everyone, I think, recalls the mysteriousness of that first scene. The cold middle of the night on the castle platform, the muffled sentries, the uneasy atmosphere of apprehension, the challenges leaping out of the dark, the questions that follow the challenges, feeling out the darkness, searching for identities, for relations, for assurance. "Bernardo?" "Have you had quiet guard?" "Who hath relieved you?" "What, is Horatio there?" "What, has this thing appeared again tonight?" "Looks 'a not like the king?" "How now, Horatio! . . . Is not this something more than fantasy? What think you on 't?" "Is it not like the King?" "Why this same strict and most observant watch . . ?" "Shall I strike at it with my partisan?" "Do you consent we shall acquaint [young Hamlet] with it?"

We need not be surprised that critics and playgoers alike have been tempted to see in this an evocation not simply of Hamlet's world but of their own. Human beings in their aspect of bafflement, moving in darkness on a rampart between two worlds, unable to reject, or quite accept, the one that, when they face it, "to-shakes" their dispositions with thoughts beyond the reaches of their souls—comforting themselves with hints and guesses. We hear these hints and guesses whispering through the darkness as the several watchers speak. "At least, the whisper goes so" (1.1.), says one. "I think it be no other but e'en so," says another. "I have heard" that on the crowing of the cock "Th' extravagant and erring spirit hies/To his confine," says a third. "Some say" at Christmas time "This bird of dawning" sings all night, "And then, they say, no spirit dare stir abroad." "So have I heard," says the first, "and do in part believe it." However we choose to take the scene, it is clear that it creates a world where uncertainties are of the essence.

From Maynard Mack, *Everybody's Shakespeare*. Rpt. Lincoln: U of
    Nebraska, 1994.

Norman Holland: Reader-Response

In the following excerpt from a famous and influential essay, Norman Holland considers what his favorite five lines from Hamlet *tell us—not only about the play, but about Norman Holland.*

*H*amlet is a huge play, Shakespeare's longest. An uncut performance takes from five to six hours. To tell you my reactions to all of it would take weeks, but I can tell you about my five favorite lines from the thirty-nine hundred or so that make up the tragedy as a whole. They are:

   O, what a rogue and peasant slave am I (2.2.550)

> *What's Hecuba to him, or he to Hecuba,*
> *That he should weep for her? (2.2.559-60)*
>
> *How all occasions do inform against me*
> *And spur my dull revenge!   (4.4.32-33)*

What do these lines permit me to do which is so satisfying?. . . .

In short, these sentences begin with a simplicity, move into something full of alternatives and complexities, and come around to a simplicity again. This is, of course, the pattern of the tragedy as a whole. On seeing the ghost, Hamlet resolves purely and simply to set the times right. As you know, we then go into three long and involved acts in which he does anything but. He does not return to his task of revenge until the final scene of the play when he accepts his destiny. "If it be now, 'tis not to come; if it be not to come, it will be now; if it be not now, yet it will come. The readiness is all."

> *There's a divinity that shapes our ends,*
> *Rough-hew them how we will.*

Could I not say then that I find in each of these lines the combination of risk-ing and security I enjoy in the tragedy as a whole? They make it possible for me to explore alternatives, but, finally, from their regularity and completion and endstops, I can make a mastery of those alternatives. There is, if not a divin-ity that shapes their ends, at least a sense for me of regularity and order. . . .

Notice, too, that all three of these favorite sentences are attacks on a per-son, two on Hamlet himself, one on his surrogate, the actor. They denigrate—I am a rogue and peasant slave. Or they dehumanize—my revenge is a horse; occasions are spies, Hecuba is something to him—what? Yet this killing anger of Hamlet's is turned inward from its real object—his parents. It feels to me as though Hamlet can tolerate his anger toward them better than their anger toward him. They angry at me? No, it is I who am angry at them. Have they left something undone? No, it is I who have left something undone. In effect, by what he does say, Hamlet tells me what he cannot say. My parents are angry at me. My parents are indifferent to me. They value me as a word or a thing. . . .

Words in this tragedy are, for me certainly and perhaps also for Ham-let and Shakespeare, a kind of potential space in which I can create alter-natives and possibilities instead of being faced with violent action or parental indifference. We have sampled but five, yet there are nearly four thousand lines, each one of which, to some degree, allows me to use words to work out alternatives and so control my very deep fears. I fear that par-ents or parent-figures will be angry at me—I would rather be angry at them. I fear that they will ignore me—I would rather ignore them. Although I enjoy risking these possibilities, I want, finally, to have them controlled as easily as one can control words. All it takes is a line of verse or a phrase as regular in scansion as "That he should weep for her" or "And spur my dull revenge."

Hamlet has been described as a "great neurotic," a term whose meaning I'm not sure of. I am sure, however, that Hamlet allows me a great counter-transference. And that is the secret of the greatness of this tragedy and, final-ly, of all great works of art: they permit us to become creators ourselves.

From *"Hamlet—My Greatest Creation." Journal of the American Academy of Psy-choanalysis* 3 (1975): 419-427.

Coppelia Kahn: Cultural and Political Criticism

In this brief passage, Coppelia Kahn draws our attention to the status of Hamlet's father as a cuckold (the victim of his wife's infidelity). Kahn suggests how this fact illuminates Hamlet's reaction.

The Ghost in *Hamlet* is so poignantly powerful in his injured majesty that it seems ungracious to remember that he is also a cuckold. He himself obliquely notes it when he calls Claudius "that incestuous, that adulterate beast," distinguishing incest, the fact of his brother's sexual liaison with Gertrude, from its timing, which made it adultery (I.v.42). Hamlet's awareness of this ignominious aspect of his father's grievance, though only indirectly revealed to us, shapes his attitude toward the great task of revenge by complicating his identification with his father.[1] A mighty wrong has been done to a noble king; as he is noble, so must his anger and his cause be great. But insofar as part of that wrong is cuckoldry, his nobility is diminished, his anger impotent, and his cause an embarrassment. Viewed in this context, Hamlet's well-known misogyny and preoccupation with Gertrude's faults are an outlet for the rage mingled with shame he feels at his father's situation. He must bury or disguise his awareness of it, because to admit it would damage severely his idealized image of that father. So long as he can blame a woman's frailty for the indignity his father suffers, as the conventions of cuckoldry enable him to do, that image can be saved. But at the same time, his concern with his mother's crime diverts him from revenge and inevitably reminds him of his father's weakness: King Hamlet, like the most ordinary cuckold, was hoodwinked by his own wife. Thus to the extent that Hamlet sees his father as a cuckold, his anxiety and propensity to delay revenge are increased by a paralyzing ambivalence.[2]

From Coppelia Kahn, *Man's Estate: Masculine Identity in Shakespeare.* Berkeley: University of California Press, 1981.

Elaine Showalter: Psychological and Feminist Criticism

The following passage by Elaine Showalter considers how Ophelia has been betrayed in various productions. Prior to 1960, Showalter says, Ophelia's psychology was usually seen in Freudian terms—that is, in part that her insanity, in other words, is the result of her female sexuality, as her rejection by Hamlet leads to hysteria. After 1960, Freud's model of female hysteria, as Showalter points out, has been replaced by a modern view of feminine madness rooted in

[1]Cf. Avi Erlich's interesting argument in *Hamlet's Absent Father* (Princeton: Princeton UP, 1978). He contends that Hamlet delays his revenge because he is waiting for his absent, ghostly father to prove his strength by returning to kill Claudius himself. The source of Hamlet's perception of his father as weak and absent, Erlich holds, is his unconscious fantasy that his father was castrated by Gertrude in a primal scene. I see evidence of a different kind of castration, in the fact rather than the fantasy of King Hamlet's cuckoldry. [Kahn's note.]

[2]Richard Flatter, in his *Hamlet's Father* (New Haven: Yale UP, 1949), argues that Hamlet's delay is largely caused by the Ghost's prohibition against harming his mother, for Hamlet cannot properly revenge his father's murder until he discovers whether his mother was complicit in it. Flatter dismisses the question of Gertrude's adultery, saying that it has been partly absolved by time and her subsequent marriage, and stresses the problem of her complicity. But he does show, in a penetrating analysis of the closet scene, how obsessed Hamlet is with the connection between the adultery and the murder, and how the purposes of the father, to conceal this connection, and of the son, to discover it, diverge. [Kahn's note.]

schizophrenia. Showalter mentions examples of this schizophrenic Ophelia on the stage, and then acknowledges that since the 1970s a feminist Ophelia has emerged, presenting the madwoman as a social protestor. The different performances of Ophelia, Showalter notes, reflect different attitudes "toward women and madness."

Since the 1960s, the Freudian representation of Ophelia has been supplemented by an antipsychiatry that represents Ophelia's madness in more contemporary terms. In contrast to the psychoanalytic representation of Ophelia's sexual unconscious that connected her essential femininity to Freud's essays on female sexuality and hysteria, her madness is now seen in medical and biochemical terms, as schizophrenia. This is so in part because the schizophrenic woman has become the cultural icon of dualistic femininity in the mid-twentieth century as the erotomaniac was in the seventeenth and the hysteric in the nineteenth. It might also be traced to the work of R. D. Laing on female schizophrenia in the 1960s. Laing argued that schizophrenia was an intelligible response to the experience of invalidation within the family network, especially to the conflicting emotional messages and mystifying double binds experienced by daughters. Ophelia, he noted in *The Divided Self,* is an empty space. "In her madness there is no one there. . . . There is no integral selfhood expressed through her actions or utterances. Incomprehensible statements are said by nothing. She has already died. There is now only a vacuum where there was once a person" (195n).

Despite his sympathy for Ophelia, Laing's readings silence her, equate her with "nothing," more completely than any since the Augustans; and they have been translated into performances which only make Ophelia a graphic study of mental pathology. The sickest Ophelias on the contemporary stage have been those in the productions of the pathologist-director Jonathan Miller. In 1974 at the Greenwich Theatre his Ophelia sucked her thumb; by 1981, at the Warehouse in London, she was played by an actress much taller and heavier than the Hamlet (perhaps punningly cast as the young actor Anton Lesser). She began the play with a set of nervous tics and tuggings of hair which by the mad scene had become a full set of schizophrenic routines—head banging, twitching, wincing, grimacing, and drooling.

But since the 1970s too we have had a feminist discourse which has offered a new perspective on Ophelia's madness as protest and rebellion. For many feminist theorists, the madwoman is a heroine, a powerful figure who rebels against the family and the social order; and the hysteric who refuses to speak the language of the patriarchal order, who speaks otherwise, is a sister. In terms of effect on the theater, the most radical application of these ideas was probably realized in Melissa Murray's agitprop play *Ophelia,* written in 1979 for the English women's theater group "Hormone Imbalance." In this blank-verse retelling of the Hamlet story, Ophelia becomes a lesbian and runs off with a woman servant to join a guerrilla commune.

While I've always regretted that I missed this production, I can't proclaim that this defiant ideological gesture, however effective politically or theatrically, is all that feminist criticism desires or all to which it should aspire. When feminist criticism chooses to deal with representation, rather

5

than with women's writing, it must aim for a maximum interdisciplinary contextualism, in which the complexity of attitudes toward the feminine can be analyzed in their fullest cultural and historical frame. The alternation of strong and weak Ophelias on the stage, virginal and seductive Ophelias in art, inadequate or oppressed Ophelias in criticism, tells us how these representations have overflowed the text and how they have reflected the ideological character of their times, erupting as debates between dominant and feminist views in periods of gender crisis and redefinition. The representation of Ophelia changes independently of theories of the meaning of the play or the Prince, for it depends on attitudes toward women and madness.

From Elaine Showalter, "Representing Ophelia: Women, Madness, and the Responsibilities of Feminist Criticism." In Patricia Parker and Geoffrey Hartman, eds. *Shakespeare and the Question of Theory.* London: Routledge, 1985, pp. 236-237.

Janet Adelman: Psychological and Feminist Criticism

In this excerpt, Janet Adelman looks at the character of Gertrude: should we see her as wicked or as confused? What is the meaning of her death? Adelman considers what her ambiguity means for Hamlet's fantasies and for the power of the play.

Given her centrality in the play, it is striking how little we know about Gertrude; even the extent of her involvement in the murder of her first husband is left unclear. We may want to hear her shock at Hamlet's accusation of murder—"Almost as bad, good mother, / As kill a king and marry with his brother" (3.4.28-29)—as evidence of her innocence; but the text permits us to hear it alternatively as shock either at being found out or at Hamlet's rudeness. The ghost accuses her at least indirectly of adultery and incest—Claudius is "that incestuous, that adulterate beast" (1.5.42)—but he neither accuses her of nor exonerates her from the murder. For the ghost, as for Hamlet, her chief crime is her uncontrolled sexuality; that is the object of their moral revulsion, a revulsion as intense as anything directed toward the murderer Claudius. But the Gertrude we see is not quite the Gertrude they see. And when we see her in herself, apart from their characterizations of her, we tend to see a woman more muddled than actively wicked; even her famous sensuality is less apparent than her conflicted solicitude both for her new husband and for her son. She is capable from the beginning of a certain guilty insight into Hamlet's suffering ("I doubt it is no other but the main, / His father's death and our o'er-hasty marriage" (2.2.56-57). Insofar as she follows Hamlet's instructions in reporting his madness to Claudius (3.4.189-90;4.1.7), she seems to enact every son's scenario for the good mother, choosing his interests over her husband's. But she may of course believe that he is mad and think that she is reporting accurately to her husband; certainly her courageous defense of her husband in their next appearance together—where she bodily restrains Laertes, as 4.5.122 specifies—suggests that she has not wholly adopted Hamlet's view of Claudius. Here, as elsewhere, the text leaves crucial aspects of her action and motivation open. Even her death is not quite her own to define. Is it a suicide designed to keep Hamlet from danger by dying in his place? (Gertrude drinks the cup knowingly in Olivier's film of *Hamlet.*) She knows that Claudius has prepared the cup for Hamlet, and she shows unusual determination in disobeying Claudius's command not to drink it ("Gertrude, do not drink. / I will, my lord" [5.2.294–95]). In her last moment, her thoughts seem to be all for Hamlet; she cannot spare Claudius even the attention it would take to blame him ("O my dear Hamlet! / The drink, the drink! I am poison'd" [5.2.315–16].) Muddled, fallible, fully human, she seems ultimately to make the choice that Hamlet would have her make. But even here she does not speak clearly; her character remains relatively closed to us.

The lack of clarity in our impressions of Gertrude contributes, I think, to the sense that the play lacks, in Eliot's famous phrase, an "objective correlative." For the character of Gertrude as we see it becomes for Hamlet—and for *Hamlet*—the ground for fantasies quite incongruent with it; although she is much less purely innocent than Richard III's mother, like that mother she becomes the carrier of a nightmare that is disjunct from her characterization as a specific figure. This disjunction is, I think, the key to her role in the play and hence to her psychic power: her frailty unleashes for Hamlet, and for Shakespeare, fantasies of maternal malevolence, of maternal spoiling, that are compelling exactly as they are out of proportion to the character we know, exactly as they seem therefore to reiterate infantile fears and desires rather than an adult apprehension of the mother as a separate person.

These fantasies begin to emerge as soon as Hamlet is left alone onstage:

> *O that this too too sullied flesh would melt,*
> *Thaw and resolve itself into a dew,*
> *Or that the Everlasting had not fix'd*
> *His canon 'gainst self-slaughter. O God! God!*
> *How weary, stale, flat, and unprofitable*
> *Seem to me all the uses of this world!*
> *Fie on't, ah fie, 'tis an unweeded garden*
> *That grows to seed; things rank and gross in nature*
> *Possess it merely. That it should come to this!*
> *But two months dead. . . .*   *(1.2.129–38)*

This soliloquy establishes the initial premises of the play, the psychic conditions that are present even before Hamlet has met with the ghost and has been assigned the insupportable task of vengeance. And what Hamlet tells us in his first words to us is that he feels his own flesh as sullied and wishes to free himself from its contamination by death, that the world has become as stale and unusable to him as his own body, and that he figures all this deadness and staleness and contamination in the image of an unweeded garden gone to seed—figures it, that is, in the familiar language of the fall. And he further tells us that this fall has been caused not by his father's death, as both Claudius and Gertrude seem to assume in their conventional consolations, but by his mother's remarriage, the "this" he cannot specify for fourteen lines, the "this" that looms over the soliloquy, not quite nameable and yet radically present, making his own flesh—"this. . . flesh"—dirty, disrupting his sense of the ongoing possibility of life even as it disrupts his syntax.

From Janet Adelman, "Man and Wife Is One Flesh': *Hamlet* and the Confrontation with the Maternal Body." From *Suffocating Mothers: Fantasies of Maternal Origin in Shakespeare's Plays.* New York: Routledge, 1992.

John Updike: Creative "Interpretation"

This excerpt is from John Updike's Gertrude and Claudius, *a compelling novel that tells the Hamlet story. Updike is richly imagining a conversation that does not occur in Shakespeare's play, as we see how Gertrude and Claudius come to be married only a month after her husband's death.*

The King was irate. "I com*mand* that he come back to Denmark!" Claudius announced to Gertrude. "His insolent self-exile mocks our court and undermines our fledgling rule. He stays away to do just that. Though we have named him the next to take the throne, our own seat thereupon having been, in part, compelled by his prolonged withdrawal from Denmark, and urged upon me by my colleagues on the *rad* and ratified by the *thing*, swiftly convened in Viborg—for all of this, he sulks in absentia and, when he does deign appear, seems skittish to the point of madness. So belatedly did he attend his father's funeral, and so readily leave once the great bones were interred, that his friend Horatio—a *cap*ital fellow, I've asked him to stay as long as he desires, and to give the crown his counsel at his pleasure—Horatio never had the chance to greet him! His best friend was ignored, and the populace could take no impression of an apparition so fleeting. Hamlet plays the ghost, a presence spun of rumor, to spite me, for the people have ever had him in their favor, and his absence at Elsinore purposely saps our reign of credibility!"

Gertrude was not yet accustomed to hearing her lover speak like this, at such length, with such pomp. Even in their privacy now he spoke as if there were others about them, courtiers and emissaries, the human furniture of rule. Two weeks had passed since her husband had perished in the orchard, unattended, unshriven, like some nameless pauper who eked his living on a Baltic beach, or like some soulless little rag of a woodland prey snatched up in sharp talons. Already Fengon, to her eye, had become bulkier, more majestic. He had named himself Claudius at the coronation, and Corambis, following his master into the imperial dignity of Latin, had taken the name of Polonius. "I think he means no harm to you or to Denmark," she began, half-heartedly defending her son.

"Denmark and I, my dear, are now synonymous."

"Of course—I think it's wonderful! But as to little Hamlet, there have been so many sudden changes, and he really did adore his father, though they weren't much alike, in subtlety or education. The boy needs time, and he feels at ease in Wittenberg, has companions there, and his professors—"

"Professors professing seditious doctrines—humanism, usury, market values, the monarchy as something less than the pure gift of God—the boy is thirty, it's time he came home to reality. Do you *really*," he went on, in a tyrannical accusatory vein that reminded her sadly of his predecessor on the throne, "think he *is* in Wittenberg? We have no idea if he is or not. 'Wittenberg' is just his word for 'elsewhere'—elsewhere than Elsinore!"

Gertrude blurted, "It's not you he's avoiding. It's me."

"You, his own mother? Why?"

"He hates me, for wishing his father dead."

The King blinked. "Did you?"

5

Her voice was thickening; the habit of tears had been reëstablished   10
in her eyes these two weeks, and now she felt them warmly gathering
once more. "My grief wasn't enough to suit him. I didn't want to die
myself—to throw myself on his father's pyre, so to speak, though of
course they don't have pyres any more, that was barbaric, these poor
drugged slave girls. . . . And I couldn't stop myself from thinking that
now there was no chance of Hamlet's, my husband Hamlet's, finding out
about *us*. I dreaded that, though I pretended not to, I didn't want to
worry *you*. I was re*lieved*. I hate myself, admitting it. Even dead, Hamlet
has a way of making me feel guilty, for being less good and public-spirited
than he was."

"Yes, well. I lived with that all my life—you just married into it."

"Now little Hamlet has it, that same gift. Of making me feel dirty and
ashamed and unworthy. I have a confession. No, it's too terrible to say." She
waited to be coaxed, then went on, uncoaxed. "All right, I'll *tell* you: I'm
glad the child isn't at Elsinore. He would sulk. He would try to make me feel
shallow, and stupid, and wicked."

"But how would he know. . . anything?"

How like a man, Gertrude thought. *They want you to do everything to them, but then are too fastidious to name it. Claudius just
wants things all to go smoothly, now that he is king, the past sealed
off, history. But history isn't dead like that; it lives in us, it got us here.*
"Children just *know*," she said. "We're all they have to study at first; they
become experts. He senses everything; I've terribly disappointed him. He
wanted me to *die*, to be the perfect stone statue of a widow, guarding the
shrine of his father for him forever, because it has his childhood sealed
up in it also. Adoring his father for him is a kind of self-adoration. They
were two of a kind—too good for this world. The night we were married, Hamlet didn't even look at me naked. He was too drunk. You, bless
you, *looked*."

His wolfish teeth showed a smile in the dark fleece of his beard, a flash   15
of white like the white spot in his hair. "No man could have helped looking,
my love. You were, are, sublime in every part."

"I'm a fat spoiled forty-eight-year-old, but being called sublime feels
somehow *right*. As a kind of *play*. Hamlet—big Hamlet—didn't know how
to *play*."

"He played only to win."

Gertrude suppressed the observation that Claudius, too, in his new
majesty, showed an inclination to win. But, then, having spent her life in the
company of kings, Gertrude knew that for a king losing usually meant losing your life. High position entailed a precipitous fall.

"I'm fond of him, actually," Claudius said. "Young Hamlet. I think I can
give him something he never had from his own father—he and I are fellow
victims of that obtuse bruiser—that Koll-killer. We're alike, your son and I.
His subtlety, which you mentioned, is much like my own. We both have a
shadow-side, and a yen to travel, to get away from this foggy hinterland,
where the sheep look like rocks and the rocks look like sheep. He wants
more, to learn more."

"I thought you said he doesn't really go to Wittenberg."   20

"He goes *somewhere*, and learns *something*, that gives him dissatisfaction. I tell you I *feel* for him. We're both victims of Danish small-mindedness—

Viking blood-hunger crammed into the outward forms of Christianity, which no one up here has ever understood, from Harald Bluetooth on; for him it was just a way to preëmpt a German invasion. Christianity turns grim in lands of frost; it is a Mediterranean cult, a religion of the grape. Truly, I am certain I can make the Prince love me. I appointed him my successor on my own impulse."

"He may resent that he remains a prince, while you occupy his father's throne."

"How could he resent that? He was never *here,* he showed no interest in learning the art of rule—of all that threatens and upholds a government. Some whisper," Claudius told Gertrude with lowered voice and subdued expression, "that he is mad."

She shivered. "He is sane, and shrewd," she said, "but still I cannot grieve on his absence. If he comes home, I sense that he will bring unhappiness."

"But come he must, lest a rebel faction form outside Elsinore's walls, and here is the scheme to bring him: marry me."   25

Her impulse was to greet his words with joy; but these disrupted times shaded their import somberly, and like little weights they took her heart lower. "My husband, your brother, is but two weeks dead."

"Another two, and it will be a month—lag enough for such seasoned meat as we. Gertrude, don't deny me the natural outcome of my long and perilous devotion. Our present situation, scattered awkwardly through Elsinore's royal apartments, is too curious; we must sneak and tryst as if your husband's ghost keeps jealous guard over your virtue. Our union will settle all jangling gossip and give Elsinore a solid base—a master and a mistress." *And cement my hold on the throne,* Claudius did not say.

"I doubt it will settle Hamlet," said the Queen. The name's persistent doubleness—father, son; king, prince—brought a lump to her throat, as if it were too large to swallow.

"I wager the contrary," said Claudius, bluff and headlong in his decisions as kings must be. "It will restore his mother to the highest status, and supply an uncle in place of a father. Our wedded example will strengthen and steady his courtship of Ophelia, which you and Polonius both desire—you for the sake of your son's health and sanity, he to gain his daughter high estate. I do not begrudge the old man that boon of perpetuation; he served our own wooing well."

His speaking brusquely of their "wooing" touched a sensitive area in   30
Gertrude. Though she had been bold and brazen enough in placing herself at a lover's disposal while still wedded to the King, when the ruthless irregularity of her behavior could be lightly scanned by her conscience as the enactment of a romance such as had beguiled her betranced days of married boredom, her escapade took on a live soreness since the King's death: she felt her fall had somehow caused the adder in the orchard to sting the sleeping cuckold. At the same time, Sandro had disappeared, and she wondered if there was a reason she didn't know. Claudius, questioned, had said the boy had become homesick with winter's onset, so he had let him go south, with a tolerant bonus. It was strange this had been done so suddenly, without her knowing. Claudius in his old guise had spoken to her with the careless freedom of one with nothing to hide; now there was a certain formality, a pregnant circumspection. Yes, it would be good to bundle and hide the whole affair—the lakeside lodge, the small troop

enlisted in their deceit, the hectic gratification of belonging to two men at once, the pagan shamelessness—within the unimpeachable, unbreakable contract of a royal marriage. Blushing as if once again garlanded in virginity, Gertrude consented.

Claudius clapped his hands: a politic and lucrative bargain had been struck. The date was set. Messengers—to Wittenberg, to Laertes in Paris, to the capitals of friendly powers—were sent posting on their way. Even with so muted a celebration in prospect, a marriage draped in mourning, Gertrude found these narrowing November days brightened. What we once did imperfectly, we yearn to perfect in the second doing.

From John Updike, *Claudius and Gertrude*. New York: Knopf, 2000, pp. 163–169.

Suggestions for Writing

1. It's often useful to say in your own words what you think a particular critical passage is saying, being sure to refer specifically to what the critic says, quoting enough to support your interpretation.
2. Once you are familiar with a critical argument, you might want to identify the critical approach (or approaches) being employed in one or more of the critical excerpts provided. Support your characterization with specific support from the text, explaining what a particular critic says and how he or she manages to say it. Include your own assessment of how persuasive and effective you consider the critic's argument to be.
3. Agree or disagree (or both) with one of the critical excerpts.
4. Look very closely at a passage from the play: as the large body of criticism on *Hamlet* demonstrates, interesting things can be said about virtually any aspect of the play. Then attempt a reading of the passage, employing one of the critical stances discussed in this book (or some other). If you find yourself with little to say, try another passage. Eventually you'll hit on a passage (or grouping of passages) that you'll have something to say about.
5. Compare a scene from two different versions of the play, or compare one film version to your own imagined staging of the scene.
6. If you had to select one or two lines as the real heart of the play, its essence in a sense, what line or lines would you pick? Support your selection by linking it to other passages in the play.

A Midsummer Night's Dream

Reading Shakespeare attentively, you're bound to enlarge your vocabulary and sensitivity to language. Shakespeare's verbal dexterity is astonishing. You also can't avoid thinking about human nature: Shakespeare is clearly fascinated by the problem of motivation—why people do and don't do certain things, how we control and don't control our desires. You'll surely learn something about Elizabethan England and perhaps other historical periods as well. Toward these ends and others, *Midsummer Night's Dream (MSD)* seems an attractive choice to expand your engagement with Shakespeare.

For starters, *MSD* has played a key role in the expanding awareness of critical strategies in the past thirty years or so. As Gary Jay Williams put it recently, "the play has been extraordinarily responsive in the theatre to the cultural energies in every era" (*Our Moonlight Revels*, p. xi). The play's use of dreams, and dreams within dreams, and plays within the play, encourages psychological approaches that high-light the shifting natures of illusion and reality, of conscious and unconscious mind. Recent fiction and film have been particularly concerned with these perennial issues, with movies like *The Matrix* and *The Truman Show* exposing the potential-ly illusive nature of reality. The importance of the "rude mechanicals" in the play unavoidably raises issues of class and economy, as Bottom and his friends are han-dled both satirically and affectionately. Cultural materialist, Marxist, and new histori-cist readings of the play have stimulated discussion, and oftentimes helped focus feminist criticism, which would seem to be shooting fish in a barrel in a play in which a father invokes a law allowing him to choose his daughter's husband—or command her death.

Yet the play's sexual issues are more complex than they might seem at first glance, and gay, lesbian, and queer approaches have insisted, to the discomfort of some, that we cannot ignore Oberon's obsessive desire for the young Indian boy in Titania's possession any more than we can ignore the intense relationship that Tita-nia invokes with the boy's mother. Many productions in the past forty years or so, particularly in the 1960s and 1970s, have emphasized the play's potential for sexual promiscuity and perversity, with the four lovers interchanging partners (what hap-pens in the woods?) and Titania enjoying man-ass Bottom, whose name suggests a lot. A play that is so self-consciously involved with play-making invites deconstruc-tive interest, which has revealed a swirling number of binary oppositions that are challenged and called into question—good and evil, law and desire, husband and wife, noble and commoner, and so forth. These tensions have even continued to be resolved in interesting uses of traditional close reading, or New Criticism. Since a main tenet of this textbook is that readers at all levels need (and are able) to control a variety of critical strategies, it seems reasonable to select a play that has responded already to a wide variety of approaches.

This diverse critical attention has resulted, fortunately, in some brilliant literary criticism—which is another reason to choose *MSD,* as these focus chapters are designed to bring together comprehensible and complementary excerpts from diverse critical sources.

Yet another reason to choose *MSD* is simply this: it's the most important, best Shakespearean play that most students are unlikely to have read. You've probably read at least one tragedy (most likely *Hamlet* or *Romeo and Juliet,* but perhaps *Othello,* or *Macbeth,* or even possibly *King Lear*). The comedies and romances typically get less attention, and we might argue that they deserve more. One interesting indication of this view, and of the perceived importance of *MSD,* is the adoption of this play, and only two others, by the English National Curriculum in Great Britain in the 1990s. Stu-dents who are thinking of pursuing English studies in Great Britain, in other words, are required to read *MSD.* Rereading Shakespeare, I want to reassure you, is even more rewarding than reading him. So, if this is your first time through *MSD,* don't let it be your last. Toward that non-end, lets consider a few more suggestions.

Your Shakespeare

The first suggestion is this: see some version of the play on video, if you can—until you can get to a live production. Watching more than one version would be espe-cially desirable, and enjoyable too since there are so many excellent and strikingly different productions available on video. Readily available videos include a luxuri-ously dreamy, briskly comic 1999 version starring Kevin Kline and Michelle Pfeiffer, directed by Michael Hoffman; a classic 1935 film, star-studded with James Cagney,

Dick Powell, Mickey Rooney (as Puck), directed by Max Reinhardt and William Dieterle, which is amusing in part because of its cultural distance; and the Royal Shakespeare Company's fantastical and romantic 1996 version, directed by Adrian Noble. If you're reading or viewing the play on video for the first time, you'll likely be tempted to stop and reread or replay some scenes. First, read the play straight through—experience the story as a whole rather than try to make sense of every detail and, as a result, lose sight of the bigger picture. On subsequent readings and viewings, you can concentrate on particular scenes.

To better enjoy the play as a whole, you may find it helpful to have a sense of the story. If you'd rather be surprised, and encounter the plot as it unfolds, then please skip over the next few paragraphs.

Act 1, scene 1.   Theseus, the ruler of Athens, has conquered the Amazons and captured Hippolyta, whom he plans to marry in four days. They meet four people: Egeus, father of Hermia, who loves Lysander; and Demetrius, who loves Hermia, and has been chosen by Egeus to be her husband. According to Athenian law, which Theseus explains, Hermia must accept her father's choice, Demetrius. If she doesn't, then she must become a nun or be put to death. The Duke gives her until the night before his own wedding to decide. Given this choice, Hermia and Lysander decide to run away together. They tell their plan to Helena, who loves Demetrius, who formerly loved her. With questionable logic, Helena decides to tell Demetrius that Hermia is running away, hoping that he will appreciate her loyalty to him. Helena plans to follow Demetrius into the woods.

The relationships will be clearer as you see or read the play, but here's the love triangle, or rectangle, once more: Hermia loves Lysander; Lysander loves Hermia; Demetrius loves Hermia, but used to love Helena; Helena loves Demetrius. Egeus insists that Hermia marry Demetrius, even though she loves Lysander.

Act 1, scene 2.   The working-class characters, who generate most of the play's comedy, are planning to perform a play to entertain Theseus and Hippolyta. Peter Quince is their leader; Bottom is the most theatrical and absurd; Flute, Snout, Starveling, and Snug complete the troupe. They plan to meet the next night in the woods to rehearse without distractions.

Act 2, scene 1.   In the woods outside Athens, we learn that Oberon (king of the fairies) dearly wants Titania (his queen) to give him an Indian boy. Titania, who loved the boy's mother, refuses. Oberon sends Puck in search of a magic flower; he plans to charm Titania into giving him the boy.

Helena has indeed told Demetrius, and when he comes on stage he is looking for Hermia and Lysander; he is himself being pursued by Helena. Oberon, pitying Helena, instructs Puck to use the flower's magical juice to make Demetrius love Helena, while Oberon himself goes to charm Titania.

Act 2, scene 2.   After Oberon bewitches Titania (she will fall in love with the next creature she sees), Puck bewitches the sleeping Lysander, thinking he is Demetrius. Helena awakens Lysander, and the magic potion causes him to love Helena most passionately (Hermia is now dogmeat, as far as he's concerned). Helena thinks he's making fun of her. When Hermia awakens and finds herself alone, she goes in search of Lysander. At this point, things are pretty messed up: Helena loves Demetrius, who loves Hermia; Hermia loves Lysander, who now loves Helena; Lysander loves Helena, who loves Demetrius; Demetrius loves Hermia, who loves Lysander. But wait!

Act 3, scene 1.   Puck sees the workmen rehearsing their ridiculous play, and he transforms Bottom into an ass, just for fun. Bottom of course awakens Titania, who falls immediately in love with the grotesque Bottom, and she has her fairies carry him to her bower, where she can enjoy him.

Act 3, scene 2.   Oberon and Puck observe the effects of the botched charming: now both men, Lysander and Demetrius, love Helena, who thinks they are making fun of her; and Hermia comes to think her friend has stolen her love, and turns on her. Lysander and Demetrius charge off to find a place to fight, and Helena runs away from the enraged Hermia. Puck, amused by this confusion, is ordered by Oberon to keep the humans from hurting each other, and to redo the charm so that Lysander once again loves Hermia.

Act 4, scene 1.   Oberon reveals that he now has the boy he wanted from Titania, and he releases her from the spell. Titania is of course horrified to find herself in the arms of an ass (named Bottom), and she and Oberon leave together, after Puck removes the ass's head from Bottom. The human lovers awaken, with Lysander and Hermia, and Demetrius and Helena, happily paired up.

Act 4, scene 2.   Bottom sends the cast to practice; their play has been selected for performance.

Act 5.   Theseus and Hippolyta and their court watch the workers mangle the tragic story of Pyramus and Thisbe. After the play, the fairies bless all three marriages, and Puck asks for the audience's good will.

Finally, if you're curious about the play's initial production, you're not alone. We simply don't know when and where *MSD* was first acted, although scholars are pretty sure it was written about the same time as *Romeo and Juliet*, about 1595 or 1596. It may have been to honor a wedding; Queen Elizabeth may have been in the initial audience (there are lines that seem to allude to her); but really no one knows.

WILLIAM SHAKESPEARE (1564–1616)

A Midsummer Night's Dream

[Dramatis Personae

Theseus, Duke of Athens
Hippolyta, Queen of the Amazons, betrothed to Theseus
Philostrate, Master of the Revels
Egeus, father of Hermia

Hermia, daughter of Egeus, in love with Lysander
Lysander, in love with Hermia
Demetrius, in love with Hermia and favored by Egeus
Helena, in love with Demetrius

NOTE ON THE TEXT: This text of *A Midsummer Night's Dream* is taken from the First Quarto of 1600. Edited by David Bevington.

Oberon, King of the Fairies
Titania, Queen of the Fairies
Puck, or Robin Goodfellow
Peaseblossom,
Cobweb,
Mote,   } *fairies attending Titania*
Mustardseed,
Other fairies attending

Peter Quince, a carpenter,   *Prologue*
Nick Bottom, a weaver,   *Pyramus*
Francis Flute, a bellows mender,   *representing*   *Thisbe*
Tom Snout, a tinker,   } *representing*   *Wall*
Snug, a joiner,   *Lion*
Robin Starveling, a tailor,   *Moonshine*
Lords and *Attendants* on *Theseus* and *Hippolyta*

Scene: *Athens, and a wood near it]*

Act I

Scene I [Athens. Theseus' Court.]

> *Enter Theseus, Hippolyta, [and Philostrate,] with others.*

Theseus: Now, fair Hippolyta, our nuptial hour
　　　Draws on apace. Four happy days bring in
　　　Another moon; but, O, methinks, how slow
　　　This old moon wanes! She lingers* my desires,
　　　Like to a stepdame* or a dowager*   5
　　　Long withering out* a young man's revenue.
Hippolyta: Four days will quickly steep themselves* in night;
　　　Four nights will quickly dream away the time;
　　　And then the moon, like to a silver bow
　　　New bent in heaven, shall behold the night   10
　　　Of our solemnities.*
Theseus:　　　　　　　　Go, Philostrate,
　　　Stir up the Athenian youth to merriments.
　　　Awake the pert and nimble spirit of mirth.
　　　Turn melancholy forth to funerals;
　　　The pale companion* is not for our pomp.*   [*Exit Philostrate.*]   15
　　　Hippolyta, I wooed thee with my sword*
　　　And won thy love doing thee injuries;
　　　But I will wed thee in another key,
　　　With pomp, with triumph,* and with reveling.

---

4 *lingers* postpones, delays the fulfillment of   5 *stepdame* stepmother.   a *dowager* i.e., a widow
(whose right of inheritance from her dead husband is eating into her son's estate)   6 *withering out*
causing to dwindle   7 *steep themselves* saturate themselves, be absorbed in   11 *solemnities* festive
ceremonies of marriage   15 *companion* fellow.   *pomp* ceremonial magnificence   16 *with my*
sword i.e., in a military engagement against the Amazons, when Hippolyta was taken captive
19 *triumph* public festivity

Theseus's impressive palace in the 1900 production in London, directed by
Sir Herbert Beerbohm Tree, helped no doubt to underscore the contrast
between the legal authority exerted within the city and the carnival trangres-
sions in the woods.

Enter Egeus and his daughter Hermia, and Lysander, and Demetrius.

Egeus: Happy be Theseus, our renownèd duke!   20
Theseus: Thanks, good Egeus. What's the news with thee?
Egeus: Full of vexation come I, with complaint
    Against my child, my daughter Hermia.—
    Stand forth, Demetrius.—My noble lord,
    This man hath my consent to marry her.—   25
    Stand forth, Lysander.—And, my gracious Duke,
    This man hath bewitched the bosom of my child.
    Thou, thou Lysander, thou hast given her rhymes
    And interchanged love tokens with my child.
    Thou hast by moonlight at her window sung   30

With feigning* voice verses of feigning* love,
And stol'n the impression of her fantasy*
With bracelets of thy hair, rings, gauds,* conceits,*
Knacks,* trifles, nosegays, sweetmeats—messengers
Of strong prevailment in* unhardened youth.   35
With cunning hast thou filched my daughter's heart,
Turned her obedience, which is due to me,
To stubborn harshness. And, my gracious Duke,
Be it so* she will not here before Your Grace
Consent to marry with Demetrius,   40
I beg the ancient privilege of Athens:
As she is mine, I may dispose of her,
Which shall be either to this gentleman
Or to her death, according to our law
Immediately* provided in that case.   45
Theseus: What say you, Hermia? Be advised, fair maid.
To you your father should be as a god—
One that composed your beauties, yea, and one
To whom you are but as a form in wax
By him imprinted, and within his power   50
To leave* the figure or disfigure* it.
Demetrius is a worthy gentleman.
Hermia: So is Lysander.
Theseus: In himself he is;
But in this kind,* wanting* your father's voice,*
The other must be held the worthier.   55
Hermia: I would my father looked but with my eyes.
Theseus: Rather your eyes must with his judgment look.
Hermia: I do entreat Your Grace to pardon me.
I know not by what power I am made bold,
Nor how it may concern* my modesty   60
In such a presence here to plead my thoughts;
But I beseech Your Grace that I may know
The worst that may befall me in this case
If I refuse to wed Demetrius.
Theseus: Either to die the death* or to abjure   65
Forever the society of men.
Therefore, fair Hermia, question your desires,
Know of your youth, examine well your blood,*
Whether, if you yield not to your father's choice,
You can endure the livery* of a nun,   70
For aye* to be in shady cloister mewed,
To live a barren sister all your life,

---

31 *feigning* (1) counterfeiting (2) faining, desirous   32 *And . . . fantasy* and made her fall in love
with you (imprinting your image on her imagination) by stealthy and dishonest means   33 *gauds*
playthings.   *conceits* fanciful trifles   34 *Knacks* knickknacks   35 *prevailment in* influence on
39 *Be it so* if   45 *Immediately* directly, with nothing intervening   51 *leave* i.e., leave unaltered.
disfigure obliterate   54 *kind* respect. *wanting* lacking. *voice* approval   60 *concern* befit   65 *die
the death* be executed by legal process   68 *blood* passions   70 *livery* habit, costume   71 *aye* ever.
mewed shut in. (Said of a hawk, poultry, etc.)

Chanting faint hymns to the cold fruitless moon.
Thrice blessèd they that master so their blood
To undergo such maiden pilgrimage;
But earthlier happy* is the rose distilled*   75
Than that which, withering on the virgin thorn,
Grows, lives, and dies in single blessedness.

Hermia: So will I grow, so live, so die, my lord,
Ere I will yield my virgin patent* up   80
Unto his lordship, whose unwishèd yoke
My soul consents not to give sovereignty.

Theseus: Take time to pause, and by the next new moon—
The sealing day betwixt my love and me
For everlasting bond of fellowship—   85
Upon that day either prepare to die
For disobedience to your father's will,
Or* else to wed Demetrius, as he would,
Or on Diana's altar to protest*
For aye austerity and single life.   90

Demetrius: Relent, sweet Hermia, and, Lysander, yield
Thy crazèd* title to my certain right.

Lysander: You have her father's love, Demetrius;
Let me have Hermia's. Do you marry him.

Egeus: Scornful Lysander! True, he hath my love,   95
And what is mine my love shall render him.
And she is mine, and all my right of her
I do estate unto* Demetrius:

Lysander: I am, my lord, as well derived* as he,
As well possessed;* my love is more than his;   100
My fortunes every way as fairly* ranked,
If not with vantage,* as Demetrius';
And, which is more than all these boasts can be,
I am beloved of beauteous Hermia.
Why should not I then prosecute my right?   105
Demetrius, I'll avouch it to his head,*
Made love to Nedar's daughter, Helena,
And won her soul; and she, sweet lady, dotes,
Devoutly dotes, dotes in idolatry
Upon this spotted* and inconstant man.   110

Theseus: I must confess that I have heard so much,
And with Demetrius thought to have spoke thereof;
But, being overfull of self-affairs,*
My mind did lose it. But, Demetrius, come,
And come, Egeus, you shall go with me;   115
I have some private schooling* for you both.

---

76 *earthlier happy* happier as respects this world. *distilled* i.e., to make perfume   80 *patent* privilege   88 *Or* either   89 *protest* vow   92 *crazèd* cracked, unsound   98 *estate unto* settle or bestow upon   99 *as well derived* as well born and descended   100 *possessed* endowed with wealth   101 *fairly* handsomely   102 *vantage* superiority   106 *head* i.e., face   110 *spotted* i.e., morally stained   113 *self-affairs* my own concerns   116 *schooling* admonition

For you, fair Hermia, look you arm* yourself
To fit your fancies* to your father's will,
Or else the law of Athens yields you up—
Which by no means we may extenuate*—   120
To death or to a vow of single life.
Come, my Hippolyta. What cheer, my love?
Demetrius and Egeus, go* along.
I must employ you in some business
Against* our nuptial, and confer with you   125
Of something nearly that* concerns yourselves.

Egeus: With duty and desire we follow you.

Exeunt [all but Lysander and Hermia].

Lysander: How now, my love, why is your cheek so pale?
How chance the roses there do fade so fast?
Hermia: Belike* for want of rain, which I could well   130
Beteem* them from the tempest of my eyes.
Lysander: Ay me! For aught that I could ever read,
Could ever hear by tale or history,
The course of true love never did run smooth;
But either it was different in blood*—   135
Hermia: O cross!* Too high to be enthralled to low.
Lysander: Or else misgrafted* in respect of years—
Hermia: O spite! Too old to be engaged to young.
Lysander: Or else it stood upon the choice of friends*—
Hermia: O hell, to choose love by another's eyes!   140
Lysander: Or if there were a sympathy* in choice,
War, death, or sickness did lay siege to it,
Making it momentany* as a sound,
Swift as a shadow, short as any dream,
Brief as the lightning in the collied* night   145
That in a spleen* unfolds* both heaven and earth,
And ere a man hath power to say "Behold!"
The jaws of darkness do devour it up.
So quick* bright things come to confusion.*   150
Hermia: If then true lovers have been ever crossed,*
It stands as an edict in destiny.
Then let us teach our trial patience,*
Because it is a customary cross,
As due to love as thoughts, and dreams, and sighs,
Wishes, and tears, poor fancy's* followers.   155
Lysander: A good persuasion.* Therefore, hear me, Hermia:

117 *look you arm* take care you prepare   118 *fancies* likings, thoughts of love   120 *extenuate*
mitigate, relax   123 *go* i.e., come   125 *Against* in preparation for   126 *nearly that* that closely
130 *Belike* very likely   131 *Beteem* grant, afford   *blood* hereditary station   136 *cross* vexation
137 *misgrafted* ill grafted, badly matched   139 *friends* relatives   141 *sympathy* agreement
143 *momentany* lasting but a moment   145 *collied* blackened (as with coal dust), darkened
146 *in a spleen* in a swift impulse, in a violent flash. *unfolds* reveals   149 *quick* quickly; also,
living, alive. *confusion* ruin   150 *ever crossed* always thwarted   152 *teach . . . patience* i.e.,
teach ourselves patience in this trial   155 *fancy's* amorous passion's   156 *persuasion* doctrine

I have a widow aunt, a dowager
Of great revenue, and she hath no child.
From Athens is her house remote seven leagues;
And she respects* me as her only son.   160
There, gentle Hermia, may I marry thee,
And to that place the sharp Athenian law
Cannot pursue us. If thou lovest me, then,
Steal forth thy father's house tomorrow night;
And in the wood, a league without* the town,   165
Where I did meet thee once with Helena
To do observance to a morn of May,*
There will I stay for thee.

Hermia: My good Lysander!
I swear to thee by Cupid's strongest bow,
By his best arrow* with the golden head,   170
By the simplicity* of Venus' doves,*
By that which knitteth souls and prospers loves,
And by that fire which burned the Carthage queen*
When the false Trojan* under sail was seen,
By all the vows that ever men have broke,   175
In number more than ever women spoke,
In that same place thou hast appointed me
Tomorrow truly will I meet with thee.

Lysander: Keep promise, love. Look, here comes Helena.

Enter Helena.

Hermia: God speed, fair* Helena! Whither away?   180
Helena: Call you me fair? That "fair" again unsay.
Demetrius loves your fair.* O happy fair!*
Your eyes are lodestars,* and your tongue's sweet air*
More tunable* than lark to shepherd's ear
When wheat is green, when hawthorn buds appear.   185
Sickness is catching. O, were favor* so,
Yours would I catch, fair Hermia, ere I go;
My ear should catch your voice, my eye your eye,
My tongue should catch your tongue's sweet melody.
Were the world mine, Demetrius being bated,*   190
The rest I'd give to be to you translated.*
O, teach me how you look and with what art
You sway* the motion* of Demetrius' heart.
Hermia: I frown upon him, yet he loves me still.
Helena: O, that your frowns would teach my smiles such skill!   195

160 *respects* regards   165 *without* outside   167 *do . . . May* perform the ceremonies of May Day
170 *best arrow* (Cupid's best gold-pointed arrows were supposed to induce love; his blunt leaden
arrows, aversion.)   171 *simplicity* innocence. *doves* i.e., those that drew Venus' chariot
173, 174 *Carthage queen, false Trojan* (Dido, Queen of Carthage, immolated herself on a funeral
pyre after having been deserted by the Trojan hero Aeneas.)   180 *fair* fair-complexioned
(generally regarded by the Elizabethans as more beautiful than a dark complexion)   182 *your fair*
your beauty (even though Hermia is dark-complexioned). *happy fair* lucky fair one   183 *lodestars*
guiding stars. *air* music   184 *tunable* tuneful, melodious   186 *favor* appearance, looks
190 *bated* excepted   191 *translated* transformed   193 *sway* control. *motion* impulse

Hermia: I give him curses, yet he gives me love.
Helena: O, that my prayers could such affection* move!*
Hermia: The more I hate, the more he follows me.
Helena: The more I love, the more he hateth me.
Hermia: His folly, Helena, is no fault of mine.   200
Helena: None, but your beauty. Would that fault were mine!
Hermia: Take comfort. He no more shall see my face.
    Lysander and myself will fly this place.
    Before the time I did Lysander see
    Seemed Athens as a paradise to me.*   205
    O, then, what graces in my love do dwell,
    That he hath turned a heaven unto a hell?
Lysander: Helen, to you our minds we will unfold.
    Tomorrow night, when Phoebe* doth behold
    Her silver visage in the watery glass,*   210
    Decking with liquid pearl the bladed grass,
    A time that lovers' flights doth still* conceal,
    Through Athens' gates have we devised to steal.
Hermia: And in the wood, where often you and I
    Upon faint* primrose beds were wont to lie,   215
    Emptying our bosoms of their counsel* sweet,
    There my Lysander and myself shall meet,
    And thence from Athens turn away our eyes
    To seek new friends and stranger companies.*
    Farewell, sweet playfellow. Pray thou for us,   220
    And good luck grant thee thy Demetrius!
    Keep word, Lysander: We must starve our sight
    From lovers' food till morrow deep midnight.
Lysander: I will, my Hermia. (*Exit Hermia.*) Helena, adieu.
    As you on him, Demetrius dote on you!   225

                           Exit Lysander.

Helena: How happy some o'er other some can be!*
    Through Athens I am thought as fair as she.
    But what of that? Demetrius thinks not so;
    He will not know what all but he do know.
    And as he errs, doting on Hermia's eyes,   230
    So I, admiring of* his qualities.
    Things base and vile, holding no quantity,*
    Love can transpose to form and dignity.
    Love looks not with the eyes, but with the mind,
    And therefore is winged Cupid painted blind.   235
    Nor hath Love's mind of any judgment taste;*

197 *affection* passion. *move* arouse   204–205 *Before . . . to me* (Hermia seemingly means that love
has led to complications and jealousies, making Athens hell for her.)   209 *Phoebe* Diana, the
moon   210 *glass* mirror   212 *still* always   215 *faint* pale   216 *counsel* secret thought
219 *stranger companies* the company of strangers   226 *o'er . . . can be* can be in comparison to
some others   231 *admiring of* wondering at   232 *holding no quantity* i.e., unsubstantial,
unshapely   236 *Nor . . . taste* i.e., nor has Love, which dwells in the fancy or imagination, any
taste or least bit of judgment or reason

Wings and no eyes figure* unheedy haste.
And therefore is Love said to be a child,
Because in choice* he is so oft beguiled.*
As waggish* boys in game* themselves forswear,   240
So the boy Love is perjured everywhere.
For ere Demetrius looked on Hermia's eyne,*
He hailed down oaths that he was only mine;
And when this hail some heat from Hermia felt,
So he dissolved, and showers of oaths did melt.   245
I will go tell him of fair Hermia's flight.
Then to the wood will he tomorrow night
Pursue her; and for this intelligence*
If I have thanks, it is a dear expense.*
But herein mean I to enrich my pain,   250
To have his sight thither and back again.

Exit.

Scene II [Athens.]

Enter Quince the carpenter, and Snug the joiner, and Bottom the weaver, and Flute the bellows mender, and Snout the tinker, and Starveling the tailor.

Quince: Is all our company here?

Bottom: You were best to call them generally,* man by man, according to the scrip*.

Quince: Here is the scroll of every man's name which is thought fit, through all Athens, to play in our interlude* before the Duke and the Duchess on his wedding day at night.   5

Bottom: First, good Peter Quince, say what the play treats on, then read the names of the actors, and so grow to* a point.

Quince: Marry,* our play is "The most lamentable comedy and most cruel death of Pyramus and Thisbe."

Bottom: A very good piece of work, I assure you, and a merry. Now, good Peter   10
Quince, call forth your actors by the scroll. Masters, spread yourselves.

Quince: Answer as I call you. Nick Bottom,* the weaver.

Bottom: Ready. Name what part I am for, and proceed.

Quince: You, Nick Bottom, are set down for Pyramus.

Bottom: What is Pyramus? A lover or a tyrant?   15

Quince: A lover, that kills himself most gallant for love.

Bottom: That will ask some tears in the true performing of it. If I do it, let the audience look to their eyes. I will move storms; I will condole* in

---

237 *figure* are a symbol of   239 *in choice* in choosing. *beguiled* self-deluded, making unaccountable choices   240 *waggish* playful, mischievous. *game* sport, jest   242 *eyne* eyes. (Old form of plural.)   248 *intelligence* information   249 *a dear expense* i.e., a trouble worth taking on my part, or a begrudging effort on his part. *dear* costly   2 *generally* (Bottom's blunder for "individually.").   *scrip* scrap (Bottom's error for "script.")   4 *interlude* play   7 *grow* to come to   8 *Marry* (A mild oath; originally the name of the Virgin Mary.)   12 *Bottom* (As a weaver's term, a *bottom* was an object around which thread was wound.)   18 *condole* lament, arouse pity

some measure. To the rest—yet my chief humor* is for a tyrant. I could
play Ercles* rarely, or a part to tear a cat* in, to make all split*.   20

> "The raging rocks
> And shivering shocks
> Shall break the locks
>   Of prison gates;
> And Phibbus' car*   25
> Shall shine from far
> And make and mar
>   The foolish Fates."

This was lofty! Now name the rest of the players. This is Ercles' vein, a
tyrant's vein. A lover is more condoling.   30

Quince: Francis Flute, the bellows mender.

Flute: Here, Peter Quince.

Quince: Flute, you must take Thisbe on you.

Flute: What is Thisbe? A wandering knight?

Quince: It is the lady that Pyramus must love.   35

Flute: Nay, faith, let not me play a woman. I have a beard coming.

Quince: That's all one.* You shall play it in a mask, and you may speak as small*
as you will.

Bottom: An* I may hide my face, let me play Thisbe too. I'll speak in a monstrous little voice, "Thisne, Thisne!" "Ah Pyramus, my lover dear! Thy   40
Thisbe dear, and lady dear!"

Quince: No, no, you must play Pyramus, and Flute, you Thisbe.

Bottom: Well, proceed.

Quince: Robin Starveling, the tailor.

Starveling: Here, Peter Quince.   45

Quince: Robin Starveling, you must play Thisbe's mother. Tom Snout, the
tinker.

Snout: Here, Peter Quince.

Quince: You, Pyramus' father; myself, Thisbe's father; Snug, the joiner, you,
the lion's part, and I hope here is a play fitted.   50

Snug: Have you the lion's part written? Pray you, if it be, give it me, for I am
slow of study.

Quince: You may do it extempore, for it is nothing but roaring.

Bottom: Let me play the lion too. I will roar that I will do any man's heart
good to hear me. I will roar that I will make the Duke say, "Let him roar   55
again, let him roar again."

Quince: An you should do it too terribly, you would fright the Duchess and
the ladies, that they would shriek; and that were enough to hang us all.

All: That would hang us, every mother's son.

Bottom: I grant you, friends, if you should fright the ladies out of their wits, 60
they would have no more discretion but to hang us; but I will aggravate*
my voice so that I will roar you* as gently as any sucking dove;* I will
roar you an 'twere* any nightingale.

---

19 *humor* inclination, whim.   *Ercles* Hercules (The tradition of ranting came from Seneca's
Hercules Furens.)   20 *tear a cat* i.e., rant. *make all split* i.e., cause a stir, bring the house down
25 *Phibbus' car* Phoebus', the sun god's, chariot   37 *That's all one* it makes no difference. *small*
high-pitched   39 *An* if. (also at line 57)   61 *aggravate* (Bottom's blunder for "moderate.")
62 *roar you* i.e., roar for you. *sucking dove* (Bottom conflates *sitting dove* and *sucking lamb*, two
proverbial images of innocence.)   63 *an 'twere* as if it were

Quince: You can play no part but Pyramus; for Pyramus is a sweet-faced man,
a proper* man as one shall see in a summer's day, a most lovely gentle-   65
manlike man. Therefore you must needs play Pyramus.

Bottom: Well, I will undertake it. What beard were I best to play it in?

Quince: Why, what you will.

Bottom: I will discharge* it in either your* straw-color beard, your orange-
tawny beard, your purple-in-grain* beard, or your French-crown-color*   70
beard, your perfect yellow.

Quince: Some of your French crowns* have no hair at all, and then you will play
barefaced. But, masters, here are your parts. [*He distributes parts.*] And I
am to entreat you, request you, and desire you to con* them by tomorrow
night, and meet me in the palace wood, a mile without the town, by moon-   75
light. There will we rehearse; for if we meet in the city, we shall be dogged
with company, and our devices* known. In the meantime I will draw a bill*
of properties, such as our play wants. I pray you, fail me not.

Bottom: We will meet, and there we may rehearse most obscenely* and
courageously. Take pains, be perfect.* Adieu.   80

Quince: At the Duke's oak we meet.

Bottom: Enough. Hold, or cut bowstrings.*   *Exeunt.*

Act II

Scene I [A Wood Near Athens.]

Enter a Fairy at one door, and Robin Goodfellow [Puck] at another.

Puck: How now, spirit, whither wander you?

Fairy:

> *Over hill, over dale,*
> *   Thorough* bush, thorough brier,*
> *Over park, over pale,**
> *   Thorough flood, thorough fire,*   5
> *I do wander everywhere,*
> *Swifter than the moon's sphere;**
> *And I serve the Fairy Queen,*
> *To dew* her orbs upon the green.*
> *The cowslips tall her pensioners* be.*   10
> *In their gold coats spots you see;*
> *Those be rubies, fairy favors;**
> *In those freckles live their savors.**

I must go seek some dewdrops here
And hang a pearl in every cowslip's ear.   15

65 *proper* handsome   69 *discharge* perform. *your* i.e., you know the kind I mean   70 *purple-in-grain* dyed a very deep red. (From *grain*, the name applied to the dried insect used to make the dye.)   *French-crown-color* i.e., color of a French crown, a gold coin   72 *crowns* heads bald from syphilis, the "French disease"   74 *con* learn by heart   77 *devices* plans.   *draw a bill* draw up a list   79 *obscenely* (An unintentionally funny blunder, whatever Bottom meant to say.)   80 *perfect* i.e., letter-perfect in memorizing your parts   82 *Hold . . . bowstrings* (An archer's expression, not definitely explained, but probably meaning here "keep your promises, or give up the play.")
3 *Thorough* through   4 *pale* enclosure   7 *sphere* orbit   9 *dew* sprinkle with dew. *orbs* circles, i.e., fairy rings (circular bands of grass, darker than the surrounding area, caused by fungi enriching the soil)   10 *pensioners* retainers, members of the royal bodyguard   12 *favors* love tokens   13 *savors* sweet smells

Farewell, thou lob* of spirits; I'll be gone.
Our Queen and all her elves come here anon.*
Puck: The King doth keep his revels here tonight.
Take heed the Queen come not within his sight.
For Oberon is passing fell* and wrath,*   20
Because that she as her attendant hath
A lovely boy, stolen from an Indian king;
She never had so sweet a changeling.*
And jealous Oberon would have the child
Knight of his train, to trace* the forests wild.   25
But she perforce* withholds the lovèd boy,
Crowns him with flowers, and makes him all her joy.
And now they never meet in grove or green,
By fountain* clear, or spangled starlight sheen,*
But they do square,* that all their elves for fear   30
Creep into acorn cups and hide them there.
Fairy: Either I mistake your shape and making quite,
Or else you are that shrewd* and knavish sprite*
Called Robin Goodfellow. Are not you he
That frights the maidens of the villagery,*   35
Skim milk,* and sometimes labor in the quern,*
And bootless* make the breathless huswife* churn,
And sometimes make the drink to bear no barm,*
Mislead night wanderers,* laughing at their harm?
Those that "Hobgoblin" call you, and "Sweet Puck,"*   40
You do their work, and they shall have good luck.
Are you not he?
Puck: Thou speakest aright;
I am that merry wanderer of the night.
I jest to Oberon and make him smile
When I a fat and bean-fed* horse beguile,   45
Neighing in likeness of a filly foal;
And sometimes lurk I in a gossip's* bowl
In very likeness of a roasted crab,*
And when she drinks, against her lips I bob
And on her withered dewlap* pour the ale.   50
The wisest aunt,* telling the saddest* tale,
Sometimes for three-foot stool mistaketh me;
Then slip I from her bum, down topples she,

16 *lob* country bumpkin   17 *anon* at once   20 *passing fell* exceedingly angry. *wrath* wrathful
23 *changeling* child exchanged for another by the fairies   25 *trace* range through   26 *perforce*
forcibly   29 *fountain* spring. *starlight sheen* shining starlight   30 *square* quarrel   33 *shrewd*
mischievous. *sprite* spirit   35 *villagery* village population   36 *Skim milk* i.e., steal the cream.
quern hand mill (where Puck presumably hampers the grinding of grain)   37 *bootless* in vain
(Puck prevents the cream from turning to butter.) *huswife* housewife   38 *barm* head on the ale
(Puck prevents the barm or yeast from producing fermentation.)   39 *Mislead night wanderers*
i.e., mislead with false fire those who walk abroad at night (hence earning Puck his other names
of Jack o' Lantern and Will o' the Wisp)   40 *Those . . . Puck* i.e., those who call you by the names
you favor rather than those denoting the mischief you do.   45 *bean-fed* well fed on field beans
47 *gossip's* old woman's   48 *crab* crab apple   50 *dewlap* loose skin on neck   51 *aunt* old woman
saddest most serious

And "Tailor"* cries, and falls into a cough;
And then the whole choir* hold their hips and laugh,   55
And waxen* in their mirth, and neeze,* and swear
A merrier hour was never wasted* there.
But, room,* fairy! Here comes Oberon.
Fairy: And here my mistress. Would that he were gone!

> *Enter [Oberon] the King of Fairies at one door, with his train, and*
> *[Titania] the Queen at another, with hers.*

Oberon: Ill met by moonlight, proud Titania.   60
Titania: What, jealous Oberon? Fairies, skip hence.
   I have forsworn his bed and company.
Oberon: Tarry, rash wanton.* Am not I thy lord?
Titania: Then I must be thy lady; but I know
   When thou hast stolen away from Fairyland   65
   And in the shape of Corin* sat all day,
   Playing on pipes of corn* and versing love
   To amorous Phillida. Why art thou here
   Come from the farthest step* of India,
   But that, forsooth, the bouncing Amazon,   70
   Your buskined* mistress and your warrior love,
   To Theseus must be wedded, and you come
   To give their bed joy and prosperity.
Oberon: How canst thou thus for shame, Titania,
   Glance at my credit with Hippolyta,*   75
   Knowing I know thy love to Theseus?
   Didst not thou lead him through the glimmering night
   From Perigenia,* whom he ravishèd?
   And make him with fair Aegles* break his faith,
   With Ariadne* and Antiopa?*   80
Titania: These are the forgeries of jealousy;
   And never, since the middle summer's spring,*
   Met we on hill, in dale, forest, or mead,*
   By pavèd* fountain or by rushy* brook,
   Or in* the beachèd margent* of the sea,   85
   To dance our ringlets* to* the whistling wind,

54 *Tailor* (possibly because she ends up sitting cross-legged on the floor, looking like a tailor, or
else referring to the *tail* or buttocks.)   55 *choir* company   56 *waxen* increase. *neeze* sneeze
57 *wasted* spent   58 *room* stand aside, make room   63 *wanton* headstrong creature   66, 68 *Corin,
Phillida* (Conventional names of pastoral lovers.)   67 *corn* (Here, oat stalks.)   69 *step* farthest
limit of travel, or, perhaps, *steep*, "mountain range"   71 *buskined* wearing half-boots called
buskins   75 *Glance . . . Hippolyta* make insinuations about my favored relationship with
Hippolyta   78 *Perigenia* i.e., Perigouna, one of Theseus's conquests. (This and the following
women are named in Thomas North's translation of Plutarch's "Life of Theseus.")   79 *Aegles* i.e.,
Aegle, for whom Theseus deserted Ariadne according to some accounts   80 *Ariadne* the daughter
of Minos, King of Crete, who helped Theseus to escape the labyrinth after killing the Minotaur;
later she was abandoned by Theseus. *Antiopa* Queen of the Amazons and wife of Theseus;
elsewhere identified with Hippolyta, but here thought of as a separate woman   82 *middle
summer's spring* beginning of midsummer   83 *mead* meadow   84 *pavèd* with pebbled bottom.
rushy bordered with rushes   85 *in* on. *margent* edge, border   86 *ringlets* dances in a ring. (See
orbs in line 9.)   *to* to the sound of

A sinister and magical Oberon (Powys Thomas) and Titania (Muriel Pavlov) appeared in the 1954 Stratford-upon-Avon production, directed by George Devine. The notion that fairies can fly is dramatically emphasized by their appearance as exotic birds.

But with thy brawls thou hast disturbed our sport.
Therefore the winds, piping to us in vain,
As in revenge, have sucked up from the sea   90
Contagious* fogs which, falling in the land,
Hath every pelting* river made so proud
That they have overborne their continents.*
The ox hath therefore stretched his yoke* in vain,
The plowman lost his sweat, and the green corn*
Hath rotted ere his youth attained a beard;   95
The fold* stands empty in the drownèd field,
And crows are fatted with the murrain* flock;
The nine-men's morris* is filled up with mud,
And the quaint mazes* in the wanton* green
For lack of tread are undistinguishable.   100
The human mortals want* their winter* here;
No night is now with hymn or carol blessed.
Therefore* the moon, the governess of floods,
Pale in her anger, washes* all the air,
That rheumatic diseases* do abound.   105
And thorough this distemperature* we see
The seasons alter: hoary-headed frosts
Fall in the fresh lap of the crimson rose,
And on old Hiems'* thin and icy crown
An odorous chaplet of sweet summer buds   110
Is, as in mockery, set. The spring, the summer,
The childing* autumn, angry winter, change
Their wonted liveries,* and the mazèd* world
By their increase* now knows not which is which.
And this same progeny of evils comes   115
From our debate,* from our dissension.
We are their parents and original.*
Oberon: Do you amend it, then. It lies in you.
Why should Titania cross her Oberon?
I do but beg a little changeling boy   120
To be my henchman.*
Titania: Set your heart at rest.
The fairy land buys not the child of me.
His mother was a vot'ress of my order,*
And in the spicèd Indian air by night

---

90 *Contagious* noxious   91 *pelting* paltry   92 *continents* banks that contain them   93 *stretched his yoke* i.e., pulled at his yoke in plowing   94 *corn* grain of any kind   96 *fold* pen for sheep or cattle   97 *murrain* having died of the plague   98 *nine-men's morris* i.e., portion of the village green marked out in a square for a game played with nine pebbles or pegs   99 *quaint mazes* i.e., intricate paths marked out on the village green to be followed rapidly on foot as a kind of contest. *wanton* luxuriant   101 *want* lack. *winter* i.e., regular winter season; or, proper observances of winter, such as the *hymn or carol* in the next line (?)   103 *Therefore* i.e., as a result of our quarrel   104 *washes* saturates with moisture   105 *rheumatic diseases* colds, flu, and other respiratory infections   106 *distemperature* disturbance in nature   109 *Hiems'* the winter god's   112 *childing* fruitful, pregnant   113 *wonted liveries* usual apparel. *mazèd* bewildered   114 *their increase* their yield, what they produce   116 *debate* quarrel   117 *original* origin   121 *henchman* attendant, page   123 *was . . . order* had taken a vow to serve me

Full often hath she gossiped by my side   125
And sat with me on Neptune's yellow sands,
Marking th' embarkèd traders* on the flood,
When we have laughed to see the sails conceive
And grow big-bellied with the wanton* wind;
Which she, with pretty and with swimming* gait,   130
Following—her womb then rich with my young squire—
Would imitate, and sail upon the land
To fetch me trifles, and return again
As from a voyage, rich with merchandise.
But she, being mortal, of that boy did die;   135
And for her sake do I rear up her boy,
And for her sake I will not part with him.

Oberon: How long within this wood intend you stay?

Titania: Perchance till after Theseus' wedding day.
If you will patiently dance in our round*   140
And see our moonlight revels, go with us;
If not, shun me, and I will spare* your haunts.

Oberon: Give me that boy, and I will go with thee.

Titania: Not for thy fairy kingdom. Fairies, away!
We shall chide downright, if I longer stay.   145

Exeunt [Titania with her train].

Oberon: Well, go thy way. Thou shalt not from* this grove
Till I torment thee for this injury.
My gentle Puck, come hither. Thou rememb'rest
Since* once I sat upon a promontory,
And heard a mermaid on a dolphin's back   150
Uttering such dulcet* and harmonious breath*
That the rude* sea grew civil at her song,
And certain stars shot madly from their spheres
To hear the sea-maid's music?

Puck: I remember.

Oberon: That very time I saw, but thou couldst not,   155
Flying between the cold moon and the earth
Cupid, all* armed. A certain* aim he took
At a fair vestal* thronèd by* the west,
And loosed* his love shaft smartly from his bow
As* it should pierce a hundred thousand hearts;   160
But I might* see young Cupid's fiery shaft
Quenched in the chaste beams of the watery moon,
And the imperial vot'ress passèd on,
In maiden meditation, fancy-free.*
Yet marked I where the bolt* of Cupid fell: 165

---

127 *traders* trading vessels. *flood* flood tide   129 *wanton* (1) playful (2) amorous   130 *swimming* smooth, gliding   140 *round* circular dance   142 *spare* shun   146 *from* go from   149 *Since* when   151 *dulcet* sweet. *breath* voice, song   152 *rude* rough   157 *all* fully. *certain* sure   158 *vestal* vestal virgin. (Contains a complimentary allusion to Queen Elizabeth as a votaress of Diana and probably refers to an actual entertainment in her honor at Elvetham in 1591.) *by* in the region of   159 *loosed* released   160 *As* as if   161 *might* could   164 *fancy-free* free of love's spell   165 *bolt* arrow

It fell upon a little western flower,
Before milk-white, now purple with love's wound,
And maidens call it love-in-idleness.*
Fetch me that flower; the herb I showed thee once.
The juice of it on sleeping eyelids laid   170
Will make or man or* woman madly dote
Upon the next live creature that it sees.
Fetch me this herb, and be thou here again
Ere the leviathan* can swim a league.

Puck: I'll put a girdle round about the earth   175
    In forty* minutes.   [*Exit.*]

Oberon: Having once this juice,
    I'll watch Titania when she is asleep
    And drop the liquor of it in her eyes.
    The next thing then she waking looks upon,
    Be it on lion, bear, or wolf, or bull,   180
    On meddling monkey, or on busy ape,
    She shall pursue it with the soul of love.
    And ere I take this charm from off her sight,
    As I can take it with another herb,
    I'll make her render up her page to me.   185
    But who comes here? I am invisible,
    And I will overhear their conference.

    Enter Demetrius, Helena following him.

Demetrius: I love thee not; therefore pursue me not.
    Where is Lysander and fair Hermia?
    The one I'll slay; the other slayeth me.   190
    Thou toldst me they were stol'n unto this wood;
    And here am I, and wood* within this wood
    Because I cannot meet my Hermia.
    Hence, get thee gone, and follow me no more.

Helena: You draw me, you hardhearted adamant!*   195
    But yet you draw not iron, for my heart
    Is true as steel. Leave you* your power to draw,
    And I shall have no power to follow you.

Demetrius: Do I entice you? Do I speak you fair?*
    Or rather do I not in plainest truth   200
    Tell you I do not nor I cannot love you?

Helena: And even for that do I love you the more.
    I am your spaniel; and, Demetrius,
    The more you beat me I will fawn on you.
    Use me but as your spaniel, spurn me, strike me,   205
    Neglect me, lose me; only give me leave,
    Unworthy as I am, to follow you.

---

168 *love-in-idleness* pansy, heartsease   171 *or . . . or* either . . . or   174 *leviathan* sea monster,
whale   176 *forty* (Used indefinitely.)   192 *and wood* and mad, frantic (with an obvious word play
on *wood*, meaning "woods")   195 *adamant* lodestone, magnet (with pun on *hardhearted*, since
adamant was also thought to be the hardest of all stones and was confused with the diamond)
197 *Leave you* give up   199 *speak you fair* speak courteously to you

What worser place can I beg in your love—
And yet a place of high respect with me—
Than to be usèd as you use your dog?   210
Demetrius: Tempt not too much the hatred of my spirit,
     For I am sick when I do look on thee.
Helena: And I am sick when I look not on you.
Demetrius: You do impeach* your modesty too much
     To leave* the city and commit yourself   215
     Into the hands of one that loves you not,
     To trust the opportunity of night
     And the ill counsel of a desert* place
     With the rich worth of your virginity.
Helena: Your virtue* is my privilege.* For that*   220
     It is not night when I do see your face,
     Therefore I think I am not in the night;
     Nor doth this wood lack worlds of company,
     For you, in my respect,* are all the world.
     Then how can it be said I am alone   225
     When all the world is here to look on me?
Demetrius: I'll run from thee and hide me in the brakes,*
     And leave thee to the mercy of wild beasts.
Helena: The wildest hath not such a heart as you.
     Run when you will. The story shall be changed: 230
     Apollo flies and Daphne holds the chase,*
     The dove pursues the griffin,* the mild hind*
     Makes speed to catch the tiger—bootless* speed,
     When cowardice pursues and valor flies!
Demetrius: I will not stay* thy questions.* Let me go!   235
     Or if thou follow me, do not believe
     But I shall do thee mischief in the wood.
Helena: Ay, in the temple, in the town, the field,
     You do me mischief. Fie, Demetrius!
     Your wrongs do set a scandal on my sex.*   240
     We cannot fight for love, as men may do;
     We should be wooed and were not made to woo.

                                                   [*Exit Demetrius.*]

     I'll follow thee and make a heaven of hell,
     To die upon* the hand I love so well.   [*Exit.*]
Oberon: Fare thee well, nymph. Ere he do leave this grove,   245
     Thou shalt fly him, and he shall seek thy love.

     Enter Puck.

     Hast thou the flower there? Welcome, wanderer.

---

214 *impeach* call into question   215 *To leave* by leaving   218 *desert* deserted   220 *virtue* goodness
or power to attract. *privilege* safeguard, warrant. *For that* because   224 *in my respect* as far as I
am concerned, in my esteem   227 *brakes* thickets   231 *Apollo . . . chase* (In the ancient myth,
Daphne fled from Apollo and was saved from rape by being transformed into a laurel tree; here it is
the female who *holds the chase*, or pursues, instead of the male.)   232 *griffin* a fabulous monster
with the head and wings of an eagle and the body of a lion.   *hind* female deer   233 *bootless*
fruitless   235 *stay* wait for, put up with. *questions* talk or argument   240 *Your . . . sex* i.e., the
wrongs that you do me cause me to act in a manner that disgraces my sex   244 *upon* by

Puck: Ay, there it is.   [*He offers the flower.*]
Oberon: I pray thee, give it me.
I know a bank where the wild thyme blows,*
Where oxlips* and the nodding violet grows,   250
Quite overcanopied with luscious woodbine,*
With sweet muskroses* and with eglantine.*
There sleeps Titania sometimes of* the night,
Lulled in these flowers with dances and delight;
And there the snake throws* her enameled skin,   255
Weed* wide enough to wrap a fairy in.
And with the juice of this I'll streak* her eyes
And make her full of hateful fantasies.
Take thou some of it, and seek through this grove.

                                             [*He gives some love juice.*]

A sweet Athenian lady is in love   260
With a disdainful youth. Anoint his eyes,
But do it when the next thing he espies
May be the lady. Thou shalt know the man
By the Athenian garments he hath on.
Effect it with some care, that he may prove   265
More fond on* her than she upon her love;
And look thou meet me ere the first cock crow.
Puck: Fear not, my lord, your servant shall do so.

                                             Exeunt [*separately*].

Scene II [*The Wood.*]

Enter Titania, Queen of Fairies, with her train.

Titania: Come, now a roundel* and a fairy song;
Then, for the third part of a minute,* hence—
Some to kill cankers* in the muskrose buds,
Some war with reremice* for their leathern wings
To make my small elves coats, and some keep back   5
The clamorous owl, that nightly hoots and wonders
At our quaint* spirits. Sing me now asleep.
Then to your offices, and let me rest.

Fairies sing.

First Fairy: You spotted snakes with double* tongue,
                        Thorny hedgehogs, be not seen;   10
                   Newts* and blindworms, do no wrong;
                        Come not near our Fairy Queen.

---

249 *blows* blooms   250 *oxlips* flowers resembling cowslip and primrose   251 *woodbine*
honeysuckle   252 *muskroses* a kind of large, sweet-scented rose. *eglantine* sweetbrier, another
kind of rose   253 *sometime of* for part of   255 *throws* sloughs off, sheds   256 *Weed* garment
257 *streak* anoint, touch gently   266 *fond on* doting on   1 *roundel* dance in a ring   2 *the
third . . . minute* (Indicative of the fairies' quickness.)   3 *cankers* cankerworms (i.e., caterpillars
or grubs)   4 *reremice* bats   7 *quaint* dainty   9 *double* forked   11 *Newts* water lizards
(considered poisonous, as were *blindworms*—small snakes with tiny eyes—and spiders)

Chorus [*dancing*]: Philomel,* with melody
        Sing in our sweet lullaby;
       Lulla, lulla, lullaby, lulla, lulla, lullaby.   15
        Never harm
        Nor spell nor charm
       Come our lovely lady nigh.
       So good night, with lullaby.

First Fairy: Weaving spiders, come not here;   20
        Hence, you long-legged spinners, hence!
       Beetles black, approach not near;
        Worm nor snail, do no offense.*

Chorus [*dancing.*]: Philomel, with melody
        Sing in our sweet lullaby;   25
       Lulla, lulla, lullaby, lulla, lulla, lullaby.
        Never harm
        Nor spell nor charm
       Come our lovely lady nigh.
       So good night, with lullaby.   30

                              [*Titania sleeps.*]

Second Fairy: Hence, away! Now all is well.
        One aloof stand sentinel.*

             [*Exeunt Fairies, leaving one sentinel.*]

     Enter Oberon [*and squeezes the flower on Titania's eyelids*].

Oberon: What thou seest when thou dost wake,
   Do it for thy true love take;
   Love and languish for his sake.   35
   Be it ounce,* or cat, or bear,
   Pard,* or boar with bristled hair,
   In thy eye that shall appear
   When thou wak'st, it is thy dear.
   Wake when some vile thing is near.   [*Exit.*]   40

     Enter Lysander and Hermia.

Lysander: Fair love, you faint with wandering in the wood;
       And to speak truth, I have forgot our way.
      We'll rest us, Hermia, if you think it good,
       And tarry for the comfort of the day.
Hermia: Be it so, Lysander. Find you out a bed,   45
   For I upon this bank will rest my head.
Lysander: One turf shall serve as pillow for us both;
   One heart, one bed, two bosoms, and one troth.*
Hermia: Nay, good Lysander, for my sake, my dear,
   Lie further off yet. Do not lie so near.   50
Lysander: O, take the sense, sweet, of my innocence!*

---

13 *Philomel* the nightingale. (Philomela, daughter of King Pandion, was transformed into a
nightingale, according to Ovid's *Metamorphoses* 6, after she had been raped by her sister Procne's
husband, Tereus.)   23 *offense* harm   32 *sentinel* (Presumably Oberon is able to outwit or
intimidate this guard.)   36 *ounce* lynx   37 *Pard* leopard   48 *troth* faith, trothplight
51 *take . . . innocence* i.e., interpret my intention as innocent

This watercolor, *Fairies Making an Arc of Flowers* by T. Grieve, emphasizes
the spectacular potential of the fairy kingdom. A representation of the lavish
1856 production by Charles Kean, it shows the meeting of Oberon and Titania.
After 1843, the fairy king Oberon was often played by women. Here, Puck,
played by the famous actress Ellen Terry, is sitting near Oberon. Music and
dance clearly played a major role in this production.

> Love takes the meaning in love's conference.*
> I mean that my heart unto yours is knit,
> So that but one heart we can make of it;
> Two bosoms interchainèd with an oath—   55
> So then two bosoms and a single troth.
> Then by your side no bed-room me deny,
> For lying so, Hermia, I do not lie.*
> *Hermia:* Lysander riddles very prettily.

52 *Love . . . conference* i.e., when lovers confer, love teaches each lover to interpret the other's
meaning lovingly   58 *lie* tell a falsehood (with a riddling pun on *lie*, "recline")

Now much beshrew* my manners and my pride   60
If Hermia meant to say Lysander lied.
But, gentle friend, for love and courtesy
Lie further off, in human* modesty.
Such separation as may well be said
Becomes a virtuous bachelor and a maid,   65
So far be distant; and good night, sweet friend.
Thy love ne'er alter till thy sweet life end!
Lysander: Amen, amen, to that fair prayer, say I,
And then end life when I end loyalty!
Here is my bed. Sleep give thee all his rest!   70
Hermia: With half that wish the wisher's eyes be pressed!*

[*They sleep, separated by a short distance.*]

Enter Puck:

Puck: Through the forest have I gone,
               But Athenian found I none
               On whose eyes I might approve*
               This flower's force in stirring love.   75
               Night and silence.—Who is here?
               Weeds of Athens he doth wear.
               This is he, my master said,
               Despisèd the Athenian maid;
               And here the maiden, sleeping sound,   80
               On the dank and dirty ground.
               Pretty soul, she durst not lie
               Near this lack-love, this kill-courtesy.
               Churl, upon thy eyes I throw
               All the power this charm doth owe.*   85

[*He applies the love juice.*]

               When thou wak'st, let love forbid
               Sleep his seat on thy eyelid.
               So awake when I am gone,
               For I must now to Oberon.   *Exit.*

Enter Demetrius and Helena, running.

Helena: Stay, though thou kill me, sweet Demetrius!   90
Demetrius: I charge thee, hence, and do not haunt me thus.
Helena: O, wilt thou darkling* leave me? Do not so.
Demetrius: Stay, on thy peril!* I alone will go.   [*Exit.*]
Helena: O, I am out of breath in this fond* chase!
The more my prayer, the lesser is my grace.*   95
Happy is Hermia, wheresoe'er she lies,*
For she hath blessèd and attractive eyes.
How came her eyes so bright? Not with salt tears;

---

60 *beshrew* curse. (But mildly meant.)   63 *human* courteous (and perhaps suggesting "humane,"
the Quarto spelling)   71 *With . . . pressed* i.e., may we share your wish, so that your eyes too are
pressed, closed, in sleep   74 *approve* test   85 *owe* own   92 *darkling* in the dark   93 *on thy peril*
i.e., on pain of danger to you if you don't obey me and stay   94 *fond* doting   95 *my grace* the
favor I obtain   96 *lies* dwells

If so, my eyes are oftener washed than hers.
No, no, I am as ugly as a bear,   100
For beasts that meet me run away for fear.
Therefore no marvel though Demetrius
Do, as a monster, fly my presence thus.*
What wicked and dissembling glass of mine
Made me compare* with Hermia's sphery eyne?*   105
But who is here? Lysander, on the ground?
Dead, or asleep? I see no blood, no wound.
Lysander, if you live, good sir, awake.

Lysander [*awaking*]: And run through fire I will for thy sweet sake.
Transparent* Helena! Nature shows art,*   110
That through thy bosom makes me see thy heart.
Where is Demetrius? O, how fit a word
Is that vile name to perish on my sword!

Helena: Do not say so, Lysander, say not so.
What though he love your Hermia? Lord, what though?   115
Yet Hermia still loves you. Then be content.

Lysander: Content with Hermia? No! I do repent
The tedious minutes I with her have spent.
Not Hermia but Helena I love.
Who will not change a raven for a dove?   120
The will* of man is by his reason swayed,
And reason says you are the worthier maid.
Things growing are not ripe until their season;
So I, being young, till now ripe not* to reason.
And, touching* now the point* of human skill,*   125
Reason becomes the marshal to my will
And leads me to your eyes, where I o'erlook*
Love's stories written in love's richest book.

Helena: Wherefore* was I to this keen mockery born?
When at your hands did I deserve this scorn?   130
Is 't not enough, is 't not enough, young man,
That I did never—no, nor never can—
Deserve a sweet look from Demetrius' eye,
But you must flout my insufficiency?
Good troth, you do me wrong, good sooth,* you do,   135
In such disdainful manner me to woo.
But fare you well. Perforce I must confess
I thought you lord of* more true gentleness.*
O, that a lady, of* one man refused,
Should of another therefore be abused!*   *Exit.*   140

Lysander: She sees not Hermia. Hermia, sleep thou there,
And never mayst thou come Lysander near!

102–103 *no marvel . . . thus* i.e., no wonder that Demetrius flies from me as from a monster
105 *compare* vie. *sphery eyne* eyes as bright as stars in their spheres   110 *Transparent* (1) radiant
(2) able to be seen through, lacking in deceit. *art* skill, magic power   121 *will* desire   124 *ripe not*
(am) not ripened   125 *touching* reaching. *point* summit. *skill* judgment   127 *o'erlook* read
129 *Wherefore* why   135 *Good troth, good sooth* i.e., indeed, truly   138 *lord of* i.e., possessor of.
gentleness courtesy   139 *of* by   140 *abused* ill treated

> For as a surfeit of the sweetest things
> The deepest loathing to the stomach brings,
> Or as the heresies that men do leave   145
> Are hated most of those they did deceive,*
> So thou, my surfeit and my heresy,
> Of all be hated, but the most of* me!
> And, all my powers, address* your love and might
> To honor Helen and to be her knight!   *Exit.*   150

Hermia [*awaking*]: Help me, Lysander, help me! Do thy best
> To pluck this crawling serpent from my breast!
> Ay me, for pity! What a dream was here!
> Lysander, look how I do quake with fear.
> Methought a serpent ate my heart away,   155
> And you sat smiling at his cruel prey.*
> Lysander! What, removed? Lysander! Lord!
> What, out of hearing? Gone? No sound, no word?
> Alack, where are you? Speak, an if* you hear;
> Speak, of all loves!* I swoon almost with fear.   160
> No? Then I well perceive you are not nigh.
> Either death, or you, I'll find immediately.

> *Exit. [The sleeping Titania remains.]*

Act III

Scene I *[The Action Is Continuous.]*

Enter the clowns [Quince, Snug, Bottom, Flute, Snout, and Starveling].

Bottom: Are we all met?

Quince: Pat,* pat; and here's a marvelous convenient place for our rehearsal. This green plot shall be our stage, this hawthorn brake* our tiring-
house,* and we will do it in action as we will do it before the Duke.

Bottom: Peter Quince?   5

Quince: What sayest thou, bully* Bottom?

Bottom: There are things in this comedy of Pyramus and Thisbe that will
never please. First, Pyramus must draw a sword to kill himself, which
the ladies cannot abide. How answer you that?

Snout: By 'r lakin,* a parlous* fear.   10

Starveling: I believe we must leave the killing out, when all is done.*

Bottom: Not a whit. I have a device to make all well. Write me* a prologue, and
let the prologue seem to say, we will do no harm with our swords, and
that Pyramus is not killed indeed; and for the more better assurance, tell
them that I, Pyramus, am not Pyramus but Bottom the weaver. This will   15
put them out of fear.

145–146 *as . . . deceive* as renounced heresies are hated most by those persons who formerly were
deceived by them   148 *Of . . . of* by . . . by   149 *address* direct, apply   156 *prey* act of preying
159 *an if* if   160 *of all loves* for all love's sake   *stage direction: clowns* rustics   2 *Pat* on the dot,
punctually   3 *brake* thicket.   *tiring-house* attiring area, hence backstage   6 *bully* i.e., worthy,
jolly, fine fellow   10 *By 'r lakin* by our ladykin, i.e., the Virgin Mary.   *parlous* perilous, alarming
11 *when all is done* i.e., when all is said and done   12 *Write me* i.e., write at my suggestion (*Me* is
used colloquially.)

Quince: Well, we will have such a prologue, and it shall be written in eight
and six.*

Bottom: No, make it two more: let it be written in eight and eight.

Snout: Will not the ladies be afeard of the lion?   20

Starveling: I fear it, I promise you.

Bottom: Masters, you ought to consider with yourself, to bring in—God
shield us!—a lion among ladies* is a most dreadful thing. For there is not
a more fearful* wildfowl than your lion living, and we ought to look to 't.

Snout: Therefore another prologue must tell he is not a lion.   25

Bottom: Nay, you must name his name, and half his face must be seen through
the lion's neck, and he himself must speak through, saying thus or to the
same defect:* "Ladies," or "Fair ladies, I would wish you," or "I would request
you," or "I would entreat you, not to fear, not to tremble; my life for yours.*
If you think I come hither as a lion, it were pity of my life.* No, I am no such   30
thing; I am a man as other men are." And there indeed let him name his
name, and tell them plainly he is Snug the joiner.

Quince: Well, it shall be so. But there is two hard things: that is, to bring the
moonlight into a chamber; for, you know, Pyramus and Thisbe meet by
moonlight.   35

Snout: Doth the moon shine that night we play our play?

Bottom: A calendar, a calendar! Look in the almanac. Find out moonshine,
find out moonshine.

[They consult an almanac.]

Quince: Yes, it doth shine that night.

Bottom: Why then may you leave a casement of the great chamber window   40
where we play open, and the moon may shine in at the casement.

Quince: Ay; or else one must come in with a bush of thorns* and a lantern and
say he comes to disfigure,* or to present*, the person of Moonshine. Then
there is another thing: we must have a wall in the great chamber; for
Pyramus and Thisbe, says the story, did talk through the chink of a wall.   45

Snout: You can never bring in a wall. What say you, Bottom?

Bottom: Some man or other must present Wall. And let him have some plaster, or some loam, or some roughcast* about him, to signify wall; or let
him hold his fingers thus, and through that cranny shall Pyramus and
Thisbe whisper.   50

Quince: If that may be, then all is well. Come, sit down, every mother's son,
and rehearse your parts. Pyramus, you begin. When you have spoken
your speech, enter into that brake, and so everyone according to his cue.

Enter Robin [Puck].

17–18 *eight and six* alternate lines of eight and six syllables, a common ballad measure   23 *lion
among ladies* (A contemporary pamphlet tells how, at the christening in 1594 of Prince Henry,
eldest son of King James VI of Scotland, later James I of England, a "blackamoor" instead of a
lion drew the triumphal chariot, since the lion's presence might have "brought some fear to the
nearest.")   24 *fearful* fear-inspiring   28 *defect* (Bottom's blunder for "effect.")   29 *my life for
yours* i.e., I pledge my life to make your lives safe   30 *it were . . . life* i.e., I should be sorry, by
my life; or, my life would be endangered   42 *bush of thorns* bundle of thornbush faggots (part of
the accoutrements of the man in the moon, according to the popular notions of the time, along with
his lantern and his dog)   43 *disfigure* (Quince's blunder for "figure.") *present* represent
48 *roughcast* a mixture of lime and gravel used to plaster the outside of buildings

Puck [*aside*]: What hempen homespuns* have we swaggering here
    So near the cradle* of the Fairy Queen?   55
    What, a play toward?* I'll be an auditor;
    An actor, too, perhaps, if I see cause.
Quince: Speak, Pyramus. Thisbe, stand forth.
Bottom [*as Pyramus*]:
    "Thisbe, the flowers of odious savors sweet—"
Quince: Odors, odors.   60
Bottom: "—Odors savors sweet;
    So hath thy breath, my dearest Thisbe dear.
    But hark, a voice! Stay thou but here awhile,
      And by and by I will to thee appear."   *Exit.*
Puck: A stranger Pyramus than e'er played here.*   [*Exit.*]   65
Flute: Must I speak now?
Quince: Ay, marry, must you; for you must understand he goes but to see a
    noise that he heard, and is to come again.
Flute [*as Thisbe*]: "Most radiant Pyramus, most lily-white of hue,
    Of color like the red rose on triumphant* brier,   70
    Most brisky juvenal* and eke* most lovely Jew,*
    As true as truest horse that yet would never tire.
    I'll meet thee, Pyramus, at Ninny's tomb."
Quince: "Ninus'* tomb," man. Why, you must not speak that yet. That you
    answer to Pyramus: You speak all your part* at once, cues and all. Pyra-   75
    mus, enter. Your cue is past; it is "never tire."
Flute: O—"As true as truest horse, that yet would never tire."

    [*Enter Puck, and Bottom as Pyramus with the ass head.**]

Bottom: "If I were fair,* Thisbe, I were* only thine."
Quince: O, monstrous! O, strange! We are haunted. Pray, masters! Fly, mas-
    ters! Help!

    [*Exeunt Quince, Snug, Flute, Snout, and Starveling.*]   80

Puck: I'll follow you, I'll lead you about a round,*
    Thorough bog, thorough bush, thorough brake, thorough brier.
    Sometimes a horse I'll be, sometimes a hound,
      A hog, a headless bear, sometimes a fire;*
    And neigh, and bark, and grunt, and roar, and burn,
    Like horse, hound, hog, bear, fire, at every turn.   *Exit.*   85
Bottom: Why do they run away? This is a knavery of them to make me
    afeard.

---

54 *hempen homespuns* i.e., rustics dressed in clothes woven of coarse, homespun fabric made from
hemp   55 *cradle* i.e., Titania's bower   56 *toward* about to take place   65 *A stranger . . . here*
(Either Puck refers to an earlier dramatic version played in the same theater, or he has conceived
of a plan to present a "stranger" Pyramus than ever seen before.)   70 *triumphant* magnificent
71 *brisky juvenal* lively youth. *eke* also. *Jew* (An absurd repetition of the first syllable of *juvenal,*
and an indication of how desperately Quince searches for his rhymes.)   74 *Ninus* mythical
founder of Nineveh (whose wife, Semiramis, was supposed to have built the walls of Babylon where
the story of Pyramus and Thisbe takes place)   75 *part* (An actor's *part* was a script consisting
only of his speeches and their cues.)   *stage direction: with the ass head* (This stage direction,
taken from the Folio, presumably refers to a standard stage property.)   78 *fair* handsome. *were*
would be   81 *about a round* roundabout   84 *fire* will-o'-the-wisp

From the 1888 Augustin Daly production: Otis Skinner as Lysander; Virginia Dreher as Hermia; Ada Rehan as Helena; John Drew as Demetrius.

Enter Snout.

Snout: O Bottom, thou art changed! What do I see on thee?

Bottom: What do you see? You see an ass head of your own, do you?

                                                   [Exit Snout.]

Enter Quince.

Quince: Bless thee, Bottom, bless thee! Thou art translated.*   *Exit.*   90

Bottom: I see their knavery. This is to make an ass of me, to fright me, if they
    could. But I will not stir from this place, do what they can. I will walk
    up and down here, and will sing, that they shall hear I am not afraid.

                                                   [He sings.]

        The ouzel cock* so black of hue,
           With orange-tawny bill,   95
        The throstle* with his note so true,
           The wren with little quill*—

Titania [awaking]: What angel wakes me from my flowery bed?

Bottom [sings]:

        The finch, the sparrow, and the lark,
           The plainsong* cuckoo gray,   100
        Whose note full many a man doth mark,
           And dares not answer nay*—

90 *translated* transformed   94 *ouzel cock* male blackbird   96 *throstle* song thrush
97 *quill* (Literally, a reed pipe; hence, the bird's piping song.)   100 *plainsong* singing a melody
without variations   102 *dares . . . nay* i.e., cannot deny that he is a cuckold

For, indeed, who would set his wit to* so foolish a bird? Who would
give a bird the lie,* though he cry "cuckoo" never so?*

Titania: I pray thee, gentle mortal, sing again.   105
Mine ear is much enamored of thy note;
So is mine eye enthrallèd to thy shape;
And thy fair virtue's force* perforce doth move me
On the first view to say, to swear, I love thee.

Bottom: Methinks, mistress, you should have little reason for that. And yet, to   110
say the truth, reason and love keep little company together nowadays—
the more the pity that some honest neighbors will not make them
friends. Nay, I can gleek* upon occasion.

Titania: Thou art as wise as thou art beautiful.

Bottom: Not so, neither. But if I had wit enough to get out of this wood, I   115
have enough to serve mine own turn.*

Titania: Out of this wood do not desire to go.
Thou shalt remain here, whether thou wilt or no.
I am a spirit of no common rate.*
The summer still doth tend upon my state,*   120
And I do love thee. Therefore go with me.
I'll give thee fairies to attend on thee,
And they shall fetch thee jewels from the deep,
And sing while thou on pressèd flowers dost sleep.
And I will purge thy mortal grossness* so   125
That thou shalt like an airy spirit go.
Peaseblossom, Cobweb, Mote,* and Mustardseed!

Enter four Fairies [Peaseblossom, Cobweb, Mote, and Mustardseed].

Peaseblossom: Ready.
Cobweb: And I.
Mote: And I.
Mustardseed: And I.
All: Where shall we go?
Titania: Be kind and courteous to this gentleman.   130
Hop in his walks and gambol in his eyes;*
Feed him with apricots and dewberries,*
With purple grapes, green figs, and mulberries;
The honey bags steal from the humble-bees,
And for night tapers crop their waxen thighs   135
And light them at the fiery glowworms' eyes,
To have my love to bed and to arise;
And pluck the wings from painted butterflies
To fan the moonbeams from his sleeping eyes.
Nod to him, elves, and do him courtesies.   140
Peaseblossom: Hail, mortal!

---

103 *set his wit to* employ his intelligence to answer   103–104 *give . . . lie* call the bird a liar. *never
so* ever so much   108 *thy . . . force* the power of your unblemished excellence   113 *gleek* jest
116 *serve . . . turn* answer my purpose   119 *rate* rank, value   120 *still . . . state* always waits
upon me as a part of my royal retinue   125 *mortal grossness* materiality (i.e., the corporeal
nature of a mortal being)   127 *Mote* i.e., speck. (The two words *moth* and *mote* were pronounced
alike, and both meanings may be present.)   131 *in his eyes* in his sight (i.e., before him)
132 *dewberries* blackberries

In this stunning scene from the 1935 film, the influence of Mendelssohn's 1843 incidental music (including the famous Wedding March) is clearly evident. Titania's fairies are not in the least threatening; they're flowing, sensual, forces of nature. (Turner Entertainment Company)

Cobweb: Hail!
Mote: Hail!
Mustardseed: Hail!
Bottom: I cry your worships mercy,* heartily. I beseech your worship's name.   145
Cobweb: Cobweb.
Bottom: I shall desire you of more acquaintance,* good Master Cobweb. If I cut
    my finger, I shall make bold with you.*—Your name, honest gentleman?
Peaseblossom: Peaseblossom.
Bottom: I pray you, commend me to Mistress Squash,* your mother, and to   150
    Master Peascod,* your father. Good Master Peaseblossom, I shall desire
    you of more acquaintance too.—Your name, I beseech you, sir?
Mustardseed: Mustardseed.
Bottom: Good Master Mustardseed, I know your patience* well. That same
    cowardly, giantlike ox-beef hath devoured many a gentleman of your   155
    house. I promise you, your kindred hath made my eyes water* ere now.
    I desire you of more acquaintance, good Master Mustardseed.
Titania: Come wait upon him; lead him to my bower.

145 *I cry . . . mercy* I beg pardon of your worships (for presuming to ask a question)
147 *I . . . acquaintance* I crave to be better acquainted with you   147–148 *If . . . you* (Cobwebs
were used to stanch bleeding.)   150 *Squash* unripe pea pod   151 *Peascod* ripe pea pod
154 *your patience* what you have endured. (Mustard is eaten with beef.)   156 *water* (1) weep for
sympathy (2) smart, sting

The moon methinks looks with a watery eye;
And when she weeps,* weeps every little flower,   160
Lamenting some enforcèd* chastity.
Tie up my lover's tongue,* bring him silently.

[*Exeunt.*]

Scene II [The Wood.]

Enter [Oberon,] King of Fairies.

Oberon: I wonder if Titania be awaked;
Then, what it was that next came in her eye,
Which she must dote on in extremity.

[*Enter*] *Robin Goodfellow* [*Puck*].

Here comes my messenger. How now, mad spirit?
What night-rule* now about this haunted* grove?   5
Puck: My mistress with a monster is in love.
Near to her close* and consecrated bower,
While she was in her dull* and sleeping hour,
A crew of patches,* rude mechanicals,*
That work for bread upon Athenian stalls,*   10
Were met together to rehearse a play
Intended for great Theseus' nuptial day.
The shallowest thickskin of that barren sort,*
Who Pyramus presented,* in their sport
Forsook his scene* and entered in a brake.   15
When I did him at this advantage take,
An ass's noll* I fixèd on his head.
Anon his Thisbe must be answerèd,
And forth my mimic* comes. When they him spy,
As wild geese that the creeping fowler* eye,   20
Or russet-pated choughs,* many in sort,
Rising and cawing at the gun's report,
Sever* themselves and madly sweep the sky,
So, at his sight, away his fellows fly;
And, at our stamp, here o'er and o'er one falls;   25
He "Murder!" cries and help from Athens calls.
Their sense thus weak, lost with their fears thus strong,
Made senseless things begin to do them wrong,
For briers and thorns at their apparel snatch;
Some, sleeves—some, hats; from yielders all things catch.*   30
I led them on in this distracted fear

160 *she weeps* i.e., she causes dew   161 *enforcèd* forced, violated; or, possibly, constrained (since
Titania at this moment is hardly concerned about chastity)   162 *Tie . . . tongue* (Presumably
Bottom is braying like an ass.)   5 *night-rule* diversion or misrule for the night. *haunted* much
frequented   7 *close* secret, private   8 *dull* drowsy   9 *patches* clowns, fools. *rude mechanicals*
ignorant artisans   10 *stalls* market booths   13 *barren sort* stupid company or crew
14 *presented* acted   15 *scene* playing area   17 *noll* noddle, head   19 *mimic* burlesque actor
20 *fowler* hunter of game birds   21 *russet-pated choughs* reddish brown or gray-headed
jackdaws. *in sort* in a flock   23 *Sever* i.e., scatter   30 *from . . . catch* i.e., everything preys on
those who yield to fear

And left sweet Pyramus translated there,
When in that moment, so it came to pass,
Titania waked and straightway loved an ass.

Oberon: This falls out better than I could devise.   35
But hast thou yet latched* the Athenian's eyes
With the love juice, as I did bid thee do?

Puck: I took him sleeping—that is finished too—
And the Athenian woman by his side,
That, when he waked, of force* she must be eyed.   40

Enter Demetrius and Hermia.

Oberon: Stand close. This is the same Athenian.
Puck: This is the woman, but not this the man.

[*They stand aside.*]

Demetrius: O, why rebuke you him that loves you so?
Lay breath so bitter on your bitter foe.

Hermia: Now I but chide; but I should use thee worse,   45
For thou, I fear, hast given me cause to curse.
If thou hast slain Lysander in his sleep,
Being o'er shoes* in blood, plunge in the deep,
And kill me too.
The sun was not so true unto the day   50
As he to me. Would he have stolen away
From sleeping Hermia? I'll believe as soon
This whole* earth may be bored, and that the moon
May through the center creep, and so displease
Her brother's* noontide with th' Antipodes.*   55
It cannot be but thou hast murdered him;
So should a murderer look, so dead,* so grim.

Demetrius: So should the murdered look, and so should I,
Pierced through the heart with your stern cruelty.
Yet you, the murderer, look as bright, as clear   60
As yonder Venus in her glimmering sphere.

Hermia: What's this to* my Lysander? Where is he?
Ah, good Demetrius, wilt thou give him me?

Demetrius: I had rather give his carcass to my hounds.

Hermia: Out, dog! Out, cur! Thou driv'st me past the bounds   65
Of maiden's patience. Hast thou slain him, then?
Henceforth be never numbered among men.
O, once* tell true, tell true, even for my sake:
Durst thou have looked upon him being awake?
And hast thou killed him sleeping? O brave touch!*   70
Could not a worm,* an adder, do so much?
An adder did it; for with doubler* tongue
Than thine, thou serpent, never adder stung.

---

36 *latched* fastened, snared   40 *of force* perforce   48 *Being o'er shoes* having waded in so far
53 *whole* solid   55 *Her brother's* i.e., the sun's. *th' Antipodes* the people on the opposite side of
the earth (where the moon is imagined bringing night to noontime)   57 *dead* deadly, or deathly
pale   62 *to* to do with   68 *once* once and for all   70 *brave touch!* fine stroke! (Said ironically.)
71 *worm* serpent   72 *doubler* (1) more forked (2) more deceitful

Demetrius: You spend your passion* on a misprised mood.*
    I am not guilty of Lysander's blood,   75
    Nor is he dead, for aught that I can tell.
Hermia: I pray thee, tell me then that he is well.
Demetrius: And if I could, what should I get therefor?*
Hermia: A privilege never to see me more.
    And from thy hated presence part I so.   80
    See me no more, whether he be dead or no.   *Exit.*
Demetrius: There is no following her in this fierce vein.
    Here therefore for a while I will remain.
    So sorrow's heaviness doth heavier* grow
    For debt that bankrupt* sleep doth sorrow owe;   85
    Which now in some slight measure it will pay,
    If for his tender here I make some stay.* *[He] lie[s] down [and sleeps].*
Oberon: What hast thou done? Thou hast mistaken quite
    And laid the love juice on some true love's sight.
    Of thy misprision* must perforce ensue   90
    Some true love turned, and not a false turned true.
Puck: Then fate o'errules, that, one man holding troth,*
    A million fail, confounding oath on oath.*
Oberon: About the wood go swifter than the wind,
    And Helena of Athens look* thou find.   95
    All fancy-sick* she is and pale of cheer*
    With sighs of love, that cost the fresh blood* dear.
    By some illusion see thou bring her here.
    I'll charm his eyes against she do appear.*
Puck: I go, I go, look how I go,   100
    Swifter than arrow from the Tartar's bow.*   *[Exit.]*
Oberon [applying love juice to Demetrius' eyes]:
        Flower of this purple dye,
        Hit with Cupid's archery,
        Sink in apple* of his eye.
        When his love he doth espy,   105
        Let her shine as gloriously
        As the Venus of the sky.
        When thou wak'st, if she be by,
        Beg of her for remedy.

      Enter Puck:

Puck: Captain of our fairy band,   110
           Helena is here at hand,

---

74 *passion* violent feelings. *misprised mood* anger based on misconception   78 *therefor* in return
for that   84 *heavier* (1) harder to bear (2) more drowsy   85 *bankrupt* (Demetrius is saying that
his sleepiness adds to the weariness caused by sorrow.)   86–87 *Which . . . stay* i.e., to a small
extent, I will be able to "pay back" and hence find some relief from sorrow, if I pause here awhile
(*make some stay*) while sleep "tenders" or offers itself by way of paying the debt owed to sorrow
90 *misprision* mistake   92 *that . . . troth* in that, for each man keeping true faith in love
93 *confounding . . . oath* i.e., breaking oath after oath   95 *look* i.e., be sure   96 *fancy-sick* lovesick.
cheer face   97 *sighs . . . blood* (An allusion to the physiological theory that each sigh costs the
heart a drop of blood.)   99 *against . . . appear* in anticipation of her coming
101 *Tartar's bow* (Tartars were famed for their skill with the bow.)   104 *apple* pupil

                      And the youth, mistook by me,
                      Pleading for a lover's fee.*
                      Shall we their fond pageant* see?
                      Lord, what fools these mortals be!   115

Oberon: Stand aside. The noise they make
                      Will cause Demetrius to awake.
Puck: Then will two at once woo one;
                      That must needs be sport alone.*
                      And those things do best please me   120
                      That befall preposterously.*

                                        [They stand aside.]
        Enter Lysander and Helena.

Lysander: Why should you think that I should woo in scorn?
      Scorn and derision never come in tears.
      Look when* I vow, I weep; and vows so born,
      In their nativity all truth appears.*   125
      How can these things in me seem scorn to you,
      Bearing the badge* of faith to prove them true?
Helena: You do advance* your cunning more and more.
      When truth kills truth,* O, devilish-holy fray!
      These vows are Hermia's. Will you give her o'er?   130
      Weigh oath with oath, and you will nothing weigh.
      Your vows to her and me, put in two scales,
      Will even weigh, and both as light as tales.*
Lysander: I had no judgment when to her I swore.
Helena: Nor none, in my mind, now you give her o'er.   135
Lysander: Demetrius loves her, and he loves not you.
Demetrius [awaking]: O Helen, goddess, nymph, perfect, divine!
      To what, my love, shall I compare thine eyne?
      Crystal is muddy. O, how ripe in show*
      Thy lips, those kissing cherries, tempting grow!   140
      That pure congealèd white, high Taurus'* snow,
      Fanned with the eastern wind, turns to a crow*
      When thou hold'st up thy hand. O, let me kiss
      This princess of pure white, this seal* of bliss!
Helena: O spite! O hell! I see you all are bent   145
      To set against* me for your merriment.
      If you were civil and knew courtesy,
      You would not do me thus much injury.
      Can you not hate me, as I know you do,
      But you must join in souls* to mock me too?   150
      If you were men, as men you are in show,

113 *fee* privilege, reward   114 *fond pageant* foolish spectacle   119 *alone* unequaled
121 *preposterously* out of the natural order   124 *Look when* whenever
124–125 *vows . . . appears* i.e., vows made by one who is weeping give evidence thereby of their
sincerity   127 *badge* identifying device such as that worn on servants' livery (here, his tears)
128 *advance* carry forward, display   129 *truth kills truth* i.e., one of Lysander's vows must
invalidate the other   133 *tales* lies   139 *show* appearance   141 *Taurus* a lofty mountain range in
Asia Minor   142 *turns to a crow* i.e., seems black by contrast   144 *seal* pledge
146 *set against* attack   150 *in souls* i.e., heart and soul

You would not use a gentle lady so—
To vow, and swear, and superpraise* my parts,*
When I am sure you hate me with your hearts.
You both are rivals, and love Hermia,   155
And now both rivals, to mock Helena.
A trim* exploit, a manly enterprise,
To conjure tears up in a poor maid's eyes
With your derision! None of noble sort*
Would so offend a virgin and extort*   160
A poor soul's patience, all to make you sport.
Lysander: You are unkind, Demetrius. Be not so.
For you love Hermia; this you know I know.
And here, with all good will, with all my heart,
In Hermia's love I yield you up my part;   165
And yours of Helena to me bequeath,
Whom I do love, and will do till my death.
Helena: Never did mockers waste more idle breath.
Demetrius: Lysander, keep thy Hermia; I will none.*
If e'er I loved her, all that love is gone.   170
My heart to her but as guestwise sojourned,*
And now to Helen is it home returned,
There to remain.
Lysander: Helen, it is not so.
Demetrius: Disparage not the faith thou dost not know,
Lest, to thy peril, thou aby* it dear.   175
Look where thy love comes; yonder is thy dear.

   Enter Hermia.

Hermia: Dark night, that from the eye his* function takes,
The ear more quick of apprehension makes;
Wherein it doth impair the seeing sense,
It pays the hearing double recompense.   180
Thou art not by mine eye, Lysander, found;
Mine ear, I thank it, brought me to thy sound.
But why unkindly didst thou leave me so?
Lysander: Why should he stay, whom love doth press to go?
Hermia: What love could press Lysander from my side?   185
Lysander: Lysander's love, that would not let him bide—
Fair Helena, who more engilds* the night
Than all yon fiery oes* and eyes of light.
Why seek'st thou me? Could not this make thee know
The hate I bear thee made me leave thee so?   190
Hermia: You speak not as you think. It cannot be.
Helena: Lo, she is one of this confederacy!
Now I perceive they have conjoined all three
To fashion this false sport in spite of me.*
Injurious Hermia, most ungrateful maid!   195

153 *superpraise* overpraise. *parts* qualities   157 *trim* pretty, fine (Said ironically.)   159 *sort*
character, quality   160 *extort* twist, torture   169 *will none* i.e., want no part of her
171 *to . . . sojourned* only visited with her   175 *aby* pay for   177 *his* its   187 *engilds* gilds,
brightens with a golden light   188 *oes* spangles (here, stars)   194 *in spite of me* to vex me

Have you conspired, have you with these contrived*
To bait* me with this foul derision?
Is all the counsel* that we two have shared—
The sisters' vows, the hours that we have spent
When we have chid the hasty-footed time   200
For parting us—O, is all forgot?
All schooldays' friendship, childhood innocence?
We, Hermia, like two artificial* gods,
Have with our needles created both one flower,
Both on one sampler, sitting on one cushion,   205
Both warbling of one song, both in one key,
As if our hands, our sides, voices, and minds
Had been incorporate.* So we grew together,
Like to a double cherry, seeming parted,
But yet an union in partition,   210
Two lovely* berries molded on one stem;
So with two seeming bodies but one heart,
Two of the first, like coats in heraldry,
Due but to one and crownèd with one crest.*
And will you rend our ancient love asunder,   215
To join with men in scorning your poor friend?
It is not friendly, 'tis not maidenly.
Our sex, as well as I, may chide you for it,
Though I alone do feel the injury.
Hermia: I am amazèd at your passionate words.   220
I scorn you not. It seems that you scorn me.
Helena: Have you not set Lysander, as in scorn,
To follow me and praise my eyes and face?
And made your other love, Demetrius,
Who even but now did spurn me with his foot,   225
To call me goddess, nymph, divine, and rare,
Precious, celestial? Wherefore speaks he this
To her he hates? And wherefore doth Lysander
Deny your love, so rich within his soul,
And tender* me, forsooth, affection,   230
But by your setting on, by your consent?
What though I be not so in grace* as you,
So hung upon with love, so fortunate,
But miserable most, to love unloved?
This you should pity rather than despise.   235
Hermia: I understand not what you mean by this.
Helena: Ay, do! Persever, counterfeit sad* looks,
Make mouths* upon* me when I turn my back,
Wink each at other, hold the sweet jest up.*

196 *contrived* plotted   197 *bait* torment, as one sets on dogs to bait a bear
198 *counsel* confidential talk   203 *artificial* skilled in art or creation   208 *incorporate* of one
body   211 *lovely* loving   213–214 *Two . . . crest* i.e., we have two separate bodies, just as a coat
of arms in heraldry can be represented twice on a shield but surmounted by a single crest
230 *tender* offer   232 *grace* favor   237 *sad* grave, serious   238 *mouths* i.e., mows, faces,
grimaces. *upon* at   239 *hold . . . up* keep up the joke

This sport, well carried,* shall be chronicled.   240
If you have any pity, grace, or manners,
You would not make me such an argument.*
But fare ye well. 'Tis partly my own fault,
Which death, or absence, soon shall remedy.
Lysander: Stay, gentle Helena; hear my excuse,   245
My love, my life, my soul, fair Helena!
Helena: O excellent!
Hermia [to Lysander]: Sweet, do not scorn her so.
Demetrius [to Lysander]: If she cannot entreat,* I can compel.
Lysander: Thou canst compel no more than she entreat.
Thy threats have no more strength than her weak prayers.   250
Helen, I love thee, by my life I do!
I swear by that which I will lose for thee,
To prove him false that says I love thee not.
Demetrius [to Helena]: I say I love thee more than he can do.
Lysander: If thou say so, withdraw, and prove it too.*   255
Demetrius: Quick, come!
Hermia: Lysander, whereto tends all this?
Lysander: Away, you Ethiope!*

        [*He tries to break away from Hermia.*]

Demetrius: No, no; he'll
Seem to break loose; take on as* you would follow,
But yet come not. You are a tame man. Go!
Lysander [to Hermia]: Hang off,* thou cat, thou burr! Vile thing, let loose,   260
Or I will shake thee from me like a serpent!
Hermia: Why are you grown so rude? What change is this,
Sweet love?

Lysander: Thy love? Out, tawny Tartar, out!
Out, loathèd med'cine!* O hated potion, hence!
Hermia: Do you not jest?
Helena: Yes, sooth,* and so do you.   265
Lysander: Demetrius, I will keep my word with thee.
Demetrius: I would I had your bond, for I perceive
A weak bond* holds you. I'll not trust your word.
Lysander: What, should I hurt her, strike her, kill her dead?
Although I hate her, I'll not harm her so.   270
Hermia: What, can you do me greater harm than hate?
Hate me? Wherefore? O me, what news,* my love?
Am not I Hermia? Are not you Lysander?
I am as fair now as I was erewhile.*
Since night you loved me; yet since night you left me.   275

240 *carried* managed   242 *argument* subject for a jest   248 *entreat* i.e., succeed by entreaty
255 *withdraw . . . too* i.e., withdraw with me and prove your claim in a duel. (The two
gentlemen are armed.)   257 *Ethiope* (Referring to Hermia's relatively dark hair and
complexion; see also *tawny Tartar* six lines later.)   258 *take on as* act as if, make a fuss as if
260 *Hang off* let go   264 *med'cine* i.e., poison   265 *sooth* truly   268 *weak bond* i.e., Hermia's
arm (with a pun on *bond*, "oath," in the previous line)   272 *what news* what is the matter
274 *erewhile* just now

Why, then you left me—O, the gods forbid!—
In earnest, shall I say?

Lysander: Ay, by my life!
And never did desire to see thee more.
Therefore be out of hope, of question, of doubt;
Be certain, nothing truer. 'Tis no jest   280
That I do hate thee and love Helena.

Hermia [to Helena]: O me! You juggler! You cankerblossom!*
You thief of love! What, have you come by night
And stol'n my love's heart from him?

Helena: Fine, i' faith!
Have you no modesty, no maiden shame,   285
No touch of bashfulness? What, will you tear
Impatient answers from my gentle tongue?
Fie, fie! You counterfeit, you puppet,* you!

Hermia: "Puppet"? Why, so!* Ay, that way goes the game.
Now I perceive that she hath made compare   290
Between our statures; she hath urged her height,
And with her personage, her tall personage,
Her height, forsooth, she hath prevailed with him.
And are you grown so high in his esteem
Because I am so dwarfish and so low?   295
How low am I, thou painted maypole? Speak!
How low am I? I am not yet so low
But that my nails can reach unto thine eyes.

[*She flails at Helena but is restrained.*]

Helena: I pray you, though you mock me, gentlemen,
Let her not hurt me. I was never curst;*   300
I have no gift at all in shrewishness;
I am a right* maid for my cowardice.
Let her not strike me. You perhaps may think,
Because she is something* lower than myself,
That I can match her.

Hermia: Lower? Hark, again!   305

Helena: Good Hermia, do not be so bitter with me.
I evermore did love you, Hermia,
Did ever keep your counsels, never wronged you,
Save that, in love unto Demetrius,
I told him of your stealth* unto this wood.   310
He followed you; for love I followed him.
But he hath chid me hence* and threatened me
To strike me, spurn me, nay, to kill me too.
And now, so* you will let me quiet go,
To Athens will I bear my folly back   315
And follow you no further. Let me go.
You see how simple and how fond* I am.

---

282 *cankerblossom* worm that destroys the flower bud, or wild rose   288 *puppet* (1) counterfeit
(2) dwarfish woman (in reference to Hermia's smaller stature)   289 *Why, so* i.e., Oh, so that's how
it is   300 *curst* shrewish   302 *right* true   304 *something* somewhat   310 *stealth* stealing away
312 *chid me hence* driven me away with his scolding   314 *so* if only   317 *fond* foolish

Hermia: Why, get you gone. Who is 't that hinders you?
Helena: A foolish heart, that I leave here behind.
Hermia: What, with Lysander?
Helena: With Demetrius. 320
Lysander: Be not afraid; she shall not harm thee, Helena.
Demetrius: No, sir, she shall not, though you take her part.
Helena: O, when she is angry, she is keen* and shrewd.*
    She was a vixen when she went to school;
    And though she be but little, she is fierce. 325
Hermia: "Little" again? Nothing but "low" and "little"?
    Why will you suffer her to flout me thus?
    Let me come to her.
Lysander: Get you gone, you dwarf!
    You minimus,* of hindering knotgrass* made!
    You bead, you acorn!
Demetrius: You are too officious 330
    In her behalf that scorns your services.
    Let her alone. Speak not of Helena;
    Take not her part. For, if thou dost intend*
    Never so little show of love to her,
    Thou shalt aby* it.
Lysander: Now she holds me not. 335
    Now follow, if thou dar'st, to try whose right,
    Of thine or mine, is most in Helena.   *[Exit.]*
Demetrius: Follow? Nay, I'll go with thee, cheek by jowl.*

                  [Exit, following Lysander.]

Hermia: You, mistress, all this coil* is 'long of* you.
    Nay, go not back.*
Helena: I will not trust you, I, 340
    Nor longer stay in your curst company.
    Your hands than mine are quicker for a fray;
    My legs are longer, though, to run away   *[Exit.]*
Hermia: I am amazed and know not what to say.   *Exit.*

           [Oberon and Puck come forward.]

Oberon: This is thy negligence. Still thou mistak'st, 345
    Or else committ'st thy knaveries willfully.
Puck: Believe me, king of shadows, I mistook.
    Did not you tell me I should know the man
    By the Athenian garments he had on?
    And so far blameless proves my enterprise 350
    That I have 'nointed an Athenian's eyes;
    And so far* am I glad it so did sort,*
    As* this their jangling I esteem a sport.
Oberon: Thou seest these lovers seek a place to fight.

323 *keen* fierce, cruel. *shrewd* shrewish   329 *minimus* diminutive creature *knotgrass* a weed, an infusion of which was thought to stunt the growth   333 *intend* give sign of   335 *aby* pay for 338 *cheek by jowl* i.e., side by side   339 *coil* turmoil, dissension. *'long of* on account of   340 *go not back* i.e., don't retreat (Hermia is again proposing a fight.)   352 *so far* at least to this extent. *sort* turn out   353 *As* that

Hie* therefore, Robin, overcast the night;   355
The starry welkin* cover thou anon
With drooping fog as black as Acheron,*
And lead these testy rivals so astray
As* one come not within another's way.
Like to Lysander sometimes frame thy tongue,   360
Then stir Demetrius up with bitter wrong;*
And sometimes rail thou like Demetrius.
And from each other look thou lead them thus,
Till o'er their brows death-counterfeiting sleep
With leaden legs and batty* wings doth creep.   365
Then crush this herb* into Lysander's eye,   [giving herb.]
Whose liquor hath this virtuous* property,
To take from thence all error with his* might
And make his eyeballs roll with wonted* sight.
When they next wake, all this derision*   370
Shall seem a dream and fruitless vision,
And back to Athens shall the lovers wend
With league whose date* till death shall never end.
Whiles I in this affair do thee employ,
I'll to my queen and beg her Indian boy;   375
And then I will her charmèd eye release
From monster's view, and all things shall be peace.
Puck: My fairy lord, this must be done with haste,
For night's swift dragons* cut the clouds full fast,
And yonder shines Aurora's harbinger,*   380
At whose approach ghosts, wand'ring here and there,
Troop home to churchyards. Damnèd spirits all,
That in crossways and floods have burial,*
Already to their wormy beds are gone.
For fear lest day should look their shames upon,   385
They willfully themselves exile from light
And must for aye* consort with black-browed night.
Oberon: But we are spirits of another sort.
I with the Morning's love* have oft made sport,
And, like a forester,* the groves may tread   390
Even till the eastern gate, all fiery red,
Opening on Neptune with fair blessèd beams,
Turns into yellow gold his salt green streams.
But notwithstanding, haste, make no delay.
We may effect this business yet ere day.   [*Exit.*]   395

355 *Hie* hasten   356 *welkin* sky   357 *Acheron* river of Hades (here representing Hades itself)
359 *As* that   361 *wrong* insults   365 *batty* batlike   366 *this herb* i.e., the antidote (mentioned in
2.1.184) to love-in-idleness   367 *virtuous* efficacious   368 *his* its   369 *wonted* accustomed
370 *derision* laughable business   373 *date* term of existence   379 *dragons* (Supposed by Shakespeare
to be yoked to the car of the goddess of night or the moon.)   380 *Aurora's harbinger* the morning star,
precursor of dawn   383 *crossways . . . burial* (Those who had committed suicide were buried at
crossways, with a stake driven through them; those who intentionally or accidentally drowned (in
floods or deep water), would be condemned to wander disconsolate for lack of burial rites.)
387 *for aye* forever   389 *the Morning's love* Cephalus, a beautiful youth beloved by Aurora; or
perhaps the goddess of the dawn herself   390 *forester* keeper of a royal forest

Another indication of the creativity *MSN* calls forth: Puck (Joseph Marcell) is surrounded by fairy puppets in this 1981 Stratford-upon-Avon production, including a puppet that looks like himself.

Puck:

> Up and down, up and down,
> I will lead them up and down.
> I am feared in field and town.
> Goblin,* lead them up and down.   400

    Here comes one.

    Enter Lysander.

Lysander: Where art thou, proud Demetrius? Speak thou now.
Puck [mimicking Demetrius]:
    Here, villain, drawn* and ready. Where art thou?
Lysander: I will be with thee straight.*
Puck: Follow me, then,
    To plainer* ground.

        [Lysander wanders about, following the voice.]*

    Enter Demetrius.

Demetrius: Lysander! Speak again!   405
    Thou runaway, thou coward, art thou fled?
    Speak! In some bush? Where dost thou hide thy head?
Puck [mimicking Lysander]:
    Thou coward, art thou bragging to the stars,

399 *Goblin* Hobgoblin. (Puck refers to himself.)   402 *drawn* with drawn sword   403 *straight* immediately   404 *plainer* more open.   *stage direction: Lysander wanders about* (Lysander may exit here, but perhaps not; neither exit nor reentrance is indicated in the early texts.)

Telling the bushes that thou look'st for wars,
And wilt not come? Come, recreant;* come, thou child,
I'll whip thee with a rod. He is defiled   410
That draws a sword on thee.
Demetrius: Yea, art thou there?
Puck: Follow my voice. We'll try* no manhood here.

                                                                        Exeunt.

        [*Lysander returns.*]

Lysander: He goes before me and still dares me on.
    When I come where he calls, then he is gone.
    The villain is much lighter-heeled than I.   415
    I followed fast, but faster he did fly,
    That fallen am I in dark uneven way,
    And here will rest me. [*He lies down.*] Come, thou gentle day!
    For if but once thou show me thy gray light,
    I'll find Demetrius and revenge this spite.   [*He sleeps.*]   420

        [*Enter*] Robin [*Puck*] *and* Demetrius.

Puck: Ho, ho, ho! Coward, why com'st thou not?
Demetrius: Abide* me, if thou dar'st; for well I wot*
    Thou runn'st before me, shifting every place,
    And dar'st not stand nor look me in the face.
    Where art thou now?
Puck: Come hither. I am here.   425
Demetrius: Nay, then, thou mock'st me. Thou shalt buy* this dear,*
    If ever I thy face by daylight see.
    Now, go thy way. Faintness constraineth me
    To measure out my length on this cold bed.
    By day's approach look to be visited.   430

                                        [*He lies down and sleeps.*]
        Enter Helena.

Helena: O weary night, O long and tedious night,
    Abate* thy hours! Shine comforts from the east,
    That I may back to Athens by daylight
    From these that my poor company detest;
    And sleep, that sometimes shuts up sorrow's eye,   435
    Steal me awhile from mine own company.

                                        [*She lies down and*] sleep[*s*].

Puck: Yet but three? Come one more;
            Two of both kinds makes up four.
            Here she comes, curst* and sad.
            Cupid is a knavish lad,   440
            Thus to make poor females mad.

        [*Enter Hermia.*]

Hermia: Never so weary, never so in woe,
    Bedabbled with the dew and torn with briers,

---

409 *recreant* cowardly wretch   412 *try* test   422 *Abide* confront, face. *wot* know   426 *buy* aby,
pay for. *dear* dearly   432 *Abate* lessen, shorten   439 *curst* ill-tempered

I can no further crawl, no further go;
   My legs can keep no pace with my desires.   445
Here will I rest me till the break of day.
Heavens shield Lysander, if they mean a fray!

                                [She lies down and sleeps.]

Puck: On the ground
           Sleep sound.
           I'll apply   450
           To your eye,
      Gentle lover, remedy.

                 [He squeezes the juice on Lysander's eyes.]

           When thou wak'st,
           Thou tak'st
           True delight   455
           In the sight
Of thy former lady's eye;
And the country proverb known,
That every man should take his own,
In your waking shall be shown: 460
   Jack shall have Jill;*
   Naught shall go ill;
The man shall have his mare again, and all shall be well.

              [Exit. The four sleeping lovers remain.]

Act IV

Scene I [The Action Is Continuous. The Four Lovers Are Still Asleep* Onstage.]

    Enter [Titania,] Queen of Fairies, and [Bottom the] clown, and Fairies; and [Oberon,] the King, behind them.

Titania: Come, sit thee down upon this flowery bed,
    While I thy amiable* cheeks do coy,*
    And stick muskroses in thy sleek smooth head,
    And kiss thy fair large ears, my gentle joy.

                               [They recline.]   5

Bottom: Where's Peaseblossom?
Peaseblossom: Ready.
Bottom: Scratch my head, Peaseblossom. Where's Monsieur Cobweb?
Cobweb: Ready.
Bottom: Monsieur Cobweb, good monsieur, get you your weapons in your
    hand, and kill me a red-hipped humble-bee on the top of a thistle; and,   10
    good monsieur, bring me the honey bag. Do not fret yourself too much
    in the action, monsieur; and, good monsieur, have a care the honey bag
    break not. I would be loath to have you overflown with a honey bag,
    signor. [*Exit Cobweb.*] Where's Monsieur Mustardseed?

---

461 *Jack shall have Jill* (Proverbial for "boy gets girl.")   *stage direction: still asleep* (Compare with the Folio stage direction:"They sleep all the act.")   2 *amiable* lovely. *coy* caress

Mustardseed: Ready. 15

Bottom: Give me your neaf,* Monsieur Mustardseed. Pray you, leave your
courtesy,* good monsieur.

Mustardseed: What's your will?

Bottom: Nothing, good monsieur, but to help Cavalery* Cobweb* to
scratch. I must to the barber's, monsieur, for methinks I am marvelous 20
hairy about the face; and I am such a tender ass, if my hair do but tickle me I must scratch.

Titania: What, wilt thou hear some music, my sweet love?

Bottom: I have a reasonable good ear in music. Let's have the tongs and the
bones.*

[*Music: tongs, rural music.**]

Titania: Or say, sweet love, what thou desirest to eat. 25

Bottom: Truly, a peck of provender.* I could munch your good dry oats.
Methinks I have a great desire to a bottle* of hay. Good hay, sweet hay,
hath no fellow.*

Titania: I have a venturous fairy that shall seek
The squirrel's hoard, and fetch thee new nuts. 30

Bottom: I had rather have a handful or two of dried peas. But, I pray you, let none
of your people stir* me. I have an exposition of* sleep come upon me.

Titania: Sleep thou, and I will wind thee in my arms.
Fairies, begone, and be all ways* away.

[*Exeunt Fairies.*]

So doth the woodbine* the sweet honeysuckle 35
Gently entwist; the female ivy so
Enrings the barky fingers of the elm.
O, how I love thee! How I dote on thee!

[*They sleep.*]

Enter Robin Goodfellow [Puck].

Oberon [coming forward]: Welcome, good Robin. Seest thou this sweet sight?
Her dotage now I do begin to pity. 40
For, meeting her of late behind the wood
Seeking sweet favors* for this hateful fool,
I did upbraid her and fall out with her.
For she his hairy temples then had rounded
With coronet of fresh and fragrant flowers; 45
And that same dew, which sometime* on the buds
Was wont to swell like round and orient* pearls,
Stood now within the pretty flowerets' eyes

---

16 *neaf* fist   16–17 *leave your courtesy* i.e., stop bowing, or put on your hat   19 *Cavalery*
cavalier. (Form of address for a gentleman.)   *Cobweb* (Seemingly an error, since Cobweb has been
sent to bring honey, while Peaseblossom has been asked to scratch.)   23–24 *tongs . . . bones*
instruments for rustic music. (The tongs were played like a triangle, whereas the bones were held
between the fingers and used as clappers.)   *stage direction: Music . . . music* (This stage direction
is added from the Folio.)   26 *peck of provender* one-quarter bushel of grain   27 *bottle* bundle
28 *fellow* equal   32 *stir* disturb. *exposition of* (Bottom's phrase for "disposition to.")   34 *all ways*
in all directions   35 *woodbine* bindweed, a climbing plant that twines in the opposite direction
from that of honeysuckle   42 *favors* i.e., gifts of flowers   46 *sometime* formerly   47 *orient pearls*
i.e., the most beautiful of all pearls, those coming from the Orient

Like tears that did their own disgrace bewail.
When I had at my pleasure taunted her,   50
And she in mild terms begged my patience,
I then did ask of her her changeling child,
Which straight she gave me, and her fairy sent
To bear him to my bower in Fairyland.
And, now I have the boy, I will undo   55
This hateful imperfection of her eyes.
And, gentle Puck, take this transformèd scalp
From off the head of this Athenian swain,
That he, awaking when the other* do,
May all to Athens back again repair,*   60
And think no more of this night's accidents
But as the fierce vexation of a dream.
But first I will release the Fairy Queen.

[He squeezes an herb on her eyes.]

    Be as thou wast wont to be;
    See as thou wast wont to see.   65
    Dian's bud* o'er Cupid's flower
    Hath such force and blessèd power.
Now, my Titania, wake you, my sweet queen.
Titania [waking]: My Oberon! What visions have I seen!
    Methought I was enamored of an ass.   70
Oberon: There lies your love.
Titania: How came these things to pass?
    O, how mine eyes do loathe his visage now!
Oberon: Silence awhile. Robin, take off this head.
    Titania, music call, and strike more dead
    Than common sleep of all these five* the sense.   75
Titania: Music, ho! Music, such as charmeth* sleep!   *[Music.]*
Puck [removing the ass head]:
    Now, when thou wak'st, with thine own fool's eyes peep.
Oberon: Sound, music! Come, my queen, take hands with me,
    And rock the ground whereon these sleepers be.   *[They dance.]*
    Now thou and I are new in amity,   80
    And will tomorrow midnight solemnly*
    Dance in Duke Theseus' house triumphantly,
    And bless it to all fair prosperity.
    There shall the pairs of faithful lovers be
    Wedded, with Theseus, all in jollity.   85
Puck: *Fairy King, attend, and mark:*
    I do hear the morning lark.
Oberon: *Then, my queen, in silence sad,**
    Trip we after night's shade.
    We the globe can compass soon,   90

59 *other* others   60 *repair* return   66 *Dian's bud* (Perhaps the flower of the *agnus castus* or
chaste-tree, supposed to preserve chastity; or perhaps referring simply to Oberon's herb by which
he can undo the effects of "Cupid's flower," the love-in-idleness of 2.1.166–168.)
75 *these five* i.e., the four lovers and Bottom   76 *charmeth* brings about, as though by a charm
81 *solemnly* ceremoniously   88 *sad* sober

	Swifter than the wandering moon.	
Titania:	*Come, my lord, and in our flight*	
	Tell me how it came this night	
	That I sleeping here was found	
	With these mortals on the ground.	95

Exeunt. [Oberon, Titania, and Puck].

Wind horn [within].
Enter Theseus and all his train; [Hippolyta, Egeus].

Theseus: Go, one of you, find out the forester,
For now our observation* is performed;
And since we have the vaward* of the day,
My love shall hear the music of my hounds.
Uncouple* in the western valley; let them go.   100
Dispatch, I say, and find the forester.   *[Exit an Attendant.]*
We will, fair queen, up to the mountain's top
And mark the musical confusion
Of hounds and echo in conjunction.
Hippolyta: I was with Hercules and Cadmus* once,   105
When in a wood of Crete they bayed* the bear
With hounds of Sparta.* Never did I hear
Such gallant chiding;* for, besides the groves,
The skies, the fountains, every region near
Seemed all one mutual cry. I never heard   110
So musical a discord, such sweet thunder.
Theseus: My hounds are bred out of the Spartan kind,*
So flewed,* so sanded;* and their heads are hung
With ears that sweep away the morning dew;
Crook-kneed, and dewlapped* like Thessalian bulls;   115
Slow in pursuit, but matched in mouth like bells,
Each under each.* A cry* more tunable*
Was never holloed to nor cheered* with horn
In Crete, in Sparta, nor in Thessaly.
Judge when you hear. [*He sees the sleepers.*] But soft!*
What nymphs are these?   120
Egeus: My lord, this is my daughter here asleep,
And this Lysander; this Demetrius is;
This Helena, old Nedar's Helena.
I wonder of* their being here together.
Theseus: No doubt they rose up early to observe   125
The rite of May, and hearing our intent,
Came here in grace of our solemnity.*

---

97 *observation* i.e., observance to a morn of May (1.1.167)   98 *vaward* vanguard, i.e., earliest
part   100 *Uncouple* set free for the hunt   105 *Cadmus* mythical founder of Thebes. (This story
about him is unknown.)   106 *bayed* brought to bay   107 *hounds of Sparta* (A breed famous in
antiquity for their hunting skill.)   108 *chiding* i.e., yelping   112 *kind* strain, breed   113 *So
flewed* similarly having large hanging chaps or fleshy covering of the jaw. *sanded* of sandy color
115 *dewlapped* having pendulous folds of skin under the neck   116–117 *matched . . . each* i.e.,
harmoniously matched in their various cries like a set of bells, from treble down to bass   117 *cry*
pack of hounds.   *tunable* well tuned, melodious   118 *cheered* encouraged   119 *soft* i.le., gently,
wait a minute   124 *wonder of* wonder at   127 *in . . . solemnity* in honor of our wedding ceremony

But speak, Egeus. Is not this the day
That Hermia should give answer of her choice?
Egeus: It is, my lord.   130
Theseus: Go, bid the huntsmen wake them with their horns.

                                                   [*Exit an Attendant.*]

Shout within. Wind horns. They all start up.

Good morrow, friends. Saint Valentine* is past.
Begin these woodbirds but to couple now?
Lysander: Pardon, my lord.   [*They kneel.*]
Theseus: I pray you all, stand up.   [*They stand.*]
I know you two are rival enemies;   135
How comes this gentle concord in the world,
That hatred is so far from jealousy*
To sleep by hate and fear no enmity?
Lysander: My lord, I shall reply amazedly,
Half sleep, half waking; but as yet, I swear,   140
I cannot truly say how I came here.
But, as I think—for truly would I speak,
And now I do bethink me, so it is—
I came with Hermia hither. Our intent
Was to be gone from Athens, where* we might,   145
Without* the peril of the Athenian law—
Egeus: Enough, enough, my lord; you have enough.
I beg the law, the law, upon his head.
They would have stol'n away; they would, Demetrius,
Thereby to have defeated* you and me,   150
You of your wife and me of my consent,
Of my consent that she should be your wife.
Demetrius: My lord, fair Helen told me of their stealth,
Of this their purpose hither* to this wood,
And I in fury hither followed them,   155
Fair Helena in fancy* following me.
But, my good lord, I wot not by what power—
But by some power it is—my love to Hermia,
Melted as the snow, seems to me now
As the remembrance of an idle gaud*   160
Which in my childhood I did dote upon;
And all the faith, the virtue of my heart,
The object and the pleasure of mine eye,
Is only Helena. To her, my lord,
Was I betrothed ere I saw Hermia,   165
But like a sickness did I loathe this food;
But, as in health, come to my natural taste,
Now I do wish it, love it, long for it,
And will forevermore be true to it.
Theseus: Fair lovers, you are fortunately met.   170

132 *Saint Valentine* (Birds were supposed to choose their mates on Saint Valentine's Day.)
137 *jealousy* suspicion   145 *where* wherever; or, to where   146 *Without* outside of, beyond
150 *defeated* defrauded   154 *hither* in coming hither   156 *in fancy* driven by love
160 *idle gaud* worthless trinket

Of this discourse we more will hear anon.
Egeus, I will overbear your will;
For in the temple, by and by, with us
These couples shall eternally be knit.
And, for* the morning now is something* worn,   175
Our purposed hunting shall be set aside.
Away with us to Athens. Three and three,
We'll hold a feast in great solemnity.*
Come, Hippolyta.

[*Exeunt Theseus, Hippolyta, Egeus, and train.*]

Demetrius: These things seem small and undistinguishable,   180
    Like far-off mountains turnèd into clouds.
Hermia: Methinks I see these things with parted* eye,
    When everything seems double.
Helena: So methinks;
    And I have found Demetrius like a jewel,
    Mine own, and not mine own.*
Demetrius: Are you sure   185
    That we are awake? It seems to me
    That yet we sleep, we dream. Do not you think
    The Duke was here, and bid us follow him?
Hermia: Yea, and my father.
Helena: And Hippolyta.
Lysander: And he did bid us follow to the temple.   190
Demetrius: Why, then, we are awake. Let's follow him,
    And by the way let us recount our dreams.   [*Exeunt the lovers.*]
Bottom [*awaking*]: When my cue comes, call me, and I will answer. My
    next is, "Most fair Pyramus." Heigh—ho! Peter Quince! Flute, the bellows
    mender! Snout, the tinker! Starveling! God's* my life, stolen hence and   195
    left me asleep! I have had a most rare vision. I have had a dream, past the
    wit of man to say what dream it was. Man is but an ass if he go about*
    to expound this dream. Methought I was—there is no man can tell what.
    Methought I was—and methought I had—but man is but a patched*
    fool if he will offer* to say what methought I had. The eye of man hath   200
    not heard, the ear of man hath not seen, man's hand is not able to taste,
    his tongue to conceive, nor his heart to report,* what my dream was. I
    will get Peter Quince to write a ballad* of this dream. It shall be called
    "Bottom's Dream," because it hath no bottom;* and I will sing it in the
    latter end of a play, before the Duke. Peradventure, to make it the more   205
    gracious, I shall sing it at her* death.

[*Exit.*]

175 *for* since. *something* somewhat   178 *in great solemnity* with great ceremony
182 *parted* i.e., mproperly focused   184–185 *like . . . mine own* i.e., like a jewel that one finds
by chance and therefore possesses but cannot certainly consider one's own property
195 *God's* may God save   197 *go about* attempt   199 *patched* wearing motley, i.e., a dress of
various colors.   *offer* venture   200–202 *The eye . . . report* (Bottom garbles the terms of
1 Corinthians 2:9)   203 *ballad* (The proper medium for relating sensational stories and
preposterous events.)   204 *hath no bottom* is unfathomable
206 *her* Thisbe's (?)

Scene II [*Athens.*]

Enter Quince, Flute, [Snout, and Starveling].

Quince: Have you sent to Bottom's house? Is he come home yet?
Starveling: He cannot be heard of. Out of doubt he is transported.*
Flute: If he come not, then the play is marred. It goes not forward. Doth it?
Quince: It is not possible. You have not a man in all Athens able to dis-   5
      charge* Pyramus but he.
Flute: No, he hath simply the best wit* of any handicraft man in Athens.
Quince: Yea, and the best person* too, and he is a very paramour for a sweet
      voice.
Flute: You must say "paragon." A paramour is, God bless us, a thing of naught.*

Enter Snug the joiner.

Snug: Masters, the Duke is coming from the temple, and there is two or   10
      three lords and ladies more married. If our sport had gone forward, we
      had all been made men.*
Flute: O sweet bully Bottom! Thus hath he lost sixpence a day* during his
      life; he could not have scaped sixpence a day. An the Duke had not
      given him sixpence a day for playing Pyramus, I'll be hanged. He would   15
      have deserved it. Sixpence a day in Pyramus, or nothing.

Enter Bottom.

Bottom: Where are these lads? Where are these hearts?*
Quince: Bottom! O most courageous day! O most happy hour!
Bottom: Masters, I am to discourse wonders.* But ask me not what; for if I tell
      you, I am no true Athenian. I will tell you everything, right as it fell out.   20
Quince: Let us hear, sweet Bottom.
Bottom: Not a word of* me. All that I will tell you is that the Duke hath dined.
      Get your apparel together, good strings* to your beards, new ribbons to
      your pumps;* meet presently* at the palace; every man look o'er his part;
      for the short and the long is, our play is preferred.* In any case, let This-   25
      be have clean linen; and let not him that plays the lion pare his nails, for
      they shall hang out for the lion's claws. And, most dear actors, eat no
      onions nor garlic, for we are to utter sweet breath; and I do not doubt but
      to hear them say it is a sweet comedy. No more words. Away! Go, away!

                                                            [*Exeunt.*]

Act V

Scene I [*Athens. The Palace of Theseus.*]

Enter Theseus, Hippolyta, and Philostrate, [lords, and attendants].

Hippolyta: 'Tis strange, my Theseus, that* these lovers speak of.
Theseus: More strange than true. I never may* believe

---

2 *transported* carried off by fairies; or, possibly, transformed   4 *discharge* perform   6 *wit*
intellect   7 *person* appearance   9 *a . . . naught* a shameful thing   11–12 *we . . . men* i.e., we
would have had our fortunes made   13 *sixpence a day* i.e., as a royal pension   17 *hearts* good
fellows   19 *am . . . wonders* have wonders to relate   22 *of* out of   23 *strings* (to attach the
beards)   24 *pumps* light shoes or slippers. *presently* immediately   25 *preferred* selected for
consideration   1 *that* that which   2 *may* can

These antique* fables nor these fairy toys.*
Lovers and madmen have such seething brains,
Such shaping fantasies,* that apprehend*   5
More than cool reason ever comprehends.*
The lunatic, the lover, and the poet
Are of imagination all compact.*
One sees more devils than vast hell can hold;
That is the madman. The lover, all as frantic,   10
Sees Helen's* beauty in a brow of Egypt.*
The poet's eye, in a fine frenzy rolling,
Doth glance from heaven to earth, from earth to heaven;
And as imagination bodies forth
The forms of things unknown, the poet's pen   15
Turns them to shapes and gives to airy nothing
A local habitation and a name.
Such tricks hath strong imagination
That, if it would but apprehend some joy,
It comprehends some bringer* of that joy;   20
Or in the night, imagining some fear,*
How easy is a bush supposed a bear!

Hippolyta: But all the story of the night told over,
And all their minds transfigured so together,
More witnesseth than fancy's images*   25
And grows to something of great constancy;*
But, howsoever,* strange and admirable.*

Enter lovers: Lysander, Demetrius, Hermia, and Helena.

Theseus: Here come the lovers, full of joy and mirth.
Joy, gentle friends! Joy and fresh days of love
Accompany your hearts!

Lysander: More than to us   30
Wait in your royal walks, your board, your bed!

Theseus: Come now, what masques,* what dances shall we have,
To wear away this long age of three hours
Between our after-supper and bedtime?
Where is our usual manager of mirth?   35
What revels are in hand? Is there no play
To ease the anguish of a torturing hour?
Call Philostrate.

Philostrate: Here, mighty Theseus.

Theseus: Say, what abridgment* have you for this evening?
What masque? What music? How shall we beguile   40
The lazy time, if not with some delight?

Philostrate [giving him a paper]:

---

3 *antique* old-fashioned (punning too on *"antic," "strange," "grotesque"). fairy toys* trifling stories
about fairies   5 *fantasies* imaginations. *apprehend* conceive, imagine   6 *comprehends*
understands   8 *compact* formed, composed   11 *Helen's* i.e., of Helen of Troy, pattern of beauty.
brow of Egypt i.e., face of a gypsy   20 *bringer* i.e., source   21 *fear* object of fear
25 *More . . . images* testifies to something more substantial than mere imaginings   26 *constancy*
certainty   27 *howsoever* in any case. *admirable* a source of wonder   32 *masques* courtly
entertainments   39 *abridgment* pastime (to abridge or shorten the evening)

There is a brief* how many sports are ripe.
Make choice of which Your Highness will see first.
Theseus [*He reads*]: "The battle with the Centaurs,* to be sung
  By an Athenian eunuch to the harp"?   45
  We'll none of that. That have I told my love,
  In glory of my kinsman* Hercules.
  [*He reads.*] "The riot of the tipsy Bacchanals,
  Tearing the Thracian singer in their rage"?*
  That is an old device;* and it was played   50
  When I from Thebes came last a conqueror.
  [*He reads.*] "The thrice three Muses mourning for the death
  Of Learning, late deceased in beggary"?*
  That is some satire, keen and critical,
  Not sorting with* a nuptial ceremony.   55
  [*He reads.*] "A tedious brief scene of young Pyramus
  And his love Thisbe; very tragical mirth"?
  Merry and tragical? Tedious and brief?
  That is, hot ice and wondrous strange* snow.
  How shall we find the concord of this discord?   60
Philostrate: A play there is, my lord, some ten words long,
  Which is as brief as I have known a play;
  But by ten words, my lord, it is too long,
  Which makes it tedious. For in all the play
  There is not one word apt, one player fitted.   65
  And tragical, my noble lord, it is,
  For Pyramus therein doth kill himself.
  Which, when I saw rehearsed, I must confess,
  Made mine eyes water; but more merry tears
  The passion of loud laughter never shed.   70
Theseus: What are they that do play it?
Philostrate: Hardhanded men that work in Athens here,
  Which never labored in their minds till now,
  And now have toiled* their unbreathed* memories
  With this same play, against* your nuptial.   75
Theseus: And we will hear it.
Philostrate: No, my noble lord,
  It is not for you. I have heard it over,
  And it is nothing, nothing in the world;
  Unless you can find sport in their intents,

42 *brief* short written statement, summary   44 *battle . . . Centaurs* (Probably refers to the battle
of the Centaurs and the Lapithae, when the Centaurs attempted to carry off Hippodamia, bride of
Theseus' friend Pirothous. The story is told in Ovid's *Metamorphoses* 12.)
47 *kinsman* (Plutarch's "Life of Theseus" states that Hercules and Theseus were near kinsmen.
Theseus is referring to a version of the battle of the Centaurs in which Hercules was said to be
present.)   48–49 *The riot . . . rage* (This was the story of the death of Orpheus, as told in
Metamorphoses 11.)   50 *device* show, performance   52–53 *The thrice . . . beggary* (Possibly an
allusion to Spenser's *Teares of the Muses*, 1591, though "satires" deploring the neglect of learning
and the creative arts were commonplace.)   55 *sorting with* befitting   59 *strange* (Sometimes
emended to an adjective that would contrast with *snow*, just as *hot* contrasts with *ice*.)
74 *toiled* taxed. *unbreathed* unexercised   75 *against* in preparation for

Extremely stretched* and conned* with cruel pain   80
To do you service.
Theseus: I will hear that play;
For never anything can be amiss
When simpleness* and duty tender it.
Go, bring them in; and take your places, ladies.

[*Philostrate goes to summon the players.*]

Hippolyta: I love not to see wretchedness o'ercharged,*   85
And duty in his service* perishing.
Theseus: Why, gentle sweet, you shall see no such thing.
Hippolyta: He says they can do nothing in this kind.*
Theseus: The kinder we, to give them thanks for nothing.
Our sport shall be to take what they mistake;   90
And what poor duty cannot do, noble respect*
Takes it in might, not merit.*
Where I have come, great clerks* have purposèd
To greet me with premeditated welcomes;
Where I have seen them shiver and look pale,   95
Make periods in the midst of sentences,
Throttle their practiced accent* in their fears,
And in conclusion dumbly have broke off,
Not paying me a welcome. Trust me, sweet,
Out of this silence yet I picked a welcome;   100
And in the modesty of fearful duty
I read as much as from the rattling tongue
Of saucy and audacious eloquence.
Love, therefore, and tongue-tied simplicity
In least* speak most, to my capacity.*   105

[*Philostrate returns.*]

Philostrate: So please Your Grace, the Prologue* is addressed.*
Theseus: Let him approach.   [*A flourish of trumpets.*]

Enter the Prologue [*Quince*].

Prologue: If we offend, it is with our good will.
That you should think, we come not to offend,
But with good will. To show our simple skill,   110
That is the true beginning of our end.
Consider, then, we come but in despite.
We do not come, as minding* to content you,
Our true intent is. All for your delight
We are not here. That you should here repent you,   115
The actors are at hand; and, by their show,
You shall know all that you are like to know.

80 *stretched* strained. *conned* memorized   83 *simpleness* simplicity
85 *wretchedness o'ercharged* social or intellectual inferiors overburdened   86 *his service* its
attempt to serve   88 *kind* kind of thing   91 *respect* evaluation, consideration
92 *Takes . . . merit* values it for the effort made rather than for the excellence achieved
93 *clerks* learned men   97 *practiced accent* i.e., rehearsed speech; or, usual way of speaking
105 *least* i.e., saying least. *to my capacity* in my judgment and understanding
106 *Prologue* speaker of the prologue. *addressed* ready   113 *minding* intending

Theseus: This fellow doth not stand upon points.*
Lysander: He hath rid* his prologue like a rough* colt; he knows not the stop.*
    A good moral, my lord: it is not enough to speak, but to speak true.   120
Hippolyta: Indeed, he hath played on his prologue like a child on a
    recorder;* a sound, but not in government.*
Theseus: His speech was like a tangled chain: nothing* impaired, but all dis-
    ordered. Who is next?

> *Enter Pyramus [Bottom], and Thisbe [Flute], and Wall [Snout], and*
> *Moonshine [Starveling], and Lion [Snug].*

Prologue: Gentles, perchance you wonder at this show;   125
    But wonder on, till truth makes all things plain.
This man is Pyramus, if you would know;
    This beauteous lady Thisbe is, certain.
This man with lime and roughcast doth present
    Wall, that vile wall which did these lovers sunder;   130
And through Wall's chink, poor souls, they are content
    To whisper. At the which let no man wonder.
This man, with lantern, dog, and bush of thorn,
    Presenteth Moonshine; for, if you will know,
By moonshine did these lovers think no scorn*   135
    To meet at Ninus' tomb, there, there to woo.
This grisly beast, which Lion hight* by name,
The trusty Thisbe coming first by night
Did scare away, or rather did affright;
And as she fled, her mantle she did fall,*   140
    Which Lion vile with bloody mouth did stain.
Anon comes Pyramus, sweet youth and tall,*
    And finds his trusty Thisbe's mantle slain;
Whereat, with blade, with bloody, blameful blade,
    He bravely broached* his boiling bloody breast.   145
And Thisbe, tarrying in mulberry shade,
    His dagger drew, and died. For all the rest,
Let Lion, Moonshine, Wall, and lovers twain
At large* discourse, while here they do remain.

> *Exeunt Lion, Thisbe, and Moonshine.*

                                             150
Theseus: I wonder if the lion be to speak.
Demetrius: No wonder, my lord. One lion may, when many asses do.
Wall: In this same interlude* it doth befall
    That I, one Snout by name, present a wall;
    And such a wall as I would have you think
    That had in it a crannied hole or chink,   155
    Through which the lovers, Pyramus and Thisbe,
    Did whisper often, very secretly.

---

118 *stand upon points* (1) heed niceties or small points (2) pay attention to punctuation in his
reading. (The humor of Quince's speech is in the blunders of its punctuation.)
119 *rid* ridden. *rough* unbroken.   *stop* (1) the stopping of a colt by reining it in (2) punctuation
mark   121 *recorder* a wind instrument like a flute   122 *government* control   123 *nothing* not at
all   135 *think no scorn* think it no disgraceful matter   137 *hight* is called   140 *fall* let fall
142 *tall* courageous   145 *broached* stabbed   149 *At large* in full, at length   152 *interlude* play

This loam, this roughcast, and this stone doth show
That I am that same wall; the truth is so.
And this the cranny is, right and sinister,*   160
Through which the fearful lovers are to whisper.

Theseus: Would you desire lime and hair to speak better?

Demetrius: It is the wittiest partition* that ever I heard discourse, my lord.

[*Pyramus comes forward.*]

Theseus: Pyramus draws near the wall. Silence!

Pyramus: O grim-looked* night! O night with hue so black!   165
    O night, which ever art when day is not!
    O night, O night! Alack, alack, alack,
        I fear my Thisbe's promise is forgot.
    And thou, O wall, O sweet, O lovely wall,
        That stand'st between her father's ground and mine,   170
    Thou wall, O wall, O sweet and lovely wall,
        Show me thy chink, to blink through with mine eyne.

                    [*Wall makes a chink with his fingers.*]

    Thanks, courteous wall. Jove shield thee well for this.
        But what see I? No Thisbe do I see.
    O wicked wall, through whom I see no bliss!   175
        Cursed be thy stones for thus deceiving me!

Theseus: The wall, methinks, being sensible,* should curse again.*

Pyramus: No, in truth, sir, he should not. "Deceiving me" is Thisbe's cue: she
    is to enter now, and I am to spy her through the wall. You shall see, it
    will fall pat* as I told you. Yonder she comes.   180

    Enter Thisbe.

Thisbe: O wall, full often hast thou heard my moans
        For parting my fair Pyramus and me.
    My cherry lips have often kissed thy stones,
        Thy stones with lime and hair knit up in thee.

Pyramus: I see a voice. Now will I to the chink,   185
        To spy an* I can hear my Thisbe's face.
        Thisbe!

Thisbe: My love! Thou art my love, I think.

Pyramus: Think what thou wilt, I am thy lover's grace,*
        And like Limander* am I trusty still.

Thisbe: And I like Helen, till the Fates me kill.   190

Pyramus: Not Shafalus* to Procrus* was so true.

Thisbe: As Shafalus to Procrus, I to you.

Pyramus: O, kiss me through the hole of this vile wall!

Thisbe: I kiss the wall's hole, not your lips at all.

Pyramus: Wilt thou at Ninny's tomb meet me straightway?   195

Thisbe: 'Tide* life, 'tide death, I come without delay.

---

160 *right and sinister* i.e., the right side of it and the left; or, running from right to left,
horizontally   163 *partition* (1) wall (2) section of a learned treatise or oration
165 *grim-looked* grim-looking   177 *sensible* capable of feeling. *again* in return   180 *pat* exactly
186 *an* if   188 *lover's grace* i.e., gracious lover   189, 190 *Limander, Helen* (Blunders for
"Leander" and "Hero.")   191 *Shafalus, Procrus* (Blunders for "Cephalus" and "Procris," also
famous lovers.)   196 *'Tide* betide, come

[Exeunt Pyramus and Thisbe.]

Wall: Thus have I, Wall, my part dischargèd so;
    And, being done, thus Wall away doth go.   *[Exit.]*

Theseus: Now is the mural down between the two neighbors.

Demetrius: No remedy, my lord, when walls are so willful* to hear without   200
    warning.*

Hippolyta: This is the silliest stuff that ever I heard.

Theseus: The best in this kind* are but shadows;* and the worst are no
    worse, if imagination amend them.

Hippolyta: It must be your imagination then, and not theirs.   205

Theseus: If we imagine no worse of them than they of themselves, they may
    pass for excellent men. Here come two noble beasts in, a man and a lion.

    Enter Lion and Moonshine.

Lion:
    You, ladies, you, whose gentle hearts do fear
        The smallest monstrous mouse that creeps on floor,
    May now perchance both quake and tremble here,   210
        When lion rough in wildest rage doth roar.
    Then know that I, as Snug the joiner, am
    A lion fell,* nor else no lion's dam;
    For, if I should as lion come in strife
    Into this place, 'twere pity on my life.   215

Theseus: A very gentle beast, and of a good conscience.

Demetrius: The very best at a beast, my lord, that e'er I saw.

Lysander: This lion is a very fox for his valor.*

Theseus: True; and a goose for his discretion.*

Demetrius: Not so, my lord; for his valor cannot carry his discretion, and the   220
    fox carries the goose.

Theseus: His discretion, I am sure, cannot carry his valor; for the goose carries
    not the fox. It is well. Leave it to his discretion, and let us listen to the moon.

Moon: This lanthorn* doth the hornèd moon present—

Demetrius: He should have worn the horns on his head.*   225

Theseus: He is no crescent,* and his horns are invisible within the circum-
    ference.

Moon: This lanthorn doth the hornèd moon present;
    Myself the man i' the moon do seem to be.

Theseus: This is the greatest error of all the rest. The man should be put into
    the lanthorn. How is it else the man i' the moon?   230

Demetrius: He dares not come there for the candle, for* you see it is already
    in snuff.*

---

200 *willful* willing   200–201 *without warning* i.e., without warning the parents (Demetrius makes
a joke on the proverb "Walls have ears.")   203 *in this kind* of this sort. *shadows* likenesses,
representations   213 *lion fell* fierce lion (with a play on the idea of "lion skin")
218 *is . . . valor* i.e., his valor consists of craftiness and discretion   219 *a goose . . . discretion* i.e.,
as discreet as a goose, that is, more foolish than discreet   224 *lanthorn* (This original spelling,
lanthorn, may suggest a play on the *horn* of which lanterns were made, and also on a cuckold's
horns; however, the spelling *lanthorn* is not used consistently for comic effect in this play or
elsewhere. At 5.1.133, for example, the word is *lantern* in the original.)   225 *on his head* (as a
sign of cuckoldry)   226 *crescent* a waxing moon   231 *for* because of, for fear of
232 *in snuff* (1) offended (2) in need of snuffing or trimming

Hippolyta: I am aweary of this moon. Would he would change!

Theseus: It appears, by his small light of discretion, that he is in the wane;
but yet, in courtesy, in all reason, we must stay the time.   235

Lysander: Proceed, Moon.

Moon: All that I have to say is to tell you that the lanthorn is the moon, I, the
man i' the moon, this thornbush my thornbush, and this dog my dog.

Demetrius: Why, all these should be in the lanthorn, for all these are in the
moon. But silence! Here comes Thisbe.   240

> *Enter Thisbe.*

Thisbe: This is old Ninny's tomb. Where is my love?

Lion [*roaring*]: O!

Demetrius: Well roared, Lion.

> [*Thisbe runs off, dropping her mantle.*]

Theseus: Well run, Thisbe.

Hippolyta: Well shone, Moon. Truly, the moon shines with a good grace.   245

> [*The Lion worries Thisbe's mantle.*]

Theseus: Well moused,* Lion.

> [*Enter Pyramus; exit Lion.*]

Demetrius: And then came Pyramus.

Lysander: And so the lion vanished.

Pyramus: Sweet Moon, I thank thee for thy sunny beams;
I thank thee, Moon, for shining now so bright;   250
For, by thy gracious, golden, glittering gleams,
I trust to take of truest Thisbe sight.
But stay, O spite!
But mark, poor knight,
What dreadful dole* is here?   255
Eyes, do you see?
How can it be?
O dainty duck! O dear!
Thy mantle good,
What, stained with blood?   260
Approach, ye Furies* fell!*
O Fates,* come, come,
Cut thread and thrum;*
Quail,* crush, conclude, and quell!*

Theseus: This passion, and the death of a dear friend, would go near to   265
make a man look sad.*

Hippolyta: Beshrew my heart, but I pity the man.

Pyramus: O, wherefore, Nature, didst thou lions frame?
Since lion vile hath here deflowered my dear,
Which is—no, no, which was—the fairest dame   270

246 *moused* shaken, torn, bitten   255 *dole* grievous event   261 *Furies* avenging goddesses of
Greek myth. *fell* fierce   262 *Fates* the three goddesses (Clotho, Lachesis, Atropos) of Greek myth
who spun, drew, and cut the thread of human life   263 *thread and thrum* i.e., everything—the
good and bad alike; literally, the warp in weaving and the loose end of the warp   264 *Quail*
overpower. *quell* kill, destroy   265–266 *This . . . sad* i.e., if one had other reason to grieve, one
might be sad, but not from this absurd portrayal of passion

That lived, that loved, that liked, that looked with cheer.*
    Come, tears, confound,
    Out, sword, and wound
The pap* of Pyramus;
    Ay, that left pap,   275
    Where heart doth hop.   [*He stabs himself.*]
Thus die I, thus, thus, thus.
    Now am I dead,
    Now am I fled;
My soul is in the sky.   280
    Tongue, lose thy light;
    Moon, take thy flight.   [*Exit Moonshine.*]
Now die, die, die, die, die.   [*Pyramus dies.*]
Demetrius: No die, but an ace,* for him; for he is but one.*
Lysander: Less than an ace, man; for he is dead, he is nothing.   285
Theseus: With the help of a surgeon he might yet recover, and yet prove an ass.*
Hippolyta: How chance Moonshine is gone before Thisbe comes back and
    finds her lover?
Theseus: She will find him by starlight.

    [*Enter Thisbe.*]

    Here she comes, and her passion ends the play.   290
Hippolyta: Methinks she should not use a long one for such a Pyramus. I
    hope she will be brief.
Demetrius: A mote* will turn the balance, which Pyramus, which* Thisbe, is
    the better: he for a man, God warrant us; she for a woman, God bless us.
Lysander: She hath spied him already with those sweet eyes.   295
Demetrius: And thus she means,* videlicet:*
Thisbe: Asleep, my love?
    What, dead, my dove?
      O Pyramus, arise!
    Speak, speak. Quite dumb?   300
    Dead, dead? A tomb
Must cover thy sweet eyes.
    These lily lips,
    This cherry nose,
These yellow cowslip cheeks,   305
    Are gone, are gone!
    Lovers, make moan.
His eyes were green as leeks.
    O Sisters Three,*
    Come, come to me,   310
With hands as pale as milk;

---

271 *cheer* countenance   274 *pap* breast   284 *ace* the side of the die featuring the single pip, or
spot (The pun is on *die* as a singular of *dice*; Bottom's performance is not worth a whole *die* but
rather one single face of it, one small portion.). *one* (1) an individual person (2) unique
286 *ass* (with a pun on *ace*)   293 *mote* small particle *which . . . which* whether . . . or
296 *means* moans, laments (with a pun on the meaning, "lodge a formal complaint"). *videlicet* to
wit   309 *Sisters Three* the Fates   313 *shore* shorn

Lay them in gore,
Since you have shore*
With shears his thread of silk.
   Tongue, not a word.   315
   Come, trusty sword,
Come, blade, my breast imbrue!*   [*She stabs herself.*]
   And farewell, friends.
   Thus Thisbe ends.
Adieu, adieu, adieu.   [*She dies.*]   320

Theseus: Moonshine and Lion are left to bury the dead.

Demetrius: Ay, and Wall too.

Bottom [*starting up, as Flute does also*]: No, I assure you, the wall is down
that parted their fathers. Will it please you to see the epilogue, or to
hear a Bergomask dance* between two of our company?   325

[*The other players enter.*]

Theseus: No epilogue, I pray you; for your play needs no excuse. Never excuse;
for when the players are all dead, there need none to be blamed. Marry, if
he that writ it had played Pyramus and hanged himself in Thisbe's garter, it
would have been a fine tragedy; and so it is, truly, and very notably dis-
charged. But, come, your Bergomask. Let your epilogue alone. [*A dance.*]   330
The iron tongue* of midnight hath told* twelve.
Lovers, to bed, 'tis almost fairy time.
I fear we shall outsleep the coming morn
As much as we this night have overwatched.*
This palpable-gross* play hath well beguiled   335
The heavy* gait of night. Sweet friends, to bed.
A fortnight hold we this solemnity,
In nightly revels and new jollity.   *Exeunt.*

   Enter Puck [*carrying a broom*].

Puck: Now the hungry lion roars,
        And the wolf behowls the moon,
      Whilst the heavy* plowman snores,   340
        All with weary task fordone.*
      Now the wasted brands* do glow,
        Whilst the screech owl, screeching loud,
      Puts the wretch that lies in woe   345
        In remembrance of a shroud.
      Now it is the time of night
        That the graves, all gaping wide,
      Every one lets forth his sprite,*
        In the church-way paths to glide.   350

317 *imbrue* stain with blood   324–325 *Bergomask dance* a rustic dance named from Bergamo,
a province in the state of Venice   331 *iron tongue* i.e., of a bell. *told* counted, struck ("tolled")
334 *overwatched* stayed up too late   335 *palpable-gross* palpably gross, obviously crude
336 *heavy* drowsy, dull   341 *heavy* tired   342 *fordone* exhausted   343 *wasted brands*
burned-out logs   349 *Every . . . sprite* every grave lets forth its ghost   352 *triple Hecate's*
(Hecate ruled in three capacities: as Luna or Cynthia in heaven, as Diana on earth, and as
Proserpina in hell.)

And we fairies, that do run
   By the triple Hecate's* team
From the presence of the sun,
   Following darkness like a dream,
Now are frolic.* Not a mouse   355
   Shall disturb this hallowed house.
I am sent with broom before,
To sweep the dust behind* the door.

*Enter [Oberon and Titania,] King and Queen of Fairies, with all
their train.*

Oberon: Through the house give glimmering light,
   By the dead and drowsy fire;   360
Every elf and fairy sprite
   Hop as light as bird from brier;
And this ditty, after me,
Sing, and dance it trippingly.

Titania: First, rehearse* your song by rote,   365
To each word a warbling note.
Hand in hand, with fairy grace,
Will we sing, and bless this place.

                                           [Song and dance.]

Oberon: Now, until the break of day,
Through this house each fairy stray.   370
To the best bride-bed will we,
Which by us shall blessèd be;
And the issue there create*
Ever shall be fortunate.
So shall all the couples three   375
Ever true in loving be;
And the blots of Nature's hand
Shall not in their issue stand;
Never mole, harelip, nor scar,
Nor mark prodigious,* such as are   380
Despisèd in nativity,
Shall upon their children be.
With this field dew consecrate*
Every fairy take his gait,*
And each several* chamber bless,   385
Through this palace, with sweet peace;
And the owner of it blest
Ever shall in safety rest.
Trip away; make no stay;
Meet me all by break of day.   390

---

355 *frolic* merry   358 *behind* from behind, or else like sweeping the dirt under the carpet.
(Robin Goodfellow was a household spirit who helped good housemaids and punished lazy ones,
but he could, of course, be mischievous.)   365 *rehearse* recite   373 *create* created
380 *prodigious* monstrous, unnatural   383 *consecrate* consecrated   384 *take his gait* go his way
385 *several* separate

Peter Brook's 1970 production, for the Royal Shakespeare Company, startled audiences with its stark set and animalistic sexuality. Brook, under the influence of Jan Kott, emphasized the play's connections to dreams and the unconscious.

Exeunt [Oberon, Titania, and train].

Puck [to the audience]: If we shadows have offended,
      Think but this, and all is mended,
      That you have but slumbered here*
      While these visions did appear.
      And this weak and idle theme,   395
      No more yielding but a dream,*
      Gentles, do not reprehend.
      If you pardon, we will mend.*
      And, as I am an honest Puck,
      If we have unearnèd luck   400
      Now to scape the serpent's tongue,*
      We will make amends ere long;
      Else the Puck a liar call.
      So, good night unto you all.
      Give me your hands,* if we be friends,   405
      And Robin shall restore amends.*   *[Exit.]*

[About 1594–1595]

393 *That . . . here* i.e., that it is a "midsummer night's dream"   396 *No . . . but* yielding no more than   398 *mend* improve   401 *serpent's tongue* i.e., hissing   405 *Give . . . hands* applaud   406 *restore amends* give satisfaction in return

Questions

Act I

1. How are the opening scenes' two pending marriages—Theseus and Hippolyta, Hermia and Lysander or Demetrius—related? Think about the freedom of the women in each marriage. How are women represented in this scene?
2. Look carefully at Helena's speech beginning at line 226. Make a list of the qualities of "Love" revealed in her speech. How does her view of love compare to your own?
3. Is Helena's desire to "enrich my pain" believable? That is, would a real person make such a declaration? Explain.
4. The scene with Quince, Bottom, and the other artisan players may seem unrelated to the various lovers presented in the preceding scenes. What is the connection? (What is the occasion of their performance? Can you guess at this point what kind of performance it will be?)

Act II

1. Lysander's observation that "The course of true love never did run smooth," seems to be accurate even on the supernatural level. Is the conflict between Oberon and Titania similar to the difficulties between the human lovers? Explain.
2. What sort of a creature is Puck? How would you describe Puck's relationship with Oberon? (How many characters are in some sense enslaved to another character?)
3. What is your response to Hermia's speech at the conclusion of this act (lines 151–163)? Is Hermia, alone in the woods in the dark, in any real danger? Is the audience supposed to fear for her? Explain.

Act III

1. Could Bottom's comment to Titania that "reason and love keep little company," be considered the unifying theme of *A Midsummer Night's Dream?* Explain.
2. How do you think Shakespeare intended his audiences to respond to Titania's speech beginning at line 130 (act III, scene i)? What is your response? Explain the difference, if any.
3. Why does Puck recount his adventures, telling Oberon what the audience has already just seen? (Why do you sometimes retell a story, even though your audience may already know what happened?) Consider the artfulness of Puck's story.
4. Puck's exclamation, "Lord, what fools these mortals be," is famous. Does the play support that sentiment without exception? Is the fairy court more impressively rational than the human court? At this point in the play, how do the two courts compare?
5. We know that Hermia is mistaken when she charges that Demetrius has murdered Lysander in his sleep. This isn't a tragedy; it isn't *Hamlet.* So why does Shakespeare allude to such a violent world? Does Hermia's assertion

damage the atmosphere of comedy and romance? What other hints of darkness appear in the play?

6. Helena's complaint, beginning at line 151, "If you were men. . . ," is particularly ironic in Elizabethan theatre. (Who would be playing Helena and Hermia?) How does the play define and complicate our notions of "man," "woman," "human," and "not-human"? (See Helena's speech, for starters.)

7. Oberon says, "we are spirits of another sort" (388). Explain what he means. What sort of spirits are they?

Act IV

1. What do you make of Oberon's request for the changeling child? How much of the night's misadventures can be traced back to this dispute between Oberon and Titania? What conclusions might one draw here?

2. Egeus invokes the law at line 148. Will the law resolve this situation? What will straighten things out?

3. Shakespeare is playing with the distinction between dreaming and waking. What other distinctions are called into question in the play?

Act V

1. What do the lunatic, the lover, and the poet have in common? Is this a plausible grouping? Is it persuasive?

2. Comment on the reference at line 57 to "tragical mirth." Does this phrase apply to the play as a whole?

3. Explain Theseus's speech in lines 89–105. Relate his remarks to the "transformations" throughout the play.

4. Oberon says about the players that "the best in this kind are but shadows." Does this observation undermine the value of theater? What about Puck's concluding speech to the audience? To what extent is Puck picking up on themes raised throughout the play?

5. All ends happily, it appears. Are there any loose ends still left, however? What about Demetrius? The changeling boy? Puck? What conclusions can you draw from the ending?

Critical Viewpoints

Sidney Homann: The Director's View

This excerpt by Sidney Homann offers an interesting glimpse backstage and provides a surprising answer to the question of how actors and directors get inside the heads of characters and develop a scene. In this case, an accident becomes the key to how a scene is played.

With his frail body plagued by arthritis, unsteady on his feet, our Egeus brought onstage an enormous large black law book, so large that it dwarfed him and he had great difficulty carrying it. On "And, my gracious Duke" (38), he managed to unload the volume on Theseus, who later, on "Either to die the death, or to abjure" (65), turned to the specific section where these harsh edicts were inscribed. I suggested that halfway through the conversation between the Duke and Hermia, Hippolyta cross to stage-left and, while the Duke was talking to Hermia on the left, take the volume from him, crossing back with it to her downstage-right position. She chose Theseus' "For disobedience to your father's will" (87) for that cross. Absorbed in his conversation with Hermia, Theseus could still feel her lift the book from his right arm, would catch her in the periphery of his eye and, distracted by Hippolyta, falter a bit on his next line. His subtext here was something like: "I'm not sure why you interrupted me in the middle of my talk with Hermia. Why would you, a woman, want to look at a law book? Well I can't deal with this now; we'll talk about it later—in private." As our stage manager suggested, Theseus has something of the E. H. Hutton mentality: when he speaks, everyone listens. Now back in her space downstage-right, Hippolyta could thumb through the law book, reading there a confirmation of her suspicions about Theseus' supposedly brave new world. Every once in awhile she would look up from her reading, sympathizing with her sisters, feeling for Lysander, looking contemptuously at Egeus and Demetrius and—most certainly—showing increasing doubts about the man who, at the top of the scene, had reminded her of the consummation four days away.

One day in rehearsal Hippolyta accidentally slammed the law book shut on Theseus' "Or else the law of Athens yields you up" (119), making a sound that, given the size of the book, boomed across the stage. Startled, the actor playing Theseus looked in her direction, and I promptly suggested that he deliver the next line to Hippolyta (they were twenty-five feet apart): "Which by no means we may extenuate." With the line said to Hippolyta rather than Hermia, Theseus' subtext was: "Why did you slam that book, right in the middle of my speech? Why did you take it in the first place? Don't you understand that I'm just doing my job? I can't ignore or water down ('extenuate') the law. I'm the Duke. It's my job to enforce the laws in that book you're reading. What I personally think about the law is not relevant. We'll speak about this later."

He crossed stage-right to Hippolyta on "Come, my Hippolyta" (122); his line to her, "What cheer, my love?" had the modern sense of: "Why so glum? Why out of spirits?" After his final four lines, where he promises to confer with Egeus and Demetrius on "something nearly that concerns" them, Theseus, facing upstage with his profile to stage-right, offered his left arm to Hippolyta, his eyes saying: "It's time to go, and I need to discuss this strange behavior of yours as soon as we are in private quarters." Turning toward him, her profile to stage-left, Hippolyta, instead of linking her arm with his as he expected, put the law book in Theseus' left hand, the action speaking loudly: "Snuggle up with that tonight, honey." He glared at her, angry that she was embarrassing him in front of the courtiers, who were now whispering among themselves on stage-left. Then she glanced down at whatever women were in the front row's audience left—we added this Brechtian touch the second week of rehearsals—as if addressing them: "Sisters, this male will wait an eternity for me until I give him my right arm [Theseus had since passed the book to his right arm and was conspicuously holding his left arm open in invitation]. What do you think I should do? What would you do, if you were I?" Then, much to Theseus' relief but, by the delay, asserting her integrity and such power as a woman could have in this patriarchal world, she gave him her arm so they could exit.

From Sidney Homann "'What Do I Do Now?': Directing *A Midsummer Night's Dream.*" In Jay Halio and Hugh Richmond, eds. *Shakespearean Illuminations: Essays in Honor of Marvin Rosenberg.* Newark: U of Delaware P, 1998, pp. 284–286.

C. Walter Hodges: Reader-Response Criticism

These drawings by C. Walter Hodges indicate how he imagined staging Act 2, scene 2; Act 3, scene 1; and Act 4, scene 1. This exercise is interesting and instructive, and these drawings are included here primarily to encourage you to attempt a similar depiction. Your artistic skills may be better or worse than Hodges; the point is not to produce a pretty drawing, but rather to think concretely about what a particular scene should look like.

11 Possible ways of staging Titania's bower (Act 2, Scene 2 and Act 3, Scene 1), by C. Walter Hodges. 11 *a* shows the bower at 2.2.91 and 11 *b* at 3.1.107. Titania's bower is described by Oberon at the end of 2.1 as canopied with flowers, and in 2.2 Titania sleeps in it. A curtained projection from the rear centre of the stage may have been used (see 2.2.30 SD and n.). The lovers then enter, Lysander and Hermia sleep, Demetrius and Helena quarrel, and all exit separately. There is no break in the action between Acts 2 and 3, and in 3.1, after the rehearsal of 'Pyramus and Thisbe' is interrupted by Puck, Titania wakes to hear Bottom (see 3.1.107 and n.). The audience is aware throughout of Titania as supposedly in her bower

Drawing of Act 2, Scene 1, and Act 3, Scene 1, by C. Walter Hodges. Source: New Cambridge Shakespeare, A Midsummer Nights Dream, edited by R.A. Foakes, 1984, p. 34. © Cambridge University Press.

A Midsummer Night's Dream   36

12   Possible ways of staging Act 4, Scene 1, by C. Walter Hodges. In this complex scene at least four areas of the stage are in use for different groups, and, until Bottom is left alone on stage at the end of the scene, there are always between ten and fifteen actors on stage. The lovers lie down separately to sleep at the end of Act 3, and 12a shows how the stage may have appeared at the opening of Act 4, when Titania sits with Bottom on a 'flowery bed'. 12b shows the entry of Theseus and Hippolyta with their 'trains' in procession at 4.1.125. (For further comment, see 4.1.0 SD and n.)

Drawing of Act 4, Scene 1, by C. Walter Hodges. Source: New Cambridge Shakespeare, A Midsummer Nights Dream, edited by R.A. Foakes, 1984, p. 36. © Cambridge University Press.

David Bevington: New Criticism

In the following three excerpts, the prominent Shakespearean scholar David Bevington assumes that the play itself tells us how to read its portrayal of love. Bevington is responding to the work of Jan Kott, who in 1964 (in Shakespeare Our Contemporary) had exaggerated (in Bevington's view) the play's dark side. For Kott, MSD is about sexual instinct and man's animal nature: Oberon wants Titania's boy because he is a bisexual pedophile, and Titania enjoys Bottom because he has the enormous sexual equipment of an ass. Bevington thinks that Kott, as well as Peter Brook's 1970 production based upon Kott, goes too far, and he searches for the harmonious balance in the play's depiction of sexuality and love.

When Oberon instructs Puck in Act III, scene ii of *A Midsummer Night's Dream*, to overcast the night with "drooping fog as black as Acheron," and to lead the "testy rivals" Demetrius and Lysander astray so that they will not actually harm one another in their rivalry, while Oberon for his part undertakes to obtain the changeling boy from Titania whom he will then release from her infatuated love of Bottom, Puck replies that the two of them will have to work fast. Such fairy doings need to be accomplished by night, insists Puck. With the approaching break of day, and the shining of Aurora's harbinger or morning star, ghosts and damned spirits will have to trip home to churchyards and their "wormy beds" beneath the ground. Puck's implication seems clear: he and Oberon, being spirits of the dark, are bound by its rules to avoid the light of day.

Just as clearly, however, Oberon protests that Puck is wrong in making such an assumption. "But we are spirits of another sort," Oberon insists.

> *I with the Morning's love have oft made sport,*
> *And, like a forester, the groves may tread*
> *Even till the eastern gate, all fiery red,*
> *Opening on Neptune, with fair blessed beams*
> *Turns into yellow gold his salt green streams.*

> (III.ii.388–93)[1]

Oberon may frolic until late in the dawn, though by implication even he may not stay abroad all day. The association of Oberon with sunlight and dawn is thus more symbolic than practical; it disassociates him from spirits of the dark, even though he must finish up this night's work before night is entirely past. He concedes to Puck the need for hurry: "But notwithstanding, haste; make no delay. / We may affect this business yet ere day." The concession implies that Oberon has made his point about sporting with the dawn not to refute Puck's call for swiftness, but to refute Puck's association of the fairies with ghosts and damned spirits.[2]

This debate between Oberon and Puck reflects a fundamental tension in the play between comic reassurance and the suggestion of something dark and threatening. Although the fairies act benignly, Puck continually hints at a good deal more than simple mischief. The forest itself is potentially a place of violent death and rape, even if the lovers experience nothing more than fatigue, anxiety, and being torn by briars. In the forest,

[1] Quotations are from *A Midsummer Night's Dream*, The Pelican Shakespeare, edited by Madeleine Doran (Baltimore, 1959). My title for this essay somewhat resembles that of Marjorie B. Gaber in her chapter, 'Spirits of another sort', from *Dream in Shakespeare* (New Haven, CT, 1974), but our critical purposes are essentially different. [The notes are Bevington's.]

[2] Roger Lancelyn Green, 'Shakespeare and the Fairies', *Folklore*, 73 (1962), 89–103, stresses his belief that the fairies of this play are not evil or malicious, like many spirits of folklore. So does K. M. Briggs (*The Anatomy of Puck* [London, 1959]). M. W. Latham (*The Elizabethan Fairies* [New York, 1930]) contend also that the fairies in *A Midsummer Night's Dream* are unthreatening, though he concedes that Shakespeare demonstrates in other plays a power among the fairies for troublemaking. David Young (*Something of Great Constancy* [New Haven, CT, 1966]), on the other hand, ably shows what is threatening about Puck; see, for example, p. 28. See also W. Moelwyn Merchant, '*A Midsummer Night's Dream*: a Visual Re-creation' in *Early Shakespeare*, ed. John Russell Brown and Bernard Harris, Stratford-upon-Avon Studies, 3 (London, 1961), pp. 165–83; G. K. Hunter, *William Shakespeare: The Late Comedies* (London, 1962), p. 16; and Michael Taylor, 'The Darker Purpose of *A Midsummer Night's Dream*', *Studies in English Literature*, 9 (1969), 257–73.

moreover, the experience of love invites all lovers to consider, however briefly, the opportunity for sexual revelling freed from the restraints of social custom. Of late, Jan Kott has shown to us most forcefully this dark side of love; indeed, he has done so too forcefully, and with an often exaggerated effect upon contemporary productions of this and other plays.[3] Still, his insight has something to commend it. If his overstated emphasis on the dark side of love can perhaps be seen as a manifestation of the new sexual freedom of the 1960s, the sometimes overheated reactions against Kott can perhaps be related to the reluctance of most of us to give up the romanticised and sentimentalised nineteenth-century reading of the play (epitomised in Mendelssohn's incident music) to which Kott is addressing his attack. Even today, we find it distasteful to speak openly of sexual longing in this comedy, for fear of dealing grossly with the play's delicately understated portrayal of Eros. My purpose, however, is to suggest that in its proper context the dark side of love is seldom very far away in this play. . . .

Repeatedly in this play, a presumption of man's licentiousness is evoked, only to be answered by the conduct of the lovers themselves. This representation of desire almost but not quite satisfied is to be sure a titillating one, but it looks forward as do the lovers themselves to legitimate consummation in marriage and procreation. At the very end, the lovers do all go to bed while Oberon speaks of the issue that will surely spring from their virtuous coupling. Earlier, Theseus has proposed to await the marriage day for his consummation, even though he captured his wife through military force; why else should he complain of the aged moon that "lingers" his desires "Like to a stepdame or a dowager"? (Hippolyta, with a maiden's traditional reluctance, seems more content with the four-day delay than does her amorous bridegroom.) The tradesmen's play serves as one last comic barrier to the achievement of desire, although it is mercifully brief and can be performed without epilogue in the interest of further brevity. Such waiting only makes the moment of final surrender more pleasurable and meaningful.

The conflict between sexual desire and rational restraint is, then, an essential tension throughout the play reflected in the images of dark and light. This same tension exists in the nature of the fairies and of the forest. The ideal course seems to be a middle one, between the sharp Athenian law on the one hand with its threat of death or perpetual chastity, and a licentiousness on the other hand that the forest (and man's inner self) proposes with alacrity, but from which the lovers are saved chiefly by the steadfastness of the women. They, after all, remain constant; it is the men who change affections under the effect of Oberon's love potion. (In the fairy plot, to be sure, we find a reverse symmetry that is surely intentional: the woman is inconstant, since it is Titania, the fairy queen, who takes a new lover. With a similar reversal the obstacle to love in the fairy plot is internal, since the king and queen are divided by their own quarrel for mastery in love, whereas in the plot of the four lovers the original obstacle is the external one of parental opposition.)[8]

This tension between licentiousness and self-mastery is closely related also to the way in which the play itself constantly flirts with genuine disaster but controls that threat through comic reassurance. Hermia is threatened

---

[3]Jan Kott, *Shakespeare Our Contemporary*, trans. Boleslaw Taborski (New York, 1964). . . .

[8]Young (*Something of Great Constancy*) discusses 'mirroring' of this sort on pp. 95ff.

with death in Act I, or with something almost worse than death—perpetual maidenhood, and yet we know already from the emphasis on love and marriage that all such threats to happiness are ultimately to prove illusory. Lysander and Hermia speak of "War, death, or sickness" and of other external threats to love, but are resolved on a plan of escape that will avoid all these. Repeatedly in the forest the lovers fear catastrophe only to discover that their senses have been deceiving them. "But who is here?" asks Helena as she comes across a sleeping man, Lysander, on the ground: "Dead, or asleep?" (II.ii.100–1). When, shortly afterwards, Hermia awakes to find herself deserted, she sets off after her strangely absent lover: "Either death, or you, I'll find immediately" (I.156). The choice seems dire, but the comic sense of discrepancy assures us that the need for such a choice is only a chimera. Later, again, when Helena concludes that all her erstwhile friends have turned against her for some inexplicable reason, she determines to leave them: "'Tis partly my own fault, / Which death or absence soon shall remedy" (III.ii.243–4). Only in the story of Pyramus and Thisbe, with its hilarious presentation of the very tragedy of misunderstanding that did not occur in *A Midsummer Night's Dream,* does comic reassurance fail. Instead of Helena's "Dead, or asleep?" the order is reversed. "Asleep, my love?" asks Thisbe as she finds Pyramus on the ground. "What, dead, my dove?" (V.i.316–17).[9]. . .

Titania does of course undergo an experience of misdirected love that is analogous to human inconstancy in love and that is prompted by the same love-juice applied to the eyes of Demetrius and Lysander. To confound her with a mortal is, however, to follow Kott's erroneous lead of imagining her as a white-skinned Scandinavian in Paris coupling with a dark-skinned man. That anachronistic image may well convey to us an aura of the exotic and bizarre, but in doing so it introduces a false note of sexual perversity and compulsion. Titania abundantly demonstrates that she is motivated by no such human drive. Her hours spent with Bottom are touchingly innocent and tender. Like the royal creature that she is, she forbids Bottom to leave her presence. Even if he is her slave, however, imprisoned in an animal form, she is no Circean enchantress teaching him enslavement to sensual appetite. Instead, her mission is to "purge thy mortal grossness so / That thou shalt like an airy spirit go" (III.i.145–6). It is because she is prompted by such ethereal considerations that she feeds him with apricots and dewberries, fans the moonbeams from his sleeping eyes, and the like. As Oberon reports later to Puck, having kept close watch over Titania, she graces the hairy temples of Bottom's ass's head "With coronet of fresh and fragrant flowers" (IV.i.51). Rather than descending into the realm of human passion and perversity, she has attempted to raise Bottom into her own. Bottom, for his part, speaking the part of the wise fool, has noted the irrationality of love but has submitted himself to deliciously innocent pleasures that are, for him, mainly gastronomic. Titania, and Shakespeare too, have indeed purged his mortal grossness, not by making him any less funny, but by showing how the tensions in this play between the dark and the affirmative side of love are reconciled in the image of Titania and the ass's head.

From David Bevington, "'But We Are Spirits of Another Sort'; The Dark Side of Love and Magic in *A Midsummer Night's Dream.*" *Medieval and Renaissance Studies* 13 (1975): 80–92.

[9]On 'Pyramus and Thisbe' as 'a foil to the entire play of which it is a part', see R. W. Dent, 'Imagination in *A Midsummer Night's Dream*', *Shakespeare Quarterly,* 15 (1964), 115–29.

Norman Holland: Reader-Response and Psychological Criticism

In the following excerpts, Holland combines reader-response and psychological assumptions. He believes that readers create meanings by bringing their own individual identities to the text. That may sound unavoidable and unremarkable, but Holland takes this notion further by assuming that each reader has certain identity themes—recurrent interests, needs, values— that shape whatever he or she is reading. The text may change, in other words, but a particular reader is always looking for the same things, as Holland sees it. Thus, Holland's reading of Hermia's dream is most remarkable for what it reveals about Holland, and for what it suggests about how we might interact with great works on a personal level. The occasion of Hermia's dream, you will recall, is that she and Lysander have become exhausted in the woods. They lie down to sleep; Lysander is bewitched by Puck, awakes to see Helena, and goes off in pursuit of her. Then Hermia wakes up alone.

When we first hear the dream, it is still going on. That is, I think she is still dreaming when she first speaks about it. As with so many nightmares, she is having trouble waking:

> *Help me, Lysander, help me! do thy best*
> *To pluck this crawling serpent from my breast!*
> *Ay me, for pity!*

And only now, I think, is she beginning to come out of it:

> *Ay me, for pity! what a dream was here!*
> *Lysander, look how I do quake with fear.*
> *Methought a serpent eat my heart away,*
> *And you sate smiling at his cruel prey.*
> *Lysander! what, remov'd? Lysander! lord!*
> *What, out of hearing gone? No sound, no word?*
> *Alack, where are you? Speak, and if you hear!*
> *Speak, of all loves! I swoon almost with fear.*
> *No? Then I well perceive you are not nigh.*
> *Either death, or you, I'll find immediately.*
>
> (II.ii.145–56)

In effect, as Hermia tells the dream, she splits it into two parts. In the first, we hear the dream actually taking place. In the second, Hermia reports the dream to us after it is over. In the first part she makes a plea for help, but in the second we learn that Lysander wasn't interested in helping at all—he was just smiling and watching the serpent eat Hermia. Further, if we take the most obvious Freudian meaning for that serpent—a penis or phallus—the masculinity in the dream is split between the attacking, crawling serpent and her lover Lysander, smiling at a distance.

Among the fifty-one topics Erikson suggests considering in a full dream analysis, let me be merciful and select just one:'methods of defence, denial, and distortion', which might be considered a variation on another topic, 'mechanisms of defence', itself a subtopic of 'ego identity and life-plan'.[1] I see in this dream something I think is fundamental to Hermia's character.

---

[1] Erik H. Erikson, 'The Dream Specimen of Psychoanalysis', in *Psychoanalytic Psychiatry and Psychology: Clinical and Theoretical Papers, Austen Riggs Center,* ed. Robert P. Knight and Cyrus R. Friedman (New York, 1954), pp. 131–70, 144–5. [All notes are Holland's.]

If I go back to the first things Hermia says and look just at her speeches as an actor would, I see a recurring pattern.[2] After hearing her father, Theseus admonishes her, 'Demetrius is a worthy gentleman', and Hermia replies with her first words in the play, 'So is Lysander' (an alternative). But, replies Theseus, since Demetrius has your father's approval, he 'must be held the worthier'. 'I would my father look'd but with my eyes', answers Hermia. Next she begins a long speech by begging Theseus' pardon, wondering why she is bold, and worrying lest, by revealing her thoughts, she impeach her modesty. But, she says:

> . . . I beseech your Grace that I may know
> The worst that may befall me in this case,
> If I refuse to wed Demetrius.
>
> (I.i.62–4)

I hear in all these speeches a distinct, recurring pattern. Call it a concern for alternatives, for other possibilities, or for an elsewhere: Lysander as alternative to Demetrius, her judgement as an alternative to her father's, her boldness contrasted with her modesty, or the alternatives the law allows her. We could say that Hermia's personal style or character consists (in the theoretical language of Heinz Kohut) of creating self-objects.[3] Thus, after her dialogue with Theseus, the lovers are left alone, and Hermia uses a variety of examples and legends from the elsewhere of classical mythology to illustrate and buttress their love. Then, to Helena, who loves Demetrius, she describes how she and Lysander will run away, again looking for an elsewhere, an alternative to Athens: 'To seek new friends and stranger companies.' I would phrase Hermia's personal style as the seeking of some alternative in order to amend something closer to herself.

Her last speeches as well as her first show this sense of alternatives. Theseus, Egeus, and the rest have come upon the lovers and wakened them. However, the lovers are not sure they aren't still dreaming. Says Hermia:

> Methinks I see these things with parted eye,
> When every thing seems double.
>
> (IV.i.189–90)

Demetrius starts checking reality and asks: 'Do you not think/The Duke was here, and bid us follow him?' And Hermia, for her last word in the play, offers one final alternative; 'Yea, and my father.'[4] . . .

---

[2]For a more elaborate example of this method, see Norman N. Holland, 'A Touching of Literary and Psychiatric Education', *Seminars in Psychiatry*, 5 (1973), 287–99.

[3]Heinz Kohut, *The Analysis of the Self: A Systematic Approach to the Psychoanalytic Treatment of Narcissistic Personality Disorders* (New York, 1971), pp. xiv–xv and passim.

[4]Most Shakespeareans regard Hermia and Helena as interchangeable, except for height and colour (III.ii.290ff. and II.ii.114). Reading their 'sides', though, as an actress would (see n. 3 above), I detect a characterological difference. As in the text, Hermia speaks and acts through 'amendment by alternative' (to compress her identity into a theme). Helena tries to cope (I think) by establishing a contradiction or opposition and then seeking to become that opposite. See, for example, her speeches in I.i.: 'Call you me fair? That fair again unsay', and 'O that your frowns would teach my smiles such skill.' She would give everything, she tells her rival Hermia, 'to be your translated'. And she adds: 'How happy some o'er other some can be.' All these lead to her explication of the emblem of Cupid in terms of reversals and her decision at the end of the scene to convert Demetrius' pursuit of Hermia in the wood to his presence with herself. Compare her last words in the play, 'And Hippolyta' (Theseus' opposite) to Hermia's, 'and my father' (Theseus' parallel).

For me, the two images of Hermia's dream, the eating snake and the smiling lover, evoke large questions of fidelity and possession between men and women that I find puzzling and troubling as I watch my students struggling to find and maintain stable relationships or as I see in my own generation yet another friend's marriage break up. That is, Hermia's dream, her very presence in the forest with Lysander, builds on the mutual promises she and Lysander made, a contract sealed by a dangerous elopement, a pledge of faith that her lover, at the very moment of her dream, has abandoned. Her dream begins from his infidelity.

As I visualise the dream, I see a small snake at a distance—yes, like a penis in the classic Freudian symbolism—but I also remember a picture from a book of nature photographs of a snake's wide open mouth with long, curved fangs under a pink, arched palate, one demonic eye showing behind the furious jaws. The head is all mouth, really, there is so little else besides that act of biting. Hermia describes the snake as 'crawling', and we have already guessed at her associations. Mine are to a baby who is all helpless, inarticulate demand. For me, then, Hermia's image of the snake sets up the idea of possession, the way a lover or a penis can make a total demand as an animal or a baby demands food. . . .

Nowadays, people reject the idea that love entitles you to possess another person. I too reject that kind of possessiveness—at least I consciously do. Yet the opposite possibility, a cool distant love, does not satisfy me as a solution. I believe in a fidelity of mutual trust, an exchange of promises that I will be true to you and you will be true to me. I realise that contemporary patterns of marriage and sex deeply question this style of relationship. Many people believe they can and do love more than one person passionately and sexually at the same time.

No matter how contemporary I like to think myself in sexual matters, however, I have to admit that, deep down, I do not feel that the mutual pledge of loving or of sexual promises is the kind of contract one can negotiate like a lease on an apartment, with provisions for termination, renegotiation, or repairs. Nor do I believe one can hold several such leases at once. To be intimate is to risk oneself with another, and it is difficult, for me at least, to feel free to open myself up to another person without being able to feel that that opening up will be one-to-one, that neither of us will compromise our intimacy by sharing it with some third person. Somewhere inside me I deeply fear that I would be made small and ridiculous, like a child, were my lover to share our one-to-oneness with another lover. Hence I perceive Lysander's smiling as a cruel ridicule. . . .

10

Thus I read Hermia's dream as having three parts. First, the snake preys on a passive Hermia's heart in an act of total, painful, destructive possession—hard on Hermia, but satisfying to that masculine snake. That possessiveness is one possibility open to me in relating to a woman or a play.

Second, Lysander smilingly watches the woman he so recently loved being possessed by another. His smile signals to me another kind of cruelty—dispassion, distance, indifference—another way of relating to a play or a lover. The snake is fantastic and symbolic, whereas Lysander presents a far more realistic lover whom I can interpret all too well through our century's alternatives to romantic commitment.

Then there is a third aspect to the dream, as I view it. It is a nightmare. The dream has aroused anxieties too great for Hermia to sleep through. She wakes, and we never learn how she might have dreamed that a loving Lysander plucked away a possessive snake. Instead, we are left with his deserting her for another woman.

For me, the sense of incompleteness is particularly strong, because I very much need to see a coherence and unity in human relations. I want a happy ending for this comedy. I want these couples married at the end, but I don't see—I don't trust, really—the way the comedy gets them together. Out of infidelity comes fidelity—but how? Hermia trusts Lysander, but he is unfaithful and leaves her alone and terrified: 'I swoon almost with fear.' It is hard for me to trust that there will be a happy outcome despite his cruel and contemptuous abandonment.

When I confess my uneasiness because the dream is incomplete and the play is silent on the creation of trust, I am working through something about myself I have faced many times before. It's hard for me simply to trust and to tolerate uncertainty or absence or silence. I question both Hermia's dream and the sexual revolution of our own time because I need to *know* things, particularly about human relations. I need to feel certain.

None of this, of course, do Lysander or the other lovers say. They talk about feelings of love and jealousy we can all share, but they do so within the conventions of Renaissance marriage. You and I, however, read what they say from a perch in our own culture, with its many marital and non-marital and extra-marital possibilities, all challenging the traditional limits on relations between the sexes. Where Shakespeare's lovers proceeded in their own day to a sure and socially structured Renaissance conclusion, now I feel they are opening up all kinds of twentieth-century uncertainties without, naturally, saying much about them. In particular, Hermia's dream images the tension between possessiveness and distance and the—to me at least—unknown way trust will resolve that tension. . . .

Hermia's dream is not simply a dream dreamed for us. Rather, we dream her dream for ourselves, and as we know ourselves so we know the dream, until its local habitation is here and its name is us.

From Norman Holland, "Hermia's Dream." From *Annual of Psychoanalysis* 7 (1979): 369–389.

Richard Wilson: Political Criticism

In this excerpt Richard Wilson discusses Karl Marx's fascination with MSD and suggests the sort of moves involved in an economical view of the play.

Whenever Karl Marx contemplated British politics he was reminded of *A Midsummer Night's Dream,* and when he considered Britain's token opposition he thought of the bathetic mew of Snug the Joiner. Victorian parliamentarians who imagined themselves as earth-shakers, he joked, were like Shakespeare's craven craftsman, unconvincingly acting out the rage of the British lion; while the thunder of a *Times* editorial was a charade to which the only possible response was Demetrius's ironic applause for Snug's fox-like valour: 'Well roar'd lion!' The secret of British compromise, Marx deduced, was contained in the discretion with which the workers and nobles defer for each other in Shakespearean Athens; and if modern France had gone from revolutionary tragedy to constitutional comedy, this was because Napoleon III had learned from Duke Theseus to manage politics 'as a masquerade in which grand costumes, words, and postures serve only as masks,' and the Paris mob played its part 'as Nick Bottom plays that of the lion,' *sotto voce* and roaring 'as gently as any sucking dove' (I.ii.87). After 1848, Marx considered, conservative rule throughout Europe was 'like the lamentable comedy of Pyramus and Thisbe performed by Bottom and his friends': a pitiful burlesque. History repeats itself the second time as farce in a parliamentary system, he inferred, because sovereignty and subversion are both neutralised in the synthesis that is predicted in Shakespeare's play: 'It is like the lion in *Midsummer Night's Dream*, who calls out: "I am a lion!" and then whispers "I am not a lion, but only Snug". Thus every extreme is one time the lion of contradiction, at another the Snug of mediation.' Representing bloody tragedy as a comic game, therefore, parliament tames the revolution; and if Shakespeare remained, Eleanor Marx reported, her father's Bible, that was in part because of the uncanny way in which the plot of *A Midsummer Night's Dream* seemed to him to premonitor this historic reversal.

From *Essays and Studies* 46 (1993): 1–24.

Shirley Nelson Garner: Feminist Criticism

Since MSD *involves a daughter being forced to marry against her will, and a male ruler who is marrying his conquered captive, not to mention a fairy king who humiliates and dominates his fairy queen, it is not surprising that feminist critics have been interested in this play. In this essay Shirley Nelson Garner makes two persuasive points: the play ultimately "affirms patriarchal order and hierarchy," and heterosexuality is tenuous, threatening to break down if patriarchal order is not maintained. Garner's purpose seems not to be an attack on the way men have oppressed women and feared women's bonding with each other; rather, Garner seems to be engaged in an analysis of how social and sexual order is maintained. For Garner, in other words, that is what the play is about: Shakespeare is exposing the forces that threaten social and sexual order, and the mechanisms that keep these forces in check.*

> *Jack shall have Jill;*
> *Nought shall go ill;*
> *The man shall have his mare again,*
> *and all shall be well.*

More than any of Shakespeare's comedies, *A Midsummer Night's Dream* resembles a fertility rite, for the sterile world that Titania depicts at the beginning of Act II is transformed and the play concludes with high celebration, ritual blessing, and the promise of regeneration. Though this pattern is easily apparent and has often been observed, the social and sexual implications of the return of the green world have gone unnoticed. What has not been so clearly seen is that the renewal at the end of the play affirms patriarchal order and hierarchy, insisting that the power of women must be circumscribed, and that it recognises the tenuousness of heterosexuality as well. The movement of the play toward ordering the fairy, human, and natural worlds is also a movement toward satisfying men's psychological needs, as Shakespeare perceived them, but its cost is the disruption of women's bonds with each other. . . .

Titania's attachment to the boy is clearly erotic. She 'crowns him with flowers, and makes him all her joy', according him the same attentions as those she bestows on Bottom when, under the spell of Oberon's love potion, she falls in love with the rustic-turned-ass. She has 'forsworn'

Oberon's 'bed and company' (II.i.62). Whatever the child is to her as a 'love-ly boy' and a 'sweet' changeling, he is ultimately her link with a mortal woman whom she loved. Oberon's passionate determination to have the child for himself suggests that he is both attracted to and jealous of him. He would have not only the boy but also the exclusive love of Titania. He needs to cut her off from the child because she is attracted to him not only as boy and child, but also as his mother's son. Oberon's need to humiliate Titania in attaining the boy suggests that her love for the child poses a severe threat to the fairy king. . . .

Like the fairy king, the two men in power in the human world, Theseus and Egeus, want to attain the exclusive love of a woman and, also, to accommodate their homoerotic desires. In order to do so, they, like Oberon, attempt to limit women's power, and their success or failure to do so affects their participation in the comic world. . . .

Though Theseus is less severe than Egeus, he is, from the outset, unsympathetic toward women. The first words he speaks, voicing the play's first lines and first image, must be taken as a sign: the moon 'lingers' his desires, he tells Hippolyta, 'Like a stepdame, or a dowager,/Long withering out a young man's revenue.' He utterly supports Egeus as patriarch, telling Hermia:

> To you your father should be as a god,
> One that composed your beauties; yea, and one
> To whom you are but as a form in wax
> By him imprinted and within his power
> To leave the figure or disfigure it.
>
> (I.i.47–51)

As a ruler, he will enforce the law, which gives Egeus control over Hermia's sexuality and embodies patriarchal order. Though he has heard that Demetrius has won Helena's heart but now scorns her, and has meant to speak to him about it, 'My mind did lose it' (I.i.114). A lover-and-leaver of women himself, he undoubtedly identifies with Demetrius and forgets his duty toward Helena. He exits inviting Egeus and Demetrius to follow and talk confidentially with him, suggesting his spiritual kinship with them. . . .

It is significant that the woman whom he at last will marry is not traditionally feminine. She has been a warrior, and in her new role as the fiancée of the Athenian Duke, we see her as a hunter. Nostalgically, she recalls her past experiences:

> I was with Hercules and Cadmus once,
> When in a wood of Crete they bayed the bear
> With hounds of Sparta. Never did I hear
> Such gallant chiding; for, besides the groves,
> The skies, the fountains, every region near
> Seemed all one mutual cry. I never heard
> So musical a discord, such sweet thunder.
>
> (IV.i.113–19)

Her androgynous character appears to resolve for Theseus the apparent dissociation of his romantic life, the sign of which is his continual desertion of women who love him.

Having found an androgynous woman, Theseus captures her and brings her home to be his wife. By conquering and marrying this extraordinarily powerful woman, he fulfils his need for the exclusive love of a woman while gratifying his homoerotic desires. Unlike Oberon, however, he finds satisfaction for his desires merged in one person. If we imagine Hippolyta played by a male actor who, though cast as a woman, dresses and walks like a man ('buskined mistress', 'bouncing Amazon'), Hippolyta and Theseus must have looked more like homosexual than heterosexual lovers. Hippolyta's androgynous appearance is further confirmed by the fact that in Renaissance fiction and drama men were occasionally disguised as Amazons, e.g. lovers, like Sidney's Zelmane, in the *Arcadia,* who wished to be near his lady.

. . . Whereas the separation of Hippolyta and Titania from other women is implied or kept in the background, the breaking of women's bonds is central in the plot involving the four young lovers. Demetrius and Lysander are divided at the outset, but the play dramatises the division of Hermia and Helena. Furthermore, their quarrelling is more demeaning than the men's. And once Demetrius and Lysander are no longer in competition for the same woman, their enmity is gone. Hermia and Helena, on the contrary, seem permanently separated and apparently give over their power to the men they will marry. Once their friendship is undermined and their power diminished, they are presumably 'ready' for marriage.

Hermia's fond recollection of her long-standing and intimate friendship with Helena calls attention to Helena's disloyalty, occasioned by the latter's desire to win Demetrius's thanks and to be near him. Telling her friend that she intends to run away with Lysander, Hermia recalls:

> *And in the wood, where often you and I*
> *Upon faint primrose beds were wont to lie,*
> *Emptying our bosoms of their counsel sweet,*
> *There my Lysander and myself shall meet.*
> (I.i.214-17)

Just as Helena breaks her faith with Hermia to ingratiate herself with Demetrius, so later she will believe that Hermia has joined with men against her. Deeply hurt, Helena chastises Hermia:

> *Is all the counsel that we two have shared,*
> *The sister's vows, the hours that we have spent,*
> *When we have chid the hasty-footed time*
> *For parting us—O, is all forgot?*
> *All school days friendship, childhood innocence?*
> *We, Hermia, like two artificial gods,*
> *Have with our needles created both one flower,*
> *Both on one sampler, sitting on one cushion,*
> *Both warbling of one song, both in one key;*
> *As if our hands, our sides, voices, and minds,*
> *Had been incorporate. So we grew together,*
> *Like to a double cherry, seeming parted,*
> *But yet an union in partition,*
> *Two lovely berries moulded on one stem;*
> *So, with two seeming bodies, but one heart;*
> *Two of the first, like coats in heraldry,*
> *Due but to one and crowned with one crest.*
> *And will you rent our ancient love asunder,*
> *To join with men in scorning your poor friend?*
> *It is not friendly, 'tis not maidenly.*

Our sex, as well as I, may chide you for it,
Though I alone do feel the injury.

(III.ii.198-219)

In a scene that parallels in its central position Titania's wooing of Bottom, the rupture of their friendship becomes final. They accuse and insult each other, with Hermia calling Helena a 'juggler', 'canker blossom', 'thief of love', 'painted maypole'; and Helena naming her a 'counterfeit' and a 'puppet' (III.ii.282-96). Their quarrel becomes absurd as it turns on Hermia's obsession, taken up by both Lysander and Helena, that Lysander has come to prefer Helena because she is taller. Though no other women characters in Shakespeare's plays come close to fighting physically, Hermia threatens to scratch out Helena's eyes (III.ii.297-8). Her threat is serious enough to make Helena flee (II. 340-3). Lysander is made equally ridiculous in his abrupt change of heart; yet he and Demetrius are spared the indignity of a demeaning quarrel and leave the stage to settle their disagreement in a 'manly' fashion, with swords. Even though Puck makes a mockery of their combat through his teasing, they are not so thoroughly diminished as Hermia and Helena.

From *Women's Studies* 9 (1981): 48-63.

Douglas Green: Queer Theory

In the following excerpt Green considers how the play reveals alternative sexualities and then attempts to curb them. By considering (in the second excerpt) Oberon's reaction to Titania and Bottom's union, Green argues that "perversion" cannot be entirely contained by the "the illusions of total order and control."

In 1985 Liviu Ciulei, artistic director of the Guthrie Theater in Minneapolis, mounted a production of *A Midsummer Night's Dream*. His version of the play was, as the program notes attest, greatly informed by modern commentary on the play, including that of such notable feminist critics as Shirley Nelson Garner.[1] This essay has its genesis in a particular aspect and effect of that production. In interludes between several scenes, accompanied by music and covered by enormous, beautiful gauze runners on a set solely of black, white, and red, some of the principal actors would join in a variety of pantomime sexual encounters—straight, gay, lesbian, bisexual, single-partner, multiple-partner, etc. As the play proceeded, these comparatively random unions rose with the confusions of the lovers and gradually sorted themselves out as the "true lovers" found each other. What I experienced at this production was a metatheatrical illustration of the well-known way in which this and other Shakespearean comedies represent disruptions of social order—ones that at times for twentieth-century viewers and readers seem liberating—only to

[1]See Thomas Clayton's polemical review of this production, "Shakespeare at the Guthrie: *A Midsummer Night's Dream," Shakespeare Quarterly* 37 (1986): 229 36. Clayton praises Ciulei's *Dream* as "a major production by any measure and certainly one of the most systematically conceived," but apparently regrets the vision of Shakespeare's play as "a dark comedy about patriarchal abuses of power in a reading Ciulei said was prescribed by the imperatives of our time" (230).

accommodate that order, usually by reasserting some slightly modified version of it at the end.

For me Ciulei's *Dream* exposed how "it is our cultures that imagine that when heterosexual relations occur beside homosexual relations, the straight relation must win out—as if a biological destiny were asserting itself."[2] The Guthrie production suggested simultaneously the erotic possibilities (officially) proscribed by the societies of Shakespearean Athens, Elizabethan England, and Reaganite America that the text temporarily brings into play and the naturalized reassertion of those proscriptions. In so doing, Ciulei exposed one likely aspect of *Dream's* ideological effect in our time, if not in early modern England: the play is designed to foreclose all erotic unions that do not lead to socially sanctioned (i.e., marital) procreation; in a time that had witnessed simultaneously radical feminism and the reassertion of "family values," gay rights and the cruel effects of mass paranoia about HIV and AIDS, Ciulei's production had exposed how a bit of high humanist culture like *A Midsummer Night's Dream*, despite its seeming tolerance and expansiveness, contributes to the ideological work of contemporary conservatism. If finally the text curbs the willful exercise of paternal power by Egeus, it still ends with the erasure of Amazons, the paternal sanctioning by Theseus of desired unions to ensure or enhance procreation, and the curbing too of Puckish pleasures in "those things. . . . / That befall prepost'rously" (3.2.120–21).[3]

. . . What is it that so frightens and/or disgusts Oberon as he surveys the love-making of Titania and her Bottom? The scene enacts a crucial *méconnaissance,* really a complex series of misrecognitions by Oberon: of his own sodomitical intentions toward the changeling boy, of his own misogynistic fears of female power and desires, of the residence of his honor in Titania and of his resentment of its disposition outside himself, of Titania's "lesbianism" as bestiality and hence as sodomy, of his own desires to be desired (by Titania) and to control desires, of his own sadistic voyeurism, etc. It exposes analogically the justification for Theseus's abduction of the Amazon: what women do when not subject(ed) to men is beyond the pale. Metatheatrically, it may represent (masculine) Elizabethan incomprehension in the face of the queen, who has the power to dispose of herself and to act on her own desires—Elizabeth as sodomite, her imagined transgressiveness,

[2]Alan Sinfield, *Cultural Politics—Queer Reading* (Philadelphia: University of Pennsylvania Press, 1994), 10.

[3]See, for instance Shirley Nelson Garner, "*A Midsummer Night's Dream:* 'Jack Shall Have Jill; / Nought Shall Go Ill,'" *Women's Studies* 9 (1981): 47–63. Garner holds the view "that the renewal at the end of the play affirms patriarchal order and hierarchy, insisting that the power of women must be circumscribed, and that it recognizes the tenuousness of heterosexuality," which needs, therefore, to be enforced (47). I am indebted to Garner's essay throughout, particularly for its feminist analysis of homoerotic elements in the play and of what Adrienne Rich, in "Compulsory Heterosexuality and Lesbian Existence," *Signs* 5 (1980): 631–60, calls "compulsory heterosexuality." The sodomitical import of "preposterousness" is discussed later in this essay; see Jonathan Goldberg, *Sodometries: Renaissance Texts, Modern Sexualities* (Stanford: Stanford University press, 1992), 180–81, on the meaning of "preposterous venus." . . .

whether seeking a husband or furtively fulfilling carnal desires with men (or women) not her equals.[4]

The full comic force of the scene derives precisely from the inexpressibility of the "undoings" of this moment where what is inconceivable finds its representation in what is proscribed: thus the scene may constitute from Oberon's voyeuristic position a reenactment of the unthinkable (lesbian) love of Titania for her votaress (mother of the disputed changeling boy), now displaced onto the manifest bestiality of Titania's embrace of an "ass," whose name—Bottom—may well conjure the anatomical pun, which introduces the (other) "sodomy" that is never mentioned or recognized as such but implied in Oberon's obsession with the changeling boy.[5] In this case, what Foucault says of power's masking itself in order to succeed applies as forcefully to the self-delusion of the ruler as it does to the blinding of the ruled: "power is tolerable only on condition that it mask a substantial part of itself. Its success is proportional to its

[4]I am indebted in general here to Goldberg's discussion of Puttenham (*Sodometries*, 29–61), especially the subsidiary analysis of the *Sieve Portrait* of Elizabeth (43–47). Goldberg builds on but also raises questions about new historicist views of the anxiety elicited by the queen's sexuality and power (see, for example, Louis Adrian Montrose, "*A Midsummer Night's Dream* and the Shaping Fantasies of Elizabethan Culture: Gender, Power, Form," in *Rewriting the Renaissance,* eds. Margaret W. Ferguson, Maureen Quilligan, and Nancy J. Vickers [Chicago: University of Chicago Press, 1986], 65–87 and 329–34, and "'Shaping Fantasies': Figurations of Gender and Power in Elizabethan Culture," in *Representing the English Renaissance,* ed. Stephen Greenblatt [Berkeley: University of California Press, 1988], 31–64). See Gregory W. Bredbeck's discussion of the monarch's "two bodies" and its implications for writing (about) *Edward II* (50–60), especially the implicit "recognition of a space between power and person that can be narrowed or widened depending on the circumstances" (53); this space has a good deal to do, I think, with the way that through Titania concerns about the English queen's political powers are shifted to the sexual appetites of the temporal woman. Equally significant is James L. Calderwood's discussion of the double meaning of Titania's lines about the moon's "lamenting some enforced chastity" (3.1.198–200), delivered as she prepares to have Bottom hauled off to her bower (Calderwood, 421–22); the phrase, at least in its secondary meaning as compulsory chastity, calls up both the nunnery to which Hermia would be sent and the ostensible condition of the Virgin Queen herself.

[5]As Bray stresses, social and economic context and power determined how sodomitical relationships were both perceived and conducted: "What determined the shared and recurring features of homosexual relationships [in Renaissance England] was the prevailing distribution of power, economic power and social power, not the fact of homosexuality itself" (Bray, *Homosexuality in Renaissance England,* 56). Traub sees a "maternal" bond between Titania and her devotee through the boy ("[In]significance," 158–59), but I would suggest that the embrace of Titania and Bottom-the-ass is a "male" metaphor for female-female relations, exchanges, and bonds. If so, was the substitution of this human ass for another woman somehow a less threatening displacement (for Shakespeare) or a sadistic, misogynistic one—a sign of confusion in the face of "lesbian" sexuality or one of anxiety? Still, I agree with Traub about Oberon's feelings of superfluousness in the face of relations that simply do not require him ("[In]significance," 159). To the extent that one does see tensions between an image of Oberon and Titania as squabbling over an adoptive son and those of the boy as embodiment of intersecting sexual relations (Titania-[votaress], Titania-boy, Oberon-boy), one might speculate also on incest as a key site of the contradiction between the family as a "deployment of alliance" and as "a hotbed of constant sexual incitement" (Foucault, 180–109) and what that might do, if not to likely Renaissance views of the dispute over the boy, then at least to some of ours: it might suggest, among other things, incest as a sign of "perverse" desire that cannot otherwise be represented.

ability to hide its own mechanisms."[6] Interestingly, the scene's allusion to sodomy marks multiple social frontiers. Among others, it indicates and—from and through Oberon's perspective—castigates, even negates, the possibilities of unrestrained female desires of any sort and their enactment ("Be as thou wast wont to be; / See as thou wast wont to see" [4.I.71–72]); ignores the supposedly impossible aspirations of subordinate classes and their realization, reducing them to "the fierce vexation of a dream" (4.I.69); and misconstrues and/or displaces erotic desires and practices of his own—"And now I have the boy" (4.1.62)—that he does not or cannot recognize as sodomy.

Not surprisingly, this is one of those moments of disorder in which Oberon hauls out another potion, a theatrical *deus ex machina,* to contain the explosive representations that derive originally from his own intervention in the affairs of those around him: "But first I will release the Fairy Queen" (4.1.70). We might recognize here the tension between the play's expansiveness and its containment: the very system of power relations that enables a Theseus or Oberon to intervene in and arrange the affairs of others leads to situations that belie their attempts to maintain order; the solution to those situations in turn lies with changes in the rulers themselves—a proposition at once seemingly radical in identifying the source of the problem (the rulers' having ruled poorly) and yet hopelessly contained within and supportive of the status quo.

And yet the genie cannot quite be squeezed back into the bottle. As Oberon's agent, Puck represents that slippage between power and its exercise that affords some space, however minimal, for interests, desires, pleasures, and practices other than those consonant with dominant ideology. Thus Oberon scolds Puck: "Of thy misprision must perforce ensue / Some true love turn'd, and not a false turn'd true" (3.2.90–91). Though the *OED* glosses this usage as "a misunderstanding" or "a mistake," both the legalistic sense, having to do with "a misdemeanor or failure of duty on the part of a public official," and the wholly separate substantive meaning of "scorn" or "contempt" are possible and likely operative here. Such Puckish "misprision" embodies what Dollimore calls the "paradoxical perverse," in which "the most extreme threat to the true form of something comes not so much from its absolute opposite or its direct negation, but in the form of its perversion; somehow the perverse threat of (or rather because of) that connection, also the utter contradiction of the true and authentic."[7] Like Bottom, whose imagination is unfathomable and hence, if not threatening, still not ordered as Theseus would have it, Puck signals in the fairy world the possibility of disorder or, put another way, the un- or mis-recognized possibility of preposterous pleasures: "And those things do best please me / That befall prepost'rously" (3.2.120–21). If it is on such misrecognitions, on such blind spots, that the illusions of total order and control—of Oberon and, by extension, of Theseus—are constructed, it is nevertheless through the "perverse dynamic" of Puckish agency that these illusions are exposed.[8]

5

---

[6]Foucault, 86.

[7]Dollimore, 121.

[8]According to Dollimore, "the perverse dynamic signifies the potential of those [perverse] paradoxes to destabilize, to provoke discoherence" (121).

From Douglas Green, "Preposterous Pleasures: Queer Theories and *A Midsummer Night's Dream*." In Dorothea Keller, ed. *A Midsummer Night's Dream: Critical Essays*. New York: Garland, 1998, pp. 369-400.

Philip McGuire: Deconstruction and Historical Criticism

With deconstruction's emphasis on opening up texts, in part by listening carefully for what is not being said, it's not surprising that Philip McGuire is especially interested in Hippolyta's silence in the play's opening moments. Her absence of lines opens up a space for actors and directors to create her part, and thus McGuire looks at four different productions of MSN from different historical moments. He finds strikingly divergent readings of the play issuing from this silence, supporting the deconstructive assumption that meaning cannot be controlled—by authors, readers, or the text. This slipperiness of meaning is not, as McGuire notes, necessarily a bad thing as it enables the different productions' variety of interpretations.

Four specific productions of *A Midsummer Night's Dream* between 1959 and 1980 demonstrate the range of meanings and effects that Hippolyta's silence can generate without contradicting the words of Shakespeare's playtext. During Peter Hall's 1959 production at the Shakespeare Memorial Theatre in Stratford-upon-Avon, Hippolyta's silence confirmed the harmony between her and Theseus that was expressed during the opening dialogue. She and Theseus sat side by side as he listened to Egeus' accusation and Hermia's reply. After warning Hermia to 'take time to pause', Theseus stood and raised an unresisting Hippolyta to her feet. As they walked toward the staircase that dominated the set, Theseus stated that Hermia's decision must be made 'by the next new moon – / The sealing day betwixt my love and me / For everlasting bond of fellowship' (II.83-5). They reached the staircase and stood there together while Theseus set forth the third of Hermia's alternatives: 'on Diana's altar to protest / For aye austerity and single life' (II.89-90). The consistent pairing of Theseus and Hippolyta underscored the contrast between what that 'sealing day' would bring for Hippolyta and what it would bring for Hermia. Their movements together also established that both Theseus and Hippolyta were oblivious to the contrast.

That pairing was interrupted briefly later in the scene, when Theseus walked away from Hippolyta and toward Hermia while advising her to 'arm yourself / To fit your fancies to your father's will' (II.117-18), but the interruption did not signify any breach in the relationship between Theseus and Hippolyta. Having warned Hermia that the Athenian law sentenced her 'to death or to a vow of single life' if she failed to obey her father, Theseus turned immediately to the woman who was soon to become his bride and said, 'Come, my Hippolyta' (I.122). Hippolyta's silent response was a model of the very type of obedience that Hermia had outspokenly refused to accept. Without hesitation, Hippolyta crossed toward Theseus and he toward her and, hands joined, they walked together toward the exit as he asked solicitously, 'What cheer, my love?' (I.122).

Hall's production, in which Hippolyta's silence conveyed her untroubled, obedient acquiescence in the sentence imposed on Hermia, stands in pointed contrast to the production of *A Midsummer Night's Dream* that

John Hirsch directed at the Stratford (Ontario) Shakespearean Festival in 1968. In Hirsch's production, the opening exchange between Theseus and Hippolyta established that theirs was a relationship marked by conflict rather than by harmony. Theseus was a nearly doddering old man in military dress uniform of the late nineteenth century; Hippolyta was a desirable woman of middle years who entered carrying a red rose and wearing a black dress that, in contrast to what Hermia and Helena wore, showed her shoulders. As Hippolyta spoke of how quickly 'the night of our solemnities' would arrive, she stepped away from Theseus and stood, downstage right, on the lower of the two steps around most of the perimeter of the Festival Theatre's thrust stage. Theseus followed her, and when he ordered Philostrate to 'stir up the Athenian youth to merriments' (I.12)—an order that took on sexual overtones and stressed his own age—Hippolyta again distanced herself from him. Using the bottom step, she crossed to the downstage left corner, where she sat on the first step. Theseus followed her again and, dropping to his hands and knees, tried to kiss her at the conclusion of his pledge to wed her 'with pomp, with triumph, and with revelling'. Hippolyta avoided the kiss by drawing back without rising—a gesture that conveyed both her distaste and Theseus' awkward, futile amorousness as he sought to convert his military victory over the queen of the Amazons into a sexual conquest. The entrance of Egeus, Hermia, Demetrius, and Lysander caught Theseus unprepared. His failure as a wooer was obvious to them, and his subsequent exercise of ducal power became in part a compensation for that failure.

Hirsch's production intensified the conflict between Theseus and Hippolyta by using her silence to emphasise Hippolyta's recognition of the affinities between herself and Hermia. In this production, in contrast to Hall's, Hippolyta was not at Theseus' side as he listened to and acted upon Egeus' complaint against Hermia. Theseus, standing centre stage, addressed himself to Hermia, who stood at the downstage right corner while Hippolyta remained seated on the top step at the downstage left corner. That triangular configuration aligned the two women in their resistance to male authority, and that alignment eventually became a pairing. Hippolyta stood up when Demetrius called for Hermia to 'relent' (I.91), and when Lysander defiantly asked, 'Why should not I then prosecute my right?' (I.105), Hippolyta moved toward Hermia along the same step that she had earlier used to dodge Theseus. The pairing of the two women was completed following Hippolyta's response to Theseus' words, "Come, my Hippolyta'. She crossed not to Theseus but to Hermia. Although he stood holding his hand out toward her, Hippolyta turned her back to him and handed to Hermia the red rose she had carried since her entrance. She then exited, leaving Theseus to ask, 'What cheer, my love?' to her departing back. Hippolyta's demonstration that she felt neither duty toward nor desire for Theseus gave a special flavour to the words Egeus used when he and Demetrius obeyed Theseus' order to accompany him as he exited after Hippolyta: 'With duty and desire we follow you' (I.127).

The rose that Hippolyta passed to Hermia extended the correspondences between the two women beyond the fact that both faced marriages that were being imposed on them by men whose control rested on law or military conquest. That rose made it easier for the audience to realise that Hippolyta's life among the Amazon women is analogous to that

5

'single life' available to Hermia if, resisting her father's will, she elects 'to abjure / For ever the society of men' (II.65-6) and to live instead among women 'in shady cloister mewed' (I.71). The use of the rose to draw attention to the analogy was particularly appropriate because Theseus uses the rose metaphorically when he dismisses a life lived among women and without men:

> *Thrice blessed they that master so their blood*
> *To undergo such maiden pilgrimage;*
> *But earthlier happy is the rose distilled*
> *Than that which, withering on the virgin thorn,*
> *Grows, lives, and dies in single blessedness.*
>
> *(II.74-8)*

Passed from Hippolyta to Hermia and then to Helena, the only woman in the opening scene whom no man seeks to marry, that rose came to signify the 'single blessedness' that Theseus dismisses. Hermia's response to his words is a defiant vow to undertake 'such maiden pilgrimage':

> *So will I grow, so live, so die, my lord,*
> *Ere I will yield my virgin patent up*
> *Unto his lordship whose unwished yoke*
> *My soul consents not to give sovereignty*
>
> *(II.79-82)*

The sovereignty that Hermia explicitly refuses to accept is the sovereignty that, in Hirsch's production, the conquered Queen of the Amazons resisted in silence, and the life of a 'barren sister' (I.72) that Hermia prefers to wedded life with Demetrius points toward the life in sisterhood that Hippolyta lost when Theseus triumphed in battle.

Celia Brannerman's 1980 production of *A Midsummer Night's Dream* for the New Shakespeare Company at the Open Air Theatre in Regent's Park, London, endowed Hippolyta's silence with quite different meanings and effects. Theseus once again wore a military dress uniform of the late nineteenth century, but he was middle-aged and vigorous; Hippolyta wore vaguely near-Eastern garb, including what one reviewer called 'Turkish harem pants'. Hippolyta did not move away when, kneeling on one knee, Theseus declared, 'But I will wed thee in another key, / With pomp, with triumph, and with revelling.' That posture suggested that the conqueror was submitting to the conquered, and thus Theseus' words became a conciliatory pledge rather than a self-aggrandising announcement of his capacity to shift styles as martial affairs gave way to marital concerns.

Standing side by side, Theseus and Hippolyta both found Egeus' complaint against Hermia and Lysander amusing at first. Egeus concluded his initial speech by opening a book he carried and citing the law that entitled him, as Hermia's father, to 'beg the ancient privilege of Athens':

> *As she is mine, I may dispose of her,*
> *Which shall be either to this gentleman*
> *Or to her death, according to our law*
> *Immediately provided in that case.*
>
> *(II.41-5)*

Theseus himself checked Egeus' citation and handed the book, still open, to Hippolyta, before he turned to Hermia and said, 'Be advised, fair maid, / To you your father should be as a god' (II.46–7). As Theseus listened to Hermia's reply, Hippolyta stood slightly away from him studying the book of laws. When Hermia asked to 'know / The worst that may befall me in this case / If I refuse to wed Demetrius', Theseus replied, 'Either to die the death, or to abjure / For ever the society of men' (II.62–6). Having different characters consult the book of laws brought into focus the fact that Theseus here allows Hermia an alternative that her father had not mentioned when he called for either her obedience or her death, 'according to our law / Immediately provided in that case'. In offering Hermia the opportunity to live a life outside 'the society of men', Theseus made the first of several efforts to mollify the silent woman who would soon be his wife and who had been until very recently the head of a society that consisted entirely of women.

On hearing Theseus fix as Hermia's deadline 'the sealing day betwixt my love and me / For everlasting bond of fellowship', Hippolyta angrily and loudly snapped shut the book of laws—a gesture sharply different from the actions of Hippolyta and Theseus at the comparable point in Hall's production, when their gestures demonstrated their unbroken fellowship. Theseus rose and raised Hippolyta to her feet, after which they walked hand in hand toward the staircase as he set the deadline. The Theseus of Brannerman's production tried again to mollify a Hippolyta whose displeasure was unspoken but also unconcealed as he spoke his final words of counsel to Hermia:

> For you, fair Hermia, look you arm yourself
> To fit your fancies to your father's will;
> Or else the law of Athens yields you up
> (Which by no means we may extenuate)
> To death, or to a vow of single life.
>
> (II.117–21)

In most productions of *A Midsummer Night's Dream,* the words 'which by no means we may extenuate' are spoken to Hermia and emphasise the certainty of 'death' or 'single life' if she persists in defying her father's will. Brannerman's Theseus, however, addressed the words to Hippolyta rather than to Hermia, and they become, because of that interpretation, an effort by Theseus to ease Hippolyta's displeasure by explaining his own inability to mitigate the workings of Athenian legal processes. The effort failed. Hippolyta responded to the next words Theseus spoke ('Come, my Hippolyta') by stepping toward him, slapping the book of laws into his hands, and proceeding to exit without him. He was left to ask after her, in a last, futile effort at reconciliation, 'What cheer, my love?' In Brannerman's production, Hippolyta's silence was part of a process whereby, as she witnessed Theseus' handling of Hermia's predicament, Hippolyta suspended her initial receptiveness to marriage with Theseus.

In his much acclaimed 1970 production of *A Midsummer Night's Dream* for the Royal Shakespeare Company (RSC), Peter Brook used Hippolyta's silence to deepen a split between her and Theseus that was present but muted during the play's opening dialogue. Theseus and Hippolyta stood together during that exchange, and Hippolyta did not give the word

10

'quickly' an overtly hostile emphasis, but she walked away, crossing from stage right to stage left after Theseus voiced his pledge to wed her 'with pomp, with triumph, and with revelling'.

When Egeus presented his case against Hermia and Lysander, Theseus and Hippolyta remained apart, seated downstage right and downstage left, respectively. That configuration fixed and emphasised their separation. Hippolyta stayed seated until after Hermia's declaration that she would not marry Demetrius, to 'whose unwishèd yoke / My soul consents not to give sovereignty'. A sustained pause followed the word 'sovereignty', during which no one moved or spoke. Then Hippolyta rose to her feet. The timing of her movement brought into focus her unspoken resistance to the sovereignty over her that Theseus had won in battle and would now exercise in marriage. That resistance, in turn, sharpened the words with which Theseus broke the stillness that followed the word 'sovereignty'. 'Take time to pause', he cautioned Hermia. He then set the deadline for Hermia's decision, and in the specific context of Brook's production, this announcement of that deadline was also a declaration of his resolve to demonstrate his sovereignty over Hippolyta. Hermia must decide 'by the next new moon', which would also be, Theseus stressed, 'the sealing day betwixt my love and me / For everlasting bond of fellowship.'

Another distinct pause followed Theseus' final warning to Hermia that if she chose to resist her father's authority and did not marry Demetrius, the law of Athens would yield her up 'to death, or to a vow of single life'. That pause ended when Theseus said, 'Come, my Hippolyta'. Hippolyta, however, stood motionless as Theseus crossed toward her, and before reaching her, he stopped to ask, 'What cheer, my love?' When she still did not step toward him or speak, he turned in embarrassed anger to address Demetrius and Egeus. The Queen of the Amazons continued to stand motionless and silent as he spoke to the two men, and she did not join Theseus when he exited through the door upstage right. Instead, Hippolyta walked alone toward the door upstage left, silently challenging Theseus' claim that she is '*my* Hippolyta', '*my* love' (emphasis added). On reaching the doors, Theseus and Hippolyta stopped and looked briefly at one another before each exited separately. With 'duty and desire', Egeus and Demetrius then followed Theseus through the door upstage right. Their eager compliance with his order to 'go along' gave a final definition to Hippolyta's silent and Hermia's explicit refusal to submit to the sovereignty that men claimed over them.

Another way of demonstrating the impact that Hippolyta's silence can have is to consider a production—Elijah Moshinsky's in 1981 for BBC-TV—that obliterated it. Moshinsky split Shakespeare's single opening scene into several 'scenes' set in different locations. The first of Moshinsky's scenes opened by having the camera show Hippolyta, dressed in black, pacing restlessly, even angrily, in front of a line of attendants who stood along one wall of a room. The voice of Theseus speaking the play's first lines intruded as the audience watched Hippolyta. Then the camera showed him, still wearing armour, standing in front of his attendants, ranged along the opposite wall. Facing him across that intervening space, Hippolyta replied without in any way narrowing the distance, both physical and emotional, between them. After Hippolyta finished speaking, Theseus first ordered Philostrate to 'stir up the Athenian youth to merriments', then crossed until he stood face to face with an unsmiling, defiant Hippolyta. In an assertion of his will and dominance, he declared to her his resolve to wed her 'with pomp, with triumph, and with revelling'.

Moshinsky's production then shifted directly to the arraignment of Hermia, which, set in a different room, became a scene distinct from the exchange between Theseus and Hippolyta that began the play. Hippolyta was not present during this second scene to watch in silence as Theseus heard the 'complaint' against Hermia and passed judgement. Her absence negated all possibility of establishing visual correspondences between Hippolyta's situation and Hermia's, and Moshinsky squandered the potential established by his interpretation of the opening dialogue between Theseus and Hippolyta. Moshinsky thus wasted the opportunity presented by the silence that Shakespeare's words impose on Hippolyta—the same opportunity that Hall, Hirsch, Brannerman, and Brook exploited in sharply divergent ways.

From Philip McGuire, *Speechless Dialect: Shakespeare's Open Silences.* Berkeley:
    U of California P, 1985. pp. 1–18.

Leonard Tennenhouse: New Historical Criticism

This excerpt, by Leonard Tennenhouse, though a challenging piece of writing, is a good example of new historical criticism. Tennenhouse is looking for patterns in the play that reflect patterns in the Elizabethan culture Shakespeare inhabited. He finds that challenges to authority in the play are ultimately made part of a reassertion of that authority. The play turns things upside only to reaffirm the order in place at the outset. Queen Elizabeth, Tennenhouse goes on to say, employed the same sort of strategies, containing and authorizing challenges to authority.

If we take the example of *Midsummer Night's Dream,* a play surely characteristic of Shakespeare's romantic comedies, we can see that the problem which authority has to master is a problem with authority itself, authority grown archaic. At the outset, the law seems to serve only the will of the father. A comedic resolution obviously requires either the independence of the law or the generosity of the father. It requires, in other words, a more inclusive order. Given that romantic comedy invariably poses this problem only one form of resolution will do, the formation of an authority figure who overrules the existing law of the father. Oberon represents the traditional alternative to patriarchal law. He is the figure of carnival, and the introduction of this principle into the play triggers a series of inversions.[1] As if Titania's playing the role of an unruly woman were not enough to tell what this is all about, Puck reproduces similar forms of inversion among

[1] My discussion of the rhetorical figures of carnival and misrule owes a debt to Mikhail Bakhtin's *Rabelais and His World,* trans. Helene Iswolsky (Cambridge: MIT Press, 1968) and Michel Foucault's *Surveiller et Punir: Naissance de la prison* (Paris: Gallimard, 1975). For Bakhtin in particular, carnival represents those cultural practices which oppose the norm enforcing ceremonies and institutions of the State. In this critical tradition, then, carnival is neither a literary phenomenon nor an archetypal one. It is a means of describing certain material practices of the body as they underwent literary displacement—or resisted it—in the making of modern society. Throughout this essay I am indebted to the work of Peter Stallybrass and Allon White who have traced this process of the displacement of carnival from the Renaissance to the modern period in their forthcoming *The Politics and Poetics of Trangression.* The authors very generously allowed me to consult portions of their book in manuscript and to cite their research.

the Athenians—both lovers and mechanicals—who have wandered into the woods.[2] Such inversions—of gender, age, status, even of species— violate all the categories organising Elizabethan reality itself. This Renaissance nightmare can occur precisely because patriarchal law is initially so closely identified with political authority that to violate the will of the father is to return to what Hobbes would later represent as the horrors of a state of nature.

The figures of festival operate to break down the hierarchical distinctions organising Elizabethan society, only—in the end—to be taken within the social order where they authorise a new form of political authority.[3] This mutually transforming exchange places disorder within the framework of festival and displaces it on to art, as illustrated by 'the story of the night told o'er', Bottom's 'dream', as well as the mechanicals' production of the tragedy of Pyramus and Thisbe. When Theseus and his party come upon the sleeping couples lying intermingled on the ground, the Duke surmises, 'No doubt they rose up early to observe / The rite of May. . .' (IV.i.132–3).[4] By identifying the lovers as revellers, Theseus does more than decriminalise their transgression of the law; he identifies their state of disarray with the order of art. 'I know you two for rival enemies,' he says to the young men, 'How came this gentle concord in the world. . . ?' (IV.i.142–3). At the same time, however, the inclusion of filial disobedience within a field of permissible illegalities, changes the construction of political authority. What had been a violation of the father's law, in other words, thus becomes a scene of harmony. Indeed, when Egeus presses Theseus to punish the youthful offenders, the Duke overrules the father.

But if Theseus authorises certain inversions of power relations by situating them within the framework of festival and art, then it is also true that the introduction of disorder into the play ultimately authorises political authority. Once Theseus includes the rites of May within the domain of the permissible, the revellers in turn fall on their knees before him. Thus brought together, revellers and Duke can comprise a harmonious political body where the juridical power of the monarch exists independently from that of the patriarch. When Theseus overrules the angry father, juridical power can no longer be identified with patriarchal power. A new set of political conditions appears where competing bases for authority are held in equipoise by the Duke. That is, his ideal role is an improvement, in terms of the play, over the punitive power he threatened to exercise at its opening. The entire last act of the play consequently theorises the process of inversion whereby art and politics end up in this mutually authorising relationship. This process is then reproduced on the stage in the form of an Elizabethan tragedy which has been converted into comedy as rude

[2]For a discussion of the 'unruly woman' as a feature of carnival, see Natalie Zemon Davis, "Women on Top', in *Society and Culture in Early Modern France* (Stanford University Press, 1975), pp. 124–51.

[3]The many references to festival and misrule in this play have been discussed in a different fashion by C.L. Barber, *Shakespeare's Festive Comedy: a Study of Dramatic Form and its Relation to Social Custom* (Princeton University Press, 1959), pp. 155–62.

[4]*The Riverside Shakespeare* (Boston: Houghton Mifflin, 1974). All citations of the plays are to this edition.

mechanicals play a range of parts from those of noble lovers to the creatures and objects of the natural world.

The popularity of such inversions becomes clear when we see how
Elizabeth herself used various forms of authority against one another. It is
not enough to say that the transfiguration of authority in romantic comedy
resembles Elizabeth's actual style of exercising power. To be sure, she used
her power as a patron to affect the power of the ruling families and thus set
economically-based political authority in opposition to that based on
blood. Yet this strategy was more than personal ingenuity on her part, for
her characteristic strategies for expressing power were just as dependent
upon the political conditions of the time as the form of a comedy such as
Midsummer Night's Dream.

From Leonard Tennenhouse, "Strategies of State and Political Plays: *A Midsummer
Night's Dream, Henry IV, Henry V, Henry VIII.*" In Jonathon Dollimore and
Alan Sinfield, eds. *Political Shakespeare: New Essays in Cultural Materialism.*
Manchester: Manchester UP, 1985. pp. 109–129.

Louis Montrose: New Historical Criticism

*These brief excerpts by Louis Montrose suggest how new historicist critics connect literary works
to cultural and economic history. Montrose, an important Renaissance scholar, finds an interesting link between Bottom and Shakespeare in the first passage; in the second, he relates the
play to courtly entertainments.*

The immediate reason for the presence of Bottom and his companions in
A Midsummer Night's Dream is to rehearse and perform an 'interlude
before the Duke and the Duchess, on his wedding-day at night' (1.2.5–7).
However, their project simultaneously evokes what, only a generation
before the production of Shakespeare's play, had been a central aspect of
civic and artisanal culture in England—namely, the feast of Corpus Christi,
with its ceremonial procession and its often elaborate dramatic performances. The civic and artisanal status of the amateur players is insisted upon
with characteristic Shakespearean condescension: Puck describes them to
his master, Oberon, as 'rude mechanicals, / That work for bread upon Athenian stalls' (3.2.9–10); and Philostrate describes them to his master, Theseus,
as 'Hard-handed men that work in Athens here, / Which never laboured in
their minds till now' (5.1.72–3). In the most material way, Bottom's name
relates him to the practice of his craft—the 'bottom' was 'the core on which
the weaver's skein of yarn was wound' (Arden *MND*, p. 3, n. 11); and it also
relates him to his lowly position in the temporal order, to his social baseness. Furthermore, among artisans, weavers in particular were associated
with Elizabethan food riots and other forms of social protest that were
prevalent during the mid-1590s, the period during which *A Midsummer
Night's Dream* was presumably written and first performed. Thus, we may
construe Bottom as the spokesman for the common in the play—but with
the proviso that this *vox populi* is not merely that of a generalised *folk*. Bottom is primarily the comic representative of a specific socio-economic
group with its own highly articulated culture. He is not the voice of the dis-
possessed or the indigent but of the middling sort, in whose artisanal, civic
and guild-centred ethos Shakespeare had his own roots. During his childhood in Stratford, Shakespeare would have had the opportunity and the

occasion to experience the famed Corpus Christi play that was performed annually in nearby Coventry. Bottom himself, the most enthusiastic of amateur thespians, makes oblique allusion to the figures and acting traditions of the multi-pageant mystery plays. Thus, Bully Bottom, the weaver, is an overdetermined signifier, encompassing not only a generalised common voice but also the particular socio-economic and cultural origins of William Shakespeare, the professional player-playwright—and, too, the collective socio-cultural origins of his craft. *A Midsummer Night's Dream* simultaneously acknowledges those origins and frames them at an ironic distance; it educes connections only in order to assert distinctions.

. . . As has long been recognised, *A Midsummer Night's Dream* has affinities with Elizabethan royal iconography and courtly entertainments. The most obvious features are Shakespeare's incorporation of a play performed in celebration of an aristocratic wedding, and Oberon's allusion to 'a fair vestal, throned by the west. . . . the imperial votaress' (2.1.158, 163)—the latter being invoked in a scenario reminiscent of the pageantry presented to the queen on her progresses. From early in the reign, Elizabeth had been directly addressed and engaged by such performances at aristocratic estates and in urban centres. In these pageants, masques and plays, distinctions were effaced between the spatio-temporal locus of the royal spectator/actress and that of the characters being enacted before her. Debates were referred to the queen's arbitration; the magic of her presence civilised savage men, restored the blind to sight, released errant knights from enchantment, and rescued virgins from defilement. Such social dramas of celebration and coercion played out the delicately balanced relationship between the monarch and the nobility, gentry and urban elites who constituted the political nation. These events must also have evoked reverence and awe in the local common folk who assisted in and witnessed them. And because texts and descriptions of most of these processions, pageants and shows were in print within a year—sometimes within just a few weeks—of their performance, they may have had a cultural impact far more extensive and enduring than their occasional and ephemeral character might at first suggest. Such royal pageantry appropriated materials from popular late medieval romances, from Ovid, Petrarch and other literary sources; and when late Elizabethan poetry and drama such as Spenser's *Faerie Queene* or Shakespeare's *A Midsummer Night's Dream* reappropriated those sources, they were now inscribed by the allegorical discourse of Elizabethan royal courtship, panegyric and political negotiation. Thus, the deployment of Ovidian, Petrarchan and allegorical romance modes by late Elizabethan writers must be read in terms of an intertextuality that includes both the discourse of European literary history and the discourse of Elizabethan state power.

From Louis Montrose, "A Kingdom of Shadows." In Dorothea Keller, ed. *A Misummer Night's Dream: Critical Essays.* New York: Garland, 1998, pp. 217–240.

Suggestions for Writing

1. Summarize the argument of an excerpt and assess its persuasiveness. Do you agree?
2. Compare two or more critical approaches, articulating the different underlying assumptions, and how these assumptions influence what is said about the play.

3. Attempt to add a paragraph to any of the excerpts provided. The key here will be to imagine how the article's line of argument might be extended. (Find the entire article in your library or online, and compare your work to the real thing.)

4. Explore the rich resources for Shakespearean study on the Internet, and write a report for your classmates on what you found. Although any search engine will turn up a wealth of starting points, I suggest you use one of the following at the outset:

a. http://daphne.palomar.edu/shakespeare/—This site, created by Terry Gray at Palomar College, is very thorough: biographies of Shakespeare, discussions of the Elizabeth theater, and especially links to other sites and scholarly articles.

b. http://www.uelen.com/shakespeare—The page on *Star Trek* references to Shakespeare makes this site worth visiting, but you'll also find a study guide for *MSN,* lesson plans for teaching Shakespeare, lots of photographs of costumes, and an introduction to studying the Great Bard, "Shakespeare 101."

c. http://www.jetlink.net/~massij/shakes/—This site, by J.M. Massi, has a nice list of film versions, a Shakespearean FAQ, and links to other useful sites.

d. http://www.reading.ac.uk/globe/—This site has lots of pictures: Shakespeare in performance, the Old Globe Theater, and the New Globe Theater.

19

More Plays

All the world's a stage,
And all the men and women merely players. . . .

——Shakespeare, *As You Like It*

Someday, with any luck, a computer will pass the Turing Test, and arguments will intensify over whether machines can think, and whether this computer or any computer could be "alive." The idea of the Turing Test, proposed by Alan Turing in 1950, is that a computer may be said to be thinking when its responses cannot be distinguished from the responses of a human being. In other words, if you're talking to a computer and you don't know it, then according to the Turing Test the computer is thinking. To fool us into thinking it's a person, the computer will have to lie—and lie cleverly. It will have to say, for instance,

"No, no, no! You're like, 'I really, really love you,' and you're like, 'Whatever.'"

that it's just come back from the store and blueberries were on sale—and if its conversationalist knows the stores were closed, or blueberries are out of season, it will have to make something up to cover itself.

One essential behavior that a machine will have to learn how to simulate is simulation itself: pretending and acting appear to be woven into the fabric of being human. Perhaps this ability to fool people, even if momentarily, even if partially, helps to explain why actors and the theatre have for centuries had a somewhat disreputable reputation. How can one tell if an excellent actor is lying? How do we know that our friends, family, political leaders, teachers, aren't fine actors? By the same token, if computers ever develop the ability to lie, how can we tell? Won't things get interesting then!

This issue—of pretending, playing, acting, even lying as human essentials—is important in part because it suggests that all the world is a stage, as Shakespeare so famously said, and that every day we are all involved in a very large theatre in a kind of role-playing—just as we are also cast as dramatic critics everyday. For making sense of the world, and determining who is a real person and who isn't, who is putting us on and who's telling the truth, the study of drama is excellent preparation.

This chapter provides a small sampling of the artificial persons and worlds that drama presents. In these brief, modern, extremely accessible and engaging plays, the characters are somehow concerned with fooling someone, with covering something up, with determining what is real, with pretending to be something or someone they are not; and they involve the audience so vividly and convincingly in their quests that we momentarily may take them for real people.

MARSHA NORMAN (1947–)

Marsha Norman grew up in Louisville, Kentucky, the daughter of a fundamentalist Methodist mother who restricted her from watching movies or television, and isolated her from other children. Norman did experience some local theatre, and went on to Agnes Scott College in Georgia to major in philosophy. After working as a journalist, reviewing books, plays, and films for the Louisville Times, Norman wrote Getting Out, *a play based on her experiences with disturbed youth at the Kentucky Central State Hospital. This play's success allowed her to move to New York and to focus on writing plays. Norman won the Pulitzer Prize and other awards for* 'night, Mother *(1983). She has also published a novel,* The Fortune Teller *(1987), along with other plays.*

The Laundromat *began its artistic life as the first act of* Third and Oak, *a two-act play that premiered in 1978.* The Laundromat *was presented as a stand-alone one-act play in 1979 at the Ensemble Studio Theatre in New York, and it was later filmed for HBO by Robert Altman.*

The Laundromat

Characters

Alberta, a reserved woman in her late fifties.
Deedee, a restless twenty-year-old.
Shooter, a black disc jockey in his late twenties.
Willie, a black man in his late fifties.

Time and Place

This play takes place in a laundromat and the pool hall next door, at the corner of Third and Oak, in the middle of the night.
    The time is the late seventies.

    Lights come up on a standard, dreary laundromat. There are tile floors, washers, dryers, laundry baskets on wheels, and coin-op vending machines for soaps, soft drinks and candy bars. There is a bulletin board on which various notices are posted. There is a table for folding clothes, a low table covered with dirty ashtrays and some ugly chairs littered with magazines. A clock on the wall reads three o'clock and should continue to run throughout the show. One side of the laundromat will be used as a window looking out onto the street. The song "Stand By Your Man" is playing over the radio. The door to the attendant's room is slightly ajar.

Shooter's voice *(On the radio, over the final chords of the song)*: And that's all for tonight, night owls. This is your Number One Night Owl saying it's three o'clock, all right, and time to rock your daddy to dreams of de-light. And mama, I'm comin' home. And the rest of you night owls gonna have to make it through the rest of this night by *yourself,* or with the help of *your* friends, if you know what I mean. And you know what I mean. 5

The radio station goes dead, music replaced by an irritating static. Alberta opens the door tentatively, looks around and walks in. She has dressed carefully and her laundry basket exhibits the same care. She checks the top of a washer for dust or water before putting her purse and basket down. She takes off her coat and hat. She walks back to the door marked Attendant, *and is startled briefly when she looks in.*

Alberta: Hello? *(Steps back, seeing that the attendant is asleep)* Sleep? Is that how you do your job? Sleep? What they pay you to do, sleep? Listen, it's fine with me. Better, in fact. I'm glad, actually. *(She leans in and* 10 *turns off the radio. She walks back toward the basket, talking to herself)* Do you want him out here talking to you? *(Procrastinating)* You came to do your wash so do your wash. No, first. . . . *(She takes an index card out of her purse. She tacks it up on the bulletin board. We must see that it is very important to her)* There. Good. *(She opens a* 15 *washer lid and runs her fingers around the soap tray, taking out lint and depositing it in one of the coffee cans. As she does this, she accidently knocks over her purse)* It's okay. Nothing breakable. Clean it up, that's all. You've been up this late before. Nothing the matter with you, just nerves. . . and gravity. 20

Alberta bends down and begins to put the things back in her purse. She cannot see as Deedee backs in the door of the laundromat. Deedee is a wreck. She carries her clothes tied up in a man's shirt. She trips over a wastebasket and falls on her laundry as it spills out of the shirt.

Deedee: Well, poo-rats!

Alberta stands up, startled, hesitates, then walks over to where Deedee is still sprawled on the floor.

Alberta: Are you all right? *(She is angry that Deedee is there at all, but polite nevertheless)*

Deedee *(Grudgingly)*: Cute, huh?

Alberta *(Moving the wastebasket out of the way)*: Probably a wet spot on the floor. *(Goes back to her wash)* 25

Deedee: I already picked these clothes off the floor once tonight. *(No response from Alberta)* We been in our apartment two years and Joe still ain't found the closets. He thinks hangers are for when you lock your keys in your car. *(Still no response, though she is expecting one)*

I mean, he's got this coat made of sheep's fur or somethin' and my
mom came over one day and asked where did we get that fuzzy little
rug. *(She is increasingly nervous)* Joe works at the Ford plant. I asked
him why they call it that. I said, "How often do you have to water a Ford
plant?" It was just a little joke, but he didn't think it was very funny.   30

Alberta (Her good manners requiring her to say something): They prob-   35
ably do have a sprinkler system.

Deedee: Shoulda saved my breath and just tripped over the coffee table.
He'd laughed at that. *(No response)* Well, *(Brightly)* I guess it's just you
and me.

Alberta: Yes. *(Makes a move to get back to her wash)*   40

Deedee: Guess not too many people suds their duds in the middle of the night.

Alberta: Suds their duds?

Deedee: I do mine at Mom's. *(She begins to put her clothes in two washers, imitating Alberta)* I mean, I take our stuff over to Mom's. She got
matching Maytags. She buys giant-size Cheer and we sit around and   45
watch the soaps till the clothes come out. Suds the duds, that's what
she says. Well, more than that. She wrote it on a little card and sent it in
to Cheer so they could use it on their TV ads.

Alberta (Pleasantly): Gives you a chance to talk, I guess. Visit.

Deedee: She says, "Just leave 'em, I'll do 'em," but that wouldn't be right, so   50
I stay. Course she don't ever say how she likes seeing me, but she holds
back, you know. I mean, there's stuff you don't have to say when it's
family.

Alberta: Is she out of town tonight?

Deedee: No, probably just asleep. *(Alberta nods. She reads from the top of*   55
the washer) Five cycle Turbomatic Deluxe. *(Punching buttons)* Hot
wash-warm rinse, warm wash-warm rinse, warm wash-cold rinse, cold
wash-cold rinse, cold wash, delicate cycle. *(Now lifts the lid of the
washer)* What's this? Add laundry aids.

Alberta: Your mother does your laundry.   60

Deedee: You don't have a washer either, huh?

Alberta (Too quickly): It's broken.

Deedee: Get your husband to fix it. *(Looking at Alberta's mound of shirts)*
Got a heap of shirts, don't he?

Alberta: It can't be fixed.   65

Deedee: Where are *your* clothes?

Alberta: Mine are mostly hand wash.

Deedee: We just dump all our stuff in together.

Alberta: That's nice.

Deedee: Joe can fix just about anything. He's real good with his hands.   70
(Relaxing some now) I've been saying that since high school. *(Laughs)*
He makes trucks. God, I'd hate to see the truck I'd put together. *(Now a
nervous laugh)* He had to work the double shift tonight. *(Going on
quickly)* They do all kinds out there. Pickups, dump trucks. . . they got
this joke, him and his buddies, about what rhymes with pickle truck, but   75
I don't know the end of it, you know, the punch line. Goes like. . . "I'll
come to get you baby in a pickle truck, I'll tell you what I'm wantin' is
a—*(Stops, but continues the beat with her foot or by snapping her fingers)* See, that's the part I don't know. The end. *(Shrugs)*

Alberta: Overtime pays well, I imagine.   80

Deedee: It's all-the-time, here lately. He says people are buyin' more trucks 'cause farmers have to raise more cows 'cause we got a population explosion going on. Really crummy, you know? People I don't even know having babies means Joe can't come home at the right time. Don't seem fair.   85

Alberta: Or true.

Deedee: Huh?

Alberta: The population explosion is over. The birthrate is very stable now.

Deedee: Oh.

Alberta: Still, it's no fun to be in the house by yourself.   90

Deedee: See, we live right over there, on top of the Mexican restaurant. *(Going over to the window)* That window with the blue light in it, that's ours. It's a bunch of blueberries on a stalk, only it's a light. Joe gave it to me. He thinks blue is my favorite color.

Alberta: So the restaurant noise was bothering you.   95

Deedee: They got this bar that stays open till four. That's how Joe picked the apartment. He hates to run out for beer late. He don't mind running down. *(Broadly)* Old Mexico Taco Tavern. Except Joe says it's supposed to be Olé Mexico, like what they say in bullfights.

Alberta: Bullfights are disgusting.   100

Deedee: You've seen a real bullfight?

Alberta: We used to travel quite a bit.

Deedee (Excited, curious, demanding): Well, tell me about it.

Alberta: There's not much to tell. The bull comes out and they kill it.

Deedee: What for? *(Putting her clothes in the washer)*   105

Alberta (Pleased at the question): Fun. Doesn't that sound like *fun* to you?

Deedee (Encouraged): Your husband works nights too?

Alberta: Herb is out of town. Did you mean to put that in there?

Deedee (Peering into her washer): Huh?

Alberta: Your whites will come out green.   110

Deedee (Retrieving the shirt): Joe wouldn't like that. No sir. Be like when Mom's washer chewed this hole in his bowling shirt. Whoo-ee! Was he hot? Kicked the chest of drawers, broke his toe. *(No response from Alberta)* And the chest of drawers too. *(No response)* Is Herb picky like that?   115

Alberta: Herb likes to look nice. *(Reaches for her soap)*

Deedee: Hey! You forgot one. *(Picking the remaining shirt out of Alberta's basket)* See? *(Opens it out, showing an awful stain)* Yuck! Looks like vomit.

Alberta: It's my cabbage soup.   120

Deedee: Well, *(Helping)* in it goes. *(Opening one of Alberta's washers)*

Alberta: No!

Deedee: The other one? *(Reaching for the other washer)*

Alberta (Taking the shirt away from her): I don't want to. . . it's too. . . that stain will never. . . *(Enforcing a calm now)* It needs to presoak. I forgot   125
the Woolite.

Deedee: Sorry.

Alberta: That's quite all right. *(Folding the shirt carefully, putting it back in the basket. Wants Deedee to vanish)*

Deedee: One of those machines give soap?   130

    Alberta points to the correct one and Deedee walks over to it.

Deedee: It takes nickels. I only got quarters.

Alberta: The attendant will give you change. *(Pointing to the open attendant door, putting her own coins in her washers)*

Deedee (Looking in the door): He's asleep.

Alberta: Ah.

Deedee: Be terrible to wake him up just for some old nickels. Do you have any change?   135

Alberta: No.

Deedee: Looks like he's got a pocket full of money. Think it would wake him up if I stuck my hand in there? *(Enjoys this idea)*   140

Alberta (Feeling bad about not helping and also not wanting the attendant awake): Twenty years ago, maybe. *(Deedee laughs)* Here, I found some.

Deedee walks back, gives Alberta the quarters; she counts out the change.

Alberta: That's ten, twenty, thirty, forty, fifty.

Deedee (Putting the nickels in the soap machine): He shouldn't be sleeping like that. Somebody could come in here and rob him. You don't think he's dead or anything, do you? I mean, I probably wouldn't know 145
it if I saw somebody dead.

Alberta: You'd know. *(Starts her washers)*

Deedee (Pushing in the coin trays, starting her washers): Okay. Cheer up! *(Laughs)* That's what Mom always says, "Cheer up." *(Looks at Alberta)* 150
Hey, my name is Deedee. Deedee Johnson.

Alberta: Nice to meet you.

Deedee: What's yours?

Alberta: Alberta.

Deedee: Alberta what?   155

Alberta (Reluctantly): Alberta Johnson.

Deedee: Hey! We might be related. I mean, Herb and Joe could be cousins or something.

Deedee: Yeah. I guess there's lots of Johnsons.

Alberta (Looking down at the magazine): Yes.   160

Deedee: I'm botherin' you, aren't I? *(Alberta smiles)* I'd talk to somebody else, but there ain't nobody else. 'Cept Sleepy back there. I talk in *my* sleep sometimes, but him, he looks like he's lucky to be breathin' in his. *(Awkward)* Sleep, I mean.

Alberta: Would you like a magazine?   165

Deedee: No thanks. I brought a Dr. Pepper. *(Alberta is amazed)* You can have it if you want.

Alberta: No thank you.

Deedee: Sleepy was one of the seven dwarfs. I can still name them all. I couldn't tell you seven presidents of the United States, but I can say the 170
dwarfs. *(Very proud)* Sleepy, Grumpy, Sneezy, Dopey, Doc and Bashful. *(Suddenly very low)* That's only six. Who's the other one?

Alberta: (Willing to help): You could name seven presidents.

Deedee: Oh no.

Alberta: Try it.   175

Deedee: Okay, *(Takes a big breath)* There's Carter, Nixon, Kennedy, Lincoln, Ben Franklin, George Washington. . . uh. . .

Alberta: Eleanor Roosevelt's husband.

Deedee: Mr. Rooscvclt.

Alberta: Mr. Roosevelt. That's seven. Except Benjamin Franklin was never   180
president.

Deedee: You're a teacher or something, aren't you?

Alberta: I was. Say Mr. Roosevelt again.

Deedee: Mr. Roosevelt.

Alberta: There. Teddy makes seven.   185

Deedee: Around here? *(Alberta looks puzzled)* Or in the county schools?

Alberta: Ohio. Columbus.

Deedee: Great!

Alberta: Do you know Columbus?

Deedee: Not personally.   190

Alberta: Ah.

Deedee: I better be careful. No ain'ts or nuthin'.

Alberta: You can't say anything I haven't heard before.

Deedee: Want me to try?

Alberta: No.   195

Deedee: What does Herb do?

Alberta (Too quickly): Is Deedee short for something? Deirdre, Deborah?

Deedee: No. Just Deedee. The guys in high school always kidded me about
my name. *(Affecting a boy's voice)* Hey, Deedee, is Deedee your name
or your bra size?   200

Alberta: That wasn't very nice of them.

Deedee: That ain't the worst. Wanna hear the worst? *(Alberta doesn't
respond)* Ricky Baker, Icky Ricky Baker and David Duvall said this one.
They'd come up to the locker bank, David's locker was right next to
mine and Ricky'd say, "Hey, did you have a good time last night?" And   205
David would say, "Yes. In Deedee." Then they'd slap each other and
laugh like idiots.

Alberta: You could've had your locker moved.

Deedee: I guess, but see, the basketball players always come down that hall
at the end of school. Going to practice, you know.   210

Alberta: One of the basketball players I taught. . . . *(Begins to chuckle)*

Deedee (Anxious to laugh with her): Yeah?

Alberta: . . . thought Herbert Hoover invented the vacuum cleaner.

> *Alberta waits for Deedee to laugh. When she doesn't, Alberta steps
> back a few steps. Deedee is embarrassed.*

Deedee: Why did you quit. . . teaching.

Alberta: Age.   215

Deedee: You don't look old enough to retire.

Alberta: Not my age. Theirs.

Deedee: Mine, you mean.

Alberta: Actually, Mother was very sick then.

Deedee: Is she still alive?   220

Alberta: No.

Deedee: I'm sorry.

Alberta: It was a blessing, rcally. There was quite a lot of pain at the end.

Deedee: For her maybe, but what about you?

Alberta: She was the one with the pain.   225

Deedee: Sounds like she was lucky to have you there, nursing her and all.

Alberta: I read her *Wuthering Heights* five times that year. I kept checking different ones out of the library, you know, *Little Women, Pride and Prejudice,* but each time she'd say,"No, I think I'd like to hear *Wuthering Heights.*" Just like she hadn't heard it in fifty years. But each time, I'd read the last page and look up, and she'd say the same thing.

Deedee: What thing?

Alberta: She'd say,"I still don't see it. They didn't have to have all that trouble. All they had to do was find Heathcliff someplace to go every day. The man just needed a job. *(Pause)* But maybe I missed something. Read it again."

Deedee: My mom thinks Joe's a bum. *(Somehow she thinks this is an appropriate response, and Alberta is jolted back to the present)* No really, she kept paying this guy that worked at Walgreen's to come over and strip our wallpaper. She said, "Deedee, he's gonna be manager of that drugstore someday." Hell, the only reason he worked there was getting a discount on his pimple cream. She thought that would get me off Joe. No way. We've been married two years last month. Mom says this is the itch year.

Alberta: The itch year?

Deedee: When guys get the itch, you know, to fool around with other women. Stayin' out late, comin' in with stories about goin' drinkin' with the boys or workin' overtime or. . . somethin'. Is that clock right?

Alberta: I think so.

Deedee: Bet Herb never did that, huh?

Alberta: Be unfaithful, you mean? *(Deedee nods)* No.

Deedee: How can you be so sure like that? You keep him in the refrigerator?

Alberta: Well, I suppose he could have. . . *(Doesn't believe this for a minute)*

Deedee: Like right now, while he's up in wherever he is. . .

Alberta: Akron. *(Surprised at her need to say this)*

Deedee: Akron, he could be sittin' at the bar in some all-night bowling alley polishin' some big blonde's ball.

Alberta: No.

Deedee: That's real nice to trust him like that.

Alberta: Aren't you afraid Joe will call you on his break and be worried about where you are?

Deedee: You got any kids?

Alberta: No.

Deedee: Didn't you want some?

Alberta: Oh yes.

Deedee: Me too. Lots of 'em. But Joe says he's not ready. Wants to be earning lots of money before we start our family.

Alberta: That's why he works this double shift.

Deedee: Yeah. Only now he's fixin' up this '64 Chevy he bought to drag race. Then when the race money starts comin' in, we can have them kids. He's really lookin' forward to that—winnin' a big race and havin' me and the kids run out on the track and him smilin' and grabbin' up the baby and pourin' beer all over us while the crowd is yellin' and screamin'. . .

Alberta: So all his money goes into this car.

Deedee: Hey. I love it too. Sundays we go to the garage and work on it. *(Gets a picture out of her wallet)* That devil painted there on the door, that cost two hundred dollars!

Alberta: You help him?

Deedee: He says it's a real big help just havin' me there watchin'.   280

Alberta: I never understood that, men wanting you to watch them do whatever it is. . . I mean. . . Well *(Deciding to tell this story, a surprise both to her and to us)* every year at Thanksgiving, Herb would watch over me, washing the turkey, making the stuffing, stuffing the turkey. Made me nervous.   285

Deedee: You coulda told him to get lost. *(Offers fabric softener)* Downy?

Alberta nods yes, accepting Deedee's help, but is still nervous about it.

Alberta: Actually, the last ten years or so, I sent him out for sage. For the dressing. He'd come in and sit down saying "Mmm boy was this ever going to be the best turkey yet" and rubbing his hands together and I'd push jars around in the cabinet and look all worried and say "Herb, I don't think I have enough sage." And he's say, "Well, Bertie, my girl, I'll just go to the store and get some."   290

Deedee (Jittery when someone else is talking): I saw white pepper at the store last week. How do they do that?

Alberta: I don't know.

Deedee: Is Dr. Pepper made out of pepper?   295

Alberta: I don't know.

Deedee: And what did Herb do, that you had to watch, I mean.

Alberta: He gardened. I didn't have to watch him plant the seeds or weed the plants or spray for pests or pick okra. But when the day came to turn over the soil, that was the day. Herb would rent a rototiller and bring out a lawn chair from the garage. He'd wipe it off and call in the kitchen window, "Alberta, it's so pleasant out here in the sunshine." And when he finished, he'd bring out this little wooden sign and drive it into the ground.   300

Deedee: What'd it say?   305

Alberta: Herb Garden. *(Pauses)* He thought that was funny.

Deedee: Did you laugh?

Alberta: Every year.

Deedee: He's not doing one anymore? *(Walking to the window)*

Alberta: No.   310

Deedee (Looks uneasy, still staring out the window): Why not?

Alberta: What's out there?

Deedee: Oh nothing.

Alberta: You looked like—

Deedee: Joe should be home soon. I turned out all the lights except the blueberries so I could tell if he comes in, you know, when he turns the lights on.   315

Alberta: When is the shift over?

Deedee (Enforced cheer now): Oh, not for a long time yet. I just thought. . . He might get through early, he said. And we could go have a beer. Course, he might stop off and bowl a few games first.   320

Alberta gets up to check on her wash. Deedee walks to the bulletin board.

Deedee (Reading): "Typing done, hourly or by the page. Cheer." What on earth?

Alberta: Must be cheap. *(Laughs a little)* It better be cheap.

Deedee (Taking some notices down): Most of this stuff is over already. Hey!   325
    Here's one for Herb. "Gardening tools, never used. Rake, hoe, spade and
    towel."

Alberta: Trowel.

Deedee (Aggravated by the correction): You got great eyes, Alberta.   330
    (Continues reading) "459-4734. A. Johnson." You think this A. John-
    son is related to us? *(Laughs)* No, that's right, you said Herb wasn't
    doing a garden anymore. No, I got it! This A. Johnson is you. And the
    reason Herb ain't doin' a garden is you're selling his rakes. But this says
    "never used." Alberta, you shouldn't try to fool people like that.   335
    Washin' up Herb's hoe and selling it like it was new. Bad girl.

Alberta: Actually, that is me. I bought Herb some new tools for his birthday
    and then he. . . gave it up. . . gardening.

Deedee: Before his birthday?

Alberta: What?   340

Deedee: Did you have time to go buy him another present?

Alberta: Yes. . . well, no. I mean, he told me before his birthday, but I didn't
    get a chance to get him anything else.

Deedee: He's probably got everything anyhow.

Alberta: Just about.   345

Deedee: Didn't he get his feelings hurt?

Alberta: No.

Deedee: Joe never likes the stuff I give him.

Alberta: Oh, I'm sure he does. He just doesn't know how to tell you.

Deedee: No. He doesn't. For our anniversary, I planned real far ahead for this   350
    one, I'm tellin' you. I sent off my picture, not a whole body picture, just
    my face real close up, to this place in Massachusetts, and they painted,
    well I don't know if they really painted, but somehow or other they *put*
    my face on this doll. It was unbelievable how it really looked like me.
    'Bout this tall *(Indicates about two feet)* with overalls and a checked   355
    shirt. I thought it was real cute, and I wrote this card sayin' "From one
    livin' doll to another. Let's keep playin' house till the day we die."

Alberta: And he didn't like it?

Deedee: He laughed so hard he fell over backward out of the chair and
    cracked his head open on the radiator. We had to take him to the   360
    emergency room.

Alberta: I'm sorry.

Deedee: We was sittin' there waitin' for him to get sewed up and this little kid
    comes in real sick and Joe he says to me, *(Getting a candy bar out of
    her purse and taking a big anxious bite out of it)* I brought this doll   365
    along, see, I don't know why, anyway Joe says to me. . . "Deedee, that lit-
    tle girl is so much sicker than me. Let's give her this doll to make her feel
    better." And they were takin' her right on in to the doctors 'cause she
    looked pretty bad, and Joe rushes up and puts this doll in her arms.

Alberta: They let her keep it?   370

Deedee: Her mother said, "Thanks a lot." Real sweet like they didn't have
    much money to buy the kid dolls or something. It made Joe feel real
    good.

Alberta: But it was your present to him. It was your face on the doll.

Deedee: Yeah, *(Pause)* but I figure it was his present as soon as I gave it to   375
    him, so if he wanted to give it away, that's his business. But *(Stops)* he

didn't like it. I could tell. *(Walks to the window again)* They need to wash this window here.

Alberta: I gave Herb a fishing pole one year.

Deedee (Not interested): He fishes.   380

Alberta: No, but I thought he wanted to. He'd cut out a picture of this husky man standing in water practically up to his waist, fishing. I thought he left it out so I'd get the hint.

Deedee: But he didn't?

Alberta: Oh, it was a hint all right. He wanted the hat.   385

Deedee: Right.

Alberta (Seeing that Deedee is really getting upset): Do you like the things Joe gives you?

Deedee: I'd like it if he came home, that's what I'd like.

Alberta: He'll be back soon. You'll probably see those lights go on as soon   390
as your clothes are dry.

Deedee: Sure.

Alberta: People just can't always be where we want them to be, when we want them to be there.

Deedee: Well, I don't like it.   395

Alberta: You don't have to like it. You just have to know it.

Deedee (Defensive): Wouldn't you like for Herb to be home right now?

Alberta: I certainly would.

Deedee: 'Cause if they were both home where they should be, we wouldn't have to be here in this crappy laundromat washin' fuckin' shirts in the   400
middle of the night!

> *Deedee kicks a dryer. Alberta is alarmed and disturbed at the use of the word "fuckin'."*

Deedee: I'm sorry. You probably don't use language like that, well, neither do I, very often, but I'm *(Now doing it on purpose)* pissed as hell at that sunuvabitch.

> *Alberta picks up a magazine, trying to withdraw completely. She is offended, but doesn't want to appear self-righteous. Now, Shooter pushes open the front door. Deedee turns sharply and sees him. She storms back and sits down beside Alberta. Both women are somewhat alarmed at a black man entering this preserve so late at night. Shooter is poised and handsome. He is dressed neatly, but casually. He is carrying an army duffel bag full of clothes, a cue case and a sack of tacos. He has a can of beer in one pocket. He moves toward a washer, sets down the duffel bag, opens the cap on the beer. He is aware that he has frightened them. This amuses him, but he understands it. Besides, he is so goddamned charming.*

Shooter (Holding the taco sack so they can see it): Would either of you   405
two ladies care to join me in a taco?

Alberta (Finally): No thank you.

Shooter (As though in an ad): Freshly chopped lettuce, firm vine-ripened New Jersey beefsteak tomatoes, a-ged, shred-ded, ched-dar cheese, sweet slivers of Bermuda onion and Ole Mexico's very own, very hot   410
taco sauce.

Deedee: That's just what they say on the radio.

Shooter: That's because I'm the "they" who says it on the radio.

Deedee: You are?

Shooter (Walking over): Shooter Stevens. *(Shakes her hand)*   415

Alberta (As he shakes her hand): Nice to meet you.

Deedee: You're the Number One Night Owl?

Shooter (As he said it at the beginning of the act): . . . sayin' it's three o'clock,
     all right, and time to rock your daddy to dreams of de-light.

Deedee: You are! You really are! That's fantastic! I always listen to you!   420

Shooter (Walking back to his laundry): Yeah?

Deedee: Always. Except when. . . I mean, when I get to pick, I pick you. I
     mean, your station. You're on late.

Shooter: You got it.

Deedee (To Alberta): Terrific. *(disgusted with herself)* I'm telling him he's on   425
     late. He knows he's on late. He's the one who's on late. Big news, huh?

Shooter: You a reporter?

Deedee (Pleased with the question): Oh no. *(Stands up, stretches)* Gotten
     so stiff sitting there. *(Walks over)* Don't you know what they put in
     those things?   430

Shooter: The tacos?

Deedee: Dog food.

Shooter (Laughing): Have to eat 'em anyway. Good business. I keep stop-
     pin' in over there, they keep running the ad. Gonna kill me.

Deedee: No kidding. We take our. . . *(Quickly)* My garbage cans are right   435
     next to theirs and whatta theirs got in 'em all the time? Dog-food cans.

Shooter (He smiles): Maybe they have a dog.

Alberta: It could be someone else in the building.

Shooter: See?

Deedee: She didn't mean they have a dog. She meant some old person in   440
     the building's eatin' dog food. It happens. A lot around here.

Shooter (To Alberta): You her mom?

Alberta: No.

Deedee: We just met in here. She's Alberta Johnson. I'm Deedee Johnson.

Alberta: Shooter is an unusual name.   445

Shooter (Nodding toward the pool hall next door): I play some pool.

Deedee (Pointing to the cue case): What's that?

Shooter: My cue.

Deedee: You any good?

Shooter: At what?   450

Deedee: At pool, dummy.

Shooter (Putting his clothes in the washer): I do okay.

Deedee: You must do better than okay or else why would you have your
     own cue?

Shooter: Willie says, Willie's the guy who owns the place, Willie says pool cues   455
     are like women. You gotta have your own and you gotta treat her right.

Deedee (Seeing a piece of clothing he's dropped in): Did you mean to put
     that in there?

Shooter (Pulling it back out): This?

Deedee: Your whites will come out green.   460

Shooter (Dropping it back in the washer): Uh-uh. It's nylon.

Alberta: Your work sounds very interesting.

Shooter: Yes, it does.

Deedee: What's your real name?

Shooter: G.W. 465

Deedee: That's not a real name.

Shooter: I don't like my real name.

Deedee: Come on. . .

Shooter (Disgusted): It's Gary Wayne. Now do I look like Gary Wayne to you? 470

Deedee (Laughs): No.

Shooter: Mom's from Indiana.

Alberta: From Gary or Fort Wayne?

Deedee: Alberta used to be a teacher.

Shooter: It coulda been worse. She coulda named me Clarksville. *(Deedee* 475
laughs) Hey! Now why don't the two of you come over and join us for
a beer?

Alberta: No thank you.

Shooter (Pouring in the soap): It's just Willie and me this time of night.

Alberta: No. 480

Deedee (With a knowing look at Alberta): And watch you play pool?

Shooter: Actually, what we were planning to do tonight was whip us up a
big devil's food cake and pour it in one of the pool tables to bake. Turn
up the heat real high. . . watch it rise and then pour on the creamy
fudge icing with lots of nuts. 485

Deedee: You're nuts.

Shooter: Get real sick if we have to eat it all ourselves. . .

Deedee: I've never seen anybody play pool.

Shooter: The key to pool's a. . . *(Directly seductive now)* real smooth
stroke. . . the feel of that stick in your hand. . . 490

Deedee: Feels good?

Shooter: You come on over, I'll show you just how it's done.

Deedee: Pool.

Shooter: Sure. *(Smiles, then turns sharply and walks back to Alberta,
depositing an empty soap box in the trash can)* Willie always keeps 495
hot water. You could have a nice cup of tea.

Alberta (A pointed look at Deedee): No.

Deedee: Our wash is almost done. We have to—

Shooter: We'll be there quite a while. Gets lonesome this late, you know.

Deedee: We know. 500

> *And suddenly, everybody feels quite uncomfortable.*

Shooter (To Alberta): It was nice meeting you. Hope I didn't interrupt your
reading or anything.

Deedee: She used to be a teacher.

Shooter: That's what you said. *(Walking toward the door)* Right next door,
now. Can't miss it. *(To Deedee)* Give you a piece of that fudge cake. 505

Deedee: Yeah, I'll bet you would.

Shooter (Closing the door): Big piece.

> *Alberta watches Deedee watch to see which direction Shooter takes.*

Deedee (After a moment): I thought we'd had it there for a minute, didn't
you? *(Visibly cheered)* Coulda been a murderer, or a robber or a rapist,
just as easy! *(Increasingly excited)* We coulda been hostages by now! 510

Alberta: To have hostages you have to commit a hijacking. You do not hijack
a laundromat.

Deedee: Depends how bad you need clean clothes.

Alberta: I didn't like the things he said to you.

Deedee: He was just playin'. 515

Alberta: He was not playing.

Deedee: Well, what does it hurt? Just words.

Alberta: Not those words.

Deedee: You don't miss a thing, do you?

Alberta: I'm not deaf. 520

Deedee: Just prejudiced.

Alberta: That's not true.

Deedee: If that was a white DJ comin' in here, you'd still be talkin' to him, I bet. Seein' if he knows your "old" favorites.

Alberta: If you don't want to know what I think, you can stop talking to me. 525

Deedee: What you think is what's wrong with the world. People don't trust each other just because they're some other color from them.

Alberta: And who was it who said he could be a murderer? That was you, Deedee. Would you have said that if he'd been white?

Deedee: It just makes you sick, doesn't it. The thought of me and Shooter 530 over there after you go home.

Alberta: It's not my business.

Deedee: That's for sure.

> *Alberta goes back to reading her magazine. Deedee wanders around.*

Deedee: You don't listen to him on the radio, but I do. And you know what he says after "rock your daddy to dreams of de-light"? He says, "And 535 mama, I'm comin' home." Now, if he has a "mama" to go home to, what's he doing washing his own clothes? So he don't have a "mama," and that means lonely. And he's loaded, too. So if he's got a wife, she's got a washer, so don't say maybe they don't have a washer. Lonely.

Alberta: All right. He's a nice young man who washes his own clothes and 540 is "friendly" without regard to race, creed or national origin.

Deedee: I mean, we're both in here in the middle of the night and it don't mean we're on the make, does it?

Alberta: It's perfectly respectable.

Deedee: You always do this when Herb is out of town? 545

Alberta: No.

Deedee: You don't even live in this neighborhood, do you?

Alberta: No.

Deedee: Know how I knew that? That garden. There ain't a garden for miles around here. 550

Alberta: You've been reading Sherlock Holmes.

Deedee (Knows Alberta was insulting her): So why did you come over here?

Alberta (Knows she made a mistake): I came for the same reason you did. To do my wash.

Deedee: In the middle of the night? Hah. It's a big mystery, isn't it? And you 555 don't want to tell me. Is some man meetin' you here? Yeah, and you can't have your meetin' out where you live 'cause your friends might see you and give the word to old Herb when he gets back.

Alberta: No. *(Pauses)* I'm sorry I said what I did. Go on over to the pool hall. I'll put your clothes in the dryer. 560

Deedee (Easily thrown off the track): And let him think I'm all hot for him. No sir. Besides, Joe might come home.

Alberta: That's right.

Deedee: Might just serve him right, though. Come in and see me drinkin'
beer and playin' pool with Willie and Shooter. Joe hates black people.   565
He says even when they're dancin' or playin' ball, they're thinkin' about
killin'. Yeah, that would teach him to run out on me. A little dose of his
own medicine. Watch him gag on it.

Alberta: So he *has* run out on you.

Deedee: He's workin' the double shift.   570

Alberta: That's what you said.

Deedee: And you don't believe me. You think he just didn't come home, is
that it? You think I was over there waitin' and waitin' in my new night-
gown and when the late show went off I turned on the radio and ate a
whole pint of chocolate ice cream, and when the radio went off I   575
couldn't stand it anymore so I grabbed up all these clothes, dirty or not,
and got outta there so he wouldn't come in and find me cryin'. Well,
(Firmly) I wasn't cryin'!

Alberta (After a considerable pause): I haven't cried in forty years.

Deedee: Just happy I guess.   580

Alberta (With a real desire to help now): I had an Aunt Dora, who had a
rabbit, Puffer, who died. I cried then. I cried for weeks.

Deedee: And it wasn't even your rabbit.

Alberta: I loved Aunt Dora and she loved that rabbit. I'd go to visit and she'd
tell me what Puffer had done that day. She claimed he told her stories,   585
Goldilocks and the Three Hares, The Rabbit Who Ate New York. Then
we'd go outside and drink lemonade while Puffer ate lettuce. She grew
lettuce just for him. A whole backyard of it.

Deedee: Little cracked, huh?

Alberta: I helped her bury him. Tears were streaming down my face.   590
"Bertie," she said, "stop crying. He didn't mean to go and leave us all
alone and he'd feel bad if he knew he made us so miserable." But in the
next few weeks, Aunt Dora got quieter and quieter till finally she wasn't
talking at all and Mother put her in a nursing home.

Deedee: Where she died.   595

Alberta: Yes.

Deedee: Hey! Our wash is done. *(Alberta seems not to hear her)* Look, I'll
do it. You go sit.

Alberta (Disoriented): No, I . . .

Deedee: Let me, really. I know this part. Mom says you can't blow this part,   600
so I do it. She still checks, though, finds some reason to go downstairs
and check the heat I set. I don't mind, really. Can't be too careful.

*Deedee unloads the washers and carries the clothes to the dryers.
Alberta walks to the window, seeming very far away.*

Deedee (Setting the heat): Regular for you guys, warm for permos and
undies. Now Herb's shirts and shorts get hot. Pants and socks get . . .

Alberta: Warm.   605

Deedee: What's Herb got left to wear anyhow?

Alberta: His gray suit.

Deedee (Laughs at how positive Alberta is about this): What color tie?

Alberta: Red with a silver stripe through it.

Deedee (Still merry): Shirt?   610

Alberta: White.

Deedee: Shoes?

Alberta (Quiet astonishment): I don't know.

Deedee: Well I'm glad. Thought you were seeing him all the way to Akron, X-ray eyes or something weird. Alberta. . .   615

Alberta: Yes? *(Worried, turning around to face her now, afraid Deedee will know her secret)*

Deedee: You got any dimes?

Alberta (Relieved): Sure. *(Walks to her purse)* How many do we need?

Deedee: Two each, I guess. Four dryers makes eight. *(As Alberta is getting*   620
them out of her wallet) I don't know what I'd have done if you hadn't been here. I didn't think. . . before I. . .

Alberta: You'd have done just fine. Don't forget Sleepy back there.

Deedee: I wish Mom were more like you.

Alberta: Stuck up?   625

Deedee: Smart. Nice to talk to.

Alberta: Thank you, but. . .

Deedee: No, really. You've been to Mexico and you've got a good man.

> *Alberta takes off her glasses, still very upset.*

Deedee: Mom's just got me and giant-size Cheer. And she don't say two words while I'm there. Ever. I don't blame her I guess.   630

Alberta: Well. . .

Deedee: Yeah.

Alberta (Back in balance now): But you're young and pretty. You have a wonderful sense of humor.

Deedee: Uh-huh.   635

Alberta: And you'll have those children someday.

Deedee: Yeah, I know. *(Gloomily)* I have my whole life in front of me.

Alberta: You could get a job.

Deedee: Oh, I got one. This company in New Jersey, they send me envelopes and letters and lists of names and I write on the names and   640
addresses and Dear Mr. Wilson or whatever at the top of the letter. I do have nice handwriting.

Alberta: I'm sure.

Deedee: I get so bored doing it. Sometimes I want to take a fat orange crayon and scribble *(Making letters in the air)* EAT BEANS, FATSO, and   645
then draw funny faces all over the letter.

Alberta: I'm sure the extra money comes in handy.

Deedee: Well, Joe don't know I do it. I hide all the stuff before he comes home. And I keep the money at Mom's. She borrows from it sometimes. She says that makes us even for the water for the washing   650
machine. See, I can't spend it or Joe will know I got it.

Alberta: He doesn't want you to work.

Deedee (Imitating Joe's voice): I'm the head of this house.

Alberta: He expects you to sit around all day?

Deedee: I guess. *(With good-humored rage)* Oh, I can wash the floor if I   655
want.

Alberta: You should tell him how you feel.

Deedee: He'd leave me.

Alberta: Maybe.

Deedee (After a moment): So what, right?   660

Alberta: I just meant, if you give him the chance to understand—

Deedee: But what would I say?

Alberta: You'd figure something out. I'm sure.

Deedee: I don't want to start it. I don't want to say I want a real job, 'cause
   then I'll say the reason I want a real job is I gotta have something to   665
   think about besides when are you coming home and how long is it
   gonna be before you don't come home at all. And he'll say what do you
   mean don't come home at all and I'll have to tell him I know what
   you're doing, I know you're lying to me and going out on me and he'll
   say what are you gonna do about it. You want a divorce? And I don't   670
   want him to say that.

Alberta: Now. . . you don't know—

Deedee (Firmly): I called the bowling alley and asked for him and the bartender said, "This Patsy? He's on his way, honey." I hope he falls in the
   sewer.   675

Alberta: Deedee!

Deedee: I hope he gets his shirt caught in his zipper. I hope he wore socks
   with holes in 'em. I hope his Right Guard gives out. I hope his baseball cap
   falls in the toilet. I hope she kills him. *(Pushing one of the carts, hard)*

Alberta: Deedee!   680

Deedee: I do. Last night, I thought I'd surprise him and maybe we'd bowl a
   few games? Well, I was gettin' my shoes and I saw them down at lane
   twelve, laughin' and all. He had one of his hands rubbing her hair and
   the other one rubbing his bowling ball. Boy did I get out of there
   quick. I've seen her there before. She teaches at the Weight Control   685
   upstairs, so she's probably not very strong but maybe she could poison
   him or something. She wears those pink leotards and even her hair
   looks thin. I hate him.

Alberta: I'm sure you don't really.

Deedee: He's mean and stupid. I thought he'd get over it, but he didn't.   690
   Mean and stupid. And I ain't all that smart, so if I know he's dumb, he
   must really be dumb. I used to think he just acted mean and stupid.
   Now, I know he really *is*. . .

Alberta: . . . mean and stupid.

Deedee: Why am I telling you this? You don't know nuthin' about bein'   695
   dumped.

Alberta: At least you have some money saved.

Deedee: For what?

Alberta: And your mother would let you stay with her till you got your own
   place.   700

Deedee: She's the *last* person I'm tellin'.

Alberta: I'll bet you'd like being a telephone operator.

Deedee: But how's he gonna eat? The only time he ever even fried an egg,
   he flipped it over and it landed in the sink. It was the last egg, so he
   grabbed it up and ate it in one bite.   705

Alberta: One bite?

Deedee: I like how he comes in the door. Picks me up, swings me around in
   the air. . .

Alberta (Incredulous): He stuffed a whole egg in his mouth?

Deedee: You're worse than Mom. *(Angrily)* He's gonna be a famous race car   710
   driver someday and I want to be there.

Alberta: To have him pour beer all over you.

Deedee: Yes, to have him pour beer all over me.

Alberta (Checking the clothes in one of her dryers, knowing she has said
      too much): He could have come in without turning on the lights. If you   715
      want to go check, I'll watch your things here.
Deedee: You want to get rid of me, don't you?
Alberta: I do not want to get rid of you.
Deedee: So why don't *you* go home? Go get the Woolite for that yucky shirt
      you didn't wash. You not only don't want to talk to me, you didn't even   720
      want me to touch that shirt. Herb's shirt is too nice for me to even
      touch. Well, I may be a slob, but I'm clean.
Alberta: I didn't want to wash it.
Deedee: That ain't it at all. Herb is so wonderful. You love him so much. You
      wash his clothes just the right way. I could never drop his shirt in the   725
      washer the way you do it. The stain might not come out and he might
      say what did you do to my shirt and you might fight and that would
      mess up your little dream world where everything is always sweet and
      nobody ever gets mad and you just go around gardening and giving
      each other little pecky kisses all the time. Well, you're either kidding   730
      yourself or lying to me. Nobody is so wonderful that somebody else
      can't touch their shirt. You act like he's a saint. Like he's dead and now
      you worship the shirts he wore.
Alberta: What do I have to do to get you to leave me alone?
Deedee (Feeling very bad): He is dead, isn't he?   735
Alberta: Yes.
Deedee: I'm so stupid.
Alberta: You. . . .
Deedee: What? Tell me. Say something horrible.
Alberta (Slowly, but not mean): You just don't know when to shut up.   740
Deedee: Worse that that. I don't know how. *(Hates what she has done)*
Alberta: But you are not dumb, child. And don't let anybody tell you you
      are, okay? *(Takes off her glasses and rubs her eyes)*
Deedee: I'm sorry, Mrs. Johnson, I really am sorry. You probably been plannin'
      this night for a long time. Washin' his things. And I barged in and spoiled   745
      it all.
Alberta: I've been avoiding it for a long time.

      Deedee feels terrible, she wants to ask questions, but is trying very
      hard, for once, to control her mouth.

Alberta: Herb died last winter, the day before his birthday.
Deedee: When you got him the rakes.
Alberta: He was being nosy, like I told you before, in the kitchen. I was mak-   750
      ing his cake. So I asked him to take out the garbage. He said, "Can't we
      wait till it's old enough to walk?"
Deedee: How. . .
Alberta: I didn't miss him till I put the cake in the oven. Guess I thought he
      was checking his seedbeds in the garage. I yelled out, "Herb, do you   755
      want butter cream or chocolate?" And then I saw him. Lying in the
      alley, covered in my cabbage soup. It was his heart.
Deedee: Did you call the. . .
Alberta: I picked up his head in my hand and held it while I cleaned up as
      much of the stuff as I could. A tuna can, coffee grounds, eggshells. . .   760
Deedee (Carefully): You knew he was dead, not just knocked out?

Alberta: He'd hit his head when he fell. He was bleeding in my hand. I knew
   I should get up, but the blood was still so warm.
Deedee: I'm so sorry.
Alberta: I don't want you to be alone, that's not what I meant before.   765
Deedee: Looks like I'm alone anyway.
Alberta: That's what I meant.
Deedee: Sometimes I bring in a little stand-up mirror to the coffee table
   while I'm watching TV. It's my face over there when I look, but it's a
   face just the same.   770
Alberta: Being alone isn't so awful. I mean, it's awful, but it's not that awful.
   There are harder things.

*The dryers stop. Deedee watches Alberta take a load of clothes from
the dryer, holding them up to smell them.*

Deedee: I'd probably eat pork and beans for weeks.
Alberta (Her back to Deedee): I found our beachball when I cleaned out
   the basement. I can't let the air out of it. It's *(Turning around now)* his   775
   breath in there. *(Sees Deedee is upset)* Get your clothes out. They'll
   wrinkle. That's amazing about the shoes.
Deedee: The shoes?
Alberta: Remember I was telling you what Herb had on? Gray suit. . .
Deedee: . . . white shirt, red tie with a silver stripe through it. . .   780
Alberta: I hang onto the shirt he died in, and I don't even know if he's got
   shoes on in his coffin.
Deedee: Well, if he's flyin' around heaven, he probably don't need 'em.
   (Pauses) You bought him all black socks.
Alberta: It was his idea. He thought they'd be easier to match if they were   785
   all the same color.
Deedee: Is it?
Alberta: No. Now I have to match by length. They may be all black, but they
   don't all shrink the same. I guess I don't really have to match them
   now, though, do I? *(Continues to match them)*   790
Deedee: I'd like to lose all Joe's white ones. *(Holding them up over the
   trash can, then thinking maybe it's not such a good idea)*
*Alberta (Going back for her last load of clothes, looking toward the win-
   dow):* Deedee. . . your lights are on. In your apartment. All the lights
   are on now.   795
Deedee: You sure?
Alberta: Come see.

Deedee walks over to the window.

Deedee: You're right.
Alberta: Yes.
Deedee: So what do I do now?   800
Alberta: I don't know.
Deedee: Should I rush right home? Ask Joe did he have a good time bowling a few games after his double shift? Listen to him brag about his
   score? His score he didn't make in the games he didn't bowl after the
   double shift he didn't work? Well I don't feel like it. I'm going next   805
   door. Play some pool. Make him miss me.

Alberta: You should go home before you forget how mad you are. You don't have to put up with what he's doing. You can if you want to, if you think you can't make it without him, but you don't have to.

Deedee: But what should I say? Joe, if you don't stop going out on me, I'm   810
not ever speaking to you again? That's exactly what he wants.

Alberta: What you say isn't that important. But there is something you have to remember while you say it.

Deedee: Which is?

Alberta: Your own face in the mirror is better company than a man who   815
would eat a whole fried egg in one bite. *(Deedee laughs)* But it won't be easy.

Deedee (Cautiously): Are you gonna wash that other shirt ever?

Alberta: The cabbage-soup shirt? No, I don't think so.

Deedee: Yeah.   820

Alberta (Loading up her basket): Maybe, in a few months or next year sometime, I'll be able to give these away. They're nice things.

Deedee: People do need them. Hey! *(Leaving her laundry and going to the bulletin board)* I told you there ain't a garden for miles around here. You better hang onto these hoes. It's getting' about time to turn   825
over the soil, isn't it?

Alberta: Another two weeks or so, yes it is. Well, *(Taking the card)* that's everything. I'll just get my soap and. . .

Deedee (Hesitantly): Mrs. Johnson?

Alberta: Alberta.   830

Deedee: Alberta.

Alberta: Yes?

Deedee: I'm really lonely.

Alberta: I know.

Deedee: How can you stand it?   835

Alberta: I can't. *(Pauses)* But I have to, just the same.

Deedee: How do I. . . how do you do that?

Alberta: I don't know. You call me if you think of something. *(Gives her a small kiss on the forehead)*

Deedee: I don't have your number.   840

Alberta (Backing away toward the door): I really wanted to be alone tonight.

Deedee: I know.

Alberta: I'm glad you talked me out of it.

Deedee: Boy, you can count on me for that. Hey! Don't go yet. I owe you some money.   845

Alberta: No. *(Fondly)* Everybody deserves a free load now and then.

Deedee (Trying to reach across the space to her): Thank you.

Alberta: Now, I suggest you go wake up Sleepy back there and see if there's something he needs to talk about.

Deedee: Tell you the truth, I'm ready for a little peace and quiet.   850

Alberta: Good night. *(Leaves)*

Deedee (Reaching for the Dr. Pepper she put on the washer early on): Yeah, peace and quiet. *(Pops the top on the Dr. Pepper)* Too bad it don't come in cans.

Lights go down as she stands there looking out the window.

[1978]

Questions

1. Norman has chosen (or rather invented) Deedee and Alberta with some care. How are they different? How are they similar? Point to particular moments in the play when the distance between them is obvious, and also to moments when they are connecting on a personal level.
2. Norman provides concise but crucial instructions regarding the scene when the play opens. Discuss the scene. Why, for example, is "Stand By Your Man" on the radio? Would the play work as well if it were set in a new laundromat? Why couldn't Deedee and Alberta meet in an all-night diner?
3. What is your response to Alberta in the opening minutes of the play? How do you see her as the play ends? What has happened?
4. What is the most important line in the play? What is Norman's point? What is the play really about?
5. What does the role of Shooter add to the play? Is the race issue related to the play's main point? How?
6. What is the significance of the sleeping attendant? What does this non-role add to the play? (Consider especially the ending.)
7. When Deedee says, at the end, "I don't have your number," Alberta has just taken a card with her number on it off the bulletin board. Why doesn't Alberta hand the card to Deedee?

DAVID IVES (1950–)

A Chicago native, who attended Catholic schools and then Northwestern University and the Yale Drama School, David Ives is famous for his innovative short plays. Sure Thing was one of six brief comedies first staged together as All in the Timing *in 1993; for 1995–96, this grouping of plays was performed in the United States more often than any other play, excluding only Shakespeare. Ives also writes short fiction, television and movie screenplays, and opera.*

Sure Thing

Characters

Betty
Bill

> Scene. A café.

> *Betty, a woman in her late twenties, is reading at a café table. An empty chair is opposite her. Bill, same age, enters.*

Bill: Excuse me. Is this chair taken?
Betty: Excuse me?
Bill: Is this taken?
Betty: Yes it is.
Bill: Oh. Sorry.
Betty: Sure thing.

> *(A bell rings softly.)*

Bill: Excuse me. Is this chair taken?
Betty: Excuse me?

5

Bill: Is this taken?

Betty: No, but I'm expecting somebody in a minute.   10

Bill: Oh. Thanks anyway.

Betty: Sure thing.

    (A bell rings softly.)

Bill: Excuse me. Is this chair taken?

Betty: No, but I'm expecting somebody very shortly.

Bill: Would you mind if I sit here till he or she or it comes?   15

Betty (glances at her watch): They do seem to be pretty late. . . .

Bill: You never know who you might be turning down.

Betty: Sorry. Nice try, though.

Bill: Sure thing.

    (Bell.)

    Is this seat taken?   20

Betty: No it's not.

Bill: Would you mind if I sit here?

Betty: Yes I would.

Bill: Oh.

    (Bell.)

    Is this chair taken?   25

Betty: No it's not.

Bill: Would you mind if I sit here?

Betty: No. Go ahead.

Bill: Thanks. *(He sits. She continues reading.)* Everyplace else seems to be
    taken.   30

Betty: Mm-hm.

Bill: Great place.

Betty: Mm-hm.

Bill: What's the book?

Betty: I just wanted to read in quiet, if you don't mind.   35

Bill: No. Sure thing.

    (Bell.)

    Everyplace else seems to be taken.

Betty: Mm-hm.

Bill: Great place for reading.

Betty: Yes, I like it.   40

Bill: What's the book?

Betty: The Sound and the Fury.

Bill: Oh. Hemingway.

    (Bell.)

    What's the book?   45

Betty: The Sound and the Fury.

Bill: Oh. Faulkner.

Betty: Have you read it?

Bill: Not . . . actually. I've sure read *about* it, though. It's supposed to be great.

Betty: It is great.   50

Bill: I hear it's great. *(Small pause.)* Waiter?

    (Bell.)

    What's the book?

Betty: The Sound and the Fury.

Bill: Oh. Faulkner.

Betty: Have you read it?   55

Bill: I'm a Mets fan, myself.

    (*Bell.*)

Betty: Have you read it?

Bill: Yeah, I read it in college.

Betty: Where was college?

Bill: I went to Oral Roberts University.   60

    (*Bell.*)

Betty: Where was college?

Bill: I was lying. I never really went to college. I just like to party.

    (*Bell.*)

Betty: Where was college?

Bill: Harvard.

Betty: Do you like Faulkner?   65

Bill: I love Faulkner. I spent a whole winter reading him once.

Betty: I've just started.

Bill: I was so excited after ten pages that I went out and bought everything
    else he wrote. One of the greatest reading experiences of my life. I   70
    mean, all that incredible psychological understanding. Page after page
    of gorgeous prose. His profound grasp of the mystery of time and
    human existence. The smells of the earth . . . What do you think?

Betty: I think it's pretty boring.

    (*Bell.*)

Bill: What's the book?   75

Betty: *The Sound and the Fury.*

Bill: Oh! Faulkner!

Betty: Do you like Faulkner?

Bill: I love Faulkner.

Betty: He's incredible.   80

Bill: I spent a whole winter reading him once.

Betty: I was so excited after ten pages that I went out and bought every-
    thing else he wrote.

Bill: All that incredible psychological understanding.

Betty: And the prose is so gorgeous.   85

Bill: And the way he's grasped the mystery of time—

Betty: —and human existence. I can't believe I've waited this long to read him.

Bill: You never know. You might not have liked him before.

Betty: That's true.

Bill: You might not have been ready for him. You have to hit these things
    at the right moment or it's no good.   90

Betty: That's happened to me.

Bill: It's all in the timing. (*Small pause.*) My name's Bill, by the way.

Betty: I'm Betty.

Bill: Hi.

Betty: Hi. (*Small pause.*)   95

Bill: Yes I thought reading Faulkner was . . . a great experience.

Betty: Yes. (*Small pause.*)

Bill: *The Sound and the Fury* . . . (*Another small pause.*)

Betty: Well. Onwards and upwards. (*She goes back to her book.*)

Bill: Waiter—?   100

(Bell.)

You have to hit these things at the right moment or it's no good.

Betty: That's happened to me.

Bill: It's all in the timing. My name's Bill, by the way.

Betty: I'm Betty.

Bill: Hi.   105

Betty: Hi.

Bill: Do you come in here a lot?

Betty: Actually I'm just in town for two days from Pakistan.

Bill: Oh. Pakistan.

> *(Bell.)*

My name's Bill, by the way.   110

Betty: I'm Betty.

Bill: Hi.

Betty: Hi.

Bill: Do you come in here a lot?

Betty: Every once in a while. Do you?   115

Bill: Not so much anymore. Not as much as I used to. Before my nervous
breakdown.

> *(Bell.)*

Do you come in here a lot?

Betty: Why are you asking?

Bill: Just interested.   120

Betty: Are you really interested, or do you just want to pick me up?

Bill: No, I'm really interested.

Betty: Why would you be interested in whether I come in here a lot?

Bill: I'm just . . . getting acquainted.

Betty: Maybe you're only interested for the sake of making small talk long   125
enough to ask me back to your place to listen to some music, or because
you've just rented this great tape for your VCR, or because you've got
some terrific unknown Django Reinhardt record, only all you really want
to do is fuck—which you won't do very well—after which you'll go into
the bathroom and pee very loudly, then pad into the kitchen and get   130
yourself a beer from the refrigerator without asking me whether I'd like
anything, and then you'll proceed to lie back down beside me and confess that you've got a girlfriend named Stephanie who's away at medical
school in Belgium for a year, and that you've been involved with her—*off
and on*—in what you'll call a very "intricate" relationship, for the past   135
seven YEARS. None of which *interests* me, mister!

Bill: Okay.

> *(Bell.)*

Do you come in here a lot?

Betty: Every other day, I think.

Bill: I come in here quite a lot and I don't remember seeing you.   140

Betty: I guess we must be on different schedules.

Bill: Missed connections.

Betty: Yes. Different time zones.

Bill: Amazing how you can live right next door to somebody in this town
and never even know it.   145

Betty: I know.

Bill: City life.

Betty: It's crazy.

Bill: We probably pass each other in the street every day. Right in front of this place, probably.   150

Betty: Yep.

Bill (looks around): Well the waiters here sure seem to be in some different time zone. I can't seem to locate one anywhere. . . . Waiter! (*He looks back.*) So what do you—(*He sees that she's gone back to her book.*)

Betty: I beg pardon?   155

Bill: Nothing. Sorry.

    (Bell.)

Betty: I guess we must be on different schedules.

Bill: Missed connections.

Betty: Yes. Different time zones.

Bill: Amazing how you can live right next door to somebody in this town   160
and never even know it.

Betty: I know.

Bill: City life.

Betty: It's crazy.

Bill: You weren't waiting for somebody when I came in, were you?   165

Betty: Actually I was.

Bill: Oh. Boyfriend?

Betty: Sort of.

Bill: What's a sort-of boyfriend?

Betty: My husband.   170

Bill: Ah-ha.

    (Bell.)

    You weren't waiting for somebody when I came in, were you?

Betty: Actually I was.

Bill: Oh. Boyfriend?

Betty: Sort of.

Bill: What's a sort-of boyfriend?   175

Betty: We were meeting here to break up.

Bill: Mm-hm . . .

    (Bell.)

    What's a sort-of boyfriend?

Betty: My lover. Here she comes right now!   180

    (Bell.)

Bill: You weren't waiting for somebody when I came in, were you?

Betty: No, just reading.

Bill: Sort of a sad occupation for a Friday night, isn't it? Reading here, all by yourself?

Betty: Do you think so?   185

Bill: Well sure. I mean, what's a good-looking woman like you doing out alone on a Friday night?

Betty: Trying to keep away from lines like that.

Bill: No, listen—

    (Bell.)

    You weren't waiting for somebody when I came in, were you?   190

Betty: No, just reading.

Bill: Sort of a sad occupation for a Friday night, isn't it? Reading here all by yourself?

Betty: I guess it is, in a way.

Bill: What's a good-looking woman like you doing out alone on a Friday   195
night anyway? No offense, but . . .

Betty: I'm out alone on a Friday night for the first time in a very long time.

Bill: Oh.

Betty: You see, I just recently ended a relationship.

Bill: Oh.   200

Betty: Of rather long standing.

Bill: I'm sorry. (*Small pause.*) Well listen, since reading by yourself is such
a sad occupation for a Friday night, would you like to go elsewhere?

Betty: No . . .

Bill: Do something else?   205

Betty: No thanks.

Bill: I was headed out to the movies in a while anyway.

Betty: I don't think so.

Bill: Big chance to let Faulkner catch his breath. All those long sentences
get him pretty tired.   210

Betty: Thanks anyway.

Bill: Okay.

Betty: I appreciate the invitation.

Bill: Sure thing.

(*Bell.*)

You weren't waiting for somebody when I came in, were you?   215

Betty: No, just reading.

Bill: Sort of a sad occupation for a Friday night, isn't it? Reading here all by
yourself?

Betty: I guess I was trying to think of it as existentially romantic. You
know—cappuccino, great literature, rainy night . . .   220

Bill: That only works in Paris. We *could* hop the late plane to Paris. Get on
a Concorde. Find a café . . .

Betty: I'm a little short on plane fare tonight.

Bill: Darn it, so am I.

Betty: To tell you the truth, I was headed to the movies after I finished this   225
section. Would you like to come along? Since you can't locate a waiter?

Bill: That's a very nice offer, but . . .

Betty: Uh-huh. Girlfriend?

Bill: Two, actually. One of them's pregnant, and Stephanie—

(*Bell.*)

Betty: Girlfriend?   300

Bill: No, I don't have a girlfriend. Not if you mean the castrating bitch I
dumped last night.

(*Bell.*)

Betty: Girlfriend?

Bill: Sort of. Sort of.

Betty: What's a sort-of girlfriend?   305

Bill: My mother.

(*Bell.*)

I just ended a relationship, actually.

Betty: Oh.

Bill: Of rather long standing.

Betty: I'm sorry to hear it.   310

Bill: This is my first night out alone in a long time. I feel a little bit at sea, to   315
tell you the truth.

Betty: So you didn't stop to talk because you're a Moonie, or you have some
weird political affiliation—?

Bill: Nope. Straight-down-the-ticket Republican.

(Bell.)

Straight-down-the-ticket Democrat.   320

(Bell.)

Can I tell you something about politics?

(Bell.)

I like to think of myself as a citizen of the universe.

(Bell.)

I'm unaffiliated.

Betty: That's a relief. So am I.

Bill: I vote my beliefs.   325

Betty: Labels are not important.

Bill: Labels are not important, exactly. Take me, for example. I mean, what
does it matter if I had a two-point at—

(Bell.)

three-point at—

(Bell.)

four-point at college? Or if I did come from Pittsburgh—   330

(Bell.)

Cleveland—

(Bell.)

Westchester County?

Betty: Sure.

Bill: I believe that a man is what he is.

(Bell.)

A person is what he is.   335

(Bell.)

A person is . . . what they are.

Betty: I think so too.

Bill: So what if I admire Trotsky?

(Bell.)

So what if I once had a total-body liposuction?

(Bell.)

So what if I don't have a penis?   340

(Bell.)

So what if I spent a year in the Peace Corps? I was acting on my
convictions.

Betty: Sure.

Bill: You just can't hang a sign on a person.

Betty: Absolutely. I'll bet you're a Scorpio.   345

(Many bells ring.)

Listen, I was headed to the movies after I finished this section. Would
you like to come along?

Bill: That sounds like fun. What's playing?

Betty: A couple of the really early Woody Allen movies.

Bill: Oh.   350
Betty: You don't like Woody Allen?
Bill: Sure. I like Woody Allen.
Betty: But you're not crazy about Woody Allen.
Bill: Those early ones kind of get on my nerves.
Betty: Uh-huh.   355

    (Bell.)

Bill: Y'know I was headed to the—
Betty (*simultaneously*): I was thinking about—
Bill: I'm sorry.
Betty: No, go ahead.
Bill: I was going to say that I was headed to the movies in a little while, and . . .   360
Betty: So was I.
Bill: The Woody Allen festival?
Betty: Just up the street.
Bill: Do you like the early ones?
Betty: I think anybody who doesn't ought to be run off the planet.   365
Bill: How many times have you seen *Bananas*?
Betty: Eight times.
Bill: Twelve. So are you still interested? (*Long pause.*)
Betty: Do you like Entenmann's crumb cake . . . ?
Bill: Last night I went out at two in the morning to get one. Did you have   370
    an Etch-a-Sketch as a child?
Betty: Yes! And do you like Brussels sprouts? (*Pause.*)
Bill: No, I think they're disgusting.
Betty: They are disgusting!
Bill: Do you still believe in marriage in spite of current sentiments against it?   375
Betty: Yes.
Bill: And children?
Betty: Three of them.
Bill: Two girls and a boy.
Betty: Harvard, Vassar, and Brown.   380
Bill: And will you love me?
Betty: Yes.
Bill: And cherish me forever?
Betty: Yes.
Bill: Do you still want to go to the movies?   385
Betty: Sure thing.
Bill and Betty (together): Waiter!

    Blackout

                                                [1988]

Questions

1. Explain the function of the bell in this play. What other devices might Ives
   have chosen? How do you imagine the audience reacting to the bell as the
   play unfolds?
2. What is the source of the play's comedy? Does the play have a serious
   point? What is it? How does the title contribute to both the comedy and the
   theme of the play?

3. What is your reaction to the ending? What is the relationship of the ending to the rest of the play?

AUGUST WILSON (1945–)

August Wilson grew up in a slum in Pittsburgh with his five siblings and his mother, Daisy Wilson, a maid. His white father, Frederick August Kittle, a baker, never lived with Wilson's family. After flunking out of the ninth grade, August Wilson worked at blue-collar jobs, educating himself in public libraries, and then began writing dramatic skits for the Science Museum of Minnesota. In 1968 he founded the Black Horizon Theatre Company in Pittsburgh, and began writing plays. By the 1980s, Wilson was recognized as a leading playwright, and he has now won two Pulitzer Prizes and many other honors.

The Janitor

Characters

Sam
Mr. Collins

Setting: A Hotel Ballroom

> *(Sam enters pushing a broom near the lectern. He stops and reads the sign hanging across the ballroom.)*

Sam: National. . . Conference. . . on. . . Youth.

> *(He nods his approval and continues sweeping. He gets an idea, stops, and approaches the lectern. He clears his throat and begins to speak. His speech is delivered with the literacy of a janitor. He chooses his ideas carefully. He is a man who has approached life honestly, with both eyes open.)*

Sam: I want to thank you all for inviting me here to speak about youth. See. . . I's fifty-six years old and I knows something about youth. The first thing I knows. . . is that youth is sweet before flight. . . its odor is rife with speculation and its resilience. . . that's its bounce back. . . is remarkable. But it's that sweetness that we victims of. All of us. Its sweetness. . . and its flight. One of them fellows in that Shakespeare stuff said, "I am not what I am." See. He wasn't like Popeye. This fellow had a different understanding. "I am not what I am." Well, neither are you. You are just what you have been. . . whatever you are now. But what you are now ain't what you gonna become. . . even though it is with you now. . . it's inside you now this instant. Time. . . see, this how you get to this. . . Time ain't changed. It's just moved. Or maybe it ain't moved. . . maybe it just changed. It don't matter. We are all victims of the sweetness of youth and the time of its flight. See. . . just like you I forgot who I am. I forgot what happened first. But I know the river I step into now. . . is not the same river I stepped into twenty years ago. See. I know that much. But I have forgotten the name of the river. . . I have forgotten the names of the gods. . . and like everybody else I have tried to fool them with my dancing. . . and guess at their faces. It's the same with everybody. We don't have to mention no names. Ain't nobody innocent. We are all victims of ourselves. We have all had our

5

10

15

20

hand in the soup. . . and made the music play just so. See, now. . . this what I call wrestling with Jacob's angel. You lay down at night and that angel come to wrestle with you. When you wrestling with that angel you bargaining for you future. See. And what you need to bargain with is that sweetness of youth. So. . . to the youth of the United States I says. . . don't spend that sweetness too fast! 'Cause you gonna need it. See. I's fifty-six years old and I done found that out. But it's all the same. It all comes back on you. . . just like reaping and sowing. Down and out ain't nothing but being caught up in the balance of what you put down. If you down and out and things ain't going right for you. . . you can bet you done put a down payment on your troubles. Now you got to pay up on the balance. That's as true as I'm standing here. Sometimes you can't see it like that. The last note on Gabriel's horn always gets lost when you get to realizing you done heard the first. See, it's just like. . . .   25   30   35

Mr. Collins: (*Entering*) Come on, Sam. . . let's quit wasting time and get this floor swept. There's going to be a big important meeting here this afternoon.   40

Sam: Yessuh, Mr. Collins. Yessuh.

(Sam goes back to sweeping as the lights go down to—)

Black

Questions

1. What is Sam's point? How is it related to the idea of "I am not what I am"?
2. Does Sam make his point effectively? What is surprising about his "speech"?
3. Explore Sam's allusion to Jacob's Angel. The story appears in Genesis 32: 24–32. How does it apply to Sam's speech?
4. What is the effect of Mr. Collins's interruption? How would the play be different if Sam had simply lost interest in what he was saying, or run out of things to say?
5. Should Mr. Collins hear any of Sam's speech? If yes, how much? Explain.

Catherine Celesia Allen

Cathy Celesia Allen has written seven full-length plays and numerous one-acts. She won a 1993 Beverly Hills Theatre Guild Award for The Essence of Being.

Anything for You

Anything for You was originally produced at the Circle Repertory Lab in New York City, June 1993. Scott Segall directed the following cast:

> Lynette   Johanna Day
> Gail   Jo Twiss

Characters

Lynette: thirtyish, stylish
Gail: same age, a bit more conservative
Time: the present
Place: an urban café

At Rise: Lynette sits alone at a table for two, staring into her drink. Gail approaches the table, a bit harried. She kisses the preoccupied Lynette on the cheek, sits.

Gail: Sorry I'm late. I was just about to walk out when this rap artist of ours plops himself in the outer office, announces he's not leaving until somebody acknowledges his artistic crisis. This is a kid, nineteen years old mind you, who has a house in the Hamptons and a hot tub for every day of the week, and he's having an artistic crisis. That needs acknowledgment. *(She picks up a menu.)* Have you ordered yet?   5
(perusing the menu) So I have to sit there for twenty minutes trying to sound sincere when I tell him "It's not so bad, Roger. Money doesn't compromise your art. It just makes it more affordable." When what I really wanted to say was, This is the legal department. We work here. You're feeling screwed up or dysfunctional, go to artistic, bother them.   10
So anyway. . . the squab looks good. What do you think?

(Gail continues to study the menu. Lynette leans forward in her chair.)

Lynette: I need to have an affair.
Gail: Hmm? did you say something?
Lynette: I said, Gail, that I need to have an affair.
Gail: (looking up) You don't mean that.   15
Lynette: Yes I do.
Gail: An affair?
Lynette: Yes.
Gail: You?
Lynette: Uh-huh.   20
Gail: But you and Richard—
Lynette: I know.
Gail: Then I don't understand.
Lynette: Neither do I.
Gail: So basically you're sitting here telling me for no good reason that you   25
    want to—
Lynette: Not want. Need. Capital N. The big guns.
Gail: Why?
Lynette: I don't know. An overwhelming biological necessity for alternate
    body types. I don't know.   30
Gail: I don't think this is the place we should be discussing this.
Lynette: This is exactly the place. You are exactly the person. Gail. If I don't
    sleep with someone other than my husband very soon, I won't be
    responsible for myself.
Gail: Lynette.   35
Lynette: Time bomb. Tick tick tick.
Gail: Don't you think you're being a little overdramatic?
Lynette: No. Tick.
Gail: Have you met someone?
Lynette: No. Although when you get right down to it, everybody's a candidate.   40
Gail: You're kidding, right? All right, joke's over, very funny, ha ha, you're
    kidding.
Lynette: Gail, you don't know what it's like. I can't work. I can't sleep. All I
    know is I want a hot roll in the hay. That's the extent of my cognizant
    abilities.   45

Gail: I think you should try to show a little control.

Lynette: Yesterday I looked at a clock. I forgot how to tell time.

Gail: What are you drinking?

Lynette: I'm losing my mind.

Gail: You certainly are. Richard—   50

Lynette: Is sweet and kind and good, I know. He adapts, no matter how crazy I am. "You're right honey, I'll be more careful, I'll try not to let my heels touch the floor in that irritating manner anymore." I could tell him I want to chuck it all for a sugar cane farm in Borneo and he'd be researching farming techniques and plane fares within the hour.   55

Gail: So it seems to me you have nothing to complain about.

Lynette: I'm not complaining. But God, if I don't find someone to sear me to the bones I am going to explode. Little pieces of me flying out my office window and over New York, settling on some old ladies in the park. Explode.   60

Gail: I don't know what to say. You've put me in a difficult position. I love Richard.

Lynette: I do too.

Gail: He and George are best friends.

Lynette: Like brothers.   65

Gail: And you're my best friend—

Lynette: (expectantly) Yes?

Gail: Yes what?

Lynette: I'm your best friend.

Gail: Yes.   70

Lynette: You'd do anything for me.

Gail: Of course I would, you know that. What are you driving at?

Lynette: Sleep with me.

Gail: What?!

Lynette: Sleep with me, Gail. Make love to me until I beg you to stop.   75

Gail: You can't be serious.

Lynette: I couldn't live with myself if I did it with another man, not to mention what it would do to Richard if he found out. But you—

Gail: Are astonished.

Lynette: You're a woman, Gail. It wouldn't be cheating. It would be experimenting.   80

Gail: You're out of your mind.

Lynette: Will you do it?

Gail: Of course not.

Lynette: Why not?   85

Gail: In the first place, no offense, but I'm not physically attracted to you.

Lynette: Liar.

Gail: What did you call me?

Lynette: You're lying. You've wanted me from the day we met.

Gail: Oh, now I agree with you, Lynette, you have gone over the deep end.   90

Lynette: You stare at me. You watch my mouth when I speak. When we kiss hello you let your nose linger in my hair a little bit longer than necessary and you breathe in.

Gail: I can't really have this conversation anymore, okay? Can we order? *(pause)* I think you should see a doctor.   95

Lynette: You're angry.

Gail: I'm not, I'm flabbergasted. To think that after all these years of what I
thought was a close friendship you would suddenly come up with this
insane notion that I—that we—I'm married, Lynette.

Lynette: I know.   100

Gail: And I love George. Not to mention I'm one hundred percent
heterosexual.

Lynette: I'm going out of my mind.

Gail: I wish I could help you. I really do.   105

Lynette: You love me.

Gail: Of course I do. But that doesn't mean I desire you in a sexual manner.

Lynette: What about New Year's Eve?

Gail: (after a pause) What about it?

Lynette: New Year's Eve, 1991. The four of us spent it together. I drank too   110
many peach margaritas.

Gail: I remember.

Lynette: I got sick. Richard ended up carrying me into the bathroom and
you stayed to help.

Gail: You were so sick. Richard was so angry.   115

Lynette: I thought I'd never stop throwing up. When I finally did, I laid down
on the bathroom floor, closed my eyes, and you kissed me. On the mouth.

Gail: I didn't.

Lynette: You did. For a good long time.

Gail: You must have dreamt it, Lynette, I think I would remember—   120

Lynette: I remember thinking, "how soft her mouth is." You held my lower
lip for an extra second. Then you let go and the air hissed out of me like
a balloon.

Gail: I did not kiss you, Lynette. I mean, I may have given you a peck on the
cheek because I felt sorry for you, but beyond that, you are mistaken.   125

Lynette: I felt your tongue.

Gail: Lynette! *(She looks around, lowers her voice.)* This is really inappropriate.

Lynette: Why are you so against this? You have me, I have my fling—everybody
wins.

Gail: Except Richard, and George.   130

Lynette: We don't tell them. This is a secret between friends. Inviolable.

Gail: It's not that simple.

Lynette: Why not?

Gail: Lynette, look—do you want me to fix you up with someone? There
are a lot of lesbians in the music business.   135

Lynette: I want you.

Gail: No you don't.

Lynette: I do. You're my friend, I can trust you, there's no danger of falling
in love. I was going to say you're honest but you can't even admit to
kissing me when we both know—   140

Gail: All right, all right, I kissed you, I kissed you! I'd had a little to drink
myself that night— *(to an unseen patron)* Can I help you?

Lynette: You were stone cold sober. The antibiotics, remember?

Gail: (helplessly) You looked so pretty. Lying there with your hair spread
out over the mat. So vulnerable and so. . . beautiful, actually.   145

Lynette: Sleep with me, Gail.

Gail: I can't.

Lynette: Why not?

Gail: Because I'm in love with you.

Lynette: What?   150

Gail: I'm in love with you, Lynette. You think I go around kissing drunken
    smelly women on the mouth because it's a thing of mine?

Lynette: But I thought—

Gail: That my heart couldn't possibly leap every time I see you? That I don't
    feel profound jealousy when you and Richard reach for each other like   155
    any other happily married couple? That my feelings can't be real?

Lynette: No, I mean. . .

Gail: What, Lynette? What did you think?

Lynette: I don't know. A harmless crush. Like schoolgirls.

Gail: Not exactly.   160

Lynette: No. *(pause)* So where does this leave us?

Gail: I don't know.

Lynette: (after a pause) Maybe I do drink too much.

Gail: Maybe.

Lynette: I have a problem.   165

Gail: Yes.

Lynette: And you have a problem.

Gail: Yes.

Lynette: What do you think we should do?

Gail: I think we should order.   170

      (They return to looking at their menus.)

                End

                          [1993]

Questions

1. A recent production of this play included a waiter who, according to the
   review, added "comic relief." What might the waiter do, and do you think
   such comedy would be an asset or not?

2. How adept is Lynette with language? How does her use of language affect
   the way the audience perceives her?

3. What is the turning point of this play? Is it prepared for? That is, do you
   believe what happens? Explain.

4. Discuss the ethics of each woman. Does this play encourage promiscuity,
   discourage promiscuity, or focus on some other issue?

5. What will happen next? Is Gail's comment, "I think we should order," in any
   way a resolution—or a hint at a resolution?

6. Would this play work with two men? What about with a gay man and a heterosexual woman? Explain.

MILCHA SANCHEZ-SCOTT (1950–)

*Born in Bali, the daughter of a Colombian-Mexican father and an Indonesian mother, Milcha
Sanchez-Scott grew up in South America, Mexico, and Britain. Her family moved to San Diego
when she was fourteen. Sanchez-Scott has worked as a writer primarily in Los Angeles,
although she has also worked as a maid and an actress, among other things.*

*This play contains many passages that are in Spanish. In performance, no translation would be
provided, and a translation here would be distracting. With very little Spanish, you should*

make out much of what is said; if you understand no Spanish, you'll still be able to grasp what is going on. Just keep going: the context will usually make clear what is being said.

The Cuban Swimmer

Characters

Margarita Suárez, the swimmer
Eduardo Suárez, her father, the coach
Simón Suárez, her brother
Aída Suárez, the mother
Abuela, her grandmother
Voice of Mel Munson
Voice of Mary Beth White
Voice of Radio Operator
Setting. *The Pacific Ocean between San Pedro and Catalina Island.*
Time. *Summer.*

   Live conga drums can be used to punctuate the action of the play.

Scene I

   Pacific Ocean. Midday. On the horizon, in perspective, a small boat enters upstage left, crosses to upstage right, and exits. Pause. Lower on the horizon, the same boat, in larger perspective, enters upstage right, crosses and exits upstage left. Blackout.

Scene II

   Pacific Ocean. Midday. The swimmer, Margarita Suárez, is swimming. On the boat following behind her are her father, Eduardo Suárez, holding a megaphone, and Simón, her brother, sitting on top of the cabin with his shirt off, punk sunglasses on, binoculars hanging on his chest.

Eduardo *(Leaning forward, shouting in time to Margarita's swimming.):*
   Uno, dos, uno, dos. Y uno, dos. . . keep your shoulders parallel to the water.
Simón: I'm gonna take these glasses off and look straight into the sun.
Eduardo *(Through megaphone.): Muy bien, muy bien.* . . but punch those
   arms in, baby.   5
Simón *(Looking directly at the sun through binoculars.):* Come on, come
   on, zap me. Show me something. *(He looks behind at the shoreline and ahead at the sea.)* Stop! Stop, *Papi!* Stop!

   (Aída Suárez and Abuela, the swimmer's mother and grandmother, enter running from the back of the boat.)

Aída and Abuela: Qué? Qué es?
Aída: Es un shark?   10
Eduardo: Eh?
Abuela: Que es un shark dicen?

   (Eduardo blows whistle. Margarita looks up at the boat.)

Simón: No, *Papi,* no shark, no shark. We've reached the halfway mark.
Abuela *(Looking into the water.):* A dónde está?
Aída: It's not in the water.   15

Scene from the University of Colorado's production of
The Cuban Swimmer.

Abuela: Oh, no? Oh, no?

Aída: No! A *poco* do you think they're gonna have signs in the water to say
you are halfway to Santa Catalina? No. It's done very scientific. *A ver,
hijo,* explain it to your grandma.

Simón: Well, you see, Abuela—*(He points behind.)* There's San Pedro. *(He* 20
points ahead.) And there's Santa Catalina. Looks halfway to me.

*(Abuela shakes her head and is looking back and forth, trying to
make the decision, when suddenly the sound of a helicopter is heard.)*

Abuela (Looking up.): Virgencita de la Caridad del Cobre. Qué es eso?

(Sound of helicopter gets closer. Margarita looks up.)

Margarita: Papi, Papi!

*(A small commotion on the boat, with everybody pointing at the
helicopter above. Shadows of the helicopter fall on the boat. Simón
looks up at it through binoculars.)*

Papi—qué es? What is it?

Eduardo (Through megaphone.): Uh. . . uh. . . uh, *un momentico. . . mi*   25
    hija. . . . Your *papi's* got everything under control, understand? Uh. . .
    you just keep stroking. And stay. . . uh. . . close to the boat.

Simón: Wow, *Papi!* We're on TV, man! Holy Christ, we're all over the fuck-
    ing U.S.A.! It's Mel Munson and Mary Beth White!

Aída: Por Dios! Simón, don't swear. And put on your shirt.   30

    (Aída fluffs her hair, puts on her sunglasses and waves to the heli-
    copter. Simón leans over the side of the boat and yells to Margarita.)

Simón: Yo, Margo! You're on TV, man.

Eduardo: Leave your sister alone. Turn on the radio.

Margarita: Papi! Qué está pasando?

Abuela: Que es la televisión dicen? (She shakes her head.) Porque como
    yo no puedo ver nada sin mis espejuelos.   35

    (Abuela rummages through the boat, looking for her glasses. Voices of
    Mel Munson and Mary Beth White are heard over the boat's radio.)

Mel's Voice: As we take a closer look at the gallant crew of *La Havana.* . . and
    there. . . yes, there she is. . . the little Cuban swimmer from Long Beach,
    California, nineteen-year-old Margarita Suárez. The unknown swimmer is
    our Cinderella entry. . . a bundle of tenacity, battling her way through the
    choppy, murky waters of the cold Pacific to reach the Island of   40
    Romance. . . Santa Catalina. . . where should she be the first to arrive,
    two thousand dollars and a gold cup will be waiting for her.

Aída: Doesn't even cover our expenses.

Abuela: Qué dice?

Eduardo: Shhhh!   45

Mary Beth's Voice: This is really a family effort, Mel, and—

Mel's Voice: Indeed it is. Her trainer, her coach, her mentor, is her father,
    Eduardo Suárez. Not a swimmer himself, it says here, Mr. Suárez is head
    usher of the Holy Name Society and the owner-operator of Suárez Trea-
    sures of the Sea and Salvage Yard. I guess it's one of those places—   50

Mary Beth's Voice: If I might interject a fact here, Mel, assisting in this swim
    is Mrs. Suárez, who is a former Miss Cuba.

Mel's Voice: And a beautiful woman in her own right. Let's try and get a
    closer look.

    (Helicopter sound gets louder. Margarita, frightened, looks up again.)

Margarita: Papi!   55

Eduardo (Through megaphone.): Mi hija, don't get nervous. . . it's the
    press. I'm handling it.

Aída: I see how you're handling it.

Eduardo (Through megaphone.): Do you hear? Everything is under con-
    trol. Get back into your rhythm. Keep your elbows high and kick and   60
    kick and kick and kick. . .

Abuela (Finds her glasses and puts them on.): Ay sí, es la televisión. . . (She
    points to helicopter.) Qué lindo mira. . . (She fluffs her hair, gives a big
    wave.) Aló América! Viva mi Margarita, viva todo los Cubanos en los
    Estados Unidos!   65

Aída: Ay por Dios, Cecilia, the man didn't come all this way in his helicop-
    ter to look at you jumping up and down, making a fool of yourself.

Abuela: I don't care. I'm proud.

Aída: He can't understand you anyway.

Abuela: Viva. . . (She stops.) Simón, *cómo se dice viva?*   70

Simón: Hurray.

Abuela: Hurray for *mi Margarita y* for all the Cubans living *en* the United States, *y un abrazo. . .* Simón, *abrazo. . .*

Simón: A big hug.

Abuela: Sí, a big hug to all my friends in Miami, Long Beach, Union City,   75
except for my son Carlos, who lives in New York in sin! He lives. . . *(She crosses herself.)* in Brooklyn with a Puerto Rican woman in sin! *No decente. . .*

Simón: Decent.

Abuela: Carlos, *no decente.* This family, *decente.*   80

Aída: Cecilia, *por Dios.*

Mel's Voice: Look at that enthusiasm. The whole family has turned out to cheer little Margarita on to victory! I hope they won't be too disappointed.

Mary Beth's Voice: She seems to be making good time, Mel.

Mel's Voice: Yes, it takes all kinds to make a race. And it's a testimonial to the   85
all-encompassing fairness. . . the greatness of this, the Wrigley Invitational Women's Swim to Catalina, where among all the professionals there is still room for the amateurs. . . like these, the simple people we see below us on the ragtag *La Havana,* taking their long-shot chance to victory. *Vaya con Dios!*   90

(Helicopter sound fading as family, including Margarita, watch silently. Static as Simón turns radio off. Eduardo walks to bow of boat, looks out on the horizon.)

Eduardo (To himself.): Amateurs.

Aída: Eduardo, that person insulted us. Did you hear, Eduardo? That he called us a simple people in a ragtag boat? Did you hear. . . ?

Abuela (Clenching her fist at departing helicopter.): Mal-Rayo los parta!

Simón (Same gesture.): Asshole!   95

(Aída follows Eduardo as he goes to side of boat and stares at Margarita.)

Aída: This person comes in his helicopter to insult your wife, your family, your daughter. . .

Margarita (Pops her head out of the water.): Papi?

Aída: Do you hear me, Eduardo? I am not simple.

Abuela: Sí.   100

Aída: I am complicated.

Abuela: Sí, demasiada complicada.

Aída: Me and my family are not so simple.

Simón: Mom, the guy's an asshole.

Abuela (Shaking her fist at helicopter.): Asshole!   105

Aída: If my daughter was simple, she would not be in that water swimming.

Margarita: Simple? *Papi. . . ?*

Aída: Ahora, Eduardo, this is what I want you to do. When we get to Santa Catalina, I want you to call the TV station and demand an apology.

Eduardo: Cállete mujer! Aquí mando yo. I will decide what is to be done.   110

Margarita: Papi, tell me what's going on.

Eduardo: Do you understand what I am saying to you, Aída?

Simón (Leaning over side of boat, to Margarita.): Yo Margo! You know
   that Mel Munson guy on TV? He called you a simple amateur and said
   you didn't have a chance.   115

Abuela (Leaning directly behind Simón.): Mi hija, insultó a la familia.
   Desgraciado!

Aída (Leaning in behind Abuela.): He called us peasants! And your father
   is not doing anything about it. He just knows how to yell at me.

Eduardo (Through megaphone.): Shut up! All of you! Do you want to   120
   break her concentration? Is that what you are after? Eh?

   (Abuela, Aída and Simón shrink back. Eduardo paces before them.)

   Swimming is rhythm and concentration. You win a race *aquí.*
   (Pointing to his head.) Now. . . *(To Simón.)* you, take care of the boat,
   Aída *y Mama.* . . do something. Anything. Something practical.

   (Abuela and Aída get on knees and pray in Spanish.)

   Hija, give it everything, eh?. . . *por la familia. Uno.* . . *dos.* . . . You   125
   must win.

   *(Simón goes into cabin. The prayers continue as lights change to in-
   dicate bright sunlight, later in the afternoon.)*

Scene III

   *Tableau for a couple of beats. Eduardo on bow with timer in one
   hand as he counts strokes per minute. Simón is in the cabin steering, wearing his sunglasses, baseball cap on backward. Abuela and
   Aída are at the side of the boat, heads down, hands folded, still muttering prayers in Spanish.*

Aída and Abuela (Crossing themselves.): En el nombre del Padre, del
   Hijo y del Espíritu Santo amén.

Eduardo (Through megaphone.): You're stroking seventy-two!

Simón (Singing.): Mama's stroking, Mama's stroking seventy-two. . . .

Eduardo (Through megaphone.): You comfortable with it?   5

Simón (Singing.): Seventy-two, seventy-two, seventy-two for you.

Aída (Looking at the heavens.): Ay, Eduardo, *ven acá,* we should be grateful that *Nuestro Señor* gave us such a beautiful day.

Abuela (Crosses herself.): Sí, gracias a Dios.

Eduardo: She's stroking seventy-two, with no problem *(He throws a kiss to*   10
   the sky.) It's a beautiful day to win.

Aída: Qué hermoso! So clear and bright. Not a cloud in the sky. *Mira! Mira!*
   Even rainbows on the water. . . a sign from God.

Simón (Singing.): Rainbows on the water. . . you in my arms. . .

Abuela and Eduardo (Looking the wrong way.): Dónde?   15

Aída (Pointing toward Margarita.): There, dancing in front of Margarita,
   leading her on. . .

Eduardo: Rainbows on. . . *Ay coño!* It's an oil slick! You. . . you. . . *(To*
   Simón.) Stop the boat. *(Runs to bow, yelling.)* Margarita! Margarita!

   [DL]](On the next stroke, Margarita comes up all covered in black
   oil.)

Margarita: Papi! Papi. . . !   20

(Everybody goes to the side and stares at Margarita, who stares back. Eduardo freezes.)

Aída: *Apúrate,* Eduardo, move. . . what's wrong with you. . . *no me oíste,* get my daughter out of the water.

Eduardo *(Softly.):* We can't touch her. If we touch her, she's disqualified.

Aída: But I'm her mother.

Eduardo: Not even by her own mother. Especially by her own mother. . . .   25
You always want the rules to be different for you, you always want to be the exception. *(To Simón.)* And you. . . you didn't see it, eh? You were playing again?

Simón: *Papi,* I was watching. . .

Aída *(Interrupting.): Pues,* do something Eduardo. You are the big coach,   30
the monitor.

Simón: Mentor! Mentor!

Eduardo: How can a person think around you? *(He walks off to bow, puts head in hands.)*

Abuela *(Looking over side.): Mira como todos los* little birds are dead.   35
(She crosses herself.)

Aída: Their little wings are glued to their sides.

Simón: Christ, this is like the La Brea tar pits.

Aída: They can't move their little wings.

Abuela: *Esa niña tiene que moverse.*   40

Simón: Yeah, Margo, you gotta move, man.

(Abuela and Simón gesture for Margarita to move. Aída gestures for her to swim.)

Abuela: *Anda niña, muévete.*

Aída: Swim, *hija,* swim or the *aceite* will stick to your wings.

Margarita: *Papi?*

Abuela *(Taking megaphone.):* Your *papi* say "move it!"   45

(Margarita with difficulty starts moving.)

Abuela, Aída and Simón *(Laboriously counting.): Uno, dos. . . uno, dos. . . anda. . . uno, dos.*

Eduardo *(Running to take megaphone from Abuela.): Uno, dos. . .*

(Simón races into cabin and starts the engine. Abuela, Aída and Eduardo count together.)

Simón *(Looking ahead.): Papi,* it's over there!

Eduardo: Eh?   50

Simón *(Pointing ahead and to the right.):* It's getting clearer over there.

Eduardo *(Through megaphone.):* Now pay attention to me. Go to the right.

(Simón, Abuela, Aída and Eduardo all lean over side. They point ahead and to the right, except Abuela, who points to the left.)

Family *(Shouting together.): Para yá! Para yá!*

(Lights go down on boat. A special light on Margarita, swimming through the oil, and on Abuela, watching her.)

Abuela: *Sangre de mi sangre,* you will be another to save us. En Bolondron, where your great-grandmother Luz Suárez was born, they say one day it   55
rained blood. All the people, they run into their houses. They cry, they

pray, *pero* your great-grandmother Luz she had *cojones* like a man. She run outside. She look straight at the sky. She shake her fist. And she say to the evil one, "*Mira. . . (Beating her chest.) coño, Diablo, aquí estoy si me quieres.*" And she open her mouth, and she drunk the blood.   60

Blackout.

Scene IV

Lights up on boat. Aída and Eduardo are on deck watching Margarita swim. We hear the gentle, rhythmic lap, lap, lap of the water; then the sound of inhaling and exhaling as Margarita's breathing becomes louder. Then Margarita's heartbeat is heard, with the lapping of the water and the breathing under it. These sounds continue beneath the dialogue to the end of the scene.

Aída: Dios mío. Look how she moves through the water. . . .

Eduardo: You see, it's very simple. It is a matter of concentration.

Aída: The first time I put her in water she came to life, she grew before my eyes. She moved, she smiled, she loved it more than me. She didn't want my breast any longer. She wanted the water.   5

Eduardo: And of course, the rhythm. The rhythm takes away the pain and helps the concentration.

(Pause. Aída and Eduardo watch Margarita.)

Aída: Is that my child or a seal. . . .

Eduardo: Ah, a seal, the reason for that is that she's keeping her arms very close to her body. She cups her hands, and then she reaches and digs, reaches and digs.   10

Aída: To think that a daughter of mine. . . .

Eduardo: It's the training, the hours in the water. I used to tie weights around her little wrists and ankles.

Aída: A spirit, an ocean spirit, must have entered my body when I was carrying her.   15

Eduardo (To Margarita.): Your stroke is slowing down.

(Pause. We hear Margarita's heartbeat with the breathing under, faster now.)

Aída: Eduardo, that night, the night on the boat. . .

Eduardo: Ah, the night on the boat again. . . the moon was. . .

Aída: The moon was full. We were coming to America. . . . *Qué romantico.*   20

(Heartbeat and breathing continue.)

Eduardo: We were cold, afraid, with no money, and on top of everything, you were hysterical, yelling at me, tearing at me with your nails. *(Opens his shirt, points to the base of his neck.)* Look, I still bear the scars. . . telling me that I didn't know what I was doing. . . saying that we were going to die. . . .   25

Aída: You took me, you stole me from my home. . . you didn't give me a chance to prepare. You just said we have to go now, now! Now, you said. You didn't let me take anything. I left everything behind. . . . I left everything behind.

Eduardo: Saying that I wasn't good enough, that your father didn't raise you so that I could drown you in the sea.   30

Aída: You didn't let me say even a good-bye. You took me, you stole me,
     you tore me from my home.

Eduardo: I took you so we could be married.

Aída: That was in Miami. But that night on the boat, Eduardo. . . . We were   35
     not married, that night on the boat.

Eduardo: No pasó nada! Once and for all get it out of your head, it was
     cold, you hated me, and we were afraid. . . .

Aída: Mentiroso!

Eduardo: A man can't do it when he is afraid.   40

Aída: Liar! You did it very well.

Eduardo: I did?

Aída: Sí. Gentle. You were so gentle and then strong. . . my passion for you
     so deep. Standing next to you. . . I would ache. . . looking at your
     hands I would forget to breathe, you were irresistible.   45

Eduardo: I was?

Aída: You took me into your arms, you touched my face with your finger-
     tips. . . you kissed my eyes. . . *la esquina de la boca y. . .*

Eduardo: Sí, Sí, and then. . .

Aída: I look at your face on top of mine, and I see the lights of Havana in   50
     your eyes. That's when you seduced me.

Eduardo: Shhh, they're gonna hear you.

     (Lights go down. Special on Aída.)

Aída: That was the night. A woman doesn't forget those things. . . and later
     that night was the dream. . . the dream of a big country with fields of
     fertile land and big, giant things growing. And there by a green, slimy   55
     pond I found a giant pea pod and when I opened it, it was full of little,
     tiny baby frogs.

     *(Aída crosses herself as she watches Margarita. We hear louder
     breathing and heartbeat.)*

Margarita: Santa Teresa. Little Flower of God, pray for me. San Martín de
     Porres, pray for me. Santa Rosa de Lima, *Virgencita de la Caridad del
     Cobre,* pray for me. . . . Mother pray for me.   60

Scene V

     *Loud howling of wind is heard, as lights change to indicate unsta-
     ble weather, fog and mist. Family on deck, braced and huddled
     against the wind. Simón is at the helm.*

Aída: Ay Dios mío, qué viento.

Eduardo (Through megaphone.): Don't drift out. . . that wind is pushing
     you out. *(To Simón.)* You! Slow down. Can't you see your sister is
     drifting out?

Simón: It's the wind, *Papi.*   5

Aída: Baby, don't go so far. . . .

Abuela (To heaven.): Ay Gran Poder de Dios, quita este maldito viento.

Simón: Margo! Margo! Stay close to the boat.

Eduardo: Dig in. Dig in hard. . . . Reach down from your guts and dig in.

Abuela (To heaven.): Ay Virgen de la Caridad del Cobre, por lo más tú   10
     quieres a pararla.

Aída (Putting her hand out, reaching for Margarita.): Baby, don't go far.

(Abuela crosses herself. Action freezes. Lights get dimmer, special on Margarita. She keeps swimming, stops, starts again, stops, then, finally exhausted, stops altogether. The boat stops moving.)

Eduardo: What's going on here? Why are we stopping?

Simón: Papi, she's not moving! Yo Margo!

(The family all run to the side.)

Eduardo: Hija!. . . Hijita! You're tired, eh?   15

Aída: Por supuesto she's tired. I like to see you get in the water, waving your arms and legs from San Pedro to Santa Catalina. A person isn't a machine, a person has to rest.

Simón: Yo, Mama! Cool out, it ain't fucking brain surgery.

Eduardo (To Simón.): Shut up, you. *(Louder to Margarita.)* I guess your   20
mother's right for once, huh?. . . I guess you had to stop, eh?. . . Give your brother, the idiot. . . a chance to catch up with you.

Simón (Clowning like Mortimer Snerd.): Dum dee dum dee dum ooops, ah shucks. . .

Eduardo: I don't think he's Cuban.   25

Simón (Like Ricky Ricardo.): Oye, Lucy! I'm home! Ba ba lu!

Eduardo (Joins in clowning, grabbing Simón in a headlock.): What am I gonna do with this idiot, eh? I don't understand this idiot. He's not like us, Margarita. *(Laughing.)* You think if we put him into your bathing suit with a cap on his head. . . *(He laughs hysterically.)* You think any-   30
one would know. . . huh? Do you think anyone would know? *(Laughs.)*

Simón (Vamping.): Ay, mi amor. Anybody looking for tits would know.

(Eduardo slaps Simón across the face, knocking him down. Aída runs to Simón's aid. Abuela holds Eduardo back.)

Margarita: Mía culpa! Mía culpa!

Abuela: Qué dices hija?

Margarita: Papi, it's my fault, it's all my fault. . . . I'm so cold, I can't   35
move. . . . I put my face in the water. . . and I hear them whispering. . . laughing at me. . . .

Aída: Who is laughing at you?

Margarita: The fish are all biting me. . . they hate me. . . they whisper about me. She can't swim, they say. She can't glide. She has no grace. . . .   40
Yellowtails, bonita, tuna, man-o'-war, snub-nose sharks, *los baracudas*. . . they all hate me. . . only the dolphins care. . . and sometimes I hear the whales crying. . . she is lost, she is dead. I'm so numb, I can't feel. *Papi!* Am I dead?

Eduardo: Vamos, baby, punch those arms in. Come on. . . do you hear me?   45

Margarita: Papi. . . *Papi*. . . forgive me. . . .

(All is silent on the boat. Eduardo drops his megaphone, his head bent down in dejection. Abuela, Aída, Simón, all leaning over the side of the boat. Simón slowly walks away.)

Aída: Mi hija, qué tienes?

Simón: Oh, Christ, don't make her say it. Please don't make her say it.

Abuela: Say what? *Qué cosa?*

Simón: She wants to quit, can't you see she's had enough?   50

Abuela: Mira, para eso. Esta niña is turning blue.

Aída: Oyeme, mi hija. Do you want to come out of the water?

Margarita: Papi?

Simón (To Eduardo.): She won't come out until *you* tell her.

Aída: Eduardo. . . answer your daughter.   55

Eduardo: Le dije to concentrate. . . concentrate on your rhythm. Then the rhythm would carry her. . . ay, it's a beautiful thing, Aída. It's like yoga, like meditation, the mind over matter. . . the mind controlling the body. . . that's how the great things in the world have been done. I wish you. . . I wish my wife could understand.   60

Margarita: Papi?

Simón (To Margarita.): Forget him.

Aída (Imploring.): Eduardo, *por favor.*

Eduardo (Walking in circles.): Why didn't you let her concentrate? Don't you understand, the concentration, the rhythm is everything. But no,   65
you wouldn't listen. *(Screaming to the ocean.)* Goddamn Cubans, why, God, why do you make us go everywhere with our families? *(He goes to back of boat.)*

Aída (Opening her arms.): Mi hija, ven, come to *Mami. (Rocking.)* Your *mami* knows.   70

> *(Abuela has taken the training bottle, puts it in a net. She and Simón lower it to Margarita.)*

Simón: Take this. Drink it. *(As Margarita drinks, Abuela crosses herself.)*

Abuela: Sangre de mi sangre.

> *(Music comes up softly. Margarita drinks, gives the bottle back, stretches out her arms, as if on a cross. Floats on her back. She begins a graceful backstroke. Lights fade on boat as special lights come up on Margarita. She stops. Slowly turns over and starts to swim, gradually picking up speed. Suddenly as if in pain she stops, tries again, then stops in pain again. She becomes disoriented and falls to the bottom of the sea. Special on Margarita at the bottom of the sea.)*

Margarita: Ya no puedo. . . I can't. . . . A person isn't a machine. . . *es mi culpa.* . . Father forgive me. . . *Papi! Papi!* One, two. *Uno, dos. (Pause.)*
Papi! A dónde estás? (Pause.) One, two, one, two. *Papi! Ay, Papi!*   75
Where are you. . . ? Don't leave me. . . . Why don't you answer me? *(Pause. She starts to swim, slowly.) Uno, dos, uno, dos.* Dig in, dig in. *(Stops swimming.) Por favor, Papi! (Starts to swim again.)* One, two, one, two. Kick from your hip, kick from your hip. *(Stops swimming. Starts to cry.)* Oh God, please. . . . *(Pause.)* Hail Mary, full of   80
grace. . . dig in, dig in. . . the Lord is with thee. . . . *(She swims to the rhythm of her Hail Mary.)* Hail Mary, full of grace. . . dig in, dig in. . . the Lord is with thee. . . dig in, dig in. . . . Blessed art thou among women. . . . *Mami,* it hurts. You let go of my hand. I'm lost. . . . And blessed is the fruit of thy womb, now and at the hour of our death.   85
Amen. I don't want to die, I don't want to die.

> *(Margarita is still swimming. Blackout. She is gone.)*

Scene VI

> *Lights up on boat, we hear radio static. There is a heavy mist. On deck we see only black outline of Abuela with shawl over her head. We hear the voices of Eduardo, Aída, and Radio Operator.*

Eduardo's Voice: La Havana! Coming from San Pedro. Over.

Radio Operator's Voice: Right, DT6–6, you say you've lost a swimmer.

Aída's Voice: Our child, our only daughter. . . listen to me. Her name is Margarita Inez Suárez, she is wearing a black one-piece bathing suit cut high
in the legs with a white racing stripe down the sides, a white bathing   5
cap with goggles and her whole body covered with a. . . with a. . .

Eduardo's Voice: With lanolin and paraffin.

Aída's Voice: Sí. . . con lanolin and paraffin.

(*More radio static. Special on Simón, on the edge of the boat.*)

Simón: Margo! Yo Margo! (*Pause.*) Man don't do this. (*Pause.*) Come
on. . . . Come on. . . .(*Pause.*) God, why does everything have to be so   10
hard? (*Pause.*) Stupid. You know you're not supposed to die for this.
Stupid. It's his dream and he can't even swim. (*Pause.*) Punch those
arms in. Come home. Come home. I'm your little brother. Don't forget
what Mama said. You're not supposed to leave me behind. *Vamos,* Margarita, take your little brother, hold his hand tight when you cross the   15
street. He's so little. (*Pause.*) Oh Christ, give us a sign. . . . I know! I
know! Margo, I'll send you a message. . . like mental telepathy. I'll hold
my breath, close my eyes, and I'll bring you home. (*He takes a deep
breath; a few beats.*) This time I'll beep. . . I'll send out sonar signals
like a dolphin. (*He imitates dolphin sounds.*)   20

(*The sound of real dolphins takes over from Simón, then fades into
sound of Abuela saying the Hail Mary in Spanish, as full lights
come up slowly.*)

Scene VII

*Eduardo coming out of cabin, sobbing, Aída holding him. Simón
anxiously scanning the horizon. Abuela looking calmly ahead.*

Eduardo: Es mi culpa, sí, es mi culpa. (*He hits his chest.*)

Aída: Ya, ya viejo. . . . it was my sin. . . I left my home.

Eduardo: Forgive me, forgive me. I've lost our daughter, our sister, our
granddaughter, *mi carne, mi sangre, mis ilusiones.* (*To heaven.*) *Dios
mío,* take me. . . take me, I say. . . Goddammit, take me!   5

Simón: I'm going in.

Aída and Eduardo: No!

Eduardo (*Grabbing and holding Simón, speaking to heaven.*)*:* God, take
me, not my children. They are my dreams, my illusions. . . and not this
one, this one is my mystery. . . he has my secret dreams. In him are the   10
parts of me I cannot see.

(*Eduardo embraces Simón. Radio static becomes louder.*)

Aída: I. . . I think I see her.

Simón: No, it's just a seal.

Abuela (*Looking out with binoculars.*)*: Mi nietacita, dónde estás?* (*She
feels her heart.*) I don't feel the knife in my heart. . . my little fish is not   15
lost.

(*Radio crackles with static. As lights dim on boat, Voices of Mel and
Mary Beth are heard over the radio.*)

Mel's Voice: Tragedy has marred the face of the Wrigley Invitational
Women's Race to Catalina. The Cuban swimmer, little Margarita Suárez,

has reportedly been lost at sea. Coast Guard and divers are looking for
her as we speak. Yet in spite of this tragedy the race must go on   20
because. . .

Mary Beth's Voice (Interrupting loudly.): Mel!

Mel's Voice (Startled.): What!

Mary Beth's Voice: Ah. . . excuse me, Mel. . . we have a winner. We've just
received word from Catalina that one of the swimmers is just fifty   25
yards from the breakers. . . it's, oh, it's. . . Margarita Suárez!

(Special on family in cabin listening to radio.)

Mel's Voice: What? I thought she died!

*(Special on Margarita, taking off bathing cap, trophy in hand,
walking on the water.)*

Mary Beth's Voice: Ahh. . . unless. . . unless this is a tragic. . . No. . . there
she is, Mel. Margarita Suárez! The only one in the race wearing a black
bathing suit cut high in the legs with a racing stripe down the side.   30

(Family cheering, embracing.)

Simón (Screaming.): Way to go, Margo!

Mel's Voice: This is indeed a miracle! It's a resurrection! Margarita Suárez,
with a flotilla of boats to meet her, is now walking on the waters,
through the breakers. . . onto the beach, with crowds of people cheering her on. What a jubilation! This is a miracle!   35

(Sound of crowds cheering. Lights and cheering sounds fade.)

Blackout.

[1984]

Questions

1. This play clearly poses some interesting challenges for the director and set
   designer. What problems do you see, and how might they be solved? (Consider the photograph on page 1088.)
2. Is this play really about Eduardo? About a certain kind of fatherhood? Assess
   the significance of the different issues raised by the play. (For instance, are
   issues regarding gender or ethnicity raised?) What do you think is its center,
   its main point?
3. How does the role of Simon affect the viewer's evolving response?
4. What do you make of the ending? Does the ending deconstruct in some
   way the rest of the play, or does it resolve the play satisfactorily? Are we supposed to believe that Margarita is really "walking on the waters" after her
   "resurrection"? Is this ironic? Or just overstatement on the part of Mel?
5. Why does Sanchez-Scott leave significant stretches of Spanish in the play,
   knowing that some readers/viewers will not speak Spanish?

Appendix A

Research and Documentation

But the whole thing, after all, may be put very simply. I believe that it is better to tell the truth than to lie. I believe that it is better to be free than to be a slave. And I believe that it is better to know than to be ignorant.

—H. L. Mencken

Investigating the Work

You are free to walk into any one of thousands of libraries, to access many thousand websites, seeking the truth about whatever you wish, dispelling the mists and fogs of ignorance. In the history of civilization, at no time or place have so many people had such a freedom and privilege.

When a research paper assignment actually compels you to venture forth into the forests of available knowledge, it's all too easy to forget how spectacularly fortunate we are, and instead to feel overwhelmed and lost. Once you get into a project, as veteran investigators know, doing research can be interesting, satisfying, and even exciting. You do need some patience, however, and a plan, and some patience, and the flexibility to adapt your plan, and some more patience, and some focused effort. Doing research is a lot like doing detective work, and just think how patiently the great detectives—Sherlock Holmes, Father Brown, Columbo—sift through the evidence, exploring different theories, waiting for the facts to fit together.

Although luck often plays some role in any sort of investigation, successful detectives and researchers don't rely on it; they depend instead upon their own intelligence and certain time-proven strategies, upon certain standard conventions and authorities. You'll need to supply the patience and the luck; this chapter will get you started on the strategies and conventions for doing a research paper. Specifically, this chapter will take you through the evolution of a sample research paper, considering along the way how topics and research questions are found, how sources are located, used, and credited, and how drafts are generated and revised.

The Purposes of Research

Why do writing-about-literature courses at every level often include research papers? In order to help you learn how to use the astonishing resources of modern libraries, certainly; also to deepen your understanding of authors, readers, and texts; and, to allow you an important opportunity to write and to improve your writing. Even if a research paper is seen as a mere exercise, an artificial endeavor, it is an exercise that employs and refines extremely valuable skills, no matter what sort of career you have in mind. Few things can be considered more important today than the ability to find information, to analyze and interpret it, and to articulate your findings clearly. A research paper is a piece of writing, not a cut-and-paste collage, and it will call for the same kind of drafting and revising you'd put into an original essay, poem, or short story.

In the world of work, the writing tasks you'll face can be divided, ideally, into two kinds. In one kind, what you're supposed to do is fairly explicit and specific: "Review our advertising campaign so far and summarize it for the client"; "Research the clinic's records and explain to the drug company how patients have responded to the combination therapy"; "Find out what happened to Mr. Landry's contract, and write an apologetic letter to him." In another kind of research task, you're on your own, without explicit guidance: you define the purpose, the audience, the materials, the presentation. It's sometimes tricky, in reality, knowing which kind of task you have: you might think the guidelines are quite rigid and prescribed, when you were actually expected to be more creative. You might think you're completely on your own, when actually your supervisor assumes you'll follow a standard form and procedure.

Classroom assignments can be divided into the same two groups, with the same possibilities for misunderstanding. Clearly, it is crucial for you to determine which kind of assignment you're dealing with. Is your task explicitly spelled out? Or perhaps *implicitly* restricted? Likewise, if an audience is not indicated, is one implied or expected to be understood? Are you given guidelines on the materials to use, and the format for your paper? If you aren't given guidelines, should you use your own judgment? Or are there guidelines that everyone takes for granted? Clearly, in talking about the process of writing a research paper, we need to consider both kinds of assignments (and the fuzzy in-between ones too), starting with the topic. And if you're at all unsure about your assignment, don't hesitate to ask your teacher for help.

The Topic and the Task

The researcher, like the detective, may have only a vague idea of what he or she is looking for at the outset; indeed, figuring out what you're looking for is often at least as important and difficult as finding it. If you're responsible for inventing your own topic, then the usual textbook advice says to begin by choosing a broad topic that interests you, and then narrowing it down. That advice sounds quite reasonable. But where does one find a list of broad topics from which to select an interesting one, and what if none of the broad topics seem stimulating?

From nothing you get nothing, as the old saying goes, and you may have to do some reading, thinking, talking, brainstorming, and writing in order to generate a list of potential topics. Let's say you're trying to come up with some possible topics for a research paper in a Shakespeare course. You might go to the library and browse through some recent articles or books on Shakespeare; even an encyclopedia entry would probably give you some ideas. You might think about the class discussions and what you've found intriguing or puzzling. You might ask someone who's an expert for some suggestions—or even ask someone who's not an expert, "What would you like to know?" You might free-associate or free-write, letting your brain roam around for ten minutes or so. If you're willing to supply *something*, virtually *anything* can lead you to some potential topics.

Don't believe it? You need go no further than what you're likely to be sitting on right now to find some possible topics. Are there any chairs in Shakespeare? (Can't think of any, but there are lots of thrones.) What makes a chair into a throne? (The king, or maybe the queen, is sitting on it?) How many thrones appear in *Hamlet*? (Two? One for Claudius and one for Gertrude?) What do they signify? (Power, to Claudius; a lost father, to Hamlet; what, for Gertrude?) What should they look like on stage? Who gets to sit on them? By this point, lots of broad topics may have occurred to you from these specific questions: The idea of "the king" in Shakespeare; the politics of succession to the throne in Shakespeare's time; the importance of furniture or other stage properties in Shakespeare; the importance of setting in Shakespeare, or even the importance of *sitting*; and many more. The idea here is that there really aren't any rules for coming up with topics. You can start anywhere asking questions, and just keep on thinking until you hit something potentially interesting.

Once you have some broad topics to consider, there are really only two ways to narrow them: you can limit them in space, or limit them in time. The conventional wisdom says, for instance, that you shouldn't try to write on "Religion in Shakespeare's England," which is far too broad. Rather than all of Shakespeare's England, why not focus on "Religion in *Hamlet*"? That's still a pretty large topic, so perhaps you should restrict yourself to "Church Doctrine in *Hamlet*." The topic still seems large, so perhaps you could focus on one aspect of church doctrine that you connect to one aspect of Shakespeare's play—maybe "Church Doctrine and Hamlet's Ghost."

You should limit your topic, in other words, to a subject that might not take years to research and several books to cover, that you might realistically be able to get control of in the time and space available. There are, however, some things to consider regarding this commonsensical "narrow down" advice. For one thing, the advice appears to doom students to think always on a small scale. Someone who finds the admittedly expansive idea of "Religion in Shakespeare's England" truly fascinating, may think that "Church Doctrine and Hamlet's Ghost" is too esoteric and constricting to have much appeal. Certainly we all need to be encouraged to think about large things and small, about both the meaning of life and the cost of cabbages. Yet, on the other hand, what student can hope to cover "Religion in Shakespeare's England" satisfactorily in a single research paper? Just imagine all the religious books published in Shakespeare's day, all the different churches and personalities in England at that time, the whole history of religion beforehand and its influence on Shakespeare's England.

It is often possible, however, to think about particular aspects of a large topic, to focus your vision rather than giving it up. You might consider a paper, for example, summarizing and evaluating some of the recent scholarship on religion in Shakespeare's England. Your paper then focuses on part of the scholarship about a subject rather than on the subject itself. You get to think about religion in Shakespeare's England, but in a manageable framework. Or, you might remind yourself and your reader of the potential connection between your narrowed topic and the larger one—how church doctrine regarding ghosts, as it influences Shakespeare's *Hamlet*, may well be an important clue to religious beliefs in Shakespeare's day. Guidance from your instructor, always worth seeking, is especially valuable in such ambitious research projects.

The "narrow down" advice, however you decide to implement it, may seem to require you to restrict your focus before you've done any research: quite simply, you may not know *how* to narrow a topic most intelligently until you've researched the topic. To many people, "Religion in Shakespeare's England" certainly sounds like a fascinating topic, something interesting to pursue. But if you try to narrow the topic down before you've learned anything about it, you might end up with, say, "Presbyterianism in *Hamlet*" or "Religion in Shakespeare's London." The first would appear to be impossible to research; the second doesn't reduce your task much at all.

This might look like a catch-22 situation—where you can't do research until you've done research; you can't narrow your topic until you've narrowed the topic. In truth, you probably just need to do some basic fly-by research first—by reading an encyclopedia entry, a general overview, a portion of some important work; or by talking with an expert, or at least someone familiar with the subject.

Part of this preliminary research should include investigating yourself, exploring what you already know and feel about the topic. This self-research needn't be anything elaborate: just sit down for ten minutes and write out whatever your mind can generate on the topic—questions, suspicions, concerns, observations, whatever. You may find, to your surprise, that you know more about the topic, or have more interest in it, than you might have imagined at the outset. Or you might find that you have even less interest or knowledge than you thought. In any event, this self-inventory likely will help to reveal what you need to do in order to make the topic your own—to get yourself intellectually engaged in the subject, and to get the project to the launch pad.

If writing a research paper is like writing anything else, then it's usually messy, not proceeding in any simple linear fashion, but rather jumping all around from one task to another to three others all at once. You can't expect to go through a neat series of steps, choosing your topic, locating sources, collecting information, finding a thesis, making an outline, writing a draft, revising. You might actually start off with a fully formed thesis, before you've even done any research; or you might find, as you're making an outline, that you need more sources; or you might discover as you're revising that you're actually writing about the wrong topic; or whatever. The logical sequence of activities described here is really a fiction.

Still, selecting a topic would seem to be a considerably neater process if you're given a specific assignment. Imagine, for instance, that you've been given this assignment:

1. Using at least five different sources, provide information about Yeats's life around the time of "Sailing to Byzantium." Limit your paper to about eight pages, including documentation.

The topic here appears to be defined clearly enough: Yeats's life about the time of "Sailing." But is the researcher's *task* made clear? A topic designates an area for investigation, but the writer's task in a research paper involves more than just the topic: the writer needs to consider the audience, the materials, the *purpose* of the research.

Compare this assignment to the first one:

2. In a formal research paper addressing your classmates and other interested students, discuss how Yeats's life helps us to understand "Sailing to Byzantium." Use at least five different sources, including at least two biographies, one critical essay, and one other poem. Eight pages maximum.

In this assignment, the writer's task is delineated; the audience, the materials, and the purpose are laid out. Not only must the writer locate, organize, and present relevant facts, he or she should use this biographical information to read the poem. The assignment also makes clear enough which critical stance the writer should think most immediately about adopting. The assignment doesn't say "perform an act of biographical criticism," but the student who understands the fundamentals of that critical approach should be sitting pretty.

Consider, by way of contrast, this assignment:

3. In a formal research paper addressing your classmates and other interested students, provide your own original close reading of Yeats's "Sailing to Byzantium." Compare/contrast your reading to at least three other interpretations. At least two of these other readings should be published in scholarly journals or books.

Or this one:

4. Identify two conflicting interpretations of Yeats's "Sailing to Byzantium" and attempt to provide biographical, historical, or textual support for both readings. Do not try to resolve the conflicts; instead, try to convince an audience of general readers that the two readings cannot be resolved.

Or this one:

5. Relying primarily on sources published in Yeats's lifetime, consider how Yeats's contemporaries might have responded to "Sailing to Byzantium." How might their responses differ from the response of a reader today?

As you can see, these last three assignments call for critical stances distinctively different from each other and from the previous assignments. To understand the task involved in an assignment, the researcher needs to understand the critical theory essentially involved: for number 3, for instance, the researcher needs to employ New Critical strategies; number 4 calls for a deconstructive attitude; number 5 invokes reader-response and historical approaches. Even if the assignment is one that you are giving to yourself (an open topic, in other words), it's essential for you to consider the nature of the critical approach involved in the task. Otherwise, you won't know what to do with the materials you've so patiently and brilliantly captured.

A brief review of what this section has covered might be helpful before we move on:

The Topic:

- If you can choose the topic, generate lots of possibilities before you settle on one that appeals to you.
- Resist narrowing your topic until you've done some basic research, including a self-inventory.
- Be patient and flexible, adapting and evolving your topic as your research unfolds.

The Task:

- Be sure you understand or clarify the audience, the format, the materials, and the purpose for your research. What question, for whom, and how, are you trying to answer?
- Identify the critical strategies appropriate to the task.

In their classic book on *The Craft of Research*, Wayne Booth, Gregory Colomb, and Joseph Williams suggest that researchers attempt to fill in the blanks in the following sentence:

1. I am studying _____,
2. because I want to find out who/how/why _____,
3. in order to understand how/why/what _____.

Attempting to complete this sentence can give you a good indication of whether you clearly grasp your topic and your task. Just don't expect to be able to fill in the blanks definitively before you move on to do your research. As Booth, Colomb, and Williams indicate, you may be far into your project before you're sure what you're doing. Doing research is an act of faith, believing not only that you can find the resources to answer your questions, but believing also that you can somehow find out the questions.

How To Do Research

In the process of writing a research paper on a literary topic, when is it appropriate to consult secondary sources (that is, works about or related to your subject, the primary source)? Most textbooks will advise you to wait until you're thoroughly familiar with the primary work(s), and have formed some detailed ideas of your own before consulting secondary works. But, as the foregoing discussion of topics and tasks has just emphasized, the evolution of a research project is rarely simple or straightforward. The logic underlying the conventional wisdom is transparent enough: if you, an impressionable student, read too much *about* a work before you've formed your own opinions, then your own ideas will be influenced and shaped by the secondary sources you've consulted. The idea is that you'll ruin your chances of ever thinking for yourself.

Obviously, you should follow your teacher's direction in this matter, and there are certainly situations when it makes sense to think on your own. But, generally, secondary resources are often so helpful that you might move to them as quickly and deeply as possible. To be sure, if you only skim through the primary work, or ignore it altogether, and read only biographies, histories, criticism, or commentaries, then one can easily imagine how the secondary sources would stunt your learning. But the resources you are consulting should naturally take you back to the primary work, again and again, as your understanding expands in the wake of more information and more points of view.

For some works, like Yeats's "Sailing to Byzantium," you probably won't be able to read more than a fraction of the relevant scholarship. But the more you read, the more you will know even about those secondary works you haven't read, because critical discussion of a work is like a conversation. In a lively conversation, you can often listen carefully at any number of points and have a pretty good idea what has already been said. Some authorities are likely to be mentioned again and again in a conversation—those clearly are resources you'll most want to see.

Getting some idea what has already been said does two things. Ideas of your own may be sparked, and you can place your ideas within the context of what others have said. The reader will be interested in knowing, for example, if your interpretation of a poem is totally different from what anyone else has said, or if it is similar to the mainstream reading, or if it falls into one of several camps. By situating your insights in the context of other voices, you'll also be convincing your readers that you are informed and worth listening to.

How do you find secondary sources to skim, sift, and devour? Let's talk about the different kinds available.

Background Sources

Encyclopedias, readers' guides, dictionaries, and other such general references are available in a modern college library. Many general sources are also accessible on the Internet, but there may be no librarian to assure you that the source is reputable. These kinds of references are likely to be especially useful early in a project, but may prove valuable at any point. Since these works are shelved in the reference area and do not circulate, they have the added advantage of never being checked out. The *New Encyclopedia Brittanica* offers especially helpful and authoritative background information and can guide you to other sources. But many other encyclopedias also offer more specialized coverages. The *Oxford Companion* series, for instance, features expert overviews on a wide range of subjects. I have, at shoulder's length from my keyboard, *The Oxford Companion to English Literature*, *The Oxford Companion to American Literature*, *The Oxford Companion to Medicine* (two volumes), *The Oxford Companion to the Mind*, and *The Oxford Companion to Philosophy*. There's an *Oxford Companion* for many more subjects; they're probably in your library's reference area, along with other encyclopedic works such as the *Encyclopedia of Asian History* or *The New Princeton Encyclopedia of Poetry and Poetics*. For literary research, *The Reader's Encyclopedia* is especially worth noting, since it covers characters, authors, books, and terms.

These encyclopedic works include biographical entries, but there are also volumes devoted only to biography. The two most famous biographical references in English are the *Dictionary of National Biography*, for Great Britain, and the *Dictionary of American Biography*, for the United States. The *Dictionary of Literary Biography*, or *DLB* as it's affectionately known, has numerous volumes devoted to particular biographical interests. Volume 67, for example, edited by Gregory Jay, has extended entries for twenty-seven *Modern American Critics Since 1955*. Volume 57, edited by William Thesing, covers *Victorian Prose Writers after 1867*. If there is a *DLB* volume relevant to your topic, you'll most probably find a wealth of information; it's certainly worth checking. *The Atlantic Brief Lives* is a wonderful compendium of biographies of writers, artists, composers, written by a leading authority on each figure. Many rather specialized biographical sources exist—*Chicano Scholars and Writers* for example. Again, a reference librarian can direct you.

Literary handbooks and literary histories can also provide valuable background information. The standards: *The Oxford History of English Literature* (thirteen volumes), and Spillers's *Literary History of the United States* (two volumes); Holman and Harmon's *Handbook to Literature*, Roger Fowler's *Dictionary of Modern Critical Terms*, and *The Johns Hopkins Guide to Literary Theory and Criticism*.

You won't want to cite such general sources in your paper usually: they're just part of your preliminary research, providing you with whatever is common knowledge. (And as a rule, "common knowledge" does not require documentation, even if it's news to you, unless you use the words or phrasing of the original. When in doubt, ask your teacher—or go ahead and provide the citation.)

Bibliographies and Indexes

As you zero in on, or circle around, your topic and task, you'll likely want to move at some point beyond general background sources. Bibliographies and indexes tell you where to look. The *MLA Bibliography*, which is updated annually, is arguably the most important guide to literary scholarship, and the place I'd look first. In most university libraries, the *MLA Bibliography of Books and Articles* is available electronically, allowing you to search quickly and thoroughly for a particular author, work, subject, or combinations thereof. The *Reader's Guide to Periodical Literature* is another extremely useful resource, similar in scope to the MLA guide. By beginning with the most current year, and working backward in these indexes, you can get a wealth of materials to consult. Usually you'll be able to tell from the title whether the citation will be relevant to your topic. You should also know that *The Essay and General Literature Index* has the particular virtue of including references to essays published in collections.

Reviews of books are often particularly useful, not only providing a brief summary of a book's contents, but also leading to other resources. To find book reviews, consult the *Index to Book Reviews in the Humanities*, the *Book Review Digest*, or the *Book Review Index*.

You can also consult specialized bibliographies. For a major author, it's likely that someone has published a bibliography devoted to that author and related matters. For Samuel Johnson, for instance, you could consult Clifford and Greene's *Samuel Johnson: A Survey and Bibliography of Critical Studies*, which has an opening essay discussing all the scholarship on Johnson up to 1970, and then lists hundreds and hundreds of books and articles under various headings, such as "General Comment on Johnson,""Johnson's Views and Attitudes on Various Subjects," and "Johnson's Prose Style." For scholarship on Johnson after 1970, you'd want to see Greene and Vance's *Bibliography of Johnsonian Studies, 1970-85*.

For references to criticism on poems or short fiction, consult *Poetry Explication: A Checklist of Interpretation since 1925 of British and American Poems Past and Present* and *Twentieth-Century Short Story Explication: Interpretations 1900-1975, of Short Fiction Since 1800*. There are also bibliographies on particular subjects (science fiction, the medieval romance, prose fiction in seventeenth-century magazines). There is even a bibliography of bibliographies, edited by Trevor Howard-Hill. The publication dates of such bibliographies should be noted, since some will be more current than others.

Such guides and bibliographies are often convenient and thorough, but to find books on a particular subject, you simply need access to your library's catalog and a good grasp of the alphabet. If the library's holdings are listed online, then you can create your own bibliography simply by searching for an author, a text, or a subject. You may also be able to connect by computer to the databases of other libraries and access their holdings. Your reference librarian can help you determine what, if anything, a computer search would cost, and whether it might be worth it. Most major libraries today have sites on the World Wide Web, allowing access to their card catalogs through such web sites. The Library of Congress, for example, has an incredibly useful (and busy) web site, consulted by scholars and researchers around the world, in industry and academia. As for universities, for example, the University of South Carolina has a web site that allows you to jump to the library's holdings, for instance; or, you can mouse-click to the English department's home page and get information on the faculty's various research interests.

To find information on the Internet, you will want to use some kind of search engine, like Alta Vista, Yahoo, Excite, or others. Unlike some computer searches available only to subscribers (DIALOG, Lexus/Nexus), these searchers are free and widely available from Internet access providers. But if you know anything about the Internet, then you're likely to be familiar with these tools, and you're also likely to know that all sorts of stuff gets onto the Net. While you want to look carefully at the credibility of all your sources (a university-press book is probably more reliable than a privately printed one; a scholarly journal article probably has more clout than a newspaper or popular magazine), you'll need to look especially carefully at material that comes to you electronically. In the case of published articles or books, someone with expertise, supposedly, has validated the research. But it's possible for anyone to "publish" anything on the Web without anyone else's approval: one only has to be smart enough to get the material posted, not necessarily smart enough to get the facts right. You should use the Internet to pick up references or to bat around ideas via e-mail or interest groups, but you should base your research on books and articles published by established places.

Indeed, you won't need to consult all or even most of the background sources or indexes mentioned or alluded to here. When you locate just one good source, it will likely cite other good sources, which will all cite more useful sources, and so forth. Most research projects seem to start slowly but pick up momentum rather quickly. With only a little effort, you'll have no trouble finding more material than you can use for almost any topic. And more references than you can use is usually the right amount you need, because some sources may not be available (checked out, lost, otherwise unavailable); others may be redundant, incomprehensible, or off-target.

Securing Resources, Taking Notes, Finding a Thesis

It's absolutely crucial that you get into the library as soon as possible. Some students put off going to the library because they're afraid they'll get lost or won't know how to find things. But that's the whole point: of course you'll get lost, and of course you don't know how to find everything. I've spent many hours prowling the stacks of many libraries, and I've yet to see the bleached bones of a lost student. You will get lost but you'll find your way around eventually, and you'll run into who-knows-what adventures in the meantime; you won't know where things are, but you'll find them, if they can be found. The sooner you get started, the more time you'll have to process the materials you do find, and to track down those you can't immediately locate.

After you get yourself to the library, the next most important thing to remember is this: the reference librarian can tell you how to find just about anything. Reference librarians are paid to help patrons find things, so it is wise to consult them whenever you need help. Obviously they can't do your research, but you'll likely be amazed at the help they can give.

Once you're in the library, and you've smiled pleasantly at the reference librarian, you're ready to start tracking down sources. I suggest that you alternate between two activities: identifying materials to consult, and actually getting these materials into your hands. Since it may take time to get some resources, which might be checked out, misplaced, or available only through inter-library loan, go ahead and get some materials into the pipeline. Also, by going for some materials to examine as soon as possible, you may be able to search more efficiently and effectively than if you relied solely on indexes, websites, bibliographies, general reference works, the card catalog, and the like.

My own favorite research strategy at the beginning of a project is what I think of as "strategic browsing." I go to the card catalog and find out the call numbers for a few books about the author or subject I'm working on. Then I go into "the stacks" and find those books. They'll likely be shelved with similar books, and so I start browsing. I look for extremely worn books, which means they're probably important, and for rather new books, which means the references to other works should be fairly up-to-date. I look at the tables of contents and in the indexes of the books I've picked up, and I skim very quickly any material that seems promising. I carry notecards with me, and I make a card for the most promising sources I find.

However you identify potential sources, do fill out a notecard for each item—one item per notecard. For a book, list the author, title, publisher, place of publication, date, and the page numbers (if appropriate). Like this:

```
Jay, Gregory. America the Scrivener. Ithaca: Cornell
UP, 1990.
```

For a journal article, list the author, title, name of the journal, date of publication, volume number, and page numbers. Like this:

```
Thesing, William. "The Inevitable Demise of Victorian
Scholarship." Victorian Studies 87 (May 1997): 43-813.
```

It's important to record this information accurately: you'll use it not only to find the resource, but also to make your list of Works Cited, the bibliography for your project.

To find an item, first consult your library's card catalog, searching by author, title, or subject. When you find an item, you'll see a screen or card that looks something like this:

```
AUTHOR: Williams, Annette
TITLE: Samuel Johnson after Deconstruction: Rhetoric and the
Rambler
EDITION: 1st ed.
PUBLISHER: Carbondale: Southern Illinois University Press, 1992.
DESCRIPTION: x, 192 pages, notes, bibliography, index.
SUBJECTS: 1. Johnson, Samuel, 1709-1784. 2. Rambler (London,
England: 1750-52). 3. Rhetoric—1500-1800. 4. Deconstruction.
LOCATION: Cooper Library
CALL #: PR3537.T4L96 1992
STATUS: Checked out; due back 4/1/97
```

The call number is your key to finding an item. Print out the screen's information, if that's possible; or add the call number and anything else you need to your index card. If the item's available, don't hesitate: go get it. If not, and you need to see it, then request it immediately.

Journal articles will ordinarily be available if your library subscribes to the journal. Check the card catalog or database under the journal's title. If you don't have time to read the journal article in the library, you can probably photocopy it.

Once you begin to get some research materials in your own hands, what should you do with them—aside from handling with care? Early in a research project, it's often hard to know what's important and what isn't; but as you become more familiar with your topic, zeroing in on your task and the research questions you're trying to answer, it will become much easier to decide what to skim, what to read carefully, and what to ignore. You can quickly make some tentative judgments about the value of a source, assessing its relevance for your project, its readability, the prestige of the publisher, the date of the material, and the topics actually covered.

As you poke around patiently, you'll no doubt encounter striking ideas, passages, sentences, even phrases. Write them down. Keep careful track of what you're quoting, what you're summarizing, what you're supplying yourself in reaction. And be sure to write down the page numbers where material appears. You're trying to create a storehouse of materials to draw upon, quotations to insert, and ideas to develop or bounce off of. You shouldn't have to go back later and try to figure out where a particular idea or quotation came from. Below you'll see a sample notecard from a research project on Robert Heinlein, which records an idea and a quotation, as well as the page number and the source. Full information on the source appears on another card—giving you two kinds of cards or, if you prefer, computer files: notecards, with identifying tags and page numbers; and bibliographical cards, with full publishing information about each source.

Notecard:

```
Like Robert Louis Stevenson, Heinlein had tuberculosis.
Another parallel: both "early demonstrated their talent
in juvenile fiction." (I wonder: are Heinlein's early
works really juvenile fiction? How are they different
from other science fiction of the time? Isn't all sci-
ence fiction "juvenile" in a sense?)
    Stover 3
```

Bibliographical card:

```
Stover, Leon. Robert A. Heinlein. Boston: Twayne, 1987.
PS 3515 .E288 Z88 1987
```

It may be helpful, especially as your project progresses, to supply a subject heading for each notecard, so that you can begin to group related notes together. But you probably don't want to start fitting your notecards into any sort of set order too soon, before you've had a chance to explore your subject adequately. As you take more notes and shuffle through your cards or computer entries, you'll have a better sense of how your materials will fit together.

As you begin to make connections, it will be crucial to keep in mind that your research paper is not simply a string of quotations and paraphrases: it is an argument. It's easy enough for students, as their secondary resources pile up, to forget about their own essential role in writing the research paper. You've got all these interesting quotations and ideas, and it may seem that your job is simply to introduce them and bring them on stage. But for most research projects, you're more than the master of ceremonies: The critics and documents that you bring on stage are there to support and illuminate *your* discussion. How does a research project become your property, your intellectual offspring?

As you move from defining your topic and your task, locating and working with your research materials, taking notes and contemplating, at some point you will need to evolve a thesis—a main point that will organize and focus your research paper. Your thesis may be evident to you even before you begin the project—in which case, you'll want to strive to keep an open mind as you delve through the research. Or your thesis may slowly emerge as you work with the materials. Or the point you want to make may not be clear until after you've written a draft, or even more, of the entire project. In any event, sooner or later, the purpose of your research will become clear to you: your thesis, unavoidably, will eventually find you. If your research project is a response to an assignment, then your thesis will be the answer to the research question implied or stated in the assignment. If you've invented your own project, then your thesis will be the answer to the research questions you've invented—and sometimes, as veteran researchers will confirm, it is only with the discovery of your thesis that you'll realize precisely what questions you've been attempting to answer.

How do you know if you have a thesis yet? A thesis should be an assertion, an idea that can be stated as a sentence. It should be an original idea, not a mere echo of someone else's thinking (although you certainly may rely on others' ideas). A thesis should also be arguable—meaning that you are *able* to support it, or argue for it, with evidence; and also that you *need* to support it, or argue for it, because not everyone will immediately agree with your idea, without seeing your argument, that is. A thesis should also unify your materials, as the driving force behind your project. Once you have this thesis—an original and arguable assertion that pulls your material together—then you're ready to start drafting in earnest.

The Writing Process

You don't need to begin with your introduction, move to the main body, and then write a conclusion. If you can do that, fine. But oftentimes it's hard to write the introduction until *after* you've written the body and the conclusion, and then you can see exactly what you're introducing. Of course, taking a shot at the introduction may help you see how to shape the main body. Then again, one could argue that writing the conclusion first allows you to see what you're working toward. The real key is to allow yourself enough time to play around with your research essay—to create a lot of mess, make adjustments large and small, reorganize and rethink, revise, polish, and wait for the applause.

Many writers find that making an outline is helpful in the drafting phase. Making a formal and detailed outline too early in the process of writing, before you have a good sense of what you're doing, is probably a waste of time for most projects. But there are always exceptions. A sketchy outline that simply lists the points you're going to make can be useful, especially if you view such an outline as a chance to try out a plan. You need not stick to any outline religiously, however, because you might close off some brilliant line of thinking that occurs to you as you write. Writing is, after all, a very powerful tool for thinking. But occasionally and repeatedly trying to imagine how the project as a whole is going to fit together—that has often proved very helpful to scholars at all levels.

Principles of Documentation

It's essential to keep in mind, as you're drafting, that your reader should be able to see instantly and unambiguously which ideas are yours and which ideas have some other source. Your reader, as we noted, is ultimately interested *in what you have to say,* not in how many quotations and references you can string together. So make sure that you give yourself appropriate credit. But also make sure that you give your supporting cast appropriate credit. Using the words or ideas of someone else without clearly acknowledging the source is plagiarism. Deliberate plagiarism, knowingly stealing someone else's words or ideas, is an extremely serious academic offense.

Since the principles of documentation are fairly simple and straightforward, it's easy enough to avoid any potential problems. You do *not* need to identify a source for common knowledge—information that any informed person already knows, or that is available in a number of sources. You also don't have to give anyone else credit for your own ideas and findings. What does require citation?

1. Direct quotations, where you use someone else's words. Put their words inside quotation marks, and make sure the page number and the source of the quotation are clear.
2. Ideas, insights, illustrations, lines of argument—*anything* that you take from someone else. You may summarize without quotation marks, if the wording is your own; but you may not rely on anyone else's thinking without attribution.
3. Assistance from other people, including friends, teachers, experts. If you're talking about your paper, and a friend offers an idea you can use, be sure to recognize his or her contribution.

Occasionally you may be unsure whether some information is common knowledge, or whether some insight is your own, or something you might have read late at night as you were dozing off. If you're in doubt, err on the side of giving credit. It's even possible to have a note like this one, which appears somewhere in the published works of Morse Peckham: "I regret to say that I am unable to identify the source of this information."

To illustrate more specifically how to reference sources appropriately, let's look at some examples. The following illustrations deal with this famous poem.

WILLIAM BUTLER YEATS (1865–1939)

Sailing to Byzantium

That is no country for old men. The young
In one another's arms, birds in the trees
—Those dying generations—at their song,
The salmon-falls, the mackerel-crowded seas,
Fish, flesh, or fowl, commend all summer long
Whatever is begotten, born, and dies.
Caught in that sensual music all neglect

5

Monuments of unaging intellect.

An aged man is but a paltry thing,
A tattered coat upon a stick, unless   10
Soul clap its hands and sing, and louder sing
For every tatter in its mortal dress,
Nor is there singing school but studying
Monuments of its own magnificence;
And therefore I have sailed the seas and come   15
To the holy city of Byzantium.

O sages standing in God's holy fire
As in the gold mosaic of a wall,
Come from the holy fire, perne in a gyre*,
And be the singing-masters of my soul.   20
Consume my heart away; sick with desire
And fastened to a dying animal
It knows not what it is; and gather me
Into the artifice of eternity.

Once out of nature I shall never take   25
My bodily form from any natural thing,
But such a form as Grecian goldsmiths make
Of hammered gold and gold enameling
To keep a drowsy Emperor awake;
Or set upon a golden bough to sing   30
To lords and ladies of Byzantium
Of what is past, or passing, or to come.

                                                        1927

First, imagine that you notice and copy a passage from pages 171–72 of a second-ary source, Albert Ketcheman's *William Butler Yeats*. Here's the passage:

> And the poems, even the most crucial one, "Sailing to Byzantium," are clear enough. The reader's only real problem in that poem is to see why Byzantium itself was so attractive to Yeats.

And here's what your notecard might look like:

```
Clarity, attractiveness of Byzantium

Ketcheman 171-72:
"And the poems, even the most crucial one, 'Sailing
to Byzantium,' are clear enough. The reader's only
real problem in that poem is to see why Byzantium
itself was so attractive to Yeats."
```

You also copy down another passage, this one from page 199 of Clark's *Yeats*, as your notecard indicates:

19 *perne in a gyre* spin down a spiral

```
     Clarity, beginning lament

Clark 199:

"The movement of 'Sailing to Byzantium' is quite
clear, and so are its essential terms. The poem begins
with the familiar lament for lost bodily vigor and
sexuality, a regret not overcome by the compensating
sense of increased wisdom, a Yeatsian obsession which,
in the earlier fragment, is exceedingly blunt."
```

Now, imagine that you write the following sentence in a draft:

1. Some critics might think that "Sailing to Byzantium" is quite clear, but at least three terms in the poem are ambiguous.

The critical context is vaguely presented in your sentence: do critics actually think that, and who are they? It's also not entirely clear if the assertion of ambiguity is your own idea, or a contradictory supplement to some critics' thinking. The reference isn't very fair or helpful.

So you revise the sentence, coming up with this more explicit statement:

2. Albert Ketcheman says "Sailing to Byzantium" is "clear enough" (171), and Justin Clark says its "movement" and "essential terms" are "quite clear" (199), but at least three terms in the poem are ambiguous.

This version is definitely better, but the significance of your assertion is still not directly stated. It's not really clear who says that three terms are ambiguous.

Here's another revision:

3. Typical opinions are offered by Ketcheman, who says "Sailing to Byzantium" is "clear enough" (171), and by Clark, who says its "movement" and "essential terms" are "quite clear" (199). I find, however, at least three terms that these critics explain in contradictory terms, and which remain ambiguous and puzzling.

Now this is starting to sound good. In this version both the critical context and your place within that context are made clear. There's no question who's saying what, and there's no question that you've got something interesting to add to the critical discussion.

In a writing-about-literature course, the format for documenting your research sources will likely be the new Modern Language Association (or MLA) style. Check with your teacher to be sure. Other styles of documentation are also available, each with its own advantages and admirers. The goal for all documentation styles is the same: to clearly identify the writer's sources. You can learn a great deal about documentation just by paying attention to how it is handled in your sources: notice how authors are quoted, how ideas are attributed, how works and writers are named and cited.

While the scope of this chapter won't allow me to cover the different styles for documenting a research paper, you will get to see in a moment how a sample research paper is put together using the MLA style. The *MLA Handbook for Writers of Research Papers* (2004; 5th edition), which should be available in any reference area and just about any bookstore, provides a clear and extremely thorough explanation of how to use the MLA style.

A Sample Research Paper

Now let us actually trace, in brief, the process of writing a sample research paper. Here is the assignment:

> In research format, writing for your classmates and other interested readers, briefly discuss at least two different interpretations of Yeats's "Sailing to Byzantium" and compare these readings to your own.

And here is how one hypothetical student, Anna Olivia Williams, proceeded.

Getting Ideas

First Source. Anna immediately charges into the library and starts browsing through various sources, identified by looking in the *MLA Bibliography*, which happens to be on-line in her school's library. Skimming through the first four articles that look promising, Anna notices that Cleanth Brooks's study of this poem is often mentioned. So she locates *The Well-Wrought Urn* and makes a "Works Cited" entry for it in a computer file or on a notecard.

```
Brooks, Cleanth.
The Well-Wrought Urn. New York: Holt, 1947.
```

She then reads through the essay, making the following notes:

```
Brooks 178-191

The tension for Brooks:

nature vs art

becoming vs being

sensual vs intellectual

here vs Byzantium

aging vs timelessness
```

Anna doesn't put any quotation marks here because this set of oppositions is her own interpretation of Brooks's argument. She has noticed that he repeatedly identifies oppositions in the poem, and so she lists them. Can you see these oppositions? In the first stanza, for instance, Yeats discusses the world of nature ("fish, flesh, or fowl," "sensual music"), and he concludes that those in the world of nature neglect art ("monuments of unageing intellect").

Anna puts the page numbers where this discussion occurs at the top of the card. This is a good idea because she might forget to put down the page number after she's made the note. Then she'd have to hunt around to find the material later.

```
Brooks 188-189: "artifice" and unity

"The word 'artifice' fits the prayer at one level after
another; the fact that he is to be taken out of nature;
that his body is to be an artifice hammered out of
```

> gold; that it will not age but will have the finality
> of a work of art."
>
> Brooks thus believes Yeats favors the latter items in
> the list of elements in tension.

You'll notice that Anna uses quotation marks for part of the note: these are Brooks's words. It's crucial to keep straight what is your summary of the criticism, and what is quoted. Otherwise, you may use the critic's phrasing, thinking it's your own. Anna has also put a tag word at the top to suggest what the note is about. As her notecards pile up, these tags will allow her to sort them and move them around more easily. As she understands how her paper is going to develop, she may add to or alter these tags.

> Brooks 189: "artifice" and irony
>
> "But 'artifice' unquestionably carries an ironic
> qualification too. The prayer, for all its passion,
> is a modest one. He does not ask that he be gathered
> into the 'artifice of eternity.' The qualification
> does not turn the prayer into mockery, but it is all-
> important: it limits as well as defines the power of
> the sages to whom the poet appeals."

Brooks's focus on irony here should suggest that his stance is indeed New Critical.

> Brooks 186–187: thesis
>
> "To which world is Yeats committed? Which does he choose?
>
> The question is idle—as idle as/ the question that the
> earnest schoolmarm puts to the little girl reading for
> the first time 'L'Allegro—Il Penseroso': which does
> Milton *really* prefer, mirth or melancholy? . . .
> Yeats chooses both and neither."

On this card Anna has a slash after "as" to let her know where the page break comes in Brooks's essay. If she needs to quote only a part of this passage, she'll know which page(s) to cite. She has also left out material, indicated by the ellipsis.

Brooks's point here suggests the complexity of Yeats's poem, refusing easy categorization into one thing or the other.

> Brooks 189–190: irony of the golden bird—both natural
> and supernatural
>
> "The irony [of the poem] is directed, it seems to me,
> not at our yearning to transcend the world of nature,
> but at the human situation itself in which supernatural
> and natural are intermixed—the human situation which is
> inevitably caught between the claims of both natural
> and supernatural. The golden bird whose bodily form the
> speaker will take in Byzantium will be withdrawn from

> the flux of the world of becoming. But so withdrawn, it
> will sing of the world of becoming—'Of what is past, or
> passing, or to come."

Brooks's New Critical stance is clear here, as he finds irony, unity, complexity. Using her notecards, Anna sketches out what she might say about Brooks:

> Operating as a New Critic, Cleanth Brooks identifies
> a number of tensions in Yeats's poem—between nature
> and art, becoming and being, the sensual and intellec-
> tual, "here" and Byzantium, aging and timelessness
> (178–191). How Yeats manages to unify these tensions
> is epitomized for Brooks by the word "artifice" in the
> third stanza. The word suggests that Yeats's speaker
> will be taken out of nature (188–189), but it occurs
> in a phrase that ironically qualifies this suggestion:
> the speaker will become an "artifice of eternity,"
> rather than genuinely a part of eternity (189). Thus,
> Brooks says, of the oppositions set up by the poem,
> Yeats "chooses both and neither" (187). The poem is
> unified by the idea that the golden bird, like "the
> human situation," is "inevitably caught between the
> claims of both natural and supernatural" (189–190).

You'll notice that Anna names the source, Brooks, and simply puts the page reference where the quotation or reference ends. She is following the MLA style of documentation. The works cited page at the end of her essay will give the reader the bibliographical information needed to find the source.

Second Source.   In the card catalog, Anna comes across a work by Brenda Webster, *Yeats: A Psychoanalytic Study*—obviously a distinctive approach. Here are the notes she makes while reading Webster, which turns out to be a difficult work to understand:

> Webster, Brenda.
> *Yeats: A Psychoanalytic Study*. New York: Macmillan, 1973.

Here are some of the few sentences Anna thinks she understands:

> Webster 213–214: bird as defense
> "The bird functions as a defense against anxieties
> unconsciously raised by the poem—not just the fear of
> aging and thwarted sexuality . . . , but the overarching
> fear of a loss of integrity."

> Webster 214: Yeats's operation
> "Sailing" was written before Yeats had a "Steinach oper-
> ation, which increased his sense of sexual vitality."

Anna makes a note to find out what a Steinach operation is.

> Webster 214: union with the mother
>
> "The old man's frustrated sexual desire is the visible
> strand of what we shall see is a submerged theme or
> fantasy of union with the mother." A few sentences
> later: "in the works by Yeats that embody incestuous
> fantasies, the hero is often symbolically castrated or
> mutilated by the mother figure before he can be loved.
> In 'Sailing' Yeats endows the aging process itself
> with the threatening qualities of a cruel mother. Now
> it is age that sexually frustrates the old man and
> threatens him with disintegration and loss of self."

Then she sketches out what she might say about Webster:

> According to Brenda Webster, Yeats's speaker wants to
> become a golden bird as "a defense against anxieties
> unconsciously raised by the poem" (113). Yeats's fears
> included, Webster says, aging and thwarted sexuality;
> soon after the poem Yeats would have a Steinach opera-
> tion, increasing his sexual vitality (Webster 214).
> But the most important anxiety, Webster believes, was
> Yeats's fear of "a loss of integrity" (214). Yeats
> dreams of becoming a golden bird so that he might have
> an ageless body. But this desire is part of a deeper
> one: he wants to reunite with his mother, and removing
> his manhood by becoming a golden bird is, so Webster
> says, part of that process.
>
> But I don't see how a golden bird can join with the
> mother any more easily than a grown man, or a wooden
> pig, or a crystal do-do bird.

Third Source.   Anna's teacher has mentioned one source in class, "The Practice
of Theory" by Lawrence Lipking. Anna gets this essay and finds that Lipking examines Yeats's poem from a deconstructive perspective in order to show what is
wrong with deconstruction. For the essay itself she makes a card:

> Lipking, Lawrence. "The Practice of Theory." In
> *Literary Theories in Praxis*. Ed. Shirley Staton.
> Philadelphia: U of Pennsylvania P, 1987. 426-440. Rpt.
> from *College Forum* 14: 23-29.

Then, for each point that she thinks she might use, Anna also makes a card:

> Lipking 431: Singing—pro or con?
> Lipking asks why should soul "louder sing/ For every
> tatter in its mortal dress"? He sees two possibilities.
> 1. The soul is singing to distract itself from the

tatters of its mortal dress (for example, sore
throats, hemorrhoids, arthritis). 2. The soul is
singing in celebration of its body falling apart
because the tatters bring the soul closer to eternity
and separation from the body. Lipking concludes there
is no way to tell which of these meanings is right,
and therefore "the line does not make sense," if by
"sense" we mean that a statement cannot mean one
thing and the opposite thing at the same time.

Lipking 431: singing school—yes or no?

Lipking asks if there is a singing school. If "Nor is
there singing school" means there isn't one, then how
come the speaker wants some singing masters in the
next verse? The lines are contradictory: the poem
doesn't make sense.

Lipking 432: Status of eternity?

Lipking asks if the artifice of eternity is "something
permanent (an eternal artifice) or something evanes-
cent (an illusion without any substance)." He says he
can't decide based on the poem.

Lipking 432: "That"

Lipking points to the uncertainty of the opening
"That." Yeats himself, Lipking points out, said it
"was the worst syntax he ever wrote."

Lipking 432–433: the bird—obvious contradiction

Lipking finds one contradiction in the poem "so important and obvious that it is noticed by a great many
students, and even some critics." Namely, the speaker
cannot claim he will "never take/ My bodily form from
any natural thing" because, Lipking says, "every bodily
form must be taken from nature, whether the form of a
bird or simply the golden form embodied by an artist."

At this point, Anna tries to write a quick summary of what she has learned. This step is useful, but too often passed over; it allows you to work with your materials, to evolve your own ideas before you actually start trying to write the paper itself. Here is what Anna writes:

In "The Practice of Theory" Lawrence Lipking simply
says what nearly every student who has read Yeats's
poem carefully thinks—the poem does not make sense.

The reference of the opening "That" is never made
clear, as Lipking says (432). Nor can the reader tell
if there is a singing school or not: as Lipking
notes, "Nor is there singing school" seems to say
there is no singing school, but then the speaker
immediately desires to have singing masters in the
next verse (431). The lines are thus contradictory.

Lipking also points to the uncertainty involved in the
assertion that the soul should "louder sing/ For every
tatter in its mortal dress." Does this statement mean
that the soul should sing to distract itself from the
decay of the body, its "mortal dress"? Or does it mean
that the soul should sing in celebration of its body
falling apart, since such disintegration brings the
soul closer to eternity and separation from the body?
Lipking concludes there is no way to tell which of
these meanings is right, and therefore "the line does
not make sense," if by "sense" we mean that a statement cannot mean one thing and the opposite thing at
the same time (431). Likewise, Lipking notes that the
speaker cannot carry out his declaration to "never
take/ My bodily form from any natural thing" because
"every bodily form must be taken from nature, whether
the form of a bird or simply the golden form embodied
by an artist" (432-433).

In pointing out these problems in the poem, Lipking's
point is not that Yeats's poem is a poor one. The
problem, Lipking says, is that when we adopt a deconstructive stance, we are inevitably committed to seeing how a work fails to make sense. Language always,
if we read closely enough, fails to make sense.

Organizing

At this point Anna determines she's got plenty of secondary sources to satisfy the
assignment. Now she needs to work on her own reading. Her first reaction to "Sailing" was quite different from any of the critics she has read. She did not find the
speaker of the poem to be appealing. Yeats, or his spokesman, strikes Anna as self-
absorbed, fretful, whining, and even a bit pompous. She decides that her view is so
different that it should be interesting to her readers, and she determines after looking over the poem again that her reading can be supported. So she writes the following rough draft of her reading:

1. I'd like to see what a feminist critic would do with this poem. Women appear
    only as the imaginary "ladies of Byzantium" who no doubt drop grapes and
    cherries into the mouths of the lords of Byzantium. Women are conspicuous
    by their absence. Yeats doesn't even consider whether "That" country, what-
    ever it is, is a place for old women or even old people. It's just no country for
    old men. An "aged man" is "a paltry thing," but an aged woman apparently
    isn't worth considering.

2. Why is Yeats so self-absorbed and depressed that he desires the ridiculous transformation into a singing golden bird? (Is this the best paradise he can come up with?) Given three wishes, he wants to be a bird? And not even a real bird?

    Yeats frets because he is obsessed with aging. But what aspect of aging? Sex appeal, it seems. He focuses on "The young/ In one another's arms," and the other images relate to sexuality: salmon struggling upstream to reproduce and die; mackerel crowded together to mate. The "birds in the trees" are linked in our culture to romance. The reference to "dying generations" compresses the problem: he is dying while generations continue to be produced.

3. When he perceives his sexual appeal is waning, an older man today might buy a Porsche and chase younger women. Yeats's solution is even more desperate and absurd. He aims to do away with the physical altogether. Yeats changes sex into music: the transition is the reference to "sensual music." So he wants to leave the world of the sensual, passing from sensual music to music alone. As a golden bird, his sensual music will be outside nature. He will avoid the male horror of aging. Why can't our culture be more comfortable with life's natural processes?

Drafting

At this point Anna is ready to put it all together. With this much preparation, she simply needs to introduce the critical statements, refine them, and link them together. How can these statements be related?

She could simply describe how they relate to one another and contrast them to her own position. A more ambitious approach would be to present the other positions in some sort of sequence leading up to her ideas. What kind of sequence could there be? Brooks's New Critical reading sees some oppositions, and he argues that they are unified by the ironic status of the golden bird, both within and without nature. Lipking's deconstructive reading, however, refuses to allow such a resolution, identifying logical problems that cannot be explained away. And Webster's psychological study suggests why Yeats's logic should fail: he is attempting to deal with an impossible desire, the Oedipal impulse to rejoin his mother. Anna's point is a variation of Webster's position: the poem's problems do stem from Yeats's psychological distress, but that distress is not so weird as an Oedipal obsession. It is simply the fear of growing old and sexually unattractive.

After a draft or two and a close revision, the following paper emerges:

```
Anna Olivia Williams
Professor Callie Taylor
March 24, 2002


Five Views of Yeats's "Sailing to Byzantium"

    W. B. Yeats's "Sailing to Byzantium," one of the most-
read poems in the English language, is also one of the
most challenging. Yeats scholars keep insisting that the
```

poem is clear, yet various interpretations keep appearing.[1] The syntax of the poem can be difficult. Yeats, in fact, said the opening line was "the worst syntax he ever wrote" (qtd. in Lipking 432). But even after the reader has determined what the lines mean, certain difficulties remain. Perhaps the most crucial question is how the poem resolves the opposing forces it sets up. Every reader perceives that nature and art, youth and age, and a number of other elements are opposed. But how does Yeats's desire to become a golden bird, an "artifice of eternity," resolve the poem's tensions?

A persuasive discussion of how the poem's oppositions are resolved occurs in Cleanth Brooks's New Critical reading. Brooks argues that they are unified by the ironic status of the golden bird. He means that the bird is, as Yeats puts it, an "artifice," and it is therefore outside of nature. His body will not age, but will have "the finality of a work of art" (189). Brooks reveals here his adherence to the New Critical idea that the work of art has a stable presence and permanence. But "artifice," as Brooks recognizes, is qualified by Yeats, who wants to become an "artifice of eternity." About this qualification, Brooks says the following:

> The qualification does not turn the prayer into mockery, but it is all-important: it limits as well as defines the power of the sages to whom the poet appeals. (189)

Thus Brooks believes the poem is unified by this balancing of its various oppositions.

But Brenda Webster strives to discover why such a complex process of unifying opposites would appeal to Yeats, and her Freudian reading finds the answer in, of course, the Oedipus complex. For Webster, the golden bird

is not an ironically unifying device; it is rather "a
defense against anxieties unconsciously raised by the poem—
not just the fear of aging and thwarted sexuality . . . ,
but the overarching fear of a loss of integrity" (213-214).
Yeats overcomes this fear of self-loss, Webster argues, by
desiring a union with his mother, a kind of return to the
womb. The symbol of the golden bird is part of this desire,
Webster says, because in Yeats's other works involving
"incestuous fantasies, the hero is often symbolically
castrated or mutilated by the mother figure before he can
be loved" (214). But, Webster tells us:

> In "Sailing" Yeats endows the aging process itself
> with the threatening qualities of a cruel mother.
> Now it is age that sexually frustrates the old man
> and threatens him with disintegration and loss of
> self. (214)

For Lawrence Lipking, and I must confess for me, such
psychoanalytical explanations are not satisfying. Lipking
simply admits that crucial lines in the poem do not make
sense (431). Lipking sees two possible answers to the
question of why the soul should "louder sing/ For every
tatter in its mortal dress." On the one hand, perhaps the
soul is singing to distract itself from the tatters of its
mortal dress. On the other hand, perhaps the soul is
singing in celebration of its body falling apart because
the tatters bring the soul closer to eternity and
separation from the body. Lipking concludes there is no
way to tell which of these meanings is right, and
therefore "the line does not make sense," if by "sense" we
mean that a statement cannot mean one thing and the
opposite thing at the same time (431).

Lipking likewise considers whether there is a singing
school in the poem. The line "Nor is there singing

school" seems to say there is no such school, but the speaker desires some singing masters in the next verse. Rather than attempting some ingenious explanation, Lipking simply acknowledges that the lines are contradictory and the poem at every point deconstructs itself. Brooks's unification of the poem, Lipking would say, simply overlooks the evidence, engaging in wishful thinking. The golden bird, rather than being key to the poem's unity, involves it in an obvious contradiction, "so important and obvious that it is noticed by a great many students, and even some critics" (432). Namely, the speaker cannot claim he will "never take/ My bodily form from any natural thing" because, Lipking says, "every bodily form must be taken from nature, whether the form of a bird or simply the golden form embodied by an artist" (433).

I agree with Webster and Lipking that this much-honored poem contains hopeless contradictions, but I think the explanation is less hidden than an Oedipus complex and less shocking than the deconstructive idea that all language is contradictory. Instead, Yeats is undergoing the sort of crisis many older men undergo when they perceive themselves to be aging and growing unattractive. He wants to become a golden bird because he wants to be beautiful, but he does not want to engage in sexual competition for women.

This retreat from sexuality is prepared for in the first stanza, where Yeats focuses on "The young/ In one another's arms." Other images also relate to sexuality: salmon struggling upstream to reproduce and die; mackerel crowded together to mate. And the "birds in the trees" are linked in our culture to romance. The problem Yeats faces is compressed into the reference to "dying generations": he is dying while generations continue to be produced.

Yeats is so intent on escaping the sexual that he
cannot even consider whether "That" country, whichever it
is, is a place for old women or even old people. All he
can consider is that it is no country for old men—really,
for one old man in particular. An "aged man" is "a paltry
thing," but an aged woman apparently is not worth
considering. Thus, Yeats aims to do away with the physical
altogether. He combines sex and music in the "sensual
music," and in becoming the golden bird he will make the
transformation complete, turning his sexual being into
music alone. As a golden bird, his sensual music will be
outside nature, and he will avoid the horror—which is for
him, strictly masculine, strictly his own—of aging.

Note

[1]See for instance Ketcheman, who says "Sailing to
Byzantium" is "clear enough"(171), and Clark, who says its
"movement" and "essential terms" are "quite clear"(199).
They disagree however on several points.

Works Cited

Brooks, Cleanth. *The Well-Wrought Urn*. New York: Holt,
    1947.
Clark, Donald. *Yeats*. New York: Basic Books, 1962.
Ketcheman, Albert. *William Butler Yeats: A Life*. New York:
    Harper, 1958.
Lipking, Lawrence. "The Practice of Theory." *College Forum*
    14: 23-29.
Webster, Brenda. *Yeats: A Psychoanalytic Study*. New York:
    Macmillan, 1973.

Appendix B

Editing and Revising

Editing

An editor helps a writer recognize which aspects of a text are finished, and which aspects need more work. Sometimes editors make suggestions and corrections themselves, but their job mainly is to bring virtues and flaws to the writer's attention.

Although most writers aren't lucky enough to have professional editors, it is nonetheless useful in some ways to think of editing and revising as separate jobs. An editor doesn't have to worry about how to fix the problems he or she finds (that's the writer's problem), and so editors may be more likely to decide this or that *is* a problem. Also, although there are always exceptions, good editors are often not that worried about the writer's ego or feelings. Their concern is with the finished product. It doesn't really matter how long the writer worked on a piece; if it stinks, it stinks; and the writer can deal with it.

When you have a draft in pretty good shape, it's time to become an editor. What should you look for? Anything and everything, but very simple questions— such as What do you like most? What do you like least? What needs more work?— can produce very useful feedback. But besides such general concerns, there are specific stylistic flaws that good editors regularly look for.

But before we look at such flaws, a word of caution: general advice regarding style is risky, simply because an effective style is so sensitive to the particular context— the purpose, the audience, the image the writer wants to project. Good writers sometimes violate rules and principles, but they at least know they're violating them, and why.

Tightening

On a stylistic level, an editor's prime directive might be this: *Cut the Fat.* Editors just assume that your prose can be tighter, leaner. They try to eliminate any sentences, phrases, words, even syllables you don't need. They want every word to earn its keep, and if a simpler word or phrase will do the same job, they want you to choose the shorter, simpler wording—unless you have a reason to do otherwise. For example,

John Trimble of the University of Texas, author of the classic *Writing with Style*, is a superb editor. John likes to count the words in the original and the revision. He likes to point out that if you can tighten twenty words to fifteen words, then you can cut a two hundred page text to one-fifty. We'd save a lot of trees if everyone edited so astutely.

How do you find the flab to cut? Here are some tips to help you.

- *Look at the subjects of your sentences.* Is every one *really* the proper subject? That is, does the subject of each sentence accurately reflect its focus? Are you saying "The kind of situation involved here is one of mis-communication between the engineer and the architect"? Or are you putting the real actor and action in the subject and verb positions, as in "The architect misled the engineer"? Richard Lanham's *Revising Prose* (or *Revising Business Prose* if you prefer marketplace examples) can provide extensively detailed help on getting the parts of your sentences organized. A few examples, however, can illustrate much of Lanham's method.

The following sentences are adapted from an essay discussing waste disposal problems (by Elizabeth Royte, in *Harper's*, June 1992). Consider this one:

> The situation is one in which still more landfills will be forced to close, following the EPA requirements introduced last September.

Although it is possible that "the situation" is where the writer actually wants the focus, it seems unlikely. The real subject of the sentence, I would suggest, is either "more landfills" or "EPA requirements." To decide which one to use, you'd need to look at the context in which the sentence occurs. Notice how changing the subject changes the sentence in each case:

> More landfills will be forced to close, following the EPA requirements introduced last September.
> EPA requirements introduced last September will force still more landfills to close. (Royte's version)

Notice that the first version has 22 words; the second has 14; and the third has 11, which is cutting the original in half. Imagine if everything you read were half as long as it is—if your physics text were 125 pages instead of 250, if your IRS instructions were 8 pages instead of 16!

Some sentences begin not with the wrong subject, but without one—or with a subject that is essentially empty:

> There are scarred hillsides of this valley that provide a good vantage point from which to view the nation's garbage wars.

The first word here, "there," is just a pointing word, linked by "are" to the rest of the sentence. Sometimes you do want simply to point out a situation or a fact, and beginning with "There are" or "It is" is a good idea. But oftentimes the sentence will seem more effective, not to mention more direct, when the subject position is occupied by a real subject:

> Scarred hillsides of this valley provide a good vantage point from which to view the nation's garbage.

Here's another tip to help you find the fat:

- *Look for phrases that can be replaced by a word or at least a shorter phrase*. Consider, for example, this sentence: "The shift in voter loyalty is due to the fact that the economy grew even worse." Is there a familiar phrase in this sentence? Yes, of course, it's "due to the fact that." What happens if you try to replace that phrase?

The shift in voter loyalty occurred because the economy grew even worse.

Or, changing the subject of the sentence, we have this leaner and more direct version:

Voter loyalty shifted because the economy grew even worse.

Another tip:

- *Look for prepositional phrases that can be collapsed or eliminated*, especially where you have a string of prepositional phrases. For instance: "The imbalance of chemicals in the liver of the patient caused problems for the intern of the evening watch." If we try to remove some of the prepositional phrases, what happens?

The chemical imbalance in the patient's liver caused problems for the evening-watch intern.

We've gone here from nineteen words to fourteen, making the sentence a little tighter.

And another piece of advice:

- *Watch out for large words and stilted phrasings*. One clue to wordiness may be the flowering of words ending in *-ion*. For instance: "The institution told those directly involved in the educational profession that consultation would be forthcoming." I think this sentence means simply:

The administrators told the teachers they would be consulted.

That's fifteen words converted to nine—saving over a third. Plus, the revision just sounds friendlier, more like a person talking. If you cannot imagine yourself *saying* what you've written, then ask yourself how you would say it. Then write that down instead.

Here are some other examples and revisions (see if you can explain the principle behind the revision):

Original #1:

It is largely because of the fact that Grant caused such widespread destruction that many Southerners dislike the North even to the present time.

Revision #1:

Grant caused such widespread destruction that many Southerners dislike the North even today.

Or,

Many Southerners dislike the North even today because Grant caused such widespread destruction.

Original #2:

In the event that a hurricane hits Charleston again, the new construction regula-tions codes will have been applied for the purpose of making buildings stronger.

Revision #2:

If a hurricane hits Charleston again, the new building codes to make buildings stronger will have been applied.

Original #3:

If economists take into consideration only the purchasing capability of Argentineans of the upper class, the recent period of inflation in the double digits will seem rather mild.

Revision #3:

If economists consider only the buying power of upper-class Argentineans, the recent period of double-digit inflation will seem rather mild.

Brightening

Editors also look for opportunities to make your style livelier, more vigorous, more appealing. What makes prose more engaging? Try some of the following (but not all at once in every sentence!):

- *Include comparisons.* Ask yourself, "What is this like?" When the U.S. Army was debating whether they should hire Indian warriors to track and catch Apache warriors like Geronimo, one officer said, "Using standard methods is like trying to hunt down a deer with a marching band." The (disturbing) comparison made the case powerfully, and the Indian scouts were hired. In his "Travels in Georgia," John McPhee talks about a turtle that was "run over like a manhole cover, probably with much the same sound." When a sheriff puts the turtle out of its misery, McPhee says "the gun made an absurdly light sound, like a screen door shutting." A friend of McPhee's carries the dead turtle down to the pond "like a heavy suitcase with a broken strap." These comparisons bring the idea to life, making us see one thing in terms of another, enriching our grasp. "Oh, so *that's* what it sounded like," we say. (As you may know, when you use "like" or "as," the comparison is called a "simile." If you don't use "like" or "as," it is known as a "metaphor.")

- *Replace weak verbs with more active, more vivid, more precise verbs.* Instead of saying "he walked slowly along," you might want to say "he *meandered* along." Instead of "the new recipe is better than the old one," you might want to say, "the new recipe grabs your taste buds, while the old one just teased them." Most teachers and style guides will tell you to watch out for "to be" or linking verbs—"is," "are," "am," "was." These verbs certainly are useful, and oftentimes they are fine to use. But when most of your sen-tences simply say that "X is Y," then likely your prose is not very vivid or active. So, as you're revising, see if some of your linking verbs should be con-verted into active verbs.

- *Add details.* Perhaps "She went to work" should be changed to "Mary Catherine crawled out of bed and stumbled over to her computer, deter-mined to write up the annual report despite her mind-boggling hangover." One of the most common student shortcomings in writing classes is saying too little, taking for granted that the reader can see or understand whatever is clear to the writer.

One effective way to add details is to use appositives. An appositive adds information by renaming a noun: Instead of "Samuel Johnson said many witty things," you write "Samuel Johnson, the eighteenth-century author, said many witty things." Or, going further, you might say "Samuel Johnson, the eighteenth-century author, the subject of Boswell's great biography, said many witty things."

- *Be specific*. Instead of "After a boring day, he went home," you might want to say this: "After a lengthy and lumbering discussion of the toilet paper allotment, an unnecessary and uneventful meeting with his assistant, and four hours of staring out his window at the building next door, he went home."

- *Use a few startlingly short sentences, even one- or two-word sentences.* Absolutely. (Just like that; and also try some parenthetical comments on what you've just said.) Also try some dashes, semicolons, and colons. Bullet dots are also effective when you want to list items. Magazine writers do all sorts of things to liven up the page. Look closely at writing that aspires to be popular and try to do what you see those writers doing, even at the level of punctuation.

Connecting

Good writing flows. Readers like to find themselves moving smoothly along, as each sentence seems to be connected to the preceding sentences. This connectedness is often referred to as "coherence," the property of bonding together. Good editors are on the lookout for gaps in coherence. A number of strategies contribute to this quality, which some readers refer to as "flowing," but mainly you want to link every sentence in some way to what has gone before and what is coming up. To see how a passage holds together, let's look at an example by Francis Davis:

> What used to appeal to listeners, both black and white, about black performers like James Brown, Ray Charles, Aretha Franklin, and even such Motown smoothies as Marvin Gaye and Smokey Robinson, was their "authenticity," the indisputable realness of their music and the cultural values it embodied. By comparison, recent black performers, including the comic-strip militants Public Enemy, have transformed themselves into self-caricatures as insubstantial as the "Toons" in the 1988 movie *Who Framed Roger Rabbit?*, who were understood to be standing in for racial minorities. A glance at any Guns N' Roses video should be enough to persuade us that black performers aren't contemporary pop's only Toons. But because pop music plays such a large part in shaping both black self-image and white perceptions of black culture, more is at stake in the persona of a performer who is black.

> —from Francis Davis, "Toons," in *The Atlantic* (April 1992)

What features of coherent writing can we notice here?

First, coherent writing often involves repeating words and phrases, or using synonyms, antonyms, or other variations of words. Such repetition keeps the reader's attention focused on the subject. In Davis's passage, notice how the repetition of the word "black" in every sentence helps to link the sentences together: the paragraph focuses on what "black" means. Also, notice how "realness" is contrasted to "Toons" (a cartoon being of course the opposite of real): this opposition also helps knit the passage together.

Second, coherent writing often involves using pronouns and pointing adjectives. In the previous example, notice how "their" and "themselves" helps to create coherence. Third, coherent writing often involves repeating a construction or phrase. The phrase "black performers," for instance, reappears in the passage. Fourth, coherent writing often involves explicit transitions. In Davis's example, "By comparison" and "But" point out relationship.

Using any sort of technique to improve your coherence will be ineffective if your thinking is not coherent. As you're drafting, it is inevitable that ideas will interrupt the progression of your thought, taking you down tangential lines of development, leading you to associate the current topic with some other. In editing, you'll want to look for these distracting or interrupting ideas, and revise them by grouping related ideas together. Coherent writing (usually) doesn't require the reader to make leaps of logic or to fill in narrative omissions. The writing goes step by step, as sentences are linked and related.

Once you're satisfied the ideas really do fit together and are in the proper order, then you want to make sure the reader is able to see the progression. Here is a brief guide to some explicit connecting devices:

- Similar ideas can be explicitly connected by "likewise," "similarly," "by the same token," "in the same way," and "also."

- Contrasting ideas can be explicitly connected by "but," "yet," "however," "still," "even so," "on the other hand," and several other connectors.

- Items in sequence can be explicitly connected by numerical ordering: "first," "second," "third," and so forth.

- An idea can be connected to preceding material by being simply added to it, using "and," "in addition," "furthermore," "also," "besides," and other linking words.

- An idea that acknowledges what your reader already knows, or that there are other points of view, can be explicitly connected by "of course," "granted," "to be sure," "even though," and other words.

- Illustrations can be explicitly connected by "for example," "for instance," and "in particular."

- Conclusions can be explicitly linked by "therefore," "thus," "hence," "consequently," and other words.

Notice how many of the features mentioned contribute to the coherence of the following paragraph, from "The Next New Deal" by Neil Howe and Phillip Longman (*The Atlantic*, April 1992):

Finally, there was the program originally designed to offer all Americans what President Franklin Roosevelt's brain trusters called "a floor of protection" against destitution in old age. But over the course of more than half a century Social Security had evolved into something radically different. By 1991 the system was distributing more than $55 billion a year, or more than a fifth of its benefits, to households with incomes above $50,000. For that much money the government could have provided every American with cradle-to-grave insurance against poverty—including the one American child in twenty who lived in a household reporting a cash income during 1991 of less than $5,000.

Revising

For too many students, "revising" means simply "changing a few words, checking the spelling, and looking for typing errors." But for writers, including teachers of writing, revising means much more. "Revision" means "re-seeing," looking at anew—rethinking and rewriting. You may change a word, a phrase, a sentence; you may well find that whole sections need to be reworked, or deleted, or created.

Thus, the first step in revising is in a sense not a step at all but an attitude: once you have assumed the attitude of an editor, taking for granted that your writing can be improved, then you also need to be willing to make changes, even large ones, even trying an entirely different approach. In the age of word processing, it is easy enough to make some back-up copies, and then play with your draft. Indeed, aggressive and effective revising involves a certain degree of playfulness: you have to be willing to try something else out, to fiddle, to start over.

Probably the worst attitude for revising is one of personal commitment to the way you said it the first time. It's always possible that the first draft is exactly perfect; but experienced writers will tell you that such a possibility rarely comes into being. It doesn't hurt to change your words. View it as a game, a puzzle, an opportunity to get something just right. That's the virtue of writing over speaking, isn't it? We get the chance to take it back and put it another way before the audience has even heard it. And if you don't like the changes, you can always put it back the way it was. Once you've assumed that your work can be changed and possibly improved, what should you do?

The Hard-to-Please Reader

Since most of us tend to have a certain affection for whatever we have managed to produce, there is a natural tendency to overlook problems and weaknesses, and to like whatever we see as we read over the current draft. Most readers, however, aside from your family and loved ones, are not necessarily so enamored with what you've written. Therefore, as your editing identifies words, sentences, or passages to work on, you should *imagine a hard-to-please reader*, one who doubts whatever you say unless it's obvious or nailed down, who is impatient for you to get to your point, who picks your writing apart at every opportunity. Imagine you are rewriting your draft *for that reader*, who is challenging your text in every way you can think of. Try to pull that tough reader in by acknowledging and anticipating alternative points of view, by tightening and brightening your prose, by eliminating distractions of any sort, including grammatical slip-ups. Especially look for assertions that might be controversial or ambiguous without more support or elaboration. What is quite clear to you may be very confusing to a reader.

How about an example? Let's see what happens when we look to rewrite a passage with our hard-to-please reader in mind. Here is the first paragraph from a student essay called "Where Did Man Really Come From?":

```
Ever since the beginning of modern times, people have
always wondered about the origin of humankind. For some, this
question of ancestry is a large puzzle with many missing
pieces. For others, the solution does not seem unreachable.
In fact, many feel that it is just a matter of time before
man's origins are completely revealed. Among these optimistic
```

```
people are anthropologists, archaeologists, and many other

scientists. Though anthropologists only have various clues

and guesses to work with today, they do have enough evidence

to give a rather clear picture of man's history and

development. Whether this evidence leads to the discovery of

man's origins in the future is still to be seen.
```

Through the eyes of its creator, or similarly uncritical sight, this paragraph may seem fine. It's okay. But what would our hard-to-please (htp) reader say about it? Let's take it sentence by sentence. As we move along, pay close attention to both the attitude and the strategies being employed in revising.

```
1. Ever since the beginning of modern times, people have

    always wondered about the origin of humankind.
```

Does this first sentence seem somehow familiar? Our htp reader has seen lots of essays that make some huge claim like this one, and the htp reader always wonders if the writer really knows what he or she is talking about. "Always" is one of those exhaustive terms, like "never," "completely," "entirely," "totally," "continuously" and others, that are sometimes used imprecisely, when the category really isn't exhaustive. Our htp reader would likely ask, "Do you really mean to say that human beings have devoted themselves solely to wondering about their origin, or that all their wondering has been so focused? I doubt it."

You've got to admit: "often" would be more accurate than "always." Similarly imprecise is "Ever since the beginning of modern times." What does that mean? "Quick," the htp reader says, "tell me exactly when did 'modern times' begin?" With television? The automobile? The steam engine? The rise of science? The recovery of classical civilization? Or classical civilization itself? Or maybe Egyptian civilization? With the discovery of fire? We have a span of many, many centuries here, and no way really to say within a few thousand years or so what the writer means.

Obviously the sentence should be edited, perhaps to say precisely when modern times began and people started wondering; but I suspect that the writer really means something like "I don't know when people started wondering about this, but I bet it was a good while ago." If that's the case, and the writer doesn't know, then maybe it would be better just to move on to the topic: "People have often wondered about the origin of humankind."

I fear that this sentence, however, still would not engage our htp reader, who would find this opening obvious: "Of course they have; it goes without saying. What's your point?" Remembering the advice about openings, the writer might well want to avoid this gesture toward a sweeping generalization at the outset, delete the first sentence, and move instead swiftly toward the topic. Do the next two sentences head that way?

```
2. For some, this question of ancestry is a large puzzle

    with many missing pieces.

3. For others, the solution does not seem unreachable.
```

These sentences do seem to be heading somewhere. Sentence 2 sets up one category for whom the origin of humanity is a puzzle with missing pieces, and sentence 3 sets up another category for whom "the solution" is not reachable. The htp reader, looking carefully, might wonder about these two categories: the writer says, "For some" and "For others," but are they really separate? Don't the people who think that a solution is reachable also necessarily believe that there is a large puzzle with many missing pieces to begin with? If they don't believe there is a puzzle, how can they think there may be a solution? The two categories of people, actually, would appear to be "those who think we can solve the question of man's origin" and "those who don't," since it is presumably a large puzzle for anyone. Thus far, one could argue, the paper really has said only this much:

> *Some people believe the question of mankind's origin, a large puzzle with many missing pieces, can be solved.*

In deleting the first sentence, we have lost the idea that this question has been around for some time (the writer isn't sure how long; maybe no one is), and so "the question of mankind's origin" might be altered to "the ancient question of mankind's origin." Also, an htp reader might worry over having a question "solved": questions are answered. The word "solved" really applies better to the puzzle, but the grammatical subject of "solved" is "question." Simply change "question" to "problem":

> *Some people believe the ancient problem of mankind's origin, a large puzzle with many missing pieces, can be solved.*

What will our htp reader have to say about the next two sentences?

4. In fact, many feel that it is just a matter of time before man's origins are completely revealed.

5. Among these optimistic people are anthropologists, archaeologists, and many other scientists.

What does sentence 4 do for the reader, htp or otherwise? If we already know that some people believe the problem can be solved, don't we also already know that they believe it is "just a matter of time" before that happens? Sentence 4 does shift from "some" to "many," which raises the question of what the writer really wants to say: what in fact is meant by "some" and "many"? Are these just vague because the writer doesn't know, or do they actually refer to something meaningful?

Sentence 5 suggests that the writer does have something fairly specific in mind, including "anthropologists, archaeologists, and many other scientists." Since sentence 4 doesn't provide additional information, it can be deleted. Here then is what we have so far:

> *Some people believe the ancient problem of mankind's origin, a large puzzle with many missing pieces, can be solved. Among these optimistic people are anthropologists, archaeologists, and many other scientists.*

Since sentence 5 essentially explains who "some people are," the writer might consider combining these two sentences, like this:

> *Some people, including anthropologists, archaeologists, and many other scientists, believe the ancient problem of mankind's origin, a large puzzle with many missing pieces, can be solved.*

1136   Appendix B / Editing and Revising

On the other hand, this revision loses the reference to "these optimistic people," a characterization the writer might want to keep, depending on the rest of the paper. Continuing:

```
6. Though anthropologists only have various clues and
   guesses to work with today, they do have enough
   evidence to give a rather clear picture of man's
   history and development.
```

Even our htp reader would have to say that this sentence conveys important information. Is there anything at all that isn't entirely clear about it? Perhaps the htp reader might wonder exactly what is meant by "clues and guesses." Unless you've studied anthropology, you might have no idea what is meant here.

There is also something slightly worrisome about what each part of the sentence says: the first part says anthropologists have only "various clues and guesses to work with today," but the second part says they can "give a rather clear picture of man's history and development." The htp reader may well wonder if the writer, by pointing to the "various clues and guesses" (which seem slight), intends to undermine the anthropologists' "rather clear picture" of mankind's story. Can one draw a rather clear picture of all human history from "various clues and guesses"? Does the writer mean to be ironic?

To decide, we need to know what sentence 6 is supposed to accomplish. It stands between the statement that some scientists believe the problem of humanity's origin can be solved, and this statement:

```
7. Whether this evidence leads to the discovery of man's
   origins in the future is still to be seen.
```

Examined in context, the connecting role of sentence 6 seems clear: some scientists believe the origin can be found; they have already explained the history and development (this is sentence 6); but it still isn't clear if an understanding of the history and development will lead to an understanding of the origin.

Now that we understand the function of sentence 6, the htp reader may wonder if it can be improved. Is everything clear? Can the reader say precisely what is being referred to? What, for instance, are the "clues and guesses"? Although readers with anthropological training probably have a good idea what these clues and guesses are, the rest of us probably don't. Are they related to the "large puzzle with many missing pieces"? Yes, upon consideration, it seems clear that the anthropologists are observing clues from and making guesses about the large puzzle with missing pieces. How might the writer help the reader to make this identification? The connecting role of sentence 6 could be made more explicit by continuing the puzzle comparison from the previous sentence, and by inserting the word "already," to highlight the progress made toward solving the problem mentioned in the first sentence. Here's how the revised passage looks so far:

Some people, including anthropologists, archaeologists, and many other scientists, believe the ancient problem of mankind's origin, a large puzzle with many missing pieces, can be solved. Though anthropologists only have bits and pieces of the whole picture today, they already can describe rather clearly man's history and development. Whether this evidence leads to the discovery of man's origins in the future is still to be seen.

In the last sentence, sentence 7, the phrasing of "the discovery of man's origins in the future" is worth noting because it is paradoxical: "origins in the future"? Does the phrase actually work, or is it just interesting but ultimately distracting? If it is determined to be distracting, "in the future" can easily enough be moved, like this: "Whether this evidence will lead in the future to the discovery of man's origins is still to be seen."

But the sentence is still puzzling to any reader who looks carefully, I think, because it seems to say that scientists will discover humanity's origins simply by continuing to look at "this evidence" they already possess. What seems more likely, and what I suspect the writer means to say, is that scientists may possibly find more evidence in the future that will help them understand the past better, perhaps even unlocking the secret of humanity's origin. What kind of evidence? No doubt the kind that anthropologists uncover, since they are mentioned: ancient artifacts, human and animal remains, ancient ruins and debris.

Since the idea in the last sentence seems so directly related to the puzzle metaphor, why not continue the image all the way through? So, changing the "past in the future" phrase, making clear that there may be more evidence uncovered, adding the puzzle metaphor, we arrive at this revised sentence:

Whether enough pieces will be found in the future to complete the puzzle and understand humanity's origin is still to be seen.

And here is the entire passage revised under the eye of our htp reader:

```
    Some people, including anthropologists, archaeologists,
and many other scientists, believe the ancient problem of
mankind's origin, a large puzzle with many missing pieces,
can be solved. Though anthropologists only have bits and
pieces of the whole picture today, they already can describe
rather clearly man's history and development. Whether enough
pieces will be found in the future to complete the puzzle
and understand humanity's origin is still to be seen.
```

To help you appreciate the significant difference between these two passages, compare the revision to the original:

```
    Ever since the beginning of modern times, people have

always wondered about the origin of humankind. For some, this

question of ancestry is a large puzzle with many missing

pieces. For others, the solution does not seem unreachable.

In fact, many feel that it is just a matter of time before

man's origins are completely revealed. Among these optimistic

people are anthropologists, archaeologists, and many other

scientists. Though anthropologists only have various clues

and guesses to work with today, they do have enough evidence

to give a rather clear picture of man's history and

development. Whether this evidence leads to the discovery of

man's origins in the future is still to be seen.
```

The rewrite is not only shorter (70 words versus 113), it is tighter and therefore easier to read. How was the revision created?

I've gone through the process here in such detail in order to show you, as much as possible, how it happened. Now it may seem, as you reflect on what has happened, that it has taken a tremendous amount of time and effort just to revise this one paragraph. Keep in mind that it doesn't take nearly as long to do something as it takes to describe what you're doing. Also, some paragraphs won't need as much work; but some will need more, and some will need to be ditched entirely. The most important thing to note here is that it does take a little patience to revise successfully. Beyond that, for the most part, you just have to become a hard-to-please reader, use your common sense, and try various ways of saying something, or saying something else.

Actually, you really need only to be willing to ask some basic and commonsense questions as you write and rewrite and write and rewrite and write some more:

- Is it clear? (Should it be?) Can it be clearer? (Should it be?)
- Is it concise? (Should it be?) Can it be more concise? (Should it be?)
- Is it engaging? (Should it be?) Can it be more engaging? (Should it be?)

In considering revising, we've pretty much been pretending it is a separate step that occurs after you have a draft. Such an illusion is helpful because it helps keep you from tinkering too much with what you're writing as you're first trying to get it down. But, in reality, revising occurs all along, not just as an ending activity. Writing and rewriting are pretty much indistinguishable in practice, as a writer works, even though they are usefully distinguished in theory.

Proofing

You've written and rewritten and edited and rewritten and written some more, and now your text is finished. Yet there is one more thing you need to do—and then you might need to do some more. You need to proofread your text, catching errors and infelicities, large and small, before they slip into print.

One of the difficulties in proofreading, however, once you've decided to do it, is that the paper is so familiar to you that you see what you think it says, not what is really on the page. A cure for this problem is to read the paper backward, proofreading the last sentence first, then the next-to-last sentence, and so forth. That way, it's harder for you to think about what the text is saying, and you're more likely to look at what it says—the spelling, the grammar, the complete thoughts, and such. You can also tell a good bit by reading your paper aloud. This strategy isn't as helpful for finding typing or spelling errors, but it helps you determine if sentences make sense and sound okay.

It's much better to make marks on your final copy, correcting errors or clearing up obscurities, than to turn in a beautiful paper with errors and obscurities remaining. Try to catch those problems before you print out or type up the final version, but most people do not mind edited copy—as long as the changes aren't too numerous or too messy. Very few manuscripts sent to publishers are typed perfectly; and if they are, the publisher's editors will very quickly mark them up, adding questions, marking the copy for the printer, making suggestions and corrections.

In addition, your teacher is almost certainly going to write on your paper, perhaps making some of the same corrections you might make. So, proofread and edit your final copy, and don't hesitate to make marks on it.

For proofreading texts, writers and editors have evolved over the years certain symbols. The marks shown here are taken from *Webster's Tenth Collegiate Dictionary*,

PROOFREADERS' MARKS

⌐ϑ or ૪ or ⁊ delete; take it out

◡ close up; print as o ne word

ϑ̸ delete and close up

∧ or ϒ or ⅄ caret; insert here (something

insert a space

eq # space evenly where indicated

stet let marked text stand as set

tr transpose change order the

/ used to separate two or more marks and often as a concluding stroke at the end of an insertion

⌐ L set farther to the left

⌐ set ⌐ farther to the right

⌒ set æ or fl as ligatures æ or fl

= straighten alignment

‖ ‖ straighten or align

✗ imperfect or broken character

▢ indent or insert em quad space

¶ begin a new paragraph

(sp) spell out (set 5 lbs as five pounds)

cap set in capitals (CAPITALS)

sm cap or s.c. set in small capitals (SMALL CAPITALS)

lc set in lowercase (lowercase)

ital set in italic (italic)

rom set in *roman* (roman)

bf set in boldface (**boldface**)

= or -/ or ⌃ or /H/ hyphen

$\frac{1}{N}$ or en or /N/ en dash (1965-72)

$\frac{1}{M}$ or em or /M/ em—or long—dash

∨ superscript or superior (∨ as in πr^2)

∧ subscript or inferior (∧ as in H_2O)

∨ or ∧ centered (◇ for a centered dot in p · q)

∧ comma

∨ apostrophe

⊙ period

; or ;/ semicolon

: or ⊙ colon

" " or ∨ ∨ quotation marks

(/) parentheses

[/] brackets

OK/? query to author: has this been set as intended?

⌐ or ⊥ [1] push down a ▮ work-up

⊙ [1] turn over an inverted letter

wf [1] wrong font; a character of the wrong size or csp. style

[1] The last three symbols are unlikely to be needed in marking proofs of photocomposed matter.

but these are standard: editors around the world recognize these symbols. The most useful ones are those for deleting, adding, and letting something stand in the original version after it has been changed. You should memorize these symbols and practice using them.

Format and Appearance

Common sense will help you here. You want the paper to make a good impression. It should be easy to read, and what you're saying should be the focus. If you're using a printer, be sure to use the best-quality setting. Don't make your reader strain to see what you're saying (after dozens of papers, small difficulties start to seem larger). Make all corrections clearly, with black or blue-black ink. If you're writing by hand, use your best handwriting, and skip lines.

About the paper: don't use onion-skin paper. It tends to float off the table with the least little breeze. Also, don't use a colored paper. Just plain white is strongly preferred. Follow whatever directions your teacher or supervisor or project leader has given you about the format, but be sure to put your name and the page number on every page. Also, a date on the first page is helpful, as is information about the course, just in case the paper gets separated from you or your teacher. (See the sample first page here.)

Jacob Schimpf
Professor Lindstedt
Paper #1
September 25, 1996

You should also make sure you have an effective title. All too often, students omit titles for their essays, or call them "Paper #2" or something equally unrevealing and unappealing. A title like "Melville's *Moby Dick*" or "Pope's *Dunciad*," for instance, tells the reader very little. Is the novel itself going to follow? Will the essay cover every possible aspect of the novel? Also, notice that the actual title is not enclosed in quotation marks unless it is a quotation; when you refer to a title, you do use quotation marks in order to tell the reader, "This is the actual title; I'm using the author's words, so it's in quotation marks." Most teachers do not want a cover sheet with only the title and your name. So the first page of a paper, usually, will look something like this:

Jacob Schimpf
Professor Lindstedt
Paper #1
September 25, 1996

Blowing Smoke: Cigarette Advertising and Health Issues

Testifying recently before the U.S. Occupational
Safety and Health Administration (OSHA), an
environmental health expert noted that a non-smoker who
works for one month near one smoker takes in as much
NDMA, which is particularly potent cancer-causing
compound, as someone who has smoked 75 cigarettes.[1] But
the R. J. Reynolds Company's recent advertising

And here's how the second page might look:

```
                                                        Schmipf 2

while "sidestream" smoke, the technical term for the smoke

that curls off the end of a burning cigarette, contains

higher levels of carcinogens than the "mainstream" smoke

that is exhaled by the smoker.
```

Having a meaningful title is really important. It's not just a formality; titles are very powerful. As your own experience as a reader will no doubt indicate, the title of a piece often determines whether or not you will read it. Perhaps students often ignore titles because they know that in a school setting the reader usually feels compelled to read what they have written no matter what. But it is certainly to your benefit even in such compulsory situations if the reader *wants* to read what you've written.

The title not only can draw readers in, but it also can prepare them for what is to follow. In some recent issues of *Esquire*, a magazine consistently noted for excellent writing, the following titles appear: "A Nation of Crybabies: What Japan Thinks of Us"; "Rocket Launches, Lust, Croquet, and the Fall of the West"; and "Inhuman Architecture, Bad Food, Boredom, and Death by Fun and Games." These titles range from being fairly descriptive ("What Japan Thinks of Us") to intriguingly strange (what do rocket launches, lust, and croquet have to do with the fall of the West?). They are designed to grab a reader's attention with odd juxtapositions and striking assertions.

In some contexts, however, your title should be entirely informational. The third quarter report for your company shouldn't be called "Trouble in Paradise" or "We're in the Money." Instead, "Reorganization Planned" or "Dramatic Increases in Earnings" would be more appropriate.

In your English classes, especially when you are writing argumentative essays (about literature or any other topic), your title should probably be informative and engaging but not cute. For instance, an article by Marshall Brown in *PMLA*, by some accounts the leading journal of literary scholarship, is called "Unheard Melodies: The Force of Form." The first part of the title is an allusion (an implied reference, specifically to these lines in Keats's *Ode on a Grecian Urn*: "Heard melodies are sweet, but those unheard/ Are sweeter"). Brown's use of this line is interesting because "form" is a part of a work that is not "heard." It is the arrangement of the parts, not their expression; form is an abstraction. Brown's title is then descriptive and interesting. This kind of two-part title that Brown uses appears fairly often, especially in academic discourse: one part (usually the first) provides an engaging and suggestive hook; the other part, usually following a colon, provides more information.

How can you find a good title? Your first resource is the paper itself. Is there perhaps a quotation that has a phrase you can use in your title? Is there a sentence of your own that can be converted into the title? Titles are often in one way or another responses to other works and their titles, so the more widely you read, the more materials you can draw on for your title.

For your convenience, here's a countdown checklist before your paper leaves the launchpad.

✔ Revising Checklist

- ❑ Check the subjects of your sentences.
- ❑ Look for phrases that can be replaced by a word or at least a shorter phrase.
- ❑ Look for prepositional phrases that can be collapsed or eliminated.
- ❑ Watch out for large words and stilted phrasings.
- ❑ Include comparisons.
- ❑ Replace weak verbs.
- ❑ Add details.
- ❑ Consider adding quotations, a startlingly short sentence, dashes, parentheses, or other engaging techniques.
- ❑ Check for gaps in coherence.
- ❑ Proofread, reading the paper backward.
- ❑ Use proofreader's marks.
- ❑ Make sure the paper is easy to read (lines are skipped, on plain white paper).
- ❑ Follow the assigned or appropriate format.
- ❑ Use an effective title.
- ❑ Have a chocolate-chip cookie (or other suitable indulgence) to celebrate!

Appendix C

Brief Biographies of Selected Poets

DANNIE ABSE (1923–), born in Cardiff, Wales, attended the University of Wales, and then did his medical training at King's College in London and at Westminster Hospital. He is both Jewish and Welsh, physician and poet. Drawing on his medical experience and private life, he has published ten volumes of poetry, plays, essays, and three novels. Now retired from medical practice, Abse has continued to write poetry.

DIANE ACKERMAN (1948–), author of six collections of poetry and a series of nonfiction books, is currently a staff writer at *The New Yorker*. She received her MFA and PhD from Cornell University and has taught at several universities. Praised by readers and critics alike, she received the Academy of American Poets' Lavan Award in 1985. Most recently, she was awarded the Art of Fact Award for Creative Nonfiction (2000) and had a molecule (*dianeackerone*) named after her.

MAYA ANGELOU (1928–) is a poet, essayist, historian, playwright, actress, director, producer, memoirist, and civil rights activist who is fluent in six languages (what does she do in her spare time?). She holds a lifetime appointment as Reynolds Professor of American Studies at Wake Forest University.

JOHN ASHBERRY (1927–) grew up on a farm near Lake Ontario. Graduating from Harvard in 1949 he went to France as a Fulbright Scholar from 1955 to 1957, then returned to France from 1958 to 1965 as an art critic. In 1976, Ashberry enjoyed the stunning achievement of winning the Pulitzer Prize, the National Book Award, and the national Book Critics Circle Award. His poetry is usually said to be both difficult and playful, and it has been compared to the art of Jackson Pollock, in the sense that the process of its construction is exposed, and also in the sense that its meaning, however forcefully asserted, remains elusive, a series of suggestive and fleeting moments and gestures. The author of twenty volumes of poetry, along with a novel, art criticism, and other items, he has taught at Brooklyn College and worked as art critic for *Newsweek*. His many awards include recognition as a MacArthur Foundation "genius."

MARGARET ATWOOD (1939–) was born in Ottawa and educated at the University of Toronto and Radcliffe College. Her poetic reputation was made by *The Circle Game* in 1966, which won the Governor General's Award. She has published poetry, novels, children's books, criticism, and short stories. She won another Governor General's Award in 1985 for the science-fiction novel *The Handmaid's Tale,* which was made into a major film. She lives and writes in Toronto.

WYSTAN HUGH AUDEN (1907–1973) was born in York, England, moved to Birmingham in childhood, and attended Oxford University (Christ's Church). At Oxford, Auden became friends with Christopher Isherwood and Stephen Spender, and his talent was quickly evident. By 1930, with a collection entitled simply *Poems,* Auden had established himself as a major new poet. After much travel and service in the Spanish Civil War, Auden moved in 1939 to the United States and became an American citizen. Producing essays, plays, and edited volumes, in addition to poems, Auden cultivated an interest in modern Christian theology. He lived in New York and Austria, dying in Vienna.

Well-known poet and playwright **AMIRI BARAKA** (LeRoi Jones) (1934–) received his BA from Howard University. His writing is known for its political flavor, reflecting on contemporary issues of ethnicity, class, and power. He has received the PEN/Faulkner Award, a Guggenheim Fellowship, and a grant from the National Endowment for the Arts. He has taught at various universities and has been a professor of Africana Studies at the State University of New York in Stony Brook since 1985.

APHRA BEHN (1640–1689), the author of twenty plays, is widely considered the first professional woman writer. She also published two collections of poetry and several novels. Before establishing herself as an author, Behn was a spy for King Charles II in Antwerp, Belgium, and later spent time in English debtor's prison. Behn is best known for her play *The Rover* and her novel *Oroonoko.* Most of her works deal with love, sex, and power, but very little is known about her private life.

LOUISE BOGAN (1897–1970) worked for thirty-eight years as a poetry critic for *The New Yorker.* She also served as Poet Laureate of the United States from 1945–1946. She lived in New York for the majority of her life, where she published three original books of poetry as well as several collections of her verse. Bogan is known for her mastery of formal verse, a stark contrast to the modern free verse of her contemporaries. Her poems deal with the themes of grief and love, silence and language.

JOHN BREHM is a freelance writer, a resident of New York City, and a visiting writer at Cornell University.

ANNE BRADSTREET (1612–1672) was born into an English Puritan household, and studied literature and history in five languages. When she was eighteen, her family sailed to America and settled in Massachusetts. There, Bradstreet endured the hardships of both wilderness and patriarchal power, which forced her to live entirely in the domestic sphere. Her poetry is extremely private, written mostly for herself. During her lifetime, only one volume of poetry was published, perhaps without her consent. After her death, an additional volume appeared.

GWENDOLYN BROOKS (1917–2000) is a Pulitzer Prize-winning poet, renowned for her innovative and socially conscious verse. Her work is featured in Chapter 12, where you'll find more biographical information along with a sampling of her work.

After traveling in France and Italy, BRUEGHEL (1520–1569) painted his major works, depicting peasant life vividly, in Brussels.

WILLIAM CULLEN BRYANT (1794–1878) published his first poem at age ten and composed his famous poems "Thanatopsis" and "To a Waterfowl" before age twenty-one. As an adult, Bryant practiced law before becoming the editor of the *New York Evening Post*. Throughout his lifetime he continued publishing poetry and critical essays, as well as respected translations of the *Iliad* and the *Odyssey*. He is considered to be a forefather of American Romanticism, given his belief in the principles of naturalism and spontaneity.

ROBERT BURNS (1759–1796), the most famous Scottish poet, worked mostly as a farmer during his lifetime. He was raised in a poor farming family, but his father educated him, exposing him to both Scottish and English literature. Burns is known for his use of Scottish dialect. In addition to publishing a successful volume of poetry, *Poems, Chiefly in the Scottish Dialect,* Burns journeyed throughout the Highlands collecting folk songs to publish. He died at the age of thirty-seven from severe rheumatic heart disease.

JOHN BURNSIDE (1955–) is a Scottish poet and novelist who is interested, among other things, in ecology and the environment. He has won the Scottish Arts Council Book Award for both *The Hoop* (1988) and *Common Knowledge* (1991), and his *Feast Days* (1992) was awarded the Geoffrey Faber Memorial Prize. His first novel, *The Dumb House* (1997), is the disturbing story of a father who locks up his children as part of a scientific experiment. He has been doing research, according to a recent interview in *The Guardian,* on a Scottish explorer who led an expedition to the North Pole.

THOMAS CAMPION (1567–1620) was a physician, composer, and poet (in Latin and English). Although his life is somewhat obscure, we know he practiced medicine in London, never married, and died with only twenty-three pounds to his name, despite having associated with the elites of King James's England.

MARGARET LUCAS CAVENDISH (1623–1673) was born in Essex, England, about seven years after Shakespeare's death, the eighth child of Sir Thomas Lucas and Elizabeth. She was taught only the basics of reading and writing, along with needlework, dancing, music, singing, and the other essential skills for upper-class ladies. But Cavendish had a powerful desire to write, producing poetry, essays, letters, plays, biography, autobiography, fiction, scientific treatises, even science fiction. She amazed her contemporaries with her outlandish clothing, her energy, her vanity, her extravagance. "Earth's Complaint" is clearly related to her imaginative interest in the "new" science that was just beginning to transform the world. More information about this fascinating woman and related links are available at the following site: http://www.luminarium.org/sevenlit/cavendish/.

HELEN CHASIN (1938–) taught English at Emerson College in Boston, after studying with Robert Lowell at Harvard. She has published two collections of poems, *Casting Stones* (1975) and *Coming Close and Other Poems* (1968).

AMY CLAMPITT (1920–1994) grew up in Iowa, graduated from Grinnell College, and worked in New York City as a secretary for Oxford University Press, an Audubon Society librarian, and a freelance editor. She began to focus on writing poetry in her forties, and her first collection, *The Kingfisher,* was published when she was sixty-three; it was followed by six books in the ensuing years. Winner of MacArthur, Guggenheim, and other prizes, she taught at the College of William and Mary, Amherst College, and Smith College.

LUCILLE CLIFTON (1936–) was born in Depew, New York, and her poetry both reflects and transcends the civil rights movement that she has lived through. Although she said "I am a black woman poet, and I sound like one," Clifton also said that she writes about "being human," and she invites anyone who has "ever been human" to "share" in her poetry. She had the good fortune to be in a writer's group with Ishmael Reed, who showed some of her work to Langston Hughes, who included her in his landmark anthology, *Poetry of the Negro* (1970). She has published at least ten books of poetry and sixteen books for children, winning the National Book Award, an Emmy, and many other prizes. Most recently she has been serving as Distinguished Professor at St. Mary's College of Maryland.

STEPHEN CRANE (1871–1900) was born in Newark, New Jersey. In his brief life, Crane was a war correspondent and writer, remembered today especially for *The Red Badge of Courage* (1895), an unforgettable story of the Civil War, and for *Maggie: A Girl of the Streets* (1893), although he also wrote poems and short stories.

COUNTEE CULLEN (1903–1946) graduated from New York University and went on to become one of the leading figures in the Harlem Renaissance. He published seven volumes of poems that reveal his increasingly conservative views on poetry. He often used the traditional sonnet form. Cullen received a Guggenheim Fellowship, which allowed him to travel between the United States and France. For the last twelve years of his short life, Cullen taught English, French, and Creative Writing at Frederick Douglass Junior High School in New York.

e.e. cummings (1894–1962) is best known for his play with language—his experiments with syntax, spelling, punctuation, and imagery in the eleven collections of poetry published during his lifetime. He received an MA from Harvard University and later won both a Guggenheim Fellowship and an Academy of American Poets Fellowship. During World War I, cummings volunteered to work as an ambulance driver in France, where he endured a three-month imprisonment in a French detention camp on false charges.

KWAME DAWES (1963–) was born in Ghana, raised in Jamaica, and studied in New Brunswick, Canada, where he also began to teach. He is a prolific writer, publishing twelve books of poetry, plays, an anthology of reggae poetry, as well as literary criticism. He currently directs the MFA Program in Creative Writing at the University of South Carolina.

ALAN DEVENISH's work has appeared in *Poetry Northwest* and *College English,* among other places. He and his wife live and teach in New York.

JAMES DICKEY (1923–1997), born in Atlanta, attended Clemson College in South Carolina in 1942, but his football and college career were cut short when he left after a year to enlist in the Air Force. Dickey flew combat mis-sions in the Pacific and read poetry. After the war, he enrolled in Vanderbilt University, and was encouraged to write poetry. He pursued graduate work in English at Vanderbilt, and then at Rice. After the Air Force recalled him to train pilots for the Korean War, he taught briefly at the University of Florida. When a poem he read to a women's group created a controversy over its propriety, Dickey resigned and went into advertising, in 1956. By 1961, Dickey had established himself as a poet, winning a Guggenheim Fellowship and publishing *Helmets* in 1964 and *Buckdancer's Choice* (National Book Award) in 1965. After serving as Poetry Consultant to the Library of Congress from 1966 to 1968, Dickey joined the faculty at the University of South Carolina, where he taught until his death. A major poet, Dickey also wrote several novels, including the blockbuster *Deliverance* (1970).

EMILY DICKINSON (1830–1885) lived almost her entire life in Amherst, Massachusetts. She attended Mount Holyoke Female Seminary for a year, but by the 1860s she had become reclusive, rarely leaving home and seeing few visitors, although she did read widely and carried on a lively correspondence with many people. She was a very productive poet, and has become a major literary figure, but in her own lifetime she was virtually unknown. Her first book of poems was not published until 1890, four years after her death. There are many excellent resources on Dickinson, including several recent and fascinating biographies. A good website (among many) can be found at http://www.iath.virginia.edu/dickinson/.

FRED DINGS (1962–) earned an MFA from the famed University of Iowa Writer's Workshop, and a PhD in Eng-

lish (creative writing) from the University of Utah. He has published poems in many prestigious journals and magazines, as well as two complete books of poems. He is currently teaching at the University of South Carolina.

GREGORY DJANIKIAN (1949–), born in Egypt, came to the United States at the age of eight. His first language is Armenian, although his father speaks seven other languages, and his mother speaks four others. Djanikian's parents, he has said, might have two or three different languages swirling around in a conversation, which has made for a certain difficulty with idioms: "an expression such as 'he's a tall drink of water' may find itself altered to 'he's a thin drinking glass,' something a little odder though perhaps no less descriptive" (in *The Best American Poetry 2000,* ed. Rita Dove [New York: Scriber, 2000], p. 215). Djanikian has published four books of poetry. Recently he has been directing the undergraduate creative writing program at the University of Pennsylvania.

JOHN DONNE (1572–1631), one of England's greatest poets, was born into a Catholic family in London in a period of political, scientific, and theological ferment and unrest. He studied at both Cambridge and Oxford, but he did not graduate in order to evade the required pledge of loyalty to the Anglican Church, the official Church of England. But after his brother died in prison, serving time for his Catholic faith, Donne did join the Anglican Church. In the 1590s, he studied law, served in a naval expedition against Spain (two years), and wrote love poems, satires, and some religious poems. In 1601 he secretly married the sixteen-year-old niece of his patrons. His displeased father-in-law had him imprisoned briefly and refused to provide any dowry or support. The

Donnes lived in poverty and dependency until Anne died in 1617, shortly after giving birth to their twelfth child. The *Holy Sonnets,* which include "Death, be not proud," are thought to have been written around this time. After joining, under some pressure, the Anglican ministry in 1615, Donne went on to become dean of Saint Paul's Cathedral in 1621, and one of England's most celebrated preachers.

RITA DOVE (1952–) is the youngest person and the only African American artist to hold the position of Poet Laureate of the United States. Dove has also received the Pulitzer Prize in Poetry and the Duke Ellington Lifetime Achievement Award. She is the author of seven collections of poetry, as well as a book of short stories, a novel, a collection of essays, a play, and a song cycle. She received her MFA from the University of Iowa and currently holds the chair as Commonwealth Professor of English at the University of Virginia in Charlottesville.

JOHN DRYDEN (1621–1700) was educated at Westminster and Trinity College, Cambridge. He moved to London in 1657 to begin his career as a professional writer. He was appointed Poet Laureate of England in 1668, but later lost the position because he refused to denounce his Catholic faith. In addition to poetry, Dryden wrote almost thirty works for the stage, as well as numerous critical essays. He is buried in Westminster Abbey next to Chaucer.

RICHARD EBERHART (1904–) was born in Minnesota, and his childhood on the large estate, Burr Oaks, provided him with themes and imagery for his later poetry. He studied briefly at the University of Minnesota, and then Dartmouth College, working after graduation in various jobs, including deckhand on a steamship. After earning a second degree from England's Cambridge University, and serving as private tutor for the son of King Prajadhipok (of what was then Siam), he entered Harvard University for graduate work, married, served in the Naval Reserve during World War II, and then worked for the Butcher Polish Company for six years. In the 1950s, he began to focus upon writing poetry and teaching (at a wide range of universities). His prizes include a Pulitzer, a National Book Award, the Frost Medal, and many others.

JAMES FENTON (1949–) was born in Lincoln, England. He began publishing poetry while earning his BA (1970) from Oxford University, and later worked as a theatre critic, then book reviewer for the *Sunday Times. Children in Exile* (1985) brought attention to his poetry, and *The Snap Revolution,* a book of essays (1986), and *All the Wrong Places: Adrift in the Politics of the Pacific Rim* (1988), a book of political analysis, indicated Fenton's range. He was appointed Professor of Poetry at Oxford in 1994.

ROBERT FRANCIS (1901–1987), according to Robert Frost, was the greatest of all the great neglected poets. From 1926 until his death, Francis lived alone in a three-room house in Amherst, Massachusetts, crafting engaging poems that (like the poems of Dickinson and Frost, also residents of Amherst) often have a surprising depth. He won the Shelley Memorial Award in 1939 and the Rome Award in 1957; he taught and lectured at various workshops, conferences, and universities. He served as Phi Beta Kappa poet at both Tufts University and Harvard, and taught at the American University in Beirut, Lebanon. He was the author of ten volumes of poetry, a novel, and an autobiography.

CAROLINE FRASER, formerly on the staff of *The New Yorker*, has published poems in the best literary magazines. She has also published (in 1999) a book severely critical of Christian Scientists' treatment of sick children, *God's Perfect Child: Living and Dying in the Christian Science Church.*

LOUISE GLÜCK (1942–), born in New York City, has won many prizes for her poetry, including the Pulitzer Prize for *The Wild Iris* in 1992. She teaches at Williams College and lives in Cambridge, Massachusetts. Her collection of essays, *Proofs and Theories: Essays on Poetry* (1994), an exceptionally readable exploration, won the PEN/Martha Albrand Award for Nonfiction.

ROBERT GRAVES (1895–1985) was born at Wimbledon, England. He saw much action in World War I, and was reported to have been killed in action at one point. Graves married Nancy Nicholson near the end of war, but she (Graves said) soon included him in her universal condemnation of men. After studying at Oxford, Graves moved to Majorca with the American poet Laura Riding, who revived him intellectually, leading to his extraordinarily productive career as a novelist, anthropologist, and poet.

THOM GUNN (1929–), born in England, moved to California (after studying at Cambridge) in 1954. Teaching at the University of California at Berkeley, Gunn has won many major prizes for his often-sensual poetry (more than thirty books), including MacArthur and Guggenheim Awards.

THOMAS HARDY (1840–1928), born in Dorset, England, studied architecture and wrote poems that no one would publish. Turning to the novel, Hardy produced a series of highly successful works, mostly tragic and increasingly dark. He continued, however, occasionally, to write poetry.

MICHAEL HARPER (1938–) studied creative writing at the University of Iowa, where he was the only African American student in his classes. He currently teaches at Brown University and serves as the Poet Laureate for the state of Rhode Island. Author of eight collections of poetry, Harper has received a fellowship from the Guggenheim Foundation as well as a grant from the National Endowments for the Arts. He has been nominated twice for the National Book Award.

SEAMUS HEANEY (1939–), the last of nine children, was raised on his parents' farm, Mossbawn, in County Derry in Northern Ireland. He began publishing under the name "Incertus" while a teacher at St. Joseph's College in Belfast, producing his first volume, *Eleven Poems,* in 1965. His breakthrough came the next year, when his first son was born, with *Death of a Naturalist,* which won several prizes. By 1973, Heaney had four books of poetry, three children, and enough fame to allow him to devote his time to giving many readings in England and the United States, writing poetry, editing two anthologies, and accepting more awards, including eventually the Nobel Prize for Literature in 1995. He returned to teaching in 1975, first at Carysfort College in Dublin, then at Harvard as a chaired professor, while continuing to publish important and popular poetry. His recent translation of *Beowulf* (2000) is stunning. "Digging" is one of a significant number of poems Heaney has written in memory of his father or mother.

ANTHONY HECHT (1923–) was born in New York City. After graduating from Bard College in 1944, he served in the army in Europe and Japan. He has published many well-received books of poetry, including *The Hard Hours* (1967), which won the Pulitzer Prize, one of many prizes his work has garnered. Hecht taught at the University of Rochester, and lives in Washington, D.C.

ROBERT HERRICK (1591–1674), born in London, became an ordained Anglican minister in 1623. He was removed from his position in Devon in 1647 because of his support for Charles I (overthrown, and in 1649 beheaded). His most important religious and secular writings appeared primarily in *Hesperides* (1648). Herrick was reinstated during the Restoration (1660).

GERARD MANLEY HOPKINS (1844–1889) was born in London and studied at Oxford, where he became a Catholic (influenced by the Oxford Movement) in 1866. He became a Jesuit priest in 1877, and Professor of Greek at Dublin in 1884. Not a single poem of his was published in his lifetime, and the first posthumous collection, in 1918, was not embraced. An expanded collection in 1930 was celebrated, however, and his work has continued to gain respect.

A.E. HOUSMAN (1859–1936) excelled at his studies of classical languages at Oxford, but he did not graduate after he failed his final exams. There is speculation that this failure resulted from his unrequited love for a fellow student. Despite this academic setback, Housman published several scholarly articles and established a good reputation. He was appointed as the Chair of Latin at University College, London, and later Kennedy Professor of Latin at Cambridge University. He published three collections of poetry during his lifetime.

LANGSTON HUGHES (1902–1967) was born in Joplin, Missouri, and raised by his grandmother. At age twelve, he moved to Lincoln, Illinois, to live with his mother and her husband. Although Hughes began writing poetry in high school, he went to Columbia University to study engineering, but he dropped out after a year (with a B+ average). He then traveled to Mexico, Africa, and Europe before moving to Harlem in 1924. *The Weary Blues,* his first book of poetry, was published in 1926 by Knopf, a major publisher, and Hughes went on to play a key role in the Harlem Renaissance, that flowering of artistic talent in the 1920s. Over his rich career, Hughes wrote sixteen books of poems, as well as novels, short stories, essays, plays, children's poetry, autobiographies (three of them), songs and musicals, and radio and television scripts. He also supported other black authors, editing four anthologies and encouraging writers in various ways. His home in Harlem is a cultural landmark by order of the New York City Preservation Commission.

TED HUGHES (1930–1998), one of the twentieth century's most controversial and important poets, was named the British Poet Laureate in 1984. Noted especially for his poems about animals, Hughes also wrote for children, including *The Iron Man* (1968; called *The Iron Giant* in the United States). He was married to Sylvia Plath, the noted American poet who committed suicide.

LUISA IGLORIA (1961–) is originally from Baguio City in the Philippines. She has received the National Book Award as well as eleven Palanca Awards (the Philippine equivalent of the Pulitzer Prize) for her poetry, short fiction, and essays. She previously published under the names Maria Luisa A. Cariño and Maria Luisa B. Aguilar. She currently teaches at Old Dominion University in both the English Department and the Institute for the Study of Minority Issues.

ROBINSON JEFFERS (1887–1962) was a nature-lover who studied forestry, medicine, and other subjects at various universities (after graduating from Occidental College in 1905). He married Una McCall Kuster in 1913, and they settled on the coast of California at Carmel, where Jeffers helped to build their famous Tor House. He later built himself the stone Hawk Tower as a retreat for Una and a playhouse for his sons. Jeffers wrote all his major poetry in this wild and dramatically beautiful setting. The website for the Tor House Foundation (www.torhouse.org) features pictures and other good links.

BEN JONSON (1572–1637), as Shakespeare's contemporary and competitor (Shakespeare was in the cast of Jonson's *Every Man in His Humour* in 1598), produced an influential group of plays and a host of imitators (the "tribe of Ben," as they were called).

JOHN KEATS, in his brief life (1795–1821), produced a major body of important poems, along with some of the most renowned letters in any language. Born in London, Keats studied medicine from 1815–1817, and published his first book of poems in 1817. He died in Rome, seeking relief from tuberculosis in the Italian climate.

GALWAY KINNELL (1927–) was born in Providence, Rhode Island, and studied at Princeton and the University of Rochester. He has won both the Pulitzer Prize and the National Book Award (for *Selected Poems* in 1980). In addition to a significant body of poetry, he has also published important translations. He has served as a chaired professor of creative writing at New York University, and is currently a Chancellor of The Academy of American Poets.

KENNETH KOCH (1925–2002) was born in Cincinnati, Ohio, and he studied at Harvard and Columbia University (where he was later a professor). Koch was associated with the New York School, who were inspired by the paintings of Jackson Pollock, Willem de Kooning, and Larry Rivers. Critics found his early work obscure, but often praised his later poetry for its clarity and humor. The winner of many literary prizes for his poetry, Koch also wrote plays, books for helping children write poetry, and a libretto.

PHILLIP LARKIN (1922–1985) was the author of nine collections of poetry, as well as a published scholar of American jazz. He graduated from St. John's College, Oxford, and made his living as a librarian throughout England and Ireland. He received the Queen's Gold Medal for Poetry and the Order of the Companion of Honour. He was offered the position of Poet Laureate for England but declined because he didn't want to lead a public life.

LI-YOUNG LEE (1937–), after moving to America from Indonesia, was educated at the universities of Pittsburgh and Arizona, and the State University of New York. Author of three collections of poetry, Lee received the Lamont Poetry Selection of the Academy of American Poets for his second book (in 1990). He is also the recipient of a grant from the National Endowment for the Arts and a Guggenheim Fellowship. Lee has taught at several universities, including Northwestern and the University of Iowa.

DENISE LEVERTOV (1923–1997), born in Essex, England, was the daughter of an Anglican parson who had been raised a Hasidic Jew. At age five, she had determined to be a writer; at twelve, she sent some of her poetry to T. S. Eliot, who responded with generous encouragements and suggestions; at seventeen, she published her first poem in *Poetry Quarterly.* She was a civilian nurse in World War II, and moved to New York City in 1948, having married Mitchell Goodman, an American writer. She was associated for a time with the Black Mountain group of poets (in North Carolina), but she moved beyond any allegiance in the 1960s, with a series of works focused on feminism and political activism relating to the Vietnam War. She published more than twenty volumes of poems, establishing her position as a major modern poet.

C. DAY LEWIS (1904–1972) was born in Ballintubber, Ireland, and studied at Oxford. As a teacher and writer, Day Lewis was involved in left-wing politics. He abandoned communism in 1939 and became Professor of Poetry at Oxford in 1951 (until 1956). He became Poet Laureate of England in 1968.

STEPHEN SHU NING LIU (1930–) was born in China and graduated from the University of Nanking in May 1948. After leaving China, he attended Wayland Baptist College, in Plainview, Texas, earning his BA in English in 1956. He received an MA degree from the University of Texas in Austin in 1959; his PhD from the University of North Dakota was awarded in 1973. He has taught at many schools, including the University of North Dakota and Clark County Community College.

RICHARD LOVELACE (1618–1658), one of the English Cavalier poets, led a highly political life. He came from a wealthy family and studied at Oxford. He was close to King Charles and a key figure in his court. After presenting a Royalist petition to Parliament in 1642, he was imprisoned for two months. During the English civil war, he served with the French army. Lovelace spent his family's fortune supporting his royalist sympathies and died in poverty in 1658.

AMY LOWELL (1871–1925) won the Pulitzer Prize in 1926, the year after her death, for *What's O'Clock.* Unfortunately, Lowell, whose lifestyle offended many critics of the time, never received such honors during her life. A masculine-dressing, cigar-smoking woman, Lowell was self-confident and a good businesswoman. She is credited for importing the Imagist movement to America, a school of poetry that prized economy of words, clarity of language, and a naturalness of form, avoiding traditional rhyme and meter.

ROBERT LOWELL (1917–1977) was born into a prominent Boston family. He attended Harvard, then transferred to Kenyon College, then did graduate work at Louisiana State University. Lowell was fortunate enough to study with three legendary figures, John Crowe Ransom, Robert Penn Warren, and Cleanth Brooks. His second book, *Lord Weary's Castle,* won the Pulitzer Prize in 1946, when Lowell was only thirty. Jailed during World War II, because of his antiwar activism, Lowell also protested vigorously against the Vietnam War. His marital and psychological difficulties (manic depression) increasingly became subjects for his poetry, and with *Life Studies* (1959) Lowell appears to have moved much modern poetry toward a more "confessional" mode. By the time he died suddenly of a heart attack at age sixty, he was established as one of the most influential poets of the twentieth century.

ARCHIBALD MacLEISH (1892–1982), born in Illinois, finished first in his class at Harvard Law School after attending Yale. He was an ambulance driver and field artillery captain in World War I, returning after the war to Boston to practice law. Increasingly, he desired to write poetry full-time, so he gave up his law practice in 1923 on the same day that he became a partner in his firm. He published four books in the next four years, and by 1932 he had won the Pulitzer Prize. MacLeish became politically active in the 1930s, working as an editor at *Fortune* magazine, as librarian of Congress from 1939–1944, and as an informational director in the War Department. After World War II, he moved into academia, teaching at Harvard (1949–1962) and at Amherst (1963–1967). He won a second Pulitzer in 1952 for his *Collected Poems,* and a third Pulitzer for *J.B.,* a play in verse, in 1958. He also won a National Book Award, the Bollingen Prize, and even an Academy Award for his work on *The Eleanor Roosevelt Story.* After this extraordinarily rich career, MacLeish died in Boston in 1982, more than ninety years old.

ELI MANDEL (1922–) was born in Estevan, Saskatchewan. He has published a significant body of poetry, winning the Governor General's Poetry Award in 1968, but he has also influenced Canadian poetry by editing anthologies and teaching young poets at the Universities of Alberta, Victoria, Toronto, and York.

CHRISTOPHER MARLOWE (1564–1593) was born at Canterbury, in Kent, England. After studying at Cambridge, he became Shakespeare's rival as a playwright, indicating what might be done in blank verse. Marlowe was stabbed in a tavern brawl, which may have been a cover for his murder.

CLAUDE MCKAY (1890–1948) was one of the earliest and most prominent figures of the Harlem Renaissance. He grew up in Jamaica and moved to the United States in 1912. His first book of poetry, published when he was twenty, heavily used Jamaican dialect. McKay was a proponent of political

writing, and his poetry reflects this; he traveled to England, the Soviet Union, and France to study political systems, including communism. He published three collections of poetry during his lifetime.

WILLIAM MEREDITH (1919–), born in New York City, has published nine books of poetry, winning the National Book Award, a Guggenheim, a Pulitzer, and other honors. Selected prose pieces have also been released as *Poems Are Hard to Read* (1991). He graduated from Princeton in 1940, served as an aviator in World War II, and taught at Connecticut College from 1955 to 1983.

W.S. MERWIN (1927–) was born in New York City. He won the Yale Younger Poets Award for his earliest poetry collection, *A Mask for Janus.* Since then he has won the Pulitzer Prize, the Bollingen Prize, and the Ruth Lilly Poetry Prize, among many others, as well as fellowships from The Academy of American Poets, the Guggenheim Foundation, the National Endowment for the Arts, and the Rockefeller Foundation. He is the author of more than fifteen books of poetry and twenty books of translation. He currently lives and works in Hawaii.

DIANE MIDDLEBROOK, after graduating from Washington University, earned her PhD in English from Yale in 1969. A poet and a scholar, Middlebrook has published an important biography of Anne Sexton and an excellent introduction to poetry, among other works. She taught at Stanford from 1966 to 2002, and is now Professor Emerita.

EDNA ST. VINCENT MILLAY (1892–1950) was born in Maine and attended Vassar College. In the 1920s in Greenwich Village, New York, Millay lived in an eight-foot-wide attic, writing in a variety of forms and winning the

Pulitzer Prize in 1923. In that same year, she married Eugen Boissevain, but she continued to be involved intimately with women.

PAUL MULDOON (1951–) was born in Northern Ireland, where he attended St. Patrick's College and Queen's University. After working for the BBC radio and television, he devoted himself to writing and teaching poetry in 1986. He became Professor of Poetry at Oxford at 1999.

HOWARD NEMEROV (1920–1991) was a poet and fiction writer. He was born in New York City and graduated from Harvard University. During World War II, he served as a pilot in the U.S. Air Force. He taught at several universities and was the Distinguished Poet in Residence at Washington University. Author of six collections of poetry, Nemerov received grants from the Guggenheim Foundation and the Academy of American Poets, as well as a grant from the National Endowment for the Arts. He was Poet Laureate of the United States from 1988 to 1990.

MICHAEL ONDAATJE (1943–) was born in Sri Lanka and moved to Canada by way of England in 1962. Most widely known for his novel *The English Patient* (1992), which became an acclaimed film, Ondaatje has published highly regarded fiction and poetry since the 1960s, and has taught at York University since 1971.

WILFRED OWEN (1893–1918) was educated in a strictly evangelical school in Great Britain. He began writing poetry when he was seventeen. He moved to the continent to teach, first in Bordeaux and then in the Pyrenees. He returned to England in 1915 to enlist in World War I. Owen was injured in 1917 and taken to a war hospital, where he wrote many of his best-known poems during his conva-

lescence. Owen returned to battle in June 1918 and was killed in November of that year. He was awarded the Military Cross for bravery.

DOROTHY PARKER (1893–1967) had her first poem published in *Vanity Fair* when she was twenty-one. Two years later, she was hired at *Vanity Fair,* where she became New York's only female drama critic. Parker contributed poetry and drama reviews to the premiere issues of *The New Yorker;* she later became the book reviewer for the magazine. In addition, Parker wrote screenplays, living for a time in Hollywood, and she won an academy award for cowriting *A Star Is Born.* Parker was inducted into the American Academy of Arts and Letters in 1959.

LINDA PASTAN was born in New York City; she graduated from Radcliffe in 1954 and earned an MA from Brandeis in 1957. Her poems have appeared in leading venues (*The New Yorker, The Atlantic Monthly,* and many others); her eleventh book of poetry, *The Last Uncle,* was published by Norton in 2002. She was Poet Laureate for the state of Maryland from 1991 to 1995 and worked on the staff of the prestigious Breadloaf Writers Conference for twenty years.

SYLVIA PLATH (1932–1963) was born in Boston and attended Smith College, where she graduated *summa cum laude* despite a breakdown after her junior year. In 1955 she won a Fulbright award and attended Cambridge University where she met and married the poet Ted Hughes (see page 1150), and had two children. She committed suicide in 1963, and the poems that were collected and published posthumously established her as a major poet. They are usually called "confessional" poems, reflecting an autobiographical introspection, an emotional intensity, and brilliantly startling imagery.

SIR WALTER RALEIGH (1552–1618) (also spelled "Ralegh") was born in Devon, England. After studying at Oxford, he became a favored courtier in Elizabeth I's court. Knighted in 1584, Raleigh organized three expeditions to America. He was imprisoned when Elizabeth discovered his affair with one of her maids-in-waiting, Bessy Throckmorton, whom he married upon his release. After Elizabeth's death, Raleigh's enemies convinced James I that he was traitorous, but his death sentence was commuted to life in prison. However, after Raleigh made an unsuccessful expedition to Orinoco, seeking a gold mine, the death sentence was reinstated and carried out.

DUDLEY RANDALL (1914–2000) had his first poem published when he was thirteen years old. He worked several jobs and served in the Army before completing his bachelor's degree in 1949, and going on to earn a Master's from the University of Michigan. Randall then worked as a librarian at several universities, including the University of Detroit, where he also served as poet-in-residence. He published five collections of poetry during his lifetime. In 1965, Randall founded Broadside Press to give a voice to African American writers.

JOHN CROWE RANSOM (1888–1974) graduated from Vanderbilt University at the age of fifteen and worked as a high school teacher until he moved to Oxford University on a Rhodes Scholarship to study classics. Ransom then returned to teach English and write poetry as a professor at Vanderbilt. In 1937 he moved to Kenyon College, where he founded *The Kenyon Review* and served as editor from 1939 to 1959. During his lifetime, Ransom won the Bollingen Prize for Poetry and received a National Book Award.

HENRY REED (1914–1986) was born in Birmingham, England, and graduated from Birmingham University. He served in the British Army for two years during World War II. He then worked as a freelance journalist, foreign office staff member, and professor at the University of Washington, Seattle. He also served as a broadcaster, journalist, and radio writer for the British Broadcasting Company (BBC).

ADRIENNE RICH (1929–) graduated from Radcliffe in 1951 and won the Yale Younger Poets Award for her first book. Author of nearly twenty volumes of poetry, Rich has also received the National Book Award, two Guggenheim Fellowships, and an Academy of American Poets fellowship; she was also the first-ever recipient of the Ruth Lilly Poetry Prize. Her poetry reflects her political and feminist involvement. In 1997, Rich declined a National Medal for the Arts because of her political views.

THEODORE ROETHKE (1908–1963) grew up in Michigan, spending time in his father's greenhouse, soaking up imagery and ideas that would influence his poetry. Although Roethke was unhappy attending the University of Michigan and Harvard and took ten years to write his first book of poems, he went on to teach at various universities and to publish a solid body of work. He won the Pulitzer Prize for *The Waking* in 1954. Not only has Roethke influenced other poets, but composers have also used his words. A musical setting of his poem "Snake," for example, is available online at http://www.pbs.org/wnet/ihas/poet/roethke.html.

GJERTRUD SCHNACKENBERG (1953–), born in Tacoma, Washington, has moved from the intensely personal poems of her first book, a moving memoir of her father that included "Supernatural Love," to an extended meditation on the story of Oedipus in her most recent book, the award-winning *Throne of Labdacus* (2001). Schnackenberg has won numerous awards, including the prestigious Guggenheim and National Endowment for the Arts fellowships, as well as the Rome Prize in Literature, the American Academy and Institute of Arts and Letters Award, and the Lavan Younger Poets Award.

PERCY BYSSHE SHELLEY (1792–1822) was the eldest son in a wealthy family in Sussex, England. Attending Eton College, then Oxford University, he published a Gothic novel, *Zastrozzi* (1810), some burlesque verse, and a collaborative volume of poems with his sister, Elizabeth. But he was expelled from Oxford and alienated from his father for his part in writing and circulating a pamphlet, "The Necessity of Atheism." At nineteen, Shelley married Harriet Westbrook, who was sixteen, and shortly thereafter published *Queen Mab: A Philosophical Poem,* which reflects the influence of William Godwin. By 1814, Shelley had fallen in love with Godwin's daughter, Mary (who would soon write *Frankenstein*). After Harriet committed suicide in 1816, Mary and Percy were married, but custody of Harriet's children did not go to Percy because of his "free love" philosophy. Mary and Percy's friendship with George Gordon, Lord Byron, deeply influenced the writing of all three. In one of the most remarkable periods of productivity in literary history, Shelley wrote his major works during the last four years of his life. He drowned, before turning thirty, while sailing off the coast of Italy in a storm.

"Stevie Smith" is the pen name of FLORENCE MARGARET SMITH (1902–1971), who was born in Hull, England, and worked in publishing in London before she began writing. After publishing a novel in 1936, she began a successful career as a poet with *A Good Time Was Had By All* in 1937.

GARY SNYDER (1930–) was born in San Francisco and has served as a professor of English at the University of California, Davis. He is the author or editor of sixteen books of poetry and prose, and the winner of numerous prizes, including a Guggenheim Foundation fellowship.

CATHY SONG (1955–) was born in Honolulu, Hawaii, and educated at Wellesley College and Boston University. She has taught at various universities, but her permanent home is in Hawaii.

ROBERT SOUTHWELL (1561?–1595), born in Norfolk, England, was raised a Catholic and became a Jesuit priest in 1584, assigned to missionary work in Anglican England. Southwell lived in various Catholic houses, keeping his religious work hidden. His poetry and prose were popular, and sold openly. Shakespeare, it is generally agreed, was familiar with Southwell's poetry. If he was involved in any political intrigue, the evidence has never surfaced, but in 1592 he was arrested, tortured on at least thirteen occasions, and spent three years in a filthy dungeon. He was finally hung and quartered in 1595.

WILLIAM STAFFORD (1914–1992) began graduate studies in English at the University of Kansas and then was drafted for the Vietnam War. He worked as a conscientious objector in various positions within the United States, completing, after the war, his MA and PhD at the University of

Iowa. Stafford received a National Book Award and fellowships from the National Endowment for the Arts and the Guggenheim Foundation. He taught at Lewis and Clark College in Oregon for thirty-two years.

WALLACE STEVENS (1879–1955), born in Reading, Pennsylvania, attended Harvard and earned a law degree from New York Law School. He then worked in the insurance industry, becoming vice president of Hartford Accident and Indemnity Co. in 1934. He began publishing poems in 1914, writing as he commuted to work and in the evenings, developing a startlingly original voice and style. His greatness was not widely recognized until near the end of his life, but it is clear in retrospect that *Ideas of Order* (1935), *The Man With the Blue Guitar* (1937), and *Notes Towards a Supreme Fiction* (1942) establish Stevens as a major poet.

MARK STRAND (1934–) won the Pulitzer Prize in 1999 for the poetry in *Blizzard of One* (1998), his tenth book of poems. He has also published children's books, translations, and essays on various topics, and he has won many of the most prestigious prizes for literature, including serving as Poet Laureate of the United States. He was born on Prince Edward Island in Canada, but he grew up in the United States and South America. The transcript of an interesting PBS interview, following the Pulitzer announcement, is available at http://www.pbs.org/newshour/bb/entertainment/jan-june99/pulitzer_4-15.html.

JONATHAN SWIFT (1667–1745) was born in Ireland and graduated from Trinity College in Dublin with a Masters degree. He worked as a secretary and tutor in England, but became increas-

ingly involved with religious affairs when he returned to Ireland in 1699. He served as an emissary for Irish clergy in London and later became Dean of St. Patrick's Cathedral. He wrote political and satirical pieces for journals and took over the Tory journal *The Examiner* in 1710. Swift suffered, in his later years, from some kind of dementia (possibly Alzheimer's) and died at the age of seventy-eight.

ALFRED, LORD TENNYSON (1809–1892) was born in Lincolnshire, England, and studied at Cambridge. His first poems, which appeared in 1829, did not find a very receptive audience, but a revised collection in 1842 established him as a major poet. In 1850, he became Poet Laureate (succeeding Wordsworth), and continued to write poems and plays until his death.

DYLAN THOMAS (1914–1955) published his first volume of poetry at the age of twenty. He had already been fired from a reporter position at the *South Wales Evening Post,* but he then began working as a radio broadcaster for the BBC in London. This occupation suited him, and he made a meager living as a freelance broadcaster. During World War II, after he was evaluated as medically unfit to serve, Thomas worked with a documentary film unit. Thomas died at the age of thirty-nine from alcohol poisoning. He was the recipient of the Foyle Prize for literature.

CHARLES TOMLINSON (1927–), born in Stoke-on-Trent, England, studied at Queen's College, Cambridge, and taught at the University of Bristol for thirty-six years. He began as a painter, but he published his first book of poems in 1951—followed by over twenty more, often dealing with various aspects of nature and the environment. He is also a noted translator and scholar.

DAVID WAGONER (1926–), born in Massillon, Ohio, has published ten novels and fourteen volumes of poetry. He is the editor of *Straw for the Fire: From the Notebooks of Theodore Roethke, 1943–63* (1972), and also editor of the influential literary magazine, *Poetry Northwest,* which he began editing in 1966. *The Escape Artist,* a novel, was made into a movie by Francis Ford Coppola, and Wagoner's poetry has been honored by many awards. A photo, more information, and other poems can be found at www.poets.org.

DEREK WALCOTT (1930–) was born in the West Indies. He graduated from the University of the West Indies, before receiving a Rockefeller Fellowship to study American drama in 1957. Walcott founded the Trinidad Theatre Workshop, and his own plays have been widely and successfully produced. Among the many honors for Walcott's poetry, plays, and essays: the 1992 Nobel Prize in Literature, the Queen's Medal for Poetry, and a MacArthur Foundation "genius" award. He teaches creative writing at Boston University in the fall and lives in St. Lucia the rest of the year.

WALT WHITMAN (1819–1892) was born and raised in New York. He taught for three years before becoming a journalist, founding a weekly newspaper, *The Long-Islander,* and editing other various newspapers, including the Brooklyn *Daily Eagle* and the New Orleans *Crescent.* While a journalist, he published the first edition of *Leaves of Grass.* He would publish seven more editions of this work as well as four other collections of poetry during his lifetime. He later worked for the

Department of the Interior in Washington D.C., making a meager living as a clerk.

RICHARD WILBUR (1921–) has been a New Englander for most of his life, born in New York City and teaching at various universities there (Harvard, Wellesley, Wesleyan for twenty years, Smith for ten). In World War II, Wilbur was transferred from cryptography school to the front lines, reportedly because of his involvement in leftist politics, and he saw action in Italy, France, and Germany. He has been a prolific poet and translator, winning just about every major award possible, including being named the second Poet Laureate of the United States. A particularly revealing interview with Wilbur is available online at http://www.theatlantic.com/unbound/poetry/wilbur.html.

WILLIAM CARLOS WILLIAMS (1882–1963), born in Rutherford, New Jersey, decided in high school to be a writer and a doctor. After attending the University of Pennsylvania Medical School, he returned to his hometown to practice pediatric medicine and write. Also a novelist, essayist, and playwright, Williams is best known for his poetry, which deals primarily with fresh perspectives on everyday life. He won the Pulitzer Prize for Literature in 1963, the same year he died.

WILLIAM WORDSWORTH (1770–1850), born in Cockermouth in northwest England, educated at Cambridge, altered the history of English poetry with his poems and writings about poetry. After an affair in France in 1790 with Annette Vallon, which resulted in a daughter, Wordsworth lived with his sister, Dorothy, and developed the ideas that would help usher in Romanticism. He married Mary Hutchinson in

1802, but his sister remained his life-long companion.

JAMES WRIGHT (1927-1980), after graduating from Kenyon College, won the Yale Younger Poets Award before completing his PhD at Washington University. He then received a Fulbright scholarship and studied in Vienna for a year. Wright received the Pulitzer Prize for his *Collected Poems* and a Guggenheim Fellowship. He taught at Hunter College for fourteen years and was the author of eleven volumes of poetry.

WILLIAM BUTLER YEATS (1865-1939), born in Dublin, Ireland, turned to writing poems and plays after training as an artist. He received the Nobel Prize for Literature in 1923, and his best-known poems are from the 1920s. He served as a senator of the Irish Free State from 1922-1928.

Glossary of Literary and Critical Terms

Absence   Deconstruction in particular draws attention to the significance of what is missing in a text. What is absent is sometimes as telling as what is present. The idea of absence can be useful, however, in any critical approach. A reader-response approach may note how missing information, for instance, must be supplied by the reader.

Absurd   As a critical term, the "absurd" is most often associated with the twentieth-century theatre of the absurd. Conventions of plot are violated as the meaninglessness of life is depicted. Samuel Beckett's *Waiting for Godot* (1954) is an early and influential work in the absurd tradition.

Accent   In poetry, the emphasis or stress placed on a syllable. In the phrase "Dallas Cowboys," English speakers place the accent on "Dal-" and "Cow-." *See meter.*

Act   An act is a significant portion of a play. Playwrights divide plays into acts for many reasons—to allow for a shift in the setting, to signal the end of one sequence of events and the beginning of another, to suggest the passage of time, and much more. Acts may be divided into scenes. Shakespeare followed the Roman practice of dividing plays into five acts, but later playwrights have used four, three, or two acts. And some have preferred to ignore acts altogether, dividing the action into scenes only.

Affective Fallacy   A key term in New Criticism, referring to the confusion between what a poem is and how it affects a particular reader. It is a fallacy, William Wimsatt and Monroe Beardsley argued in 1946, to focus on a work's effects. Compare this term to the "intentional fallacy," also coined by Wimsatt and Beardsley. It is also a fallacy, they argued, to conflate the poem and the author's intentions. The poem itself should be the object of the reader's attention.

Affective Stylistics   Stanley Fish's invented term for a way of reading that embraced the affective fallacy: The literary work is the response to it, Fish argued in 1970, as he revealed how various works guide the response of attentive readers.

African-American Criticism   A way of approaching texts, including but not limited to literary texts, that focuses upon the representation and participation of African-Americans. Like feminist criticism, African-American criticism can draw upon many disciplines, including history, biology, philosophy, psychology, and anthropology.

Allegory   A kind of story or description in which characters, or objects, or even actions stand for abstract ideas. A character whose name is Susan Student might be entertained at a bar by Danny Drinking and Lucy Laziness.

Alliteration   Repeated sounds in words. Usually alliteration refers to the repetition of consonant sounds at the beginning of words, as in Danny Drinking and Lucy Laziness.

Allusion   An allusion is a kind of reference that depends upon the reader's prior knowledge. If someone says that a fighter can "float like a brick and sting like a noodle," he is alluding to Mohammed Ali's famous declaration that he could "float like a butterfly" and "sting like a bee."

Ambiguity   This term points to the possibility of more than one meaning being assigned to a particular text. A text that is subject to more than one plausible interpretation has ambiguity. Ambiguity is not a virtue in many texts (medical textbooks, newspaper articles, instructions). But in literary texts, especially for New Critics, multiple meanings are often valued as part of the richness of literature. As William Empson put it in *Seven Types of Ambiguity* (1930), "The machinations of ambiguity are among the very roots of poetry."

Anabasis   A Greek term, literally "a going up," which refers to the rising action leading to the climax in a play or story.

Anachronism   Literally "back-timing" in Greek, this term refers to something that is out of place in time. For instance, Shakespeare refers to the clock in *Julius Caesar* (the clock had not been invented in Caesar's day).

Anagnorisis   The term used by Aristotle to indicate a character's moment of understanding. It is the Greek word for "recognition."

Anagram   The rearranged letters of one word forming another word: for instance, "rats" is an anagram of "star."

Analysis   The careful assessment of the parts of a work and how they relate to each other. An analysis is a close study.

Anapest   Two unstressed syllables and one stressed. Coleridge offers this illustration in his *Metrical Feet* (I insert the slashes to divide the anapests): "With a leap / and a bound / the swift A/napests throng." "With a leap" offers two unstressed syllables ("with a") and one stressed ("leap"), and the rhythm of the rest of the line repeats that sequence. *See meter.*

Anaphora   The technical term for the repetition of a word at the beginning of successive phrases or sentences.

Antagonist   The character (or other entity) who opposes the main character, the protagonist. In Amy Tan's "Two Kinds," the antagonist is the narrator's mother. In *Hamlet,* the antagonist is Claudius.

Anticlimax   What comes after the *climax.* An anticlimax can be amusing: The hero slays a dragon without suffering a scratch, then returns to his castle and cuts off his finger slicing up a turkey. An anticlimax can also be awkward, when a story goes on even though the main issue has been resolved.

Antihero   A protagonist who is lacking in heroic qualities—who is, in fact, the opposite of heroic.

Antistrophe   The stanza that follows the strophe. In a Greek tragedy, the chorus moved from right to left, singing the strophe; they then moved from left to right while singing the antistrophe.

Antithesis   The opposition of two ideas.

Apostrophe   A literary device whereby a speaker addresses some one or thing who is not physically present or capable of responding. Keats speaks to a star in "Bright Star"—an apostrophe.

Archetype   A symbol that is (supposedly) universally recognized. Some would argue that the snake is an archetype of evil.

Aside   The dramatic convention that allows a character to speak to the audience while other characters apparently do not hear what is being said.

Assonance   The repetition of vowel sounds.

Aubade   A poem or song dealing with lovers parting at dawn.

Authorial Intention   What an author intends for a reader to understand. Different critical approaches give different weight to what an author may have intended.

Autobiography   The story of the writer's own life.

Ballad   A poem or other work that is designed to be sung, and that tells a story.

Ballad Stanza   Four lines, alternating eight and six syllables. The second and fourth lines rhyme, usually.

Bathos   Absurdly inflated language. When a writer unsuccessfully strives, or pretends to strive, for an elevated, noble, sublime emotion—the result is bathos.

Bildungsroman   A novel about growing up, gaining insight and maturity.

Binary   Having two parts. In deconstruction, binary oppositions are crucial to the making of meaning. We don't know "bad" unless we know "good" also.

Biographical Criticism   The critical approach that focuses on using information about the author to help illuminate his or her work.

Blank Verse   Unrhymed verse. Usually "blank verse" is used to mean unrhymed iambic pentameter, which is generally considered to be the poetic meter closest to spoken English. *See Iambic Pentameter.*

Bucolic   Related to the *pastoral*. From the Greek word for "cowherd." "Bucolic" poems have to do with rural scenes or styles.

Cacophony   The opposite of *euphony*. A cacophony is an uproar, a mixture of harsh and unpleasant sounds.

Caesura   A pause within a line of poetry. In marking the rhythm, a caesura is indicated by this symbol: ‖

Canon   In the Christian tradition, those books of the Bible that are considered to be divinely inspired. Since the fourth century, "canon" has referred to these accepted works. In literary study, "canon" refers similarly to those works that are widely accepted as "classics." Various branches of political criticism, in the past few years, have challenged the traditional canon, bringing neglected works (often by women and minorities) to the attention of readers.

Carpe diem   Literally, "snatch the day." This Latin phrase appears in Horace's *Odes* and other classical sources, and it has come to stand for an attitude of enjoying oneself now, while it's still possible. In post-classical literature, especially in Christian and moral writings, the *carpe diem* theme takes on a very different twist, as readers are exhorted to seize the present moment in order to prepare for eternity.

Catharsis (also Katharsis)   The effect of tragic drama upon an audience. The Greek term means "purgation" or "purification," and it is used by Aristotle in *The Poetics* (about 330 BCE) to describe the beneficial effects of viewing a tragedy. Instead of feeling depressed or appalled by the tragic events they witness, the audience feels exalted or relieved at the end of a tragedy. The idea of catharsis, Aristotle believes, explains why: By experiencing the emotions of pity and fear as they view a tragedy, the audience is able to purge or purify these feelings (Aristotle is not clear which—or is it both?).

Character, Characterization   A character is an agent or actor in a literary work. Most characters represent human beings, but dogs, aliens, Death, or any entity can be a character. Characterization concerns how the attributes of the character are conveyed to the reader. The writer may *tell* the reader about the character; or, put the character in motion and *show* the reader. Characters are typically divided into *flat* or *round* ones. The critic E. M. Forster first made this distinction, noting how some characters represent one idea or quality (and hence are flat), while other characters are quite complex and realistic (round). Flat characters may be considered *caricatures,* simplistic distortions of a real person. They may also be called *stock* characters, fitting predetermined and stereotypical notions (the sleazy lawyer, the dumb blonde, for instance). Characters who change are considered to be *dynamic,* and critics may consider whether their evolution is motivated and plausible. Characters who do not change are said to be *static.*

Chiasmus   The technical term for a verbal pattern in which the key elements are expressed, then reversed. For instance: "In war, he's a lover; in love, he's a warrior."

Chorus   From the Greek word for "dance," the chorus in a Greek tragedy was a group of performers who, in some plays, commented on the action, and in other plays participated. The chorus in many plays appears to have moved across the stage and back (strophe and antistrophe) in a choreographed fashion while chanting. Roman theatre copied the idea of a Chorus, but later dramatists have rarely used a chorus—although important exceptions have used a single actor as a chorus, commenting on the action.

Class   Various kinds of political criticism focus on class in literary works—how it is represented, how it is criticized or reinforced. Class may be the result of birth, but in modern times is more often an economic or social matter. Karl Marx distinguished two classes in capitalist cultures, the proletariat and the bourgeoisie. Other schemas separate blue-collar from white-collar workers; or middle class from upper and lower class—or even "working class."

Cliché   An expression that has been overused. "Cool as a cucumber" and "hot as a pistol" were once fresh and arresting comparisons, but they have become stale.

Climax   The point in a plot when the action reaches the highest point of tension. The climax is related to the *crisis,* which is the turning point in the action.

Close Reading   Popularized by the New Critics, close reading is the careful attention to the details of a work, noting the richness of their relationship. Close reading is sometimes called *explication.*

Closet Drama   A play that is meant to be read, not performed. Such plays are often written in verse. John Milton's *Samson Agonistes* is a famous example of a closet drama.

Comedy   Any work that is amusing. Comedy, which ends happily, is usually contrasted with tragedy, which ends in disaster. In comedies, events threaten to turn out disastrously, but do not. In tragedy, it may appear that dangers and problems can be averted, but they are not. Comedy is often divided into high comedy, which is primarily verbal, and low comedy, which stresses physical, slapstick humor. *Seinfeld,* the television show, by this distinction, was largely a "high" comedy, but the comic antics of the Kramer character brought a balancing "low" humor. Other kinds of comic works include: sentimental comedy, which follows the amusing aspects of a troubled love affair; satiric comedy, which advances some social commentary by means of humor; comedy of manners, which focuses on the rules of behavior for men and women; comedy of intrigue, which features a complex plot with twists and surprises; and farce, which presents absurd and outrageous clowning.

Comic Relief   Comedy that interrupts a serious scene or work, providing "relief" from the tragic tension. A classic example is the gravedigger's scene in *Hamlet.*

Conceit   An extended and unlikely comparison between two things. In "A Valediction: forbidding mourning," John Donne compares two lovers' souls to compasses—a startling analogy.

Conflict   Refers, as a literary term, to a struggle between characters or forces. Conflict drives the plot.

Connotation   The implied meanings or associations of a word, as opposed to the literal meaning. The connotations of a word may be altered or colored by the context of its use. The word "clever," for instance, may be a positive or a shady quality, depending upon the context of its use.

Consonance   A kind of rhyme created by the repetition of consonant sounds, separated by different vowels: "sit" and "sat" for instance.

Convention   A practice in a literary work that is understood by an audience because it has, over time, become a familiar technique. Harp music and a wavy picture have come to mean that the audience is about to see a flashback, or a shift from the real world to a dream world, or some other similar shift. This convention can be exploited for comic effect, as in the Wayne's World segments from *Saturday Night Live.*

Couplet   Two lines of rhyming poetry, one after the other. Browning's famous poem, "My Last Duchess," is written in couplets.

Crisis   The turning point in a plot. Complications pile up until there is a decisive turn toward the plot's resolution: The technical term for that turning point is the crisis.

Criticism   Literary criticism is simply discourse about literature. Criticism may have many different aims. Certainly, one possible goal of criticism is helping other readers better appreciate, understand, or evaluate a literary work, or grouping of works. But criticism, especially in the last few decades, has played a significant role in cultural analysis and political activism. Criticism has also aspired to make philosophical contributions, using literary analysis as the occasion for broader concerns. And some literary critics, clearly, have endeavored to entertain their readers, closing the gap between creative writing and critical writing.

Cultural Studies   An emerging field that lacks a distinctive theory, subject area, principle, or method. "Culture" can encompass virtually anything (from physics to rock music), and the approaches used in cultural studies have been borrowed from existing fields—art theory, literary criticism, linguistics, psychology, anthropology, sociology, political science, philosophy, musicology, and more. What is distinctive about cultural studies appears to be an interest in power—in understanding how any given aspect of "culture" relates to political power and social action. More specifically, the umbrella of cultural studies has consistently been employed to advance a radical or progressive set of political commitments and actions. In this sense, cultural studies is simply the term for one kind of political criticism in a wide range of fields. That kind of political criticism is the subset devoted to analyzing and altering structures of power, especially in first-world capitalist societies.

Dactyl   A kind of meter that has one stressed syllable and two unstressed syllables. One of the most famous poems to employ a dactylic meter is Tennyson's "Charge of the Light Brigade," which contains these lines:

> Cannon to right of them,
> Cannon to left of them,
> Cannon in front of them
> Volleyed and thundered.

The first three lines each contain two dactyls—a stressed then two unstressed syllables. The Beatles' song "Lucy in the Sky with Diamonds" is primarily dactylic in its rhythm.

Deconstruction   Rigorously close and often playful reading of a text, exposing how a text fails to make sense, or makes contradictory senses, or makes some unexpected or startling sense.

Denotation   The literal meaning of a word, as opposed to the *connotation*, or associative meanings.

Dénouement   French for "unknotting," this term refers to that part of the plot when the complications are resolved.

Deus Ex Machina   Latin for "a god from the machine," referring to the practice of resolving the conflicts in a play by lowering an actor onto the stage, who, playing the part of a god, will save the day. Such a rescue is not considered a feature of the best playwriting, as it allows the writer as well as the characters to escape by implausible means.

Dialect   Speakers in different regions have different accents, different vocabulary, even different sentence structures. Social and economic class, as well as educational level, may also be reflected in one's language. Writers use dialect to convey efficiently information about a character who is talking.

Dialogue   Talk between and among characters. Skillful writers can often use dialogue to convey necessary background information as well as to advance the action.

Diction   The writer's choice of words. Diction is usually divided into informal, middle, and formal diction—ranging from ordinary, everyday language to elevated, ornate language. A distinction is also made between poetic diction and common speech.

Différance   A term invented by the French theorist Jacques Derrida, it suggests both "to differ" and "to defer," suggesting the slipperiness of meaning. Meaning is always deferred, never fully and entirely arriving with the reader. Also, statements differ from themselves, as the process of deconstruction can tease out conflicting meanings from a text.

Dirge   A funeral poem or song, commemorating a person's death. An elegy may mourn an individual or a general loss, and an elegy is also thought of as a more formal work than a dirge.

Double Rhyme   A rhyme involving two syllables—stressed, then unstressed. For instance, "standing" and "landing."

Drama   From the Greek word "dram," which means "to perform." A drama is any work meant to be performed on a stage—although, to be sure, a *closet drama* is performed on the mind's stage.

Dramatic Irony   The gap between what a character believes and what the audience knows. When Oedipus vows to hunt down the murderer no matter what, the audience knows—as he does not—that he is talking about himself.

1166 Glossary of Literary and Critical Terms

Dramatic Monologue   A lyric poem in which the speaker is addressing a silent listener. The speaker thus reveals the situation, the events, everything—including perhaps the character of the listener.

Dramatis Personae   The list of characters in a play. In the printed play, such a list precedes the text of the play, and may give brief descriptions of each character.

Dystopia   Greek for "a bad place," the opposite of *utopia,* an ideal place. In more than one *Star Trek* episode, what appears to be a utopia later turns out to be a dystopia.

Eclogue   A pastoral poem usually involving a conversation between two shepherds.

Electra Complex   In Greek myth, Electra seeks revenge for the death of her father, Agamemnon, by plotting the death of her mother. Hence, the Electra Complex is used to describe the daughter's version of the *Oedipus Complex.*

Elegy   A poem mourning the loss of someone, something, or loss more generally.

Encomium   A poem that praises a person, place, event, or thing.

End Rhyme   The most common kind of rhyme in poetry: The last word of a line rhymes with the last word of the next line. In internal rhyme, words within the lines create the rhyme.

End-Stopped Line   Having a pause at the end of the line. In poetry, lines are either end-stopped, or they exhibit *enjambment,* continuing without pause from one line to the next.

English Sonnet   Also called a Shakespearean sonnet, the English sonnet has fourteen lines with the following rhyme scheme: abab cdcd efef gg.

Enjambment   The continuation of a poetic statement from one line to the next. Enjambment is distinguished from end-stopped lines.

Epic   An epic is a major poem telling the story of heroic deeds. Epics are often associated with the character of a nation or group of people.

Epigram   A brief witty poem or group of lines. Epigrams in classical times were inscriptions placed on tombstones or buildings.

Epigraph   Lines that are printed at the beginning of a work, or the beginning of a section of a work. Epigraphs are usually quotations from an earlier work.

Epilogue   The ending part of a work. In a play, the epilogue may be a speech by an actor following the end of the action, and often commenting on the play and asking for a generous appreciation by the audience.

Epiphany   Originally a term used to indicate the incarnation of divinity, but introduced into literary studies by James Joyce, who uses "epiphany" to refer to a sudden profound insight. When Joyce's character, Stephen Dedalus, suddenly understands (or believes he understands) the essence of some matter, he has an epiphany, "a sudden spiritual manifestation" revealing the deeper meaning of the everyday.

Episode, Episodic   An episode is a unit in a larger narrative. An episode can stand alone to some degree, but it also assumes that the audience will experience additional episodes. An episode of a television show has an ending that (usually) resolves the problems raised in a particular story, but the particular episode is more meaningful and enjoyable when it is seen as part of a larger "work." A particular episode of *Seinfeld,* say, is self-contained but part of a larger whole. An episodic work is one, then, that exhibits a series of units that are both independent and connected. The audience should feel satisfied at the end of an episode, but also eager to return for the next episode.

Epistolary   Relating to correspondence (that is, letters or epistles). A novel that unfolds its story by means of letters exchanged between and among characters is said to be "epistolary."

Euphony   The opposite of cacophony, "euphony" refers to language that is harmonious and pleasant.

Exegesis   Explanation; the close reading and analysis of a text.

Exposition   That part of a work that provides necessary background information. Usually, exposition comes near the beginning of a work. More skillful writers (usually) provide exposition in an unobtrusive way, providing the needed background as the story is unfolding.

Fable   A story with a moral. A fable is usually brief, and may be in verse or prose. The moral may be explicitly stated or clearly implied. Aesop's *Fables* are the most famous.

Falling Action   That part of a plot following the crisis and climax, leading to the resolution.

Farce   Comedy that is based on absurd situations, physical humor, crude language. Farce is thought of as "low" comedy: its apparent goal is not to stimulate the audience intellectually, but simply to evoke laughter.

Feminist Criticism   A way of approaching texts, including but not limited to literary texts, in which the representation and participation of women is focused upon. Feminist criticism can draw upon many disciplines, including history, biology, philosophy, psychology, and anthropology. See *Gender Criticism.*

Fiction   Any narrative that is in some respect a work of the imagination. To oppose fiction and reality, or fiction and truth, is too simple: any work, even one aspiring to the strictest standards of historical or scientific fact, may include much imagination and speculation. By the same token, works we consider to be "fiction" may contain much we also consider to be in some sense true. Still, the distinction remains useful as a kind of license for the writer and a kind of cue for the audience's reception.

Figurative Language   Language that is not literal, not ordinary, is said to be figurative. For instance, "Larry swallowed Sam's story" is probably not literal (unless Larry actually ate Sam's manuscript or computer disk), but it is instead a comparison: Sam offered a story, and Larry so completely accepted it that it was as if he had "swallowed" it. As Stanley Fish (among others) has pointed out, however, all language ultimately is figurative because words are not equal to things. Still, most people would say that "my darling girl" and "my car," when used to describe the same entity, are not equally literal.

Figures of Speech   Uses of language that are not literal, not ordinary language, may be termed "figures of speech." Among the most familiar figures are metaphor and simile (comparing one thing to another), synecdoche and metonymy (substituting one item for another), and figures that appeal to the ear and eye: rhyme, or chiasmus, for instance. Numerous figures have been identified over the centuries, and various strategies for organizing them have been proposed.

First-Person Point of View, First-Person Narrator   This term refers to stories that are told by an "I," a character who (seemingly) speaks directly to the reader. Such first-person narrators are usually assumed to be speaking truthfully—presenting things as they remember them or experience them. But first-person narrators can be *unreliable*. The narrator may be fallible, remembering inaccurately, or willfully misleading. The narrator may also be *naive*, imperfectly understanding what he or she (or perhaps it) is relating to the reader.

Fixed Form   A predetermined shape or pattern for a form. A sonnet, for instance, is a fixed form: A sonnet should have fourteen lines and specific sequence of rhymes.

Flashback   A scene interrupting a story in order to present an earlier scene. After the flashback, the narrative may continue on from the point of interruption.

Flat Character   A character with simple qualities or traits; the opposite of a *round* character, who seems more complex and realistic.

Foil   A contrasting character, one who illuminates another character. Fortinbras may be seen as a foil to Hamlet, highlighting Hamlet's procrastination because he takes decisive action to avenge his father. Laertes, another injured son, may also be seen as a foil to Hamlet.

Foot   A unit of rhythm used to divide verse: A foot, in English poetry, may have stressed or unstressed syllables. Five kinds of feet are commonly used to describe poetic rhythms: an *iamb* (one unstressed, then one stressed); a *trochee* (one stressed, then unstressed); an *anapest* (two unstressed, then one stressed); a *dactyl* (two stressed, then one unstressed); and a *spondee* (two stressed syllables).

Foregrounding   To draw attention to something that would not otherwise be prominent. Foregrounding can therefore be an activity of the literary text, or the literary critic.

Foreshadowing   Something in a work that hints at something to come. A character may mention his fear of heights, thus foreshadowing a scene later when he must be on a ladder.

Form   The shape of a work. Form may be seen as the structure into which the work's content is poured, but most theorists today would assert that form and content are bound together. What a writer can say is determined to some degree by the form available; the form of the work is determined to some degree by what the writer is saying. Although some literary works do follow a predetermined form, for others the form appears to be ad hoc—invented for this particular work. For the reader, discovering the work's form is thus key to discovering its meaning. Since intelligent readers may reasonably differ in their descriptions of a work's form, the status of this form is uncertain (Is it in the work? Created by the reader? Is it stable?).

Frame Story   A story that sets up the occasion for another story (or stories). The most famous use of a frame story is probably *The Arabian Nights,* in which Queen Shahrazad tells story after story to avoid being executed by her King.

Free Verse   Poetry that does not follow a prescribed pattern. Free verse does not have a rhyme scheme; it does not have a metrical pattern; even the lines are not any certain length.

Freytag's Pyramid   According to Gustav Freytag, the structure of the characteristic five-act tragic drama has five parts: introduction, rising action, climax, falling action, and catastrophe.

Gay and Lesbian Criticism   A critical strategy that focuses on the representation of homosexual people, as well as the recovery and assessment of work by gay and lesbian writers. An extension, in a sense, of feminist criticism, examining the relationship between gender and sexuality as it relates to gay and lesbian issues.

Gender Criticism   Related to feminist criticism, and to gay and lesbian criticism, gender criticism approaches literature and other artifacts with a particular goal: to question the idea that gender is natural, inevitable, innate. Gender criticism explores the idea that gender is a construct, perpetuated by culture. Gender critics have promoted the idea that human beings are not simply divided into opposing pairs, masculine and feminine, but that a more accurate depiction of human sexuality would be a complex spectrum, involving a wide range of behaviors. Whether this behavior is biological or social in nature, or both, is a crucial question. Some critics, Judith Butler for instance, have argued that sex, apart from obvious anatomical differences, is a cultural construct. Most critics distinguish sex from gender (biology from culture), allowing them to assume that women are essentially different from men, and that women's writing and reading are essentially different also. This essentialist position contrasts with the constructionist view: If gender is constructed (not to mention sex), then men should be able to write as women, and vice versa. If gender is constructed, then homosexuality, one might posit, is somehow the effect of social and psychological processes. This position would appear to contradict recent brain studies showing that men and women process information quite differently (women appear to devote more of their brains to processing emotions, and have larger structures for integrating right and left hemispheres), as well as studies that suggest structural differences in the brains of homosexual versus heterosexual men.

Genre   From the French term for "type," this term refers to the kind of work something is perceived to be. Science fiction and detective fiction are perceived to be distinct and different genres. Readers approach them (and any other genre) with different expectations. There will not necessarily be any crime committed and solved in a science fiction story; a detective story doesn't have to have some extrapolation from an existing condition into some future development. Writers are not obligated, of course, to follow the conventions of any particular genre: There are science fiction detective stories, for instance (Isaac Asimov has written some wonderful ones featuring a robot detective). And a writer may well violate some convention of the genre to great effect. But the idea of a genre is useful because readers then know what conventions are being invoked. The traditional genres include tragedy, comedy, epic, lyric, pastoral, and satire. Other categorizations, suggesting the range of use of "genre" as a concept, include autobiography, the western, vampire stories, the essay, Star Trek novels, pornography.

Gothic   In general, a term used to indicate a style of architecture dominant in the middle ages (roughly 1200 to 1400 AD), and featuring stained glass windows, elaborately detailed woodwork, arches, spires, vaulted ceilings, and gargoyles (grotesque figures). In literature, the gothic suggests gloom, horror, decay, mystery—embracing in a sense an orientation toward the aesthetic qualities of gothic architecture. Goth Rock in the 1980s and 1990s popularized an indulgent and provocative cultivation of the morbid and grotesque.

Haiku   A verse form adapted from Japanese, consisting of three lines containing, usually, five, seven, and five syllables. The unrhymed lines are typically concerned with nature and convey some sort of spiritual awe or awareness. Some modern poets have sometimes varied the syllabic count, calling any very brief poem that evokes a certain attitude a "haiku."

Hamartia   From the Greek for "error," the term as used by Aristotle refers to an error in judgment that leads to the downfall of a tragic hero. In modern criticism, the term is also often used to describe the hero's frailty or flaw that leads to the fatal error in judgment. Whether it designates the flaw or the flawed judgment, the hero's hamartia may well be an error only in some particular circumstances. A dedication to the truth, family pride, military courage—these may all be seen as virtues, but they may all also be the hamartia that leads to disaster, given the right (or rather wrong) conditions. It is this crucial involvement of fate that makes for tragedy: If an evil man performs an evil deed, his downfall is not tragic. If a basically good man is led by his character to do something that causes his own downfall—that is the realm of tragedy.

Harlem Renaissance   A flowering of artistic achievement by African Americans, beginning in the 1920s in the Harlem area of New York City. Langston Hughes, Zora Neale Hurston, and Duke Ellington, for example, were part of the Harlem Renaissance.

Heptameter   A line of poetry having seven "feet" or metrical units. *See Meter.*

Hero, Heroine   Usually thought of as the main character of a work. "Hero" and "heroine" differ from "protagonist" in this way: A work may have both a hero and a heroine, but by definition only a single protagonist.

Heroic Couplet   Two successive rhyming lines, following the metrical pattern of an iambic pentameter (that is, unstressed, then stressed; with five such units or feet). This pattern is called "heroic" because it was so often used to write about heroic, and then in the eighteenth century, mock-heroic subjects.

Hexameter   A line of poetry having six metrical "feet." *See Meter.*

Historical Criticism   That critical strategy that employs historical research to understand and assess literary works. All critical strategies, including even New Criticism and deconstruction, may draw usefully upon historical research. Historical criticism may also draw on literary texts to illuminate history. And, historical orientations may also raise questions about the context of a work's publication (and thus assist in a type of reader-response criticism).

Hubris   Excessive pride leading to disaster. For tragic heroes, hubris is often the tragic flaw or contributes to the tragic flaw.

Hyperbole   Overstatement or exaggeration to the point of absurdity. "I could eat a cow" is hyperbole.

Hypertext   An electronic text that allows the reader (or user) to gain access to additional, secondary texts by mouse-clicking on designated parts of the text. For writers, hypertext may allow the creation of multiple versions of a story or different experiences of the same story. For literary critics, hypertext has allowed scholars to create flexible research tools, with additional information on terms or illustrations available, for readers who desire them, but hidden for readers who do not. The ability to search electronic texts has also altered the way that scholars may work with texts. Hypertext thus allows for—and may require—a more active reader.

Iamb   A metrical unit consisting of an unstressed, then a stressed syllable.

Iambic Pentameter   A line of verse containing five metrical units (or feet), each one (or most of them anyway) containing an unstressed, then stressed syllable.

Id   For Freud, that part of the mind responsible for basic desires—hunger and sensuality, for instance. The id seeks pleasure without restraint. The superego is the source of social constraints that may discipline the id; the ego attempts to negotiate between the drives of the id and the controls of the superego.

Ideology   The underlying beliefs and assumptions of some identifiable group. To function as an ideology, this set of beliefs must seem somehow natural and right. When an ideology begins to be called into question, to the extent that it is questioned, it begins to fail as an ideology. Indeed, one could say that for a culture to exist as an identifiable culture, the participants in that culture must hold some common ideology. For communism, or capitalism, or Christianity, or animism to function as an ideology, for instance, that particular set of beliefs must seem true to some group of people. Literature is an important resource for studying ideology because literature is unavoidably an artifact of an ideology, and because literature is also a force for articulating and reinforcing and perpetuating an ideology.

Image, Imagery   A text (word, phrase, sentence, sentences) that appeals to the reader's senses, especially but not exclusively sight, is said to be an image. Literary critics can look for patterns of images, or imagery, that create unity and meaning.

Imitation   *See Mimesis.*

Implied Author   The character that a real author presents to the reader. Invented by Wayne Booth, the term usefully reminds readers that an author reveals certain aspects of himself or herself and conceals or ignores others. Readers can draw inferences about an author, based on reading his or her text, but this author is implied by the text. It is not the real author.

Implied Reader   The reader that the writer imagined would be reading his text. Invented by Wolfgang Iser, this term distinguishes a real reader from the reader that the text itself implies. If part of a text in English contains passages that are in Spanish, for instance, and it seems clear that the reader needs to understand these Spanish passages, then the implied reader is bilingual, among other things.

In Medias Res   "In the middle of things" literally (Latin). The device of beginning a story, not at the beginning, but in the middle.

Influence   In literary history, the way that one writer or group of writers affects subsequent writers. The later writer may adopt some aspects of the earlier writer(s), and attempt to alter or undermine or ignore some other aspects. The idea of influence thus allows critics to think about how a particular writer or work is original, and how a writer or work is in a particular tradition or sequence of works.

Intention   What an author aimed to do in a work. An intention may be stated, implied, or obscure, but some literary critics have turned to the idea of intention as the grounding for a particular interpretation. Biographical study, from this point of view, is important because information about an author allows readers to say more plausibly whether a particular intention fits the work. For E. D. Hirsch, the meaning of a text is what its author intended it to mean. There are at least three problems with such a limit: An author's intention may be impossible to recover, especially given the possibility of unconscious intentions; it seems impossible to prove that one has discovered an author's intention; a work may have value or interest beyond what its author intended, and such a limit seems therefore unnecessary.

Intentional Fallacy   The error, according to W. K. Wimsatt and Monroe Beardsley, of basing interpretation on authorial intention. Such a practice is a fallacy, as the New Critics argued, because the object of the critic's attention should be the text itself, the literary work.

Intertextuality   This term points to the way that any given text is connected to many other texts. A reader who is unaware of an allusion, for instance, can fundamentally misunderstand the alluding text. A reader who has no experience with a certain genre will be unable to appreciate a work written within that genre.

Irony   Although irony is a complex and elusive term, its various meanings can be traced back to an incongruity or contradiction between appearance and reality. "Irony" comes from a Greek word for lying or pretending, but the gap between appearance and reality is meant to be perceived in irony. Someone who says "Lovely day," stepping out into a driving rain, is probably being ironic—and means to be seen as ironic. For New Critics, irony is a crucial term, drawing attention to the difference between the surface of a work and its levels of meaning and significance. Among the varieties of irony, the following kinds are generally distinguished. Verbal irony occurs when a speaker says one thing and means another. Situational irony occurs when what is expected to happen is not what happens. Dramatic irony occurs when a character says one thing and the audience knows that the statement means more than the character knows. When this discrepancy occurs in a tragedy, it may be called tragic irony. Cosmic irony occurs when a character aims to do some thing that fate (or God) prevents.

Limerick   A comical poem with five lines and an aabba construction; lines 1, 2, and 5 usually have three feet, and lines 3 and 4 contain two feet.

Line   In poetry, words are arranged on the page in lines. Line lengths are named for the number of feet they contain: Monometer = one foot. Dimeter = two feet. Trimeter = three feet. Tetrameter = four feet. Pentameter = five feet. Hexameter = six feet. Heptameter = seven feet. Octameter = eight feet.

Lyric   In contrast to a narrative poem, which tells a story, a lyric poem presents a speaker's thoughts and emotions. Lyric poems are brief; they are presented in first person (using "I," in other words); they are characteristically imaginative and melodic. The sonnet, the elegy, the ballad, the haiku, the ode are all kinds of lyric poems.

Marxist Criticism   The approach to literature that focuses on issues of economy and class. Inspired by the writings of Karl Marx, but not limited to communist ideas, Marxist criticism has survived the demise of Soviet-style communism by viewing texts as material products in an economy. Marxist critics see a political role for literary criticism, exposing oppression and injustice—characteristically, and perhaps ironically, in capitalistic societies (which have historically allowed open critique).

Melodrama   Literally, a melodrama is a drama with song (the Greek word "melos" means "song"). A melodrama pits a thoroughly evil villain against a thoroughly good protagonist. The excitement and entertainment of a melodrama is based primarily on plot development rather than character. The happy ending of a melodrama occurs, often at the last possible minute, characteristically after surprising plot twists and impending disasters. "Melodrama" has come to be a negative term.

Metaphor   A figure of speech that attempts to represent one thing more effectively by comparing it to another. For example, "He has an eggshell ego" compares someone's ego to an eggshell, providing a more vivid way of saying that his ego is fragile. In this metaphor, the ego is called the *tenor*—the target of the comparison; the eggshell is called the *vehicle*—the means by which the idea is being conveyed. A *direct metaphor* makes the comparison explicitly by articulating both tenor and vehicle: "Sally was a rocket running down the track." The tenor is "running," and "rocket" is the vehicle. An *indirect metaphor* provides only the vehicle: "Sally rocketed down the track." Sally's running, the tenor, is not explicitly stated; the vehicle, "rocketed," implies the tenor. A *dead metaphor* occurs when the comparison is so familiar that it is no longer noticed: "Let's snag some lunch" probably does not create a comparison between getting some lunch and fishing, or any other activity, for most people. A *mixed metaphor* involves multiple comparisons: "The rocketing track star squirted down the track." The star's running is compare to a rocket, and to a liquid squirting, and the end result is confusion. An *extended metaphor* is a comparison that runs through a significant portion or even of all the text.

Meter   The pattern of rhythm in a poem, based on accented and unaccented sylla-bles. Meters can be identified by the number of feet in a line, from a monome-ter with one foot per line, up to at least an octameter with eight feet per line. (*See Line.*) Meters are also designated by the characteristic pattern of stressed and unstressed syllables in the poem's feet: The most common feet are the iamb, trochee, anapest, dactyl, spondee, and pyrrhic. (*See Foot.*) When a poem is identified as being written in, say, iambic pentameter, not every single foot of every line has to be in an iambic form, and every single line does not have to have five feet. Poets may vary the pattern to avoid monotony. The meter of a poem is then the dominant metrical pattern. *Rising meter* means simply that the lines tend to move from unstressed to stressed syllables; *falling meter* means that the lines move from stressed to unstressed syllables.

Metonymy   A *figure of speech* that represents one thing by another that is associ-ated with it. The British government might be represented, for example, by referring to the prime minister's residence on Downing Street in London: "The word from Downing Street is optimistic" means that the prime minister's gov-ernment feels optimistic.

Mimesis, Mimetic Criticism   A Greek term used by critics to indicate the repre-sentation or mirroring of reality in literature. Aristotle in the *Poetics* (about 330 BCE) says that the purpose of literature is to imitate reality selectively, rep-resenting nature truthfully in a way that benefits humanity. In the Romantic period, literature was celebrated increasingly not for its ability to imitate reali-ty, but for its expressiveness and originality. Mimetic Criticism assesses literary works on the accuracy of their portrayal of reality.

Motif   Any element in a work that runs through it, helping to unify the work, such as symbols, images, themes.

Mythological Criticism   A critical strategy that focuses upon various aspects of myths as they appear in literary works. A myth is a story that somehow explained (or continues to explain) a fundamental truth for a cultural group. For C. G. Jung, the dramatic similarities among myths all over the world point to the existence of a collective unconscious. All human beings, Jung argues, somehow inherit common mythic patterns and elements. Mythological critics attempt to look beyond the surface differences of literary works to find under-lying common patterns of mythic characters, plots, and meanings.

Narrative, Narrative Poem   A narrative is a story—a sequence of events with a discernible beginning, middle, and end. Narratives may be fictional or factual, or both.

Narrator   The speaker, created by the author, who tells a story (a narrative). Read-ers experience the story from this speaker's *point of view*. The narrator is often a character within the story, but not necessarily. Most stories are told from a single point of view, but multiple narrators have been famously and successfully used (Faulkner's *The Sound and Fury*, for instance). Various kinds of narrators have been distinguished. A third-person narrator who knows everything is called an *omniscient narrator*: "William thought he was handsome, but Sally didn't agree, even though no one else knew her opinion." A third-person narrator who knows and reveals some things but not others is called a *limited omniscient narrator:* "William thought he was handsome, but he didn't know what Sally thought." A *first-person narrator* tells a story directly to the reader—his own story, in the narrative autobiographical: "I'm William, and I think I'm handsome. But I wasn't sure until last Tuesday what Sally thought about my appearance." A first-person narrator who doesn't understand what he or she is revealing is called a *naive narrator.* And a first-person narrator who misleads his or her audience is called an *unreliable narrator.*

Naturalism   *See Realism.*

New Criticism   A critical strategy that emphasizes close reading of texts in order to reveal their complexity and unity. New Critics focus on the work itself, and not the author's intention (the intentional fallacy) or the reader's response (the affective fallacy). New Criticism rose to prominence in the 1940s, but it remains (arguably) the most widely used approach in high schools and colleges.

New Historicism   The critical approach that focuses on an individual work within the context of its time. New Historicists see history as a text, and literature as not only a record of history, but also as a force shaping history. New Historicists thus can read a wide variety of texts in order to provide the richest possible historical context for a work.

Octave   A group, or stanza, of eight lines; the first eight lines of a sonnet.

Ode   A serious, elevated, lengthy poem on a serious subject. Odes do not have a particular pattern.

Oedipus Complex   Sigmund Freud's term for a young boy's normal desire to possess his mother and remove his father. As part of their psychological development, boys must work through this complex, relinquishing their maternal desire, recognizing the father's prior and superior claim.

Omniscient Point of View   *See Narrator.*

Onomatopoeia   A word that sounds like what it means: "Buzz" and "hiss" are commonly cited examples.

Orientalism   As used by Edward Said in *Orientalism* (1978), and adopted by other critics, a term referring to the process of inventing ideas and images about the Eastern world. The Eastern and Middle-Eastern people, Said argued, have often been portrayed in ways that promoted their colonization by Europe.

Overstatement   *See Hyperbole.*

Oxymoron   The figure of speech that places contradictory words side by side; a compressed paradox. For instance, an ugly beauty, a peaceful war, or a dismal success.

Pantomime   Silent acting. A pantomime is also called "a dumb show." Shakespeare's *Hamlet* features a famous pantomime in the play-within-the-play scene.

Parable   A brief story designed to convey a moral to a particular audience. Parables such as the prodigal son and the lost sheep are employed by Jesus in the New Testament.

Paradox   A contradictory statement that nonetheless makes sense, as in Yogi Berra's assertion that a particular restaurant was "so popular and crowded that no one goes there anymore." New Critics are especially mindful of the power of paradox to convey rich meanings.

Parallelism A rhetorical device in which units of language—words, phrases, sentences, paragraphs—are arranged in parallel structures. For instance, in this passage from Winston Churchill's report to the House of Commons, October 8, 1940, parallelism structures both sentences: "Death and sorrow will be the companions of our journey; hardship our garment; constancy and valor our only shield. We must be united, we must be undaunted, we must be inflexible."

Paraphrase A restatement of another's ideas; putting a text into one's own words. Oftentimes, a paraphrase is a prose version of a poetic original. For the New Critics, a poem could not be paraphrased without substantial loss of meaning.

Parody An imitation for comic effect. *Saturday Night Live,* for instance, has often created parodies of White House news conferences, television game shows, and other events. The parody must contain enough of the original's elements to be recognizable. Anthony Hecht's "Dover Bitch" is a well-known parody of Arnold's "Dover Beach."

Pastoral A work in a rural setting, celebrating a bucolic lifestyle. Traditionally, pastoral poems involved surprisingly articulate and artistic shepherds, who were often engaged in singing contests.

Pathos Greek for "passion," this term refers to the sorrow aroused in the reader or audience. Pathos is associated with witnessing innocent suffering. When pathos is heavy-handed or implausible, it often slips into *bathos.*

Patriarchal "Father-ruled." A term employed primarily by feminist critics to refer to a masculine-centered society. The complementary term, "matriarchal" or "mother-ruled," has applied to a few societies.

Persona From the Latin for "mask," a persona is the "mask" or public face one presents to others.

Personification A figure of speech assigning human qualities to something not human. For instance, a "beckoning chair" or a "soft-spoken merlot wine" gives human qualities (people beckon and speak softly) to a chair and a wine.

Play, Playwright A play is a story performed on stage by actors for an audience. A playwright is the creator of such a performance.

Plot The arrangement of the events of a story.

Point of View Every story is told by some speaker, who is situated somewhere. This stance is called the *point of view.* A *first-person narrator,* using "I," may be a participant in the story, intimately or remotely; an observer; or simply a reporter. Although uncommon, a first-person plural narrator, using "we," is also possible. A *third-person narrator* is also quite flexible, allowing for a speaker who knows everything (an *omniscient* point of view), or one who is more *limited.* The point of view may also be from an *unreliable narrator,* who misleads the reader (knowingly or not), or a *naive* narrator, who relates what he or she (or perhaps it) may not fully understand.

Political Criticism Any approach to a text that starts from and is motivated by a political stance. In a sense, all criticism is inevitably political because every reader unavoidably occupies some political position. But some criticism pursues an identifiable political agenda and can therefore be usefully distinguished as political criticism. Feminist criticism, for example, approaches a text especially interested in how it may represent women and perhaps reinforce their oppression or subjugation. Gay and Lesbian criticism approaches a text interested in how the text represents gay and lesbian people. A text may "represent" a political group or concept in many ways: by being written by a member of that group, by depicting a member, or even by failing to include depiction of that member. In theory, any discernible faction of people could engage in political criticism: Some people might engage in left-handed criticism in order to examine the stereotypes of left-handed people that are perpetuated in literary texts.

Portmanteau   A word invented by combining two words. In Lewis Carroll's "Jabberwocky," "slithy" results from combining "slimy" and "lithe," according to Humpty Dumpty.

Postcolonial Criticism   An approach that might best be seen as a combination of political and historical strategies, examining literary texts in terms of the relationship between colonial and colonizing cultures. For instance, British writers on India might be studied to see how they represented Indian culture during or after colonial rule. Indian writers might be studied to see how they represented their own culture, and the impact upon it of British rule. Postcolonial criticism generally finds that colonizing cultures tend to distort the colonial culture for political purposes. Exposing the history of that distortion, as reflected in literary texts, is thus an act of political intervention.

Postmodern, Postmodernism   Relating to a literary and philosophical movement that focuses upon the alienation and ultimate meaninglessness of life. The postmodern, which followed World War II, pushes beyond *Modernism,* which emerged as an intellectual movement from 1910 to 1930. While modernists like T. S. Eliot, for example, may have considered the world to be fragmented, incoherent, enthralled by tradition, they did also generally believe that literature could play a transforming and reintegrating role. Postmodernists have no such illusion; at most, literature can distract us momentarily from the absurdity and emptiness at the core. Deconstruction is a critical approach that grows out of a postmodern outlook.

Prologue   A speech spoken at the beginning of a play. More generally, any preliminary speech or activity coming before a main event.

Protagonist   The leading character; usually the hero. The protagonist is opposed by the antagonist, and this conflict drives the plot.

Psychological Criticism, Psychoanalytical Criticism   Psychological criticism looks at literary texts in terms of human psychology. Psychological critics may focus upon the author's psychology, the psychology of characters, or the psychology of the reader. Psychoanalytic criticism is that kind of psychological criticism that derives from psychoanalysis and Freud.

Pun   A play on words, in which one word sounds like or looks like another word. Often used to comic effect. For instance: A Russian man named Rudolph engages in an argument with his American girlfriend over whether it is raining or snowing, until he finally says, "Rudolph the Red knows rain dear." The punch line (using the term loosely) is an extended pun.

Quatrain   A stanza (that is, a grouping of lines) that contains four lines. The lines may be rhymed or unrhymed and still be considered a quatrain.

Queer Theory   An outgrowth of gay and lesbian criticism that applies deconstructive strategies to categories of sex and gender. Queer theory calls into question the whole idea of stable categories of sexual identity. It has been especially active in studying Renaissance texts.

Race   A social construct based on perceived physical variations in human beings. Biologically, race is a flawed concept because there is in reality a spectrum of human differences and similarities rather than distinct categories. The variation across the range of people termed "black," for instance, is greater than the variation between those termed "black" and those termed "white." The construction of race allows for the stereotyping of individuals, but at the same time allows for the creation of cultural conventions and communities.

Reader-Response Criticism   An approach to literary criticism that focuses on the way readers react to texts. Reader-response criticism includes a wide range of interests: For instance, on the one hand, investigating how contemporary readers may respond differently to a text than readers at some other period; and on the other hand, exploring the most subjective and personal responses to a particular text. Reader-response critics may argue for a best or ideal response to a text; or they may simply strive to articulate the whole spectrum of responses. Reader-response techniques have been employed very successfully by critics aligned with various political approaches, including especially feminist critics.

Realism   Depicting accurately the ordinary or everyday life; focusing on details and events rather than thoughts and feelings. Realism can be usefully distinguished from *romanticism,* which values the subjective and imaginative. Realism can also be distinguished from *naturalism,* which assumes that human beings are controlled by external forces (of biology, economy, class). Thus, realism and naturalism both try to represent an objective and detailed view of ordinary reality; in realism, characters have some measure of free will, but in naturalism they do not. As literary movements, realism and naturalism can be seen as reactions to romanticism, which celebrated the individual, free will, creativity, emotions, and originality. Most scholars date the Romantic period from the late eighteenth century through much of the nineteenth century. Realism and naturalism developed in the later part of the nineteenth century and both continued to evolve into the twentieth century.

Recognition   The moment in a story when a character suddenly realizes the significance of the moment, as when Oedipus realizes that he indeed killed his father and married his mother. Also called *anagnorisis.*

Renaissance   A literary period usually considered to extend from about 1500 to 1660. Shakespeare is the dominant writer of this period.

Representation   Anything that stands for another thing is in a sense a "representation" of that second thing. A map is a representation of the land it depicts. A short story set in the pre-Civil War south can be seen as a "representation" of that region. New historicists are especially sensitive to the ways that representations shape and perpetuate a culture's values and perceptions.

Resolution   The concluding action of a plot.

Revenge Tragedy   A kind of tragedy popular during Shakespeare's day, in which some enormous injury was revenged. *Hamlet* has many elements of a revenge tragedy, but it greatly surpasses other works in this genre. These elements include a ghost or spirit calling for revenge, hesitations and delays in carrying out the revenge, tricks to deceive the villain, violence and gore, sensuality and high emotions, and philosophical reflections on the action. The movie *Cyborg,* starring Jean-Claude Van Damme, has some elements of a revenge tragedy. Although a ghost is lacking, the protagonist does experience flashbacks in which he sees his murdered family and draws renewed power. There is also very little philosophical reflection on the part of the protagonist (Van Damme's dialogue is severely limited), but the movie as a whole does promote philosophical reflection about civilization's future.

Reversal   The point of the plot when the protagonist's fortunes turn around. If things are going well, they turn for the worse; if they are going poorly, they turn suddenly for the better.

Rhetoric, Rhetorical Criticism   Often, especially in modern times, a term of disparagement, suggesting that a statement is not true or substantive, but is rather contrived to produce an effect. In a more general, and more broadly historical sense, rhetoric is concerned with the resources of language—how writers and speakers persuade audiences. Rhetorical criticism draws attention to the devices of persuasion. Such devices may be blatantly obvious (as in the use of rhyme and rhythm in Johnnie Cochran's defense of O. J. Simpson: "If it doesn't fit, you must acquit"), or very subtle (as in the use of alphabetizing, spacing, font, cover, and much else in a phone book, persuading us that the phone company is trustworthy and excellent).

Rhyme   The repetition of vowel sounds and all following sounds in two or more words, as in ring, king, bing, sing; or together, whether, leather. Rhymes may be distinguished in several ways. By placement in a poetic line: end-rhyme (the rhyming words are at the end of the line of course), internal rhyme, and beginning rhyme. By stresses: A masculine rhyme has one stressed syllable, and a feminine rhyme has two or three stressed syllables. By degree: A perfect rhyme involves words that rhyme exactly: cough and off. A half-rhyme (or near rhyme, or slant rhyme) involves words with syllables that sound similar, but are not perfect rhymes: cough and laugh. And eye rhymes involve words that might appear to be rhymes, but are not when pronounced: cough and through. Rhyme schemes are described by using lower-case letters to stand for rhyming words. An *abac* rhyme scheme would have the first and third lines rhyming, and the second and fourth lines ending with different sounds.

Rhythm   As any language is spoken, the flow of words is varied by stresses and pauses. "Rhythm," which is Greek for "flow," refers to this pattern of stresses and pauses. Rhythm occurs in prose and poetry. *Meter* refers to the more formal patterns in verse.

Rising Action   That portion of the plot that leads to the climax or crisis, as the plot becomes more complicated.

Romanticism   *See Realism.*

Round Character   In E. M. Forster's formulation, round characters have the kind of complexity and depth that make them seem like real people.

Sarcasm   An extreme form of irony, sarcasm is designed to ridicule and attack its object. "Parents who have violent children just need to give them a good beating every day."

Satire   Satire exposes absurdity by being absurd. Jonathan Swift's famous satire, "A Modest Proposal," ridicules the English oppression of the Irish by proposing the most absurd oppression—that the English should eat the Irish children.

Scene   A unit of action, usually in a play, although a "scene" can occur in any narrative. A scene usually begins and ends when the setting changes, or when characters enter or exit.

Script   The written version of a play.

Sentimentalism   Marked by an excessive appeal to an audience's emotions. A work is said to exhibit sentimentalism when rousing feelings of pity and sympathy seem to be the author's primary (or only) goal, or when the author seems willing to lower artistic standards to make such an appeal.

Sestet   A six-line stanza, or poem.

Sestina   A poem with thirty-nine lines divided into six *sestets* and a concluding *envoy* (of three lines).

Setting   The time, place, and context in which a story occurs. (All these conditions may be plural: times, places, contexts). In the play, the setting is the space created on the stage (the scenery and the props).

Shakespearean Sonnet   A sonnet having three quatrains and a couplet in the following rhyme scheme: *abab cdcd efef gg*. This form was made famous by (you guessed it) Shakespeare.

Simile   An explicit comparison using "like," "as," or a similar comparative term. "His manners stood out like little piles of cow manure on a manicured golf course."

Soliloquy   In a play, a speech revealing a character's thoughts and/or emotions directly to the audience, as if he or she were thinking aloud.

Sonnet   A poem containing fourteen lines. *See Shakespearean Sonnet.*

Spondee   A metrical foot containing two stressed syllables.

Stage Directions   What the playwright says, in the script, about how to perform some part of the play. Stage directions may address tone, pacing, movement, anything.

Stanza   A group of lines in a poem, usually set off by a line of space.

Stock Character   A character who is a recognizable type, having qualities that an audience has seen in other characters in other works. The computer nerd, for instance, is a stock character: glasses taped together, greasy hair, unfashionable clothes, socially awkward.

Stream-of-Consciousness   A literary technique that presents what appears to be the unedited flow of thoughts of the writer, or narrator, or character. The style may be choppy, incoherent, contradictory, dreamy—whatever might flow through someone's mind.

Stress   Some syllables in spoken English are given an emphasis, while others are not. This sequence of stressed and unstressed syllables results in a rhythm. For poems, the pattern of stresses determines the dominant *meter.*

Style   The words that a writer chooses, and the way the words are arranged, add up to the style of a text. Ernest Hemingway, for instance, is known for his terse, clear style, with simple sentences and ordinary words. William Faulkner, on the other hand, is noted for his ornately convoluted sentences and rich vocabulary.

Subplot   A story line that is secondary to the main plot. The subplot may contrast with the main plot, or reinforce it, or provide some counterpoint, or any number of other things.

Suspense   The audience's tension or concern regarding the events unfolding. In action-adventure movies, for instance, suspense builds primarily by means of the increasing danger that the protagonist faces.

Symbol   Something that stands for or refers to something else. A person, place, action, or object may serve as a symbol. A flag, for instance, may stand for a country; a white whale may stand for evil. A *conventional symbol* is one that is generally shared by a community or culture. A *contextual* or *literary symbol* acquires its symbolic meaning within the literary work.

Synecdoche   A figure of speech that uses a part of something to represent the whole (or, sometimes, vice-versa). For instance, "I have forty hands working in the field" points to the workers by referring to them as a part of their bodies.

Tenor   *See Metaphor.*

Tercet   A three-line stanza.

Terza rima   A difficult rhyme scheme that uses interlocking three-line stanzas, like this: *aba bcb cdc ded efe* etc. Dante Alighieri made *terza rima* famous with

The Divine Comedy (in Italian), but in English the form is not used often. Robert Frost's "Acquainted with the Night" uses this form.

Theme　An assertion that arguably articulates the message or meaning of a literary work. A theme is therefore key to the unity of a work. *Theme* can be usefully distinguished from the subject. The subject of *Hamlet* might be expressed as "a son's delayed revenge." The theme might be expressed this way: "In some situations, a greater moral obligation requires one to violate lesser moral obligations."

Thesis　The main idea of an essay. A thesis should be a sentence, and it should be arguable (not obvious), supportable (facts can be presented), and comprehensive (it should apply to the entire work, not just a portion).

Tone　Attitude as revealed in style. An author's orientation toward his or her subject matter or reader can be revealed in word choice and syntax. Tone, especially in writing, can be difficult to convey and discern. The differences for instance between a playful and a mocking tone can be quite subtle even in person, much less in writing.

Tragedy　A drama that characteristically ends in disaster. Tragedy can be traced back to the fifth-century BC Greeks, especially Aeschylus, Euripedes, and Sophocles. Aristotle's definition of tragedy, in the *Poetics* (about 330 BC), has been widely accepted. According to Aristotle, a tragedy imitates a serious and important action that elicits fear and pity in the audience, producing *catharsis*. The tragic hero should be mostly good and of high standing, but the hero's fall from high standing is the result of a tragic flaw that leads to an error in judgment (or *hamartia*). This tragic flaw is often excessive pride (or *hubris*).

Tragic Flaw　The fault in a tragic hero that leads to an error in judgment.

Tragicomedy　A drama that includes both comic and tragic elements.

Triplet　Three lines, a tercet, that all rhyme.

Troche　A metrical foot that consists of one stressed syllable, then an unstressed syllable.

Understatement　A rhetorical strategy that involves saying less than one intends. For instance, after surviving a plane crash, someone says "Yes, we had trouble with our flight."

Undecidability　The quality in texts that defeats any stable articulation of meaning. Deconstruction seeks to expose the undecidability of texts, showing how different competing readings are equally plausible.

Unreliable Narrator　A narrator who misleads the reader, whether intentionally or not. The narrator may have incomplete information, or misunderstand the information, or deliberately distort or obscure the story being told.

Utopia, Utopian　Referring to an ideal place. From the Greek for "no place" (*outopia*), utopian fiction describes some kind of paradise that may be placed in the past, future, or undiscovered space.

Verse　Any metrical composition. Some critics distinguish between "verse," which includes even greeting card rhymes and the most awful patterned compositions, and "poetry," which implies a certain level of quality in a rhythmical composition.

Villanelle　A French verse form with nineteen lines: five tercets and then a quatrain, with this rhyme scheme: *aba aba aba aba aba abaa.*

Acknowledgments

Abse, Dannie. "Brueghel in Naples" from *Selected Poems* by Dannie Abse. Copyright © 1994 by Daniel Abse. Reprinted by permission of Penguin Putnam, Inc.

Ackerman, Diane. "Driving Through Farm Country at Sunset" from *Jaquar of Sweet Laughter: New and Selected Poems* by Diane Ackerman. Copyright © 1991 by Diane Ackerman. Used by permission of Random House, Inc.

Adams, Douglas. From *Original Hitchhiker Radio Scripts* by Douglas Adams. Copyright © 1995 by Serious Productions Ltd. Used by permission of Harmony Books, a division of Random House, Inc.

Adelman, Janet. "'Man and Wife Is One Flesh?': *Hamlet* and the Confrontation With the Maternal Body" in *Suffocating Mothers: Fantasies of Maternal Origin in Shakespeare's Plays,* 1992.

Aguilar-Cariño, Maria Luisa B. "Dinakdakan," from *Returning a Borrowed Tongue: Poems by Filipino and Filipino American Writers,* edited by Nick Carbo. Copyright © 1995 by Coffee House Press. Reprinted with the permission of Coffee House Press, Minneapolis, Minnesota.

Al-Shaykh, Hanan. Translated by Catherine Cobham, "Keeper of the Virgins" from *I Sweep the Sun off Rooftops* by Hanan Al-Shaykh, translated by Catherine Cobham. Copyright © 1998 by Doubleday, a division of Random House, Inc. Used by permission of Doubleday, a division of Random House, Inc.

Allen, Catherine Celesia. *Anything for You* by Catherine Celesia Allen. Copyright © by Catherine Celesia Allen.

Angleou, Maya. "My Arkansas" from *And Still I Rise* by Maya Angelou. Copyright © 1978 by Maya Angelou. Used by permission of Random House, Inc.

Ashberry, John. "Paradoxes and Oxymorons" from *Shadow Train* by John Ashberry. Copyright © 1980, 1981 by John Ashberry. Reprinted by permission of Georges Borchardt, Inc., for the author.

Atwood, Margaret. "Siren Song" from *Selected Poems 1966–1984* by Margaret Atwood. Copyright © Margaret Atwood 1990. Reprinted by permission of Oxford University Press, Canada.

Atwood, Margaret. "Siren Song" from *Selected Poems, 1965-1975* by Margaret Atwood. Copyright © 1976 by Margaret Atwood. Reprinted by permission of Houghton Mifflin Company. All rights reserved.

Atwood, Margaret. "Spelling" reprinted by permission of Margaret Atwood, from the collection *True Stories* © 1981 by Margaret Atwood, first published in Canada by Oxford University Press and in the United States by Simon & Shuster.

Atwood, Margaret. "Variation on the Word 'Sleep'" from *Selected Poems II, 1976-1986* by Margaret Atwood. Copyright © 1987 by Margaret Atwood. Reprinted by permission of Houghton Mifflin Company. All rights reserved.

Atwood, Margaret. "Variation on the Word 'Sleep'" from *Selected Poems 1966-1984* by Margaret Atwood. Copyright © Margaret Atwood 1990. Reprinted by permission of Oxford University Press, Canada.

Auden, W. H. "In Memory of W. B. Yeats," copyright 1940 and renewed 1968 by W. H. Auden, from *W. H. Auden: The Collected Poems* by W. H. Auden. Used by permission of Random House, Inc.

Auden, W. H. "Musée des Beaux Arts," copyright 1940 and renewed 1968 by W. H. Auden, from *W. H. Auden: The Collected Poems* by W. H. Auden. Used by permission of Random House, Inc.

Baldwin, James. "Sonny's Blues." Copyright © 1965 by James Baldwin. Originally published in *Partisan Review*. Copyright renewed. Collected in *Going to Meet the Man*, published by Vintage Books. Reprinted by arrangement with the James Baldwin Estate.

Baraka, Amiri. "Preface to a Twenty Volume Suicide Note" by Amiri Baraka. Copyright © 1964 by Amiri Baraka. Reprinted by permission of Sterling Lord Literistic, Inc.

Beer, Janet. From *Kate Chopin, Edith Wharton and Charlotte Perkins Gilman: Studies in Short Fiction* by Janet Beer. Copyright © 1997 by Janet Beer. Reprinted by permission of Palgrave Macmillan.

Bevington, David. "'But We Are Spirits of Another Sort': The Dark Side of Love and Magic in *A Midsummer Night's Dream*" from *Medieval and Renaissance Studies, Number 7: Proceedings of the Southeastern Institute of Medieval and Renaissance Studies, Summer* 1975, edited by Siegfried Wenzel. Copyright © 1978 by the University of South Carolina Press. Used by permission of the publisher.

Footnotes from *Hamlet* from *The Complete Works of Shakespeare, 4th Edition* by David Bevington. Copyright © 1992 by HarperCollins Publishers. Reprinted by permission of Pearson Education, Inc.

Bogan, Louise. "Women" from *The Blue Estuaries* by Louise Bogan. Copyright © 1968 by Louise Bogan. Copyright renewed 1996 by Ruth Limmer. Reprinted by permission of Farrar, Straus and Giroux, LLC.

Boyle, T. Coraghessan. "The Hit Man" from *The The North American Review.* Copyright © 1980 by *The North American Review.* Reproduced with permission of *The North American Review* via Copyright Clearance Center.

Brehm, John. "Sea of Faith." Copyright © 1999 by John Brehm. First appeared in *The Southern Review*. Reprinted by permission of the author.

Brinson, Claudia Smith. "Einstein's Daughter." First appeared in *Kalliope*. Copyright © by Claudia Smith Brinson. Reprinted by permission of the author.

Brooks, Gwendolyn. "A Bronzeville Mother Loiters in Mississippi. Meanwhile a Mississippi Mother Burns Bacon" from *Blacks* by Gwendolyn Brooks. Reprinted by consent of Brooks Permissions.

Brooks, Gwendolyn. "And Shall I Prime My Children?" from *Blacks* by Gwendolyn Brooks. Reprinted by consent of Brooks Permissions.

Brooks, Gwendolyn. "Do Not Be Afraid of No" from *Blacks* by Gwendolyn Brooks. Reprinted by consent of Brooks Permissions.

Brooks, Gwendolyn. "First Fight, Then Fiddle" from *Blacks* by Gwendolyn Brooks. Reprinted by consent of Brooks Permissions.

Brooks, Gwendolyn. "Gay Chaps at the Bar" from *Blacks* by Gwendolyn Brooks. Reprinted by consent of Brooks Permissions.

Brooks, Gwendolyn. "God Works in Mysterious Ways" from *Blacks* by Gwendolyn Brooks. Reprinted by consent of Brooks Permissions.

Brooks, Gwendolyn. "Langston Hughes" from *Blacks* by Gwendolyn Brooks. Reprinted by consent of Brooks Permissions.

Brooks, Gwendolyn. "Sadie and Maude" from *Blacks* by Gwendolyn Brooks. Reprinted by consent of Brooks Permissions.

Brooks, Gwendolyn. "The ballad of chocolate Mabbie" from *Blacks* by Gwendolyn Brooks. Reprinted by consent of Brooks Permissions.

Brooks, Gwendolyn. "The Bean Eaters" from *Blacks* by Gwendolyn Brooks. Reprinted by consent of Brooks Permissions.

Brooks, Gwendolyn. "The Mother" from *Blacks* by Gwendolyn Brooks. Copyright © 1944, 1945, 1949, 1959, 1960, 1963 by Gwendolyn Brooks Blakely. Reprinted by permission of the Estate of Gwendolyn Brooks.

Brooks, Gwendolyn. "The Sundays of Satin-Legs Smith" from *Blacks* by Gwendolyn Brooks. Reprinted by consent of Brooks Permissions.

Brooks, Gwendolyn. "We Real Cool" from *Blacks* by Gwendolyn Brooks. Reprinted by consent of Brooks Permissions.

Brooks, Gwendolyn. "What Shall I Give The Children?" from *Blacks* by Gwendolyn Brooks. Reprinted by consent of Brooks Permissions.

Brooks, Gwendolyn. "*The Chicago Defender* Sends A Man to Little Rock" from *Blacks* by Gwendolyn Brooks. Reprinted by consent of Brooks Permissions.

Burnside, John. "The Sand Merchant's Wife" by John Burnside. Copyright © by John Burnside. Reprinted by permission of the author.

Carroll, Lewis. "Jabberwocky" from *Alice's Adventures in Wonderland* by Lewis Carroll, copyright © 1982 by Bear Run Publishing, Inc., reprinted by permission of Harcourt, Inc.

Carver, Raymond. "Catherdral" from *Cathedral* by Raymond Carver, copyright © 1983 by Raymond Carver. Used by permission of Alfred A. Knopf, a division of Random House, Inc.

Chasin, Helen. "The Word Plum" from *Coming Close and Other Poems* by Helen Chasin. Copyright © 1968 by Helen Chasin. Reprinted by permission of Yale University Press.

Cheever, John. "Reunion" from *The Stories of John Cheever* by John Cheever, copyright 1978 by John Cheever. Used by permission of Alfred A. Knopf, a division of Random House, Inc.

Cheever, John. "The Country Husband" from *The Stories of John Cheever* by John Cheever, copyright © 1978 by John Cheever. Used by permission of Alfred A. Knopf, a division of Random House, Inc.

Cheever, John. "The Swimmer" from *The Stories of John Cheever* by John Cheever, copyright © 1978 by John Cheever. Used by permission of Alfred A. Knopf, a division of Random House, Inc.

Cisneros, Sandra. "One Holy Night" from *Woman Hollering Creek.* Copyright © 1991 by Sandra Cisneros. Published by Vintage Books, a division of Random House Inc. and originally in hardcover by Random House Inc. Reprinted by permission of Susan Bergholz Literary Services, New York. All rights reserved.

Clampitt, Amy. "Lindenbloom" from *The Collected Poems of Amy Clampitt* by Amy Clampitt, copyright © 1997 by the Estate of Amy Clampitt. Used by permission of Alfred A. Knopf, a division of Random House, Inc.

Clampitt, Amy. "Nothing Stays Put" from *The Collected Poems of Amy Clampitt* by Amy Clampitt, copyright © 1997 by the Estate of Amy Clampitt. Used by permission of Alfred A. Knopf, a division of Random House, Inc.

Clifton, Lucille. "Forgiving My Father" Copyright © 1980 by Lucille Clifton. First appeared in *Two-Headed Woman,* published by The University of Massachusetts Press. Now appears in *Good Woman,* published by BOA Editions, Ltd. Reprinted by permission of Curtis Brown, Ltd.

Cowley, Malcolm. "Frost: A Dissenting Opinion." *New Republic.* September 11, 1944, and September 18, 1944. pp. 312–13 and 345–47.

Cullen, Countee. "Incident" originally published in *On These I Stand,* copyright 1947 by Harper & Row. Reprinted by permission of Thompson & Thompson.

cummings, e. e. "anyone lived in a pretty how town." Copyright 1940, © 1968, 1991 by the Trustees for the e. e. cummings Trust, from *Complete Poems: 1904–1962* by e. e. cummings, edited by George J. Firmage. Used by permission of Liveright Publishing Corporation.

Davis, Amanda. "Louisiana Loses Its Cricket Hum." Copyright © 2001 by Amanda Davis. Reprinted by permission of Dunow & Carlson Agency.

Dawes, Kwame. "Umpire at the Portrait Gallery" from *Midland* by Kwame Dawes. Copyright © 2001 by Kwame Dawes. Reprinted by permission of Ohio University Press, Athens, Ohio and Goose Lane Editions.

Dickey, James. "The Sheep Child" from *Poems 1957-1967* by James Dickey. Copyright © 1978 by James Dickey. Reprinted by permission of Wesleyan University Press.

Dickinson, Emily. Poems # 185, 303, 357, 392, 465, 585 reprinted by permission of the publishers and the Trustees of Amherst College from *The Poems of Emily Dickinson*, Thomas H. Johnson, ed., Cambridge, Mass.: The Belknap Press of Harvard University Press. Copyright © 1951, 1955, 1979 by the President and Fellows of Harvard College.

The Dimensions of Robert Frost, Reginald L. Cook, 1958, New York University Press.

Dings, Fred. "The Divers." Copyright © 2002 by Fred Dings. Reprinted by permission of the author.

Dings, Fred. "Chains of Change" from *Eulogy for a Private Man* by Fred Dings. Copyright © 1999 by Fred Dings. Reprinted by permission of the Author.

DiRenzo, Anthony. From "The Last Laugh and the Liberty of December" in *American Gargoyles: Flannery O'Connor and the Medieval Grotesque* by Anthony DiRenzo. Copyright © 1993 by the Board of Trustees, Southern Illinois University, reprinted by permission of the publisher.

Djanikian, Gregory. "Immigrant Picnic." First appeared in *Poetry* July 1999.

Dove, Rita. "Motherhood" from *Selected Poems,* Pantheon Books, © 1993 by Rita Dove. Reprinted by permission of the author.

Dove, Rita. "The Vibraphone" from *Fifth Sunday,* Callaloo Fiction Series, No. 1, © 1985 by Rita Dove. Reprinted by permission of the author.

Eberhart, Richard. "The Fury of Aerial Bombardment," from *Collected Poems, 1930-1976* by Richard Eberhart. Copyright © 1976 by Richard Eberhart. Used by permission of Oxford University Press, Inc.

Eberhart, Richard. "The Groundhog" from *Collected Poems 1930-1986* by Richard Eberhart. Copyright © 1960, 1976, 1987 by Richard Eberhart. Reprinted by permission of Oxford University Press, Inc.

Ehrenreich, Barbara and Deirdre English, "The 'Sick' Women of the Upper Classes," reprinted from *Complaints and Disorder: The Sexual Politics of Sickness.* Copyright © 1973 by Barbara Ehrenreich and Deirdre English, by permission of the Feminist Press at the City University of New York, www.feministpress.org.

Engle, Paul. From "Chicago Can Take Pride in New, Young Voice in Poetry." First appeared in the *Chicago Tribune Book Review,* 1945. Reprinted by permission of Hualing Nieh Engle.

Erdrich, Louise. "Wild Geese" from *Love Medicine* by Louise Erdrich. Copyright © 1984 by Louise Erdrich. Reprinted by permission of Henry Holt and Company, LLC.

Faulkner, William. "A Rose for Emily." Copyright 1930 and renewed 1958 by William Faulkner, from *Collected Stories of William Faulkner* by William Faulkner. Used by permission of Random House, Inc.

Feldstein, Richard. Reprinted from "Reader, Text, and Ambiguous Referentiality in 'The Yellow Wallpaper',", in *Feminism and Psychoanalysis,* Richard Feldstein and Judith Roof, eds. Copyright © 1989 by Cornell University. Used by permission of the publisher, Cornell University Press.

Fenton, James. "God, A Poem" from *Children in Exile* by James Fenton. Copyright © 1972 by James Fenton. Reprinted by permission of Sterling Lord Literistic, Inc.

Fetterly, Judith. "Reading About Reading: 'A Jury of Her Peers,' 'The Murders in Rue Morgue,' and 'The Yellow Wallpaper'" (pp. 159–160) in *Gender and Reading: Essays on Readers, Texts and Contexts* edited by Elizabeth Flynn and Patrocino Schqeikert. Copyright © 1986 by Johns Hopkins University Press. Reprinted by permission of Johns Hopkins University Press.

Fitzgerald, F. Scott. "Babylon Revisited" reprinted with permission of Scribner, an imprint of Simon & Schuster Adult Publishing Group, from *The Short Stories of F. Scott Fitzgerald,* edited by Matthew J. Bruccoli. Copyright 1931 by the Curtis Publishing Company. Copyright © renewed 1959 by Frances Scott Fitzgerald Lanahan.

Francis, Robert. "Catch," from *The Orb Weaver.* Copyright © 1960 by Robert Francis and reprinted by permission of Wesleyan University Press.

Francis, Robert. "The Pitcher," from *The Orb Weaver.* Copyright © 1960 by Robert Francis and reprinted by permission of Wesleyan University Press.

Fraser, Caroline. "All Bears" from *The New Yorker* 1991. Copyright © 1991 by Caroline Fraser. Reprinted by permission of the author.

Frost, Robert. "Choose Something Like a Star," from *The Poetry of Robert Frost* edited by Edward Connery Lathem. Copyright 1949, © 1969 by Henry Holt and Company. Reprinted by permission of Henry Holt and Company, LLC.

Frost, Robert. "Desert Places," From *The Poetry of Robert Frost,* ed. Edward Connery Lathem. Copyright 1928, 1930, 1939 © 1969 by Henry Holt and Co., © 1964, 1967, 1970, 1975 by Lesley Frost Ballentine. Copyright 1936, 1942, 1951, 1956, 1958 by Robert Frost. Reprinted by permission of Henry Holt and Company, LLC.

Frost, Robert. "Design," from *The Poetry of Robert Frost* edited by Edward Connery Lathem. Copyright 1947, © 1969 by Henry Holt and Co., copyright 1936 by Robert Frost, copyright © 1964, 1975 by Lesley Frost Ballentine. Reprinted by permission of Henry Holt and Company, LLC.

Frost, Robert. "It Bids Pretty Fair" from *The Poetry of Robert Frost* edited by Edward Connery Lathem. Copyright 1947, © 1969 by Henry Holt and Co., copyright 1936 by Robert Frost, copyright 1964, 1975 by Lesley Frost Ballentine. Reprinted by permission of Henry Holt and Company, LLC.

Frost, Robert. "Mending Wall," "The Road Not Taken," "After Apple Picking," "Birches," "Out, Out—," "Fire and Ice," from *The Poetry of Robert Frost,* ed. Edward Connery Lathem. Copyright 1928, 1930, 1939 © 1969 by Henry Holt and Co., © 1964, 1967, 1970, 1975 by Lesley Frost Ballentine, copyright 1936, 1942, 1951, 1956, 1958 by Robert Frost. Reprinted by permission of Henry Holt and Company, LLC.

Frost, Robert. "Stopping by Woods on a Snowy Evening," From *The Poetry of Robert Frost*, ed. Edward Connery Lathem. Copyright 1928, 1930, 1939 © 1969 by Henry Holt and Co., © 1964, 1967, 1970, 1975 by Lesley Frost Ballentine, copyright 1936, 1942, 1951, 1956, 1958 by Robert Frost. Reprinted by permission of Henry Holt and Company, LLC.

Frost, Robert. Excerpt from "The Figure a Poem Makes," from *The Selected Prose of Robert Frost*, edited by Hyde Cox and Edward Connery Latham. Copyright 1939, © 1967 by Henry Holt and Company. Reprinted by permission of Henry Holt & Company, LLC.

Gabbin, Joanne. From "Blooming in the Whirlwind: The Early Poetry of Gwendolyn Brooks," from *The Furious Flowering of African American Poetry* by Joanne Gabbin. Reprinted by permission of the University of Virginia Press.

Gaines, Ernest. "Just Like a Tree," from *Bloodline* by Ernest J. Gaines, copyright © 1963, 1964, 1968 by Ernest J. Gaines. Used by permission of Doubleday, a division of Random House, Inc.

Gentry, Marshall Bruce. From "Dancers in the Furnace," from *Flannery O'Connor's Religion of the Grotesque* by Marshall Bruce Gentry (Jackson, MS: University Press of Mississippi, 1986) pp. 42–43. Reprinted by permission.

Gill, Brendan. "The Knife." Originally published in *The New Yorker*, March 16, 1940. Reprinted by permission of the Estate of Brendan Gill.

Gill, Brendan. From *Here at the New Yorker* by Brendan Gill. Copyright © 1975 by Brendan Gill. Used by permission of Random House, Inc.

Gionne, Richard. From *Flannery O'Connor: Hermit Novelist*. Copyright © 2000 by Board of Trustees of the University of Illinois. Used with permission of the University of Illinois Press.

Glaspell, Susan. *Trifles* by Susan Glaspell. Copyright 1951. Reprinted by permission of Baker's Plays.

Glück, Louise. "The Apple Trees" from *The First Four Books of Poems* by Louise Glück. Copyright © 1968, 1971, 1972, 1973, 1974, 1975, 1976, 1977, 1978, 1979, 1980, 1985, 1995 by Louise Glück. Reprinted by permission of HarperCollins Publishers, Inc.

Graves, Robert. "Down, Wonton, Down" from *Collected Poems of Robert Graves* by Robert Graves. Copyright © 1988. Reprinted by permission of Carcanet Press Limited.

Green, Douglas. "Preposterous Pleasures: Queer Theories and *A Midsummer Night's Dream*" in *A Midsummer Night's Dream: Critical Essays*, edited by Dorothea Keller, 1998. Copyright © 1998. Reprinted by permission of Taylor & Francis Books, Inc.

Grenier, Donald. From "Preface" in *Robert Frost: The Poet and His Critics*. Copyright 1942 by American Library Association. Reprinted by permission of American Library Association.

Gunn, Thom. "Moly" from *Collected Poems* by Thom Gunn. Copyright © 1994 by Thom Gunn. Reprinted by permission of Farrar, Straus, and Giroux, LLC.

Hamburger, Michael. "A Poet's Progress" is taken from *Michael Hamburger: Collected Poems 1941-1994* published by Anvil Press Poetry in 1995.

Hardy, Thomas. "The Oxen," reprinted with the permission of Scribner, an imprint of Simon & Schuster Adult Publishing Group, from *The Complete Poems of Thomas Hardy,* edited by James Gibson (New York: Macmillan, 1978).

Harjo, Joy. "For Anna Mae Pictou Aquash" from *In Mad Love and War,* copyright © 1994 by Joy Harjo and reprinted by Wesleyan University Press.

Harper, Michael S. "Dear John, Dear Coltrane" by Michael S. Harper. Copyright © 1970, 1985 by Michael S. Harper. Reprinted by permission of the author.

Heany, Seamus. "Digging" from *Death of a Naturalist* by Seamus Heany. Copyright © by Seamus Heany. Reprinted by permission of Faber & Faber Ltd.

Heany, Seamus. "Digging" from *Opened Ground: Selected Poems, 1966-1996* by Seamus Heany. Copyright © 1998 by Seamus Heany. Reprinted by permission of Farrar, Straus and Giroux, LLC.

Hecht, Anthony. "The Dover Bitch," from *Collected Earlier Poems* by Anthony Hecht. Copyright © 1990 by Anthony Hecht. Used by permission of Alfred A. Knopf, a division of Random House, Inc.

Hedges, Elaine. "Afterword" to *The Yellow Wallpaper,* copyright © 1973 by Elaine R. Hedges, by permission of the Feminist Press at the City University of New York, www.feministpress.org.

Hemingway, Ernest. "A Very Short Story" reprinted with permission of Scribner, a division of Simon & Schuster, Inc. from *In Our Time* by Ernest Hemingway. Copyright 1925, 1930 by Charles Scribner's Sons. Copyright renewed 1953, © 1958 by Ernest Hemingway.

Hogan, James. "Oedipus the King: The Theban Plays," pages 19-21, from *A Commentary on the Plays of Sophocles* by James C. Hogan. Copyright © 1991 by the Board of Trustees, Southern Illinois University, reproduced by permission of the publisher.

Holland, Norman. Pages 119-122 from *The Dynamics of Literary Response* by Norman Holland. Copyright © 1975 by Norman Holland. Reprinted by permission of Sterling Lord Literistic.

Homann, Sidney. "'What Do I Do Now?': Directing *A Midsummer Night's Dream*," in Jay Halio and Hugh Richmond, *Shakespearean Illuminations: Essays in Honor of Marvin Rosenberg,* 1998

Horvath, Brooke Kenton. From "The Satisfaction of What's Difficult in Gwendolyn Brooks's Poetry." *American Literature* 62, No. 4, 606-16. Copyright © 1990 Duke University Press. All rights reserved. Used by permission of the publisher.

Hospital, Janette Turner. "Morgan, Morgan" reprinted from *Dislocations* by Janette Turner Hospital. Copyright © 1987 by Janette Turner Hospital. Reprinted by permission of Louisiana State University Press and the Blanche C. Gregory, Inc. Literary Agency.

Hughes, Gertrude Reif. From "Making It Really New: Hilda Doolittle, Gwendolyn Brooks, and the Feminist potential of Modern Poetry." *American Quarterly* 42:3

Kennard, Jean. "Convention Coverage or How to Read Your Own Life." *New Literary History,* 13:1 (1981) 74–78. Copyright © New Literary History, University of Virginia. Reprinted with permission of The Johns Hopkins University Press.

Kilkup, Karen. Pages 45–48 from *Robert Frost and Feminine Literary Tradition* by Karen Kilkup. Copyright © 1998 by University of Michigan Press. Reprinted by permission.

Kinnell, Galway. "Saint Francis and the Sow," from *Mortal Acts, Mortal Words* by Galway Kinnell. Copyright © 1980 by Galway Kinnell. Reprinted by permission of Houghton Mifflin Company. All rights reserved.

Kinnell, Galway. "The Bear," from *Body Rags* by Galway Kinnell. Copyright © 1968 by Galway Kinnell. Reprinted by permission of Houghton Mifflin Company. All rights reserved.

Knox, Bernard, M.W. Pages 19–21, from *Oedipus at Thebes* by Bernard M.W. Knox. Copyright © 1957 by Yale University Press. Reprinted by permission.

Koch, Kenneth. "Variations on a Theme by William Carlos Williams," by Kenneth Koch. Reprinted by permission of Kenneth Koch Literary Estate.

Larkin, Philip. "A Study of Reading Habits," from *Collected Poems* by Philip Larkin. Copyright © 1988, 1989 by the Estate of Philip Larkin. Reprinted by permission of Farrar, Straus and Giroux, LLC.

Larkin, Philip. "A Study of Reading Habits," from *Collected Poems* by Philip Larkin. Reprinted by permission of Faber & Faber Ltd.

Lee, Li-Young. "Persimmons," from *Rose.* Copyright © 1986 by Li-Young Lee. Reprinted with the permission of BOA Editions, Ltd.

Lessing, Doris. "A Woman on the Roof" from *Stories* by Doris Lessing. Copyright © 1978 by Doris Lessing. Reprinted by permission of Jonathan Clowes Ltd.

Levertov, Denise. "Advent 1966," by Denise Levertov from *Relearning the Alphabet.* Copyright © 1970 by Denise Levertov. Reprinted by permission of New Directions Publishing Corp.

Levertov, Denise. "O Taste and See," from *Poems 1960–1967.* Copyright © 1964 by Denise Levertov. Reprinted by permission of New Directions Publishing Corp.

Levertov, Denise. "To the Snake," by Denise Levertov, from *Collected Earlier Poems 1940–1960.* Copyright © 1946, 1956, 1958 by Denise Levertov. Reprinted by permission of New Directions Publishing Corp.

Lowell, Robert. "For the Union Dead," from *For the Union Dead* by Robert Lowell. Copyright © 1959 by Robert Lowell. Copyright © renewed 1987 by Harriet Lowell, Caroline Lowell, and Sheridan Lowell. Reprinted by permission of Farrar, Straus, and Giroux, LLC.

Mack, Maynard. "The Readiness is All," reprinted from *Everybody's Shakespeare* by Maynard Mack. Copyright © 1993 by University of Nebraska Press. Reprinted by permission.

MacLeish, Archibald. "Ars Poetica" from *Collected Poems 1917–1982* by Archibald MacLeish. Copyright © 1985 by The Estate of Archibald MacLeish. Reprinted by permission of Hougton Mifflin Company. All rights reserved.

MacPike, Loralee. From "Environment as Psychopathological Symbolism in 'The Yellow Wallpaper'" *American Literary Realism,* 8.3 (1975): 286–287. Reprinted by permission of the editors of *American Literary Realism.*

Malphrus, Ellen. "Thanksgiving on the Chicken Bone Express." Copyright © 1993 by Ellen Malphrus. Reprinted by permission of the author.

Mandel, Eli. "Houdini," from *The Other Harmony: The Collected Poems of Eli Mandel,* Andrew Stubbs and Judy Chapman, ed., 2000. Canadian Plains Research Center.

Marcus, Mordicai. From *The Poems of Robert Frost: An Explication.* Copyright © 1991 by G. K. Hall. Reprinted by permission of The Gale Group.

McGuire, Philip. Pages 1–18, from *Speechless Dialect: Shakespeare's Open Silences* by Philip McGuire. Published by University of California Press. Copyright © 1985 by Philip McGuire. Reprinted by permission of the author.

McNally, Terence. *Andre's Mother.* Copyright © 1994 by Terrence McNally. Reprinted by permission of William Morris Agency, Inc. on behalf of the Author.

Meredith, William. "A Major Work" is reprinted from *Effort at Speech: New and Selected Poems* by William Meredith, published by TriQuarterly Books/Northwestern University Press in 1997. Copyright © 1997 by William Meredith. All rights reserved; used by permission of Northwestern University Press and the author.

Merwin, W. S. "For the Anniversary of My Death," by W. S. Merwin. Copyright © 1967 by W. S. Merwin. Reprinted by permission of The Wylie Agency.

Merwin, W. S. "Leviathan," by W. S. Merwin. Copyright © 1956 by W. S. Merwin. Reprinted by permission of The Wylie Agency.

Middlebrook, Diane. "February Afternoon, In a Boat in the Seine," (draft) From "Making the Poem" from *Worlds Into Words: Understanding Modern Poems* by Dianne Middlebrook. Copyright © 1978 by Diane W. Middlebrook. Used by permission of W. W. Norton & Company, Inc.

Millay, Edna St. Vincent. "Never May the Fruit be Plucked," by Edna St. Vincent Millay from *Collected Poems,* HarperCollins. Copyright 1923, 1951 by Edna St. Vincent Millay and Norma Millay Ellis. All rights reserved. Reprinted by permission of Elizabeth Barnett, literary executor.

Millay, Edna St. Vincent. Sonnett XXX of *Fatal Interview,* by Edna St. Vincent Millay. From *Collected Poems,* HarperCollins. Copyright © 1931, copyright © 1958 by Edna St. Vincent Millay and Norma Millay Ellis. All rights reserved. Reprinted by permission of Elizabeth Barnett, literary executor.

Miller, R. Baxter. From "'Does Man Love Art?': The Humanistic Aesthetic of Gwendolyn Brooks." *Black American Literature and Humanism.* Ed. R. Baxter Miller. Lexington: UP of Kentucky, 1981.

Montrose, Louise. *A Midsummer Night's Dream: Critical Essays,* edited by Dorothea Keller, 1998.

Ransom, John Crowe. "Bells for John Whiteside's Daughter," from *Selected Poems, Third Edition, Revised and Enlarged* by John Crowe Ransom. Copyright 1924, 1927 by Alfred A. Knopf, Inc. and renewed 1952, 1955 by John Crowe Random. Used by permission of Alfred A. Knopf, a division of Random House, Inc.

Reed, Henry. "Naming of Parts," from *Collected Poems* by Henry Reed, edited by Jon Stallworthy. Copyright © 1991. Reprinted by permission of Oxford University Press.

Rich, Adrienne. "Aunt Jennifer's Tigers." Copyright © 2002, 1951 by Adrienne Rich from *The Fact of a Doorframe: Poems Selected and New 1950-2001* by Adrienne Rich. Used by permission of W. W. Norton & Company, Inc.

Roethke, Theodore. "My Papa's Waltz," from *The Collected Poems of Theodore Roethke,* by Theodore Roethke. Copyright 1942 by Hearst Magazines, Inc. Used by permission of Doubleday, a division of Random House, Inc.

Roethke, Theodore. "Root Cellar." Copyright 1943 by Modern Poetry Association, Inc. from *The Collected Poems of Theodore Roethke,* by Theodore Roethke. Used by permission of Doubleday, a division of Random House, Inc.

Sanchez-Scott, Milcha. "The Cuban Swimmer," from *Dog Lady and the Cuban Swimmer.* Copyright © 1984, 1988 by Milcha Sanchez-Scott. Reprinted by permission of William Morris Agency, Inc. on behalf of the author.

Schnackenberg, Gjertrud. "Supernatural Love," from *The Lamplit Answer* by Gertrude Schnackenberg. Copyright © 1985 by Gertrude Schnackenberg. Reprinted by permission of Farrar, Straus and Giroux, LLC.

"'Shaping Fantasies': Figurations of Gender and Power in Elizabethan Culture," 1983. *Representations* Vol. 2 (Spring 1983), 133-135.

Showalter, Elaine. "Repressing Ophelia: Women, Madness and the Responsibilities of Feminist Criticism," in *Shakespeare and the Question of Theory* edited by Patricia Parker and Geoffrey Hartman. Copyright © 1985. Reprinted by permission of Taylor & Francis.

Shu-ning Liu, Stephen. "My Father's Martial Art." Copyright © 1981 by the Antioch Review, Inc. First appeared in *The Antioch Review,* Vol. 39, No. 3. Reprinted by permission of the Editors.

Smith, Stevie. "How Cruel is the Story of Eve" from *Collected Poems of Stevie Smith.* Copyright © 1972 by Stevie Smith. Reprinted by permission of New Directions Publishing Corp.

Smith, Stevie. "Not Waving But Drowning," from *Collected Poems of Stevie Smith.* Copyright © 1972 by Stevie Smith. Reprinted by permission of New Directions Publishing Corp.

Snyder, Gary. "Some Good Things to Be Said for the Iron Age," from *Left Out in the Rain* by Gary Snyder. Copyright © 1986 by Gary Snyder. Reprinted by permission of North Point Press, a division of Farrar, Straus and Giroux, LLC.

Song, Cathy. "Waterwings" from *Frameless Windows, Squares of Light: Poems* by Cathy Song. Copyright © 1988 by Cathy Song. Used by permission of W.W. Norton & Company, Inc.

Stafford, William. "Traveling through the Dark." Copyright © 1962, 1998 by the Estate of William Stafford. Reprinted from *The Way It Is: New and Selected Poems* with the permission of Graywolf Press, Saint Paul, MN.

Steinbeck, John. "Chrysanthemums." Copyright 1937, renewed © 1965 by John Steinbeck, from *The Long Valley,* by John Steinbeck. Used by permission of Viking Penguin, a division of Penguin Putnam Inc.

Stevens, C. Ralph. From "Introduction" to *The Correspondence of Flannery O'Connor and the Brainard Cheneys,* by C. Ralph Stevens. Copyright © 1989 by the University of Mississippi Press. Reprinted by permission.

Stevens, Wallace. "The Anecdote of the Jar," from *The Collected Poems of Wallace Stevens* by Wallace Stevens, copyright © 1954 by Wallace Stevens and renewed 1982 by Holly Stevens. Used by permission of Alfred A. Knopf, a division of Random House, Inc.

Strand, Mark. "Eating Poetry," from *Reasons for Moving* by Mark Strand. Copyright © 1968 by Mark Strand. Reprinted by permission of The Wylie Agency.

Strand, Mark. "Keeping Things Whole" from *Keeping Things Whole,* by Mark Strand. Copyright © 1968 by Mark Strand. Reprinted by permission of The Wylie Agency.

Strand, Mark. "The Garden" from *Keeping Things Whole,* by Mark Strand. Copyright © 1978 by Mark Strand. Reprinted by permission of The Wylie Agency.

Tallach, Douglas. From *The Nineteenth Century American Short Story: Language, Form and Ideology,* by Douglas Tallach. Copyright © 1993. Reprinted by permission of Taylor & Francis.

Tallent, Elizabeth. "No One's a Mystery," from *Sudden Fiction* by Elizabeth Tallent. Copyright © 1985 by Elizabeth Tallent. Reprinted by permission of The Wylie Agency, Inc.

Tan, Amy. "Two Kinds," from *The Joy Luck Club* by Amy Tan. Copyright © 1989 by Amy Tan. Reprinted by permission of Penguin Putnam, Inc.

Tennenhouse, Leonard. "Strategies of State and Political Plays: *A Midsummer Night's Dream, Henry IV, Henry VIII* " in *Political Shakespeare: New Essays in Cultural Materialism,* edited by Jonathan Dollimore and Alan Sinfield. Used by permission of the publisher, Cornell University Press.

Thomas, Dylan. "Do Not Go Gentle Into That Good Night," from *The Poems of Dylan Thomas.* Copyright 1945 by The Trustees for the Copyrights of Dylan Thomas. Reprinted by permission of New Directions Publishing Corp.

Thomas, Dylan. "Fern Hill," from *The Poems of Dylan Thomas.* Copyright 1945 by The Trustees for the Copyrights of Dylan Thomas. Reprinted by permission of New Directions Publishing Corp and David Higham Assoicates.

Thurber, James. "The Catbird Seat" from *The Thurber Carnival.* Copyright © 1945 by James Thurber. Copyright renewed 1973 by Helen Thurber and Rosemary A. Thurber. Reprinted by arrangement with Rosemary A. Thurber and The Barbara Hogenson Agency.

Tomlinson, Charles. "On a Pig's Head" from *Selected Poems* by Charles Tomlinson. Copyright © 1997 by Charles Tomlinson. Reprinted by permission of Oxford University Press, Inc.

Turner, Margaret. Excerpt from "Conversations With Flannery O'Connor," by Margaret Turner. Copyright © 1960 by *Atlanta Journal-Constitution.* Reproduced with permission of *Atlanta Journal-Constitution* via Copyright Clearance Center.

Updike, John. "A & P," from *Pigeon Feathers and Other Stories,* by John Updike. Copyright © 1962 and renewed 1990 by John Updike. Used by permission of Alfred A. Knopf, a division of Random House, Inc.

Updike, John. "Deaths of Distant Friends," from *Trust Me* by John Updike. Copyright © 1987 by John Updike. Used by permission of Alfred A. Knopf, a division of Random House, Inc.

Updike, John. "Ex-Basketball Player," from *The Carpentered Hen and Other Tame Creatures,* by John Updike. Copyright © 1982 by John Updike. Used by permission of Alfred A. Knopf, a division of Random House, Inc.

Updike, John. Pages 163–169, from *Claudius and Gertrude,* by John Updike. Copyright © 2000 by John Updike. Used by permission of Alfred A. Knopf, a division of Random House, Inc.

Wagoner, David. "This is a Wonderful Poem," from *Traveling Light: Collected and New Poems.* Copyright © 1999 by David Wagoner. Used by permission of the poet and the University of Illinois Press.

Walcott, Derek. "Frederiksted, Dusk," from *Sea Grapes,* by Derek Walcott. Copyright © 1976 by Derek Walcott. Reprinted by permission of Farrar, Straus & Giroux, LLC.

Walcott, Derek. "Frederiksted, Dusk," from *Sea Grapes,* by Derek Walcott published by Jonathan Cape. Used by permission of The Random House Group Limited.

Wayman, Tom. "Did I Miss Anything," from *Did I Miss Anything? Selected Poems 1973-1993,* by Tom Wayman. Copyright © 1993. Reprinted by permission of Harbour Publishing, Madiera Park, BC.

Webster, Harvey. From "Pity the Giants." Reprinted with permission from the September 1, 1962 issue of *The Nation.*

Whitt, Margaret Earley. From *Understanding Flannery O'Connor,* by Margaret Earley Whitt. Copyright © 1995. Reprinted by permission of University of South Carolina Press.

Wilbur, Richard. "A Late Aubade," from *Walking to Sleep: New Poems and Translations.* Copyright © 1968 and renewed 1996 by Richard Wilbur. Reprinted by permission of Harcourt, Inc. Originally appeared in *The New Yorker.*

Wilbur, Richard. "The Death of a Toad," from *Ceremony and Other Poems.* Copyright 1950 and renewed 1978 by Richard Wilbur, reprinted by permission of Harcourt, Inc.

Wilbur, Richard. "The Writer," from *The Mind-Reader.* Copyright © 1971 by Richard Wilbur. Reprinted by permission of Harcourt, Inc.

Williams, Kenny Jackson. "Gwendolyn Brooks," from *The Oxford Companion to African-American Literature*, edited by William Andrews, et al. Copyright © 1997 by Oxford University Press, Inc. Used by permission of Oxford University Press, Inc.

Williams, William Carlos. "Raleigh Was Right," from *Collected Poems 1939-1962, Vol. II*. Copyright © 1944 by William Carlos Williams. Reprinted by permission of New Directions Publishing Corp.

Williams, William Carlos. "The Dance," and "Spring and All," from *Collected Poems 1939-1962*, Vol. 2. Copyright 1944 by William Carlos Williams. Reprinted by permission of New Directions Publishing Corp.

Williams, William Carlos. "The Red Wheelbarrow," by William Carlos Williams from *Collected Poems: 1909-1939, Vol. I*. Copyright 1938 by New Directions Publishing Corp. Reprinted by permission of New Directions Corp.

Williams, William Carlos. "This Is Just to Say," by William Carlos Williams, from *Collected Poems, 1909-1939 Vol. I*. Copyright 1938 by New Directions Publishing Corp. Reprinted by permission of New Directions Publishing Corp.

Wilson, August. "The Janitor." Copyright © 1985 by August Wilson. Reprinted by permission of August Wilson.

Wilson, Richard. From "The Kindly Ones: The Death of the Author in Shakespearean Athens." *Essays and Studies* 46 (1993): 1-24.

Wolff, Tobias. "Say Yes" from *Back in the World*, by Tobias Wolff. Copyright © 1996 by Tobias Wolff. First published by Vintage Books, a division of Random House, Inc. Reprinted by permission of International Creative Management, Inc.

Wright, James. "A Blessing," from *Above the River: The Complete Poems*. Copyright © 1990 and reprinted by permission of Wesleyan University Press.

Yeats, William Butler. "The Second Coming." Reprinted with the permission of Scribner, an imprint of Simon & Schuster Adult Publishing Group, from *The Collected Works of W.B. Yeats, Volume 1: The Poems, Revised*, edited by Richard J. Finneran. Copyright 1924 by The Macmillan Company; copyright renewed © 1952 by Bertha Georgie Yeats.

Yeats, William Butler. "Adam's Curse," reprinted with the permission of Scribner, an imprint of Simon & Schuster Adult Publishing Group, from *The Collected Works of William Butler Yeats, Volume I: The Poems, Revised*, edited by Richard J. Finneran (New York: Scribner, 1977).

Photo Credits

Page 7: AP/Wide World Photos, Inc. Page 14: Nancy Crampton. Page 60: *Margaret Cavendish, Duchess of Newcastle* (1624-1674) (engraving) by English School, (17th century). Private Collection/Bridgeman Art Library. Page 62: Photograph by Hulleah Tsinhnahjinnie. Courtesy of Joy Harjo. Page 65: Robert Holmes/CORBIS. Page 97: Yale Collection of American Literature, Beinecke Rare Book and Manuscript Library. Page 136: Photo. No. EH2665 in the John F. Kennedy Library. Page 145: Cornell Capa/TimePix.

Index of First Lines
of Poems

Index of Authors
and Titles